basic Drama Projects

9th Edition

Annotated Teacher's Edition

by Fran Averett Tanner, Ph.D.

Perfection Learning®

Editorial Director Julie A. Schumacher, Carol Francis

Senior Editor Gay Russell-Dempsey

Permissions Meghan Schumacher, Oliver Oertel

Text Writers **Donald Abramson,** Playwright, Theatre Writer, Editor, Skokie, IL

Anthony Adler, Co-founder: The Actor's Gymnasium, Theatre Critic, Evanston, IL

Lisa Dillman, Playwright, Teacher, Education Writer, Chicago, IL

Elaine Malone, High School Drama Teacher, Durham, NC

Joan McElroy, Ph.D., Education Writer, North Providence, RI

Carmen McElwain, High School Drama Teacher, Plano, TX

Sheri Reda, Education Specialist, Chicago, IL

Kim Rubinstein, Professor of Theatre Arts, University of San Diego, La Jolla, CA

Design **Herman Adler Design,** Evanston, Illinois,

Randy Messer, Art Director, Perfection Learning,

Tobi Cunnningham, Jane Wonderlin and **Cameron Peterson,** Designers, Perfection Learning

The editors would like to thank Peter Hay for permission to use material from his books *Theatrical Anecdotes* and *Broadway Anecdotes,* both published by the Oxford University Press (1987 and 1989, respectively).

© 2015 by Perfection Learning®
www.perfectionlearning.com

When ordering this book, please specify:

Hardcover: ISBN 978-0-7891-8903-5 or **9407402**
Ebook edition (2014): ISBN: 978-0-7891-8907-3 or **94074D**

Basic Drama Projects

Projects

9th Edition

Perfection
Learning®

Editorial Director **Julie A. Schumacher, Carol Francis**
Senior Editor **Gay Russell-Dempsey**
Illustrations **Mike Aspengren**
Picture Research **Lisa Lorimor, Anjanette Houghtaling**
Permissions **Meghan Schumacher, Oliver Oertel, Karyn Morrison**
Text Writers **Sheri Reda,** Education Specialist, Chicago, Illinois
      Lisa Dillman, Playwright, Teacher, Education Writer, Chicago, Illinois
      Joan McElroy, Ph.D., Education Writer, North Providence, Rhode Island
Handbook Writer **Ric Averill,** Composer, Playwright, Drama Program Director for Lawrence Arts Center,
      Lawrence, Kansas
Design **Herman Adler Design,** Evanston, Illinois, **Randy Messer,** Art Director, Perfection Learning
      Tobi Cunnningham, Jane Wonderlin and **Cameron Peterson,** Designers,
      Perfection Learning

Acknowledgments
Text Credits

Excerpt from "The Actor's Nightmare" by Christopher Durang from *Christopher Durang Explains It All for You.* Copyright ©1983 by Christopher Durang. Used by permission of Grove/Atlantic, Inc.

Any third party use of this material, outside of this publication, is prohibited.

Excerpt from "After Cages" by CinSalach. Copyright ©1996 by CinSalach. Reprinted by permission of Tia Chucha Press.

Excerpt from *Blood Wedding* by Federico Garcia Lorca. Translation by James Graham-Lujan and Richard L. O'Connell, from *Three Tragedies.*

Copyright ©1947 by New Directions Publishing Corp. Reprinted by permission of New Directions Publishing Corp.

Excerpt from *Blithe Spirit* by Noël Coward. *Blithe Spirit* copyright © NC Aventales AG 1942 by permission of Alan Brodie Representation Ltd. www.alanbrodie.com

(Acknowledgments continued on page 624)

Copyright © 2015 by Perfection Learning® Corporation
www.perfectionlearning.com

1 2 3 4 5 6 7 RRD 20 19 18 17 16 15 14

[print] ISBN-13: 978-0-7891-8896-0
[digital] ISBN-13: 978-0-7891-8897-7

Basic Drama Projects

9th Edition

Projects

Perfection
Learning®

by Fran Averett Tanner, Ph.D.

Technical Theatre Consultant

The editors are indebted to **Dana Taylor,** director of technical theatre and vocal music at Mt. Vernon High School Fine Arts Academy in Mt. Vernon, Indiana, and Technical Editor for *Dramatics* and *Teaching Theatre* magazines. Mr. Taylor is also a recipient of the Distinguished Achievement Award in Education from the United States Institute for Theatre Technology. Mr. Taylor provided expert consultation and writing for the expanded Technical Theatre unit in the 9th Edition of *Basic Drama Projects.*

Review Board

The Editors also thank the following teachers who helped create this book and who give tirelessly on behalf of theatre students around the country.

Jeanne Averill
Drama Teacher
Lawrence High School
Lawrence, Kansas

Tracy Boylan
Drama Teacher
La Salle-Peru Township High School
LaSalle, Illinois

Deborah Clark
Drama Teacher
Hollywood Hills High School
Hollywood, Florida

Robert Kallos
Drama Teacher
The Galloway School
Atlanta, Georgia

Andrea Kidd
Drama Teacher
Pembroke Pines Charter High School
Pembroke Pines, Florida

Elaine Malone
Drama Teacher
Durham Academy
Durham, North Carolina

Carmen McElwain
Drama Teacher
Plano, Texas

Kim Rubinstein
Professor of Theatre Arts
University of California San Diego
La Jolla, California

Nan Zabriski
Professor of Theatre Arts
De Paul University
Chicago, Illinois

Student Actors

We would also like to thank the following student actors for their help in making the photographic images in this book lively and instructive.

Emmett Adler	Lauren Gray
Max Adler	Yasmeen Kheshgi
Stephon Albert	Christa Koskosky
Gail Amornpongchai	Lizzie Laundy
Paige Azuma	Henry Marcus
Calvin Baptiste, Jr.	Mghnon Martin
Bryan D. Blaney	Tatyana Pramatarova
Peter Bloom	Alex Rosenfield
Elaine Coladarci	Isaac Simpson
Amanda Georgantas	Eileen Spangler
Alex Goode	Hilary Ubando

Additional thanks go to Lost Era Costumes, Chicago, Illinois, for their generous help in costuming; Joe Silvestri of Lake Forest Academy for allowing use of theatre space and student models; Shauna Thieman of Western Michigan University Theatre Department, Lee Ann Bakros from the Des Moines Community Playhouse, and Christina Faison of North High in Des Moines, Iowa, for the use of photographs from their productions.

Welcome to Drama Class!

We think you're going to enjoy your stay!
Basic Drama Projects offers you just what the name suggests: engaging, challenging, creative, and fun projects that provide an introduction to theatre basics. Here are hands-on, action-packed assignments—from improv and character development to writing and directing to creating props and planning and building sets. *Basic Drama Projects* also provides a collection of monologues and scenes for performance as well as a handbook for all aspects of theatrical production.

Success in this class will not necessarily lead to a starring role on Broadway or a career in costume design or sound engineering. Instead, it is a place where you can tap into your own creativity, gain self-confidence, and experience working collaboratively with others. You will discover that working in the theatre almost always means being part of a team.

This is a class where teamwork and dependability aren't just words—they are tools of the trade. And speaking of words, whether your first language is English or another language, the feature in this book called "The Language of Theatre" will help you develop a working vocabulary for the world of theatre. As you gain a broader theatre background, you will also develop other skills that have application to college and careers in and beyond the theatre. You will learn to become a critical listener and viewer and a creative problem solver—qualities that will serve you well no matter where your future takes you.

Contents

Contents

Contents

Contents

Unit Seven

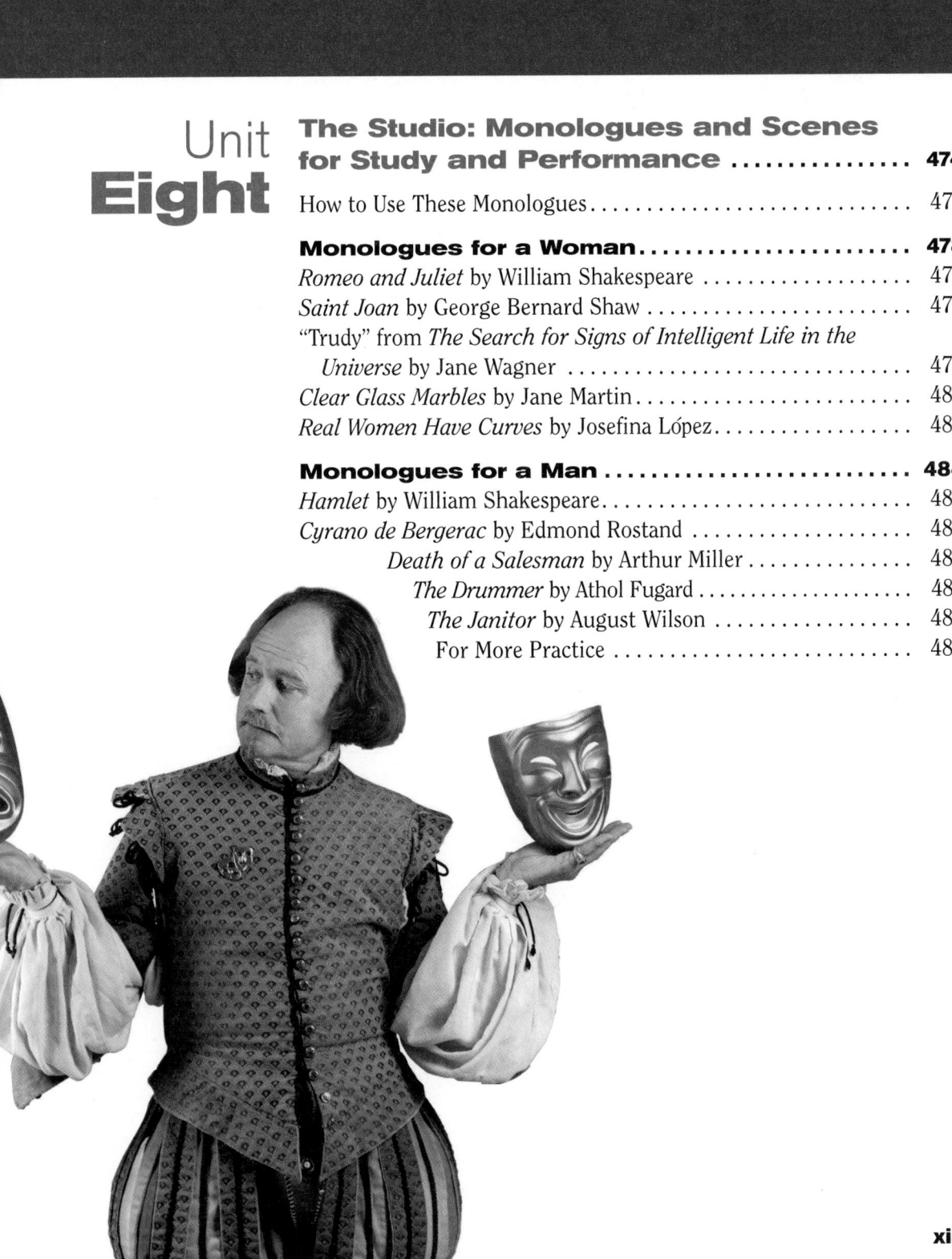

Contents

Unit One

Begin with the Basics

Unit One offers students experiential learning about the basics of performance, including warm-ups, the use of observation and experience, the elements of pantomime, and the principles of improvisation. Projects in this unit will help students learn to trust themselves and each other as performers and will introduce students to the kinds of work that underpin effective performances.

Project Preview

Chapter 1 The Theatre and You
Re-creating powerful memories

Chapter 2 Warm Up
Creating a warm-up routine

Chapter 3 Observation
Giving a detailed description

Chapter 4 Pantomime
Preparing a pantomime

Chapter 5 Improvisation
Performing an improvisation

Note: The Theatre Information Pack (or TIPack)
In putting together this program, the editors learned that every teacher has his or her own idea as to what material should be included in the early chapters of the student book. Teachers' varied requests demonstrated the organic nature of theatre and presented an interesting challenge.

In response to teachers' concerns, a set of fourteen blackline masters has been compiled that provide basic information for theatre students. This introductory material, which is found in the Teacher's Resource Binder, can be duplicated and taught as a preview chapter at the beginning of the year, or given to students as a reference tool.

In addition, each of the pages in the Theatre Information Pack is referenced in the appropriate chapter as a TIPack page.

Unit One

Begin with the Basics

Quotable

Use the quote below as a journal writing prompt, discussion starter, or for your own enjoyment.

On the stage you're exploring the limits of yourself. How loud and how strong and how big and how wide is the human entity? How much are we like giants and kings?

Ruby Dee, Actor

Discussion Questions

The following questions are intended to tap into students' **prior knowledge** and attitudes about the subject matter of the unit.

- What do people get out of a theatre experience?

- How would you describe your unique creativity?

- What do you do to relax? How does your body feel when it is relaxed?

- Have you ever participated in an organized sport of any kind? What did you or your teammates do to prepare for a game?

- What do you think of when you hear the term *warm-up?* How do you think this phrase can be applied to theatre?

- Who is your favorite athlete or dancer? What qualities does that person display in performance?

- Some people experience the world primarily through their eyes. Others are more attuned to smells or sounds. What sense do you feel predominates in your experience of the world?

- What is the most vivid sense memory you can call up at will?

- Was there a time when someone's body language tipped you off to what they were thinking? Explain.

- What do you think your physical presence communicates about you?

- What have you experienced as the advantages and disadvantages of working with partners?

ACTivity Gather the students to pose for a group picture. First, ask them to pose for a formal shot. Then have them pose for an informal shot. You also may want to challenge the students to pose as a group of characters from a particular play.

Theatre Journal

Suggest that students choose one of the characters in the photograph on this page and write a short biography of this character. Then have them compare their biography to those of their classmates.

Visual Cue

The image above shows a scene from the New York production of *Rent.* Based on the opera *La Boheme, Rent* was written by composer Jonathan Larson, who died at 35 of an aneurysm the night before the musical made its off-Broadway debut. *Rent* won both the Tony Award and the Pulitzer Prize in 1996. The following prompts can be used to exercise **critical viewing skills.**

- Describe the people in the picture. What can you tell about them based on their costumes?

- Study the picture, then close your eyes and try to describe three of the people in it.

ACTivity Have the students describe the positioning of the actors on stage. Then have them work in groups of five to come up with and demonstrate a unique and appealing placement of actors singing together.

Chapter 1

The Theatre and You

This chapter asks students to explore the idea of creativity and identify creative processes in theatre and in their own lives.

Objectives

1 to recognize creativity in self and others

2 to recognize theatre as a creative art form

3 to recognize theatre's social value and influence on society

4 to use memory in a creative context

Project Specs

This chapter requires students to create performances using their own personal memories. In the case of highly sensitive students, this may feel a bit invasive. Stress that the choice of what to include is strictly their own and that they should share only personal information they are comfortable with others knowing.

ELL Support

The concepts may be complex to communicate to some English Language Learners. Make time to give these students a bit more in-depth instruction, and use The Language of Theatre feature with them for additional support.

On Your Feet

Knock, Knock. Before you begin the activity, ask students what live sounds they might use to create an interesting rhythm pattern. Responses might include finger snapping, knocking, stomping, toe tapping, drumming, and more. Then, as you move through the activity, ask students to use all these sounds and add different monosyllabic sounds or words to enhance the percussive elements.

Chapter

1 The Theatre and You

Think about a time when you had a moment of pure inspiration—when a new idea or solution suddenly occurred to you out of nowhere. These moments can seem almost magical, yet creativity is a natural part of every person's life. Creativity is also a cornerstone of personal expression in the arts, including theatre.

Project Specs

Project Description For this project, you will create and perform a one- to three-minute presentation based on three powerful personal memories.

Purpose to recognize links among creativity, individuality, and performance

Materials a list of three memories that serve as the basis of your presentation; the Theatre and You Activity Sheet your teacher provides

On Your Feet

Your teacher will start a simple vocal rhythm accompanied by clapping, knocking, or stomping. Next, the whole group picks up the rhythm and keeps it going. Then the teacher points to someone to take a turn creating a brand new beat, which the whole group then picks up. When the beat becomes firmly established, the second person points to someone else, and so on. Be ready to change the beat when your turn comes. **Collaborate** with your classmates to work as an **ensemble** by listening, concentrating fully, and moving smoothly from one rhythm to the next.

Theatre Terms

collaborate
creativity
empathy
ensemble
ephemeral
immediacy
performing arts
set
technical elements

Theatre Terms

collaborate to work jointly with another person or group to produce or create something

creativity ability to discover or invent something

empathy ability to relate to feelings that are experienced by someone else

ensemble a group that performs together to achieve an overall effect

ephemeral lasting only a short time

immediacy directness

performing arts artistic processes that are performed in front of an audience

set stage environment

technical elements effects in a performance that are not created by the onstage performers, including lighting, recorded sound, costuming, etc.

The Theatre as an Art Form

The art of theatre has been around since the dawn of human history. At first, theatre was ritual based and had more to do with religion than entertainment. Theatre as we think of it in Western culture began with the Greeks about 2,500 years ago when civic festivals made a transition from publicly performed religious rites to the form we now identify as plays. Since then the art of theatre has bounced in and out of public favor—sometimes revered as high-culture and other times declared illegal and shunned by "proper" society. Even today, some people question the value of theatre. Defenders of the art, however, know that it inspires individuals to heights of greatness in all aspects of theatre and allows people to understand themselves, others who are different from them, and society in a uniquely empathic way.

The Performing Arts

Theatre is one of the performing arts, along with music and dance. What separates these from other art forms is that they are **ephemeral**, meaning that what the artist creates in front of an audience does not exist beyond the performance. Unlike visual arts such as drawing, painting, and sculpture—or literary arts such as poetry or prose—the performing arts leave no physical trace. Once a performance is over, it lives on only in the hearts and minds of those who performed and those who observed.

Analyzing the Arts Within an Art

While watching a play, audiences are usually focused on the actors and storyline. Whether they realize it or not, however, they are at the same time responding to the work of offstage artists who created the production's **technical elements**. For example, the stage environment, or **set**—whether it depicts a living room, a cornfield, or the surface of the moon—is the result of hours of work by the set designer. The lighting designer's contribution doesn't simply make the stage visible; it also provides subtle information about the play's time period, place, mood, and tone. Each technical element—set, lights, costumes, props, special effects, sound, painted backdrops, make-up, masks, and more—is an art unto itself, carefully crafted to blend and be interdependent with the other production elements and enrich the audience's understanding of the play.

Elements in Art Forms

Each art form relies on its own elements to communicate. You can compare and contrast them below. In many theatrical productions, all the arts play a role in communicating meaning.

- **Visual arts:** Color, shape, line, texture, form, light, shadow, medium (paint, chalk, photography, sculpture, for example), perspective, subject matter

- **Music:** Pitch, rhythm, melody, harmony, dissonance, instrumentation or vocal arrangement, lyrics, dynamics, structure, imitation, tempo

- **Dance:** Movement, parts of the body, gestures, choreography, music, rhythm, story, direction, pace, physicality

- **Film:** Color, camera angle, editing, different kinds of shots (long, close-up, establishing), story, acting, music, structure, perspective

Chapter 1 The Theatre and You **5**

The Theatre as an Art Form

Tell students that an audience enters the theatre as a group of individuals. But by the end of the show they have all taken part in a communal experience.

They have provided the actors with their attention and their emotional responses. They, this group of individual audience members, have bonded with each other and with the performers and formed a small one-night-only family.

Elicit class discussion on students' feelings about the responsibility they have as audience members.

The Performing Arts

Ask students to discuss the differences between what they feel and see in a theatre setting as opposed to film and television. They should compare and contrast what each has to offer in terms of immediacy, intimacy, action, spectacle, storytelling, and so on. You might want to create a chart on the board and list their observations.

Resource Binder

- Student Contract, TIPack, p. A
- Letter to Parents or Caregivers, TIPack, p. B
- Dealing with Stage Fright, TIPack, p. C
- The Theatre and You Activity Sheet, p. 4
- Theatre Elements Worksheet, p. 5
- Critique Sheet: Three Powerful Memories, p. 6
- The Theatre and You Test, p. 7

To Have on Hand

- Copies of scenes from Tennessee Williams's *The Glass Menagerie* and Athol Fugard's *Master Harold . . . and the Boys*.
- Video or DVD versions of one or both plays.

Theatre as Mirror

Read aloud Tom's opening monologue from *The Glass Menagerie*. Ask the class to discuss the information Tom doles out to the audience here, as he reveals both the particular onstage world and the historical backdrop of the play. For example,

- How does he describe the larger world? What has been going on in American society at the time of Tom's memory?
- What details does he reveal about himself, his family, and his deeply held beliefs about the world?
- What technical elements does he mention?

To guide students toward the chapter project, ask them to think about what the opening words of their own memory play might consist of. What might they want to tell an audience right at the outset?

Theatre as Mirror

Although theatre shares some traits with the other performing arts, it is unique in one important way. It is the only art form where the means of communication and the subject are one and the same. In other words, theatre is about human beings—their feelings and actions—presented by human beings in the presence of other human beings. As such, theatre is the live performance medium that most closely mirrors our day-to-day lives. The **immediacy** and intimacy of the live theatre experience allow audiences to imagine the world through new eyes and to develop kinship with and empathy for other people and places.

Here's an example. Imagine you're sitting in a darkened auditorium. As the lights come up onstage, an actor enters and begins to give a bit of the background of the play you're watching. In the play, the time is the late 1930s, and Americans are still suffering the aftershocks of the Great Depression. The actor, playing a character named Tom, goes on to talk about two of the other characters in this play—his mother, Amanda, and his sister Laura. He lets you know that this story will be told from his own point of view, that it is in fact a "memory play." Eventually he steps into an area you realize is a room from his past, where you soon meet the other people he has described. So begins one of the best-loved plays in American theatre history, Tennessee Williams' *The Glass Menagerie*. By the time the actor begins to interact with the other characters, you and the rest of the audience are fully engaged. Sitting together in the dark, you have all been taken back in time, transported to another place, another family—directly into someone else's personal and cultural memory, in fact—a very different world from your own, yet recognizable and relatable.

Tom Wingfield (Hans Fleischmann) and Amanda Wingfield (Maggie Cain) in *The Glass Menagerie* at Mary-Arrchie Theatre Co. (Chicago, 2013) Projection Design by Anna Henson.

Totally Quotable ...

"I regard the theatre as the greatest of all art forms, the most immediate way in which a human being can share with another the sense of what it is to be a human being."

—playwright Oscar Wilde

Broadway production of
Master Harold . . . and the Boys

The Social Value of Theatre

Theatre can help you understand aspects of your own life by taking you inside other cultures as well. South African playwright Athol Fugard's play *Master Harold . . . and the Boys*, for example, portrays an encounter between two black waiters and an entitled white teenager to reveal some ugly truths about South Africa during the time of institutionalized racism known as apartheid. Fugard's play was banned in his homeland when apartheid was still the law, so the play was first produced at Yale Repertory in New Haven, Connecticut, in 1982. Soon after that, the play moved to Broadway, where it ran for 344 performances. A battle cry against apartheid, Fugard's play became a global sensation. While *Master Harold . . .* was certainly not the reason apartheid was abolished in 1990, the play's blunt discussion of the loss of dignity and humanity of apartheid did help to open eyes and minds all over the world.

Theatre's Influence and Role

As the example of *Master Harold . . . and the Boys* demonstrates, theatre has a role in influencing our values. A theatrical production draws audience members into the drama and by so doing engages both the emotions and the intellect. Audiences watching the musical *Les Misérables,* for example, sympathize with the characters facing injustice and in so doing heighten their awareness of injustice more generally. Live theatre also influences personal values as it displays for all the world to see the glories and shames of humans and all the gray areas in between.

Live theatre also plays a role in everyday cultural life. Popular plays spawn reactions from other art forms and are also referred to in parodies that appear in such shows as *Saturday Night Live* or *The Simpsons*.

The Social Value of Theatre

Explain to students that *apartheid* is an Afrikaans word meaning "the state of being apart" or "aparthood." In South Africa, apartheid, which is depicted to dramatic effect in *Master Harold . . . and the Boys,* lasted from 1948 until 1994. The laws separating whites and blacks reached into every aspect of society. Whites made up the ruling class, while blacks were considered and treated as the lowest rung of the social ladder.

Ask students to think about the title of Fugard's play as they study the photo on this page. The following prompt can be used to exercise **critical viewing skills.**

- In this shot of a curtain call from the play, does Master Harold (left) appear to be the dominant character? Explain your answer.

Theatre's Influence and Role

Remind students that part of the theatre's influence stems from the fact that it gives audiences a compressed view of life. After all, we go to the theatre to see ourselves reflected, but we don't go to see smaller versions of human behavior. We go to see people doing big things and taking chances we ourselves perhaps would not. As Alfred Hitchcock once put it, "Drama is life with the dull bits cut out."

Totally Quotable ...

"The theatre was created to tell people the truth about life and the social situation."

—actor and teacher Stella Adler

"The theatre on its own can't and doesn't change society, but plays can define a moment. The Marriage of Figaro did seem to predict a revolution, but I doubt it sent anybody into the streets."

—director Nicholas Hytner

You as a Creative Being

Remind students that while some of them might not consider themselves creative, every person has natural creative ability. For example, though they might not be playwrights, each person in the room creates an entire day's worth of dialogue every day as a normal part of living and interacting with others. Creating flip videos, posting on social media, and working on new projects for school, home, work, or hobby—each of these things requires some degree of creativity.

A Few Traits of Creative People

Elicit student discussion of their own experiences in the context of these traits. Then ask volunteers to interpret the following quotes from well-known creative people.

- "Every child is an artist; the problem is staying an artist when you grow up." –Pablo Picasso, artist
- "Imagination is the beginning of creation. You imagine what you desire, you will what you imagine, and at last, you create what you will." –George Bernard Shaw, playwright
- "Creativity is just connecting things. When you ask creative people how they did something, they feel a little guilty because they didn't really do anything–they just saw something. It seemed obvious to them after a while."   –Steve Jobs, entrepreneur and inventor

You as a Creative Being

Renowned 20th-century Russian theatre director Konstantin Stanislavski once wrote, "Love the art in yourself, not yourself in art." His words encourage actors to pursue their creative goals not for the praise they might receive but out of love and respect for their art. In another sense, though, loving "the art in yourself" might be taken to mean accessing your own **creativity** in the name of personal expression.

A Few Traits of Creative People

- Deep curiosity
- Ability to concentrate and problem solve
- Ability to think outside the box
- Drive to succeed
- Willingness to take risks including possible failure

So what is creativity? Simply put, it is the ability to discover or invent something original. A moment of creativity might result in something as significant as a revolutionary scientific theory or as ordinary as a delicious new sandwich variety.

Creativity in personal expression can reveal itself in all kinds of ways, depending on a person's talents, temperament, background, and outside interests. One person may have the natural disposition and interpersonal and verbal skills to connect easily to the role of an actor. Another may have no interest or aptitude whatsoever for being onstage, but may instead have the skills needed for set design or maskmaking. To analyze, explore, and evaluate your own creativity, consider your special strengths. Do you tend to excel in the visual dimension with drawings and graphics? Or are you more comfortable with language, showing your strength in writing, speaking, and listening? Are you very logical, depending on reason and

Historical Note: Masks in Ancient Greece

Refer students to the photo at the bottom of this page. Tell them that masks have been part of theatrical tradition since the earliest days of Greek theatre. At that time, theatrical performances featured from one to three actors, and each actor used a variety of masks to switch back and forth among multiple characters. Theatre was performed in enormous outdoor spaces called *amphitheatres*, which were similar to today's sports stadiums. This meant that the features of each mask had to be greatly exaggerated so as to be seen by even distant audience members. Ask students to discuss the various uses of masks in contemporary theatre and culture.

calculation to solve problems? Sometimes people overlook the talents they actually have because they are overly focused on the things they don't do well, or they fear they might fail. But successful professionals from all walks of life will tell you that taking any truly creative step means risking failure. The trick is to keep trying and not let failure derail your efforts. That perseverance requires self-discipline—the ability to overcome personal weaknesses to do what is required. It also requires artistic discipline—the commitment to studying your art and expressing your creativity in increasingly developed ways.

The Personal Value of Theatre

Studying and participating in theatre and theatre-related courses can help you develop your creativity, but it can also improve your academic skills. You may find that the theatre connects to and enhances your understanding of social studies, history, current events, psychology, and many other subjects.

Theatre, like literature, can also help you gain insights into yourself and be sensitive to other people. When you watch a play, you identify with the characters, vicariously experiencing what they experience and in that way stretching your powers of empathy. In a similar way, when you act in a play, you delve inside the characters and learn what makes them tick—again building on your ability to empathize. Such deep understanding can influence your own behavior if you find yourself in situations similar to those portrayed in drama.

The Language of
THEATRE

Work with a partner to express ideas and feelings as you prepare the chapter project.

- Use single words or short phrases to express ideas and feelings about a strong memory. Add gestures and facial expressions to help express the *immediacy* of the memory.

- Use complete sentences to express ideas and feelings about your chosen memories. Say how the memories spark your *creativity*.

- Practice a presentation of one of your chosen memories with your partner. Express your feelings in a way that creates *empathy*.

- After choosing your three memories, have an extended discussion about the ideas and feelings you want to express. Use the discussion as a way to *collaborate* on your presentations.

As a quick creativity exercise, have students to look at the photo for a few moments. What is the girl in the photo doing? Why? What does the flower in her mouth represent? Based on her expression, is she tearing her hair out or simply pushing it back from her face? What does her expression signify? Ask students to create a caption for the photo. There are no right or wrong answers here. Student interpretations can be silly, serious, or somewhere in between. Ask for volunteers to read their captions aloud.

The Personal Value of Theatre

Challenge students to think about characters in plays they have seen or read that have made them feel empathy. Remind them that empathy, the ability to share a specific emotional state with another person, is different from sympathy, which is simple concern for the well-being of another person without a shared emotional state. For example, when you feel sympathy for someone in pain, you might feel sorry for him or her and wish the pain would go away; if you feel empathy for that person, you imagine yourself in similar circumstances feeling the same thing he or she does.

The Language of
THEATRE

Let students know that listening carefully is one key to positive in-class partner interactions. During the preparation period for this chapter project, remind them that if they fail to understand something a partner says, they should politely ask to have the statement repeated or clarified.

From the Field: The Heart of Art

I've noticed that there is always a group of kids who, while not stellar students in other areas, shine when it comes to acting, directing, painting, and just plain creating. Students need theatre, and the arts in particular, to have this place to shine, to know that they can make positive contributions, and to understand how art impacts not only the brain, but the soul.

Steve Jones, Teacher, Hartford, Connecticut

Career Focus

Go through the items in the Career Focus feature with students. Encourage them to think at this point about what area of theatre (acting, writing, directing, criticism, design, stage crew) is most interesting to them. What skills and talents do they already possess that might help them excel in this area? For example, a student with skill at drawing, painting, or construction might gravitate to the technical or design side of theatre. If a student has leadership skills and strong interpersonal and interpretive skills, directing might turn out to be a good path. Make it clear that interests are just as important as natural talents and skills. Just because a person has never been in a play before doesn't mean that person lacks the means to become an actor.

Career Focus

Throughout this book, you'll read about higher education opportunities and careers that theatre skills can enhance. Here are just a few examples:

- Reading and discussing plays can help you build your powers of concentration, analysis, and critical thinking, which could serve you well in a career such as law, business, or politics.

- Performing in plays can improve your confidence, memory, and communication skills, all of which are needed in any career that requires public speaking, management, and teamwork.

- Understanding and working on the technical side of theatre such as stage scenery, costumes, lighting, or sound techniques can strengthen visual and theoretical skills that are key to careers including architecture, engineering, and design.

- Directing or coaching others builds empathy as well as leadership, collaboration, and team-building skills that are central to careers in business and management.

As you read about possible career opportunities, you may want to use a checklist like the one below to analyze and evaluate them.

For careers/avocations within the theatre

- Analyze and evaluate the training needed. Find out what specific training is needed. How might you go about getting that training? Have you had any such training already?

- Analyze and evaluate the skills needed. Look carefully at the skills you already have and those you will need. What will it take to attain those skills? What professionals might be able to give you more information about how to attain these skills?

- Analyze and evaluate the self-discipline needed. Do you have the self-discipline you need? What specific actions can you take to build your self-discipline?

- Analyze and evaluate the artistic discipline needed. Are you a person with strong artistic discipline? If not, how can you improve your discipline?

- Make judgments about a career after analyzing the training, skills, self-discipline, and artistic discipline it requires. Looking at everything you love to do, is theatre at the top of the list? Is a career in theatre what you want to be doing in ten years? twenty?

For careers/avocations beyond the theatre

- What skills and experiences gained in theatre can help you succeed in such careers as law, medicine, business, politics, and diplomacy?

For higher education beyond studies in theatre

- What skills and experiences gained in theatre can help you succeed in college or in another post-high school learning environment?

As you rack up accomplishments in this theatre class and any productions you take part in, hold onto artifacts of your work, such as photos, blueprints, and scripts. Use them to compile a résumé and portfolio that demonstrate your work.

Notes

_____
_____
_____
_____
_____
_____
_____
_____

PREPARE

Mine Your Memories

This project gives you a chance to explore your creativity as it relates to personal expression. You will use words, gestures, and facial expressions to create a presentation of three memories that have meaning or importance to you. First, take several minutes to write down some memories. Be creative and don't censor yourself. Work as quickly as you can, and try not to spend too much time on any single memory; at this point, you should only need a few words or phrases to solidify each one in your mind. Remember: these don't have to be the most important memories of your life. They are simply moments you remember clearly that have some special meaning.

When the time is up, select three memories from the list you created. Try to recall vivid details about each. Use your five senses to capture specific details in your mind. Think about how you will present them to the class. You can separate the three memories from one another in any way you like; the idea is to keep each one very specific and distinctive from the others. You may find it helpful to sketch out the order and other details about how you plan to present your work. Finally, come up with a title for your presentation.

PRESENT

Re-Create the Times of Your Life

When your turn comes, calmly enter the playing area. You can take your notes with you if you like. Give yourself a moment to breathe and center yourself. Stand up straight with your feet planted slightly apart. Try not to hold onto too much muscular tension, but bear in mind that a little bit of nervous energy can actually serve to strengthen your presentation. Introduce the title of your presentation, pause a moment, and begin. Try to enjoy sharing the memories. They are personal expressions of moments from your life, and that makes them important.

When you have finished, take a brief pause and then quietly leave the playing area. Remember that your presentation is not complete until you have returned to your seat.

PREPARE

Mine Your Memories

Encourage students to begin writing their lists of memories right away. Reassure them that the three memories they end up choosing from the list need be neither the greatest hits nor a trio of deepest, darkest moments. Often the simplest memories work best—playing baseball with friends, making a video for a class, or just hanging around the house on a hot summer day.

Tell them to think of this assignment as painting three small memory snapshots with words. Warn them that self-censorship is the single greatest obstacle to success with this project.

PRESENT

Re-Create the Times of Your Life

Remind students that their goal is to re-create their three memories with the class in a format of their own choosing. Some students may have performance anxiety and consequently need to read directly from their notes; others may go more fully into the performance aspects of the project, adding choreographed movements or sound effects to their descriptions. Any way students choose to depict their three memories is valid.

Using Sensory Images

A technique that some actors use to conjure emotional moments is sense memory, which allows them to recall and draw on the physical sensations surrounding a past emotional state or event, rather than the emotion itself.

Though students are not likely to select highly charged emotional memories for this project, tell them that using sensory images (those that use sight, hearing, smell, taste, and touch) will help them create more vivid moments.

CRITIQUE

Evaluate a Classmate's Presentation

Hand out the Critique Sheet for this project or have students use their own paper.

Discuss with students the rubrics that they will use to make their evaluations. Let them know that you will be assessing them using the same rubric and that you will also be paying attention to how well they assess each other's work.

As this is the first assignment, pay special attention to any students having difficulty presenting themselves in front of the class. Speak privately to these students about techniques they might use to make themselves more comfortable in this area.

CRITIQUE

Evaluate a Classmate's Presentation

As you watch your classmates' presentations, take notes on how effectively they illustrate their selected memories. How effectively were they able to take you inside those moments? Choose one presentation to evaluate. Consider both the successful and the not-so-successful aspects of the performance. Your evaluation should be based on a scale of 1 to 5, in which 1 means "needs much improvement" and 5 means "outstanding." As you craft your evaluation, ask yourself questions like the following.

- Did the presentation hold your interest and/or make you think of your own life?

- Were the three memories specific and distinct from one another? Were the transitions between the three memories clear?

- Was the presentation focused and well paced?

- Did the presenter speak clearly?

- Did the movements add interest and/or clarity to the presentation?

- Was the presentation the correct length?

Write a paragraph defending your scoring.

Remind the class that critiquing a fellow student's presentation depends on both honesty and empathy. It can be difficult to negotiate this balance, but fairness is key. As author Edgar Allan Poe once put it, "In criticism I will be bold, and as sternly, absolutely just with friend and foe. From this purpose nothing shall deter me."

Additional Projects

1 In small groups, define, identify, analyze, and evaluate your individual creativity. Also provide feedback to your group members about strengths you see in them. Discuss ways in which each person could express and explore his or her creativity in theatre class and in a theatrical production. For example, students who excel in visual arts could bring their creativity to the design of sets and props.

2 Imagine a room in your home as a possible setting for a play. Think about elements of this room that reflect the particular time, place, culture, and relationships of the people in your household. Analyze aspects of the room such as architecture, furniture style, lighting, and decorations including art, photographs, or knickknacks. Write a brief summary with a conclusion that portrays theatre as a reflection of particular times, places, and cultures.

3 Work with a partner to create a PowerPoint presentation recognizing, analyzing, and defending the value and power of theatre as an art form. In your presentation, analyze the elements of the art of theatre. Look for examples of how theatre may have influenced values and behavior in everyday life.

4 Using computer graphics or art supplies, create a poster or chart analyzing and evaluating how theatre training in specific disciplines such as acting, directing, or technical theatre might prepare a person to work and interact effectively in different careers or fields of study.

5 Read the scene between Nora and her husband in *A Doll's House* by Henrik Ibsen found in Unit Eight. Analyze this scene in terms of what it reveals about the time period and culture in which the characters live.

6 Analyze and research the impact and influence of live theatre on contemporary society. Synthesize your findings in an essay about whether or not theatre has the ability to bring about social change. Give clear reasons for your view.

7 Theatre Journal Think of three works of art that you know well in different mediums. For example, you might know Vincent Van Gogh's painting *Starry Night*, the movie *The Hobbit: The Desolation of Smaug*, and *The Nutcracker* ballet. In your journal, compare and contrast the elements each work uses to communicate. Refer to the chart on page 5 for ideas.

The Theatre and You Test

The test for this chapter is available in blackline master form in the Resource Binder, page 7.

For More Information

Books
Cameron, Julie, *The Artist's Way*, Tarcher, 2002.

Lamott, Anne. *Bird by Bird: Some Instructions on Writing and Life*, Anchor Books, 1995.

Other Media
21st Century Skills: Promoting Creativity and Innovation in the Classroom, DVD, Association for Supervision and Curriculum Development, 2009.

Apps
Evernote
Idea Sketch
lino
Paper by FiftyThree
Popplet
SyncSpace

Theatre Journal
If appropriate, encourage students to keep their journals digitally. Free online journal tools are widely available, as are a variety of apps for various mobile devices. Students can also check their word-processing programs to find out if journal templates are included.

Substitute Teacher Activities

The suggestions below are intended for the substitute teacher when you are out of the classroom for a day or two.

- Assign the Theatre Elements Worksheet on page 5 of the Resource Binder.

- Assign students one or more of the Additional Projects on this page.

- Have students work in pairs. Ask them to use four to six memories (two to three from each of them) to create a collaborative memory collage.

Chapter 2

Warm Up

This chapter introduces students to the basics of relaxing and warming up before rehearsing or performing. An effective performer has a flexible body and a pliable mind. The relaxation techniques and warm-up exercises students learn now will be useful throughout their lives.

Objectives

1 to develop and practice preparation and warm-up techniques

2 to increase flexibility and body control

3 to improve articulation

4 to create and perform a two- to three-minute warm-up routine

Project Specs

Explain to students that most disciplines, even those as diverse as auto mechanic, weaver, and mountain climber, require the right tools and proper guidelines. These are known as *specifications,* or *specs.* In this book, the specs for each project are listed on the first page of the chapter.

Special Needs Students

Note that students who are physically challenged may need to have some exercise and warm-up routines modified for their use.

On Your Feet

Choose one of the tongue twisters and demonstrate it for the class. You may want to have a competition in which students take turns saying a tongue twister clearly as many times as possible. Students who can say a given tongue twister three times quickly without an error enter "playoffs." The winner is declared "Twister Wizard."

Chapter

2 Warm Up

Actors relax and warm up in order to be alert and responsive as they perform. Warm-ups help increase the actor's ability to direct the nervous energy that arises before going onstage. By relaxing and warming up before a performance, you too can safely prepare your voice and body for the strenuous work ahead.

Project Specs

Project Description You and a partner will create and perform a two- to three-minute warm-up routine using techniques and exercises learned in class.

Purpose to develop and practice preparation and warm-up techniques that help increase flexibility, body control, relaxation, and vocal articulation

Materials loose-fitting, comfortable clothing; a list of the elements in your routine or the Warm-Up Activity Sheet your teacher provides

On Your Feet

To begin exercising clear speech, or **articulation,** try to say one or more of the following tongue twisters rapidly without mispronouncing any words:

- Two teamsters tried to tag twenty-two keys.
- She makes a proper cup of coffee in a copper coffee pot.
- Red leather, yellow leather, red leather, yellow leather (repeat)
- Would Wheeler woo Wanda while Woody snoozed woozily?

Theatre Terms

adrenaline
articulation
pliable
professionals
routine
stage fright
vocalizing

Theatre Terms

adrenaline a hormone that produces the feeling of sudden increased energy

articulation the clear pronunciation of words

pliable supple, flexible

professionals people who make a living in their chosen line of work

routine a series of actions that may be repeated

stage fright feeling nervous before or during a performance

vocalizing singing without words

PREVIEW

The Actor Prepares

Like all disciplined **professionals,** good actors make what they do look effortless. They seem to inhabit the characters they play. Their bodies, minds, voices, and emotions are their tools, and they use them expertly to create the effects they desire. Some actors undergo rigorous physical training to maximize their capabilities onstage. Some do not. However, all serious actors warm up before rehearsals and performances. This preparation will help them to be alert and responsive to stage directions, other actors, and their own physical, mental, and emotional needs.

Actors who warm up become alert and physically prepared for the demands

Actors warm up before a performance.

of acting. They also direct the normal nervous energy that arises before a performance. Instead of spiraling into fright, actors who loosen up can put increased energy into the demands of their roles and the performance at hand.

Actors are often called upon to perform very vigorous movement, such as dancing, fighting, or wrestling. Singing, yelling, and other **vocalizing** may also be called for. If you learn these skills and practice them as part of your everyday **routine,** your voice and body will become strong, **pliable,** or adaptable, and disciplined, and they will be safe from strain. As a bonus, you will be ready and qualified for that physically demanding, once-in-a-lifetime role.

Why Warm Up?

Just as athletes do not take to the court or the field without doing warm-up exercises, neither do actors. The warm-ups help you in a number of ways: they relax you, they help clear your mind, and they prepare you to use your voice and body effectively and safely. In other words, they take the nervous energy that arises naturally and put it to work as you portray your character onstage. Additionally, these exercises build confidence and expand your range of communication and movement. Gaining mastery over your body's expressive ability can be exhilarating. It also helps you appreciate the work of those actors who make it look easy.

Chapter 2 Warm Up   **15**

Resource Binder

- Dealing with Stage Fright, TIPack, p. C
- Warm Up Activity Sheet, p. 8
- Trust Exercises Worksheet, p. 9
- Critique Sheet: Warm-up Routine, p. 10
- Warm Up Test, p. 11

> **Handbook Connections**
> pages 567–568, 572, 577–578

To Have on Hand

- Extra sweatshirts and sweatpants for students who are not dressed for physical activity
- Prize for the winner of the tongue-twister challenge
- CD or MP3 player for those who want to put routines to music
- A large mirror students can look in when trying a new movement or position

---

PREVIEW

The Actor Prepares

Discuss the fact that actors must rely on the body, mind, and voice as the tools and instruments of their craft. Unlike other crafts, in which a person can get a new tool whenever one is needed, the actor can only improve his or her instrument by honing personal skills.

Ask students who play a sport to demonstrate things they do to warm up before playing. Ask the same question of students who play a musical instrument or sing. Then discuss the similarities between the various warm-ups.

Why Warm Up?

Talk to students about the many injuries that athletes and dancers suffer each year. Discuss how warming up can prevent such injuries. Tell students that muscular stiffness disappears as the body is conditioned and that awkwardness subsides also.

Show, Don't Tell Because some students may think that athletic ability is required of them, demonstrate an effective stretching routine that almost anyone can do. Encourage the students to copy your moves. If you have a daily exercise routine, teach it to your students. Invite students who dance or practice yoga or the martial arts to talk about what they enjoy about these endeavors.

Visual Cue

Use these prompts to help students exercise **critical viewing skills.**

- Where do the people in the picture appear to be?
- How close to actually performing do you think they were when photographed?
- Do you think these actors are athletic? Why or why not?

Chapter 2 Warm Up   **15**

Relaxation Techniques

If technology is available, you might want to have students perform relaxation techniques to various kinds of music.

ACTivity Encourage students to suggest names for the poses they take while performing the relaxation techniques and the warm-ups. Tell them that in yoga, particular poses are often named for animals.

ACTivity **Beginning Students** To encourage slow movements, have students perform the rag doll technique to the count of ten and the head movements to a count of five or more. Remind students that moving slowly helps avoid injuries. At the end of these movements, students should gently shake out their right wrist, left wrist, right ankle, left ankle, and so on to a count of four.

ACTivity **Advanced Students** Invite students to suggest alterations or adaptations that will help them maximize stretches safely. Mention again that some people find motivation in moving to music or naming positions so that they are easy to visualize and remember.

Warm-up Exercises

Relaxation techniques are different from warm-up exercises. Warm-up exercises are best done after putting the body into a relaxed state; therefore, they usually come after relaxation techniques. Some movement specialists recommend doing relaxation techniques both before and after warm-ups.

Show, Don't Tell Demonstrate breathing in to a count of four while swinging your arms slowly forward, then breathing out to a count of four while swinging arms slowly backward. This heightens relaxation during warm-ups by controlling the breath during the exercises.

The following warm-up routines will prepare you physically and vocally for the stage—and for the demands of everyday life.

Relaxation Techniques

- With feet apart in a comfortable balance, stretch up tall. Then bend over like a rag doll by rolling down slowly, beginning with your head. Hang loosely from the waist with your relaxed arms and hands dangling to the floor. Keep your arms, hands, and head completely relaxed. Slowly roll back up, keeping relaxed. Repeat.

- Breathe in as your teacher or director counts to eight. Take a deep breath, bringing air in through your nose, then into your throat, your chest, and your lungs. Feel your middle expand as your breath fills your body. Then breathe out slowly through your mouth for the count of eight. Repeat several times.

The rag doll: Stretch and collapse gently.

- With your neck relaxed and your chin close to your chest, slowly move your head to the left, back to the front, to the right, and up. Then reverse the rotation. Be sure to move very slowly and cautiously. Keep your neck relaxed, letting your head slowly roll like a dead weight in a socket.

- Lie quietly on your back. Close your eyes and make your mind a blank slate. Chase all thoughts away, concentrating only on relaxing your body. Listen to the rhythm of your heartbeat as, one at a time, you relax every part of your body—from your toes, to your legs and arms, and up to your head. Feel your body melt into the floor. Remain in this relaxed position for a few moments before you begin your warm-up exercises.

Warm-up Exercises

- Swing your relaxed arms in large circles, one at a time.

- Lie on your back and tuck in your knees, holding them to your chest with your hands. Roll gently from side to side. Do this ten times.

From the Field: Don't Look at Me!

Relaxation techniques can also be strong self-awareness tools. A few years ago I began having my students face each other for five to seven minutes and just look into one another's eyes. For many students, all the tension goes out of the body as they establish a connection to the other.

The first time I tried this exercise, though, two of my students kept clenching their fists. I thought perhaps they were nervous, but then they both said they had become increasingly angry. For them, this was not a relaxation technique at all—but a tension-builder! After some discussion, we realized that all the staring must have elicited a fight response.

It was an insightful moment in which the whole class got to explore the range of human responses.

Patti Interrante, Assistant Professor of Speech and Theatre, Oakton College, Des Plaines, Illinois

- Sit on your ankles, keeping your back straight. Stretch up, with your arms extended, as high as you can go. Keep your body straight. Do this four times.

- Use your entire body to draw huge numbers, from one to ten, in the air. Use as much space as you can. Bend, stretch, and travel around the room as you write. Do this for about three minutes.

- Play "imaginary jump rope." By yourself or with two partners (to hold the imaginary rope), jump an imaginary rope until you are tired. You might want to try using a few different rhythms, changing your jumping pattern accordingly—alternating feet together and feet apart, and so on.

- Lie on your back and then extend your entire lower body into a shoulder stand, placing your hands on your back and your elbows on the floor. Stay in this position for a count of twenty. Next, roll your legs back and over your head, letting your feet touch the floor. Keep your legs straight. Only go back as far as is comfortable. Then one vertebra at a time until you are flat on your back again. Repeat.

- Stand with your feet slightly apart. Begin to shake your hands. Shake them more and more vigorously. When your teacher yells, "Freeze!" stop all movement. Then begin to tense the same muscles in your hands. Repeat this exercise several times.

- Stretch your tongue. Try to touch the tip of your tongue to your nose. Don't be discouraged if you can't do it—only one in 1000 people can. Repeat several times.

When in a play, create your own warm-ups to suit your role. If your character sword fights, you may want to prepare with warm-ups based on lunges and broad arm movements. Check with a coach to make sure your warm-up is safe.

Be careful to keep your back straight as you do this exercise. Do not overdo it.

ACTivity Some students may struggle with anxiety and others may suffer from boredom while doing slow, careful movements. To keep students focused and engaged, invite volunteers to give meaning to the movements by weaving a story around them.

Vocabulary Enhancement

It can be helpful for students to understand something about anatomy in order to exercise properly. For example, those who lead theatrical warm-ups often tell actors to stretch and bend one vertebra at a time. *Vertebrae* are the individual small bones that comprise the backbone.

Similarly, voice teachers often advise actors where to place the tongue in relation to the *palate*. The palate is the roof of the mouth. The bony part is known as the *hard palate* and the soft part is known as the *soft palate*.

Notes

_____

_____

_____

_____

_____

_____

_____

_____

Here's How

Remind students that even something as simple as a warm-up activity can be dangerous without some attention to safety. Invite them to discuss the first two bullet points in greater detail. Reinforce the idea that breathing and relaxation techniques should play a role in any warm-up routine. Encourage students to think of warm-up combinations that warm up the voice and the body simultaneously. For example they might: Take a deep breath and then let it out in an elongated "ahhhh" sound, while gently bending their knees.

Vocal Exercises

Show, Don't Tell To encourage a sense of camaraderie, have students stand in a circle while doing these exercises. The circle shape keeps the atmosphere relaxed and the interaction intimate. Join the circle and demonstrate each vocal exercise for the students before asking them to try it.

It might help some students to do the "ahhh" and "oooo" sounds by thinking about making as big a face as possible for the "ahhh" and as small a face as possible for the "oooo."

ACTivity Challenge students to try an activity called "chewing your face." Demonstrate exaggerated stretches while going through the vowels: AAA—EEE—III—OOO—UUU.

Invite students to try these exercises with and without sound.

If your students enjoy tongue twisters, give them a few more:

• Unique New York
• Tie twine to three tree twigs.
• Four furious friends fought for the phone.

If time permits, challenge students to develop and teach the class their own tongue twisters.

Here's How
To Stay Safe in the Theatre

Throughout this book, you will encounter information on ways to stay safe in your dramatic and theatrical work. As an overview, however, take note of the following safe and appropriate theatre practices and their importance in successful theatre experiences.

• To avoid physical strain and injury, always do warm-ups before a performance. Demonstrate safe use of your body both in class and out.

• Protect your voice through vocal warm-ups.

• Express your character's emotions safely. If your character breaks dishes in a rage, work out ahead of time with the props crew how to perform this act safely with specially designed dishes.

• Devise sets and stage movements that limit the possibilities of trips or falls.

• Handle all props safely and be sure they are in good repair.

• If you are part of a technical crew, know the safety issues of the area in which you are working—construction, lights, sound, costumes, makeup.

Serious injuries can result if you do not take safety in the theatre seriously at all times. Note all the safety information you will find in this book and never take chances that could put you or your theatre team in any danger.

Vocal Exercises

• Smile! Smile with great exaggeration, letting your teeth show and drawing your lips as tightly as possible. Say "eeeee." Then exaggerate a pucker and say "ooooo." Repeat these two motions and sounds ten times in quick succession. Then add consonants to create sound combinations such as "me-moo," "tee-too," "bee-boo," "gee-goo," and "lee-loo."

• Begin a slow yawn and make the sound "ahhhh" as you exhale. Remember the open quality of the sound you are making. Aim for it in all your speech.

• Open wide. Open your mouth as wide as possible. Say "ahhh" as you exhale. Now close your mouth, saying "oooo" as you exhale. Repeat "ahhh-oooo" several times. Take care to open your mouth as wide as possible.

• Read the rhyme below with clarity and emphasis. Start off slowly, then increase your speed as you read it two more times.

To sit in solemn silence in a dull dock
In a pestilential prison with a life long lock
Awaiting the sensation of a short sharp shock
From a cheap and chippy chopper on a big black block.
—W. S. Gilbert from *The Mikado*

Backstage Gossip: Acting 8, Basketball 3

Actor Cherry Jones once described a conversation with William Peterson about the rigors of theatrical performance, saying, "Billy Peterson, when we were doing *Night of the Iguana*, said, 'I think what we do is harder than what professional athletes do.' He said, 'Those basketball players only play three games a week. We play eight, back to back.'"

from *The Actor's Art*, edited by Jackson R. Bryer and Richard A. Davison

PREPARE

Work Out Your Warm-up Routine

Your teacher will assign you a partner or ask you to find a partner for this project. Have your partner read the various routines and exercises described on the previous pages while you follow the directions for doing them. Then you do the same for your partner. Repeat the exercises until you feel comfortable doing them all.

Together, decide whether you will use both physical and vocal elements to create your routine. Next, determine the order of the elements you will include for your two- to three-minute routine using a list or the Activity Sheet your teacher provides.

Plan how you will present the routine to the class: Will one of you instruct the class while the other demonstrates the routine? Will you both demonstrate the routine while you give instructions? Remember that you are demonstrating safe use of the body. Plan on pointing out safety matters while giving instructions.

You may want to use music to accompany your routine. If you do, be sure the music has the appropriate rhythm and mood for what you are trying to achieve.

When you have completely worked out your preparation and warm-up routine, time it to be sure it is no longer than three minutes and no shorter than two minutes. Practice at least five times before you actually present your routine.

PRESENT

Be the Instructor

When your turn comes, stand still for a second with your partner and take a deep breath, bringing air into your lungs. Introduce yourselves to the class and then demonstrate your routine. Encourage your classmates to join in the routine. Have fun, smile, and harness all that nervous energy!

When you are finished, pause and then quietly leave the playing area. Remember to maintain a sense of physical and vocal control from the time you leave the playing area until you return to your seat.

The Language of THEATRE

Listen closely as a teacher or partner speaks to distinguish sounds and intonation patterns using some of the theatre terms on page 14.

- Listen for the different *s* sounds and hear the difference between a statement and a question: *Professionals* design *dresses. Professionals* design *dresses?*

- Listen for the common sound that is found in the words *articulation* and *professionals*. Listen for the differences between a statement, a question, and a command in sentences using these words.

- Listen to the warm-up tongue twisters on page 14 that help exercise articulation. Distinguish the sounds that make each one a tongue twister. Identify whether they are statements or questions.

- Listen to and follow the instructions for the Vocal Exercises on page 18 as part of your warm-up routine project. How does the intonation in the instructions help you to follow them?

PREPARE

Work Out Your Warm-up Routine

Invite students to add music to their routines, as well as other physical elements not introduced in this book. Invite them to find additional elements through dance, yoga, martial arts, and other physical exercise programs. Have music available for their use.

ACTivity Students who have access to video and/or sound equipment can use that equipment to help them develop and rehearse their routines.

PRESENT

Be the Instructor

Students who have made a video of their routines can join the class as participants in following their own routines.

ACTivity Urge students to be active teachers. After demonstrating their routines, they can break them down into movements and teach each one to the class—first performing the movement and then asking the class to perform it.

Consider using students' warm-ups throughout the year, thereby demonstrating the usefulness of the assignment and reinforcing its importance in theatre.

The Language of THEATRE

Encourage everyone to speak clearly and distinctly to make it easier for all classmates to understand what they hear. Invite students to ask for words or phrases to be repeated if necessary to help them develop their understanding of spoken English.

Notes

_____

_____

_____

_____

_____

_____

_____

CRITIQUE

Compare Two Warm-up Routines

Hand out the Critique Sheet for this project or have students use their own paper. (You will probably want to have two Critique Sheets available, as the students are comparing two routines.) Be sure students understand that the critique activity involves several steps, including note-taking, scoring, and writing. It will be helpful to assign the two people each student will evaluate so that no one is overlooked.

Introduce students to the concept of the nonjudgmental critique. Critiquing is different from criticizing in that it is aimed at helping someone improve their performance rather than simply pointing out weaknesses. Therefore, it is a good idea for students to indicate what they like about a performance before making suggestions for improvement. Such suggestions should include ways to make a weak area as strong as the student's best work.

After you have reviewed students' critiques, trim off the evaluator's name and hand out the sheets to the subjects of the evaluations.

Spotlight on

Stage Fright Relaxation techniques and warm-ups do help alleviate stage fright, but in extreme cases students may want to try one or more of the following:

- After doing routine warm-ups, run in place for two to three minutes. The running will put some of the extra adrenaline to use.

- Some actors consciously try to exaggerate movements, such as shaking the knees or hands for a short period, in order to get those movements out of their systems.

- Never lock your knees or stiffen up when nervous. If you find yourself stiff in any way, tense and relax that part of the body.

CRITIQUE

Compare Two Warm-up Routines

As you watch your classmates' warm-up routines, take notes as to how well the routines are presented. Use a scale of 1 to 5, with 5 being "outstanding" and 1 being "needs much improvement." Ask yourself questions such as those below as you evaluate the routines.

- Were the instructions clear and easy to do?

- Did the instructors speak clearly?

- Was the routine the correct length?

- Was the routine effective in warming up and relaxing the participants?

- How would you use this routine to prepare for a performance?

Compare how well two separate pairs of presenters created and presented their routines. Write a paragraph explaining the reasons for the scores you gave.

Spotlight on

Stage Fright

According to a nationwide survey, speaking in front of others is the number one fear of Americans. We experience **stage fright**–dry mouth, shaky knees, trembling hands, sweaty palms, and queasy stomach–because we suspect we won't do well. Minor stage fright can be helpful to a performer because it releases extra **adrenaline,** a chemical our bodies produce to help us deal with unfamiliar situations. The surge of adrenaline provides the performer with increased energy, enthusiasm, and animation. A heightened sense of awareness is useful to the actor, but uncontrolled stage fright can derail a performer. Below are a few tips for managing stage fright.

Be Prepared. When we are prepared we automatically feel more comfortable and confident. If you find your hands are shaky or your mouth is dry, take a moment to remind yourself that you know exactly what you're doing.

Use Good Posture. Good posture provides a strong base for movement and vocal production. Your good posture will give the audience an impression of confidence–and it just might make you feel more confident as well.

Breathe. Don't forget to breathe! Inadequate breath can lead to a shaky voice and a feeling of physical insecurity. If necessary, take a couple of deep breaths to ground yourself before you begin speaking.

Give Yourself Time. Remember that most people who experience stage fright usually warm up after a short time. The more public speaking you do, the easier it becomes.

Backstage Gossip: The Reverse Kidnapping

It seems even college professors can succumb to stage fright. One summer Harold J. Kennedy employed a local college professor to perform in a production of *Captain Brassbound's Conversion*. He was thrilled to find that the professor was a marvelous actor. In fact, the professor had only one flaw: He had never overcome his stage fright.

On opening night, the professor entered on cue, opened his mouth, and—began shaking. He could not make words come out of his mouth. Actor Jane Cowl, who was supposed to be his kidnap victim, finally saved the day by asking, "Do you want to take me to the mountains?"

The professor nodded, dumbly, and Cowl took his hand. "Let's go!" she said, and ran with him off stage.

from *No Pickle, No Performance* by Harold J. Kennedy

Additional Projects

1. Say "ahhhhh." Sustain a comfortably pitched tone. Then create variations by increasing the volume, decreasing the volume, and bringing the volume back to start. Repeat with pitch: make the sound higher in pitch, then lower in pitch, then bring it back to start.

2. With a partner, carry on an animated conversation in gibberish or a pretend "foreign language," using only nonsense or invented words. If you find it difficult to make up words or sounds, use the syllables "da-da-shoon" repeatedly. Sincerely try to communicate through this new language.

3. Say a sentence such as "Now is the time," or "There goes the last one," in each of the following ways: sternly, eagerly, worriedly, soothingly, shyly, drowsily, angrily, sadly, and happily.

4. Imagine that you are a balloon. Blow yourself up. You can be completely inflated with three large inhalations. Expand in three stages, until you are completely expanded, like a balloon. Ask a partner or classmate to "pop" you. Then deflate as a balloon might.

5. With a partner, think of a scene from a play, movie, or book that has considerable movement in it. Some examples are a lightsaber fight from *Star Wars*, any dance from *Grease,* and the flight of the "fellowship" from the dragon in *The Lord of the Rings*. Discuss how you could prepare for that scene if you were acting in it. Then create a safe warm-up routine for those movements and practice it with your partner. Demonstrate your routine to the class.

6. Create a graphic showing safe theatre practices and their importance.

7. Memorize part of Biff's monologue from *Death of a Salesman* by Arthur Miller, found in Unit Eight. Imagine that Biff is doing sit-ups or bouncing a ball during the scene. Then perform the movements of this activity while speaking the lines from the scene. Allow the words to accompany the movement. If you prefer, memorize a monologue of your own choosing and work out your own activity to accompany it.

8. **Theatre Journal** Make a list of the things you do in your everyday life that could help prepare you for performing on the stage. Examples might be singing in the chorus or playing basketball. Write a short explanation of the ways in which these activities help you prepare both physically and emotionally.

> If possible, keep your journal digitally. You can find free online journal tools as well as apps for a variety of mobile devices. Many word processing programs also have templates for journals.

Warm Up Test

The test for this chapter is available in blackline master form in the Resource Binder, page 11.

For More Information

Books
West, Edie, *210 Icebreakers*, McGraw Hill, 1997.

Other Media
Borysenko, Joan, *The Beginner's Guide to Meditation,* Audio CD, Hay House, 2006.

Elaine, Tiffany, *Teen Tone,* DVD, Four Crossings Entertainment, 2007.

Get Real with Shaun T: Brand New Fun Workout Program Designed for Young People, DVD, Beachbody, [no date].

Kaminoff, Leslie, *Freeing the Breath: Health, Relaxation, and Clarity Through Better Breathing*, Audio CD, Sounds True, 2010.

Muldaur, Maria, *Developing Your Vocal Performing Style*, DVD, Homespun, 2005.

Pei, Chris, *Qi Gong for Beginners*, DVD, Body Wisdom, 2009.

Apps
Being in Voice
Yoga By Teens

Theatre Journal

Use the following as an additional or substitute prompt.

Make a list of the various stretches and movements involved in achieving the everyday actions, chores, and other activities you perform regularly.

Substitute Teacher Activities

Here are suggestions for one or more days when you will be out of the classroom:

- Assign the Trust Exercises Worksheet on page 9 of the Resource Binder.

- Discuss the information found in the Student Handbook concerning Physical Warm-ups (p. 572), Movement (pp. 567–568), and Voice (pp. 577–578).

- Assign one or more of the Additional Projects on this page.

- **Plan a Relaxation Teach-In**. Assign the students to groups and ask each group to research and select one good relaxation tip. Have each group present their tip. The class will then gather all these tips and create a series of relaxation techniques based upon them. The entire class can then practice these techniques together.

Chapter 3
Observation

This chapter introduces students to the discipline of observation. It awakens them to the power of the senses and the importance of memory in helping to create believable characters.

Objectives

1 to improve the memory

2 to strengthen the powers of observation

3 to practice recalling observed objects through the senses

4 to give a detailed description of an object

Project Specs

Special Needs Students
Researchers have determined that children learn in at least seven different ways. Many are predominantly visual, for example, while others are aural, tactile, or kinesthetic. The project designated for this chapter should prove rewarding for aural, tactile, or kinesthetic learners.

On Your Feet

Show, Don't Tell In order to demonstrate engagement of the senses and memory, allow students to choose an item in the room for you to observe. Have the students show you the object for one minute, then take it out of sight. Describe for the students the sights, sounds, physical sensations, smells, tastes, movements, and memories the object evokes for you.

Chapter
3 Observation

Acting is said to be the study of human behavior. So, in addition to their own memories and imaginations, actors must depend on their powers of **observation.** As an actor, you must become aware of how other people feel, move, speak, think, and behave. You must be able to recall what you observe, and use it to build believable characters.

Project Specs

Project Description For this assignment, you will give a detailed one- to three-minute description of an object.

Purpose to learn the skills of observation and recall

Materials a list of the characteristics of your chosen object or the Observation Activity Sheet provided by your teacher

Theatre Terms

conscious
emotional recall
observation
recall
sensory recall
spontaneous
subconscious
visualize

On Your Feet

To test your powers of observation, look around the classroom and choose an object, such as a poster, and quietly observe it for one minute. Concentrate on the colors, shapes, printed words, and textures. Also pay attention to how the item makes you *feel*. Now close your eyes and try to re-create the object in your mind. Now, without looking at the object, write down every detail you remember. Compare what you have written to the object. Did you miss anything?

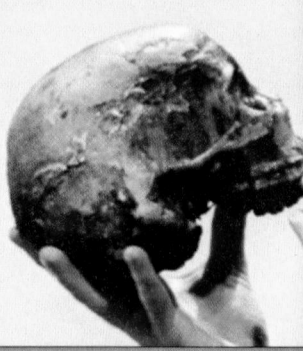

22 Unit One Begin with the Basics

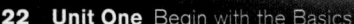

Theatre Terms

conscious aware (of in the mind)

emotional recall recall that uses remembered feelings to recapture an experience

observation the act of recognizing or noticing an object, a fact, or event

recall to remember a fact or event so as to re-create it

sensory recall recall that uses all the senses to recapture an experience

spontaneous not planned

subconscious existing in the mind just below the level of consciousness

visualize picture in one's mind

Someone once said that only through the specific can we reveal the universal. This is especially relevant in the theatre. As actors are called upon to create believable characters and situations, the value of observation becomes very clear. Remembered observations, both physical and emotional, form the backbone of realistic characters.

As an actor you must become a keen observer—a student of the world around you. That's because to portray any character believably, you have to create a complex and specific human being made up of hundreds of key details. That might sound difficult, but using your powers of observation can help. You can start off with something less complicated than a human being—an inanimate object.

Celia Keenan-Bolger played the shy Laura Wingfield in the 2013 Broadway revival of *The Glass Menagerie.*

Plays are often about people's relationship with their possessions—or their relationship with *other* people's possessions. In Tennessee Williams's play *The Glass Menagerie,* a painfully shy young woman named Laura seeks refuge from the outside world in her collection of delicate glass animals. When playing this character, an actor must have a specific *relationship* with the members of the tiny glass menagerie. After all, if the figurines mean nothing to Laura, they won't mean much to an audience either.

Alan Cumming, as Hamlet, focuses on the skull of Yorick in the 1993 London production.

Chapter 3 Observation **23**

Explain to the students that no actor has sufficient personal experience to play all types of people onstage. So, in addition to a powerful imagination, actors must depend on their powers of observation. They must become aware of how others feel, move, think, speak, behave, and experience their environments.

They must also be able to retain what they observe so that they can use it to build characters outside their own personal experience.

ACTivity To make your point, invite a volunteer to walk across the front of the classroom using his or her own natural gait. Then challenge that person to imitate your gait or the gait of a celebrity known to the class. With the class, analyze the similarities and differences between the two ways of walking.

 **Visual Cues**

The two images on this page show actors in relationship to inanimate objects that are central to their characters. You may want to use the following prompts to help students exercise **critical viewing skills.**

- In the top photograph, Celia Keenan-Bolger's character invests meaning in her glass animal. As an actor, what might you do to prepare to create this character?

- In the bottom photograph, Alan Cumming performs a scene in which Hamlet remembers his dead friend Yorick. What emotions might the actor draw upon in this scene?

- What senses are these actors using in their observation of objects?

Resource Binder

- Basic Theatre Terminology, TIPack, p. D
- Observation Activity Sheet, p. 12
- Tapping Your Inner Resources Worksheet, p. 13
- Critique Sheet: Describe an Object, p. 14
- Observation Test, p. 15

Handbook Connections
pages 568–569

To Have on Hand

Have ready a set of fairly familiar objects for display. Make sure a number of the objects have qualities or associations related to the senses of taste, hearing, and smell.

You may want to keep some objects covered with a napkin or cloth so that sounds or smells do not dissipate.

PREPARE

Your Observations and Impressions

Point out to the students that objects and events that people find memorable or remarkable often lodge themselves into the brain unconsciously. Some students will find they have very good recall abilities.

A Test Run

Beginning Students

Students with little experience might benefit from ignoring the time limit at first and simply writing as much as possible. Once they have included sufficient detail, they can pare down their description to fit the time limit. Encourage them to read their descriptions aloud.

Advanced Students

Challenge advanced students to improvise their descriptions and present them extemporaneously instead of using preparation time.

Vocabulary Enhancement

To help establish the emotional reality of a scene, actors use the principle of *recall*. When actors recall events in their own lives that provoke the same emotions their characters experience, they use what is called *emotional recall*.

The Language of THEATRE

Encourage students to keep a language notebook for the terms they learn in this class. They may want to make entries on individual cards so they can sort the terms alphabetically later. The entries should include the word, its meaning, and a sentence using the word.

PREPARE

Your Observations and Impressions

In this assignment you will describe a familiar object and provide your impressions and feelings about it. You will draw on **sensory recall**—using all five senses to recapture an experience—to describe the physical object in detail. You will draw on **emotional recall**—remembered feelings—to reveal to your audience what the object means to you.

Suggestions for Objects

- a piece of jewelry
- a photograph
- an article of clothing
- a trophy or plaque
- a piece of art
- a musical instrument

Suppose, for example, that you decide upon a treasured toy from your early childhood. Using your powers of observation, you will **recall** or re-create this item in such a way that your audience will **visualize** the object you describe. You should also share other details and memories, such as how you felt when you first saw the toy or what it meant to you at a particular time in your life. Perhaps the toy evokes memories of a holiday with a loved one who is no longer living. Or it might bring to mind an innocent childhood joy or surprise over receiving a toy you wanted very much.

You can choose any object—but make sure it's one that means something to you or meant something to you in the past. In order to describe your object so that your audience will actually be able to see it, ask yourself the following questions and keep a list of your answers:

- What does the object look like?
- How does it smell?
- How does it feel?
- How does it/might it taste? (if applicable)
- How does it sound?
- What does it remind me of?
- What makes it important to me?

A Test Run

Set a timer for three minutes. Rehearse describing your chosen object and its impact on you. You do not have to memorize what you will say. Because the object has personal meaning for you, the words to describe it should be **spontaneous**. Stay within the one- to three-minute time limit.

The Language of THEATRE

Work with a partner to help you understand the meanings of any unfamiliar theatre terms on page 22.

- Look for shorter words you know within longer new words. For example, *visualize* contains the word *visual*, a word you might know or have experienced in another text.

- Discuss other words you know with similar meanings. For example, *remember* is like *recall*. Recall a sense memory and share it with your partner.

- Discuss where you may have encountered the word *spontaneous* in other contexts and times you were spontaneous in taking an action.

- In an extended conversation, explain why *conscious* is a key word in relation to *observation*. Share experiences in which your skill in observation proved useful.

Backstage Gossip: Seeing Is Believing

John Gielgud often used observation to help create a character.

Once when I was rehearsing *Crime and Punishment*—it was a very hot day, I was walking through St. James Park—I saw a tramp lying down with his head buried in the dirty grass, filthy hands

and everything, and he was absolutely relaxed. I thought, "This is the way that Raskolnikov must lie on the bed," and immediately it gave me a kind of line on the part.

from Theatrical Anecdotes by Peter Hay

Here's How
To Improve Your Sense Memory

You look at thousands of things every day without really *seeing* them. You can improve your powers of observation by using a few simple techniques.

1 **Relax.** Don't strain to focus on the details you think you're most likely to remember. Instead, try to look at the world around you with fresh eyes.

2 **Observe in segments.** For instance, if you look at an object, an ornate vase for example, you might focus on its outline, then the color, the texture, the weight, and the way it feels to the touch. Notice the associations that you make. Let your observation take in not only what your eyes tell you, but also what your other senses reveal. These associations can be very important for later recall.

3 **Use your journal** to record your impressions and observations. This gets you into the habit of paying attention to what you notice—and what you don't. Writing down what you observe can help you hold it in your **conscious** mind as well as in your **subconscious**—the part of the brain just below your awareness—so you can use it later. You can write about almost anything: what you saw on a walk, what a chocolate shake tastes like, what the air smells like after a rainstorm, and so on.

PRESENT
Describe Your Object

When your name is called, hand in your list or Activity Sheet and walk to the playing area.

Begin by telling the audience what your chosen object is. This can be a simple, objective statement, such as "I'm going to describe my trumpet."

As you begin your presentation, remember to keep your body relaxed and to breathe deeply to avoid excessive nervousness. Don't hurry. Concentrate on specifics. Don't worry that you're not including everything. Speak naturally and try to be completely truthful. After all, you are talking about something you know very well.

When you have finished, ask the audience if they have questions about the object you've just described. Set a limit of three questions. Afterward, thank your audience and return to your seat.

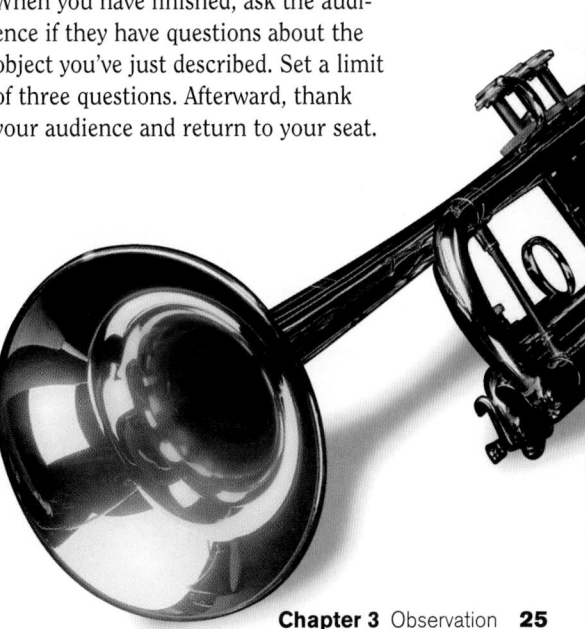

Chapter 3 Observation **25**

Here's How

Relax. Encourage students to relax by daydreaming about using an object or experiencing an event. Invite them to imagine encountering the object or event as a newcomer to this country or an alien from another planet.

Observe in segments. Unbidden associations are often the most fruitful, but students who are stuck might benefit by a conscious, formal exercise in word association. Have them state an obvious observation and then free associate around that word.

Use your journal. Encourage students to write at least one description a day in their journals. Point out that their descriptions can serve as references to enrich their acting roles.

PRESENT
Describe Your Object

Reassure students with performance anxiety by asking all students to make sure they place the emphasis on the objects they are describing, not their performance style in describing it.

Nevertheless, you may want to allow students to experiment with presentation style by speaking in the first person, as if they were the object they are describing, or by presenting their object by creating a riddle.

Show, Don't Tell Demonstrate the presentation activity by being the first to perform. To clarify and model your expectations, describe the object using one sentence for each of the five senses. Use at least one simile or metaphor. Also talk about the emotions the object evokes in you.

From the Field: Look at Me!

Early in the semester I advise students to start observing each other for an upcoming exercise. Then, several weeks later, I ask them to stand onstage, one at a time. The student onstage listens to what classmates have noticed about him or her. (Observers are to make only supportive, positive statements.)

At first, students find it painful to be observed. Soon, however, they become more comfortable. I tell them that they should come to expect—and that they deserve—positive attention.

The exercise has two more benefits: It builds community among the classmates, and it counteracts the tendency in performers to snipe at each other.

Kathleen Carot, Assistant Professor of Speech and Theatre, Oakton College, Des Plaines, Illinois

CRITIQUE

Evaluate a Classmate's Description

Hand out the Critique Sheet for this project or have students use their own paper.

As you evaluate presentations, let students know that you will be using the same rubrics for them as they are using for each other. In addition to their presentations, you may also wish to evaluate students on how well they assess each other's presentations.

After you have reviewed students' critiques, trim off the evaluator's name and hand each sheet to the subject of the evaluation.

ACTivity You may want to select three judges for each description to allow for more variety of response to each student's work.

Spotlight on

Peer Evaluation To be useful and effective, peer evaluation requires that each student put himself or herself in the place of the performer. Students must learn to think of themselves as collaborators on a creative project rather than competitors.

- Talk to students about "PIP," the Positive/Improvement/Positive approach to evaluation. Urge them to begin their critiques by stating something positive about the performance. Then they follow with a statement about something that can be improved. That is then followed by another positive statement about the work.

- Introduce the concept of speaking in "I" statements. Rather than making a statement about a performance as if it were an objective fact, such as "You never make eye contact," students should frame comments in terms of their own personal responses, such as "I didn't see you make eye contact."

CRITIQUE

Evaluate a Classmate's Description

Choose one of the descriptions presented in class to evaluate. Think about both the successful and unsuccessful aspects of your classmate's performance. Your evaluation should be based on a scale of 1 to 5, in which 1 is equal to "needs much improvement" and 5 is equal to "outstanding." Your evaluation should answer these questions:

- How did the person involve all five senses in the description of the object?
- Did you believe that the object meant something specific to the person?
- Could you visualize the object?
- Was any one sense emphasized while another was ignored?

Write a paragraph defending your scoring.

Spotlight on

Peer Evaluation

Peer evaluation, the act of looking critically at the work of your classmates, is beneficial to the evaluator as well as to the performers. When you critique the work of your peers, you have the opportunity to compare your work to that of others whose performance level is similar to your own. You will also participate in an exchange of ideas as you communicate your point of view, and your insights may have an impact on another's work. When your peers evaluate you, you gain worthwhile information regarding your work as well as a number of ideas for growth and improvement.

An effective peer evaluation often tells the performer what you understand to be the purpose or meaning of the work, what you enjoyed, what was especially effective or well done, and anything that confused or disturbed you. If possible, conclude with a final comment about the work as a whole.

When you are evaluating your classmates, maintain a positive, but objective, attitude. Keep an open mind—give your classmates the benefit of any doubt—and try not to be overly critical. State any suggestions for improvement in an even, upbeat manner, and never say anything that would unnecessarily hurt someone's feelings. As the receiver of feedback, also keep an open mind. Take the good suggestions to heart and revise your personal work in light of the specific comments. Ask questions to clarify any feedback you don't understand, and remember that no performance is ever perfect!

Backstage Gossip: Educating the World

Actor Julie Walters, in discussing her role in *Educating Rita*, referred to the pleasure of using recall of her own past.

"I loved . . . being able to talk about the class system, which always made me feel inadequate in life, giving voice to feelings I couldn't give voice to in life . . . oh, awful! It was wonderful playing those scenes because of the feelings I've always felt and forgotten I felt. It all came dredging out."

from *Actress to Actress* by Rita Gam

Additional Projects

1 A simple action, when analyzed in minute detail, can be hilarious. Describe a familiar action, such as eating an orange, sharpening a pencil, or washing your hair. See yourself performing the action. Describe it in as much detail as you can.

2 Write a one-page monologue in which a character uses observation and recall to describe a specific moment from the distant past.

3 Work with a partner to play the "mirror game." Stand face-to-face about one foot apart. Choose which of you will be the leader. This person will initiate movements, which the other person will mirror. In other words, the follower will perform the exact same gestures as if seeing himself or herself in a mirror. If the leader's left hand goes into the air, the follower makes the same gesture but uses the right hand. Work together for several minutes. By observing each other very closely, you should be able to create a very convincing mirror image.

4 On YouTube or another video file-sharing site, find a dramatic scene with acting that is especially effective in bringing a character to life. Use that clip as part of a PowerPoint or other digital presentation that explains the purpose and value of observation, sensory recall, and emotional recall in theatre.

5 With a partner, write and present a short scene in which one actor provides feedback to another about a performance. In your scene, show how to give and receive constructive peer criticism effectively.

6 Read the scene between Nora and her husband in *A Doll's House* by Henrik Ibsen, found in Unit Eight. Consider what Nora has observed about their relationship, and write a short summary.

7 Theatre Journal Read the scene from *A Doll's House* again. Choose either Nora or her husband and write about what observations and sensory and emotional recollections you might draw on to portray that character in that scene.

Harpo Marx and Lucille Ball play the "mirror game."

Observation Test
The test for this chapter is available in blackline master form in the Resource Binder, page 15.

For More Information
Books
Lawrence, Gale, *A Field Guide to the Familiar: Learning to Observe the Natural World*, UPNE, 1998.

McGaw, Charles J., *Acting Is Believing*, Wadsworth, 2008.

Other Media
Secrets of Body Language, DVD, A&E Home Video, 2009.

Apps
Many cell phones already come equipped with a digital camera. Students may wish to take photos and movies to help develop their observation skills.

IMotion HD
Paper by FiftyThree

Theatre Journal
Use the following as an additional or substitute prompt.

Students with a penchant for comedy or for the absurd might enjoy writing a love letter to the object they selected for this chapter project, telling it what they find thrilling about it.

Substitute Teacher Activities

Here are suggestions for one or more days when you will be out of the classroom:

- Assign the Tapping Your Inner Resources Worksheet on page 13 of the Resource Binder.

- Teach the Creating Believable Action section of the Student Handbook, p. 568.

- Assign one or more of the Additional Projects on this page.

- **Plan a Shared Descriptions Session.** Using objects set out for display, have students write a thorough description of an object and then discuss the thoughts or memories it evokes. Invite students to share their descriptions, thoughts, and memories with the class. This exercise strengthens powers of observation while promoting student interaction.

Theatre **Then** and Now

Stanislavski and Chekhov

The work of Konstantin Stanislavski is inextricably linked with the work of Anton Chekhov, because the two helped bring out the best in each other's work. Stanislavski's Moscow Art Theatre began putting on plays in the summer of 1898, but it did not distinguish itself until it produced Chekhov's *The Seagull* in December of that year.

The play had been a miserable failure when it was performed two years earlier in St. Petersburg. Stanislavski decided to give the play another chance, however, and he put his masterful directing in the service of the play's mood and storyline. The play was a success, the unique identity of the Moscow Art Theatre was established, and Chekhov was encouraged to write more plays.

Other Cultures, Other Times

Until Stanislavski developed his system, actors paid less attention to their own inner reality than to the external requirements of a play.

In classical Greek theatre, Japanese Noh, and Kabuki, actors worked like other tradespeople in apprenticeship programs designed to teach them the proper stylized movements and expressions for individual plays and for their craft in general.

Classical European acting styles, which were popular into the 19th century, were based on presenting symbolic pictures of emotions such as grief, envy, anger, or love. Actors played a ruling emotion rather than expressing the complexity of the character. Using this system, actors specialized in "types," which could be played in much the same way from production to production. Actors often played one or two types for their entire careers.

Theatre **Then** and Now

Stanislavski's System/ The Actors Studio

The Stanislavski System

Russian actor, director, teacher, and author Konstantin Stanislavski (1863–1938) co-founded the Moscow Art Theatre, which was regarded during his lifetime as one of the world's greatest theatre companies. But he is best remembered for creating a type of theatre training that influenced generations of actors around the world, a program known as the Stanislavski System. Through experimentation he came to believe that even those who were not born with artistic genius could achieve great acting.

One of Stanislavski's main concepts was that the actor who uses imagination as well as sense memory to recall experiences will be able to substitute them for those of the character—thus achieving believability. The script's reality or truthfulness becomes secondary to the emotional reality of the actor. It all depends on what Stanislavski called the "magic if." The actor must try to answer the question "What would I do *if* I were . . ." Thus, the actor is not forced into trying to believe that he or she is the person

"Live truthfully in imaginary circumstances."

—*Stanislavski*

in these actual circumstances, but rather what he or she would do given the same situation.

Stanislavski's system had the following goals:

1 to make the external behavior—movement and voice—natural and convincing

2 to know and carry out the *objectives* or inner needs of a character

3 to make the life of the character onstage continuous, with a past and a future, and a life in between the scenes onstage

4 to commit to action (behaving in ways to get character's objective) and reaction (listening and responding to the other characters)

Backstage Gossip: An Abbreviated Rehearsal

When Theresa Helburn, executive director of New York's new Theatre Guild, visited Konstantin Stanislavski in Russia, she was impressed. She immediately asked Stanislavski whether he might come to the United States and direct a play for the Guild. Stanislavski was interested. So Helburn asked, "How long would you need to rehearse a play?"

"Two years," said Stanislavski.

"Two years for one play!" exclaimed Helburn. "But that's impossible!"

"Well, in that case," replied Stanislavski, "How about two weeks?"

from *Broadway Anecdotes* by Peter Hay

Stanislavski's system, based on the actor's own experience and emotions, helped create an onstage reality that revolutionized the theatre. He later cautioned against adapting his system, however, without accounting for the differences in the actors' cultural backgrounds and artistic sensibilities.

The Actors Studio

Stanislavski and his company took the American theatre world by storm when the Moscow Art Theatre performed in New York City. Among the American admirers Stanislavski won over were actors from the famed Group Theatre (1931–1941). When three members of the Group (Cheryl Crawford, Robert Lewis, and Elia Kazan) decided to create an actor training center in 1947, the basis of the program was the Stanislavski System. They called this training center the Actors Studio. In 1952, Lee Strasberg took over as head of the program, which he ran for the next thirty years. During that time Strasberg refined, developed, and branched out from Stanislavski's ideas. Strasberg's new technique would eventually become known simply as "The Method."

The Actors Studio, through Pace University in New York City, offers a three-year graduate training program in play-writing, acting, and directing. It is also the subject of the popular cable television show *Inside the Actors Studio*.

Some Distinguished Alumni of the Actors Studio

Alec Baldwin
Marlon Brando
James Dean
Robert De Niro
Shirley MacLaine
Marilyn Monroe
Paul Newman
Sidney Poitier

Recent graduates of the Actors Studio include Bradley Cooper and Sean Penn.

Vivien Leigh and Marlon Brando in the film adaptation of Tennessee Williams's *A Streetcar Named Desire*.

The Actors Studio

As Artistic Director of the Actors Studio, Lee Strasberg established the Actors Studio Theatre in the 1960s. From the start, it was plagued with difficulties, and it closed after only a year and a half. Despite the problems with the theatre, Strasberg continued to train actors in The Method at the Actors Studio. The training center turned out to be Strasberg's great contribution to theatre. Under the workshop conditions created by his program, actors could develop their craft without the pressures of a particular production. Strasberg retained his position as director until his death in 1982.

For More Information

Books

Carnicke, Sharon M., *Stanislavski in Focus*, Routledge, 1998.

Hirsh, Foster, *A Method to Their Madness: The History of the Actors Studio*, Da Capo Press, 2002.

Stanislavski, Constantine, *An Actor Prepares*, Theatre Arts Books, 2002.

Stanislavski, Constantine, *Building a Character*, Theatre Arts Books, 2002.

Stanislavski, Constantine, *Creating a Role*, Theatre Arts Books, 2002.

Strasberg, Lee, *A Dream of Passion: The Development of the Method*, New American Library Trade, 1990.

Other Media

Creating Physical Theater: The Body in Performance, DVD, Insight Media, 2006.

The Group Theatre, DVD, Insight Media, 1967.

Hethmon, Robert H., ed., *Strasberg at the Actors Studio: Tape Recorded Sessions*, Theatre Communications Group, 1993.

Inside the Actors Studio: Leading Men, DVD, Shout!Factory, 2007.

The Stanislavsky Century, DVD, Films Media Group, 1993.

Visual Cue

The image on this page shows Vivien Leigh and Marlon Brando in a scene from the film *A Streetcar Named Desire*.

- Who seems to have the upper hand in this scene?

- In what ways, if any, does the scene look contrived? In what ways, if any, does the scene look real?

- How might you update this scene if you were to direct it today?

Chapter 4

Pantomime

This chapter offers students a chance to integrate relaxation, warm-up, and observation techniques to create a pantomime.

Objectives

1 to develop an awareness of body language

2 to use movement and body language as a means of communication

3 to understand the principles of pantomime

4 to pantomime an activity

Project Specs

Special Needs Students
Students with physical disabilities may perform this activity to whatever extent they are able to maintain control over the body. Facial expressions alone can communicate a story.

Advanced Students
Students who are adept at movement and observation can work together to link their individual pantomimes into an episodic story.

On Your Feet

Show, Don't Tell Jump-start this class period by letting students walk in on—and participate in—a performance in process. Pretend that you have laryngitis and that you need help getting ready for class. Using pantomime alone, request that students find particular objects or props and either put them somewhere or perform a particular task.

After the tasks are completed, tell students you'd like to discuss pantomime. Ask them what they found easy and what they found difficult about communication through pantomime.

Chapter

4 Pantomime

You face your audience with an important message, but you must communicate without words! By using **pantomime**—gestures, body movement, and facial expressions—you can get your ideas across quite well. You need not be an accomplished mime to be an actor, but training and practice in the art of pantomime will certainly help.

Project Specs

Project Description For this assignment, you will prepare a one- to three- minute pantomime of an activity.

Purpose to develop actions that are believable to both actor and audience

Materials a 50- to 100-word outline of your pantomime or the Pantomime Activity Sheet your teacher provides

On Your Feet

To begin your study of pantomime, think of a way you can express to a partner the following ideas without saying a word:

"Everything is OK."
"Please, help me out here."
"Don't say another word!"
"I haven't a clue."

Theatre Terms
body language
clown white
mime
pancake makeup
pantomime

Street mimes perform for passersby.

Theatre Terms

body language communicating thoughts and feelings through body movements (crossing arms, furrowing brow, etc.)

clown white white makeup often used by mimes and clowns

mime an actor who communicates through movements of the body and face without speaking; also, the activity of the mime

pancake makeup thick, water soluble makeup usually applied with a damp sponge

pantomime body movement and expression without dialogue

Make-believe and Acting

The basis of acting is literally a matter of "make-believe." It requires the ability to pretend—an ability that nearly everyone possesses to some degree. You can probably recall the fun you had as a child playing a game in which you were a heroic astronaut or a professional athlete. Your pleasure was great because you gave yourself over completely to the game. You were believing.

The belief that a child brings to pretending is similar to the belief that an actor must bring to a part. Like children playing make-believe, actors must become the characters they play. This is a difficult task because, unlike children who enjoy the unrestrained freedom of play for its own sake, actors must

communicate to an audience. In order to make an audience believe, the actor must believe!

The Basics of Pantomime

Mime is one of the oldest forms of theatre—the dramatic art of representing life through expressive movements of the body and face. The English word *mime* comes from the ancient Greek *mimos,* meaning "to imitate" or "to mimic." *Pantomime* usually refers to the mimed dramatic sketch as a whole. The actor performing a pantomime must communicate without words, using precise gestures and exact movements to convey ideas. Like all actors, the mime's objective is to make the audience believe in the world he or she is creating. As you learn the basic techniques of mime, you will learn how to employ consistently such physical techniques as posture, facial expression, gestures, movement, and stance to express thoughts, feelings, and actions nonverbally. You will also come to appreciate the importance of nonverbal communication and **body language**—how body positioning and movement reflect thoughts and feelings.

Try It on for Size

On the following pages are just a few of the many techniques employed by students of the art of pantomime. Take the time to study the images carefully, thinking about the instructions as they relate to the pictures. Then practice these movements yourself.

Chapter 4 Pantomime **31**

PREVIEW
Make-believe and Acting

While some students will find freedom in omitting spoken language from their performances, others will worry about their skill level in pantomime and its implication for their abilities as actors. Make it clear that one need not be an accomplished mime to be an actor. Pantomime is a good way of training the body, but to learn it well takes more time than is available in a comprehensive drama class.

Explain that in acting, we begin with actions because of the truth in the adage "actions speak louder than words." Acting is not about what you are saying but what you are communicating. Sometimes, what a person does communicates something far more important than what he or she says.

ACTivity Invite students to relive the days of childhood by pretending that they are astronauts, cowhands, professional athletes, dancers, and so forth. Call out occupations one at a time and have students participate by wordlessly communicating that role.

The Basics of Pantomime

When discussed as forms of theatre, pantomime and mime are similar, but still distinct. Both are skilled activities that require warm-ups, especially of the wrists and ankles. But they differ in their effects. Pantomime is true to life. Mime is stylized. It often is blown up larger than life to communicate an idea, emotion, or theme. Both types of wordless performance require a clean approach to movement.

Resource Binder

- Pantomime Activity Sheet, p. 16
- Mime Games Worksheet, p. 17
- Critique Sheet: Pantomime, p. 18
- Pantomime Test, p. 19

Handbook Connections
pages 569–570

To Have on Hand

- White pancake makeup
- Small sponges
- Makeup brush
- Black grease pencil or paint
- Red grease pencil or paint
- Baby powder
- White athletic sock
- Small painter's brush
- Freestanding mirror

 sual Cue

The image on this page shows street mimes whose work has a political theme.
- What do you think the issue they are addressing might be?
- How would you identify the different figures in this photograph?
- What physical details support your opinion?

The Chest

Show, Don't Tell Strut around the room with your head high and chest out and ask students to identify your prevailing attitude (pride, egotism, self-assurance, and so on). Try a few other postures and have students guess what emotions or attitudes you are conveying.

ACTivity Work with the students to create a list of emotions and the physical expressions and movements that go with them. For example, you might write *despair* on the board and ask students to stand and try to express this emotion without words, paying particular attention to the upper body and chest.

The Face and Head

Show, Don't Tell Squint your eyes and frown and say, "You are very bright students." Ask the class if they were surprised by what you said and whether they believed your words. Discuss their impressions. Then use your face and head to create a few more emotions or attitudes and have the students write sentences that say in words what your face and head convey silently.

ACTivity Ask the class to stand. Then call out various emotions at random and have students try to demonstrate them using only the head and face.

Vocabulary Enhancement

The word *mime* is pronounced MYM. The Greek word *mimos* is pronounced MEE mohs.

The Chest

The chest is an essential element in all movement in pantomime. It harbors the body's center of gravity and is often the moving force behind emotion.

This mime stands with chest expanded. This connotes pride, sophistication, nobility, or confidence.

If the chest is pushed forward more dramatically, aggressiveness and determination are suggested.

The chest is now curved inward, indicating weakness, old age, shyness, or exhaustion.

The Face and Head

The face is unique; it is what identifies us to others. We can communicate a lot with just a little effort of the facial muscles—a subtle downturn of the mouth to show displeasure or the angry flair of the nostrils. While these small facial movements speak volumes, learning how to control them may not be easy. The mime must learn to do just that, however, in order to tell his or her story. A mime often wears **clown white,** a kind of white makeup, to highlight the face and its movements.

This mime's open and upturned lips, wide eyes, arched brows, and raised head indicate happiness–or sometimes surprised delight.

Notes

A downturned mouth, narrowed eyes, with the head thrust forward, can indicate anger or threat.

With the mouth in a straight line, eyes wide, eyebrows arched, and head raised and to the side, the mime appears to be listening, attentive, or curious.

Here's How
To Use White Makeup

Although it is not essential that you wear clown white to perform pantomime, the white, along with the black that outlines the eyes and brows, helps the audience focus on your face.

1 Dip the sponge in water, squeeze, then rub it into the white pancake makeup.

2 Apply the white over your face, excluding the lips. Gently blot the face to remove any streaks.

3 Apply red grease pencil or paint to lips.

4 Apply black grease pencil or paint to the area above eyebrows, above and below the eyes, and around eyes for emphasis.

5 Fill the sock with baby powder and tap your face to set the makeup. Brush away excess powder.

The Makeup Kit
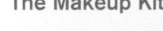

- White **pancake makeup**
- Small sponge
- Makeup brush
- Black grease pencil or paint
- Red grease pencil or paint
- Baby powder
- White athletic sock
- Small painter's brush

Here's How

Advise students that caution is needed during every step of this process. It is always advisable to begin by using too little rather than too much of anything. Students can always add more water to the pancake makeup, but if they add too much at the beginning, the makeup will be runny and hard to use.

Similarly, if they paint too narrow or light a line above the eyebrows, they can add to it. But if they paint too broad a line, they will have to wash their faces and start over. Powder should also be applied gently so as not to collect on one area of the face.

If you decide to have students experiment with mime makeup, make sure that each person has his or her own sponge. As an alternative, you may wish to demonstrate the makeup application using one student as a model.

The Makeup Kit

Eyeliner and lipstick might replace grease pencils or paint in a pinch. Pancake makeup and baby powder are always necessary, however.

Backstage Gossip: Speak Up

In Mel Brooks's 1976 film *Silent Movie,* a producer decides that the public is ready to once again embrace the silent movie. It was an interesting premise, but Brooks couldn't quite pull it off. Most viewers agree, however, that the highlight of the film is the scene in which the world-famous mime Marcel Marceau speaks the only word in the film—"Non."

The Legs and Feet

Show, Don't Tell Sit in front of the class with your legs crossed. As you discuss a subject of your choice with the students, move your leg or foot back and forth nervously. Speak in your normal tone. After a few minutes, ask the students what they noticed about you as you spoke, and what their impressions were. Discuss other ways you could relay nervousness or excitement by using your legs and feet. Ask students to demonstrate how they might do it.

ACTivity Have students use only leg and feet movements to communicate a character's personality. Class members then suggest situations for the character, and the student must assume poses that reflect the suggestions, paying particular attention to the legs and feet.

ACTivity **Advanced Students** Students who are ready might carry the above exercise a bit further by adding more details to the movement. For example, you might suggest that a student who has created the body language of an angry, impatient man make a phone call to his mother. You might ask a student in a carefree toddler's pose to pour milk into a small glass. If, at any time, the volunteer forgets to remain in character, students should call out "Character" as a reminder. Allow the volunteer to complete the action in a brief demonstration or let it unfold into a story.

ACTivity **Special Needs Students** Invite students to duplicate the leg and feet positions of the young man in the photos on this page. If they seem ready, ask these students for other ways they might use their legs and feet to show shyness or a threatening posture.

The Legs and Feet

We walk, run, hop, jump, sit, stand, and even lie down using our legs and feet. We jiggle them when nervous or bored and stamp them when we are angry or upset. Have you ever noticed that when you are impatiently waiting for someone you tap your foot in irritation? And when you are excited or happy about something your feet almost dance? The mime can express character and personality through movement of the legs and feet just as with the face and chest. Try to imitate a few of the poses below.

One leg crossed over the other with the body leaning indicates a relaxed, casual, and sometimes, arrogant personality.

Feet turned in or one leg bent behind the other indicates a shyness or timidity.

Feet apart and legs straight show strength and confidence. Add a head held very high with the hands on the hips and you create a feeling of scorn, threat, or contempt.

Backstage Gossip: The Triumph of Mrs. Siddons

Charles Young remembers how a great actor inspired others on the stage.

I remember Mrs. Siddons coming down the stage in the triumphal entrance of her son, Coriolanus, when her dumb-show drew plaudits that shook the house. She came alone, marching and beating time to the music; rolling . . . from side to side, swelling with the triumph of her son. Such was the intoxication of joy which flashed from her eye, lit up her whole face, that the effect was irresistible. She seemed to me to reap all the glory of that procession to herself.

from Theatrical Anecdotes by Peter Hay

The Arms and Hands

Never underestimate the power of the arms, hands, and fingers in conveying emotion or telling a story. Mimes create invisible walls, stroke, caress, or push away using hands and arms. The joints of the elbow, wrist, and hand give the mime the flexibility to manipulate invisible objects. Practice the hand positions used in the photographs, combining them with various face, body, and leg movements.

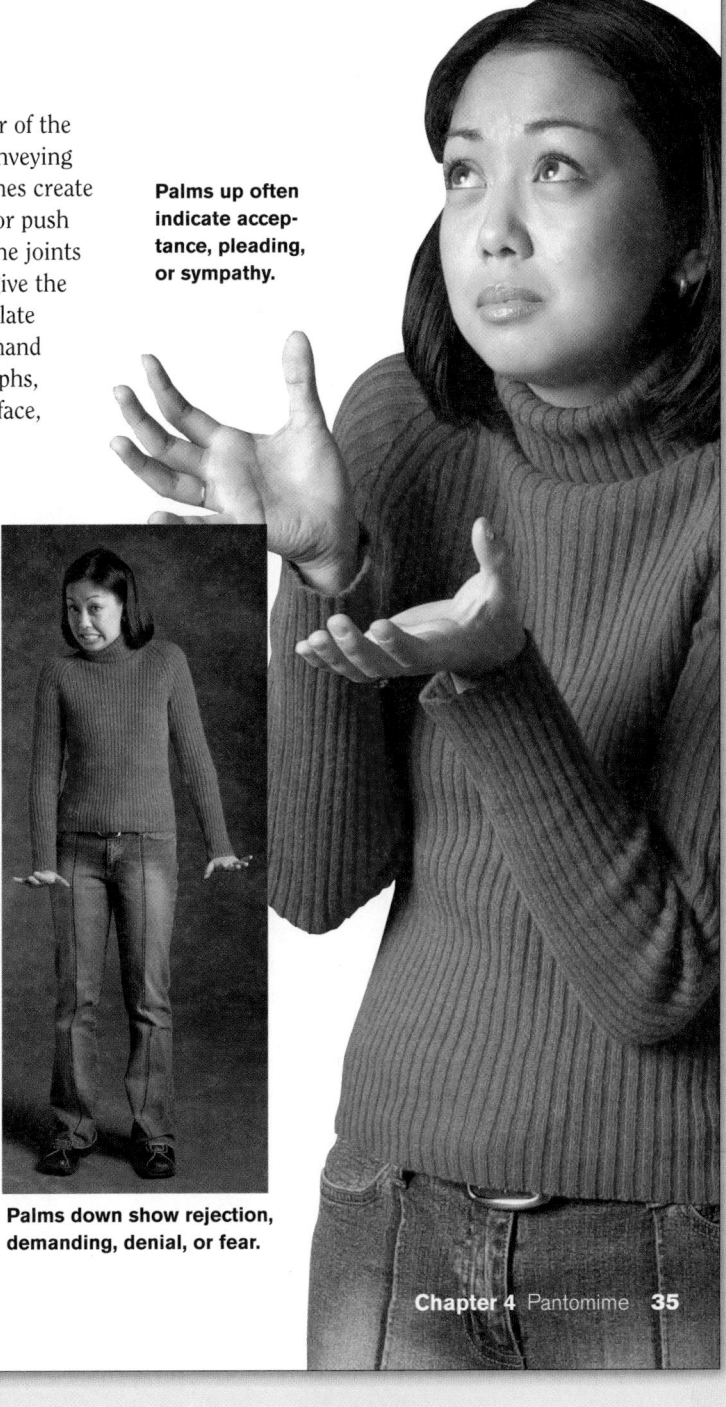

Palms up often indicate acceptance, pleading, or sympathy.

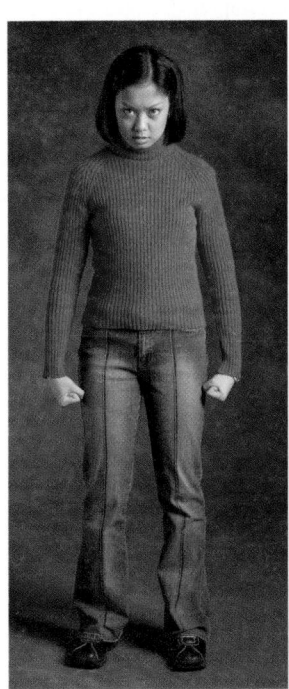

Clenched fists indicate anger, threat, or forced control.

Palms down show rejection, demanding, denial, or fear.

The Arms and Hands

Show, Don't Tell To highlight the importance of the arms and hands, tell a story using only your arms and hands and just a few choice words. Have students continue adding to the plot, as you continue using your arms and hands to tell the main story.

ACTivity **Advanced Students**
Direct volunteers to affect expressions and body language to define a character as in the activity on the previous page. Then extend the activity by suggesting events that change the mood or attitude of the character. Encourage the performers to go through the changes they think are appropriate to their characters.

Suggest to the students that they make their original expressions and body language the default positions for their characters.

ACTivity **Special Needs Students**
Ask students to duplicate the arm and hand positions of the young woman in the photos on this page. If they seem ready, ask students for other ways they might use the hands and arms to indicate anger or fear.

Notes

PREPARE

Visualize and Focus on Your Pantomime

Suggest to the students that they focus on the actions and objects in their pantomimes rather than concentrating on their own movements. Point out that they don't think about the way they are moving in ordinary life; they simply move to accomplish what they want to accomplish. The same should be true of their pantomimes.

To help them focus on the object in their pantomimes, remind them that an object not only has size and shape, but texture and weight. Students can use observation and sense memory to recall the characteristics of the object. You can also supply prompts such as the following:

- How does the weight of the object feel?

- Is the object pleasant or unpleasant to the touch?

- How must I pick up and put down the object?

- What dangers are there in handling the object?

ACTivity Allow students to brainstorm a list of thirty to forty actions to pantomime. They may then use any of the actions listed or choose other actions of their own.

The Language of THEATRE

Analyzing photographs and other visuals helps students build visual literacy and English vocabulary at the same time. Encourage them to identify familiar objects in visuals with English words. Guide students as needed to the visuals that are most relevant to understanding the theatre terms.

PREPARE

Visualize and Focus on Your Pantomime

In this project you will focus all of your attention on your pantomime. See the situation and objects in your mind's eye and work within that imaginary setting until it becomes believable.

Suggestions for Pantomimes

- Play a computer game.
- Build a campfire.
- Row a boat.
- Go fishing.
- Eat a meal.
- Clean your room.
- Play a sport.
- Prepare a meal.
- Build something.
- Get ready for school.

Suppose that you choose bowling for your pantomime. You must "see" the alley, see where the balls are stored, and see where you keep score. You must visualize the action of bowling: wiping your hands on the towel; picking up the ball as you walk up to the starting line. Begin your approach on the proper foot. Feel the weight of the imaginary ball as you swing it back and then forward. Feel its size, shape, and texture. Then feel the release of the ball, and watch it travel down the alley or gutter. Follow through with your reaction. Make everything you do believable. Remember, you are doing the action in your own person, not as a character in a play. Be the real you. Your teacher and classmates will be observing how true your actions are to the situation. Work through the following steps.

1. **Think of an action** you want to pantomime. Choose an activity that you have performed many times. See the suggestions at the left.

2. **Outline each step** in the action. Divide each main step into smaller actions until you have a complete series of movements. Remember that your purpose is a well-planned action that is believable. Visualize your surroundings. Then think about the action and see it. If you cannot recall the exact action, perform the action or observe someone else doing it. Record the details and movement.

To refresh your understanding of observation and sensory and emotional recall, reread Chapter 3, pages 24–25.

The Language of THEATRE

Use visuals and context to help you understand spoken language as you and a partner take turns reading aloud.

- Listen to each of the theatre terms on page 30 and look for visuals in the chapter that help you understand them in the context of the theatre.

- Listen to the sentences that introduce each of the boldface theatre terms in the chapter. Look for visuals to help you understand what you heard.

- Listen to the captions for the examples of body language on pages 32–35 without looking at the pictures. Then look at the visuals and see how they increase your understanding of the captions.

- Listen to the Preview text on page 31 with your book closed. Then look at the visuals on pages 30–31 and notice how they deepen your understanding of the text and the terms *mime* and *body language*.

Quotable

Use the quote below as a writing prompt, discussion starter, or for your own enjoyment.

If an actor can find the personal rhythm of a character, he's home free. And one of the best ways to do that is to follow a person down the street, unbeknownst to him. Pick up his walk, imitate it and continue it, even after he's out of sight. As you're doing it, observe what's happening to you. By zeroing in on a guy's personal rhythm, you'll find that you've become a different person.

Dustin Hoffman, Actor
from *The Films of Dustin Hoffman* by Douglas Brode

PRESENT

Perform Your Pantomime

Begin your presentation with a short, well-worded introduction to awaken audience curiosity. Then present your pantomime. Take your time and include each detail. If you are immersed in the task at hand, intent on doing the action in a believable way, you will not be worried about what the audience thinks of you.

At the conclusion of your scene, pause, give a slight bow, and then quietly leave the playing area. Remember, you cannot make an audience believe in something you do not believe in yourself.

To pantomime an action, first visualize it step by step.

CRITIQUE

Evaluate a Classmate's Pantomime

Imagine that you are a drama critic and write a short review of a classmate's pantomime. Include strong points as well as areas that could be improved. Use a scale of 1 to 5, with 5 equaling "outstanding" and 1 equaling "needs much improvement." Review Peer Evaluation on page 16 for further help.

Ask yourself these questions:

- Was the pantomime well planned?
- What important details did the actor include or leave out?
- How did the actor make you believe in the dimensions of the imaginary objects used?
- What did the actor do to help you believe that he or she was actually engaged in this action?

Write a short explanation of how you arrived at the score you gave.

PRESENT

Perform Your Pantomime

Show, Don't Tell Describe the beginning of a great play you saw recently. Be as succinct as possible and leave a lot to the students' imaginations. When they have questions, explain that the introduction you gave was meant to whet their appetites. Similarly, their introductions should serve only to whet the audience's appetite—not to explain the scene. Point out that a pantomime, however short, is a story. To build interest in the story, they should introduce it without telling it or giving away the ending.

ACTivity If you feel your students need practice at such introductions, have them say a few words about a favorite book or movie. Encourage students to tell just enough to make others want to experience it for themselves.

CRITIQUE

Evaluate a Classmate's Pantomime

Hand out the Critique Sheet for this project or have students use their own paper.

It will be helpful to assign the person each student will evaluate so that everyone receives a peer evaluation.

Let students know that you will be using the same rubrics for them as they are using for each other. In addition to their presentations, you may also wish to evaluate students on how well they assess each other's presentations.

After you have reviewed students' critiques, trim off the evaluator's name and hand out the sheets to the subjects of the evaluations.

From the Field: Well-Oiled Machines

I use many of Viola Spolin's games to get students working together. Often, I start out simple and then add elements as we go along.

For example, I might have a student go onstage and begin doing a movement a machine might do. One by one, I ask students to join the first student. After the whole group is working together, I will ask students to describe what the machine is doing.

After they come to a consensus, I ask them to keep their function in mind while I prompt the machine to speed up, slow down, or alter its movement in any number of ways. Starting slowly, they are able to use their imaginations, take direction, and work together—all at the same time.

Rick Karlin, Teacher, Chicago, Illinois

Pantomime Test

The test for this chapter is available in blackline master form in the Resource Binder, page 19.

For More Information

Books

Alberts, David, *Talking About Mime*, Heinemann, 1994.

Feder, Jack, *Mime Time: A Book of Routines and Performance Tips*, Meriwether Publishing, 1992.

Kipnis, Claude, *The Mime Book*, Meriwether Publishing, 1988.

Stoltzenberg, Mark, *Exploring Mime*, Sterling Publishing, 1979.

Other Media

Body Language, DVD, Insight Media, 2012.

Mime Over Matter, DVD, Insight Media, 1988.

www.mime.info/

Apps

Ultimate Charades

Theatre Journal

Use the following as an additional or substitute prompt. Write about the ways you are similar to and different from the person you observe in the activity.

- How is the way you move different from the way this person moves?
- What gestures do you both employ?

Additional Projects

1 Using an imaginary rope, play tug-of-war. Teams of equal number should stand in front of each other in a line, facing a similarly positioned team. In your mind, see and feel the rope. Pull together as hard as you can to take the rope from the other team. Be careful that the rope does not stretch. If one side gets the advantage, the other side must give. Make the game so believable to you, that at the end of it, you feel tired from the strong physical exertion.

2 In a one- to two-minute scene, make believable your efforts to escape from a place where you are trapped—perhaps a cave or an elevator. Visualize the area in which you are trapped. Then use your whole body in trying to escape. Strain, grunt, claw, climb, and dig. Make yourself and your audience believe your endeavors. Continue your efforts until your teacher calls, "Cut."

3 Play "Statues" with a group of classmates. Each person takes a turn dancing freely about the room until someone calls, "Stop!" The dancer then freezes into a statue that shows a specific emotion, such as anger, pain, fear, or joy. The others must guess the feeling being expressed. If people have trouble determining the emotion, try to discover the reason, and rework the statue until it fully captures the emotion being expressed.

4 Read all the stage directions for *The Drummer* by Athol Fugard, found in Unit Eight. Use pantomime to tell the whole story, employing physical techniques consistently to express thoughts, feelings, and actions without words.

5 Read about Kabuki Theatre and Asian American Theatre on pages 40–41. With additional research, create a multimedia presentation identifying the key figures and trends associated with both Japanese Kabuki and contemporary Asian American drama and theatre.

6 **Theatre Journal** Observe someone participating in an everyday activity. Watch carefully and record the steps in the activity in a numbered list.

Substitute Teacher Activities

Below are suggestions for one or more days when you will be out of the classroom:

- Assign the Mime Games Worksheet on page 17 of the Resource Binder.
- Assign one or more of the Additional Projects on this page.
- Teach the Mime and Pantomime section of the Student Handbook, pp. 569–570.

- **Plan a First Meeting Pantomime.** Give students five or ten minutes to record details about the first new person they met at your school. Suggest that they consider how they felt walking into the school that day, what they were wearing, and whether they were in a hurry or not. Then have them take turns performing a pantomime of this meeting. Point out that their own expressions will be extremely important, since there will not be an actor representing the other person.

Master of the Craft
Marcel Marceau

Marcel Marceau (1923–2007) was undoubtedly the most famous mime in the world. He usually performed on a bare stage with few or no props. The clown-white makeup he wore highlighted every subtle facial expression. Marceau had the ability to make his audience feel what his character was feeling and to see the imagined world that he created.

Marceau's interest in pantomime began when he was quite young. He would imitate with gestures anything that captivated his imagination. His admiration for such silent screen artists as Charlie Chaplin and Buster Keaton inspired his pursuit of silence as a profession.

In his essay "The Poetic Halo," Marceau said this about his profession: "When the actor-mime sustains his dramatic action with the inspiration of his thought, the sensitive response he induces is the echo of his soul, and the gesture becomes a silent inner song."

His most famous pantomimes include "The Cage," "Walking Against the Wind," and "In the Park."

In 1947, Marceau created Bip, the clown who became his most famous and most beloved character.

For More Information

Books
Marceau, Marcel, *Bip in a Book,* Stewart, Tabori & Chang, 2001.

Martin, Ben, *Marcel Marceau: Master of Mime,* Viking Penguin, 1979.

Other Media
Charlie Rose with Marcel Marceau (September 27, 2000), DVD, Charlie Rose, Inc., 2006.

Marcel Marceau Speaks, Audio CD, Times Two Audio, 2000.

Master of the Craft
More About Marcel Marceau

Marcel Marceau was born Marcel Mangel in Strasbourg, France, on March 22, 1923. His father died in Auschwitz during World War II, but Marceau and his brother escaped capture by the Nazis, changed their names, and joined the French Resistance.

In 1946, he enrolled as a student at the Sarah Bernhardt Theatre in Paris, where he studied with the great master of mime, Etienne Decroux. Decroux invited Marceau to join his company, casting him as Arlequin in a pantomime entitled "Baptist," which launched Marceau's career.

Marceau attracted international attention at the Berlin Festival of 1951. He then launched a tour of thirty-six countries, which made him world-famous.

Marceau also founded a school, L'Ecole International de Mimodrame de Paris Marcel Marceau, to educate aspiring mimes from around the globe.

Masters Past and Present

Marceau's acclaim rests on his virtuosity and on the way he has continued a proud tradition in French pantomime. Bip, the clown character Marceau developed, is based on a touching white-faced clown created by Jean-Gaspard Deburau (1796–1846), the originator of French mime. Deburau's clown, named Pierrot, was a pale fellow, lovesick but hopeful, who became one of the most popular characters in French theatre. Deburau, in turn, is often associated with the mime of the same name in director Marcel Carné's 1946 film *Children of Paradise (Les Enfants du Paradis),* which presents a fascinating portrait of theatre folk in early 19th-century France. It was a noisy, rude, haphazard theatre, with audiences often on the brink of riot; a theatre where poor and hungry actors forged friendships with thugs; and a theatre in which a sad, passionate mime could create magic from it all. This classic film is available on video and DVD.

Cultural Heritage

Japanese Kabuki Theatre

Kabuki was a form of entertainment that appealed to all the classes in Japan. Samurai and ladies attended Kabuki performances along with merchants, workers, monks, and students. The higher classes sat in covered seats, while the lower classes sat out in the open air.

Government authorities in Japan looked down upon Kabuki performers and even refused them civil rights. The general public, on the other hand, idolized them. Over time, the acting profession became hereditary. Families established acting dynasties, some of which are still viable. For example, Japan's Danjuro XII, an actor born in 1946, continues a family tradition that extends back to the 17th century.

Originally, Kabuki was comprised of improvised sketches inserted into dance performances. Over time, the sketches developed into plays, and in 1670, the first important Kabuki writer emerged. By the 1800s, Kabuki was written by teams consisting of a writer and several assistants. Even so, Kabuki writing is considered to be largely a blueprint for action, rather than a form of literature in its own right.

From the mid-17th century to the mid-19th century, Kabuki performances were about twelve hours long. In 1868, they were shortened to eight hours. Since World War II, most Kabuki performances are four hours long—but most theatres offer two shows a day.

Cultural Heritage

Japanese Kabuki Theatre

Probably the best known drama form of traditional Japanese theatre is Kabuki. In the early 17th century a female dancer named O-kuni is said to have developed a new form of dance and drama. When she danced in the dry riverbeds of Kyoto, the capital, O-kuni caused a sensation, and soon she had many imitators. From this Kabuki was born.

Another early form of Kabuki, seldom performed today, was a simple silent performance that lasted no longer than ten minutes—much like a short pantomime. Over the years, Kabuki became more and more elaborate, stylized, and intricate. Eventually women were banned from Kabuki performance and

This male actor portrays a woman in a Kabuki play.

certain men became specialists in portraying women. To this day only males perform traditional Kabuki.

Traditional Kabuki performances are distinctive for the elaborateness of their costuming, makeup, and staging. Costumes are highly stylized and colorful, and the traditional white makeup and elaborate hairstyles help create Kabuki's richness.

Actors on a traditional Kabuki stage.

For More Information

Books

Ariyooshi, Sawako, trans. I. James Brandon, *The Kabuki Dance,* Kodansha International, 1994.

Leiter, Samuel L., *A Kabuki Reader: History and Performance,* Sharp, Armonk, 2001.

Other Media

Acting Techniques of the Noh Theatre of Japan, DVD, Insight Media, 1980.

Kagamijishi: Kabuki Dance, DVD, Films for the Humanities & Sciences, 2004.

Kabuki for the West, DVD, Insight Media, 2009.

Selected Scenes from the Japanese Noh Theatre, DVD, Insight Media, 2010.

The Tradition of Performing Arts in Japan, DVD, Insight Media, 1990.

Asian American Theatre

Kabuki took an interesting turn at the end of the twentieth century in its partnership with such Western drama classics as *Macbeth* and *Medea*. Western plays with strong, universal themes such as pride and revenge lend themselves well to Kabuki interpretation. These productions featured Western actors playing Asian characters who were based on characters from the Western classics.

White actors made up to look Asian had been common in American theatre in the 1950s. In addition, Asian characters were often limited to a few stereotypes, such as a mysterious detective or an innocent war bride. Starting in 1965, Asian Americans protested against these practices and created their own theatres, such as the East West Players, the Asian American Theatre Workshop, and the Pan Asian Repertory Theatre. Today many such theatres exist on both coasts and in Midwestern cities, such as Theatre Mu in Minneapolis.

Asian American playwrights began to gain prominence with the off-Broadway production of Frank Chin's *The Chickencoop Chinaman*

in 1972. David Henry Wang became the first Asian American to win a Tony award in 1988, for his Broadway smash *M. Butterfly*. Wang continued to win awards for later works. He and numerous other Asian Americans are part of an increasingly diverse American theatre that reflects the global culture. Subjects in Asian American drama have evolved from issues of Asian American identity to richly multicultural and universal themes.

A scene from *M. Butterfly*.

Asian American Theatre

Asian American theatre companies were originally centered in areas with large concentrations of Asian immigrants, including Los Angeles, Seattle, San Francisco, and New York. East West Players began in Los Angeles in 1965 and has since produced premiers of more than 100 plays and musicals that reflect the Asian Pacific American experience. About 44 percent of the theatre's audience is non-Asian, reflecting the company's desire to build bridges between East and West. Across the country in New York City, the Pan Asian Repertory Theatre was founded in 1977 by Artistic Producing director Tisa Chang. The theatre offers new works by Asian American playwrights along with translations of classics in Asian theatre and Western classics with an Asian twist. These companies and others across the country have provided a springboard for Asian American performers who have built careers in theatre, film, and television. The theatres also provide training and opportunities for young actors, directors, and technical artists. As Asian American theatre continues to evolve there will likely be a trend to produce more plays that reflect a mixture of many cultures. Americans and others in the West are increasingly aware of Asian culture as Asian nations play a larger role in many aspects of their lives.

For More Information

Books

Lee, Esther Kim, *A History of Asian American Theatre*, Cambridge University Press, 2011.

Lee, Josephine, ed., *Asian American Plays for a New Generation*, Temple University Press, 2011.

Yew, Chay, ed., *Version 3.0: Contemporary Asian American Plays*, Theatre Communications Group, 2011.

Other Media

David Henry Hwang, DVD, Insight Media, 2002.

Hwang, David Henry, *M. Butterfly*, DVD, Warner Home Video, 2009.

Chapter 5

Improvisation

This chapter introduces students to the principles of improvisation. Improvisation is a challenging activity. Students are not expected to master it at this point, but rather to understand the basics of this performance genre. We will return to improvisation in later chapters of this book.

Objectives

1 to understand the basics of improvisation

2 to understand the value and purpose of concentration and cooperation

3 to work collaboratively with others

4 to use movement, voice, and body to create an improvisation

Project Specs

ELL Students
Students who are less familiar with the English language may need to work out on paper or kinesthetically the various uses of the word *set*. Use The Language of Theatre feature on page 45 for additional support.

Advanced Students
For the activities in this chapter, advanced students should not be set apart in any way. In fact, advanced students may find their most significant and meaningful challenges in improvising with students who are less at home onstage.

On Your Feet

Before the students begin working with their partners on this exercise, tell them that one of them will portray a character of some kind and will have to figure out the scenario as they go along.

---

5 Improvisation

One of the most demanding things an actor can be called upon to do is to **improvise**—to make up the words in the **dialogue** and the action while playing out a scene. No lines to learn, no planned movement, just you (and your fellow actors) going wherever your imagination leads you.

Project Specs

Project Description You and a partner (or partners) will perform a three- to five-minute improvisation.

Purpose to learn introductory improvisation skills in order to develop concentration and focus

Materials a 50- to 100-word sentence outline of your group improvisation or the Improvisation Activity Sheet your teacher provides

On Your Feet

To practice working with a partner, play a round of "Who Am I?" with your classmates as the audience. Your partner will decide what kind of person he or she wants to play without telling you. For example, he or she might play a traffic cop arresting you for speeding or a babysitter looking after you, the child. Based on how your partner acts toward you, you must guess who that person is and try to respond accordingly.

Theatre Terms

collaboration
concentration
cooperation
dialogue
ensemble
improvise
set

Theatre Terms

collaboration working with others toward a common goal

concentration focusing the mind intensely on a particular object or idea

cooperation acting together with others for a common purpose

dialogue conversation among characters

ensemble a group of actors working together to create an artistic whole rather than stressing individual players

improvise to make up the dialogue and action of a scene as you go along

set (1) establish definite movements and lines (2)* scenery used onstage

*this definition is used in another chapter

Yes, and . . .

Improvisation means acting without a script. It means creating a scene on the spot that you and your fellow actors— the **ensemble**—compose together. Improvisation requires a great deal of **collaboration** and trust. You must share ideas, believe that your partners will support you, and work together to create something all your own.

Successful improvisers say "yes, and. . . ." In other words, they embrace a situation or comment presented to them and react to it, add to it, and make it into a character or scene. They understand the value of listening carefully to their partners and the

purpose of that careful listening in building an improvised "reality." They understand the value of **concentration** and its purpose in sustaining spontaneously-created reality. And they understand the value of **cooperation,** recognizing that without the mutual support of partners, improvisation—or any dramatic endeavor, for that matter— would be impossible. When faced with a problem onstage, they use their wits through listening, concentration, and cooperation to solve it.

The most effective improvisations reflect the basic dramatic structure of characters working their way through some kind of problem or conflict. When working on a scene, follow these principles of improv.

- Always remain open to your partner(s), the plot, and your own ideas.

- Listen carefully and respond to your partner(s) onstage.

- Show, rather than tell, how you feel.

- Take chances! Don't be afraid to fail.

- Trust yourself and your partner(s).

Members of The Second City improvise a skit suggested by an audience member.

Resource Binder

- Audience Etiquette, TIPack, p. E

- Improvisation Activity Sheet, p. 20

- Improv Guidelines and Games Worksheet, p. 21

- Critique Sheet: Short Scene Improvisation, p. 22

- Improvisation Test, p. 23

Handbook Connections
pages 565–566

To Have on Hand

- Three or four chairs or cubes that can be used as chairs

- A table or a cube that can be used as a table

- Personal props such as hats, ties, scarves, purses, jackets, backpacks, and briefcases to help students get into character

Yes, and . . .

Inform students that improvisations generally fall into two basic categories—situation centered and character centered—but that most improvisations use elements of both. As improvisers, they can begin by creating characters and putting them into situations, or they can begin by developing situations and acting out a response to these situations.

ACTivity Hand out 3" x 5" cards and ask students to describe characters and situations that interest them. Collect the cards for use in scenes.

ACTivity To give students practice at responding positively and building on others' ideas, read the ideas on the 3" x 5" cards and ask students how they might go about creating a scene and characters.

Beginning Students
Call on students to add details to the situation or specific mannerisms for the characters already discussed in class.

Advanced Students
Challenge students to act out the situations presented in class and then to improvise what would happen next.

The image on this page shows a group of actors in the midst of an improvisation.

- How would you describe the characters in this photograph?

- How would you describe the situation?

- What might the standing character or the squatting characters say to begin the scene?

PREPARE

Commit to the Reality of Improv

To increase students' comfort levels regarding improvisation, point out that they should not try to be funny. Much of the comedy that comes out of improvisation is derived from the situations the characters find themselves in. If students simply commit to finding solutions within the context of the scene, humor will come.

ACTivity Storytelling activities can offer a gentle introduction to improvisation techniques. Begin a fictional narrative of any kind. Science fiction and fantasy are good for a start. Ask students to add to the story you are telling in any way that moves the narrative forward. As students gain confidence, you can use increasingly realistic beginnings. Encourage the students to transform ordinary beginnings into fantastic or outlandish improvisations.

If time and space permit, you might want to call for volunteers to act out the story elements as they arise.

ACTivity Allow each improv group to warm up by playing "bus stop" or "movie line." In either improvisation, one person waits at a bus stop or in a movie line and is then joined by unique characters who appear one at a time.

Easing into It

Discuss with students the necessity of conveying in clear, concise, effective language any directorial information that will help the group achieve their goal.

ACTivity Expand the activity in which students try to find a new use for an everyday object. After a student finds a novel use for the object, invite other students to come on the scene with other ways to use the object. Allow students to improvise a scene based on the object and the additional characters' ways of using it.

PREPARE

Commit to the Reality of Improv

This assignment will require that you respond naturally and immediately to any suggestion that pops into your mind or the mind of your partner(s). You will need to commit to the reality of an imaginary circumstance no matter how silly or impossible it seems.

Suppose, for example, that you and your partner or team are building a fire. One of your improv partners says, "I'm getting freezer burn from this fire!" Don't argue about whether freezer burn is possible; it already has happened. Your partner said it, so it's true. Instead of denying the idea, put yourself in a world where freezer burn from a fire is possible—or even common. Respond to your partner's predicament.

This does not mean you can't ever argue in an improvisation. You can blame your partner for getting freezer burn. You can berate your partner for bringing you to Jupiter in the first place. You can claim that your injury or problem is even worse than your partner's. You must, however, buy into your partner's reality. No matter what, you must remain "in the scene."

Easing into It

Unfortunately, there's no such thing as "easing into it"! You'll have to jump in with both feet. How do you make sense out of a leap into the void? These tips can help orient you:

- Remember that trust in the team is essential. Your improv partners will enter any reality you propose. They will believe your characters are real. They will build on the plot you imagine. You are not alone.

- You can develop a character from a gesture, a voice, an expression, a piece of clothing, and so on.

Career Focus
The Improv Group

If you are an aspiring actor, belonging to an improv group can hone your skills. If you want to be a doctor, lawyer, teacher, executive, sales rep, or any other person who deals with the public, improv can help you relax, be self-confident, and have a sense of humor about yourself. Collaboration and the ability to think on your feet are useful skills for many college majors.

Established improv groups frequently offer training and workshops. At many colleges, students can take classes in improvisation and join improv groups to develop and practice skills. Refer to the chart on page 10 for more ways to evaluate this career.

Backstage Gossip: It's for You

Improvisation skills can come in handy even during a performance of Shakespeare. During a production of *Julius Caesar*, actors Joseph Mahar and John Tillinger had pulled out their daggers and were just about to kill Caesar when the stage manager's phone rang. The ringing phone could be heard on stage and into the house. Aware that the audience had heard the phone, Mahar turned to Tillinger and asked, "What shall we do if it's for Caesar?"

The audience roared.

from *Broadway Anecdotes* by Peter Hay

Two students improvise a game of baseball.

- You can develop an activity—and spark a plot idea—by finding a new use for an everyday object, such as turning a pot into a helmet or an umbrella into a baseball bat.

- You can open dialogue by repeating a cliché, a line from a poem, or a bit of slang.

- After you have developed a scene, or even part of a scene, you can retain, or **set,** the parts of the scene that were effective. Then you can do the scene again with your partner, letting new ideas come to the surface. Again, set the material that works. Eventually, the material that is set gives you a framework in which to perform.

- Your scene, once you set it, will have the familiarity of a memorized script. But refrain from setting the scene in stone. Go ahead and improvise words, phrases, and new moments in any scene—even one that is "finished."

PRESENT

Perform an Improvisation

When your names are called, hand in your outlines or Activity Sheets, then with your partner or partners walk to the playing area. Be aware that it is perfectly normal to be nervous. Trust your partners to help you, try to relax, and enjoy the moment. When you have finished your improvised scene, turn to the audience and ask, "What happens next?" Take a suggestion and continue the improvisation for another minute.

When you are finished, pause and then bow politely before leaving the playing area.

The Language of
THEATRE

Work with a partner to show that you can identify and use formal and informal English.

- Improvise a short *dialogue* in informal, everyday English. Then say two sentences that you would use in a school assignment using more formal English.

- Discuss why *dialogue* is usually a good example of informal English. Identify an example of formal English in your textbook and discuss why it is appropriate there.

- Discuss why *collaboration* and *cooperation* are important when an ensemble improvises. Use a mixture of formal and informal English in your discussion.

- *Improvise* a *dialogue* to use in your improvisation project that uses informal English. After you have presented your project, write a formal paragraph about how you *set* different parts of the scene.

PRESENT

Perform an Improvisation

Show, Don't Tell To break the ice, ask students to call out a situation for you and a partner of your choosing to improvise. Suggest to the students how you would think through the scenario, the kinds of characters involved, and the direction the scene might take, and then do a short improv with your partner.

ACTivity When it comes time for the presenters to ask, "What happens next?" you might want to open the question to the entire class and ask volunteers to share their ideas for continuing the scene.

The Language of
THEATRE

Pair English learners with strong English speakers who can help them identify and understand the differences between informal English used in conversation and formal English used in classroom interactions and materials.

Vocabulary Enhancement

A given character or situation in an improvisation is called a *set up.*

From the Field: Taking Risks

Improvisation is part of the acting technique I learned from Stella Adler in New York. The cornerstone of her technique is improvisation, and to develop a sense of adventure in actors, she worked hard making the theatre a place where it is safe to explore.

We did lots of exercises to build trust and a sense of community. After the exercises, we'd work with a script to explore our characters' goals and objectives. Then we'd create improvisations in which we'd go after the objectives using our own words. By using improvisation in this way, actors can use their own experience as a way of pursuing a character's goals. Then, actors can go back to the text, and bring their own experience to it.

Dameon Carot, Actor, New York, New York

CRITIQUE

Evaluate Your Classmates' Improvisation

Hand out the Critique Sheet for this project or have students use their own paper. In either case, be sure students understand that the critique activity involves several steps, including note-taking, scoring, and writing.

This might be a good time to have pairs or groups of students compare, analyze, and evaluate their differing critiques in order to better understand other interpretations of similar dramatic presentations.

Spotlight on

Experimentation Remind students that experimentation may go in many directions within the two broad areas suggested. The purpose of experimentation is to continue to let the creative process of the improvisation flow.

- When researching styles, it may be especially useful for students to see scenes from productions in different styles using online videos or DVDs. Parody may be a more scripted form of experimentation with a style, but some aspects of parody might be applied to improvisation as well.

- Model one or more of the technical theatre experiments suggested to give students a feel for how they might use them in their own improvisations.

CRITIQUE

Evaluate Your Classmates' Improvisation

Choose one of the improvisations presented in class and evaluate it. Use a scale of 1 to 5, with 5 being "outstanding" and 1 being "needs much improvement." Ask yourself these questions:

- In what way did the actors remain true to the improvisational principle of "yes, and. . ."?

- How did the performers display trust and acceptance?
- How did the performers build on each other's suggestions?
- How well did the performers listen and respond to each other as they built dramatic structure into their scene?
- How did the partners show, rather than tell, their feelings?
- In what way did the performers keep you interested in the outcome of the scene?

Write an explanation of how you arrived at this score.

Spotlight on

Experimentation

In a sense, all improvisation is an experiment. When you are comfortable with basic improvisation, however, you can stretch your skills by experimenting in the following ways.

- **Experiment with different styles.** For example, try the scene you have worked out for this project as if it were a scene from a play by Shakespeare or a musical by Andrew Lloyd Webber. Do some research into theatrical genres and choose a few that interest you especially. Try to figure out some of the key elements in each style so you can work them into an improvisation in that style. No matter the style, however, do not lose sight of creating believable characters. Even in the world of improv, characters need to have recognizable and credible traits.

- **Experiment with technical theatre elements.** If you have picked up everyday objects and turned them into something creative in the act of improvising, you have already done some experimenting with technical elements—props, in this case. Try experimenting safely with other technical elements, such as set, sound, and lighting. For example, using projection, you could display changing scenes and adjust your improv to reflect the changes. In a similar way, you could provide a soundtrack mix that changes mood quickly and adjust your improv accordingly. Or you could change lighting randomly and improvise a meaning for the changes.

Backstage Gossip: If Only They'd Boo!

Modern audiences who don't like a play usually sit in stony silence. Once in a while, they boo. Audiences in the 19th century were often more forthcoming about their displeasure. Once, when Edmund Kean was touring, disaffected audience members tore out their seats and smashed the theatre lights in what came to be known as the "Boston Riot."

Additional Projects

1 Work with a team to improvise a comic scene showing what happens when an improv group fails to follow fundamental principles. Show the improv "fail" that results when group members fail to listen to one another, fail to concentrate, and fail to cooperate. Create a dramatic structure to serve as a framework for the improvisation, and refine your scene before presenting it to the class.

2 Form a discussion panel with four or more classmates. Have each participant represent the line of clothes of a particular designer, a magazine in a publishing house's stable, or a piece of furniture in a housewares store. Each improviser should adopt the personality of the item represented. The teacher or a classmate can serve as the moderator, asking various panel members questions, which they must answer in character.

3 Host a party for unusual superheroes, such as Yapping-Dog Man, Backwards Girl, or Bionic Bellower. The host should be a superhero, too. Have each superhero guest arrive at the party individually and reveal who he or she is. To provide dramatic structure to the scene, once all have arrived, the host should announce that he or she needs them to solve a world problem. Have the group of superheroes collaborate to solve the problem. Then repeat the scene, experimenting in a different style.

4 Bring to the front of the class an everyday object, such as a tennis racket, a paper bag, or a broom. Take turns with your classmates, one by one, experimenting to find a new use for the object. Then display that use for the class.

5 Read the scene between Argan and Louison in *The Imaginary Invalid* by Molière, found in Unit Eight. With a partner, improvise another scene in which Argan tries to extract information from Louison.

6 In a short multimedia project, explain how the skills needed for improvisation can be applied to college and career settings.

7 **Theatre Journal** Next time you go to a restaurant, park, or mall, sit for a moment and listen to the activity around you. Then jot down interesting fragments of conversation you overhear. Such fragments can make great opening lines in an improvisation.

Improvisation Test

The test for this chapter is available in blackline master form in the Resource Binder, page 23.

For More Information

Books

Caruso, Sandra, *The Young Actor's Book of Improvisation: Dramatic Situations from Shakespeare to Spielberg*, Heinemann, 1998.

Cassady, Marsh, *Spontaneous Performance: Acting Through Improv*, Meriwether Publishing, 2000.

Davies, Gil, *Staging a Pantomime*, A&C Black, 1995.

Spolin, Viola, *Improvisation for the Theater: A Handbook of Teaching and Directing Techniques*, 3rd. ed., Northwestern University Press, 1999.

Other Media

Collins, Rives, *Creative Drama and Improvisation*, DVD, Insight Media, 1990.

Improvisation for the Theatre, DVD, Insight Media, 2003.

Apps

The Amazing Improv Generator
Improv Suggestifier

Theatre Journal

Use the following as an additional or substitute prompt. Ask students to describe the people whose conversations they overhear and then to write about how they might use these characters in an improvisation.

Substitute Teacher Activities

Below are a few suggestions for one or more days when you will be out of the classroom:

• Assign the Improv Guidelines and Games Worksheet on page 21 of the Resource Binder.

• Teach the Improvisation section of the Student Handbook, pp. 565–566.

• Assign one or more of the Additional Projects on this page.

• **Plan a Journal Writing Session.** Encourage students to record an event or write about a person that captured their attention. Tell them to free write imaginatively about the person or event by adding a paragraph or more that begins with the words "What if . . . ."

Theatre **Then** and Now

Commedia Dell'arte

Commedia was an art form popular with the common people, as opposed to the literary plays attended by nobles and royalty. It required little in the way of props or technical elements, and the professional actors who performed it played equally well on both court stages and market squares.

In *commedia,* as in later forms of European theatre, actors often played one stock type their entire lives. They were completely familiar with the range of their character's expressions and thus could react quickly and creatively to any improvised circumstance.

Because *commedia* was so successful and adaptable, it spread rapidly throughout Europe. Actors simply adopted the stock characters and added their own scenarios and words.

Other Cultures, Other Times

It seems that elements of *commedia* have punctuated comedy as long as comedy has existed. Ancient Greek theatre and mime differ from classic *commedia* in that they were scripted. Nevertheless, the text of an ancient Greek mime found in Egypt has many of the elements later developed in *commedia*:

- Its text was a domestic comedy of love and adultery.
- It used stock comic characters.
- The script included gaps in which stage business could take place.
- It had outrageous plot elements that offended moralists.

Visual Cues

The images on this page show Pierrot and two players in the play *Scapin,* adapted from a Molière play.

- Describe the two figures in the photograph from *Scapin*.
- What elements identify them as stock characters?

Theatre **Then** and Now

Improvisation in the 1500s

Commedia Dell'arte

Developed in Italy from pantomimes that may have been remnants of ancient Roman comedy, *commedia dell'arte* (comedy of art) was flourishing in the middle 1500s. It was a highly-improvised comedy performed in the streets for the masses. A company, consisting usually of seven men and three women, would improvise action, dialogue, song, and dance around a familiar plot—one that usually involved love and intrigue. Actors had to be clever and inventive to keep the plot moving, and an athletic, agile body was necessary for the fights, acrobatic stunts, and dances that were required.

Commedia dell'arte is still performed around the world with many of the stock characters that were familiar to 16th-century Italians. A few of the most famous characters are the clever, witty, and mischievous Harlequin; the flirtatious and pretty Columbine; Pantalone, the gullible father; and Pierrot, the clown.

This recent performance of *Scapin* is based on Molière's adaptation of a *commedia dell'arte* play.

Pierrot, the clown, is often lovelorn and moody.

For More Information

Books

Grantham, Barry, *Playing Commedia: A Training Guide to Commedia Techniques,* Heinemann, 2000.

Kozlowski, Rob, *The Art of Chicago Improv: Shortcuts to Long-Form Improvisation,* Heinemann, 2002.

Novelly, Maria C., et al., *Theatre Games for Young Performers: Improvisations and Exercises for Developing Acting Skills,* Meriwether Publishing, 1985.

Rudin, Jeffrey, *Commedia dell'arte: A Handbook for Troupes,* Routledge, 2001.

Sweet, Jeffrey, *Something Wonderful Right Away,* Limelight Editions, 2004.

Other Media

Commedia dell'Arte: The Story, the Style, DVD, Insight Media, 2007.

Spirit of Commedia, DVD, Insight Media, 2005.

The Second City—First Family of Comedy, DVD, Acorn Media, 2007.

Improvisation Today

The Second City and Beyond

In 1955, a group of students, musicians, and actors rented a storefront attached to a bar. They fashioned a house and stage that featured a few nondescript chairs. And they called themselves the Compass Players.

The Compass Players wanted to try something no one else was doing. They wanted to improvise scenes from thin air. So they walked on stage and whipped up sketches about mothers and daughters, husbands and wives, dating, taxes, social issues, and anything else that came to mind. Sometimes they were hilarious. Sometimes they were terrible. No one—not even the actors—knew what would happen next.

Audiences loved the thrill of watching actors in process. And so, the idea caught on and led to the creation in 1959 of the most successful improv group to date—The Second City, named after the city in which it was born, Chicago, Illinois. The Second City is still a thriving theatrical event and is also a well-respected school in Chicago, with branches in Toronto, Cleveland, and Los Angeles. Talent for the long-running *Saturday Night Live* sketch comedy show was often recruited from The Second City. Early cast members from The Second City included John

Belushi, Dan Akroyd, and Bill Murray. More recent alumni include Tina Fey and Jason Sudeikis. Will Ferrell and Kristin Wiig are graduates of another improv theatre and school begun in 1974 in Los Angeles, The Groundlings.

Jordan Black, a former member of The Groundlings improv company, created an improv show called *The Black Version*. The premise is simple: audience members shout out movie titles, the director chooses one, and the all-black cast takes to the stage to improvise "the black version" of the movie.

Both Chicago and Los Angeles have continued to nurture improv talent as actors draw on their cultural heritage for comedy. In 2002, Salsation Theater Company was founded by Latino actors from Chicago's improv community. In the same year, Room to Improv was established in Los Angeles "to create a space for Asian Americans to tell stories" that appeal to diverse audiences.

The Second City and Beyond

The Second City took its name from its status as second to New York in population, size—and theatrical importance. But the success of The Second City made improvisation a theatrical industry in Chicago and elsewhere. Second City alumnus Del Close was at the forefront of many of these efforts. In the late 1960s, he helped organize an improv group known as the Committee. There, he began developing techniques for long-form improvisation, which Second City had begun exploring in 1962.

The Groundlings took its name from the members of the lower class who stood to watch plays during Shakespeare's time. Since its founding, the theatre has become a prime source of comedy talent for television and film. *The Black Version* is a show created by several of the troupe's African American actors. Their first "black version" was of the movie *E.T.*

Salsation Theatre Company uses both written sketch comedy shows and improvisation to tell stories of Latino life and heritage. The group performs in English and Spanish.

The image on this page shows improvisational actors in action.

- What attitude does the man on the far right seem to have?
- What might the man in the white jacket be looking at?
- How might these actors improvise a black version of a popular film?

Backstage Gossip: Alas, Poor Del!

Del Close once played the part of Polonius in a production of *Hamlet.* He won a Joseph Jefferson award for his performance, and he was grateful, but he jokingly claimed the role he really wanted to play was Yorick. When he died, his colleagues in the theatre were startled to learn that Close had willed his own skull to the Goodman Theatre, in the hope that it would be used in future theatrical productions of *Hamlet.*

Unit One Review

PREVIEW

1. Students should note the ability of theatre to activate empathy in audiences, resulting in better understanding of ourselves and others in society as a whole and in personal lives. Further, theatre raises consciousness on important issues facing society, and it serves as a mirror for both the greatness and foibles of humans.

2. Actors should warm up to relax, master the body, build confidence, and use up nervous energy.

3. Observation aids the imagination and the memory so that actors can play the reality of various scenes.

4. Students should demonstrate as well as explain their answers.

5. Answers may vary. Actors and children both give themselves over to the scenes they enact.

6. Answers will vary. Mimes primarily wish to communicate without words.

7. Student demonstrations should include body language such as a frown and clenched fists.

8. Answers will vary. Students should note that in real life, people adjust to new circumstances constantly and their remarks are not rehearsed.

9. Saying "Yes, and . . . " moves the action forward so that a scene can build, and advances the improvisation rather than shutting it down.

PREPARE

10. Answers will vary but should reflect an understanding of working effectively with a partner.

11. Answers will vary but should reflect collaboration.

Unit One Review

PREVIEW

Examine the following key concepts previewed in Unit One.

1. What is the value of theatre, both socially and personally?

2. Why it is important for actors to warm up before a rehearsal or performance?

3. How does observation help you as an actor?

4. If you were to play a character devoted to a pet, how would you speak to, touch, and talk about that pet? Give examples.

5. How is a child's game of make-believe similar to an actor playing a role?

6. What is the mime's objective?

7. Without using words, indicate that you are angry about something.

8. How is improvisation like real life?

9. Why is it important to say "Yes, and . . ." in improvisation?

PREPARE

Assess your response to the preparation process for projects in this unit.

10. Was it easier to prepare with a partner you chose or one that your teacher chose for you? Why?

11. When working with a partner, how did you decide which tasks you would take on and which your partner would be responsible for?

12. Were you able to fully utilize all five senses when using your sensory recall? Which senses seemed easier to call upon and why?

13. What techniques did you use to visualize your pantomime project?

14. Did you find it more difficult to prepare for your pantomime or your improvisation project? Why?

PRESENT

Analyze the experience of presenting your work to the class.

15 Were you able to have fun while presenting your childhood memories and your warm-up routine? Why or why not?

16 In describing your object, were you able to help your audience see it clearly? Did you forget any important elements?

17 Were you able to become fully immersed in the pantomime you presented, or did you lose focus? What did you find distracting? How did this feel?

18 When the audience gave a suggestion for continuing your improvisation, were you able to do this to your satisfaction or would you do it differently now? If so, in what way?

CRITIQUE

Evaluate how you go about critiquing your work and the work of others.

19 What were the major stumbling blocks to remaining fair, impartial, or constructive while critiquing your classmates' presentations?

20 In what way did critiquing your classmates help you critique your own performances?

21 What strategies do you use or can you develop to make the most of constructive feedback from your peers on your own performances?

EXTENSIONS

- Look at the image to the left. Use your powers of observation and sensory and emotional recall to perform a short pantomime of someone eating this sundae.

- Practice standing in positions that show the following feelings, and then choose one to present to the class: impatience, sorrow, hope, delight, concern, contempt, anticipation, support.

Resource Binder
Unit One Test, p. 24

---

12 Answers should demonstrate an awareness of the five senses.

13 Answers should reflect the use of recall techniques.

14 Answers will vary.

PRESENT

15 Answers will vary but should reflect an analytical approach to the presentation of the childhood memories and warm-up routine.

16 Answers should reflect an awareness of the use of the senses in description.

17 Answers will vary but students should describe the situation rather than blame themselves or others.

18 Answers should display thought about the student's work.

CRITIQUE

19 Answers should display self-reflection.

20 Answers should reflect an understanding of objective criteria.

21 Answers should reflect an understanding of the benefits of receiving constructive feedback from peers.

EXTENSIONS

Encourage students to take chances in these extensions. Remind them that they will not know if they have worked to the extent of their abilities unless they fail once in a while.

Unit **Two**

Elements of Acting

Unit Two, along with Unit Three, will give students a clear picture of how actors prepare for a role and how they, along with other members of the production team, work together to create an artistic, meaningful, and unified whole. Projects in this unit will help students move comfortably on the stage and understand how they can improve their vocal production and articulation.

Project Preview

Chapter 6 Movement
Creating stage movement for a scene

Chapter 7 Stage Directions
Plotting stage crosses

Chapter 8 Voice Production and Articulation
Demonstrating a vocal exercise

Chapter 9 Ensemble Work
Performing as part of an ensemble

Unit **Two**   Elements of Acting

Quotables

Use the quotes below as journal writing prompts, discussion starters, or for your own enjoyment.

The performer's art is as much intellectual as physical; there is meaning in his movements; every gesture has its significance.

Lucien of Samosata, 2nd-century Greek Writer

Language springs out of the inmost parts of us. No glass renders a man's likeness so true as his speech.

Ben Jonson, 17th-century Dramatist and Poet

53

The following questions are intended to tap into students' **prior knowledge** and attitudes about the subject matter of this unit.

- Have you ever been on a stage for any kind of production? Describe the experience.

- How did you feel when you moved on the stage? Awkward? Comfortable? Confused?

- Who told you where to move? Did they use any special terminology such as *upstage* or *stage right*?

- Have you ever spoken to a group or an audience? Was it a class presentation? Speech? Acting role? Other?

- What happened to your voice in this speaking situation? Did you try to enunciate more clearly? Did you mumble? Did your throat tighten up? Could your audience hear you?

- As an audience member, what kinds of listening experiences have you had?

- What kind of team or group have you been a part of? Sports team? Singing group? Cooperative learning project? Debate club? Theatrical production? Family event?

- Describe your experiences in the team or group. Did you work well together or not?

Theatre Journal

Have students write a short dialogue for the characters in the photo. They should consider the following: What is the situation? Are the man and woman at odds with one another, or are is there someone else not pictured who is part of the conflict? How do you know?

Visual Cue

The image above shows actors in the acclaimed 2013 Bangladesh production of *Muktodhara*, written by Nobel Laureate Rabindranath Tagore in 1922, one theme of which is humans vs. machines.

- Describe the people in the picture. What kinds of characters are they playing?

- What emotion might the actors be expressing? How do you know?

- How do the actors' bodies show this emotion?

ACTivity Have pairs of students stand and replicate the actors' stances and facial expressions. On the count of three, they should assume another position that they feel shows the same emotion.

ACTivity Have pairs of students work out an improvisation that begins with them taking on the characters and stances of the actors in the picture.

Chapter 6

Movement

This chapter introduces students to the importance of natural movement on the stage and how movement communicates important information about a character.

Objectives

1 to understand how to execute natural body movements on stage

2 to learn how to incorporate stage business into a scene

3 to understand how natural, believable movement enhances characterization

4 to plan and execute a scene incorporating stage movement

Project Specs

Special Needs Students
This project may need to be simplified. Have ready preplanned scenarios that incorporate a few easy movements.

Advanced Students
Instruct students to perform the same movement scene again, incorporating music that reflects the mood of the scene. They should determine if the music changed the way the characters moved or heightened the scene's emotion.

On Your Feet

Show, Don't Tell Choose a capable student as your partner, and demonstrate how to communicate the way in which two strangers riding in an elevator might behave.

---

6 Movement

Whether you're the lead or one of the supporting players, whether you have long monologues or no lines to speak at all, the one thing you will be doing as an actor on stage is *moving*. How, when, and where to move takes some practice, so get moving!

Project Specs

Project Description You and a partner will plan and present stage movement for a two- to four-minute scene.

Purpose to practice moving naturally onstage

Materials a written scenario that details the movement needed for the scene or the Movement Activity Sheet provided by your teacher

Theatre Terms

cheating out
gestures
muscular memory
offstage
onstage
scenario
stage business
upstaging

On Your Feet

With a partner, use only movement to communicate the actions, thoughts, and feelings for the situations below. Stand about five feet apart. Depending on the situation you are enacting, you will move toward or away from your partner and use body language to add further texture to the moment.

- a surprise meeting between friends who haven't seen each other in a long time
- two strangers pretending not to notice each other
- friends or siblings who have just had a big argument
- friends saying good-bye knowing they will not meet again

Theatre Terms

cheating out playing toward the audience while seemingly conversing with others on stage

gestures movements of parts of the body, such as shrugging the shoulders

muscular memory having an action appear effortless and natural due to repeating the movement many times

offstage the part of the stage that the audience cannot see

onstage the part of the stage that is visible to the audience

scenario an outline of a play that includes details about the plot, movement, and gestures

stage business any small action that the actor performs without major movement

upstaging drawing the audience's attention to yourself when it should be focused on another character

The Magic of Movement

In daily life you probably don't pay all that much attention to the way you move. But **onstage** as an actor, you must persuade the audience that the small environment is whatever the scene calls for—a ship, a living room, a faraway galaxy, or a doctor's waiting room—and that you are a real person interacting within that environment.

To be physically believable and natural onstage, you will need solid stage movement techniques to consistently express actions, thoughts, and feelings nonverbally. The safe and appropriate techniques that follow will help you convey real meaning through your stage movements.

Moving on Stage

Entering Make sure you are in position and ready to enter the stage in character and on cue. Enter with your head up, unless your character's thoughts or emotions demand otherwise. Know the exact point at which you

A scene from *The Mikado* by the English National Opera, September 1994.

become visible to the audience. You don't want the audience to see you when you think you're hidden **offstage**—it takes away from the magic of the performance.

Walking Your normal walking movement should be rhythmical and smooth. As you walk, look ahead. To portray certain characters, however, your walk may be slow, labored, jittery, and so on.

Standing Keep your weight on the balls of your feet. Unless you have a motivated movement to make, stand still. An actor's shuffling feet reveal nervousness and inexperience and can make the audience uncomfortable.

Turning When turning on stage, keep the audience in mind and turn toward them. The only exception to this rule is when such a turn would be obviously awkward because you are already in a position facing mostly away from the audience.

Sitting If the scene calls for you to sit, place yourself in a comfortable position, but make sure you are poised to get up when you need to. Never slouch unless the role specifically calls for it. If you must back up to the chair to sit down, do so until you touch it with the back of your leg, and then sit.

Chapter 6 Movement **55**

The Magic of Movement

"Actions speak louder than words." Write this phrase on the chalkboard and ask the students to discuss what it means. Assuming this statement is true, how a character moves must reveal just as much if not more about the character than what he or she actually says. Discuss the ways in which we communicate nonverbally with body language, facial expressions, and gestures.

ACTivity Have volunteers stand before the class and give them a specific ensemble movement to perform. Then give each individual volunteer a specific emotion to portray and ask them to express their emotion while still performing the ensemble movement.

Moving On Stage

Show, Don't Tell Demonstrate for the students the proper way to execute the stage movements of entering, walking, standing, turning, sitting, rising, gesturing, and exiting.

ACTivity Select a scene from a play that incorporates several movements. Have the students perform the scene using the stage movements discussed in the text.

Visual Cues

The Mikado, with music by Arthur Sullivan and lyrics by W. S. Gilbert, is arguably the most popular opera ever written. This comic opera opened on March 14, 1885, and has been delighting audiences ever since. The pictured 1994 production was a controversial performance because director Jonathan Miller changed the setting from Japan to a 1920s English seaside hotel.

- How are the characters expressing their individuality through their gestures?

- What different emotions can you see portrayed by the characters in the photograph?

Resource Binder

- Movement Activity Sheet, p. 28

- Stage Business Worksheet, p. 29

- Critique Sheet: Movement, p. 30

- Movement Test, p. 31

Handbook Connections
pages 567–569

To Have on Hand

- A stopwatch to time the movement scene—for practice and performance

- A playing space and one or two chairs so that the students may incorporate the proper way to stand, sit, and rise into their movement scene presentations

- Scripts or playbooks with movement written into them for advanced extensions of the assignment

- Cards with situations on them for the On Your Feet assignment—have pairs of students draw a situation and perform

Moving forward before rising helps you get up with ease.

The gestures and the expressions of the actors above show their feelings.

Rising When getting up from your seat, anticipate the move by slowly easing forward on the chair. Keep your spine straight and rise with your weight on one foot and then shift it to the other to ensure balance.

Gesturing Gestures are bodily actions, such as shrugging, pointing, or raising the eyebrows, that express thoughts, emotions, and actions. Gestures should be definite and clear. Halfhearted gestures show a lack of experience or focus.

Exiting Be sure you stay in character until you are offstage and invisible to the audience.

Practice these stage movement techniques until you can use them so effectively that they appear effortless to the audience. Only through sustained practice will you be able to move naturally onstage without having to think about it constantly. This constant repetition of motion helps you develop **"muscular memory."**

The Language of
THEATRE

Work with a partner to tell a story that includes specific and detailed description.

- Tell a brief story about a familiar activity, such as running to catch up with friends. Use movements and *gestures* along with words to tell the story.

- Share a story in which someone walks into class late. Describe the scene, including the movement and *gestures* of the people involved in as much detail as you can.

- Narrate a detailed story in which you describe someone getting on a bus or getting up from a sunken couch. Discuss how you might develop *muscular memory* if you were presenting the story *onstage*.

- Describe how a movement you have noticed in people *offstage* might be adapted for a scene *onstage*. Discuss a detailed *scenario* in which that movement might be used.

Backstage Gossip: The Plot Sickened

On the whole, actors like to arrive on stage on cue and leave in an orderly manner as rehearsed. It isn't always possible. George Sanders appeared in a play when he was coming down with gastric flu. In the middle of his last scene, he suddenly announced to the rest of the company that he was popping out for a breath of fresh air. He left the stage in great haste—while the other characters stayed where they were—dumbfounded—and returned less than a minute later having thrown up in the wings. He then completed his performance as usual.

from *Great Theatrical Disasters* by Gyles Brandreth

Working Out the Scene: Beginning, Middle, and End

With a partner, you are to perform a two- to four-minute scene that incorporates basic movement principles and action. You will have to coordinate the onstage movement between you and your partner. You will perform a scene that shows what both characters want (their intentions), a conflict, and a resolution—in other words, it will have dramatic structure. Your scene will have a beginning, middle, and end.

Create a Scenario

You will not need to create dialogue for this scene. You will convey meaning and communicate all actions, feelings, and thoughts through movements, gestures, and facial expressions. However, you and your partner will have to collaborate to write a detailed **scenario**—an outline that includes information about the plot, what each character wants, how their intentions conflict, and what they do about it.

You can use one of the suggestions at the right as a jumping-off point, or you can create a scenario of your own. As your scenario takes shape, write down each action and each major shift in the two characters' intentions using as much detail as possible.

Add the Movement

Once you have written the scenario, experiment with movement, gestures, and facial expressions. For example, if one character enters a scene in which the other character is already onstage, from what direction does the entering actor come? Where is the onstage actor standing (or sitting)? How do the actors greet each other? Do they smile or frown? Indicate movement with specific notations such as these:

Character 1 moves from left to right and opens the door. Character 2 enters.

After they exchange pleasantries, Character 1 motions for Character 2 to sit in the chair on the left side of the playing area.

Character 2 sits in the right-hand chair instead.

Character 1 looks displeased and sits opposite Character 2.

Discuss what meaning you want to convey with each stage movement or gesture you create. For example, when Character 2 doesn't sit in the recommended chair, what effect does this have on each character—and on the scene? Have a specific reason for each movement you devise. Take the scene as far as you can.

Possible Scenarios

- You wait for a competitive friend to come and play chess. When your friend arrives, you begin to play. Show what happens during and after the game.
- You are typing a research paper when there is a knock at the door. A pushy neighbor who wants to sell you tickets to a school carnival enters. You don't want to buy any tickets. What happens next?
- You enter a shoe store and sit down to be waited on. You tell the tired clerk the type of shoe you want. He brings three pairs. You begin trying on shoes. What does the clerk do? What do you do? Do you buy any shoes?

PREPARE

Working Out the Scene: Beginning, Middle, and End

Discuss with the students the plot structure of a play, focusing on the idea of opposing goals or intentions that create a conflict between characters.

ACTivity Using a familiar fairy tale such as *Goldilocks and the Three Bears*, break down the elements of the story. For example:

Beginning—The bears leave home and Goldilocks walks into their house.

Middle—Goldilocks proceeds to eat their food and use their house as though it were her own, finishing Little Bear's porridge and breaking his chair.

End—The bears return home to find Goldilocks in Little Bear's bed. She awakens and runs away.

Follow up by discussing the conflict and resolution of the story.

Create a Scenario

Invite students to give examples of other scenario outlines of well-known stories. Have different students describe the beginning, middle, and end of each story, followed by a discussion of various characters' goals and conflicts.

Add the Movement

ACTivity Using the example scenarios students have contributed, ask volunteers for suggestions on movement notations—how the characters move, if gestures are needed, what facial expressions might be appropriate, and so on.

Possible Scenarios

Encourage students to explore the emotions of the people in each of the possible scenarios presented. How would the person awaiting a chess match feel? How might his or her gestures and movements reveal these feelings to the audience?

Notes

_____

_____

_____

_____

_____

_____

_____

_____

Rehearse the Scene

After explaining how to rehearse the scene, hand out the Movement Activity Sheet and show the students how to use it. Give the students a time limit for completing the preparation of their presentations. Keep a stopwatch handy to help students stay within the time limit. If students are having artistic disagreements, help them work through any problems by suggesting ways to compromise and collaborate effectively.

Here's How

Have students demonstrate stage business techniques they would incorporate into these scenes:

- Reading a newspaper on a hot July evening

- Preparing a picnic by the sea

- Waiting for a long-overdue bus

- Cooking dinner at a campsite

- Walking home with a friend on a snowy day

 sual Cue

The following prompts can be used to exercise **critical viewing skills.**

- What makes this stage picture interesting?

- Discuss the various types of movement on the stage.

- What do you think is happening in this scene? What is it about the characters' body language that leads you to this conclusion?

ACTivity Have students create stage pictures like the one in the photo above. Ask a volunteer to begin by freezing into an interesting pose. Have the class study the pose and think about how they could compliment the stage picture. When students have an idea, they enter the picture and strike a new pose. Eventually, the entire class should be part of the portrait.

Each of the actors in this scene has a good sense of his motivation and position onstage.

Rehearse the Scene

Practice your scene with your partner. Watch each other's movements, gestures, and facial expressions. Is everything clear? Does the scene make sense? Does the movement illustrate the characters' thoughts, feelings, and actions as well as their relationship and the situation? Make and accept suggestions for improvement. Go through the scene again. This time, make sure you are staying within the two- to four-minute time frame. When you have shaped the scene to the best of your ability, think of a title for it. Then work out the technical details of how you will set up for the scene, which of you will introduce the scene, and what you will do once you've finished performing.

Remember that no move you make will matter if the audience can't see it. Successful actors develop an innate sense of their positioning onstage in relationship to the audience.

Here's How
To Incorporate Stage Business

Any small action that the character performs without major movement is called **stage business.** Sometimes stage business is written into the script as directions, but generally it is added by the director and actor. If your character continually knits or is forever whittling a piece of wood, this reveals something about his or her nature. Stage business may communicate the time of day or the season. If you toast bread at the table, it suggests morning. Fanning yourself with a newspaper indicates a hot day in summer. Business can also create atmosphere or add interest to the play. Whatever specific business is used, it should be planned early in the rehearsals and practiced at each one. Remember, you must have a good reason for performing all stage business.

58   Unit Two Elements of Acting

From the Field: See It with Your Elbow!

Viola Spolin's phrase "See it with your elbow!" is one I use to express to the students the importance of total body awareness. The whole body must react and feel what the character is experiencing. If the character is feeling sad, the audience must then see sadness in the way the character enters the room, in the walk, the gestures, and facial expressions. I encourage students to get their entire bodies into the scene—from head to toe.

Carmen McElwaine, Drama Instructor, Plano, Texas

Spotlight on

The Rules of Stage Movement

Become familiar with these six basic principles of stage movement.

1 Onstage, movement should always be *motivated* by the intentions of the actors in the scene. Make sure that when you move onstage you know exactly *why* you are doing so. React as though experiencing a stimulus to which you respond instinctively.

2 Movement must be *simplified*. There is no point in creating busy traffic patterns onstage. Simpler is best.

3 Movement must be *heightened* from real life. In real life you might wander into a room for no apparent reason and promptly walk back out again. In a scene onstage, however, each action counts.

4 Movement must *delineate* character. Movement tells the audience a great deal about characters and their relationship to one another. Make sure your movement is in keeping with your character's thoughts and feelings.

5 Movement must be *toward the audience.* To create realistic interactions actors must have contact with the other people onstage. However, keeping an "open" position—one that turns you slightly toward the audience—works best. Often this is referred to as **cheating out.**

6 To maintain balanced and pleasing stage pictures an actor must *adjust to the movement of others*. Taking out a handkerchief on stage while another actor is the focus of the scene or angling your body so that your scene partner must turn away from the audience to speak to you is called **upstaging.** It is rude. Never do it.

Actors cheating out

The Rules of Stage Movement

ACTivity To help students work on motivated intentions when moving onstage, write the following sentence on the chalkboard:

David didn't tell me you were invited to the party.

Then have students create a movement while saying this line with one of the following intentions:

• to charm the person

• to intimidate the person

• to ridicule the person

• to indicate a social error has been made

• to show surprised delight

• to show stunned outrage

Tell students they may approach the scene in a serious or humorous way, but remind them that they must move and speak naturally and convincingly— no overacting.

ACTivity Have students practice cheating out by standing together in the playing area and carrying on a conversation.

Backstage Gossip: Bad Stage Business

John Barrymore (grandfather of Drew Barrymore) once played a father who strongly disapproved of his daughter's fiancé. In one scene, as the fiancé left the stage, the daughter would ask her father what he thought of his future son-in-law. Barrymore was supposed to answer, "I think he is a dirty dog." One night, when the fiancé walked off stage, he accidentally tipped over a pitcher of water. An awkward moment of silence followed as everyone watched a puddle form. The daughter asked on cue, "What do you think of Tom, father?" To which Barrymore replied, "I think he is a dirty dog. And what's more, he isn't even housebroken!"

from the Web site *www.anecdotage.com*

PRESENT

Perform a Scene Using Stage Movement

Before beginning the movement scenes, remind the students to hand in their Activity Sheets when their names are called. Tell students who are watching, that proper audience behavior begins as soon as the Activity Sheet is handed in. They should remain quiet and attentive for the duration of the performance. Have a stopwatch ready to time each scene.

CRITIQUE

Evaluate Classmates' Scenes

Hand out the Critique Sheet for this project or have students use their own paper. In either case be sure the students understand that the critique activity involves several steps including note-taking, scoring, and writing. It will be helpful to assign the scenes that each student will evaluate so that everyone receives a peer evaluation.

As you evaluate presentations, let the students know that you will be using the same rubrics for them as they will be using for each other. In addition to their presentations, you may also wish to evaluate students on how well they assess the other presentations.

When projects have been completed, cut off the names of the reviewers and hand the Critique Sheets back to the students being reviewed.

PRESENT

Perform a Scene Using Stage Movement

When your name is called, hand in your scenario or Activity Sheet and walk to the playing area. Deliver your introduction to the scene as you and your partner rehearsed it. Then pause a moment to focus on your character, and then perform your two- to four-minute scene for the class.

At the end of the scene, turn to your classmates and ask, "What just happened here?" If you have performed well, they should be able to track the plot of your scene.

Allow only two minutes for the discussion. When you are finished, thank your audience and bow politely before leaving the playing area. Remember to retain a professional demeanor until you have reached your seat.

CRITIQUE

Evaluate Classmates' Scenes

Evaluate one or two of the scenes presented in class. Begin your critique by listing all the positive aspects of the scene. Then move on to the areas that in your view needed improvement, including anything that seemed unclear in the scene. Then, using the following rating scale, give the scene a number score: "outstanding" = 5; "well done" = 4; "fair" = 3; "needs some improvement" = 2; "needs much improvement" = 1.

To give an accurate, well-supported critique, ask yourself these questions:

- Did the scene have a beginning, middle, and end?
- How did each character make his or her intentions clear?
- Did each performer respond to what the other was doing?
- Were movements motivated by the characters' intentions?
- Did the movement seem appropriate and spontaneous, or was there unnecessary business?
- Were you interested in the outcome, or resolution, of the scene?

Write a paragraph explaining why you gave the score or scores you did.

Notes

Additional Projects

1 Determine basic movement that you can use to communicate the thoughts, feelings, and actions of the following characters: a loudmouthed, ignorant person; a nervous, high-strung person; a vigorous athlete; an extremely weak or tired person; a timid, self-conscious person; and one other of your choice. Pay particular attention to mannerisms and gestures, the placement of your weight, and the degree of tension in your movements. If you are up for the challenge, try doing one or two of the above without any facial expression.

2 Experiment with stage movements by trying to apply animal movements to humans. Visit a zoo, farm, wooded area, or park near your home. Select a bird or animal to observe. Note the individual movements of this creature's paws, head, eyes, tail, wings, and so on. Pay close attention to specific mannerisms. In class, portray the animal's action. Then transfer those characteristics into human action. Your human portrayal should maintain the basic movements, rhythm, and patterns of the animal and convey thoughts, feelings, and actions.

3 Think of a situation that involves waiting—waiting in line, waiting for a bus, or waiting for a friend's arrival. Choose an age at least ten years older or younger than your current age. Then go to the playing area and portray a person of that age in your chosen situation. Make sure you incorporate the body rhythm, facial expressions, and the basic movements and attitudes of that age group. Keep your movements selective and specific.

4 Read the scene from *You Can't Take It With You* by Moss Hart and George F. Kaufman found in Unit Eight. With several partners, devise stage movements for the character of Kirby that convey his thoughts, feelings, and actions. Model those movements for the class.

5 Theatre Journal Keep notes on what you observe about the way people move when doing various things, such as walking down stairs or describing something large and impressive.

"One onstage movement can convey pages of thought and yet the same movement—overdone—has a hammy meaning all its own."

—Actor Richard Basehart

Substitute Teacher Activities

Here are suggestions for one or more days when you will be out of the classroom.

- Assign the Stage Business Worksheet on page 29 of the Resource Binder.

- Teach the Motivation, Movement, and Creating Believable Action sections of the Student Handbook, pp. 566–568.

- Assign one or more of the Additional Projects on this page.

- Play **"What's My Move?"** On 3" x 5" cards list a number of situations, such as "You've just been cut from the team" or "You are out on a date with the most boring person on earth." Students must demonstrate the movements that would accompany the situation.

Movement Test

The test for this chapter is available in blackline master form in the Resource Binder, page 31.

For More Information

Books

Evans, Mark, *Movement Training for the Modern Actor*, Routledge, 2008.

King, Nancy, *A Movement Approach to Acting*, Prentice Hall, 1981.

Kline, Peter, *Physical Movement for the Theatre*, Rosen Publishing Group, 1971.

Lecoq, Jacques, *The Moving Body: Teaching Creative Theatre*, Theatre Arts Books, 2002.

Sabatine, Jean, *Movement Training for the Stage and Screen: The Organic Connection Between Mind, Spirit, and Body*, Watson-Guptill Publishing, 1995.

Wangh, Andre Gregory, *An Acrobat at the Heart*, Vintage Books, 2000.

White, Edwin C., et al., *Acting and Stage Movements: A Complete Handbook for Amateurs and Professionals*, Meriwether Publishing, 1985.

Other Media

Body Language, DVD, Insight Media, 2012

Body Language for Actors: Portraying Different Cultures, DVD, Insight Media, 2007.

Apps

Rehearsal 2
Theater Blocking

Theatre Journal

Use the following as an additional or substitute prompt.

As you watch people move in their various activities, think about what emotion each person must be feeling.

Discuss possibilities as to what may have happened to the person before the moment that you began observing them, leading to the emotion they are now portraying.

Theatre **Then** and Now

Ritual Dance Movement

Ritual dance was performed with the intention of influencing or controlling events important to society, such as desired rainfall, success in battle, and so on. Rituals were also performed with the intention of glorifying deities, ancestors, or an important victory. Masks, costumes, and body paint were often worn in order to call forth a higher power or to represent an animal in the hunt. These rituals contained great spectacle, and as a result became a form of entertainment to society.

A common Native American dance was the bull dance, in which the costumes consisted of actual buffalo heads as headdresses and buffalo skins.

In 1808, playwright James Nelson Barker wrote a romantic drama about Pocahontas, *The Indian Princess,* which became the first play about Native Americans to reach the stage. On the whole, American plays of the 19th century presented American Indians as "noble savages."

In 1871 a new and unfortunate trend began when Augustin Daly's play *Horizon* presented Native Americans as villains. Finally, in the middle 1900s, more realistic and historically accurate plays began to appear, such as *Black Elk Speaks,* based on the life of a Sioux holy man, written for the stage by Christopher Sergel.

Dancing is an important part of Native American society.

Theatre **Then** and Now

Ritual Dance Movement

Dance and music have been important parts of human interaction since the beginning of recorded time. Sound, rhythm, and exuberant physical movement are as much a part of theatre today as they were thousands of years ago.

The theatre as we know it is believed to have evolved from shamanism and ritual dance. A shaman was a priest figure common to almost all very early cultures. Part of the shaman's job was to communicate with the gods on behalf of his community. This communication often took the form of physical imitation of animals and symbolic movements depicting weather systems or crop growth. As early as 2500 B.C., rituals merged with traditional dance to form elaborate theatrical ceremonies.

 **Visual Cue**

Have students study the image of the Native American dancer and then respond to the following questions:

• What challenges, responsibilities, and gratification would dancing in authentic costume offer the Native American dancer?

• How do costumes affect the way we move on stage? Would an actor move differently depending on the costume?

Modern Movement

In the Canadian town of Gaspe, a group of stilt walkers, jugglers, and specialty performers created a new kind of circus—a mesmerizing blend of theatre, circus techniques, street performance, high-tech lighting and sound, and eye-popping costumes. The year was 1984 and they called themselves **Cirque du Soleil** (Circus of the Sun). Their goal was nothing less than to "reinvent the circus." Pure physical movement and music form the common language that allows audiences to journey with Cirque du Soleil to a place of dreams and wonder. Cirque du Soleil has also made films of its shows for television and IMAX theatres. For more information, visit their Web site at www.cirquedusoleil.com.

The Blue Man Group features three bald-headed, blue-faced characters who take their audience through a fast-paced, multisensory experience that blends slapstick, music, art, and science into a thrilling new theatrical form. The group's award-winning theatrical productions have been described as "ground-breaking," "visually stunning," and "musically powerful." Their props include Jell-O, marshmallows, rolls and rolls of toilet paper, and

Cirque du Soleil shines on.

cans of paint, among other things. These inventive blue fellows have a unique style of percussion music, which they play primarily on invented instruments—such as large plastic tubing, flexible fiber rods, gigantic gongs, and sheets of aluminum.
Visit their entertaining Web site at www.blueman.com.
Blue Men move to the beat of their own drums.

Modern Movement

In addition to Blue Man Group and Cirque du Soleil, another exciting group found audience favor in the 1990s. The best way to describe them is to say that *Stomp* is a unique blend of percussion, movement, and visual comedy. Its creators, Luke Cresswell and Steve McNicholos, first presented the show on the streets of Brighton, England, where a group of street performers, commonly known as "buskers," tried to attract people's attention by their performances. Busking is a custom in England dating back to the Middle Ages.

Stomp contains no dialogue nor plot, but replaces it with the everyday sounds of garbage can lids, pipes, brooms, and so on, creating an incredible display of music and movement. The show premiered in England to high acclaim and eventually began its run at the Orpheum Theatre in New York in February of 1994.

 Play excerpts from various kinds of music and ask students to write a description of the movement that comes to mind as they listen. Discuss with students how music can affect the telling of a story, the expressing of an emotion, or the way characters move on stage. If there is time, have students get up and move as the music is played again.

Visual Cue

- In the top photo, what do you think is the most important physical attribute of the person on the ring?

- In the bottom photo, do you think the blue makeup encourages the audience to focus more on the men's faces or their movements?

- Would the visual impact be different if they were Green Man Group?

For More Information

Books
Burton, Bryan, *Moving Within the Circle, Contemporary Native American Music and Dance,* World Music Press, 1993.

Vial, Veronique, *Varekai: Cirque du Soleil,* Harry N. Abrams, 2003.

Vial, Veronique, *Wings: Backstage with Cirque du Soleil!!!,* Arena Editions, 1999.

Other Media
Cirque du Soleil—Flow, DVD, Columbia/Tristar, 2007.

Cirque du Soleil—Worlds Away, DVD, Paramount, 2013.

Dance of the Spirits: Mask Styles and Performance, DVD, Insight Media, 1988.

The World of American Indian Dance, DVD, Insight Media, 2003.

www.stomponline.com

Chapter **7**

Stage Directions

This chapter introduces students to the stage areas, the effect of the actor's body position on stage, and movement across the stage.

Objectives

1 to understand and practice body positioning

2 to become familiar with the areas of the stage

3 to use movement to create expression of thought, feeling, and character

4 to plot and execute stage directions

Project Specs

Tape or draw the floor of the playing area into nine sections representing the stage areas shown on p. 66.

Special Needs Students

Note that students with dyslexia may need extra help with the "backwards" left and right stage terminology in this chapter.

Advanced Students

To complete the project, have students use a real script that combines dialogue as well as crosses.

On Your Feet

Show, Don't Tell Before the game begins, demonstrate *stage left* and *stage right* for students. You may wish to have a small prize for the last person standing.

7 Stage Directions

Don't just stand there—do something! Theatre is all about dramatic action. The action and excitement in a play are both supported by—even created by—movement. Effective stage movement is an indispensable part of a gripping production, and the actor must know how to follow stage directions every step of the way.

Project Specs

Project Description You will plot three stage crosses for a classmate to execute and then perform a classmate's three stage crosses in two to three minutes.

Purpose to learn to create and follow stage directions and to assume body positions accurately and with confidence

Materials a drawing showing three stage crosses or the Stage Directions Activity Sheet your teacher gives you

On Your Feet

Play "Simon Says Staging!" with a small group. A "director" calls out directions in which the group must move either "stage right" or "stage left" while facing the director. For example, "Hop stage left" or "Kick stage right."

Theatre Terms

backstage
counter-cross
cross
downstage/upstage
full back/full front
profile
quarter turn
raked
sightlines
stage left/stage right
three-quarter turn

Theatre Terms

backstage behind the stage; out of view

counter-cross moving in the opposite direction of an actor making a cross

cross movement across the stage

downstage toward the audience

full back/full front facing or completely turned away from the audience

profile sideways to the audience

quarter turn halfway between full front and stage left/right

raked slanted

sightlines imaginary lines indicating visibility of stage areas

stage left/stage right the actor's left or right as he or she faces the audience

three-quarter turn halfway between full back and stage left/right

upstage toward the back of the stage

A Look at the Stage

The stage didn't always look the way it does today. Early on in theatre history, players discovered that people could see them better on a **raked,** or slanted, surface. So they built their playing areas on an incline. The back of the playing area was actually higher than the front. Thus, the back part of the stage became known as "upstage," while the front part of the stage was called "downstage." So back when the audience was on a flat level, the stage was raked. As the audience seating became raked, as it is today, the stage got flatter.

Even today, some stages have a small incline, or rake, to improve visibility, or **sightlines,** for the audience. Whether they do or not, however, the tradition remains, and actors everywhere move away from the audience to be **upstage** and toward the audience to be **downstage.**

Where Am I?

When directors and choreographers sketch an acting area, they generally divide it into nine locations, as seen on page 66.

Generally, the downstage area is considered a "strong" position, or a position of power. That's because it is near the audience and thus has a greater impact than other positions.

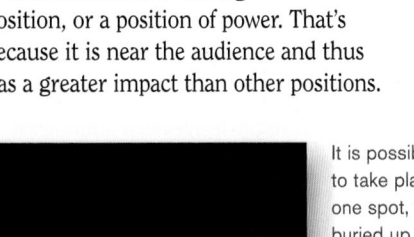

Upstaged!

You've heard of upstaging—and you know it's NOT the thing to do, but do you know where the term originated? When actors deliver lines from upstage, they steal the focus by forcing the other actors to turn with their backs to the audience in order to speak to the upstage actors.

It is possible for a play to take place entirely in one spot, with the actor buried up to her neck in sand, as in *Happy Days* by Samuel Beckett, but it happens rarely.

Chapter 7 Stage Directions **65**

Resource Binder

Handbook Connections

To Have on Hand

- Tape or chalk for marking the playing area
- Prize for winner of the "Simon Says Staging" game
- Images of various types of stages
- Scripts or playbooks with stage crosses marked on them
- Cards with the eight body positions
- A box for collecting the list of students' stage crosses and diagrams or Activity Sheets

A Look at the Stage

Find as many images of various stages from around the world as possible. Talk to students about stage configurations. Discuss the shape, size, height, and width of each. Where are the seats in relation to the stage? Is there a curtain? What kind of play would you imagine being performed on this stage? Compare these stages to the one on page 66. Then use this image to show which part of the stage would be higher if it were raked.

Upstaged!

Show, Don't Tell Use students to demonstrate how one actor can upstage another. Have students read a favorite scene in twos or threes with one actor speaking his or her lines to the others from an upstage position. Instruct the other actors to speak their lines to the upstage actor. Ask the class for their impressions of this exchange. Point out that while beginning actors often unwittingly upstage another actor, only a truly selfish performer would intentionally try to steal the focus from another.

Visual Cue

Discuss the image in the student book using the following prompts:

- What kind of challenges would face an actor who couldn't move?
- If you couldn't move, how would you develop a character?
- Would you enjoy this kind of role? Why or why not?

ACTivity Ask volunteers to portray emotions such as anger, sympathy, or excitement without moving their bodies in any way. They could improvise some lines or use an excerpt from Unit Eight.

Where Am I?

ACTivity Practice body position with students by reading from various plays and asking students to demonstrate how they would position their bodies in the scene. Discuss what the actors who are not speaking would be doing while other actors are speaking. Ask students to suggest body positions for the following scenarios:

- an engaged couple planning their wedding
- a neighbor eavesdropping
- four friends planning a party
- three kids walking to school
- parents arguing with their child
- an angry teenager

Ask students to suggest other scenarios that will help them practice their body positioning.

ACTivity **Beginning Students**
If you have not already done so, draw or tape a simulated stage outline on the floor. Divide the stage into nine areas. Have the students line up along a wall. One by one, call out a stage direction and have students stand on the appropriate area of the stage. Practice until the class is comfortable with each of the nine positions.

ACTivity **Advanced Students**
Use the activity above, but call out the abbreviations (UR, CR, DC, CS, etc.) at a faster and faster pace. Once all the spaces are occupied, call out two positions for quick exchanges ("DR to UR!") and have those students switch spots.

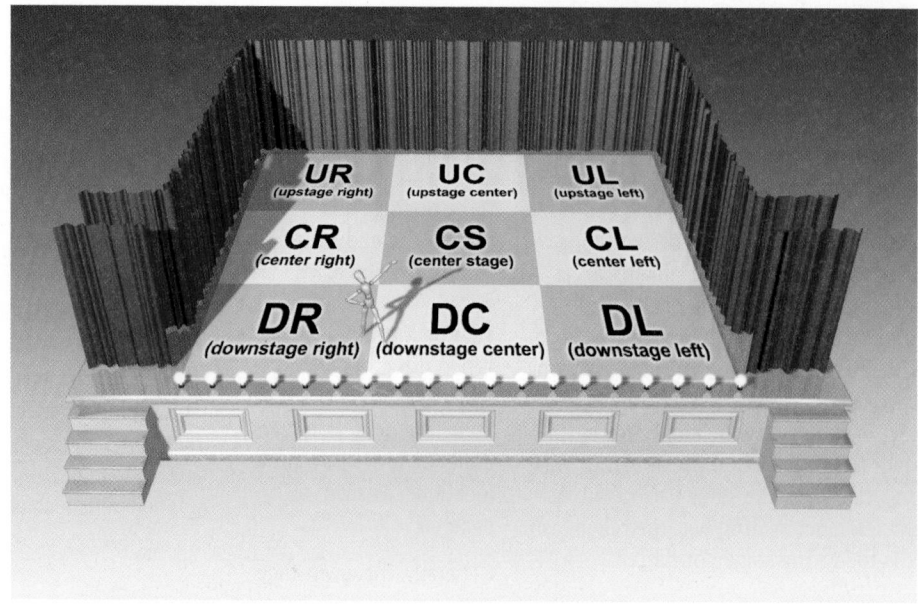

The many areas of the stage. **Backstage** is the area behind the stage that the audience cannot see.

Stage right is a stronger position than **stage left** because Western audiences are conditioned by reading to look from left to right. Thus, they tend to look stage right for the flow of action or the drama's movement. Because of the strength of downstage and stage right, important scenes will often be played there, and strong characters will tend to settle there.

The following body positions also affect the strength of one's character onstage:

1 Actors who share a scene equally often use a **quarter turn** toward each other. This places their bodies so that the audience can easily see them.

2 If a scene becomes intense, actors may turn in **profile** to the audience. This tightens their focus on each other and the audience's focus on them.

3 When one character's lines are especially important, other actors might make a **three-quarter turn** toward that actor, in order to "give" that actor focus.

4 For monologues and asides to the audience, actors often stand **full front,** facing the audience.

5 In unusual circumstances, an actor might turn his or her **full back** to the audience.

Backstage Gossip: Don't Cross Me!

Ruth Gordon once described to George Kaufman a new play in which she was appearing: "In the first scene I'm on the left side of the stage, and then the audience has to imagine I'm eating dinner in a crowded restaurant. Then in scene two I run over to the right side of the stage and the audience imagines I'm in my own drawing room." Kaufman listened, then mused: "And the second night you have to imagine there's an audience out front."

from *Theatrical Anecdotes* by Peter Hay

PREPARE

Getting Your Bearings

A **cross** is a movement from one stage area to another. The director will indicate a stage cross as an "X" on paper. Generally, the actor takes the shortest, most direct route, which is straight across some portion of the stage. Sometimes, however, a director will call for a complicated cross. That's because straight crosses tend to imply strength and decisiveness. A director may want to convey feelings of indecision, casualness, grace, or ease.

Following a complicated cross is not really that hard. How many times have you gone to the refrigerator for a drink, stopping first at the cabinet for a glass and then pausing to look for something to eat? Still, you will want to practice a complicated cross before performing it for an audience so that it looks natural.

The director's notations on this script indicate that Me (Meryl) stays where she is while W (Win) enters from the upper left (the porch). Win then crosses left to Meryl.

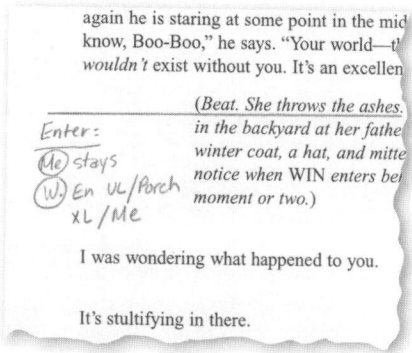

> again he is staring at some point in the mid
> know, Boo-Boo," he says. "Your world—th
> *wouldn't* exist without you. It's an excellen
>
> Enter: (*Beat. She throws the ashes.*
> (Me) stays   in the backyard at her fathe
> (W.) En UL/Porch   winter coat, a hat, and mitte
>   XL/Me   notice when WIN *enters be*
>   moment or two.*)
>
> I was wondering what happened to you.
>
> It's stultifying in there.

The five body positions.

Labels in photo: one quarter left, full front, three quarter left, profile left, full back

Getting Your Bearings

ACTivity Practice crosses with the students by setting up a few pieces of furniture (or drawing them with chalk or using cardboard cutouts). Let students write a short script with directions such as, "Clarice saunters from the sofa to the desk and picks up the letter" or "Harvey leaps up from his chair, dances over to the door, and waltzes out of the room." Ask the students to direct one another in the crosses needed to fulfill the directions in the scripts.

Try to gather scripts or playbooks in which crosses and other directions have been marked. Talk about the marks and what they mean. Ask students to demonstrate the various crosses and other stage directions you find.

ACTivity Ask five students to stand on the simulated chalk stage in the positions shown on this page. Have large cards ready with all eight of the possible body positions written on them: "one quarter right," "three quarter left," and so on. One by one, have students pick new designated positions that they must quickly change to. When the first group has mastered all the positions, call up five new students.

Vocabulary Enhancement

Let students know that the off-stage areas on either side of the acting area are called the *wings.*

The auditorium where the audience sits is called the *house.*

From the Field: Collision Course

Well-planned crosses are not just necessary for the actor. The stage crew members who change scenery between scenes also need to plan their moves, especially when the change is quick and the stage is dark. We learned this the hard way when a member of our stage crew who was exiting quickly with a tray full of glasses and dishes ran into another stagehand who was entering with a heavy antique table. Both the tray and the table were dropped with a terrific crash. Fortunately the only things broken were the glasses.

Julie Nobles, Teacher, Chicago, IL

ACTivity Have students continue to practice crossing by asking them to sit in a chair, stand, and cross to a certain point on the stage or in the classroom. Check to be sure that each student rises from the chair with back straight and one foot extended. Remind students to start on the foot facing in the direction they are heading.

Add to the activity by asking several students to stand on stage while one student executes the crosses you ask for. Next, give the student who is moving a few lines of dialogue to speak while crossing. Check to be sure that the students without lines or movement stay in character but do not move or talk when the cross is going on.

Here's How

Have students practice each of the Here's How tips in order until they are very comfortable with them.

- crossing while speaking

- remaining still while another crosses

- crossing behind a speaking actor

- standing downstage while speaking more lines

- standing upstage while speaking fewer lines

- counter-crossing when someone moves toward you

PREPARE

Like people in all other walks of life, some actors learn through action. They learn by doing the crosses they need to do. Others learn visually. They are more comfortable seeing the movements on paper first.

In order to keep your body turned to the audience, begin a cross by stepping forward on the foot nearest your destination. For example, if you are standing stage right and making a cross to stage left, you should take your first step with the left foot. (Most people do this naturally.)

If you are speaking while you make your cross, go ahead and walk in front of the other characters. Generally, it's best to avoid moving when another character is talking, as your movement will steal attention away from the speaker. But if you need to cross when others are speaking, cross quietly behind them while staying in character.

Here's How
To Move Without Crashing into Anyone

1 The moving figure dominates! If you are the speaking character and must cross, walk in front of the other characters.

2 If another character is talking, do not move. However, if the script calls for you to move during another character's lines, cross behind that person while staying in character.

3 If two actors cross the stage together, the one with more lines should be downstage, a short step ahead of the other actor.

It is usually necessary for actors to adjust to one another's crosses by using a **counter-cross.** If you find yourself in the direct path of another's cross, you may "counter" by giving way a little and then by adjusting your position after the cross, as in the diagram.

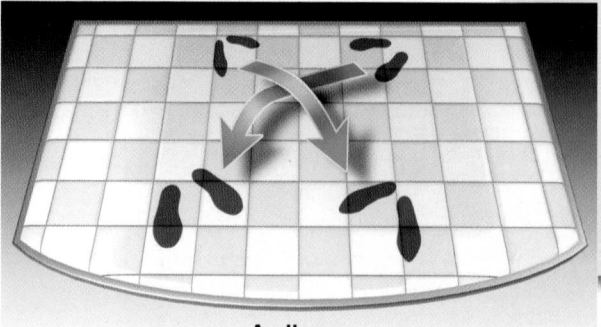

Audience

The speaker (green arrow) crosses right in front of the listener. The listener (purple arrow) "counters" by moving in the opposite direction and turning toward the speaker. Both should finish moving at the same time.

Notes

PREPARE

Plot Three Stage Crosses

On the Activity Sheet for this chapter, which your teacher will provide, or on a separate piece of paper, list three stage crosses and body positions and plot them on a stage diagram. You may list any combination of crosses and positions you wish. The following should serve only as an example.

Sample Directions:

a X DR; stand quarter position left; raise right hand

b X UC; stand in a full front position; bow

c X UR; stand in a one-quarter position left; click your heels twice

d X DC; stand in a profile, face left; raise both arms as high as you can

e X DL; stand in a three-quarter position, face right; twist from your waist

f X UL; stand in a full front position; turn right; sit down

Be sure your name appears on both the top and bottom sections of your paper. Divide the page by cutting it in two (or along the dashed lines of the Activity Sheet) and place it in a box along with your classmates' directions for stage crosses.

PRESENT

Read Aloud and Execute Three Stage Crosses

When your teacher calls your name, rise and draw at random a set of directions from the box. Be sure you do not get your own. Hand the directions to the person who wrote them. Then go to the playing area, and as your classmate calls out directions, follow them as though you were on stage. Be sure you begin each cross on the foot nearest your destination and cross to the correct stage area as directed. Finish each cross by assuming the proper body position.

When a classmate selects your set of directions from the class box and hands them to you, read each clearly. Proceed to the next direction only after your classmate has correctly followed your previous order.

The Language of THEATRE

Work in small groups to respond to questions and requests about stage directions.

- Play the "Simon Says Staging" game on page 64 by responding to directions to move *stage left* or *stage right*. Answer questions, such as "Where is stage left?" using words or gestures.
- Take turns responding to requests to demonstrate *profile, quarter turn,* and *three-quarter turn.* Then take turns answering questions, such as "What is a quarter turn?"
- Take turns responding to simple stage *crosses,* such as "Move from downstage to upstage." Then take turns answering questions about the theatre terms on page 64, such as "What is a *raked* stage?"
- Perform three stage *crosses* by responding to a classmate's directions as described in the chapter project. Then answer questions, such as "Which directions were most challenging?"

Chapter 7 Stage Directions **69**

PREPARE

Plot Three Stage Crosses

Draw a stage diagram like the one on page 66 on the board for all the students to see. Write the directions for a stage cross on the board next to the stage diagram. For example, X DL or X DC. Indicate by drawing an X and a line to the DL position and then the DC position on the stage diagram that this is where the actor would move on the stage.

ACTivity Ask various students to come to the board. Indicate a start position for the student to place the chalk. Then ask another student to call out a cross. The student must then draw a line ending in an X to the place designated. Continue with other students, giving each a different starting position. Let all students have a turn at the chalkboard.

Finally, hand out the Stage Directions Activity Sheet and show students how to use it. Have a box ready to collect these sheets when students are done.

PRESENT

Read Aloud and Execute Three Stage Crosses

Make sure students understand that they will be picking a classmate's stage crosses from the box and executing them and not reading their own directions.

The Language of THEATRE

Model for students how to answer questions by turning the form of a question into the form of a response. For example, an answer to the question "Where is stage left?" could begin with the sentence frame "Stage left is . . . ."

Backstage Gossip: A Starring Roll

During the rehearsal of one of his musicals, composer Jerome Kern was becoming increasingly irritated by a mannered actress who was constantly rolling her *r*'s. She had once more interrupted the rehearsal to ask:

"You want me, Mr. Kern, to cr-r-ross the stage, but I'm behind the table here. How can I get acr-r-oss?"

"It's simple," Kern suggested, "just r-r-roll over on your *r*'s."

from *Broadway Anecdotes* by Peter Hay

CRITIQUE

Evaluate a Classmate's Stage Crosses

Hand out the Critique Sheet for this project or have students use their own paper.

After you have reviewed student critiques, trim off the evaluator's name and hand out the sheets to the subjects of the evaluations.

Spotlight on

Taking Your Bows There are almost as many ways to conduct a curtain call as there are theatres, but every curtain call should be as professional as the rest of the performance.

- *Always* rehearse the curtain call.
- Some theatres have predetermined that there will be only one (or two) calls regardless of the amount of applause.
- Theatres with a strong ensemble ethic usually have the entire cast take part in each bow.
- Large cast and Broadway-type shows usually start the curtain call with the bit players and work up to the leads or "stars" who take individual bows.
- Small casts generally just line up and take simple bows. Large casts, especially musicals, may have elaborately choreographed curtain calls complete with musical reprises.

Vocabulary Enhancement

Manipulating the curtain and/or the lights to produce more clapping and curtain calls than the audience really wants to give is called *milking the applause*.

CRITIQUE

Evaluate a Classmate's Stage Crosses

Choose one of the sets of stage crosses performed by your classmates and evaluate it. Think about the impression your classmate would make if he or she were moving in ordinary life. Rate the crosses on a scale of 1 to 5, with 1 being "needs much improvement" and 5 being "outstanding." Your critique should answer these questions:

- Did the performer move to the correct locations?
- Did the performer end up in the proper body position?
- Did the performer move with confidence?
- Did the performer move with the proper foot first?
- Did the performer's movements seem natural and in character?

Write a paragraph defending your reasons for the rating you gave.

Spotlight on

Taking Your Bows

The curtain closes and the lights go up, but the show isn't over until the actors take their bows. The type of bow they perform depends on the style of the play and the particular production. Most often, actors perform a humble bow, standing straight, then bending the head and back slightly forward.

Sometimes you may be asked to perform a more genteel bow, in which you bend at the hips, keeping your back straight and your head dropped slightly.

Rarely, an actor will be asked to curtsey. To do a bob curtsey, keep your feet close together, swing one foot slightly behind the other, bend your knees quickly, and bob your head. A court curtsey is similar, but deeper and slower.

Remember to take your bows seriously. They are your way of telling the audience you are honored to perform for them and appreciate their attendance and applause.

Backstage Gossip: Philosophy Pays

Joan Rivers began her career in small off-Broadway shows, one of which led to an actor's nightmare—no applause! Rivers felt she was doing an excellent job in this show and invited every agent and show–business person she could in hopes of furthering her career. Naturally, everything that could go wrong, did. Doors stuck, props vanished, actors didn't connect, engine fumes filled the theatre, endless fire trucks went by, Rivers began to stutter, and a poor young actor whose role was to sit in a cage, shook the bars so hard they came apart in his hand. As she recalls: "Now the poor schlep had to hold the cage together and after my big speech about how this boy's spirit must go free . . . and I'm going to let him go now, the boy just handed me the bars and slunk away.

"At the end . . . the cast appeared for the curtain call. Then my philosophy class at Barnard finally paid off. I understood the proposition of one hand clapping."

Additional Projects

1 Go to the stage area and make several crosses, ending with varied body positions. Challenge your classmates to identify each stage area you are in and the body position you are assuming.

2 With two partners, plot a series of crosses that might define a character type, such as a CEO at a successful board meeting, a criminal under indictment, a shy immigrant, a couple quarreling, or a child with something to hide.

3 With a partner, plot crosses for a two-person scene. You can use stage directions from an existing play or plot movements of your own. Once you have mastered the scene, try reversing the staging. What do the different crosses do to the relationship between the characters?

4 Cooperate with one or more partners to plot the movement, including crosses, for the scene from *A Raisin in the Sun* by Lorraine Hansberry found in Unit Eight. Decide when to walk while speaking a line and when to walk between lines. Make sure to keep the focus on the proper actor in the scene.

5 Read about theatre architecture through history on pages 72–73. Write a summary that explains the historical development of theatre architecture from the ancient arenas to the intimate spaces of today.

6 **Theatre Journal** Next time you're in a public place, such as a sports or cultural venue, watch the unconscious movements of people in a group. Do some people in the group upstage others? Who gets the most focus? Who do the group members seem to think is their audience? Write about what you observe.

The director, on the left, is helping the actor who is playing an apologetic young man cross to the actor who is playing his angry friend.

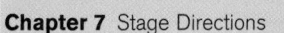

Stage Directions Test
The test for this chapter is available in blackline master form in the Resource Binder, page 35.

For More Information

Books
Bloom, Michael, *Thinking Like a Director,* Faber & Faber, 2001.

King, Nancy, *A Movement Approach to Acting,* Prentice Hall, 1981.

Kline, Peter, *Physical Movement for the Theatre,* Rosen Publishing Group, 1971.

White, Edwin C., et al., *Acting and Stage Movements: A Complete Handbook for Amateurs and Professionals,* Meriwether Publishing, 1985.

Other Media
Blocking a Scene: Basic Staging with Actors, DVD, Insight Media, 1990.

Body Language: Beyond Words, DVD, Insight Media, 2008.

Apps
Rehearsal 2
Theater Blocking

Theatre Journal
Use the following as an additional or substitute prompt.

As you observe people in a public place, try to decide what their mood is from watching how they move. Choose two or three moods and describe the kind of movements that go with them.

Substitute Teacher Activities

- Assign the Moving in Character Worksheet on page 33 of the Resource Binder.

- Teach the Movement section, pp. 567–568, and/or the Storytelling section, pp. 575–576, of the Student Handbook.

- Assign one or more of the Additional Projects on this page.

- **Plan a Fairy Tale Festival.** Divide the class into small groups and assign a well-known fairy tale to each group. "Cinderella," "The Three Pigs," "Little Red Riding Hood," "Goldilocks and the Three Bears," and "Hansel and Gretel" are all good candidates. Have the group choose a narrator and then work together to plan how the narrator should move as he or she tells the story.

Theatre **Then** and Now

The Actor Onstage

The Theatre of Dionysus was created in honor of Dionysus, the fertility god. It contained two performance areas: the dancing circle (or orchestra) and the area backed by the scene building (or *skene*). The chorus performed in the dancing circle. Statues were used to decorate such theatres, often glorifying a ruler or important battle.

Other Cultures, Other Times

There were two types of Medieval stages, the *fixed stage* and the *movable* stage. The most well-known fixed stage was constructed in 1547, at Valenciennes in northern France, and contained a rectangular platform with two areas. One area contained huts, which served as the plays' different locations, and the other was the *platea*, an extended playing space. The actor went from hut to hut to show change of location as there were no set changes.

The most famous of Elizabethan theatres was the Globe Theatre, built in 1599, which consisted of an open-air building with a platform stage in the middle surrounded on three sides by open standing room. A large enclosed balcony covered by small roofed galleries surrounded the theatre, offering seating for those that could afford the fee. The back of the stage contained a multilevel façade. The stage was covered by a roof supported by two columns. The underside, called the *heavens*, was painted with moons, stars, and planets. For more about the Globe, see pages 454–455.

ACTivity Gather pictures of playbills and posters that depict characters from theatrical productions. Using the pictures, discuss what the posture, mannerisms, and facial expressions of the characters portray about them. Make comparisons between the way the Romans integrated the arts and how we integrate the arts today.

Theatre **Then** and Now

The Actor Onstage

With flexibility, creativity, and a good concept, theatre can be performed almost anywhere. In ancient times, outdoor theatre was the norm. Excavations in ancient Crete and the mainland nearby have uncovered evidence of early outdoor performance spaces that consisted of a rectangular area flanked by rows of stone seats.

Ancient Arenas

The Theatre of Dionysus in Athens was the West's first public *theatron,* or seeing-place. It was situated on a hillside below the Acropolis. Originally people simply sat or stood on the hillside to watch choral performances. As time went on and choral performances turned into full-length tragedies, terraces were built into the hillsides. Wooden seats were added, and when those deteriorated, stone seats were built. The stone auditorium completed sometime around 330 B.C. could seat 14,000 to 17,000 people. Some historians believe stages were built into the theatres; others do not.

Nevertheless, historians agree that the audience—and the performances—remained outdoors. Music and dancing were an integral part of productions. And as time went on, spectacle became increasingly important. Indeed, some productions after the Romans conquered the Greeks became little more than loud and gory spectacle.

Under these conditions, actors relied heavily on pantomime and large gestures. Roman actors studied great orators and made extensive use of stylized movements, including stock placement of the head, hands, and feet, along with special intonations to signal specific emotions. Tragic acting involved slow, stately movements befitting the dignity of the characters and subject matter. Comic plays always included running, fighting, beatings, and physical humor. These acting conventions persisted through the Elizabethan age and into the 19th century.

This Roman statuette of a comic actor is from around the 1st century. It is from the collection of The Newark Museum.

isual Cues

The following prompts can be used to discuss the Roman statuette and the photo from *Tony 'n Tina's Wedding.*

- How does the facial expression of the statuette show a comedic role rather than a dramatic one?

- As an audience member or actor, would you enjoy being a part of *Tony 'n Tina's Wedding* or would you be uncomfortable?

Today's Intimate Spaces

Today, arenas are reserved for sporting events and large-scale entertainment such as rock concerts. Big musicals like *Stomp, Rent,* or *Wicked* might play to houses that seat 2000 to 3000 people. But most commercial theatre takes place in smaller, indoor houses that seat 200–1200. Off-Broadway and off-off-Broadway shows might take place in storefronts that seat 50 or fewer audience members.

As a result, stages have been scaled back. So have conventions in movement, gesture, and intonation. Actors in most plays today don't seek to impress the audience. Their movements tend to be smaller, realistic, even intimate.

Tragedy might include simple stillness or tears. Comedy might include the broad physical humor of an earlier burlesque, but it might rely instead upon quick, witty wordplay such as that perfected by playwrights David Mamet or Tom Stoppard.

Today it is not uncommon for actors who are entering or exiting to wind their way through the house. And sometimes audience members are invited to become part of the play, as in *Tony n' Tina's Wedding,* shown below.

The audience joins the conga line during the play *Tony n' Tina's Wedding,* which ran in New York for 22 years.

Today's Intimate Spaces

The most popular type of stage, the proscenium stage, developed during the Italian Renaissance of the early 17th century. The proscenium arch is designed to frame the stage and hide what is going on backstage, separating the audience from the actors, creating the illusion of a self-contained world on the stage. The advantage of the "picture-frame stage" is that it allows for large scenery. The disadvantage is that it keeps the audience at a distance.

The arena stage, also called *theatre in the round,* can locate audiences on all four sides of the stage, allowing for an intimate setting but restricting scenery to minimal sets. Margo Jones pioneered the arena stage in 1947 by establishing Theatre 47 in Dallas, Texas.

The thrust stage, a variation of the proscenium, emerged in America after WWII. The actors perform on a platform that thrusts out into the audience.

The black box stage is a type of minimal performance space emerging from the 1960s. Usually painted black and containing complex overhead lighting and moveable audience seating, the black box theatre is very flexible. The audience may be placed on one, two, three, or even all four sides of the playing area, while entrances and exits can be placed on either side of the stage space or through the audience.

For More Information

Books

Arnott, Peter D., *The Ancient Greek and Roman Theatre*, Random House,1971.

Ball, James, *The Greek Theatre*, Old Vicarage Publications, 1983.

Elder, Eldon, *Will It Make a Theatre? Find, Renovate, and Finance the Non-Traditional Performance Space*, Allworth Press, 1997.

McAuley, Gay, *Space in Performance: Making Meaning in the Theatre*, University of Michigan Press, 2000.

Other Media

The Design of the Modern Theatre: Adolphe Appia's Innovations, DVD, Insight Media, 1993.

The Role of Theatre in Ancient Greece, DVD, Films for the Humanities and Sciences, 1989.

Stages of Theatre: From the Greeks to Shakespeare, DVD, Films for the Humanities and Sciences, 2005.

Chapter 8

Voice Production and Articulation

This chapter introduces the importance of the voice to the actor and of training and using it properly.

Objectives

1 to learn how to build and use proper breathing and articulation to produce vocal tone

2 to understand how to communicate emotions and develop a character through the voice

3 to understand the foundation for daily vocal practice and to perform a vocal exercise

Project Specs

Beginning Students
Have selections available for students who are having difficulty locating them.

Advanced Students
Encourage students to choose a scene from Shakespeare or a similarly challenging piece of writing.

ELL Students
Have selections available that incorporate minimal vocal challenges. Allow students to practice tongue twisters in their first languages.

On Your Feet

Show, Don't Tell Using another word, such as "Yes" or "No," demonstrate how to communicate each situation using the word.

Chapter

8 Voice Production and Articulation

It has been said that good stage actors can make a "person in the last row wearing earplugs hear them clearly." In this chapter, you will learn how to train and exercise your voice for just that purpose.

Project Specs

Project Description For this assignment, you will have two minutes to perform a vocal exercise, or exercise for the voice, which will be one part of a foundation for daily vocal practice.

Purpose to develop, practice, and demonstrate effective voice and diction to express thoughts and feelings safely

Materials a written description of your chosen vocal exercise or the Voice Production and Articulation Activity Sheet your teacher provides

Theatre Terms
audible
circumflex
diaphragm
inflection
larynx
pitch
project
rate
resonance
volume

On Your Feet

Use the word "Oh" to communicate each of the following thoughts and feelings:

- sudden understanding
- great shock or horror
- irritation
- happiness or joy
- extreme sadness

Note the differences in the volume and tone of your voice for each.

Theatre Terms

audible able to be heard

circumflex a combination of rising and falling inflection

diaphragm the muscle below the rib cage

inflection variety of vocal pitch

larynx the area of the throat that contains the vocal cords

pitch the relative highness or lowness of the voice

project to send the voice out to the audience

rate the speed at which one speaks

resonance a rich, warm speaking quality

volume the relative loudness of your voice

Your Voice Is Your Key

As an actor, you know that your voice is a basic element of your craft. In addition to having enough **volume**, or strength, to be **audible** to the audience no matter what size the theatre, you can develop your voice to be flexible enough to add subtle layers of character, emotional texture, and meaning to your lines by expressing both thoughts and feelings. And it must be strong enough to withstand long rehearsals and intense performances.

Unless you have serious vocal problems that need a specialist's attention, you can do much to build vocal audibility and flexibility by practicing vocal exercises every day. Some professional

John Hall performs in a 1995 production of Shakespeare's A Midsummer Night's Dream.

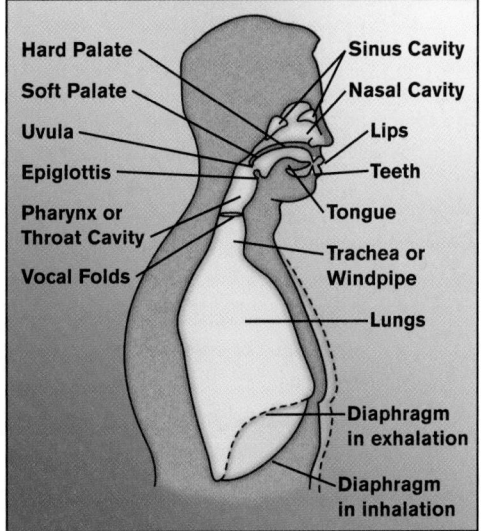

These areas of the body are involved in voice production.

actors work for years with vocal coaches and teachers to develop the most versatile voice they can and keep it safe. The following sections provide information on safe and appropriate techniques for developing and using your voice. Employ these techniques to achieve emotional expression in your acting.

Voice Production

Technically, speech sounds are produced by air that has been forced through the lungs by the action of certain rib muscles and the **diaphragm,** a flat muscle that separates the chest from the abdominal cavity. The exhaled air vibrates the vocal cords in the **larynx,** which is found in the pharynx.

Chapter 8 Voice Production and Articulation   **75**

Because the theatre generally employs actors who have worked extensively on their vocal quality, it is extremely important to train your voice properly if you are to find work on the stage. Most actors achieve an undergraduate degree, and many go on to acquire advanced degrees. Students must understand that not only does acting require talent and training, but also time to develop one's voice. The time to start is now.

Voice Production

Show, Don't Tell Study the diagram on this page with the students. Discuss intake and exhalation of air and how it affects the diaphragm. Demonstrate the process for the students. Next, demonstrate how words are formed by the various articulators. Show how the letter *t* is formed by the tongue, how *th* is formed on the teeth, and so on.

ACTivity Instruct the students to form a circle, standing with feet a shoulder width apart, hands on the diaphragm. As a group say, "Oooooohhhhhh," "Aaaaaauuuuuu," and "Eeeeeeeeeeeee." Remind the students to use their whole mouth—remembering to stretch the lips, the jaw, and cheeks. Start a slow pattern and then gradually increase the pace, being careful to continue stretching.

Visual Cue

Shakespeare's *A Midsummer Night's Dream* is thought to be written for a wedding couple. It is one of his most famous comedies. Here, John Hall plays Snug, the joiner, in his role as the lion in the play within the play.

- What does Hall's facial expression tell you about this scene?
- What type of character do you think he is portraying?

Resource Binder

- Voice Production Diagram, TIPack, p. F
- Voice Production and Articulation Activity Sheet, p. 36
- Vocal Exercises Worksheet, p. 37
- Critique Sheet: Vocal Exercise, p. 38
- Voice Production and Articulation Test, p. 39

Handbook Connections
pages 577–578

To Have on Hand

- A stopwatch to time the vocal exercise presentations
- Several candles in holders
- Matches
- A selection of vocal exercises for the Try This activity on p. 78

Proper Breathing

Breathing is the basis of the voice. The actor's goal is to breathe "normally" while under the pressure of a performance. The actor's breath must originate from the abdomen, not from the chest. Deep breaths give the voice the support it needs for the stage.

ACTivity Have students recite the poem "Jack and Jill," as follows:

Jack and Jill went up the hill
To fetch a pail of water.
Jack fell down and broke his crown
And Jill came tumbling after.

The poem should be recited in one slow breath. Instruct students to maintain a volume and rate appropriate to the poem and to articulate each word carefully.

Here's How
To Protect Your Voice

Vocal training begins by taking care of the voice you have. After all, you can *improve* your voice, but you can't *exchange* it. Demonstrate safe use of your voice both in and beyond this class by following these simple rules.

- Always warm up your voice before a performance or even a class presentation.

- Eat well, get enough sleep, and exercise regularly to avoid colds and other respiratory illnesses; they present a serious threat to your voice.

- Don't smoke or drink alcohol. There are many reasons to avoid these substances, but the chemicals and toxins in them are exceptionally harmful to the voice.

- Never strain your voice by shouting when you have a cold or by singing in an improper range.

  - Never shout yourself hoarse. Such strain makes throat membranes sore and invites infection that can lead to permanent damage. When in doubt, don't shout. If you are playing a character who shouts or has to talk loudly, be sure to support your voice with breath from the diaphragm.

The sound produced is modified by the resonators (throat, nose, mouth, and sinuses) and formed into vowels and consonants by the articulators (tongue, jaw, teeth, cheeks, lips, and hard and soft palates).

When exercising your voice you will be working to achieve controlled breathing and **resonance,** or a rich, warm sound quality. In addition, variety in **pitch,** volume, **inflection,** and **rate** is important. Clear articulation, or way of speaking, and proper pronunciation round out the important elements of voice production. The diagram on page 75 shows all the areas of your body that contribute to the sound of your voice.

Proper Breathing

Actors and singers know that to have the necessary air control for a performance they must breathe from the diaphragm. This means that the chest cavity stays relatively still, while the waist expands and contracts, and the lower ribs rise and fall slightly. Once you have mastered diaphragmatic breathing, you will notice that it requires less effort than chest breathing, allows you to breathe more deeply, and provides the control you need to project long passages without running out of breath. Breathing from your diaphragm might feel strange at first. To get comfortable with this type of breathing, practice daily.

Notes

Here's How
To Employ Effective Voice and Diction

You can effectively express thoughts and feelings with voice and diction.

- Imagine you are in a conflict with a friend and you think it's time to make up. Your voice can express that thought. You might say, "I don't think we're getting anywhere" with tone, volume, and inflection that communicates you are ready to put the conflict behind you. Try saying that sentence to a classmate, finding the tone, volume, and inflection that offers your thought of peace. Next try saying that to express not the thought of peace but the feeling of anger. You will notice the tone, volume, and inflection to be very different, and very effective at expressing your feeling.

- Diction also expresses thoughts and feelings. Try saying "Put the top on the cookie jar" to express the thought that putting the top on will solve the problem of keeping the cookies fresh. Next try saying that to express the feeling of great annoyance with a child who has been nagging you. You will likely enunciate much more deliberately to the child.

In your acting, employ effective voice and diction to express your character's thoughts and feelings.

Richer Tone

Tone depends on many factors, including the shape and size of your vocal mechanism, which you will not be able to change. However, you can learn to make the most of what you've got by keeping your throat open and controlling your breath. If your voice sounds harsh or raspy, it is usually the result of a closed throat. If your voice sounds breathy, you are probably using more breath than you need.

To relax your throat and improve your tone safely, try this exercise:

Yawn exaggeratedly. Take a deep breath, stretch, and then yawn again. With your throat open and relaxed, quietly and slowly say the following while prolonging the vowel sounds: "Ma-a-ah, blo-o-oh, fla-a-aw, pla-a-ay, be-e-e, t-o-o." Yawn again to relax, then continue with other vowel sounds.

Try This

1 Lie flat on your back with one hand on your abdomen and the other on your chest. Keep your chest still. The abdomen should move up when you inhale and down when you exhale. Now stand up and try the identical action. Gradually speed up your breathing until you are panting like a dog. Remember to use only your abdomen—try to keep your chest still.

2 Using your diaphragm, take a deep breath and see how far you can count as you exhale. Do not force or speed up the count. If you start to get tense, breathe normally, and start again. Practice this until you can exhale to a count of sixty.

Richer Tone

The yawn is the perfect form of breath because it comes from a relaxed body. Most of the time when people yawn, they breathe in air from the abdomen, not from the chest, exactly where the actor's breath must come from. When an actor is feeling nervous and experiencing stage fright, breathing becomes shorter and shallower. Therefore, actors must train themselves to take deep breaths—allowing good vocal support and ensuring a relaxed speaking voice.

Try This

ACTivity After performing the first two exercises, instruct students to walk around the room, making sure their arms, shoulders, and necks are loose, breathing in deep breaths, and being conscious not to breathe from the chest but from the abdomen.

ACTivity Have students loosen their facial and vocal muscles by using the following exercises:

1 Open the mouth and eyes as wide as possible and then close them as tightly as possible.

2 Slowly and silently count to ten, exaggerating the mouth, using the tongue and lips. Add sound.

3 Silently speak the scale (do, re, me, fa, so, la, ti, do), exaggerating the mouth, using the tongue and the lips. Add sound.

Backstage Gossip: A Violet Velvet Voice

When Laurence Olivier played Othello in 1964, he felt his natural voice was inadequate for the task.

"I did go through a long period of vocal training especially for it, to increase the depth of my voice, and I actually managed to attain about six more notes in the bass. I never used to be able to sing below D, but now, after a little exercising, I can get down to A, through all the semitones; and that helps at the beginning of the play, it helps the violet velvet that I felt was necessary in the timbre of the voice."

from *Theatrical Anecdotes* by Peter Hay

Show, Don't Tell For this experiment in tone techniques, model one of the words for the students. Say "Oh" in a sarcastic tone and have students tell you what emotion they think you are conveying, and so on.

Pitch, Inflection, Volume, and Rate

Actors can take the same line and change its meaning simply by where they choose to place the inflection. It is important for actors to understand inflection and to use it to convey meaning.

Try This

Have two candles at the front of the room and ask students to come forward two at a time to test their breath control. Depending on the fire codes in your school, you may have to go outside the building.

Inflection Marks

Show, Don't Tell Draw a chart with the three headings below on the chalkboard and model for students under which head one of the emotions listed should be placed. Then write on the board a sentence that reveals this emotion, adding the proper inflection mark. Finally, say the sentence using the correct inflection.

- Rising Inflection
- Lowering Inflection
- Sustained Inflection

Nervousness	*Boredom*
Calm	*Despair*
Excitement	*Disgust*
Anger	*Sarcasm*
Fear	*Doubt*

Continue working on inflection using the rest of the list.

Read a passage from your literature book, prolonging the vowels.

Tone is the vocal element you use to create different emotional colors when you speak or sing. Try these simple techniques to experiment with tone:

1 Say each of these words—*oh, yes, well, really, possibly*—to convey each of these emotions or states of being: happiness, pride, fatigue, fright, anger, suspicion, innocence, pleading, and sorrow.

2 Reproduce the tone color of these words by making your voice sound like the word's meaning: *bang, crackle, swish, grunt, tinkle, roar, coo, thin, wheeze, bubble, buzzy, splash, clang, gurgle.*

Pitch, Inflection, Volume, and Rate

Pitch is the relative highness or lowness of your voice. You can produce a medium pitch by relaxing your throat. This is the easiest pitch to project and the easiest for an audience to listen to. In acting, high pitch indicates nervousness, excitement, anger, or fear. A low pitch conveys despair or disgust.

Try This

Test yourself for breathlessness. Light a candle and hold it about five or six inches away from your face. Speak directly toward the flame. If the candle flickers or goes out, you are using too much breath. When you produce a clear tone, you actually use very little breath—the candle flame will move only a tiny bit, if at all.

Inflection, in combination with pitch, allows you to glide from high to low on a single word, syllable, or phrase. Rising inflection connotes questioning. Falling inflection signifies finality. **Circumflex** is a combination of the two, expressing sarcasm, doubt, and innuendo.

Inflection Marks

Laura:
Oh, Jack! What are you doing?
[rising inflection]

Damon:
Jack always has a reason.
[sustained inflection]

Lateefa:
Stay out of this, Jack.
[falling inflection]

Volume is the relative loudness of your voice. To send, or **project,** their voices to all areas of the theatre, performers often must speak very loudly, yet they must seem to the audience to be speaking at a normal volume. Breathing from the diaphragm is the key to vocal projection.

Rate is the speed at which you speak. Rate of speech can indicate many things about a person or a character. For example, a slow rate usually indicates old age, important ideas, and/or a state of sorrow or exhaustion. A faster rate indicates youth and/or the emotions of excitement, happiness, and anger.

Notes

Articulation and Pronunciation

Proper breathing, great tone, and perfect pitch will make no difference at all if you have poor articulation, also called *diction*. After all, the audience has to understand what you're saying. Poor diction is generally the result of carelessness and sluggish speech; it can make you sound as if you have a mouthful of oatmeal. Actors need to develop and practice effective diction so that onstage, where every word counts, they can express thoughts and feelings through their voices.

Using proper pronunciation means making sure you know how to say each word you speak. If you do not know the meaning of a word you read, or you are unsure of its pronunciation, look it up *before* you say it in front of an audience! Practice effective diction as you rehearse your lines so that you can express thoughts and feelings clearly but with subtlety.

On pages 14 and 18 of Chapter 2, you tried a few tongue twisters to practice articulation. Repeat those once again and then try the additional phrases below. Remember to open your mouth wide as you say each one. Pick up speed as you gain control.

- Six slim sleek saplings stood silently.
- She sells seashells by the seashore.
- A big black bug bit a big black bear.
- Fill the sieve with thistles; then sift the thistles through the sieve.
- Better buy the bigger rubber baby buggy bumpers.

PREPARE

Choose Your Exercise

Choose one of the exercises suggested below and on the following page to perform in front of the class. Write down your ideas for presenting this exercise or use the Activity Sheet your teacher provides. Practice your selection several times, demonstrating safe use of your voice as well as effective voice and diction to express thoughts and feelings. Use proper breathing, a medium pitch, sufficient volume, and clear articulation. Remember that your presentation should not exceed two minutes.

Feel free to adapt any of the suggestions in an imaginative way.

- Choose a favorite childhood poem or song lyrics such as "My Shadow" or "She'll Be Comin' 'Round the Mountain" to recite.

Practice articulation and pronunciation so that you are prepared when you go onstage.

Articulation and Pronunciation

Special Needs and ELL Students Allow these students to say either simplified tongue twisters or tongue twisters in their first languages.

Show, Don't Tell Write a few lines from one of Shakespeare's plays on the board. Begin by modeling *scansion*, the analysis of the verse for emphasis. When scanning, look for things such as *glottal sounds* (consonants caused by air held back, such as in *g* and *k*), *alliteration* (repetitive consonants), and *sibilants* (hissing sounds). Read the passage to the students and have them discuss your articulation and pronunciation.

ACTivity Write the following from *Macbeth* on the chalkboard:

If it were done when 'tis done, then 'twere well
It were done quickly. If th' assassination
Could trammel up the consequence and catch
With his surcease, success that but this blow
Might be the be-all and the end-all here,
But here, upon this bank and shoal of time,
We'd jump the life to come.

Have a volunteer scan for glottal sounds, alliteration, and sibilants, marking them on the board. Then give the class a few minutes to practice the passage silently, being careful to stress the things they found during scansion. Ask volunteers to perform the passage aloud.

PREPARE

Choose Your Exercise

Remind the students of the importance of using proper breathing, pitch, volume, and articulation.

Show, Don't Tell Model for the students how you would choose and prepare one of the suggested exercises.

Backstage Gossip: Isn't He a Scream?

Dustin Hoffman, an actor who likes to totally transform himself into a character and to hide his own personality traits as much as possible, actually locked himself in a room and screamed for more than five hours . . . in order to make his voice sound like the 121-year-old man in the film *Little Big Man.*

from *Introducing Theatre* by Joy H. Reilly and M. Scott Phillips

Special Needs Students

Have a simple poem or paragraph available for students who might have a difficult time finding one of their own.

PRESENT

Perform Your Vocal Exercise

Before students begin presenting their vocal exercises, remind them to hand in their Activity Sheet or description when their name is called. Also remind the students who are watching that proper audience behavior begins as soon as the Activity Sheet is handed in. The audience should remain quiet and attentive for the duration of the performance. Have a stopwatch ready to time each scene.

The Language of THEATRE

Encourage students to pause the recordings or replay certain sections as needed to understand what they hear. Students may work with a partner who is a strong English speaker for additional support.

Breathe from your diaphragm as you practice saying the lines from memory. Work toward saying the poem or lyric with clear enough diction to express subtle thoughts and feelings. Try to finish one stanza on a single exhalation. Control your breath so that you don't run out of air in the middle of a phrase or sentence.

- Choose a dramatic paragraph from the text of a literature book or from your personal reading. Alternatively, you may write a paragraph of your own. Practice reading the paragraph aloud varying your pitch, volume, and rate and employing effective voice and diction to convey thoughts and feelings. Remember to use proper breathing technique. Keep your throat relaxed and open to achieve the best tone possible, and read with feeling.

- Select an excerpt from one of Shakespeare's monologues or scenes found in Unit Eight of this book. Read it over, and then read it aloud for the class employing effective voice and diction to express the thoughts and feelings in the scene. You will need a partner for the scene.

- Create a new tongue twister consisting of two to four lines. Use the tongue twisters on pages 14, 18, and 79 as a guide. Share the tongue twister you create with the class.

PRESENT

Perform Your Vocal Exercise

When your name is called, hand your description of your vocal exercise or Activity Sheet to your teacher, and then proceed to the playing area. Perform your exercise for the class, demonstrating safe use of your voice. Remember to take your time. Every word and breath counts.

When you have finished your presentation, try not to make faces or shrug your shoulders if you feel you didn't do well. Your presentation doesn't truly end until you sit down.

The Language of THEATRE

Listen to a variety of media to build and reinforce theatre concepts and language.

- Listen to a brief recording by a famous actor or orator. Notice the *rate* and the *volume* of his or her speech. When are they speaking fast or slow? loud or soft?

- Listen to two recordings by famous actors or orators. Compare the *pitch*, *rate*, and *volume* used by the different speakers.

- Listen to several recordings by famous actors and orators. Discuss with a partner how the speakers create *resonance* and use *inflection* to communicate different ideas or emotions.

- Listen to recordings by famous actors and orators and a recording of your own voice. Then write an analysis of what you hear. Use the *inflection* marks on page 78 to help you remember the sounds.

From the Field: Voice, Movement, Gesture

I have my theatre arts students take positions throughout the auditorium. Once an order has been determined in a crisscross pattern, the first actor calls out the name of the person who is next, accompanied by a sweeping gesture toward the person, followed by a resounding "Hah." The order can be changed and eventually lines from scenes they are working on can be substituted for the vocalized "Hah." Moving the students outdoors to work on this exercise adds additional space between them and requires greater movement and a louder voice.

Richard Steggerda, Teacher, Bristol, VT

CRITIQUE

Evaluate Classmates' Vocal Exercises

Take notes as you watch your classmates' vocal presentations. Use a scale of 1 to 5, with 5 being "outstanding," 4 being "very good," 3 being "good," 2 being "needs some improvement," and 1 being "needs much improvement." Ask yourself the questions below as you evaluate.

- Did the performer use proper breathing?

- How audible was the performer's presentation?

- How clearly did he or she articulate?

- Did the performer speak at the proper rate—neither too fast nor too slow?

- Did the performer demonstrate safe and effective techniques for vocal expression?

Choose two of the presentations you have already critiqued and write a paragraph explaining why you gave each the score you did. Use the answers you wrote to the questions above to help in your evaluation.

Career Focus

Voice-over Actor

Many stage actors supplement their theatre careers by working as voice-over performers. Though you may never have seen a voice-over actor, you hear them all the time. Typical voice-overs are radio spots, television commercials, corporate training films, and documentary and educational film narration. New digital technologies provide additional opportunities, such as voices on phones, video games, podcasts, and webinars. College students develop voice-over skills while working on multimedia presentations. Aspiring voice-over actors start by making a professional digital demo of their voice to send to prospective clients.

A career in voice-over requires a strong, supple voice; a personable, professional demeanor; and the ability to do dialects and/or impressions. A musical background can also be very helpful.

Evaluate the self-discipline and artistic discipline this career requires. For example, keeping the voice strong and supple requires self-discipline and care not to strain the voice in daily life. In addition, expanding the range of voices an actor can do requires artistic discipline and dedication to the craft. Refer to the chart on page 10 for more ways to evaluate this career.

Being able to convey a strong personality is an asset to the voice-over actor.

CRITIQUE

Evaluate Classmates' Vocal Exercises

Hand out Critique Sheets for this project or have students use their own paper. You might prefer to assign two exercises for each student to evaluate in order to insure that everyone gets evaluated.

Career Focus

There are many different areas where the voice-over actor can find work. In addition to those mentioned in the student book, sports teams announcers and voice-overs for movie trailers are other examples. Web sites, such as *voices.com* and *voiceovers.co.uk* are available to support the actor in finding work. A very popular type of voice-over work is animation, where actors become the voices of cartoon characters. *Shrek,* a popular 2001 animated film based on the children's book by William Steig, featured the voices of Mike Myers, Eddie Murphy, Cameron Diaz, and John Lithgow. *Shrek 2,* released in 2004, had many of the same popular voices as well as such stars as Julie Andrews, Antonio Banderas, and Rupert Everett. Justin Timberlake joined the mix in 2007 in *Shrek the Third.* In *Shrek Forever After* in 2010, Walt Dohrn and Jon Hamm added their voices.

The following prompts can be used to begin a discussion about the photo on this page.

- What are the challenges an actor would face when totally dependent on the voice?

- Do you think this voice-over actor has made an attempt to memorize his lines? Why would he do this?

Notes

_____

_____

_____

_____

_____

_____

_____

_____

Voice Production and Articulation Test

The test for this chapter is available in blackline master form in the Resource Binder, page 39.

For More Information

Books

Alburger, James, *The Art of Voice Acting: The Craft and Business of Performing for Voice-Over,* Focal Press, 1998.

Berry, Cicely, *Voice and the Actor,* John Wiley & Sons, 1991.

Cohen, Robert, *Acting One,* McGraw-Hill, 2001.

Hogan, Harlan, *VO: Tales and Techniques of a Voice-Over Actor,* Palgrave Macmillan, 2002.

Jones, Chuck, *Make Your Voice Heard: An Actor's Guide to Increased Dramatic Range Through Vocal Training,* Back Stage Books, 1996.

Other Media

Developing Your Voice: Skills in Vocal Improvement, DVD, Insight Media, 2001.

History of Vocal Teaching, DVD, Insight Media, 2008.

Human Speech: Articulation, DVD, Insight Media, 2003.

The Voice Theatre Lab Collection, DVD, Insight Media, 2011.

Voice Skills, DVD, Insight Media, 2002.

Apps

Being in Voice
Tongue Twisters

Theatre Journal

Use the following as an additional or substitute prompt.

Record your own voice as you recite a poem or monologue. Then listen and take notes about what you would correct. Record your voice again and try to implement the vocal corrections.

Additional Projects

Warm up your voice before starting any vocal project on this page so you can do it safely.

1 With a partner, select a two- to four-minute scene in which two characters exchange dialogue. In reading the scenes, employ the various vocal techniques you have learned. Try to go further with a particular element than you have gone before.

2 Employ and demonstrate effective voice and diction as you say the following lines aloud, using the inflection indicated in brackets. Determine the thoughts and feelings in each line and use voice and diction to communicate them effectively.

- I'm sorry, but I must decline your invitation. [falling inflection]
- What's the big idea? [rising inflection]
- So you took my new sweater! [rising inflection]
- I think I've solved the problem. [sustained inflection]

3 Read aloud two poems that feature contrasting emotional content. Imagine that you are delivering these poems in a large crowded auditorium. Experiment with your volume, diction, inflection, tone, and the flexibility of your voice. Use your voice to convey as precisely as possible the thoughts and feelings in the poems. As always, demonstrate safe use of your voice and employ safe and appropriate techniques for vocal expression.

4 Practice projecting your voice to the last row in the classroom. Stand up and focus your eyes on the back wall. Say your name, the name of your street, and the name of your favorite song. Repeat all of this information using only vowels; then do the same using only consonants. Finally, repeat your name, street name, and favorite song articulating and projecting to the best of your ability.

5 Rehearse the monologue from *Clear Glass Marbles* by Jane Martin found in Unit Eight. Use all the techniques you have learned in this chapter to give your reading as much emotional color as possible. Experiment with a number of different accents. Time yourself to make sure the monologue will fit within a four-minute time period.

6 Read about John Leguizamo on the next page and griots and American storytelling on pages 84–85. Choose one of those topics to research to explore how the people and traditions represented have influenced theatre and drama in the United States.

7 In a brief essay, explain why self-discipline is particularly important for a voice-over actor. Use plenty of examples to support your point.

8 **Theatre Journal** To some extent, improving your voice is based on listening. Listen to the way others speak. Listen to recordings by famous actors and orators. Note and describe any unusual speech inflections you hear as you casually observe life around you. Then consider how you could make those unique inflections "stage-ready"— that is, presented with proper breathing, projection, and diction.

"Speech finely framed delighteth the ears."
—2 Maccabees.II, 39

Substitute Teacher Activities

- Assign the Vocal Exercises Worksheet on page 37 of the Resource Binder.

- Teach the Voice section of the Student Handbook, pp. 577–579.

- Assign one or more of the Additional Projects on this page.

- **Play "A Twist of the Tongue."** Repeat a few of the tongue twisters on page 79 for students. Then, divide the class into groups of four and have each group write two tongue twisters. Ask each group to present its tongue twisters to the class. Have the class stand and repeat the tongue twisters with the originators.

Master of the Craft

John Leguizamo: Man of Many Voices

"I see the new Latin artist as a pioneer, opening up doors for others to follow. And when they don't open, we crowbar our way in . . . . "

—*John Leguizamo*

As it turns out, John Leguizamo doesn't need a crowbar. Instead, he has become a major star by way of his talent and ambition. Born in Bogota, Colombia, in 1964 and raised in New York City, he was voted Most Talkative in his high school class. But this charming chatterbox went on to become a respected comedian and serious actor, writer, and director. No matter what the role, he has won fans with his sharply observed takes on the life and times of Latinos; he pokes fun at stereotypes as he merrily shatters them.

Leguizamo studied acting at New York University where he was the only Latino in his class. Later, he enrolled at the Lee Strasberg Institute. Leguizamo studied

John Leguizamo in hi one-man show.

with Strasberg for only one day before the legendary teacher died. He then began his stand-up comedy career in clubs in and around New York City. From there he began getting small roles in movies.

In 1991 his first one-man show, *Mambo Mouth*, premiered off Broadway and became

a runaway hit. He received multiple awards for his rendition of seven different Latino characters. In several later one-man shows, he continued to use his stamina, razor-sharp timing, versatile voice, and one-of-a-kind storytelling to create multifaceted characters that move audiences to both tears and laughter.

While receiving his greatest praise for the one-man shows, Leguizamo has appeared in a number of highly acclaimed films. In 2001 he played Toulouse-Lautrec in the film *Moulin Rouge* alongside Nicole Kidman. Since then he has acted in *The Take* (2007), *Miracle at St. Anna* (2008), and *The Lincoln Lawyer* (2011), among others. His voice work as Sid the Sloth is very popular in the *Ice Age* movies.

Master of the Craft

More About John Leguizamo

John Leguizamo grew up in what he calls "the big melting pot of America" where every accent was at his "beck and call." This explains why he became a fine mimic with a great ear for the nuances of human speech and interaction. Leguizamo can transform instantly into a 65-year-old man, an unruly teenager, a small child, or even a young woman. Since winning the film role of Chi Chi Rodriguez in the film *To Wong Foo: Thanks for Everything, Julie Newmar,* he has continued to score bigger and better roles. In 1996 he played Tybalt in Baz Luhrmann's film adaptation of William Shakespeare's *Romeo and Juliet* with Leonardo DiCaprio and Claire Danes. A favorite starring role was in Spike Lee's *Summer of Sam* in 1999. His role as a voice-over actor in the 2002 animated film *Ice Age*, in which he played Sid the Sloth, was well received. He reprised the role in subsequent films in the series. In 1999, he won the Emmy for Outstanding Performance in a Variety or Music Performance for his role in *Freak*.

Masters Past and Present

Ray Romano began his career at sixteen when he formed a comedy troupe titled *No Talent*. After attending Queens College, he began performing in the late-night comedy circuit while holding a day job. Finally in 1987, Romano decided to pursue work in the entertainment industry full time. In 1991, Romano's dream was realized when he performed on the *Tonight Show* with the legendary host Johnny Carson. His 1995 appearance on *Late Night With David Letterman* prompted the idea of developing a sitcom. The comic's offbeat domestic observations struck a chord with audiences and critics alike in the hit television series *Everybody Loves Raymond*, which is now in reruns. Like Leguizamo, Romano had a vocal role in the *Ice Age* series of movies.

For More Information

Books
The Works of John Leguizamo: Freak, Spic-o-rama, Mambo Mouth, and Sexaholix, Harper Paperbacks, 2008.

Other Media
Live, [Explicit Lyrics] John Leguizamo, CD, RCA, 2001.

Mambo Mouth, DVD, Uni/Polar, 1992.

John Leguizamo: Tales From a Ghetto Klown, DVD, PBS Home Video, 2012.

Theatre **Then** and Now

Storytellers Across Time

The word *story* comes from the Latin word *historia*, meaning *history*. Before written history, people told stories in order to understand the past and the present. Many people believe that storytelling played an important part in the birth of theatre. Men would go off to hunt for food or to battle an enemy and then come back to those anxiously awaiting to hear what had happened. Storytelling was the means for passing history down from generation to generation.

 Have the students select a short story to read to the class. Instruct the students to also select music that will enhance the mood and spirit of the story. Remind the students that not only do they need to incorporate the vocal techniques learned in this chapter in their presentation, but they also need to use facial expressions and body language.

The Griot

A popular griot school is located in Gambia, a small country in West Africa. The man in the photo, Dembo Jobarteh, is the general manager and main teacher of the school. He is also a master at the kora and the drums.

Theatre **Then** and Now

Storytellers Across Time

The Griot

The ancient griots were native West African storytellers. They fulfilled a wide variety of roles in African society, serving not only as the keepers of a community's oral tradition, but also as genealogists, teachers, masters of ceremonies, and advisors. Some historians believe that through their efforts to mediate conflicts and take part in ceremonies, griots became a form of social glue that worked to keep African societies united. Griots were present at births, weddings, sports events, and governmental meetings, and also spread the word to others. In short, they played a vital part in every aspect of society. No other profession in any part of the world comes close to the intricate and intimate ties the griots had to their people.

The griot is not simply a cultural and historical oddity. Modern-day griots have become extremely popular, thanks in part to the 1970s television miniseries "Roots." In it, author Alex Haley authenticated the story of his ancestry by listening to village history told to him by an African griot. Since then, African griots, weaving a spellbinding collage of spoken word, song, and movement, have played to packed houses in New York, London, and elsewhere around the world.

Gambian griot Dembo Jobarteh tuning his kora. The instrument's body is made from a gourd that is cut in half and partially covered with cow skin. Fishing line is used for the twenty-one strings.

Visual Cues

Use the prompts below to discuss the images on this and the next page.

- How do you think Dembo Jobarteh uses his kora when telling a story?

- What instruments might storytellers from other nations use to tell their stories?

- What emotion do you think the Moth storyteller is trying to convey? What leads you to this conclusion?

- What advantages and disadvantages would a storyteller have if he or she were to use a microphone on a stand during a presentation?

The Moth

Of course, storytelling has played a key part in almost every culture. In the United States, the American Indians had an extensive oral tradition. The immigrants who came to America from all over the world brought their oral traditions with them. Storytelling in the United States today is alive and well. Many cities and educational organizations see ethnic storytelling events as a way to build community and encourage generations to come together. A number of organizations are completely devoted to the fine art of storytelling. One such organization is The Moth.

The brainchild of poet and novelist George Dawes Green, The Moth started small. Green wanted to recreate his childhood evenings of storytelling in rural Georgia in an urban environment. He had seen that stories that focused on a tale of woe about some unlucky character drew the listeners in like moths to a flame. Green started in 1997 with just a few friends in his living room. But The Moth, as he called it, quickly developed a following. Soon the event moved to Joe's Pub at New York's Joseph Papp Public Theatre and later to the Brooklyn Academy of Music and the Players Club. Now The Moth appears around the country, drawing a broad, culturally diverse audience of approving spectators and storytellers. In 2013, The Moth hosted its first High School Grand Slam of storytelling in New York City.

Because the storytellers at The Moth usually are not professional performers, and because most of them tell stories from their own lives, audiences find the stories exhilarating, fresh, and unique. Since 2009, *The Moth Radio Hour* has reached millions of listeners on public radio and in podcasts. In 2010, the program received a Peabody Award for broadcasting excellence for reinvigorating the ancient art of storytelling. You can learn more about The Moth by visiting www.themoth.org.

Moth storyteller Taylor responds to the theme "Face to Face."

Photo courtesy of Jason Falchook

The Moth

The goal of the storytellers at the Moth is twofold: to entertain and to spark a story in people watching. The Moth believes that everyone has a story to tell. The Moth is actively looking for fresh stories. The Moth link themoth.org/tell-a-story provides a way for people to record and submit a story pitch online. Story ideas are then voted on by visitors to the website. Or submit a pitch over the phone by calling 1-877-799-MOTH (1-877-799-6684). You can also prepare a five-minute story, show up at a Moth Storyslam, and hope to be one of 10 people chosen to tell their story. The website offers storytelling tips and directions for taking part in a Storyslam.

ACTivity Instruct the students to read or remember a story from childhood. They should use the vocal techniques learned in this chapter to present the story to the class.

Advanced Students

Encourage students to tell a story they make up themselves. A story of creation or an important event would be good choices. Suggest that they visit the Moth Web site for more information.

For More Information

Books

Geisler, Harlynne, *Storytelling Professionally,* Libraries Unlimited, 1997.

Hale, Thomas A., *Griots and Griottes: Masters of Words and Music,* Indiana University Press, 1999.

Walsh, John, *The Art of Storytelling: Easy Steps to Presenting an Unforgettable Story,* Moody Publishing, 2003.

Other Media

Distant Voices, Thunder Words, DVD, Insight Media, 2001.

Jay O'Callahan: A Master Class in Storytelling, DVD, Insight Media, 1983.

Storytelling the Navajo Way, DVD, Insight Media, 2006.

Storytelling: Voicework and the Ensemble Experience – Sound and Range, DVD, Insight Media, 2003.

Chapter 9

Ensemble Work

This chapter will teach students the importance of working together as an ensemble. Students will learn how to enhance their characters by developing concentration and listening skills, learning how to react and how to play off the other characters in the scene.

Objectives

1 to understand the importance of ensemble acting

2 to develop the concentration, skill, trust, teamwork, and courtesy necessary to work in an ensemble

3 to perform an improvised ensemble scene with several partners

Project Specs

Advanced Students
Have students use a real script that combines movement and planned dialogue as well as ensemble acting.

On Your Feet

Show, Don't Tell Demonstrate with student volunteers how to perform a short improvised scene. Encourage students to look again at the rules of improvisation found on page 43.

Advanced Students
Have students use the suggested situations but give each character a physical obstacle (sick to one's stomach, waiting to sneeze, an uncontrollable itch, etc.) that occurs every time the character tries to achieve the goal. Have the students discuss the challenge of trying to achieve a goal with the added physical difficulty.

---

9 Ensemble Work

What if every night of your life were a one-person show? What if every conversation ended in a monologue? Life would be quite dull. Human beings are social creatures. We want to know all about the nooks and crannies of one another's lives. We want to be involved in those lives too—not as onlookers, but as participants—as part of the ensemble.

Project Specs

Project Description For this assignment, you and several partners will perform a three- to five-minute improvised ensemble scene.

Purpose to develop the concentration, skill, teamwork, and courtesy necessary to explore creativity in an ensemble

Materials an annotated list of your character's relationship with other characters in a scene or the Ensemble Work Activity Sheet your teacher provides

Theatre Terms

emoting
ensemble ethic
fall
going up
illusion of the first time
interplay
step on
supporting roles

On Your Feet

With one to three partners, improvise one of the scenes below:

- Four of you are in the family room at home. Two of you want to clean up the clutter; the other two try to find ways out of the job.

- A boy attempts to make a date with a girl he just met. She likes him but doesn't think she should accept. He is determined, however.

- One of you is packing a suitcase, determined to take a trip. Two friends try to keep you from packing.

Theatre Terms

emoting expressing oneself emotionally

ensemble ethic working for the good of the group rather than for the individual

fall when an actor does not stay in character

going up forgetting ones lines or actions

illusion of the first time a mental technique that allows performers to repeat their scenes again and again with freshness and spontaneity

interplay interaction between characters

step on to cut off or interrupt another character by speaking over his or her lines

supporting roles roles that support main characters

Ensemble Acting

Acting demands **interplay,** or interaction, between all of the characters. To be realistic, characters must play off one another in an interactive way. They must pay attention to everything going on around them. Every time an actor speaks, his or her words should seem new and interesting to the others onstage. The actor must communicate the **illusion of the first time,** which means that the action must seem spontaneous and fresh even after hours and hours of practice. When your character is not speaking, you must react as though you are hearing the other characters for the first time. It takes practice. Watch carefully as the other actors speak and move. You'll find yourself

more engrossed in the nuances of what the other actors are doing than you are in yourself.

When you interact purposefully with your fellow actors, you begin to develop a working relationship based on trust and respect. You become not just an individual, but an important part of the whole. That's what the **ensemble ethic** is all about.

The Ensemble Actor's Safety Net

It is empowering to be part of a mutually supportive group onstage. Interacting wholeheartedly with others offers the ensemble actor the benefits articulated below.

- Your close ties to the other characters won't let you **"fall"** out of character or forget your lines.

- You won't have time for your own private speculations or fears.

- If you have learned your lines well, the reality of your situation won't allow you to forget them.

- You can collectively explore creativity to become a whole greater than its parts.

In the play *Experiment with an Airpump*, each member of the ensemble contributes a unique individual interpretation that impacts the dynamics of the entire group.

Chapter 9 Ensemble Work **87**

Discuss the importance of the *illusion of the first time* to the believability of a performance.

The Ensemble Actor's Safety Net

Discuss the importance of developing trust among an ensemble. The students must trust each other and feel the environment is "safe" before they will feel truly comfortable. Remind students that trust builds slowly and is destroyed quickly.

ACTivity Have ten to twelve students at a time stand in a tight circle facing inward. One person stands in the center with his or her arms crossed in front of the chest. Students comprising the circle face the person in the middle, palms up, ready to catch the person. When everyone is ready, the center student falls backward and is caught by the other students. Slowly, the center student is passed around the circle. No one student in the circle should ever have the weight of the center student alone. Everyone should have a chance to be in the center.

An Experiment with an Airpump, by Shelagh Stephenson, explores the issue and moral questions behind scientific research. The setting of the play shifts back and forth from 1799 to 1999, between two families who occupy the same house two hundred years apart.

- What do you think is happening in the picture? What leads you to this conclusion?

- Pick one character in the group and write a short description of his or her life. Read it for the class.

Resource Binder

- Performers' Etiquette, TIPack, p. G
- Crew Etiquette, TIPack, p. H
- Safety Rules and Reminders, TIPack, p. I
- Ensemble Work Activity Sheet, p. 40
- Guidelines for the Ensemble Worksheet, p. 41
- Critique Sheet: Ensemble Work p. 42
- Ensemble Work Test, p. 43

Handbook Connections
page 573

To Have on Hand

- A stopwatch to time the ensemble scene presentations for practice and performance

- A playing space and possibly one or two chairs to help the students have different levels in their ensemble

- Scripts or playbooks for several actors with movement and dialogue for advanced extensions of the assignment

PREPARE

Choose Your Situation

Discuss with the students the plot structure of a play and what should be incorporated in the beginning, middle and end of a scene. Review the rules and guidelines of improvisation. If you wish, divide the students into groups in advance, or you can allow the students to pick their own groups.

Special Needs and ESL Students

These students may need help with this project. You may want to discuss with them in advance the characters they choose and the characters' objectives. Additionally, try to pair these students with advanced students who are willing to help them develop their characters and the characters' objectives as they work on their scene.

ACTivity Select two students to begin a "Freeze-'n-go" improv activity. Give the actors a situation and a location in which to begin their scene. As the actors begin their improvisation, the audience should watch for interesting body positions to spark an idea in which to start a new improv. When an audience member has an idea, he should call "Freeze" and then go onstage and tap the person he would like to replace. He should then assume the exact body position of the frozen actor and begin the scene establishing a new situation and location.

Beginning Students

Perform the same exercise, but instead the instructor will call "Freeze" and the name of a student to replace an actor on stage. It might be necessary to help the student think of a new situation and location to begin the new scene. Have the class offer ideas.

PREPARE

Choose Your Situation

Divide into mixed groups of five. (Your teacher may wish to assign groups, scenes, and roles.) With your partners, choose a group of characters and situations from the following chart, or explore group creativity and invent a detailed situation with characters of your own.

Location	Character	Objective/Intention/Need
A spring garage sale in an empty building downtown	Antique dealer	Hopes to find something of value
	Old woman	Has to crochet 50 baby booties for bazaar
	Theatre prop person	Looking for a cane
	Real estate salesman	Needs a commission
	Young man	Has no place to live
An airport in which a boarding flight has been delayed	Ticket agent	Trying to help customers
	Business executive	Has to keep an important appointment
	Orphan	Going to meet new foster family
	College student	Heading back to school
	Foreign visitor	Anxious to get back home
A living room on prom night	Young man	Just meeting his date's parents
	Young woman	Anxious about her parents' reaction to her date
	Mother	Anxious about her daughter
	Father	Not impressed with his daughter's date
	Younger brother	Getting in the way
A lakeside resort full of vacationers	Older woman	Wealthy, concerned with social position
	Personal assistant	Works for the wealthy woman
	Reporter	Looking for a scoop
	Competitive swimmer	Training for the next Olympics
	Manager of the resort	Trying to keep everyone happy
A drawing room in a Victorian mansion where a murder has just occurred	Detective questioning those assembled	Wants to solve this murder before dinner
	Butler	Named in the will
	Business partner of the deceased	Was being sued by the deceased
	Brother of the deceased	Argued with the deceased recently
	Neighbor	Disliked the deceased

From the Field: Building Trust

Arthur Bartow, author of *The Director's Voice,* approached Gordon Davidson, a celebrated but controversial director, and asked, "How do you build trust?" Davidson replied, "I really do believe that the work is a collaboration, that it is not a judgmental situation, that the actors absolutely have the right to experiment and fail. I feel that there is as much chance that they are going to teach me something about the event or the character as there is that I'm going to be able to teach them."

from *The Director's Voice* by Arthur Bartow

Developing Relationships

In an ensemble, all the parts are **supporting roles,** or roles that support another role. When working on any of your group projects in drama, make a point of encouraging all members to contribute by exploring their individual creativity—which in turn inspires creativity within the ensemble as a whole. Respect everyone's ideas, even if they differ markedly from your own. Strong discussions and disagreements are healthy and productive within the group. Getting angry or insulting others' opinions, however, is not.

Working with the Group

With your group, decide on the situation you are going to improvise together. Choose your parts and decide what your various objectives will be. Play off one another's creativity. You should each be keeping a list of your own character's relationship to the other characters in the scene (or using the Activity Sheet provided by your teacher). Briefly discuss how your characters' relationships assist in telling the story, being sure to consider carefully what your partners have to say.

Working Alone

In your journal, quickly sketch out in more detail what your character thinks of the other characters in your scene, as well as how your character sees himself or herself. Think about the kind of person your character will be and how your character might move, speak, and gesture.

Back with the Group

When you all think you have a fairly good understanding of your characters, meet again as a group. Decide upon the opening line in your scene. To ensure that all characters play a part in the

The Language of
THEATRE

Monitor your understanding and ask for clarification of any spoken language in the classroom you don't understand.

- Listen as a classmate or teacher offers simple definitions of the theatre terms on page 86, such as "*Interplay* means interaction among actors." Notice which words you understand and ask for help understanding unfamiliar words.

- Listen to your partners during the On Your Feet exercise on page 86. Do not *step on* someone else's lines and ask your partners to clarify unfamiliar words.

- Listen as a classmate or teacher reads the instructions on page 88 as you prepare to work on your project. Discuss with your partners how to develop an *ensemble ethic* and ask for help with unfamiliar language.

- Listen to your partners as you create your ensemble project. With an understanding that all roles are *supporting roles*, ask for clarification of unfamiliar language or ideas.

Even with such a large cast, everyone's role is equally important.

Developing Relationships

ACTivity Divide the class into groups of five. Each group will be assigned a task to perform without verbal communication. Tasks might range from moving an imaginary sofa to preparing an invisible enchilada. Give each group time to discuss strategy. When performing, the group must rely on nonverbal skills to communicate to the audience what they are doing.

Working with the Group

Help students decide which character they will play and how to map out their objectives. Encourage students to think about which roles they would be best suited for or which roles might offer a new challenge.

ACTivity Divide the class into two circles. Have each group create a pattern by throwing a ball to someone in the group until everyone has received the ball just once. When the ball gets back to the person who began the activity, they repeat the pattern until they have it down smoothly. Next, they reverse the pattern. Once the reversed pattern is smooth, a second ball is added, maintaining the same pattern. Continue to add balls. The object is to see how many balls the group can add and still maintain the pattern.

The Language of
THEATRE

Allow students to signal their understanding of spoken English by using a thumbs-up or thumbs-down signal as you introduce new vocabulary. Invite students who have signaled thumbs up to clarify the term for classmates.

Backstage Gossip: Ghost on Strike

A company of players producing a Shakespearean repertoire were in desperate straits when they one day announced a performance of *Hamlet* in a small town. Salaries had been unpaid for many weeks, and there was much dissatisfaction in the company. All went well with the performance until Hamlet's line about his father's ghost: "Perchance 'twill walk again." Here the ghost broke into the scene from off-stage with the loudly-voiced answer: "Nay, 'twill walk no more until its salary is paid."

from *Theatrical Anecdotes* by Peter Hay

Back with the Group

After explaining how to develop and rehearse the scene, hand out the Ensemble Work Activity Sheets and show the students how to use them. Give the students a time limit to go through the steps to complete the preparation of their presentations. Time students as they practice to see that they stay within the three- to five-minute time limit.

ACTivity Have several actors line up on one end of the stage. Ask them to walk as a character completely different from themselves—someone much older or younger, or someone of the opposite sex. Ask the students to use recall or actual observation as they practice at home. Remind students that the goal is to master an accurate portrayal, not necessarily a comic portrayal, though the walk could naturally be amusing.

Career Focus

Entertainment papers and resources can be found best by searching the Web. Listed below are helpful Web sites.

New York
www.backstage.com

Los Angeles
www.variety.com
www.backstage.com

Dallas
www.dallasobserver.com
www.stage-online.org

Chicago
www.performink.com
www.leagueofchicagotheatres.org

Unions
www.actorsequity.org
www.sagaftra.org

Audition Material
www.stageplays.com

General Information
www.onlinetalentdirectory.com

scene, sketch out a sequence of events that includes dialogue for each of the characters. As a group, describe the dramatic structure of the scene—the development and outcomes. Use your individual and group creativity.

If you feel confident with what you have established this far, continue by working on how each of your characters will move throughout the scene. When you have created a scene to your satisfaction, practice it a few times, making sure you do not exceed five minutes. Remember, this project is improvisational. Don't go over it so often that you memorize it. You are now ready to present your ensemble scene.

Dominic West rises to the actor's ultimate challenge: playing a character of the opposite sex (in Caryl Churchill's *Cloud Nine*).

Career Focus
Stage Actor

The best way to become an actor is to act! To develop your skills as an actor, you can begin by acting in school plays, teen acting classes, community theatres, and small professional companies. These are ways to build skills and a résumé. The experiences of concentration, teamwork, and critiquing that you gain in the theatre can also be applied to many other college majors and careers.

Some actors join with others to form scene study groups. They choose a scene from a play to work on together. Members of the group take turns acting and critiquing one another's work.

In addition to ensemble scene study, select a monologue or two to memorize and rehearse as a solo performance piece. Look for audition calls in local or entertainment media in print or online. Be prepared not to get every job you audition for, but approach each audition as a chance to learn about the process and receive feedback. Each time you audition, more people are becoming familiar with you and your work.

And remember, Broadway isn't the only place where a serious actor can find a place on the stage. All over the country regional theatre is alive and well and drawing audiences. Many actors earn a good living in cities with a strong cultural and theatrical base. Refer to the chart on page 10 for more ways to evaluate this career.

Visual Cue

In 1979 Caryl Churchill received wide notice for *Cloud Nine,* a satirical play involving farcical moments in the relationships between characters cast in a cross-gender fashion.

- What challenges would an actor face when trying to play someone of the opposite sex?

- Can you think of a greater challenge than playing this kind of role?

Backstage Gossip: Show Me the $$$

When Tom Cruise was starting out, he was told by a TV executive, "You're too intense and you're not pretty enough for television. You should try features." Shortly thereafter Cruise announced his plan to move to New York to seek his fortune as an actor. His concerned stepfather asked a question which later became the source of amusement— "How much is this gonna cost me?"

from the Web site *anecdotage.com*

Spotlight on

Roles, Responsibilities, and Production Etiquette

Understanding and respecting the roles, responsibilities, and efforts of all those you work with on stage is an important part of the collaboration needed in theatre work. Whether you are a beginner or a seasoned professional, you can go a long way toward winning the respect of your colleagues by simply being courteous and following the rules below.

Actor

- Be on time for rehearsals and performances—don't make others wait for you.
- Know your lines.
- Pick up your cues on time. Don't miss your lines or say them too late.
- Don't **step on** another actor's lines (cut them off) or upstage another actor.
- Avoid stealing focus by moving, gesturing, or **emoting** too much (overacting) while another actor is speaking.
- Find ways to cover for an actor who gets lost in a scene or goes blank, called **"going up."**

Director

- Try to set the schedule at least one week in advance, and stick to it.
- Listen respectfully to the thoughts and opinions of the actor, as well as the design and tech crews. Your leadership is important and helps set the tone of the production.
- Use positive and encouraging words.

Designer

- Work with the director to develop a workable design that reflects the director's concept.
- Talk to the cast and crew before finalizing the design.
- Consider altering your design according to cast and crew feedback.

Technical Professionals

- Always keep tools in their proper location when not in use.
- Maintain respect for the needs of other professionals at work.
- Be very careful with tools while working around others (see Safety Rules on page 256).

Spotlight on

Roles, Responsibilities, and Production Etiquette An important part of ensuring that a play's rehearsals and performances run smoothly is setting up an atmosphere of professionalism and communication. It is important that everyone involved in the show arrives at rehearsal prepared and ready to work. Actors must listen to the director and be ready to take and use constructive criticism. Actors must also listen and respond to the other actors in the scene so as not to miss cues or step on lines.

Vocabulary Enhancement

"To do nothing" refers to a situation where an actor is expected to look as though he belongs in the scene, but to not steal the focus of the scene away from where it belongs. The challenge for the actor is to find ways to make the audience accept his or her presence as a part of the scene, but not become guilty of scene stealing. This is a very important technique to master for the ensemble actor.

Backstage Gossip: Line Going Up!

John Barrymore used to tell of the confusion that prevailed in an old stock company with which he had once played in repertory. The vast number of plays and the frequency and inconsistency with which they were performed, rendered confusion more or less inevitable. One evening Barrymore found himself unable to remember his lines. Faking a piece of business, he sidled over into the wings and hastily called to the director, "What's the line, what's the line?" The director sighed wearily and asked, "What's the play?"

from *Theatrical Anecdotes* by Peter Hay

PRESENT

Perform Your Ensemble Scene

Before they begin their ensemble scenes, remind students to hand in their Activity Sheets when their group is called. Once they have handed in their sheets, they should stand before the class in a professional manner. One group member should introduce the scene, briefly describing the location, the situation, and the characters, as well as who will be playing them.

Remind the audience that as soon as the Activity Sheets are in and the group enters the playing area, the audience should remain quiet and attentive for the duration of the performance. Have a stopwatch ready to time each scene.

CRITIQUE

Evaluate Your Classmates' Scene

Hand out the Critique Sheet for this project or have students use their own paper. In addition to their presentations, you may also wish to evaluate students on how well they critique others. Later, discuss with them any problems you see with their critiques.

Here's How

Show, Don't Tell Use student volunteers to set up an example situation of a scene gone off track. Then show the students how you would use the techniques in that situation to get the scene back on the right track.

PRESENT

Perform Your Ensemble Scene

Before your name or the name of someone in your group is called, decide which member of the group will introduce the scene. Give your lists or Activity Sheets to your teacher. The group member who has agreed to do the introduction should briefly describe the location of the scene, the characters and the situation, as well as indicating who plays which character. Perform your scene for the class, demonstrating your creativity and its effect on the audience. When you have finished, bow politely.

Here's How
To Keep Your Ensemble on Track

If you think a scene is going off track, remind yourself or the other actors of your relationship in one of the following ways:

1 **State the relationship outright.** Say something such as, "You may be my boss, but . . ." or "I know you are angry about my being five hours late, Dad, and . . . ."

2 **Use a gesture or action** that reinforces your relationship to a character. Hug or strong-arm someone, flirt, or shoot a glance of withering scorn.

3 **Pause.** Take a breath. It's better than rushing headlong out of control.

CRITIQUE

Evaluate Your Classmates' Scene

Choose one of the ensemble scenes presented in class to critique. As you watch and take notes, ask yourself the following questions:

• Could I describe each character's objective in the scene and the tactics used to get what he or she wanted?

• Could I outline each character's relationship and attitude to the other characters in the scene?

• Did any one character stand out among the others? Why?

• Did all the characters have some action, event, relationship, or motivation in common?

• In what ways was creativity evident in the scene? Analyze the creative elements and their effect on the audience.

Use a scale of 1 to 5 to rate the scene, with 5 being "outstanding" and 1 being "needs much improvement." After you have rated the scene, write a short paragraph explaining why you gave the rating you did.

Meet with your ensemble after receiving feedback on your performance. Part of strengthening an ensemble is reflecting on group work and understanding how it can be improved. Discuss ways you could improve your ensemble work, always recognizing that *everyone* is responsible for success.

Backstage Gossip: One-Night Stand

A road company at the end of the 19th century and its financial resources arrived in Waco, Texas, hoping to stay for a while and recoup. They failed to take the town by storm, which was put into perspective the next morning in the local paper: "Rain-storm in Galveston, lasted twenty minutes. Hail storm in Beaumont, ten minutes. Wind-storm in Langtry, two days. Barnstorm in Opera House, one night."

from *Theatrical Anecdotes* by Peter Hay

Additional Projects

1 Choose a partner and wait onstage for your partner to enter the scene. Based on the way in which your partner acts toward you and responds to you, try to determine what your relationship is. When you respond correctly, your partner should let you know and end the scene.

2 Choose a three-person scene and rehearse it with your partners. Then, at the moment of performance, switch characters and perform one another's parts.

3 Work with a group to make a simple task into an ensemble job. For example, make use of six actors to build a birdhouse, make a stew, or get someone a job. Make sure each group member has an equally important role. Use and demonstrate creativity as a group. After each group performs, analyze the creativity the group displayed and the efffect of that creativity on the audience.

4 To enhance your teamwork and listening skills, play the following alphabet game in a large group. Starting with *A*, each player names a person, place, and object—always repeating everything said previously. So, for example, player number four would say, "*Anna* lives in the *attic* with an *apple, Bob* lives in a *boat* with a *bicycle, Carl* lives in a *cabin* with a *cat,*" and might add, "*Doris* lives in a *dungeon* with a *duck.*" As you continue through the alphabet, try to be dramatic and expressive, and don't forget anything you've heard!

5 Evaluate the kinds of training and experience that are most valuable to someone pursuing a career as a stage actor. Does the career appeal to you? Would you enjoy the training? Write your thoughts in an essay.

6 Read more about ensembles on pages 94–95. Use the information as a springboard to analyze and research the influences of multicultural heritage of drama and theatre in the United States. Use technology to document your information and present your findings in a clear, coherent manner.

7 Perform a staged reading of the scene from *Blithe Spirit* by Noel Coward found in Unit Eight. Take into account the way the comedy depends upon listening and precise responses between each actor in the scene.

8 **Theatre Journal** Reflect in your journal on your ensemble work. Articulate the importance of both leadership and collaboration in the activities you did with your ensemble. Analyze the ways creativity develops within an ensemble.

> "*We were never cute, I think that still holds true. Everyone always liked everyone's work, and that's what also kept it together. There was very much a shared sensibility . . . but also a respect for one another's work.*"
>
> —John Malkovich, discussing his work as a member of Chicago's Steppenwolf Theatre Company

Ensemble Work Test

The test for this chapter is available in blackline master form in the Resource Binder, page 43.

For More Information

Books
Bonczek, Rose Burnett and David Storck, *Ensemble Theatre Making: A Practical Guide*, Routledge, 2012.

Gwinn, Peter Campbell, and Charna Halpern, *Group Improvisation: The Manual of Ensemble Improv Games*, Meriwether Publishing, 2003.

Kozlowski, Rob, *The Art of Chicago Improv: Short Cuts to Long-Form Improvisation*, Heinemann, 2002.

Wilk, John R., *The Creation of an Ensemble: The First Years of the American Conservatory Theatre*, Southern Illinois University Press, 1986.

Other Media
Ensemble Building, DVD, Insight Media, 2006.

Stage for a Nation, DVD, Films for the Humanities and Sciences, 1986.

Substitute Teacher Activities

Here are suggestions for one or more days when you will be out of the classroom.

- Assign the Ensemble Guidelines Worksheet on page 41 of the Resource Binder.
- Teach the Group Readings section of the Student Handbook, p. 573.
- Assign one or more of the Additional Projects on this page.
- Divide the class into groups of four or five to **Present a Play Called** *Trapped.*

Members of the group will be trapped somewhere, and they must decide Who, What, When, and Where. Who are the characters, What happened to cause them to become trapped, How do they manage to get out, When does the scene occur (time period, time of day, time span), and Where does it occur? The plot should have a *beginning* that shows the action as they become trapped, a *middle* that shows them trying to get out, and an *end* that shows how they escape.

Cultural Heritage

English and European Ensembles

Anton Chekhov lived from 1860 to 1904. He began his career with short stories and then went on to writing plays. His play *The Sea Gull* opened in 1896, but was a failure because the actors neither understood their roles nor learned their lines. In later years, he provided the Moscow Art Theatre with *Uncle Vanya* in 1899, *The Three Sisters* in 1901, and *The Cherry Orchard* in 1904. All four plays reveal the monotonous and frustrating life of Russian characters who hope for a more meaningful life but don't know how to obtain it.

Some found Chekhov's plays dark and obscure, but the great director Konstantin Stanislavski worked hard to illuminate Chekhov's work. He would carefully study each play before rehearsals began, often visiting the locale of the play. He and the Moscow Art Theatre were the perfect match for Anton Chekhov.

Other Cultures, Other Times

The longest continuously running professional theatre in Australia, the *Ensemble Theatre* of Sydney, has strived to entertain as well as challenge its audiences for over forty years. Founded in a north Sydney location in the 1950s, it moved to its current location on Sydney Harbor's Careening Cove in 1960. This location was converted into Australia's first theatre-in-the-round stage, where fine theatre continues to be produced.

Visual Cue

- By studying the picture of *The Three Sisters* performance, what conclusions do you come to about what is going on in the scene?

- What is it about the stage picture that makes the scene visually interesting?

- Does any one character stand out more than another? Why?

Cultural Heritage

English and European Ensembles

Elizabethan Actors

Elizabethan England saw theatre grow from an occasional, itinerant art form to a commercial enterprise complete with permanent playhouses and professional acting companies. These early companies embraced a star system, by which the most celebrated actors won leading, sympathetic roles, while other actors specialized in playing particular types. Leading Elizabethan actors like Richard Burbage learned more than 50 plays and performed about 70 roles in rotation—over and over again—during a typical three-year period. This system encouraged actors to think in terms of generalized types and to play to the audience rather than to each other.

19th-Century European Actors

In the 19th century, however, things began to change. New playwrights like George Buchner in Germany and Anton Chekhov in Russia began experimenting with naturalistic and expressionistic plays. Directors like Duke George II of Meiningen and Stanislavski of the Moscow Art Theatre began asking actors to work closely together to create a unified, realistic picture onstage. Companies began working together for weeks, even months on end, to develop a unified approach to a single play. Stars still emerged, but they gave themselves over to each production's social or artistic ideals.

Chekhov's *The Three Sisters*, one of the earliest ensemble productions, has been produced continually since its debut in 1901.

For More Information

Books

Dauphin, Sue, *Houston by Stages: A History of Theatre in Houston,* Eakin Publications, 1981.

Grote, David, *The Best Actors in the World: Shakespeare and His Acting Company,* Greenwood Publishing Group, 2002.

Peterson, Bernard L., *The African American Theatre Directory 1816-1960: A Comprehensive Guide to Early Black Theatre Organizations, Companies, Theatres, and Performing Groups,* Greenwood Press, 1997.

Skrebneski, Victor, *Steppenwolf Theatre Company: Twenty-Five Years of an Actor's Theatre,* Sourcebooks Trade, 2000.

Other Media

The Negro Ensemble Company, DVD, Films for the Humanities and Sciences, 1987.

The Renaissance Theatre, DVD, Insight Media, 2005

Shakespeare's Globe, DVD, Insight Media, 2005.

Diverse U.S. Ensembles

Steppenwolf Theatre Company

Many theatre companies today work entirely as ensembles, such as Steppenwolf Theatre in Chicago. Plays there reflect the artistic vision and theatrical values that the company members hold. Steppenwolf members are strong, determined actors willing to "look the fool" and take on unusual roles and off-beat characters.

Ensemble Theatre of Houston

The Ensemble Theatre of Houston promotes collaboration among theatre professionals of all races, genders, and ethnicities. Too often in the past, African American actors, directors, and crew members had trouble finding a place in the theatre. Over the years, however, this ensemble has helped to encourage and preserve African American artistic expression. The core troupe is African American, but the ensemble is committed to maintaining a "color-blind" approach to casting (see page 333), as well as to hiring directors, designers, and playwrights. They are unified in their theatrical values, their social vision, and their artistic mission.

Other Ensembles

Latina women also found limited opportunities in traditional theatre companies. Founded in 2004, Breath of Fire Latina Theatre Ensemble in Santa Ana, California, produces world premieres relevant to the Latina community. Like the Ensemble Theatre of Houston, Cornerstone Theater Company in Los Angeles is a multi-ethnic ensemble. There theatre professionals work with members of various communities to tell their stories in parking lots, factories, and schools, as well as in theatres.

Community members Lorinda Hawkins and Renée Günter starred in Cornerstone Theater Company's production of *SEED: A Weird Act of Faith*. Oct. 25–Nov. 18, 2012 @ Chuco's Justice Center. Written by Sigrid Gilmer. Directed by Shishir Kurup. Photo by Kevin Michael Campbell.

Diverse U.S. Ensembles

Steppenwolf Theatre Company

The nationally acclaimed not-for-profit Steppenwolf Theatre Company first performed in a church basement in 1974. It began under the leadership of Terry Kinney, Jeff Perry, and Gary Sinise but has grown into an ensemble that includes forty-three artists. The company is committed to ensemble collaboration and taking artistic risks. Located in Chicago's Lincoln Park area and in its fourth decade, the company has performed over 200 works and continues to thrive.

Ensemble Theatre of Houston

One of the oldest and most distinguished professional theater companies, the Ensemble Theatre in Houston, Texas, is dedicated to the African American experience. Financing the theatre with his own money, George Hawkins, an accomplished stage and film actor, founded the theatre in 1976. Though Hawkins died in 1990, the theatre remains dedicated to giving artists a place to work and grow.

Other Ensembles

Sara Guerrero, a director, producer, and playwright, is the Founding Artistic Director of Breath of Fire Latina Theatre Ensemble. Its more than twenty world premiers include Cherríe Moraga's Digging Up the Dirt. For more than 25 years, Los Angeles–based Cornerstone Theatre has collaborated with people with varying levels of theatre experience to tell stories about crucial community issues.

Visual Cue

The play *Seed: A Weird Act of Faith*, by Sigrid Gilmer, focuses on an urban community fighting for sustainable food choices.

By looking at the facial expressions of the women in *Seed: A Weird Act of Faith*,

what conclusions can you draw about what might be happening?

- What about the stage picture makes it visually interesting? Would it change if the actors were facing each other?

Unit Two Review

PREVIEW

1 When standing naturally, you should put your weight on the balls of your feet.

2 **scenario** an outline of a play that includes details about the plot, movement, and gestures

cheating out playing toward the audience while seemingly conversing with others on stage

stage business any small action that the character performs without major movement

upstaging drawing the audience's attention to yourself when it should be focused on another character

3 The strongest stage positions are *downstage,* because it is close to the audience, and *stage right,* because we are trained to read from left to right, and so the audience's eye will look left first.

4 The person is standing in a *full front* body position.

5 X DL means *cross down left.*

6 Emoting is NOT essential to voice production. Emoting means to overact.

7 Ask students to say these sentences aloud in class and discuss the results.

8 The most important thing an ensemble actor must learn is the *ensemble ethic*, developing a working relationship based on trust and respect.

9 Discipline is what drives the actor to take care of his "instrument" and improve his skills. It is also what drives the actor back to another audition when he has been rejected. Trust and courtesy are vital components of a successful ensemble. It is NOT important for the actor to have good looks.

Unit Two Review

PREVIEW

Examine the following key concepts previewed in Unit Two.

1 Where should you put your weight when you stand naturally?

2 Define the terms below.
  a. scenario   b. stage business   c. cheating out   d. upstaging

3 Of the following, which are the stronger positions, and why?
  upstage or downstage   stage right or stage left

4 In what body position is the person below standing?

5 What does X DL mean?

6 Which of the following is NOT essential to voice production and articulation?
  pitch   volume   articulation   emoting   inflection

7 Say this sentence using rising inflection, falling inflection, and sustained inflection: *You always go for a run in the park before you eat breakfast.*

8 What would you say is the most important thing an ensemble actor must learn?

9 Which of these are important qualities for a good actor, and why?
  discipline   trust   good looks   courtesy

PREPARE

Assess your response to the preparation process for projects in this unit.

10 How did you and your partner work together to create the scenario and add the movement to your stage movement project?

11 When working on voice and articulation, which aspect of the process did you find most difficult and why?

12 What advice would you give to others learning about stage crosses?

13 Were you able to fully trust the people in your ensemble? Why or why not?

14 Were you and your partner or partners able to work together smoothly and efficiently to prepare your ensemble improvisation?

PRESENT

Analyze the experience of presenting your work to the class.

15 Which project did you find the most rewarding? Why?

16 Did you find it easier to write the three stage crosses or to execute them? Why?

17 Were you happy with the vocal exercise you chose to do, or do you now wish you'd chosen another one? Explain your feelings.

18 Were you able to present your ensemble improvisation in an atmosphere of trust and support?

CRITIQUE

Evaluate how you go about critiquing your work and the work of others.

19 Did you find it easier to critique your classmates in terms of movement, vocal presentation, or ensemble work?

20 Ask a classmate who critiqued one of your presentations to share the critique with you. How balanced and insightful do you find it to be?

21 Evaluate the critiques you wrote in this unit. In what way could they have been more balanced and helpful?

EXTENSIONS

- Read each group of letters below until you understand their meaning. Then play with pitch and inflection as you say them aloud.

  I C U R A Q T   I N V U   G U R O K   P T S N X T C

- Create gestures for the following sentiments:

  I'm really tired and need to get some sleep.
  This is one mighty boring conversation.
  Stop lecturing me, please.
  This guy is definitely not telling the truth.
  The dog needs to go for a walk, and I'm not in the mood to do it.
  These dirty dishes have been sitting on the counter for five days!

Unit Two Review **97**

Resource Binder
Unit Two Test, p. 44

PREPARE

10–14 These questions should be answered honestly and thoughtfully by students. Discuss with students any answers that are not satisfactory.

PRESENT

15–18 Discuss with students their feelings about the presentation process: What they enjoy about it, what they would do differently, and what they learned.

CRITIQUE

19–21 Talk to students about their impressions of the critique process. Have them share both positive and negative experiences.

EXTENSIONS

- I SEE YOU ARE A CUTIE.
  I ENVY YOU.
  GEE, YOU ARE OK or GEE, YOU ROCK!
  PETE'S IN ECSTASY, or PETEY IS IN ECSTASY.

- Have students present their gestures to the class. Ask them to discuss the ones that they found the most inventive and effective.

Unit **Three**

Creating a Character

Unit Three teaches students to analyze characters from clues in the play's text and gives students tools to use in the development of characters in a variety of comic and dramatic roles.

Project Preview

Chapter 10 Character Analysis
Creating distinct characters in an improvised scene

Chapter 11 Character Development
Developing characters and performing a scene

Chapter 12 Dramatic Roles
Writing and performing a dramatic scene

Chapter 13 Comic Roles
Writing and performing a comic scene

Unit **Three**

Creating a Character

Quotable

Use the quote below for a journal writing prompt, discussion starter, or creating a class lesson.

Observation (of human behavior) is like breathing . . . I believe we have a camera lens inside our heads and when something is required in a character that I haven't personally experienced, I find that at some time I have observed a similar characteristic in another person which remains in my subconscious . . . .

Judi Dench, Actor

Discussion Questions

The following questions are intended to tap into students' **prior knowledge** and stimulate ideas about what it means to create a character for a play.

- Who are your favorite dramatic actors? Why do you admire their work?

- List five traits about yourself that you feel define who you are at present. Choose a character from a play and do the same. Is it easier to create a list about yourself or a character? Why?

- What would you do to discover the important details about a character's circumstances if you have never experienced them?

- Do you think it is more difficult to play a character very similar to you or very different? Why?

- Create two lists: one titled COMIC and the other DRAMATIC. What qualities and abilities are necessary to play each kind of role? Write them on the list.

- Do you think it is more challenging to play a comic or a dramatic role? Why?

- Faye Dunaway said on the PBS television program *Inside the Actors Studio* that to be an actor one needs "to be willing to excavate your mind and soul." What do you think she meant by that? Do you think you would be willing to do that to create a character? Why or why not?

Theatre Journal

Search through magazines to find images of people that represent either a comic or dramatic point of view. Make a collage of comic characters and one of dramatic characters. Compare their qualities, physical mannerisms, and other characteristics.

Visual Cue

The above image shows a performance of the comic opera *Platee* at Covent Garden in London, England.

- Do you think the characters in this production are comic or dramatic characters? What visual clues give you this impression?

- What do the actors' body positions, gestures, expressions, and costumes tell you about their characters?

- Which characters seem to have the highest and lowest status? How can you tell?

ACTivity Ask students to write a short speech for the froglike character at the left of the photo. Have volunteers read their speeches using the voice, gestures, and movement as they envision it for the character.

Chapter 10
Character Analysis

In this chapter students will learn to use the text to uncover a character's circumstances, characteristics, and objectives. They will create distinct characters with articulated goals.

Objectives

1 to detect clues about character from the dramatic text, including physical and emotional traits

2 to delineate and specify emotional, mental, and spiritual aspects of character

3 to articulate with precision character motivation, objective, and obstacle

4 to prepare and perform a scene involving distinct characters

Project Specs

Explain to students that analyzing a character can be as involved, challenging, rigorous, and enjoyable as they make it. Many actors do outside research to gather information on a character's background, historical period, psychological underpinnings, and so on. Other actors just take the script and go from there.

On Your Feet

ACTivity After the interview, have each student write a character description of himself or herself for a dramatic or comic play based on the partner's interview notes. Tell students to use vivid language that will stimulate the imagination of the actor playing the role. Have the class mix up the descriptions and read them aloud, guessing whom each description is based upon.

Chapter

10 Character Analysis

To be a good actor, you must become a student of humanity. Your knowledge of people is one of the most valuable assets you have when it comes to creating a believable character. As you analyze and develop a role, you will draw upon the text of the play, your own experiences, and remembered observations of people you meet, read about, or see on film.

Project Specs

Project Description You and a partner will each create distinct characters with specific goals in a three- to five-minute improvised scene.

Purpose to analyze a character in terms of internal and external traits, motivation, objectives, and stakes

Materials a list of shared information between your own and your partner's character, a list of your character's internal and external traits, or the Character Analysis Activity Sheet provided by your teacher

Theatre Terms
artistic selectivity
conflict
dual role
external traits
internal traits
motivation
objectives
obstacle
outcome
stakes

On Your Feet

Spend two minutes interviewing a partner. Ask questions about his or her background, family, friends, personal preferences, hobbies, accomplishments, and so on. Take notes and try to create a composite of the person. At the end of two minutes, look over your notes and tell your partner about himself or herself. Then switch roles.

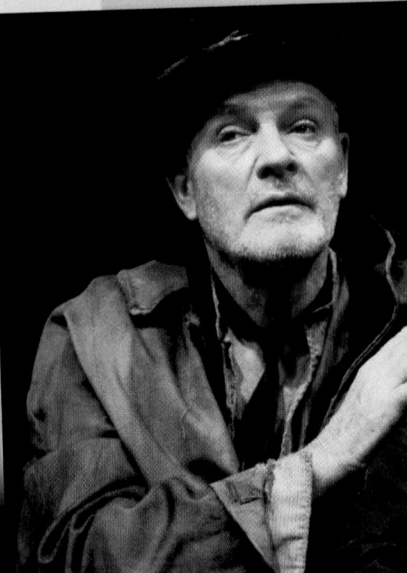

Theatre Terms

artistic selectivity selecting the optimum amount of information necessary to portray a character

conflict dramatic opposition of the protagonist with society, peers, or himself/herself

dual role the two aspects of acting: the actor-as-character and the actor-as-actor

external traits characteristics that make up physical appearance

internal traits characteristics that make up personality

motivation reason for a behavior or action

objectives goals or needs

obstacle anything that gets in the way of reaching an objective

outcome result

stakes level or degree of importance in getting objectives met

PREVIEW

The Actor and the Character

As an actor in a play you have a **dual role.** You are both the actor-as-character and the actor-as-actor. If you are to be convincing onstage, you must use your imagination—and the work you've done analyzing and developing your character—to maintain your belief in what you as the character are doing, feeling, and saying. You should think as the character thinks and concentrate on fulfilling his or her goals, or **objectives.** On the other hand, as an actor you must maintain technical control and a professional attitude at all times. You the actor and you the character must work as a unit to create the delicate balance of believable characterization. This may sound like a demanding job—and it is. But characterization shouldn't be a

strain. Relax and enjoy the process as you create a believable individual onstage.

Developing the Actor-as-Character

To be an effective onstage presence you will need to know hundreds of things about your character—much more than you will actually be able to portray onstage. Your job then becomes one of **artistic selectivity.** What are the really important aspects of this character? How can you effectively communicate the essentials of the character? At the same time, remember that none of the work you do while developing your character is wasted. The more you know about the character, the more textured your performance will be.

And you must harness your character's emotions and avoid overacting, which offends both the audience and your fellow actors. The hundreds of things you understand about your character will reveal themselves through the various layers and colors you are able to bring to the role.

Julian Glover and Alan Doble create distinctive characters in the Piccadilly Theatre production of *Waiting for Godot.*

Chapter 10 Character Analysis **101**

Actors have a unique artistic advantage over many other artists: They require no canvas, paint, paper, or other tools of the trade. All an actor really needs is his or her own body—and the ability to move, speak, and think. Let students know from the start that acting is certainly gratifying and exciting work, but it is also very demanding—and often difficult. Acting requires hours of hard physical and emotional dedication and a great deal of discipline—the result of which, ironically, should be conveyed in a relaxed and seemingly effortless way. What separates the good actor from the great actor is how well he or she can use the imagination to make a character live and breathe.

Developing the Character

Suggest to students that instead of asking how much they can do with their parts to decide how *little* they can do and still communicate the necessary ideas and emotions. Instill in them the belief that as artists creating a role, they must:

- Select
- Combine
- Discard

Vocabulary Enhancement

Theatregoers and critics alike often speak of a fine actor's *stage presence,* which is the ability to seem perfectly at ease onstage, as if he or she belonged there.

Resource Binder

Handbook Connections
pages 560–562

To Have on Hand

Have examples of well-written scenarios from various sources on hand, including some written by high school students.

Motivation and Conflict

Draw three columns on the chalkboard and write the words *WHAT* and *WHY* at the top of the first two. Then ask students to think about times in the last week when they had a strong need to do something. Ask them to tell you what it was as you write it on the board. Next ask them to explain why they wanted what they did. Write that on the board also. Explain that WHAT is the goal, or OBJECTIVE, and WHY indicates the MOTIVATION. Discuss the motivations and objectives that the students expressed.

Now add the last title, *HOW,* to the third column, and ask students what they did to achieve their goals. Tell them that the means they used to achieve their objectives are called TACTICS. Write down the tactics that they used. Discuss other tactics that might have been used to achieve the same objectives.

ACTivity Make a list of objectives with the class using verbs that stimulate an emotional response. Examples: to *incite* a riot, to *seize* power, to *hypnotize* into submission, to *abscond* with funds, etc. Once the list is complete, one student at a time acts out a movement or short scene using one verb and its objective.

The Character Inside and Out

ACTivity Suggest to students that they create a character notebook for a specific character from a play. This can be done as a project over several days. Have them create a biography of the character that describes the character's history, occupation, family status, and any other circumstances.

Some of this information will come directly from the text, some will come from research, and some will come from the imagination.

Motivation and Conflict

In real life people often do and say things for no apparent reason. A character in a play, however, needs a specific reason, or **motivation,** for doing or saying anything. Motivation determines your character's objectives. Whatever is standing in the way of your character's objectives is an **obstacle.**

This is the essence of **conflict,** which in turn is the basis of drama. The **outcome** of a conflict is the result of the steps the characters take to overcome their obstacles. What the characters may gain or lose as a result of the outcome are the **stakes.** The higher the stakes are in a play, the greater the character's motivation; the more powerful the conflict, the more important the outcome.

The Character Inside and Out

To find your way into the mind and body of a character, you must know the role inside and out. That means you must understand both the character's internal and external traits.

To determine a character's **internal traits,** challenge yourself to discover what he or she is like inside. Find out the character's background—that is, his or her family circumstances, environment, occupation, level of education, hobbies, and so on—and his or her emotional reactions to all of these circumstances. You can break internal traits into three basic categories.

1 **Mental characteristics** Is the character intelligent, clever, dull, slow, or average?

2 **Spiritual qualities** What are the character's ideals, ethical codes, and beliefs? What is his or her attitude toward other people and toward life in general?

3 **Emotional characteristics** Is the character confident, outgoing, happy, and poised or sullen, confused, nervous, cynical, and timid? What are his or her likes and dislikes? How does he or she respond to others? (One good technique when analyzing emotional characteristics is to ask yourself how a character's temperament is similar to and different from your own.)

After answering all these questions, determine your character's motivating desire within the play or scene. In other words, what does your character *want*? You may have to do the additional work of imagining the circumstances that led to the events of the play or scene.

Quotable

Acting is the life of the human soul receiving its birth through art.

from *Acting: The First Six Lessons* by Richard Boleslavski

To play the title role in *Mary Stuart* convincingly, actor Jenny Bacon must convey the motivation and obstacles faced by the Scottish queen.

A character's **external traits** have to do with outward appearance and what that appearance says about him or her. Draw on your physical awareness to develop the external traits of your character, such as the following.

1 **Posture** Does the way the character sits and stands suggest confidence, timidity, awkwardness, or grace?

2 **Movement and gestures** Does the character's movement and gait reveal poise, nervousness, weakness, or strength? What does the character's movement reveal about his or her age, health, or general attitude?

3 **Mannerisms** Does the character have any tics or little habits that provide keys to his or her personality? Examples might be nail biting, gum chewing, head scratching, or table tapping.

4 **Voice** Does the character have a specific regional dialect or any vocal mannerisms?

5 **Mode of dress** Is the character's appearance neat, casual, prim, or sloppy? Are the clothes clean or dirty? Are they in good taste?

Chapter 10 Character Analysis **103**

Suggest also that they answer the questions below about the character.

- What is your character's deepest fear?
- What is your character's deepest desire?
- What is the biggest obstacle in the way of your character getting his or her desire?
- Does your character have any odd habits?
- What songs or poems remind you of this character?
- Is there an aspect of your character that you know nothing about? Research this information and include it in your notebook.

Also have students include any photographs, artwork, lyrics, or poetry that suggest their character's traits— external and internal.

ACTivity Place five chairs in a row in the playing area and ask five students to sit down. Ask them to experiment with different postures that reveal character. Have the class suggest what each posture tells them about the person.

ACTivity Invite other students to be seated and add an environment and circumstances to the mix, such as sitting in a hospital waiting room or a police station. Each person in a chair creates the posture based on one sentence that represents his or her character, i.e., "I'm very worried about these headaches" or "Keep clear, I'm tough."

ACTivity **Advanced Students** Add more dimensions to the seated characters. Two are from the South, one is from England, one has a peculiar habit, and so on. Continue to challenge advanced students to create characters whose actions reveal both internal and external characteristics.

ACTivity **Advanced Students** Ask students to choose two or three gestures they have seen people make and memorize them so that they have a "choreography of gestures." When they are ready, ask these students to show their choreography of gestures to the class. Discuss the characters created by these gestures.

Chapter 10 Character Analysis **103**

 **sual Cue**

Friedrich Schiller's 19th-century play, *Mary Stuart,* brings to the stage the last three days of the life of Mary, Queen of Scots. Imprisoned for eighteen years in England, she was finally beheaded for her supposed involvement in an attempt on the life of Queen Elizabeth I. The play revolves around Mary and Elizabeth and their followers, who exhibit different perspectives on almost every important idea of their age.

- In what way does the character's attire suggest who she is?

- Does the character exhibit the bearing of a queen? Explain.

- What does the actress's posture suggest about the queen's circumstances?

- Imagine that you are Queen Elizabeth I standing before Mary Stuart. How would you approach her? What might you say?

Developing the Actor-as-Actor

Review the skills of listening, observing, and concentrating that students learned in Chapter 3. Point out that actors must listen to and observe one another in a scene while concentrating on staying in character and responding to the situation in a believable way. Invite students to discuss how they apply these skills in everyday situations. For example, how do they concentrate on what a partner is saying when other people are speaking in the classroom?

Tell students that the "outside in" approach to acting is sometimes called the classical approach because it was the technique used by actors for centuries. Such actors begin by perfecting movement and voice. Then they work to visualize how their character uses those qualities in a believable way within the context of the play. Some actors who use this approach are Laurence Olivier, Jim Carrey, and William Shatner.

The Language of THEATRE

Show students short videos of Laurence Olivier and Marlon Brando performing scenes from Shakespeare.

- Invite students to express their opinions about how believable each performer was, using words or short phrases.
- Invite students to express their opinions in complete sentences, using frames such as "This character is believable [not believable] because . . . ."
- Explain to students that Olivier is more of an "outside in" actor and Brando an "inside out" actor. Invite them to express their opinions about these techniques in a discussion with a partner.
- Ask students to discuss their opinions of the different techniques used by the two actors to reveal *external* and *internal traits*, supporting their opinions with evidence from the video clips.

When analyzing and developing a character's external qualities, you'll want to avoid stereotypes. For example, you don't necessarily want to choose a cartoonlike drawling "hick" voice simply because your character is supposed to be uneducated. Try to make the more interesting, less obvious choice.

Developing the Actor-as-Actor

Actors have a lot of experience as *people*, as do you! You, like all actors, have developed a keen sense of awareness in several dimensions. Suppose you walk into a room full of people. Your physical awareness—the attention to your body and its relation to the environment— helps you size up the physical details of the room. Your intellectual awareness tells you where you are and why and tunes you in to your thoughts. Your emotional awareness, attention to your feelings and the feelings of others, lets you "pick up on" subtle cues from others and gauge the emotion in the room. Your social awareness helps you grasp interactions between people and gauge the dynamics in the room.

You, like everyone else, also have many, many interactions with people. You have physical interactions with others—high-fives, hugs, hand-holding, tickling. You have intellectual interactions with others—debates about politics or collaboration on a project. You have emotional interactions with others—conflicts and resolutions, times of tears and times of laughter. And you have social interactions—you relate to others in a variety of situations, such as school, home, sports, and church.

Actors use the physical, intellectual, emotional, and social awareness and interactions they have learned through their life experience and apply them in their acting as they convey stories and portray believable characters.

Actors also draw on a variety of skills, techniques, and concepts to create believable characters and tell a story. You have already been developing some of these in earlier projects.

Skills Listening, observing, and concentrating are some of the most important skills an actor has. Listening and observing allow an actor to respond sensitively to the emotional and physical environment of the play. However, even on a small stage, there are so many things to listen to and observe that an actor must also have strong skills in concentration. Concentration helps actors know how to focus their attention.

Actors also need the skills of voice projection, diction, inflection, physical movement, and stage awareness to make sure they are seen and heard clearly as they portray the thoughts, actions, and feelings of their characters

Notes

_____

_____

_____

_____

_____

_____

To play the title role in *Mary Stuart* convincingly, actor Jenny Bacon must convey the motivation and obstacles faced by the Scottish queen.

A character's **external traits** have to do with outward appearance and what that appearance says about him or her. Draw on your physical awareness to develop the external traits of your character, such as the following.

1 **Posture** Does the way the character sits and stands suggest confidence, timidity, awkwardness, or grace?

2 **Movement and gestures** Does the character's movement and gait reveal poise, nervousness, weakness, or strength? What does the character's movement reveal about his or her age, health, or general attitude?

3 **Mannerisms** Does the character have any tics or little habits that provide keys to his or her personality? Examples might be nail biting, gum chewing, head scratching, or table tapping.

4 **Voice** Does the character have a specific regional dialect or any vocal mannerisms?

5 **Mode of dress** Is the character's appearance neat, casual, prim, or sloppy? Are the clothes clean or dirty? Are they in good taste?

Suggest also that they answer the questions below about the character.

• What is your character's deepest fear?

• What is your character's deepest desire?

• What is the biggest obstacle in the way of your character getting his or her desire?

• Does your character have any odd habits?

• What songs or poems remind you of this character?

• Is there an aspect of your character that you know nothing about? Research this information and include it in your notebook.

Also have students include any photographs, artwork, lyrics, or poetry that suggest their character's traits—external and internal.

ACTivity Place five chairs in a row in the playing area and ask five students to sit down. Ask them to experiment with different postures that reveal character. Have the class suggest what each posture tells them about the person.

ACTivity Invite other students to be seated and add an environment and circumstances to the mix, such as sitting in a hospital waiting room or a police station. Each person in a chair creates the posture based on one sentence that represents his or her character, i.e., "I'm very worried about these headaches" or "Keep clear, I'm tough."

ACTivity **Advanced Students** Add more dimensions to the seated characters. Two are from the South, one is from England, one has a peculiar habit, and so on. Continue to challenge advanced students to create characters whose actions reveal both internal and external characteristics.

ACTivity **Advanced Students** Ask students to choose two or three gestures they have seen people make and memorize them so that they have a "choreography of gestures." When they are ready, ask these students to show their choreography of gestures to the class. Discuss the characters created by these gestures.

 **Visual Cue**

Friedrich Schiller's 19th-century play, *Mary Stuart,* brings to the stage the last three days of the life of Mary, Queen of Scots. Imprisoned for eighteen years in England, she was finally beheaded for her supposed involvement in an attempt on the life of Queen Elizabeth I. The play revolves around Mary and Elizabeth and their followers, who exhibit different perspectives on almost every important idea of their age.

• In what way does the character's attire suggest who she is?

• Does the character exhibit the bearing of a queen? Explain.

• What does the actress's posture suggest about the queen's circumstances?

• Imagine that you are Queen Elizabeth I standing before Mary Stuart. How would you approach her? What might you say?

Developing the Actor-as-Actor

Review the skills of listening, observing, and concentrating that students learned in Chapter 3. Point out that actors must listen to and observe one another in a scene while concentrating on staying in character and responding to the situation in a believable way. Invite students to discuss how they apply these skills in everyday situations. For example, how do they concentrate on what a partner is saying when other people are speaking in the classroom?

Tell students that the "outside in" approach to acting is sometimes called the classical approach because it was the technique used by actors for centuries. Such actors begin by perfecting movement and voice. Then they work to visualize how their character uses those qualities in a believable way within the context of the play. Some actors who use this approach are Laurence Olivier, Jim Carrey, and William Shatner.

The Language of THEATRE

Show students short videos of Laurence Olivier and Marlon Brando performing scenes from Shakespeare.

- Invite students to express their opinions about how believable each performer was, using words or short phrases.
- Invite students to express their opinions in complete sentences, using frames such as "This character is believable [not believable] because . . . ."
- Explain to students that Olivier is more of an "outside in" actor and Brando an "inside out" actor. Invite them to express their opinions about these techniques in a discussion with a partner.
- Ask students to discuss their opinions of the different techniques used by the two actors to reveal *external* and *internal traits*, supporting their opinions with evidence from the video clips.

When analyzing and developing a character's external qualities, you'll want to avoid stereotypes. For example, you don't necessarily want to choose a cartoonlike drawling "hick" voice simply because your character is supposed to be uneducated. Try to make the more interesting, less obvious choice.

Developing the Actor-as-Actor

Actors have a lot of experience as *people*, as do you! You, like all actors, have developed a keen sense of awareness in several dimensions. Suppose you walk into a room full of people. Your physical awareness—the attention to your body and its relation to the environment—helps you size up the physical details of the room. Your intellectual awareness tells you where you are and why and tunes you in to your thoughts. Your emotional awareness, attention to your feelings and the feelings of others, lets you "pick up on" subtle cues from others and gauge the emotion in the room. Your social awareness helps you grasp interactions between people and gauge the dynamics in the room.

You, like everyone else, also have many, many interactions with people. You have physical interactions with others—high-fives, hugs, hand-holding, tickling. You have intellectual interactions with others—debates about politics or collaboration on a project. You have emotional interactions with others—conflicts and resolutions, times of tears and times of laughter. And you have social interactions—you relate to others in a variety of situations, such as school, home, sports, and church.

Actors use the physical, intellectual, emotional, and social awareness and interactions they have learned through their life experience and apply them in their acting as they convey stories and portray believable characters.

Actors also draw on a variety of skills, techniques, and concepts to create believable characters and tell a story. You have already been developing some of these in earlier projects.

Skills Listening, observing, and concentrating are some of the most important skills an actor has. Listening and observing allow an actor to respond sensitively to the emotional and physical environment of the play. However, even on a small stage, there are so many things to listen to and observe that an actor must also have strong skills in concentration. Concentration helps actors know how to focus their attention.

Actors also need the skills of voice projection, diction, inflection, physical movement, and stage awareness to make sure they are seen and heard clearly as they portray the thoughts, actions, and feelings of their characters

Notes

in a convincing, expressive way. And without the skill of cooperating, an actor would be unable to "play off" other characters or support an ensemble effort.

Actors use and apply their physical, intellectual, emotional, and social awareness and interactions as they apply all of these acting skills to convey a story and portray believable characters.

Techniques Actors also use a variety of techniques to create convincing characters. You read about the Actors Studio on pages 28–29 and the approach pioneered by Stanislavski. That approach is sometimes known as the "inside out" approach, since it depends on the actor drawing on sensory and emotional recall to bring a character to life. That contrasts with the "outside in" approach in which an actor concentrates on the external qualities of a character—voice, body, and movement—and uses those to develop the inner character's thoughts and feelings. Many actors integrate these and other techniques to create believable characters rather than use one single approach. Once again, no matter the technique they use, actors draw on their physical, intellectual, emotional, and social awareness and interactions to portray believable characters and convey stories.

Concepts Actors also draw on a variety of concepts to create believable characters and portray a meaningful story. One,

the "magic if" (see page 28), calls on actors to ask what they would do or feel or say if they were the character. Another acting concept is associated mainly with improvisation—"Yes, and . . . " (see page 43), which helps create a mindset to accept and expand on an improvised reality. When applying any acting concept, actors will use their physical, intellectual, emotional, and social awareness and interactions to help further the story they are conveying and give the characters the breath of real life.

Draw on your awareness as you put your acting skills, techniques, and concepts to work. Use your intellectual awareness when portraying your character's mental characteristics and spiritual qualities. Use your emotional awareness to portray the feelings of a believable character facing a conflict. Use your physical awareness to bring the external qualities of your character to life. And use your social awareness to craft your character's relationship to other characters and to society as a whole.

Also draw on your interactions as you apply acting skills, techniques, and concepts. Applying your physical, intellectual, emotional, and social interactions to the characters you portray will help convey a story with three-dimensional characters that spring to life.

Notes

_____

_____

_____

_____

_____

_____

_____

_____

_____

_____

ACTivity Ask students to review an earlier project where they created characters for improvised scenes. Invite them to choose one and write a brief analysis of the skills, techniques, and concepts they applied in that situation. Then have them share their analysis with a partner.

Show, Don't Tell To make the four types of awareness more concrete for students, model how you might apply each one to create a specific character. For example, you might refer to Marlon Brando's portrayal of Julius Caesar and discuss his mental state as a powerful ruler, the conflicts he faced, his physical attributes, and his relationship with Marc Antony and Brutus. Or invite students to choose a character and apply the same process.

The Language of
THEATRE

Have students work in pairs to express ideas about awareness as it relates to creating believable characters.

- Invite students to share words or short phrases that they associate with each type of awareness.
- Invite students to share four sentences about how they might use each type of awareness.
- Invite students to discuss how each type of awareness contributes to _artistic selectivity_ in creating a character.
- Invite students to discuss how actors might use the four types of awareness differently depending on the techniques and concepts they apply to develop _motivation_.

ACTivity Have students return to the character notebooks they created and make notes about specific skills, techniques, and concepts they might use to make the character believable. Encourage them to review their notes in light of the four types of awareness to see if they have covered all aspects of the character.

PREPARE

Create a High-Stakes Scenario

Show, Don't Tell As you discuss some aspect of the work involved for this chapter, incorporate a mannerism of some kind, such as biting a lip or wrinkling your nose. Do not indicate that you are upset in words but by gesture or manner alone. Continue until students indicate in some way that they are aware of this physical tic. Ask them to discuss what they thought as you repeated this movement. What did it reveal about you and what you might be feeling or thinking?

Discuss with the class the scenario for two siblings presented on this page. Does it have a familiar ring? Which sibling do they think should realistically come out on top, and why? Suggest ways in which disagreements over the outcome of this scenario might be resolved, including tossing a coin, asking an arbitrator, compromising on the time each uses the line, or giving up use of the phone line altogether. Have students suggest other possibilities. Encourage them to be willing collaborators as they exchange ideas with their partners for their own scenarios.

ACTivity Have pairs of students face one another. Ask them to choose two opposite words, such as *summer/winter* or *big/small*. Each of them has one minute to describe to the other all the positive aspects of one of these words. Then each has two minutes to explain to the class why their word is a better one. Students should use as many tactics as possible to win.

Mannerisms can tell you a lot about your character.

The Language of THEATRE

Learn and use basic vocabulary by listening and speaking.

- Listen to and use the basic vocabulary needed to ask questions for the On Your Feet activity on page 100: who, what, when, where, why, and how. Ask "why" questions to discover *motivation*.

- Listen as a teacher or partner models simple questions for the On Your Feet activity. Then ask a partner these questions to learn about his or her *internal traits*.

- Complete the On Your Feet activity with a partner as you listen to and use the basic vocabulary needed to understand some *obstacles* or *conflicts* your partner has faced.

- Work with a partner to develop a high-*stakes* scenario as outlined on pages 106–107. Listen to and respond with the appropriate vocabulary to develop the characters' *objectives*.

PREPARE

Create a High-Stakes Scenario

You are now going to work with a partner to improvise a scenario in which the stakes are high for each of your characters. You will need to think of a situation in which two characters come into conflict over a physical object of some kind (perhaps a bag of money, a legal document, or a treasured family heirloom). Decide when and where your scene takes place and what the relationship between your characters should be. Then agree upon a bit of their shared history (if any). Write down everything you decide upon. Here's an example:

Scenario for Two Siblings
Characters: Rita and Joe
Relationship: Sister and Brother
Ages: Rita is 15; Joe is 14
Situation: Rita desperately needs to use the laptop; Joe is searching online and has been tying up the laptop for an hour.
Time of year: Just after Thanksgiving
Time of day: 10 p.m.

Decide which character will ultimately achieve his or her objectives. This will serve as the outcome of the scene. DO NOT determine what your characters will say and do in the scene ahead of time—you are to improvise your actual exchange.

The Language of THEATRE

Display a graphic organizer showing the 5 Ws and an H to introduce the basic vocabulary needed to conduct an interview. Explain that Who refers to people, What refers to things or actions, When refers to time, Where refers to place, Why refers to motivation, and How refers to the way something is done.

sual Cue

Have students look at the picture at the top of the page. Use the following prompts.

- What do the mannerisms of the student on the left tell you about him?

- What does the posture of the student on the right indicate about her?

- What other habit might someone have involving glasses?

After you have come up with your shared situation and history, take some time to work independently. Both of you should come up with external and internal traits for your character, as well as motivations (Rita: Why does she need to use the laptop? Joe: Why does he have to be online?), objectives (Rita: How will she get Joe offline? Joe: How will he distract Rita until he can finish what he is doing?), and stakes (Rita: What will happen if she doesn't have access to the laptop? Joe: What will happen if he doesn't finish what he is doing?).

At the right are a few other possible scenarios. You can use one of them or create your own. The important thing

is to be specific about your shared history and your character's internal and external traits, motivation, and objectives. Rehearse your scene so that you know only the basic shape of the improvisation. Don't write down specific lines you want to say; keep this improvisation spontaneous. Time yourselves to make sure you will come within the three- to five-minute time frame.

As the students work independently on their scenarios, continue to use the example of the two siblings to help them along. They should, at this point, know enough about their partner's character to be able to explore how they will continue with their encounter and what will happen next.

As the students begin to rehearse their scenarios, remind them to remain open to new ideas—their own and their partner's. They should not be using any specific words, but they should have a specific direction.

Suggestions for Scenarios

If students choose any of these scenarios, instruct them to put themselves into the place of the character and try to imagine how they would feel and to what lengths they would go to reach their objective in the scene.

Visual Cue

Glengarry Glen Ross remains one of David Mamet's most admired plays. It was made into a film in 1992, starring Jack Lemmon, Al Pacino, Ed Harris, Alan Arkin, Kevin Spacey, and Alec Baldwin, among others.

- What do their postures say about how these two men are relating to one another?
- Which man appears to have the upper hand?
- Judging by the set, what might have happened in this real estate office?

Two characters clash over a high-stakes real estate deal in David Mamet's *Glengarry Glen Ross.*

Chapter 10 Character Analysis **107**

Backstage Gossip: The Greatest Motivator

Early in 1962 Noel [Coward] was the guest of honor one Sunday at a dinner given by the Gallery First-Nighter's Club. Beginning his speech, "Desperately accustomed as I am to public speaking,"

he continued, "you ask my advice about acting? Speak clearly, don't bump into people, and if you must have motivation think of your pay packet on Friday."

from *Theatrical Anecdotes* by Peter Hay

PRESENT

Perform Your High-Stakes Scene

It always helps to add a time limit to a scene in order to heighten the stakes and the feeling of urgency. You might want to watch the presentations with watch in hand, letting the actors know when they have four, three, two, and then one minute left to achieve their goals. Tell students to create for themselves a motivation for the time limit; for example, in the scenario on page 94 it might be that the siblings have only a few minutes to end their confrontation before their parents get home.

It might also be helpful to coach students into trying different tactics or working harder to reach their objective as they work through their scenes. Remind them also to be sure they respond to the other character's demands, and so on.

CRITIQUE

Evaluate Your Classmates' Scene

Hand out the Critique Sheet for this activity or have students use their own paper. If you have counted down the time for the students, ask how they think this affected their work on the scene.

If you have focused on tactics, you might want to add an additional question about what tactics were used by each of the partners, which ones were successful, and why.

PRESENT

Perform Your High-Stakes Scene

When your or your partner's name is called, give your lists or Activity Sheets to your teacher. Then take a few moments to set up your scene (arrange chairs if you need them, for example). Do not rush.

Remember to keep the stakes high with the choices your character makes during the scene. If one method doesn't work, try another. Each character must work hard to achieve the goal. When you perform your scene, you will no doubt find out things about the other character that you didn't know. You must respond to these things in the moment. Try to make everything clear within the scene. You will not be using an introduction for this activity.

Remember to keep yourself open to the audience, both physically and emotionally, as you perform your scene. And draw on your intellectual, emotional, physical, and social awareness as you apply your skills, techniques, and concepts to make your characters believable as they work through the story arc of your scene. When you have finished your scene, turn to the audience and bow politely before returning to your seat.

CRITIQUE

Evaluate Your Classmates' Scene

Choose one of the scenes presented and evaluate it on a scale of 1 to 5, with 5 being "outstanding" and 1 being "needs much improvement." Your critique should answer these questions:

- How old were these two characters?
- What was their relationship to one another?
- What was each character's objective?
- How high were the stakes for each character?
- What did each character do to get what he or she wanted?
- Which character got what he or she wanted—and how was this achieved?
- Did one character appear stronger than the other? If so, in what way?

Write a paragraph detailing the reasons for the score you gave.

Quotable

The actor is an artist, not a critic. His job is not to explain a text, but to bring a character to life. To understand as an intelligent man and to understand as an artist are two completely different things . . . .

Paul Claudel, French Poet and Playwright

Additional Projects

1 Select newspaper human-interest stories to analyze. In groups, supply the necessary characters for the action of the story. Establish the characters' physical, intellectual, emotional, and social dimensions. Then improvise a scene built around them. Use your awareness of the characters' dimensions to create believable characters who interact in believable ways.

2 In groups, build a scene around a historical event, such as Lewis and Clark's first meeting with Sacajawea, General Lee's surrender to Ulysses S. Grant at Appomattox Courthouse, or the Lincoln/ Douglas debates. Be sure your story has characters in conflict, high stakes, a clear outcome, and historical accuracy.

3 Choose a hand prop or costume accessory such as a pair of long white gloves, an oversized umbrella, a colorful silk handkerchief, a pocket watch, or a stuffed bird. Create a brief scene in which you portray a character who is wearing this accessory or holding this prop. Use movement as well as words to express thoughts, feelings, and actions inspired by the prop or accessory. Keep safety in mind when using the prop, and remember to practice safe vocal and physical expression as well.

4 Work with a partner to create a scene. Character A goes on stage and waits for Character B to enter. A decides upon a definite character relationship with B but does not tell B what it is. B must discover who he or she is strictly through the way A talks and behaves toward him or her. B responds as sensibly as possible until his or her identity becomes clear.

5 Read the scene from *A Star Ain't Nothin' But a Hole in Heaven* by Judi Ann Mason found in Unit Eight of this book. With two partners, choose a part and read the scene through together. As you read, be aware of each character's motivation, obstacles, and stakes in this particular scene.

6 **Theatre Journal** Go to a public place such as a museum, a park, or a mall. Sit down on a bench and do a bit of people watching. Take note of the way people walk and the expressions on their faces. Imagine what the lives of these people might be like. Choose one passerby to use as the basis for a character. Write a history for this character. Use what you see and your imagination to create a rich character study.

This image might help you build a scene around one of the debates between Abraham Lincoln and Stephen A. Douglas that took place throughout Illinois in 1858. It is possible to find transcripts of these debates at your library or on the Internet.

Chapter 10 Character Analysis **109**

Character Analysis Test

The test for this chapter is available in blackline master form in the Resource Binder, page 51.

For More Information

Books
Adler, Stella, *The Techniques of Acting,* Bantam Books, 1992.

Boleslavski, Richard, *Acting: The First Six Lessons,* Routledge, 2003.

Cohen, Robert, *Acting One,* McGraw-Hill, 2001.

Meisner, Sanford, *Acting,* Vintage Books, 1987.

Stanislavski, Constantine, *Creating a Role,* Theatre Art Books, 2002.

Other Media
Controversy in American Acting, DVD, Insight Media, 2007.

How to Use the Stanislavski System, DVD, Insight Media, 2004.

Sanford Meisner Master Class, DVD, Insight Media, 2007.

Apps
2b Acting
Actor Audtion App by Scott Sedita
Stop Acting! The Audition Class with Margie Haber

Theatre Journal
Use the following as an additional or substitute prompt.

Ask students to use their character studies to present a short scene in which their character introduces himself or herself.

Remind them that it may be more convenient to keep their journals online, using a journal app or software program.

Substitute Teacher Activities

Here are some suggestions for the days that you will be out of the classroom.

• Assign the Finding Your Motivation Worksheet on page 49 of the Resource Binder.

• Discuss the information concerning Characterization found on pages 560–562 in the Student Handbook.

• Assign one or more of the Additional Projects on this page.

• **Play "Who Am I?"** Students give pertinent internal and external characteristics of a famous person in fiction, film, or television without revealing the character's name in any way. Classmates must guess the person's name.

Theatre Then and Now

Henrik Ibsen

When Ibsen's *A Doll's House* was first performed in Norway, it was said that when Nora leaves her husband and children at the end of the play and slams the door, it was "a slam heard around the world." No one in a play had ever left her family before, and it shocked the world.

Many theatre experts believe that the last scene in the play is one of the most perfectly crafted scenes in theatre. They believe that when Nora asks her husband Torvald to "sit down and talk," naturalism and realism were born in the theatre. For the first time, people sat down and discussed their problems.

For More Information

Books

Adler, Stella, Barry Paris, ed. *Stella Adler on Ibsen, Strindberg, and Chekhov,* Knopf, 1999.

Gosse, Edmund, *Henrik Ibsen,* University Press of the Pacific, 2003.

Shaw, George Bernard, *The Quintessence of Ibsenism,* Dover Publications, 1994.

Templeton, Joan, *Ibsen's Women,* Cambridge University Press, 2001.

Other Media

Mabou Mines' Dollhouse, DVD, Insight Media, 2008.

Theatre Then and Now

Ibsen and Miller— Appointment with Humanity

Henrik Ibsen and Arthur Miller both wrote plays with universal themes about the human condition. They created flesh-and-blood, flawed characters on desperate quests for meaning and fulfillment. A testimony to this universality is the fact that much of Ibsen's work is still produced more than 110 years after it was written, and *Death of a Salesman,* a play that celebrated its sixty-fifth birthday in 2014, remains one of the world's most produced plays.

Cate Blanchett played the unhappy Hedda Gabler in this 2004 production at The Wharf Theatre in Sydney, Australia

Henrik Ibsen (1828–1906)

Throughout history, playwrights have struggled to define and illustrate what it means to be human. The Greeks gave the world classical tragedy, a form that depicted a noble-born person who, through a flaw in his own character, brings about his own ruin. William Shakespeare's dramas also focused on highborn individuals whose character flaws brought them down.

In the mid- to late-1800s the Norwegian writer Henrik Ibsen created a series of social dramas about middle-class people. These were plays of such psychological depth that Ibsen later became known as

and the social order of the day.

In his 1890 play *Hedda Gabler,* the formidable but desperately unhappy title character sets about changing and destroying the lives of those around her as a way of fulfilling her own dreams of freedom and independence. Hedda is a strong, intelligent woman who is trapped by the role society has created for her.

Ibsen created characters whose desperate need to live differently drove them to self-destruction while also ruining the lives of others.

Backstage Gossip: Ibsen's Open Drain

When Henrik Ibsen's play *Ghosts* was first produced in 1881, the fact that it dealt with hereditary venereal disease and took the view that the social conventions of the day laid personal happiness to waste caused the *Daily Telegraph* in London to label it "an open drain; a loathsome sore unbandaged" and a "a dirty act done publicly . . . ."

Arthur Miller (1915–2005)

Nearly sixty years after *Hedda Gabler* was written, playwright Arthur Miller's 1949 masterpiece, *Death of a Salesman,* took the American theatre by storm. The play focuses on Willy Loman, a salesman long past his prime, who is still waiting in vain for his small corner of the American Dream. Like Ibsen, Miller was interested in how society affects the individual. Willy Loman is a complex blend of desperation and bravado. At his core, he knows he is a failure, but he spends much of the play trying to convince himself and those around him that he is just about to make a comeback as the great salesman he once was.

As the play progresses, it becomes clear that Willy is reinventing his past and that in fact he was never a great salesman. He has always been an average man with unreachable dreams. Toward the end of the play, Willy realizes that his failure as a salesman is mirrored in his failure as a husband and father. The American dream has escaped his grasp, and, like Hedda Gabler, Willy Loman makes a desperate final statement.

> *"I think now that the great thing is not so much the formulation of an answer for myself, the theatre, or the play—but rather the most accurate possible statement of the problem."*
>
> —Arthur Miller

The role of Willy Loman has attracted many fine actors over the years, including Dustin Hoffman, above.

> *"My main goal has been to depict people, human moods and human fates, on the basis of certain predominant social conditions and perceptions."*
>
> —Henrik Ibsen

Arthur Miller

Arthur Miller won the Pulitzer Prize in 1949 for *Death of a Salesman,* which has come to be regarded as one of the great dramas of American theatre. His plays, particularly the early ones, are produced throughout the world.

When it was first performed, however, the play caused heated arguments as to its status as a tragedy. Some critics believed that Willy Loman was too ordinary and petty to cause the pity and fear instilled in audiences of great tragic drama. Willy's small life and sorry aspirations could not stand up against such tragic heroes as Antigone or Oedipus, they argued. Miller defended his work by saying that any character willing to sacrifice his life to secure his own dignity was a worthy successor to the tragic tradition.

Visual Cue

In the *Death of a Salesman* photograph, all three characters seem to have strong objectives.

- Describe the relationship of these three men based on their body postures and shapes.
- How high do the stakes seem, and how can you tell?

For More Information

Books

Gottfried, Martin, *Arthur Miller,* DaCapo Press, 2003.

Miller, Arthur, et al., *Echoes Down the Corridor: Collected Essays, 1994-2000,* Viking Press, 2000.

Miller, Arthur, *On Politics and the Art of Acting,* Viking Press, 2001.

Other Media

A Conversation with Arthur Miller, DVD, Films for the Humanities and Sciences, 1997.

Four Plays by Arthur Miller, DVD, Insight Media, 2002.

Backstage Gossip: But What About Marilyn?

When David Merrick was first introduced to Arthur Miller, who had been an idol to him, the playwright was accompanied by Marilyn Monroe, then at the height of her glamorous fame. It says something about the stature of both men that the producer forever remembered the impact of this meeting: "I just couldn't stop staring at Arthur Miller."

from *Broadway Anecdotes* by Peter Hay

Chapter 11

Character Development

In this chapter students learn to analyze and deepen their understanding of character by placing the character in the larger context of the world of the play and its style.

Objectives

1 to understand a character in relationship to the play as a whole

2 to understand the style of the play and how it affects character choices

3 to learn traditional play structure and how it reveals the character's journey

4 to act in a scene incorporating specific character choices based on text analysis

Project Specs

Special Needs Students
Choose scenes for these students carefully, making sure they can be successful in the playing of the characters. Choose contemporary characters that are close to their age.

On Your Feet

Advanced Students
After the students have created this "portrait" of a family member or friend, have them present that character portrait in different styles and/or time periods. The styles can be realistic and representational, such as a soap opera or an Ibsen play, or they can be nonrealistic and presentational, such as a Greek tragedy or a French farce.

---

11 Character Development

An old theatre adage states, "There are no small roles— only small actors." Even roles with very few lines are important to a play. No matter what size your role, you will need to develop your character in detail. This chapter will provide you with some tools to help you through the process.

Project Specs

Project Description For this assignment, you and a group of classmates will perform a seven- to ten-minute scene from a play involving three or more characters.

Purpose to sharpen your analytical skills and develop a vivid characterization

Materials an analysis of your character's attributes or the Character Development Activity Sheet your teacher provides

On Your Feet

Think of a close friend or family member. Try to re-create this person using only your posture, vocal rhythm and tone, facial expression, and a few key phrases.

Rebecca Wisocky creates the character Bananas, the wife in John Guare's *House of Blue Leaves.*

Theatre Terms

cue
cue pickup
denouement
fourth wall
nonrealistic play
presentational
realistic play
representational
subtext

Theatre Terms

cue the last few words of a character's lines that precede another character's lines

cue pickup the term for when a character begins to speak

denouement the outcome of the main problem in a drama

fourth wall the imaginary wall through which the audience views the play

nonrealistic play a play in which the characters and/or events are exaggerated

presentational a direct address approach, in which the actor speaks directly to the audience

realistic play a play that imitates real life

representational an indirect address approach, in which the actors seem "unaware" that the audience is watching through the fourth wall

subtext information that is thought and felt but not stated by a character

Using the Right Tools

In Chapter 10 you learned how to analyze a character's internal and external traits, motivation, and objectives. But when you act in a play you must also understand the relationship your character has to the play as a whole. A thorough study of the play's other characters and its plot, structure, theme, and genre—such as comedy or drama—will give you the tools you need to portray your character believably and effectively.

Staying in Style

As an actor onstage, you must understand and analyze the style and genre of the play you're performing. Plays can be realistic or nonrealistic. A **realistic play** imitates real life—it shows recognizable

characters in dramatic situations. Examples of realistic plays include Henrik Ibsen's *A Doll's House*, Cheryl L. West's *Jar the Floor* (see Unit Eight for scenes from these plays), and Rebecca Gilman's *Spinning into Butter*. Typically, realistic plays utilize the convention of the **fourth wall**, meaning the audience looks and listens in on the action through an imaginary wall. The actors in these plays perform in a **representational** style—in other words, as if they are unaware that there is an audience watching.

In a **nonrealistic play**, the characters and/or situations are exaggerated or depart from real life. Nonrealistic plays include such genres as fantasies in which plants and animals talk as well as people; symbolic plays where the characters and setting represent ideas; and romantic plays where life is pictured ideally and imaginatively, dreams come true, and the language is often poetic. Examples of nonrealistic plays include Christopher Durang's *The Actor's Nightmare* (fantasy and symbolic), Rostand's *Cyrano de Bergerac* and Shakespeare's *A Midsummer Night's Dream* (romantic), and Caryl Churchill's *Far Away* (fantasy and symbolic). In many nonrealistic plays, actors use a **presentational**, or direct address, approach—meaning that they break the stage illusion by speaking directly to the audience.

Show, Don't Tell To help students recognize a variety of play styles that are realistic and nonrealistic, comic and dramatic, bring in an assortment of videos or DVDs and show clips from the film that best illuminates each style. *The Diary of Anne Frank* or *The Miracle Worker* would work well as representatives of a realistic style. A good representation of a nonrealistic play might be *Kiss of the Spider Woman* or *A Midsummer Night's Dream*. Thornton Wilder's *The Skin of Our Teeth* should stimulate an interesting discussion of a nonrealistic play that uses a presentational approach. When you have selected the plays you will discuss, focus on the style, whether it is realistic or not, and the specific characteristics of that particular style.

John Guare's *House of Blue Leaves* takes place in the 1960s and is a serious drama wrapped up in a slapstick farce. It tells the story of Artie, an aspiring songwriter; his loopy wife, the aptly named Bananas; and his mistress, Bunny—among others. In the mix are James Dean, Marilyn Monroe, JFK, the Pope, and the Vietnam War. The plot reflects America's most fervent dream: to be somebody. Guare's America is a place where, as the starstruck Bunny says, "when famous people sleep at night, it's us they dream of."

- What do the background images in the photo tell you about the time period of the play and the people who inhabit the space?

- How would you describe Bananas?

Resource Binder

- Character Development Activity Sheet, p. 52

- Finding the Subtext Worksheet, p. 53

- Critique Sheet: Characterizations in a Group Scene, p. 54

- Character Development Test, p. 55

- Actor's Script Analysis, p. 162

Handbook Connections
pages 559–561

To Have on Hand

- A box of available props and costumes for the students to use in their scenes

- Mood music to play under a scene to help create meaning and emotion

- Special set pieces (or students can bring these to class the day before their scene)

- Online videos or DVDs of films representing various styles

Plot and Structure

Draw the bell-shaped outline of the basic structure of a traditional play on the chalkboard so that all students can see it. Write the words *Turning Point, Rising Action, Resolution, Falling Action,* and *Conflict* on the board and have students come to the board and label the diagram appropriately, starting with *Conflict* and ending with *Resolution.* Discuss each element in turn with students and then break down these elements in a short story they are familiar with, such as *The Lottery* by Shirley Jackson or *To Build a Fire* by Jack London.

Note that while the bell-shaped diagram reflects the structure of traditional plays, some modern works do not follow this pattern.

ACTivity Use the plot of *The Wizard of Oz* or *Harry Potter and the Sorcerer's Stone* and call on various students to identify the plot elements in order, from conflict to resolution. If there is time, ask students to suggest additional stories.

Surreal scenic elements and lighting reveal the mood of David Saar's play *The Yellow Boat,* about Saar's real-life son's death from AIDS.

Plot and Structure

To analyze your character effectively, you must analyze and evaluate the play's plot and structure. Like any good work of literature, a play's plot is made up of a series of incidents linked by a theme. It involves conflict (struggle) that is revealed through action, which leads to the dramatic turning point, or climax, and then to a logical conclusion, or resolution.

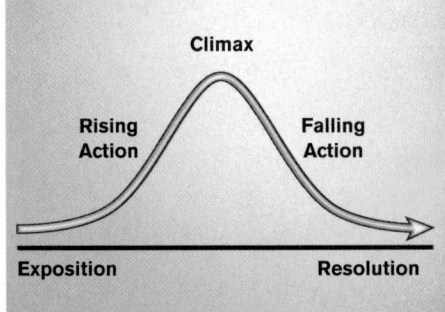

The basic structure of most plays includes these five elements.

sual Cue

The Yellow Boat was written as an affirmation of a child's life and of the courage and wonder of all children. Benjamin Saar, the son of David and Sonja Saar, was eight years old when he died in 1987 of complications from AIDS. While he lived, Benjamin's imagination and artistic gifts transformed his physical and emotional pain into beautiful, deftly colored drawings.

- Do you think this scene reflects the son's or the parents' point of view?

- Why do you think a playwright's story of his son's life and death would contain surreal elements?

The Actor and the Traditional Play Structure

In order to really understand drama, an actor must understand the importance of a play's structure. The structure of a play is what holds together the characters' actions and words. By analyzing the elements of a story's structure, the actor has important insight into the plot, the theme, and his character's motivations. Evaluate the elements that follow as they relate to the actor.

1 **Exposition** The exposition serves to establish the play's setting and introduce the characters and a conflict—a problem or struggle of some sort. The conflict may be between characters, between a character and some object or event, or between a character and the character's inner self. It is often set in motion by an inciting incident, at which point the action begins to rise. It is your job as an actor to assess your character's role in the conflict and to determine how your character should act and react as the conflict intensifies.

2 **Rising Action** (or complications) Any additional events that stem from the conflict are important elements for you to be aware of and to think about in terms of the forward movement of the play and your character's role in it.

3 **Climax** This is the highest point of emotional intensity in the drama. It usually occurs near the end of the play. Here, the main character will most likely take an action to end the conflict. All the play's action leads to this point, and again, as an actor, you must be aware of the momentum that has been generated to this point and adjust your performance intensity accordingly.

4 **Falling Action** These are the events that happen after the climax. As an actor, you must adjust your performance to the change in atmosphere.

5 **Resolution** (or denouement) Here is where the complications are worked out. And, although the play is at this point winding toward its conclusion, be careful not to lose your energy as an actor or to slide into sluggish line delivery or posture. Stay with the rhythm and flow of the play, but keep your performance energy high.

Some contemporary playwrights may omit one or more of these elements.

Mood

The mood of a play is its emotional texture. The audience should sense the play's mood early on—during the rising action. Nearly every aspect of the play contributes to the mood—from the characters to the plot to the design elements.

When you have analyzed and evaluated the plot, mood, and structure of the play or scene in which you've been cast, you

The Actor and the Traditional Play Structure

ACTivity It will be helpful to use a play the group is familiar with or a play you are working on in class as you discuss play structure with students. *Romeo and Juliet* is a good choice because most students are familiar with the story.

Together, isolate, analyze, and discuss each element of the traditional play structure within the text you chose. Then follow one character, Juliet for example, through the play's structure and analyze how her character is revealed through her actions during the rising action, the turning point, and so on. Example: What is Juliet's *conflict* and what does she do to solve it during the *rising action*?

Beginning or ELL Students
You can help any student who is not familiar with *Romeo and Juliet* or any other play under discussion to understand plot structure by using a familiar movie instead. Help the student understand the conflict in the story, the actions that lead to a decisive moment, the turning point, and the resolution of the story.

Mood

Ask students to make a list of three pervasive moods that alter all they see and everything they may do. Under each mood ask them to describe its tempo, rhythm, colors, sounds, music, weather, or temperature. Advise them that when they are working on their scene, they should use the mood that underlies the scene and incorporate this into the development of their characters.

Quotable

When in doubt, make a fool of yourself. There is a microscopically thin line between being brilliantly creative and acting like the most gigantic idiot on earth.

Cynthia Heimel, Actor

Sound is a strong way to affect mood. Have groups of students create silent improvisations within a specific environment and situation (who, what, where) using sound effects or music. Example: Use music and improvisation to depict a city bar at 2 A.M. after the city's team has won a big game. Each actor chooses a character with a motivation and objective for the scene. During the silent scene, use different sound effects and music to alter the mood. Body language and movement should change with the changing mood created by the sound.

Characterization

Share with students a few of the techniques below and on the following page, which are helpful when working through a script.

- Ask a friend to record your cue lines. Leave the right amount of empty space on the recording for you to speak your lines before the next cue line. Practice your lines using the recording for the cues. You can also ask your friend to cue you in person as you practice your lines. Several apps, including some listed on page 121, are also designed to help actors learn lines.

- Do a physical activity while reading the script out loud: jog, bounce a ball, do sit-ups, and so on. Let the words travel through the physical activity and out your mouth. Let the activity naturally change the way you say the lines. By memorizing lines this way, you are learning them deep into your system.

The Language of
THEATRE

Before any activity, ask students what they already know about a given topic. Determine which theatre terms are familiar and which ones are unfamiliar and tailor instruction accordingly.

Light, setting, and the actor's body language all create a mood of defeat in this scene from *Death of a Salesman*.

can at last begin to focus on your particular character and how he or she fits into the play.

After you have read the play once to understand all of its elements, read it again to identify with your specific role. Visualize the action through your character's eyes. Understand your character's behavior and dialogue in view of his or her motivation.

The Language of
THEATRE

Listen for unfamiliar terms as a partner or your teacher reads the theatre terms on page 112 aloud.

- Listen to hear if any words or word parts of the theatre terms on page 112 are familiar. For example, *fourth wall* contains two words that may be familiar from other contexts and topics.

- Listen to the theatre terms and identify which ones are familiar and unfamiliar. Listen to brief definitions that relate the terms to the context of theatre and the topic of character development.

- Listen as someone reads the complete descriptions of the terms *realistic play* and *nonrealistic play* on page 113 to understand them in the context of theatre and their relationship to the topic of character development.

- As you prepare your ten-minute scene, listen to your classmates so you recognize your *cues* and deliver *cue pickups* that are appropriate in the context of the character's role in the play.

Characterization

In previous chapters, you've learned that making observations, drawing upon your own experience, using your imagination, and investigating the character's internal and external traits all help you understand a character. To know your character through and through, use the steps below as you read through and memorize your script. After following the steps, you should be able to describe your character's physical, intellectual, emotional, and social dimensions.

- Use clues from the script to analyze your character's internal and external traits (see pages 102–103). Think about people who remind you of your character. Discover ways in which your character is like and unlike you. Research aspects of your character that are unknown to you.

 **V**isual Cue

In this scene from Arthur Miller's classic drama, Willy Loman has arrived home after a sales trip. Ask students to use their **critical viewing skills** to answer the following questions:

- How does the lighting affect the impression given in this scene?

- What do you imagine the character to be thinking?

- What do you think the actor will do once he is inside the house?

- Have a clear sense of what happened to your character before the events depicted in the play. Some actors make complete histories of their character's family life, employment, friendships and alliances, and so on as a way of delving as deeply as possible into the person they are playing.

- Ask yourself what your character wants and what he or she does to get it. Does the character want different things from different people?

- Figure out whose side your character is on. Is yours the central character? Or does your character oppose the central character in some way? Or does your character assist the central character? Most characters fall into one of these categories.

- In addition to the dialogue (what your character *says*), you should pay close attention to the stage directions to figure out what your character *does*—and why.

- Pay attention to what the other characters say about your character and how they behave toward him or her.

- Think about how your character *changes* over the course of the play. Does the character experience a major shift—a change of attitude or circumstance? How will you convey this?

- Remember that plays, like real life, are mostly about what *isn't* said. The dialogue of a play can be compared to the tip of an iceberg. What's said represents only a part of the whole story. The information that is implied but not stated by a character is called the **subtext.** For example, consider the character who tells another character, "I hate you! I'm leaving!" but proceeds to stay onstage. What the character *does* contradicts what he or she says—so you can be fairly certain the character is experiencing something besides hatred—perhaps even its exact opposite! The subtext a character conveys is often much more important than what the character actually says.

- Pay special attention to your character's rhythms. Does he or she speak in a staccato manner (short, choppy sentences and fragments) or in long, fluid sentences? The way the character speaks is likely to reflect the way the character moves.

Love Your Character!

Acting teachers often tell their students they must "love" their characters. By this they mean that you must respect, understand, and empathize with a character in order to bring life to the role. This does not mean that you as a person would make the same choices the character does, nor does it mean you necessarily approve of the character's actions. But you must attempt to live inside the character's skin—and that's impossible to do if you stand outside and judge him or her. Above all, remember that if you're not fascinated by your character, no one else will be either.

- Practice your lines with your scene partner while doing a shared activity such as throwing a ball back and forth or arm wrestling. Again, allow the lines to be connected to and fall out of the action.

Share the following questions that actors should ask when creating a character:

- Who am I?
- What is my goal, and what will I do to achieve it?
- What are my obstacles?
- What are my circumstances?
- What are my relationships?

ACTivity **Advanced Students**
Have students create a silent improvisation in groups of six to eight. Give them the circumstances of a scene, such as "It is Paris in the spring at midday in a romantic café." The actors choose the characters' circumstances—why they are at the café and what they want to have happen while they are there (objectives). Play music to create mood. At different moments throughout the improv, freeze the group and ask one character to speak his or her subtext or inner monologue out loud. Return to the group action for a while, then repeat with another actor.

In order to listen well onstage, it is important to know what you are listening for. When you know your character's motivation and objective, you must relate them to what the other character(s) onstage do or say or feel.

From the Field: Death by the Spoonful

We enjoy warming up in class with a game we like to call "The Spoon of Death." The class passes a spoon around until I call either "Poison!," "Swordfight!," or "Heart Attack!" The person left holding the spoon must die the appropriate death, in a tragic or comic manner. The designated student may use dialogue—and subtext is encouraged.

Kay Jacobs, Drama Instructor,
San Francisco, California

Love Your Character!

Discuss with students how they would go about trying to "love" despicable characters such as Shakespeare's *Richard III* or Beatrice in Paul Zindel's *The Effect of Gamma Rays on Man-in-the-Moon Marigolds.* Talk about the rich depth of character to be discovered in villains and the necessity not to overdo their evil ways.

Spotlight on

Cues, Cue Pickup, and Memorization Picking up cues takes a bit of practice. Demonstrate cue pickup with a volunteer. Then have students pair off and read a two-character scene of their own choosing. Encourage students to memorize part of the scene. After they have worked on their scenes for a time, ask volunteers to demonstrate their memorization skills and their ability to pick up their cues correctly.

Visual Cue

Anton Chekhov's play *The Good Doctor* is a riotous romp in which a woman demands that a bank manager pay compensation for her husband's disability. The play involves a great deal of physical humor.

- Who seems to be in control of this situation?
- If you were playing the man, what tone of voice might you be using?

The Language of
THEATRE

Support students in learning new language structures in the classroom.

- As students work on picking up cues, encourage them to listen for the type of sentence that signals their cue. Is it a question or a statement?
- Invite students to listen to classmates model a cue pickup in an interrupted sentence. Ask them what clues they heard in words or pauses to indicate where the interruption occurred.
- Have students work in groups of four. As one pair models dialogue from a scene of their choosing, the other pair listens for language or sentence structures that signal the cues.
- Encourage students to listen closely to their classmates' presentations to hear the language structures that signal cues and cue pickups.

Spotlight on

Cues, Cue Pickup, and Memorization

Cues are the last few words of the speech that precedes yours. Sometimes a sound or movement will be your cue, but generally you take your cue from someone else's lines. A **cue pickup** occurs the minute you begin saying your lines. To pick up your cues at the correct time, you should learn to take a breath before the other actor has finished speaking, so that you are ready to come in with your line.

Most plays call for quick cue pickup, a tempo that holds audience interest and simulates real-life conversation. Quick cue pickup does *not* mean you should race through your lines. Vary each line according to the ideas and emotions it expresses.

Never anticipate your cue. Picking up the phone before it rings or bursting into tears before you hear a piece of bad news can render your acting ridiculous.

If the script indicates an interrupted sentence—in other words, one actor cutting off another actor's line—give special attention to this timing. If someone is to cut in on your speech, make sure that you have a completion for the line handy in case your scene partner doesn't come in on cue!

As you memorize your lines, you will also be memorizing your cues. Develop your memorization skills with these techniques.

- Repeat, repeat, repeat.
- Move around while learning your lines. The movement helps lock in the memory.
- Make a recording of the play section by section. Read your lines quietly and the lines of the other characters in a louder voice. When you play back the recording, you can then practice your lines with the cues.
- Divide scenes into "beats," chunks that develop or pertain to one main topic or emotion. For example, if your character is in dialogue about a decision that has to be made, and then the doorbell rings and a new character is introduced, the first beat would be the decision dialogue and the next beat would be the chunk with the new character. Dividing a scene into beats will help give it a logic and flow in your memory.

Practice your memorization skills at every chance you get.

In this scene from *The Good Doctor*, the actors must pick up their cues even in unusual body positions.

Backstage Gossip: She's the Top!

Famed teacher Alvina Krause of Northwestern University hated extra pausing in a scene, which she felt killed the pacing of a play. She used the concept of "topping in" as a way to pick up one's cues. The concept involves starting to speak your line on the last word of the cue lines that come right before yours. Many of her students thought it was quite exciting, but some were perhaps less pleased when Krause would stop a play in performance by standing up in the audience and screaming "TOP IN!"

PREPARE

PREPARE

Choose a Play and a Character

Get together with several classmates and choose a ten-minute play, a scene from a one-act play, or a scene from a full-length play (your teacher may wish to assign a scene to you). Try to read the entire play to analyze and evaluate its structure, style, and genre. With your group, discuss the mood, basic action, and climax of the play. DO NOT concentrate on your specific role at this time. Work to understand the play as a whole. Then analyze the characters together. Decide how the scene you have chosen relates to the play as a whole.

Next, each of you should study your individual role in the scene. Identify your character's actions, feelings, and words. Work hard to create a vivid character with believable intellectual, emotional, physical, and social dimensions. Use research and script analysis to revise the physical, vocal, and physiological choices you make to enhance the believability of your character and the relevance of the dramatic work.

Rehearse the Scene

The next step is to come together again to rehearse the scene. As a group, create basic movements and stage business for the scene. When you are not speaking your lines, listen in character to your fellow actors.

After you have read the scene together a few times, have someone time it to be sure you are not exceeding the ten-minute limit.

Memorize Your Lines

Finally, you must memorize your dialogue in the scene. It's impossible to achieve complete character concentration when you still have the script in your hand. Use the techniques on the previous page to cement your lines and cues in your memory. When you and your partners have memorized the scene to the point where it runs smoothly, you are ready to perform.

Listening closely to others helps actors remain in character while allowing the audience to focus on the speaker.

Choose a Play and a Character

Help students decide which plays would be appropriate for them based on their skill level and degree of sophistication. Discuss with students the need to be sensitive to others in their selections. Advise them to avoid choosing plays that some students would consider offensive.

Go over the tips for evaluating the script and the characters in it. Have students break into groups to choose the play and the scene they will present.

As students study their individual roles, be available to answer any questions as to characterization, author's intent, background history, and so on.

Rehearse the Scene

Students may need extra time in or after class to rehearse their scenes. Be available to help them time their scene as well as to discuss any questions regarding interpretation or stage business.

Memorize Your Lines

Remind students to use a digital recorder or ask for a friend's or family member's help in memorizing their lines. Then be sure that all members of the group have a place to rehearse their scene together.

Visual Cue

Chief Inspector Foot (of the Yard) tries to crack the case in Tom Stoppard's play *After Magritte* at the Bridewell Theatre in London.

• Which character do you think is Inspector Foot?

• Who seems to be the focal point of this scene, and how do you think he feels about it?

• Who do you think is about to speak next? Why?

PRESENT

Perform Your Group Scene

Give any students who would like to dress in costume the time needed to do so. Be sure that each group has any props they may need ready in the playing area before they begin their scene.

CRITIQUE

Evaluate Your Classmates' Scene

Hand out the Critique Sheet for this project or have students use their own paper. (You may want to use two Critique Sheets, as the students are evaluating both the scene and a particular actor from the scene.)

Go over the questions that students should ask for the group presentation and the individual actor. Note that the critique for the group focuses on how well the actors worked together, picked up cues, and maintained relationships. The questions about the actor's performance focus more on goals and character representation.

PRESENT

Perform Your Group Scene

Choose one person to introduce your scene. This person will also set the scene by providing a bit of background about how this section fits into the larger play. This need not be long; just make sure the audience has enough information to know what's going on within the context of the play. Make sure you have all the necessary props. Once the designated person has introduced the play and given the audience a bit of background, play the scene as you rehearsed it. Stay focused and remain in character throughout.

CRITIQUE

Evaluate Your Classmates' Scene

Evaluate a presentation by one group of classmates. Because the scene represents a team effort, you should evaluate the ensemble as well as the individual performances. Your critique should answer these questions about the group:

- Did the actors work together as an ensemble?

- How did they develop and maintain viable characters?

- What did the actors do to make their characters' motivations and intentions clear?

- Did the actors pick up their cues?

- In what way did the actors establish a consistent mood in the scene?

- Were the relationships between the characters clear?

- Did the actors maintain a consistent style and tone?

Then choose one actor from the scene and evaluate his or her performance using a rating of 1 to 5, with 5 representing "outstanding," 4 representing "very good," 3 representing "good," 2 representing "needs some improvement," and 1 representing "needs much improvement." Use the criteria below to help in your evaluation.

Did the actor
- have a specific goal within the scene?

- listen and respond in character?

- embody the character both physically and vocally?

- have clearly established external traits?

- provide information as to the scene's subtext?

Write a short paragraph explaining why you gave this particular actor the score you did.

As you listen to feedback on your performance, make notes about how you can refine your range of acting skills to build a believable and sustainable performance. With research in reliable sources, create a collection of acting exercises you can use to refine your technique. Be prepared to justify why you chose the exercises you did.

Quotable

Acting is not about dressing up.
Acting is about stripping bare.
The whole essence of learning lines is to forget them so you
can make them sound like you thought of them that instant.

Glenda Jackson, Actor

Additional Projects

1 Write a prose biography of the character you portrayed in the class project. Include as many facets of the character as possible; for example, you might include family background, level of education, leisure activities, employment status, favorite food, favorite color, most memorable experience, greatest disappointment, and so on. Base your writing on your interpretation of details in the play. Your biography should give a good description of your character's intellectual, emotional, physical, and social dimensions.

2 Read a full-length play and write an analysis of its style, mood, characters, plot, genre, and structure and evaluate the impact those have on characterization.

3 It is sometimes said that a majority of plots are about one of two things: either a stranger coming to town or a character going on a journey. Write a scene in which three distinctive characters take part in one of these basic plots.

4 Read the scene from *Macbeth* by William Shakespeare found in Unit Eight. Get together with two classmates and choose different parts. Discuss the subtext of this short scene and the emotions and motivations of the characters, as well as its realism and romanticism. Work on the scene together. Identify the memorization techniques from page 118 that work best for you and practice using them to memorize your lines in this scene. Apply all you have learned to present a convincing character with convincing interactions:

- warm up before your scene so you can use your voice and body safely

- create and devise stage movement to express thoughts, feelings, and actions

- experiment safely and effectively with props, scenery, sound, and/or lighting

- employ effective voice projection, inflection, and diction to express thoughts and feelings

- listen carefully, not only for your cues but also for staying present in the scene and responding appropriately

5 **Theatre Journal** When you create a character, you build a whole new world for yourself. And that means you must learn to look at the world from a different point of view. As an exercise, try to re-examine a very familiar person in your life. Try to see this person in a fresh, new way. Then write about what you notice.

Character Development Test

The test for this chapter is available in blackline master form in the Resource Binder, page 55.

For More Information

Books
Harrop, John, and Sabin Epstein, *Acting with Style,* Pearson Allyn & Bacon, 1999.

Jones, Brie, *Improve with Improv: A Guide to Improvisation and Character Development,* Meriwether Publishing, 1993.

Perry, John, *The Encyclopedia of Acting Techniques,* Betterway Publications, 1997.

Stanislavski, Constantine, *Building a Character,* Theatre Arts Books, 2002.

Other Media
Building a Character, DVD, Insight Media, 1988.

Char-ac-ter, DVD, Insight Media, 2012.

Apps
2b Acting
Actor Audtion App by Scott Sedita
Line Learner
Line Please
Scene Partner
Stop Acting! The Audition Class with Margie Haber

Theatre Journal

Use the following as an additional or substitute prompt. Write a short scene in which you use the impressions you gathered about a familiar person you re-examined. Have this person exhibit the new characteristics you uncovered.

Substitute Teacher Activities

- Assign the Finding the Subtext Worksheet on page 53 of the Resource Binder.

- Discuss the information concerning Acting Types and Characterization found on pages 559–561 in the Student Handbook.

- Assign one or more of the Additional Projects on this page.

- **Play "What's My Subtext?"** Students are given written copies of various sentences, such as "Hello, dear, I see you've been shopping again." or "Is that a new tie? What color would you call that?" The actor must pick a sentence and then quickly say the line and convey the subtext. Students must guess what the actor is really saying.

Theatre **Then** and Now

William Shakespeare and the Elizabethan Drama

William Shakespeare was born in 1564 in Stratford-upon-Avon, England. He married Anne Hathaway, with whom he had three children. He decided to pursue a professional career in the theatre, which prompted his move to London between the years of 1587 and 1588. While in London he became a member of an acting troupe called The Lord Chamberlain's Men. He was part owner of two famous theatres, The Blackfriar's Theatre and the original Globe Theatre. Shakespeare wrote thirty-seven plays, two long poems, and many sonnets. His plays are classified as historical, comedic, and tragic.

The back of the stage of the Globe Theatre contained a tiring house on top, where the actors changed clothes, and a multileveled façade that was part of the tiring house. The stage was covered by a roof supported by two columns, and the underside, called the *heavens,* was painted with moons, stars, and planets.

Theatre **Then** and Now

Elizabethan Drama to Epic Theatre

William Shakespeare and the Elizabethan Drama

The Elizabethan period began in 1558 with the coronation of Queen Elizabeth I of England. The period ended with her death in 1602. Although many people think of William Shakespeare (1564–1616) as *the* Elizabethan dramatist, there were a number of other fine playwrights creating work during this period, such as Christopher Marlowe and Ben Johnson. Marlowe (1564–1593) was considered by many of his contemporaries to be Shakespeare's equal. Unfortunately, Marlowe died in a barroom knife fight at the age of twenty-nine.

Because there was no artificial lighting, performances were often held outdoors in the afternoon. Performances that took place at night were lit by huge standing torches. No women were allowed to perform in the plays. Young boys often played female roles as it was thought they could better assume the character and movement of a woman. They would speak in lighter voices and use exaggerated feminine gestures.

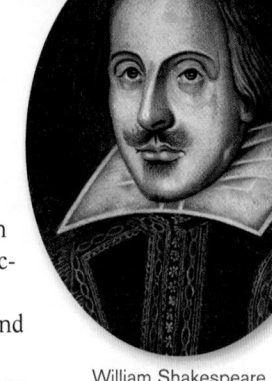

William Shakespeare

Shakespeare's plays featured many highborn or noble characters. The language is rich and layered with images. Low-born characters were often used for comic relief or as the hero's sidekick.

The style of acting during Shakespeare's time was much more overblown than actors use today. Actors were not much concerned with rendering subtle emotions. They tended to shout their lines, which in fact was usually necessary given the size of the theatre. The actors concentrated on getting the play's words and ideas across. After all, as Hamlet says, "The play's the thing . . . ."

Many of Shakespeare's plays were first seen in the original Globe Theatre.

For More Information

Books
Bradley, David, *From Text to Performance in the Elizabethan Theatre: Preparing the Play for the Stage,* Cambridge University Press, 1992.

Day, Barry, and John Gielgud, *This Wooden 'O,' Shakespeare's Globe Reborn: Achieving an American Dream,* Limelight Editions, 1998.

Dillon, Janette, *Theatre, Court and City 1595-1610: Drama and Social Space in London,* Cambridge University Press, 2002.

Hodges, Walter C., *Globe Restored: Study of the Elizabethan Theatre,* Native American Books, 1990.

Other Media
Shakespeare's Globe, DVD, Insight Media, 2005.

Shakespeare High, DVD, Insight Media, 2011.

Shakespeare for Students, DVD, Insight Media, 2009.

Bertolt Brecht and the Epic Theatre

Bertolt Brecht (1898–1956) was a German poet and playwright. His plays were openly political and usually addressed issues such as poverty, war, and class struggle. He rejected the principles of classical drama and realism and did not believe a play needed a dramatic climax. He often employed direct address to the audience as well as songs to comment on the play's action. His theory of drama came to be known as epic theatre. It is best illustrated in his plays *Mother Courage, The Good Woman of Setzuan,* and *The Caucasian Chalk Circle.* Above all, Brecht believed that drama should not try to create the illusion of reality but should exist on its own terms. Rather than attempting to persuade the audience of a play's reality, Brecht tried to distance viewers. In this way, he thought that the audience would think for themselves.

Achieving this type of alienation effect, as it came to be called, required a highly stylized performance method. Brecht believed in the idea of argument as opposed to plot. Traditional plots, Brecht believed,

attempted to implicate the viewer in the action as opposed to allowing the viewer to remain an outside spectator. In Brecht's view, the epic theatre's detached methods aroused the viewer to take action—to take a side in the argument. Brecht's views on characterization are perhaps best illustrated by this quote: "The actor has to discard whatever means he has learnt of getting the audience to identify itself with the characters which he plays . . . . At no moment must he go so far as to be wholly transformed into the character played . . . ."

A classic of epic theatre, Brecht's *Mother Courage* depicts the lengths to which people will go to survive during wartime.

Bertolt Brecht and the Epic Theatre

Author, director, teacher, and performer Paul Sills is the creator of Story Theatre, a storytelling venue that has appeared on and off Broadway. Story Theatre is a descendent of Brecht's Epic Theatre. Sills applied the concept of stepping out of the play and speaking directly to the audience.

ACTivity Have the students repeat their group scene. At any time, one of the actors can step out of the scene, face the audience, and speak directly to them about what is going to happen next in story-theatre style. Or add a third actor who narrates the scene as a commentator might narrate a sporting event.

For More Information

Books

Brecht, Bertolt, Tom Kuhn, ed., *Brecht on Art and Politics,* Methuen Publishing, 2003.

Brecht, Bertolt, John Willett, trans., *Brecht on Theatre: The Development of an Aesthetic,* Hill & Wang, 2001.

Ewen, Frederic, *Bertolt Brecht: His Life, His Art and His Times,* Citadel Press, 1992.

Sills, Paul, *Story Theatre: Four Shows,* Applause Books, 2000.

Other Media

Brecht Practice Pieces, DVD, Insight Media, 1964.

College Brecht, DVD, Insight Media, 2012.

Theater of War, DVD, Lorber Films, 2010.

Chapter 12
Dramatic Roles

In this chapter students will be introduced to a brief history of dramatic literature and how to prepare for a role in a dramatic scene.

Objectives

1 to learn something of the history and range of dramatic roles

2 to understand three types of dramatic literature

3 to use imagination and memory to stimulate the emotional responses necessary to play a dramatic scene

4 to write a short dramatic scene with detailed characters

Project Specs

For this chapter it is important that you choose whether to guide your students towards using personal stories to create their short dramatic plays, or whether you want them to create more from fiction or imagination.

On Your Feet

Show, Don't Tell Demonstrate how you would capture the emotion of a tragic event, such as the destruction of the World Trade Center in New York, using only one line. Ask students to comment on your posture and facial expression.

Chapter
12 Dramatic Roles

Many actors believe that dramatic roles are the real "meat" of acting. Plays that treat their subject seriously are placed into three broadly defined categories—tragedy, social drama, and melodrama. While exploring each of these dramatic forms, you will acquire the tools to take on serious dramatic roles yourself.

Project Specs

Project Description For this assignment, you and a classmate will create, write, and perform a three- to five-minute dramatic scene.

Purpose to use strong characterization and controlled emotional intensity

Materials an outline of your scene or the Dramatic Roles Activity Sheet your teacher provides

Theatre Terms
antagonist
catharsis
melodrama
protagonist
regional accent
social drama
tragedy
tragic flaw

On Your Feet

Think about a difficult, sad, or dramatic event that happened to a friend or family member. Capture the emotions that event holds for you in one sentence. Practice saying the sentence out loud, taking on the character of your friend or family member. Create a specific posture and facial expression for the character, and then repeat the line until you can "hear" the person on whom you based the character.

Chiwetel Ejiofor creates one of the most dramatic roles of all time as the title character in *Othello*.

Theatre Terms

antagonist the character who is the opposing force to the protagonist, or main character

catharsis the sense of calm that comes after experiencing intense emotions

melodrama a play that focuses more on cliff-hanging action and intense emotions than on character development

protagonist the main character in a work of literature

regional accent the sound of speech from a particular region

social drama a play that focuses on serious, real-life problems of ordinary people

tragedy a drama in which a protagonist struggles against some force, usually making a sacrifice before going down in defeat

tragic flaw a weakness of personality that ultimately causes a character's destruction

The Elements of Drama

Dramas are categorized in three ways: as tragedy, social (or serious) drama, or melodrama. Each genre has its own unique characteristics and requires its own set of acting skills to bring out the characters' physical, intellectual, emotional, and social dimensions. As an actor or critic, evaluate the genre of a work to understand its special traits and its impact on performance and understanding.

Greek Tragedy

Considered to be the highest form of drama, **tragedy** magnifies the intensity of profound human emotions to tell the story of a person who achieves a sense of nobility by means of unswerving sacrifice and/or suffering. In classic Greek tragedy, the **protagonist** (or main

character) struggles with a particular problem or an opposing force (the **antagonist**) and eventually goes down in defeat—usually death—but not before achieving an aura of dignity. Because of the depth of a tragedy's emotion, the audience tends to experience horror, pity, and deep sadness, which are typically followed by a **catharsis,** the sense of calm that comes from purging such emotions.

In Greek tragedy, a tragic hero comes into conflict with the gods. The audience always knew the plot of these classic myths but was eager to see how a particular playwright would handle the relationship between the gods and the hero. Violence, as such, was never witnessed by the audience in these tragedies. The chorus or a messenger would report the violent action. The tragedies of Sophocles (c. 495–406 B.C.), such as *Oedipus Rex* and *Antigone,* are perfect examples of classic Greek tragedy.

Shakespeare's Tragedies

The Elizabethan playwrights ignored the classical tragic form, for the most part. The tragedies of William Shakespeare (1564–1616) often focused on a protagonist at odds with himself. This often highborn hero has a **tragic flaw,** a weakness of character, which ultimately brings about his or her own destruction. Shakespeare and his contemporaries often mixed comedy into their tragedies; and music, song, and

Chapter 12 Dramatic Roles **125**

The Elements of Drama

ACTivity Ask various students to read pivotal soliloquies from *Hamlet, Othello, Julius Caesar, Macbeth,* or another of Shakespeare's tragedies. Discuss the students' interpretations of the scenes as they relate to each character's tragic flaw.

Visual Cue

In Shakespeare's *Othello,* a powerful man is led astray by an insidious friend and his own false pride. Ask students to use their critical viewing skills to answer the questions below.

- What does the actor's expression tell you about the character?

- How would you describe the actor's costume?

The Language of
THEATRE

Support students in learning new and essential language by using accessible language in the classroom.

- Use accessible language with terms such as "main character" and "enemy" to introduce the theatre terms protagonist and antagonist.

- Read aloud the first paragraph on Greek Tragedy on page 125 as students follow along in the text. Point out how the boldface words are explained with simpler terms in each sentence.

- Encourage students to use context clues that explain the theatre terms in more accessible language as they read the chapter.

- Encourage students to look for more accessible language in the context of a sentence or paragraph to help them understand unfamiliar terms or concepts as they read the chapter.

Resource Binder

- Dramatic Roles Activity Sheet, p. 56

- Regional Accents Worksheet, p. 57

- Critique Sheet: Dramatic Scene, p. 58

- Dramatic Roles Test, p. 59

Handbook Connections
pages 559–563, 568–569, 577–579

To Have on Hand

- One-act plays for the students to use as inspiration or guides for the plays they write, such as the ten-minute plays published by Smith and Kraus, Inc., under the title *Humana Festival Plays*

- Recording device

- Stopwatch to time student performances

- Soliloquies from Shakespeare's tragedies

- Scenes from social dramas

Serious Drama Today

Read scenes from contemporary social dramas of the last fifty years, including *All My Sons, Look Back in Anger, Spinning into Butter, Angels in America, Ruined,* and *Water by the Spoonful.* Discuss the issues raised in these plays with students.

 **Advanced Students**

Have pairs or groups of students choose a scene from a social drama they admire and perform the scene for the class. Ask the class to discuss the social issues addressed in the scene.

Building a Dramatic Character

Discuss with students how they would order the four elements in terms of difficulty. Is it harder for an actor to convey motivation or emotional intensity? Why?

Visual Cue

Arthur Miller's *The Crucible* was written in 1953, during the time of the McCarthy hearings when many Americans were accused of and tried for being Communists. The play follows events during the famous witch hunts in 17th-century Salem, Massachusetts.

- These two people are husband and wife. What do their costumes tell you about them?

- What do their postures and expressions tell you about their relationship?

---

dance were sometimes part of a scene as well. Dialogue that was intellectual or meaningful would be presented in iambic pentameter (ten syllables with five stresses to the line); the uneducated or foolish often spoke in prose. The tragic universe of Shakespeare's plays often highlights a disrupted life that seeks to regain order within a spiritual context. *Hamlet, Macbeth,* and *King Lear* are fine examples of Shakespearean tragedy.

Actors at the College of Central Florida portray the complex moral attitudes of the Keller family in Arthur Miller's *All My Sons.*

Serious Drama Today

Of course, actors are still taking on the plays of the Greeks and Elizabethans, but there are many contemporary plays that investigate issues similar to those in the tragedies of the past. This serious drama, also called **social drama,** tackles subjects that do not fall strictly into the category of tragedy—the everyday struggles and failures of ordinary folk in the hard-edged landscape of the 20th and 21st centuries. Arthur Miller's heroes, in such plays as *All My Sons* and *Death of a Salesman,* struggle to maintain their dignity and humanity while acting in immoral ways. Lawrence and Lee's *Inherit the Wind* and Rebecca Gilman's *Boy Gets Girl* also explore important contemporary issues. In *Waiting for Godot* and *Endgame,* Samuel Beckett's antiheroes come to realize the modern world is meaningless and chaotic.

All of these dramatists point out the problems people face today, without necessarily suggesting solutions to them.

Building a Dramatic Character

There are four essential elements when it comes to acting in a tragedy or a serious drama.

The actor must convey

1 strong characterization

2 emotional intensity

3 simplicity of objective

4 motivation

Backstage Gossip: You're Not Serious!

Having written a string of hit comedies, Philip Barry tried his hand at serious, socially significant dramas. After one of these failed, director and critic Harold Clurman said to drama critic Brooks Atkinson: "We should encourage him to remain superficial."

from *Broadway Anecdotes* by Peter Hay

In serious and tragic plays, the characters are usually fully drawn individuals who have one dominant trait that the actor must project. Hamlet is indecisive; Othello is jealous; Anne Sullivan in *The Miracle Worker* is determined. The protagonist of just about any tragedy or serious play is in some definable way very impressive. This is not only because of the character's indomitable spirit but also because he or she has the courage to stand up against a great obstacle. The antagonist must also be played with strength to provide an adequate conflict for the protagonist. Keep this in mind as you prepare to write your scene.

Using Emotion

The intense emotions called for in dramatic roles must be portrayed with utter conviction and sincerity while maintaining the poise necessary to put the play across. To create these emotions, you may need to use emotional recall. This is the process by which you use the memory of emotional incidents from your own past and transfer them to your character's situation. To do this, you must focus on the details of the past event and try to visualize and feel the emotion all over

Gay Nineties melodramas such as *Lily, the Felon's Daughter* feature stock characters such as Lord Monty, played by Kent Streed, a suitor with slicked-down hair and an offering of roses.

again. Then try to create that same emotion in the character. (See Chapter 3 for more on recall.)

Melodrama

Melodrama is a type of play that focuses more on cliff-hanging action and tugging on the heartstrings than on character development or society's real problems. The purpose of a melodrama is to create great suspense and excitement in the

Using Emotion

You may want to have students reread pages 24–25 in which recall is discussed. Then ask them to re-create an emotion in their minds. Suggest that students imagine how they would feel in similar circumstances and go from there. Volunteers may wish to share this emotion with the class.

Melodrama

Though melodrama is not as popular as it once was, many contemporary plays are in some ways derived from this early form. Read excerpts from the melodrama *The Bad Seed* to the students. Then compare it to the Gay Nineties melodrama *Lily, the Felon's Daughter*. Discuss the heightened emotions, simple plots, and one-dimensional characters.

If it is difficult for the students to grasp the idea of the melodrama, show them a silent film video or DVD with dramatic content, such as D. W. Griffith's *Broken Blossoms*, Erich von Stroheim's *Greed*, or F. W. Murnau's *Sunrise*. Be sure you discuss the fact that from our contemporary perspective these films may seem highly melodramatic, but give proper credit to the fact that in the hands of these skilled early directors, the stories are still very moving and the film work quite compelling.

ACTivity **Advanced Students**
Ask these students to analyze and write a short dramatic scene in all three styles of drama: tragedy (Greek or Shakespearean), social drama, and melodrama.

Visual Cue

Tom Taggart's play *Lily, the Felon's Daughter* is a classic American melodrama of the Victorian era. Even today audiences continue to boo the villain and cheer the hero while the piano plays a rollicking tune.

- How would you describe Lord Monty?

- Do you think Monty is a hero or a villain?

ACTivity What contemporary music sounds might be associated with the three types of drama? An example might be Janis Joplin as Greek drama, Tom Waits or Eminem as social drama, and Loretta Lynn as melodrama. Ask students to bring in music that they feel has the sound, feel, and texture of each type and share it with the class.

Using Regional Accents

Discuss with the class the variations in how English is spoken in America. Consider the South, the East, the West, and the Midwest, as well as differences between city speakers and rural speakers. Suggest that, in general, urban dwellers speak with a quicker pace and rural speakers may have a more nasal twang. Note the drawl and the light, lingering *AH* instead of long *I* used in the South, and the loss of the *r* sound in certain areas such as Boston (where *car* is pronounced *cAH*). Tell them to resist any temptation to fall back on stereotypes when creating a character from a region with which they have limited knowledge.

ACTivity Have the class work on their British accents by practicing the broader vowel range and higher pitch of the typical speaker of British English. Ask students to practice Eliza Doolittle's "The rain in Spain falls mainly in the plain. In Hampshire hurricanes hardly happen." And then add "I know you are right, Sir Henry," first in Standard English, then in Cockney English. The chart below should help.

Standard Sound
face pronounced fAs
slow pronounced slO
ice pronounced Is
right pronounced rIt
help pronounced help

Cockney Sound
face pronounced fIs
slow pronounced sLOU
ice pronounced OIs
right pronounced roYIt
help pronounced elp

audience. It was very popular in the United States in the early 1800s and is still performed by small theatre groups and high school drama groups across the country. Most melodramas have a happy ending. Examples of contemporary melodramas include Frederick Knott's *Dial M for Murder,* Agatha Christie's *The Mousetrap,* and Maxwell Anderson's *The Bad Seed.*

A subcategory of melodrama are the Gay Nineties melodramas (meaning they were written and first performed during the 1890s). These plays have exaggerated values of right and wrong. They feature such stock types as the mustachioed villain and the sweet, innocent heroine. Though modern audiences find these plays humorous, in their time such works also aroused tears.

Using Regional Accents

A **regional accent** is the particular sound of speech of a region. Inexperienced actors are not usually cast in roles for which an accent is necessary, but even actors with plenty of experience can be frustrated by tricky regional speech patterns. If you are cast in a role that requires you to speak with an accent of a certain region, you can, of course, get a book on the subject, but a better choice would be to listen to a native speaker, either in person or recorded.

To do a credible accent, you will need to develop your ear. For example, imagine that you have been cast as the cockney flower girl, Eliza Doolittle, in *Pygmalion* by George Bernard Shaw (or *My Fair Lady,* the musical version of that play). You might get a video of the play, or you might find an audio recording that includes a lower-class urban English accent. Listen for specific sounds and rhythms in the accent and think about how they differ from your normal speech. Figure out the phonetic differences so that you can re-create them consistently. In fact, consistency is the most crucial element when it comes to developing a believable accent. When you perform, give the suggestion of the accent rather than concerning yourself with making every sound recognizable as being from a particular place. The important thing is that you be clearly understood.

Most actors take on the acquisition of an accent privately, not during rehearsal time. However, professional theatres sometimes employ coaches to help the actors in this regard. These experts work with the cast to hone and perfect their speech and create the kind of consistent accents that audiences expect.

Notes

_____

_____

_____

_____

_____

_____

_____

Here's How
To Stay in Control

When acting in an intense dramatic play, you may feel the need to drain yourself completely during the climactic scene. Resist this impulse! To present the strongest characterization possible, you need to maintain control. Always hold something in reserve. Some acting teachers suggest that you "give it ninety percent—and hold back ten percent." If you do this, the audience will think you're acting with abandon, when in reality you will be in complete control—able to stay focused and aware.

And don't turn on those water works, either. Many young actors feel that they must work themselves up to tears to get the audience to feel the emotion of a sad scene. But good actors know that succumbing completely to tears can have a distancing effect on the audience. Uncontrolled tears can also lead to inaudibility. The better choice for an actor is almost always to work against breaking into tears. An actor struggling against falling apart creates tension; that tension draws the audience into the emotional moment.

PREPARE
Ready, Set, Write!

What is one of the most tragic events that could happen to someone? You can dramatize your idea in this presentation as you devise an imaginative scenario that you can turn into a short script.

First, work with a partner to brainstorm your scene. The suggestions on the following page may help you. Then improvise back and forth, and outline the scene and some of the dialogue for both characters. Your dialogue should reveal the characters' motivations and portray them in a believable way. You may wish to record your improvisations so that you can remember your best lines. When you have finished writing the outline of your scene, reshape it so that each moment is clear and distinct. Then refine the outline into a working script.

Ready, Set, Act!

Now rehearse. Create basic movement to express your characters' thoughts, feelings, and actions nonverbally as well as through your script. If some of the lines do not sound quite right as you rehearse, edit them accordingly.

Use emotional and sensory recall to help you fully realize the situation, but to portray the emotions, concentrate on what your character *does*. Stay in character, focus on the objectives, and respond to your partner. Time your scene and stay within the three- to five-minute time range.

Chapter 12 Dramatic Roles **129**

PREPARE
Ready, Set, Write!

Encourage students to use their own ideas to find a subject for their dramatic scene, but ask them to go over it with you before they proceed. Try to have some type of recording device available for students who wish to use one.

Here's How

To really understand control, this might be a good time to have interested students experience the dramatic equivalent of being out of control by taking on a bit of Shakespeare. Ask students to read the lines below from *A Midsummer Night's Dream.* These lines are spoken in full bombast by Bottom, who is acting the character Pyramus in the play *Pyramus and Thisbe.* His approach knows not the word *control.*

Approach ye Furies fell!
O Fates, come, come
Cut thread and thrum;
Quail, crush, conclude, and quell. . .

[Tell students to read this line with an awareness of the force of the alliteration.]

Thus die I, thus, thus, thus.
Now am I dead.
Now am I fled;
My soul is in the sky.
Tongue lose thy light;
Moon take thy flight.
Now die, die, die, die, die.

[Advise students that as they perform the death scene, Bottom, as Pyramus, does not hold back in any way. This death would involve lots of swooning, falling, getting up, dropping again, writhing, jerking, and so on.]

When students have performed this short scene, discuss the process, the outcomes, and the limitations of this type of acting.

Backstage Gossip: Sense Memory

Stella Adler's teaching method was Stanislavian but it led her to major differences with Lee Strasberg and the method as practiced at the Actors Studio. When he died in 1982 she spoke to her class. . . .

"A man of the theatre died last night," she intoned, having asked her class to stand for a moment of silence. "It will take a hundred years before the harm that man has done to the art of acting can be corrected."

from *Ned Sherrin's Theatrical Anecdotes*

PRESENT

Act in a Dramatic Scene

Remind the students presenting their scenes that the "moment before" not only allows them to focus and relax before they begin, it also gives the audience a chance to settle down and focus. Tell them that they should not begin a presentation until they have the attention of the entire audience.

CRITIQUE

Evaluate Your Classmates' Dramatic Scene

Before they begin their evaluations, let the students in the audience discuss each scene. How did the presentation make them feel? Did the scene elicit in them feelings of empathy, catharsis, or agitation? Was this what the playwright intended to elicit? Encourage give-and-take between the audience and the writers/presenters.

The Language of THEATRE

Invite students to add pictures or other graphic aids to their vocabulary cards or notebooks to help them remember the academic vocabulary and its meaning. Provide support as needed to help students with pronunciation.

PRESENT

Act in a Dramatic Scene

When either your own or your partner's name is called, give the outline of your scene or the Dramatic Roles Activity Sheet to your teacher before you begin your presentation. Then introduce your scene briefly. You only need to give the audience enough information to allow them to understand the basic situation.

Take a moment before you begin. This "moment before" is a handy tool for actors. It allows you to focus more completely before you launch into a scene, and it allows the audience time to settle down.

Perform your scene. Stay focused and remain in character. Consistently employ the physical techniques you developed as you wrote the script to help make the characters believable. When you are finished, take a brief bow and return to your seat.

Suggestions for Dramatic Scenes

- A mother learns that her only child is critically injured.
- A brilliant painter finds that she is going blind.
- A young man about to be married finds out he has a terminal disease.
- A father is sentenced to life in prison for a crime he did not commit.
- A woman with a proud family background discovers that her brother has committed a serious crime.

CRITIQUE

Evaluate Your Classmates' Scene

Evaluate a presentation by one pair of your classmates using a scale of 1 to 5, with 5 being "outstanding" and 1 being "needs much improvement." Your evaluation should be confined to the performance, not the writing. Ask yourself these questions:

- How were the presenters able to convey the drama of the scene?
- How well did the actors convey their characters' objectives?
- In what way did the actors' movements and gestures impact the scene?
- Did the actors stay in character, listen to each other, and respond throughout the scene?

Write a short paragraph explaining why you gave this pair the score you did.

The Language of THEATRE

Use the new academic language in the chapter in writing and speaking activities.

- Write each of the theatre terms on page 124 on an index card or in a vocabulary notebook, breaking each term into syllables. Then say each term aloud.
- Write each of the theatre terms and its definition on an index card or in a notebook. Then take turns with a partner saying sentences using each term.
- Work with a partner to write and perform a dramatic scene (see pages 129–130). As you work on the scene, use the appropriate theatre terms from page 124 to discuss what you plan to do. Write up your plan using those terms.
- Write a critique of a scene performed by one pair of classmates (see above) using appropriate theatre terms from page 124. Then present your feedback orally in a constructive manner.

From the Field: Just Do It

The playwright Maria Irene Fornes teaches young playwrights to write their plays in a "trance state." Giving them meditation exercises first, with suggestions of what to be thinking about that will help create the play, she then asks them to sit down and write for twenty minutes without any pauses to evaluate or think. Just write. She has written her plays this way.

Spotlight on

The Worst Romeo Ever

Over the course of history, plenty of actors have made a mess of Shakespeare's lines. But many theatre historians agree that Robert Coates was perhaps the worst offender. Coates (1772–1848) had no talent but plenty of money—enough to finance vanity productions in which he would star. He produced *Romeo and Juliet* often and, to the utter despair of his various Juliets, he always played Romeo. Audiences loved Coates or, more accurately, they loved to use him for target practice by lobbing rotten fruits and vegetables at him during the show. In the scene in which Romeo discovers that Juliet has killed herself, audiences would jeer at Coates and yell such comments as "Why don't YOU die?"

The critics weren't kind to Coates either. Reviews of his performances were often descriptions of the rioting audience and the flying foodstuffs.

Robert Coates

Spotlight on

The Worst Romeo Ever In his 1995–1996 diary, *My Name Escapes Me*, Alec Guinness uses his eye for observation as well as his own reflections to describe a life well lived. In the book, Guinness, who died in 2000, writes of enjoying Baz Luhrmann's film adaptation of William Shakespeare's *Romeo and Juliet*, adding ruefully that the worst Romeo ever was, in fact, "none other than me."

John Gielgud also struggled with the part of Romeo when he and Laurence Olivier alternated the roles of Mercutio and Romeo. Says Gielgud, "I was directing and I bullied him a great deal about his verse-speaking, which he admitted himself, he wasn't happy about. I was rather showy about mine, and fancied myself very much a verse-speaker, and I became very mannered in consequence. But I was so jealous, because not only did he play Romeo with tremendous energy, but he knew just how to cope with it and select. I remember Ralph Richardson saying to me, 'But you see, when Larry leans against the balcony and looks up, then you have the whole scene immediately.'

"Because he had this wonderful plastique, which is absolutely unself-conscious, like a lithe panther or something. I had been draping myself around the stage for weeks, thinking myself very romantic as Romeo, and I was rather baffled and dismayed that I couldn't achieve the same effect at all."

Notes

_____
_____
_____
_____
_____
_____
_____
_____

Dramatic Roles Test

The test for this chapter is available in blackline master form in the Resource Binder, page 59.

For More Information

Books

Blumenfield, Robert H., *Accents: A Manual for Actors*, Limelight Editions, 2002.

Brook, Peter, *The Open Door*, Theatre Communications Group, 2001.

Perry, John, *The Encyclopedia of Acting Techniques*, Betterway Publications, 1997.

O'Neill, Cecily, and Alan Lambert, *Drama Structures: A Practical Handbook for Teachers*, Heinemann, 1990.

Shapiro, Mel, *An Actor Performs*, Wadsworth Publishing, 1996.

Waxberg, Charles, *The Actor's Script: Script Analysis for Performers*, Heinemann, 1998.

Zucker, Carole, ed., *In the Company of Actors: Reflections on the Craft of Acting*, Routledge, 2000.

Other Media

Acting with Accent, Audio CDs, Insight Media, 1979.

Acting in Tragedy with Brian Cox, DVD, Hal Leonard, 2011.

Apps

The Real Accent App
Rehearsal 2
Shakespeare
Stop Acting! The Audition Class with Margie Haber

Theatre Journal

Use the following as an additional or substitute prompt.

Turn your short account of a newspaper event into a monologue. Act out the part of a witness to the event telling the audience the important details about what happened.

Additional Projects

1 Dramatize a dramatic event from your life or from your family history. Use emotional and sensory recall to create and perform your dramatization.

2 Devise and improvise serious group scenes that reflect dramatic structure and build to a climax. Refine your scenes so that they include classical, contemporary, realistic, and non-realistic elements. Here are some suggestions for sample scenes:

- A group of miners working underground senses something is wrong. As they prepare to go up, rocks begin to cave in on them.

- A group of striking workers is demonstrating outside an office building. They see that other workers have arrived and are crossing the picket line. Shouting ensues.

- A political speaker is heckled at an outdoor rally until bedlam breaks loose.

- A bus driver picks up various passengers. One woman appears to have wings. A man is able to read the minds of other passengers.

3 Write a short dramatic monologue (a long speech given by one character) and present it to the class. Use all your acting tools—voice projection, diction, inflection, physical movement, and emotional and sensory recall—to portray a believable character.

4 Memorize either the monologue from *Saint Joan* by George Bernard Shaw or the monologue from *The Janitor* by August Wilson found in Unit Eight. Consider the cultural and historic contexts and integrate these with your own personal experiences to create a believable character. Develop an accent to help convey your character. Present the monologue to the class.

5 **Theatre Journal** Skim through the news. Find a story that has serious elements, such as a fire, a car accident, or some other life-or-death incident. In your journal, write a short account of the event from the point of view of someone either directly or peripherally involved. Try to think about the events as they might seem to that person.

Substitute Teacher Activities

Here are some suggestions for the days that you will be out of the classroom.

- Assign the Regional Accents Worksheet on page 57 of the Resource Binder.

- Discuss the information concerning Acting Types and Characterization found on pages 559–561 and Accents found on page 577 in the Student Handbook.

- Assign one or more of the Additional Projects on this page.

- **Play "Name That Character."** Students act out a character in fiction, film, or television by moving, gesturing, and speaking like that character. Classmates must guess who the person is.

Master of the Craft
Kenneth Branagh

Born in 1960 in Belfast, Ireland, actor Kenneth Branagh was the second of three children born to a working-class family. When he was still a boy, his family moved to England. When Branagh was fifteen, a crucial event took place in his life: He saw English theatre legend Derek Jacobi play Hamlet. From then on, he knew he wanted to be an actor.

At eighteen he was accepted into one of the best theatre schools in the world—the Royal Academy of Dramatic Art. Once out of school he was immediately cast in a play on the West End (London's version of Broadway). The Royal Shakespeare Company subsequently hired him into its repertory company, and, at the age of twenty-three, he took on the pivotal role of Prince Hal in Shakespeare's *Henry V.* He became an immediate sensation, winning many awards for his performance.

Kenneth Branagh, as Hamlet, with Kate Winslet.

In 1987, Branagh and a friend started a theatre company of their own, the Renaissance Theatre Company. Branagh's productions of the Shakespeare plays *Twelfth Night* and *Much Ado About Nothing* won rave reviews. Then Branagh fulfilled one of his many ambitions by playing Hamlet. Shortly thereafter, in 1989, he directed and starred in a film version of *Henry V.* The success of the film brought Branagh unexpected international fame.

He was quickly signed to make several more films.

Kenneth Branagh has, of course, had some failures along the way, but he is an artist whose ambition is evenly balanced with his great talent. He continues to challenge himself as an artist, acting in and directing film, television, and theatre. In 2001, he won multiple awards for *The Play What I Wrote*. He received critical acclaim and numerous award nominations for his portrayal of Laurence Olivier in the 2011 film *My Week with Marilyn*.

Branagh as Prince Hal in *Henry V.*

Master of the Craft
Masters Past and Present

ACTivity Make a large class collage of masters of the craft of acting. Have students bring in pictures of actors and actresses they feel are masters at dramatic acting. They can be cut from magazines, photocopied from books, or printed from online sources. Ask them to also cut out or bring in typed words that describe qualities that make these people masters. On a large piece of cardboard, create a collage with the pictures and quotes.

For More Information
Books
Branagh, Kenneth, *Beginning*, W. W. Norton, 1990.

Crowl, Samuel, *Shakespeare at the Cineplex: The Kenneth Branagh Era*, Ohio University Press, 2005.

White, Mark, *Kenneth Branagh: A Life*, Faber & Faber, 2005.

Quotable

I said I'm a kid from Brooklyn, and I'm not supposed to be able to do this [Othello]. Then Kenneth Branagh said, 'I'm an Irish kid from Belfast, and I'm not supposed to be able to do this either.' But Shakespeare was an actor first. Those words were written to be spoken. And once you do that a couple of times, you think, 'That's pretty! I want to say that again! Where can I get more?'

Laurence Fishburne, Actor

Theatre Then and Now

A Role for All Eras

Other actors who have played Hamlet through the ages include John Gielgud, Richard Burton, David Wagner, Kenneth Branagh, and even Sarah Bernhardt. Film stars who have played the role include Mel Gibson and Leonardo DiCaprio.

For More Information

Books

Branagh, Kenneth. *Hamlet: Screenplay, Introduction and Film Diary,* W. W. Norton, 2013.

Proctor, Bryan W., *The Life of Edmund Kean,* Arno Press, 1970.

Shakespeare, William, *Hamlet: A Parallel Text Edition,* Perfection Learning, 2003.

Shakespeare, William, Harold Jenkins, ed., *Hamlet: Playgoer's Edition,* Arden, 1997.

Shattuck, Charles Harlen, *The Hamlet of Edwin Booth,* University of Illinois Press, 1969.

Smith, Gene A., *American Gothic: The Story of America's Legendary Theatrical Family: Junius, Edwin, and John Wilkes Booth,* Touchstone Books, 1993.

Other Media

Hamlet Study Guide—Timeless Shakespeare, CD-ROM, Saddleback Educational Publishing, 2010.

Olivier's Shakespeare (Henry V, Hamlet, Richard III), DVD, Criterion Collection, 2006.

William Shakespeare's Hamlet, DVD, Warner Home Video, 2007.

Theatre Then and Now

A Role for All Eras: Hamlet, Prince of Denmark

For more than 300 years, actors have coveted the role of Hamlet, the brilliant, angry, indecisive title character of Shakespeare's tragedy. The role's richness, humor, and emotional depth have challenged generations of actors.

Edmund Kean (1787–1833) was the leading English actor of the early 1800s. He specialized in tragic roles and was best known for his many portrayals of Hamlet. He had many opportunities to sharpen his skills in this role—he first played it when he was only fourteen years old. Extremely charismatic, Kean brought romanticism to every role. His acting was once described by a critic as "quietly imploding before his audience." The great poet Coleridge said of Kean, "Seeing him act was like reading Shakespeare by flashes of lightning." Kean's reputation as a great interpreter of Shakespeare was ensured. His excessive drinking and wild lifestyle earned him quite another reputation, however, and eventually it took its toll. He died in his mid-forties.

Edwin Booth (1833–1893) "An actor is a sculptor who carves in snow." So said Edwin Booth with regard to the fleeting nature of the theatre: Once a scene is played, it is gone forever.

Edwin Booth played the role of Hamlet for a remarkable 100 consecutive nights. The melancholy Dane was a role for which Booth's appearance, voice, and bearing were ideally suited. Slender and darkly handsome, Booth possessed a voice that was both musical and tempered with a natural air of reserve. His acting style, quieter than most other actors of his day, became increasingly sensitive and subdued.

His career was tarnished in 1865 when his brother, John Wilkes Booth, assassinated President Lincoln. After that, Edwin did not reappear onstage until January 1866, when he again played Hamlet. The audience's applause after this performance showed their conviction that the glory of one Booth brother had not been eclipsed by the infamy of the other. Edwin Booth's final stage appearance was in Brooklyn, New York, as Hamlet in 1891.

Backstage Gossip: Who's in Charge?

William Macready (1793–1873) was an actor with a notoriously violent temper. During rehearsals for *Hamlet*, he angered the actor playing King Claudius, and, on opening night, the latter chose to die in the same spot onstage that the Prince of Denmark had selected as his own. "Die farther upstage!" Macready whispered. No answer. "Die farther upstage, sir!" Macready demanded more loudly. The corpse sat up and, to the audience's delight, said, "I'm King here, and I'll die where I damned well please!"

Sir Laurence Olivier (1907–1989)

"If I wasn't an actor, I think I'd have gone mad. You have to have extra voltage, some extra temperament to reach certain heights. Art is a little bit larger than life, and I think you probably need a little touch of madness." These are the words of legendary English actor Laurence Olivier. He began his career in 1926 as a member of the Birmingham Repertory Theatre. He was known for his physical athleticism and his dazzling vocal ability and range—particularly in Shakespearean roles. There is a famous story that shines a light on Olivier's acting technique. While making the 1976 film *Marathon Man,* Olivier found out that his costar, American actor Dustin Hoffman, had been preparing for his role by going without food and sleep. Hoffman wanted to look and feel just like the character he was playing—a torture victim. Olivier, mystified, asked Hoffman, "My dear boy, why don't you just *act*?" Olivier's film version of *Hamlet,* which he starred in and directed, is available on DVD.

Laurence Olivier as Hamlet in 1948.

It won Oscars for Best Picture and Best Actor in 1948. In 1970, Olivier was made a lord, the first member of the theatrical profession to receive such an honor. Olivier's extraordinary ability to illuminate the words and ideas of Shakespeare won him a well-deserved place in theatre and film history.

Edwin Booth as Hamlet, the "Melancholy Dane."

Sir Laurence Olivier

It has been said that to prepare to play Hamlet every night Sir Laurence Olivier would try to push down the walls of the theatre with all of his might. When he was at the height of physical and emotional frustration, he would enter the stage as Hamlet.

Other Cultures, Other Times

A Hamlet for Russia

In 1971, at Moscow's Taganka Theater, a production of *Hamlet* premiered that ran for over ten years, ending with the early death of Vladimir Vysotsky, the poet-singer-actor who played Hamlet. This production was innovative in its use of film montage as well as the ever-present image of a moving curtain. More important was the spiritual and cultural influence Vysotsky's performance gave the play.

Before playing Hamlet, Vysotsky was already a popular proponent of conscience and freedom, and he was much loved throughout the country. When he died, many of his countrymen participated in a spontaneous memorial service.

For More Information

Books

Coleman, Terry, *Olivier,* Henry Holt, 2006.

Lewis, Roger, *The Real Life of Laurence Olivier,* Applause Books, 2000.

Mer, Nathan, *Vladimir Vysotsky: 1938–1980,* International University Press, 1991.

Olivier, Laurence, *On Acting,* Simon & Schuster, 1986.

Olivier, Laurence, *Confessions of an Actor: Laurence Olivier, an Autobiography,* Simon & Schuster, 1985.

Other Media

You can find videos of Vladimir Vysotsky singing on YouTube.

Backstage Gossip: A Peripheral Actor

Laurence Olivier talks about creating the role of Richard III.

I began to build up a character, a characterization. I'm afraid I do work mostly from the outside in. I usually collect a lot of details, a lot of characteristics, and find a creature swimming about somewhere in the middle of them . . . .

Some people start from the inside, some people start from the periphery. I would say, at a guess, that Alec Guinness is what we would call a peripheral actor. I think I'm the same. The actor who starts from the inside is more likely to find himself in the parts he plays, than to find the parts in himself.

from *Theatrical Anecdotes* by Peter Hay

Chapter 13

Comic Roles

In this chapter students will learn about several different comedy genres and some proven comedy techniques for the stage. They will practice writing and performing their own comic monologue.

Objectives

1 to recognize and perform different genres of theatrical comedy

2 to experiment with age-old comic techniques for the stage and try out their effectiveness

3 to understand the difference between playing comedy and drama

4 to create a comic character and then write and perform a monologue for that character

Project Specs

Talk to students about the quote from Lynn Fontanne on page 139. Would they agree?

Show, Don't Tell Pick a selection that you think would illustrate how a passage can be played for drama or for laughs. Read the passage with dramatic intent and ask students to comment. Then read the same passage in a comedic way and discuss the result with students.

On Your Feet

Ask volunteers to read their funny stories to the class before your work on this chapter begins. Return to these stories later and ask students how they might change them in light of what they have learned.

---

13 Comic Roles

It is said that tragedy is when you fall down the stairs and comedy is when someone else does. It's not that we enjoy seeing others suffer—it's that we know how to laugh at ourselves—after it stops hurting. Good comedy requires perspective: The comic actor presents a character's misfortune while providing just enough emotional distance to let us laugh. It's a juggling act, but when it works, it's magic.

Project Specs

Project Description You will write, refine, and perform a comic monologue of three to five minutes in length.

Purpose to develop a sense of comic presentation and timing

Materials a list of character traits that describe your character or the Comic Roles Activity Sheet your teacher provides

Theatre Terms

burlesque
comedy of manners
farce
high comedy
hold
low comedy
middlebrow comedy
parody
rule of three
satire
travesty

On Your Feet

Think of a funny story from your childhood. It can be an actual experience or something funny you once read or saw. Practice telling the story, then tell it to a friend and ask for feedback as to what the friend found funny.

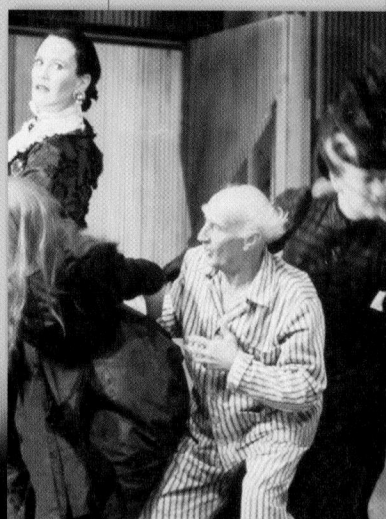

The play *A Flea in Her Ear* employs elements of burlesque to create its comic effect.

Theatre Terms

burlesque physical comedy that uses exaggeration

comedy of manners comedy that makes fun of upper-class pretentiousness

farce physical comedy that exaggerates situations until they are hardly believable

high comedy comedy that pokes fun at political situations and social standards

hold the pause required after a character delivers a funny line

low comedy comedy that is physical and sometimes vulgar

middlebrow comedy comedy based on plot and sentimental situations

parody to imitate in a humorous way

rule of three the belief that comedic routines designed to make the audience laugh are only funny three times in a row

satire comedy that makes fun of people to try to change their foolish behavior

travesty a humorous imitation

PREVIEW

What's So Funny?

No two people have funny bones in exactly the same spot. What some people find hilarious, others find painful or sad. What sends you rolling on the floor might only nudge a smile out of the person next to you. In fact, humor varies so greatly that it can be classified in several different genres. Evaluate the genre of any comedy you are performing or studying to appreciate its conventions and their implications for the entire creative team.

Low comedy, which is physical and sometimes vulgar, includes outlandish, exaggerated forms of humor such as **farce** and **burlesque.** Both genres make use of oddly harmless violence. Farce stretches common plots to the very edge of believability through exaggeration and surprise. Burlesque uses a great deal of exaggeration too—but it's directed at a person, custom, artifact, or event. A

burlesque can take the form of a **travesty** and poke fun at respected subjects. It can **parody** a famous work by imitating the author's style in a humorous way. The loftier the subject, the more likely it will become a target for burlesque. As you may have guessed, burlesque and farcical characters tend to be fairly extreme in their appearance, movements, and reactions. They often don't think they are being funny, but their circumstance and habits are laughable.

Arsenic and Old Lace is an example of a middlebrow situation comedy.

Middlebrow comedy includes more plot-based, sentimental genres, such as romantic comedy, situation comedy, and sentimental comedy. These genres may provoke chuckles and smiles, but they also encourage weeping and other emotional responses. Characters in these comedies are more realistic, though their situations and responses can still be quite broad.

High comedy includes **satire** and **comedy of manners.** Satire makes fun of individual people and their follies in an attempt to change their foolish behavior. A comedy of manners, such as Sheridan's *The School for Scandal*, often makes fun of upper-class pretentiousness and the accepted standards of the wealthy. Both these genres appeal to the intelligence of

Chapter 13 Comic Roles **137**

Resource Binder

- Comic Roles Activity Sheet, p. 60
- Analyzing Humor Worksheet, p. 61
- Critique Sheet: Comic Monologue, p. 62
- Comic Roles Test, p. 63

Handbook Connections
pages 559–563, 568–569, 577–579

To Have on Hand

It is always a good idea to have a collection of good examples of the different kinds of comedy you will be studying in the form of online videos or audio recordings, CDs, and DVDs. Spalding Gray's recording *It's a Slippery Slope* is a fine example of a comedy monologue. Films of some of the great teams such as the Marx Brothers and George Burns and Gracie Allen, along with the performances of stand-up comics such as Robin Williams, Richard Pryor, and Ellen DeGeneres are good ways to see how comic timing operates.

PREVIEW

What's So Funny?

Discuss with students what makes them laugh and why other people laugh at things that don't seem funny to the observer.

Show, Don't Tell Show the students part or all of a Charlie Chaplin or Buster Keaton silent film. Then show them part or all of a Jim Carrey film or Mike Myers as Austin Powers. Ask students to compare and contrast these comedies and to talk about what they found funny in each. Discuss how elements of these films could be categorized as farce, parody, or satire.

ACTivity Play a storytelling game. In turn, have students sit at the head of the class. Each one tells a comic story that is either true or invented. The audience votes whether they have told a true or fictitious story. Tabulate the votes, then ask the teller to reveal whether it was truth or fiction. Ask the class to discuss whether the teller's behaviors seem truthful. Did storytellers seem more comfortable telling a true or a made-up story?

Beginning Students
To accomplish the activity above, you may want to give students a theme to base their stories on, such as "Tell about your most embarrassing moment."

Visual Cue

A Flea in Her Ear, Georges Feydeau's classic French farce, is a mad romp in which a wife tries to trap her innocent husband in a love tryst. A film version, starring Rex Harrison and Rosemary Harris, is also available.

- Describe two of the people in the photo.

- Look at the man in the striped costume at the left. Imitate the way he would move and speak.

The Rule of Three

Show, Don't Tell Watch videos of one of the films mentioned previously, such as one of the Marx Brothers' popular movies or clips from the Burns and Allen TV show and try to catch them using the rule of three.

Advanced Students

Ask students to write and perform the two forms of comedy below.

- **Stand-up Comedy in a Comic Persona** You might want to set up a "comedy club" in the classroom with an audience, stage, and perhaps a live drummer.
- **Comic Parody** Have students write and perform a comic parody that imitates some other theatrical form.

Engaging the Audience

Discuss with the students how the comic actor engages an audience. How might an actor walk the fine line between making the audience feel superior to the character while at the same time identifying with the character?

Vocabulary Enhancement

Commedia dell'arte, the popular comedy born in 16th-century Italy that has been discussed in previous chapters, often contained improvisations called *lazzi.* These comic routines incorporated acrobatics, slapstick, and repetition. *Lazzi* are the ancestors of *schtick.*

Visual Cue

Oscar Wilde's *The Importance of Being Earnest* is just as popular today as it was in the 1890s. Indeed, a film version starring Reese Witherspoon, Judi Dench, and Colin Firth is available on video and DVD.

- When you look at this photo, how can you tell it's a comedy?
- How would you read a book in a comic way?
- Would you rather play a comic or dramatic role?

The Rule of Three

If there is one thing comic writers and comedians hold sacred, it's the **rule of three.** It goes like this: Pratfalls, accidents, mis-understandings, and simi-lar "schticks" are funny only three times in a row. After that, they tend to fall flat. No one knows why exactly; they just know that a fourth time won't get a laugh.

What's the exception to the rule? The rule of three times three. Sometimes, a play offers an opportunity to use the rule of three on three separate occasions. On the third occasion, you might get away with adding a fourth surprise—repetition. After the third set of three, you may actually go for a fourth time. The schtick is funny the fourth time because it's not expected.

Oscar Wilde's *The Importance of Being Earnest* is a perfect example of a comedy of manners.

their audience. They poke fun at political situations, cultural habits, and entrenched attitudes. The more you know about the subject of a satire and how these comedies approach this subject, the more you can appreciate the characters' sly and subtle sarcasm. Characters in these genres must be fairly realistic and restrained, yet quirky and witty enough to provoke laughter.

What do almost all comic actors have in common? Commitment. No matter how ridiculous their situation. . . they take their acting seriously!

Engaging the Audience

Obviously, drama and comedy have some things in common. However, some necessary techniques are particu-lar to comedy. A comic writer and performer must engage an audience in the comic character, employing at least some of the elements below.

- Be sure that the audience identifies with your character.
- The audience should feel that it knows something your character doesn't.
- Help the audience feel superior to your character.
- Throw in the unexpected just when the audience is least expecting it.
- Invert the logic of a situation by doing what seems illogical. For example, two enemies might hug in the middle of an argument.

Quotable

So why do we laugh at comic situations? Because laughter comes from a feeling of superiority. Whether we laugh at danger, weakness, inadequacy, meanness, deformity, or simply because we feel good, laughter is an indication that we are not intimidated by life.

from *Introducing Theatre* by Joy Reilly and M. Scott Phillips

- Juxtapose two opposite things to heighten confusion. For example, pair a short, fat person with a tall, thin one, or create a character who loves kittens but is full of rage.

- Use rapid-fire dialogue and movement.

- Remember the Rule of Three.

Once an audience starts to respond, the actor must remember to **hold** for laughs. This means you must pause a bit to wait until the laughing dies down. If you speak and act over the laughing, the audience will start to restrain their laughter in order to follow the action, or they may lose an important point in the dialogue. If, however, you freeze—while staying in character and focusing on the situation at hand—you can continue when the laughter subsides. This allows the laughter to build and, perhaps, fill the house.

PREPARE

The Comic Edge

Comic playwrights such as Oscar Wilde and Tom Stoppard have created characters full of wit, charm, and snappy dialogue to comment on the social pretensions of their times. While making fun of his characters in *The Importance of Being Earnest,* Wilde also imbued them with such charm and grace that the audience couldn't help but be fond of them. Stoppard's brilliant use of language in *Rosencrantz and Guildenstern Are Dead* also endears the audience to this pair of rogues.

Good comedy stays on the edge of what is considered safe and polite. Too polite equals boring, and too edgy may offend the audience. The comic character must hold the audience in a tenuous balance between the two. A good comedy makes fun of the foibles and pretensions of the audience while also recognizing that we all share these faults.

Gary Oldman, Tim Roth, and Richard Dreyfuss in *Rosencrantz and Guildenstern Are Dead.*

Remind them that when performing comedy, actors must know how to hold for laughs. The standard rule is to hold only until the laugh has reached its peak. When the actor hears the laugh begin to subside, he or she should begin—or continue—speaking at a slightly increased volume. This gets easier with experience.

Advanced Students

Have capable students throw in gestures and movement as they practice their rapid-fire comic readings.

Vocabulary Enhancement

Comic timing refers, in part, to the ability of actors to speak in rapid-fire dialogue, often in one breath. At the ends of each line they lift the last word and then pause with some kind of take or gesture that releases the joke. This is also called *"serving up the joke."*

The popular television comedies *Whose Line Is It Anyway?* and *The Gilmore Girls* were known for the effective way they juxtaposed opposite character types and used dialogue that incorporated fast-paced give-and-take to create a comic effect. Share examples with students of these two shows or your current favorites available online.

Quotable

I think comedy is more difficult to play . . . If you are capable of playing tragedy it means you have a great well of emotion in you—and you just push yourself off and roll downhill . . . Comedy—you really have to have that ear out and that eye on yourself. You have to be very up and brilliant . . .

Lynn Fontanne, Actor

PREPARE

The Comic Edge

As students prepare to create their comic characters, recap what they have learned about types of comedy, how to engage an audience, and how laughs are created and sustained.

Find Your Comic Character

Help students as they first find their characters and then create lists and outlines of their characters' traits. Urge them to be as specific as they can be in their descriptions. Share first drafts with students after they have read them to family members and friends. Encourage them to rework their drafts as many times as needed.

Special Needs Students

These students may be best at oral comic storytelling in which they practice their story orally without having to write it down. You might also want to start these students with a comic story from their own lives told in first person before asking them to create a comic character.

ACTivity Play the "Hidden Problem Game." Students choose a physical problem that they must hide. Examples are bad breath, a huge pimple, having to go to the washroom, cramps, etc. They then improvise a scene in which they are being interviewed for a job while having to hide their problem from the audience. Ask them to first do this in a realistic way and then in a very exaggerated and comic way.

The Language of THEATRE

Create a word wall by posting the new theatre terms for the chapter in groups on the wall. Use the text to see what words can be grouped together. Then invite students to add words related to each of the terms based on the activities in the student book.

Find Your Comic Character

You too must try to create in your comic character someone who is flawed in some way—silly, vain, snobbish, gossipy, for example—but who also draws the audience in and arouses their interest as a believable character. At the left are a few suggestions to help you find your character and devise an imaginative scenario with dramatic structure that you can turn into a script for your monologue.

Think about yourself as the character in your monologue. How is your character different from the other characters that might be in this situation? How can you emphasize the uniqueness of your character? What surprises can you inject into your character's speech or actions?

Make a list of your character's traits or use the Comic Roles Activity Sheet provided by your teacher. Refer to these notes as you write a rough description of your character's activities in the scene. You can write this first draft more as an outline than a monologue. Then read your first draft aloud to a family member or friend. Based on what was funny and what was not funny, refine your script by writing a new draft with specific lines and stage directions. It may take several drafts to get the comic monologue you are excited to present.

Rehearse your monologue until you are sure of your character, actions, and lines. Your audience will enjoy the scene only if they can relax—confident that you are well prepared. Do not exceed the five-minute time limit.

Suggestions for Comedy Characters

- a prim person visiting a tattoo or piercing parlor
- Beethoven at a rave
- a sedate man buying women's lingerie in an exclusive store
- a parent with four children, arms full of bundles, trying to find change for the bus
- a tourist in Hawaii eager to learn the hula
- a parent teaching a sixteen-year-old to drive the family car
- a person trying to build a bookcase using directions in a foreign language

The Language of THEATRE

Work with a partner to use new basic language in writing and speaking activities.

- Brainstorm words related to comedy. Say each word aloud and write it in a word web on the board or in a notebook. Say and write the phrases *high comedy* and *low comedy*.
- Individually write three sentences to define *low comedy*, *middlebrow comedy*, and *high comedy*. Then read a sentence and ask your partner to say what kind of comedy has been defined.
- Discuss the differences between *farce* and *satire* with your partner. Then individually write a paragraph summarizing your discussion.
- Individually write a comic monologue as directed on this page. Then practice your monologue with your partner, noticing where to *hold* to allow for laughter.

Notes

_____

_____

_____

_____

_____

_____

PRESENT

Perform a Comic Monologue

When your turn comes, give your list of character traits and monologue script or the Activity Sheet to your teacher and walk quietly to the playing area.

Present your comic scene to the class, with the physical movements that make your character funny and believable. When you have finished your monologue, pause, and then bow politely before leaving the playing area.

Here's How
To Deal with the Giggles

Of course, if you remain focused, you will not get the giggles during a comic performance. But momentary lapses happen to everyone. If it happens to you, bring yourself back into your character using any of the following methods:

1 Tell yourself the situation is laughable. Let your character be overtaken by disbelief.

2 As the character, tell yourself—and communicate by your actions or gestures—that you simply cannot believe the circumstances. If you must, repeat them to yourself, in order to bring your character's situation back to the center of your awareness.

3 Turn your laughter into a character trait. Become a character who laughs, cries, and reacts uncontrollably.

CRITIQUE

Evaluate a Classmate's Monologue

Choose one of the monologues presented in class and evaluate your classmate's comedy performance. Use a rating system based on 5 points in your evaluation, with "outstanding" being a 5; "well done" being a 4; "fair" being a 3; "needs some improvement" being a 2; and "needs much improvement" being a 1. To give an accurate, well-supported critique, ask yourself these questions:

- Was this a performance of a low, middlebrow, or high comedy?

- What genre or genres of comedy could I identify in this performance?

- What elements of humor did the performer use (for example, the rule of three, sarcasm, and so on)?

- Was one moment particularly funny? Which one, and why?

Write an explanation of how you arrived at the score you gave.

PRESENT

Perform a Comic Monologue

Before they begin, discuss with students the fact that their comic monologue should reflect all aspects of their character—the words, the voice, the gestures, the movements, and so on, should all play into their comic intent.

ACTivity Before each student presents his or her comic monologue, have the student make a funny face just as the character might do.

Here's How

Discuss with students the possibility that in some situations breaking up in front of an audience may serve to heighten the fun. The idea being that the comedy must be good if it cracks up the comedian.

CRITIQUE

Evaluate a Classmate's Monologue

Hand out the Critique Sheet for this project or have students use their own paper. Quickly go over the elements of humor and what to look for in a strong comic monologue.

After you have reviewed student critiques, discuss with the subjects of the evaluations any recurrent suggestions for improvement.

Backstage Gossip: Rx for Giggles

Laurence Olivier's stage career almost ended before it began because he could not stop giggling onstage. He was finally cured by Noel Coward during a seven-month run of *Private Lives.* Every night during performance, Coward and co-star Gertrude Lawrence would think up another way to try and break Olivier up until he was finally able to control himself.

Comic Roles Test

The test for this chapter is available in blackline master form in the Resource Binder, page 63.

For More Information

Books

Aitken, Maria, *Style: Acting in High Comedy*, Applause Books, 1996.

Helitzer, Mel, *Comedy Writing Secrets*, Writers Digest Books, 1992.

Perret, Gene, *The New Comedy Writing Step by Step: Revised and Updated with Words of Instruction, Encouragement, and Inspiration from Legends of the Comedy Profession*, Quill Driver Books, 2007.

Robinson, Davis Rider, *The Physical Comedy Handbook*, Heinemann, 1999.

Roche, Jenny, *Comedy Writing*, McGraw-Hill, 1999.

Seyler, Athene, *The Craft of Comedy*, Theatre Arts Books, 1990.

Vorhaus, John, *The Comic Toolbox: How to Be Funny Even if You're Not*, Silman-James Press, 1994.

Other Media

Comedy, DVD, Insight Media, 2004.

Drama: Comedy, DVD, Insight Media, 1995.

Gene Wilder in Conversation with Wendy Wasserstein, DVD, The 92nd Street Y, 2009.

Political and Social Satire through Caricature, DVD Films for the Humanities and Sciences, 1985.

Theatre Journal

Use the following as an additional or substitute prompt.

In tragedies, the protagonist often has a "tragic flaw." In comedies the protagonist often has a "comic foible." Comic foibles are character traits that we recognize in ourselves and exaggerate. Write about your comic foible and how it affects your life. Or write about the comic foibles of two other people you know. Then write a comic foible for the character you are working on for your comic monologue.

Additional Projects

1 Translate the funny story you told at the beginning of this lesson—or some other funny experience—into a humorous scene with believable characters and dramatic structure. Write a draft, refine it, and then ask a group of students to perform it with you.

2 With a partner, research a media library in order to find and learn a classic comedy routine. Rehearse it thoroughly and then perform it for the class.

3 In a group with two or three others, read a classic farce such as *Tartuffe* by Molière or *What the Butler Saw* by Joe Orton and discuss the humorous elements it contains. Evaluate the effect of the genre on the way characters would be portrayed. Work on a scene you find particularly funny, and then present it to the class.

4 Read a comedy of manners. Then memorize and present a humorous two- to three-minute monologue from it. The following plays are possible sources for monologues: *The Women* by Clare Boothe Luce, *Blithe Spirit* by Noël Coward, *The Importance of Being Earnest* by Oscar Wilde, or *The School for Scandal* by Richard Brinsley Sheridan.

5 Read the scene from *The Importance of Being Earnest* by Oscar Wilde or the scene from *The Imaginary Invalid* by Molière found in Unit Eight. Choose and analyze a character, and then write a short description of how you would play this character based on the style, genre, and historic and cultural context. Describe the intellectual, emotional, physical, and social dimensions of the character.

6 Read about comic playwrights on pages 144–145. Do further research to compare and contrast the comedies of Molière with those of Neil Simon. Write an informative essay analyzing and evaluating the influence of the historical and cultural environment in which they were created and how they in turn influenced theatre and society. In your essay, explain why Molière is known as the father of modern comic drama, and why Neil Simon is described as the most successful playwright in theatre history.

7 **Theatre Journal** Next time you embarrass yourself, stop as soon as you are able and make a note of the event. Analyze what it was that made the event funny to others. Think about the kinds of characters who might find themselves in such a situation and the circumstances in which it might occur. Consider ways to make the event funnier—and then rehearse it as a comic bit!

"Laughter seems like a trifle, yet it has a power . . . that is well-nigh irresistible; it often changes the tendency of the greatest affairs, as it very often dissipates hatred and anger."

–Quintilian, Roman orator

Substitute Teacher Activities

- Assign the Analyzing Humor Worksheet on page 61 of the Resource Binder.

- Assign one or more of the Additional Projects on this page.

- **Create a Comedy Club.** Rearrange the space so that it looks like a club with a small stage and mike in the center or front. An emcee should be designated, and the students can work on the following acts to perform at the Club:

1 Stand-up comedy, either as self or in character
2 Improv scenes as in The Second City or *Saturday Night Live*
3 Comic storytelling from a life story
4 Parodies or satires of songs, TV shows, or life events
5 Political satires
6 Burlesque show that uses song, dance, pratfalls, slapstick, and other schtick

You can even serve refreshments!

Master of the Craft

Lily Tomlin

"All my life, I always wanted to be somebody. Now I see that I should have been more specific."
—Lily Tomlin

Mary Jean Tomlin didn't know she wanted to be a famous comedian when she was growing up in Detroit, Michigan, but she did enjoy gags. In fact, when she ordered gag items from the back of a comic book and couldn't pay for them, her mother paid for the package and made her do odd jobs until she could pay the money back. Such is the price of comedy.

When she got older, Tomlin didn't try acting until her second year of college at Michigan's Wayne State University. She appeared in student productions, including a variety show, where she presented a character called "The Tasteful Lady," which she still plays today.

Tomlin left Wayne State after her junior year and moved to New York. Beginning in 1960, she worked during the day at temporary jobs and performed in cabarets at night. Tomlin's career caught fire in 1969, when she was cast in the television comedy revue *Laugh-In.* There, she developed some of her classic characters, including Ernestine, the obnoxious telephone operator, and Edith Ann, the precocious child who tells outlandish stories ending with "And that's the truth!"

Tomlin has appeared in comic and dramatic roles in movies and television since 1975. She had a recurring role on TV's *The West Wing,* and she continues to tour and perform onstage. Her most celebrated work is her one-woman show entitled *The Search for Signs of Intelligent Life in the Universe,* which was written for her by Jane Wagner.

If flexibility and creativity are keys to a successful life, then Lily Tomlin has a pocketful of keys. But she is not overly impressed with success. "The trouble with the rat race," says Tomlin, "is that even if you win, you're still a rat!"

Lily Tomlin as Ernestine.

Master of the Craft

More About Lily Tomlin

Lily Tomlin cut her teeth on the television comedy-variety show *Rowan & Martin's Laugh-In,* which ran from 1968 to early 1973.

Other regulars included Flip Wilson, Sammy Davis Jr., Goldie Hawn, Arte Johnson, Henry Gibson, and Jo Anne Worley. On *Laugh-In,* Tomlin developed her sarcastic, nasal-voiced telephone operator, Ernestine, as well as Edith Ann, a child philosopher whose monologues always ended in the phrase "and that's the truth," followed by raspberries.

Tomlin's charming Web site, *www.lily tomlin.com/intro.htm* gives just about all the information you could possibly want concerning the versatile Lily.

For More Information

Books

Sorensen, Jeff, *Lily Tomlin: Woman of a Thousand Faces,* St. Martin's Press, 1989.

Wagner, Jane, *The Search for Intelligent Life in the Universe,* Perennial Press, 1991.

Other Media

The Best of Lily Tomlin: 20th Century Masters - The Millennium Collection, Audio CD, Polydor, 2003.

Lily Tomlin: The Search for Signs of Intelligent Life in the Universe, DVD, Laugh.com, 2005.

Lily Tomlin: This Is a Recording, MP3 Album, Universal, 2011.

Notes

_____
_____
_____
_____
_____
_____
_____

Cultural Heritage

Great Comic Playwrights

William Shakespeare is thought to be the greatest playwright of all time, and with good reason. Not only did he write elegant, thrilling drama and create memorable characters in his tragedies and histories, he also fashioned fascinating characters and inventive, witty dialogue in a number of comedies. Many of these comedies have a dusting of fairy folk and fools who have been beloved by audiences from his time to ours. No fool is more hilarious than Nick Bottom and no fairy so wry and mischievous than Puck in *A Midsummer Night's Dream*. Puck finds delight in playing tricks on mortals, and Bottom is inept enough to fall victim to Puck's spell.

A Midsummer Night's Dream, thought to have been written for a wedding couple, is perhaps Shakespeare's most sparkling comedy. In addition to the fools and fairies, there are two pairs of scrambled lovers, the wedding of a duke, and a hilarious play-within-a-play. It all takes place on the night before Midsummer Day, a night often associated with a crazed, albeit temporary, state of mind. The witty dialogue, frantic pace, and matrimonial mix-ups all come together to bring us a play that has had audiences laughing for hundreds of years.

Cultural Heritage

Comic Playwrights

Molière at work.

Comedy and France's Classical Age

In the mid 1600s, King Louis XIV of France was Europe's most powerful monarch. Nicknamed the Sun King, he gathered about him a glittering court. A great patron of the arts, Louis XIV sponsored a blossoming of French culture known as the Classical Age. This product of cultural and historical forces would help produce the playwright known as the father of comic drama—Molière.

Modeled on the classics of ancient Greece and Rome, the new classicism (or "neoclassicism") stressed order, clarity, social responsibility, and emotional restraint. Plays were expected to adhere to the three "unities" outlined by the ancient Greek philosopher Aristotle: unity of time (taking place in a day or less), unity of place (occurring in a single locale), and unity of action (having just one main story, with all scenes related to it). Two fine French playwrights of the Classical Age, Corneille and Racine, focused on tragedy; their colleague Molière, however, is renowned for brilliant comedy.

Molière, born Jean-Baptiste Poquelin in 1622, founded a traveling acting troupe known as the Illustrious Theatre. In 1658 the company was invited to perform for King Louis XIV. Its production of *The Love-Sick Doctor*, a play Molière himself had written, so delighted the king that he helped support the troupe.

Over the next twenty-four years, Molière's plays ripened from clever farces to brilliant comedies of manners. Among the most famous are *The Imaginary Invalid, The Misanthrope, The School for Wives*, and *Tartuffe*. Ridiculing powerful courtiers, clerics, and actors of the day, Molière's comedies made him dangerous enemies, but his popularity survived. They had a lasting impact on theatre by elevating comedy to a new level of respect as a genre able to powerfully portray human nature and society. Molière's plays continue to be widely performed today.

"The more we love our friends, the less we flatter them. It is by excusing nothing that pure love shows itself."

—Molière

For More Information

Books

Beaudin, Beth, *Molière*, Chelsea House, 2003.

Knutson, Harold C., *The Triumph of Wit: Molière and Restoration Comedy*, Ohio State University Press, 1988.

Leon, Mechele, *Molière, The French Revolution, & the Theatrical Afterlife*, University of Iowa Press, 2009.

McCarthy, Gerry, *The Theatres of Molière*, Routledge, 2002.

Scott, Virginia, *Molière: A Theatrical Life*, Cambridge University Press, 2002.

Other Media

Le Bourgeois Gentilhomme, DVD and VHS, Films for the Humanities and Sciences, 2001.

Modern Molière: Tartuffe, DVD, Insight Media, 2007.

Yiddish Theatre and Its Heirs

In the multicultural heritage of the United States, Jewish Americans are inextricably associated with the development of comedy. The historical and cultural influence of centuries of persecution may have led European Jews to turn to comedy as a kind of coping mechanism.

When European Jews fled to America, they brought this tradition with them. Many went first to New York's Lower East Side, which at the turn of the twentieth century became a Jewish cultural mecca. In thriving neighborhood theaters, plays were performed in Yiddish, the language of most Eastern European Jews. They included not only comedies by great humorists such as Sholem Aleichem but serious plays such as *The Dybbuk.* As the population became more Americanized, Jewish playwrights moved on to English-language venues.

Jewish humor continues to be a vibrant force in American comedy. Wendy Wasserstein (1950–), known for exploring feminist issues, drew frequently on her Jewish-American background in plays such as *The Sisters Rosensweig,* which she infused with Jewish culture and humor even amid serious themes. Neil Simon (1927–), one of modern America's finest comic playwrights, also relies heavily on his Jewish-American heritage. From it have come several semi-autobiographical works, including *Come Blow Your Horn, Biloxi Blues,* and *Lost in Yonkers.* Other Simon comedies, such as *The Odd Couple* and *The Sunshine Boys,* depict characters and relationships that seem straight out of Jewish-American comedy routines of old.

Neil Simon

" . . . Jews . . . laugh at their predicament, and it's what blacks do, too. I do my funniest writing when I'm in a predicament."

—Neil Simon

Molly Picon, one of Yiddish Theatre's great stars, later appeared in the film version of Neil Simon's *Come Blow Your Horn.*

Along with Neil Simon, David Ives is one of the most brilliantly comic playwrights living today. He is well known for the series of imaginative, delightful, and often loony one-act comedies that have been entertaining playgoers for years. *All in the Timing,* which ran over 600 performances during the 1995–96 off-Broadway season, was described by *The New York Times* as ". . . one-act plays that percolate with comic brio." The plays from this collection are said to be the most performed plays in the country (not counting the works of Shakespeare).

Lives of the Saints and *Mere Mortals* are two other popular collections of Ives' plays. David Ives was awarded a Guggenheim Fellowship in playwriting in 1995.

Sholom Aleichem (1859–1916) is the pen name of Sholem Rabinovitsh and relates to the Hebrew phrase shalom aleichem, which means "peace be with you." The Yiddish Art Theatre in New York presented adaptations of his work in their early years. The libretto for the musical *Fiddler on the Roof* drew on his Tevye and the Dairyman stories.

For More Information

Books
Berkowitz, Joel. *Yiddish Theatre: New Approaches,* Littman Library Of Jewish Civilization, 2008.

Simon, Neil, *The Play Goes On: A Memoir,* Simon & Schuster, 2002.

Simon, Neil, *Rewrites: A Memoir,* Simon & Schuster, 1998.

Other Media
The Drama of Creation: Writers on Writing, DVD, Insight Media, 2006.

A Yiddish World Remembered, DVD, Insight Media, 2002.

Backstage Gossip: On Second Thought

Harold Clurman was introduced at a party to Neil Simon's business manager. Clurman told him that he had just written an article called "In Defense of Neil Simon."

"That's wonderful," said the manager, "I look forward to reading it." They went their separate ways, but a little while later, the man came back to ask Clurman:

"I don't quite understand why a man who earns forty thousand dollars a week needs a defense."

from *Broadway Anecdotes* by Peter Hay

Unit Three Review

PREVIEW

1 An actor's "dual role" means that the actor is the character while also being the actor.

2 External traits are: a) posture, c) mode of dress, and e) voice.

3 The fourth wall is the space between the actors on stage and the audience, which the audience looks through as if it were a window to the scene.

4 The five elements of plot structure are conflict, rising action, turning point (or climax), falling action, and resolution (or denouement).

5 Implied information is b) subtext.

6 The protagonist is the person the audience cares about, often a hero, but not always. The antagonist is any force, often a person, that opposes the protagonist.

7 Social drama is serious drama that focuses on the hopes and struggles of ordinary people, while melodrama is much less realistic in its attempt to create excitement and suspense.

8 Lowbrow comedies use outlandish and sometimes vulgar humor to elicit laughs while middlebrow comedies are more refined, sentimental, and plot-based.

9 Characters in a comedy do not have c) a tragic flaw.

PREPARE

10 Answers will vary, but students should support their reasons for choosing character traits or motivation as the most difficult part of analyzing a character.

11 Most students will probably say it was easier to work out the feelings than the actions and easier to work out the actions than the words in the scene.

Unit Three Review

PREVIEW

Examine the following key concepts previewed in Unit Three.

1 Describe an actor's "dual role."

2 Which of the following are a character's external traits?
   a. posture   c. mode of dress   e. voice
   b. spiritual qualities   d. mental characteristics

3 What is the fourth wall?

4 Name the five elements of plot structure.

5 What do we call information that is implied but not stated by a character?
   a. subculture   b. subtext   c. secret script   d. innuendo   e. gossip

6 Explain how a protagonist differs from an antagonist.

7 Compare social drama to melodrama.

8 What is the difference between low and middlebrow comedies?

9 Which of the following is NOT important when engaging an audience in a comedy?
   a. the audience feels superior to your character
   b. the character can be easily identified with
   c. the character has a tragic flaw
   d. something happens when least expected

PREPARE

Assess your response to the preparation process for projects in this unit.

10 In analyzing your character for the high-stakes scenario, was it easier to determine the character's traits or motivation? Explain why.

11 As you prepared a scene from a play, was it easier to work out the character's actions, words, or feelings? Why?

12 How did you go about finding your comic character while preparing for your comic monologue?

13 Was it easier to prepare your dramatic scene or your comic monologue? Why?

14 Did you find it more satisfying to work out a character on paper or on stage?

PRESENT

Analyze the experience of presenting your work to the class.

15 When you performed your high-stakes scenario, could you feel the audience responding to your situation? How were you able to keep the audience interested?

16 Was it difficult to remain in character while presenting a dramatic scene?

17 Which presentation in this unit did you find the most challenging? Why?

18 Which was more satisfying: acting in a scene you wrote yourself or acting in a scene written by another? Explain why.

CRITIQUE

Evaluate how you go about critiquing your work and the work of others.

19 Did you find it easier to evaluate a comedy or a dramatic work? Why?

20 Describe an insightful critique you received from your teacher or classmate and how it helped your performance.

21 What one thing did most performers have trouble with in creating a character, and what could they do to improve their performance?

EXTENSIONS

- Choose a monologue from Unit Eight to perform. As you prepare to present it, synthesize ideas from research, script analysis, and context to create a performance that is believable, authentic, and relevant. That is, the character should be believable, the interpretation and performance should be true to the genre and style, and the presentation should be relevant to the context of the play and to universal human concerns.

- Look at the photograph at the right. Write a list of all the things you know about this character just from her appearance.

Unit Three Review **147**

Resource Binder

Unit Three Test, p. 64

---

12 Answers will vary but should show an understanding of the preparation process in putting together a comic monologue.

13 Most students will probably agree that it was easier to prepare a dramatic scene than to prepare a comic monologue.

14 Answers will vary. Actors will probably say the onstage work was more satisfying; writers will say the writing was more satisfying.

PRESENT

15 Answers will vary, but most students will probably say that they could feel the audience responding, and that they worked harder if they thought they were losing the audience.

16 Some students may admit to difficulty in staying in character; others will have no problem.

17 Answers will vary.

18 Most students will probably say that acting in a scene they wrote themselves was more satisfying.

CRITIQUE

19 Most students will say the comedy was harder to evaluate.

20 Descriptions will vary.

21 For most students, staying fresh and giving the illusion of the first time causes the most problems. Continuing to practice helps.

EXTENSIONS

- Evaluate the performance on its believability, authenticity, and relevance

- She is elderly and probably wealthy. She has a strong sense of herself. She likes to dress with style and flair. She doesn't mind overdoing it a bit. She has good posture and probably lots of confidence. She likes to strike a pose, and so on.

Unit **Four**

The Play: From Vision to Reality

Unit Four will allow students to explore what it takes to get a play from the page to the stage. Projects in this unit will help students analyze and understand the elements of drama, the personnel involved in a typical production, the ways in which directors orchestrate physical action onstage, and the experience of actually attending a play.

Project Preview

Chapter 14 The Playwright
Creating a scenario

Chapter 15 The Director and Producer
Analyzing a play as a director would

Chapter 16 The Cast
Creating a rehearsal schedule

Chapter 17 Blocking
Blocking a scene with more than one actor

Chapter 18 Review a Play
Presenting a talk show about a play you attend and critique

Unit **Four**

The Play: From Vision to Reality

Quotables

Use the quotes below as writing prompts, discussion starters, or for your own enjoyment.

Speak the speech, I pray you, as I pronounced it to you, trippingly on the tongue. But if you mouth it, as many of our players do, I had as lief the town crier spoke my lines . . . .

from *Hamlet* by William Shakespeare

Don't tell me anything's impossible. Let's try it first.

Joseph Papp, Director and Producer

Discussion Questions

The following questions are intended to tap into students' **prior knowledge** and attitudes about the subject matter of the unit.

- Have you ever seen a play or film and thought you might want to write one yourself someday? What was it that inspired you?

- Have you ever been cast in a play or worked as a member of a stage crew? Describe the experience.

- To whom did you report in your capacity as an actor or crew member? What kinds of responsibilities did you have?

- Have you ever been in charge of a group of people? What was it like?

- Have you ever worked as a member of a team? How did that experience make you feel about yourself and the other team members?

- Have you ever had to learn specific physical movements, such as dance steps? Who taught you? What techniques helped you learn the movements?

- Have you ever been to a theatre production? What was the experience like?

Theatre Journal

Write a short two-character scene that evokes an emotional state similar to the one in the photograph.

Visual Cue

The image above shows actor Ben Miles as Thomas Cromwell and Lydia Leonard as Anne Boleyn in the 2014 London adaptation of two books by Hilary Mantel, *Wolf Hall* and *Bring Up the Bodies.* The following prompts can be used to exercise students' **critical viewing skills.**

- What is a possible relationship between the two characters in the picture?

- What do the actors' positions reveal about their emotional states?

- How would you describe to another person the moment portrayed in this photo?

ACTivity Have students improvise three or four lines of a monologue for one of these two characters.

ACTivity Have two students at a time simulate the positions of the people in the photograph. Then ask them to assume positions that show the opposite of those in the photo.

Chapter 14
The Playwright

This chapter introduces students to Aristotle's *Poetics* and the structural components of a play. Students will learn how to create a scenario for an original play.

Objectives

1 to understand the six elements of drama

2 to learn and recognize the structural components of a drama

3 to understand theatre as a collaborative storytelling process

4 to create a dramatic scenario based on standard play structure

Project Specs

Have students pair off to act out the sample scene on p. 154 to solidify their understanding of conflict.

Special Needs Students
Students with visual or developmental impairments may be unable to complete this assignment as written. Be sensitive to these students by allowing them to work with a partner to record their scenarios instead of writing them and presenting them aloud.

Advanced Students
Have students create an entire act from their scenario.

On Your Feet

Some students may confuse what happens in the play (plot) with what the play is about (theme). Help students determine the play's theme, if it seems vague or confusing to them.

---

14 The Playwright

Theatre requires more collaboration than any other art form. The playwright, director, designers, actors, and crew must combine their talents to create a final production. The script is the blueprint for the work. In this chapter you will take on the role of playwright.

Project Specs

Project Description You will write and present a five-to ten-minute scenario for a play—complete with theme, plot, and characters in conflict.

Purpose to understand basic dramatic concepts and the structural elements of a play

Materials a one- or two-page scenario for an original play or The Playwright Activity Sheet your teacher provides

Theatre Terms

archetype
climax or turning point
crisis
diction
epic
exposition
inciting incident
plot
resolution
spectacle
staged readings
theme
workshop

On Your Feet

Think about a play you have seen or read. Ask yourself what happened in the play. (What was the plot?) Now ask yourself what the play was about. (What was the main idea, or theme?) Share the play's plot and theme with your classmates.

Theatre Terms

archetype a character who represents a certain type or idea

climax (or **turning point**) the high point of the play, when a decision is made

crisis an event that occurs just when it seems things could either resolve or worsen

diction the vocal style, dialect, rhythm, and words of the characters

epic a long narrative poem about a hero

exposition the information telling the *who,* *what, when, where,* and *why* of a play

inciting incident the event to which all other actions in the play can be traced

plot the story of the play

resolution the end of the story when the conflict is resolved

spectacle everything the audience sees

staged readings readings that are roughly blocked

theme the underlying meaning of a play

workshop to discuss, analyze, and revise a play in collaboration with others

Writing a Drama

Theatre is as old as humankind itself. The earliest forms of theatre emerged from religion and ritual. Ancient people used to act out the success of a hunt or a harvest as well as rituals having to do with life events such as birth, coming of age, and death. Many of these accounts were handed down orally and didn't achieve written form until around 500 B.C., the beginning of the classical age of Greek drama.

The Greeks developed a written body of work, including the **epic** (a long narrative poem that told the story of legendary heroes and their travels and exploits), all of which originated with the oral tradition. The Greeks then developed ways of dramatizing some of these stories for performance. The great

philosopher Aristotle (384–322 B.C.) was one of the first to analyze these plays. From watching and reading, Aristotle came up with six basic elements of drama, which he defined in a text called the *Poetics*. These elements still serve as guideposts for playwrights today.

Aristotle's Elements of Drama

Plot The **plot** is the story of the play, or the actions of the main character, called the *protagonist*, as he or she comes in conflict with an opposing force. The actions of a protagonist while dealing with this force are what illuminate the play's theme.

Character According to Aristotle, characters should be good, believable people who accurately reflect their circumstances in life and who act consistently.

Diction The language, or the **diction** as Aristotle called it, includes the style, dialect, rhythm, and the actual words of the characters.

Thought This is the central idea the playwright is exploring, which embodies a truth about life. Today, this is usually referred to as the **theme**.

American playwright Arthur Miller shares his ideas about the theatre.

Resource Binder

- The Playwright Activity Sheet, p. 70
- Aristotle's Elements of Drama Worksheet, p. 71
- Critique Sheet: Scenario for a Play, p. 72
- Playwright Test, p. 73

Handbook Connections
pages 575–576

To Have on Hand

- Photos of and biographical information on great American playwrights, directors, and producers
- A full rehearsal schedule from a professional or community theatre
- Flash cards with the elements of drama listed on one side and the definitions on the other, which can be used by students to quiz one another
- A list of local or regional theatres students might attend

Writing a Drama

Students might be interested to know that one of the early Greek playwrights, **Sophocles** (496–406 B.C.), began his career as an actor and performed in many of his own plays. However, his voice was relatively weak, and eventually he gave up acting to focus on playwriting and other artistic pursuits. His most famous works, *Oedipus the King, Antigone,* and *Electra,* are still performed today.

Aristotle's Elements of Drama

Although the protagonist is the play's main character, he or she need not be a heroic or admirable person. Remind students that, personality aside, the protagonist is the character who changes, and is changed by, the course of the play's action because of the way he or she deals with the conflict.

Show, Don't Tell With a very capable student, read a two-person scene from *Glengarry Glen Ross* by David Mamet for the students and ask them to think about the diction—including Mamet's staccato style, the overlapping rhythm of the interchange, and the precise word choices. You may want to choose a passage that is free of language that might be offensive to some students.

ACTivity Have students discuss plays they have read or seen in which the language seemed unusual or particularly effective. Have them discuss the rhythm, dialect, and word choices of the play.

Visual Cue

Discuss with students the photograph of Arthur Miller.

- What special insights might the playwright bring to the rehearsal process?
- As a cast member, what sorts of questions might you ask of the playwright?
- As an actor, would you appreciate the playwright being on hand during play rehearsal? Explain.

The spectacle of the play *Camino Reál* is a treat for the eyes.

Sound Everything the audience hears in the play—from the words to the music to the sound effects—is included in the sound.

Spectacle Everything the audience sees—including scenery, costuming, dance, pantomime, and swordplay— is included in the **spectacle.**

Note that the first four elements are also found in other literary forms, such as novels and short stories. The last two elements, however, are unique to the theatre.

Why Is It Called a Play?

The answer is simple. A play is exactly that—an event carried out with the spontaneity, intense concentration, and commitment of children at play.

But *writing* a play requires planning the entire course of action—what happens and why. The play will involve a central character who becomes involved in a conflict. As in other literary genres, a

play's conflict and the progress of the central character can include an **archetype** or two—a character who represents a certain type. An archetype can symbolize universal ideas about human behavior.

There are lots of different ways to write a play. But every playwright must discover a plot (characters in conflict); choose a central course of action that illuminates the theme; select diction appropriate to the desired time period and style; and use sound, scenery, and spectacle to bring the play to vibrant life.

152 Unit Four The Play: From Vision to Reality

Backstage Gossip: August Wilson Interviews Himself

In May 2003 August Wilson, a preeminent American playwright and two-time Pulitzer Prize winner, took to the Seattle Repertory Theatre stage to present a one-man show called *How I Learned What I Learned*. In this autobiographical work, Wilson more or less interviewed himself, presenting an in-depth look at his past and present and his thoughts on everything from race to family to music.

You might want to have your students use a self-interview process to find elements of their own lives on which to base a play.

PREPARE

Gather Ideas for Your Scenario

Many playwrights claim that they do not choose what to write about—instead, they say, ideas and subject matter choose them! You may find the same thing yourself. However, to jump-start your process, try the following writing exercises to develop an idea for a play.

1 **Find a Subject.** Think of a starting point for your play—a challenging question, an interesting character, or a problem to solve—and write it at the top of a sheet of paper. You may take your idea from a newspaper article, a person you know, an incident from your own life, a story you heard, and so on. Once you have chosen your starting point, take five to ten minutes to freewrite about everything you can think of that might be included in the play. For example, if your idea has to do with a robbery, ask and answer questions for yourself about the perpetrators, the victims, the bystanders, and so on. Where did the robbery take place? Why? What time of year? What time of day? How might personal circumstances drive a person to commit a robbery? What are the consequences of such an action—both legally and morally? Be specific, and include every detail and question you think you might be able to use later.

2 **Create a Character.** Using the information you've created about the subject, think of a character to represent a part of the idea. In the example of the robbery, you might choose the robber, the victim, a relative of either of these, a bystander, and so on. Take five minutes to write a short monologue from this character's point of view. This should open up other areas of thought. It may lead you in any number of directions. For example, you may decide that your play is about how witnessing a crime affects a bystander's life. Or you might decide that it's about the events that led up to the robbery or made it seem necessary. You can write a play about almost anything, as long as your characters and your situation are specific and meaningful to you.

3 **Develop a Conflict.** This is a simple exercise based on the same principles used in many improvisations. Your job here is to let the audience know the "Ws." *Who* is in the scene? *Where* are they? *What* are they doing? The *What* should be the conflict, which creates a problem to be solved. Remember that conflict results when one character's objective, or goal, bumps into an obstacle.

PREPARE

Gather Ideas for Your Scenario

Before students begin to write about their ideas for a play, share with them that many playwriting teachers advocate writing in groups. They claim that the energy generated by a room full of writers can stimulate the entire group's process even though no words are exchanged. After your students have written for the allotted time, discuss whether anyone felt the group energy as they worked.

Find a Subject. If students are having trouble finding a subject, have them look through current newspapers or back over their journals for ideas.

Create a Character. Have students close their eyes and try to visualize their characters. Then ask them to write a short description of the character.

Develop a Conflict. To help them develop a conflict, ask students to think about the kinds of situations this particular character would get into. What problems might result for the character, his or her family, or society as a whole?

ACTivity Assign students a situation for their character, such as waiting for a bus, sitting at a counter in a diner, or attending a family reunion. Each student improvises a short scene in which his or her character assesses what is happening in the situation. This short monologue can help to bring out interesting character traits.

From the Field: The Passive Playwright

In his book *The Dramatist's Toolkit*, playwright Jeffrey Sweet claims that autobiographical characters—those based upon the writer's own life—tend to be the most passive characters in a play. They often comment wryly or stand off to the side of the action rather than taking an active role in the play's conflict.

Remind students that drama is based on conflict. If they put themselves into their own play, they need to explore what that character wants within the context of the scene.

Sample Scene

Review with students that a character's *objective* is his or her *goal*—the thing this character wants more than anything else. The *obstacle* is a person or situation that gets in the way of the character's objective and does everything possible to thwart it. In the sample scene, Ray's objective is to get the car keys from Molly. Molly's refusal is Ray's obstacle.

ACTivity **Beginning Students**

Have pairs of students read through the sample scene. Encourage them to make strong vocal and physical choices. Then allow them to discuss their reasons for making the choices they did.

ACTivity **Advanced Students**

Most students will interpret the scene as one in which Molly tries to help her son Ray. Ask students to think about the scene in another way. What if Molly's motivations weren't quite so selfless? Have them play the scene using this new interpretation.

The Language of
THEATRE

Encourage students to monitor their understanding of spoken language in the classroom.

- Tell students to notice how much they understand when they listen to your instructions or when they interact with classmates. Encourage them to ask for clarification as needed.
- When providing instruction, pause frequently to allow students time to monitor their level of understanding and ask for repetition or clarification as needed.
- Invite students to briefly summarize instructions and mirror back classmates' language ("What I hear you saying is . . .") to monitor whether they have understood what they heard.
- Encourage students to continue to monitor their understanding of spoken English, especially when new concepts and vocabulary are used in the classroom.

Sample Scene
(A small, cluttered kitchen [where]. MOLLY [who] sits at the table clipping coupons. RAY [who] enters suddenly from outside. He has a cut on his forehead and is very agitated.)

RAY. Ma, I gotta use the car *[what/objective].*

MOLLY. Raymond.

RAY. I got no time to talk, Ma. Give me the keys.

MOLLY. What's happened?

RAY. Listen, I gotta get out of town for a couple days *[what/objective].* I'll call you. Keys?

(A silence. RAY shifts uncomfortably under his mother's steady gaze.)

MOLLY. You're not taking my car. You're not going anywhere till you tell me what's going on here, Raymond Joseph *[what/obstacle].*

(A siren sounds in the distance.)

RAY. You want me to go to jail?! Is that it?

MOLLY. No.

RAY. Then give me the keys.

(He spies the keys on the table and makes a grab for them. MOLLY snatches them away and puts them in her pocket.) [what/obstacle]

MOLLY. Talk to me, Raymond . . . You know I am trying to help you. Please . . .

Read the sample scene above. In a small amount of space, it clearly outlines the situation, reveals character, and begins to move the plot along. Good dialogue accomplishes all of the following purposes:

- it reveals character motivation
- it advances the plot
- it provides **exposition,** information so the audience knows what's going on (see page 156)
- it reveals theme

Create a one- to two-page scene of your own using the subject, main character, and conflict you devised in the three steps just discussed on page 153. Then add a second or third character. Make sure that your situation is driven by conflict between the characters or between a character and some obstacle. Write your dialogue so that it reveals character motivation, provides exposition, advances the plot, and helps the audience understand the theme.

From the Field: Points for Participation

I give my students ten points each day for participation. They learn that these points average in to have a significant impact on their grades. This ensures student involvement in the day's activities.

Tanya Dean Hoyle, Drama Teacher, Tuscumbia, AL

Think About a Scenario

Where will your play go from here? That depends on the statement you are trying to make and the story you want to tell. Now that you have a basic situation, two or more characters, and the conflict or obstacles they must face, you are ready to think about a whole play that might stem from them.

You and a partner were asked to create a scenario for your project in Chapter 6, Movement. For the project in this unit, you will create a more detailed scenario that applies Aristotle's elements of drama. First, you will need to develop the theme. Based on the example of a robbery given previously, the theme might be that crime doesn't pay. Or it might be that desperate situations call for desperate solutions. It could be both of these—and more. Above all, the theme you choose should contain ideas that you care about and that interest you.

Then you must decide who your characters are and what they are trying to do in the play. No matter what your theme is, you must tell a story in which the characters are believable or interesting enough to draw the audience into the play.

As you write your scenario, think about all of the elements on the following page.

You will need a plot, the beginning of which you have already created while developing the play's conflicts. What happens next? What happens after that?

Your scenario must reflect dramatic structure (see next page) by showing that the action arises logically from the conflict and leads to a crisis and climax. You have probably discovered the characters' ways of speaking while exploring the theme, the characters themselves, and their conflicts. Also keep in mind the spectacle and sound of your play— in other words, what it will look and sound like.

Keeping all these principles in mind will help you create, write, and refine a scenario that structures the progression of your idea for a play. In Chapter 11, you learned about play structure from the perspective of an actor working on character development. Now we will add a few more elements and look at the play from the perspective of the playwright creating a new work.

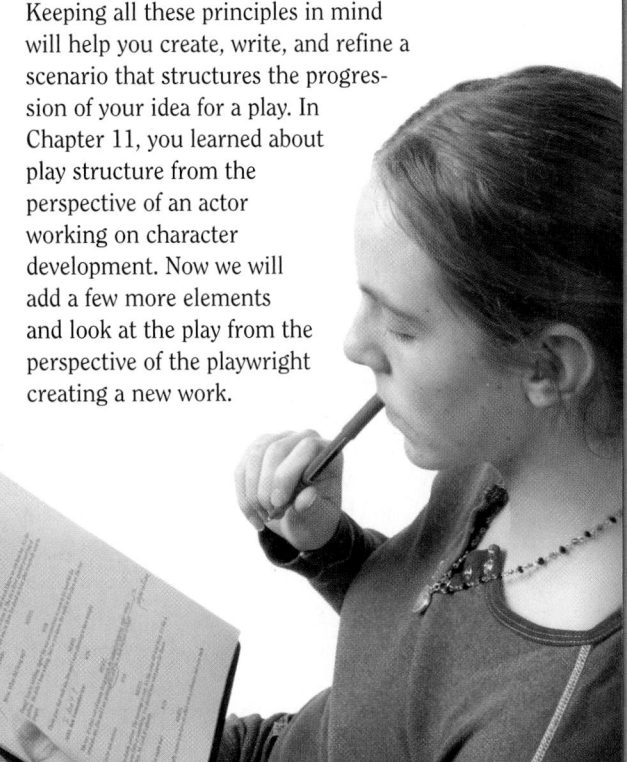

Think About a Scenario

Ask students to think about how to categorize the play they would like to write. Is it

- personal?
- political?
- sociological?
- comic?
- tragic?

ACTivity Have students write a brief paragraph that reveals the thematic statement they want their play to make.

Show, Don't Tell On the board, draw a plot structure diagram like the one on page 157 labeled *Exposition, Inciting Incident, Rising Action, Crisis, Climax, Falling Action,* and *Resolution.* Have students take turns coming to the board and plotting each of the seven structural elements of a play with which they are all familiar. Then create a flowchart together that tells in sentence form each of these important elements of the play.

ACTivity Have students create flowcharts that depict the important elements they plan for their plays using the seven structural components you have listed on the chalkboard (a complete list is also available on page 156).

From the Field: To Right (and Write) a Wrong

Lisa Loomer, discussing her play *The Waiting Room,* once said: "I definitely write from a need to try, in my own two hours, to right a wrong. My little play is inconsequential in terms of whether or not we have health care, but it may affect the way people who see the play think about the issue."

Have students use the sample script from page 154 and the Plot Structure diagram on page 157 to continue plotting out the short scenario involving Molly and Ray. Students may come up with ideas similar to the ones below.

1 **Exposition:** Ray has committed armed robbery. Though no one was hurt, the police are after him.

2 **Inciting Incident:** He goes to see his mother, who refuses to give him the keys to her car.

3 **Rising Action:** The police arrive at the door and Ray hides.

4 **Crisis:** The police believe Molly is withholding information about Ray and they threaten to take her down to the station for questioning.

5 **Climax:** Ray enters with a gun. It turns out to be a squirt gun. His mother points this out and Ray surrenders to the police.

6 **Falling Action:** The police take Ray away in handcuffs.

7 **Resolution:** Molly puts on her coat and hat calling, "Don't worry, Ray. I'm coming too. You know I want to help you."

Encourage students to be imaginative in getting to the resolution. Remind them that the characters do not have to be heroic or even good-hearted. Above all the characters must work hard to fulfill their objectives. Whether they accomplish these objectives or not is another matter.

Write Your Scenario

Remind students that the rules of playwriting structure can be applied to a great many, but not all, plays.

1 **Exposition** This is the setup of the play. You learned about the three Ws of exposition previously (Who, Where, and What), and it is important that as a playwright you have a clear idea what your characters' lives were all about before the events of your play begin. In the sample scene on page 154, the exposition informs us that Molly is Ray's mother. The scene takes place in her house. It also allows us to see that Ray may have committed a crime. This is not stated, but it is strongly implied by the playwright's dialogue and by the actions created in the stage directions for Ray.

2 **Inciting Incident** The event that sets the action on its course is called the **inciting incident.** In the example, the inciting incident is Molly's refusal to give Ray her car keys. Here is where the conflict begins. The playwright must be sure that this conflict has enough dramatic impetus to carry the scene forward, because the rest of the play will spin out from it.

3 **Rising Action** The playwright must carefully build the dramatic tension as characters encounter obstacles to their goals. It is important for the playwright to keep the drama tight and to give the characters ways to help the audience understand how they rationalize their feelings and actions.

4 **Crisis** As the play continues, the playwright must create an event that

occurs just at the moment when it seems things could either resolve or get much worse. This is the **crisis.** The playwright must be sure not to infuse in the crisis too much emotional intensity, as this could make the climax to follow seem anticlimactic.

5 **Climax** In the **climax,** which is the high point of the play, the playwright creates a situation in which the protagonist makes an irrevocable decision. The playwright must strive to convince the audience that this highly emotional event will either result in victory or in some way bring an end to the conflict. The climax is also called the *turning point.*

6 **Falling Action** The events after the climax must seem logical and true to the play. This is where the playwright wraps up any loose ends and moves toward the outcome of the play.

7 **Resolution** The end of the story, in which the conflicts are resolved, is called the **resolution.** It takes a light touch in terms of writing. At this point, the playwright must be sure that the audience can see clearly the result of the choice or action of the protagonist.

Write Your Scenario
You are now ready to write your scenario. Go back to your seed idea, and then begin to make choices. There is

Quotable
Use the quote below as a prompt, discussion starter, or for your own enjoyment.

Usually you can't write ten lines without someone wanting something. Even if you don't know it.

Lanford Wilson, Playwrigh

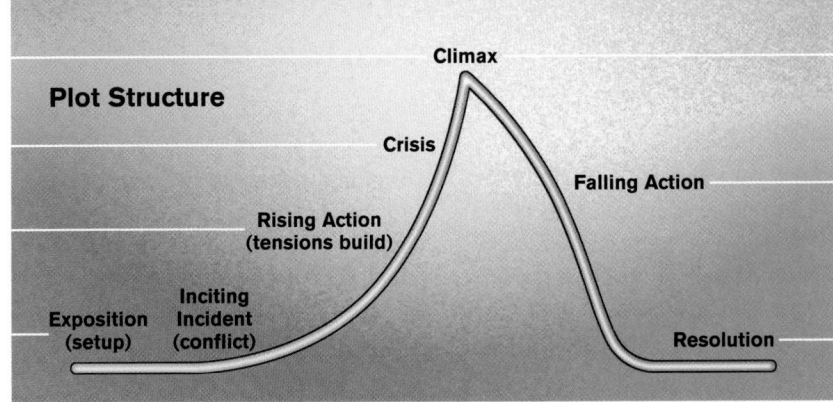

Plot Structure

Climax

Crisis

Falling Action

Rising Action
(tensions build)

Inciting
Incident
(conflict)

Exposition
(setup)

Resolution

Your scenario should include these plot elements. Be aware that not all plays contain all elements.

a benefit to restricting yourself by making strong choices. Each time you make a decision about the play, you rid yourself of other elements that no longer need your focus. For example, once you decide that your play takes place in a kitchen, you need no longer worry about other scenic considerations. If your play features only two characters, you know who's going to be doing the talking and when. Once you have boxed in the essential ideas of the play, you have effectively boxed out other nonessential ideas—you've given your play a direction. Your goal is to set up the play's structure so effectively that it will have a logical, effective, and satisfying ending—the seeds of which were planted in the beginning.

You will need to make the following choices:

- **Who is in the play?**
- **Where does it take place?**
- **Who is the protagonist?**
- **Who or what is the antagonistic force?**

- **Where do these two meet?** (the inciting incident)
- **What does the protagonist decide to do** about it?
- **What is the response of the antagonistic force?**
- **What is the critical choice or action of the protagonist** that brings the play to its logical conclusion?
- **What happens after the play ends?** (This should be clear from what happens within the play.)

Your scenario should be a scene-by-scene telling of the story in narrative form. Be sure to come up with a title.

When you have completed your writing, exchange your scenario with a classmate. Discuss each other's work in terms of the progression of the story and the clarity of the theme. Make any necessary changes and create a clean copy.

Practice reading your scenario aloud, and time yourself to be sure it is between five and ten minutes long.

In such great plays as Samuel Beckett's *Waiting for Godot* and Eugene Ionesco's absurdist classic *The Bald Soprano,* there are no clear-cut answers to the question of who is the protagonist and who or what is the antagonistic force. Harold Pinter rose to fame by eliminating any semblance of exposition in such plays as *The Caretaker* and *The Birthday Party.* It is very difficult to tell the players without exposition; we find it hard to tell the villains from the heroes in these plays. This was one of the points Pinter probably wanted to make.

Remind students that as in most endeavors, it is important to *know* the rules before making the decision to diverge from them.

ACTivity Have pairs of students exchange their scenarios while the work is still evolving. Have them determine how well the scenario follows the elements of good plot structure. Remind students that collaboration should consist of constructive feedback presented in a positive manner. They should respond to the work they read, not the work they would like to have written themselves or the work they feel should have been written.

Vocabulary Enhancement

The resolution is also referred to as the *denouement* (day new MAH), which comes from a French word meaning "to untie."

Backstage Gossip: Earache

When Mr. Boaden had read his unsuccessful drama *Aurelio and Miranda* in the green room, he observed that he knew nothing so terrible as reading a piece before such a critical audience. The actress Mrs. Powell who was present said she knew one thing much more terrible. "What can that be?" demanded the author. "To be obliged," said she, "to sit and hear it."

from *Theatrical Anecdotes* by Peter Hay

PRESENT

Share Your Drama Scenario

Help students understand that they can use their voices to build excitement as they share their scenarios. They may wish to review some of the techniques discussed in Chapter 8, Voice Production and Articulation.

ACTivity Many larger communities have theatre companies that workshop new plays. Call your local theatre. You may be able to set up a time for your students to see a staged reading. Or you might be able to obtain a copy of a script in development. Workshops and readings are very different from productions and would provide students with an entirely different view of the playwriting process.

CRITIQUE

Evaluate a Classmate's Scenario

Hand out the Critique Sheet for this project or have students use their own paper. Quickly go over the elements to look for in a strong scenario and leave the plot structure diagram on the chalkboard.

After you have reviewed student critiques, discuss with the subjects of the evaluations any recurrent suggestions for improvement.

PRESENT

Share Your Drama Scenario

When your name is called, hand in a copy of your scenario or the Activity Sheet and walk to the playing area. As always, take a moment to gather yourself by drawing a deep relaxing breath before you begin.

Begin by telling the audience the title of your play. Then read through your scenario. Rhythm and pacing are important when you're reading aloud. Avoid speaking in a monotone! Remember that you are telling a story. Vocally emphasize the most important or interesting parts of that story. It's important to establish a connection with the audience, so make eye contact with your listeners periodically.

When you have finished, thank your audience, and return to your seat.

CRITIQUE

Evaluate a Classmate's Scenario

Choose one of the scenarios presented in class and evaluate it on a scale of 1 to 5, with 5 being "outstanding" and 1 being "needs much improvement." Ask yourself the questions below to help focus your evaluation.

- What details did the playwright use to make the plot clear?

- How would you describe the theme (or themes) of the play?

- What was the conflict, and was it strong enough?

- What changes to the play would you suggest based on this scenario?

- In what way did the speaker's manner of presentation impact your appreciation of the scenario?

Write a paragraph that details your evaluation and explains the rating you gave. After receiving feedback on your own scenario, write a paragraph summarizing your classmate's response, commenting on each point made. Explain how you can use this constructive criticism in your future work.

Quotable

When you go to the theatre you want to know who the main character is, and you want to be able to see what they want, see what's against them, and see whether they get it or not. Then you want to go home.

Marsha Norman, Playwright

Spotlight on

Collaboration

Unlike the novelist or the poet—who can work alone—playwrights are dependent upon the artistic vision of others to bring their work to life. Collaboration is a vital aspect of a playwright's job. First-time playwrights should seek out directors who enjoy working on new plays and actors who are eager to create a role for the very first time. These collaborators can often help the playwright create more vibrant and believable scenes. Above all, plays are meant to be seen and heard. They can be developed and refined through private and public readings and through productions.

"The Eugene O'Neill Center National Playwrights Conference is dedicated to the development of new work for the theatre . . . ." So begins the mission statement of one of the most prestigious theatre organizations in the United States. Founded in 1964, the Eugene O'Neill Theater Center has set a high standard for new play development. Named after one of America's greatest playwrights, the O'Neill Center is a haven where playwrights can develop their craft free from the pressures of the marketplace. It offers many different programs, but perhaps the most famous is the annual summer workshop known as the National Playwrights Conference. Each year, playwrights from all over the country compete for a workshop slot there. Located in Waterford, Connecticut, the conference typically receives 650 play submissions annually. Of these, only 12 to 15 are selected for participation. Each selected play is assigned a director and a group of actors. Together with the playwright, these artists **workshop** the play—discussing, analyzing, and reading it aloud many times over the course of one month. The playwright has the opportunity to revise and rewrite the play. The process, culminating in two public **staged readings,** is designed to take a good script and make it stronger and more producible.

Over the years, many of the country's most distinguished writers have developed their plays at the O'Neill—including John Guare, August Wilson (see the Master of the Craft on page 161), Edwin Sanchez, and Kia Corthron.

Three artists collaborate on a play at the Eugene O'Neill Theater Center.

Spotlight on

Collaboration In addition to the O'Neill Theatre Center, there are several other organizations around the country devoted to new-play development. Here are just a few of them:

- Humana Festival of New American Plays, Actors Theatre of Louisville, KY (actorstheatre.org)

- The Playwrights' Center, Minneapolis, MN (pwcenter.org)

- New Dramatists, New York, NY (newdramatists.org)

- Chicago Dramatists, Chicago, IL (chicagodramatists.org)

- Sundance Institute Theatre Program, Sundance, UT (*www.sundance.org/programs/theatre*)

Visit these Web sites yourself and encourage students to visit them as well to find out more about the collaborative process of each organization.

Vocabulary Enhancement

Tell students that staged readings and workshops fall under the general heading of *development,* the process through which many new plays must go before they are deemed ready for full production.

Visual Cue

The following prompts can be used to help students exercise **critical viewing skills.**

- What do you think the interpersonal dynamic is like among these three artists?

- Which one do you think is the playwright? What makes you think so?

- If you had to describe this scene using only one sentence, what would you say?

The Playwright Test

The test for this chapter is available in blackline master form in the Resource Binder, page 73.

For More Information

Books

Here are some excellent text resources on playwriting fundamentals:

Dunne, Will, *The Dramatic Writer's Companion: Tools to Develop Characters, Cause Scenes, and Build Stories*, University of Chicago Press, 2009.

Garrison, Gary, *Perfect 10: Writing and Producing the 10-Minute Play*, Heinemann, 2001.

Hatcher, Jeffrey, *The Art and Craft of Playwrighting*, Heinemann, 2001.

McLaughlin, Buzz, *The Playwright's Process: Learning the Craft from Today's Leading Dramatists*, Back Stage Books, 1997.

Sweet, Jeffrey, *Solving Your Script: Tools and Techniques for the Playwright*, Heinemann, 2001.

Sweet, Jeffrey, *The Dramatist's Toolkit: The Craft of the Working Playwright*, Heinemann, 1993.

Other Media

Links to playwriting opportunities for young people can be found at:

www.aate.com

www.youngplaywrights.org

Dramatists Play Service, Inc. recommends The 52nd Street Project Kid Theatre Kit. Visit www.dramatists.com or call (212) 683-8960 for information.

Theatre Journal

Use the following as an additional or substitute prompt.

Think about the jobs in theatre production that do not involve acting, and choose one that interests you. Think about why this position interests you, and write about it in your journal.

Additional Projects

1 Write a one-act play from the scenario you created. When you have finished it, collaborate with a small group of classmates to refine and act out the script. Check to be sure it has these characteristics:

- It reflects dramatic structure (see pages 156-157).

- It conveys meaning to the audience through its dramatic structure and believable characters.

- The dialogue reveals character motivation, advances the plot, provides exposition, and reveals theme.

You may wish to perform your new play for the entire class.

2 Read a full-length play and then write a two-page scenario for it. Include a statement of the play's style and genre, theme, a summary of its plot and conflict, and brief sketches of each character describing their intellectual, emotional, physical, and social dimensions.

3 Put on a playreading for your classmates. You can read something you've written or select a published work. Perform the play as a sit-down reading. Cast the reading and make sure you have someone to read the stage directions.

4 If you have written a play, enter it in a playwriting contest. You can find a wealth of information about writing contests on the Internet. You might start with the Young Playwrights Inc.'s National Playwriting Contest, begun by Stephen Sondheim in 1981.

5 Suppose your community parks and recreation department offers workshops in acting, set design and construction, lighting, and costumes, but not on playwriting. Write a proposal for such a workshop to get them to fund it. In your proposal, define the role of all artistic partners, including playwrights, so their contribution to a dramatic production is clearly appreciated.

6 Read about playwrights on pages 162–163 and review the information on pages 40–41, 110–111, and 144–145 as well. With a partner, create spreadsheets, timelines, or tables about cultural heritage in theatre. One item should show key figures, works, and trends in world drama and theatre. A second should show key figures, works, and trends in the multicultural heritage of United States drama and theatre.

7 Read *The Drummer* by Athol Fugard, which can be found in Unit Eight. Re-create this simple pantomime as a two-character scene with dialogue that motivates the action.

8 **Theatre Journal** As a playwright, you are a student of human nature—and what better human can you practice on than yourself? Spend some time analyzing an incident from your life. Perhaps it was a comment someone made to you that bothered or confused you. Maybe you did something that made you proud or that you regret. In your journal, write about the incident until you feel that you have a handle on why it happened and what it means to you.

Substitute Teacher Activities

Here are ideas for the substitute teacher when you are out of the classroom.

- Assign the Aristotle's Elements of Drama Worksheet on page 71 of the Resource Binder.

- Assign one or more additional projects on this page.

- Teach the Script on pages 575–576 of the Student Handbook.

- **Have a Class Discussion About Play Structure** by comparing theatre and film. Ask students which aspects of playwriting structure are common to both plays and movies. Create a Venn diagram illustrating the similarities and differences.

Spotlight on

Collaboration

Unlike the novelist or the poet—who can work alone—playwrights are dependent upon the artistic vision of others to bring their work to life. Collaboration is a vital aspect of a playwright's job. First-time playwrights should seek out directors who enjoy working on new plays and actors who are eager to create a role for the very first time. These collaborators can often help the playwright create more vibrant and believable scenes. Above all, plays are meant to be seen and heard. They can be developed and refined through private and public readings and through productions.

"The Eugene O'Neill Center National Playwrights Conference is dedicated to the development of new work for the theatre . . . ." So begins the mission statement of one of the most prestigious theatre organizations in the United States. Founded in 1964, the Eugene O'Neill Theater Center has set a high standard for new play development. Named after one of America's greatest playwrights, the O'Neill Center is a haven where playwrights can develop their craft free from the pressures of the marketplace. It offers many different programs, but perhaps the most famous is the annual summer workshop known as the National Playwrights Conference. Each year, playwrights from all over the country compete for a workshop slot there. Located in Waterford, Connecticut, the conference typically receives 650 play submissions annually. Of these, only 12 to 15 are selected for participation. Each selected play is assigned a director and a group of actors. Together with the playwright, these artists **workshop** the play—discussing, analyzing, and reading it aloud many times over the course of one month. The playwright has the opportunity to revise and rewrite the play. The process, culminating in two public **staged readings,** is designed to take a good script and make it stronger and more producible.

Over the years, many of the country's most distinguished writers have developed their plays at the O'Neill—including John Guare, August Wilson (see the Master of the Craft on page 161), Edwin Sanchez, and Kia Corthron.

Three artists collaborate on a play at the Eugene O'Neill Theater Center.

Spotlight on

Collaboration In addition to the O'Neill Theatre Center, there are several other organizations around the country devoted to new-play development. Here are just a few of them:

- Humana Festival of New American Plays, Actors Theatre of Louisville, KY (actorstheatre.org)

- The Playwrights' Center, Minneapolis, MN (pwcenter.org)

- New Dramatists, New York, NY (newdramatists.org)

- Chicago Dramatists, Chicago, IL (chicagodramatists.org)

- Sundance Institute Theatre Program, Sundance, UT (*www.sundance.org/programs/ theatre*)

Visit these Web sites yourself and encourage students to visit them as well to find out more about the collaborative process of each organization.

Vocabulary Enhancement

Tell students that staged readings and workshops fall under the general heading of *development,* the process through which many new plays must go before they are deemed ready for full production.

Visual Cue

The following prompts can be used to help students exercise **critical viewing skills.**

- What do you think the interpersonal dynamic is like among these three artists?

- Which one do you think is the playwright? What makes you think so?

- If you had to describe this scene using only one sentence, what would you say?

The Playwright Test

The test for this chapter is available in blackline master form in the Resource Binder, page 73.

For More Information

Books
Here are some excellent text resources on playwriting fundamentals:

Dunne, Will, *The Dramatic Writer's Companion: Tools to Develop Characters, Cause Scenes, and Build Stories*, University of Chicago Press, 2009.

Garrison, Gary, *Perfect 10: Writing and Producing the 10-Minute Play*, Heinemann, 2001.

Hatcher, Jeffrey, *The Art and Craft of Playwrighting*, Heinemann, 2001.

McLaughlin, Buzz, *The Playwright's Process: Learning the Craft from Today's Leading Dramatists*, Back Stage Books, 1997.

Sweet, Jeffrey, *Solving Your Script: Tools and Techniques for the Playwright*, Heinemann, 2001.

Sweet, Jeffrey, *The Dramatist's Toolkit: The Craft of the Working Playwright*, Heinemann, 1993.

Other Media
Links to playwriting opportunities for young people can be found at:

www.aate.com

www.youngplaywrights.org

Dramatists Play Service, Inc. recommends The 52nd Street Project Kid Theatre Kit. Visit www.dramatists.com or call (212) 683-8960 for information.

Theatre Journal

Use the following as an additional or substitute prompt.

Think about the jobs in theatre production that do not involve acting, and choose one that interests you. Think about why this position interests you, and write about it in your journal.

Additional Projects

1 Write a one-act play from the scenario you created. When you have finished it, collaborate with a small group of classmates to refine and act out the script. Check to be sure it has these characteristics:

- It reflects dramatic structure (see pages 156-157).

- It conveys meaning to the audience through its dramatic structure and believable characters.

- The dialogue reveals character motivation, advances the plot, provides exposition, and reveals theme.

  You may wish to perform your new play for the entire class.

2 Read a full-length play and then write a two-page scenario for it. Include a statement of the play's style and genre, theme, a summary of its plot and conflict, and brief sketches of each character describing their intellectual, emotional, physical, and social dimensions.

3 Put on a playreading for your classmates. You can read something you've written or select a published work. Perform the play as a sit-down reading. Cast the reading and make sure you have someone to read the stage directions.

4 If you have written a play, enter it in a playwriting contest. You can find a wealth of information about writing contests on the Internet. You might start with the Young Playwrights Inc.'s National Playwriting Contest, begun by Stephen Sondheim in 1981.

5 Suppose your community parks and recreation department offers workshops in acting, set design and construction, lighting, and costumes, but not on playwriting. Write a proposal for such a workshop to get them to fund it. In your proposal, define the role of all artistic partners, including playwrights, so their contribution to a dramatic production is clearly appreciated.

6 Read about playwrights on pages 162–163 and review the information on pages 40–41, 110–111, and 144–145 as well. With a partner, create spreadsheets, timelines, or tables about cultural heritage in theatre. One item should show key figures, works, and trends in world drama and theatre. A second should show key figures, works, and trends in the multicultural heritage of United States drama and theatre.

7 Read *The Drummer* by Athol Fugard, which can be found in Unit Eight. Re-create this simple pantomime as a two-character scene with dialogue that motivates the action.

8 **Theatre Journal** As a playwright, you are a student of human nature—and what better human can you practice on than yourself? Spend some time analyzing an incident from your life. Perhaps it was a comment someone made to you that bothered or confused you. Maybe you did something that made you proud or that you regret. In your journal, write about the incident until you feel that you have a handle on why it happened and what it means to you.

Substitute Teacher Activities

Here are ideas for the substitute teacher when you are out of the classroom.

- Assign the Aristotle's Elements of Drama Worksheet on page 71 of the Resource Binder.

- Assign one or more additional projects on this page.

- Teach the Script on pages 575–576 of the Student Handbook.

- **Have a Class Discussion About Play Structure** by comparing theatre and film. Ask students which aspects of playwriting structure are common to both plays and movies. Create a Venn diagram illustrating the similarities and differences.

Master of the Craft

August Wilson: Master Playwright

Frederick August Kittel was born in Pittsburgh, Pennsylvania, in 1945. At an early age, he knew he wanted to be a poet. He dropped out of school in the tenth grade but went on to educate himself—at the library and on the street. His father essentially abandoned the family, and in 1965 the young August changed his last name to Wilson—his mother's maiden name.

In 1978, Wilson took a job in St. Paul, writing scripts for the Science Museum of Minnesota. The move put him in close proximity to The Playwrights' Center, a Minneapolis-based play development organization, which granted Wilson a fellowship in 1980. In 1982, Wilson's play *Ma Rainey's Black Bottom* was selected for participation in the O'Neill

Theater Center's National Playwrights Conference. There Wilson met the center's artistic director, Lloyd Richards. It was a fruitful alliance. Richards went on to direct six of Wilson's plays on Broadway.

In an interview with the *New York Times* in 1984, Wilson said, "My generation of blacks knew very little about the past of our parents. They shielded us from the indignities they suffered." Wilson began to throw light on that shadowy past with an ambitious series of plays, each set in a different decade of the 20th century and focused specifically on black issues.

Fences, Joe Turner's Come and Gone, Two Trains Running, and *Seven Guitars* are some of these plays.

His roots as a poet are evident in each of Wilson's dramas. His work is explosive and fiercely beautiful—the language is alive and real, yet lyrical. In a 1990 review of *The Piano Lesson, New York Post* critic Clive Barnes stated, "This is a play in which to lose yourself—to give yourself up . . . to August Wilson's thoughts, humors, and thrills, always talking the same language of humanity."

Wilson died in 2005.

Pulitzer Prize-winner August Wilson

Backstage Gossip: Wilson Versus Brustein

In 1997 a feud sprang up between playwright August Wilson and director, writer, and critic Robert Brustein. Their disagreement over matters such as color-blind casting and funding for African American writers led to a public debate between the two men.

Wilson said in part: "We reject any attempt to blot us out, to reinvent history and ignore our presence . . . . We want you to see us. We are black and beautiful.

We have an honorable history in the world of men . . . . We do not need color-blind casting; we need some theaters to develop our playwrights."

Brustein responded by questioning whether there should perhaps be "some kind of statute of limitations on white guilt and white reparations." He further berated Wilson for having "fallen into a monotonous tone of victimization."

More About August Wilson

Wilson said that he was fiercely opposed to color-blind casting—casting that does not take race into account, or that uses racial casting dynamics other than those called for in the script. He found the idea of an all-black *Death of a Salesman* "an assault on our presence, an insult to our [African American] intelligence."

Encourage a class discussion on what might be the pros and cons of color-blind casting as well as the social and artistic impact of under representing certain ethnic and racial groups.

ACTivity August Wilson honed his craft at development organizations such as The Playwrights' Center and the Eugene O'Neill Center. As a long-term project, encourage your students to write one-act plays and workshop them in small groups. Students should offer constructive feedback and suggestions about character, plot, and structure.

Masters Past and Present

August Wilson's plays are set in past decades, but their themes resonate with modern viewers. When writing a play set in the past, there must be a connection between the events of the play and the world we live in today.

Below are playwrights who have also worked from historical perspectives.

- William Shakespeare, despite a lack of both formal education and world travel, wrote many plays set in ancient times and exotic places, including *Antony and Cleopatra, Julius Caesar,* and *Titus Andronicus.*

- In *Life of Galileo,* Bertolt Brecht (1898–1956) wrote about the famous 16th-century Italian astronomer Galileo Galilei.

- Jean Anouilh (1910–1987) wrote a version of *Antigone,* an ancient play by Sophocles.

- Caryl Churchill (1938–) wrote about English colonial Africa during the time of Queen Victoria in her play *Cloud Nine.*

Cultural Heritage

Early Playwrights: West and East

The plays presented at festivals to honor Dionysus included the Great Dionysia at Athens, held in the spring; the Rural Dionysia, held in the winter; and the Lenaea, which followed the Rural Dionysia and was also held in the winter. Every year the festival held three competitions for playwriting. One was for comedy; another for dithyramb, an elaborate choral form that typically featured fifty or more singers; and one for tragic plays. From these ancient contests sprang some of the world's greatest drama.

The oldest existing comedies are by Aristophanes. His writing is a mixture of satirical attacks on public figures of the time and bawdy jokes.

Other Cultures, Other Times

Among the most famous of the early 20th-century Indian playwrights was **Rabindranath Tagore** (1861–1941). Born into a wealthy and artistically inclined Calcutta family, Tagore wrote plays, poems, and songs, most of which were originally performed by the many talented members of his immediate family. In 1913 Tagore won the Nobel Prize for literature. He also wrote the Indian national anthem. Tagore's best-known play is *The Post Office*, written in 1931. This poignant play, about a dying boy who is restricted to his home and denied the joys of the outdoors by a rigid-minded doctor, is still performed throughout the world. The child longs to enter life and believes that the king will send him a message through the post office opposite his window. When a message finally comes, it is blank.

 Obtain a copy of *The Post Office* and have a group of students perform it as a staged reading. You can download a copy of the play from *www.gutenberg.org/ebooks/6523*.

Cultural Heritage

Early Playwrights: West and East

Sophocles

In ancient Greece, a playwriting competition was held at a yearly festival in honor of the patron of Greek theatre, the god Dionysus. From these ancient contests sprang some of the world's greatest drama. Euripides (484–406 B.C.) wrote 90 plays, but only 18 remain, including *Medea*. His plays mine the deep sorrow of the human condition. Aeschylus (525–456 B.C.) is believed to have written 90 tragedies. Of these, only 7 remain, including the Oresteia trilogy. Sophocles (496–406 B.C.) wrote perhaps 125 tragedies, of which only 7 survive, including *Antigone* and *Oedipus Rex*. These great classical tragedies continue to influence playwrights.

Zeami: Father of Japanese Noh Drama

Centuries later and on another continent, playwriting flourished in Japan through Zeami Motokiro (1363–1443). As the son of an itinerant actor, Zeami joined the world of the theatre at an early age. When he was eleven, he performed with his father's company at a shrine in Kyoto. His audience that day included Yoshimitsu, the ruler of Japan. Yoshimitsu was so taken with the performance of young Zeami that he set up the troupe in his palace and thereby became their financial protector. Over the course of his life, Zeami became an accomplished playwright, penning more than 100 plays that would form the basis of Noh drama.

What this 14th-century pioneer created was a dramatic form written in the upper-class language of the time that based its stories on people and situations of an earlier period. The result was a series of plays of poetic richness and universality. Many of these works are regularly performed today. Young actors still study Zeami's teachings on the skills and methods of the Noh actor.

Noh drama is still performed in much the same way it was more than 600 years ago.

Visual Cue

Use the questions that follow to help students use **critical viewing skills**.

- What can you tell about the Noh actor just from looking at the picture on this page?

- What do the picture on this page and the photo from *Tontlawald* on page 163 have in common?

Contemporary U.S. Playwrights from Diverse Cultures

Today playwrights from diverse cultural backgrounds enrich the American stage. Rajiv Joseph, an Indian American from Cleveland, Ohio, received funding to develop his play, *Bengal Tiger at the Baghdad Zoo,* in 2009. A finalist for the Pulitzer Prize in 2010, the play explores the effects of war in Iraq from a variety of perspectives. After its regional debut in Los Angeles, the play moved to Broadway in 2011. Joseph has received numerous awards for his ongoing work.

Tarell Alvin McCraney is best known for his trilogy *The Brother/Sister Plays,* coming-of-age stories set in a fictional African American community in Louisiana. McCraney draws on his experiences as a young black man in the inner city of Miami, casting everyday experiences in mythic terms. After their development at the McCarter Theatre in Princeton, New Jersey, the plays have been performed at the Public Theater in New York, Steppenwolf Theatre in Chicago, and in numerous theaters around the world. McCraney received a MacArthur Foundation "genius grant" in 2013.

Eugenie Chan draws on her heritage as a fifth-generation Chinese American from San Francisco to write works that blend tradition, language, and history. She has written numerous dramas and comedies ranging from one-act to full-length plays, including *Madame Ho* and *Kitchen Table,* and a new ensemble work, *Tontlawald,* based on an Estonian folktale. Her works have been commissioned by and performed at numerous theatres across the country, ranging from the Public Theater and Pan Asian Rep to the Houston Grand Opera.

Actor Marilet Martinez plays Lona, finding her way through the "ghost forest" in the 2012 world premiere of *Tontlawald* at San Francisco's Cutting Ball Theater. Eugene Chan wrote the text, and Paige Rogers and Annie Paladino directed. Photo by Annie Paladino.

Contemporary U.S. Playwrights from Diverse Cultures

Playwrights from diverse cultures are well-represented among Pulitzer Prize winners and finalists. Ayad Akhtar, a Pakistani American, won in 2013 for his play *Disgraced.* Quiara Alegría Hudes drew on family stories from her Puerto Rican and Jewish heritage in her winning 2012 play, *Water by the Spoonful,* and her 2007 finalist, *Eliot, A Soldier's Fugue.* Her musical about Latino immigrants in New York City, *In The Heights,* was a finalist in 2009. In that same year, the winner was African American playwright Lynn Nottage for *Ruined.* Stephen Karam's *Sons of the Prophet,* about a Lebanese-American family, was a finalist in 2012.

Resources for Young Playwrights

The Web site of Young Playwrights, Inc., founded in 1981 by Stephen Sondheim, offers links to numerous competitions for high school-age playwrights, including contests for different regions of the county. See www.youngplaywrights.org/competitions.

Insight for Playwrights is a monthly marketing newsletter with the latest submission information for theatres, contests, fellowships, residencies, and other development programs for dramatic writers. *Insight* offers sixteen pages a month of important submission information: "We scour the trades and the Internet for playwriting opportunities . . . so you can concentrate on your writing." See www.writersinsight.com for information about electronic or paper subscriptions.

From the Field: Write What You Know

When I work with student playwrights, I begin with the idea that they must write about what they know and, more importantly, what they have experienced.

I have found that the biggest problems kids have with writing scenes (or stories) is finding the material. I feel that if I can get them to look at their own lives and believe that it is a great (possibly the greatest) source for their writing, they can then truly begin to work and explore.

It is a lesson that really sticks with them because it tells them right away that they must be emotionally connected to their writing or it has little real value.

Joel Drake Johnson, Playwright and Teacher, Chicago, IL

Chapter 15

The Director and Producer

This chapter helps students to understand the personnel and the team effort that go into producing a play. Students will learn how to analyze a play as a director would.

Objectives

1 to understand the specific duties of the director and the producer

2 to understand the role of other members of the production team

3 to use analytical skills to make casting and staging decisions

4 to use the structural elements of drama to analyze a play

Project Specs

For this chapter, encourage students to use their imaginations to visualize a performance of their selected play as they read it.

ELL Students
Note that ELL students may need extra help with some of this chapter's vocabulary. The Language of Theatre feature on page 170 provides additional support.

Advanced Students
For extra credit, students may wish to contact a local or regional theatre and interview a director, producer, or house manager.

On Your Feet

Instead of a list, students may want to create a graphic showing the responsibilities and duties of each member of the production team they can think of. They can leave some blank space where they can add personnel when they complete this chapter.

Chapter

15 The Director and Producer

The production of a play represents the talent and commitment of many people. Whether on the stage or in the wings, you should have an understanding and appreciation of all phases of the production process. This chapter will give you more information about each job—focusing particularly on the work of the director and the producer.

Project Specs

Project Description For this assignment, you will analyze a play as a director would and give a three- to five-minute presentation.

Purpose to hone your skills at play analysis and interpretation and to understand some of the basic elements of directing a play

Materials a written breakdown or a graphic representation of the important elements of a play you would like to direct or the Director and Producer Activity Sheet your teacher provides

On Your Feet

With a classmate, discuss what you think the director and producer do to make a play happen. Who else is necessary for the production of a play? Make a list of who does what on a play. When you finish working on this chapter, compare your list to what you have learned.

Director Jean-Pierre Vincent, right, and actor Daniel Auteuil discuss the leading role in Molière's *That Scoundrel Scapin* for the annual theatre festival in Avignon, France.

Theatre Terms

director a person who interprets a play, casts, blocks, and helps actors create their roles

dramaturg a person who performs a variety of tasks to assist with the production of a play, such as script evaluation and historical research

general admission when seating is not assigned and audience members can sit where they like

producer a person who finds financing for a play, chooses the director, and oversees the day-to-day business activities

prompt book a three-ring binder or other notebook that holds the annotated script along with the director's ideas

royalties the money paid to the rights holder of a play

strike disassembling of the set

symbol a concrete image that is used to represent an abstract concept or principle

The Director

It is the responsibility of the **director** to create a cohesive group that will work together to accomplish a successful dramatic presentation. In high school, the director is often the theatre teacher, but students should also have the opportunity to try out their directing skills. A director has responsibilities to everyone involved in every aspect of a production, as the chart to the right shows.

A Short List of the Director's Duties

If you choose to be a director, you have a big job ahead of you. Following are five key areas in which the director must demonstrate leadership and responsibility.

A Director's Responsibilities

- To the playwright: understanding and appreciation of the author's intent

- To the script: respect for its artistic integrity; sensitivity to the historical and cultural context

- To the actors: understanding and careful interpretation of the characters; leadership to keep the cast working effectively

- To the designers: clear communication of concepts and respect for ideas

- To the technicians: clear communication; efficient use of rehearsal time

- To the audience: commitment to providing a worthwhile theatrical experience

1 Getting Started The director selects the play, sets the dates for auditions, rehearsals, and the performance, and develops the artistic vision for the play. The chosen script should be well written and of high artistic quality, and the director should connect with it strongly. The theme should truthfully reveal some important element of the human experience. The play should feature strong characters, cohesive dialogue, and an interesting plot. It should be suitable to the school and community audience as well as the available talent pool and the school's technical capabilities. The fact is, if you don't have the necessary casting pool and facilities, you should not produce the play.

Chapter 15 The Director and Producer **165**

PREVIEW

The Director

The best stage directors, through their creative vision, inspire the people on a production to do their best, most imaginative work. Remind students that it is hard to inspire others if you are not inspired and excited yourself. Good directors bring an infectious enthusiasm to all phases of the production process.

ACTivity Have students work in pairs on a directing activity. One student reads a passage from a play, novel, or poem. The other student offers suggestions on how to present the material more expressively. The "director" may suggest movements or vocal adjustments, changes of rhythm and volume, and so on. After the "actor" has rehearsed the material with the director, the two students switch places.

Vocabulary Enhancement

Casting an actor who has very similar characteristics to those of the character is called *typecasting*. The term *typecast* is often used to describe an actor who is constantly cast in similar and/or stereotypical roles, e.g., the smirking lawyer, the lusty girlfriend, the crusty old-timer with a bad temper, etc.

Resource Binder

- Who's Who: Flow Chart, TIPack, p. J
- Who's Who: Job Descriptions, TIPack, p. K
- Director and Producer Activity Sheet, p. 74
- Profiles of Management Personnel Worksheet, p. 75
- Critique Sheet: Director's Presentation, p. 76
- Director and Producer Test, p. 77
- Director's Script Analysis: Plot/Theme, p. 163 and Character/Setting, p. 164
- Production Budget Form, p. 165

To Have on Hand

- Books or magazine articles with information about well-known theatre directors and producers

- Anthologies from which students may select their plays

Handbook Connections
pages 580–586

A Short List of the Director's Duties

Tell students that while reading and rereading the script, the director may enlist the aid of any number of other resources to gain a thorough understanding of the world of the play.

The director will probably also research the characters' professions, religions, ethnic customs, and so on.

Assembling the Team In addition, the director must be able to project his or her vision of the play to the design team and the actors, for they are the ones who will be bringing that vision to life.

Assembling the Tools Many plays can be obtained through the Samuel French organization. French publishes and licenses Broadway and off-Broadway hits as well as plays from London's West End and original scripts submitted by untested authors. Visit their Web site www.samuelfrench.com/ for details.

The Producer

A good way for a student to learn about all aspects of the theatre is to assist a producer. At the high school level, you might do well to select one or two students to assist you as you direct and produce a play. If there are good nonprofit or community theatre groups in your area, contact them about having students job-shadow various theatre personnel for a week or two.

A Short List of the Producer's Duties

Tell students that in the professional theatre, particularly for Broadway-scale musicals, there is often a team of producers who work together to either invest the money themselves or to find a larger group of investors willing to take on the risk. Remind them that producing theatre on any level is a risk in terms of finding an audience, winning critical praise, and making a profit. Therefore, producers must be more than just money people. They should also have a deep belief in the artistic product and the creative team.

2 **Reading and Researching** The director studies the play through multiple readings. If the play takes place in a different historical period, the director should also check a number of references to learn more about how people who lived during that time looked, spoke, worked, and so on. Often the director gets help from a **dramaturg** (see the box on page 169).

3 **Assembling the Team** The director enlists the aid of the production team to establish both continuity of design and a production schedule.

4 **Assembling the Tools** The director or stage manager prepares a **prompt book** using a three-ring loose-leaf binder. Each page of the prompt book contains a page of the script, glued onto a piece of paper. The wide margins allow the director to write detailed notations about movement, technical cues, and so on. Think of the prompt book as the entire production written down on paper.

5 **Getting Down to It** The director conducts auditions, casts the play, and schedules and conducts rehearsals.

The Producer

In addition to appreciating the director's role, recognize the roles of theatre management. The key theatre management role is that of producer. Most high school drama groups do not have a producer, but they are very common in the legitimate theatre. The producer finds the people who are willing to invest money in the show and creates a budget. The producer also hires the director and the staff who will work on the production. And while the producer will have help from members of the crew in running the advertising campaign, he or she is responsible for its direction. In many high schools, the producer is also the director.

A Short List of the Producer's Duties

While the director is analyzing the script, creating the preliminary prompt book, and thinking about all the other onstage aspects of the production, the producer is hard at work on the business end. He or she finds investors, pays bills, oversees the budget, and works closely with a variety of different production crews. Here are some of the production areas for which the producer is ultimately responsible.

1 **Getting Permission** The producer must figure out a budget that takes into consideration the costs of producing the play, including the payment of **royalties,** money paid to the author for the use of the script. The box office receipts should help to pay the royalties, which can sometimes involve a great deal of money. Be sure to check the royalty fees before committing to any play. (It should go without saying that even schools

Backstage Gossip: New Play, Anyone?

When actor Sidney Poitier brought Lorraine Hansberry's brand new script *A Raisin in the Sun* to fledgling director Lloyd Richards, Richards fell in love with it. But for a long time neither he nor producer Phil Rose could find a theatre willing to take a chance on staging it.

A Raisin in the Sun finally premiered at the Ethel Barrymore Theatre in New York in February 1959 to great critical and popular acclaim. It has had hundreds of productions since then and is widely regarded as one of the best American plays of the 20th century.

must pay the necessary royalties. Failure to do so is a criminal offense.) To secure the royalties, the producer must contact the play's publisher by mail, fax, or email. Rights cannot be secured by telephone. Information the producer gives to the publisher includes performance dates, number of seats, ticket price, and type of theatre (in the case of a school, nonprofessional/educational).

2 Getting an Audience A large part of the producer's job is to bring in a crowd—to let the school and community know about the production and to get them excited about attending. This involves:

- Creating and distributing posters/flyers advertising the show. Posters should be put up at least two or three weeks before opening night.
- Announcing the play through the school's channels: newsletters, Web site, e-mails, calendars.
- Writing public service announcements (PSAs) for local radio and TV stations. These brief announcements are typically made free of charge.
- Sending press releases to local newspapers. With planning and imagination, a producer can sometimes wrangle a feature story from the newspaper or a public radio station.
- Running an ad in the paper or on the radio (if the school's budget allows for this). The ad must be turned in far enough in advance so that it will do some good. The approved copy should be submitted at least two weeks before opening night. The copy should be edited and proofread to make sure all the information a potential ticket-buyer will need is included.
- Selling program ads. The money from these ads goes to pay for the program printing and to fund other areas of the production.

3 The Program The producer is also in charge of creating the program. There should be artistic continuity between the program and the advertising, posters, and flyers. Per the royalties agreement, the program must credit the playwright. Each publisher provides the guidelines for this credit, so check the agreement carefully. The program recognizes each cast and production team member. Programs may include a "Special Thanks To" section in which people and organizations that have made contributions to the production are credited. Depending on the budget, the program may be anything from a single sheet of paper folded in half that lists the names and roles of the cast and crew to an elaborate document that includes biographies (and sometimes photographs).

Sometimes shows are funded through corporate sponsorship. A theatre's marketing personnel often try to find a link between a particular play and a sponsor's product or service. For example, a play about a food critic might receive funding from a national food-services corporation or even a local restaurant.

Remind students that the closer the show gets to opening night, the more the producer may have to fill in for the director with regard to offstage production details both large and small.

ACTivity Have students choose a play and write a brief public service announcement (PSA) about a production of it. Specify a length of 150 words or less. Then have students exchange their PSAs with a partner and read them aloud.

ACTivity ELL Students These students can create a PSA in their native language, if they wish.

ACTivity Advanced Students These students may wish to create both a PSA and a radio ad. Encourage them to record their ads using background music. Play the finished recordings for the class.

ACTivity Special Needs Students Have students read or watch a play and discuss the type of sponsor who might be interested in providing financial backing for it.

Show, Don't Tell If possible, bring in programs from various theatre productions (professional, community, school) and compare the different elements of each. Discuss with students which ones they think have the most impact, and why. Discuss the importance of including all the necessary information in a program.

ACTivity Have students choose a well-known play and create their own program for the play.

Quotable

What a playwright needs most is a director, because a good director lifts the play off the page into radiant life. The playwrights who've succeeded have had that director. To my mind, it's the most important collaboration in the theatre.

Tina Howe, Playwright

The Production Team

Tell students that the set, lighting, sound, makeup, and costume designers' ideas are carried out during production by the various production crews. Each designer creates drawings and or models of his or her designs. These are then built and maintained by the assigned crew members. For example, the set designer creates plans, drawings, and a scale model of the set for the play. The set crew then builds the set based on these specifications.

In the professional theatre and at many schools, the stage manager serves as the prompter during rehearsals, but during performances professional theatres (and most schools) do not use a prompter at all. If an actor forgets a line, he or she—sometimes with the help of other cast members—is responsible for getting the show back on track.

 **Advanced Students**

Obtain a copy of *Stage Design: A Practical Guide* by Gary Thorne (Crowood Press, 1999). It contains information on how to create scale models. Have interested students choose a play from which to create a scale model of a set design.

Vocabulary Enhancement

Let students know that forgetting one's lines is called *going up.* An actor might say, for example, "I completely went up in scene one!"

Visual Cue

Have students look at the photo of the production team. Then use the following prompts to exercise their **critical viewing skills.**

- What skills do you think are necessary for the work these members of the production team are doing?
- What seems to be the attitude of these crew members?

The production team works to prepare for an upcoming play.

4 Running Interference The duties of the director and the producer overlap at times. The producer's role often expands as the director gets deeper into the rehearsal process. A good producer stays in very close contact with the director—and picks up the slack when needed!

The Production Team

The director, producer, designers, and actors may have the jobs with the highest profiles, but they wouldn't get far without the production team. Following is a list of backstage and off-stage personnel and their duties to help you understand and appreciate their collaborative relationships.

The *assistant director* helps the director in conducting rehearsals, making phone calls, and sometimes doing research or taking on the role of a dramaturg (see the box at the right).

The *stage manager,* who fulfills another theatre management role, is in charge of all stage crews. He or she also assists the director. During rehearsals, the stage manager takes notes, records the actors' movements, informs the production team of the director's needs, and helps with scheduling. During final rehearsals and performances, the stage manager has complete supervision of the stage. He or she calls cues for lights, special effects, and curtains. When the play closes, the stage manager helps with the **strike** (disassembling) of the set.

The *prompter* must attend every rehearsal to become completely familiar with the script and all its cues and pauses. The prompter is responsible for feeding actors their lines should they forget them. The prompter also makes sure the rehearsal room or theatre is ready, and during rehearsals he or she holds the prompt book, noting all movements assigned by the director. (For more on prompting and the rehearsal process, see Chapter 16.)

Stage crews build, paint, and set up stage scenery. The stage crew on site during performances also shifts scenery when needed, and after the performance, sets up for Act I of the next night's show.

Backstage Gossip: Whose Line Is It Anyway?

Kenneth Tynan, in *Persona Grata,* tells of an occasion during a London production of a Lunt-Fontanne vehicle when that wonderfully proficient team suddenly stopped in mid-scene. The prompter, after a first astonished moment, threw the next line to them, and Mr. Lunt responded charmingly, "It's not that we don't know the line, old boy. We just can't remember which one of us says it."

They also help with strike after the final show. (See Chapters 19 and 20 for more on set design and the stage crew.)

The *light crew* uses the lighting charts and cue sheets to properly hang and focus the lights. The crew then runs the lights during the show. The light crew assists with strike. (See Chapter 21 for more about lighting design and the light crew.)

The *sound effects crew* works on the sound cue sheet and provides the necessary sound effects. Under the direction of the sound designer, they may help select music to enhance the scene transitions and the mood of the play. (See Chapter 22 for more about sound design.)

The *costume crew* supplies the costumes and assigns dressing rooms. During the run of the play, the costume crew keeps the costumes clean, organized, mended, and pressed. (See Chapter 23 for more about costuming.)

The *makeup crew* plans makeup for each actor, obtains necessary supplies, and arranges for a separate makeup room if possible. During the final rehearsals and the run of the show, the makeup crew assists the actors in applying their makeup. (See Chapter 24 for more about makeup design and the makeup crew.)

Spotlight on

The Dramaturg

What is a dramaturg? You may not have heard this word before, but a dramaturg plays a vital part in many production teams. He or she may serve as a script reader in the theatre's literary department, evaluating plays that are under consideration for production. The dramaturg often does research into the historical or societal issues of a play and shares that information with the director and cast. Most dramaturgs know a great deal about playwriting structure, so they are particularly useful during productions of world premiere plays.

Although dramaturgs have been a part of the theatre scene since the 1800s, it has only been relatively recently that their place within the American production process has been clearly defined. Twenty or so years ago, most American theatres did not work with a dramaturg. Now these multifaceted professionals represent a strong creative component in theatre productions large and small.

Spotlight on

The Dramaturg Many schools do not use dramaturgs. For those that do, the dramaturg is often a history teacher. He or she generally prepares a presentation for the cast and crew about the playwright, the time period, and the issues the play deals with. Ask teachers at your school with expertise on the subject or time period of a play you are working on (or the play or playwright) to come to a rehearsal to make a presentation to your students. List this person's name in the program as the production dramaturg.

A good dramaturg functions as a third set of eyes for the playwright and the director. When working on a new play, the dramaturg asks questions about character, structure, and plot to help create a tightly molded concept of the work. For the actors, designers, and director, a good dramaturg provides historical/religious/political/socio-cultural research to help put the play into a proper context, all the while remaining focused on the text.

From the Field: Mallaturgy

I've found that the best dramaturgy occurs through what I call "mallaturgy"—the time when another theatre artist and a dramaturg can spend some time together outside the theatre setting—perhaps in the mall—talking about the piece and its background in more universal terms.

Michele Volansky, Dramaturg, Chair and Professor of Drama at Washington College

The *properties (props) crew* prepares detailed props lists for each scene and locates all props and furniture, including those props that will not be used in performance but are used during rehearsal. The head of the props crew assigns each crew member specific props to set and strike for each act. The crew organizes the props, keeping those for each scene in a separate basket or on a separate table. Although actors are expected to check their individual props, the props crew is responsible for making sure the props are in the correct spot for the actor to check. (See Chapter 25 for more about props.)

The *business manager,* also fulfilling a role in theatre management, is in charge of the money. In a school setting, this person is often a faculty member. He or she serves as public relations officer and supervises the publicity, ticket sales, and program issues.

The *publicity crew* advertises the show by giving the school and local papers various news stories concerning performance dates, people involved, and information about the play, the playwright, and so on. This crew identifies and designs marketing products for the play, such as posters and flyers. The crew also remains alert for possible feature stories engendered by the rehearsal process and arranges for photographers or arts and community reporters to have access to the cast. The crew puts up posters in the community and sends out postcards and flyers. The work of the publicity crew is crucial when it comes to attracting an audience.

The Language of THEATRE

Develop learning strategies and use support as needed to understand oral language.

- Listen to the theatre terms *director* and *producer* as the teacher or a classmate says them aloud and notice what pattern they share with the word *actor*. Work with a teacher or partner to use this pattern to understand the meaning of the terms.

- Use reasoning and your knowledge of basic vocabulary to predict the meaning of the expressions *general admission* and *prompt book* when you hear them. Ask for clarification if needed.

- Listen to a partner read about a producer's job regarding *royalties* on pages 166–167. Use strategies such as reasoning and analyzing to understand what is said. Ask for clarification if needed.

- As you listen to your classmates' presentations, use a repertoire of learning strategies to help you understand what they are saying about the plays' *symbols*. Ask for clarification if needed.

Backstage Gossip: A Brilliant Publicity Move

When Murray Mednick's *The Coyote Cycle* premiered at Santa Fe, New Mexico's Theatre in the Red in 1984, the producers needed a way to entice the public into coming to an epic outdoor show—one that had never before been produced. During the months leading up to the opening, the savvy producers hung flyers all over town that simply read "Coyote is Coming."

As a result of this low-cost advertising ploy, by the time the show opened, Santa Fe was abuzz with the question, "What the heck *is* Coyote?"

Another theatre management role to recognize is that of the house manager. The *house manager* is responsible for the seating and comfort of the audience during performances. The house manager sees to it that the auditorium is cool enough or warm enough, that the doors open on time, and that there are plenty of programs for distribution. He or she also supervises the ushers.

Ushers escort the audience members to their seats. If the performance is **general admission** (meaning that no seats are assigned and audience members can sit where they like), the ushers' main duty is to hand out programs and present an upbeat and courteous attitude. Ushers ask latecomers to wait in the lobby until the next scene change to avoid disturbing others (including the actors who are performing onstage). After the audience has left the auditorium, the ushers are responsible for picking up any trash or programs that may have been left behind.

Symbolic Elements of Drama

In previous chapters, we have looked at characters in conflict and analyzed the elements of plot. But to direct a play, you must also understand its theme (or themes) and the symbols it employs.

A **symbol** is a concrete image that is used to represent an abstract concept or principle. In Arthur Miller's *Death of a Salesman,* Willy Loman's vegetable patch represents the old way of life with its opportunities for growth and renewal. In Jane Martin's *Clear Glass Marbles,* a bowl of marbles represents the waning days of a dying mother's life. In August Wilson's *The Piano Lesson,* a piano symbolizes for one character the need to remember the past; for another character, it represents the key to a new future. A play's setting can often be symbolic as well. Think about what the following settings might convey.

- cemetery
- dining room
- train
- corporate boardroom
- museum
- Las Vegas

Symbolic Elements of Drama

ACTivity Ask students to think about the symbolism in some of the plays they have read. Then have them choose one play and make a list of its symbols. Before they begin, remind them that very often a prop or a place has special symbolic significance. For example, Belle Reeve, the family plantation Blanche speaks of in *A Streetcar Named Desire,* is a symbol of Blanche's loss, not only of her home, but also of her youth and the promise of love.

Quotable

Use the quote below as a writing prompt or discussion starter.

I regard the theatre as the greatest of all art forms, the most immediate way in which a human being can share with another the sense of what it is to be a human being.

Oscar Wilde, Playwright

Technical Elements of Drama

ACTivity Ask students to think about the cultural, social, and political aspects in some of the plays they have seen, either in person or in a video. Then have small groups choose one play and discuss how the technical elements of the play were used to reflect those aspects. Invite students to create short multimedia presentations to summarize their discussion for the class, using examples from the play to demonstrate their main ideas.

The Language of THEATRE

Support students with linguistically accommodated content area material as needed.

- Allow students to use a play in their native language to prepare their chapter project.
- Invite students to use a script that features both their native language and an English translation as they prepare their chapter project.
- Encourage students to read a play in English for their project and provide them with annotations as needed to accommodate their growing English proficiency
- Encourage students to read a play in English for their project with little or no linguistic accommodation.

The set for the Lyric Stage Company of Boston's production of *Nicholas Nickleby*, based on a novel by Charles Dickens, shows some of the drabness of life in 19th century England. (l to r) Jason Powers as Smike, Jack Cutmore-Scott as Nicholas Nickleby, and Nigel Gore as Mr. Squeers. Photo by Mark S. Howard. Graphic Design by Melissa Wagner O'Malley.

Technical Elements of Drama In addition to themes, symbols, and settings, a director must also take other considerations of a script into account to determine technical elements and assignments. These include cultural, social, and political aspects as well as styles and genres.

Cultural Aspects From what culture does the play derive? What are the conventions of that cultural tradition, and what technical elements—sets, props, lighting, sound, makeup—are required to represent that culture accurately?

Social Aspects What was society like in the time and place the play was written? How can you reflect the times and place in the technical elements of the production? For example, a dramatization of a novel by Charles Dickens might reflect the poverty and lack of upward mobility of the working class in 19th century London through a drab set with a narrow, crowded street.

 **V**sual Cue

The following prompts can be used to exercise students' **critical viewing skills**.

- What can you tell about the cultural and social aspects of the play based on the photo?

- What do you think might be happening in the scene?

Political Aspects What was the political climate in the world of the play? How can that be represented through the characters, set, music, lighting, and makeup? What choices might a director make about how best to reflect the political overtones? Take, for example, two productions of David Hare's political play *Stuff Happens*, which features real-life characters at the highest levels of government—including President George W. Bush, Secretary of Defense Colin Powell, Secretary of State Condoleezza Rice—in the lead-up to the U.S. war in Iraq. When the play was first staged in London, the setting was on an epic scale, as if to match the global power of the players involved. However, several years later when it was staged in New York, the production was scaled down, so that the audience was not viewing larger-than-life characters from a distance but now experiencing them as real people, and themselves almost as participants.

Styles and Genres A director should recognize that the function of technical elements varies from one theatrical style or genre to another. For example, a lifelike and recognizable living room would be an appropriate set for a realistic play. In a nonrealistic play, however, the function of the set might be more symbolic and serve to convey a more abstract idea appropriate to the play's themes.

Also research the styles of directors whose work you respect. Study the choices those directors made and determine if you can apply them to your directing.

PREPARE

Put on Your Director's Hat

Your first task is to analyze and evaluate a play the way a director would. Follow the steps below.

1 Select a play you think you will like and read through it carefully. Pay close attention to what the characters say and do.

2 Read the play a second time. Look for its themes and symbols. Ask yourself questions as you go along. If you notice a recurring idea, track that idea all the way through to the end of the play. Also consider the play's time and place and the cultural, social, and political aspects that might affect how you would direct the play. Take notes. Be sure this is a play you are excited about directing.

3 When you have finished analyzing and evaluating the play, you should be able to do all of the following.
   • Name the protagonist.
   • Name the antagonistic force.
   • Explain the major plotline.
   • Specify the conflict.
   • Define the play's theme.
   • List one or more symbols.
   • Explain how the play's setting, time, literary style, genre, characters, themes, and cultural, social, and political issues affect technical considerations.
   • Explain why you want to direct this play.
Next, you may either write a one- or two-page paper that illuminates all of the

PREPARE

Put on Your Director's Hat

Remind students that directing a play is hard work. There is no point in a director working on a play that doesn't excite him or her deeply. Ask students to analyze what it is about their chosen play that they find so intriguing. Is it hilarious, frightening, uplifting, or disturbing? Does it relate to their own life issues? At some point early in the rehearsal process, directors usually share their vision of the play with the actors and crew. The more personal the play is to the director, the more capable he or she will be of stimulating the cast and the other members of the production team.

Quotable

The theatre is the best way of showing the gap between what is said and what is seen to be done, and that is why, ragged and gap-toothed as it is, it has still a far healthier potential than some poorer, abandoned arts.

David Hare, Playwright and Director

Rehearse Your Presentation

Get together with students who are using visual aids before the time assigned for their presentations and go over with them how they will proceed. Let them practice using computers and any other audiovisual equipment they plan to employ. Help them run through their presentations until all elements flow together seamlessly.

Career Focus

Contact your local professional or community theatre and invite a stage director to come and speak to your class or to give students a tour of the theatre facility. If possible, ask your visitor to provide a short presentation (similar to the one students are working on) about a play he or she recently directed.

The following prompts can be used to help students build their **critical viewing skills.**

- What interpersonal skills do you think this director might be using to get a point across to the actor?

- What does the actor's body language tell you about how the director's words are being received?

- How important do you think openness is to the rehearsal process?

points on the previous page or create a digital presentation that illustrates your points graphically. Your teacher may supply a Director and Producer Activity Sheet, which you may also use to work through this assignment. Whichever way you decide to handle your preparation, be sure that you cover each of the elements listed in the previous paragraph.

Rehearse Your Presentation

If you have written a paper, practice reading it aloud a few times, making sure you have covered each of the assignment's points and that you don't go over three minutes. Be sure to include time for about two minutes of questions from the audience. You should be familiar enough with the material that questions about theme, symbolism, plot, character, and your vision of the play will not throw you.

If you present your project by means of a digital presentation, make sure you can explain each element and how it is linked to the other elements. Cover the same elements you would cover in a written essay. If you need any special equipment, arrange this with your teacher ahead of time. Make sure your presentation does not exceed five minutes, including questions from the audience.

Career Focus

Stage Director

As is the case in so many areas of the theatre, becoming a successful stage director takes more than just talent. Directors must have drive, self-discipline, and artistic discipline to succeed. They must educate themselves in all areas of the theatre, read and analyze both new plays and classics, and be comfortable in the rehearsal room.

Many professional directors begin training in their craft in high school and college and go on to obtain master of fine arts degrees in directing. Some directors begin their careers as actors and gradually shift their focus to directing. Acting helps strengthen their understanding of the collaborative process.

If you are interested in becoming a director, evaluate the training needed. Have you begun training by participating in school and community productions? Are you willing to continue your training in college? Is the training in acting the way you would go? For that all-important real-world experience, you might apply to train as an apprentice at a local theatre as an assistant director. Refer to the chart on page 10 for more ways to evaluate this career.

Notes

_____

_____

_____

_____

_____

_____

PRESENT

Share Your Director's Vision

When your name is called, make certain your information is in order and step to the playing area. Hand in any written material or the Activity Sheet to your teacher. Take a moment before introducing your presentation to breathe and focus. Tell the class the name of the play and its author before you begin. Once you begin, keep up the pace, but make sure you cover each point. When you have finished, ask the audience if they have questions. Set a limit of three questions. If someone asks you a question for which you simply have no answer, admit that you don't know, but try to suggest ways that one might find the answer. After you have answered the third question, thank your audience and return to your seat.

The stage director discusses a scene with a lead actor while other actors rehearse.

CRITIQUE

Evaluate a Classmate's Presentation

Choose one of the class presentations to review. Evaluate the presenter using a scale from 1 to 5, with 5 being "outstanding," and 1 being "needs much improvement." To begin, ask yourself the questions below.

For written/verbal presentations:
- Was the presenter's overall vision of the play clear and insightful?
- Did the presenter cover the play's theme adequately?
- How well did the presenter convey an understanding of the play's symbols?
- Was the statement of the conflict clear?
- How did the presenter handle the plot description?
- In what way did the presenter answer the questions from the audience?

For digital presentations:
- How did the graphics convey the play's plot and theme?
- In what way did the presenter involve conflict, symbols, and character?
- Were you able to get a good sense of the play?
- How comfortable did the presenter appear while answering questions?

Write a paragraph explaining why you gave the presenter the rating you did.

PRESENT

Share Your Director's Vision

Before students begin to share their work, remind them that their presentations start the moment their names are called. Approaching the playing area with a calm but confident gait and expression will go a long way toward keeping the presenter focused and will set the tone for the presentation.

CRITIQUE

Evaluate a Classmate's Presentation

Hand out the Critique Sheet for this project or have students use their own paper. Be sure the students understand what they will be looking for in the verbal presentations, including what theme entails, what symbols in a play encompass, and the seven elements of a plot. You might want to have information on these points written on the chalkboard for the students.

With regard to the graphic presentation, remind students that they are evaluating how well any charts, graphs, or other aids convey the presenter's points. Are the graphics easy to understand and helpful to the presentation?

After you have read the critiques, share them with students, allowing them to analyze and evaluate the critical comments. Discuss with students any points that they feel will help the further development of their work.

Quotable

It's not a field, I think, for people who need to have success every day: If you can't live with a nightly sort of disaster, you should get out. I wouldn't describe myself as lacking in confidence, but I would just say that the ghosts you chase you never catch.

John Malkovich, Actor and Director

The Director and Producer Test

The test for this chapter is available in blackline master form in the Resource Binder, page 77.

For More Information

Books

Bogart, Anne, *A Director Prepares: Seven Essays on Art in Theatre*, Routledge, 2001.

Botto, Louis, and Robert Viagas, *At This Theatre: 100 Years of Broadway Shows, Stories and Stars*, Applause Theatre Book Publishers, 2002.

Brook, Peter, *The Empty Space: A Book about Theater*, Simon & Schuster, 1995.

Fliotsos, Anne, and Wendy Vierow, *American Women Stage Directors of the Twentieth Century*, University of Illinois Press, 2008.

Frick, John W., editor, and Stephen Valliool, editor, *Theatrical Directors: A Biographical Dictionary*, Greenwood Press, 1994.

Grippo, Charles, *The Stage Producer's Business and Legal Guide*, Allworth Press, 2002.

Hauser, Frank, and Russell Reich, *Notes on Directing*, RCR Creative Press, 2003.

Other Media

Director and Actor—Passions, Process and Intimacy, DVD, Insight Media, 2012.

From Page to Stage: A Guide to Student Productions, DVD, Insight Media, 2009.

Working Forensically: Collaborative Directing in Contemporary Theatre, DVD, Insight Media, 2012.

Theatre Journal

Use the following as an additional or substitute prompt.

Think about the choice you made of theatre-related jobs. What jobs outside the theatre might employ the same basic skills? Describe some of these jobs.

Additional Projects

1 Cast and direct two classmates in the performance of a scene. Encourage your classmates to read through the scene silently several times before reading it aloud. Once they have read the scene aloud, work together to clarify its theme. Give your classmates notes on character and physical/vocal presentation. When the three of you have rehearsed the scene to your satisfaction, present it to the class.

2 With a partner, create an organizational chart on a poster board or on the computer of all the participants in a theatrical production, including theatre management. Recognize and define the role of each in one or two sentences. With arrows or another graphic of your choice, demonstrate your understanding and appreciation by indicating the collaborative relationships among all the participants.

3 Write character sketches for each character in the play you worked on for this chapter's project. Analyze the play thoroughly to create the most detailed sketches you can. Include their intellectual, emotional, physical, and social dimensions, taking into account the time and place in which the play was written or takes place.

4 Select a full-length period play to research. Your research should focus on a wide-ranging issue, such as the politics of the time, the social issues, or some other issue inherent to the play. Write a paper outlining your dramaturgic findings.

5 In an essay, explain the director's responsibilities to the author's intent, the script, the actors, the designers, the technicians, and the audience. In your explanation, also address why self-discipline and artistic discipline are needed to supplement the theatre skills and experience gained in higher education in order to become a successful stage director.

6 Select one of the longer excerpts from the monologues and scenes in Unit Eight. Analyze and evaluate the script and discuss the excerpt in terms of how you might direct the scene. Think about the play's theme, plot, symbols, major conflict, and the classmates you would cast to play the various parts. Thoroughly research the play and evaluate how the play's setting, time, literary style, genre, characters, themes, and cultural, social, and political aspects would affect technical considerations, functions, and artistic roles in mounting the play. Using your knowledge, present the scene for an audience of family members of your class. Be prepared to justify the choices you made based on interpretations of data from your research.

7 Identify and design marketing products you might use to attract people to attend a performance of the play containing the monologue or scene you chose in the previous activity.

8 Define the following standard vocabulary terms of theatre management and demonstrate their proper use by writing a brief explanation of what theatre management entails: *business manager, house manager, producer, public relations, publicity, ushers.*

9 **Theatre Journal** Think about the jobs in theatre production that do not involve acting, and choose one that interests you. Think about why this position interests you, and write about it in your journal.

Substitute Teacher Activities

Below are a few ideas that will help the substitute teacher.

- Assign the Profiles of Management Personnel Worksheet on page 75 of the Resource Binder.

- Teach portions of the Directing and Producing section of the Student Handbook found on pages 580–586.

- Assign one or more of the Additional Projects on this page.

- **Create a Production Checklist.** Encourage students to discuss the various duties of the production team. Assume that *The Little Foxes* by Lillian Hellman has been selected for production. Students must create a list of all the things that must be done to prepare the play, including obtaining performance rights, casting the play, assembling the production team, advertising the play, scheduling rehearsals, and so on.

Master of the Craft
Peter Brook (1925–)

Peter Brook is an English theatrical producer and director who became known in the 1950s for his experimental productions with London's Royal Shakespeare Company. As a young man, he directed a startling variety of plays—from Shakespeare to musical comedy—with skill and ingenuity.

His early work was inspired by the theories of experimental theatre; these plays and theatrical events defied the notions of realistic and naturalistic acting and pushed the boundaries of the stage. In one memorable Brook production of Shakespeare's *Titus Andronicus,* actress

A scene from *The Persecution and Assassination of Jean-Paul Marat as Performed by the Inmates of the Asylum of Charenton Under the Direction of the Marquis de Sade.*

Vivien Leigh spouted a seemingly endless length of bright red ribbon in a scene in which her character's tongue was cut out. Such visual touches would influence a generation of theatre practitioners.

Over the course of his more than seventy years in the theatre, Brook has acquired a well-deserved reputation as the greatest living inventor of the modern stage. But by his own admission, he has never lost his sense of being an apprentice to his craft. "I think you can't lose this, because a craft has no end. A craft is a ladder. There

Peter Brook

always has to be another level to everything . . ."

Brook's work is challenging, physical, electrifying, and visually alive. He values the audience's intelligence. "In being aware of what holds an audience and what loses them, you develop more and more the awareness that rhythm, space, all the physical sides of theatre are playing on the audience, and it is in this way you develop your tools."

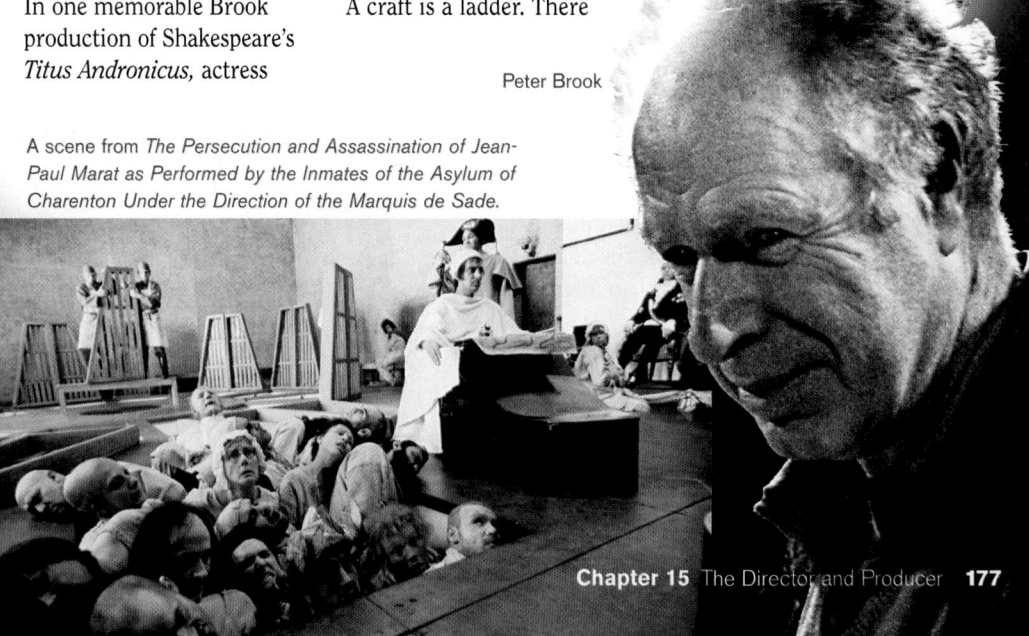

Backstage Gossip: Sheer Terror

Peter Brook is known for spending weeks of rehearsals with improvisations. One of the best-known theatrical stories concerns his production of Seneca's *Oedipus* . . . Brook had made the distinguished cast go through many days of primal screaming, imitating various animals—everything except work on the text. One day he asked the actors to prepare a short

improvisation based on the most terrifying experience they could possibly imagine. When it came to Sir John Gielgud's turn, he did nothing . . . . Brook asked whether there was nothing terrifying that he could think of. "Actually, Peter, there is," replied Sir John quietly: "we open in two weeks."

from *Theatrical Anecdotes* by Peter Hay

Master of the Craft
More About Peter Brook

Peter Brook often tests new work, particularly his reimaginings of Shakespeare's texts, on student audiences. About two-thirds of the way through a rehearsal process, when his actors have learned all their lines, he has them improvise a segment of the text for students. This puts the emphasis on the storytelling aspects of the play and lets him know if the progression is clear. Brook claims that students are honest in their reactions and if they're bored, they usually don't try to hide it. He listens to the "quality of their silences" during the performance, as well as to what they tell him afterward.

Tell your students that many artists who are considered geniuses in their particular art form claim that they, like Peter Brook, maintain a lifelong sense of being a student. Lead a class discussion about this idea. Ask individual students if they have anyone in their lives who has remained a student of life, of human nature, or of an art form. What other traits do these people have?

Masters Past and Present

Eva Le Gallienne (1899–1991) was a stage actress whose versatility made her one of the biggest Broadway stars of the early 1920s. But in 1926, tired of the male-dominated theatre scene, she established the first classical repertory theatre in the United States, the Civic Repertory Theatre (1926–1935). She offered the classics in rotating repertory at one-third the regular Broadway ticket price. As the Civic's producer and director, she demanded absolute loyalty from the actors she worked with. She had a sharp eye for new talent. Among her many "discoveries" were Peter Falk and Burgess Meredith.

Theatre **Then** and **Now**

The Evolution of the "Director"

Up until the end of the 19th century, there really was no such position as that embodied by the directors of today. Actors performed roles in the way they wanted to. A "director" might stand by to fulfill duties—such as choreographing entrances and exits, organizing scenic arrangements, and even coordinating costumes. But as plays became more and more psychologically complex, it became clear that an overall artistic eye was needed in the process.

The Duke of Saxe-Meiningen established a theatre troupe at his court in 1866. Historical accuracy was a hallmark of his productions, including the use of authentic costumes and sets. Rather than use painted backdrops, he helped develop settings in which the actors could be part of the environment. The Meiningen Company toured throughout the major cities of Europe, including Moscow. The realistic nature of the productions had a great influence on Stanislavski.

Theatre **Then** and **Now**

The Evolution of the "Director"

The role of the director as a creative force in the artistic process is a relatively recent phenomenon. Only since the 1870s has the director become an active, vital component in the production of the play. Before then, the "director" of a theatre troupe was typically either a kind of business manager or an actor or playwright who assumed extra responsibilities.

Pioneering Directors

Many date the emergence of the modern theatre director to George II, Duke of Saxe-Meiningen, who presented the Meiningen Company's first production in Berlin in 1874. The duke held the unified artistic vision of the company's elaborate historical dramas. These productions featured large ensembles, lavish costumes and sets, and innovations such as steps and platforms that required someone to coordinate the overall presentation. The duke also began the practice of an intensive rehearsal process.

In the 1890s, Russian actor-manager Konstantin Stanislavski established the Moscow Art Theatre. His early experiments in the use of a more psychological approach to character development also included extensive discussion of the play and long rehearsals. Over time, Stanislavsky freed the director's role from its managerial aspects as he focused on getting all members of the company to realize the playwright's intention.

After World War II, directing became a completely artistic activity as the role of actor-manager faded away. Some notable directing pioneers in the 20th century include Bertolt Brecht (Germany), Giorgio Strehler (Italy), Peter Brook and Peter Hall (Britain), Jerzy Gotkowski (Poland), and Richard Schechner and Hal Prince (United States).

Bertolt Brecht

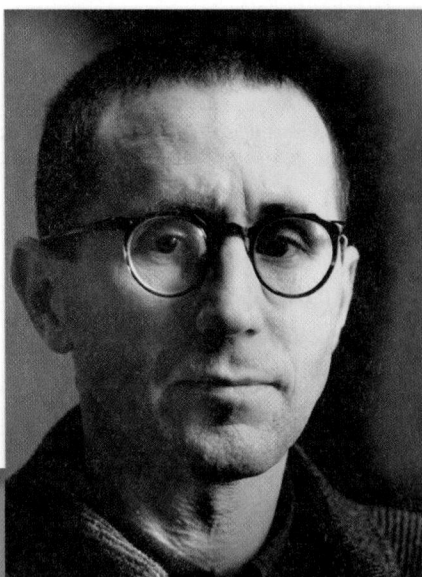

Notes

_____

_____

_____

_____

_____

_____

Hal Prince: Broadway Innovator

The *New York Times* once said that director/producer Hal Prince "may be one of the most innovative directors on Broadway. He may be the one most obsessed with craft as well . . . ."

According to Prince, he owes his success to theatrical legend George Abbott. Prince was apprenticed to Abbott at the age of twenty-five as a stage manager. But what belies Prince's modesty is the fact that, at the age of twenty-six, he co-directed a new musical called *The Pajama Game*. It became the hottest ticket in town and instantly made Prince one of the top names on Broadway.

Since that time, Hal Prince has directed more than fifty Broadway musicals. Among his hits are *Cabaret, Evita,* and *Phantom of the Opera*. His most artistically daring and groundbreaking productions, however, were the result of collaborations with composer Stephen Sondheim. Beginning in the early 1970s, these two theatre pros brought a new notion to the stage—the "concept musical," a musical play in which theme takes precedence over plot. Prince's productions of the Sondheim musicals *Company, Pacific Overtures, Sweeney Todd,* and others took the

American musical into brand-new territory. Each was different from the one before—and each challenged the notions of standard musicals to that point. Along the way, Prince picked up a record twenty-one Tony Awards.

Hal Prince approaches his craft from an intensely personal standpoint.

Mrs. Lovett sharpens her knife in a production of *Sweeney Todd*.

Visual Cue

Sweeney Todd tells the supposedly true story of a barber in London who, instead of shaving his clients' faces, slit their throats. If that tale isn't gory enough, he is additionally said to have chopped up the bodies for use in his wife's homemade meat pies. It's hard to imagine that this would be the stuff of a popular Broadway musical, but Stephen Sondheim's musical rendition is touching, funny, cautionary, and infinitely melodious.

- How would you describe Mrs. Lovett in *Sweeney Todd*?

- What do you think she is about to say? Use your best Cockney accent and say it for the class.

For More Information

Books
Brockett, Oscar G., and Franklin J. Hildy, *History of the Theatre*, 10th ed., Pearson, 2007.

Brown, John Russell, *The Oxford Illustrated History of Theatre*, Oxford University Press, 2001.

Ilson, Carol, *Harold Prince: A Director's Journey*, Limelight Editions, 2004.

Phillips, M. Scott, and Joy H. Reilly, *Introducing Theatre*, Pearson, 2014.

Other Media
American Theatre magazine, Theatre Communications Group, *www.tcg.org/ publications*

College Brecht, DVD, Insight Media, 2012.

Chapter 16

The Cast

This chapter introduces various aspects of the rehearsal process. Students will learn how to make up a rehearsal schedule based on a two-act play of their own choosing.

Objectives

1 to understand what the cast of a play does—from the audition process through opening night and beyond

2 to become familiar with the casting process

3 to understand audition etiquette

4 to organize information into a viable rehearsal schedule

Project Specs

Special Needs Students
Students with visual impairment may need to work in a larger format than the one offered on The Cast Activity Sheet. Help these students create larger-sized schedules.

Advanced Students
In addition to the chapter project, assign the Casting a Play Worksheet, p. 61, of the Resource Binder. To complete the project, have students create a rehearsal schedule for *Death of a Salesman*.

On Your Feet

Ask students whether they think it would be better to engage their fellow auditioners in conversation while waiting to audition or to remain silent. Tell them there are no specific rules about this, but that it is a good idea to be sensitive to another performer's preference, especially if he or she wants to be left alone to concentrate.

---

16 The Cast

The process of selecting actors for various roles, called **casting**, can make or break a show. Some directors consider casting to be ninety percent of their job! It's important to find the best actor for each role so that the performance will be as effective as possible. This chapter will focus on the cast as they audition and rehearse in preparation for opening night.

Project Specs

Project Description For this project, you will create and discuss for no more than six minutes a rehearsal schedule for a production of a two-act play.

Purpose to learn how to create a real-world rehearsal schedule using information from a particular play

Materials a sheet listing various personnel and duties for six weeks of rehearsal or The Cast Activity Sheet provided by your teacher; colored pens or pencils; an overhead projector and the appropriate transparency sheets

Theatre Terms

auditions
callbacks
cameo
casting
casting call
casting director
cold reading
double cast
off book
rehearsals
spiking
understudy

On Your Feet

With a partner, improvise a very short scene in which you both play actors waiting in line for the opportunity to audition for a play.

The casting director of *Martin Guerre* had to find actors who could look, speak, and move according to the parts played—from farmer to war hero.

Theatre Terms

auditions events at which actors try out for a role in a play

callbacks when actors are called back for a second audition

cameo a one-scene part

casting selecting actors for various roles

casting call an audition notice

casting director the person in charge of selecting actors for various roles

cold reading when an actor auditions for a role without having read the script

double cast selecting two actors for each role; the casts then split the performances

off book having one's lines memorized

rehearsals practices of the play in preparation for performance

spiking marking with tape where furniture will be placed onstage

understudy an actor who learns a role in case the lead actor cannot perform

Casting is usually accomplished through a series of tryouts or **auditions.** The audition time, place, and specific procedures for community tryouts are often published in local newspapers. The **casting call** for school auditions might appear in the school paper or on the school Web site, be announced over the PA system, or be posted in the school building. Scripts may be found in the school or local library, where those who are interested in auditioning may read them and prepare scenes.

Some theatres employ a **casting director** to find actors for particular parts (see page 182). Directors may sometimes prefer a **cold reading** at auditions. This means the performer is probably unfamiliar with the script and is reading the lines for the first time.

If you audition, you will usually start by filling out a casting sheet similar to the one on page 182. You will then read a scene or scenes in combination with others. The director will announce the first audition scene and assign two or more actors to perform it.

After the preliminary auditions, the director selects those actors who seem best suited to the parts. Sometimes there are as many as four people chosen as possible candidates for a role. In this

Tell students that some auditions require the actors to present one- to two-minute prepared monologues. Most professional actors have several monologues memorized so that if they are asked to present a monologue, they can do a contemporary or a classical reading, a comic or dramatic one, and so on.

To find the right cast, a director may have to look at a great many actors. And although directors take notes about most of the people who audition for them, to a large extent they must rely on their memories when deciding which actors to call back. Tell students that professional actors often wear the same clothes to both their first audition and their callback. This is thought to jar the auditor's memory of the audition that earned the actor the callback.

Visual Cue

The following prompts can be used to help students exercise their **critical viewing skills.**

- In what time period and in what part of the world might *Martin Guerre* be set?

- What type of characters make up the chorus of this musical? Are they rich? poor? Do they live in the city or the country?

- What kind of challenges would you face if you were performing in such a large group?

Resource Binder
- The Cast Activity Sheet, p. 78
- Casting a Play Worksheet, p. 79
- Critique Sheet: Rehearsal Schedule, p. 80
- Cast Test, p. 81
- Resume Form, p. 166
- Casting Sheet, p. 167
- Audition Evaluation Form, p. 168

Handbook Connections
pages 562–564 and 611

To Have on Hand
- Colored pens and pencils
- Scripts or anthologies for students from which to choose their plays

The Casting Sheet

Some casting sheets ask actors to list their weight. However, it's a good idea to leave the issue of weight out of the casting process in a school setting. There are plenty of stressors involved in auditioning and performing. Worrying about weight and other body-image issues shouldn't be among them. You may want to find other samples of casting sheets to show the students so they are aware of other points of view, however. Discuss the items on the casting sheet on this page, and make students aware they will be expected to fill them out legibly.

Show, Don't Tell Model for your students the correct way to introduce yourself at an audition. Show them the difference between a slumping posture and a confident one, a quavering voice and one that is supported from the diaphragm, a firm handshake and a weak one.

ACTivity Advanced Students

Have students choose a monologue that they would like to present as an audition piece. Remind them to look for something that fits their age range. The monologue should be less than one page long and should run no more than two minutes. Students may either memorize their monologue or read it aloud for the class.

ACTivity ELL Students

Ask students to prepare a monologue in their primary language. As students present their monologues, the rest of the class can take notes and analyze the types of emotional content being expressed.

Vocabulary Enhancement

The largest or most important roles in the show are called the *leads*. Smaller parts are *supporting roles*. Actors sometimes refer to a large or particularly juicy part as a *plum role*.

case, the director will hold **callbacks,** a second audition in which only those under serious consideration for the roles are called. At the callbacks, the director may give you suggestions as to how to perform a scene. He or she might also direct you in stage movement. You may be asked to memorize a scene or speech or to improvise a scene.

When casting, the director takes into account physical appearance, personality, level of acting, and the chemistry among possible cast members. Singing or dancing skills may also be noted. In drama class, performers are cast according to what skills they need to develop. For public presentation, the director casts the actors best suited to the roles.

The director will be looking for people with expressive, supple voices; good physical presences; and emotional intensity. In short, the director wants to find a group of actors who can engage an audience's attention and imagination, have a variety of physiques and voices, and seem to work well together.

When auditioning for a part, you may be asked to fill out a form similar to this one.

Casting Sheet

Name _____ Height _____ Year in School _____
Address _____ Female _____ Male _____
Phone _____ E-mail _____ Hair Color _____
Special Talents (sing, dance, play musical instrument, etc.) _____

Check what you would like to work on:

___ Costumes	___ Makeup	___ Publicity
___ Director's Assistant	___ Prompter	___ Stage Manager
___ Lighting & Sound	___ Props	

On back of page, please list:
1. Previous acting experience (include play, role, place)
2. Hours when you can rehearse
3. Other commitments (orchestra, sports, work, religious schedule, etc.)

Director's comments:

Appearance _____ Ability to take direction _____
Voice _____ Personality _____
Speech _____ Possible for role of _____
Interpretation _____
Movement _____

Notes

_____

_____

_____

_____

_____

_____

_____

Spotlight on

The Audition

As a beginning actor, you may not get many chances to perform for a paying audience. But you can perform for theatrical peers or professionals every time you audition.

Most auditions begin with a notice, to which you must respond by calling to make an appointment or by appearing at an open call. The notice will probably indicate whether actors will be expected to read a scene from the play, perform a serious or comic monologue from memory, sing, dance, or do any combination of these things.

In any case, it is a good idea to read the play and make note of the characters in the play. The better you know the play, the better you will be able to concentrate on acting in the scene, rather than reading or, worse, finding your place!

Once you have read the play or a description of the play, ask yourself:
- Which of these characters would I like to play?
- As which character am I likely to be cast?

Then prepare yourself for the audition by thinking about the character in the context of the play. Get a sense of the character's history and circumstances, hopes and fears, and loves and hates. Incorporate them as best you can into your monologue or scene.

As you wait for your audition, do so quietly. If you are allowed to, listen to the other readers. You may learn something that will help you in a later reading.

When you are called onstage, assume the role of a professional. Focus on the character's objective. Remember to breathe. And remember that the director wants you to do well—he or she is on your side. As you perform, be open to any acting advice the director may have. And have fun—isn't that the point?

Being relaxed and well prepared is important when auditioning.

Spotlight on

The Audition There are plenty of dos and don'ts when it comes to auditioning. Here are just a few.

- Many theatres do not allow waiting actors to listen in on other people's auditions. Instead they will ask you to wait outside the auditorium or audition space until someone summons you.

- In the Special Talents section of the casting sheet, never list a skill you do not possess. It can be very embarrassing if a director calls upon you to perform that skill at the audition or after you have been cast.

- During your audition, you may be called upon to deliver a monologue or play a scene a second time to implement an instruction from the director. If this happens, listen closely to the director's instructions, and do your best. Directors look for actors who are both flexible and able to take direction.

- No matter how you feel about your audition performance, you should thank the director and the other auditors at the end. Professionalism demands a friendly and polite presentation from beginning to end. You are not finished auditioning until you are out of the auditors' sight.

Chapter 16 The Cast **183**

Backstage Gossip: Standing Out from the Crowd

An aspiring singer auditions for a Broadway show. She is young and chatters nervously to the auditors. She's a mess; her shoes don't match, and to make matters worse, she's chewing gum. When it comes time for her to perform, she pulls the wad of gum out of her mouth and sticks it to the bottom of her chair. Then she begins to sing. The power of her voice and the confidence of her performance stun the auditors. After the young singer leaves, one of the auditors plays a hunch and checks the bottom of the chair—where there is no gum to be found.

Who was that memorable singer with the big-time voice? None other than Barbra Streisand.

Tell students that in addition to studying a major role, the understudy often has a smaller role in the show. For example, a chorus member might understudy the lead. The understudy's part is then sometimes covered by a crew member who is familiar with the show or by doubling up the chorus.

ACTivity Read Albert Einstein's quote to the class. Then have students compare it to the one in their books. How are the two quotes similar? Does one appeal to them more than the other? Why?

Rehearsals

Russian director and acting teacher Konstantin Stanislavski believed that "There are no small parts, only small actors." He believed that even cameo roles were important to a production, and the actor with the small, or bit, part had an obligation just as compelling as the star of the show.

ACTivity Read Stanislavski's quote above to students, and ask them to rephrase the sentiment in their own words. Ask them whether they think it holds true today.

The director will either contact the actors he or she has chosen or post the cast list on a bulletin board. Not getting a part you wanted can be hard, but just remember that no actor—whether famous or not—has ever gotten all the roles he or she wanted. Learning to face disappointment is part of being an actor.

To provide acting opportunities for a larger number of students, some schools **double cast.** With a double cast, two groups split the performances. However, this process takes a lot of extra rehearsal time, sometimes at the expense of a polished performance. Another choice is to select a single cast with understudies for the main roles. An **understudy** attends all rehearsals and learns a role thoroughly. If an actor becomes ill or can't perform, the understudy is able to go on in his or her place.

> **"Leave your dirty shoes at the door!"**
>
> Thus states an old rehearsal adage. It means that no matter what your mood or current situation, you must come to each rehearsal fresh and ready to do your best. Leave your worries at home.

Rehearsals

Once the play is cast, the director must organize **rehearsals,** various run-throughs of the play. A rehearsal schedule—one of several theatre systems for keeping a production on track—makes the best possible use of everyone's time. To this end, the director should group together scenes that feature the same characters. With proper attention to detail, only the necessary actors need be called for each rehearsal. This avoids the long waits that can lead to boredom and inattention. At the beginning of the rehearsal process, the director hands out a rehearsal schedule to the cast and the crew. One copy of the schedule is tacked to a board where the rehearsals take place. Often this schedule cannot be altered, so all the cast involved must meet it! Even if a role is a small **cameo,** a brief one-scene part, the actor is expected to show up to every rehearsal to which he or she is called. Being prompt and maintaining the highest standards of behavior are very important. Rehearsals are hard work, but if everyone cooperates and works as a team, the time spent will be not only fun, but also productive. After all, each member of the cast is working toward the same goal: a great show.

Rehearsal schedules vary according to the difficulty of the play, the experience of the actors, and the time available. Full-length school plays typically require at least a five- or six-week rehearsal period. That means committing five or six days a week of two to three hours each to rehearsal time. One-act plays obviously take less rehearsal time. For these shows, rehearsal generally lasts only three to four weeks with three to four sessions

Backstage Gossip: A Major Understudy

At Chicago's Goodman Theatre, when a cast member became ill and couldn't go on in the major role of Hecuba in the 2003 production of *The Trojan Women,* chorus member Laura T. Fisher stepped into the role. That left Fisher's role empty, so the production's director, Tony Award-winner and MacArthur "Genius" Grant recipient Mary Zimmerman, went on in her place until a replacement could be hired.

per week. It's important to schedule as many rehearsals as possible to maintain the highest performance standards. Some casts practice after school and some in the evenings. Cast members should count on at least two long Saturday rehearsals at some point in the schedule. The director (or teacher) may ask for a personal pledge that cast members will attend all rehearsals required of them.

The Rehearsal Sequence

The director typically provides specific goals for each rehearsal session. The following illustrates a standard rehearsal sequence.

Reading rehearsals begin right after casting is complete. Actors and designers work as a group to gain an overall understanding of the play. The director discusses his or her concept for the show—including specifics about characters, plot, and theme. The actors read through the script, after which the director may ask them questions about the play or their specific characters. Actors should also take this opportunity to ask questions about motivation and character relationships.

Blocking rehearsals are conducted onstage or in a large room where the floor plan of the set is taped onto the floor. Blocking rehearsals work out the actors' onstage movements. You will read more about blocking in Chapter 17.

Developing rehearsals begin on each act once the blocking is set. When the actors have memorized their lines, which is called being **off book,** they can fully concentrate on projecting emotion and relating to others onstage. During this stage of rehearsal, you will begin to work with rehearsal props and certain costume pieces. These rehearsals may be tailored to specific situations within the script, for example, love scenes, fights, or crowd scenes.

The Language of
THEATRE

Use learning strategies to build spoken English as you monitor and self-correct your oral language.

- Practice saying each of the theatre terms on page 180. Ask a teacher or classmate for help if needed by saying, "How do you say this word?" Then repeat the word yourself.

- Tell a partner the meaning of the terms *auditions, callbacks,* and *casting.* Use non-verbal cues or ask for help for unknown words.

- As you practice your presentation of a schedule for the *rehearsals* of a two-act play, notice where you might use synonyms or choose to describe or define something when specific words are unknown.

- When you present your schedule for the *rehearsals* of a two-act play, use synonyms or circumlocution—general explanatory words—if specific words or phrases are unavailable to you in the moment.

The Rehearsal Sequence

Students might think that actors learn their lines during rehearsal. They might be surprised to find out that most actors study their lines outside of rehearsal. They use rehearsal time to figure out important details of their character.

A typical rehearsal period for a full-length play is about 100 hours. This includes all the phases of rehearsal discussed on pages 185 through 188.

Tell students that when working on a play, the only stupid question is the one that goes unasked.

As soon as the actors are off book, the stage manager (or prompter) goes *on book* during rehearsals. If an actor loses a line, he or she calls "Line," and the stage manager says the missing line aloud to get the actor back on track. If an actor simply misses lines and keeps on going, the stage manager makes note of the missing text and reminds the actor about it later. If the actor's dropped lines cause other actors in the scene to flounder, however, the stage manager will generally clear up the problem on the spot by stopping the action.

ACTivity Have students choose a play they are familiar with and imagine that they have been cast in a production of this play. They are at the very first rehearsal. Ask them to write a list of questions—about the play, the production, or the director's vision—they might have.

The Language of
THEATRE

Explain to students that listening to strong English speakers will help them monitor and self-correct their spoken English. Encourage them to use learning strategies such as requesting assistance, employing nonverbal cues, and using synonyms and circumlocutions when exact English words are not known.

Quotables

Below are two quotes from many attributed to the great Russian director Konstantin Stanislavski. They were written in 1897.

Today Hamlet, tomorrow an extra, but even as an extra the actor must be an artist.

Arriving late at the theatre, laziness, capriciousness, hysteria, ignorance of parts, the necessity of repeating the same thing twice, are all equally harmful and must be rooted out.

Tell students that, particularly in period dramas, actors often begin to simulate their costumes or costume pieces early in rehearsal to get used to, for example, a long skirt, a corset, high-heeled shoes, knee-length boots, and so on. They do this so that when the actual costumes are provided they will make the transition more comfortably.

ACTivity Have your students read a short play, such as *The Actor's Nightmare* by Christopher Durang. Ask them to make notes about the play for a possible photo call as they read. Then have them make a list of five to ten setup shots to be taken in reverse order of the play.

Vocabulary Enhancement

If an actor must be replaced once the play has opened, the understudy is trained into the role during what is called a *put-in rehearsal* or an *understudy rehearsal*.

Polishing rehearsals are all about the little touches that make a good production great. In polishing, the director works on the actors' projection and emphasis. Murky moments between actors are cleaned up and strengthened. The pacing and rhythm of the play are perfected. Any extraneous movements are eliminated at this point, and group

Actors rehearse on a spiked stage in order to practice moving around furniture that will be positioned onstage.

scenes are tightened to allow for stronger ensemble playing. Polishing rehearsals are very important. Rehearsal schedules should be planned to allow for sufficient polishing before the show opens. Including enough time to polish the production is very important.

Technical rehearsals must be held onstage. The purpose of the technical rehearsal is to synchronize technical and performance aspects of the production. The first technical rehearsal can be long and arduous. It is often referred to as a "dry tech," meaning a rehearsal specifically to set technical cues, without actors. Also at this point, scenery shifts are choreographed and curtains are hung.

The next technical rehearsal is with the whole cast. The director asks only for those scenes requiring scene shifts, light and sound, or major prop changes. Crews now mark the furniture positions on the stage floor with masking tape, a process called **spiking.** If the schedule allows, actors do a dress parade. This means that they put on their costumes and walk across the stage under the proper lighting. This is done so that the costume crew can make any necessary adjustments.

Three dress rehearsals should be conducted in full costume. Prior to the first dress rehearsal, the director gives the cast and crew instructions—

From the Field: The Actor's Instrument

For the theatre artist, a vital part of his instrument is the voice; therefore careful consideration must be taken to protect and train it.

In his book *Acting One*, Robert Cohen writes of the importance of training; "for the actor is both the player and the instrument played; the actor therefore plays upon herself or himself in much the same way that a violinist plays upon a violin; an actor, like the violinist, can be no better than the instrument."

usually in writing—about the time, procedure, and requirements of each dress rehearsal and performance. Dress rehearsals begin on time, whether the cast and crew are ready or not! The purpose of dress rehearsal is to get the show to performance level. There is an old saying that "A bad dress rehearsal means a great opening night." Don't fall for this. A bad dress rehearsal usually only creates opening night jitters. Dress rehearsals should go smoothly, however, if everyone works efficiently.

The first dress rehearsal is the most hectic, as it coordinates sound, lights, scenery, and props. The cast wears full costumes. The director sits in the audience and watches the entire show. The prompter times the show and each scene shift. (Scene shifts should be executed within a matter of seconds.) Intermissions should be no longer than ten minutes. The only time a dress rehearsal should be interrupted is if someone is injured or a major technical problem occurs. The director gives notes on the performance at the end of the rehearsal.

The second dress rehearsal adds make-up and other technical requirements. The director also stages the curtain call—or actors' bows—at the end of the show. (See the Spotlight on Taking Your Bows on page 70 for more on this.) After this dress rehearsal, most

productions have a photo call. The director usually selects the setups in advance and hands out copies of the sequence of photos. Because the cast will be in costume for the end of the show, the photographer usually shoots the photos in reverse order. Sometimes the director will give notes after the second dress rehearsal, but many directors withhold the critique until just prior to the final dress rehearsal.

The third or final dress rehearsal should run exactly like a performance. There should be absolutely no interruptions, and every detail should be in place. Some directors make this an *invited dress,* meaning that there will be some guests in the audience. This is particularly important when the production is a comedy because the cast will need practice holding for laughs. Before this final rehearsal, there is generally a full cast-and-crew meeting backstage. At this point, the cast gives the crews a round of applause for all their hard work leading up to opening night. While the cast has been following a rehearsal calendar, the technical crews have been following their *production calendar*, another theatre system, with deadlines for each aspect of the production: set design and construction, lights, sound, scenery, props, costumes, and makeup.

During dress rehearsals, many directors move from seat to seat to watch and listen to the play from various spots around the theatre. In this way they can check to make sure that all the blocking is smooth and that the actors are visible and audible at all times.

The Language of THEATRE

Have students collaborate with peers to demonstrate their listening comprehension.

- Ask a strong English speaker to explain the different types of rehearsals. Have students say words or short phrases that explain each type.
- Have students listen to an explanation of the different types of rehearsals and collaborate with a partner on a short presentation on the topic for the class.
- Invite students to practice their presentations with a partner and give and receive feedback in order to strengthen the presentation before giving it to the class.
- Ask students to listen to classmates' presentations and then collaborate in small groups to critique one another's work.

Vocabulary Enhancement

Tell students that because actors and crew members must often maneuver scene changes in the dark, *glow tape*—tape that glows in the dark—is often used to mark sharp corners, steps, and the edge of the stage. This helps production personnel get their bearings when they are unable to see clearly.

Quotable

Use the quote below as a writing prompt or discussion starter.

We respond to a drama to that extent to which it corresponds to our dreamlife.

David Mamet, Playwright and Director

The Performance

Tell students that in the professional theatre, stage managers rarely take roll call. Instead the actors sign a call sheet when they arrive for each performance. The stage manager checks the call sheet periodically to ensure that all the actors are on hand in plenty of time for the curtain. If an actor does not make his or her scheduled call time, the stage manager must then try to locate the missing actor. Remind students that, as actors, it is their duty to be on time. If they are going to be even a few minutes late, they should call in.

After the Performance

- You might want to assign the task of tidying dressing rooms to a small group of energetic students who can complete the task quickly and efficiently.

- Personally check to see that the set is completely struck the day after the final performance.

- Go over the list of borrowed items two days after the performance to be sure they have all been returned.

- Assign various duties to all the cast and crew for bringing food and beverages to the cast party, and let everyone know when it will be.

The Performance

At last the opening night arrives. Now all the hard work on the part of the cast, crews, director, and producer will pay off in a memorable performance. Here are some final thoughts to help you prepare to create the best show possible.

Before and During the Performance

- Only those with specific jobs are allowed backstage.

- Crews should arrive early enough to have the stage set up two hours before show time.

- The cast should arrive at least one hour before curtain time to warm up, put on makeup and costumes, and check personal props. When these duties are completed, each cast member should remain quietly in the dressing room getting into character.

- The stage manager calls roll about fifteen minutes before curtain time. Then the director talks to the cast and crew. This is generally a pep talk, but most directors also remind the cast not to change anything regardless of what their friends and family members may have to say about the show.

- When you're onstage, small errors usually go unnoticed by the audience. If you make a mistake, such as calling another character by the wrong name, do not call attention to your error. Go on. If another character fails to enter on time, create inconsequential talk to fill the gap. Do not check your watch and say, "I wonder where [the missing character] is."

- As in dress rehearsal, during the production the stage manager has charge of the performance. The director sits out front and takes notes or observes the audience reaction.

- The show should always begin on time. Prompt curtain times ensure that the audience will arrive on time.

After the Performance

- The actors remove their makeup and costumes and tidy the dressing rooms. Actors should never leave a mess for the crews.

- After the final show, the crews should immediately strike the set and props.

- Borrowed items should be returned on the day following the last performance.

- Return any missing pages to the prompt book.

- Have a cast party. This is a theatre tradition; everyone is invited—cast, crews, and director. It is often held onstage after strike. If the strike is expected to go late, the party sometimes is scheduled for another night.

Notes

PREPARE

Create Your Rehearsal Schedule

Imagine that you are a director about to begin rehearsals for a two-act play. You may have a particular play in mind, or you can find one at the library. You may choose from plays listed in Unit Eight or you may be assigned a play by your teacher. Your assignment is to create a complete six-week rehearsal schedule. You may create your own calendar or list or use the Activity Sheet your teacher gives you. You may wish to make a larger copy of the Activity Sheet so that you can include all the relevant information on your rehearsal schedule. If a whiteboard is available, be prepared to display your schedule on it.

On the following page is a sample rehearsal schedule. Note that it does not include which actors are called for each rehearsal or the hours during which the rehearsal will take place.

Career Focus

Casting Director

If you're a "people person," you might consider a career as a casting director. These consultants contact and secure suitable actors to audition for various projects. They are the conduit that connects actors and their agents to the people and organizations that do the hiring.

Many professional theatre companies have full-time casting directors. But casting directors may also work on a freelance basis to cast for film, radio, and television. Some casting directors work for advertising agencies to find the right actors for television and radio spots, print ads, and voice-overs. The interpersonal, communication, and negotiating skills and experience of a casting director may transfer to other human resources careers.

Through a blend of experience, intuition, and savvy, the casting director brings the best possible actors into the audition process. Usually the casting director prescreens possible actors and secures them to audition but leaves final casting decisions to the director or producer. Once casting is complete, however, the casting director often negotiates money and scheduling with the actor's agent.

Most professional casting directors are familiar with a vast number of actors within their home city, but they also maintain connections with other casting services and talent agencies to secure the largest possible actor list. To determine whether to pursue this career, evaluate the skills needed. For example, do you have the conflict resolution skills to be a strong negotiator? Do you have the networking skills to maintain a large web of connections? Refer to the chart on page 10 for more ways to evaluate this career.

PREPARE

Create Your Rehearsal Schedule

Good examples of two-act plays students might like to work on:

- *How I Learned to Drive* by Paula Vogel
- *Collected Stories* by Donald Margulies
- *Spinning into Butter* by Rebecca Gilman
- *Holes* by Louis Sachar
- *Jar the Floor* by Cheryl West
- *Two Trains Running* by August Wilson

Tell students that there is no specific format for creating a rehearsal schedule. They can set it up however they like; but remind them that their goal is for the schedule to be as easy to read as possible.

Vocabulary Enhancement

Let students know that when an actor accidentally leaves out a sequence of lines and picks up at a point further on in the script, he or she is said to have *jumped lines* or *jumped the cue*.

Career Focus: Casting Director

ACTivity **Advanced Students**
Have students do Internet research to find out more about casting directors and, if possible, arrange an online or telephone interview. They can use the casting Web sites or contact large regional theatres that have full-time casting directors on staff.

Backstage Gossip: A Very Young Fan

After a performance one evening, Bill Cosby was visited backstage by an aide who asked him to autograph a baby book for a young couple who had recently had their first child. The book was soon returned to the couple, who excitedly searched for Cosby's signature. Unable to find it, they left the theatre rather disappointed. While looking through the book some time later, the mother saw a page entitled "Baby's first sentence." The Cos had written: "I like Bill Cosby!"

from the Web site *anecdotage.com*

Here are some tips you can share with students to help them create the most effective schedules possible.

- To fit all the information on your rehearsal schedule, you'll need to write small. Use pencil first. Then you can go over your work in pen once you've figured out the whole schedule.
- Remember to be consistent with your color coding. For example, if the color blue indicates actors, don't also use blue for designers.

Mark each rehearsal's specific goals with a star or an asterisk.

Copy the Schedule and Rehearse Your Talk

Before students copy their schedules, remind them to double-check their work against an actual calendar. In a real-life rehearsal situation, errors in the days of the week or month can be both embarrassing and problematic.

Make sure students have access to a copier, or copy the rehearsal schedules for them. Provide instruction or assistance as needed for use of a whiteboard or other projection technology.

You will create a schedule that includes the date of each rehearsal, the specific actors called for each rehearsal, the hours of the rehearsal, and the location where the rehearsal will take place (auditorium, rehearsal room, and so on). Remember that rehearsals close to opening night, especially technical and dress rehearsals, always take place on the stage where the performance will be.

Remember to schedule only those actors you will need for each rehearsal. For example, if you are only rehearsing the first half of Act I, don't call in actors who appear only in the second half of Act I. Your job is to make the most efficient use of everyone's time. Write schedule information pertaining to cast members in one color. For crew members, use a different color. For scheduling that involves both cast and crew, use a third color.

Remember that Saturday rehearsals can be longer and can take place during the day. Also bear in mind what you have learned about technical rehearsals and performances. Have a specific goal for each rehearsal on your schedule.

You will need a calendar of the current year so you can write accurate dates next to each rehearsal day.

You may decide that your schedule is for the fall or the spring production. Choose your dates accordingly. Note that on the first day of rehearsal all cast and crew members are called. For subsequent rehearsals, you may either schedule by act and scene numbers or (for smaller cast shows) by character names.

Copy the Schedule and Rehearse Your Talk

Be prepared to display your schedule on a whiteboard if available or try to make an oversized copy on a copier. Rehearse your presentation. Allow about a minute to address comments or answer questions about the play or your rehearsal schedule after your talk. The talk itself should not exceed five minutes.

This schedule calls for five rehearsals a week, two Saturday rehearsals, and three performances. Adjust your schedule to fit the needs of the play you chose.

Sample Rehearsal Schedule for a Two-Act Play

1st week:

Monday	Read complete play with all cast and crew.
Tuesday	Read first half; discussion and analysis.
Wednesday	Read second half; discussion and analysis.
Thursday	Act I: block first half; repeat to set.
Friday	Act I; block remainder; repeat to set.

Notes

_____

_____

_____

_____

_____

_____

_____

Sample Rehearsal Schedule for a Two-Act Play (Continued)

2nd week:

Monday	Act I; characterization and motivation.
Tuesday	Act II; block first half; repeat to set.
Wednesday	Act II; block remainder; repeat to set.
Thursday	Run through Acts I and II; adjust groupings if necessary.
Friday	Act II; characterization and motivation.
Saturday	Special private rehearsals for love scenes, fight scenes, etc.

3rd week:

Monday	Act I memorized; no books; work on detailed business.
Tuesday	Run through Act I (no books).
Wednesday	Act II; work on belief and response; actors should look at each other and listen to each other.
Thursday	Act II memorized; no books; work on business detail.
Friday	Run through Act II memorized; clarify business detail; use hand props.

4th week:

Monday	Run through Acts I and II memorized; work on detailed business.
Tuesday	Run through Acts I and II; work on audibility, groupings, characterization.
Wednesday	Polish Act I; business, lines, tempo, climax, props.
Thursday	Polish Act II; business, lines, tempo, climax, props.
Friday	Run through Acts I and II; concentrate on minor roles.
Saturday	Polish Acts I and II.

5th week:

Monday	Run through Acts I and II; work on audibility, unity, tempo, climax, line pickup, transitions, ensemble playing. Check for spontaneity. Actors must not anticipate lines or mouth the lines of others.
Tuesday	Polish difficult scenes, climaxes, etc.
Wednesday	Technical rehearsal without actors. Set up scenery, furniture, lights, etc. Practice shifts. Actors may run a line rehearsal with the prompter. No movement; just say lines and pick up cues readily.
Thursday	Technical rehearsal with actors. Repeat scenes needed for technical changes. Do costume review.
Friday	Run through complete show with set, lights, props.

6th week:

Monday	First dress; full costume, lights, sound, props, scenery, and shifts.
Tuesday	Second dress; as Monday, plus makeup. Plan curtain calls; take pictures.
Wednesday	Invitational dress; performance level.
Thursday	Opening night performance.
Friday	Performance.
Saturday	Performance, strike, and cast party.

Sample Rehearsal Schedule

Go through the sample schedule with your students. Ask:

- What kind of rehearsals are taking place during week one? (reading and blocking)
- During week two? (blocking and developing)
- During week three? (developing)
- During week four? (developing and polishing)
- During week five? (polishing and technical)
- During week six? (technical and performances)

Quotable

Somewhere in talking and rehearsing, there is a magical moment where actors catch a current; they're on the right road. If they really catch it, then whatever they do from then on is correct and it all comes out of them from that point on.

David Lynch, Director

PRESENT

Display and Explain Your Rehearsal Schedule

Tell students not to get too caught up in explaining the plot and other details of the play. Their project should remain focused on the schedule itself.

Remind students that they will have no more than six minutes to complete their presentations, including one minute for questions. However, if a student completes the presentation in less than a minute or two, you might step in and ask a few more questions to encourage further sharing.

CRITIQUE

Evaluate a Schedule

Prompt students to ask each presenter specific questions about details of the schedule. They should take particular note of any areas of the schedule that do not seem clear or easy to follow.

Let students know that you will be using the same rubrics for them as they are using for each other. In addition to their presentations, you may also wish to evaluate students on how well they assess each other's presentation.

Collect the student evaluations. You might wish to read a few of their evaluation paragraphs aloud.

PRESENT

Display and Explain Your Rehearsal Schedule

When your name is called, bring your rehearsal schedule or Activity Sheet to the front of the classroom. If a whiteboard is available, display your schedule on it, or use some other projection technology if available.

Your presentation will include a very brief description of the play you chose. Then take about five minutes to talk about your schedule. Be sure to mention any special rehearsal considerations the play warranted. You may wish to discuss why you broke the schedule down the way you did. Your entire presentation (with comments and questions) should not exceed six minutes. When you are finished, remove the schedule and hand it to your teacher. Then return to your seat.

CRITIQUE

Evaluate a Schedule

Select one classmate's rehearsal schedule to evaluate. Imagine that you are an actor in the play. Listen carefully to what your classmate says about the schedule. Look carefully at the way the schedule is set up and organized. You will not have time to do an in-depth analysis. You will mainly be judging this schedule on legibility, clarity of organization, color coding, and consistency. Rate the schedule on a scale of 1 to 5, with 5 being "outstanding," and 1 being "needs much improvement."

After you have rated the schedule based on the qualities suggested above, write a short paragraph explaining your evaluation.

Backstage Gossip: Department of Nightmare Auditions

Actor/singer Brian Duguay landed an audition for a production at a small theatre in Florida. They sent him two scenes to work on. When he got to the theatre, the person holding the audition said, "I don't have a reader for you today. I don't want to read it, so you read your part, and when it's time for the other character to speak, just leave space there and I'll imagine what it sounds like. We'll just pretend we hear the lines." The startled actor did the dialogue all alone.

Additional Projects

1 Read one of the following plays, and create a list of suitable actors you might cast. You can use well-known theatre, television, or film actors.

- *Medea* by Euripides
- *The Seagull* by Anton Chekhov
- *The Crucible* by Arthur Miller
- *The Heidi Chronicles* by Wendy Wasserstein
- *Arcadia* by Tom Stoppard
- *Cloud Nine* by Caryl Churchill

2 Watch a video of a play and write a review of the performance based on the casting of three characters.

3 Create two or three pages for the playbill that will accompany a play of your choice. Include interesting biographies of all the cast members.

4 In two paragraphs, evaluate the skills needed to be a casting director, and connect these skills and related theatre experiences to careers outside the theatre.

5 Review the sample rehearsal schedule on pages 190-191. For each week, describe the role of the stage manager, demonstrating your understanding of the role of theatre management skills.

6 Read the excerpt found in Unit Eight of *Does My Head Look Big in This?* by Jeff Gottesfeld and Elizabeth Wong, based on the book by Randa Abdel-Fattah. Write a short rehearsal schedule for this scene, along with the names of classmates and the roles they would play. Try to cast both males and females.

7 **Theatre Journal** Think of a character from a play you have read or seen. Looking around the classroom, think about which of your classmates might play the role in a school production. Write a short entry explaining your choice.

Scene from *Arcadia* by Tom Stoppard

The Cast Test

The test for this chapter is available in blackline master form in the Resource Binder, page 81.

Visual Cue

Use the following prompts to help students exercise **critical viewing skills.**

- What can you tell about the time period in which *Arcadia* is set?
- If you had to provide a physical description of these actors on a casting sheet, what would you write?

For More Information

Books

Cohen, Robert, *Acting One,* McGraw-Hill, 5th ed., 2007.

Kohlhaas, Karen, *Monologue Audition: A Practical Guide for Actors,* Limelight, 2004.

Kondazian, Karen, *The Actors Encyclopedia of Casting Directors: Conversations with Over 100 Casting Directors on How to Get the Job,* Lone Eagle, 2000.

Shurtleff, Michael, *Audition: Everything an Actor Needs to Know to Get the Part,* Walker and Co., 2003. (This text, originally published in 1978, remains a highly regarded handbook for auditioning actors.)

Other Media

Auditioning: An Introduction, DVD, Insight Media, 2010.

How to Audition, DVD, Insight Media, 2011.

Standby Cue 101: An Introduction to Calling Live Performances, DVD, Insight Media, 2011.

Substitute Teacher Activities

- Assign the Casting a Play Worksheet on page 79 of the Resource Binder.
- Assign one or more of the Additional Projects on this page.
- Teach the Auditions sections of the Student Handbook on pages 562–564 and 611.
- **Hold a Mock Audition** for a play the class will choose. Have four or five students be the co-directors (auditors).

They will decide whether they want those auditioning to prepare monologues or to read from the script. The remainder of the class then either selects monologues to present or chooses a scene from the play to prepare with a partner (or partners). This activity may take several days.

Make sure that each student has a chance to audition and that as many as possible take the position of auditor.

Theatre Journal

Use the following as an additional or substitute prompt.

Remind students that their casting ideas should be positively phrased. Also suggest that they think about typecasting and make an effort to avoid it. They should also avoid casting friends in major roles just because they are friends.

Theatre **Then** and Now

Talk to students about the fact that directors sometimes use *gender-blind casting*. This means that men can be cast in women's roles, and vice versa. On occasion, a playwright will do a bit of gender-bending also, as Caryl Churchill did in her play *Cloud Nine*.

In 1979, Churchill received a great deal of attention for this play, in which a female actor plays a sensitive schoolboy and a male actor plays an unfulfilled wife. The result is comic and thought-provoking. The play illustrates one of Churchill's recurrent themes—shedding light on gender distinctions.

ACTivity Ask students to find or create scenes for one male and one female actor. Then have pairs of students play the scenes with the roles reversed and discuss their experience.

Other Cultures, Other Times

- Hrotsvitha of Gandersheim, a Benedictine nun writing in the 10th century, is the first recorded female playwright. Six of her plays still survive.

- The first recorded woman playwright to write in English was Katherine of Sutton. Between 1363 and 1376 she wrote entertaining adaptations of liturgical plays.

- Mary Sidney Herbert, Countess of Pembroke, became the first woman in England to publish a play (*Antonie*, 1592).

Theatre **Then** and Now

A Leading Lady of His Time: Edward Kynaston

Edward Kynaston

Some of the greatest women's roles of all time were first played by . . . men. That's right: toward the middle of the 17th century, the most beautiful woman on the London stage was not a woman at all. And that didn't bother audiences one bit. The "leading lady" in question was actor Edward Kynaston (1619–1687), and he would go on to play an interesting role in theatre history.

At that time in England, women weren't allowed to set foot on the stage for any reason—and that included playing female characters in the plays of William Shakespeare and others. These roles were instead taken by smooth-faced, fair-skinned young men. And Kynaston was one of the best of these—he was much admired for the naturalness of his delivery, not to mention his physical beauty, in roles such as Desdemona in Shakespeare's tragedy *Othello*.

In 1660, Charles II took the throne as king of England, and with him came a new era of tolerance and religious and social reforms. In 1662, he decreed that from then on women would be allowed to play female roles in the theatre. But King Charles wasn't content to leave it at that. He also enacted a law forbidding men to play women.

And so it was that poor Edward Kynaston became the last of the great male players of women. He went from being a popular leading player to an often out-of-work actor unable to make a successful transition to male roles. In building his celebrity by playing only female roles, Kynaston effectively shut himself out of his own profession.

Contemporary playwright Jeffrey Hatcher chronicles and re-envisions the life and times of Edward Kynaston in a play called *Compleat Female Stage Beauty*.

 **Vi**sual Cue

Use the prompts below to help students broaden their **visual learning skills.**

- What physical attributes do you think Edward Kynaston might have possessed that made him the top-rated performer of women's roles?

- Do you think it would be difficult to play someone of the opposite gender? Why or why not?

A Leading Lady of Our Time: Cherry Jones

In his review of the 1995 Broadway revival of *The Heiress*, *New York Times* critic Vincent Canby called Cherry Jones "a splendid young actress who's new to me." This is a somewhat ironic quote in view of the fact that at the time Jones had more than fifty productions under her belt, a Tony nomination for *Our Country's Good* (1991), and a 1992 OBIE Award for her performance in Paula Vogel's play *The Baltimore Waltz*.

Jones received numerous awards, including her first Tony, for her performance in the lead role in *The Heiress*. In 2005, she received the Best Actress Tony for her work in *John Shanley's Doubt*. Jones continues to gain acclaim for her stage work, including a 2013 revival of *The Glass Menagerie* on Broadway. She also takes smaller roles in many prominent movies and television series, including a role as the first female president in the 2007 season of *24*.

Jones has a unique ability to disappear into a role by completely changing her voice and physical bearing. She's had plenty of opportunity to perfect this versatility. She trained at Carnegie-Mellon University and spent a year at the Brooklyn Academy of Music (BAM) before joining the American Repertory Company (Cambridge, MA) in 1980. There she performed in twenty-five plays in six seasons. She developed a reputation as a risk-taker, playing roles in everything from Shakespeare to Brecht.

Over the years, Cherry Jones has gone from a nearly anonymous actor to a major theatrical star. Her celebrity is easy to explain: She is completely dedicated to the craft of acting.

Cherry Jones

- In Italy in the 16th through 18th centuries women were closely involved with the *commedia dell'arte* not only as actresses, but also as *capocomico,* running companies and producing their own material.

ACTivity Encourage students to do library or Internet research on these leading ladies of the 19th and 20th centuries.

Sarah Bernhardt (1844–1923)

Ellen Terry (1847–1928)

Eleanora Duse (1859–1924)

Uta Hagen (1919–2004)

Marian Seldes (1928–)

Meryl Streep (1949–)

The Women's Project is a New York-based theatre devoted solely to plays written by women. The site *wptheater.org* contains information on female innovators throughout the history of theatre as well as links to other theatre-related sites. You might also find interesting information at *broadwayleague.com.*

Visual Cue

Have students look at the two images of Cherry Jones as she appears as Lysistrata (left) and as Josie in *Moon for the Misbegotten* (top). Ask the questions below.

- What kind of person do you think Jones has created as Josie in *Moon for the Misbegotten*?
- As Lysistrata, does Jones appear sexy, goofy, or one of the others of her descriptions in the quote at the left? How would you describe her?

Quotable

This is such a lark. I can be sexy. I can be goofy. I can be an old yenta. I can be young. I can be whatever I need to be at the moment and decide what that is as I go. I have done so much grim theater for so long. I love hard theater, but it is just so nice for once to get to go to work where the object is to be stupid and funny and dear and innocent—and driven to save Greece.

Cherry Jones, on her role in *Lysistrata*

Chapter 16 The Cast **195**

Chapter 17

Blocking

Students build their understanding of stage movement through the use of areas, levels, focus, and balance, and create and direct movement onstage. Because this involves both directing a scene and acting in one, you might want to schedule two or more class periods.

Objectives

1 to discover levels of meaning in movement

2 to understand the differences between functional and artistic movement

3 to create powerful stage pictures using stage positions

4 to effectively block and execute a scene with more than one actor

Project Specs

For this chapter, tape the floor of the playing area to represent the various stage areas (See page 66).

Special Needs Students
Students who have limited or impaired movement may need alternate versions of the movement exercises. Students who are unable to walk should use their hands, arms, and heads to create character-based and artistic movement.

Advanced Students
These students may wish to move beyond basic movements to more highly choreographed work.

On Your Feet

Show, Don't Tell Before students begin this exercise, use the board to demonstrate the activity by drawing a stick figure kicking a soccer ball.

Chapter

17 Blocking

The actor is here . . . and then there . . . and then here again—all the while speaking, gesturing, and doing odd bits of stage business. What helps the actor keep all this together? Blocking!

Project Specs

Project Description For this assignment, you will block a scene of four to six minutes long involving more than one actor.

Purpose to understand blocking and to apply techniques for handling complex movement onstage

Materials pencil and paper; a ground plan or the Blocking Activity Sheet your teacher provides

Theatre Terms

aesthetic balance
asymmetrical balance
blocking
counter-focus
direct focus
floor plan or
    ground plan
open stance
symmetrical balance
unity

On Your Feet

With a partner, discuss how you might break down the elements of playing a particular sport. One of you should slowly pantomime the action "frame by frame," while the other draws each step in the sequence. Then change roles. You don't have to draw well; creating stick figures will do.

Theatre Terms

aesthetic balance when the placement of actors onstage appears equally balanced

asymmetrical balance when position is used to balance characters on either side of the stage

blocking the planned movements and arrangements of actors

counter-focus when actors look from one to another, to another, and so on

direct focus when several actors look at one specific actor

floor plan or ground plan a diagram that shows the walls, doors, windows, furniture, and other architectural details onstage

open stance when an actor faces the audience directly; full front

symmetrical balance when there is an equal number of characters on each side of the stage, equidistant from the center

unity a balance in the variety and kinds of movement in a play

Blocking: Skills in Action

Theatre is a composite art. As you have begun to learn, it is not a particular skill, but a combination of technical, verbal, and visual skills. One very important element is the **blocking,** or devising the movement and arrangement of the actors within scenes and from one scene to the next. Blocking tells the actor how to get his character from one place to another on the stage. It also supports communication between the characters within the play. And it creates a visual picture that affects the experience of performing and watching the play. Thus, effective blocking creates meaningful, functional, and artistic movement.

Meaningful Movement

Of course, movement in a play must carry out the plot. Juliet must swallow the sleeping potion and Hamlet must stab Polonius if their stories are to follow the playwright's intent. But movement can also be engineered to carry information about the characters' motivations, thoughts, emotional states, and relationships. What a character does is often more important than what he or she says!

The way in which a character places a prop can telegraph his or her feelings. The way a character primps in a mirror, thumbs through a magazine, or buttons a coat may suggest details about his or her emotional life. An arrangement of characters on a sofa can reveal a wealth of details about their relationships.

The Flying Karamazov Brothers must carefully plan the blocking of their action-packed stage productions.

Resource Binder

- Blocking Activity Sheet, p. 82
- Stage Pictures Worksheet, p. 83
- Critique Sheet: Blocked Scene, p. 84
- Blocking Test, p. 85
- Blocking Shorthand, p. 161

Handbook Connections
pages 582–583

To Have on Hand

- Tape for spiking the floor of the playing area
- Images of various forms of movement expression—from disciplines such as dance, performance art, and theatre
- Scripts or anthologies from which students can select plays

PREVIEW

Blocking: Skills in Action

Tell students that blocking done well usually goes unnoticed by the audience. However, clumsy or inappropriate blocking can cause problems within a scene and within the play itself.

Although some directors allow the actors to discover their own blocking, most plot out the movement in advance and tell the actors where to move during rehearsals set aside for blocking. However, many directors allow actors to collaborate in the process. If an actor feels uncomfortable moving at a certain point—or wants to move when there is no specific blocking—the director should find out why.

Meaningful Movement

ACTivity Have students take turns miming a simple series of movements such as going to a mailbox, removing letters, and looking through them. Then give individual students a motivating statement such as, "You're waiting for a letter telling you whether you got into the college you've always wanted to attend. The letter has just arrived." Get them to think about how this piece of information might affect their blocking.

Visual Cue

The following prompts can be used to exercise **critical viewing skills.**

- What might go wrong if the movement shown in this photo weren't well blocked?
- What do you think the lines on the floor might contribute to the blocking?
- How important do you think eye contact is in this scene? Why?

ACTivity Have pairs of students face each other. Each of them tosses a tennis ball simultaneously. The other must catch it. Tell them to take their time, throw gently, and maintain eye contact. When they have perfected this, have them add one and then two more balls.

Functional Movement

Draw a large ground plan on the chalkboard. Then ask students to help position a wall, doors, windows, and furniture for a scene from a play they are all familiar with—perhaps *The Diary of Anne Frank* or *Romeo and Juliet*.

ACTivity Using the classroom as the available area, have three or four students collaborate to create a ground plan of a scene from a play of their own choosing.

Show, Don't Tell Demonstrate for students open, one-quarter, profile, three-quarter, and full back positions. Then model the difference between erect and slouched posture.

ACTivity Have students review the body positions by playing a game similar to "Simon Says." Students stand in a relaxed fashion while you call out various body positions—full front to full back—and they must assume these positions quickly and with good posture.

The Language of THEATRE

Support students in learning new expressions heard in the classroom.

- Help students learn new expressions related to functional movement by demonstrating open stance and other body positions used by actors.
- Read aloud the section The Director Plots the Blocking on pages 203–204. Encourage students to listen for new expressions and then share what they heard.
- Call on volunteers to read aloud the Prepare instructions on page 205. Then invite students to share new expressions they heard and say what they mean.
- Invite students to share new expressions they learned while working on the chapter project and explain each one in their own words.

Functional Movement

In order to fully communicate a play's meaning to the audience, you must be sure that the blocking emphasizes important characters, moments, and even objects in the play. In order to facilitate the blocking, a **ground plan,** or **floor plan,** must be created. This plan is a diagram on paper that shows the walls, doors, windows, furniture, and other important architectural details of the stage drawn to scale. The director should create a blocking plan well in advance. This saves rehearsal time and helps to keep the movement organized and unified. Even with this plan, however, changes will always be made during the evolution of the play.

A ground plan of a very symmetrical set. The ground plan is drawn as though looking down from a place high above the stage.

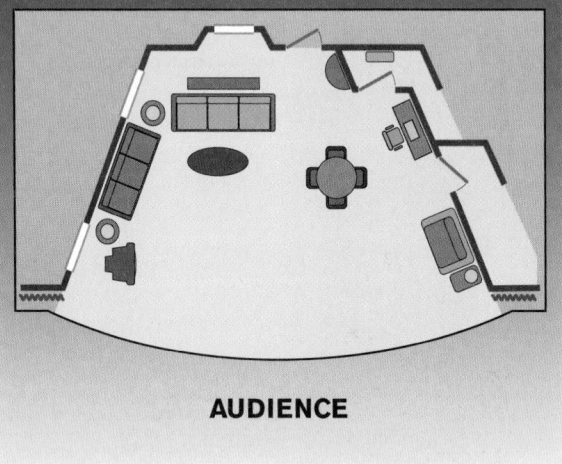

AUDIENCE

Creating a center of interest that catches and holds the audience's attention is important onstage. Usually the actor who is speaking important lines receives the emphasis. Sometimes audience attention is drawn to an inanimate object, an important line of dialogue, or significant movements that show feelings or desires. A center of interest is achieved in subtle ways so that the audience members give their attention effortlessly. The following are the director's tools for creating emphasis.

The Actor As you learned in Chapter 7, an actor will face the audience, full front, to convey important dialogue. This is called an **open stance,** and it draws attention to the character. When blocking a scene, remember that standing full front is the most emphatic stance, followed by one-quarter, profile, three-quarter, and full back stances. (See page 67 for a photograph of these.) A standing position is usually more dominant than a sitting position; sitting is more emphatic than lying down. An erect posture generally commands more attention than a slouched posture.

Stage Areas The diagram on page 199 shows the relative strength of stage areas, with number 1 being the strongest and 6 the weakest. The exception to area strength occurs when a downstage character assumes a three-quarter position in order to face an upstage character who is then emphasized.

From the Field: Mad Libs Mix-Ups

I start by having students fill out Mad Libs® together in class. Then the students act out the goofy scene they have created. Not only is this an excellent drama activity, but it is also a great review of the parts of speech.

LeAnn Gausman, Theatre Teacher, Westlake, OH

See "For More Information" on page 208 for a few Mad Lib® titles.

The director must choose the playing area according to the scene's importance. If it is a climactic scene, a strong area may be chosen. Or to weaken a strong action, such as a gory stabbing, the scene can be softened by playing it in a weaker stage area.

Some directors subscribe to the theory that each stage area has an emotional value that lends itself to certain types of scenes. You can see these connections in the following list:

Area 1 Climactic scenes
Area 2 Dignified scenes
Area 3 Love scenes
Area 4 Scenes that build tension
Area 5 Eavesdropping or foreshadowing events
Area 6 Horror and unrealistic scenes

While the link between acting area and scene can be helpful when working out a blocking plan, remember that these connections are only suggestions, not hard and fast rules. Experiment with stage movement and stage areas to achieve the effect you want.

Stage Levels The higher the level, the more attention a character receives. Not only is this because the audience can readily see raised figures, but there is also a psychological aspect of height dominating a scene. For example, the tall person dominates the short person. Elevation can be varied by using platforms and stairs, as well as by having some figures stand, sit, and kneel.

AUDIENCE

A stage mapped out with areas of strength.

Eye Focus People look where others look, so if characters A and B are looking directly at C, the audience will look at C also. This is called **direct focus.** To add variety, a director sometimes employs **counter-focus,** where A focuses on B who looks at C who looks at the speaking figure D. The audience will follow the pattern from A to B to C and finally to D. The most effective stage arrangement is the triangle, because the eyes of the audience travel along either side and focus on the figure in the middle. Generally the middle person is upstage with the downstage characters turned in three-quarter positions.

Chapter 17 Blocking **199**

In discussing the psychology behind raised stage levels, tell students that politicians and other public speakers often speak to the public from a raised platform for the same reason important characters or scenes are played on the higher stage levels.

Draw the stage with its areas of strength labeled 1 to 6 as on this page. Discuss various scenes from plays the students are familiar with in terms of where on the stage the characters would be positioned. For example, a soliloquy from Hamlet would probably be staged in area 1.

ACTivity **Advanced Students**
Have interested students choose from among the six stage areas to position characters in scenes from *Julius Caesar, A Streetcar Named Desire,* or *Death of a Salesman.* They can create floor plans with actors' positions labeled. They should write a caption telling which scene they are depicting and why they chose the stage area they did.

Show, Don't Tell Use four actors to model an example of counter-focus. A looks at B; B looks at C; C looks at D.

ACTivity Tell students to bring in images or ads from magazines that reflect the stage picture concepts depicted in this chapter. Have students work together to analyze the pictures.

Although blocking can add dimension and visual interest to talky scenes, students should be aware that "busy" blocking can detract from the scene's overall effectiveness.

Notes

_____

_____

_____

_____

_____

_____

_____

Show, Don't Tell Ask groups of students to come up to the playing area. Arrange them in various ways that indicate who is receiving the emphasis on the stage. Start with an arrangement similar to the one at the bottom of this page and proceed from there.

 Have students work together in groups of five to create a balanced stage picture, freeze, and then have one person take the focus using space, speech, or movement.

Try to bring in color photographs from actual theatrical productions to share with students. Discuss how light and color affect the scene.

Show, Don't Tell Recite a bit of dialogue from a play or a short poem for the students while standing still. Recite the same dialogue or poem again, but this time add movement that enhances what you are saying.

Alert students that movement on stage is probably one of the most challenging things they will be learning in drama class and that you will revisit creating meaningful movement again.

Visual Cue

A Clockwork Orange is based on a book by Anthony Burgess. It tells of the violent rampages of a young criminal and his gang. He is finally caught and subjected to extreme behavior modification techniques. The following prompts can be used to exercise **critical viewing skills** as students study the photo at the top of the page.

- Which actor has the primary focus? Why?
- How do you think the character in the middle is feeling? What adds to this impression?
- Who are the other people in the picture? How can you tell?
- In what way does the furniture add visual focus to the scene?

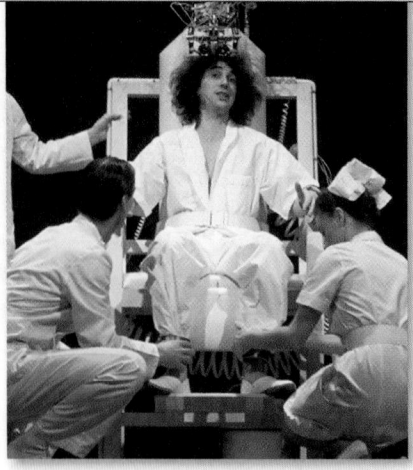

In the triangle arrangement seen here in *A Clockwork Orange,* we focus on the character in the center. While effective, avoid overusing the triangle.

Space and Contrast A character surrounded by space draws attention because of being easily seen, and the audience wonders about the isolation from the group. The more space between the character and the group, the more emphasis on the character. In the diagram below, character A receives

Because she is set apart spatially from the group, character A receives the attention of the audience.

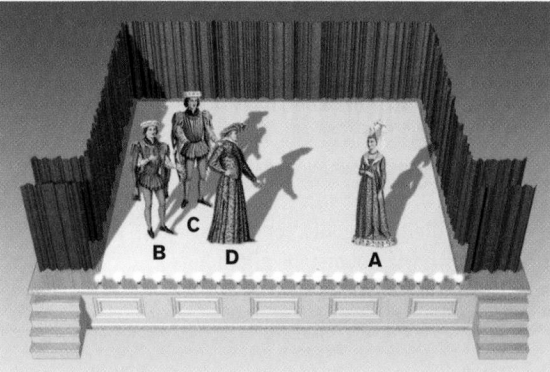

emphasis. If one actor is different from all the rest, dominance is achieved through contrast. A person who sits while others stand, who is in a full back position while others are full front, or who is dressed in one color while others are all dressed in another color will be accented through contrast.

Light and Color A character in a strong pool of light dominates those in a dim light.

The more brilliant the costume color, the more emphasis on the actor. Depending on the costume design for the play as a whole, of course, it is generally assumed that only principal characters should wear red or white, and these colors should be used with care, since they easily attract audience attention.

Speech and Movement The speaker dominates unless there is movement on stage. The moving figure always achieves emphasis. Remember that forward movement is strong; retreating movement is weak.

Scenes with a lot of dialogue can be made more interesting if you add movement. To accent certain words in the dialogue, move before the line or phrase. Movement after the line stresses the action, not the words. Movement during the line weakens the words, so it is often used when the lines are to be subordinated or "thrown away."

Notes

_____

_____

_____

_____

_____

_____

The director must choose the playing area according to the scene's importance. If it is a climactic scene, a strong area may be chosen. Or to weaken a strong action, such as a gory stabbing, the scene can be softened by playing it in a weaker stage area.

Some directors subscribe to the theory that each stage area has an emotional value that lends itself to certain types of scenes. You can see these connections in the following list:

Area 1 Climactic scenes
Area 2 Dignified scenes
Area 3 Love scenes
Area 4 Scenes that build tension
Area 5 Eavesdropping or foreshadowing events
Area 6 Horror and unrealistic scenes

While the link between acting area and scene can be helpful when working out a blocking plan, remember that these connections are only suggestions, not hard and fast rules. Experiment with stage movement and stage areas to achieve the effect you want.

Stage Levels The higher the level, the more attention a character receives. Not only is this because the audience can readily see raised figures, but there is also a psychological aspect of height dominating a scene. For example, the tall person dominates the short person. Elevation can be varied by using platforms and stairs, as well as by having some figures stand, sit, and kneel.

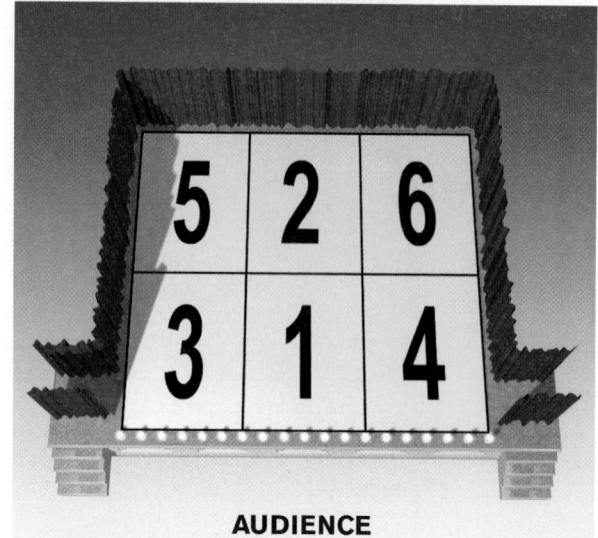

A stage mapped out with areas of strength.

Eye Focus People look where others look, so if characters A and B are looking directly at C, the audience will look at C also. This is called **direct focus.** To add variety, a director sometimes employs **counter-focus,** where A focuses on B who looks at C who looks at the speaking figure D. The audience will follow the pattern from A to B to C and finally to D. The most effective stage arrangement is the triangle, because the eyes of the audience travel along either side and focus on the figure in the middle. Generally the middle person is upstage with the downstage characters turned in three-quarter positions.

In discussing the psychology behind raised stage levels, tell students that politicians and other public speakers often speak to the public from a raised platform for the same reason important characters or scenes are played on the higher stage levels.

Draw the stage with its areas of strength labeled 1 to 6 as on this page. Discuss various scenes from plays the students are familiar with in terms of where on the stage the characters would be positioned. For example, a soliloquy from Hamlet would probably be staged in area 1.

ACTivity **Advanced Students**
Have interested students choose from among the six stage areas to position characters in scenes from *Julius Caesar, A Streetcar Named Desire,* or *Death of a Salesman.* They can create floor plans with actors' positions labeled. They should write a caption telling which scene they are depicting and why they chose the stage area they did.

Show, Don't Tell Use four actors to model an example of counter-focus. A looks at B; B looks at C; C looks at D.

ACTivity Tell students to bring in images or ads from magazines that reflect the stage picture concepts depicted in this chapter. Have students work together to analyze the pictures.

Although blocking can add dimension and visual interest to talky scenes, students should be aware that "busy" blocking can detract from the scene's overall effectiveness.

Notes

Show, Don't Tell Ask groups of students to come up to the playing area. Arrange them in various ways that indicate who is receiving the emphasis on the stage. Start with an arrangement similar to the one at the bottom of this page and proceed from there.

 Have students work together in groups of five to create a balanced stage picture, freeze, and then have one person take the focus using space, speech, or movement.

Try to bring in color photographs from actual theatrical productions to share with students. Discuss how light and color affect the scene.

Show, Don't Tell Recite a bit of dialogue from a play or a short poem for the students while standing still. Recite the same dialogue or poem again, but this time add movement that enhances what you are saying.

Alert students that movement on stage is probably one of the most challenging things they will be learning in drama class and that you will revisit creating meaningful movement again.

Visual Cue

A Clockwork Orange is based on a book by Anthony Burgess. It tells of the violent rampages of a young criminal and his gang. He is finally caught and subjected to extreme behavior modification techniques. The following prompts can be used to exercise **critical viewing skills** as students study the photo at the top of the page.

- Which actor has the primary focus? Why?
- How do you think the character in the middle is feeling? What adds to this impression?
- Who are the other people in the picture? How can you tell?
- In what way does the furniture add visual focus to the scene?

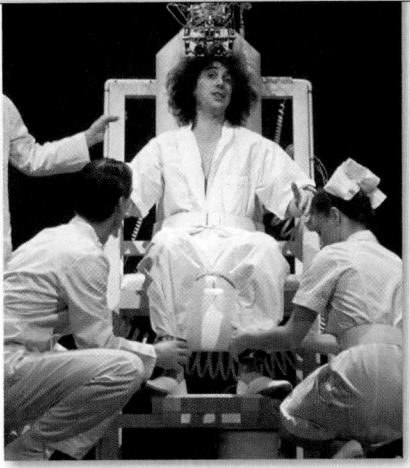

In the triangle arrangement seen here in *A Clockwork Orange*, we focus on the character in the center. While effective, avoid overusing the triangle.

Space and Contrast A character surrounded by space draws attention because of being easily seen, and the audience wonders about the isolation from the group. The more space between the character and the group, the more emphasis on the character. In the diagram below, character A receives

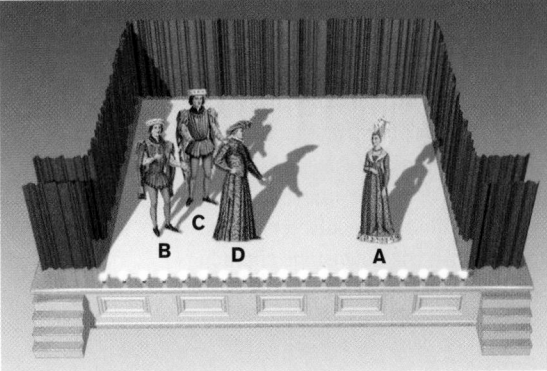

Because she is set apart spatially from the group, character A receives the attention of the audience.

emphasis. If one actor is different from all the rest, dominance is achieved through contrast. A person who sits while others stand, who is in a full back position while others are full front, or who is dressed in one color while others are all dressed in another color will be accented through contrast.

Light and Color A character in a strong pool of light dominates those in a dim light.

The more brilliant the costume color, the more emphasis on the actor. Depending on the costume design for the play as a whole, of course, it is generally assumed that only principal characters should wear red or white, and these colors should be used with care, since they easily attract audience attention.

Speech and Movement The speaker dominates unless there is movement on stage. The moving figure always achieves emphasis. Remember that forward movement is strong; retreating movement is weak.

Scenes with a lot of dialogue can be made more interesting if you add movement. To accent certain words in the dialogue, move before the line or phrase. Movement after the line stresses the action, not the words. Movement during the line weakens the words, so it is often used when the lines are to be subordinated or "thrown away."

Notes

Reinforcement Any major figure who is reinforced or backed up by minor figures achieves attention. A business executive with three secretaries hovering behind is more emphatic than one without any secretaries. The queen with her attendants or the gang leader with thugs behind him are impressive because of the reinforcement. Also, a character can be emphasized with scenery, such as being framed by an arch, a column, or a tree; or a person can be emphasized with furniture such as a high-backed chair.

Artistic Movement

Artistry in blocking means that the stage picture you create with your actors' movement is pleasing to the mind and senses. For stage movement to become satisfying, it must employ the three qualities below.

Variety By presenting various levels of emphasis and changes of mood, a play maintains variety and avoids monotony. Variety helps the audience stay focused on the elements of the plot and follow the progression of the story.

Unity There must be **unity** in the variety and kind of movement the play requires. Unity provides continuity so that a play's disparate elements come together as a whole.

Balance The elements on either side of the playing area should seem to be equal.

The aim is to move from one balanced picture to another during most scenes.

The Balanced Stage Picture

Of course, it's impossible to keep the stage balanced constantly, but the ideal is to attempt to do so. Following are three balance formats to keep in mind:

Symmetrical balance is achieved when there is an equal number of figures on each side of the stage, and all are placed

This scene from *Twelfth Night* creates an artistic picture.

Arrange students in the playing area in such a way as to illustrate scenes that show the reinforcement discussed on this page—a business executive with three secretaries, a queen and her attendants, and a gang leader with his or her thugs. Once the students get a feel for the characters and how they interact, have them move as the characters, always being aware of the need to maintain the reinforcement.

ACTivity Have students work in groups of six to create entrances that use the idea of reinforcement to highlight a specific character.

Artistic Movement

Particularly in period pieces, actors must be trained to move in ways that amplify aspects of the time and place. Sometimes directors hire a movement coach to work with the cast to ensure unity of physical presentation.

The Balanced Stage Picture

Clumsy blocking often features clumps of actors hovering on one side of the playing area or the other while a large area remains unused. To create balance, the director should aim for stage pictures that do not create too much weight on one side or the other.

Show, Don't Tell Arrange a group of students in the playing area in ways that DO NOT show balance. Discuss what is wrong with the picture and ask other students to rearrange the group to achieve a more pleasing balance.

Shakespeare's *Twelfth Night* offers the director and actors a wealth of inspiration for achieving artistic movement and a balanced stage picture. The following prompts can be used to help students **think critically** about what they see.

- What elements make this scene pleasing to the eye? Describe them.

- Is the picture symmetrically balanced? If so, how?

- Is there an element of contrast in the picture? Describe it.

Lead a group discussion of the blocking in plays or other performances in which students may have taken part. For example, mention that the school marching band uses a form of blocking to create individual and group effects. Cheerleading, debate, and other programs may also use a form of blocking to create exciting visual pictures for an audience.

Show, Don't Tell Re-create the images on this page and the next by asking students to move about in the playing area maintaining the arrangements pictured. After students have moved in asymmetrically and symmetrically balanced groups, ask them to create related characters and move as those characters would in these same arrangements.

Vocabulary Enhancement

As students learned in Chapter 5, when an actor *cheats out,* he or she turns toward the audience. In actuality, making any action onstage look realistic without actually doing what you seem to be doing is called *cheating*. When blocking a scene, a director may also call out phrases such as "Cheat left" or "Cheat right," meaning the actor should angle his or her body more to the left or to the right.

equidistant from the center. This composition is usually artificial and stylized, and it is extremely formal. It is sometimes used to indicate church, state, or courtroom scenes or with certain period plays that demand stylized acting such as Oscar Wilde's *The Importance of Being Earnest.*

Asymmetrical balance is informal. It employs the teeter-totter principle. A lighter figure on one side balances a heavier figure on the other side if the lighter figure is farther from the center. Or a character on one side can balance a group on the other side.

Aesthetic balance is sometimes called *psychological balance*. It gives the impression of equal weight on both sides of the center, even though the actual weight is not equal. For instance, one major character in the play gives the impression of outweighing several less important characters. A standing figure can balance several seated people. A speaker has more weight than a listener, and a character reinforced by scenery can balance a large group. Strong movement and bright colors also balance large masses.

No matter how you balance your stage area, one curiosity remains: if only one stage area is used for a scene and that area is balanced, the audience will be oblivious to the empty portion of the stage.

These two symmetrically balanced groups present a stylized, formal picture.

Quotable

Any smoothly functioning technology will have the appearance of magic.

Arthur C. Clarke, Science Fiction Writer

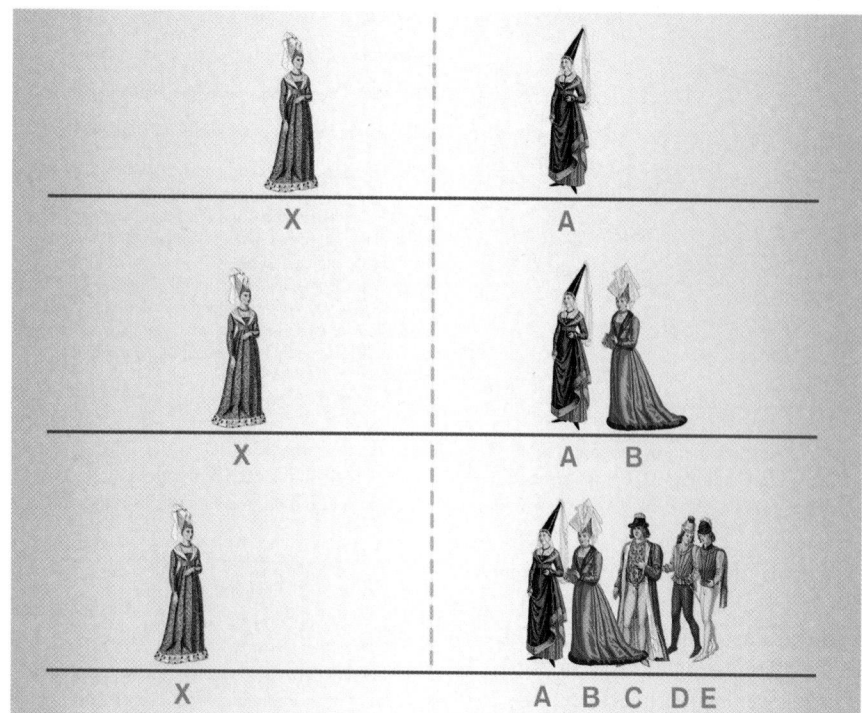

Examples of asymmetrical balance. X and A are in balance, but in order to remain in balance with A and B, X must take one step toward the side. To balance A, B, C, D, E, or more, X must take two steps to the side.

The Director Plots the Blocking

Using the ground or floor plan of the set, the director will place the furniture, being sure to keep important entrances and exits free. Furniture grouping should provide a variety of playing areas. While there should be ample space on stage for movement, there should be enough furniture to prevent the stage from looking bare, unless that is the desired effect.

Next, the director will go through each scene, creating and devising the basic crosses of each character and recording them in the margins of the prompt book. He or she will usually block the climactic scenes first to prevent repetition of the climax pictures in earlier, less important scenes. To work out the blocking, some directors use chess pieces, buttons, or inverted golf tees for characters, moving them in various positions on the floor plan.

The Director Plots the Blocking

Tell students that there has long been a debate among professional directors concerning the use of a script's stage directions. Some directors admit to deleting the playwright's stage directions entirely, while others rely on the playwright's blueprint for the blocking and tend not to change it unless it does not make sense within the parameters of the performance space and/or the set specifications.

ACTivity Have individual students block the rest of the group to illustrate such activities as waiting in a long line, cheering in the stands at a football game, watching from the ground as something amazing happens far above, and so on. Remind students to create the most intriguing stage pictures they can while still conveying the basic action of the scene. Construct the activity so that students feel free to improvise dialogue.

ACTivity **Advanced Students**
The park bench is a setting that has long been popular with playwrights. Ask students to think about possible staging problems such a setting might present. Then have them read one of these plays set on a park bench and create interesting blocking for it.

The Zoo Story by Edward Albee

A Talk in the Park by Alan Ayckbourn

The Loveliest Afternoon of the Year by John Guare

Whisper Into My Good Ear by William Hanley

Quotable

When asked how he handled rehearsals, this was the response from director Arvin Brown:

I get the actors on their feet almost immediately. I feel that that is how their instrument gets operating.

Discuss with students the relationship between the script on this page and the movements indicated in the drawing. Ask three students to play the parts of Carl, Bob, and Alice and to create the scene using the dialogue and the blocking indicated. (You might want to spike the floor to indicate where the tables, desk, and chairs will be placed.)

ACTivity Give groups of students the chance to combine the movement and dialogue in the script. Discuss their impressions of the blocking of this short scene.

ACTivity **Advanced Students**
Challenge three students to memorize the lines of the script on this page and then perform the scene using the blocking called for. You could assign the role of Alice to an advanced student and encourage a beginning, ELL, or Special Needs student to take the part of Bob.

The Language of
THEATRE

Use students' knowledge of root words, prefixes, and suffixes to help them break down complex academic vocabulary into more accessible language. As you introduce each theatre term, ask students if there are word parts they already know that will help them predict the meaning of the term.

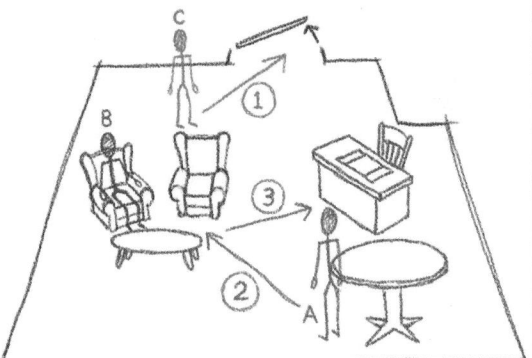

The doorbell rings.

CARL: Well, I guess I had better get that! [He exits.] **①**

BOB: So, what do you propose we do about this?

ALICE: I propose that you do nothing. I will handle it in my own way. It is obvious to me that you have no real understanding of the situation, and I feel that I can handle it. Look, Bob, **②** I don't mean to embarrass or confuse you, I am just determined to get to the bottom of things. I want to show you something that I found yesterday. I think once you see this, you will understand my concern. **③** Here, take a look at this and tell me what you think. Surely, you can't now imagine that I am being picky about this situation.

Alice (A) is standing by the round table. Bob (B) is sitting in a chair. Carl (C) is UR. For the first move ①, Carl exits UC. For the second move ②, Alice crosses to Bob. For the third move ③ Alice moves to the desk. All three movements are indicated at the appropriate place in the script.

When a movement seems effective, the director notes it in the prompt book by drawing in the margin a small rough draft of the stage floor with its furniture placement. Using a different colored pencil for each character, the character's position is labeled, and an arrow is drawn to indicate new movement. Each move is numbered using a corresponding number notated in the script at the exact place in the dialogue where the movement is to be made. Dots or crosses may be used to indicate characters. Sometimes stick figures are used to better visualize the picture and to show characters standing, sitting, and facing in certain directions.

The Language of
THEATRE

Use accessible language–words you already know– as you learn new academic vocabulary heard in the classroom.

- As you listen to a teacher or classmate say the theatre terms on page 196, use words that you know to say whether you know any of the new terms.

- Use your knowledge of simple words such as *balance* and *plan* to help you understand the meaning of new theatre terms you hear, such as *aesthetic balance* and *floor plan*.

- As a partner reads aloud the descriptions of *symmetrical*, *asymmetrical*, and *aesthetic balance* on pages 201–202, notice how using words that are accessible to you helps you learn new terms.

- When working with classmates on your *blocking project*, listen to directions that include new theatre terms such as *counter-focus* and *open stance* and use accessible language to understand them.

Backstage Gossip: Seeing the Written Action

Many playwrights feel that the stage directions they write should be given as much consideration as the dialogue. Others write very few stage directions (or none at all) and leave the blocking entirely to the director.

Emily Mann, a well-known playwright as well as a respected director, has this to say on the subject of stage directions: "Directorial ideas are very vivid images for me, and I consider them part of the writing so that people can see it as they are reading it."

Plot the Blocking of Your Scene

Take on the director's duties by choosing and analyzing a scene and then devising stage movement for it and blocking it on paper. Your teacher may provide a Blocking Activity Sheet to help you in this. After you have planned the blocking, you will direct classmates in the scene until the movement is believable; appropriate to the dialogue; expressive of thoughts, feelings, and actions; and well executed. Follow the steps below as you work on this project:

1 Select a favorite one-act play that has literary merit and that has meaning for you.

2 Consider the theme, style, genre, mood, and structure of the play as well as the motivations and relationships of the characters.

3 Choose a four- to six-minute scene from the play, preferably one with only two or three characters in it. Copy the scene in such a way that you have wide margins for your blocking notations. Make as many copies as there are characters so that each of your actors will have a script from which to read. On a piece of paper or the Activity Sheet, complete a master floor plan using your classroom playing area as the stage size. Draw the necessary furniture, doors, and windows as near to scale as you can approximate.

4 Visualize the scene. Then, on your copy of the script, pencil in blocking notes in the margins by drawing a small, rough floor plan, labeling the characters, and indicating with arrows and lines each cross you want them to make. If the scene you have chosen has a lot of dialogue, break up the speeches with motivated movement. Remember to consider the meaning, function, and artistic effect of the movements you employ.

5 Set up makeshift furniture, and provide your actors with their scene copies. As they read the scene aloud, direct them according to the blocking you have plotted on your script. As you direct, call each actor by the character's name. Ask the actors to write down their crosses on their scripts. This will enable them to remember the blocking accurately. If necessary, explain your reasons for wanting certain movements. While your directions should be concrete, your aim is to guide, not dictate. Model leadership, but be pleasant and patient, and listen to and make changes based on the actors' ideas.

6 Work out your planned movements with the cast. Change and refine them until they work smoothly onstage. Rehearse several times until the actors feel sure of the movement. Time them to be certain the scene does not exceed six minutes.

PREPARE
Plot the Blocking of Your Scene

Provide students with a variety of colored pens and pencils to use while they work on the Blocking Activity Sheet. Remind them that not all movement is interesting and that overly busy blocking can be distracting. The blocking should enhance the scene.

Tell students that often in the professional theatre an actor may come up with an idea that solves a tricky blocking problem. Good directors listen to their actors. In the end, the blocking remains the director's decision, but remind students that theatre is a collaborative art and that the people carrying out the blocking may very well make valid contributions to the blocking process.

Allow students plenty of time to rehearse their scenes.

From the Field: Go with the Flow

When I direct a student production, I have an idea in my head how to block most scenes, but I encourage students to let movement evolve from their characters as well as the relationships among the characters in the play. With this approach, the patterns of movement are fairly well set after only a few rehearsals.

P. Yeary, Drama Coach and Choral Director, Orlando, FL

PRESENT

Introduce and Enjoy Your Blocked Scene

Tell students to simulate only the furniture that is necessary for the scene. In other words, if the scene is set in a living room but the only furniture needed is a couch and a coffee table, students should set up three or four chairs side by side (the couch) and an overturned box (the coffee table). They need not bother setting up other chairs, a simulated television set, etc. Students may wish to point out the exit areas before they begin their presentations.

Remind students that as directors their work is done once the presentation begins.

CRITIQUE

Evaluate Your Classmate's Blocked Scene

Hand out the Critique Sheet for this project or have students use their own paper. Remind students that evaluating others involves taking good notes, scoring using the rubric, and writing an explanation of the scoring.

It will be helpful to assign the person each student will evaluate so that everyone receives a peer evaluation.

You might want to help students who had obvious trouble with blocking by going over their scene with them once again, making suggestions, and showing them the movements you believe would have been more effective.

PRESENT

Introduce and Enjoy Your Blocked Scene

In order for you to present your scene and act in someone else's, this project will probably take several class periods to complete. When your teacher calls for your scene, hand in a copy of your script and ground plan or the Activity Sheet. Set up any furniture that will be needed in the playing area.

Briefly discuss which of the principles provided in the Preview section you used to block this scene. Then introduce your cast and announce the play's title. Finally, join the audience, watching your scene objectively.

Your instructor may offer to show more effective movement for your scene. Accept any suggestions cheerfully.

CRITIQUE

Evaluate Your Classmate's Blocked Scene

Choose one of the scenes presented in class, and evaluate the blocking. Your evaluation should be based on a scale of 1 to 5, in which 1 is equal to "needs much improvement" and 5 is equal to "outstanding." Your evaluation should answer these questions:

- Which character was made to seem most important to the action of the scene, and why?

- How did the blocking help focus attention on the character emphasized in the scene?

- Did you feel that this emphasis was true to the script?

- In what way was the stage picture balanced?

- What did the blocking tell you about the emotional states and relationships of the characters?

Write a short explanation for the rating you gave this scene.

Notes

Spotlight on

Stage Combat

Actors in a play that involves violence must perform realistic movements safely. Through the use of stage combat, they can make it appear that they are dueling, hitting, punching, pulling hair, or even throwing each other around a room. What they are actually doing is more like dancing than fighting, however. Because it makes use of quick, sharp movements and near misses, stage combat can be dangerous. *Do not attempt stage combat without special training and careful preparation.* Even with special training and preparation, be careful to demonstrate safe use of your body in any stage combat.

Stage combat is choreographed much like a dance. Like dance, it requires a good deal of rehearsal to get the moves just right.

Hair Pulling One actor grasps the other actor's hair. The second actor hangs on to the wrists of the first and shouts as if hair is being pulled.

Slaps and Punches One actor aims a slap or punch near the victim. The other performs a hidden clap to simulate contact, then reels backward as if hit.

Stabbing An actor shows a knife, dagger, or sword, then turns so that it is hidden to the audience. He or she then plunges forward, thrusting the weapon under the armpit or in some other spot near, not on, the victim. The victim recoils as if stabbed. The weapon is withdrawn with more force than it took to plunge it in and is then disposed of so the audience won't notice the lack of blood.

Falling The secret of falling is to stay relaxed. To lessen the shock, actors break their falls a little at a time—knees, torso, arms, and then head. Whenever possible, they land on soft furniture!

Dying A person who's been shot, stabbed, or beaten tenses immediately, inhales, and doubles toward the wound. The dying person who speaks is generally short of breath, speaking in broken lines with a voice that suggests weakness.

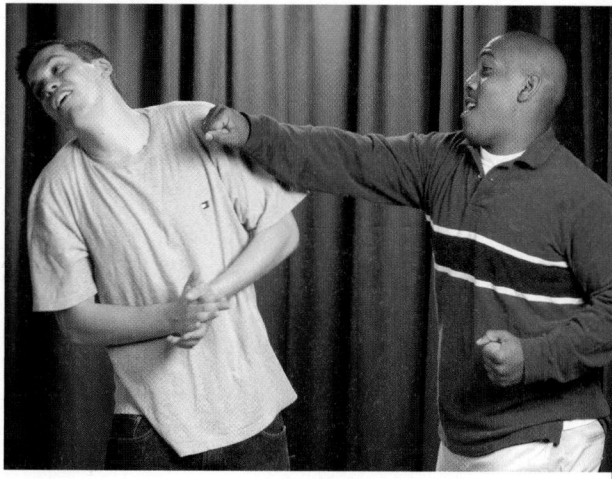

Spotlight on

Stage Combat Share these tips about stage combat with your students.

- **Look your scene partner in the eye.** Eye contact is very important in stage combat.

- **Keep in constant communication.** There is an unspoken communication between actors involved in stage combat. Counting and using physical signals is how many actors continually check in with one another to achieve the most realistic-looking combat possible.

- **Make noise.** Much of the realistic look and sound of stage combat comes from the noises the actors make. They gasp and grunt and scream and bellow as the fight progresses. These sounds also make up for the sounds that might be present in a real fight (cracking bones, the thud of a head against a wall, and so on).

- **Never change the fight choreography** without first rehearsing the change with your partner.

- Always remember, **safety first!**

Backstage Gossip: A Little Too Real

The 1991 Broadway production of Paul Rudnick's *I Hate Hamlet* starred eccentric British actor Nicol Williamson as the ghost of legendary thespian John Barrymore. The play featured a scene in which the ghost duels with his young protégé, played by Evan Handler. One night Williamson, who had already been ad-libbing up a storm during that performance, changed the choreography during the swordfight and wound up nicking Handler and drawing blood. Outraged, Handler promptly stormed offstage in mid-performance.

Blocking Test

The test for this chapter is available in blackline master form in the Resource Binder, page 85.

For More Information

Books

Barranger, Milly S., *Theatre: A Way of Seeing,* Wadsworth Publishing Company, 2005.

Price, Roger, and Leonard Stern, *Best of Mad Libs,* Price Stern Sloan, 2008.

Price, Roger, and Leonard Stern, *Cool Mad Libs,* Price Stern Sloan, 2001.

Price, Roger, and Leonard Stern, *Straight "A" Mad Libs,* Price Stern Sloan, 2003.

Snow, Jackie, *Movement Training for Actors,* Book and DVD, Bloomsbury Methuen Drama, 2013.

Wright, Edwin C., and Marguerite Battye, *Acting and Stage Movement,* Meriwether Publishing, Ltd., 1985.

Other Media

Basic Stage Combat, DVD, Educational Video Network, 2004.

Blocking a Scene: Basic Staging with Actors, DVD, Insight Media,1990.

Movement for the Actor, DVD, Insight Media,1993.

Period Movement: Early and Late Renaissance, DVD, Insight Media, 2005.

Period Movement: Restoration, DVD, Insight Media, 2005.

The Stage Fight Director, DVD, Insight Media, 1990.

Super Swordfighting: Advanced– Multiple Weapons and Opponents, DVD, Insight Media, 2008.

Unarmed Stage Combat, DVD, Insight Media, 2006.

For more information about blocking, movement, and stage combat, visit:

www.actorsmovementstudio.com

www.safd.org

Additional Projects

1 Using one big sofa or overstuffed armchair, see how many varied groupings you can achieve with two characters.

2 Experiment with different stage movements to block scenes that reveal the following situations:

- three people whispering
- two people quarreling
- four people looking for something
- a messenger bringing good news to a group
- three people shopping
- five people showing surprise
- three people telling a story to four others

3 Study famous paintings, and identify the artist's use of balance and emphasis. Write an essay relating this technique to the theatre. Suggested paintings:

- Cézanne's *Card Players*
- De Hooch's *A Dutch Courtyard*
- da Vinci's *The Last Supper*
- Hopper's *Nighthawks*

4 Ask your teacher for help in performing an element of stage combat to express actions nonverbally. Practice the technique, under supervision, until you can execute it safely and well. Then demonstrate your technique and the safe use of your body for the class.

5 Devise stage movement and block a scene from a period play such as *Macbeth* by William Shakespeare or a stylized play such as *A Waitress in Yellowstone* by David Mamet. You can find scenes from these plays in Unit Eight of this book.

6 **Theatre Journal** When you next find yourself at a large dinner—or in the school lunchroom—sketch the seating arrangement at a table that holds your interest. Then answer these questions: Who appears to be drawing the most attention at the table? Who appears to be drawing the least attention? What effect does closeness to the center of attention have upon the dynamics of the conversations and behaviors at the table?

Cézanne's *Card Players*

Substitute Teacher Activities

Here are suggestions for one or more days when you will be out of the classroom.

- Assign the Stage Pictures Worksheet on page 83 of the Resource Binder.

- Assign one or more of the Additional Projects on this page.

- Teach the Blocking and Stage Composition section of the Student Handbook, pp. 582–583.

- **Create Stage Movement** based on animals. Have students look at pictures of animals in motion. Then have each student choose an animal and create stage movement to depict it. The movement may be highly choreographed and stylized or it may be a more realistic simulation of the animal's movement patterns. Students can present one-minute interpretations of their chosen animal. The rest of the class tries to guess what animal is being portrayed.

Master of the Craft

Anne Bogart

Method actors are generally directed to first find meaning in a script and let that meaning direct their movements. "Viewpoints," a technique developed by Mary Overlie and made famous by director Anne Bogart, begins with actions and gestures, using them to stimulate emotion and meaning. In intensely physical, expressive stage productions such as *Bob* and *Going, Going, Gone*, Bogart has created a radical and influential new way of putting together a play.

Drawing on Overlie's influences as well as Martha Graham, the pioneer of modern dance, and Japanese director Tadashi Suzuki, Bogart has created a distinctive body of work. She once told *American Theatre* magazine that "Viewpoints is a way to practice creating fiction using time and space." It allows actors to create as they rehearse. Thus, they collaborate rather than simply follow directions.

In her actor training workshops, Bogart has actors use Viewpoints to develop a common language of movement. The technique calls for actors to relate to time and space in nine different ways. The four time elements are: tempo, duration, kinesthetic response, and repetition of a movement.

The five elements of space are shape, gesture, architecture, topography, and spatial relationships. The technique unifies the actors and the production. The movements that emerge become part of the play's choreography, so that the physical, mental, and emotional components develop at the same time.

Bogart declares that Viewpoints is not THE way to produce a play; it is ONE way. She is committed to letting every actor—and every production—develop in its own unique way.

"Depending on the point of view, Anne Bogart is either an innovator or a provocateur assaulting a script."

–Mel Gussow, *New York Times*

A scene from Bogart's *Dispute*

Anne Bogart

Master of the Craft

More About Anne Bogart

For complete information about Anne Bogart's SITI Company, visit *www.siti.org*. This site provides not only a history of the company and biographies of its members, but also links to other interesting sites related to movement for the stage.

Masters Past and Present

Theatre originally sprang from religious festivals involving dance. It therefore makes sense that some of the greatest innovators in movement for the stage were dancers.

- O-kuni (exact dates unknown, although some sources claim she died in 1613 at the age of 87) performed at Kitano Shrine in Kyoto, Japan. The dances she and her companions performed, a mixture of folk and religious movements, were the beginning of the Kabuki theatre tradition. (For more on O-kuni and Kabuki, see page 40.)

- Isadora Duncan (1878–1927) was a dancer whose style and methods ushered in the era of modern dance and signaled a revolution in contemporary stage movement. (For more on Isadora Duncan read her autobiography, *My Life*, revised and updated edition, published by Liveright, 2013.)

Quotables

Share with your students these quotes from Isadora Duncan, the first lady of modern dance.

Movement is life.

The dancer of the future will be one whose body and soul have grown so harmoniously together that the natural language of that soul will have become the movement of the body.

If I could say it, I wouldn't have to dance it.

Theatre **Then** and Now

The Ancient Greek Chorus

The Greek chorus represented a unique blend of empathy and aloofness. On the one hand, the chorus rejoiced in human good and flailed in sorrow at the flaws of humankind and the fickleness of the gods. On the other hand, it stood apart, somewhat removed from both triumph and tragedy, commenting on the action rather than taking part in it. In a sense, the chorus showed the audience how to respond to the events of the play.

Other Cultures, Other Times

Around 1485, Italian rulers began to finance productions of ancient Roman plays. These productions used a fifteen-member chorus, the same number the ancient Romans used.

Theatre **Then** and Now

The Ancient Greek Chorus

In ancient Greece, being a member of the chorus was an important role. Early Greek tragedies featured only one actor, who often exited to change costumes, leaving the chorus to continue the story until he returned. The chorus learned about half the lines in the play, all the songs, and all the dances. And every play included dances.

Most often, the Greek chorus made its entrance on stage in a stately march. Chorus members sang and danced in unison and recited their lines together. Occasionally, the chorus would be split into groups. The groups would enter separately and take turns performing.

This Greek chorus in the National Theatre of London's production of the Oresteia trilogy was made up entirely of men.

lines, the songs, and the movement of the chorus represented the voice, the sentiment, and the action of society. Greek theatre was about the common good.

Visual Cue

A Chorus Line began when dancers were tape-recorded as they talked about their personal and professional lives. A musical libretto was pieced together from their stories. Marvin Hamlisch composed the music, and Edward Kleban wrote the lyrics. Michael Bennett then choreographed the show, resulting in staging, songs, dialogue, and dance that segued beautifully one into the other.

Ask students to look at the image from *A Chorus Line* and respond to the following prompts.

- Although this is obviously a chorus number, which performer or performers have the focus?

- Is the stage picture balanced?

- Is there unity?

A Chorus Line

While the common good in Greek drama was represented by a group that acted as one person, most contemporary work emphasizes the individual who represents one aspect of society. At least, that's the message that comes through in Michael Bennett's *A Chorus Line,* a musical production that opened on Broadway in 1975 and ran continuously for fifteen years.

A Chorus Line celebrates the individual talents and dreams that converge whenever dancers audition for parts in a Broadway chorus line. It allowed the members of a chorus line to present their individual stories before being subsumed into the collective of the Broadway chorus. By the last scene, when the light fades on a kick-line that shows no sign of ending, the audience has come to appreciate the individuals in the chorus line as much as the line itself.

A Chorus Line opened the way to a new sub-genre of musical plays that celebrate creative interchange between the individual and the community. *Rent,* for example, celebrates the power of community to help individuals survive a crisis. In *Stomp,* group members use sticks, brooms, pipes, and trash can lids to create a percussive orchestra celebrating the power of individuals to come together in a collaborative effort. Each of these productions endeavors to portray a community respectful of all its contributors.

Watching *A Chorus Line,* the audience is entertained by the group's precision dancing but is also touched by the life stories of its individual members.

For More Information

- The 1985 film version of *A Chorus Line,* starring Michael Douglas, is available through Amazon.com.

- For information about the Broadway production of *A Chorus Line,* including an interview with one of the stars, visit ibdb.com/production.php?id=3752. In addition, there are videos of selections from the play on YouTube.

- For a modern example of a play that uses a Greek-style chorus, see Paula Vogel's *How I Learned to Drive,* published by Dramatists Play Service, 1998.

Chapter 18

Review a Play

This chapter focuses on students attending a play and evaluating it using critical skills and emotional reactions.

Objectives

1 to explore active listening

2 to understand the experience of seeing a live performance

3 to evaluate a live performance using critical principles

4 to present thoughts and reactions in a group-discussion format

Project Specs

For this chapter, you may have to do some research to find out about the highest-quality, most easily accessible, and most affordable theatres in your region or community.

Special Needs Students

Although many theatres are now wheelchair accessible, remind students with disabilities that it's important to ask about accessibility when making reservations.

On Your Feet

Ask students to think about these elements of audience etiquette:

- cell phones
- candy wrappers
- whispering
- taking pictures

Chapter

18 Review a Play

"All the world's a stage," says Jacques in Shakespeare's *As You Like It.* Today that statement may seem particularly appropriate in view of the global world in which we live. While you probably feel very comfortable with television and movies, your experience with live theatre may be limited. This is about to change!

Project Specs

Project Description For this chapter's project, you and a group of friends will attend and review a local theatre production and then present a ten-minute improvised talk show based on the performance.

Purpose to understand the experience of seeing a live performance and to evaluate the production critically

Materials the program from a local theatre production; a two-page written review or the Attend a Play Activity Sheet provided by your teacher

Theatre Terms

active listening
amphitheatre
audience participation
metaphoric
suspend disbelief

On Your Feet

With your classmates, demonstrate several things you should and should not do as an audience member. Develop a checklist of appropriate audience behavior and etiquette at different kinds of performances.

Theatre Terms

active listening using what you hear to build meaning and to answer questions about characters and plot developments

amphitheatre a round structure arranged around an open space with tiered seating

audience participation when the audience participates in the action of the play

metaphoric representative

suspend disbelief the ability of viewers to forget they are watching a show and to accept what they see and hear as real life

Interdependence of Theatrical Elements

It is often said that theatre requires three things: *a story, someone to tell it,* and *someone to listen and respond.* Analyzing these three facets and evaluating how they relate to one another will show how each aspect of a theatrical production is interdependent on all the others to create the final effect.

A Story

You have read about the role of the playwright in a dramatic presentation. (See Chapter 14.) Without the story and the script that conveys it, there would be no production at all.

Someone to Tell It

Who tells the playwright's story? As you have read, many artistic partners collaborate in the telling of the story and depend on one another for their contribution to be meaningful. The director has an overall vision, but without the actors to portray the characters, the designers to envision the world of the play, the technicians to build and light that world and provide sound for it, and the costume, makeup, and props artists to give it authenticity and flash, the director would be powerless. How do all these separate theatre personnel work in concert to deliver a single vision for the play by opening night? One way is to use standard theatre systems, such as rehearsal calendars and production schedules, to move the play along in an organized way. Another is to use time-honored methods through which the various technical crews communicate with the director and with one another. You have already read about the

Audience members enjoy an open-air performance in Oberammergau, Bavaria. What they are watching is the result of interdependent artistic partners, from the playwright to the stage crews, collaborating to create one artistic vision.

Resource Binder

- Review a Play Activity Sheet, p. 86
- Be a Theatre Critic Worksheet, p. 87
- Critique Sheet: Talk Show Performance, p. 88
- Review a Play Test, p. 89

To Have on Hand

- A stopwatch that students can borrow during the talk show
- Well-written theatre reviews as examples
- Style guides that include information on how to write criticism

Interdependence of Theatrical Elements

Invite students to share their experiences of reading a story or play and seeing a play or film based on the story. Discuss how these experiences reflect the importance of the collaboration of artistic partners involved in telling a story in a theatrical format.

ACTivity Choose a particular play or film mentioned by the students and ask them to identify the single vision for the play and suggest the contributions of different artists to telling the story.

Vocabulary Enhancement

The phrase *suspend disbelief* refers to an explanation by Samuel Taylor Coleridge in his 1817 *Biographia Literaria,* in which he discusses theories of the creative imagination: " . . . my endeavours should be directed to persons and characters supernatural, or at least romantic; yet so as to transfer from our inward nature a human interest and a semblance of truth sufficient to procure for these shadows of imagination that willing suspension of disbelief for the moment, which constitutes poetic faith."

 ### Visual Cue

Oberammergau is famous for its Passion Play (based on the life of Christ), which dates back to 1634. In 1634 and 1635, an outbreak of the plague killed 15,000 people in nearby Munich. The villagers vowed that if they were spared they would do something in which everyone, rich and poor, could take part—and the Passion Play fulfilled this promise. The townspeople survived, and since that time the people of Oberammergau have presented the play every ten years (except during WWII).

Use the following prompts to help build **critical viewing skills.**

- What type of play do you think is being performed in the picture?
- What can you infer about the vision the artistic partners had for this production?

Someone to Listen and Respond

Encourage students to share with the class their experiences attending theatre in the past. Elicit discussion of how it felt to be in an audience, how the audience behaved during the play, the moments they remember about the performance, and so on.

ACTivity Ask students to discuss the differences between what they feel and see in a theatre setting as opposed to film and television. They should compare and contrast what each has to offer in terms of immediacy, intimacy, action, spectacle, storytelling, and so on. You might want to create a chart on the board and list their observations.

ACTivity Ask students to think about what questions they might ask themselves as they watch the first scene of a play unfold. Write their responses on the board.

Elicit class discussion on students' feelings about the responsibility they have as audience members.

The Language of
THEATRE

Pay special attention during classroom instruction to the use of expressions that are only common in the United States. Use synonyms or descriptions to make these expressions more easily understood by English learners.

---

prompt book, one such communication method. Recognize other communication methods as well—costume and light plots, prop lists, and design renderings and models. All these communicate information essential to creating a single vision. The stage manager is always on hand to make sure that vision is conveyed smoothly to the audience. The creative collaboration among all participants forms a wave of energy that reaches the audience.

Someone to Listen and Respond

As an audience member, you play a role in a theatrical production through your **active listening.** You can look anywhere on the stage at any time, depending on what draws your attention. It may be a costume, the look on an actor's face, a particular bit of business, or a painted backdrop upstage. *You* can create the environment in your mind rather than have it focused by a movie camera's lens and the editing process. Your concentration and participation are vital to the actors onstage. When their wave of creativity reaches the audience, your engagement reflects it back to them, heightening the energy even more.

The immediacy of theatre gives the audience a **metaphoric** statement of life, the feeling that what is happening in that moment onstage represents the events of real life. While we watch a play, we are suspended in an intensified illusion of reality. We don't turn to the dramatic

arts to see smaller interpretations of our lives; we come to see larger ones. Yet what we see must appear truthful and believable in the moment. The characters, events, and dialogue must remain consistent and true. The viewers must accept what they see and hear. This is often called the ability to **"suspend disbelief,"** and good critics must be able to do this to give the dramatic work a proper understanding.

The Language of
THEATRE

Learn new language structures and expressions heard in the classroom.

• Listen for the common sound in the words *amphitheatre* and *metaphoric*. As you listen to instruction and interact with classmates, notice other words that contain that same sound and the expressions those words appear in.

• Listen to the compound nouns *active listening* and *audience participation*. Notice that the first expression combines an adjective and a noun and the second combines two nouns.

• Use *active listening* when your teacher talks about attending a play. Notice the sentence structures that the teacher uses and any new expressions you hear.

• Use *active listening* when your classmates present their talk shows about the *metaphoric* experience of live theatre. Notice variations in sentence structure and new expressions that you hear.

From the Field: The Heart of Art

I've noticed that there is always a group of kids who, while not stellar students in other areas, shine when it comes to acting, directing, painting, and just plain creating. Students need theatre, and the arts in particular, to have this place to shine, to know that they can make positive contributions, and to understand how art impacts not only the brain, but the soul.

Steve Jones, Teacher, Hartford, Connecticut

Spotlight on

Audience Participation

Some shows use the audience as part of the act. Many improv troupes, for example, ask audience members to shout out ideas for the improvisers to use as the basis for sketches. Obviously, in these cases, audience etiquette follows very different rules. Nonetheless, audience responses must be polite and respectful.

Audience participation is a big part of the fun at the Chicago-based performance phenomenon known as *Too Much Light Makes the Baby Go Blind*. For this show, a small group of improvisers, the Neofuturists, performs "thirty plays in sixty minutes." The material changes from week to week; the performers spend the days in between performances writing batches of new, extremely short plays. During the show the company performs the plays at breakneck speed. The numbers 1 through 30 are pinned onto a clothesline. The audience shouts out a number and the actors rip it down and perform the sketch to which that number was assigned. The Neofuturists also ask questions of the audience, sometimes demanding feedback, sometimes bringing members of the audience onto the stage to participate.

As a special audience-participation bonus, after every sold-out performance, the cast members order pizza for the audience.

By means of a unique blend of performance velocity, improvisation, and sharp writing, the Neofuturists and their ever-changing show *Too Much Light Makes the Baby Go Blind* have become an international phenomenon.

Chapter 18 Review a Play **215**

Notes

_____

_____

_____

_____

_____

_____

_____

Spotlight on

Audience Participation

Theatres are finding that audience-participation shows are popular. *Tony n' Tina's Wedding* has enjoyed long runs and sold-out houses, and the fun lies in the fact that the audience is part of the show—as wedding guests. They eat and drink and interact with each other and the cast as the play progresses.

For more information on the Neofuturists, including examples of some of the show's recurring playlets, visit *www.neofuturists.org*.

ACTivity Play an audience participation game with the students. Divide them into five groups. Each group is assigned a particular line to speak. As you read the story, pause so that players can make appropriate responses.

The Players	Their Lines
Bold Knights	"Clankety-clank"
Fair Maidens	"Help, Help"
Cruel Monarchs	"Gr-r-r-r, Gr-r-r-r"
Wicked Witches	"Cackle, Cackle"
Fierce Dragons	"Roar-r-r-r-r-r"

The Story begins: *Back in the days of bold knights _____ and fair maidens _____ , there lived two cruel monarchs _____ who had two daughters. These fair maidens _____ were the kindest in all the land. Those who passed by the castle would see the fair maidens _____ high in the castle, leaning out the window, longing for freedom. It was told about the land that these fair maidens _____ had a curse placed upon them by a covey of wicked witches _____ . Only six fierce dragons _____ that lived in the woods could set them free. Should the fierce dragons _____ look upon the fair maidens _____ , the fair maidens _____ would have the superior strength to escape their confinement. That is why the cruel monarchs _____ enlisted two bold knights _____ to slay the fierce dragons _____ .*
Have a student volunteer continue telling the story.

Goethe's Principles of Criticism

Johann Wolfgang von Goethe (GER tuh) was a poet, dramatist, novelist, and scientist. His genius led him into studies of most areas of human endeavor: law, art, music, biology, physics, politics, history, languages, and philosophy. His great dramatic poem *Faust* is considered one of the masterpieces of world literature. Go over each of the three points of Goethe's principles with the students. Discuss what each point entails and how you expect it to impact on the group's reviews.

Be prepared to expedite students' choices of shows to evaluate. You might provide a list from which students may select. It might also be wise to review students' choices before they put in a lot of work reviewing a show that might not have the breadth or depth to warrant close critical inspection. (See Goethe's third question, "Was it worth doing?")

ACTivity Often a reviewer will mention past productions of the same play or other films by the same artists so as to make comparisons. Ask students if they are more likely to trust the critical judgment of a reviewer who can make such comparisons or who has seen many productions over the years. Explain why or why not.

Intent, Structure, and Effectiveness

To create any artistic work, the artist must have a specific intent, work within a structure that reveals that intent, and be capable of rendering the structure effectively. The following questions should help you as you evaluate these and other specific elements of a dramatic presentation. Be sure to give concrete, detailed examples in support of your opinions.

Playwriting

Consider the author's intent when you critique a script. Use questions to help you analyze how effectively the intent was fulfilled. Did the work have:

- the necessary elements of its genre?
- a general appeal wide enough to interest most audience members?
- individuality and freshness of style?

Goethe's Principles of Criticism

Critics in many fields tend to agree that the principles of Goethe (1749–1832), a German philosopher, critic, and playwright, provide a sound basis for criticism. Goethe's critical methodology always used three questions:

1 **What was the artist (author, actor, director, designer) trying to do?** Did the author mean to write a tragedy? A fantasy? A farce? What was the author trying to tell us? What world was the director trying to illuminate? Was the actor showing off his or her own personality or attempting to embody a character? What was the aim of the designer?

2 **How well did the artist accomplish it?** Was the artist successful? Does the author's tragedy/fantasy/farce contain the necessary elements of that genre? Were the actor's technique and the director's methods effective?

3 **Was it worth doing?** Here you must form your own opinion as to whether or not the time and effort were worthwhile for both artists and audience. Even if the artist succeeds in achieving his or her aim, the efforts may not be of value to everyone. After considering the entire production, you must decide its worth.

These three questions provide a valuable foundation for criticism because they allow you to judge the work of an artist only after you have considered the purpose, use of technique, and intrinsic value of the individual efforts.

Backstage Gossip: "I Can Take It"

Noel Coward, playwright, songwriter, actor, and author renowned for his wit, once claimed, "I can take any amount of criticism, as long as it is unqualified praise."

Spamalot

- subtle suggestion (subtext)?
- clear structure, so that events rise to a strong climax?
- clearly drawn, believable characters who are able to arouse audience empathy?
- clear and expressive dialogue that draws the audience into the plot?
- unified effect that builds interest through variety and contrast?
- good balance of emotional climax and release?

Acting

Evaluate the following elements when considering the actor's performance:

- Was each character believable? Was each character true to the intent of the production?
- Was the acting spontaneous (did it have the illusion of the first time)?

- How did the actors project visually and verbally? Did they communicate with economy, clarity, control, and conviction?
- Were the quality, interpretation, and projection of the voice suitable for the character? Did the actors use proper tempo and rhythm in their line delivery and cue pickup?
- Were gestures and movement motivated, clear, varied, and appropriate?
- Was there a good balance between emotion and control? Were reactions true? Was the mood sustained? Were the climaxes of scenes achieved?
- Did the actors establish the proper relationships among the characters? Was there teamwork? Ensemble playing?

Chapter 18 Review a Play **217**

Visual Cue

Monty Python's *Spamalot* is a 2004 Broadway musical adaptation of the 1975 film *Monty Python and the Holy Grail*, itself a spoof of traditional stories of King Arthur and the Knights of the Round Table.

The following prompts can be used to exercise students' **critical viewing skills.**

- What can you infer about the author's intent based on the photo?
- How would you describe the relationships among the characters based on the photo?
- What do you think the actors might be communicating with their gestures?

ACTivity Listen for mentions of plays or movies on television talk shows. Are the people who talk about these productions expressing critical opinions, or are they simply promoting their own works?

Go over the playwriting questions with the students using a familiar play as your basis for discussion. Be sure students back up their answers with concrete examples and well-reasoned conclusions.

Also discuss the questions addressed to evaluating the actors. Use as an example a video, play, or television drama all the students have seen.

ACTivity Have students write a short scene that integrates several arts or media (such as incorporating computer images or video) into a play or uses television during a musical presentation.

Notes

Follow the same discussion process using the questions about directing and design work. Use a familiar television program, film, or play for this purpose.

ACTivity Share with students images of sets and costumes from a variety of nontraditional productions, cinematic as well as theatrical. Ask students to discuss their personal impressions of these designs as well as how they might impact the performance.

Here's How

ACTivity Have students look critically at one of the model reviews with the Critical Ethics at the right in mind. Ask: Are opinions backed up with valid reasons? Is the review objective and fair? Is the whole production taken into account? Does the review attempt to be constructive and not merely negative? Does the critic exhibit an arrogant cleverness at the expense of the artists involved in the performance?

Here's How
To Practice Critical Ethics

There are ethical considerations to being a good critic. Read each point below before you begin your project.

- Back up your opinions with valid reasons based on appropriate standards. Your critical opinion is only worthwhile if you can soundly substantiate it.

- Be objective and fair. Recognize your own biases and tastes and make allowances for them. Keep an open mind.

- Evaluate the whole production. Although you may choose to focus on only one or two key aspects in your review, you must evaluate the interdependence of all theatrical elements.

- Be constructive. Indicate good points along with those that need improvement. No matter what your criticism is, be diplomatic.

- Be sincere. Believe in what you say. The opinion must be your own. Although in many cases you will be guided by professional critics, you must learn to develop and stand behind your own beliefs—provided they are grounded in knowledge and understanding.

- Don't be overly negative.

- Don't try to be clever at the expense of the artist. Your job is to evaluate, not to ridicule.

- Don't sweat the small stuff. Always approach a performance with an idea that you'll enjoy it. If you constantly look for something to go wrong, you won't be able to give a fair review. You will dwell on minutiae—fluffed lines or poorly executed light cues—and miss the possible wonders of the production.

- Don't be arrogant. As a critic, you need humility, understanding, and kindness.

Directing
When assessing the work of the director, think about the following issues:

- Were all aspects unified and faithful to the author's intent?

- Was scene composition handled effectively and smoothly with proper emphasis on balance, variety, and contrast?

- Did rhythm and tempo provide the right mood, with appropriate climax and release in each scene and act?

Backstage Gossip: "How Bad Was It?"

Below are some famous examples of critics being clever rather than constructive.

George S. Kaufman: "There was scattered laughter in the rear of the theatre, leading to the belief that somebody was telling jokes back there."

Eugene Field: "All through the five acts of the Shakespearean tragedy [*King Lear*] he played the king as though under the premonition that someone was about to play the ace."

John Mason Brown: "Tallulah Bankhead barged down the aisle as Cleopatra and sank. As the serpent of the Nile she proves to be no more damaging than a garter snake."

Robert Benchley: "It is one of those plays in which all the actors unfortunately enunciated very clearly."

- Was there a good balance of aesthetic distance and empathy?

- Did each actor suit the part he or she was playing?

Technical Elements
Consider these technical aspects of the production when evaluating the staging:

- Did the set design provide appropriate background and mood?

- Did the set display design principles effectively, such as balance, emphasis, color, and texture?

- Were the costumes and makeup in harmony with the character, period, culture, mood, and style of the work?

- Were the lights, sound effects, special effects, etc., handled effectively?

Career Focus
Theatre Critic

Becoming a critic at a major newspaper, magazine, or radio or television station today typically requires a college education in theatre, dramaturgy, and/or criticism—or considerable direct experience working in the professional worlds of theatre and journalism. The personal critical thinking and writing skills and experience of a theatre critic are highly valuable for higher education and careers outside the theatre.

Many smaller media outlets do not have a full-time critic but instead deal with writers who review on a freelance basis. Some of these freelancers are highly trained and educated professionals; others are basically enlightened audience members with an interest in theatre but little or no direct education or training.

Most professional American critics are members of the American Theatre Critics Association (ATCA). The purpose of this organization, according to its bylaws, is "To make possible greater communication among United States theatre critics; to encourage absolute freedom of expression in theatre and in theatre criticism; to increase public awareness of the theatre as an important national resource; and to reaffirm the individual critic's right to disagree with his colleagues on all matters including the above."

The organization also gives awards for outstanding achievement in the theatre at its annual conference. The members vote on the Theatre Hall of Fame awards, give recommendations for the annual Tony Award for Regional Theatre, honor an emerging playwright, and give awards and citations for outstanding new plays. Refer to the chart on page 10 for more ways to evaluate this career.

Career Focus
ACTivity Ask students to choose a name from the list below and do some research on this person. Have them present their findings to the class.

Audrey Ashley

Robert Benchley

Chad Jones

Dorothy Parker

Elliott Norton

Gerald Berkowitz

Jonathan Kalb

Richard Christiansen

Susan Pellowe

Walter Kerr

ACTivity Advanced Students
Have students find a collection of reviews by two different professional critics. Tell them to read several of them and see if they can discern the particular critical principles each critic operates on. Have students analyze, compare, and evaluate the different critiques. If possible, have them find a review by each critic about the same performance. Students can then prepare their own critical analysis of the two reviews and report to the class.

Backstage Gossip: Horse Sense

[Actor Henry] Irving was putting on one of his Shakespearean pageants in which it was necessary that he should be mounted. A horse was accordingly obtained . . . and Irving, who was not much of a horseman, anxiously inquired if it was quiet. "It's as quiet as a lamb," was the reassuring answer; "it's just finished an engagement at His Majesty's Theatre carrying Mr. Beerbohm Tree in *Richard II*." At this point the horse yawned. "Ah!" said Irving, "he's a bit of a critic too, I see."

from *Theatrical Anecdotes* by Peter Hay

PREPARE

Attend the Play of Your Choice

Monitor the students' preparation for this project. A trip outside of the school grounds can be problematic in terms of travel and safety. Make certain that adequate transportation has been arranged—perhaps students' parents or guardians might volunteer to coordinate car pools.

Tell students that many people volunteer as ushers at their local theatre. They take tickets, hand out programs, and escort audience members to their seats. In exchange for these services they usually are allowed to see the show for free. Have students look into the possibility of ushering at a community or professional theatre in your area.

Depending on where your school is located, this chapter's project may be difficult, if not impossible, to carry out. If there are no theatres in your area, you can have student groups do the talk-show presentation about a play they have all read. Tell them to take notes on:

- structure
- plot
- characters
- theme

They should also think about whether the play would be producible at the school level and what kind of marketing it might need to gain an audience.

Vocabulary Enhancement

A great review is called a *rave*. A terrible review is called a *pan*.

Theatres often provide critics with *press kits*, packets of photos and text materials full of information about the theatre, the production, the playwright, the actors, and so on.

PREPARE

With a group of friends, you will attend a play. As part of the experience, you will monitor your own, your companions', and the rest of the audience's experience. You will also stand back enough from the experience to evaluate the production critically.

Before You Go

To prepare for your theatre-going experience, you and your companions should evaluate and discuss your responsibilities as thoughtful, responsive, and appropriate audience members. (See Spotlight on Audience Etiquette, below.) Also discuss, analyze, and compare appropriate behavior at various types of performances. For example, if you are at an improv event, appropriate behavior may include shouting out an idea from the audience, something that would never be appropriate during a performance of a formal, scripted play.

While You're There

Follow audience etiquette at all times. Get to the theatre early, and stay on your best behavior. Remember that appropriate behavior at one type of live performance might be inappropriate at another. So be sure to determine the behavior that suits the performance you are seeing. Monitor your behavior during the performance to make sure you are always applying appropriate behavior.

Spotlight on Audience Etiquette

To be a courteous audience member, follow the rules of etiquette below.
- Dress appropriately.
- Arrive at least fifteen minutes early to be seated and to read your program. After the curtain is up, most theatres will not seat people until a scene break, so latecomers miss part of the show. If you are allowed to enter late, you inconvenience those already seated.
- ALWAYS turn off your cell phone. Sounds from electronic devices not only disturb those around you but distract the actors as well.
- Remove your hat so that those seated behind you can see.
- NEVER put your feet on the back of the seat in front of you.
- Do not talk during the performance—not even a whisper. Save it until intermission.
- Do not take food or drink into the theatre. NEVER unwrap candy or gum during a performance.
- Don't leave during the play except in an emergency, and don't leave at the end until the house lights are turned on. It is bad manners to slip out early.
- Applaud the performers at the end of the play as they take their bows, but reserve a standing ovation for the truly outstanding performance.

Visual Cue

Use these prompts to develop students' **critical viewing skills**.

- Is it necessary to be athletic or physically strong to play the part of Charlotte?
- What is your experience when you see this image?
- What emotion do you see on the actor's face?
- How might you evaluate the effect of this image on an audience?

Enjoy the show. Leave yourself open to the possibility of both tears and laughter. Use your imagination. Suspend disbelief. Take mental notes throughout the performance about what you see and how you feel. Pay close attention to details in the performance that will help you answer the critics' questions on pages 216–219.

When You Leave the Theatre

After the play, write down your mental notes. Look through your program for any director's notes or playwright's notes that might give you further insights. Keep the program. Later, you will turn it in to your teacher.

Discuss and debate the aesthetics of the play for at least a few minutes with your companions. This discussion will help you pull your thoughts together for your part in the talk show review.

When you get home, take some private time to think about your experience at the theatre. Then, with the aid of your notes, write a two-page paper evaluating the performance on the basis of the questions on pages 216–219. Use the vocabulary included in the questions to talk about the theatrical elements. Also prepare some visuals, ideally in digital form, to reinforce your points.

You will not be reading from your paper. Instead, you will use it as the basis for a panel discussion in which you and the people with whom you attended the play will review it. Become familiar enough with your points so that you can easily chat about each.

The Talk Show Format

Choose a discussion leader (the talk show host) to help focus your group's discussion. This person will introduce each of you and tell the name of the play you attended together. He or she will then ask questions and give each participant a chance to respond. The talk show host must take part in the discussion as well, giving his or her point of view for each question. Questions should be loosely based on the notes each of you took before, during, and after the play. Panel members must answer the questions informally without reading from their notes. They must also supplement their answers with visuals prepared ahead of time.

As a group, decide in advance the order of the questions and which topics you will deal with. The talk show host will keep track of the time and make sure you don't go longer than ten minutes.

Chapter 18 Review a Play **221**

Try This

To practice answering questions and giving opinions spontaneously, ask a friend or relative to write down four or five questions for you. The questions can range from serious to silly, but they should require some thought on your part. Sit in a chair, read the questions aloud, and practice answering them. This should help prepare you for your talk show participation.

If students are reading the play instead of attending it, they can use these criteria as the basis of their two-page paper:

- a summary of the play's theme
- any particularly intriguing characters or lines
- their own emotional reaction to the writing or to character descriptions
- their own visualization of the set and lighting
- thoughts about how various audiences (under twelve, young adult, middle-aged, elderly) might respond to the play's subject matter

The Talk Show Format

Suggest that students ask if any member of their group would like to be the discussion leader. However, if you think a particular student needs a chance to work on leadership qualities, ask that student to lead the group.

Suggest also that they may wish to watch a television talk show to get a clearer idea of the style and format. Remind the group leader that he or she must do more than ask pertinent and probing questions, however. The leader of this presentation is also responsible for contributing ideas and opinions.

Give each discussion leader in turn your stopwatch to use during the group's presentation. Be sure it is returned to you when each talk show is over.

Try This

Tell students that the questions can be about any subject with which they have some familiarity. The key is to be relaxed and spontaneous.

Backstage Gossip: Is Kate Aging Badly?

In Shakespeare's day his comedy *The Taming of the Shrew* was both a box-office draw and a crowd-pleaser. But in the 20th century, some critics and audiences began to feel uncomfortable about *Shrew*. The play is about an ill-tempered, independent-minded woman named Kate and the man who "tames" her, Petruchio. First through cruelty and later through rewards, Petruchio turns Kate into a "fitting wife." Some argue that the play is antiwoman, a blatant example of male chauvinism. Apart from the antifeminist point, critics have argued about the play's artistic merits. However, many Shakespeare fans still respond favorably to the play's physical comedy and clever wordplay.

PRESENT

Put on Your Talk Show

Remind students that their goal is to be objective and well informed, not simply opinionated. Tell them that a critic is not someone who merely criticizes, but a person who studies, analyzes, and renders an informed opinion. Students should bear in mind that tone is important—sometimes it's not what one says but rather the way one says it.

Visual Cue

- Which person in the photo do you think is the host? What makes you think so?

- Does this remind you of a talk show you have seen on television? What are the similarities? How is it different?

- What might be some of the benefits of having more than two people take part in a talk show? What might be some of the disadvantages?

CRITIQUE

Evaluate a Panelist's Performance

Hand out the Critique Sheet for this project or have students use their own paper. Remind students that they are critiquing only one person in the talk show panel—it can be either the discussion leader or one of the panelists.

Discuss with students the rubrics they will be using to evaluate this person. Let them know that you will be assessing each of them in much the same way, and that you will also evaluate how well they assess others.

If you feel that a student had a particularly difficult time with the talk-show format, talk to the student about his or her impressions of the process. Suggest techniques the student can use to become more comfortable in the setting.

PRESENT

Put on Your Talk Show

When your name or another group member's name is called, give all of your papers or Activity Sheets to your teacher, along with the program and ticket stub for the play. Step into the performance area and set up your chairs in a talk show arrangement, side by side in a straight line or a semicircle.

The talk show host will introduce each of you and begin the discussion by asking a question. When it is your turn to answer, try to present as clear a picture of your experience and your review as you can. For example, if you felt excitement during the performance, convey that to the class. Acknowledge the audience's reaction to the play as well.

When nine minutes have passed, the host should start to wrap things up by asking the group for any final thoughts. At the end of the ten minutes, stop the discussion, shake hands with your fellow participants, and return to your seat.

Students present a talk show.

CRITIQUE

Evaluate a Panelist's Performance

There is a difference between playing a part and playing yourself. Some people have a much more difficult time being themselves in front of an audience than they do playing a character.

Remaining relaxed and comfortable in front of an audience without notes or a script can be nerve-wracking. You will see that some of your classmates are better at it than others. Select one classmate from a talk show panel who struck you as the most effective speaker in the group, the student you would rate as "outstanding." Write a paper explaining why. Ask yourself the questions below as you evaluate the outstanding individual in the talk show panel.

- What did the panelist do to appear physically comfortable?

- What elements (humor, enthusiasm, storytelling, etc.) did this person use to engage the audience?

- What aspects of the panelist's behavior particularly engaged you?

- How did the other participants in the presentation react to this panelist?

- What insights into the the particular performance impressed you in the panelist's critique ?

- What insights brought you to a higher level of understanding?

Backstage Gossip: Cell Phones in Traffic

Celebrated playwright and actor Sam Shepard was performing in Chicago as part of the Steppenwolf Theatre Company's Traffic series—programming that features live music and the spoken word. Early in the performance an audience member's cell phone began to ring. Shepard looked out, found the woman whose phone was ringing, and said fiercely, "Turn that thing off!" The mortified patron did.

Additional Projects

1 Attend a play, or watch a filmed version of a play of your choice. Analyze, describe, relate, and evaluate the interdependence of all the theatrical elements. Present your conclusions in a PowerPoint presentation.

2 In an improvised sketch with a small group, demonstrate the three components necessary for a theatrical experience: a story, someone to tell it, and someone to listen and respond. In your sketch, try to convey the roles and collaborative relationships of all involved. Use music or projected visuals to help you make your points in this informal presentation.

3 On a poster board or using a computer to design a graphic, visually demonstrate the collaboration of artists on a theatrical production and the theatre systems (such as production calendar) and communication methods (such as promptbook) they use to coordinate their efforts.

4 Attend another play. Before you go, review the guidelines for audience etiquette on page 220. While you are at the performance, practice appropriate audience etiquette at all times. Then apply the concepts of evaluation outlined in this chapter and write up a critical review using such theatre vocabulary as intent, structure, theme, character, setting, and effectiveness. Be sure to include consideration of technical elements as well. Plan to deliver your review orally, and avoid reading straight from your paper when you do so.

5 Prepare a brief video as a public service announcement that provides an analysis of appropriate audience behavior and etiquette in various situations, from serious plays to improvs. Use humor to get your points across. Make a point of attending several different types of live performances and follow the guidelines you give in your public service announcement for applying appropriate behavior.

6 Evaluate the career opportunities available to theatre critics and relate and appraise the value of personal theatre skills and experiences to higher education.

7 Read the scene from *The Actor's Nightmare* by Christopher Durang, found in Unit Eight of this book, and think about the nightmare aspect of this scene. Write a short scene of your own entitled *The Student's Nightmare*.

8 **Theatre Journal** The next time you are in an audience situation, pay close attention to your fellow audience members. Are they listening attentively? How can you tell? Write a definition of an active audience member behaving with appropriate etiquette.

Review a Play Test

The test for this chapter is available in blackline master form in the Resource Binder, page 89.

For More Information

For tips on audience etiquette, visit:

www.centerstagechicago.com/theatre/articles/etiquette.html

www.lifepaths360.com/index.php/theatre-etiquette-4810

www.satheatre.com/extras/18-fun-stuff/88-theatre-etiquette

For an interesting talk-show alternative, tune in to National Public Radio for interview programming such as Terry Gross's popular "Fresh Air."

Books
Brustein, Robert, *Letters to a Young Actor,* Basic Books, 2007.

Brustein, Robert, *The Theatre of Revolt: An Approach to Modern Drama*, Little, Brown, 1964.

Palmer, Richard H., *The Critics' Canon: Standards of Theatrical Reviewing in America*, Greenwood Press, 1988.

Smith, S. Stephenson, *The Craft of the Critic*, Kessinger Publishing, 2007.

Other Media
Visit the American Theatre Critics Association Web site at: *www.americantheatrecritics.org*.

Theatre Journal

Use the following as an additional or substitute prompt.

As you write your journal entry, focus not only on what a good audience member should not do, but also on what he or she should do.

Substitute Teacher Activities

The suggestions below are intended for the substitute teacher when you are out of the classroom for a day or two.

• Assign the Be a Theatre Critic Worksheet on page 87 of the Resource Binder, and have students write a review of a play, film, or television show.

• Assign one or more of the additional projects on this page.

• Go over the Audience Etiquette rules on page E of the Student TIPack.

• **Conduct a Current Events Talk Show.** Have students use the talk-show format to work in groups to discuss current events, important school activities, or other timely topics. Have each group choose a "host" who introduces and asks questions of the "guests."

• Being a good critic requires **using descriptive language.** Select five or six interesting objects in the classroom and challenge students to write paragraphs that fully describe them. Ask students to read their descriptions.

Theatre **Then** and Now

Other Cultures, Other Times

Many theatres throughout the centuries have presented outdoor plays, especially those written by William Shakespeare, during the summer months. The most famous of the outdoor Elizabethan theatres was the Globe Theatre, built in London in 1599 by Richard Burbage. It consisted of an open-air building with a platform stage in the middle surrounded on three sides by open standing room. A large enclosed balcony covered by small roofed galleries surrounded the theatre, offering seating for the few who could afford it. You might want to gather images of the old and new Globe Theatres to show students. There are also models of the Globe available that can be fairly easily assembled.

Invite a director or administrator from a local theatre that presents outdoor performances to visit the class. Ask him or her what adjustments must be made when presenting plays outside, including the technical requirements, and so on.

Bertolt Brecht (1898–1956) believed in abolishing anything artificial that separated the audience from the performers. This belief extended to the performance space. Brecht did not believe in the use of realistic sets; he preferred environmental staging, often working without even a stage.

Theatre **Then** and Now

The Roman Audience in 200 A.D.

Imagine that you are attending a play at the imposing Roman **amphitheatre** at Sabratha, around 200 A.D. You are one of thousands of people lucky enough to get a seat in the largest theatre in North Africa. By this time Roman theatres have been constructed all over Italy, Spain, and France, as well as North Africa.

Imagine the noise all these people are making. Then consider the fact that the performance is held outdoors and the performers onstage have no microphones or other artificial amplification.

In such a large performance space, subtlety won't be the first order of business. In fact, most of the actors wear masks painted with characteristic facial expressions that can be seen by audience members seated great distances away.

If you picture yourself sitting high in the stands at a football stadium watching a play going on down there on the 50-yard line, you'll have some idea of the dimensions. You should also consider that your seat is made of stone. There are no artificial lights of course, so the play is performed using that most natural of lighting systems—the sun.

For your theatre comfort, there are awnings, fruit vendors, and, if it gets particularly hot, showers of perfumed water. More likely than not, you are watching a bawdy farce full of greed, horseplay, infidelities, and women in scanty costumes. Here you are, centuries in the past, watching a performance not unlike the TV situation comedies of today!

In the theatre at Sabratha, the audience sat on the tiered stone seats at the left while the actors performed on the dark street-like area to the right.

 **Visual Cue**

Use the following prompts about the theatre at Sabratha to help students exercise their **critical viewing skills**.

- How might the shape of the theatre add to the sound quality?

- What type of modern-day facility does this amphitheatre remind you of?

- What might be the disadvantages of performing an entire play during daylight hours? Can you think of any benefits?

An Off-Broadway Audience Today

Flash forward to a typical off-Broadway theatre in the 21st century. There are anywhere from 150 to 300 seats in a performance space that seems almost intimate. You sit down on a soft-cushioned seat in a room that, no matter what the weather outdoors, is temperature-controlled for maximum comfort. You and your fellow audience members are cautioned via a high-tech sound system to turn off your cell phones for the duration of the performance.

The lights go to black. Then they rise again, and the actors begin to perform. They could be in your living room—that's how well you can hear them, thanks to that same high-tech sound system, which has tiny powerful microphones placed on, around, or above the stage. You have no problem seeing the actors, partly because they're not all that far away from you and partly because of an offstage light board, which is run by computer. The lights create subtle effects that allow you to enjoy a very realistic setting.

The acting is very natural, and the play's subject speaks to the issues of our day and the concerns of our hearts. When the play ends, the actors take their bows. You can see the pride in each of their faces.

This off-Broadway experience bears little resemblance to watching a sitcom—it is much more real and immediate. And while we may sometimes choose the farce and fantasy of TV, there's so much more being offered in live theatre.

Actor Bill Talon has created an activist performance group with his *Rev. Billy and the Church of Stop Shopping*, which performs off-Broadway as well as in the streets and even in chain stores and at demonstrations, including Occupy Wall Street.

Off-Broadway Venues

Tell students that the actors union, Actor's Equity Association (AEA), lists a special showcase code, which is available in many areas, for theatres with ninety-nine seats or less. The code usually states that actors can forgo payment in order to showcase themselves for possible future (paying) work. This allows producers to use union actors at a minimal production cost. The code generally stipulates a low ticket price and a limited run. In larger cities such as New York and Los Angeles there are many of these ninety-nine-seat houses.

In the 1960s, avant-garde theatre folk began performing in a number of unusual locations—an abandoned factory, a loft, a city bus, or the city streets—anywhere but in an actual theatre. The idea was to bring people together in unexpected and provocative ways. In this context, the play often seemed far less important than the "in-your-face" performers and the spectacle they offered. This type of theatre, sometimes called Guerilla Theatre, began to taper off toward the end of the 1960s, but it earned a place in theatre history.

For More Information

Books

Beacham, Richard C., *The Roman Theatre and Its Audience,* Harvard University Press, 1996.

Chase, Ramond G., *Ancient Hellenistic and Roman Amphitheatres, Stadiums, and Theatres: The Way They Look Now,* Peter Randall, 2003.

Farber, Donald C., *From Option to Opening: A Guide to Producing Plays Off-Broadway,* Limelight Editions, 2005.

Other Media

Ancient Theaters of Greece and Rome, DVD, Insight Media, 2005.

The Renaissance Theatre, DVD, Insight Media, 2005.

The Restoration Theater: From Tennis Court to Playhouse, DVD, Insight Media, 1996.

Stages of Theatre: From the Greeks to Shakespeare, DVD, Films for the Humanities and Sciences, 2005.

PREVIEW

1 Aristotle's six basic elements of drama are thought, plot, action, diction, spectacle, and sound.

2
1) Exposition 5) Climax
2) Inciting 6) Falling Action
  Incident 7) Resolution
3) Rising Action
4) Crisis

3 The director selects the play.

4 Royalties are payments made to the author for the right to produce the play.

5 An audition is the actor's initial tryout. The callback is the final tryout to get the role.

6 The most important thing a casting director looks for in an actor is that he or she is best suited to the role.

7 If you agree to perform in a full-length play, you can expect to be in rehearsal approximately 100 hours.

8 A ground plan allows the director to see the stage graphically and to envision the actors in motion.

9 The area where these scenes would most likely be presented:

a scene in which two lovers kiss
  Area 3

a fantasy scene
  Area 6

a scene in which two nobles meet
  Area 2

a scene that is the play's dramatic high point
  Area 1

a scene where someone listens in
  Area 5

10 Answers will vary, but students should note that theatre is ephemeral, that a theatre audience has a more complex relationship with the performance—a give-and-take of energy passing from the actors into the audience, etc.

Unit Four Review

PREVIEW

Examine the following key concepts previewed in Unit Four.

1 What are Aristotle's six basic elements of drama?

2 Put the following plot elements in the order they should occur.
Climax   Falling Action   Exposition   Inciting Incident
Crisis   Resolution   Rising Action

3 Who selects the play, the producer or the director?

4 What are royalties?

5 What is the difference between an audition and a callback?

6 The most important thing a casting director looks for in an actor is:
a. enthusiasm   b. intensity   c. best suited to role   d. a supple voice

7 If you agree to perform in a full-length play, how long might you expect to be in rehearsal?

8 How does a ground plan help block a play?

9 Match the scenes described below to the area where they would most likely be presented onstage.

a scene in which two lovers kiss	Area 1
a fantasy scene	Area 2
a scene in which two nobles meet	Area 3
a scene that is the play's dramatic high point	Area 4
a scene where someone listens in	Area 5
	Area 6

10 Compare watching a movie to attending live theatre.

PREPARE

Assess your response to the preparation process for projects in this unit.

11 Explain which of the following was the most difficult for you in preparing your dramatic scenario: finding the subject, creating the characters, or developing a conflict.

12 What was the most difficult aspect of creating a rehearsal schedule?

13 Which of the steps in blocking your scene did you find most challenging?

14 Which do you find most satisfying: writing scenes, blocking scenes, discussing scenes, or acting in scenes? Explain why.

PRESENT

Analyze the experience of presenting your work to the class.

15 In sharing your dramatic scenario, did you feel that you were connecting with the audience?

16 Do you find question-and-answer sessions after giving a presentation interesting and informative or nerve-wracking and embarrassing? Explain.

17 In your talk show discussion, did all members have an equal chance to offer their evaluation?

CRITIQUE

Evaluate how you go about critiquing your work and the work of others.

18 Did you find it easier to assess a classmate's dramatic scenario, play analysis, blocking, or talk show contribution? Why?

19 Did you feel that the presenters were asked meaningful questions during question-and-answer periods? Give two examples.

20 How did evaluating the work of others help you approach your own?

EXTENSIONS

- With a partner, block a short scene in which you play a game of imaginary darts and discuss the wonders (and flaws) of the opposite sex.

- Research and discuss additional elements of stage combat.

Unit Four Review **227**

Resource Binder

Unit Four Test, p. 90

PREPARE

11 Answers will vary. Many students will say that developing the conflict was the most challenging. Answers should be well supported.

12 Answers will vary but should reveal an understanding of each phase of the rehearsal process.

13 Answers will vary.

14 Students' answers will depend on individual preferences. Students who enjoy acting will probably indicate that acting in or blocking the scene was the most satisfying, while student writers will indicate that writing was the most satisfying.

PRESENT

15 Answers will vary depending on the audience and the presenters.

16 Question-and-answer periods can be nerve-racking and embarrassing to even experienced presenters. Students will probably indicate that while they can be informative, they are difficult.

17 Answers will vary but should show some insight into the group dynamics of the presentation.

CRITIQUE

18 Answers will vary, but students will probably indicate that the play analysis was easier to assess, particularly a familiar play.

19 Answers will vary, but students should present two well-documented examples.

20 Answers will vary.

EXTENSIONS

- The short scene should show an understanding of effective blocking while also presenting a realistic dialogue about the opposite sex.

- Invite students to demonstrate stage combat under your supervision.

Unit Five

Technical Theatre

Unit Five will give the students an overview of all the technical elements that go into the making of successful production. The students will learn how to work as part of a team to design, create, and build the lighting, the sets, the costumes, the sound, the makeup, and the props for a play. Students will learn to create the environment in which a play resides.

Project Preview

Chapter 19 Set Design
Creating a set design for a scene or a one-act play

Chapter 20 Set Construction
Understand the basics of set construction and safety in the scene shop

Chapter 21 Lighting
Creating a light design for a scene from a play

Chapter 22 Sound
Making a cue sheet and sound effects tape

Chapter 23 Costumes
Preparing three to five costume designs for a character in a play

Chapter 24 Makeup
Applying character makeup

Chapter 25 Props
Preparing a prop plot for a full-length play

Unit Five

Technical Theatre

Quotables

I am enough of an artist to draw freely upon my imagination. Imagination is more important than knowledge. Knowledge is limited. Imagination encircles the world.

Albert Einstein, Physicist

Any smoothly functioning technology will have the appearance of magic.

Arthur C. Clarke, Science Fiction Author

The following questions should tap into students' **prior knowledge** and encourage reflection on the topics discussed in this unit.

- Have you ever designed or built anything, such as a table, a box to hold your keepsakes, or a bookcase to organize your room?

- Have you ever taken an art class?

- Do you enjoy painting, drawing, or sculpting works of art?

- Is clothes-shopping high on your list of fun things to do? Do you enjoy matching garments, fabrics, and colors?

- Have you wondered how the lighting effects are created at a concert? Do you ever look toward the lights as they shift and change color?

- Are you competent with computers or other technology?

- What kind of music do you enjoy?

- Have you ever made a "favorites mix" recording of your favorite songs?

- Are you good at organizing things, helping others, and working as part of a team?

- Did you write and perform backyard or basement plays when you were younger? What did you use to create your imaginary play places? What kind of "sets" did you create?

Theatre Journal

One of the goals of Tim Supple's multilingual production of *A Midsummer Night's Dream* was to reflect the diversity of south Asia. What story might you chose to reflect the cultural diversity of the United States? What technical elements might you use in such a production to help convey the message of cultural diversity?

The image above shows the actress Archana Ramaswamy in her role as Titania in the 2007 London Roundhouse multilingual production of *A Midsummer Night's Dream* directed by Tim Supple. The following prompts can be used to help the students **identify and analyze** technical elements.

- Describe the set. What structure is in the background? What is supporting the actress? Let students know that the actress acrobatically wrapped herself into a cocoon in the billowing silk, as did other characters, for their nighttime sleep.

- Would you feel safe on this set? What does thinking about that question tell you must be an integral part of all set design and construction?

- What does Tatiana's costume suggest about both the setting of the play and her character?

- How does the lighting affect your emotional response to the scene?

Chapter 19

Set Design

This chapter introduces students to the design process, the principles of design and composition, and stage terminology. Students will learn how to design a set for a play.

Objectives

1 to learn about production concepts and the different types of sets

2 to recognize and apply the principles of design and composition in the design process

3 to create a set design for a one-act play or scene

Project Specs

It would be helpful for students to have an outline of your own stage on which to draw their designs. Give students a hands-on demonstration of the tools, makeup, lights, and props they will be using on activities in this unit.

ELL Students

Different cultures interpret colors differently. Ask students from diverse backgrounds to talk about how people in their culture respond to specific colors. For example, in China, red is the color of good luck; in Russia, red means beautiful; and in South Africa, red is the color of mourning.

On Your Feet

Giving students a handout with the outline of the school's stage and/or taping the floor to indicate the stage space might help students to visualize their designs.

Chapter

19 Set Design

The magic of theatre, like the genius of invention, is as much a matter of sweat as inspiration. Set designers use hard work, creativity, and their best collaborative skills in order to help realize a play's vision.

Project Specs

Project Description You will create a set design for a one-act play or a scene from a longer work. Then you will present your work in a five- to ten-minute talk.

Purpose to understand the basics of set design and the connection between stage design and the effectiveness of a production

Materials a hand-drawn, computer-generated, or three-dimensional design for a stage plan and/or the Set Design Activity Sheet provided by your teacher

Theatre Terms

arena stage
black box stage
box set
cyclorama
drop
elevation sketch
flats
flexible stage
incubation
proscenium stage
set pieces
teaser
thrust stage
unit set

On Your Feet

Using the materials available in the room, design a space that is especially suited to one of the following functions: a business meeting, a friendly lunch, a therapy session, a flea market. Test your design by inviting two or more students to improvise a short scene in the space you have created.

The set design for *Phantom of the Opera* is suitably atmospheric and elaborate.

Theatre Terms

arena stage a stage with seating on all four sides

black box stage a stage consisting of a large empty square with black walls

box set a set that consists of two or three walls and a ceiling

cyclorama a curtain that covers the back wall and sides of the stage

drop decorated canvas or muslin curtain that forms part of the scenery

elevation sketch a drawing that shows how the stage will look from the perspective of the audience

flats canvas stretched over wooden frames, painted, and used for scenery

flexible stage another name for black box stage; a stage that can be set up like any other stage type

The same skills that help you match your wardrobe, decorate your room, and fulfill art projects can be put into play for stage design. Learning set design principles can take you a long way toward understanding the play's meaning. Scenery is often the first thing that shows the audience something about the time, the setting, and even the purpose of the play. Some sets use little scenery and rely on the strength of the actors' interpretations and the audience's imagination to set the scene.

Set design is a creative process that begins when the director, set designer, and technical director analyze the play to determine the style, atmosphere, and color they want to create. The process involves a number of strands. One is to do research to establish historical and

Principles of Design

Lines	Mark out contours
Shape	Distinct, defined areas
Mass	Bulk and weight
Measure	Size (length, width, height)
Position	Placement of elements
Color	Use of light and pigment
Texture	Surface qualities

Principles of Composition

Unity	Oneness, cohesion
Harmony	Aesthetic order among parts
Contrast	Use of differences
Variation	Diversity, lack of monotony
Balance	Equilibrium and stability
Proportion	Proper size relationships
Emphasis	Center of attention

cultural accuracy. Unless the artistic direction calls for a different treatment, the set should accurately reflect the time, location, and culture in which it takes place. Another phase is **incubation**—that period in the creative process when ideas simmer, recombine, and sometimes give birth to new ideas and creative ways to meet challenges. After incubation, the team selects the ideas to be implemented and evaluates the effectiveness of the proposed design.

Designers must recognize and apply the principles in the chart above to create effective stage sets.

Bring in copies of several scenes from *Our Town*. Engage the students in a short rehearsal of a scene or two. After the students have a feel for the play, engage them in a discussion about set design. What do they think is the purpose of scenery? What is the job of the set designer? Students will then discuss the "minimal" sets used in productions of *Our Town*.

Engage the students in a discussion about the principles of design and composition on the stage. Bring in fine art books or images to stimulate analysis. Show the pictures and ask the students what principles of composition they recognize or how the color affects their emotional reaction to the picture.

Show, Don't Tell Make simple shapes—cylinders, square boxes, rectangular boxes, wedges, etc.— from card stock and clear tape. Define a small space in the classroom as a performance space, a desktop perhaps. Use the shapes you made in different ways inside the stage space. Ask students to describe what the different shapes do to the space. How does the stage change as the shapes are moved around?

Phantom of the Opera employs many inventive set designs. The following prompts can be used to exercise **critical viewing skills.**

- How does the set design in this scene contribute to the atmosphere of the play?

- How does the set help the actors convey the style and mood of the play to the audience?

- Research the use of "fog" onstage.

---

incubation the phase of the design process during which ideas simmer, recombine, or develop into new creative solutions

proscenium stage a stage in which the audience looks through the "fourth wall" to see the play

set pieces furniture and other three-dimensional objects

teaser a heavy curtain or frame that adjusts the height of the proscenium

thrust stage a low platform stage that juts out into the audience

unit set a set made of pieces that can be rearranged

Creativity in Technical Design

ACTivity Show still photos or video clips of movie, TV, or theatre sets. Have students work in small groups to analyze one of the sets and summarize their discussion on the creativity evident in the set design for the rest of the class.

Types of Stages

ACTivity Draw or tape the outline of the different types of stages on the floor. Divide the class into three groups. Each group will take a turn as actors and then as audience members. Give each group a funny poem to perform (Shel Silverstein's poetry works well) and tell each group which type of stage—proscenium, thrust, or arena—they will sit in to watch a performance. Assign each performance group to a specific audience configuration. Remind them that the actors must be blocked so that the audience can see the action. Give the students time to discuss the advantages and disadvantages in performing and watching a performance from each type of stage. Discuss the use of scenery and set pieces for each type.

Vocabulary Enhancement

The word proscenium (Pro SEE nee um) is from the Greek *proskenion*, which is from *pro* meaning "before" and *skene* meaning "building at the back of the stage" or the "scene" house. Our word *scene* comes from the Greek word *skene*.

The word *orchestra* (OR kes trah) is from the Greek word *orkheisthai*, meaning "to dance." The *orkheisthai* was the area in front of the stage where the Greek chorus performed. Today, it is the area where the orchestra sits during a musical.

Creativity in Technical Design

Creativity in technical design can be defined as the unique way each artist or team of artists uses the principles of design and composition to express meaning. One way to develop your own creativity in technical theatre design is to observe other performance-related design spaces—movie and TV sets, for example, or the sets of any live theatre you attend—and note what is especially effective or ineffective. But the best way to develop your own design creativity is to dig in and try your hand at it. The sections that follow will provide you with a foundation for developing your personal creative expression and communicating through design. You can demonstrate your creativity through your completed project.

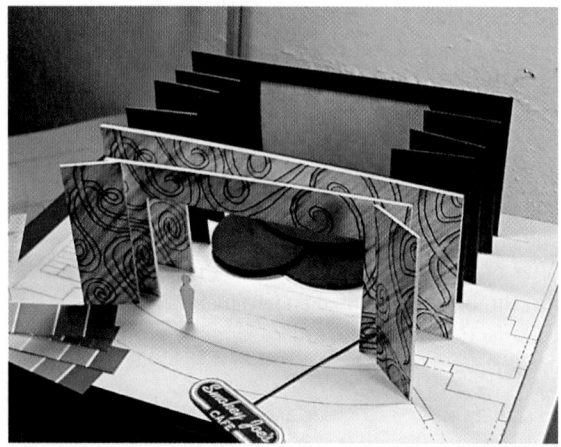

Even in a scale model, such as this one for *Smokey Joe's Cafe*, the set designer's creativity is evident.

Types of Stages

The kind of stage available for your production influences the kind of set design you can create. Get to know the different types of stages and what they can offer a production.

The Proscenium Stage The **proscenium stage** is like a picture frame. The audience sits looking into the frame to see the play. It is separated from the audience by three stage walls and an invisible "fourth wall," which the audience looks through. Proscenium productions generally require the most elaborate set designs since they cover three sides of the performance space.

The Thrust Stage A low platform stage that juts (or "thrusts") out into the audience, with seating on three sides, is called a **thrust stage.** This kind of stage offers opportunities to create several distinct acting areas. Set designs are usually minimal.

The Arena Stage Arena staging, sometimes called "theatre-in-the-round," seats the audience entirely around the playing area. An **arena stage** encourages actor-audience interaction, but it requires a set that allows for continuous movement onstage and does not block audience viewing from any side of the house. Because the audience is so close, props and scenery must look authentic.

Resource Binder

- Stage Configurations, TIPack, p. L
- Stage Diagram, TIPack, p. M
- Set Design Activity Sheet, p. 95
- Preliminary Set Design Notes Worksheet, p. 96
- Critique Sheet: Create a Set Design, p. 97
- Set Design Test, p. 98
- Set Designer's Script Analysis, p. 169

Handbook Connections pages 600–607

To Have on Hand

- Scripts or scenes from various plays
- Images of various types of sets
- Fine art books
- Cutting tools
- Tape measure and graph paper
- Pencils, erasers, colored pencils, rulers, scissors, stapler
- Color charts
- Project board, foam core, shoeboxes

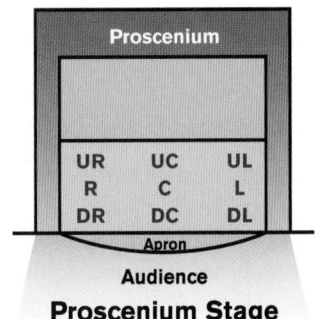

Proscenium Stage

The proscenium stage, with its grand frame, is the most common of all types of stages.

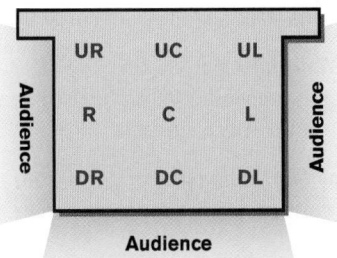

Thrust Stage

The thrust stage comes in many different shapes, but always juts out into the audience. The Globe Theatre is a thrust stage.

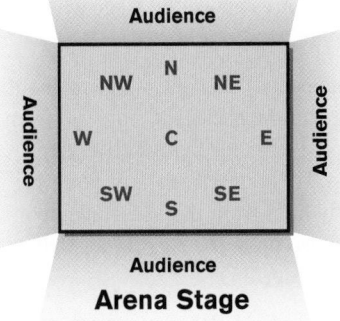

Arena Stage

The arena stage, in which only the center of the stage corresponds to traditional stage positions. Here the points of the compass are often used instead.

Black box theatre stage

A fourth type of stage is called a **black box stage** or **flexible stage**. It is called a black box stage because it is essentially a big empty square with walls painted black. It is called a flexible stage because with its simplicity it can be set up like any of the other stage types, or it can be given a completely experimental treatment. There are no permanent seats in a theatre with a black box stage; the seating of the audience can be arranged in a variety of ways to enhance audience participation or establish distance.

Communicating with Design

The ground plan (or floor plan) is one of the most important communication methods between the designer and the director. This bird's-eye view of the set—showing doors, windows, walls, stairs, platforms, ramps, and furniture placement—is also important to the people working on the design and con-

Chapter 19 Set Design **233**

Tell students that black box stages became more popular beginning in the 1960s with the blossoming of experimental theatre. Explain that the flexible nature of these stages makes them appealing to educational institutions and to theatre groups that want to adapt unconventional spaces such as a vacant warehouse, factory, or office building to performance space. Many performing arts centers that contain a variety of performance spaces include a black box stage.

ACTivity As a continuation of the previous activity, ask students from each group to suggest how they might use a black box stage to reflect the type of stage they used for performance of their poem.

ACTivity **Advanced Students**
Invite students to conduct research to find examples of black box stages or theatres in your community or in other settings around the world. Have them create a visual presentation showing examples of different set designs or different types of theatrical productions using this type of flexible stage. Ask them to include information about how technical elements such as rigging, lighting, curtains, and set pieces are accommodated.

Communicating with Design

Bring several sketches of different ground plans, elevation sketches, and color renderings. Include both hand-drafted and computer-aided designs. Discuss with students the pros and cons of both methods of designing. Encourage them to consider the look and feel of hand-drafted designs, the need to render many repeated elements, time constraints, the ability to make changes, and the need to communicate with large numbers of people. Invite students to share previous experiences using computer design programs or apps. Compare and contrast the designs you brought in based on the play and the director's concept. Can the students tell from the design what that concept is?

Notes

_____

_____

_____

_____

_____

_____

_____

_____

Stage Elements

If the cutaway stage on the next page is not like the one at your school, try to find one at another school, college, or professional theatre in your community that is. Make arrangements for the students to visit this stage. If this is not possible, try to relate the stage at your school to this cutaway drawing as best you can.

There are many schools that do not have stages this sophisticated, but the drama instructors and students create wonderful productions nonetheless. Ask the students to compare their performance space to the one pictured here. Use the vocabulary list as the focus of the discussion. Does your school use a cyc? Does your school have a fly loft? How do you adapt your sets to use the space you have to full advantage?

Even if your school doesn't have some of these elements, the students should learn about them. They may one day be in a position to work on a state-of-the-art stage and should be familiar with the terminology.

struction of the set. The ground plan should be as detailed as possible so that the stage crew can build the set to the required measurements and specifications. The designer also creates an elevation sketch, which shows how the stage will look from the audience, and a color rendering of the set. These sketches and the ground plan will go into the prompt book. Some scene designers also construct a three-dimensional scale model that is an accurate miniature reproduction of the set, showing construction, furniture, and key props.

Designers may draft their sketches by hand or use specialized computer tools. A number of apps for mobile devices now help designers create these technical theatre documents and communicate their ideas to the director and the technical crew more quickly and easily. Creating, reading, and interpreting such documents are important communication skills for theatre professionals. Demonstrate your understanding of the communication methods designers use by creating them if you are a designer or referring to them for guidance if you are on a technical crew.

Stage Elements

Knowing, understanding, and using the terms that follow will help you as you learn about designing and constructing stage sets. Some of their counterparts can be seen on the diagram on the next page.

Act Curtain (A) Curtain that masks the acting area from the audience. Sometimes called the front or grand curtain, it is opened at the beginning of the play and closed between acts or scenes. It usually parts in the middle and is a called a *traveler*.

Apron (B) Acting area between the front edge of the stage and the front curtain.

Back Wall (C) Opposite the proscenium opening; it can be used as a background for exterior sets.

Battens (D) Long pipes or poles from which curtains, lights, or flats are hung.

Cyclorama or **Cyc** Background curtain covering stage back and sides.

Drop or **backdrop (E)** A canvas or muslin curtain, usually painted, that forms part of the scenery.

Flies (F) Area above the stage where scenery is hung out of view.

Fly Gallery (G) Narrow platform about halfway up the backstage side wall from which the lines for flying scenery are worked. Without a fly gallery, you may work fly lines from the backstage floor. For a close-up of the rigging for flying flats, see page 259.

Gridiron or **Grid (H)** Framework of beams above the stage that supports riggings for flying scenery.

Notes

_____

_____

_____

_____

_____

_____

_____

Ground Cloth Canvas that covers the floor of the acting area, which may be painted to resemble bricks, stones, carpet, and so forth.

Leg (I) One of a pair of drapes hung stage right and left behind the tormentors to mask the backstage.

Locking Rail (J) Rail on the fly gallery or backstage wall to which lines are pulled and tied off. (See page 259.)

Proscenium Arch Frame or opening of a proscenium stage through which the audience views the play.

Teaser (K) Heavy curtain or canvas-covered wooden frame hung above the proscenium opening to adjust the height of the opening. Shorter curtains hung at intervals to mask lights and unused scenery are called *borders*.

Tormentors (L) Curtain or flat at each side of the proscenium opening used to regulate the width of the opening.

Trap Opening in the stage floor.

Wings The offstage area to the left and right of the stage.

ACTivity Make several game boards out of the illustration of the stage on this page using blackline master M, the labeled Stage Diagram, from the TIPack Section of the Resource Binder. Put the vocabulary words (*Act Curtain, Wings, Locking Rail,* and so on) on heavy card stock and have students make their own game pieces. Students pull one card from the deck, give the definition of the word, and place the game piece on the matching area of the diagram.

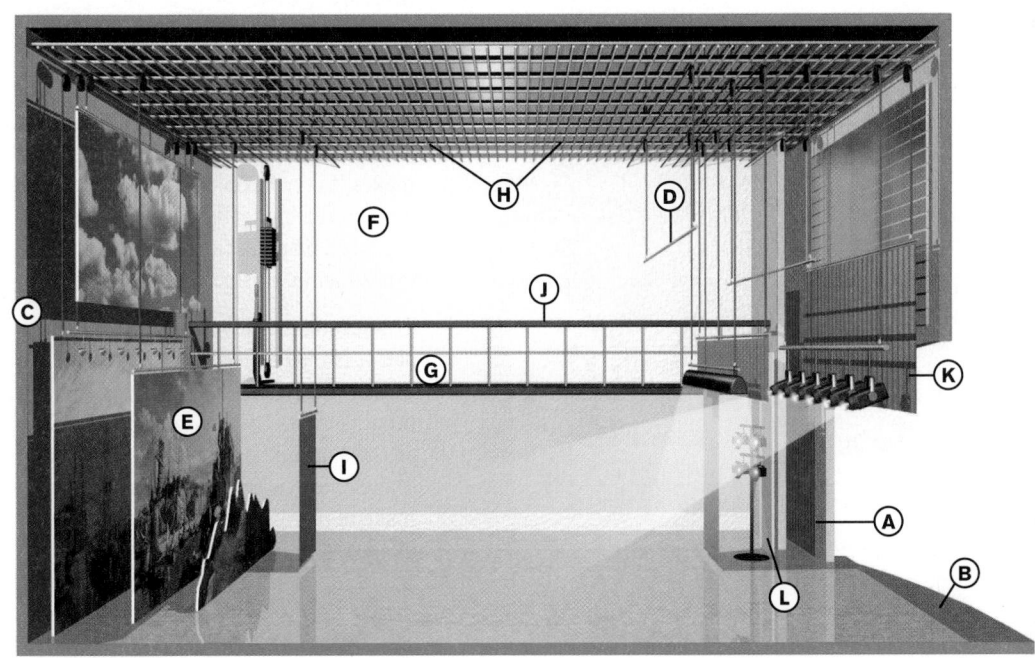

Quotable

It's better to do the design work upfront. Wood, Styrofoam, paint, and canvas can't be changed as easily as the written word. You can't put those in a word processor and play around with them. They are expensive.

Marjorie Kellogg, Set Designer

Working with the Space

Talk to students about the various sets discussed on this and the following page. Ask students to describe a theatre production they worked on or attended that used a box set. Ask how the set conveyed the style and atmosphere of the play and how color was used on the set. Was the overall design effective?

You can continue in this same way with the unit set and set variations.

ACTivity Have students make a set from a shoebox. The unit set or a set using periaktoi would be good examples to try. Use pieces of cardboard so that the set can be changed from one unit set to another. Ask students to show how the use of the unit or periaktoi allows one to change the elements of the design.

Working with the Space

Like the actor, the set must help tell the story that is being presented on stage. Sets must be effective, easy to move, and solidly built. Most important, the set must create a space in which the actor can easily move and feel in character.

Most sets are built using **flats**, which are wooden frames covered by canvas, muslin, or lightweight wood and painted. Flats can be lashed together to create walls and doorways. They can be painted in realistic or symbolic styles. They can become the backdrop for the furniture or **set pieces** (three-dimensional objects such as rocks, trees, or ramps). (See Chapter 20.)

This box set contains a number of windows and a door. Using *backing*, flats that mask the backstage area from view, makes the set seem more realistic.

To change this unit set, the balcony may be removed and a small porch added to the house, while apples or fall leaves may be attached to the tree.

There are two main kinds of sets. The most common theatrical set is the **box set,** which consists of two or three walls and perhaps a ceiling. Its simplicity makes it very flexible. It can be made to look incredibly realistic, but it can also provide a bland backdrop for experimental or surreal productions.

The second main type of set is the **unit set.** It is made of several pieces, or units, which can be rearranged to produce more than one setting. Unit sets are useful in plays requiring many scene changes. One kind of unit set is made of many individual flats that can be moved or struck completely to form a different setting. Another kind of unit set uses generic openings that can be dressed to represent doors, windows, or other elements.

Notes

_____

_____

_____

_____

_____

_____

A dramatic statement can be made in a very simple set using bold patterns and colors.

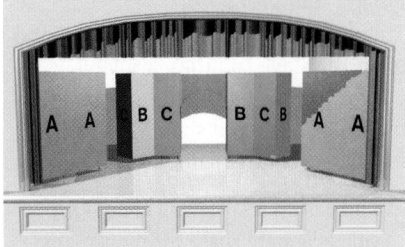

One possible arrangement of periaktoi

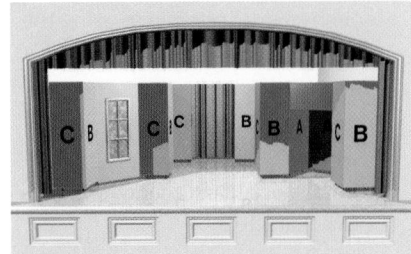

The same set with the flats rearranged

Along with other elements, the cyclorama is used to help create a formal setting.

Many set variations are possible.

- Very simple sets can be made of a few two-fold or three-fold flats that can be used to represent walls or hide and reveal furniture.

- *Periaktoi* are three-sided flats mounted on a wheeled carriage. They can be moved, and individual flats can be inserted between them to create scenic elements.

- Sometimes the cyclorama is part of the background. A few additional flats can highlight doors, fireplaces, or architectural elements, and set pieces can be arranged as if the curtains were walls and drapes.

Backstage Gossip: No Whistling Backstage

Whistling backstage is considered bad luck because, the superstition goes, it means danger. This superstition probably began years ago when sailors were hired to operate the fly system because of their experience raising and lowering the sails on boats. The sailors would raise and lower the batten on the ship upon hearing a specific whistle. Therefore, the superstition arose that if an actor or crew member whistled backstage it might cause the lowering of a batten at the wrong time, causing injury to anyone standing below.

Design Requirements

Discuss the six design requirements one at a time with the students. Note that two concern freedom of movement and safety issues while the others are concerned with artistry. Ask students which of the six they think is the most important. List the six requirements on the board as a majority of class members agree on the order of importance.

ACTivity Help students make a "set inspiration" bulletin board of pictures that communicate different times of the year, times of the day, and locations. Include both indoor and outdoor pictures. Ask them to search decorating magazines and the home section of newspapers for pictures that represent different moods and styles. Encourage them to bring in pictures that have different styles of architecture and furniture, wallpaper of varying textures, interesting landscapes, and colorful decorations. Have students arrange these pictures on the board under various headings. The students can use the images as a reference when it comes time to work on their design project.

Show, Don't Tell Select a short scene from a film or play on DVD and show it to the class. Then draw two sets on the board for the scene you just watched. Make one a realistic set and one a symbolic set. Discuss with the students the concepts of *realism* and *symbolism*. Brainstorm all the different ways the designer can use symbolism in a set design.

Design Requirements

Though your play's scenery will depend upon the stage facilities, available crew, and your budgeted time and money, your design should meet the following requirements.

- The design and setting should provide adequate space for movement, including several acting areas or levels to provide variation and interest and to motivate the actors into using the whole stage in the course of the play.

- The design and setting should communicate the time and place in which the action occurs and the cultural, social, and economic status of the characters.

- From observing the scenery with its particular color and design, the audience should immediately be able to judge the mood and style of the play.

- As the designer —and anyone involved in the technical aspects of a play—identify the technical elements in the genre and style of the play as the director has envisioned it and recognize their function in the production. The chart below shows a few selected genres and styles and how the technical elements in each may function. Through research, identify the technical elements of your play's genre and style, recognize their function, and then use them in your design and setting.

- The design and setting must be technically usable and safe. Doors and windows must open if they are to be used. Stairs, platforms, and ramps must be built firmly if they are to bear the actor's weight. If there are set changes, scenery must be planned for quick shifts carried out safely.

Technical Elements in Various Genres and Styles	
Genre	**Function**
Low Comedy	To enable and enhance physical humor/slapstick (trap doors, exaggerated props, sound effects to match pratfalls)
Greek Tragedy	To spotlight the character and fall of the tragic hero; sometimes to reflect ancient Greek conventions (full face masks, performed outdoors in natural lighting)
Style	**Function**
Realism	To give the appearance and feel of reality (familiar-looking rooms, lighting that mirrors natural lighting, normal clothing of the period)
Expressionism	To project a nonrealistic image, an expression of the director or designer's vision (sparse or incongruous sets and scenery, angular or distorted lighting, makeup to heighten the mood)
Melodrama	To heighten the villainy of the antagonist and the plight and honor of the victim (special effects to suggest natural disasters, representations of horses and dogs)

Backstage Gossip: The Real Thing

Producer David Belasco was famous for his insistence on realistic sets. For the play *The Easiest Way* he needed a cheap, boardinghouse bedroom. "We tried to build the scene in my shops, but, somehow, we could not make it look shabby enough. So I went to the meanest theatrical lodging house I could find . . . and bought the entire interior of one of its most dilapidated rooms—patched furniture, threadbare carpet, tarnished and broken gas fixtures . . . even the faded paper on the walls."

- The design and setting should be pleasing to the eye. It should be unified, balanced, and harmonious, and it should allow for the actors' faces to be readily seen. Most of all, it should be unobtrusive—except in the rare case when the characters are in conflict with their environment.

- The design should include set pieces that are functional and that contribute to the overall design of the set.

Setting the Mood

Your set can help establish the mood of your production by its angularity or softness, its luxury or sparseness, its complexity or simplicity. None of these design principles will have as immediate an effect, however, as the colors you use in your design. Scientists who have studied color have learned that various colors have specific emotional effects. Reds, oranges, and yellows, for example, are considered warm tones. They tend to be stimulating and exciting. Blues, greens, and violets are cool colors that tend to be relaxing or sobering. Of course, too much of any one tone or set of tones can be simply annoying. But careful use of color can help establish the character and overall mood in a play and influence the audience's response.

The Art of Set Design

As you can see, set design is an art unto itself, involving the creativity and skill of people who know how to express feelings and attitudes through the principles of design and composition. In fact, each aspect of technical theatre you will read about in the coming chapters—set construction, lighting, sound, costumers, makeup, and props—is an art form of its own.

Certain colors arouse specific emotions. The set designer is always aware of this.

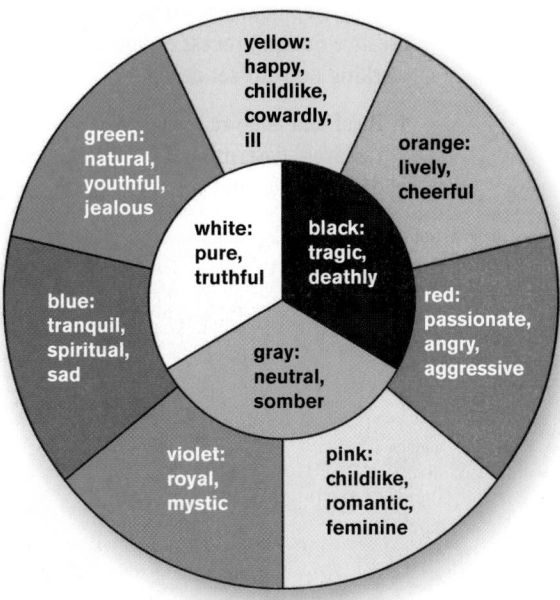

yellow: happy, childlike, cowardly, ill

orange: lively, cheerful

green: natural, youthful, jealous

white: pure, truthful

black: tragic, deathly

red: passionate, angry, aggressive

blue: tranquil, spiritual, sad

gray: neutral, somber

violet: royal, mystic

pink: childlike, romantic, feminine

Setting the Mood

Talk to the class about color. Do they have a favorite color? What is it? What emotions does this color call forth, and why?

Ask them to close their eyes and envision this color. Then have them visualize a color that feels opposite to the one they favor in emotional tone. What can they say about the "tension" they see or feel between the two colors? Have they seen a play or movie where opposite colors indicated opposite emotions? Have them explain.

ACTivity Write the names of familiar people or characters on cards—Bugs Bunny, Julia Roberts, J Lo, Whoopie Goldberg, and Homer Simpson are a few suggestions. Based on the type of person or character that is chosen, the student will assign a color that the person or character evokes. Ask the student to explain why he or she selected that particular color. Is Ben Affleck light blue, gold, or fire engine red? Why?

ACTivity Make a list of emotions or feelings. Put them on individual cards. Have the students select an emotion card and then respond to the emotion with a color. Ask the students to explain why the emotion is associated with a specific color. Is BORED blue? Is CONFUSED green? Is SILLY purple? Why or why not?

ELL Students

Using both English and the student's first language, make a list of specific locations— the beach, the mall, in the kitchen, under the sofa, etc. Ask the student what color they equate with each location, and why.

Notes

PREPARE

Work on Your Set Design

Select a play for each student (or group of students) or approve the play selected by the students. It might be interesting to use the same play for each group to see what different ideas each student or group can generate.

Go over each of the six steps, in order, with the students. You might want to give them a list of plays or make copies of the plays available to them. Note that there are lists of plays at the back of this Teacher's Edition. Be sure to hand out the Set Design and Construction Activity Sheet from page 73 of the Resource Binder at this time. Encourage students to rehearse their talks with a partner who can time the length and suggest areas for improvement.

PREPARE

Work on Your Set Design

In order to create a set design, you will first have to determine the type and size of stage you will be working on (or perhaps the size and layout of your classroom playing area). Measure the stage or acting space (see pages 250–251) and draw a ground plan using either the Activity Sheet your teacher provides, a computer program, or pencil and paper. A good scale of measure might be 1 foot equals ¼ inch. Be sure to practice proper scale as you draw your ground plan. Follow these step-by-step instructions to apply the creative design process as you continue working on your set design.

1 **Read and analyze a play.** With research, determine the kind of design, style, and color you think will best communicate the play's intent and reflect historical and cultural accuracy. Identify and recognize the function of technical elements of various styles and genres and use them in your design as appropriate to your chosen play.

2 **Review the principles of design and composition** on page 231 and color on page 239 to determine how you will apply them to your design.

3 **Make a list of your ground plan needs,** such as doors, windows, furniture, set pieces, and stairs.

4 **Fill in the Activity Sheet** or create your drawn or computer-generated ground plan, always keeping in mind your understanding of the play's theme, mood, period, and locale. Let your ideas incubate and then select, implement, and evaluate them to finish your design, refining your choices to support the story and emotional impact of the script.

5 **Prepare a five- to ten-minute talk** explaining how you applied the principles of design and composition to your plan's style, sets, and scenery and furniture placement. Tell how your set meets both the intent of the play and the design requirements discussed in this chapter. Make copies of your plan or be ready to project it from a computer.

6 **Rehearse and time your report** to present it within ten minutes.

A very minimal set can make a strong statement.

240 **Unit Five** Technical Theatre

Quotable

What is necessary ... is ... a design that has clarity without rigidity; one that could be called "open" as against "shut." This is the essence of theatrical thinking: a true theatre designer will think of his designs as being all the time in motion, in action, in relation to what the actor brings to a scene as it unfolds. In other words, unlike the easel painter, in two dimensions, or the sculptor in three, the designer thinks in terms of the fourth dimension, the passage of time—not the stage picture, but the stage moving picture.

from *The Empty Space* by Peter Brook, Producer and Director

PRESENT

Unveil Your Design

When your name is called, hand in your Activity Sheet or ground plan and walk to the playing area. Be sure to hand out copies of your ground plan to the class before you begin your talk. If you have used a computer for your design, project the ground plan as a visual aid. Remember, if you show interest and enthusiasm in what you are saying, your listeners will be interested and alert also.

The Language of
THEATRE

Work with a teacher or classmate to understand the main points and important details in spoken language.

- Listen to the theatre terms *arena stage*, *proscenium stage*, and *thrust stage* and say what is the same about them and what is different. Consider the context in which you hear the terms.

- Listen to someone read the text about Types of Stages on page 232. Say the main point and important details about each one in the context of theatre.

- Listen to someone read the text about Principles of Design and Communicating with Design on pages 231 and 233. Summarize what you hear, relating main points and important details to set design.

- Listen to your classmates' presentations of their set designs and notice the theatre terms they use. Summarize the main points and important details of one presentation.

CRITIQUE

Evaluate Your Classmate's Set Design and Presentation

Choose one of the designs presented in class and evaluate it using a scale from 1 to 5. A rating of 5 equals "outstanding," while a rating of 1 equals "needs much improvement." As you prepare your critique, think about the following questions.

- How easy to read and interpret was the set design?

- What elements necessary for a production of the play were incorporated in the ground plan?

- In what ways did the set design plan fulfill the needs of the play's theme?

- Did the set design cover all the principles of design and composition requirements?

- How did the speaker go about convincing you that this design would enhance the play?

- What were the strengths and weaknesses of the speaker's presentation style?

Write a paragraph explaining why you gave this presentation the score you did.

Repeat the evaluation process, this time using your own design as the subject. Write a second paragraph 1) explaining how you applied the design elements of theatre as an art form, and 2) evaluating yourself as a creative being.

PRESENT

Unveil Your Design

Establish with each student beforehand how he or she will be presenting the ground plan. Advise students that if they want to use the drawing they have created on the Activity Sheet, they can simply redraw it in a larger form on the chalkboard. Have the necessary computer projection technology available for students who wish to use it. Encourage these students to practice with the equipment when they are rehearsing their talk.

The Language of
THEATRE

Students may benefit from using a graphic organizer for Main Ideas and Details to take notes as they listen to spoken language in the classroom. Model how to use the graphic organizer as a student reads a section of the text.

Critique

Evaluate Your Classmate's Set Design and Presentation

Go over the evaluation rubric with the students before they begin their presentations so that they will know the criteria on which the evaluation will be based. Talk about the rating system—1 through 5.

Remind the students that they will be evaluated using the same rubric that they are using to evaluate their classmates. Also tell them to evaluate the work and not the personality. An appropriate phrase to use before the students tackle peer evaluation is "Do unto others …" And let them know if you will be evaluating them on how well they evaluate each other.

Notes

_____

_____

_____

_____

_____

_____

_____

_____

Set Design Test

The test for this chapter is available in blackline master form in the Resource Binder, page 98.

For More Information

Books

Brewster, Karen, and Melissa Shafer. *Fundamentals of Theatrical Design: A Guide to the Basics of Scenic, Costume, and Lighting Design,* Allworth Press, 2011.

Campbell, Drew, *Technical Theater for Nontechnical People,* Allworth Press, 2004.

Craig, Gordon, *On the Art of the Theatre,* Routledge, 2008.

Ingham, Rosemary, *From Page to Stage: How Theatre Designers Make Connections Between Scripts and Images,* Heinemann, 1998.

Ionazzi, Daniel A., *The Stage Craft Handbook,* Betterway Books, 1996.

Jones, Inigo, *Designs by Inigo Jones for Masques and Plays at Court,* Russell & Russell, 1966.

Other Media

Design: The Elements, DVD, Insight Media, 2010.

The Stage: Set Design and Construction, DVD, Insight Media, 1998.

Stagecraft, DVD, Films for the Humanities and Sciences, 2005.

www.usitt.org (United States Institute for Theatre Technology)

Apps

AutoCad WS
AutoQ3D
iDesign

Theatre Journal

Use the following as an additional or substitute prompt. Write a description of the colors that you associate with each season: summer, fall, winter, and spring. Include the kinds of light that are reflected in these colors. Then write a short description of an outdoor set for one of these seasons.

Additional Projects

1 Construct a model of a set you have designed. Practice the basics of measurement to make sure your model is to scale.

2 Conduct research to find an example of a technical theatre document, such as a ground plan, design rendering, or model. You might find examples at a local theatre company or online. Read and interpret the document and complete one of these activities:

  a Write a report explaining how designers and directors use such documents to communicate.

  b Give an oral presentation demonstrating an understanding of how designers and directors use such documents to communicate.

  c Use role play with a partner to model how the documents might be used by a designer and a director to communicate.

3 Choose a musical such as *Stomp* or *Rent* and demonstrate your creativity and working knowledge of the technical elements of theatre by designing on paper or computer a backdrop for the set. Go through the process of analysis, research, incubation, selection, implementation, and evaluation to create your design, refining as needed to support the story. Practice the basics of measurement applied to drafting.

4 Develop your creativity by indicating the kinds of color, design approach, kind of set, and kind of stage you would ideally use for two of the books listed below if they were brought to the stage. Explain and justify your choices in a few sentences.

Hatchet
Native Son
Great Expectations
The Catcher in the Rye

5 On paper or a computer, create a set design for *The Imaginary Invalid* by Molière based on the scene found in Unit Eight of this book. Conduct research to establish and demonstrate a working knowledge of historical and cultural accuracy based on the time period and tone of the scene. Identify and recognize the function of technical elements in this style and genre and use appropriate ones, such as screens, curtains, set pieces, furniture, and a background, in your set design. Exchange designs with a peer. Offer constructive criticism to your peer on the set design. Apply the same critical evaluation to your own work as well, making any needed adjustments.

6 **Theatre Journal** Explain and define creativity and personal expression as they relate to technical theatre and the art form of set design. Use examples of play or movie sets you are familiar with to consider how different set designers express their unique creativity in an artistic way.

Substitute Teacher Activities

Here are a few suggestions for one or more days when you will be out of the classroom:

• Assign the Set Design Activity Sheet on page 95 of the Resource Binder and allow students to try out these techniques.

• Assign one or more of the Additional Projects on this page.

• Teach the appropriate sections of Part Seven, Sets, from pages 600–607 of the Student Handbook.

• **Create a Fairy Tale Set.** Divide students into several small groups and have them select a favorite fairy tale—*Jack and the Beanstalk* or *Little Red Riding Hood,* for example. The students will then design a set and draw a color rendering for their fairy tale. Provide the students a supply of colored pencils and paper. After they have finished the design, ask each group to explain their design to the class.

Master of the Craft
G. W. "Skip" Mercier

One day, when he was an English major at the University of California at Berkeley, G. W. "Skip" Mercier walked into Henry May's office. May was a set designer who took great joy in his work and who won awards no set designer had ever won before. May's office was covered with photos and drawings, and Mercier studied them for more than an hour. He fell in love with the "visual magic" he saw on May's walls, and from that moment, his career was decided.

Mercier went on to design numerous plays on and off Broadway. Over the years, he's been nominated for a Tony Award and several Drama Desk Awards for his set design. And he's in constant demand, working on Broadway and for major regional theatres throughout the country, including Arena Stage, Alliance Theatre, and Lincoln Center. He has also taught design at the National Theatre Institute for more than 20 years.

Mercier says that his mentor, May, "showed me that being a good designer was in direct proportion to being a good man." If that's true, Mercier must be an impressive person. His set designs are creative, effective, and true to the productions they support.

G. W. Mercier

A 1" scale model set was created by Mercier for Shakespeare's *The Taming of the Shrew*, directed by Julie Taymor.

Mercier created this elegant set for *Dead Guilty*, presented at Studio Arena Theatre and directed by Jane Page.

Quotable

I hope that going to the theatre will be a national activity for all ages, one that we cannot live without. I hope that theatre and the arts will eventually take their rightful place in this country, like elections to preserve our freedom and education to nurture our minds. Art is our connection to our past and the heritage for our future . . . it provokes, it questions, it celebrates. In joy and outrage, it is the true expression of our time.

Ming Cho Lee, in his introduction to Ronn Smith's *American Set Design 2*

Master of the Craft
More About G. W. "Skip" Mercier

G. W. Mercier studied at Yale University and has since designed over 360 shows. In 1997, the year Mercier received his Tony nomination for scenic design for *Juan Darien: A Carnival Mass,* Stewart Laing took home the award for *Titanic.*

Masters Past and Present

Inigo Jones (1573–1652) was an accomplished classical architect who built homes for royalty that embodied classical proportions and the Palladian tradition. At the English courts of James I and Charles I, Jones designed costumes and sets for fanciful masques, many of which he wrote himself. He studied in Italy and brought to England scene design that included the proscenium arch, the moveable set, and painted perspective scenery.

Gordon Craig (1872–1966) has been called by some the greatest creative genius of British theatre. Craig gained fame in the early 1900s. His designs were focused on creating mood and atmosphere rather than realistic settings. He designed productions for The Abbey Theatre in Ireland and the Moscow Art Theatre, where his "white" *Hamlet* made theatre history in 1912. His conception of the play was to have Hamlet, all in black, move relentlessly through an all-white set.

Ming Cho Lee (1939–) was born and grew up in Shanghai, China. He is considered one of the leading set designers in the United States today, and many of the students he taught at Yale University during his 45-year career there have gone on to become noted designers also. Lee has designed sets for Broadway, off-Broadway, regional theatre, dance, and opera. In his set designs, which are presentational rather than representational, Lee attempts to discover the essence of the play and use iconographic symbols to represent this on the stage. Lee has said of theatre design that "the bottom line is that the set has to look good . . . If the set looks bad, all bets are off."

Theatre **Then** and **Now**

Other Cultures, Other Times

The first use of painted perspective on stage was during the Italian Renaissance. Sebastiano Serlio designed three perspectives for stage scenery, one for each of the three types of play—tragedy, comedy, and satyr plays.

During Shakespeare's time, there was very little use of scenery or props. Elizabethan theatregoers would remark that they were going to "hear" a play, not "see" a play. The language of the theatre was one of the most important elements of the theatre experience to Shakespeare's audiences. Today we frequently rely on elaborate special effects to entertain us.

In the 20th century, experiments in nontraditional production methods were developed by directors and designers such as V. E. Meyerhold (1874–1940) in Russia and Max Reinhardt (1873–1943) in Germany. Both of them explored theatre by moving outside the confines of the proscenium arch with its traditional scenery and lighting systems. Meyerhold brought his running crew out in front of the audience, who watched while the sets were shifted. His actors performed on multilevel scenery which was often extremely abstract and mechanical looking. While not uncommon today, these devices were not the usual practice in the early to middle 1900s.

Theatre **Then** and **Now**

Staging Through the Ages

Early Mechanics

Although staging in ancient Greece was simple, it did include the use of a large crane, which could lower and raise characters above the playing area. Since these "flying" characters were often gods who arrived in time to resolve a problem, the apparatus was named *deus ex machina,* or "god in the machine." The Greeks also used the three-sided *periaktoi,* discussed previously on page 237.

The Romans, whose appetite for spectacle knew no bounds, developed more elaborate special effects. In their productions, forests filled with exotic animals appeared from nowhere, and fountains spouting wine rose up from under the stage or arena floor.

Theatre died out during Europe's Dark Ages, but plays based on biblical themes began to be performed in churches during the second half of the 11th century. Large audiences and increasingly bawdy subject matter forced drama out of the churches and into the streets.

In the Middle Ages, plays were mounted on pageant wagons that traveled throughout Europe. Each scene of the play might be set on a separate wagon,

The pageant wagon rolls into town.

with machinery and costumes stored below and the playing area above. Guilds, or groups of tradesmen, sponsored these wagons and competed with one another to create elaborate effects. One device, called Hell's Mouth, resembled the jaws of a fire-breathing dragon, complete with smoke and flames.

The Renaissance, which began in Italy in the 14th century, brought a rebirth of interest in art, including theatre, and spectacular effects continued to play an important part. In England, where the Renaissance was slower to take hold, dramas were performed on simple stages with little or no scenery, but by the 17th century, England too began to experiment with trapdoors, "flying" characters, raked stages, and movable scenery.

Notes

Current Technology

The Industrial Age that spread through Europe and the United States in the late 18th and 19th centuries brought new technology to the theatre. Crews needed technical help to move heavy furniture, roll flats on and off the stage, and handle more complex scenery and theatrical effects.

Today, it is not uncommon for entire stages to rotate and for scenery to move by an unseen hand. Many professionally staged musicals include spectacular technical effects. *The Phantom of the Opera,* for example, features a computerized chandelier that swings out over the audience as well as a gondola that floats through misty, candlelit waters. (See pages 230–231.) *Les Misérables* uses massive wooden barricades that pivot in from each side of the stage and connect to become a "practical" unit onto which the actors can climb. (See page 228.) The staging for *Mary Poppins* features a four-story Edwardian house that rises and collapses. Complex mechanical effects allow Mary to work magic, such as the scene where she destroys and then restores the kitchen.

Technology is only one part of innovation in set design. Ming Cho Lee, considered the dean of American set design, introduced such innovations as scaffolding and the use of nontraditional materials. His Tony Award-winning design for the 1983 production of *K2*, a story about the efforts of two men to

Aerial rigging helps the descending angel in Tony Kushner's play *Angels in America.*

climb the world's second highest mountain, featured a 55-foot wall of "ice" made of styrofoam and plastic snow.

For More Information

Books

Aronson, Arnold, *Ming Cho Lee: A Life in Design,* Theatre Communications Group, 2014.

Carnaby, Ann J., *A Guidebook for Creating Three-Dimensional Theatre Art*, Reed Elsevier Incorporated, 1997.

Forrest, Tim, *The Bulfinch Anatomy of Antique Furniture*, Bulfinch Press, 1996.

Larson, Orville K., *Scene Design in the American Theatre from 1915 to 1960*, University of Arkansas Press, 1990.

Porter, Tom, and Sue Goldman, *Designer Primer*, Butterworth-Heinemann, 1989.

Summerson, John, *Inigo Jones*, Yale University Press, 2000.

Walton, J. Michael, editor, *Craig on Theatre*, Heinemann, 1988.

Visual Cues

Use the following prompts to generate discussion of the two images on these pages. Note that additional information on pageant wagons can be found on pages 444 and 448.

- From what you can see in the picture on page 244, describe how pageant wagons were used.

- How might the concept of pageant wagons be utilized in today's theatre productions? In what other forms of entertainment might they be used?

- Describe the image from *Angels in America* on page 245.

- Can you think of other plays where characters "fly"?

- What other unique staging have you seen or heard about?

Chapter 20

Set Construction

Objectives

1 to analyze set construction job descriptions

2 to explore the basic tools and equipment of set construction

3 to understand how to build flats and platforms

4 to apply scene-painting techniques

5 to understand the mechanics of stage rigging

Project Specs

You will probably need to set up a tour of your school's theatre facility for this project.

Special Needs Students

Although most school theatre facilities are wheelchair accessible, check the ramps and exit doors in advance to make sure that all your students will be safe and mobile during the tour.

On Your Feet

Students can do this activity either in alone or in pairs. Have several students present their lists aloud to find out where there is overlapping foreknowledge or understanding.

Chapter

20 Set Construction

So the set design is finished, and all that remains is to build it. Who is in charge of this process? Who are the people who get the job done? To paraphrase an old saying, it takes a village to build a set.

Project Specs

Project Description For this project, you will work with a small group to create a five- to seven-minute technology-based instructional guide focusing on an aspect of set construction.

Purpose to understand the basics of set design construction and safety and protocol when working backstage or in the scene shop

Materials a PowerPoint or video presentation and/or the Set Construction Activity Sheet provided by your teacher

Theatre Terms

base coat
blueprints
elevations
Hollywood flats
joinery
lauan
muslin
prime coat
rails
rigging
stiles
toggle

On Your Feet

Look around your classroom. What would it take to re-create this room as a stage set? What materials would you need? What types of tasks might be involved? With a partner create a list of the possible tasks and the kinds of materials you might need to build each of them.

The famous helicopter hovers over the actors on the stage of *Miss Saigon*.

Theatre Terms

base coat a layer of foundational paint applied after the prime coat

blueprints reproductions of technical drawings documenting a design

elevations different views of a three-dimensional area or object

Hollywood flats hard-covered flats with a frame that is perpendicular to the paint surface

joinery fasteners, bindings, and adhesives used to join together wooden or metal construction elements

lauan a type of inexpensive plywood

muslin thin fabric sometimes used to cove flats

prime coat first layer of paint

rails top and bottom sides of a flat

rigging system and hardware used to lift, lower, and hold set pieces and equipment or above the stage

stiles sides of a flat

toggle cross brace

Picture a stage buzzing with activity. One person is up on a ladder, connecting cables. A small group carries a platform and sets it down on the floor where tape marks off its correct position. High above the stage, someone is adjusting the angle of a lighting instrument. Everywhere you look there are people scurrying around carrying out their assigned tasks. This is exactly as it should be—with final technical rehearsals set to begin in just a few days, time is of the essence.

The Who's Who of Set Construction

Most of set construction involves creating a stage world based on the director's vision and the designers' specifications, but what does it take to transition from **blueprints** and scale models to a fully functioning stage set? The answer is a whole lot of teamwork and collaboration.

While there is some overlap of skills and duties, in most cases, the construction process begins with the *production manager*, who communicates closely with the director and design team, and works as a liaison among the various departments. This person is responsible for ensuring that each production element evolves as planned within the specified production schedule and budget. The *technical director* works with the set and props designers, and supervises the *master carpenter,* who in turn oversees the construction of the set. In smaller theatres, the technical director sometimes doubles as master carpenter to oversee the building crews.

Meanwhile, the *master electrician* coordinates the lighting crew as they hang and focus lights according to the lighting designer's specifications. The master electrician may also be responsible for overseeing the technicians who will later operate the light board and any special lighting instruments, such as spotlights, during performances. The *audio engineer* oversees the sound system and manages the audio crew, whose tasks include hanging speakers and microphones, and running cables to connect them to each other and to the sound console, which will relay the sound cues from the technical booth during performances. Each of these jobs relies on all the others. Together they serve to create the visual and aural world of the play.

Chapter 20 Set Construction **247**

Set up a tour of your school's theatre facility, led, if possible, by the technical director or other responsible supervisor. Check in advance to find out if there are any blueprints of the stage area or recent sets that have been built on it. If your facility or shop features storage areas for set pieces, costumes, and lighting and sound equipment, make those areas part of the tour as well. Encourage students to take notes about the theatre space.

Resource Binder

Handbook Connections
pages 600–607

The Big Picture: Know Your Theatre

Sketch It Out

Have students create scale drawings or more freeform illustrations of the theatre space at your school. They should include callouts for the dimensions of the space and note the location of lighting inventory, fire exits and extinguishers, and so on.

Make a Checklist

Create an enlarged version of the bulleted checklist on page 248, and pass out copies to the students. Ask them to use it as a checklist and fill in all the dimensions and locations for the school's or another theatre facility.

Know Your Theatre

- Stage size and dimensions
- Height of the proscenium
- Height of high and low trim for all battens
- Distances between battens
- Number of line sets and their respective weight capacities
- Location of stage electrical pockets, including floor and walls
- Location of all stage-level audio inputs and monitor outs (plugs)
- Lighting inventory: lamps, gels, cables, and accessories
- Audio inventory: microphones, cables, monitors, stands, clips, batteries
- Location of all fire extinguishers and emergency exits
- Location of documentation for fireproof and fire-retardant drapes
- Inventory of lumber
- Inventory of tools
- Location and inventory of first-aid kit

The Big Picture: Know Your Theatre

The set for each production of a play presents its own very particular physical world. Within that world, each element—scenery, lighting, sound—is dependent on all the others. In order to create a practical, well-functioning set, though—and to stay safe while you are doing so—you'll need an understanding of the larger environment you'll be working in, the theatre space itself. This is true no matter whether you are building scenery, hanging lights, or cabling speakers and setting microphones. The theatre is a work environment, one you should get to know well—from the height of the proscenium to the location of the emergency exits.

The checklist to the left shows things you should be aware of as you are working as part of a stage crew.

For efficient stage construction, the stage crew should know every nook and cranny of the stage very well.

Notes

Nuts and Bolts: Know Your Shop

The scene shop is command central for the set construction crew. It is where the bulk of the construction work is done. Most shops have high ceilings and oversized doors to allow for the easiest possible transfer of set pieces from the shop to the stage. Typically a shop has a number of workspaces for carrying out different tasks, as well as shelving, cabinets, and closets for storage of tools and materials.

Some shops are stocked with every imaginable tool; others have only a very basic assortment. No matter what tool you use, exercise caution and wear work gloves when necessary. When you have finished with a tool, be sure to put it back in its designated place.

Tools are broken into two main groups: *hand tools* and *power tools*. A hand tool is any tool that is powered by hand rather than by a motor.

- **Hammers**: claw hammer, for driving in or prying out nails; tack hammer for driving in tacks; mallet for pounding without leaving marks on the surface

- **Pliers**: needle-nose pliers, for pulling small objects; locking pliers, for locking on objects; slip-joint pliers, for clamping, gripping, and pulling

- **Screwdrivers**: standard, for driving in regular screws; Phillips, for driving in Phillips head screws, which have a cross indentation

- **Wrenches**: crescent or adjustable end, for tightening different size nuts; pipe, for use with oversize nuts or pipes; combination, for loosening any size nut in a hard-to-reach area

- **Tape measure** for measuring long distances

- **Level** for creating true horizontal or vertical surfaces

- **Chalk line**, a chalked string that, when pulled taught and snapped against a surface, leaves a straight line of chalk

- **Staple gun**, for attaching fabric or other material to wood

- **Clamps**: C-clamp, wood clamp, furniture clamp, all used for holding two or more surfaces together during work

- **Putty knife**, for applying putty and smoothing off rough edges

- **Saws**: crosscut, for wood; hack, for metal; backsaw with miter box, for angled or cross cuts

- **Plane** for smoothing off wood edges

- **File** for shaping and smoothing either wood or metal

- **Drills**: hand drill, for drilling into wood; push drill, for making starter holes

From the Field: Be Prepared

Be sure that each student knows the proper way to use all of the tools in your shop. After each student has been trained on the use of a particular tool, prepare a badge with a picture of that tool on it for that student to wear each time he or she is working in the scene shop. This will give you a quick visual reference to know that the student has been checked out on the piece of equipment he or she is currently using. You should also keep a record in your files to show which students have received training on which tools.

Elaine Malone, Drama Teacher, Atlanta, GA

The Right Tool for the Job Ask students to write short descriptions for each of the power tools mentioned on this page, detailing the kinds of tasks they might be used for in the theatre (cutting large pieces of lumber for flats or platforms; drilling holes or smoothing rough surfaces to join together; etc.).

Measure for Measure

ACTivity Divide the students into small groups. They will need to have the use of several 12' to 25' tape measures and graph paper. Using the scale of 1"= 4' (1 inch of the scale drawing represents 4 feet of the real stage), the students will measure, plot out, and draw the dimensions of the stage they usually work on. If the stage is unavailable, they can measure and draw the drama classroom. Students will gain practice in measuring and drawing stage plans.

ACTivity Working further on the activity above, students will use the stage plan they measured and graphed and build a three dimensional, accurate scale model of the stage. One of the best materials for this model is heavy project board or foam core board which can be found at a craft store or a discount retailer. Have students work on this activity before and after school hours and at home, if time does not permit working during class.

Power tools are any tools powered by a motor, including saws, drills, and sanders. Use extreme caution when working with power tools, and always store them in a designated area. Saw blades, drill bits, and sanding equipment can cause serious injury.

Many scene shops contain one or more of the following power tools.

- **Portable electric drill**, used to quickly drive or remove screws

- **Band saw** for making curved cuts in lumber

- **Circular table saw** for ripping through lumber

- **Pull-over saw** for cross and angle cuts in lumber

- **Sabre saw**, which is portable and can use any of several different blades to make curved cuts in a variety of materials, including lumber, plastic, or metal

- **Belt sander** or **disk sander** for sanding either wood or metal

Measure for Measure

The ability to take exact measurements is one of the keys to building just about anything. During set construction, sloppy measurements can result in a loss of time and materials. Always apply basic skills of measurement in construction.

Reading a Tape Measure. The most common measuring device is the measuring tape. Available in a variety of sizes, measuring tapes are typically made of cloth, plastic, or metal. The durable type used in most scene shops extends to a maximum 25 feet and has a flexible metal ribbon that pulls out and can remain stiff when extended but retracts into a coil for handy storage. It can be locked at any length. It is marked off in sixteenths of an inch, allowing for a very accurate reading.

Measuring Lumber. What do stage platforms, stair units, and frames for flats all share in common? The answer is they are most often built from lumber. A typical theatre scene shop goes through a lot of lumber each season, though much of it can be recycled and used from show to show.

You may know the term *two-by-four,* which refers to a standard size of lumber often used in set construction. But the designation is slightly confusing, as the board's true dimensions end up being slightly smaller. When the board

Career Path: Running Crew

Large professional touring events such as musicals or concerts often rely on a dedicated crew of backstage personnel that travels with a production from venue to venue. These professionals can take on such duties as driving vans and buses to and from venues, setting up equipment, rigging the lighting or sound systems specific to the show, ensuring safety and security of all equipment; setting up pyrotechnics, video, or laser effects; and monitoring health and safety issues.

is originally cut from a log it actually is 2 inches by 4 inches. But it is then put through a drying process and planed, which reduces it to a finished size of about 1½ inches by 3½ inches. So the term *two-by-four* actually refers to the dimensions of the rough cut, not the final board. Keep this in mind, and always practice proper measurement as applied to design and construction. Here are a few common lumber sizes to further illustrate this idea.

Rough Cut	Actual Lumber Size
1" x 2"	¾" x 1½"
1" x 3"	¾" x 2½"
1" x 4"	¾" x 3½"
2" x 4"	1½" x 3½"
2" x 6"	1½" x 5½"

Lumber dimensions are based on the wood's surfaces: the end, edge, and face. The edge and the end are equal in thickness. The face is the surface that defines the width.

Reading a Blueprint

A blueprint is a detailed scale drawing. Like a scale model, a blueprint is a handy tool that can help you understand—and build—a working, practical stage set. Some basic guidelines will help you read and make sense of blueprints. Always practice proper measurement and scale as applied to design or construction.

The first thing to check is the scale of the drawing. You'll find it in the lower right-hand corner of the document. This notation may say, for example, 1" = 3', which tells you that each inch on the drawing represents three feet. There may be a separate scale for the specific part of the set you will be building. If so, that scale will be written near the section in question. If specific dimensions are available, you should use those instead of the scale rule.

Next, check the **elevations**, which show different views of the three-dimensional area or object in question. There may be more than one elevation. Common elevations include:

- **Ground plan**. Also called a *plan* or *plan view*, this lets you envision the object from above. It tells you the full length and width, and shows its relationship to the rest of the set.

- **Front elevation**. This shows the view of the object as the audience sees it.

- **Section elevation**. This provides a cross-sectional view, which, when considered along with the other elevations, can give you a more three-dimensional idea of the object.

- **Detail elevation**. This blows up an important piece of the drawing to highlight important details that may not be clear from the other elevations.

If possible, bring in blueprints for the class to examine and gain practice in reading. Also find examples of ground plans for stage sets, as well as some of the common ground plan symbols for such elements as flats, doors, draperies, and stairs. You can find an example at www.dolphin.upenn.edu/pacshop/graphics.html. Then ask students to visualize a room in the school or at home they know very well. Have them describe this room to a partner in detail. Then each student will create a ground plan based on his or her partner's description. Display the students' handiwork in your classroom.

According to Scale Remind students that they are already very familiar with the use of scale to show distances and quantities on maps, charts, and graphs.

Theatre History Note

Realistic scenery has gone in and out of fashion over the course of the theatre's long history. During the days of Greek, Roman, and Elizabethan theatre, most stage settings consisted of only the rear wall of the theatre. In most plays, a scene's location was either unimportant, obvious without explanation, or stated by the actors in their dialogue. Scenery evolved further during the Italian Renaissance when the rules of drafting, perspective, and architecture were introduced in the theatre.

Fastening It All Together

Take a tour of the joinery introduced in this section. If possible, this should happen in the shop, with the technical director (or other adult in a supervisory capacity) providing a demonstration. If that is not possible, bring in a box of different kinds of joinery and have students put them into categories and note, based on stage sets they have seen, the various kinds of building projects that might require each type.

A student reviews a set of blueprints with the master carpenter, who oversees the construction of the set.

Be careful to check and then double-check blueprint information. When figuring scale, for example, make sure you understand what is being measured and the units of measurement (feet or inches) involved in a specific area. Also be aware of symbols that indicate endpoints; for example, extension lines, slashes, and arrows. Look for any general or specific notes that accompany the building project.

Fastening It All Together

How do you turn a pile of lumber sheets and boards into a platform? How do you attach flats or a stair unit to that platform? Set construction requires the fastening together of many different components. Following is a list of some of the most common **joinery** used in set construction.

- **Nails** (common, box, finishing, double head, screw, and clout) are driven into a surface using a hammer or a nail gun. Tacks, pins, brads, and spikes are also classified as nails.

- **Screws** (standard, Phillips, drywall, etc.) are driven into a surface with a screwdriver or drill.

- **Staples** are used when attaching fabric, cardboard, or other light materials to wood by means of a staple gun.

- **Glue** (wood and instant glue, wheat paste) is used to attached lighter weight materials. Hot glue is sometimes used as well; this is applied with a hot glue gun.

- **Tape** (duct, masking, electrical, gaffer's, dutchman) has a variety of uses in the theatre; among these, it can be used to spike the floor plan of the set. (Fluorescent tape referred to as "glow tape" is often used on the floor or corners of furniture and other set pieces to help actors to see the edges of obstacles during stage blackouts.)

Totally Quotable

"When you're in a show, all through rehearsals Tech Week hovers out there like a magical holy grail. In reality, Tech Week is always a train wreck of missed cues, forgotten lines, malfunctioning set pieces and short tempers."

—S. M. Stevens, Bit Players, Has-Been Actors and Other Posers

Constructing the Set

The ground plan, sketches, and model are ready. Now it is time for the building and paint crews to get to work. Most sets are built using flats, wood frames covered with cloth or sheet lumber and joined vertically to form walls. Depending on the play, flats can be painted in realistic or symbolic styles to serve as the backdrop for furniture or set pieces such as rocks, trees, or ramps. They can also be arranged in any number of different combinations to enhance lighting effects.

Building Flats: Basic Construction

With adequate equipment and know-how, and with assistance from the school's shop director, technical director, or other knowledgeable adult, you can safely build a series of functional flats that can be used to create the current set and then be stacked and stored for future use. Always understand the materials you are using and learn how to handle them safely. Apply your technical skills safely as you use the information on the following pages to demonstrate the design and building techniques of scenery.

Today, most theatres use **Hollywood flats**, which are constructed of boards turned on their edges to create thickness. When this frame is then covered with a thin sheet of wood, it becomes a strong three-dimensional box like structure. Although they can be up to 12 feet tall, a standard Hollywood flat for a stage set is 8 feet high and 4 feet wide.

1 Cut the frame

- Using 1 x 4-inch lumber, carefully measure and cut two 8-foot boards for the sides, or **stiles**. Then cut two 4-foot boards for the flat's top and bottom, or **rails**. Remember that lumber dimensions refer to the rough-cut boards, not the finished boards, which will actually be slightly smaller (approximately ¾" x 3½"). Because you have laid out the lumber on its edge, you will need to factor that into the math. The length of the stiles on an 8-foot flat will actually be 7 foot 10½ inches, which will allow for the ¾-inch rails at top and bottom.

Constructing the Set

Bring a commercial framed canvas to class. This would be a prestretched frame from a craft store that is intended for an artist to paint on. It will not be constructed exactly the way a flat needs to be—it might not have toggle rails or braces, for instance—but it will be a starting point for discussing the construction of a flat. If you have the budget, the students can make miniature flats from balsa wood (or some other very lightweight wood), glue, and inexpensive white cotton fabric.

Twine or heavy thread could be used as lash lines. The students can then paint their "flats" to be a backdrop for a play of their choosing. The students might create these flats to the same scale as the model of the stage they created previously. Then they could use the flats on the model of the stage

Vocabulary Enhancement

Techie is an affectionate nickname for any person who works behind the scenes on the technical side of theatre. This includes stage managers; lighting designers and technicians; sound designers and technicians; props designers, builders, and managers; makeup crews; dressers; and scenery movers, who are also known, collectively, as the running crew.

Backstage Chuckles

Techies enjoy coming up with backstage sayings that both celebrate and make fun of the jobs they do. Here are just a few:

You know you're a techie when ...
- you're more concerned about the location of your crescent wrench than you are about your car keys.

- you use glow tape to get around your house at night.

- you start calling the technical director "Dad."

There are a number of excellent how-to videos available for building Hollywood flats. The following three-part video will fortify the discussion of this key set construction element. Before you show the videos, let students know that Hollywood flats are also sometimes referred to as *television flats* or *TV flats*.

Part 1: www.youtube.com/
watch?v=S5uRdVBprc4

Part 2: www.youtube.com/
watch?v=urIWbrQDz7U

Part 3: www.youtube.com/
watch?v=isgawH-gopU

Toggle Rail

- You will also need to cut the cross brace, called a **toggle**, which will be the width of the flat minus the width of the two stiles. In general, you need a toggle for every 5 feet of height, so for an 8-foot flat, you'll need only one, placed at the midpoint.

2 Assemble the frame

- On the shop floor, stand the five boards up on their edges in the shape of the flat you wish to create. In other words, place the top rail above the stiles, the bottom rail below the stiles, and the toggle between the stiles.

- Now you'll need to secure the frame. Use a framing square to ensure that the corners of the frame align correctly. Then apply a layer of wood glue wherever the stiles come in contact with either a rail or a toggle.

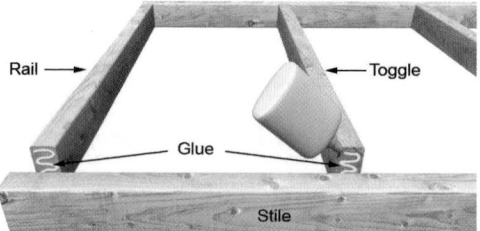

Rail — Toggle

Glue

Stile

- Follow this by screwing into the boards through the sides. When this is done the frame should be fairly sturdy. Corner braces add further stability.

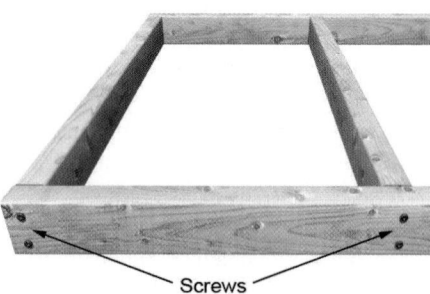

Screws

3 Cover the flat

- Next, you are going to put a cover on the flat, which will make it even stronger. The process of attaching an outer layer or covering is known as skinning the flat.

- First place the frame up on a saw-horse or large table. You will skin it with a sheet of inexpensive plywood called **lauan**, cut to the exact dimensions of the outer edge of the frame.

- Once you have the cover cut, apply a thin layer of wood glue all the way around the edges of the frame, and place the lauan cover on the frame.

- Glue is not enough to secure the cover on its own, so next you will screw the cover onto the frame. This should create a rigid three-dimensional flat with a hard surface.

Backstage Gossip: Flat Flats

Moss Hart was often asked to critique shows during their out-of-town tryouts. In Baltimore on one of these occasions, the curtain opened to show a set made of a series of green flats. Suddenly, an actor dressed as an elf came flying out on a wire and crashed into the set knocking over several flats. The curtain closed immediately in order to repair the damage. Hart's review? "It's short, but I like it!"

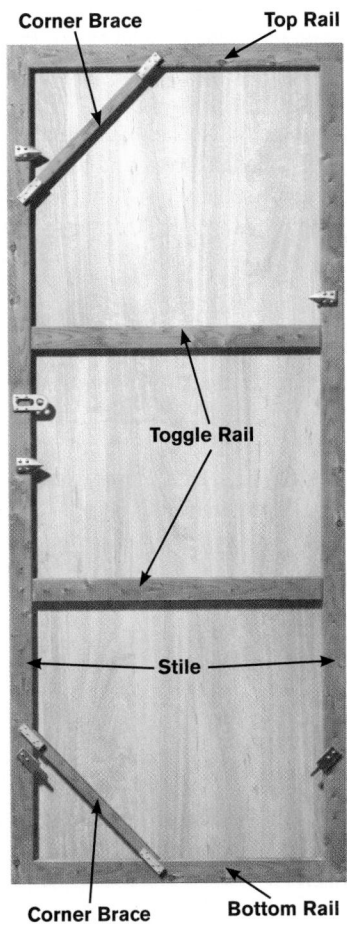

Corner Brace   **Top Rail**

Toggle Rail

Stile

Corner Brace   **Bottom Rail**

- Next, flip them over so that the surface of the joined flats is facing up. Lay a single layer of muslin over the entire surface. Taking care not to pull the muslin too tight, staple it all around the outermost edge of the joined flats.

- Next, paint the entire surface of muslin with whatever "garbage paint" is handy. (The color won't matter.) The paint will size the muslin, in effect shrinking it to fit the surface with no wrinkles, seams, or bumps where the flats are joined. From there the flats can be painted in whatever style necessary.

Hinge

Jack

Sandbag

4 Join the flats

- If you want to use flats to create an unbroken wall with no seams, you will have to apply another skin, this one made of a thin cloth called **muslin.** First put the flats face down and side by side, and screw them to one another along the stiles.

Join the Flats   Go over the steps of flat construction outlined on pages 253–255. If appropriate, demonstrate the process of joining flats together, using a piece of thin fabric over two or more student's miniature flat models.

Vocabulary Enhancement

Although today's theatres typically build and use Hollywood flats, this was not the always the case. Up until the past couple of decades, *Broadway flats* were the norm. These were lightweight flat frames covered in canvas or muslin. Though not as stable as Hollywood flats, Broadway flats were much easier to move and store in a limited storage setting.

Totally Quotable

The term "chewing the scenery" is sometimes applied to stage or film actors who overact or carry on in a generally melodramatic fashion. The critic, author, and humorist Dorothy Parker once famously used the term when, in a 1930 theatre review, she had this to say about one of the play's performers: "more glutton than actor ... he commences to chew up the scenery."

Construction Safety Tips

After students have read the safety tips on this page, have them open their journals or get out a piece of paper and choose one of the suggestions below to work on.

- Think back to the last show at your school or another school. Were all of the safety rules followed? If not, create a poster containing the necessary precautions and hang it backstage.

- Prepare a checklist of what each crew member, actor, and director should do if an emergency occurs during a rehearsal or a show at your school.

- Draw a plan of your theatre building. Locate the fire extinguishers, fire exits, and nearest phone. Do you know and can you plot on your plan the proper fire evacuation routes? Write a paragraph about how you would take charge and direct people to the nearest safe exit in an emergency.

Construction Safety Tips

Scene shops and stages abound with potential hazards. Ropes and cables are hung overhead to suspend heavy instruments that, if accidentally dropped, could cause severe injury. Often actors need to walk backstage in the dark amid furniture, properties, and lighting cable. Observe the following rules to apply your technical knowledge and skills safely when creating sets or supervising others who are working in the scene shop.

General Safety Tips

- Keep all working areas clean and organized.

- Be alert to what others are doing. As in driving, construction safety requires a defensive approach.

- Know the location of fire extinguishers on the stage, in the shop, and in the control booth, and know how to use them.

- Know the location of a well-equipped first-aid kit.

- Report all injuries or potential hazards to your instructor.

- Before raising or lowering a batten, yell "Heads up!" and wait for everyone to respond before continuing.

- Know location of Material Safety Data Sheets (MSDS).

Shop Safety Tips

- Wear protective clothing, including long pants, long sleeves, and hard-toed, rubber-soled shoes. Avoid loose clothing or jewelry that could get caught in power tools.

- Tie back long hair to prevent its being caught in power tools.

- Wear protective gear when necessary when handling tools and materials. Depending on the job, you might need goggles, earplugs, a dust mask, gloves, or a mask that filters out fumes.

- Know how to use your tools. Obey any warnings on tools. If you don't know what you are doing, don't do it!

- Pay attention. Don't talk and become distracted.

- Unplug all power tools immediately after using them.

- Look for and correct any potential hazard, such as nails sticking out of boards.

- Watch where you are going. Look up if people are working above you. Also, don't work on the floor when someone is overhead on a ladder, as tools can fall.

- Keep the shop well ventilated when dust and fumes are around.

- Use tools only as they were designed to be used. Do not improvise.

Notes

Platforms

While flats create the walls of the set, platforms are what give it levels. Platforms provide enhanced visibility and sightlines as well as added visual interest. Every platform must be durable enough to withstand the weight of its load, whether that load consists of actors, furniture, or set pieces.

A platform has three basic parts. The first is the top, referred to as the deck. The deck sits atop the frame, which features a series of cross bars, or joists, that provide extra strength and sturdiness. Finally, there are four legs, which can be any height necessary. Legs taller than 18 inches will need reinforcement with cross braces.

Building Platforms

Building a platform is in many ways comparable to building a flat. To build the most common type of 4x8-foot platform, you will use 2x4-foot stock lumber.

- Measure and cut two 7-foot by 9-inch stiles for the frame; two 4' boards for the rails, and three 3-foot by 9-inch joists.

- Lay the stiles and rails on the floor on their edges in the shape of the platform frame. Using a carpenter's square, check the accuracy of your joints. Next, use 2½" or 3" drywall or wood screws to connect one rail to the ends of two stiles. You will need two fasteners for each joint. Repeat this process for the other end. At this point, you should have a 4x8-foot frame.

- Place the joists inside the frame at intervals of 2 feet. Attach the joists, using two screws apiece on each side.

- Now, using ¾-inch plywood, carefully measure and cut the deck, and place it on top of the frame. Attach the deck (your screws should be at least 6 inches apart).

- Measure and cut the legs for your platform. Bolt the legs to the inside of the frame. To accomplish this, you will need to drill through the outside of the frame).

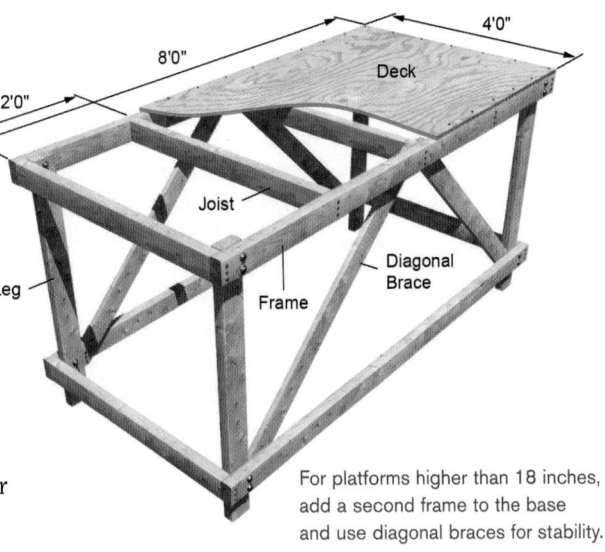

For platforms higher than 18 inches, add a second frame to the base and use diagonal braces for stability.

Vocabulary Enhancement

Classical Greek theatres sometimes employed a type of low platform known as an *eccyclema*, which could either be pushed onto the stage or revolve on an axis. The device was most often used to reveal a tableau of some offstage action to provide clarification for the onstage action. Though occasionally used in comedy, the eccyclema was most often used in tragedy, and it is considered by many theatre historians to be the earliest form of what has since evolved into the contemporary turntable or revolving set.

Painting the Set

If appropriate, have students try out the painting techniques on the miniature flat they constructed. If this does not work, ask them to create opening night cards for an upcoming play at school or elsewhere using the paint techniques they learned to decorate the back and front cover. In this latter case, they will not have to apply a prime coat. They can begin with the base coat and use small brushes, cut-up sponges, and other supplies to apply paint using the techniques of stippling, scumbling, or stenciling.

Three Stencils Have students try their hand at creating simple stencils for a number of different settings. For example, you might ask each of them to design stencils for a play set in a preschool, one set in the break room of an auto supply store, and a third set in the reception area of a veterinary clinic. When they have designed their stencils, have them cut out the forms and apply stenciling techniques to poster board or larger pieces of paper, using paints or magic markers.

Painting the Set

Ordinary flats can almost magically become marble walls or the rough-hewn interior of a log cabin or the distant vista of rugged mountains in the hands of a skilled scene painter. The following information will help you identify and apply scenic painting techniques.

Any paint job starts with the first layer, which is called a **prime coat**. This can be nearly any color or grade of paint—its purpose is only to give the flat's surface a uniform starting point. Next is the **base coat**, or foundation color. Once the base coat has been applied, any number of special techniques can add the appearance of depth, texture, and pattern to an otherwise plain surface. Some common techniques follow.

Spattering. This is accomplished by spraying droplets of paint onto a flat's surface. Standing at least three feet away from the flat, dip the brush lightly into the paint; then, with bristles facing up and tilted toward the flat's surface, slap the brush repeatedly against the heel of your hand. To be effective, spattering requires at least two different colors of paint. If the set's base coat is a dark color, use a lighter paint to spatter. If the base is a lighter color, use darker paint hues for the spatter.

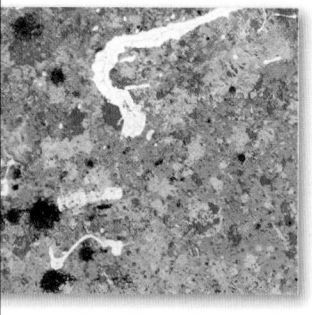

Scumbling. For this technique, you use a series of curved or straight brush strokes to blend several different colors of wet paint on the surface of the flat. This must be done very quickly, as the paint will only blend well when it is wet. To mute the blending a bit, once you finish the main work, you can run a dryer brush in a crosshatch pattern over the area.

Stenciling. With this technique you can create excellent wallpaper effects or borders by painting over commercial or handmade stencil patterns. Make sure you mark the placement of the stencil on the surface before you commit paint to it. It is best to dab the paint onto the stencil area very gently. Your goal is to cover the stencil's open area without getting any paint under the stencil form.

Stippling. With this texturing technique you use a small porous sponge dipped in paint and pat it onto the flat, platform, or other surface. You can use more than one color to give the impression of more texture.

For strategies for implementing and refining scenic painting techniques, check out page 000 in the handbook.

Video Resources

To show students some practical applications of stage painting techniques, you might share with them brief how-to videos from YouTube, such as the following:

www.youtube.com/watch?v=xJ2g5AhFmq0

www.youtube.com/watch?v=9ur59d_lb8E

www.youtube.com/watch?v=70RdiZpGaRl

www.youtube.com/watch?v=elMqGfECkFl

Rigging

Imagine you are watching a play by George Bernard Shaw. A scene ends and there is a brief bit of music as the lights dim. All of a sudden the wall of the set for the well-appointed drawing room you have only just been looking at begins to fly upward until it disappears somewhere behind the teaser curtain high above the stage. Meanwhile, another setting, this one the inside wall of a lovely seaside hotel, drifts down and settles quietly into place on the stage. In less than thirty seconds, the onstage world has completely transformed. The effect is spectacular! How does it work? The answer is simple: It's rigged.

Theatre **rigging** is responsible for many stage effects; it can close curtains and shift scenery quickly. It also gives theatre personnel a safe way to access overhead equipment, such as lighting instruments, which makes working high above the stage both easier and safer. It can even allow actors to fly.

Rigging systems can be manual, automated, or a combination of the two. Only state-of-the-art facilities typically have fully automated systems. Most high schools use a more traditional manual system. This type of rigging depends on balancing a load with steel counterweights that are shifted by means of ropes and pulleys operated by members of the backstage crew. While

Spiderman: Turn Off the Dark (2010). The production was cited for multiple safety violations when several cast members suffered serious injuries due to, among other issues, faulty rigging.

maintaining safety is important to every job in the theatre, operating a manual rigging system is perhaps the area with the greatest need for precaution. Every person operating rigging must be both well trained and authorized to do so.

Close-up of a drop with a counterweight arbor. Lines or cables run through pulleys and are tied off at the locking rail.

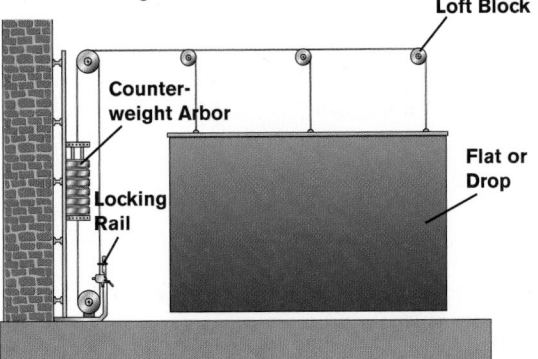

Rigging

Encourage interested students to find out more about the problems that plagued the cast and crew of the 2010 Broadway musical *Spiderman: Turn Off the Dark*. They can view a large number of articles around the production and its aftermath at the *New York Times* Web site (http://topics.nytimes.com/top/reference/timestopics/subjects/s/spiderman_turn_off_the_dark_musical/index.html).

Bring on the Wagons   In addition to stationary platforms and flying scenery, platforms and flats can also be moved on and offstage by means of rolling wagons. These have casters or rubber ties to ensure the quietest scene transitions possible. Wagons are usually used to move heavy set pieces. For some productions, entire sets are built on large rolling units, called *jackknife wagons*, which pivot onto the stage from the wings.

Backstage Gossip: A Moment of Silence

The technical problems with the production of *Spiderman: Turn Off the Dark* and the injuries resulting from them were the talk of the town in 2010. A cover for *The New Yorker* magazine featured a cartoon showing cast members from the production in hospital beds. The production and its problems were spoofed on *Saturday Night Live*, in *The Onion*, and on late-night TV. Joan Rivers began her monologues during this period with a moment of silence for "those Americans risking their lives daily—in 'Spider-Man' the musical."

PREPARE

Create a Video

Be sure to make arrangements for the video equipment well in advance. Make sure every student who will be handling the camera and any other equipment is trained to do so. You will also need to set up any backstage or scene shop tours with the technical director or whichever responsible adult operates as liaison between the classroom and the theatre facility.

PREPARE

Create a Video

In this video project you will act as a team teacher along with your fellow presenters. Your presentation will focus on either "Getting the Big Picture" of your school's theatre space or "Knowing the Nuts and Bolts" of the tools and other materials in the school's scene shop.

Reread the section of this chapter that focuses on your chosen subject area. Then take time to brainstorm the structure of your presentation.

Remember that although this is an instructional video, you can still use imagination and humor. Consider the

best way to put the information across while keeping your audience engaged and entertained.

For example, if your focus is the "Nuts and Bolts" of the scene shop, your group could:

- film a tour of the scene shop led by the technical director or shop director with each presenter asking questions that illustrate various important points

- demonstrate the right and wrong way to use various tools (but always be safe!)

- act out possible consequences of not putting tools away or of putting them away in the wrong place

- describe in detail the jobs that require power tools instead of hand tools

If your group's focus is the "Big Picture" of the theatre space, you might

- video the backstage area of your school's theatre space and point out the features listed on the checklist that appears on page 248

- with the assistance of the technical director or some other knowledgeable adult, film a demonstration of your school's rigging system

- discuss the contents and location of the theatre's first-aid kit

You can record your video on a smartphone, tablet, or inexpensive digital recorder and use any of a number of video editing programs to put together your instructional video.

Totally Quotable

"As a kid who wasn't into sports, at school I felt almost alienated at times, whereas in the theatre community there was this amazing sense of camaraderie. Early on, we would go to rehearsals with my dad, and I was like the mascot for the backstage crew. That was a big part of my childhood, so I dreamed of one day doing a play in London."

—Zach Braff

PRESENT

Show Your Video

When your group is called, walk to the playing area. The designated person should set up the video equipment. Then introduce your presentation as rehearsed and start the video. When the video is over, ask the audience if there are questions. If there are, all presenters should take turns answering them. If there are no questions, the presenters should give a brief summation of the project and leave the playing area.

The Language of THEATRE

Use support from peers and teachers to develop necessary vocabulary, grasp of language structures, and background knowledge to help you comprehend what you read.

- Review the compound nouns *prime coat, base coat,* and *Hollywood flats.* Ask for background knowledge to understand the meaning of *coat* and *Hollywood* in the context of the chapter.

- Read all the theatre terms on page 246. Notice that they are all nouns, including some compound nouns. Ask for background knowledge to help you understand their meaning.

- As you read the section Reading a Blueprint on pages 251–252, use support as needed to comprehend the different types of *elevations,* including language structures such as pronouns and antecedents.

- As you read the chapter to prepare your project with a group of classmates, ask for support as needed to comprehend any challenging language, such as the terms *joinery, lauan,* and *rigging.*

CRITIQUE

As you view your classmates' video presentations, take notes on how effectively they put across their instruction. Choose one presentation to evaluate. Consider both the successful and the not-so-successful aspects of both the video and the live presentation. Without singling any one member out, how well did the group work together? Your evaluation should be based on a scale of 1 to 5, in which 1 means "needs much improvement" and 5 means "outstanding." As you craft your evaluation, ask yourself questions like the ones below.

- Did the presentation hold your interest and/or increase your understanding of the subject?

- Did the presenters speak clearly and use descriptive examples?

- Was the presentation focused and well paced?

- Did all the presenters take part?

- Were the transitions among the speakers handled smoothly?

- Was the presentation the correct length?

Write a paragraph defending your scoring.

PRESENT

Show Your Video

To encourage viewers to comment after their fellow students' presentations, you might begin each post-presentation question-and-answer period yourself. You might ask a question that draws out one of the ideas in the presentation—for example, "Was there anything you were surprised to find out as you were shooting the video?"

CRITIQUE

Go over the evaluation rubric with students before they begin presenting their videos. Reacquaint them with the criteria they will be evaluated on as well as the rating system. Remind them that this is not a popularity contest and they should make sure they evaluate the presentations and not the personalities.

The Language of THEATRE

Suggest to students that they keep a dictionary of new theatre vocabulary words in their journals. Have them define each word; locate its root words, prefixes, or suffixes; and then try to use it in a sentence.

Notes

_____

_____

_____

_____

_____

_____

Spotlight on

The Impact of Live Theatre Lead a class discussion by asking students to share ideas they have regarding the five boldface items in the Spotlight feature. Perhaps they or a family member or close friend has been involved with a theatre production. How did that experience (or discussion of someone else's experience) change the student? Remind the class that a "change" need not be earthshaking. Simply being moved by a production—whether by anger, sadness, or joy—counts as an impact of the live theatre experience. Remembering a production days, weeks, or years later is another impact. Finding out more about the subject of a production is yet another.

Spotlight on

The Impact of Live Theatre

Many, many people are involved in the production of live theatre—from the set construction crew to the publicity manager to the actors and props team. What impact does their devoted collective work have on contemporary society? Why do they do it? Here are strategies for answering those questions.

- **Analyze the impact.** If you analyze the impact of theatre, you might identify several different areas. One area of impact is on the participants themselves—the personal satisfaction and artistic expression everyone involved in a production feels. Another is the impact on the audience. A recent study showed that the top three reasons people go to the theatre are to relax and escape, to be emotionally moved, and to learn something new. Yet a third aspect is the impact on larger society. Live theatre is an industry, providing jobs to hundreds of thousands of people. It also carries messages that often have meaning for society as a whole. (See pages 6–9 for more on the personal and social value of theatre.)

- **Evaluate the impact.** After analyzing the areas of impact, evaluate them. Does theatre provide a positive experience in each area of impact—for participants, the audience, the economy, and the social fabric?

- **Synthesize the impact.** Bring all the areas in which live theatre exerts an impact back together. What is their overall impact? As an art form that touches the lives of many people in many ways, how does theatre affect contemporary society overall?

- **Articulate the impact.** Express your analysis, evaluation, and synthesis as clearly as you can to reflect the depth and complexity of the impact of live theatre on contemporary society. Express yourself in writing, in conversation with your peers, or in a blog or online discussion group—any medium to effectively convey your thoughts.

- **Employ the impact.** Finally, as a student of theatre, use the impact of theatre to add fulfillment to your own life and to make a difference in the lives of others. Whether you are a writing the words an actor will bring to life or painting a flat to create an imaginary world, experience the power of live theatre to bring understanding and satisfaction to participants, audience members, and society as a whole.

Additional Projects

1 Create a PowerPoint presentation that illustrates necessary safety precautions for working set construction backstage or in the scene shop. Include tips on the safe handling of both tools and materials. Identify the safe use and handling of both tools and materials in scenery construction.

2 With a small group of classmates create a presentation to discuss the tools and materials commonly found in a scene shop. Each person will be responsible for discussing and/or demonstrating one of the following categories: (1) hand tools, (2) power tools, (3) measurement tools, (4) joinery, and (5) materials. In your discussion, explain how to apply technical knowledge and skills safely while using these tools or supervising others in the scene shop.

3 Demonstrate the design and building techniques of scenery using materials such as heavy cardboard, laminate, Popsicle sticks, and glue to create a 4x8-inch scale model of a Hollywood flat or a standard platform. Include each element discussed in the corresponding chapter section. Explain how you are applying the basic practices of proper measurement to make your scale model.

4 Using large sheets of paper or cardboard and different colors of paint, create an art project that identifies and applies scene-painting techniques including spattering, scumbling, stenciling, and stippling.

5 Using the information on page 247, create a flow chart showing the various technical production roles.

6 Using computer graphics or art supplies, create a poster or chart evaluating how training in set construction might benefit a person's future academic or professional life.

7 **Theatre Journal** Based on your own experiences and what you may have read, go through the strategies on the preceding page for understanding the impact of live theatre on contemporary society. Using specific examples to back up your points, analyze, evaluate, synthesize, and then articulate your conclusions in your journal. Also write about ways people can employ the impact of live theatre for the benefit of society.

Safety is always the first concern of any stage crew member.

For More Information

Books

Carter, Paul, *The Backstage Handbook,* Broadway Press, 1994.

Carver, Rita Kogler, *Stagecraft Fundamentals,* Focal Press, Inc., 2013.

Hull Miller, James, *Small Stage Sets on Tour: A Practical Guide to Portable Stage Sets,* 1987.

Ionazzi, Daniel A., *The Stagecraft Handbook,* Better Way Books, 1996.

Kaluta, John, *The Perfect Stage Crew: The Compleat Technical Guide For High School, College, and Community Theatre,* Allworth Press, 2003.

Raoul, Bill, *Stock Scenery Construction: A Handbook,* Broadway Press, 1998.

Sherwin, Stephen, *Scene Painting Projects for Theatre,* Focal Press, 2006.

Other Media

Fundamentals of Scenic Painting, DVD, Insight Media, 1989.

How Do I Paint It?, DVD, Insight Media, 1988.

Theatre Fundamentals: Backstage— Is It Safe?, DVD, Insight Media, 1983.

Apps

Technical Theatre Assistant

Substitute Teacher Activities

The suggestions below are for one or more days when you will be out of the classroom.

- Assign the Painting Techniques Worksheet on page 100 of the Resource Binder.

- Teach the Set Construction section of the Student Handbook, pp. 600–607.

- Assign one or more of the Additional Projects on this page.

Theatre **Then** and Now

Virtual Sets

More on Etienne Gaspard Robertson Phantasmagoria show-man Robertson was an innovator. He was able to improve the magic lantern's artificial light source by using a tubular wick, which created a much more powerful projection. He attached wheels to the lantern and called this new technology a Phantascope. The wheels allowed him to move the projector forward or backward at whatever speed he liked. This created an effect in many ways similar to a contemporary zoom lens on a camera. The stronger projections and the new ability to move at a higher speed paved the way for Robertson to bring his act to larger and larger venues.

Theatre **Then** and Now

Virtual Sets

From Magic Lanterns

You know from the historical development of stage technology (see pages 244–245) that set construction progressed from the very simple if nonexistent, as in Ancient Greece, to the elaborately complex today. Up until the 1600s, most theatrical events were held outside, so sets would have been subject to the elements. When theatres moved indoors, set construction became practical and widespread.

Even before then, in the early 1400s, painters in the Italian Renaissance, notably Filippo Brunelleschi, discovered the way to produce *perspective,* the representation on a flat surface of an image as the eye sees it. By the time theatre moved indoors, the technique of painting with perspective was well established, and the painted backdrop scenery for theatrical productions was often a

Images shown through rear projection were the secret to the scary effects of Phantasmagoria.

highly realistic and ornate scene using perspective.

In the mid 1600s, another development that would have an impact on theatrical sets was in the works. Christiaan Huygens—Dutch astronomer, mathematician, and philosopher—is credited with refining if not inventing a projection device known as the magic lantern. This device used a mirror behind a light source that directed light through a painted slide to project onto a surface. Magicians began to use these to trick people into believing they were witnessing apparitions during seances. In the late 1800s, people used them to stage horror shows called Phantasmagoria. The Beligian Étienne Gaspard Robertson (1763–1837) hid the projector behind transluscent curtains at the back of the stage and projected images

Notes

onto smoke, making ghosts seem to appear and move around.

To Projected Digital Sets

In the early 1900s, the Linnebach projector made it possible to use projection in theatre more easily, and several directors experimented with it during the 1920s and 1930s. In 1947, Jo Mielziner, a leading set and lighting designer, used projection in a production of the Rodgers and Hammerstein musical *Allegro*, to mixed reviews. Some thought the projections greatly added to the fluency of the show, which required many quick scene changes. Others thought they called too much attention to themselves.

Technological advances in the 1970s made projection cheaper and more effective. A turning point in its acceptance was the work of Wendall K. Harrington. Her work on the 1992 musical *The Who's Tommy* involved 54 projectors as well as video sequences, and it set the standard for theatrical projection. As digital technology exploded in the late 20th century, new kinds of projectors and new kinds of software with remarkable brightness and capabilities, including animation, were available relatively cheaply.

Projection design has become a regular part of productions today. A 2008 production of Stephen Sondheim's *Sunday in the Park with George* used projection animation to piece together bit by bit the famous impressionist painting by Georges Seurat that inspired the play. Set designer Rae Smith won a 2011 Tony Award for her work on the World War I drama *War Horse,* in which projected drawings change from the peaceful English countryside to barbed wire and skies darkened by war. Do these digital sets draw attention away from what is unique to theatre—live actors and the imagination of the audience? The debate continues.

The darkened sky is one of a series of projected drawings by Rae Smith that gave the set of *War Horse* a changing landscape.

Welcome to the Tweet Seats The fast-changing digital world has managed to make its way into live theatre both onstage and off. In 2012, Minnesota's famed Guthrie Theatre designated a new limited seating area that has become known as the "tweet seats." This section—often in the balcony or the back row of the theatre—allows audience members to use their smartphones during the show to text or tweet without disrupting other audience members. The basic idea is to use audience members' connectedness to build buzz about the production. Since 2012, many other theatres have implemented tweet seats.

From the Field: In the Blink of an Eye

Video projection designer Elaine McCarthy worked on the 2009 Broadway production of Michael Jacobs's play *Impressionism*, for which she created an onstage museum gallery of famous Impressionist artworks. Recalling her collaboration with the show's director, Jack O'Brien, McCarthy said, "Jack said at one point that it might be funny if Whistler's Mother [an iconic painting featured in the show] could wink. Three minutes later, she was winking. Jack . . . couldn't believe we could make the change so quickly."

Chapter 21

Lighting

This chapter introduces the student to the tools and equipment of the lighting designer. The function of lighting, the types of lighting instruments, and the fundamentals of safety will be covered. Students will create a lighting plot for a scene.

Objectives

1 to understand the effect that lighting has on interpretation, mood, and emphasis

2 to understand the safety issues involved in lighting

3 to analyze a scene in a play to determine the light design requirements

4 to use the tools of the designer to create a lighting plot

Project Specs

For this chapter you will need a scene or several scenes from a play. If the students have completed their set designs, you might want to have them design the lights for that set.

Beginning Students

Discuss the safety issues when working with electricity and working from heights. Let students know that if they are afraid of heights, you need to know it now, not when they are up on the ladder. Excuse any student who is uncomfortable.

On Your Feet

After students have discussed the lighting for a play or television show they saw, have them draw the scene.

Chapter

21 Lighting

You are sitting in a theatre as the house lights slowly dim. There is a hush as the audience waits in anticipation. The curtain opens and the lights rise on the scene. It's a different world up there on the stage—both magical and recognizable. The lighting is a key factor in its creation.

Project Specs

Project Description You will create a lighting plot for one scene in a play and present it to the class in a five- to ten-minute talk.

Purpose to understand the basics of stage lighting and to implement principles of visibility, mood, and color

Materials a lighting plot on paper (showing color, type, intensity, and beam of lighting) for a scene from a play or the Lighting Activity Sheet your teacher provides

On Your Feet

Think back to a play or television show you saw recently. Discuss with a partner anything you can remember about the lighting. Your discussion might consist of statements such as, "The kitchen was lighted with warm lights, including a lamp the actors could turn on and off" or "There was dim light outside the windows of the office building, which made it look like a winter afternoon."

Theatre Terms

barn doors
batten
border lights or
 strip lights
cross light
dimmers
ERS (ellipsoidal
 reflector spotlight)
floodlights
followspots
Fresnel
gelatins (gels)
gobo
moving light
practical light
roundels
scoops
solid-state
 lighting
spill
spotlights

Theatre Terms

barn doors light accessories that have moveable flaps to control the light beam

batten a pipe above the stage to hold lights or scenery

border lights (or strip lights) long, narrow, strip of lamps and reflectors

cross light when two spotlights are placed on opposite sides of the stage at a 45-degree angle

dimmers controls that change the level of lighting intensity

ERS an ellipsoidal spotlight with a strong beam that can be precisely focused

floodlights lights that illuminate broad areas of the stage

followspots spotlights that produce strong beams of light that follow an actor as he or she moves across the stage

The Functions of Lighting

Among other things, effective stage lighting provides visibility, establishes emphasis and mood, and provides logical light sources.

1 First, the audience has to be able to see the onstage action. Visibility is the number-one requirement of stage lighting. If there is too much light, the result will be a glare. If there is too little, the audience must strain to see. The goal for a lighting designer is to create a balance of intensity that allows the audience to see without being overly aware of the lights. Even if a scene is to be played "in darkness," it should start with extremely dim lighting that rises very gradually as the scene progresses.

2 Lighting also creates emphasis and mood. Bright lights tend to dominate while dim lights subordinate, so stage areas that carry the most important action usually need brighter and more dramatic lighting. The mood of the play serves as a guide for how the lights will be blended. Comedies generally require a mix of bright lights in mostly warm colors. A tragedy or serious drama usually calls for a blend of medium to low tones, shadows, and cool colors.

3 Finally, lighting should be "logical." It should accurately reproduce obvious light sources such as the sun, moon, a fireplace, lamps, and so on. By suggesting the light source, you can often imply the time of day and the weather. A cool blue apparently coming in through a window can suggest early morning. A bright, warm amber light may indicate late afternoon on a warm, sunny day.

The Williamstown Theatre Festival's production of Arthur Miller's *All My Sons* uses evocative lighting.

Chapter 21 Lighting **267**

Fresnel a spotlight whose beams create soft-edged light pools

gelatins (gels) transparent color sheets

gobo a metal sheet with a punched-out design that produces a patterned effect

moving light a programmable light able to make rapid lighting changes

practical light a light that actually works onstage, such as a lamp or candle

roundels colored glass disks

scoops lights that illuminate broad areas

solid-state lighting lighting that uses LEDs rather than incandescent or arc sources

spill unwanted light leakage

spotlights lights that produce concentrated illumination

Engage the students in a discussion of the *purpose* of lighting, using a scene from a play they have read in class. Read over the scene together. Then ask the following questions:

- How might lighting define the environment in this scene?
- What emphasis or mood should the lighting create?
- Will lighting be used to create a climate, location, time of day, or year also?
- Will the light source be from a lamp, the sun through a window, or the glow of a fireplace?
- What color should predominate in the lighting?
- Will the lights reflect an abstract concept such as the mood of the play, a specific design, or an emotion?

ACTivity Choose two students to go to the board and act as class recorders or secretaries for this exercise. Divide the rest of the class into two groups. One group is called "mood." The other is called "emphasis." Using the pictures from magazines or art books, show one picture at a time. Have the group of "mood" students call out the words they would use to describe the mood of the picture. One of the students at the board will write the words on the board. Repeat the process with the students who are called "emphasis." After going through the exercise, you will have a list of descriptive words generated by the students that they can use when they begin their lighting project.

ELL Students
Discuss with students the meaning of the words *mood* and *emphasis*. Allow them to use words in their primary language to describe the images.

268 **Unit Five** Technical Theatre

ACTivity Assign students to work in groups to take an inventory of your school's lighting instruments. Have one group determine how many Fresnels, ERS's, border lights, and followspots the theatre department has. Ask another group to start a file of this inventory, being responsible for updating it as new instruments are added and old ones are retired. A third group will keep track of instruments that need repair and will arrange to have this done, with your assistance. A fourth group might research any new lighting instruments your school needs and try to come up with ways to earn the money to buy them.

Equipment and Accessories for Lighting

Piece of Equipment	Description	
ERS (ellipsoidal reflector spotlight)	throws strong, focused light from long distance	
Fresnel	throws softer light on larger area from shorter distance	
scoop floodlight	lights large areas in strong light	
followspot	throws bright focused light on a moving actor	
border lights/strip lights	washes light over a large area	
lighting control board	the unit that controls the operation of lights	

Resource Binder

- Lighting Activity Sheet, p. 103
- Script Analysis for Lighting Worksheet, p. 104
- Critique Sheet: Create a Lighting Plan, p. 105
- Lighting Test, p. 106
- Lighting Plot, p. 171
- Lighting Cue Sheet, p. 172
- Instrument Schedule, p. 173

Handbook Connections
pages 591–595

To Have on Hand

- Art books and magazines
- Play scripts
- Stage plan showing electrical batten locations
- Gel swatch books (available from theatrical supply houses)
- Instrument symbols templates
- Pens, erasers, large paper
- Flashlights or several desk lamps
- Color charts
- Paint
- White fabric
- Scissors
- Rubber bands

Accessory Piece	Description
batten	metal pipe that holds lights
gelatins or gels	color filters for creating colored light
twist-lock connectors	connect lights to source of power
pin connectors	connect lights to source of power
gobos	metal disks with cutouts for creating patterns of light
roundels	colored glass disks used in strip lights to create color onstage

There are computer software programs that enable the designer to create a light design on his or her computer. CADD (Computer Assisted Design and Drafting) programs are expensive, so your school may not have this capability. Many colleges, universities, and professional designers have these programs. Current light design software programs can actually model and demonstrate your light design on a "virtual stage"—thus the light designer can change the design and instantly see the effect of the changes.

ACTivity Ask students to design their own gobos by creating a design on a round sheet of paper. Have students talk about their patterns and what atmosphere they intend them to create when used.

Advanced Students

These students may want to measure an actual gobo, find the correct metal stock, and create their pattern on a metal disk that will fit an ERS owned by your school.

Vocabulary Enhancement

Lighting that illuminates the actors from the front is called *frontlight*, while lighting that illuminates the actor from above and behind is called *backlight*. Backlight separates the actor from the background. *Sidelight*, lighting that illuminates the actor from the side, is often used to light dance shows and the ballet; and *downlight*, which comes from above, is used to form a pool of light. The distance between the instrument and the object to be illuminated is called the *throw*.

A good book that provides the throw distance and the beam spread for most manufacturer's lighting instruments is the *Photometrics Handbook* by the Broadway Press of Louisville, Kentucky.

From the Field: Organizing Those Gobos and Gels

Make an inventory of how many and what types of gobos your theatre has. Label a file folder with the type, manufacturer, and number of the gobo. Put each gobo in either a file drawer or designated container. Keeping the gobos stored in a logical order will make locating them each time you need them a simple matter.

Organize the gels in your inventory in the same manner. Label the color, manufacturer, and the number of each gel on the file folder. Keep the folders in a file drawer or other container. The next light hang and focus will be much easier if you can easily locate the correct gel.

Robert Kallos, Teacher, Atlanta, Georgia

Types and Elements of Lighting

Set up a light lab in your classroom or workshop or even on your stage. You can hang an ERS or two and Fresnels and then experiment with different gel colors and the different throws. A Fresnel will give a wider, softer focus, while an ERS will give a longer throw with a sharp edge.

If you have access to barn doors, the students can try controlling the light on the Fresnel with the barn door flaps. Likewise, the students can experiment with the shutters on the ERS. Remind the students never to plug in and turn on an ERS unless the shutters are in the open position.

If you do not have access to theatrical instruments, you can conduct a light color lab with several desk lamps or even flashlights. Small, high-intensity flashlights are best. Many theatrical supply houses will provide you, free of charge, with gel color swatch books. Give one to each student. Let them experiment with the small rectangles of colored gel. Also bring different fabric swatches to class to further investigate how light, color, and costume interact.

ACTivity Using gel colors, ask students to work in pairs to experiment with different effects. What do a warm color and a cool color do if they are held in front of two separate light sources and focused on a single object below? How does the effect change if they use a more saturated color? What impression does a saturated green give that light blue doesn't? How do the colors change where they overlap?

ACTivity Have the students experiment with different colored gels and different colored fabrics. How do gel colors in the light affect the fabric color?

Types and Elements of Lighting

There are four main types of stage lights. **Spotlights** produce focused illumination, while **floodlights** illuminate, or flood, broad areas of the stage. **Strip,** or **border, lights** provide a wide, uniform wash of light; **followspots** produce a strong beam of light that follows an actor moving about the stage. (These instruments and their accessories are pictured on pages 268–269.)

The main elements of these lighting instruments are:

1 a bulb, referred to as a *lamp,* which produces the light

2 a *reflector,* which reflects the light and throws it forward onto the area to be lighted

3 the *lens,* which focuses and shapes the light

4 the *housing,* or metal framework, which encloses the unit and holds the gels

5 *shutters*, used in the housing of some lights to shape the beam of light

6 the *yoke,* a metal framework used in conjunction with a C-clamp to attach a light to the batten.

Spotlights One very efficient spotlight is the **Fresnel,** which has a ridged lens, a tungsten-halogen lamp, and a spherical reflector. Beams from the Fresnel cast diffused or soft-edged light pools, which blend easily with other lighted areas. **Barn doors** are usually used with Fresnels to control the beam of light with their movable flaps.

Another type of spotlight is the **ERS (ellipsoidal reflector spot).** It features a plano-convex lens, a tungsten-halogen lamp, and an ellipsoidal-shaped reflector. Spots such as these are excellent for situations in which the light must be thrown a great distance, as the beam is strong and can be focused with extreme precision. This instrument is

The logical light in this scene comes from the fire pit.

270 Unit Five Technical Theatre

Backstage Gossip: Playing with Fire

Queen Elizabeth I almost always saw plays at night. The performances started about ten o'clock and did not end until well after midnight, which meant the use of artificial light. . . . Elizabeth was content with a general blaze from huge candelabra,

tall candle-sticks, and flaming torches which illuminated her as well as the players and helped warm the draughty spaces of the palace.

from *Theatrical Anecdotes* by Peter Hay

The starlight pattern for this scene from *Space* by Tina Landau was created using a gobo.

ideal for lighting an area without **spill**, or unwanted light leakage. The beam can be narrowed or widened to provide either a harsh or a soft edge. As a rule, ellipsoidals are hung out in the house, while Fresnels are used onstage. A **gobo**, which is a metal sheet with a punched-out design, can be placed inside the ERS to produce a patterned or textured effect.

Border lights or **strip lights** are long, narrow, metal enclosures that house a row of lamps and reflectors. These lights provide general illumination; they tone the lighted areas without changing the contrast or emphasis provided by the specific spotlighting.

Floodlights, known as **scoops**, are large fixtures—500 to 1000 watts—that are mounted in an open-faced housing.

Floodlights differ from spots in that they have no lens. They provide soft, widely diffused light, which is perfect for backdrops and the background behind doors and windows.

With the advance of technology, other types of lighting instruments are available. A **moving light**, also known as an intelligent light, mover, or wiggle light, is a programmable lighting fixture that can make quick and sometimes dramatic changes that would require many more traditional lights—and more time—to accomplish. Moving lights can be programmed to pan and tilt and to change color, focus, iris, shutters, and gobos. **Solid-state lighting,** which uses LEDs rather than incandescent or arc sources, is also gaining popularity. Solid-state lighting has a number of advantages over traditional lighting. It consumes less power, generates less heat, can be controlled by DMX, and lasts longer. However, solid-state lighting is also expensive.

A final type of light, **practical light**, is at the other end of the technology spectrum. Practical light is any light on stage such as a table lamp, chandelier, or sconce that does not light the stage but adds a layer of believability to the stage setting. The true light sources can support the belief that the practical is lighting the scene.

Gobos add texture to light, creating mood and atmosphere. They can also supply information (the name of the show) or be a part of the scenic design. If you have access to different types of gobos, bring them to class. Check Web sites of lighting companies for pictures of different types of gobos or get copies of lighting manufacturers' catalogues from a theatrical supply house. Examples might include tree branches, flowers, windows, doors, clouds, stars, and city skylines.

ACTivity Ask the students to look through a theatrical lighting supply catalogue (print or online) and choose several patterns for gobos they find interesting. Then have them write a short scene indicating the gobos they would use, and why.

Special Needs Students
Have students choose a gobo and then draw a scene that shows the effect of the gobo.

Show, Don't Tell Find examples online or in lighting design books showing moving lights used in theatre. Invite students to compare the images to the stationary lights shown in the chart on page 268. Explain that sometimes the head of the light moves and sometimes there is a mirror on a pivot that moves the beam of light. Although these lights are often called intelligent lights, the intelligence is really in the person who programs the lights. Lighting designers are usually skilled programmers but often hire a specialist who programs the lighting control console during the rehearsal phase of the play. Once the console is programmed the commands to move the lights are fairly straightforward.

sual Cue

Writer/director Tina Landau is notable for her innovative use of visual as well as physical space on stage. Ask students to use the gobos available to them as they use their **creative thinking skills** to answer the following questions.

• What other gobo might be used just as effectively in this scene?

• If these two characters were to next visit Paris, France, what gobos might you use?

Colored Light: Gels and Roundels

Have a grease pencil or china marker handy for the days you are hanging lights. After the student has cut the gel from the sheet to fit the gel holder, have the student write the name of the gel manufacturer and the gel number on the gel before he or she puts the gel into the gel frame. This will make replacing the gel or locating its storage file much easier.

Ask the students to describe how they would use light and color to create the atmosphere and mood for the following situations:

- the throne room of an evil emperor
- the forest glen of an elf in a fairy tale
- the captain's bridge of an alien spaceship
- the secret caves of the mountain ice dwellers

ACTivity If you have access to computers, ask the students to create a PowerPoint® slide of each one of the locations above and share the designs with the class. How did each design represent the topic? What colors and moods emerged?

Talk to students about the terms *saturated* color, which is a pure color or hue, and *intensity,* the brightness of the light on the stage or the amount of color. Then look at the color swatches on this page and discuss each one in terms of its intensity and whether it seems saturated or not.

ACTivity Have students keep a lighting diary for two weeks or use a section of their journals. Tell them to sit quietly for ten minutes each day and record their observations about light. They can sit on a front porch, in the backyard, in their living room, in the library, or any place that has interesting light. Ask them to write down a description of each kind of light. They might describe the color tones of a particular light. Advise them to really pay attention to what light looks like and what it does, and then to use a variety of descriptors.

Colored Light: Gels and Roundels

Several media are used to provide colored light on stage: gelatins and glass.

Gelatins (or **gels**) are transparent color sheets inserted into a frame that mounts in front of spotlights and floods. Gelatin is popular because it comes in a wide variety of colors and it is inexpensive. However, it must be replaced often because it becomes brittle and fades with use. Gelatins are available in many colors from most theatrical or lighting supply houses.

Strip lights usually have a standard color combination of red, blue, and amber or green lights. When amber

This scene from Eugene O'Neill's *Moon for the Misbegotten* suggests late afternoon by using blue lighting.

General daylight:

warm side	light scarlet
cool side	frost

Morning light:

warm side	light straw
cool side	light blue

Late afternoon light:

warm side	light amber
cool side	daylight blue

Artificial light:

warm side	light scarlet
cool side	special lavender or light blue sky

Moonlight:

warm side	steel blue
cool side	frost

Quotable

Lights are to drama what music is to the lyrics of a song. The greatest part of my success in the theatre I attribute to my feeling for colors, translated into effects of light.

David Belasco, Theatrical Producer

Color Temperature

Color temperature is measured in degrees Kelvin and is specific to every type of lamp. Within theatrical use, color temperature comes into play when your lighting design includes both tungsten and arc source lights (traditional lights and moving lights). Generally tungsten lamps have a color temperature in the 3000-3200K range while arc source lamps are between 5600-6500K. To the eyes, tungsten sources seem warmer with more red and amber while arc sources appear to have a blue cast to them. This may be most readily observed by looking at digital images or video of the two types being used side by side. The arc sources will appear considerably brighter than the tungsten sources.

and blue are mixed, they produce a nearly white light that illuminates without drastically changing costume and makeup colors. Colored glass disks called **roundels** are used in some strip lights instead of gels. However, because of their intense color, they tend to lower the illumination and make blending more difficult.

Dichroic filters, another kind of glass color filter, are found primarily in moving lights. They reflect color rather than absorbing it as standard gel does. Since they absorb no light, illumination through dichroic filters is higher than through traditional gels.

As you prepare your lighting plot, your choice of lighting colors will depend on the mood of the play and its setting (location, time of day, season). Experiment with colors until you obtain the effect you're looking for. As you experiment you may wish to try the combinations of gel colors shown on

page 272 to see how they look with the scenery and costumes. Your teacher may have sets of color samples for you to use. The popular colors seen on the previous page can create many different effects.

Be aware that these colors may appear slightly different in this textbook than they do in real life.

Connections and Controls

Lighting instruments are connected to the electric current by special stage connectors and cables. Some schools use twist-lock connectors, which provide a safe connection without the worry of accidentally pulling the connectors apart. Others prefer the more expensive pin connectors. While pin connectors must be tied with an overhand knot to ensure the connection, they are much more durable than twist locks. State electrical codes usally require the use of grounded plugs for all connections.

Color Temperature Find examples online or in lighting design books showing theatre lighting designs using tungsten and arc source lamps. Invite students to share the differences they see when looking at the different examples side by side. Ask whether they think the two types of lights create different moods.

Explain to students that incandescent light bulbs are being phased out for household use in favor of compact fluorescent bulbs and LED lighting that uses less energy. Invite students to discuss why lighting designers might be concerned if tungsten lights were no longer available for theatrical use.

Connections and Controls

Another way to ensure the connection of a pin connector is to tape the connection with gaffer's tape, readily available at theatrical supply houses.

Use the following phrases as starting points of a discussion about color and atmosphere. Ask the students to describe how they believe a lighting designer might respond to these phrases in a script and how he or she would use imagination to make them come alive onstage. Encourage students to refer to the colors on page 272 for help.

- Bright, summer morning
- Foggy afternoon
- Burnished by the sun
- Dark and stormy night
- Icy, crisp winter's morning
- Not a cloud in the sky
- Arid, dry, parched desert
- Humid, sun-drenched forest

Notes

_____
_____
_____
_____
_____
_____
_____
_____

Lighting Plots, Charts, and Cue Sheets

Go over the diagrams on this page, referring back to pages 268 and 269 to see images of the spots indicated. Discuss the areas of the stage being lighted and the kinds and positioning of the spotlights used.

Then have your students design a moon box. You will need paint, white fabric, large paper or plastic cups, rubber bands, scissors, and flashlights. Using thin, white fabric, have them draw the "face" of the moon's surface on the fabric as realistically as possible. Cut the bottom out of the paper cup. Stretch the fabric across the large end of the paper cup, securing it with a rubber band. Shine a flashlight through the small end of the cup, creating a moon image.

ACTivity Ask students to get into groups and improvise a short scene that utilizes the moon box they have created.

Help students create lighting stencils, plastic that has cutouts in the shape of theatrical lighting instruments, which they can use to trace the outline of each instrument onto their lighting plot.

Use heavy three-conductor grade cable for theatre lighting; it can carry a larger load than ordinary household cord. For school use, you should have #140-gauge cable that carries 15 amperes or #12-gauge that carries 20 amperes. Be careful not to overload the circuit. Wires can safely handle only the stated amperes.

The light board contains switches for the various lights. If possible, all instruments should be connected to **dimmers**. Dimmers regulate power to lighting instruments and other devices via a data communication system. Most systems in use today are DMX 512 (Digital Multiplex), a protocol that allows light boards to communicate with dimmers, moving lights, or other DMX devices.

Lighting Plots, Charts, and Cue Sheets

A lighting designer must be familiar with the script and know the play's mood, setting, time of day, season, weather, and any necessary special

This partial lighting plot shows which spotlights light which areas of the stage.

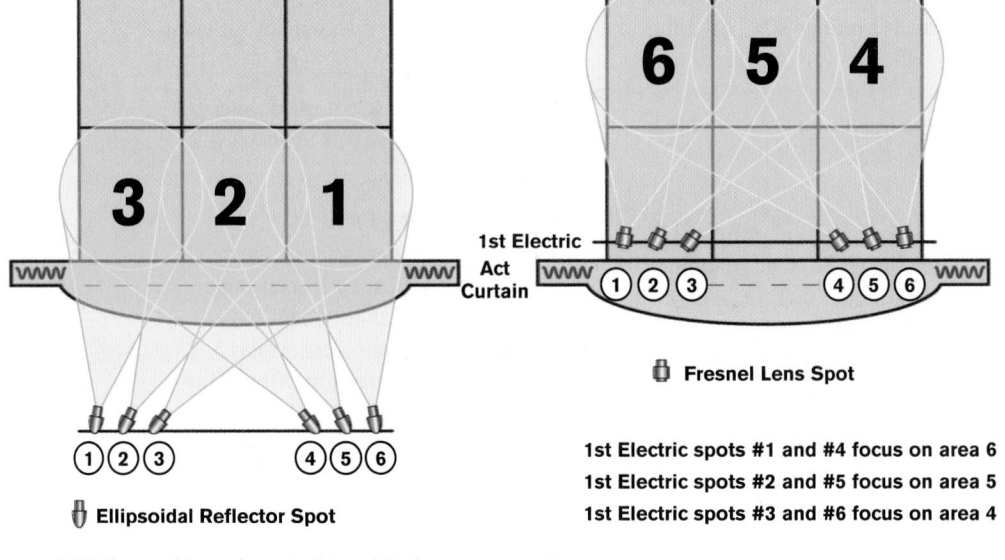

Ellipsoidal Reflector Spot

FOH (front of house) spots #1 and #4 focus on area 3
FOH spots #2 and #5 focus on area 2
FOH spots #3 and #6 focus on area 1

1st Electric
Act
Curtain

Fresnel Lens Spot

1st Electric spots #1 and #4 focus on area 6
1st Electric spots #2 and #5 focus on area 5
1st Electric spots #3 and #6 focus on area 4

Quotable

How far that little candle throws his beams! So shines a good deed in a naughty world.

William Shakespeare

effects. The lighting designer consults with the director and views the floor plan to figure out the number and location of doors and windows, the light sources, such as a fireplace or table lamps, and the color of scenery and costumes. The lighting designer also works closely with the set and costume designers to create an overall effect.

The lighting designer determines the light plot, a scale drawing, by tracing over the ground plan of the set and applying to this copy the position of

With the cue sheet, the light crew can see at a glance when to use which lights.

INSTRUMENT SCHEDULE

Number	Instrument Type	Wattage	Color	Dimmer
1	Fresnel	500	#4 Pink	A4
2	"	"	"	A7
3	"	"	"	A5
4	"	"	#17 Lau	A3
5	"	"	"	A2
6	"	"	"	A1
FOH1	ERS	1000	Frost	B1
FOH2	"	"	"	B2
C3	"	"	"	

An instrument schedule lets the light crew know which lights are being used in the production.

CUE SHEET   Act 1 Scene 1

CUE 1	House Lights full
CUE 2	Stage Lights – on
	FOH1 & FOH2 – full
	FOH2 & FOH5 – full
	FOH3 & FOH6 – up 2/3
	1st Electric Spots – full
	Border – up 2/3
CUE 3	Slowly dim house
CUE 4	Foots – up 2/3
CUE 5	Harry "I'm Tired"
	1st Electric on dimmers 4 & 6 – dim 1/2
CUE 6	

Go over the instrument schedule and cue sheet on this page with students. Note how the instrument schedule and the cue sheet both correspond to the lighting plot on the previous page.

Discuss how light can come from different directions—the front, the back, either side, and from below. Have students name specific scenes in plays where they might use light from different directions, and why. Ask them to be aware of the effects they would be trying to achieve as well. Would this scene work best with backlight, frontlight, sidelight, or downlight?

Vocabulary Enhancement

A *magic sheet* is a picture of your light plan usually drawn on the ground plan of the stage. It uses simple symbols to show where the instruments are hung, what the focus of the light is, in what direction the light is going, and the color used in the instruments. It helps the designer to conceptualize the plot by creating a picture of the design. Sometimes the magic sheet also tells the designer which dimmer controls which instrument.

Backstage Gossip: Let There Be Light

Before gas and electric lighting, candles lit the stage.

The use of candles involved the employment of candlesnuffers, who came on at certain pauses in the performance to tend and rectify the lighting on the stage . . . . The duties of a candlesnuffer were somewhat arduous. It was the custom of the audience, especially among those frequenting the galleries, to regard him as a butt with whom to amuse themselves during the pauses between the acts, hurling missiles at the unfortunate candlesnuffer.

from *Theatrical Anecdotes* by Peter Hay

Positioning Lighting Instruments

Show, Don't Tell Go over with students how to hang ERS lights and Fresnels. If you have a well-equipped stage, show them the battens where Fresnels should be hung and the beams or stands that will support the ERS lights. Point out the strip lights, if your school has them. Show the students where cross lights would be placed on each side of the stage and demonstrate a 45-degree angle.

ACTivity Have students take turns practicing cross lighting two actors standing center stage. Have actors vary their positions in order for the students to work on adjusting their cross lighting.

Encourage students to make a lighting scrapbook made up of their own designs as well as pictures from magazines. They can find interesting pictures that show various examples of light. Pictures of rooms with lamps turned on, landscape pictures with the light playing through the trees, and pictures of moonlight on a field are just a few examples. Find pictures that represent different moods and atmospheres, different climates, different directions of the light source, and different times of day. Remind students that their scrapbooks can be used as a reference when it comes time to work on their design project.

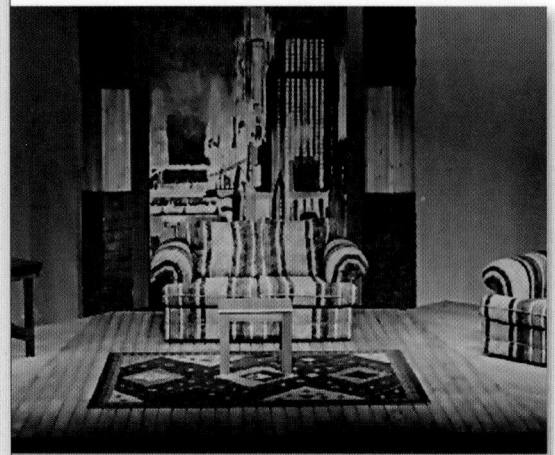 

This set is identical in each photo above, but the different lighting used in each changes the effect.

each light that will be used for each scene. He or she then numbers each light and indicates its color. The light plot shows all the light units, including foots, strips, spots, backing lights, and special lighting effects, as well as a visual representation of the throw of the spot beams. Throw is the distance from a light to what it illuminates.

Finally, the lighting designer makes a light chart or instrument schedule, listing each light, its number, type, watt, color, and dimmer connection. A light cue sheet is also prepared that tells the light level and the changes needed at exact places in the script.

Positioning Lighting Instruments

To provide adequate visibility, emphasis, and mood, lights must be properly positioned. The lighting design will be influenced by the size of the space being lit, the complexity of the action and the needs of the production. But here are some general rules.

ERS lights, with their capacity to throw light over long distances, are typically hung above the audience in Front of House (FOH) positions. These may include catwalk positions, coves, box booms, or the balcony rails. ERSs should be carefully focused to light the downstage area while avoiding spill onto either the audience or the proscenium arch. To light the upstage area, hang instruments appropriate for attaining coverage and intensity from the 1st Electric. **Battens**, the horizontal metal pipes onstage, are often designated as electrical (prewired for lights) or nonelectric (used for curtains, scenery, etc.).

sual Cues

- Compare and contrast the two pictures at the top of the page. How do they look alike, and how are they different?

- Where is the light coming from in each picture?

- Why do you think the designer chose the specific light directions for each scene?

- How would you describe the mood and the atmosphere in each picture? Why do you think the designer used these lights to define the mood and atmosphere?

Some older theatres will have strip or border lights, which allow for washes of color or for general illumination across the entire stage.

To prevent the actors' faces from being in shadow, **cross light** each stage area with two spots placed on opposite sides of the stage at a 45-degree angle. To focus these spots, position an actor in each lighting area and aim the center of the light pool at his or her face. Do not aim at the floor or the scenery. The set will be adequately lit by the spill. Cross lighting can also be used to enhance natural shadows and highlights. For this type of effect, the spots on one side of the stage should have a warmer color than the spots on the other side. For

Electrical Theory and Safety

When using any electrical device—a stage light, power tool, or audio component—demonstrate your understanding of electrical theory by following the standards associated with safe use and best practice. For stage lighting, you must be aware of the wattage of lamps and the limitations of your dimmers. In most cases, current dimmers will provide adequate power for 2400 watts (for instance, three 750w lamps) at full power and are referred to as 2.4K dimmers. You should also be aware of the amperage rating of your system. Most household circuits (and many circuits in your theatre) are likely 20 amps. For this reason you may use multiple conventional fixtures on a single circuit (each fixture may pull as few as 5 or as many as 8 amps), but many moving lights will require all 20 amps available for each fixture. Overloading amps is a fire hazard.

To figure out the watts, amps, or voltage of a lighting fixture, use the West Virginia Formula (WVA): **W**atts = **V**olts x **A**mps (120 volts x 20 amps = 2400 watts). You can also calculate **A**mps by dividing **W**atts by **V**olts (2400 watts/120 volts = 20 amps).

From the Field: A.M. to P.M.

These days, with computer boards, it's easier for the lighting designer to stay on top of script changes . . . A lighting plot has a certain amount of built-in flexibility. A plot should be specific enough that it is designed for that particular show, but general enough so that you can deal with changes. You have to deal with moving a morning scene to nighttime without rehanging all the instruments.

Allen Lee Hughes, Lighting Designer

Arrange for students to tour a nearby professional theatre or college theatre and meet with one of the lighting designers. Allow your class to ask questions about their lighting system—the types of instruments they have, the number of channels they work with, where they store and how they access their instruments. If possible, arrange for your students to see a show there. Then discuss the following questions: How effective was the lighting design? Do you think the designer captured the mood of the show?

Show, Don't Tell Select a short scene from a movie and show it to the class. Find small objects within the classroom to replicate the furnishings— a paperback book as a sofa, an eraser as a table, and so forth. Use the desk lamps from earlier in the chapter and try to replicate the light design in your scene. Ask the students for their input. Does it change the mood of the scene if you move the lamps? Does it affect the mood if you change the color?

Vocabulary Enhancement

The main source of light focused on an acting area is called the *key light*. When a *fill light* is used with the key light, it fills in the shadows and helps to blend the lights. A fill light that gives general illumination to the stage, as opposed to light that is aimed at a specific area, is called a *wash*.

Electrical Theory and Safety

If one does not already exist, have students create a lighting handbook to document the wattage of your theatre's system and of individual lighting fixtures. Have them use the West Virginia Formula to figure out the watts, amps, or voltage of each fixture and mark the information directly on the fixture or on a piece of tape attached to it.

Hanging Lighting Instruments

Before any light hang, take the time to go over all the safety rules with the students. Remind them that the "buddy system" is always in effect. They must always have a buddy with them when climbing a ladder or when they are on a scaffold or lift. Light hang and focus should only occur when a knowledgeable adult is present and supervising the work. The fly system is a dangerous and complicated system and requires that safety instructions be followed to the letter. This system is probably best left to professionals or knowledgeable adults.

Remind students that technical rehearsals are allotted to the technical crew so that they may rehearse the set changes, light cues, sound cues, or any other tasks that the crew performs to make the show run smoothly. This is the time when the actor and the tech crew practice their timing. The tech person works to turn on the light switch just as the actor's hand flips the switch and the lights come up—all with precision timing.

Lighting Crew Safety Tips

Here are a few tools that you might want to have handy when hanging the lights:

- Crescent wrench or light hang tool
- Safety cord (to attach the tool to a belt)
- Black cotton rope
- Black gaffer's tape
- The light plot

NOTE: All lighting instruments must be safety cabled to the batten.

Use a *safety cable*, a wire cable with a loop at one end and a clip fastener at the other end. Put the wire through the yolk of the instrument and around the pipe batten, attaching the clip fastener to the loop end of the cable.

example, if the spots on stage right are warm light pink, those on stage left may be cool, pale lavender. The actor's face will then have a very natural, three-dimensional appearance, as this arrangement of colors provides subtle highlights on the warm side and shadows on the cool side.

The cross lighting technique is the result of the pioneering work of American Stanley R. McCandless, known as the father of modern lighting design. McCandless left a legacy in both the artistic and technical sides of lighting, creating innovations in the use of lighting on stage as well as the design of lighting instruments themselves.

Hanging and Focusing Lighting Instruments

The lighting crew mounts and connects the lights for the play at least 10 days before performance, working when the stage is not in use. At least a week before production, the director will call a special lighting session during which the lights are focused and set. Each light cue will be rehearsed at this time. The lighting crew must make sure that all connections are securely fastened, that circuits are not overloaded, and that there is no glare from the stage into the audience.

During the week of dress rehearsal, complete stage lighting is used, and all the cues are carefully rehearsed so that

Lighting Crew Safety Tips

- Wear cotton gloves to protect your hands from heat when handling lighting equipment and materials. Grease or fingerprints on a tungsten-halogen lamp could cause it to explode when it reaches a high temperature.

- Mark the yoke of each instrument with its wattage and the type of light it is to ensure proper connections.

- Make sure that you have your tools safely pocketed or attached by clips to your clothing or tool belt. When you are working above the stage, a dropped tool could injure someone down below.

- Using a piece of tape, mark each cable to show the number of the instrument and its circuit. That way, even if the cables are ganged together, you will be able to see where each must go. It's also handy to write down the cable's length.

- Check cables periodically and replace any that are worn.

- Disconnect a plug by pulling the connector body—not the cord.

- Always wear closed-toe shoes—steel-tipped, if possible.

Notes

_____

_____

_____

_____

_____

_____

_____

the action and the lights are perfectly synchronized. The cue sheet should always be close at hand. (See page 275 for a sample cue sheet.)

On page 278 are a few safety tips to keep in mind when working with lighting components or when supervising the lighting crew.

Tools Used to Execute a Plot

These are the basic tools for carrying out the design in the light plot. Be sure to have them available.

- Work gloves (heat-resistant)
- C-wrench (attach it to a lanyard or other device in case you were to drop it)
- Ruler (for taking measurements on the light plot)
- Tape measure (for transferring those measurements to the lighting positions)
- Flashlight (it is surprisingly dark up there)
- Tie line

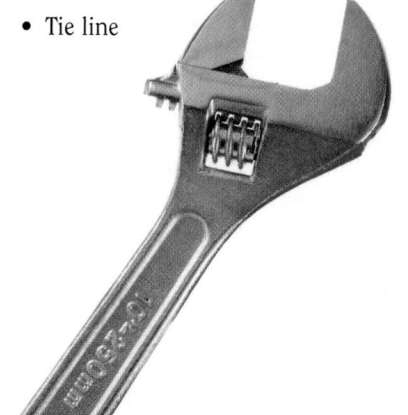

Here's How
To Create Special Lighting Effects

Special effects usually require a bit of experimentation if they are to be convincing. Try the following techniques, and refer to a specialized lighting text for additional ideas.

- *Burning logs.* Well-positioned lights can make the audience think they're seeing logs burning in a fireplace. Place an amber or orange light at the back of the logs. Attach a small tin pinwheel in front of the light. The hot air rising from the lamp will turn the pinwheel and provide the necessary flicker. You can also achieve this effect by screwing different colored lamps into flicker sockets (often used for holiday lights) that are attached to a board and placed behind the logs. A small orange or amber flood will provide a warm glow while the other lights give off a flicker.

- *Burning coals.* To simulate burning coals, place small pieces of broken amber-colored glass or crumpled orange and red gelatins over an amber lamp placed in the bottom of the grate.

- *Lighted floor lamps and table lamps.* On the stage, all floor and table lamps should only use low-wattage light bulbs. The actual light should come from stage spots focused on the area. If floor lighting is used, be sure it is clear of all flammable materials, such as curtains.

Chapter 21 Lighting **279**

Here's How

Following are a few additional suggestions for creating special lighting techniques:

- To project a rotating image onto a wall, use a roto gobo.
- To make an image move across the stage from right to left, use gobo scanners.
- To simulate candlelight, acquire electronic candles that flicker.
- Use blacklights to make any white object, including costumes, glow in the dark.
- Aquasplash is a device used to create the effect of bright, rippling water.
- Use strobe lights to create the effect of actors moving in slow motion.
- A mirror ball (using a motor) and pin spots give the effect of a disco dance floor.
- Use a police beacon and siren to simulate the approach of a police car.

Tools Used to Execute a Plot

Ask students to compare the list of tools to the Lighting Crew Safety Tips on page 278 to see how having the proper tools and using them correctly helps them to work safely.

Backstage Gossip: Temper Tantrum

John Barrymore once took drastic action when a spotlight misbehaved. During a scene between him and Constance Collier in *Peter Ibbetson*, the light lit their feet instead of their faces. Mr. Barrymore left the love scene abruptly, went offstage,

and knocked the lightman down. (He later had to pay damages . . .).

from *All Wrong on the Night* by Maurice Dolbier

Career Focus

Engage the students in a discussion of possible jobs outside the theatre in which lighting design is important. Some possible jobs are lighting industrial shows; lighting concerts, museums and exhibition halls; and lighting furniture showrooms and hotel lobbies.

Some colleges are now requiring a portfolio of student work. Much as the acting students are required to audition, technical students are required to show and discuss their portfolios. Remind your students to save copies of all of their work. In lighting design they should have copies of the light plots, instrument schedules, magic sheets, cue sheets, and any research they did. The students should also take photographs of all the shows they design and put copies in their portfolios.

Career Focus

Lighting Designer

A lighting designer can work in a variety of media, including theatre, dance, opera, television, and film. He or she might also be hired to light museum exhibits or public spaces. No matter what the media, the designer's first task is to meet with the director, or whoever is in charge of the project, to discuss the mood and action of each scene or event. The designer then develops a lighting plan that charts changes in tone and mood. Through artistic discipline, a designer develops an awareness of lighting in many settings. Artistic discipline is also required to apply the science of lighting to aesthetics.

Lighting designers often do double duty as technicians—they design the lights' placement, then hang and operate the lights. This naturally requires quite a bit of technical skill. A designer/technician must be comfortable working the rigging—in other words, he or she must be unafraid to work at great heights. This aspect of lighting requires strict self-discipline to be sure that every step of the rigging, hanging, and wiring process is fully compliant with safety standards.

Some designers thrive on the excitement of a career in theatre, film, or television.

Others prefer to work in the architectural realm, lighting building exteriors as well as residential and commercial interiors. A lighting designer may design task lighting for a modern kitchen, accent lighting for the art in an office building, or landscape lighting for gardens of all kinds.

Until recently, most theatrical lighting designers received their training on the job. Beginning as an apprentice, the budding professional gradually moved up to become a full-fledged designer. However, with more universities offering degrees in lighting design, a new breed of designer has emerged. When these designers hit the marketplace in their early twenties, they often have had a great deal of training and real-world theatre experience.

No matter which path a person takes into the business, he or she must be organized and work well with others. Designers who work in the theatre must read and analyze scripts, perform research if necessary, and often work long and inconsistent hours. These theatre skills and experiences may also be connected to success in higher education and careers outside the theatre.

If you are beginning to tackle lighting design, construct a portfolio showing your work. Refer to the chart on page 10 for more ways to evaluate this career.

280 **Unit Five** Technical Theatre

Notes

Work Out Your Lighting Plan

In this project, you are going to plan a light plot for a designated scene or play. Employ your school's lighting equipment and note any additional lights or equipment you may need.

1 Choose a play appropriate to your school's lighting capabilities. Picture the scenes as you read, and imagine the lighting you would use. You may want to draw upon the lighting in a play you have seen, deciding if you want to create a similar effect.

2 Plan your light plot. Decide the position of each light, and identify its number, color, and type of beam. Indicate all the lighting instruments you plan to use. Your cross beams should be placed at approximately 45-degree angles. Be sure the important acting areas are well lighted. Choose colors that will establish the proper mood, light source, weather, time of day, and visibility (see page 272). Provide highlighting and shadows with warm colors on one side and cool colors on the other.

3 Trace the ground plan of the set and overlay the lighting plot you planned in step two. Be sure you show each light and its number and color. Also be sure the lights overlap for proper light blending. Provide lighting for the complete scene, including any special effects lighting.

4 When your plan is finished, ask your teacher to either help you make copies for everyone in your class or create a computer-based slide show.

5 Practice your presentation so that you can talk comfortably about the choices you made in devising this plan. Do not exceed ten minutes.

The Language of THEATRE

Use visuals and context to help you read. Then orally explain in specific detail what you have read.

• Find the terms *scoop floodlight, followspot,* and *border lights* in the chart on page 268. Use key words in the description and the pictures to help you explain what each type of light does.

• Take turns with a partner reading the descriptions of each piece of equipment in the chart on pages 268–269. Use the description and pictures to help you explain each one.

• Read the text about Types and Elements of Lighting on page 270. Use the context and visuals, including the chart on pages 268–269, to help you explain what you read to a partner.

• Read the text about Lighting Plots, Charts, and Cue Sheets on pages 274–275. Use the context of the chapter and the visuals to help you understand the information. Then explain it to a partner.

Work Out Your Lighting Plan

Go over with the class your expectations for this project step by step.

• Help them select the scene for their design or suggest the same scene they used for the set design.

• Give them an inventory of light instruments to use. This can be based on the inventory your theatre program uses, if you wish.

• Hand out copies of the Lighting Plot on page 141 of the Resource Binder or have students draw their own.

• Give them the design tools they need, such as lighting templates and gel color swatches.

The Language of THEATRE

Have students preview the chapter by looking at visuals and captions to get an overview of the content. Explain how having such an overview can give them a context when they encounter new terms. Point out that many terms are defined or explained in context when they are introduced.

Quotable

There are two ways of spreading light: to be the candle or the mirror that reflects it.

Edith Wharton, Writer

PRESENT

Explain Your Lighting Plan

Help students who have enlarged any of their presentation materials or augmented their designs in any way to secure and use any necessary display tools.

Discuss the evaluation rubric with the students before they begin their presentations so that they are clear about all the criteria on which their evaluations will be based. Remind them that the rating system—1 through 5—gives 5 the highest, or "outstanding," rating.

CRITIQUE

Evaluate a Classmate's Lighting Plan Presentation

Tell students that all presentations will be evaluated using the same 1 to 5 rubric. If there is time, invite them to add another criterion they agree, as a class, should be added to the list of considerations for this presentation. Then make it clear that the class's additional evaluation question must be added to the five that are listed in their books.

Vocabulary Enhancement

The phrase "Let there be light" is a popular one in many languages, such as:

Latin	Lux fiat
French	Que la lumiére brille!
Spanish	¡Qué brille la luz!

Theatre Journal

Use the following as an additional or substitute prompt. The next time you attend a play or view a film, be aware of the lighting used to help tell the story. When you get home, write about what you saw and how the lighting design influenced the experience.

PRESENT

Explain Your Lighting Plan

When your name is called, step to the front of the room and pass out copies of your plan or use the computer to project it. Give the name of the play and tell something about the scene your plan reflects. Discuss your lighting plan in terms of how it relates to the plot, the theme, and the characters. Explain the effects you want to create in this scene. Invite your classmates to ask questions and make comments on your work. Answer any questions they might have about the decisions you made, taking care not to exceed the allotted ten minute time limit.

CRITIQUE

Evaluate a Classmate's Lighting Plan Presentation

Evaluate the work of a classmate. Rate the work on a scale of 1 to 5, with 1 being "needs much improvement" and 5 being "outstanding." Ask yourself the following questions:

- Was the presentation well organized and easy to understand?
- Did the speaker display a good understanding of lighting?
- How well did the speaker answer questions?
- How well did the speaker's lighting plan successfully reflect the play's intent?
- How clear and easy would it be to use the lighting plot?

Then write a few sentences to explain why you gave this rating. Include in your paragraph suggestions for any alternative creative choices.

Backstage Gossip: Very Funny

In a University of Minnesota production of *Daniel Boone*, when the actor playing the title role called out "The sky is red tonight" the electricians gave him a green sky, and when he urged "On to Boonesville!" a number of Indian tepees, with mischievous stagehands inside them, rose and scurried off in the opposite direction.

from *All Wrong on the Night* by Maurice Dolbier

Additional Projects

1 Familiarize yourself with the equipment on pages 268–274. Then make an instrument chart and cue sheet for the same play or scene you selected for this chapter's project.

2 On a computer, design a lighting plot for a contemporary play. Discuss your design with the class.

3 Demonstrate the effect of colored lights on costumes made of different fabrics, colors, and textures or on a made-up face. Refer to pages 272 and 328 for color information.

4 Research and report on the theory of electricity, explaining such terms as *watt, ampere, volt, circuit, direct current,* and *alternating current.* Create a graphic organizer to help explain your research. Show its relationship to theatrical lighting.

5 Interview a local lighting designer or technician about his or her early career. What did this person do to break into the field? Make a video or audio recording of your interview and play it for the class.

6 Read the excerpt from *Icarus* by Edwin Sánchez found in Unit Eight, and create a cue sheet for it.

7 With a partner, evaluate the self-discipline and artistic discipline needed to pursue career opportunities as a lighting designer and articulate connections in theatre skills and experiences to higher education and careers outside the theatre. Consider whether you and your partner have an aptitude for the work of a lighting designer or a career in which similar skills are used. Write up your evaluation in a few paragraphs.

8 With a partner, make a video explaining the safe use of lighting equipment and how you would enforce it if you were supervising the lighting crew, and then share it it with the class.

9 Under supervision, take part in a school or community production and hang and focus lighting instruments with the rest of the lighting crew, applying your technical skills safely.

10 Read about the progress in stage lighting over the centuries on pages 284–285. Identify some key figures and works in this area of technical theatre. Use this information to show how technology has changed theatre.

11 Prepare a brief report on the specialized materials used in theatrical lighting, such as scrims, gels, and dichroic filters. Include guidelines for using the materials safely.

12 **Theatre Journal** Think about a room in your house—a bedroom, a family room, or a kitchen. Describe how the lighting changes in this room over the course of a day—in the morning, at noon, and at night. Write some notes about what kinds of theatrical lighting you might use to represent this room onstage.

Lighting Test

The test for this chapter is available in blackline master form in the Resource Binder on page 106.

For More Information

Books

Essing, Linda, *The Speed of Light: Dialogues on Lighting Design and Technological Change*, Heinemann, 2002.

Keller, Max, *Light Fantastic: The Art and Design of Stage Lighting*, Prestel Publishing, 2000.

Parker, Oren W., *Scene Design and Stage Lighting with Infotrac*, International Thomson Publishing, 2003.

Pilbrow, Richard, and Hal Prince, *Stage Lighting Design: The Art, the Craft, the Life*, By Design Press, 2000.

Reid, Francis, *The Stage Lighting Handbook*, Theatre Arts Books, 2002.

Other Media

Conducting Light on a Shoestring, DVD, Tmw Media Group, 2008.

Conducting Light with Lighting Designer David Cuthbert, DVD, First Light Video Publishing, 2008.

Designing with Gobos, DVD, Theatre Arts Video Library, 1999.

Gear Guide: Gels and Lighting Modifiers, DVD, Insight Media, 2011.

Gear Guide: Tungsten and H.M.I. Fresnels, DVD, Insight Media, 2011.

Introduction to Stage Lighting: Concept, Planning, and Equipment, DVD, Insight Media, 2000.

Introduction to Stage Lighting: Rigging, Focusing, and Plotting, DVD, Insight Media, 1999.

Light 'Em Up, DVD, Insight Media, 2010.

Lighting Module, DVD, Insight Media, 2011.

Theatrical Lighting Design, CD-ROM, Insight Media, 2006.

Apps

DipSwitch
iGobo
ShowToolLD
Stagehand Pro

Substitute Teacher Activities

Below are a few suggestions for days when you will be out of the classroom:

• Assign the Script Analysis for Lighting Worksheet, p. 104.

• Discuss the information found in the Student Handbook concerning Lighting on pages 591–595.

• Assign one or more of the Additional Projects on this page.

• Divide the students into groups and play **Rhyme Light.** Students select rhymes such as "Little Jack Horner," "Humpty Dumpty," "Old King Cole," "Little Miss Muffet," and so on. Have them work together to define the mood, the environment, the emphasis, and the emotional context of the rhyme. Have them decide the kind, color, direction, and focus of the lighting for the rhyme and then describe to the class how they would light a performance of it.

Theatre **Then** and **Now**

Let There Be Light

Shakespeare's Globe Theatre used no artificial light of any kind. The plays took place in the afternoon with only natural daylight. No special lighting effects were used.

Vocabulary Enhancement

Limelight n. 1: a focus of public attention; "he enjoyed being in the limelight" [syn: *spotlight, public eye*] 2: a lamp consisting of a flame directed at a cylinder of lime with a lens to concentrate the light; formerly used for stage lighting [syn: *calcium light*]

Theatre **Then** and **Now**

Let There Be Light: From Candles to Computers

Theatre by Candlelight

Lighting has come a long way since the ancient Greeks first took to the stage. They performed only in daylight; the plays were designed to take full advantage of the sun, and performance spaces were chosen to gain the best possible natural light.

Most historians believe that the ancient Romans were the first to use torches in theatrical presentations. This allowed them to present evening performances. Medieval lighting consisted primarily of stationary torches, but there were also some that could be moved by torchbearers. Although these illumination sources created a fair amount of smoke and odor, they also produced some exciting lighting effects.

In the 18th century, stage lighting was problematic for theatres located in enclosed buildings since the smoke, odor, and flammability of open-flame light sources presented both discomfort and danger. Theatre fires were not uncommon. Later in the century, chandeliers and huge candelabras came into fashion. It was also common to use

Up until the late 1700s, theatres such as the old Covent Garden in London were lit by candles.

carefully placed reflectors to bounce the available light onto the stage. Toward the end of the century, theatres began to use scrims, gauze drops that become transparent when a light is shined from behind but that appear opaque when lit from the front.

It wasn't until the middle of the 19th century that a new invention, the gaslight, effectively snuffed out the lamps, candles, and torches that had served as standard lighting elements for hundreds of years. Gaslight was first developed in England in 1817. By 1849 it could be centrally controlled—although it also caused some major fires over the years. The first spotlight, called a *limelight* because a flame was directed on a cylinder of lime, was introduced in 1816.

For More Information

Books

Fraser, Neil, and Simon Bennison, *The Handbook of Stage Lighting*, Crowood Press, 2007.

Graves, Robert, *Lighting the Shakespearean Stage, 1567–1642*, Southern Illinois University Press, 1999.

McCandless, Stanley, *Syllabus of Stage Lighting*, Drama Publishers, 1968.

Penzel, Frederick, *Theatre Lighting Before Electricity*, Wesleyan University Press, 1979.

Rees, Terrence, *Theatre Lighting in the Age of Gas*, Society for Theatre Research, 1978.

Swift, Charles I., *Introduction to Stage Lighting: The Fundamentals of Theatre Lighting Design*, Meriwether Publishing, 2004.

Lights Up on the 20th Century

It was the invention of the incandescent bulb in 1879 and its rapid-fire use in the 20th century that brought lighting into the modern age. Perhaps the person most directly credited for creating modern stage lighting was a Swiss designer named Adolphe Appia (1862–1928). Hired to create the sets for Richard Wagner's operas, Appia rejected the tradition of the painted backdrop and instead opted for a three-dimensional set. According to his theory, shadow was as important as light as a way of creating a link between the actor and the setting. Appia's use of lighting with varying degrees of intensity, color, and mobility created a revolution in lighting and stage design.

Today, stage lighting effects are typically run by a computerized light board that can transform a stage from sunlight to moonlight to a lightning storm in seconds. Lighting has become not simply a tool but a high-tech art form all its own. With a small arsenal of scoops, ERSs, and Fresnels, a trained lighting designer can add layers of visual and atmospheric magic to any production. And although the basic principles of lighting have not changed much in recent years, the technology of illumination continues to evolve, and design trends come and go. It's impossible to know just what the stage lighting of tomorrow will bring.

Adolphe Appia is considered the father of modern stage lighting.

This scene from the play *Corners* uses computerized lighting effects to create a dramatic mood.

Chapter 21 Lighting 285

Lights Up on the 20th Century

Stanley McCandless

Stanley McCandless has been called "the founder of lighting design in the United States." McCandless was a professor at Yale University and one of the first to teach a class on stage lighting. He wrote a book, published in 1930, called *A Method of Lighting the Stage*. McCandless devised a system of lighting the stage that gave the actor a more natural look. He suggested positioning the lighting instruments on either side of the actor at a 45-degree angle and using a warm color in one instrument and a cool color in the other. The warm color became the key light; the cool color became the fill light. The McCandless system of primary source and reflected source, warm and cool tone mixed together, became the underpinning of modern light design.

Tharon Musser

Tharon Musser began her lighting design career in 1956 with the original production of *Long Day's Journey Into Night*. She subsequently received Tony Awards for Best Lighting Design for the Broadway shows *Follies*, *A Chorus Line*, and *Dreamgirls*. She was nominated for her work on *Applause*, *A Little Night Music*, *The Good Doctor*, *Pacific Overtures*, *The Act*, *Ballroom*, and *42nd Street*. Tharon Musser was honored in June of 2003 by the League of Professional Theatre Women for her distinguished career as a lighting designer.

Quotable

Twenty years ago lighting design was low man on the totem pole. Barely five percent of the programs you picked up had a credit for lighting other than "Sets and Lights by Whomever." Now, you won't pick up more than five percent of the programs that don't have 'Lighting designed by . . . . It's been very exciting to see that happen. It's exciting to see that lighting is becoming known as an art form . . . .'

Tharon Musser, Lighting Designer

Chapter 22

Sound

This chapter will introduce the student to the techniques used by the sound designer to define mood, amplify voices, and provide sound effects for a stage production. Students will learn how to use basic sound recording and playback equipment.

Objectives

1 to understand the role and the equipment of the sound designer

2 to analyze a play to determine the needs and uses of sound for that script

3 to make a sound cue sheet and a sound effects recording

Project Specs

For this chapter you will need to have several sound effects CDs or access to online sound effects libraries. The students will need access to computers, CD or digital media players, and a digital recorder or smart phone to record live sound.

Because this project involves creating appropriate sound, it should prove rewarding for the aural learner, as well as for students who learn best doing hands-on activities.

On Your Feet

To extend this listening activity, walk with your students around the school. They will need to bring a notebook and a pencil. They must maintain silence throughout the walk. Go through several hallways, past the library, the gym, and the music rooms. Be sure to go outside as well. When you return to your classroom, have the students share with the class three sounds they heard on their trip.

Chapter

22 Sound

Somewhere up there in the back of the house, maybe behind the last distant row of balcony seats, there's a small booth from which all the sound effects and music for a play are controlled. Inside this booth, a sound operator manipulates all the electronic equipment that will ensure the audience's listening pleasure.

Project Specs

Project Description With a partner, you will make and present a detailed cue sheet and sound effects recording for a scene that is no longer than fifteen minutes.

Purpose to understand the role and production of sound for theatrical presentations

Materials paper or the Sound Activity Sheet your teacher provides; a recording device and a sensitive microphone

Theatre Terms

acoustics
amplifier
body mic or lavalier mic
CD-R (compact disc, recordable)
digital audio software
equalizer
public domain
sound board, console, or mixer
transmitter

On Your Feet

Sit quietly for a few moments and listen to the sounds going on all around you. As your teacher points to individuals, each person will name a sound that he or she can hear, such as a ticking clock or people talking in the hall. List the sounds as they are named. This would be an excellent starting point for the sound design of a play set in a classroom.

Theatre Terms

acoustics the science of sound waves

amplifier a device that provides the power supply for the speakers

body mic a small microphone that can be hidden in the performer's clothing

CD-R a compact disk used for recording and playing back sound

digital audio software computer software that allows the user to mix sounds together

equalizer a device that balances the high, medium, and low frequencies from each sound source to achieve a desired blend

public domain a work that belongs to the public; free for anyone to use

sound board the device that controls all incoming sounds and allows them to be mixed or manipulated as desired

transmitter a device that sends a signal from the microphone to the receiver

Sound and the Play

Sound design has become an increasingly important element in the theatre. Like other aspects of technical theatre, sound design is an art unto itself. Advances in audio technology greatly enhance the quality of productions.

The main purpose of sound design is to support the mood and purpose of each scene. To achieve this end, sound is used:

1 To amplify the actors' voices.

2 To supply incidental or dramatic music and underscoring.

3 To provide special, realistic sound effects (crickets chirping, dogs barking, car doors slamming, children playing, for example).

The sounds that are generally used in a play are prerecorded music and sound effects from special CDs, digital recordings such as mp3, wav, or other sound file formats; sounds using compiled live music and/or sound effects; and environmental sounds recorded by the stage crew in locations such as beaches, shopping malls, or city streets. A show's sound design, like its other technical elements, should not be intrusive in any way. If the sound designer does the job right, what the audience hears will be experienced as an integral part of the world of the play.

Stomp uses sound, rhythm, and movement to create an exciting evening of theatre.

Sound and the Play

ACTivity So the students begin to develop a sound designer's vocabulary, brainstorm a list of words that have specific "sound" meaning. This will help the students as they discuss their sound design plot with their partners—or with a play director later on. The list might include *thump, crash, zing, boom, roar, snarl, bash, clang, clunk, ding, hoot,* etc. Ask the students to describe these sounds. Are they high-pitched sounds or low-pitched sounds? Are they long or short sounds? Are they happy sounds? scary sounds? Write the list on the board as the students call them out.

With its blend of percussion, movement, and visual humor, the high-energy group that comprises *Stomp* has played to rave reviews around the world.

- What objects are the cast members of *Stomp* using to create sound?

- What other objects do you think such a cast might use to produce percussive sound?

- Do you think, based on this picture, that this show uses sound as amplification, underscore, or a sound effect? Explain your ideas.

ACTivity If your classroom location permits, divide the students into groups of four or five. Using classroom items, have students improvise a two-minute piece that uses sound, rhythm, and movement as if they were the actors/musicians in *Stomp*.

Resource Binder
- Sound Activity Sheet, p. 107

- Creating a Sound Library Worksheet, p. 108

- Critique Sheet: Cue Sheet and Sound Effects, p. 109

- Sound Test, p. 110

- Sound Cue Sheet, p. 174

Handbook Connections pages 608–609

To Have on Hand
- Various electronic devices

- Hand drum, bells, a whistle, sticks, a triangle, etc.

- "Found" objects such as key rings and a box of pencils

The Sound Production Process

ACTivity Brainstorm with the students many different outdoor and indoor sounds. The list for outdoor sounds might include rain, the rustle of leaves, birds chirping, traffic, crickets, and so on. Indoor sounds might be a pot boiling on the stove, the washing machine, the garage door opening, water running in the shower, and so on.

Be sure that all students have access to some type of recording device. Then, have them go home and make a recording of two different sounds—one obtained indoors and one obtained outdoors. Have the students play their recording for the class.

Vocabulary Enhancement

Sound crews often use an electronic instrument called a *synthesizer*, usually played with a keyboard. The synthesizer generates and modifies sounds electronically and can imitate a variety of musical instruments. It allows the person playing it to compose music or devise sound effects for a play.

The Sound Production Process

The sound designer's first job is to become familiar with the script. To effectively analyze a script, the designer must read it more than once. The first reading should be for understanding; the second should be dedicated to finding the obvious places where sound effects, voice-overs, or music will be required. A third reading will typically show the designer even more areas of sound possibility and should lead to a preliminary plan for the show. After researching the music of the play's time period and consulting with the director and other technical designers about the mood and purpose of the play, the sound design is created.

The sound crew has a variety of responsibilities both before and after the show opens. Before the production goes into final rehearsals, the sound crew must put together a detailed list of cues and then find or create the necessary sounds. If recorded music is used in the show, the sound crew must either obtain the rights to the music or ascertain that the music can be used without payment of royalties because it is in the **public domain**. In other words, it belongs to the public.

During tech crew sessions, technical rehearsals, and performances, the sound crew is responsible for setting up, checking, and maintaining the microphones, speakers, recorders, and all other sound equipment used in the show. The sound crew is also responsible for the safe use of sound equipment. Cables must be properly hung so they cannot fall, and any that run on the floor must be properly attached to the surface to avoid tripping hazards. The crew must recognize the usual safety precautions in working with electricity. Additionally, the crew must control volumes at all times so that sudden loud noises do not pose a risk to hearing. If you are supervising a sound crew, make safety your number-one concern and remind the crew of safety precautions frequently.

During performances, the sound crew sees and hears everything the audience does because, for the most part, the crew must take their real-time cues from the performance in progress. Appropriate behavior for the sound crew, then, is quietly listening and paying close attention to the performance and following the sound cue sheet.

From the Field: Sounding Out the Play

I do research. It tends to be generalized research—research that has a kind of emotional value, that somehow gives a sense of the place . . . the sound you might hear in the place . . . if you can't hear the play, you really can't see the play.

Ming Cho Lee, Chairman, Yale School of Drama, Department of Design

A Basic Sound System

A workable sound system consists of equipment to produce and control sound elements. A well-equipped sound crew will need:

The **sound board,** also referred to as a **mixer** or **console,** is the heart of the sound system. It controls input from mics, playback devices such as CD players, digital media players, or other computer-based systems; allows levels and equalization to be set; adds effects such as reverberation; and sends all this to the amplifier.

Equalizers balance the high, medium, and low frequencies from each sound source (e.g., the microphones) to achieve the desired blending of the sounds.

The **amplifier** provides the power supply for the speakers.

Speakers project the sound. They are typically hung at the front of the house near the proscenium arch, facing toward the audience.

Headphones allow the crew to establish levels, check the quality of the sound, and cue up sounds.

CD players, digital media players, or computers can be used for recording, editing, and playing back sound.

Microphones are used for recording and amplifying sound. Hardwired mics are directly connected to the sound board. A **body,** or **lavalier,** mic is small enough to be hidden on the performer and has a small battery-powered **transmitter** that sends a signal to a receiver unit attached to the sound board. Handheld mics and body mics provide excellent mobility for the performer.

A **crew intercom system** allows the sound operators and other crew members to communicate with each other. It is totally separate from the main sound system.

Also used is computer-driven **digital audio software** that allows for the mixing of a wide variety of sound sources and effects. Once the desired mix is obtained, it can be downloaded from the PC to a CD-R or flash drive for playback through the sound board. You will also need a variety of smaller supplies including CD-Rs, batteries for wireless mics, and board tape for labeling the sound board's channels.

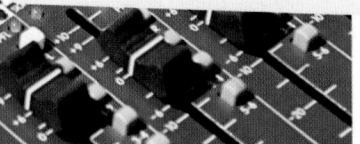

Notes

A Basic Sound System

Have students do an inventory to see if your drama department has the items listed for a basic sound system. If there are any items lacking, discuss what options you may have for substituting another device or going without the item altogether.

Each sound we hear can be interpreted on a different emotional plane. The very same sound could be interpreted very differently by individuals in the audience. To some it might sound exciting and intriguing; to others, it might seem threatening or foreboding. It is the job of the sound designer to select the sound effect that will be interpreted by the majority of the audience in the manner the script and the director intend.

ACTivity Divide the class into groups. Assign each group a category such as water, traffic, or wind. Have the students generate as many different types of sound for each category as they can. For instance, under *water* they might list *babbling brook, whitewater, waterfall, splashing fountain,* and so on. Have the students search the Internet for these sounds and write down the site addresses for possible use in their projects.

Crew Intercom Rules

Following are rules to give to students who are using an intercom system:

- Keep it clean and appropriate.
- Do not use the headsets to carry on personal conversations. Stay on the topic of the show or rehearsal.
- Be professional at all times.
- If you must leave your position and take off your headset, let the stage manager or others on the crew know by saying that you are going "off headset."

PREPARE

Have students work in pairs to explore the acoustics of different spaces in the school building. Give each pair a recording device and assign them to different spaces such as classrooms; the auditorium, gymnasium, or cafeteria; the library or media center, and office spaces. Ask them to record people's voices in the space. If the space is empty, have them record themselves speaking or singing. Invite students to play their recordings for the class and describe what they learned about acoustics.

Think About Your Sound Design

Have students pair up or assign every student a partner. Supply a good number of scripts for the students to look through. If the students have enjoyed the work of particular playwrights, see that there are other plays available by these same people. Most students find David Ives not only very amusing but fairly accessible. Paula Vogel's work is darker and may be troubling to some students. *The Actor's Nightmare* is very funny but contains allusions that beginning students may not understand.

Discuss the mood of a scene that most of the students are familiar with—perhaps the scene from *A Christmas Carol* in which Scrooge is visited by the first ghost. What sound effects music would create the mood of this scene?

The Language of THEATRE

Model different ways to ask for and share information about the theatre terms on page 286. You might invite students to share what they know about the terms and encourage them to ask you for additional information or clarification.

The Physics of Acoustics and Sound

The sound designer must understand the science of sound in the theatre and demonstrate that understanding through an effective sound design. Sound designers need to understand some principles of **acoustics**—the science of sound waves.

- How well an audience hears the important sounds of a production depends in part on the degree to which sounds are absorbed or reflected.

- Sounds are reflected from flat surfaces such as walls and floors. Sounds are absorbed by softer materials such as draperies.

- When a sound is reflected, the audience hears the original sound as well as its reflection, which gets softer the farther it travels. This prolonged sound is known as reverberation.

The acoustics of a theatre space are the result of its architectural design, but sets, curtains, props, lighting, and even the presence or absence of an audience can all affect the acoustics. Reflectors and absorbant devices represent a physical way to control acoustics; audio software is a digital way to manipulate sounds to achieve desired acoustical results. For example, adding a reverberation effect to a sound signal can mimic the feel of an empty hall.

The Language of THEATRE

Work with a partner to ask for and share information in these cooperative learning interactions.

- Listen to a brief recording of a short scene from a play. Take turns asking questions such as "What is that sound?" and "What do you hear?" Share what you hear in the recording.

- Discuss the meaning of the terms *amplifier*, *body mic*, and *public domain* by asking questions and sharing information. For example, you might ask, "Do you know any of these words?"

- As you prepare your project, discuss the kinds of digital recording technology you might use to prepare your sound effects.

- Use the Critique questions on page 294 to guide a discussion about the sound recordings you and your partner presented.

Quotable

Human beings, vegetables, or cosmic dust, we all dance to a mysterious tune intoned in the distance by an invisible player.

Albert Einstein

PREPARE

Think About Your Sound Design

You are now ready to create a simple sound design. As a sound designer you would ordinarily work closely with the director when making decisions about the show's music, voice-overs, and sound effects. For this project, you will work with a partner to analyze a one-act play or a scene from a full-length play for sound possibilities.

With your partner, choose a script that offers a number of opportunities to use sound. One example from Unit Eight of this book is Christopher Durang's *The Actor's Nightmare*. If you prefer, you can use a short scene of your own that incorporates a number of sound effects and music. Make sure your scene or play will take no longer than 15 minutes to perform.

As you read your selected scene, think about the mood it creates. Select music to reflect and enhance that mood. Almost all contemporary music is subject to copyright laws, which means you must get permission from the music publisher to use it for a theatre performance. For classroom use, however, you can feel free to use any music you like. If your selected scene does not take place in the present, try to find music that is reflective of the time period of the setting.

The Sounds of the Scene

Next, you and your partner should analyze the script. What information must be conveyed by sound? Think about where the play is set, and the sounds you would hear in this location. Suppose your scene takes place at night on the porch of a house out in the country. First look for any sounds that are specifically called for in the script. Make a list, complete with page numbers. Then try to imagine yourself in the scene. What do you hear? Crickets? The wind? A distant train whistle? The television from inside the house? Remember that your goal is to enhance the scene with sound, not to turn it into a scene *about* sound. Add the new sounds to your list. Also include ideas for background music and/or introductory music that plays before the scene begins and that fades out as the house lights dim.

Create the Sound Effects

You are now ready to create sound effects for each cue in the scene or play. Although most common sounds are available on CD, you may wish to create "live" sound effects. Many schools have a doorbell unit—a board with a button that can be pushed to activate a buzzer or other ringer. A ringing telephone can be handled the same way.

Backstage Gossip: Wondervoice

Bobby McFerrin is a performer who makes incredible vocal sounds. In his early days, McFerrin sang multiple vocal parts without any musical backing, and when he needed rhythmic accompaniment, he created it himself with his voice or body. People in Germany took to calling him "Stimmwunder," or "Wondervoice." He is often a guest conductor for symphony orchestras in the United States and abroad.

ACTivity Write "mood" words on individual cards. Words such as *mournful, intense, frightened, silly, restless,* and *joyful* might be included. The students will select a mood card from the deck and suggest a type or a piece of music that conveys the mood of that word. Write all the words on the board. If there is time, ask students to record a sound that represents one of those moods and share it with the class. The other students will guess what mood the designer has recorded.

The Sounds of the Scene

Continue using the first ghost scene from *A Christmas Carol* to discuss sound. Ask students to think about the sounds that would be heard during this encounter. Would the wind howl, would the clock tick loudly, would you hear the clinking of the chains worn by Marley's ghost? Tell students to consider all aspects of the scene they have chosen when working on the sound elements.

Create the Sound Effects

Have students who have captured sounds from the Internet share them with the class. Have sound files from the Internet or CDs available for student use. Make available recording devices for students to borrow when creating their sound effects and help them if they have trouble operating them.

ACTivity Divide the students into "Decade Groups." Have the groups research a different decade's historical phone rings. They will locate the ring pattern and tone for a typical phone of the 1950s, the 1960s, the 1970s, and so on. How has the sound changed throughout time? How is a cell phone ring different from the ring on a phone at home? Have them make a recording of their assigned ring and play it for the class.

Rent or purchase the DVD of *The Best of Victor Borge Act I and II* (available from *www.amazon.com*). Victor Borge was a comedian and classical musician from Denmark who developed a system of sounds that took the place of punctuation when he read stories to his audiences. He called his verbal punctuation marks Phonetic Punctuation.

Record Your Scene

You might want to ask students to bring in their recordings for you to preview before their presentations. That way, you can make any recommendations for re-recording sounds that are distorted or difficult to hear. Explain that they will finalize the order of the sounds in the editing process.

Edit Your Recordings

Provide support as needed as students work with the audio editing software. Go over the script while listening to the edited recording with the student to be sure that each sound or piece of music occurs in the proper order. Help any students who are having trouble chart the script according to the sound.

Make a Sound Cue Sheet

ACTivity Have the students research music associated with specific time periods. What music was popular in the 1600s, 1890s, 1920s, 1940s, and so on? What instruments predominated in each time period—harpsichord? guitar? lute? trumpet? Schedule a decade dance in your classroom. Have the students bring in examples of the music of their assigned time period and make up a dance that they think would go with each type of music.

Vocabulary Enhancement

Some theatrical productions have music playing as the audience enters. This is called *preshow music*. It is used to set the mood before the show begins and tells the audience something about the subject or style of the show.

You will probably have to experiment a bit to create your sound effects. You may wish to listen to sound effects CDs or Internet sites devoted to sound effects to decide whether you want to use any prerecorded effects.

Record Your Scene

Record all your sounds and set up any manual cues (such as a handheld doorbell that will be rung by a technician, and so on). Although your recording equipment will not be as sophisticated as a theatre system, try to record as pure a sound as possible. Record only the sound and not yourself breathing, moving the microphone, or rattling papers, all of which break the mood of the scene.

Edit Your Recordings

Using audio editing software, edit your sound files, eliminating unwanted sounds and adding effects as needed. For example, if there is a sound of a car passing by, you can add the Doppler effect, a manipulation of the sound that mimics the change in pitch and volume you hear when a car approaches and then moves away from you. In your editing, demonstrate your understanding of the physics of acoustics and apply the principles of sound as an art.

Be sure to write a cue for every sound in your scene.

Sound Cue Sheet

Name of Play _Wonder of Wonders_

Crew Members _Darlene and Calvin_

Cue No.	Script Pg.	Sound	Track No. or filename	Cue	Level	Cue to End
1	1	doorbell	5	He's 15 minutes late.	7	Finally!
2	3	crash	6	Oh, my gosh!	9	Are you OK?
3	5	music	7	Let's have some fun.	8	I'm not in the mood!
4	8	dog bark	8	Something strange is going on.	8	But we don't have a dog!

Notes

Make a Sound Cue Sheet

To guide you in operating the sound, create a cue sheet like the one on page 292 on a piece of paper or on the Sound Activity Sheet that your teacher provides. For each sound cue, you will fill in a cue number, the number of the page of the script on which it appears, the sound cue, the name of the audio file or CD track number, the spoken line or when the sound cue begins, the volume level, and the line when the sound cue ends.

Cast and Rehearse the Scene

Choose members of the class to perform in your scene, and ask them to read it through aloud. Stop the actors from speaking every time you come to a sound cue. Then play the sound for them. You will need to go over each cue several times to get the timing right.

If you have music or sound cues that are to play underneath the scene, make sure the actors are projecting enough to be heard over the sound.

Time your presentation to make sure you remain under the 15-minute time limit. Rehearse the scene at least three or four times with the sounds in place. If you need to rehearse the scene more than this to be sure that everything goes smoothly, by all means do so.

PRESENT

Play the Scene with Sound Effects

When your name is called, gather your playback equipment and other materials, and walk with your partner and actors to the playing area. Place chairs so that the actors can sit down to read. Set your own chair off to the side near a desk or table to hold your equipment. Introduce your presentation by announcing the title and author of your play. You may wish to say a few words about why you selected this particular scene and the sound challenges it presented.

Make sure your equipment is properly cued up and that your other sound tools are close at hand.

Go through your presentation exactly as you rehearsed it. If you miss a cue, do not try to go back. Instead, check your cue sheet and move ahead to the next cue. When you have finished your presentation, allow the actors to take a bow. Then hand your paper or Activity Sheet to your teacher and return to your seat.

Cast and Rehearse the Scene

Allow classtime for students to cast classmates to perform in their scenes, play the sound cues, and rehearse with the sound and music. You may want to time the final rehearsals for the students yourself.

ACTivity Have the students re-score a short scene (between two and three minutes) from an existing film on DVD. They will need to time the scene carefully, and be sure that it is a scene with a good bit of movement and facial reaction from the actors. They will turn off the sound on the film and watch the scene in silence. Then they will decide what music or sound effects they would put in place of the existing sound and record those effects or the music. Remind them to pay attention to the timing. Action must match the sound. Have them bring the film and their new score to share with the class.

PRESENT

Play the Scene with Sound Effects

You may want to go over with the students the directions for presenting their project as well as doing a sound check of the equipment.

Quotable

[In sound design] the silences—as well as the dog barks or musical underscoring—are determined by specific aesthetic decisions. Meaning and purpose are attached to everything you do as a sound designer . . . your choices for underscoring and ambience are the "sound scenery" within which the production moves.

from *Sound and Music for the Theatre* by
Deena Kaye and James LeBrecht

CRITIQUE

Evaluate the Sound Effects in the Presentation

Remind students that the evaluation rubric for the sound project is in their book. Talk about the rating system from the lowest (1) to the highest (5).

Originality is sometimes difficult for young people to judge. You might want to talk about the concept before the evaluating begins.

CRITIQUE

Evaluate the Sound Effects in the Presentation

You will be evaluating how well your classmates integrated their sound effects into the scenes they presented. The presentations will be rated on a scale of 1 to 5, with 5 being "outstanding" and 1 being "needs much improvement." As you listen to the presentations, ask yourself the following questions:

- How could the technical execution (volume, recording, etc.) be improved?

- In what way did the music and other effects fit the theme and mood of the scene?

- How good was the quality of the sound effects?

- Was the timing of sound cues appropriate to the scene?

- How original was the presentation?

Choose one of the presentations and give it a rating from 1 to 5, explaining in a few sentences your reasons for giving this score.

Career Focus

Sound Technician

A good sound technician should
- have a "good ear" for subtle sound differences
- enjoy working with electronic equipment
- be detail-oriented
- work well under pressure
- be able to make split-second decisions

There are plenty of options for a person with these qualities who chooses a career as a sound technician, or sound operator. These professionals can work in a variety of settings where live performances are staged, either as an employee of the facility or production team or as part of an entertainer's road crew. They may also find work in radio, television, in a recording studio, or in businesses that specialize in the sale and rental of sound equipment.

Sound techs must be able to determine sound requirements, build and install sound systems, set up and test equipment, service and maintain audio and recording equipment, and dub and edit recordings. In addition, they must be able to operate the controls to maintain proper sound levels.

For the right individual, the job of sound technician can be rewarding. But because many of the available jobs are oriented toward live performances, sound technicians must be willing to travel and work long hours—including evenings and weekends. Refer to the chart on page 10 for more ways to evaluate this career.

Notes

Additional Projects

1 Create a radio play using a mix of recorded and live sound effects. Create the sound, record the sound, and edit the sound so it is the most expressive and artistic it can be.

2 Create a movement-based performance that uses sound rather than dialogue to tell a story.

3 Interview a sound technician or sound designer at a local theatre. Ask about the pros and cons of the job and about the duties of the sound crew during the performance, including the safe use of sound equipment. Record your interview, and play it for the class. Based on the designer's responses, analyze appropriate behavior for a sound crew member during a performance, including paying attention to safety, and articulate that for the class. Discuss additional responsibilities of a sound crew supervisor.

4 Make an audio documentary of your class. Pick a theme—for example, first love, family relationships, or money—and create a brief series of questions. Record the members of your class as they answer one or more of these questions. Then compile their remarks and your own into the documentary.

5 In a speech, articulate career opportunities for sound technicians, evaluate the skills needed to pursue such opportunities, and articulate connections in theatre skills and experiences to careers outside of the theatre.

6 Read the "Dead Parrot" excerpt from *Monty Python's Flying Circus* found in Unit Eight, and create a sound cue sheet for the scene.

7 Theatre Journal Go to a shopping mall or supermarket. Stop and listen for three minutes. What sound effects might you record if you were the sound designer for a play set in one of these environments?

John Cleese in the "Dead Parrot" episode from *Monty Python's Flying Circus*

Chapter 22 Sound **295**

Substitute Teacher Activities

Here are a few suggestions for one or more days when you will be out of the classroom:

- Assign the Creating a Sound Library Worksheet on page 108 of the Resource Binder.

- Assign one or more of the Additional Projects on this page.

- Teach Part Eight, Sound, pages 608–609 of the Student Handbook.

- **Act Out Familiar Folktales.** Divide students into groups of four or five. Ask them to act out a folk- or fairy tale. Two or three students will be the actors, and the remaining students will be the live sound effects. For example, in *The Three Little Pigs,* the sound effects will include the fire under the pot in the pig's fireplace, the crumbling of the straw house, and the sound of running feet as the pigs scurry to the next house.

Sound Test

The test for this chapter is available in blackline master form in the Resource Binder, page 110.

ACTivity If students are familiar with *Monty Python and the Holy Grail,* ask them what those coconut shells smacking together were supposed to sound like (horses galloping down the lane). Then ask if they can think of any other movies in which the sound effects were used in so obvious and silly a manner?

Theatre Journal

Use the following as an additional or substitute prompt. Take along a small digital recorder or smart phone when you go to the mall or supermarket and record selected sounds throughout the area. Then think of a scene from a play that would be able to use these sounds.

For More Information

Books

Bracewell, John L., *Sound Design in the Theatre*, New Jersey, 1996.

Huber, David Miles, and Robert E. Runstein, *Modern Recording Techniques,* 7th ed., Focal Press, 2009.

Kaye, Deena, and James LeBrecht, *Sound and Music for the Theatre*, Third Edition, Focal Press, 2009.

White, Glenn D., *The Audio Dictionary*, Third Edition, University of Washington Press, 2005.

Other Media

Theater Sound and System, DVD, Insight Media, 2010.

Theatrical Sound Design, DVD-ROM, Insight Media, 2008.

www.soundfx.com

www.ProSoundWeb.com

www.sound-effects-library.com

Apps

Fun Sounds Free
Sound Effects!
VC Audio Pro

Theatre **Then** and **Now**

Other Cultures, Other Times

Religious rituals and ceremonies were the very first theatrical happenings. These ceremonies were filled with sound. Most rituals and ceremonies were accompanied by chanting, primitive musical instruments, and dance.

Commedia dell'arte used music before, during, and after the plays. The *commedia* is responsible for the first use of the sound effect producing "slapstick" which, when slapped together, provided a comic effect to accompany the humorous stage slaps and punches. This is the same stick still used by Punch in the Punch and Judy puppet shows.

Theatre **Then** and **Now**

Sound Effects Through Time

Early Thunder

Theatre has been using sound effects for hundreds of years. In ancient times, when a play called for thunder, for example, the sound was created by bouncing balls of lead onto stretched leather. During Shakespeare's time, the same sound came from the practice of rolling a cannon ball down a wooden chute and allowing it to hit a large drum.

In later years, another popular source of theatrical thunder was the rumble cart. This contraption consisted of a large wooden box mounted on irregularly shaped wheels and filled with heavy objects. When pulled along the floor or ground, the cart lurched along, displacing the objects inside and causing them to rumble and crash into one another.

In 1708, a playwright named John Dennis came up with yet another way to produce a thunderous sound for the stage. For one of his plays, he strung a copper sheet from wires and put a handle at one end. When the time came for the thunder effect, a stagehand would shake the copper sheet, which produced a very natural thunder effect. Soon, other theatre practitioners began using this technique themselves. It is said that Dennis, upset by the callous appropriation of his invention, routinely chided his imitators that they were "stealing his thunder." Today that phrase is used to describe situations in which someone who should be getting credit is eclipsed by the actions of another.

The rumble cart and the thunder sheet were very effective ways of producing thunderous sound.

Backstage Gossip: The Roar of Cannons

A production of *King Lear* in Washington, D.C., during the nineteenth century made use of a surplus of cannonballs in the capital to provide sound effects in the storm scene. While Lear and his companions listened to the winds blowing and cracking their cheeks, one of the stagehands pushed a wheelbarrow of cannonballs over a special uneven surface to simulate the roar of thunder. At one performance the stagehand became over-confident and, striving for a truly deafening rumble, upset the barrow. Canon balls burst through the flats and rolled down the stage towards the floodlights. The sight of the aged king leaping for his life with new-found agility provoked its own uncalled for storm of audience laughter.

from *Great Theatrical Disasters* by Gyles Brandreth

The Sound of Curly's Knuckles

Musical instruments have been a popular source of sound effects through the ages. From the 1930s through the 1940s, the Three Stooges perfected the use of the musical sound effect. Perhaps you've seen old films of the Stooges gouging and poking one another, and, when knocked unconscious, sliding down walls. Among the sound effects these film buffoons used were:

- cracking the shells of nuts to simulate crunched knuckles
- the plucking of a violin string for eye pokes
- a bang on a bass drum for a belly thump
- ratchets for twisting limbs, ears, or noses
- a slide whistle for a slide down the wall after an injury

The Three Stooges crack a nut.

Sound designer Rob Milburn recorded multiple thunderstorms and the felling of twenty trees to create just the right sound for this scene from Frank Galati's production of *The Grapes of Wrath*.

The Sounds of Today

Today, theatrical sound designers have access to a wide variety of prerecorded sound effects—or the means of producing their own. If a designer wants to simulate the sound of a waterfall, for example, he or she will have to decide just how much rushing water the effect calls for. Is it water trickling over rocks or Niagara Falls? Is the play's rainstorm a summer shower or a typhoon? Many libraries and larger professional theatres have collections of recorded sound effects that can be rerecorded onto a CD-R, and so on. The richest resource is the Internet. Many Web sites specialize in prerecorded sounds; the best ones usually charge a small fee.

Sound effects have always played an important part in our theatre enjoyment—and theatres today have more sophisticated sound effects than ever before—whether we notice them or not.

The Sounds of Today

The Foley Artist

When the credits roll after a movie, have you ever wondered what a "Foley Artist" does? The name comes from Jack Foley (1891–1967), who created sound effects for movies. Foley sounds are those sounds created to accompany the onscreen creaks, thumps, and crunches that you hear when the door opens, the cabinet shuts, or the actor walks across the gravel driveway. To provide the sound of a squeak on a stairway, Jack Foley watched the film, and as the actor descended the stars, he recorded the sound of himself, sitting in an old rocking chair, slowly rocking back. This effect was then added to the movie soundtrack.

www.marblehead.net/foley/jack.html

Quotable

[Foley is] the art of re-creating incidental sound effects (such as footsteps) in synchronization with the visual component of a movie. Named after an early practitioner. Foley artists sometimes use bizarre objects and methods to achieve sound effects, e.g., snapping celery to mimic bones being broken. The sounds are often exaggerated for extra effect—fight sequences are almost always accompanied by loud foley-added thuds and slaps.

from www.imdb.com/Glossary/F

Chapter 23

Costumes

This chapter introduces students to the methods and tools used by the costume designer. It allows the student to practice designing a costume plot for a play and offers many options for costuming a show.

Objectives

1 to understand the job of the costume designer

2 to know and utilize the tools of the costume designer

3 to analyze a play for time period, style, mood, and design

4 to create and present costume designs for a character

Project Specs

This project involves drawing costumes for a character in a play. Some students may feel uncomfortable with this assignment. Remind students that not everyone is a visual artist, but that most of us can draw well enough to convey our ideas. In this class you are not concerned with students' drawing skills, but with their concepts. Tell students you are looking for:

- careful, diligent work
- creativity
- attention to detail
- an understanding of the needs of the play

On Your Feet

Once students have brainstormed the design features from each period, ask volunteers to draw examples on the board to illustrate each one.

---

23 Costumes

Do clothes really make the man or woman? Probably not. But in the theatre, they add a visual element that enhances the audience's understanding of the character, the period, and even the theme.

Project Specs

Project Description You will prepare a set of three to five costume designs for one character from an existing play, then in a five- to ten-minute presentation, you will show your designs to the class.

Purpose to learn the basics of costume design

Materials hand-drawn or computer-based costume designs or the Costumes Activity Sheet provided by your teacher; fabric swatches, colored pencils, and appropriate paper

Theatre Terms

building
costume parade
costume plot
crinolines
modified authenticity
notions
pinking shears
silhouette
swatches
trim

On Your Feet

What do you already know about historical styles? Four classmates should go to the chalkboard and write one of these years: 1776, 1850, 1920, 1950. The rest of the class brainstorms design features from each period, which are recorded under the appropriate heading. Consider clothing, hairstyles, and footwear for both men and women.

Paul Freeman and Joanne Pierce wear costumes that reflect their characters' personalities in the Royal Shakespeare Company's production of *Cymbeline*.

Theatre Terms

building making a costume by hand

costume parade walking onstage in full costume to determine comfort, movement, and proper lighting

costume plot a list of every character and costume for each scene

crinolines full, stiff underskirts

modified authenticity the idea that clothing must give the impression of a certain time period, but it need not be absolutely authentic

notions the needles, threads, pins, and so on, used in sewing

pinking shears scissors with zigzags along the blades so that cut cloth doesn't ravel

silhouette the outline of an item

swatches small samples of fabric

trim decorative items such as buttons, lace, hats, shoes, and jewelry

Costume Design Meets Stage Design

Costume designers are an important part of the design team. Their work, like that of set, lighting, and sound designers, supports the genre, style, mood, and message of a play. This requires more than a flair for fashion; it requires careful study and planning. Before you design costumes for a play, you must first research the time period, the setting, and any relevant social situations to establish historical and cultural accuracy and then apply it in your costumes. When you understand why the fashions of a certain period developed as they did, you will also begin to understand the manners and beliefs of the time. Research can take many forms, but good sources include paintings, books, photos, and

illustrations from the period, as well as costume design books.

After a few careful readings of the play and researching the period, the costume designer meets with the director and other technical designers. Together, they discuss the theme and style of the production and decide on an approach to color, scenery, and lighting. Then, with this and the production budget in mind, the costume designer begins to develop design concepts and sketches.

The Language of THEATRE

Use visuals, vocabulary, and context to help you read the text.

- Look over all the visuals in the chapter to get an idea what the chapter is about. Then read all the headings and look for the boldface theatre terms listed on page 298.

- Review the meaning of the theatre terms on page 298 with a teacher or classmate. Then read the section Pull, Rent, Borrow, Buy, or Build on pages 300–301.

- Review the visuals and captions on pages 300–302 and predict the meaning of the terms *modified authenticity* and *silhouette*. Then read page 302 to check your predictions.

- Skim the chapter to learn the meaning of the theatre terms listed on page 298. Then as you read, use the visuals and context clues to help you understand the text.

Chapter 23 Costumes **299**

Resource Binder

- Costumes Activity Sheet, p. 111
- Costume Design Worksheet, p. 112
- Critique Sheet: Create Costumes, p. 113
- Costumes Test, p. 114
- Costume Designer's Script Analysis, p. 175
- Pull/Rent/Buy/Borrow/Build List: Costumes, p. 176
- Female Figure Outline, p. 177
- Male Figure Outline, p. 178
- Costume Plot, p. 179

Handbook Connections pages 587–590

To Have on Hand

- Costume books with various costume examples
- Paper, pencils, colored pencils, erasers
- Fabric swatches
- Box full of fabric remnants
- Tracing paper
- Thread, needles, scissors, patterns, sewing machines
- Templates from fashion Web sites

Show, Don't Tell Show students various images from costume books, theatre books, or the Internet. Focus on the types of clothing from different time periods and cultures. Have students discuss what they observe about the changes clothes have undergone throughout the ages. Ask students why they think specific clothing was used at specific times in specific locales. Examples would be the wearing of different clothing in different climates, or the fact that at one time only people above a certain station were allowed to wear the color purple.

Ask students to respond to the following questions after carefully reading the play that they are using for their project:

- Where does the play take place?
- What is the time of year, time of day, and climate?
- What is this play about?
- Is this play realistic or fanciful?
- What adjectives best describe each character?

The Language of THEATRE

Review the meaning of the theatre terms on page 298 with students before they read the chapter. Encourage them to find visuals that relate to the terms as they read.

 **isual Cue**

Shakespeare's *Cymbeline* is a very complex comedy, involving a banished husband, a faithful wife, kidnapped infants, an invented infidelity, a treacherous queen, and several murderous plots . . . all in good fun.

Use the following prompts to exercise students' **critical viewing skills**.

- What can you tell about the time period of this scene?
- What might the color choices say about the characters?

ACTivity Have the names of various time periods or styles labeled on individual index cards. Select a play that the students have read. A good choice might be *Antigone* by Sophocles. The students select two characters from the play and one card from the periods/style stack, then design two costumes based on the period/style chosen. For example, Character: Creon/Antigone; Period/Style: Early 20th century. Hand out copies of the Female and Male Outline forms (pages 147 and 148) from the Resource Binder and supply extra paper and colored pencils. Have on hand the books *Historic Costumes in Pictures* or *What People Wore* for reference. (See page 310 for more information on these books.) Students might also visit sites such as *www.costumes.org*.

Pull, Rent, Borrow, Buy, or Build?

Go over each of these terms with students until you are satisfied that they understand what each one means. Discuss productions you have worked on in terms of the costumes you pulled, rented, or borrowed for each.

Show, Don't Tell Take a little field trip to the wardrobe area or costume storage room in your school. Let the students look at the selections. Point out design elements and sewing techniques that may be of interest. Discuss color and fabric types. If you have pictures of the shows the costumes were used in, show them to the students to demonstrate the costumes under the lights and on the set.

If you have a costume rental house in your area, call to ask if you can take your class to tour the facility and to meet with the designers and seamstresses or tailors. Brainstorm with the students a list of questions that they will ask as they tour, such as "How many costumes do you have here?" or "How do you know which costumes will fit which actors?"

Pull, Rent, Borrow, Buy, or Build?

Once the designer has a concept in mind, he or she must decide how the costuming will be achieved. There are generally five ways to get the costumes needed, and all of the methods will probably have to be used at some point.

Pull Some schools and theatres are fortunate enough to have their own wardrobe of costumes from previous productions. This is the first place the designer looks—not only for appropriate costumes, but also for any items that could be modified to meet current needs.

Rent Renting can be both expensive and disappointing. Rented costumes are often ill-fitting, not available in the size and color required, or in poor condition. In addition, since rented costumes are usually available for only dress rehearsal and production, actors have little time to become used to wearing them. Still, there are times when renting is the only option. If a costume must be rented, it is best to deal with a large company with a good reputation, or better still, a local company with costumes on display.

Borrow While it is tempting to borrow costume items from friends, relatives, and neighbors, it is a risky idea. No matter how careful the costume crew

A Roman gladiator's attire from around 500 B.C.

An Egyptian costume from about 3000 B.C.

What an upper-class lady might have worn in the 1300s.

This Elizabethan costume could be that of a pirate or a nobleman.

Medieval servant presents the meal.

300   Unit Five Technical Theatre

Quotable

Sure this robe of mine does change my disposition.

William Shakespeare, *The Winter's Tale*

and the actors are, costumes take a beating onstage. Actors perspire under the lights, and it is almost impossible to avoid getting makeup on clothing. Plus, borrowed items are often fragile and easily snagged or torn. If a costume is borrowed, it must be returned promptly and in good, clean condition.

Buy It is rare to actually buy a complete costume. However, parts of costumes such as shoes, boots, shawls, and hats can often be found at secondhand stores, flea markets, and garage sales—places haunted by savvy designers. These locations, plus discount stores, are also good sources for costume jewelry, clothing that can be modified, and draperies and bed linens that can be used as fabric for making costumes.

Build Making a costume, or **building** one as it is referred to in the theatre, is the most difficult, but probably the most satisfying method of costuming. When costumes are built from scratch, the designer can get the exact look he or she has envisioned and has more creative control over color and harmony among all costumes. Costumes should not war with each other or with the scenery—unless their disharmony is part of the director's message.

After the director has approved the costume design, but before costumes

An elegant lady of the 1800s would have worn a gown like this to a formal gathering.

What a typical beggar might wear to plead for "alms."

Ben Franklin himself might have worn this American outfit from the 1700s.

This costume suits a Victorian chap of the 1890s.

A simple homespun dress suits this American prairie girl.

Chapter 23 Costumes **301**

Backstage Gossip: Fashion Casualty

Dorothy Parker, known for her caustic reviews, had this to say about an actress in The Silent Witness

Miss Strozzi . . . had the temerity to wear as truly a horrible gown as ever I have seen on the American stage. There was a flowing skirt of pale chiffon . . . a bodice of rose-colored taffeta, the sleeves of which ended shortly below her shoulder. Then there was an expanse of naked arms, and then, around the wrists, taffeta frills such as are fastened about the unfortunate necks of beaten white poodle-dogs in animal acts. Had she not luckily been strangled by a member of the cast while disporting this garment, I should have fought my way to the stage and done her in myself.

Continue discussing the costuming of various productions in which you have participated, particularly in regards to buying and building. Share any personal insights regarding either.

Alert students that when buying costume elements they should try to find bargains on fabric at local discount or fabric stores. Most fabric stores have sale tables and some fabric stores offer teachers discounts on fabric.

ACTivity With scraps of about two yards each, students can practice designing and making a simple vest or scarf. If you don't sew, see if a colleague or parent who does is willing to help the students. In addition to the fabric, students will need thread, needles, scissors, and patterns. If you can borrow five or six sewing machines, things will move along faster.

If you have a community theatre or college theatre nearby, call to see if the resident costume designer or teacher will make a presentation about building a costume to your class. Ask them to bring their portfolio to show and discuss with your students.

ELL Students
Your ELL students may find it confusing that in the theatre sewing a costume is referred to as "building." Tell them that the word is used more in the sense of "construct" or "create."

ACTivity Keep a collection of assorted costume pieces in a box in your room. This can include gloves, hats, scarves, an old sweater, a bandana, a tie, a few vests, and some assorted pieces of costume jewelry. Divide the students into small groups. Let the students select an item from the costume box. Each group of students will improvise a scene based around the wearing of their particular costume selection.

Modified Authenticity

Use the Web site *www.freepapertoys.com* to find a variety of fashionable paper dolls from different time periods. Use white paper to trace their silhouettes for the students to identify. Then ask students to use colored pencils to enhance the silhouettes.

ACTivity Have a costume contest in your room. The students will create simple costumes made of found items to wear in class. Ask colleagues to come in to act as judges. Select unusual categories for prizes. Some suggestions for titles of prizes might be Best Costume Use of the Color Red, Most Creative Use of a Hat, Best Design Using Beads and Feathers, Best Costume for a Future World.

Elements of Style

Bring in old family photos and ask students to do the same. Look them over together. How has clothing changed over the years? What did our grandparents wear to school or on outings? How did people dress when traveling? What did they wear when having a portrait taken?

ACTivity Have students interview parents, grandparents, or other older relatives or neighbors about what they wore when they were teenagers. What fashion changes have occurred over the years, and what in our society do they think caused these changes? Have students share their information with the class.

are actually built, a wise costume designer gathers **swatches,** or samples, of fabric for various costumes and tries them under the lighting in which they will be seen. Colors and patterns are also checked to make sure they work together—and with the scenic elements onstage.

Modified Authenticity

Period costumes require only **"modified authenticity."** That is, the fashions do not have to be replicated stitch by stitch, as long as prominent design elements and the basic **silhouette,** or line of the garment, that identifies the era are in place. Lines can be simplified, and elements such as hats and collars can be modified so that the audience can see the actors' faces clearly. Just a few symbolic pieces such as a cane or fan may be the only needed accessories.

Underwear often becomes important to a period costume. Greek robes require long slips to prevent "see-through" under the lights. The skirts of the Elizabethan era need special frames underneath to produce the proper shape and fullness. A dress from the Civil War period needs a hoop and **crinolines,** full stiff underskirts. A "Gay

The poodle skirt was popular with teenagers in the 1950s.

What the typical flapper wore in the 1920s.

A zoot suit of the 1940s.

This fellow from the 1970s is ready for the disco.

A typical tribal costume of Nigeria, Africa.

Backstage Gossip: Your Shift is Showing

In 1907, John Synge's comedy of rural Ireland *The Playboy of the Western World* caused a riot at the Abbey Theatre in Dublin. The play's use of such words as *shift* had the audience enraged. Five hundred police were brought in to calm the situation. And what is a *shift* anyway? It's a slip or petticoat.

Nineties" dress must have a corseted form for the snug waist and midriff.

Elements of Style

As designers build or gather costumes, these are the elements they keep in mind.

Fabric Textures and types of fabric communicate a great deal about characters. Substitutes can often stand in well for expensive fabrics. For example, instead of brocade, you can stencil designs on muslin. Unbleached muslin has another advantage too—it looks like linen at a distance. Burlap, monk's cloth, and terry cloth can substitute for wool. Instead of velvet, use heavy cotton flannel or corduroy. Silks can be made from cheesecloth and nylon chiffon. For lace collars and cuffs, use paper or plastic doilies.

Color Colors can help identify and define characters and also establish a tone for the play as a whole. Costume colors must harmonize or contrast with the set; if the costume is the same color as the background, the audience "loses" the actor. Costumes and sets must also play off each other. Especially in plays with large casts, costuming characters in different tones helps audience members identify and remember relationships between the characters.

Proper choice of color will help establish the play's mood. For example, blues and greens are restful; red conveys danger, power, or anger; black denotes

In *Romeo and Juliet*, the Montagues often wear gradations of one color, while the Capulets wear another.

tragedy or elegance; purple suggests royalty; and white is associated with purity and innocence. Principal characters should wear the more dominant colors in a show—either the brightest or the darkest on stage. Sometimes groups of characters are dressed in the same color with varying shades.

Decoration Decoration includes all the **trim**—buttons, rickrack, lace, and so on—and accessories such as hats, shoes, fans, canes, and jewelry. Each of these can be used to produce a psychological effect on the observer. As long as decorative items are used sparingly, they serve to emphasize details about the character in the play.

Essential decorations must be slightly oversized to remain visible. To keep one element from overtaking others, remember that white or light-colored tights are eye-catching, that glitter steals focus, and that the actor's personal jewelry destroys the illusion of the character, not to mention the time

Collect fabric swatches for classroom use. Use these small pieces of fabric to engage the students in a discussion of color, hue, and tint. Do some colors work together while others do not? Do the textures of some fabric seem easier to work with than others? Do some of the printed designs work well together? Does it ever work to use a plaid with a stripe?

ACTivity Give students two swatches of fabric and tell them that they must find one additional fabric swatch that will work well in the building of a costume for one of these characters: a Russian tsar, a Spanish dancer, a Native American tribal leader, a torch singer in 1930s Germany, or any others you devise. The possibilities are endless. Have the students discuss the swatch they added, and why.

ACTivity Ask students to bring in lots of trim—anything they can think of. Collect these over a period of days, then put them all in a big box and have students pick out two or three pieces without looking. The assignment: Create a small hat for a particular character using these pieces of trim (and any other fabric they care to use).

Quotable

When you don't have the money to build costumes, you start collecting costumes from other productions, other theatre companies, actors' closets, your closet. I had to wear a corduroy blazer to the opening night of Nine, *my biggest show, because all my evening clothes were being used as costumes for another show.*

William Ivey Long, Costume Designer

Here's How

Making costumes that fit the part sometimes means making costumes that are neither tasteful nor pleasing to the eye. Not every actor should look fabulous onstage. Some characters are dowdy, plain, or off-putting in appearance, and it is up to the costume designer to see that they fit the bill. The temptation to add a bit of flair or insert a little artistic "something" has to be avoided. The actor must not look like someone in a costume. The actor must look like a person inhabiting his or her own clothes.

The Question of Comfort

Tell students that costume designers must look to the director for information about any quick changes of costume that will be necessary for the show. Then the costume crew must build the costumes with that in mind. If a quick change is called for, the designer adapts the design to include Velcro™ closures instead of buttons or a zipper. You might also discuss the need for a "dresser" backstage at the crucial quick-change moments. A dresser helps the actors, either backstage or in the dressing room, whenever extra help is needed for a costume change during the show.

and place of the entire play! All actors should leave their personal jewelry at home and wear only the jewelry that will enhance their characters.

These basic principles and elements of design will help you make your costumes complement and support the mood, style, and message of a play.

Here's How
To Make the Actor Fit the Part

Sometimes the actor is built differently than the character he or she is to play. Costumes can help create the right illusion. You can use fabric, color, and line to make people appear taller, shorter, heavier, or thinner than they actually are.

Use fabric with long, vertical lines to make a person appear taller and thinner. Also, use dark colors to create a slim silhouette. Velvet, which absorbs light, tends to make people appear smaller and thinner as well. Long skirts, high hats, and v-necks add height.

Satin and other glossy fabrics add bulk to a figure, as do glaring colors, loud patterns, and horizontal lines. Placing the waistline of an outfit a bit high can obscure a small waist—and layering fabric adds actual inches.

The Question of Comfort

Actors must be able to move nimbly and perform comfortably. Their costumes should not get in the way. The costume designer should collaborate with the actors, listening to what they have to say about their characters' clothes. The actors should try on the costumes before the designer completes them. If an actor feels awkward in a costume, it will show onstage. No matter the play's time period, the goal is to have the actor look like a person inhabiting his or her own clothes.

For this reason, costumes should be ready in time for actors to rehearse in the armor, hoopskirts, tights, and corsets they will wear during the show. If this is not possible, the costume crew should provide rehearsal garments that simulate the costumes. Rehearsal shoes are a must for both men and women.

Backstage Gossip: Padding Problems

Donald Wolfit's padding for Falstaff was a monstrous piece of old-fashioned engineering. Hot, heavy, and Gothic, it caused the actor to sweat mercilessly. Between matinee and evening performances it would be hung from the flies with a powerful light shining on it, in the hope that the heat would dry it. But the worst drawback of the padding was that it had to be removed entirely if the actor was to relieve himself during the performance. Falstaff, luckily, is offstage for some length of time during the course of the play, and this provided Wolfit with the necessary opportunity. "Brilliant craftsman, Shakespeare. Knew the actor would want to pee and constructed the play accordingly. A master, a master!"

from *Theatrical Anecdotes* by Peter Hay

Keeping Track of It All

Costume designers work at the intersection of the big picture and the tiny details. They need to keep track of each costume piece for each character in every scene of a play. That's not easy under any circumstances. Following are the tools that designers use to stay organized and communicate with the director and other designers.

Costume Plot A costume designer's most valuable tool is a **costume plot.** It lists every character and costume for each scene. It also offers a way to record the stage of development for each costume. To use a costume plot effectively, make a separate page for each scene of the play. For each scene, list every character who appears in the scene, and describe his or her costume and accessories, listing each accessory separately. Some designers make a separate costume list for this purpose. Creating, reading, and interpreting costume plots are key skills for the costume designer and crew.

Acquisitions List This is a 5-column chart headed "Pull/Rent/Borrow/Buy/Build." Some theatre companies can pull items from their own stock or borrow them from other theatres. Sometimes, they build costumes from scratch. Often, however, at least some costumes and accessories must be bought, borrowed, or even rented from

costume shops. In order to keep track of what you have, what you need, and where things will come from, you keep an Acquisitions List, entering each item in the appropriate column. Some costume designers attach this list to their costume plot. Others keep it separate so they can lend it to members of the costume crew. Use it faithfully. It will help you keep the details in your grasp.

Costume Plot

Name of Play _The Crucible by Arthur Miller_

The Time _1692_ **The Place** _Salem, MASS_

Act _One_

Reverend Parris (45 years old: a righteous man):
- _Black sleeveless gown with tabs and skullcap_
- _Black Pilgrim suit with collar, hat_

Thomas Putnam (40 years old: a wealthy man):
- _Pilgrim suit of fine cloth, white collar and pilgrim hat_

John Proctor (35 years old: a farmer):
- _Leather sleeveless jerkin, rough shirt and homespun Pilgrim suit (wears coat only for Trial scene)_

Abigail Williams (17 years old: niece of Reverend Parris):
- _Typical Pilgrim dress with white collar, cap_

Betty Parris (a young girl: daughter of Reverend Parris):
- _Nightclothes_

Keeping Track of It All

Be sure each actor's name is securely attached to the inside of each piece of clothing. Dressing rooms can be hectic during a performance, and costume pieces can get lost. Having the actor's name inside the costume can help in locating lost items. At the end of each evening's performance, be sure all costumes are hung neatly and all accessories are stored in the proper container.

When you're taking your show down, you'll need to return costumes that don't belong to the theatre. So don't just mark an item as bought, rented, or borrowed. Instead, use initials that tell you where the item came from. If you can, add a label to each item that tells where it must be returned.

Also, when you return any clean borrowed items, add a thank-you card signed by the cast and crew of the show.

ACTivity To help prepare the students to work on their costume design, try this exercise as a warm-up. Read several short scenes from a play. Draw a chart on the board—another way to begin a costume plot. Ask the students to help you fill out the chalkboard plot. Begin by listing the scene numbers, then the characters' names, then the costume pieces for each character, and then any accessories. The students might pull fabric swatches from your fabric box and explain why they would build a certain character's costume in a particular color or fabric.

From the Field: Heel to Toe

I never like to know what the budget is until I'm through with my design work. I have people who must be covered up with costumes. I need to solve the design problems first and the fiscal problems later. If I have to think about how much money I've got for shoes, that will be in my way while I'm drawing a heel.

Patricia Zipprodt, Costume Designer

Be sensitive to students' concerns about weight and body image. In our culture, young people are wrestling with eating disorders. The listing of weight and dress size may not be appropriate for the measurement cards if the cards are accessible to other students. Be careful to limit access to this information.

ACTivity **Beginning Students**
Have students practice their sewing skills. Give them a needle and thread and piece of fabric, preferably fabric in a solid color. Ask them to use a series of common stitches, such as the running stitch, a basting stitch, and a slipstitch. Consult a local fabric shop for books of various stitch techniques. What stitches are used for what purpose, and why?

ACTivity **Advanced Students**
Ask the students to design the costumes for a cartoon character, but tell them that the costume must be different than the comic book costume or the movie costume. Suggested characters might be Spiderman, Batman, Catwoman, or Superman. How would they design the costume for one of these characters that expresses the traits of the character but is not the familiar costume usually associated with the character?

Safe Practices for Costume Construction

Demonstrate safe practices for sewing machine operation and for steaming or ironing costumes.

Measurement Cards Take detailed measurements of each actor, and write them on measurement cards. Even if you're not building a costume, measurements are still important. They can help you pull, rent, borrow, or buy costumes that fit.

Some costume designers are turning to 3D modeling software to help them create designs. With these programs, they can enter the exact measurements of an actor and see from all angles how a costume would appear.

Costume Spaces To encourage continued organization, assign a hanger or piece of shelf space for each costume piece. Label the space so that anyone in the production can find any piece at any time. This will not only prevent losses, it will allow the costume crew to check costumes periodically for possible repair or cleaning.

Costume Parade When the costumes are almost finished, have each actor move onstage in costume. Ask for comments about the comfort, utility, and movement of the clothes and accessories. Be aware of how the lights play on the costumes. Take notes during the costume parade, and make final alterations so that there are no surprises on opening night.

Safe Practices for Costume Construction

Costume construction involves using some specialized tools, including the sewing machine. Always follow these safety practices when operating a sewing machine.
- Follow all the instructions for use in the owner's manual.
- Keep your eyes on the machine at all times.
- Keep a margin of about an inch between the needle and your fingers as you guide the fabric through the machine.
- Make sure the presser foot is down.
- Never use bent or damaged needles.
- Move the fabric through the needle at a slow, even pace.

You may also need to steam or iron a costume. Wear safety glasses and protect your hands with gloves coated with a heat-resistant material.

If you are supervising a costume crew, be sure your team knows how to safely use these specialized tools.

Quotable

Clothes do not make the woman, and the lack of them doesn't make the actress.

Carroll Baker, Actor

PREPARE

Costume a Character and Give a Talk

For this project, you will read a play and research the time and place it portrays. Your research will allow you to accurately develop a set of wardrobe designs for a character in the play.

1 Read a one-act or full-length play that has been approved by your teacher. After you have read the play once, choose a character to costume. Go through the script again and take notes from passages that provide clues to your character.

2 Research the time period of the play.

3 Using your research and notes from the script, make a list of colors, fabric, and decorations that will help define the time, place, and character.

4 Fill in the costume chart on the Activity Sheet for this chapter, which your teacher will provide.

5 Create from three to five drawings of costumes suitable for one character in the play. Draw each costumed figure as large as you can, then complete your sketches with colored pencils, pens, watercolor, or acrylic paint. Be sure your drawings are neat and detailed. For each costume, try to include a swatch of the material you would use.

6 If you feel your completed costume drawings will be too small for your classmates to see easily, scan them so they can be projected. Your teacher can help you with this.

7 Prepare a five- to ten-minute presentation on the costumes you have sketched. Begin with a short summary of the play and a description of the character's personality, age, and social status, as well as the mood and period of the play. The body of your talk should refer to the costumes you have created. Support your presentation of the costumes by describing the styles of the period and explaining why you chose the fabric, color, line, and decoration elements you did. Conclude with a summary.

8 Rehearse your talk before class so that you can give it in an interesting, fluid way. Stay within the ten-minute time limit.

Compile Your Technical Theatre Portfolio

The costume sketches you have made are ideal candidates for your portfolio, so be sure to keep them for that purpose. You can create a digital portfolio by scanning your drawings and using one of a number of portfolio-creation software programs. Some of them are even free.

You should also be creating a résumé as you add to your theatre experiences. Keep track of titles of productions you have worked on, your role in them, and the date and place of your involvement.

PREPARE

Costume a Character and Prepare a Talk

Go over each of the eight steps that students will take to complete this project. Have plenty of plays and scenes available for them to look through.

Meet with students individually after they have completed step 4 to be sure that they have gathered all the information necessary to begin their drawings.

Students who are not comfortable with having to draw should be encouraged to think of this step as a way to visually present their understanding of the costuming needs of the play. Remind them that their artistic skills will be evaluated only in so far as they relate to their interpretations of character, mood, time period, and theme.

Some students may find this project more enjoyable if they can work on a computer. Suggest that they transfer their designs into a PowerPoint® presentation. This exercise might also be done in small groups, with students working on the part of the presentation that employs their natural strengths.

Help any students who are having trouble with the time limit. If they are running too long, suggest ways they might cut information. If their presentations are running less than five minutes, suggest areas that need strengthening.

Backstage Gossip: A Midsummer's Nightmare

Even the greats can't always manage a dignified exit. Before the war, Vivien Leigh and Robert Helpmann starred in a production of *A Midsummer Night's Dream* in Regent Park. One evening several members of the Royal Family came to see the show. At the end of the performance, Leigh and Helpmann gave a special bow to the royal party and as they did so found to their horror that their elaborate headpieces had locked together and refused to part. Miss Leigh nestled in closer to Helpmann and the two of them were then forced to back offstage, smiling inanely at the royals as they went.

from *Great Theatrical Disasters* by Gyles Brandreth

PRESENT

Show and Discuss Your Costume Designs

Be sure that any students using PowerPoint® are well acquainted with its use in presentations. Have all necessary equipment functioning and ready for them.

Remind the students that they must be as good an "audience" member as they are a "performer" or presenter. Class presentation has much in common with performing, and being an active listener in class is much like being in the audience at a show. Active listening requires good manners, quiet concentration, and reflection. Tell students that you will be evaluating how insightful their questions to the speaker are.

Keep a stopwatch on hand to time the students. If they are getting close to the ten-minute limit, give them a warning to allow them time to reach the conclusion of their presentation without rushing the final sentences.

PRESENT

Show and Discuss Your Costume Designs

When your name is called, hand your costume designs or Activity Sheet to your teacher and go to the front of the class. Pause and look at the class before you begin to speak. With poise and with a pleasant, audible voice, present your costume designs. If your drawings are large enough, or if you have reproduced them as handouts or scanned them for projection, point to elements in each design and discuss their significance. If you complete your talk before the ten-minute time limit, ask the audience for questions. Answer any questions as thoroughly as you can.

TWELFTH NIGHT
Shakespeare Repertory Theatre

OLIVIA 2
WIRED SILK KIMONO

C.D.-723
COSTUME DESIGNER

Sketch and actual costume from a production of Shakespeare's *Twelfth Night*.

From the Field: The Gravity of the Situation

Once an errant chair escaped the rear end of an actor during a production of *She Stoops to Conquer*. The actor's trousers were merely safety pinned in the back of the waistband and the pressure from the fall caused the pin to pop open. When he stood up, his trousers did not.

I like to remind everyone that the laws of nature apply on stage as well.

Jamie Bullins, Designer, Stage Manager, and Assistant Professor of Theatre and Performance at Kennesaw State University, Kennesaw, Georgia

CRITIQUE

Evaluate a Classmate's Designs and Presentation

Choose a design presentation by one of your classmates and evaluate it on a scale of 1 to 5, with 5 being "outstanding" and 1 being "needs much improvement." Think about the appropriateness of the costumes and the thoroughness of the presentation. Ask yourself these questions as you prepare your critique:

- In what way are the costumes appropriate to the time and place of the play?
- What was memorable about the costumes in terms of the play's theme?
- What mood did the costumes evoke?

- What did the costume communicate about the personality and status of the character?
- How did the presenter use fabric, color, and decoration to support conclusions about the character in the play?
- How well did the speaker understand this character based on the costumes?
- How did the speaker present the important elements of the costumes?

Write a paragraph defending the number grade you gave this presenter. In a separate paragraph, evaluate your own creativity and explain how this project helped you develop your creativity as it relates to personal expression.

Career Focus

Costume Designer

Are you
(a) visionary   (b) creative
(c) hands-on   (d) practical
(e) all of the above?
If your answer is (e), the art of costume design might be for you. Costume designers need to understand or imagine the general style of people in various times, places, social positions, and occupations. They need to harmonize the differing styles in one production. They need to develop skill at drawing or using computer programs to draw silhouettes and costumes.

They need to learn enough about sewing to understand which designs are simple and which are complex. They also need to be able to beg, borrow, and shop for the cloth, costumes, and accessories they need—usually on a budget that is too small.

To develop these skills, you can read history or fantasy, or study costume books and historical photos and paintings. Learn to sew. Hold a period costume party and provide the clothes. Then volunteer to help out in a community theatre or school production in the costume department. Refer to the chart on page 10 for more ways to evaluate this career.

CRITIQUE

Evaluate a Classmate's Designs and Presentation

Give the evaluation rubric to the students as they begin their project so that they will know the criteria on which the evaluation will be based. Discuss each of the questions they should be thinking about as they listen to their fellow classmates' presentations. Remind them that they will be asked to defend their evaluations in a written paragraph.

Career Focus

Engage the students in a discussion of possible jobs related to costume design that would mean working outside the theatre. Possibilities are tailoring, alterations, fashion design, teacher, commercial design, store displays, convention design, photography, and fashion marketing. Ask the students to see how many jobs they can think of that are related to costume design.

Backstage Gossip: Heads Up!

It was the costume designer Irene Sharaff who probably gave the greatest impetus to Yul Brynner's career. When the practically unknown actor was cast for *The King and I* (1951) he was almost bald, but with a black fringe around the back and a few strands on top.

After discussing the costumes he asked what he should do about his hair. "Shave it!" said Miss Sharaff impulsively.

"Oh no! I can't do that," Brynner protested. He was worried about a dip on the top of his head. After the designer reassured him that she could always get him a wig if the operation proved unsuccessful, Yul Brynner shaved his head, rubbed his pate with oil, which became his personal trademark, and for a while at least made baldness sexy in America.

from *Broadway Anecdotes* by Peter Hay

Costumes Test

The test for this chapter is available in blackline master form in the Resource Binder, page 114.

For More Information

Books

Braun and Schneider, *Historic Costume in Pictures*, Dover Publications, Inc., 1975.

Covey, Liz, and Rosemary Ingham, *The Costume Technician's Handbook, Third Edition*, Heinemann, 2003.

Fernald, Mary, and Eileen Shenton, *Historic Costumes and How to Make Them*, Dover Publications, 2006.

Gorsline, Douglas, *What People Wore: 1,800 Illustrations from Ancient Times to the Early Twentieth Century*, Dover Publications, 1994.

Nunn, Joan, *Fashion in Costume 1200–2000*, New Amsterdam Books, 2000.

Vogue/Butterick Step-by-Step Guide to Sewing Techniques; Rev Upd ed. Sixth&Spring Books, 2013.

Other Media

Cutting It in Costume: Design and Wardrobe Management, DVD, Insight Media, 2009.

Fashion for the Theater, DVD, Insight Media, 2002.

Historic Costume: From the Renaissance through the Nineteenth Century, CD-ROM and book, Dover Publications, 2004.

www.costumes.org

www.costumedesignersguild.com

www.fashion-era.com

Apps

History of Fashion in America
Sewing Kit

Theatre Journal

Use the following as an additional or substitute prompt: Pretend you are a bright yellow bird. Write a description of yourself based on the color yellow. How would you describe your mood and character traits? What if you were an olive green bird? What would change concerning your mood and character traits based on this different color?

Additional Projects

1 Report on a specific costume period, such as ancient Rome or China, medieval or Renaissance Europe, feudal Japan, or the 17th, 18th, or 19th century in Europe or the United States. From your research, explain the reason for the style, its basic characteristics, and its accessories. Show pictures that will help you identify and analyze the function of the costumes in your chosen style and genre.

2 Using sheets, demonstrate correct draping of a Greek or Roman costume.

3 Prepare a multimedia presentation on the safe use of basic techniques of costume construction and the specialized tools, such as the sewing machine, associated with costume construction. Include a discussion of the skills needed to supervise a costume crew.

4 Prepare a chart showing the silhouettes of basic costume periods in America.

5 Report on women's shoes or another decorative element from Greek to modern times.

6 Develop your creativity by designing and creating a period costume that you might wear in a favorite play. Evaluate your creativity and personal expression in a paragraph accompanying the costume sketch.

7 Work with a small group. Read the scene in Unit Eight from either *Cyrano de Bergerac* by Edmond Rostand or "Baucis and Philemon" by Mary Zimmerman. Each person in your group should choose a character and design a costume for that character. Collectively, create a costume plot for the scene and explain how it would be read and interpreted in a production and serve as communication with the director.

8 Construct a portfolio of your theatrical experience to date. Exchange portfolios with a classmate and offer suggestions to one another on how they can be improved to make a good impression.

9 With a partner, articulate career and avocational opportunities for costume designers and evaluate the skills needed to pursue such opportunities. Create a graphic to demonstrate your evaluation.

10 **Theatre Journal** What are the style elements of your generation? Describe, and if possible, sketch, the shape or basic silhouette of the clothes you and your friends wear. Why do you think these styles are popular?

Substitute Teacher Activities

Here are a few suggestions for one or more days when you will be out of the classroom:

• Assign the Costume Design Worksheet on page 112.

• Assign one or more of the Additional Projects on this page.

• Teach the appropriate sections of Part Three, Costumes, pages 587–590, of the Student Handbook.

• **Students Design and Create a Hat.** Provide a selection of construction paper, scissors, felt tip pens, colored pencils, glue, glitter, beads, ribbon, feathers, fabric swatches, etc. Have the students design a hat that tells the others in the class something about themselves. Are they flamboyant, crafty, organized, a dreamer? Discuss with the students what visual clues might be needed to put these ideas into a three-dimensional object.

Master of the Craft

Julie Taymor

Director, designer, puppet master, and writer, Julie Taymor is involved in every creative aspect of making plays. Her work has been informed by her studies at Oberlin and at Bread and Puppet Theatre, and it has been deeply influenced by her travels in such locales as Sri Lanka, Paris, Indonesia, and Japan. Pulling together all these influences, Taymor has developed her creative vision.

Taymor launched her first major production, *Way of Snow,* which was based on Inuit legend, using both puppets and masks. Later she designed the set, costumes, puppets, and masks for *The Odyssey* at Baltimore's Center Stage. This successful production led to work with the New York Shakespeare Festival,

> *"Imagination is much better than reality."*
> —Julie Taymor

The American Repertory Theatre, and the La Jolla Playhouse, among others.

To date, Taymor has worked on theatrical productions as diverse as Wagner's *The Flying Dutchman,* Shakespeare's *Titus Andronicus,* and Disney's *The Lion King.* In film, she is most famous for directing *Frida,* about the artist Frida Kahlo.

Taymor has been called "one of the most imaginative and provocative directors in theatre arts today." Her work is effective because she knows what is important. In *The Lion King,* for example, she recalls an argument over whether to use real glass or fake plastic beads. Taymor explains, "I knew they had to be real even if the audience couldn't tell the difference. I knew that the people wearing the beads would know, and that the spirit . . . of craftsmen would be in the fabric and materials."

That spirit infuses Taymor's entire body of work, so that in her hands, theatre regains the magic of ritual and the wonder of make-believe.

Julie Taymor and her replica of the head of Titus Andronicus.

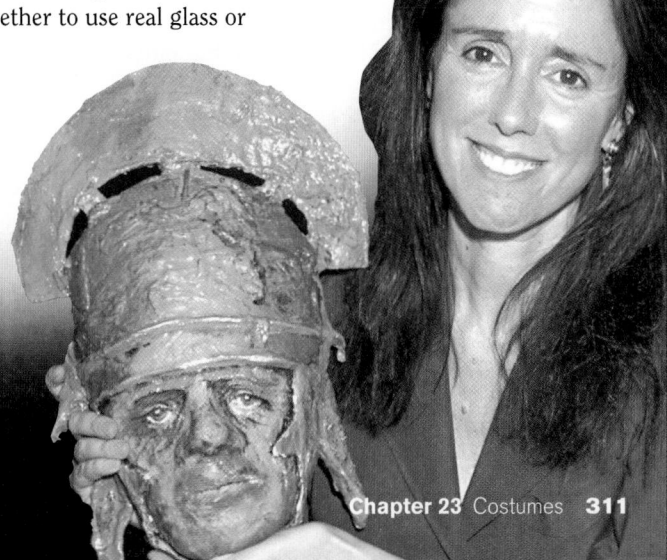

Quotable

You can lead actresses to water and drink, but you can't make them wear what they don't want to.

Edith Head, Costume Designer

Master of the Craft

More About Julie Taymor

Julie Taymor had this to say about the design of the costumes for The Lion King:

"During this developmental stage, one of my first tasks was to complete the designs of the hundreds of animals that populate the story. Having made the decision not to hide performers within animal suits or behind masks, the challenge was to convey the animals' essence while maintaining the presence of the human. I was particularly inspired by the minimalist way animals are portrayed in African art. The style meshed with my visual esthetic, and reaffirmed that one did not have to represent the whole of an animal's body in literal detail . . . The cut of the fabrics, their decorations, tones, and patterns, would evoke an animal's contours and surfaces without sacrificing the character's human qualities."

History and Costume Design: William Ivey Long

William Ivey Long is a four-time Tony winner for his costume designs for *Nine, Crazy for You, The Producers,* and *Hairspray.* In her article about Long for the Spring/Summer 2003 issue of *William & Mary,* Melissa V. Pinard states that the study of history taught Long "how to conduct historical research, which is essential for creating costumes." Long acknowledged that he would "recommend to anybody what I did—the study of history has so influenced my work."

For More Information

Books

Taymor, Julie with Alexis Green, *The Lion King: Pride Rock on Broadway,* Hyperion, 2003.

Blumenthal, Eileen, and Julie Taymor, *Julie Taymor: Playing with Fire,* 3rd ed. Harry N. Abrams, 2007.

Other Media

Behind the Scenes, Vol. 2: Theatre, Sculpture and Photography [includes Julie Taymor], DVD, First Run Features, 2002.

Theatre Then and Now
The Art of Costuming

Ancient Greece
The costumes in ancient Greek performances were quite elaborate, possibly long tunics and cloaks. The performers also wore masks that expressed a specific emotion.

Noh Drama
Stock characters were all dressed in very colorful, intricate, and elegant costumes in a Noh drama performance. Masks specific to each character were worn by the actors. The masks told the audience which character the actors were portraying.

16th-Century Italy
The stock characters of the *commedia dell'arte* wore costumes and masks that distinguished each character from the other. Dottore was a doctor or lawyer and wore an academic robe. Capitano wore a sword with his cape and an outlandishly embellished headdress. Arlecchino, or Harlequin, wore a suit with a blue, red, and green diamond-shaped design. The audience could tell what character was on stage by looking at the actor's costume.

17th-Century French Theatre
In France during the 17th century, the actors were responsible for providing their own costumes for the stage. However, this requirement was not difficult to accomplish as most costumes for the stage were contemporary clothing. Most actors could, therefore, simply wear their own garments.

Theatre Then and Now
The Art of Costuming

Costumes in the Middle Ages
Spectacle has always been part of the theatrical experience; in the late Middle Ages, it was sometimes the whole thing. Costumes were very elaborate—often intricately embroidered or bejeweled. Leather was used to clothe many a character—from the devil's body suit (equipped with tails and scales) to a young man's breeches—and angels often wore halos of gold. As the Middle Ages progressed in Europe, miracle plays, in which actors were costumed in elaborate Oriental or Byzantine costumes, evolved into morality plays, based on stories from the Bible.

In secular drama, the May Day games and Mumming plays, a kind of pantomime, of rural England drew crowds of folks to watch the antics. Tournaments in which royals and nobles could challenge each other to contests were also held in elaborate and rich costumes. Performers were often colorfully costumed as they sang and danced during the course of these tournaments.

Interludes, short and simple plays performed between longer and more serious

Mythic characters wore striking and amazing costumes in English masques, such as the costume Inigo Jones designed to represent a "Fiery Spirit."

presentations, grew ever more elaborate—and more popular. In England, they came to be called *masques*, and they were often sponsored by the court. Beginning in the early 1600s, English court masques were lavish and spectacular events held once or twice a year at court. Some of the costumes were designed by Inigo Jones, one of the most famous theatrical designers of all time.

For More Information

Books
Brooke, Iris, *English Costume from the Early Middle Ages Through the Sixteenth Century*, Dover Publications, 2001.

Buhrer, Michel, *Mummenschanz*, Rizzoli, 1986.

Cassin-Scott, Jack. *The Illustrated Encyclopedia of Costumes and Fashion from 1066 to the Present.* Cassell, 2006.

Crowfoot, Elizabeth, Frances Pritchard, and Kay Staniland, *Textiles and Clothing: Medieval Finds from Excavations in London, c.1150–c.1450*, Camden House, 2002.

Dryden, Deborah, *Fabric Painting and Dyeing for the Theatre*, Heinemann, 1993.

Norris, Herbert, *Medieval Costume and Fashion*, Dover Publications, 1999.

Thursfield, Sarah, *The Medieval Tailor's Assistant: Making Common Garments 1200–1500*, Quite Specific Media Group Ltd., 2001.

Costumes Today

Costumes serve different functions in different theatre styles and genres. Productions with simple fairy tale themes, such as *Cats, Beauty and the Beast,* and *The Lion King,* fill theaters with adults who marvel at the technical elements, including the costumes. Capes that look like wings, patterns that express character traits, and striking masks and headpieces have all contributed to the fantasy feel of the productions. William Ivey Long won a Tony Award for Costume Design in 2013 for his ingenious (and secret) way of instantly changing Cinderella's rags into a glittering ball gown right before the eyes of enchanted audiences.

Performance art and experimental theatre groups such as Mummenschanz expand the costume repertoire even further by creating costumes made of unusual materials such as brightly colored tubes and other shapes. The group has even used rolls of toilet paper to create witty and expressive costuming.

The performers in such dance-based and gritty productions as *Rent* and *Stomp* wear outfits that make extravagant use of color to define their characters.

By embracing fantasy and inventiveness, the costumes of today offer a feast not only for the eyes but for the intellect also.

Mummenschanz exhibits a creative approach to costuming.

Beth Fowler is cleverly costumed as Mrs. Potts in *Beauty and the Beast.*

ther Media

r a large selection of theatre supplies visit
ww.costumers.com and
ww.thecostumer.com.

sit the Mummenschanz group at
ww.mummenschanz.com.

Beauty and the Beast Trivia

The information that follows gives just a hint of what can be involved in a large-scale production such as *Beauty and the Beast.*

- The musical's Tony Award-winning costumes were worn and removed 201,000 times during Broadway's first 1,000 performances.

- Over the course of these same 1,000 Broadway performances, securing the 84 wigs and hairpieces that are worn during each show took 3,763 pounds of hairpins.

- The lighting design for *Beauty and the Beast* requires over 1.2 million watts—enough to light a football stadium.

- The fireball that the Enchantress uses, which transforms the prince into a beast, is a patented device that took over a year to develop, enabling her to hold the ball of fire in her hand without being burned.

- Lumiere uses about four pounds of butane fuel a month—that's an ounce of fuel per show per arm. The show uses six pounds of butane per month.

- Each of the 38-member cast wears a wireless microphone.

- When touring, the production uses 27 semitrailer trucks to move the production from city to city.

- During the first 1,000 performances on Broadway, champagne bottles in the musical number "Be Our Guest" used nearly two tons of explosives; that's 3,720 pounds of solid explosives and 187.5 pounds of liquid butane.

Chapter 24

Makeup

This chapter will introduce students to the techniques used by the makeup artist to create characters for the stage. Students will learn how to apply makeup and will discuss the process.

Objectives

1 to understand the job of the makeup artist

2 to understand the purpose of and techniques of applying makeup

3 to analyze a character for age make-up or character makeup

4 to apply character makeup creatively and safely

Project Specs

For this chapter you should have a basic supply of makeup for each student. The ideal would be to provide theatrical makeup, but that is not necessary to begin an exploration of makeup.

Advanced Students
To complete the project, the advanced student should be able to design and execute old-age makeup in addition to the character makeup required by the chapter project specs.

On Your Feet

Ask the students to continue this activity by drawing other faces with distinctive features. What emotions and disposition have the students drawn in these faces?

Chapter

24 Makeup

Women used to speak jokingly about "putting on their face." This is not a joke in the theatre, where skillfully applied makeup can enhance—even greatly alter—the image the actor projects.

Project Specs

Project Description You will apply character makeup and give a five- to ten-minute talk about the process.

Purpose to learn and use the principles of effective stage makeup

Materials hand-drawn makeup plan or the Makeup Activity Sheet provided by your teacher; standard makeup kit; character makeup items

On Your Feet

Using the chalkboard or large pad of paper, draw a face with a distinctive facial feature such as a raised eyebrow or pursed lips. Ask classmates to identify the personality characteristics they associate with the feature as you have drawn it.

Actress Kathryn Harries performs the role of the sorceress Kundry in Richard Wagner's *Parsifal*.

Theatre Terms

acetone
cake makeup
character makeup
collodion
complementary colors
creme foundation
crepe hair
makeup morgue
putty wax
spirit gum
stippling
straight makeup
water-soluble
  foundation

Theatre Terms

acetone a solvent used to remove spirit gum

cake makeup makeup that is pressed into a round container

character makeup makeup that completely changes an actor's appearance

collodion liquid used to make scars

complementary colors colors that are opposite each other on the color wheel

creme foundation a foundation with an oil base that stays on well

crepe hair artificial hair made of wool

makeup morgue a compilation of pictures of faces to use as a reference point when applying makeup

putty wax medium used to reshape areas of the body, particularly the nose

spirit gum an adhesive used for applying items such as a false beard to the face

stippling adding texture by using small, short strokes in applying makeup

straight makeup makeup that enhances natural features and coloring

water-soluble foundation makeup that can be washed off with water

Makeup: An Overview

In real life, people wear makeup to cover perceived flaws in their appearance. In the theatre, the purpose of **straight makeup,** that is, makeup that enhances natural features and coloring, is to make actors more visible and distinctive on stage. Applied well, makeup can both communicate a character's personality and enhance the actor's own features. Stage makeup can reflect the character's age, health, occupation, physical characteristics, and even attitudes. For example, a young character who plays tennis every day would probably have a ruddy or tanned face. An ancient scribe might look shriveled and wise.

The style and genre of the play and the size of the theatre space must be considered when determining how makeup

Cory Claussen wears straight makeup in this scene from the Des Moines Playhouse production of *Damn Yankees*.

is applied. If the play is realistic, the makeup should look natural to the audience. If the play is a fantasy or has many symbolic elements, then elaborate, imaginative makeup can be used to obtain special effects. If the actors are performing in a large space with strong lighting, makeup must be bold, even slightly exaggerated. Otherwise, their features may be "washed out" or made pale by the bright lights. In an intimate space, makeup should be subtle. As a rule of thumb, the objective is to create an acceptable effect for the first few rows of the audience while also making sure that the actor's face can be seen in the back rows.

Chapter 24 Makeup **315**

PREVIEW

Makeup: An Overview

First discuss with the students the difference between straight makeup and character makeup and the fact that the amount and type of makeup needed varies for a small, medium, or large stage.

ACTivity Divide the class into partners. Have a digital camera or two available to the students. Set each camera on the black-and-white mode and have students take several close-up shots of their partner's face. Print out the students' images on your computer. Ask the students to study their own photos and try to decide their face shape: round, square, oval, heart-shaped, rectangular, or diamond-shaped. Ask the students to describe what the shape of a face might mean in the design of makeup for the stage.

Visual Cue

Have students compare and contrast the pictures of Kathryn Harries in *Parsifal* and Cory Claussen in *Damn Yankees* and answer the questions that follow.

- What is the difference in their emotional states?
- How does their makeup define those emotions?
- What differences do you see in "character" makeup and "straight" makeup?
- What do you think the "style" is of both of the productions pictured?

Resource Binder
- Makeup Activity Sheet, p. 115
- Makeup Design Worksheet, p. 116
- Critique Sheet: Create Character Makeup, p. 117
- Makeup Test, p. 1180
- Character Makeup Form, p. 180

Handbook Connections pages 596–597

To Have on Hand
- Digital camera for student use
- Computer access
- Makeup kit
- Makeup books and articles
- Washcloths
- Mirrors
- Spotlight and large white paper
- Color wheel
- Gel swatches

Showing a clip from a movie that uses character makeup would be a good way to help develop interest in the topic. There are many movies that use special-effects makeup designers. Try to steer clear of too much gore, but movies such as *Planet of the Apes* and *The Lord of the Rings*™ are good examples of how makeup is used to develop character.

Applying Straight Makeup

Go over with the students the steps in applying straight makeup. You may want to choose a volunteer to work on as you model each step so the students can see how it is done. Another way to start is to have students work in groups of three, one reading the instructions, one applying the makeup, and the third being made up. They should alternate positions as they go through the steps.

ACTivity Divide the students into groups of three with the digital camera still set on the black-and-white mode. Give one of the students a large flashlight; give one of them the camera. The third student in the group will be the model. Have the student with the flashlight shine the light on the model's face to create shadows, while the student with the camera documents those shadows by taking pictures of the model's face. Let the students swap positions until each one has taken a turn at each job. Print out the pictures on your black-and-white printer. Give the students the photos of themselves. Using dark and light shades of makeup, students should make up their faces to match their photos. Remind the students that light tones and colors advance the features, while dark tones or colors make them recede.

The actor playing Elphaba in *Wicked* transforms into a youthful green-skinned witch before each performance.

While straight makeup is the norm, there are times when an actor must wear **character makeup,** additional makeup that changes his or her appearance drastically. A young person playing someone who is bald, bearded, or elderly will need character makeup, as will an actor portraying an animal, a gnome, or anyone with unusual features.

Most stage actors are closely involved in designing and applying their own makeup. They have developed a sense of facial bone structure and skin texture. They know faces. You too should try to be aware of faces—and how age, emotion, and other factors affect them. Most important of all, get to know your own face from crown to chin.

Applying Straight Makeup

Following are general instructions for applying straight makeup.

1 **Clean your face.** Remove all street makeup with either soap and water or cold cream and tissues. If you use cold cream, make sure it is completely removed before applying stage makeup. Also use a toning astringent to obtain a clean, dry face.

2 **Apply your foundation.** Use either **creme** or **water-soluble foundation** in a color that is close to your own natural skin tone. Creme, which comes in round plastic containers, blends well, holds up well when the actor sweats, and can be reworked until finally set with powder. Water-soluble foundation, also called **cake makeup,** is applied with a damp sponge, but washes off easily when sweating and is harder to blend. Most students usually find cremes easier to manage. Whichever you use, just be sure that the makeup you apply has a formula similar to your foundation. Apply creme with your fingers or a dry sponge wedge and cake with a damp sponge. Then blend smoothly and evenly. Cover all visible areas of your face, including the chin, neck, and ears. Fade out at least two inches down the neck to avoid a line at the jaw. Make sure there are no streaks.

3 **Add shadows.** Shadows of a darker color than the foundation are added to help emphasize the features of the face. This will help audience members sitting at a distance see the actor's facial features clearly. You can easily see the areas of the face that need shading:

- The cheek hollows are shaded to give them dimension.

Quotable

The most exciting kind of acting, to me, is when the actor is almost unrecognizable in the part.

Swoosie Kurtz, Actor

- Shadow below the jaw line to make it stand out from the face and neck.
- Add shadow to the crease above the eye to give the eye socket more dimension.
- Shadow the sides of the nose so it doesn't flatten.

4 **Add highlights.** Highlights of a lighter shade than the foundation are added next to further define the features of the face. Here too you can see the areas that need highlighting by following the contours of the face:

- Highlight directly under the brow to counteract the effects of overhead lights that tend to create hollows in the socket.
- Add highlights to the cheekbone to balance the shadows you added to the hollow of the cheek.
- Create subtle highlights down the ridge of the nose.
- Add subtle highlights to the chin area.

5 **Accent the eyes.** We've already shadowed the crease and highlighted the brow bone; now using an eyeliner pencil (which has a thicker form of creme), we will continue to define the eyes. Starting at the outside of the eye, draw a fine line along the roots of the lower lashes with a dark brown pencil or cake liner. Do not use black, as it looks hard and artificial. On the upper lid, start at the inside corner

With foundation and cake makeup already applied, shadows are added.

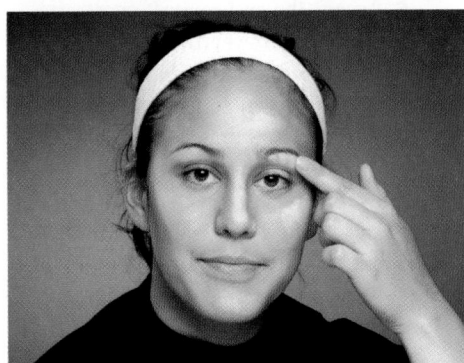

Highlights are now added to further accentuate bone structure.

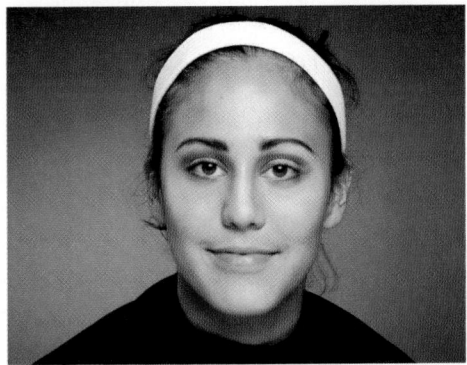

Eyeliner and mascara are added to bring out the eyes.

Chapter 24 Makeup **317**

Give students information about how the application of makeup differs depending on how close the actors are to the audience. While all actors will probably wear some kind of foundation, rouge, lipstick, and eye shadow to highlight their facial structure, the amounts will vary depending on the size of the stage.

Small Stage
Less makeup is used in general
Lighter colors for the cheeks and lips
Soft, light eye shadow

Medium Stage
More makeup in stronger colors
Highlights on the nose
Shading along the jowls

Large Stage
Same as above, but added highlights just below the brow
False eyelashes are optional

ACTivity Divide the students into small groups and let them practice applying the foundation, shadows, and highlights used for straight makeup. This will be more of a challenge for the boys, so try to pair boys with at least two girls.

ACTivity Have the students research makeup styles from past decades. What was the predominant makeup look for women in the 1920s? What did makeup look like in the 1950s? What was the most prevalent color used for eye shadow in the 1960s? How would the students describe the "punk" look from the 1970s and 80s? What is the style of makeup now?

Notes

_____
_____
_____
_____
_____
_____
_____

ACTivity Have students continue applying straight makeup to themselves. They should accent the eyebrows, apply rouge, accent the lips, and then dust the face with powder.

Once the students have completed their makeup applications, ask them to assess their work. Is everyone pleased with the results? If there are any students who felt out of their depth during this process, let them know that practice will improve the results dramatically.

ACTivity Ask students to bring in photos and works of art that they feel contain people with interesting facial structures. Using these pictures as a base, ask students to create a three-dimensional head from clay. The students can either make the head in the shape of a mask so that it can be hung on the wall, or they can create a "bust" type head to sit on a shelf. This activity will help the students become familiar with the human face and head. This is a good tool to help the students in their study of shapes, shadows, and contours.

Very basic sculpting lessons can be found at *www.kinderart.com*, and there are books available such as *Sculpting in Clay with Dale Power* available at *www.schifferbooks.com*.

(by the nose) and follow close to the lashes, extending the line about 1/4 inch beyond the outside corner. The bottom is the most important. On the lower lids, start the line at the outside and fade the line off at the middle of the eye. Do not go all around the edge. Apply one or two coats of brown mascara to all the upper lashes and to the outer portion of the lower lashes.

6 **Accent the eyebrows.** If necessary, darken your eyebrows to make them more visible. Using a medium or dark brown pencil, apply short, feathery lines drawn in the normal direction eyebrow hairs grow. Eyebrows should extend 1/4 to 1/2 of an inch beyond the eye to frame it properly. The heaviest color should be near the center, with the brows tapering at the outer end. Keep the effect soft and natural looking.

7 **Apply rouge.** Use rouge sparingly; a little goes a long way. Using your finger, dot the rouge in a crescent shape just below the cheekbone. Blend to soften all edges. The color should be strongest just below the cheekbone and should grow weaker as it moves away until it blends unnoticed into the base. There should not be a sharp delineation. For a healthy glow, males should carry rouge farther into the temples than females do, and farther down the jaw.

8 **Accent the lips.** Females should use lipstick made for stage use in a shade that matches their rouge. For a clean line, apply lipstick with a personal lipstick brush. To make lips smaller, draw the new shape using red lip-liner pencil. Then apply foundation and powder over the part of the lip you are eliminating. Men can either softly outline their lips with a brown pencil or apply a brownish-red moist rouge that they then gently wipe off, leaving only a suggestion of color.

9 **Apply the finish.** Use a powder puff to apply a thin dusting of translucent powder over the face. Remove excess powder with a powder brush. If necessary, touch up your cheeks and eyelashes.

Quotable

For an actress to be a success, she must have the face of a Venus, the brains of a Minerva, the grace of Terpsichore, the memory of [historian Thomas] Macaulay, the figure of Juno, and the hide of a rhinoceros.

Ethel Barrymore, Actor

Only amateurs appear outside the theatre in stage makeup. As soon as the play is over and curtain calls are complete, remove creme makeup with cold cream and facial tissue followed by soap and water.

Applying Character Makeup

The techniques for applying character makeup are more complex and time-consuming that those for straight make-up. Following are suggestions for the most common character makeup effects.

The Eyes and Brows With the use of shadows and liners, you can make the eyes appear larger, often indicating eagerness, innocence, or exuberance. You can make eyes appear sunken for an evil or threatening look. Eyebrows, as a natural frame to the eye, can do a lot to establish character. Changing the position or size of the eyebrows will create a character. To change the shape, you must first mask out all or part of your own brow. Block out and highlight your natural brows with foundation, or rub them with a cake of very wet soap. When they are dry, apply foundation over them and draw new brows in the desired position and shape. **Crepe hair,** artificial hair made of wool, can be added to make the brows bushier. The sketches at the right indicate a few of the eyebrows you can create.

Common Character Eyebrows

Normal

Sad/Pathetic

Evil

Surprised/Innocent

Mischievous

Applying Character Makeup

The Eyes and Brows
With the students, discuss all the character eyebrows on this page. Ask students to try to replicate these looks by manipulating their brow area. Then discuss how much more impact actually creating these eyebrows would have when playing a character with each of these characteristics.

Discuss familiar characters from plays the students have read and assign eyebrows to these characters. Examples might be:

- Puck= Mischievous
- Hamlet = Sad/Pathetic or Normal
- Iago = Evil
- Ophelia = Surprised/Innocent or Sad/Pathetic

ACTivity Have students work in pairs to create a character for one another using basic makeup and character eyebrows. They may also choose to add costume elements to create their character's look. When they are in character, the rest of the class must guess who they are.

ACTivity Divide the class into partners. Each student will take a turn as model and as artist. One student will sit in profile against the wall on which you have taped a large piece of white paper. Shine a bright light at the student so that the student's shadow is cast upon the paper. The other student will now trace the model's shadow on the paper to make a silhouette. Be sure all of the students are at about the same distance from the paper so that all the shadows will be about the same size. Hang these silhouettes on your classroom wall. Ask the students why shadow and light are important in stage makeup. Does the brightness of the light and its distance from the student affect the picture that is cast on the wall? How?

Backstage Gossip: He Knows the Nose

Actor Hal Holbrook, in his brilliant recreation of Mark Twain, is as meticulous in his makeup as in his acting. No detail is too small or too unimportant to be given careful attention each time the makeup is applied. And for every performance he devotes more than three hours to perfecting those details . . . . Mr. Holbrook says . . . . "His nose was very distinctive . . . the nose alone takes an hour . . . ."

from *Stage Makeup* by Richard Corson

The Nose, Mouth, and Hair

Discuss the various ways that the size of a nose and mouth can be changed and the materials used to help the makeup artist do so. Talk about what clues someone's hairstyle might give about that person. What era would you assume a woman with "big hair" piled high, teased, and sprayed might be representing in a play?

Show, Don't Tell Show the film *Roxanne*, starring Steve Martin. Then read the "nose" soliloquy from Edmund Rostand's *Cyrano de Bergerac*. Compare these same two scenes in the film and the play. Finally, discuss the makeup used on Steve Martin in the film to create his character's nose.

ACTivity Brainstorm with the students to make a list of all the types of noses, such as pug nose, crooked nose, witch's nose, Jimmy Durante's nose, etc. Make a "nose" art gallery for your classroom. Have the students cut noses from magazines or have the students draw pictures of different noses. Make captions for the nose gallery from various plays. Let the students find all the lines from Shakespeare that have to do with smell or noses, such as:

"A rose by any other name would smell as sweet." *Romeo and Juliet*

"I smell sweet savours . . . ."
The Taming of the Shrew

". . . and will as tenderly be led by the nose." *Othello*

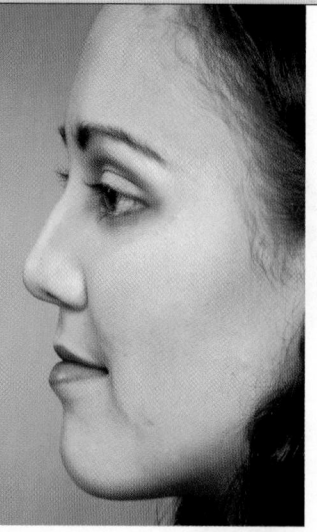

The actor with her natural nose.

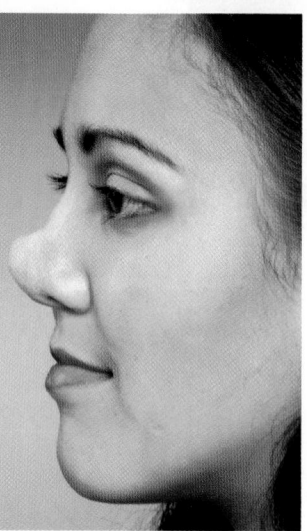

The same actor with an upturned, puckish nose.

The Nose and Mouth

You can vary nose proportions with shadow and highlighting, or you can create a three-dimensional change such as a large, upturned, or misshapen nose with **putty wax** (also called derma wax or nose putty). Prepare the putty by gently kneading it with your fingers until it is soft and pliable. Next apply **spirit gum** adhesive to a clean area of the nose. Embed a few fibers from a cotton ball into the spirit gum to create a "rug" to hold the wax onto your nose. Form the wax into the desired shape using the back of your thumb and place it over the dried spirit gum rug, molding it to the shape of your nose. Smooth out the edges until they blend into the face, and cover the wax with makeup as needed. This may take a bit of practice. Use hair gel to smooth the overall surface. To remove the nose, pull a thread tight and run it along the area under the wax.

You can alter the size of the mouth and change its expression by painting the corners up to suggest happiness or painting them down to indicate sadness, pain, or meanness.

Hair Hair can be slickly combed, messy, or elaborately coiffed as an indication of the character's personality. Women can make their hair look longer by using hairpieces or extensions. Men should get an appropriate haircut three to four weeks before performance and then let their hair grow until after the show. Sprays, gels, and pastes can be used to "mold" the hair into the desired style. To change hair color, use temporary tints found in drugstores. For gray, use a liquid hair whitener. A bald head is achieved with the use of a rubber skullcap. Since wigs are expensive to rent and difficult to fit, avoid them if possible.

Beards and Mustaches Before you apply a beard, observe men who have them. You will notice that facial hair has certain boundaries and that it grows forward under the chin and downward at the sides. It is thinner where the growth starts and becomes thicker farther down on the face. If your character hasn't shaved in a few days, create a stubble effect by **stippling,** or dabbing the face with gray-blue makeup.

Backstage Gossip: Something's Fishy

[Orson] Welles always wore a false nose when he was working on stage, largely because he hated his own and in one performance of *Moby Dick*, while Ahab was delivering one of his big speeches, the nose began to fall apart. "Tell him his nose is falling off," hissed one actor to another. It was too late. The nose had beaten them to it and was already slipping down over Welles's mouth. As the great actor screamed, "Get that white whale, men!" the nose dropped off completely, landed at his feet, and was sent curling into the audience with a deft drop-kick.

from *Theatrical Anecdotes* by Peter Hay

Here's How
To "Grow" Beards and Mustaches

To prepare crepe hair for your beard, unbraid the amount and colors you'll need. To straighten the kinks, dampen the hair, put it between two pieces of muslin or other light cloth, and press it with an iron. Since beards are rarely one solid color, combine the colors needed and then comb the pressed hair.

When applying beards:

1 Be sure the face is shaved and the part to be covered is free of foundation.

2 Define the bearded area by applying spirit gum. If you want to use the beard again, apply 2 layers of liquid latex as a base.

3 Hold a small piece of crepe hair in your hand and cut the ends on an angle. Do not use too thick a piece of hair, but have it longer than the desired finished length.

4 Paint a second coat of adhesive just above the larynx and apply a layer of hair, sticking it out toward the front. Hold until it is dry.

5 In this same manner, cut the hair, apply the adhesive, and work up in layers—like shingles on a roof—until the front of the chin is covered with hair pointing down. Continue until you reach the desired shape.

6 When completed, let spirit gum get completely dry, then gently comb out any loose hairs. Shape it into the desired style, and do a final trim. A light coat of hairspray will help it hold its shape.

7 At the top of each beard, you may need to pencil in hairs to blend the beard's edge so that it looks natural.

To create a mustache, complete steps 1–3 above. Then apply the hair at the outer corner of the lip. Work in several layers toward the center. Follow the lip line. Hold each layer in place until dry. Comb and trim.

1. Cover under the chin, pointing the hair out.

2. Add more crepe hair and cover the chin, pointing the hair down.

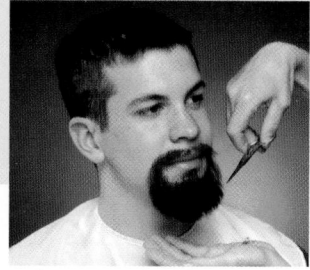

3. Cover the sides, pointing hair down, and trim to shape the beard.

Chapter 24 Makeup **321**

Here's How

Show, Don't Tell Use one of your male students as a model and show the class how you would go about building a beard. Talk about where you buy crepe hair and let them feel it before you press it. Show them how to blend colors to match your model's hair color, and then proceed to layer and trim the beard.

Have *www.anniescostumes.com* available on the class computer or give the address to the students so that they might see the images of different types of mustaches found on the site. In addition, bring in images of famous men who wore mustaches, such as Charlie Chaplin, Wyatt Earp, Theodore Roosevelt, and Fu Man Chu. Let the students study the distinctive characteristics of each. Then pass out the crepe hair.

ACTivity Pair up students, one male and one female or two males, and give them enough crepe hair to make a mustache. Ask them to research the kind of mustache they would like to create. Have them follow steps 1 through 3 to create their mustache, and encourage them to experiment. If time permits, let each of the males in a two-man pair try this activity.

Notes

Scars, Missing Teeth, and Stage Blood

Give students a chance to experiment with scars, missing teeth, and stage blood by supplying the necessary ingredients. When students have created a character using one of these elements, ask them to present a short scene involving this character (perhaps joining up with other students to create an ensemble presentation).

Aging a Face

ACTivity Have the students bring in pictures of themselves as well as pictures of the women or men (based on the gender of the student) in their families. Suggestions for a female: your mother at different ages in her life, your grandmother, your mother's sisters, you as a child, you now. Students should then compare and contrast the photos to see how the aging process works on the members of their family. Talk to your mother, father, or other family members about how they have perceived their own aging process. What does age do to skin tone and coloring? Based on your research, what might you look like when you get older?

Scars To make a fresh scar, build up the center of the scar in an irregular shape with putty wax or tissue and liquid latex. If a healed scar is desired, apply three to four coats of nonflexible, or rigid, **collodion,** a clear, thick liquid, directly to the skin, drying between each coat. Collodion will give a drawn, indented look. Collodion can irritate the skin, so be very careful and try a small test patch first. Remove collodion with **acetone,** which can be found in common nail polish remover. Follow the cleaning by applying skin moisturizer.

Missing Teeth To make teeth look like they are missing or broken, use black tooth enamel or black wax directly over the teeth.

Stage Blood Below is the standard recipe for stage blood:

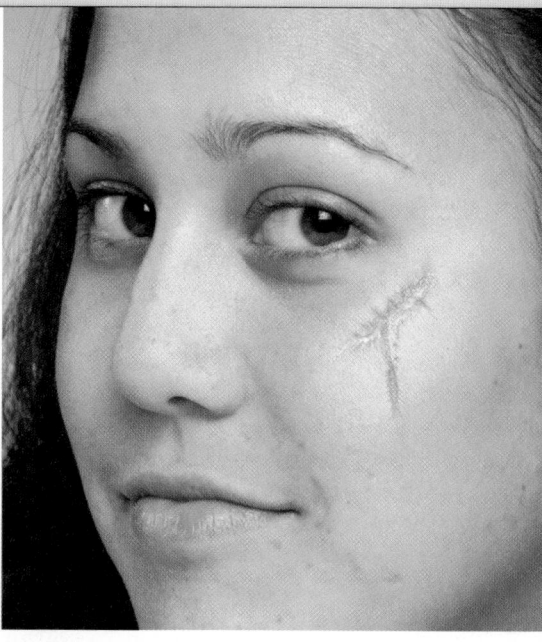

This scar was created using nonflexible collodion.

> ### Recipe for Gore
>
> One 16-oz. bottle of corn syrup
> One tablespoon red food coloring
> 1/4 cup liquid laundry detergent
> Blue food coloring
>
> - Mix first three ingredients in a jar.
> - Add blue food coloring, one drop at a time, to achieve the desired color.
> - Shake well before using.
> - Keep jar shut tightly between uses.

Aging a Face

As people age, the flesh sags around the bone structure. Wrinkles form, the texture of the skin changes, and the contours of the face shift and sag. All of these features can be reproduced on young actors through sculpting in the contours that begin to form using highlights and shadows.

Remember that age occurs gradually. When applying makeup, you must guard against making yourself look older than your character actually is. If you are playing someone who is forty or so, you will need different makeup than playing someone who is over sixty. To look in your forties, apply darker rouge lower down on the cheeks to indicate the beginning of sagging facial muscles.

Backstage Gossip: Is There a Dentist in the House?

[Actor] Richard Dennis who was appearing in *Murder by Murder* had a small pouch of stage blood secreted in his mouth so that when he was punched at the end of Act II, a trickle of blood could dribble down his chin. Unfortunately, the pouch burst at the beginning of Act II and he had to stay on the stage for forty minutes constantly apologizing to the other characters for his relentlessly bleeding gums.

from *Great Theatrical Disasters* by Gyles Brandreth

Shadow softly in the eyebag area. Begin a soft shadow in the crease that runs from your nostrils toward your mouth (the smile line). Use less lipstick if you are a female and brown liner if you are a male.

To appear in your fifties or sixties, increase the darkness of the sculpted shadows under the eyes and smile lines, follow this by adding wrinkles, which should accent the natural lines on your face. Frown and then smile, or make a characteristic expression, and then outline the natural wrinkles that appear with liner. Break up the texture of your skin by stippling the surface slightly by using a sponge and a darker base color.

Eye pouches should be more pronounced the older the character. Indicate facial hollows and sags with brown shading, and subtly highlight them with white.

Emphasize wrinkles in the forehead, around the eyes, and from the nose to the mouth. Gray the hair at the temples, and add a few gray streaks elsewhere for more aging. Apply gray to eyebrows also.

Spotlight on

The Makeup Morgue

A **makeup morgue** is a visual reference tool for creating special makeups. To create one for yourself, page through magazines and cut out any interesting faces you find. Glue each picture to a blank page, and label it with a designation that tells how you might use it, i.e., as an example of age, gender, race, skin texture, eyebrows, mouth, and so forth.

After you have gathered enough images, organize them by category and put them in a binder or accordion file. As it continues to grow, your makeup morgue will become a rich resource for future makeups.

ACTivity Have the students use makeup to practice three different designs for aging mouths, cheekbones, and chins. Have them begin with a 50-year-old person, progress to a 60-year-old, and finish with someone who is 70 years old. Have them focus on adding contours to the cheeks, chin, and mouth to show advancing age.

Spotlight on

The Makeup Morgue Bring in samples of makeup morgues for students to look through. Get them started on creating their own morgues.

ACTivity Ask students to choose a favorite character from a play, book, or movie. Have students draw an image of the character as though this character were in a play, using all they know about applying makeup.

Quotable

Father Time is the make-up man responsible for the physical changes that determine the parts the average actor is to play.

Fred Allen, Comic Actor

Create a Very Old Face

Go through each of the steps for creating a very old face with the students. You might want to use a drawing of a face on the chalkboard to illustrate some of the techniques indicated.

ACTivity Give students the opportunity to try to age a partner by following the steps for aging a face on this and the following page. Be sure they use the partner's makeup kit. Be available to assist any students having trouble getting the right effect.

Show, Don't Tell Get a copy of *Mark Twain Tonight*, starring Hal Holbrook (DVD available from *www. amazon.com*). Show selected scenes of Mr. Holbrook performing the role of Mark Twain. Mr. Holbrook was considerably younger than the character he played. Engage the students in a conversation about how they would play an old man or woman. How would makeup contribute to the aging process? What would they need to do with their bodies and voices?

Foundation and sculpting shadow is first applied to the face.

Highlights are added and blended.

Create a Very Old Face

1 Apply a pale creme foundation—lighter for a frail character and darker for a healthy character.

2 With the fingertips and a brown liner, add soft shadows to
   a eye sockets
   b indentations below the cheek bones
   c hollows at each temple
   d the sides of the nose
   e the corners of the mouth
   f under the jaw and chin
   g the depressions on both sides of the throat

3 Using off-white liner for highlights above each shadow, apply soft highlights to the bone
   a over each eyebrow
   b in each cheek
   c at the point of the chin
   d along the line of the lower jaw
   e at the throat

4 To further define wrinkles, use brown liner to create them where they naturally form
   a on the forehead
   b between the eyebrows and outer eye corners (worry lines and crow's feet)
   c in the smile lines from the nose to the corners of the mouth

5 With off-white liner on a brush, highlight below all the wrinkles.

6 With the fingertips, blend the edges of the highlight, shadow, and base.

7 Thin the lips using a dark reddish color. Stipple rouge, and apply texture (e.g., liver spots) if desired. Allow a thin portion of the natural lip to show.

Backstage Gossip: Makeup Maestro

Once during a matinee at the Haymarket Theatre, [actor Beerbohm] Tree, made up as Falstaff, met Coquelin in the wings. The great French actor was tremendously impressed by the way Tree had made up his features. "Pardon me," he said, "but how do you pad your cheeks?" Tree invited him to touch them. Coquelin did so and with a mild French oath exclaimed: "Why there is nothing!" Tree's effects were gained not by padding and such like devices, but simply by sheer skill as a grease-paint artist.

from *Theatrical Anecdotes* by Peter Hay

Lips are made thinner and hard edges are added around the eyes.

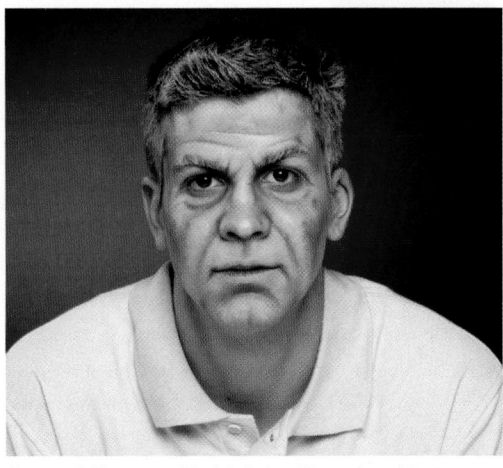

Deep wrinkles are added, hair is whitened, and liver spots can be added.

8 Whiten hair and eyebrows. Make eyebrows bushy by brushing them the wrong way. Apply whitener at temples as desired.

9 Powder creme makeup.

Makeup Essentials

Every student of acting should have his or her own makeup kit. This is not only more convenient but hygienic. Many actors outfit a fishing tackle box or toolbox. You should purchase a small makeup kit made for students. Theatrical makeup companies sell them inexpensively. Makeup can get expensive, however, so use only what is necessary, and always replace lids tightly.

The Language of THEATRE

Use visuals and context clues to help you build vocabulary and better understand what you read.

- Look for the terms *character makeup* and *straight makeup* in headings or photo captions in the chapter. Use the visuals and context to help you understand the meaning of the terms.

- Skim the section Applying Straight Makeup on pages 316–318 by reading headings, looking for boldface theatre terms, and studying the visuals and captions. Then read the section.

- Review the theatre terms on page 314 before you read the chapter. Then look for visuals and context clues as you read to enhance and confirm your understanding of their meaning.

- As you read the chapter to prepare for your *character makeup* project, notice how you use visuals and context clues to help you understand challenging language.

Makeup Essentials

Continue discussing old-age makeup and then show students your own makeup kit. Talk about the items you consider essential, how to care for each product, where you find the items, and so on.

ACTivity In class, read some selections from T. S. Eliot's *Old Possum's Book of Practical Cats* to the students. Then ask them to design the makeup for several of the cats, such as Gus the Theatre Cat, Grizabella the Glamour Cat, or Rum Tum Tugger, based on how they are described in the poems. Encourage students to see a production of Andrew Lloyd Webber's musical *Cats,* which is based on the book, onstage or on DVD or video. Compare the students' designs to the ones used in the musical.

The Language of THEATRE

Review the photo captions on pages 317–325 with students and invite them to point to the parts of each photo that relate to specific words in the captions. Ask students to notice words that are repeated in several captions and identify words that will be most useful in building their English vocabulary.

Quotable

The ideal makeup artist has the eye of the caricaturist, the hands of the sculptor, the brush of the portrait painter, and the curiosity of the student.

Greer Garson, Actor

List of Makeup Essentials

Look over the list of makeup essentials on this page with the students. Have them open their makeup kits and check to be sure they have all of the items listed—at least those for straight makeup. Let students know of stores you are aware of in town that sell any of these items at reasonable prices.

ACTivity Take your students to a play that you know incorporates a lot of makeup technique at a community or professional theatre. Tell students to pay particular attention to the actors' makeup. Then, back in the classroom, have them describe the use of makeup in the show. Did the makeup characterize the roles? Did it help the audience understand the occupation, age, lifestyle, or social status of each character? Why or why not? Was most of the makeup straight makeup, or was character makeup used also? Were the makeup choices effective for the production?

ACTivity Schedule a "wacky hands" day in your class. Ask the students to design a weird and wacky makeup application for use only on their hands. The design can complement their old-age makeup project by designing old-age hand-makeup to go with their faces. Or they can be wild and crazy and design the hands for any fantasy creature they desire. Celebrate their creativity with a "finger foods party." Have everyone wear their weird hand-makeup and bring a food item to contribute to the party.

The Essentials for Straight Makeup

1 **Foundation** in creme or cake. Include white, light, and medium shades.

2 **Liners (highlight** and **shading colors)** give the face a three-dimensional effect by providing shadows and highlights. Basic liners are black, brown, maroon, yellow, off-white, and blue.

3 **Lipsticks** in shades of red for women and a brownish shade for men.

4 **Rouge** in red or medium-red for women; reddish-brown for men.

5 **Powder (and puffs)** sets creme so it won't smudge or create a glare under the lights. Choose a shade lighter than the foundation, or use a translucent powder you can apply over any foundation.

6 **Eyebrow pencils** to darken eyebrows and line eyes. Use either medium or dark brown.

7 **Fluff brushes** to apply dry rouge, powder, and eye shadow and to remove excess powder.

8 **Lining brushes** made of sable to line the eyes and to give the appearance of wrinkles and to paint the lips. A common size is 3/16-inch or 1/4-inch.

9 **Mascara** in dark brown.

10 **Cold cream** for removing makeup.

11 **Miscellaneous** sponges, hand mirror, thread, scissors, soap, comb, tissue, brush cleaner, cotton balls, and a pencil sharpener.

The Essentials for Character Makeup

1 **Putty wax** for making false noses, warts, scars, and so forth.

2 **Liquid latex** liquid rubber that can be used for building up facial features such as chins, jowls, noses, eye pouches, and scars and for attaching crepe hair.

3 **Nonflexible collodion** a clear, thick solution used on the skin to make scars.

4 **Crepe hair** for fashioning beards and mustaches. Choose several colors, including gray and one that is close to your own color.

5 **Spirit gum** an adhesive for attaching hair, false noses, scars, and so on.

6 **Rubbing alcohol** to remove spirit gum and **acetone** to remove collodion.

7 **Hair whitener** liquid or spray.

Notes

Makeup Hygiene and Safety

For the sake of safe hygiene, it is strongly recommended that you have your own makeup kit and use only your own makeup. Be sure to have a good supply of:

- sponges
- powder puffs (or cotton balls)
- tissue
- soap or cleanser

Sponges should be thrown away after each use. Take a tissue and clean the surface of all makeup before using it. Although a liquid brush cleaner is available and is certainly effective, you may also clean your brushes in hot, soapy water. Clean them after every use. You may be tempted to borrow someone else's lipstick. This is not recommended, but if you are careful, you can use a cotton swab to remove a small amount of lipstick from another's tube (after wiping the area with a tissue first). Apply a small dab of the lipstick from the swab to your own lip brush.

Also be aware that you should never take makeup directly from containers with your fingers. Instead, squeeze a bit of makeup onto a paper towel or use a small spatula to remove a bit of makeup from jars, pots, sticks, or tubes. Always keep the lids securely closed. Wash your hands well with soap and water before applying your makeup. If you are supervising a makeup crew, help every member know and practice these rules of makeup safety.

Makeup Hygiene

Read over this section with the students to impress upon them the importance of good hygiene in drama class. Discourage sharing of any makeup. Demonstrate for them how to use a spatula for lipstick, rouge, and so on, and show them the correct way to use foundation and powder. Also be sure to alert students that they should do a patch test on the inside of the arm 24 hours before using any new product on the face.

Share the following rules with the students. You might also want to make a copy and post it in the dressing rooms.

Dressing Room Dos and Don'ts

- No food or drink in the dressing room. Water is allowed in a closed container.
- Never borrow and never share makeup.
- Go outside to use hairspray or other aerosol sprays. Do not wear perfume. Some people are allergic to strong odors—aerosol sprays can be very irritating.
- Pay attention to your own personal hygiene. Bathe every day and use a deodorant. Dressing rooms are close quarters, and running from scene to scene can make the room seem even smaller if others haven't showered.

Backstage Gossip: The Bright Blue Tin Man

Why did Jack Haley replace Buddy Ebsen as the Tin Man during the production of the film classic *The Wizard of Oz?* Because the aluminum dust in Ebsen's makeup turned him bright blue and sent him to the hospital with respiratory problems.

Always Adjust Makeup to Lighting

Bring in a large color wheel (or use the one on page 239) and discuss it with students. Tell them that a color wheel is arranged so that primary colors (red, yellow, or blue) are separated by the secondary colors (orange, violet, and green—and for the purposes of lighting, pink). Primary colors cannot be mixed from other elements, but two primaries can be mixed to obtain a secondary color.

Complementary colors are color opposites. These colors contrast with one another. They also help to make one another more active. In a color wheel, complementary colors are opposite one another. So, green and red are complements, blue and orange are complements, and violet and yellow are complements.

ACTivity Give students gel swatches and a strong light source (such as a spotlight). Have a volunteer who has been made up in either straight or character makeup position his or her face under the light. Have students experiment with the effect on the face and makeup of different colored gels. Do pink lipstick and rouge look better under the red gel? Does rouge need to be heavier under a strong amber gel? What does a green gel do to a person's face? Have students keep notes and report their findings to the class.

ACTivity For a library of ideas to use for nonrealistic makeup, have students cut out pictures of insects, flowers, animals, trees, birds, snakes, spiders, and other interesting plants or animals. They can keep these pictures in their makeup morgue for inspiration when they must devise fantasy makeup.

The illustration above shows the effect of various colored lights on a color wheel.

Always Adjust Makeup to Lighting

Colored lights dim similar colors on stage and completely darken **complementary colors** (those colors opposite each other on the color wheel). Use these techniques to adjust makeup to the existing lighting.

- A red light subdues red makeup and makes green look black. Consequently, if you have red lights on stage, you'll need to apply heavy pink base and a rouge with a blue tint.

- If you have strong amber stage lights, apply rouge heavily and use a pink base, since amber "eats up" red.
- With blue lights, the reds look purple or black, so for a blue moonlight scene use a light foundation and very little rouge.
- Since green light makes the face look ghastly, it is rarely used unless that effect is needed.

Backstage Gossip: Harry's Hoax

One day during the production of the film *Harry Potter and the Sorcerer's Stone*, Daniel Radcliffe, who played Harry Potter, arrived on the set with immense bruises all over his face. He explained that he had been in "a bit of a scuffle." According to Robbie Coltrane, who played Hagrid in the film, the makeup designer "had a minor heart attack . . . before she figured out it was a hoax."

PREPARE

Apply Your Makeup

For your project, you will apply character makeup to yourself to achieve the look of an older or unusual character. You may prefer a character who is more animal than human, such as the creatures in Edward Albee's *Seascape*. Whichever character you choose, be sure to think about this character seriously before you begin experimenting with makeup. You will want to do a bit of research into the time period of the play and read closely any descriptions of the character in the script. Keep notes, and use this information as you create your character. Follow these steps to complete the project.

1 Create a character makeup sheet like the one below or use the Activity Sheet for this chapter, which your teacher will provide. Consider what colors you should use based on your own face, the play's time period and setting, the character you are portraying, the size of the performance space, and the lighting conditions.

2 Secure a makeup kit.

3 Prepare a desk or table at home by spreading papers over it and placing it near a light source. Lay out your makeup, including cold cream, facial tissues, and a large mirror. Wear a smock or old shirt to protect your clothes. Tie your hair back if necessary.

4 Use the step-by-step procedure for applying your makeup found on the previous pages. As you proceed, keep notes as to what you are doing and why. Then practice explaining your choices to the class within the five- to ten-minute framework.

Character Makeup Sheet

Name: _____   Date: _____

Character/Description

Materials	Color	Directions
foundation		
shadows		
highlights		
eyes		
rouge		
lips		
powder		

PREPARE

Apply Your Makeup

Give students the Makeup Activity Sheet, page 97, as well as the Character Makeup form on page 150 of the Resource Binder. Before they begin to work on their makeup, go through the directions and your expectations step by step. Explain to the students that research and note-keeping are both an important part of this project. Be sure the students have an adequate supply of makeup to accomplish the goals of the design.

Remind the students to take pictures of their makeup designs and to keep them safely stored in their portfolio. A portfolio is not only a tool for college entrance; it is also a lifelong souvenir of all the work done and all the new ideas learned in the field of theatre.

From the Field: Work from the Outside In

I am the kind of person who tends to work from the outside in. I like to think of the way a person looks, and how I'm going to fit into her walk and mannerisms. Then I start building the character's inner self within that framework.

Frances Sternhagen, Actor

PRESENT

Discuss Your Makeup Choices

Keep a stopwatch on hand to time the students. If they are getting close to the ten-minute limit, give them a warning to allow them time to reach the conclusion of their presentation without rushing the final sentences.

If time allows after students have presented their makeup artistry, ask them to share with the class how they arrived at their artistic choices for this character.

CRITIQUE

Evaluate a Classmate's Makeup and Presentation

Remind students that they must be as good an "audience" member as they are a "performer" or presenter. Class presentation has much in common with performing, and being an active listener in class is much like being in the audience at a show. Active listening requires good manners, quiet concentration, and reflection.

Go over with the students the questions they should be asking themselves as they critique fellow classmates. Remind them that they are not only evaluating how well the makeup was applied, but how appropriate this makeup is to the character.

PRESENT

Discuss Your Makeup Choices

When your name is called, walk throughout the classroom in such a way that all your classmates and your teacher can get a good look at your makeup. Continue to the front of the class. Describe the character you are representing. If you prefer not to come to class in makeup, record and edit the process of applying character makeup and show it to the class with live narration. Or you could bring in "before" and "after" photographs showing your makeup process. Be prepared to explain to the class how you achieved your character's look.

Whichever way you choose to present your final character makeup, be sure to use your notes and makeup worksheet or the Activity Sheet to talk about the considerations that went in to the makeup choices you made. Be sure your talk does not exceed ten minutes.

CRITIQUE

Evaluate a Classmate's Makeup and Presentation

Evaluate a classmate's makeup as well as the reasons behind the makeup, on a scale from 1 to 5, with 5 being "outstanding," and 1 being "needs much improvement." Ask yourself these questions:

- How effective is the actor's makeup when viewed fairly closely?
- Is the effect of the actor's makeup visible from a distance?
- In what ways does the makeup represent the character?
- What other choices could have been made to better bring out the character?
- How well did the presenter explain the reasons for applying the makeup in this way?

Write a paragraph that tells why you gave this classmate the rating you did.

Career Focus

Makeup Artist

Makeup artists are employed in professional theatres and for film and video productions, as well as in photo studios that do actors' headshots and commercial photo shoots. Many makeup artists begin as photographers' assistants. Others have training as cosmetologists or hair stylists, and then apply their skills in the theatre.

You can develop your own skills as a makeup artist with practice and artistic discipline. Practice makeup techniques from books and videos. When you have gained some skill, try to replicate effects you see in still photos. Invite friends to come over in costumes, and apply makeup that matches their attire. Combine notes of the steps you use to apply makeup with photographs of your work to create a personal makeup handbook. Refer to the chart on page 10 for more ways to evaluate this career.

Backstage Gossip: Palm Reader

One evening the great actress Sarah Bernhardt was finishing her makeup for the role of Cleopatra when fellow actress Mrs. Pat Campbell entered the dressing room.

Sarah was absorbed for the moment and could spare little attention: she was painting her hands, staining the fingertips and palms with the dusky red of henna. Mrs. Campbell watched with some impatience . . . . "What you are doing will never show from the front. Nobody will see it."

"I shall see it," replied Sarah slowly. "I am doing it for myself. If I catch sight of my hand, it will be the hand of Cleopatra. That will help me."

from Theatrical Anecdotes by Peter Hay

Additional Projects

1. Apply your technical theatre skills in makeup as you demonstrate the application of putty wax to alter facial features such as the nose, ears, chin, or cheeks.

2. Report on special makeup techniques used in the movies and in television.

3. Create an "available materials" makeup. Choose any character you wish from fiction or real life. For makeup, use only the materials you have available at home other than actual makeup. Avoid anything that will stain the face, such as some food dyes. An example of available materials makeup is to create old age using white liquid glue as a base and potting soil as a beard. Or, an owl might be created with wheat paste and raw oatmeal on your face. Use your imagination.

4. Start your makeup morgue by collecting magazine pictures of various faces. Share your morgue with others in your class and discuss the ideas for makeup that you find there.

5. Imagine you are supervising a makeup crew for a production and are meeting with your team for the first time. Develop an introductory talk that covers the basics of safe makeup application.

6. Research and explain how science and technological advances have impacted set, light, sound, makeup, and costume design and implementation for the theatre.

7. Working with a partner, create one of the following on each other:

   a. A forty-year-old woman

   b. An eighty-year-old man with a beard

   c. a young rabbit

8. Read about ancient Asian and contemporary actors' faces on pages 332–333. Take notes to recognize the key figures, works, and trends in ancient Asian drama and theatre as well as in diverse United States drama and theatre.

9. Choose a specialized character from Unit Eight, such as the old woman in *Driving Miss Daisy* or Sam in *The Janitor,* and describe how you would create the makeup for this person.

10. Evaluate the training and artistic discipline needed to pursue career opportunities as a makeup artist.

11. **Theatre Journal** Observe the facial characteristics and hairstyles of the people in a public place, such as a park, mall, or supermarket. Capture a few of these people in your journal by drawing their faces and writing short descriptions of their features.

Makeup Test

A chapter test is available in blackline master form in the Resource Binder on page 118.

Theatre Journal

Use the following as an additional or substitute prompt: Observe several older people. Write your observations in your journal. Notice their movement, posture, and vocal patterns. Do older people move with ease, or are their movements slower and less sure than a younger person? What words would you use to define the older person's posture? How do the vocal timber, strength, and volume differ from someone younger?

For More Information

Books

Academy of Freelance Makeup, Makeup Is Art: Professional Techniques for Creating Original Looks, Carlton Books, 2011.

Corson, Richard, *Stage Makeup, Tenth Edition,* Pearson, 2009.

Power, Dale, *Sculpting in Clay with Dale Power,* Schiffer Publishing, 2000.

Thudium, Laura, *The Actor's Complete Step-By-Step Guide to Today's Techniques and Materials,* Back Stage Books, 1999.

Other Media

Theatrical Makeup Design, DVD, Insight Media, 2007.

www.makeupmag.com/shop/

www.stageandtheatremakeup.com

www.fun-shop.com

www.graftobian.com

www.anytimecostumes.com

Substitute Teacher Activities

Here are a few suggestions for one or more days when you will be out of the classroom:

- Assign the Makeup Activity Sheet on page 115 of the Resource Binder.

- Assign one or more of the Additional Projects on this page.

- Teach the appropriate sections of Part Five, Makeup, pages 596–597 of the Student Handbook.

- **Design a Mask.** Provide construction paper, scissors, colored pens, glue, glitter, yarn, beads, ribbon, feathers, and so on, for the students. The mask students design should reveal some aspect of their own personality. It can be affable, grumpy, proud, silly, and so on. Discuss with the students what visual clues might be needed to put these ideas into a three-dimensional object.

Cultural Heritage

Kalidasa's *Sakuntala*

Kalidasa is known as the "Shakespeare of India," and his famous play *Sakuntala*, from the *Mahabharata*, is a story of grand proportions. It is known in the West chiefly through the *Bhagavad Gita*, the magnificent dialogue between Lord Krishna and the hero Arjuna.

The story of *Sakuntala* has all the passion, intrigue, and danger of any classic drama. While hunting one day, King Dushanta arrives at the home of Sakuntala. Struck by her beauty and kindness, Dushanta asks her to marry him. Sakuntala offers a condition that the king must promise to hand over his kingdom to a son born to them, and Dushanta agrees. They marry and are happy, but the king must return to the capital. Sakuntala later gives birth to a son named Sarvadamana.

Six years pass and Dushanta has not sent for his wife or son. Sakuntala journeys to Dushanta's residence, but he has no memory of her. Sakuntala is grief-stricken. Then a heavenly voice commands Dushanta, saying, "He is your son. Accept him." The king then remembers all that has passed and acknowledges his son, who later becomes renowned as Bharata.

Other Cultures, Other Times

Makeup is very important in Japanese Kabuki theatre. The style of makeup most associated with Kabuki is called *kumadori*. The actor applies a base coat of white for most characters. Then heavy, exaggerated lines and shadows are applied that emphasize the emotion and temperament of each character. Each emotion has its own color; for example, light blue indicates calmness, while deep red indicates anger and obstinacy.

For more on Kabuki, you may want to visit *www.japan-guide.com/e/e2090.html* or *library.thinkquest.org/TQ0013420.*

Cultural Heritage

The Actor's Face

The Faces of Ancient Asia

Sanskrit drama as performed in India is probably the oldest existing classical theatre form in the world, having originated close to 2000 years ago. It is said to have come from the ancient custom of reciting poetry at social and religious gatherings. The *Natyasastra* by Bharatha Muni is the oldest text on theatre performance.

Acting in ancient India was an art that made great use of both costume and makeup. Actors were rigorously trained, adhering to strict dietary and exercise regimens. The characters they depicted included gods, kings, heroes, jesters, courtiers, and common folks. Everyone involved in the drama—actors, dancers, and musicians alike—were committed to presenting the audience with a luscious feast for the eyes and ears.

Kalidasa is generally agreed to be the greatest of Indian playwrights. He is thought to have lived between about 375 A.D. and 450 A.D. Three of his plays exist today, including *Sakuntala,* the story of a humble girl loved by King Dushanta. The couple must overcome the curse of a sage to find happiness in the final act.

Throughout India and Southeast Asia, the influence of the great Indian epics *Ramayan* and *Mahabharata,* whose stories appear in the form of dance and drama as well as puppet theatre, are still performed. In these dramatic dances, gods such as Shiva and Krishna are often integrated into the stories. The dances are very stylized and exuberant, with each dancer made up and dressed as befits the character.

The ancient theatre of India and Southeast Asia is still alive, and its faces are as beautiful and colorful as ever.

Arunja, one of the characters in the *Mahabharata,* wears the green makeup typical of the heroes of Sanskrit drama. This performance was given in Kerala, India.

Quotable

Unlike classical masks and those of China and Japan, commedia *masks did not express any particular emotion like joy or sorrow. Instead, they gave a permanent expression to the characters, such as cunning or avarice.*

from *Theatre: A Way of Seeing* by Milly S. Barranger

In choosing works to enjoy, the country in general needs to see past the notion that a piece's "universality" has anything to do with the race and culture of its characters.

David Henry Hwang

The Many Faces of Diverse America

What is the face of an American actor? The answer, of course, is that there is no single American face. American actors have faces in a wide range of skin colors and features. Nonetheless, the American stage has been dominated by white actors. Even when plays or productions included characters of color, white actors often played them in ethnic makeup. While it would be out of the question today for a white actor to play an African American, whites are still frequently hired to play Asian characters. The Asian American Performers Action Coalition researched casting and found that between 2006 and 2011, Asian Americans made up only 2% of the actors on the American stage (Broadway and nonprofit theatres), while they represent 6% of the general population and nearly 12% in the cities, where most theatrical productions are mounted and cast.

One response to the unfairness has been to adopt a colorblind or nontraditional practice of casting, a practice playwright August Wilson (see page 161) strongly protested in 1996, when Arthur Miller's *Death of a Salesman* was cast with black actors. He wrote: "It is an insult to our intelligence . . . we do not need colorblind casting; we need some theaters to develop our [black] playwrights."

The debate continues today, but the acceptance of colorblind casting may be growing. NAATCO (National Asian American Theatre Company) has twice mounted a production of William Finn's *Falsettoland,* a play about a Jewish family approaching a son's bar mitzvah, with an all-Asian American cast. The production was one of the company's most successful commercial ventures.

Actors from the NAATCO (National Asian American Theatre Company) portray a Jewish family in the 2007 production of *Falsettoland.* Critic Adam Feldman wrote, "NAATCO's cross-racial casting is able to add layers of new connotations to the piece without eroding the integrity of the story."

The Many Faces of Diverse America

The Asian American Performers Action Coalition (AAPAC) was formed in 2011 after an Asian American actor posted on Facebook his frustration about limited opportunities to even audition for many New York theatre companies. The actor wrote that he had a degree from a prestigious graduate acting program and had lived in New York for almost a decade. The response to the post was so strong that about 150 Asian American theatre professionals met the following month and decided to form the coalition. Their goal is to call attention to the issue and to increase the amount of nontraditional casting. Their research, which relied on online searches to learn the background of actors in more than 400 productions, resulted in the report "Ethnic Representation on New York City Stages." Researchers learned that Asian Americans were the only minority group that saw its roles decrease since 2007. African American and Latino actors fought for years to increase their presence on stage and in films and television programs. The members of AAPAC say they are not willing to wait another 20 years to achieve similar results. The number of plays by Asian American playwrights on Asian themes has increased, but many actors want the opportunity to play roles that are not specifically Asian.

For More Information

Books

Brandon, James R., editor, *The Cambridge Guide to Asian Theatre*, Cambridge University Press, 1997.

Kalidasa, W. J. Johnson, editor, *The Recognition of Sakuntala: A Play in Seven Acts*, Oxford World's Classics, 2008.

Debreceni, Todd, *Special Make-Up Effects for Stage and Screen*, 2nd ed. Focal Press, 2013.

Morawetz, Thomas, *Making Faces, Playing God: Identity and the Art of*
Transformational Makeup, University of Texas Press, 2001.

Sartor, David, and John Pivovarnick, *Theatrical FX Makeup*, Heinemann, 2001.

Other Media

Lars Carlsson of Sweden offers a portfolio of very interesting makeup and mask techniques on his Web site: *www.makeup-fx.com.*

Chapter 25

Props

This chapter introduces students to the methods of gathering or making props for a stage production. Students will learn methods of research and how to design, build, find, and borrow props, culminating in the creation of a prop plot.

Objectives

1 To learn the job of the prop master and prop crew

2 To analyze and research a play to determine appropriate props

3 To learn methods of building simple props

4 To develop a prop plot for a play

Project Specs

Advanced Students
In addition to a prop plot for a play, the advanced student should document his or her research and bring examples of the props to include as a part of the presentation.

ELL and Special Needs Students
Students may need help organizing and keeping track of all the new vocabulary and information involved in creating a prop plot. You might want to team these students with those who are more knowledgeable.

On Your Feet

Bring several pairs of eyeglasses to class. Have the students define a specific character type that would wear each pair of glasses. What type of character might be expected to wear a monocle? Glasses with bright red frames? Wire-rimmed "granny" glasses? How can character be defined by the props that are selected?

---

25 Props

One of the final pieces of the production puzzle is the addition of properties—or props. The right props can provide the set with crucial details that help to bring the audience into the world of the play.

Project Specs

Project Description For this assignment, you will create a prop plot (a detailed list of props) for a full-length play and describe it in a three- to eight-minute presentation.

Purpose to understand the different kinds of props, how to acquire them, and their function in the play

Materials a prop plot for a play or the Props Activity Sheet your teacher provides

Theatre Terms
decorative props
hand props
prop plot
props master
pull
set dressing
set props

On Your Feet

Look around the room and imagine that you are making a prop list for a play about this class. As your instructor calls on various people, each should name a prop that would be important to include, such as books, desks, or a chalkboard.

The Balcony, a play by Jean Genet, abounds in characters, costumes, and props.

Theatre Terms

decorative props details onstage, such as paintings, newspapers, or curtains; also called *set dressing*

hand props items used directly by the actors during the show, such as letters and telephones

prop plot a list of props needed for each scene

props master the person in charge of obtaining and organizing all of the props for a play

pull retrieve costumes or props from storage

set dressing anything onstage that adds to the visual representation, including actors

set props items used to create the set, such as furniture, carpets, and lighting fixtures

Props and What They Do

Imagine the set for a play that takes place in a dining room. On the set there are shelves of china and knickknacks, potted plants, thick brocade drapes, a mirror, paintings, and a huge table set with silverware, dishes, and goblets. There are piles of food on the plates. There are place mats, a tablecloth, and napkins. Which of these items are considered props?

The answer is—all of them. A show's props include anything the actors handle onstage as well as any furniture, draperies, carpets, or paintings on the set. To obtain suitable props, a **props master** may borrow, build, buy, rent, or **pull** them. Pulled props are those you already own—you pull them from storage.

Furniture, carpets, and lighting fixtures—known as **set props**—work along with the other technical elements of the play to establish time period, place, income level of the characters, and so on. Details such as paintings, newspapers, and curtains, which make up the **decorative props** or **set dressing,** can tell an audience a lot about the characters who inhabit this environment. Then there are the **hand props**—items used directly by the actors during the show. These might include a letter, a manuscript, a gun, a telephone, and so on. Hand props can help establish a specific character— think of the elegant heroine gazing demurely out from behind her fan or the poverty-stricken young man who, despite hardship, can't bring himself to part with his father's gold watch.

Resource Binder

Handbook Connections pages 598–599

To Have on Hand

- Paper, pencils, scissors
- Books that show historical scenes, various types of furniture, buildings, household items, etc.

Props and What They Do

Discuss the purpose of props in a play. What do props do, and why are they useful? Some suggested ideas for the discussion: How do props help define a time period? How can a prop tell the audience something about the social and economic status of the characters? In what way can a prop provide focus for a scene? How might a prop help to create a specific mood?

Show clips from films such as *You've Got Mail, Men in Black,* or *Father of the Bride.* Ask the students to discuss some of the props and what they represent for each of these films. Examples: shelf after shelf of books for *You've Got Mail;* the futuristic weapons and set pieces used in *Men in Black*; and the tents, tables, plates, glassware, silverware, and so on, used in *Father of the Bride.* Discuss the fact that for stage productions props are equally important, though not usually as abundant. For example, a shelf or two painted to look as though it has books in it, with a few actual books scattered about, would serve to suggest a bookstore like the one in *You've Got Mail.*

ACTivity Ask students to analyze a scene from one of the films above and list the props that were necessary to the scene. Then ask them to write the scene for the stage, indicating only the props that would enhance the scene's focus.

isual Cue

The following prompts can be used to exercise **critical viewing skills.**

- List three different props in the picture on this page. What is the purpose of each?

- How would you go about obtaining these three props for a production of this play at your school?

Analyzing a Script for Props

Have on hand several scripts and several prop plots from shows you have worked on. Demonstrate ways of locating and determining what props are needed for each script. Show the students how props may be hidden in the dialogue and not just listed on the page. Discuss set props and hand props and how they function in a play.

ACTivity Divide the class into small groups. Using a book like *An Illustrated Treasury of Fairy and Folk Tales,* edited by James Riordan or any other folktale source, assign the students a folktale from a culture different from their own. Examples include "The Demon of Stone Mountain" (Vietnam), "The Selkie Wife" (Scotland), "The Golden Goose" (Germany), "Children of the Wind" (Africa), or "Lotus Blossom" (China). Ask the students to research the culture in which the folktale was first told. Topics to research include climate, geography, religion, clothing, foods, ceremonies and festivals, music and dance, etc. Ask the students to use the research to draw the designs of three props to be used in performance of the folktale.

ACTivity Divide the class into groups of five. Select a short play for the students to read. Hold a production meeting in which students can choose to be the director, costume designer, light designer, sound designer, or props master for this play. The students will then discuss their ideas for staging the play. What is the director's concept? In what time period and in what style will the play take place? What style of costumes, colors for the lights, and what props will be used? The students will need to work together to come to a consensus, based on the director's vision. The students will then write a short description of the play as they each see it on the stage.

The props used in this production of Noel Coward's *Private Lives* reflect the early 1930s.

Analyzing a Script for Props

You wouldn't use a boom box as a radio prop for a play set in 1930. If your play is set in 1970, the magazines on the coffee table, if they are visible to the audience, must be from 1970 (or at least appear to be so). Even if they are not visible, some props masters insist that the authenticity of the prop is mandatory if the actors are to believe in the setting. When it comes to props, even small oversights can take the audience (and the actors) right out of the play. So it's important that the props crew analyzes the script very carefully. If necessary, the props master must do research into the time period to make sure

Be a Good Borrower!

Remember that props are used in each performance, and they can take a real beating. Check with the director and producer before borrowing anything to use onstage. Don't borrow any prop your school would be unwilling to pay to replace. Above all else, be sure to return items promptly and in good, clean condition.

that once the props crew begins to build, borrow, buy, rent, or pull existing props, they have all the information they need to get just the right articles.

Some published scripts feature a prop list that offers a breakdown of all the props needed for each scene. But if the play your school is producing doesn't have one, you will need to create your own **prop plot.** This will require that you go through each scene line by line, paying particular attention to the stage directions, and write a list of the props needed. You should code the items in terms of those already available at your school—those items you will pull. Your list should be specific. Rather than simply saying, "clock," describe the ideal clock ("contemporary clock radio with large digital numbers" or "metal alarm clock from the 1950s"). Once you have completed your prop plot, you can begin the gathering process. Note that the props crew must work closely with the set and lighting crews to make sure that furniture, rugs, and draperies don't clash with the walls, flooring, or lighting effects.

Gathering and Designing Props

If you don't have a necessary prop in storage, the easiest way to obtain it is to buy it. However, for reasons of budget and/or practicality, this is not always possible.

Large set pieces such as beds can be constructed by the set crew. Your

---

From the Field: Stripped of His Dignity

When I was in high school I was the prop master for the show *South Pacific.* The prop list given to me said "landing strip." It sounded militaristic to me so I went to the National Guard station, outside of town, and asked them if they had a landing strip. They responded with hilarious laughter.

Needless to say, it would have helped to have done a little research first.

Robert Kallos, Technical Director, Atlanta, Georgia

school may already have some smaller furniture, such as tables and chairs, in stock. Assess the school's inventory carefully. Sometimes you can make an old lamp or piece of furniture look new or different with a new shade, a coat of paint, or other decoration. If you need to make props from scratch, review the rules for the safe use of tools on page 256.

Remember, it's the illusion that counts. The audience will be sitting out in the house, not onstage. From that distance, an inexpensive, shiny-finished fabric can simulate silk, a papier-mâché vase can become a priceless marble urn, and chunks of foam covered with painted canvas can look exactly like boulders.

Prop Plot

Name of Play _What the World Needs Now_

Characters Who Handle Props:

Lisa (Sally Klein)

Kent (Damon Warner)

	Scene Description	Properties Needed
ACT I	Living Room 1950s	TV, sofa, 2 chairs, book, coffee table, 2 water glasses, newspaper, an orange
Scene No. 1		TV—wooden floor model, small screen Sofa—clean lines, wood trim 2 Chairs—wood, no arms Coffee table—glass top, metal legs with book on top
Scene No. 2		Same as No. 1 / Add orange, 2 water glasses (remove at end of scene)
Scene No. 3		Same as No. 2 / Add newspaper (remove at end of scene)
ACT II	Porch of same house 1950s	Porch swing wooden, old Shrubs
Scene No. 1		

Gathering Props

Discuss the prop plot with students and be sure they know how and when to use it. Tell them it is important that they are very familiar with the prop plot because they will soon be creating one.

As students begin to make their own prop plots, ask them to think about these questions:

- If the prop is a large item, how heavy or cumbersome is it?
- Will it have to be moved during the show?
- How many people will be needed to move the item?
- Do you have enough crew members?
- Can the prop be moved safely, quietly, and quickly?
- Can it be stored in a place that will not present a hazard to the actors or the crew?

ACTivity **Advanced Students**

Have students read a scene from _The Glass Menagerie_ in which Laura looks at her glass animals. Then give them a supply of colorful origami paper and have them read _Practical Origami_ by Rick Beech or _Paperart_ by Michael G. Lafosse or look on Web sites such as _www.origami-instructions.com_ to learn how to create origami animals. Have students read the scene using the paper props they have created. This activity should help students understand the importance of using their imaginations and creativity to build props.

ACTivity **Beginning Students**

Tell students they are producing a play called "My Room." They must list the most important props in the room and tell why they would be necessary.

Notes

Here's How

Another important aspect of being a props person is knowing what to do with your knowledge of props once you have gained it. Keeping a props scrapbook is just as important for the props master as keeping a makeup morgue is for the makeup designer. Props masters should collect images not only of the props they have created, borrowed, or rented, but of objects they might need to fabricate one day.

ACTivity Ask the students to begin to gather pictures of and articles about designs in architecture, nature, fashion, furnishings, weaponry, food products, automobiles, and so on. Have students share one that has meaning for them with the class.

Perishable Props

ACTivity Ask students to brainstorm other ways to create perishable props. Have groups of students try to create one or two of the suggestions to see if they are viable.

ACTivity Have the students experiment with papier mâché by making a small prop. For instance, they can make faux fruit, such as an apple or an orange, from a balloon and papier mâché, or they can make a bowl from the bottom of a soda bottle and papier mâché. The recipe for papier mâché and some help in designing several different items can be found at *www.frugalcrafts.com*. How-to books are available at most craft stores.

Here's How
To Search for Props

A true props person is an imaginative scavenger who can see prop potential in things other people throw away. Here are some ideas for locating items on your prop list.

- Scour secondhand stores like the Salvation Army and Goodwill.

- Become a garage sale fanatic.

- Shop at outlets and discount stores.

- Borrow from family and friends.

- Check with other theatre groups in your area, such as other high schools, colleges, and community theatres.

- Skim through books on stagecraft to see what the stage crew could build.

- Send out a list of needed items to classmates and teachers.

- Broadcast your "most wanted" list over the school PA system.

- Get yourself an interview on school or local access radio or television shows.

- Post your list on bulletin boards in school, at supermarkets, and other public locations.

- Research prices at rental stores.

- Ask local shops if you can borrow their window dressing props.

Perishable Props

Plants and food are often found on prop lists. If possible, invest in plastic or silk plants that can be reused for other shows. Real plants tend to wilt under stage lights and need constant watering and tending.

Food can be faked if the actors aren't going to be eating it onstage. For example, the Christmas roast goose on the set's dining table may be built out of papier-mâché—as long as no one has to carve or eat it. But if the play calls for the actors to actually consume the food, then it must be prepared, stored, and disposed of properly so that it doesn't spoil or attract pests, and it has to be handled safely to avoid the spread of germs. The important thing to remember about stage food is that it only needs to *appear* to be real.

Imagine that your production calls for a character to come in eating French fries. Instead of cooking up a batch of fries for each performance, you might bring in a few pieces of toast cut into the long thin shape of fries. The audience will believe these are French fries if they are told that's what they are. And cut-up dry toast won't get the

Mashed potatoes are used to simulate ice cream on stage. It doesn't melt, so it can be stored backstage and brought on at the appropriate time.

Quotable

A man who works with his hands is a laborer; a man who works with his hands and his brain is a craftsman; but a man who works with his hands and his brain and his heart is an artist.

Louis Nizer, Lawyer and Author

The fruit looks tasty in this scene from *Reflections*, but it is actually plastic.

actor's fingers greasy! Avoid using salty foods as they may cause dry mouth or even choking. In a play that requires a character to drink alcohol, the liquid in the bottle may be tea to simulate whiskey and grape or cranberry juice to be red wine. The props crew should always check with the actors who will be eating the food to see if they are allergic to anything.

During Rehearsal and Production
The props crew's work is not complete when all props have been acquired. They are also responsible for managing the props during rehearsals and the show itself. Hand props, in particular, should be obtained as quickly as possible so that actors can become used to working with them. However, an actor should never be allowed to walk away backstage with these props in hand. They need to be available and accounted for at all times. Most props masters set up a prop table on both sides of the stage. The table is covered with plain paper and all props needed on that side of the stage are placed on the table. Outlining and labeling the items with black marker will help both actors and crew keep track of the items.

The props crew also has a job to do during the run of the show. These are the people that remove and replace props between scenes and acts. They must choreograph their work with that of the stage crew so scene changes can occur quickly and quietly.

Before, during, and even after the show, the props crew has to make sure to follow practices for safe construction and handling of props and materials. Surfaces should be free of any hazardous chemicals and rough or jagged edges. Props should be checked regularly for wear and tear. Props should be matched to the age, size, and physical fitness of the actors. Open flames are to be avoided or used only near materials treated with flame retardants.

During Rehearsal and Production
ACTivity Ask students to make an inventory of the props at your school. Discuss the best way to catalogue and store them. Are there some props that need repair? What might you need to add to your basic stock? Does the budget allow for the increase in the inventory?

Have students be aware of the following questions as they prepare the prop table for a show and check over the props they have gathered.

- Are the props sturdy and safe for the actors to use and the crew to handle?
- What will be done if something breaks during the show?
- Is this a prop that is so important to the show we might need to buy or build a second one just in case?

ACTivity Ask the students to research types of musical instruments from different cultures and time periods. Books such as *The Illustrated Encyclopedia of Musical Instruments* (published by Könemann, Belgium) may be helpful. The students might research drums from Africa, bells from China, tambourines from Turkey, and mandolins from Italy. Ask the music teacher from your school to come to your class to review the research and to bring some interesting historical musical instruments to share with your class. Brainstorm about musical instruments that might be used onstage in the plays of Molière, Chekhov, or Beckett.

Notes

_____

_____

_____

_____

_____

_____

_____

PREPARE

Work on a Prop Plot and Talk

Read the scene with the students and discuss the stage directions. Practice finding props in scenes from a few other plays written in different eras. Demonstrate how you would list each prop in a scene using different colored chalk on the board:

- black for set props
- red for hand props
- blue for decorative props

As the students prepare their prop plots, ask them to verify the time period of the props they are selecting. Encourage students to use the Internet to get help answering the following questions:

- Would you have a box of Kleenex on the stage of a play set in 1923?
- Could a bottle of ketchup appear in a play written in 1920?
- If the play takes place in 1935, can an electric carving knife be used?
- Would a ballpoint pen be acceptable in a play of the 1940s?

ACTivity Have the students make an historical timeline of different props. How has the look of specific items changed throughout the years? Suggestions for the students to research might be phones, kitchen stoves, roller skates, washing machines, and radios.

PREPARE

Work on a Prop Plot and a Talk

Choose a play to use as the basis for a detailed prop plot. Read the complete play. Make a note of each prop you will need, scene by scene. For example, consider a stage direction such as this one:

(The morning sun streams in through the window. A breeze ruffles the curtains. Iris is asleep in the easy chair by the door. Clutched in her hand is a letter. Agnes enters with a can of aerosol room deodorizer. She sprays it all around the room. The noise wakes Iris, who quickly slips the letter into her pocket. Agnes snaps off the lamp on the small table next to Iris without speaking. She then moves to the portrait of their mother on the wall and straightens it ever so slightly.)

In just one stage direction, there are:
- four set props—the curtains, the easy chair, the lamp, and the small table
- two hand props—the letter and the can of aerosol room deodorizer
- one decorative prop—the portrait

These would all be listed on your prop plot. Try to be as specific as possible by providing a description of the props you see in your mind's eye. For example, is the lamp a reading lamp, a fancy glass lamp, or a fringed silk-shaded lamp? Decide and then write down that description.

When you have made your way through the play once, read it again and look for anything you may have missed. When you are sure you have recorded every prop, complete your prop plot.

Beginning with the first scene, list each prop. Use three different pens to color code your list. Use a black pen for set props, a red pen for hand props, and a blue pen for decorative props. When you get to scene two, make a new scene heading and continue listing the props.

Set props need only be listed once as long as they are not removed from the stage at any time. The same is true for decorative props. But hand props should be listed each time they appear in a new scene. So you might have to list the same letter, book, or gun in every scene of the play.

Backstage Gossip: A Stone's Throw

Of all the props that fail to work properly on stage, firearms are the worst. During a presentation of an old American melodrama . . . one character challenges another to shoot him, and is obliged. But one night the pistol failed to fire. "Why don't you shoot?" the first actor ad-libbed, while the second pulled frantically at the trigger. "Shoot, damn it, shoot!" he urged again. No luck. Desperately, the second actor looked for another weapon and found it in a prop boulder, which he tugged from the ground and threw. The papier mâché rock looked as if it weighed half a ton, but it didn't. It struck the first actor on the shoulder, and then floated gracefully to the floor like a balloon as the curtain was quickly and mercifully pulled.

from *All Wrong on the Night* by Maurice Dolbier

Once you have completed your prop list, write a synopsis of the play. Then imagine that you are the props master for a production of this play. Think about what you would say in a meeting about the play's props. What special prop challenges does the play present? What will the props add to the play's mood and tone? Where will you begin your prop search process? Can you make some of the props? What will you need to buy? Prepare a three- to eight-minute talk about these elements. Rehearse your talk a few times, being sure that you do not go over the time limit.

When students have completed their prop lists and written synopses of the play, go over their work with them using the play for reference. Be sure that the students can answer the important questions about special prop challenges, the play's mood and tone, and the search and creation of props.

Career Focus

Other jobs that a student interested in props might look into are industrial design, theme parks, themed restaurants, and retail window displays.

Career Focus
Properties Master

If you have an eye for detail and you've always enjoyed a good treasure hunt, a career as a props master might be a good fit for you. Many who work in props say that the thrill of the hunt is an integral part of the job. Let's say you need a 19th-century grandfather clock . . . and you have to get it for twenty dollars or less. Maybe your show needs an ancient samurai sword . . . one that collapses. Where will you find such things? Can you rent or borrow them? Or will you have to make them? A props master looks at these dilemmas as a challenge.

As in other technical theatre fields, props masters and their crews are responsible for hundreds of small and large tasks before, during, and after every single performance. A good memory is one prerequisite. The ability to take detailed notes is another. A props master also needs good communication skills in order to build strong relationships with prop rental houses, other theatres, and the rest of the production crew. These theatre skills and experiences connect well to higher education, too.

A career as a props master can begin with a theatre degree or with practical experience in community or professional theatre. You might begin by working as a props assistant on a play at your school or in your community. Refer to the chart on page 10 for more ways to evaluate this career.

Notes

_____

_____

_____

_____

_____

_____

PRESENT

Talk About Your Prop Plot

It might make the presentation more interesting if the students bring pictures or (if they are a manageable size) several of the actual props in to show to the class. The pictures could be displayed or on computer through a PowerPoint® presentation.

The Language of
THEATRE

Ask students to listen as you read two paragraphs aloud, one on a familiar topic related to students' lives and one from the Props chapter. Call on volunteers to identify important details in each paragraph. Explain that important details are those that develop the main idea of the paragraph.

CRITIQUE

Evaluate a Classmate's Prop Plot and Talk

Hand out the Critique Sheet for this project or have students use their own paper. You might also want to see that they have a sample of the Prop Plot handy for reference as they listen to each speaker.

After all the critiques have been turned in, ask pairs or groups of students to get together to compare and evaluate their critiques. Encourage students to be open to the ideas and suggestions of their classmates and, more importantly, to be willing to take an honest and critical look at their own work.

PRESENT

Talk About Your Prop Plot

When your name is called, hand your prop plot or Activity Sheet to your teacher and walk to the playing area. Introduce the play and give a short synopsis. Then discuss the props you plan to use, how they relate to the play's mood, and how you plan to obtain them (which you will make, which you can pull or borrow, and which you will have to rent or buy). When you have finished, thank your listeners, and return to your seat. Your instructor may wish to pass the prop plot around to your classmates.

The Language of
THEATRE

Listen for important details when topics and language are familiar or unfamiliar.

* Listen as a teacher or classmate says the theatre terms on page 334. Notice what is familiar or unfamiliar about the terms and the topic of props.

* Listen as a teacher or classmate says the definitions of the theatre terms on page 334. Notice the important details that help you distinguish between decorative props and hand props.

* Take turns reading aloud paragraphs from the Preview section with a partner. The listening partner names two important details about the paragraph, including the meaning of theatre terms.

* Listen to your classmates' presentations of their prop plots. In small groups, discuss the important details you heard in the presentations.

CRITIQUE

Evaluate a Classmate's Prop Plot and Talk

Choose one classmate's presentation to evaluate. You will rate the presentation taking into consideration several aspects of the talk. Use a scale of 1 to 5, with 5 being "outstanding," 4 being "very good," 3 being "good," 2 being "needs some improvement," and 1 being "needs much improvement." Ask yourself the following questions as you critique your classmate's presentation.

* How informative was the synopsis of the play?
* To what degree did the presenter understand the prop needs of this play?
* Was the speaker's prop plot sufficiently thorough or did it need work?
* How realistic were the speaker's plans for making, renting, borrowing, or purchasing the items?
* In what ways might the speaker make or fabricate props that he or she intends to buy or rent?
* How well did the speaker impart the information?

Remember that to do the job well, a props person must be detail-oriented. Although the presentation's time limit is short, evaluate your classmate in terms of how efficiently he or she used the allotted time. Write a paragraph explaining the rating you gave.

Backstage Gossip: The Stalking of Camille

An unexpected arrival from the wings brought a confusion to Lillie Langtry one evening when she was playing Camille. When she was onstage with her lover in the play, she noticed that the white camellia, which she was shortly to give him, was not in its usual place. She managed to sidle towards the wings and whisper "My camellia!" One of the stagehands responded instantly, and, without looking at what she had been given, Mrs. Langtry returned to her lover, saying, "Take this flower, Armand. It is rare, pale, senseless, cold—but sensitive as purity itself. Cherish it, and its beauty will excel the loveliest flower that grows, but wound it with a single touch and you shall never recall its bloom or wipe away the stain," with which she handed him a half-chewed stick of celery.

from *Theatrical Anecdotes* by Peter Hay

Additional Projects

1 Create a short pantomime on a specific theme using a few symbolic props.

2 Create a prop portrait. You can do this by copying a photograph, enlarging it, and painting over it to make it appear completely painted. Build and decorate a frame for the portrait.

3 Experiment to safely create edible and inexpensive prop foods that look like the real thing. Share your results with your classmates.

4 Evaluate the training needed to pursue career opportunities as a props master and articulate connections in theatre skills and experiences to higher education.

5 Read the scene from *The Glass Menagerie* by Tennessee Williams found in Unit Eight. Create a prop list based on this scene. Which of these props might be symbolic or emblematic?

6 Review the safe use of tools on page 256 and design a poster showing those rules

as applied to property construction. Volunteer to serve on a props crew for a school or community theatre production and use all the safe theatre practices you have learned.

7 **Theatre Journal** Think of a recent conversation you had with a friend. If your conversation were a scene in a play, what props would be needed? To answer this, you need to think about where your conversation took place. Write down everything you can remember about the setting of your conversation. Then make a list of what props and set pieces the staging of your conversation would require.

Substitute Teacher Activities

• Assign the Make Your Own Props Worksheet, p. 120.

• Discuss the information in the Student Handbook concerning Props on page 598–599.

• Assign one or more of the Additional Projects on this page.

• **Plan a Props Pantomime.** Divide the students into small groups. Decide on pantomime scenarios such as camping,

cooking dinner, or getting ready for school. The students will discuss with their group the order in which the actions need to be performed. After the students have worked out their movements, they will choose one prop to use in the performance. This activity helps students understand how much "information" props convey to an audience.

Props Test
The test for this chapter is available in blackline master form in the Resource Binder on page 122

Theatre Journal
Use the following as an additional or substitute prompt. If you could only choose five props to decorate a set meant to be a classroom, what would they be? Write about the five props and why they would be important to the set.

For More Information

Books

Beech, Rich, *Practical Origami*, Lorenz Books, 2014.

Hart, Eric. *The Prop Building Guidebook: For Theatre, Film, and TV,* Focal Press, 2013.

Lafosse, Michael G., *Paperart*, Rockport Publishers, 1998.

McGraw, Sheila, *Papier Mache Today*, Annick Press, 1991.

Riordan, James, *An Illustrated Treasury of Fairy and Folk Tales*, Xs Books, 1987.

Rossol, Monona, *The Artist's Complete Health and Safety Guide, Third Edition,* Allworth Press, 2001.

Sweet, Harvey, *Scenery, Properties, and Lighting: Scenery and Props, Vol. 1,* Pearson Allyn and Bacon, 1994.

Thurston, James, *The Theatre Props Handbook,* 2nd Rev. ed., Players Press, 2000.

Thurston, James, *The What, Where, When of Theatre Props,* 2nd ed. Players Press, 2003.

Other Media
The Prop Master, DVD, Insight Media, 2010.

www.paragonprops.com

www.frugalcrafts.com

Theatre **Then** and **Now**

Symbolic Props Across Time

The Chinese Theatre

In Chinese theatre, the Chinese property man was an important member of the company. He had thorough knowledge and an accurate understanding of all the plays in the company's repertoire. All property was brought in and removed in full view of the audience on the Chinese stage. The stagehands as well as the actors appeared on the stage during a performance.

The Elizabethan Stage

In the Elizabethan theatre, the work of the stagehand was done in part by the characters in the drama. For example, in the banquet scenes, the chairs, table, and food were brought in by the actors who played the servants.

Theatre **Then** and **Now**

Symbolic Props Across Time

14th-Century Noh Drama

In the Japanese Noh drama of the 14th century, stage props were few—but those that were used were highly symbolic and crucial to the performance. Among these props, the fan was the most important. Because the drama was presented in a formal, aristocratic language that the average viewer could not understand, the actors used fans to accentuate or illustrate almost every gesture throughout the performance.

The fan was manipulated to illustrate anything from the rising sun to a long journey. A character might open a fan to simulate a vast mountain range when mountains were described on the stage. Shortly thereafter, a character might use a closed fan to simulate a boat's oar in water—thereby symbolizing the emotions of someone who feels emotionally adrift.

The scenery in Noh plays consisted entirely of impressionistic props that formed the outlines of buildings, coaches, boats, and just about any other important object in the play. The result was a spare staging with an emphasis on precision movements and the symbolism of important props.

A Noh actor uses a fan to convey meaning.

A Japanese fan

Quotable

Some people weave burlap into the fabric of our lives, and some weave gold thread. Both contribute to make the whole picture beautiful and unique.

Anonymous

A 20th-Century Reinterpretation

Hundreds of years later, in the 1940s and '50s, German playwright and director Bertolt Brecht became intrigued with Japanese theatrical forms. He also worked with the idea of sparse but symbolic props. His plays *The Caucasian Chalk Circle* and *The Good Woman of Setzuan* reflect his great interest in Asian theatre. Like practitioners of Noh and Kabuki, Brecht was not interested in presenting a "realistic" depiction of life.

In his study of Asian theatre, Brecht saw a way to use nonrealistic sets and props to keep the audience in an intellectual state of mind. His goal was to keep the audience thinking about the characters' situations and the themes of the play. He accomplished this goal through a variety of means, among them masks and other symbolic items.

One of his favorite Asian-influenced prop tricks was to have the actors sling a board across two chairs to simulate a bridge. Brecht also favored having stage personnel bring on and take off props in full view of the audience. This technique comes from the Kabuki theatre practice of using a *kurogo* (man in black), who shifted props, costumes, and scenery, and even served occasionally as a prompter. Because the *kurogo* was not a character in the play, the audience was able to disregard him.

The chair simulates a speaker's platform in this scene from *The Caucasian Chalk Circle*.

Rooted Props

"We discovered . . . the modern trend to reduce the theatrical experience to essentials. Grotowski's 'poor theatre' and Samuel Beckett's minimalist theatre are perhaps the most widely publicized examples of this trend today. However, in the American theatre, the trend has its roots in the 1938 Broadway production of Thornton Wilder's *Our Town*. Director Jed Harris took Wilder's straightforward play about recognizable townspeople in Grover's Corner, U.S.A., and placed the actors on a bare stage framed simply by the theatre's back wall. Virtually no scenery was used, costumes were muted, and hand properties were minimal . . . The actors told the story using only those properties, such as chairs and umbrellas, that they could move on and off stage for themselves."

Milly S. Barranger, from *Theatre: A Way of Seeing, Third Edition*

For More Information

Brecht, Bertolt, Hugh Rorrison, James Stern, Tania Stern, and W. H. Auden, translators, *The Caucasian Chalk Circle*, Methuen Drama, 2012.

Holt, Michael, *Stage Design and Properties*, Phaidon Press,1994.

Hutt, Julia, and Helene Alexander, *Ogi: A History of the Japanese Fan*, Dauphin Publishing Ltd., 1992.

Konparu, Kunio, *Noh Theater: Principles and Perspectives*, Weatherhill Publishers, 1984.

Lee, Sang-Kyong, *East Asia and America: Encounters in Drama and Theatre*, Wild Peony Book Publishers, 2000.

Notes

_____

_____

_____

_____

_____

_____

_____

_____

1 Students should draw simple sketches of a proscenium, thrust, and arena stage.

2 **fly gallery** narrow platform about halfway up the backstage side wall from which the lines for flying scenery are worked.

batten long pipes from which curtains, lights, or flats are hung.

teaser heavy curtains or canvas-covered wooden frame hung above the proscenium opening to adjust its opening.

wings the offstage area to the left and right of the stage.

back wall the area opposite the proscenium opening.

trap opening in the stage floor.

drop a canvas or muslin curtain that forms part of the scenery.

3 It is a *periaktoi,* or prism set. It is a set piece that can be moved or pivoted. Each of the three sides can be a different scenic element.

4 The functions of stage lighting are to provide visibility, create emphasis and mood, and to provide logical lighting sources.

5 A few possible answers: Wear gloves to protect your hands from heat; be sure your tools are safety clipped or tied to your belt; wear appropriate clothing and close-toed shoes; inspect each instrument for damage and repair as needed; know the wattage and type of each instrument to ensure proper connections.

6 A few duties of the sound crew include putting together a detailed list of sound cues needed for the show and finding the necessary sound effects or music; obtaining the rights to use music; setting up, checking, and maintaining all of the sound equipment; supplying accurate and timely sound effects and music during the performance.

7 **pull** taking the costume from storage.

Unit Five Review

PREVIEW

Examine the following key concepts previewed in Unit Five.z

1 Draw a simple diagram of the three common stages.

2 Identify the following stage elements:
fly gallery   teaser   back wall   drop
batten   wings   trap

3 The illustration at the right is a common set piece. What is it called, and how is it used?

4 Discuss the functions of stage lighting.

5 What are the important safety issues in lighting design?

6 List a few of the duties of the sound crew.

7 What does it mean to pull, rent, borrow, buy, or build?

8 Describe the purpose of a costume parade.

9 What makeup product is used to create the appearance of a scar?

10 Why is a prop plot important?

PREPARE

Assess your response to the preparation process for projects in this unit.

11 In preparing your set design according to the ground plan, how did you keep all the elements in scale? Do you understand how to construct the set?

12 What difficulties did you encounter in working on your lighting plan?

13 What was the most inventive thing you did when preparing your sound effects for a scene?

14 In designing your costume for a character in a play, how did you determine the amout of detail to include?

15 Did you make your presentation in full makeup or did you take photos or make a video of the process? Why did you decide to do it this way?

rent renting a costume from a costume house.
borrow asking for the loan of a costume.
buy purchasing costumes.
build making your own costumes.

8 The purpose of the costume parade is to give designers feedback on the comfort, utility, and movement of the clothes and accessories and how they look under the lights so the designers can make final alterations.

9 A scar is made with putty wax or tissue and liquid latex, or with nonflexible collodion applied directly to the skin.

10 A prop plot is important because it is the list of props needed in each scene in the play, identifying the name of the character that uses the prop and describing the location in the scene. The list identifies whether the prop is available at your school or must be borrowed, built, bought, or rented.

PRESENT

Analyze the experience of presenting your work to the class.

16 Did your audience understand your intentions in creating the set design the way you did? Why or why not?

17 How did your lighting plot reflect the theme of the play?

18 Would you change anything in the costume designs you presented?

19 Were you able to convince your audience that the makeup you created for your character captured his or her spirit?

CRITIQUE

Evaluate how you go about critiquing your work and the work of others.

20 What criteria do you use to evaluate your own and others' creativity as it is expressed through the various arts of technical theatre?

21 Explain how a treatment of any of the technical elements could function very well in one style or genre and not another. Think of examples.

22 Find pictures of a set design you that appeals to you. Analyze its design principles, recognizing lines, shape, mass, measure, position, color, and texture. Then analyze its composition principles, recognizing unity, harmony, contrast, variation, balance, proportion, and emphasis. Explain the effect of each of these principles on the overall design. Apply these same principles to a set design of your own.

EXTENSIONS

• Attend (or watch) a play and write a review of the technical elements in the production. Use the questions on page 219 and the vocabulary of theatre in your review.

• Research to understand the multicultural heritage of United States theatre and identify key figures, works, and trends in technical theatre. Share the results of your research in a creative multimedia presentation.

Resource Binder

Unit Five Test, p. 123

PREPARE

11 Students should indicate that they measured each element and used a standard scale, perhaps 1' = 1/4", in preparing their set design. Answers will vary.

12 Answers will vary.

13 Answers will vary but should illustrate a creative sound element.

14 Answers will vary; the use of detail is a subjective matter.

15 Answers and reasons will vary.

PRESENT

16 Most students should say that they were able to help the audience understand their design.

17 Most students should feel that their lighting plot enhanced the play's theme.

18 Answers will vary, but some students may indicate they had ideas that were not fulfilled.

19 Answers will vary.

CRITIQUE

20 Answers will vary and students should include relevant criteria.

21 Answers should reflect an understanding of how style and genre are relevant to technical elements and include meaningful examples.

22 Answers and set designs should reflect an understanding and application of the principles of design and composition.

EXTENSIONS

• Reviews should reflect an understanding of how technical elements contributed to the play and include theatre vocabulary.

• Presentations should include key figures, works, and trends in technical theatre from the multicultural heritage of United States theatre.

Unit Six

Theatre and Its Counterparts

Unit Six covers musical theatre and other theatrical forms, including performance art, multimedia, puppet theatre, and Readers Theatre. Chapters on film, television, and electronic media help students understand the impact and influence of these media on society. Projects in this unit enable students to apply their evaluation skills to these media and to work on several mixed media presentations.

Project Preview

Chapter 26 Musical Theatre
Creating and presenting a proposal for a musical

Chapter 27 Other Theatre Forms
Creating and performing a poem for a poetry slam

Chapter 28 Film
Learning about the elements of film and reviewing a movie

Chapter 29 Television
Planning and presenting an idea for a screenplay

Chapter 30 Electronic Media
Understanding the impact of electronic media and performing a scene using digital technology

Unit Six

Theatre and Its Counterparts

Quotable

After all, there have only been three forms of musical stage entertainment in the history of Western culture that in their day have been huge money-makers and also perfected art forms. These three are Italian grand opera, the Viennese operetta, and the American musical comedy. We can be proud that one of these belongs to us.

Deems Taylor, Opera Composer and Music Critic

The following questions are intended to tap into students' **prior knowledge** about the subject matter of the unit.

- Have you ever sung and/or danced on stage? Describe the experience.

- Describe a stage or screen musical you have seen. Did you feel elated or irritated when the characters burst into song?

- Have you seen a puppet performance since you were a young child? What did you think of it?

- Have you ever read a poem aloud? How does the experience of speaking or hearing a poem differ from the experience of reading it silently?

- Have you ever seen a film that was based on a book you had read? What was good or bad about the film version?

- Have you ever daydreamed of yourself as a movie star? What kind of films do you star in?

- What kind of television shows do you most enjoy? Describe one of your favorites.

- Have you ever argued with a friend over what was good or bad about a movie? How did you settle your disagreement (or didn't you)?

Theatre Journal

The person in the photograph is a street performer. Think about the character he is portraying and then write a short monologue for this character.

349

Visual Cue

A street performer in Manchester, England, captures attention in March of 2014. Use the following prompts to help students use **critical viewing skills** as they look at this photograph.

- How would you describe the way the performer is positioned?

- How do the bystanders seem to be reacting?

- What kind of character does the actor seem to be portraying?

ACTivity Have students take turns moving across the playing area in the character portrayed in the photo. Discuss the various interpretations.

Chapter 26

Musical Theatre

This chapter gives a brief history of musical theatre, describes the functions of various musical theatre personnel, and asks students to prepare and pitch a proposal for an original musical.

Objectives

1 to understand the elements of musical theatre

2 to analyze a potential musical idea in terms of viability, characters, setting, plot, and audience appeal

3 to create and develop characters and a plot of sufficient interest and importance to carry a musical

Project Specs

As they follow the four steps on pages 358–359, students should consider how to make these elements support the one-story concept. That is, characters, setting, and plot elements should be of a consistent style, and the music should be consistent with these.

Suggest that certain stories imply certain treatments. That is, the simple cartoons on which *You're a Good Man, Charlie Brown* is based call for a small cast and simple staging, whereas the sprawling narrative of the novel *Les Misérables* demands a large cast and imposing staging.

Beginning Students

Writing a proposal for a musical may seem overwhelming. Suggest that students concentrate on a broad outline of a familiar story.

On Your Feet

As an alternative, have students write new lyrics for a familiar melody.

Chapter

26 Musical Theatre

When people hear the word *Broadway* these days, many think of musical theatre. In the mid-20th century, **straight plays** (nonmusical comedies and dramas) were a major component of Broadway theatre, but today the big musical productions are the ones that typically bring in the crowds.

Project Specs

Project Description For this assignment, you will create and present a five-minute proposal for a new musical.

Purpose to understand the elements of musical theatre

Materials written notes on the proposal or the Musical Theatre Activity Sheet provided by your teacher

On Your Feet

With a classmate, create lyrics for a short song. Alternate lines so that each of you creates some of the lyrics. Then work together to come up with a simple tune that fits the rhythm, emotions, and style of the lyrics you co-wrote.

A scene from the popular musical *Camelot*.

Theatre Terms

choreographer
chorus
musical
musical comedy
music director
pitch
principals
production numbers
straight plays

Theatre Terms

choreographer the person responsible for designing a show's dance numbers

chorus a group of singers that provides backup vocals for principal performers

musical a dramatic production accompanied by song and dance

musical comedy a comedic drama featuring song and dance

music director the person who directs the actors, singers, and dancers in a musical

pitch to try to convince a person or group to accept your proposal of an idea

principals actors in major roles

production numbers elaborate song-and-dance sequences in which most of the cast takes part

straight plays nonmusical plays

The American Musical

While other kinds of musical theatre, such as opera, have existed for centuries, the modern **musical** is a uniquely American art form. In the 1920s, musical craftsmen, such as George Gershwin, Irving Berlin, and others, wrote songs that became the perfect accompaniment for the light plots of the comedies of the day. They were called **musical comedies,** appropriately enough. The shows typically featured a slight—even silly—story, plenty of tuneful melodies, and a chorus of leggy dancers.

In 1927, musicals took a dramatic turn. Jerome Kern's *Showboat* changed everything. First, it dealt with serious

Most musicals require actors who can dance as well as sing.

subject matter: racism, spousal abuse, and abandonment. Second, it did something that was revolutionary: It tied the songs into the plot of the play. Suddenly, songs were being used not just as background and distraction, but also as a way of actually *telling* the story. Another innovation occurred in 1943, when *Oklahoma,* the Richard Rogers and Oscar Hammerstein musical, opened to rave reviews. Some consider this the true beginning of the modern musical because every element—music, dialogue, dance, and plot—were seamlessly woven together to create a totally integrated production.

Since then, musicals and musical comedies have been a favorite American theatre form. And the musical has gotten richer, more complex, and more dramatic than ever. Such award-winners as *Bye-Bye Birdie,* which incorporated rock and roll into the plot;

Chapter 26 Musical Theatre **351**

PREVIEW

The American Musical

Students may not be familiar with some of the musicals mentioned in this brief history. Find and display as many images as you can of these and other musical theatre productions showing a variety of set designs from simple to elaborate, costume designs from contemporary to fanciful, and stages from black-box to those with large, elaborate prosceniums.

Encourage students to talk about musicals they have seen on stage and in films. You might make the point that whereas a stage musical might show a scene in a stylized set piece in front of black curtains, a movie version of the same scene would almost certainly open up to a set with real-world exteriors.

Play recorded examples of different kinds of musical numbers from a variety of shows—such as the introspective solo, the love duet, and the company production number—and discuss how these songs contribute to the dramatic development of the plot.

Visual Cue

Lerner and Loewe's *Camelot,* based on T. H. White's novel *The Once and Future King,* ran from December of 1960 to January of 1963. The prompts below should help broaden students' **visual learning skills.**

- Which of these actors do you think is playing King Arthur and which is Guinevere?

- What do you think is happening in this scene?

- Which actor is the main focal point of the scene?

Resource Binder

- Musical Theatre Activity Sheet, p. 129

- From Book to Musical Worksheet, p. 130

- Critique Sheet: Pitch a Proposal for a Musical, p. 131

- Musical Theatre Test, p. 132

- Production Budget Form, p. 165

Handbook Connections
pages 563, 570–571

To Have on Hand

- Recorded clips of musical numbers for students to watch or listen to and discuss.

- Information on your school's dramatic facilities based on Here's How to Choose a Musical for Your School on page 360.

- Copies of *Pygmalion* and *My Fair Lady* (See "For More Information" on page 362.)

Share with your students the types of show songs below, identified by conductor, teacher, and author Lehman Engel.

- *Ballad* Characterized by tunefulness and a smooth quality, often speaking of love or introspection
- *Charm song* Characterized by steady rhythmic accompaniment and an optimistic feeling
- *Comedy song* Characterized by clever lyrics, often with punch lines designed to make the audience laugh out loud
- *Musical scene* Usually longer than the others and composed of several elements, characterized by a progression of emotions or a development of understanding

 Play a few minutes of music from a variety of different numbers in a wide range of popular musicals. Ask students to try to identify which of Engle's four types of show songs is being played.

Visual Cue

Ask students to look closely at this photograph from *Rent,* then have them answer the questions below.

- Try to read the body language of three of the people in the photograph. What does it tell you?
- If they were singing a song, would the lyrics speak of hope and happiness or frustrations and despair?

West Side Story, a dramatic retelling of *Romeo and Juliet* set in New York with powerful songs and dances; *Hair,* all exuberance and counter-culture; the rollicking *Jesus Christ Superstar;* and others, reflected not only the musical interests but the social issues of America.

Today's musicals often feature complex staging with multiple sets, elaborate costumes, and huge casts. It takes a lot of money and a large team of professionals to produce the kind of full-scale musical you might see on Broadway. Many communities just can't afford to produce these kinds of shows and don't have the seating capacity to draw the large-scale traveling productions. Luckily there has also been a recent movement toward smaller-cast, simpler musicals such as the popular *I Love You, You're Perfect, Now Change.* These small-cast musicals are produced on a much lower budget and consequently can charge a much lower admission price, thus helping the musical gain an even wider audience.

More and more musicals are full of singing but feature almost no dancing; for example, *Les Misérables* and *The Spitfire Grill.* Others, such as *A Chorus Line* and *Chicago,* feature an abundance of singing and dancing. And at least two

The acclaimed musical *Rent* combines catchy music and lyrics with a powerful statement about urban gentrification and homelessness.

Quotable

From the songwriter's point of view, the dirty little secret of musical theatre writing is: If the story doesn't work, nothing else you put onstage will work very well, either. Grab any passing Broadway producer by the lapels and ask him why a specific show flopped, and I guarantee he'll blink and then say, "Book problems."

Nancy Golladay, Broadway and Regional Literary Advisor

major musicals, *Contact,* directed and choreographed by Susan Stroman, and *Movin' Out,* choreographed by Twyla Tharp, are told entirely in dance. *Contact* features only a prerecorded tape of pop songs, and *Movin' Out* has a live singer at the side of the stage singing the hits of pop star Billy Joel. There are those who may not consider these two pieces musical theatre; however, *Contact* won the Tony Award for Best Musical of 2000.

Other musicals are actually modern operas—all singing and no spoken dialogue. These include *Joseph and the Amazing Technicolor Dreamcoat, Tommy, Jesus Christ Superstar,* and *Les Misérables.*

If you're going to be auditioning for a musical, it's a good idea to have some vocal and dance training and to be able to execute a few basic dance steps.

Musical Personnel

As is the case in professional theatre, high school musicals are much more complicated to produce than straight dramas. This is because musicals feature orchestral music, multiple elaborate sets, larger casts requiring huge numbers of costumes and, often, special effects. This complexity demands a larger production staff than is typically needed for a play.

Innovations and Contributions of the United States to the Performing Arts

Musical theatre is not the only one of the performing arts in which innovations and contributions of the United States are widely recognized and appreciated. Following are other examples.

- **Theatre**: Minstrel shows, vaudeville, and melodrama were three major types of theatrical performances in the 19th century.
- **Melodrama**: Soap operas were daily melodramas that began on U.S. radio in the 1930s and later ran on television. Many shows had a worldwide audience and the form is now popular in many countries.
- **Radio**: A 1910 performance of the Metropolitan Opera in New York was one of the earliest broadcasts. The Golden Age of Radio, from about 1925 to the early 1950s, featured a wide variety of music, comedy, and drama programs as radio became America's first nationwide mass media.
- **Film**: Hollywood has been the dominant force in worldwide cinema since the 1920s. American inventor Thomas Edison led the development of early technology. Walt Disney set a standard for animation, and studios such as Lucasfilm are innovators in special effects such as motion capture.
- **Television**: In the 1950s, TV spread most rapidly in the United States and brought viewers situation comedies and original dramas. The 1970s introduced the dramatic mini-series, and in 1981 MTV pioneered music videos, which had a huge influence on the music and film industries.
- **Technology**: Personal computers and mobile devices such as the iPhone and iPad allow artists to collaborate and share their work and provide new ways for people to easily listen to and watch artistic performances all over the world.
- **Electronic Media**: Internet sites such as YouTube allow amateur and professional performing artists to post videos of their work and reach a worldwide audience.

Chapter 26 Musical Theatre **353**

Musical Personnel

Discuss with students the fact that there are often nonsinging and nondancing roles in musicals, but auditions often ask that you perform one or more songs for a musical. Have students honestly analyze their own strengths in terms of vocal quality, as well as the ability to move gracefully on stage and to learn a certain amount of choreography. Talk to them about any vocal or dance training you may have had.

Additionally, talk about the idea that while most musicals try to hire actors with strong, lyrical singing voices, a number of great musical roles have starred actors with very little singing training (or ability). Rex Harrison and Richard Burton, in *My Fair Lady* and *Camelot,* respectively, did very little actual singing in their Broadway roles. What they did instead was use rhythm, cadence, emotion, and superb acting to make their parts come alive and *seem* like singing.

Talk to students about high school musicals you have directed or been a part of. What made the musical more complicated than the typical drama or comedy?

ACTivity Give students, singers and nonsingers alike, the opportunity to use their acting skills to recite one of the following songs:

- "I Wonder What the King Is Doing Tonight" from *Camelot*
- "Why Can't a Woman (Be More Like a Man)" from *My Fair Lady*
- "Just You Wait, Henry Higgins" from *My Fair Lady*
- "Can You Feel the Love Tonight?" from *Lion King*
- "All That Jazz" from *Chicago*

Notes

_____

_____

_____

_____

_____

_____

_____

Visual Cue

Based on Gregory Maguire's 1995 novel, *Wicked* tells the story of two friends, the green-skinned, brilliant Elpheba and the beautiful, popular Glinda, who grow up to be the Wicked Witch of the West and the Good Witch of the North respectively in *The Wizard of Oz*. The show opened in 2003, with Idina Menzel as Elpheba and Kristin Chenoweth as Glinda. Still running on Broadway in 2014, the musical won numerous Drama Desk and Tony awards. The show has been produced in London's West End and theatres around the world. Have students answer the questions below about the photograph.

- What technical elements create the visual picture in this scene?
- What principles of composition are evident in this scene?

Many actors get their start as members of the chorus, such as those in this scene from *Wicked*, providing backup singing for the principals.

The Actors The songs performed in musicals are typically used to convey the emotions of the characters and to heighten the emotions of the audience. Musical theatre actors must be able to bring their characters to life through song—in other words, they must have the confidence to "sell it." Of course a trained voice is also essential, but many successful musical theatre actors have interesting as opposed to traditionally beautiful voices.

Good actors who can sing are in great demand in the world of today's professional musical theatre. But many **principals** (actors in major roles) begin their careers as members of the **chorus.** This is the group of singers that provides the backup for the principals. Sometimes chorus members have short solos, but most often they are asked to harmonize and to serve in crowd scenes and production numbers.

The Director Most musicals have a director, who directs the actors onstage, and a music director, who directs the musicians (both onstage and off). The onstage director functions much as a director would in a straight play. He or she blocks the actors (except for dance numbers), coaches the actors in their non-singing scenes, and sees to the overall style and flow of the show. The director is also in charge of casting the show, although most directors collaborate with the music director on this part of the process. The director may be a teacher with a theatre background or a hired theatre professional.

Backstage Gossip: Diva Dish

For almost twenty years Ethel Merman had reigned supreme and unchallenged as the queen of musical theatre, when Mary Martin scored a sensation in *South Pacific.* Asked what she thought of the young star's performance, "Oh, she's all right," La Merman replied with a shrug, "if you like talent!"

from *Broadway Anecdotes* by Peter Hay

The Music Director The music director works with the actors, singers, and dancers throughout the rehearsal process to ensure that they are on key, up to speed, and creating the best sound possible. He or she guides the performers through the musical part of the rehearsal process and often serves as conductor during performances. The music director's job is very important to the overall effect of the show because so many of a musical's dramatic moments are conveyed through song. He or she must be able to collaborate effectively with the director and choreographer.

The music director is usually responsible for selecting the show's instrumentation. Depending on the performance space, the play, and the budget, the instrumentation might include a single piano, a small band with just a few instruments, or a full-scale orchestra. The music director usually holds special rehearsals with individual principals and periodic rehearsals for just the chorus members. He or she is typically a teacher who works with musicians in the school's band and/or orchestra programs, or is the school's music teacher (however, some schools hire outside music professionals).

The Choreographer The person responsible for designing a show's dance numbers is the **choreographer.** Many musicals feature **production numbers,** elaborate song-and-dance sequences in which almost the entire cast takes part. The choreographer must be knowledgeable about music and movement and must have a facility for working with large groups of performers all at once. At the high school level the choreographer will typically be working with individuals at a variety of experience levels and abilities. It takes both talent and patience to create a unified choreographic vision.

Designers Just as in straight plays, the set, lighting, and costume designers must contribute their creative expertise to the overall vision of the production. (See Unit Five for chapters devoted to these theatre personnel.)

Part of the thrill of a musical is the sometimes vigorous choreography in production numbers. These dancers are appearing in *Newsies*.

Chapter 26 Musical Theatre **355**

From the Field: Lip Sync/Choreography

Have the students work in pairs on this one (less intimidating). They will pick out a favorite song, school appropriate, and choreograph a dance to it. The students will perform their song, in costume, for the rest of the class. (The kids loved this one!)

LeAnn Gausman, Theatre Teacher, Parma, Ohio

One of a choreographer's great achievements is to receive an American Choreography Award. Once called the L.A. Dance Awards, this annual award is given to honor and draw attention to the art of choreography for the camera.

Each year the ACA recognizes outstanding achievements in film, television, commercials, and music videos. They also honor individuals and organizations that have made significant contributions to dance as an art and a profession, giving awards for career achievement, educational excellence, and innovation.

Past honorees have included the choreographers Michael Kidd and Bob Fosse, as well as The Gap® for their "visionary" commercials that focus on dance.

ACTivity **Advanced Students**
Ask students to choreograph a short dance sequence based on a favorite pop song, ballad, rap, classical orchestration, and so on. Emphasize that students should bring their own beliefs and cultural experiences into their work. Have them share their creations with the class, discussing their interpretations afterward.

The Producer No matter what the production level, a large-scale musical is an expensive proposition. The number of actors, sets, and production staff needed for a musical is very large compared to a straight dramatic work. A high school musical can cost anywhere from $2000 to $15,000. (A professional-level musical may cost up to $10 million.) At the front end, this means that a good producer must be very savvy about recognizing a potential show's marketability. The question is often not so much "Is it good?" as "Will it sell?"—the point being that if it won't sell, it won't matter if it's good. So

Career Focus

Choreographer

Choreographers are among the most multifaceted of all theatre professionals. Ask them how they define themselves, and they'll tell you they are dancers, actors, directors, scene designers, mediators, and more. Their creativity and leadership skills make them suited to any career where coordinating the movement of large groups is required. Choreographers work in theatre and dance companies, film and television studios, and theme parks. They also create dances for other media such as Internet and music videos. They design the movements of bands and even individual singers who know that movement in their acts helps rivet attention.

In theatre, choreographers do their most important work during the rehearsal period. They consider the mood and style of the play and look for important moments in the plot. Then they develop movements to express the emotions in those moments. When they work on musicals, choreographers develop dances and train dancers. But they also direct other movements in other kinds of productions. They design the movements for pratfalls and fight scenes and make sure the movements in every scene are effective.

If you think you might want to become a choreographer, you can begin by studying dance. You don't need to become a great dancer, but you will need to know a lot about movement.

Being a choreographer requires the self-discipline to continue to study and practice dance and to keep your body safely in top form. It also requires the artistic discipline to create new routines and to blend effectively into an ensemble when appropriate. Considering what you know about this career and your own skills, talents, and discipline, make a judgment about this career. Is it something you might pursue for yourself as either a career or an avocation? Refer to the chart on page 10 for more ways to evaluate this career.

From the Field: Exit Right . . . No, Left!

Once choreography is set, it's set. One person's wrong movement can affect all the other cast members and the outcome of the show. In a production of *Annie*, one of the little orphan girls turned offstage in the wrong direction. Because she was his cue to enter, she threw off Daddy Warbucks, and because she was on the wrong side of the stage, she bumped into scenery being moved for the next scene. That resulted in Miss Hannigan's having no desk, and the orphan's missing her next entrance cue.

To recoup, we closed the curtain and sent Rooster and Lily out front to ad-lib the rest of the scene. But the show went on!

Alisha Fran-Potter, Choreographer and Dance Teacher, Glenview, Illinois

although a high school production has a built-in audience of friends, classmates, and family members, most producers try to market the show to a larger cross-section of the community in order to ensure sufficient ticket sales to meet the budget.

Often several producers—a teacher and selected students or a group of affiliated teachers—may work together to secure funding for the production and to manage the show's marketing. The musical producer's job is made up of the same general tasks as that of a straight play producer (see Chapter 14).

The Technical Crews The crews for musicals are usually larger than those for smaller-cast straight plays. But they are similar in terms of the types of tasks they fulfill. (For more on technical crews and their functions, see Chapter 15.)

The Business Manager Like any business manager, the business manager for a musical production is in charge of the budget. Musicals, however, can present special challenges because they are often extremely expensive to produce, due to the additional cost of hiring musicians, a conductor, dancers, a choreographer, special technicians, creating lavish costumes and sets, and so

on. The business manager may decide that ticket prices have to be higher or that the advertising budget must be doubled—all in the hopes of bringing in money to finance the production.

The Language of THEATRE

Work with a teacher or classmate to tell or summarize what you read and respond to questions about it.

- Read as much as you can of the headings for the four steps to create a proposal for a musical on pages 358–359. Then say what each step is in your own words and respond to questions about them.

- Read steps 2 and 3 on pages 358–359 and summarize one of the steps for your partner. Then respond to your partner's questions about the principals or plot.

- Read the Prepare material on pages 358–359. Then summarize each step briefly for your partner. Respond to questions from your partner, e.g. What role will the chorus play?

- Read the Prepare material and create a proposal as directed. Practice your pitch with your partner and respond to questions about your proposal based on what you read.

Of course a show must be financed in order to be produced, must be produced in order to be seen, and must be seen in order to capture an audience. But gaining a production is no guarantee of quality.

Tell students that before they begin their proposals they should determine that being original and doing their best work are their main goals. You might discuss with them the age-old debate between quality and popularity. Ask them if they would rather create a work that they felt good about and that they knew represented their best efforts or a work that was popular and made money. Why?

ACTivity Have students pretend they are producers and play the Marketability Game. Give them a list of musicals, including *The Fantasticks, Cats, Into the Woods, Chicago, Grease,* and *Camelot,* and ask them to rank these shows in order as to the market potential for your high school. Remind them to consider the cost of the production in terms of the musicians you will need for each, the potential audience for each production, the numbers and talents of your student body, any extra crew or cast you may need to hire, and so on.

The Language of THEATRE

Remind students that summarizing means stating a short version of what you have read in your own words. Explain that a summary should only include the main idea and most important supporting details.

Backstage Gossip: The Gypsy Robe

It's called the *gypsy robe,* and it's a musical theatre tradition. The member of the chorus with the most Broadway credits receives the gypsy robe on opening night. Members of the show then attach something to the robe that represents some part of the show. Everyone signs it. That cast member will then take the robe to the next Broadway opening and give it to the chorus gypsy of that show who has the most credits.

PREPARE

Create a Proposal for a New Musical

To conceive of a musical show from scratch is a difficult procedure. Students are not asked to write a whole show for their project, merely a proposal. However, it may help them to focus their work if they think of a novel or play they would like to adapt.

Adaptation creates its own special problems: Students must consider carefully which characters are necessary and which might be eliminated. They must focus on the main actions, possibly eliminating subplots or extraneous actions. They also must consider whether scenes can be combined, so that—for example—only four sets are required, rather than eight.

As students work on Step 2, tell them that a main character is frequently given a "want song" that expresses what it is he or she wants. Typically, this would come rather early in the show, and it provides a good way for the audience to get to know the character and to empathize with him or her.

The want doesn't have to be overtly stated; frequently it is phrased in such a way that the audience has to infer the want from what is actually said. Either way, what a character wants should not be a matter of confusion for the audience. Suggest that students use their notes for what the character wants when they come to placing songs in Step 3.

PREPARE

Create a Proposal for a New Musical

These days, the subject of a musical can be just about anything. There are musicals about war, politics, race, immigration, parenting—even taxes! Stephen Sondheim, described as "the greatest . . . artist in American musical theatre," wrote a wildly successful musical on the unlikely topic of a murderous barber who teams up with a piemaker to dispose of his victims (*Sweeney Todd: The Demon Barber of Fleet Street*). What would *your* musical be about?

You're now going to create a proposal for an original musical that will appeal to your fellow students. Everyone in your class is a potential backer. Your musical can be comic or dramatic. You are not restricted by subject matter. Your musical can tackle any issue you would like. Of course it's always best if the subject has a special meaning for you and will interest an audience. All the proposals will be rated by the entire class, and your teacher will tabulate the votes to see who will get to "produce" his or her show.

Possible Musical Subjects

Begin by writing down some broad ideas for the subject of your musical. Possibilities might include:

- professional sports
- dating
- family relationships
- friendship
- crime and punishment
- working

Four Steps to Creating Your Proposal

1 **Decide on a Subject, Size, and Setting.** Once you have decided on the subject of your musical (something you find interesting or meaningful), you must think about its size. Will it have a small cast or be a large-scale musical? Some musicals feature only two characters; others require a cast of thirty or more. The size of the musical will strongly affect the way you tell your story. Then, decide on a setting. It might be a beach, a party, a museum, or anywhere else you can imagine.

2 **Develop the Characters.** Think about the people who will give your musical personality. Remember that, just as in a straight play, the characters in a musical must have objectives (goals or needs). Ask yourself:

- Who is the main character?
- What does he or she want?
- Who or what stands in the way of the character accomplishing the goal?
- Who are the other characters?
- What do they want?

Write a brief sketch of each character. Include his or her age, personality type, physical appearance, and anything else you feel will allow a reader to understand the character's basic qualities. If you envision a large cho-

Quotable

I learned about playwriting from the jackets of show albums because I always noticed that the first or second song in any musical was the "want" song—"All I want is a room somewhere." I want. I want.

John Guare, Playwright

rus for your musical, you don't have to write sketches for the choral roles. Just include sketches of the characters that will be crucial to the advancement of the play's main plot.

3 Write a Plot Synopsis. In order to plot your musical, ask yourself the questions below and jot down your ideas.

- Where does the story begin?
- What is its theme?
- What happens first?
- What happens next?
- What happens after that point?
- How does the story end?
- Does the main character attain his or her goal?
- Does the main character learn an important lesson?

Now write a plot synopsis. You do not need to tell every moment in the story—just chart the main course of the action. Include indications of where songs might be placed and what those songs might be about. Try to come up with titles for each song. For example: "Adrian sings 'What Next?' which expresses her shock and excitement at the incredible turn her life has taken."

4 Write a Theme Statement. Now review your character sketch and your plot synopsis. What is the dominant idea expressed? Write one sentence that sums up the play's theme.

Once you have completed your character sketches, plot synopsis, and theme statement, give your musical a tentative title. Now think about how you would use all the elements of your musical to gain interest and support for its creation. In other words, think about how you might try to sell, or **pitch**, your idea for the musical to your classmates—your potential backers. What will they find intriguing about your theme, characters, and plot? Jot down a few specifics. You can use your notes in your presentation.

Rehearse Your Proposal

You will not be required to memorize your proposal, but you should be familiar enough with it that you can cover all the necessary information in the time allotted. Use expressive language and convey your ideas in an enthusiastic manner. Your job is to excite your classmates' interest, so make every moment count. You may refer to your notes, but it's important that you don't read them aloud. Time your presentation to make sure it does not exceed the five-minute time limit.

As students work on Step 3, point out that songs should not be arbitrarily scattered throughout a show. Theoretically, a character starts singing when his or her emotions grow too large to be expressed in mere dialogue. That is why every show song should be considered as the response of a particular character to a particular dramatic situation.

At this point in the proposal process, you might want to let students exchange their plot synopses and discuss what their theme statements should be. Go over the concept of what constitutes theme if you feel the students need help with this.

Advanced Students

Give students a copy of the scripts of both *Pygmalion* and *My Fair Lady*. Have students do a scene-by-scene analysis of what was kept from the original play, what was dropped, and what was adapted when the play was turned into a musical.

Vocabulary Enhancement

Point out that the word *pitch* has multiple meanings in theatre. It can refer to the amount of slant or rake described in Chapter 7. It can also refer to a musical key. Here, of course, it means "to speak for or promote."

Rehearse Your Proposal

Before students begin the rehearsal process, be sure that they are satisfied with the proposal they have written. Meet with students who feel they need help with any aspect of the proposal. If necessary, go over the four steps to creating the proposal, focusing on any that seem especially problematic.

Special Needs Students

If students are still having trouble getting their proposals organized, use a checklist to go over the four steps with them. Check off each step when you are satisfied that this point has been covered. Then help them write the plot synopsis based on the first two steps. Finally, help students see how you can pull the theme out of the plot and come up with the sentence that sums up the theme of their musical.

Notes

_____

_____

_____

_____

_____

_____

Here's How

Unless your school has a drama club that also functions as a production agency, students may have little access to information about money or budgets. However, they can analyze available theatre space as well as potential cast, production staff, and audience. One way to choose a show that fits your particular production facilities is by studying the cast breakdowns in catalogues of play script publishers such as Samuel French.

For example, *The Fantasticks* requires a cast of seven, while *I Do, I Do* requires only two. Both can be performed in a limited space with very simple scenic elements and minimal costuming. This kind of analysis can be invaluable to any production company planning to put on a musical.

PRESENT

Pitch Your Idea for a New Musical

Point out that in their presentations, students are simply using the same skills that enhance any public presentation. Encourage them to demonstrate their own enthusiasm for their proposals; a speaker's enthusiasm has a way of infecting an audience—even an audience made up of potential theatrical backers.

Here's How
To Choose a Musical for Your School

You should always try to stage a musical that you find exciting and interesting, but there are a number of things to consider before you make a commitment. Below are a few things you should think about.

- **Money** How much will things cost (consider all the elements)? How much do you have to spend? How many tickets need to be sold to break even?

- **Space** Do you rent a space or use school facilities? Musicals require large spaces for the dance numbers. How much room will the production need both onstage and off?

- **Cast** Are there good singers, dancers, and musicians available who can handle the requirements of the show?

- **Production staff** Are a music director and choreographer available? What about a knowledgeable designer and the large, experienced tech crew you will need?

- **Audience** Will it be large enough to support the cost of the show and the efforts of everyone involved? Will the audience be receptive to the theme, style, and message of the play?

PRESENT

Pitch Your Idea for a New Musical

When your teacher calls your name, gather your notes and head to the front of the room. Take a moment to prepare. Breathe deeply and relax your muscles while maintaining good posture.

Present your proposal as you rehearsed it. Remember to stay positive, enthusiastic, and upbeat. If you lose focus for a moment, use your notes to get back on track. Remember that your class will be voting on which proposal will actually become a new musical.

When you have finished your presentation, thank your audience, give your notes or your Activity Sheet to your teacher, and return to your seat.

Quotable

Before Neil Armstrong walked on the moon....before Wilt Chamberlain completed the first of his seven consecutive years as basketball's top scorer, "Try to Remember" and "Soon It's Gonna Rain" from The Fantasticks *were part of our national culture.... And as proof that a sunny, funny musical about love has lasting value, consider that the show's original 44 investors have received a 19,465% return on their $16,500 total investment.*

from *The Fantasticks* Official Web site

CRITIQUE

Evaluate a Classmate's Pitch

The critique for this presentation will be a little different from others you have done in this drama class. This time, you will listen carefully to all the proposals your classmates present, taking notes based on the four points below: plot, characters, theme, and audience appeal. You are not evaluating the presenter's speaking ability; you are evaluating his or her ideas for a new musical. Use the scores you give for each of the four points to determine the overall rating for the proposal.

Plot

1   2   3   4   5

Characters

1   2   3   4   5

Theme

1   2   3   4   5

Audience appeal

1   2   3   4   5

Overall proposal

1   2   3   4   5

Write specific comments describing what you believe was or was not successful in each category. Keep your comments constructive and realistic. Then cast your vote for the musical you would produce and explain why you voted as you did. Base your vote on the descriptions below.

5 = Sold!

4 = I'm interested, but I would need to hear more.

3 = Has potential, but it needs work.

2 = Risky business.

1 = This one has less than a slim chance.

Hand out one Critique Sheet per student and assign the presenter that each person will critique. As this critique differs from those done previously, go over the ratings and their meanings carefully. Encourage students to take as many notes as they wish, but explain that their final votes will be based on the total of the rating numbers. Have students circle the four numbers that represent their ratings. Then have students average the four numbers to arrive at their overall proposal number, from 1 (Less than a slim chance) to 5 (Sold!).

Alert students to also think about how creative, clever, and unusual the proposal is, and whether it contains an inventive collaboration of theme and voice; and of course—would they be willing to contribute money to see it onstage?

After all the proposals have been pitched and rated, give students time to compare their own rating numbers and choose the one with the highest score. They should then vote for that proposal by class ballot and turn in their Critique Sheets.

After you have reviewed student critiques, trim off the evaluators' names and hand out the sheets to the subjects of the evaluations.

Backstage Gossip: Birth of a Musical

One day in 1949, Meredith Wilson was reminiscing to a group of friends about his boyhood in Mason City, Iowa. Among his listeners was composer Frank Loesser. Suddenly Loesser jumped to his feet. "What an idea!" he shouted. "Why don't you write a musical about it? Maybe you can start with the fire chief. Let's make him the leader of the town band. Maybe *you* can play the fire chief. And maybe instead of a pit orchestra, you can have a real brass band in the pit. And you're the leader of the band . . . . It would be real Americana!"

When Wilson opened *The Music Man* on Broadway eight years later, it bore little resemblance to this original concept, but Loesser had planted the idea in Wilson's mind.

from *The World of Musical Comedy* by Stanley Green

Musical Theatre Test

The test for this chapter is available in blackline master form in the Resource Binder, page 132.

For More Information

Books

Bordman, Gerald Martin, *American Musical Theatre: A Chronicle,* Oxford University Press, 2001.

Davis, Sheila, *The Craft of Lyric Writing,* Writer's Digest Books, 1985.

Engel, Lehman, *The Making of a Musical: Creating Songs for the Stage,* Limelight Editions, 1988.

Frankel, Aaron, *Writing the Broadway Musical,* Da Capo Press, 2000.

Jones, Tom, *Making Musicals: An Informal Introduction to the World of Musical Theatre,* Limelight Editions, 2004.

Pygmalion and My Fair Lady, Signet Classics, 1995.

Spenser, David, *The Musical Theatre Writer's Survival Guide,* Heinemann Drama, 2005.

Other Media

www.stageplays.com

The American Musical Theatre, 2 DVDs, Insight Media, 1986.

Broadway! History of the Musical, 5 DVDs, Insight Media, 1989.

Dance Composition Basics: Capturing the Choreographer's Craft, DVD, Insight Media, 2006.

Getting Your Kicks, DVD, Insight Media, 2006.

Great American Music: Broadway Musicals, DVD, Insight Media, 2006.

Musical Theater Dance, DVD, Insight Media, 2002.

Musically Acting, DVD, Insight Media, 2004.

Step by Step: an Amateurs' Guide to Choreography, DVD, Insight Media, 1992.

"Takes" on Theater Dance for Dancers of All Levels, DVD, Insight Media, 2008.

Additional Projects

1 Write the lyrics for the opening number of a musical about an aspect of your school.

2 Prepare a musical audition piece, and perform it for the class.

3 Collaborate with a classmate to perform a duet from a musical.

4 View *The Music Man* or *West Side Story* and write a review of the play, the music, and the overall production.

5 View the film version of the musical *Chicago.* Discuss the changes that might have been made to transform this stage piece into a movie. How would the film differ from the stage version?

6 Conduct research to identify examples of innovations and contributions of the United States to the performing arts in at least two fields. Write a brief essay or prepare an oral report to show your understanding and appreciation of the examples you found. Refer to the chart on page 353 for ideas.

7 Design a marketing plan for the new musical one of your classmates proposed.

8 Analyze and evaluate the skills, training, self-discipline, and artistic discipline needed for careers in choreography. In a well-developed essay, make judgments about the types of opportunities that exist within and outside of the theatre, including those in film, television, and other media.

9 Read the scene from *Promenade* by Maria Irene Fornes found in Unit Eight, and create an original song that might appear in a musical based on your chosen scene.

10 **Theatre Journal** What does it take to "sell" a song to an audience? Think about a musical performer whose work you have admired—either in a musical play or in a non-theatrical medium. What is it about this person's style that attracts and intrigues you? Write your thoughts and impressions.

Performers who can sing, dance, and act are in high demand on Broadway and in films based on Broadway productions. Pictured here is Catherine Zeta-Jones, who sang and danced along with Richard Gere and Renée Zellweger in the movie version of *Chicago.*

Substitute Teacher Activities

Here are suggestions for one or more days when you will be out of the classroom:

- Assign the From Book to Musical Worksheet on page 130 of the Resource Binder.

- Discuss the information found in the Student Handbook concerning the Musical Audition on page 563 and Musical Theatre on pages 570–571.

- Assign one or more of the Additional Projects on this page.

- **Play "What's the Rhyme?"** with students. Start them off by singing two lines in which the ends rhyme using a familiar tune. Students continue the theme and tune of the song you've started, rhyming each of their own two lines as they go.

Master of the Craft

Andrew Lloyd Webber

Ask most people to name a modern musical, and the chances are good that they will answer with a work crafted by the English composer Sir Andrew Lloyd Webber.

Born into a musical family in 1948, young Andrew began playing the violin at age three. By the age of six he was writing his own songs, and by nine, one of his pieces was published in a magazine for music teachers. An aunt introduced him to the theatre, and he was thrilled by such musicals as *My Fair Lady* and *South Pacific*.

When he was 17, Webber met the lyricist Tim Rice. A short time later, they were hired to co-write a musical for a London prep school. They chose a story from the Bible about Joseph and his coat of many colors. The resulting rock opera was *Joseph and the Amazing Technicolor Dreamcoat*. Although the music was strong, the lyrics catchy, and the story entertaining, *Joseph* didn't get much notice. Webber and Rice's next collaboration was the successful international hit *Jesus Christ Superstar*. This was followed by *Evita* in 1976, a full-scale blockbuster.

In 1981, writing the music entirely on his own, Webber wrote *Cats*, based on T. S. Eliot's *Old Possum's Book of Practical Cats*. The year 1984 brought *Starlight Express*, and two years later came the musical many consider his masterpiece, *The Phantom of the Opera*. Throughout the following decades, Webber's success continued.

Sir Andrew Lloyd Webber

The Musicals of
Andrew Lloyd Webber

*Joseph and the Amazing
  Technicolor Dreamcoat* (1968)
Jesus Christ Superstar (1970)
Jeeves (1975)
Evita (1976)
Variations (1977)
Tell Me on a Sunday (1979)
Cats (1981)
Song and Dance (1982)
Starlight Express (1984)
The Phantom of the Opera (1986)
Aspects of Love (1989)
Sunset Boulevard (1993)
By Jeeves (1996)
Whistle Down the Wind (1998)
The Beautiful Game (2000)
Bombay Dreams (2002)
The Woman in White (2004)
Love Never Dies (2010)
Stephen Ward the Musical (2013)

From an early and profound fascination with music, Andrew Lloyd Webber has become one of the world's most popular composers.

Master of the Craft

More About Andrew Lloyd Webber

It was Andrew's Aunt Vi who turned him on to the theatre and especially musical theatre. She took him to big musicals like *My Fair Lady* and movies like *Gigi* and *South Pacific*. Soon after, he built a small theatre at home and wrote musicals for it. In 1965 Andrew received a letter:

Dear Andrew, I've been told you're looking for a "with it" writer of lyrics for your songs, and as I've been writing pop songs for a while and particularly enjoy writing the lyrics I wonder if you consider it worth your while meeting me.

Tim Rice

Andrew (age 17) and Tim (age 21) started to collaborate, and their first musical became *The Likes of Us*. The musical was never produced.

Visit the Andrew Lloyd Webber Web site at: www.*andrewlloydwebber.com*

Theatre Journal

Use the following as an additional or substitute prompt.

We're often impressed by performers who can take center stage and "sell" a show-stopping song, yet that is only a small part of the musical theatre experience. Think about a quieter musical moment that impressed you in some special way.

Quotable

Musicals, whether small, medium, or big, are alive and well as long as someone wants to write one and someone wants to produce one.

Andrew Lloyd Webber, Composer

Cultural Heritage

Peking Opera

Peking Opera, which was performed in the Beijing dialect, was a blend of highly stylized action, mime, singing, stage combat, acrobatics, dance, and dialogue. The plays were divided into two categories—martial (featuring stunts and acrobatics) and civil (featuring singing). Some were a combination of both.

Traditionally the four main roles were *sheng* (male), *dan* (young female), *jing* (painted face, male), and *chou* (clown, male and female), all of which were played by men. The brightly colored facial makeup symbolized different characters and personalities. Yellow and white meant cunning; red was an indicator of uprightness and loyalty; black meant valor and wisdom; blue and green indicated the manly rebellious character of heroes; and gold and silver represented mystic or supernatural power.

Hoping to attract new and younger audiences, many Peking Opera performances now use both Chinese and Western music that has been electronically amplified. Many have added high-tech lighting and design elements.

Cultural Heritage

The Common Language of Music

Peking Opera

Peking Opera, China's most famous and popular theatrical form, isn't an opera at all. Westerners began calling it this because of the music and singing that often accompany it. The Peking Opera originated in 1790 when, at the order of the imperial court, four performance companies from Anhui Province came to Peking (Beijing) on a tour. The tour was successful, and the troupes stayed on in Beijing. Over time, the artists absorbed the music and techniques of the local opera companies. The result was a new kind of theatre—formed from the talents of many.

The Peking Opera performances were full of spectacle and included actors in brightly colored face paint. The colors of the faces signified different characters and personalities.

The music of the Peking Opera was typically graceful and pleasing to the ear. The musicians played wind, percussion, and a variety of stringed instruments including *jinghu*, which has two strings and a very high register, and *yueqin*, which has four strings and is played by plucking.

Today, as in the old days, the repertoire of Peking Opera is drawn from tales of previous ages, notable historical events, and legends of emperors, geniuses, and other important people. Having thrived for more than two centuries, Peking Opera is considered the quintessential Chinese art form.

A Peking Opera performer displays his martial arts prowess.

Notes

_____

_____

_____

_____

_____

_____

Diversity in American Musical Theatre

Rosetta LeNoire (1911-2002) made her Broadway debut in 1939 in *The Hot Mikado,* the first Broadway production that featured an all African-American cast. In 1989, the Actor's Equity Association established The Rosetta LeNoire Award, given annually to producers who use multiracial casting as she did.

For More Information

Books

Hay, John M., editor, *Boundaries in China,* Reaktion Books, 1997.

Hsia-Feng, P'An, *The Stagecraft of Peking Opera,* New World Press (China), 1995.

Kondo, Dorinne K., *About Face: Performing Race in Fashion and Theater,* Routledge, 1997.

Mackerras, Colin, *Peking Opera,* Oxford University Press, 1997.

Peterson, Bernard L., Jr., *A Century of Musicals in Black and White: An Encyclopedia of Musical Stage Works By, About, or Involving African Americans,* Greenwood Press, 1993.

Xu Chengbei, *Peking Opera,* 3rd ed. Cambridge University Press, 2012.

Other Media

Amas Musical Theatre *www.amas-musical.org* Peking Opera, DVD, Insight Media, 2004.

Porgy and Bess, DVD, Naxos of America, 2014. San Francisco Opera production.

West Side Story, DVD, MGM, 2012. 1961 film plus special features, including a documentary on the making of the film.

Bubbling Brown Sugar, featuring the music of Count Basie, Eubie Blake, Cab Calloway, Duke Ellington, Fats Waller, and other African American musicians popular during the Harlem Renaissance, had a successful 20-month run on Broadway in the mid 1970s.

Diversity in American Musical Theatre

In the United States, musical theatre reflects our multicultural nation. African Americans in the rural South (*Porgy and Bess*), fishing folk in New England (*Carousel*), Chinese immigrants to San Francisco (*Flower Drum Song*), ethnic white and Puerto Rican gangs in New York City (*West Side Story*)—these are just some of the many cultural perspectives that Broadway musicals have offered over the years.

Off Broadway productions offer even greater multicultural exploration, in repertory companies like the Amas Musical Theatre. Since its inception in 1968, Amas (Latin for "you love") Musical Theatre has been devoted to creating and staging musicals that celebrate America's diversity. Nurturing inner-city youth and other young talents, Amas brings them together with veteran artists in professional productions and offers special

training for budding directors, performers, choreographers, composers, and lyricists. With outreach programs like teen camps, Amas encourages young people from all backgrounds to participate in musical theatre.

Amas Musical Theatre is the brainchild of stage, film, and TV actress Rosetta LeNoire, who used her own savings to found it. Over the years it has mounted dozens of successful new musicals and revivals. *Bubbling Brown Sugar*, a musical based on a concept by LeNoire herself, moved on to Broadway and was nominated for three Tony Awards. More recently, the 2013 Amas production of *The Other Josh Cohen* received six Drama Desk nominations.

Backstage Gossip: Whistling the Sets

Sometimes stage design can seem to get out of hand. The lumbering movement of the gigantic set pieces used in *Les Misérables* was found to be distracting to many audience members. And a joke circulated after the opening of *Camelot* that one came out of the theatre "whistling the sets."

Chapter 27

Other Theatre Forms

This chapter covers five theatre forms that have not been dealt with in earlier chapters—performance art, multimedia, puppet theatre, Readers Theatre, and poetry slams.

Objectives

1 to explore theatrical forms outside the realm of traditional theatre

2 to utilize a variety of response strategies appropriate to the media under consideration

3 to write and perform a poem suitable for a poetry slam

Project Specs

Some students may resist the idea of performing poetry. You might assure them that performance poetry doesn't have to rhyme or contain obvious rhythms. One way to think about it might be as a soliloquy expressing the thoughts and feelings of a character—yourself.

ELL Students

Some students might find it easier to write and perform their poems in their original languages. Allow this, but then encourage them to translate their work into English and, perhaps, to perform both versions. (Don't penalize them for running overtime if they do.)

On Your Feet

Show, Don't Tell Demonstrate this activity yourself, using common words like *please, hurry,* and *why?* Show students how vocal inflection can add a meaning to a single word. With students, brainstorm and list a number of words that they can choose from for their three words.

Chapter

27 Other Theatre Forms

Although we typically associate theatre with the production of plays, there are a number of other forms that fall into the basic category of theatre.

Project Specs

Project Description You will create a multimedia performance poem and take part in a classroom poetry slam. Your performance must last no longer than three minutes.

Purpose to combine writing and performance skills, and to explore forms outside the realm of traditional theatre

Materials the text of a performance and any accompanying media or the Poetry Slam Worksheet your teacher will provide

Theatre Terms

Bunraku
multimedia
nonlinear
performance art
poetry slam
Readers Theatre

On Your Feet

Work with three other classmates to represent a common emotion or concept (loneliness, joy, curiosity, fear, political struggle, and so on) using only three words, your voice, gestures, and movement.

Suheir Hammad, Beau Sia, and Georgia Me perform in *Russell Simmons Def Poetry Jam on Broadway* at Longacre Theatre in New York.

Theatre Terms

Bunraku Japanese puppetry in which puppeteers appear onstage while manipulating the puppets

multimedia using more than one medium onstage, including TV, film, dance, etc.

nonlinear not chronological

performance art unstructured dramatic events in which movement, music, improvisation, and games are presented, often making a political statement

poetry slam a competitive poetry reading in which speakers present short, original poems

Readers Theatre a form of drama in which seated actors read aloud from a script

The "Other" Theatre

Theatre began as ritual performance, and over the centuries the art form has taken many different paths and transformed itself many times over. As you read through this section, notice the similarities as well as the differences among these various forms.

Performance Art

With its roots in music, dance, and storytelling, theatre has given rise to **performance art,** which has in turn become its own popular form. Performance art came from the "happenings" of the 1960s. Often politically charged, happenings were a spontaneous combination of movement, music, improvisation, and sometimes even theatre games. They were, for the most part, unstructured events, usually held in a venue that was not typically associated with theatre or performance—

Artist Laurie Anderson creates performance pieces that are visually and musically exciting.

public parks were often the best place to see happenings. Performance artists often experimented with the conventions of traditional theatre. Performance art is often seen in nontraditional performance spaces, such as parking garages, churches, parks, and galleries.

Performance art tends to be **nonlinear** in its structure—in other words, it does not attempt to tell a chronological story. It typically focuses on neither character nor plot, but instead concerns itself with putting across a statement that is political or in some way controversial. Many politically charged performers use humor to express their ideas. Danny Hoch, Margaret Cho, and John Leguizamo all use comedy in performing works of social, political, and artistic relevance.

Multimedia

The advent of film and video has had a lasting impact on the theatre. Early in the 20th century, innovative stage directors began using film projections

Chapter 27 Other Theatre Forms **367**

PREVIEW

The "Other" Theatre

Many students will not have experienced all the other theatrical forms described in this chapter. If you can locate video clips of innovative performance art, puppetry, or poetry slams, and so on, have them on hand.

Performance Art

Show, Don't Tell Wearing dark glasses and a sling, enter the classroom, sit in a chair facing the class, and do nothing. After four minutes, leave the classroom. When you return, explain to students that one of the avowed purposes of performance art is to cause audiences to look at common events in new and fresh ways. Ask students to share their reactions to what just happened. If students mention emotions or motivations or even bits of business, you might discuss whether they were parts of the performance or their own interpretations or expectations.

Finally, go over the text on this page and discuss why what students have seen may be considered performance art. Explain that performance art takes on a multitude of different forms and meanings. In many ways, performance art is where new forms of theatre are invented.

ual Cue

Have students look at the three poetry jam performers and use the prompts below to help them exercise **critical viewing skills.**

- Do you think these three artists are talking about the same thing?

- Name all the parts of the body they are using in the performance.

Multimedia

ACTivity Project a variety of colorful images and call on students, in turn, to improvise a short monologue or scene that relates to the image.

Resource Binder

- Other Theatre Forms Activity Sheet, p. 133

- Poetry Slam Worksheet, p. 134

- Critique Sheet: Poetry Slam Performance, p. 135

- Other Theatre Forms Test, p. 136

Handbook Connections
pages 571–572, 573

To Have on Hand

- Books of poetry

- Videos or DVDs of performance artists, poets, puppet shows, etc.

- Marionettes, puppets, and similar items

- Slide projector, screen, and slides

- Sheet

- Floor lights or spotlights

ELL or Special Needs Students

You might want to adapt the activity on page 367 to allow students to stand next to the projected image and describe what they see.

Puppet Theatre

Ask students to talk about puppets they have seen in person or on television or in the movies. Most students will probably have experienced a puppet performance at one time or another, but they might resist thinking of puppets as a serious, adult artistic medium. You might show portions of a film on video or DVD, such as *Being John Malkovich*, in which puppets (and the concept of control) play an important part, or even a movie like *Chicken Run*, in which the claymation might be thought of as a form of puppetry.

Show, Don't Tell Try to improvise a shadow puppet performance by using a sheet and floor lamps or spotlights. Demonstrate to students that you can use just about any movable object to create the shadow, including your hands, kitchen utensils, scissors, and so on. Here's where the imagination can really take over.

ACTivity Leave the sheet up and the lights on and ask volunteers to create shadow puppet shows in pairs or groups.

Despite the fact that shadow puppets are seen only as shadows by the audience, they are colorfully decorated and detailed.

as a design element in their plays. And as time went on, using more than one medium to achieve a desired effect became increasingly popular and elaborate. In addition to using film and video, **multimedia** might incorporate live painting, dance, music, puppetry, animation, and computer and laser technology on stage. More and more plays are being written in cyber collaborations—multiple playwrights working via the Internet—and some theatre groups are using the Internet as the very latest in high-tech performance space.

Puppet Theatre

Puppetry is a very old art form—some claim it is nearly as old as humankind itself. The **Bunraku** puppetry of Japan, the water puppets of Vietnam (which shoot up from underwater via long rods), and the shadow puppets of Java (which are viewed through a backlit screen), are but a few of many puppetry forms that are centuries old. (Read more about Bunraku on page 376.)

In ancient times, puppetry was closely linked to feats of magic and conjuring. Throughout history, magicians and other entertainers have used puppets in street performances and later on the stage. The puppets Punch and Judy, who battle with one another throughout their show, are famous icons throughout Europe. Puppetry has enjoyed a popular resurgence in contemporary theatre. It has moved from being primarily a children's theatre form to one that charms and mesmerizes adults as well.

With the emergence of the Bread & Puppet Theater in the early 1960s, American puppetry became politicized. The shows Bread & Puppet produced were both visually stunning and ideologically compelling. (See Theatre Then and Now on page 376.) Since then, similar puppet theatres have sprung up around the globe. Some of these puppet theatres focus on adapting literary works as well as commissioning original works. The puppets they use comprise everything from finger puppets to gigantic, incredibly complex and detailed figures that can simulate intricate human movements and expressions.

Readers Theatre

Readers Theatre is a form in which two or more actors read aloud from a script. The basis of the performance is usually a standard play script, but it can also involve anything from poetry to letters

From the Field: The Making of a Puppeteer

A nun taught us the primary colors, and a little later the public school teacher showed us the wondrous things you could do with clay and chalk and introduced us to tempera paints. What next? There came another teacher who used marionettes as an aid to teaching literature and history. We were transported! Then my twin cousins (not many years older than I) took me on a trip to the opera. We heard *Il Trovatore*, and I still am thrilled with the memory of watching that great, fringed curtain sweep open time after time to reveal caves and castles, while the massive orchestra and chorus and soloists poured their musical hearts out over the plight of Leonora and Manrico. Sixty-five years later I still take pleasure in realizing how those teachers helped form my career as an artist.

Bill Fosser, Puppeteer, Founder of Opera in Focus, Rolling Meadows, Illinois

The Bread & Puppet Theater—humans in a puppet mode.

to journals to fiction. The actors usually sit on stools and read from scripts set on music stands. Sometimes all the performers dress in similar attire.

Readers Theatre uses a stage convention that allows the actors to deliver their lines out front while reacting as if they were speaking directly to their scene partners. Many larger cities have theatres that produce Readers Theatre exclusively. A. R. Gurney, Jr.'s popular *Love Letters* is a play that is performed in Readers Theatre style. Because this play requires only two actors and no memorization, it is a popular vehicle not only for theatres but also for arts fund-raising events.

Young performers enjoy the relaxed atmosphere of Readers Theatre.

Readers Theatre

In many ways, watching a Readers Theatre performance is like listening to a radio play—the audience gets to use its imagination to create sets, costumes, and actions. Readers Theatre is not new. One of its defining productions was the acclaimed 1951 reading of *Don Juan in Hell* from G. B. Shaw's *Man and Superman* with Charles Boyer, Sir Cedric Hardwicke, Charles Laughton, and Agnes Moorehead.

ACTivity Ask students to pair up or get into groups and pick a scene from a play they would like to read to the class. Each person should have a part. Have them sit at the front of the class. Tell them to read their parts with emotion and honesty. Try to be sure that each group has a mix of talents and abilities.

The following prompts can help students exercise **critical viewing skills** while looking at the photograph at the top of this page.

- What qualifies this performance as puppetry?
- From the masks, costumes, and physical attitudes of the performers, do you think the story being told is a fanciful fairy tale or something else? What?
- What might be some advantages to acting in a mask? What might be some disadvantages?

From the Field: Puppetry Workout

There are no fat puppeteers, I can tell you. The work is too strenuous. Even a large one is at a disadvantage; there's not enough room for him backstage. If a hand puppeteer is too short, he raises himself on high cork soles. Special muscles come into play depending on what one is holding and how. We learn to talk and sing in a bent-over position while manipulating heavy marionettes. The lifting muscles in the arms of rod puppeteers become very strong—I know from personal experience.

Bil Baird, Puppeteer

Poetry Slams

If possible, try to get videos or audio-tapes of poetry slam participants in action. Discuss with students the visual and aural impact of these performances. What makes them different from a poetry reading? How do they differ from acting or other kinds of performing? How are they similar?

ACTivity To practice reading poetry before an audience, have students memorize a poem that has real meaning for them. They need not memorize the entire poem, but they should know enough of it by heart to be able to feel some emotion while reciting it. Ask students to present the poem to the class, calling on as much emotional memory and deep meaning as they can.

ELL Students

Encourage these students to recite a poem in their first language, perhaps with another student who can translate as the poem is spoken.

Career Focus

A good stage manager can make the difference between a production running smoothly and things falling apart. If an emergency arises during a performance, the stage manager has to take care of it. The stage manager keeps track of the production schedule and times rehearsals as well as the performance, often taking notes on the performances to share with cast and crew.

It is not unusual for a stage manager to be experienced in just about every area of theatre, including directing, casting, and acting.

ACTivity Ask students to choose just one aspect of the stage manager's role and make a list of all the duties that would entail for a performance of their choosing.

Poetry Slams

A **poetry slam,** another U.S. innovation to the performing arts, is a form of competitive performance poetry that was born in Chicago in 1987. Since that time, slams have become enormously popular and there are national and international competitions administered through an organization called Poetry Slam, Inc. The Nuyorican Poets Cafe, founded by Reg E. Gaines, Bob Holman, and others, in New York City is famous for its poetry slams.

At these rousing celebrations of the spoken word, poets are judged on both

Career Focus

Stage Manager

One of the hardest working people in any production is the stage manager. During rehearsals, the stage manager writes down all the blocking and sometimes writes down and hands out the director's notes to the cast between rehearsals. During performances, the stage manager takes over where the director leaves off. He or she is responsible for seeing that each performance runs smoothly. A small sample of the stage manager's duties includes:

- cueing the performers and technical crews before and during the show
- supervising the stage crew
- making sure performers and crew know their call times
- relaying notes from the director
- scheduling and overseeing meetings and rehearsals for the technical crew

Although most people learn stage management by doing it, many companies now prefer to hire someone with a college degree in theatre management, technical design, or performance. Most stage managers get their start as members of other technical crews or as assistant stage managers. Qualified stage managers are typically very much in demand.

Stage management requires organizational and project management skills to oversee all elements of a production, and it offers the experience of working with many different creative people, sometimes under pressure. Connect these skills and experiences to higher education and other careers and you can see their value beyond the theatre. Organizational and project management skills help college students juggle a busy workload and help business managers stay on top of deadlines. The experiences of working with a variety of people, even under pressure, help both college students and business people develop interpersonal strategies for success. Refer to the chart on page 10 for more ways to evaluate this career.

Notes

their writing and their performance by a panel of judges who use a 0–10 rating system.

Following are the basic rules for a poetry slam:

- Each poem must be an original work by the poet.
- Each poet gets three minutes of performance time. If the poet goes over that period of time, points will be deducted.
- Poets may not use costumes, props, or musical instruments.
- Of the scores from five judges, the highest and lowest are subtracted and the three middle scores are added together to give the poet a total score of anywhere from 0 to 30.
- The judges are selected from among the audience members.

Poetry slams are designed to be audience interactive. In other words, the audience members are free to react to the performances in any way they see fit.

PREPARE

Work on Your Poem

You are going to write an original poem and compete in a modified poetry slam. In this version you are going to add at least one additional art or media form to enhance your performance. You may choose one other student to perform with you.

As you prepare to write your poem, keep in mind that it need not rhyme, and there is no limitation in terms of style. Here's an excerpt from the performance poem "After Cages" by well-known performance poet Cin Salach:

But you are feeling the wind in your
hair, finally
After all these years
And the answer is almost too easy:
Send history packing,
But keep the future panting.
Claim this sky for yourself.
Make it sacred.
Declare it off limits to anyone
Who isn't madly in love with you.
Understand that not everyone will be.

Recite the excerpt aloud a few times. Experiment with its rhythm and sound. Choose specific words to emphasize. Think about what the poem is saying but also how it sounds as you speak it. Think about movements and other media—music, photographs, videos— that might enhance the poem.

Now you're ready to try your hand at writing your own poem.

Go over the rules for the poetry slam with students. Tell them that they will be expected to write their own poem for the slam, but remind them that three minutes to perform the poem is actually a short time. Ask them to think about a subject for their poem while you time three minutes—calling out "One, two, three" as the minutes pass. This should help them get a feel for the length of time they have to work with.

Encourage students to think carefully about the art or media form they choose to go along with their performance. Also remind them that they should be responsive to their fellow performers in a positive, encouraging way.

PREPARE

Work on Your Poem

Tell students that their performance poems will be more effective if they use their own voices. That is why it's important for students to speak their lines out loud as early as possible. Tell students to ask, "Does it sound like me?" In addition, complete sentences and correct grammar are not necessarily required. Some students may express themselves best in sentence fragments or images. Again ask, "Does it sound like me?" The most effective poems will probably have intense personal meaning to the student.

From the Field: Variety Show

Prepare a variety show containing acts such as brief one-act monologues, improvisation selections, lip-syncs, and perhaps a small sketch about the faculty.

Next have other classes sign up to view your show. Each day your variety show can be taken to new classrooms.

LeAnn Gausman, Theatre Teacher, Parma Ohio

Writing a Performance Poem

Discuss with students the idea that distinctions between types of theatrical performances have blurred over the years. Grand opera has adopted many of the design elements of the musical, which has sometimes resulted in more stylized, less cumbersome settings and quicker, smoother scene changes. Musicals, at the same time, have evolved in the direction of opera, with many musical plays now *through-sung* (with little or no spoken dialogue, as in *Evita* and *Les Misérables*). Some musicals that started out on Broadway, such as Stephen Sondheim's *Sweeney Todd*, are now being performed by opera companies.

The gap is also breaking down between performance art, stand-up comedy, and one-person concerts. HBO, MTV, and other media showcase some of the younger and often radical performers that defy easy categorization.

Suggest that interested students research some of these performance artists and new performance pieces (see Substitute Teacher Activities on page 374).

It would be a good idea to preview your students' poems before they present them to be sure they have not crossed boundaries established by you or your school for language or sexual content.

The Language of THEATRE

You may wish to ask technology-inclined students to work in small groups to create simple multimedia presentations for the class, using video and/or audio, live movement/dance, and song/spoken word.

Writing a Performance Poem

Follow the steps below to write a poem of your own.

The Language of THEATRE

Respond orally to information in a variety of media to increase your knowledge of concepts and language.

- Say what you think of when you read the term multimedia. Then watch an example of a short *multimedia* presentation and say what the term means to you now.

- With a partner, read the description of multimedia on pages 367–368. Then watch an example of a short *multimedia* presentation and discuss what the term means to you.

- Read the description of *performance art* on page 367. Then find an example of it to watch online. Share your response to the information with a partner.

- Choose two of the theatre forms presented in the chapter and read about them. Then watch an example of each online. Present an oral comparison of the two forms to a partner.

1 Relax your mind and body, and let images and words come to you. Spend five minutes writing down the images as they pass through your mind. Don't judge them; just let them in. At the end of five minutes, stop writing. Read through what you've written, and decide which image or line appeals to you most. Use that as a jumping-off point for creating your poem.

2 Make sure what you're writing is something you care about. Your poem might be about anything: a favorite photograph, a deep fear, a lonely feeling, or a great day. Whatever you choose to write about, try to come up with images that paint verbal pictures and/or make strong statements.

3 Once you've written a few lines, begin to speak them out loud. This should lead you to other images and lines.

4 Get your body into it. Performance poets tend to use their bodies expressively, so don't feel as if your feet are nailed to the floor. You can use your voice, body, and expressions to enhance the meaning of your poem.

5 Pay attention to the rhythm of your poem, and think about where you might pause or extend a moment for effect.

6 Rework your poem based on the movement you can add to it. When choosing words, think in terms of how they will help you perform the poem. Think about how the words sound as you say them aloud.

When you finish your poem, decide which art or media form to add to it and whether you will need another student, such as a dancer, to help. Be sure the art or media form is a genuine enhancement, because the judges will be evaluating the artistic elements in your performance. Give your partner, if you are using one, time to practice, and then rehearse it a few times to make sure the performance is under three minutes. Whether you choose to memorize your poem or not, you should be familiar enough with it to be able to move and create a relationship with your audience as you perform.

Notes

_____

_____

_____

_____

_____

_____

_____

PRESENT

Perform Your Poem

When your name is called, take your poem and/or your Activity Sheet with you to the front of the room. Wait as your teacher randomly chooses five judges from among your classmates. The teacher will also choose a timekeeper.

When the judges have been selected, you and your partner, if you are using one, should take a moment to center. A few deep breaths will help you. When you are ready, nod to the timekeeper, who will then begin timing your presentation. Introduce the title of your poem. Then begin to perform. Remember that this is a poetry slam—the way you perform your poem will greatly affect your score. Keep your performance fresh and energetic.

When you have finished, take a brief bow, hand in your poem and/or Activity Sheet to your teacher, and return to your seat. The judges' results regarding your performance will be tabulated at the end of the class.

CRITIQUE

Evaluate a Classmate's Poetry Performance

As a judge for the class poetry slam, listen carefully and then take a moment to create a Poetry Slam Rating Sheet similar to the one below. Be sure to evaluate the artistic elements in each performance. You will be giving an over-all rating from 0 to 10, with 10 being the best possible score. Here are some pointers from the official Poetry Slam, Inc. Web site:

- "We use the word poem to include text and performance. Some say you should assign a certain number of points for a poem's literary merit and a certain number of points for the poet's performance. Others feel that you are experiencing the poem only through the performance, and it may be impossible to separate the two. You will give each poem only one score."

- "Trust your gut; and give the better poem the better score."

- "Be fair. We all have our personal prejudices, but try to suspend yours for the duration of the slam. On the other hand, it's okay to have a prejudice that favors the true and the beautiful over the mundane and superficial, the fascinating over the boring and pedestrian."

> ## Poetry Slam Rating Sheet
>
> **Judge:**
>
> **Poet:**
>
> **Title of Poem:**
>
> **Score from 0 to 10**
>
> **Under three minutes?**
> (If NO, subtract 1 point.)
>
> **Final score:**

Chapter 27 Other Theatre Forms **373**

PRESENT

Perform Your Poem

Tell students that they have the option of making eye contact with audience members during their presentations or of maintaining a private focus. A poem that seems directly addressed to others (especially if it contains the word *you*) will benefit from the performer's making eye contact. Tell them to:

- Look directly at an audience member and establish eye contact.
- Address a few lines directly to that person.
- Find another audience member to establish eye contact with.
- Look directly at that person, and so on.

A poem that is more introspective (that is centered on the word *I*) might be performed with a private focus. Here's how:

- Find a spot on the back wall slightly above the heads of your audience.
- Keep your eyes focused in that general area as you perform.

CRITIQUE

Evaluate a Classmate's Poetry Performance

Hand out the Take Part in a Poetry Slam Critique Sheets or have students copy the Rating Sheet in their books on a piece of paper. In either case, they will be expected to give a final score of 0 to 10 and to work with the rest of the class to establish an over-all winner of the slam.

You may wish to point out that few performers will achieve a "perfect" score of 10, while 0 should probably be reserved for performers who fail completely to meet the criteria of a performance poem. (That is, merely performing may be considered worth a few points.)

Have students turn in their Rating Sheets for you to tabulate. After you have reviewed student critiques, trim off the evaluator's name and hand out the sheets to the subjects of the evaluations.

Notes

_____

_____

_____

_____

_____

_____

Other Theatre Forms Test

The test for this chapter is available in blackline master form in the Resource Binder, page 136.

For More Information

Books

Bell, John, *Puppets, Masks, and Performing Objects,* MIT Press, 2001.

Dennison, George, editor, Geoffrey Gardner, editor, Taylor Stoehr, editor, *An Existing Better World: Notes on the Bread and Puppet Theatre,* Autonomedia, 2000.

Eleveld, Mark, editor, *The Spoken Word Revolution: Slam, Hip Hop & Poetry of a New Generation,* Sourcebooks, Inc., 2003.

Jones, Brian J., *Jim Henson: The Biography,* Ballantine Books, 2013.

Smith, Marc Kelly, *Stage a Poetry Slam: Creating Performance Poetry Events,* Sourcebooks Inc., 2009.

Smith, Marc Kelly, and Joe Kraynak, *Take the Mic: The Art of Performance Poetry, Slam, and the Spoken Word,* Sourcebooks, Inc., 2009.

Tanner, Fran Averett, *Readers Theatre Fundamentals,* Clark Publishing/ Perfection Learning, 1993.

Other Media

Chinese Take Away, DVD, Insight Media, 2003.

Jamaican Storyteller/Performer Thomas Osha Pinnock, DVD, Insight Media, 2000.

Jay O'Callahan: A Master Class in Storytelling, DVD, Insight Media, 1983.

Louder Than A Bomb, DVD, Siskel/ Jacobs Productions, 2010.

www.e-poets.net/library/slam/

www.redmoon.org

Additional Projects

1 Make your own puppet. It can take any form you like: finger puppet, marionette, sock puppet, or a design of your own.

2 Collaborate with a small group of classmates to create a multimedia performance using the spoken word, live and recorded music, and movement. The work should examine a critical global issue and use your group's personal perspectives as well as community and cultural perspectives to create a message about that issue. Talk to diverse members of your community who would likely have meaningful perspectives on the issue.

3 Choose a literary selection or a collage of shorter pieces from print or online newspapers, magazines, or letters from which to create a cross-cultural Readers Theatre performance. Integrate conventions and knowledge from different art forms, such as photography, film, and music, to create a unique work. Direct the performance piece for the class, and then explain and justify your artistic choices and interpretation.

4 Make a video recording of the performance poem you created for this chapter's project. Use it to further refine your poem and your performance.

5 Evaluate how the skills, training, and experience of a stage manager connect to success in higher education and careers both in and out of the theatre. Demonstrate your evaluation in a brief video.

6 Research and write a report on a theatre counterpart such as Bunraku, shadow puppets, Punch and Judy, or other popular poetry forms such as the television program *Def Poetry.* Be prepared to present your report to the class. Include two multimedia elements in your report.

7 Choose a monologue or scene from those found in Unit Eight that reflects or questions your personal beliefs and create a performance piece based on that play, adding at least one more art or media form to enhance the meaning. Perform it for the class. Evaluate one another's performances, paying special attention to the artistic elements within it.

8 **Theatre Journal** What if someone asked you to create a performance piece about your day so far? Would you create performance art, a poem, a dance, or a monologue? Write a short description of the kind of project that would interest you.

Substitute Teacher Activities

Here are a few suggestions for one or more days when you will be out of the classroom:

- Assign the Poetry Slam Worksheet on page 134 of the Resource Binder.
- Assign one or more of the Additional Projects on this page.
- Teach the Performance Art section of the Student Handbook on pages 571–572 and the Readers Theatre section on page 573.

- Have students use the Internet to research some of these performance artists and groups: Danny Hoch, Eddie Izzard, Lisa Kron, Elevator Repair Service, and Marina Abramovic.
- Have students write a description of how they would combine at least three media to tell a news story. Students can browse news magazines and papers to find their stories.

Master of the Craft

Marc Smith: The "Slampapi"

"Smith's almost visionary on the need to rescue poetry from its lowly status in the nation's cultural life."

—*Smithsonian* magazine

Not many people can lay claim to single-handedly creating a brand-new art form. But in 1987, poet Marc Smith had a big idea. It was spawned from his feeling that poetry needed a public forum beyond the sometimes academic readings at colleges and bookstores. He wanted a forum for competitive performance poetry. The big idea began to take shape in 1987 when he persuaded the owner of Chicago's Green Mill Tavern to open its doors to the first ever poetry slam. And from that point on, the poetry slam phenomenon has just kept growing. Today more than 150 American cities host their own slams. And now there are even versions of the slam going on in England, Germany, Israel, and Sweden.

The man who made it all happen—the father of the poetry slam, or "Slampapi," as he is called in the performance community—is a terrific poet in his own right. Smith's innate sense of rhythm and his grittily realistic, urban poems tend to break poetic boundaries. His performances, both as a soloist and with his ensemble of performance poets and jazz musicians, blend the eloquence and beauty of poetry with the drama of theatre. His work has gained an international following—and Smith has become one of the most influential performance poets in the world.

In addition to a heavy touring schedule, Smith writes, performs, and continues to host and perform for the Uptown Poetry Slam's avid standing-room-only houses.

Marc Smith, aka the Slampapi

Kiss It

If you need to kiss it,
Kiss it.
If you need to kick it,
Kick it.
If you need to scream it,
Scream it.
But kiss it, kick it, scream it
Now.

—Marc Smith

Master of the Craft

More About Marc Smith

Marc Smith's first book, *Crowdpleaser*, celebrates the Green Mill Tavern and the people who frequent the poetry competitions that take place there. The book is illustrated by Michael Acerra, and it is a fascinating document filled with Smith's poetry and stories. As with Smith's best poetry slam work, *Crowdpleaser* defies labels and presents new ways of sharing the poetic form.

Visit Marc Smith's Web site at: *www. slampapi.com.*

Visit the Poetry Slam Web site at: *www.poetryslam.com.*

Theatre Journal

Use the following as an additional or substitute prompt.

Do you feel more comfortable performing in front of an audience when you are "yourself" or when you are playing a character? Many people prefer the feeling of security that can come from speaking as someone else. In your journal, explore your feelings as a performance.

Quotable

One thing, though, is for sure: Carl Sandburg jump-upstarted me. Lover, populist, Swede . . . passionate eyeball scrutinizing the world, he could be just as damn everything as everybody else . . . including careless. (That's where he connects to me.) But when there's a lot to get done, who's got enough daylight to worry about how many Ps and Qs are in the soup?

Marc Smith, Poet

Theatre **Then** and **Now**

Bunraku

Bunraku may be an ancient form, but elements of its puppetry format are still very much alive today. For example, members of the Thistle Theatre of Seattle, Washington, perform a Bunraku version of "Little Red Riding Hood." The scenes in which the Wolf opens his huge mouth to swallow Grandma and Little Red whole are especially scary—and funny.

Much Asian theatre makes use of theatrical conventions that are unfamiliar to Western culture—or are only recently coming to be appreciated. For example, in Japanese Noh theatre, stagehands dressed in black appear at appropriate times to hand an actor a fan or a sword or to position a stool for the actor to sit on. These stagehands are presumed by the experienced audience to be invisible. Likewise, the puppeteers in Bunraku—although they are fully visible at all times—are presumed to be invisible, which allows the audience to focus on the fluid and delicate movements of the puppets.

Theatre **Then** and **Now**

Puppetry for All Time

Bunraku: An Ancient Puppetry Form
Many consider Japanese Bunraku the most highly evolved form of puppetry in the world. Offering a unique combination of puppet manipulation, recitation, and music, Bunraku takes many years to master. Its name, loosely translated, means "puppets and storytelling."

Bunraku developed from an ancient Japanese tradition of traveling storytellers. At the same time there were also traveling puppeteers. It is not clear when these two art forms came together, but Bunraku is thought to have come about in 1684. That is when the first known Bunraku theatre opened in Osaka.

Bunraku puppets were about half the size of human beings. They had many moveable parts: their eyes (and eyebrows) moved, their mouths opened and shut, and their arms and hands moved in very human-looking ways.

The puppeteers in Bunraku were always visible to the audience. They brought the puppets onstage in full view of the audience. Three puppeteers were needed to operate each main character puppet.

The narrator, meanwhile, told the entire story—also in full view of the audience—using a variety of vocal techniques. In addition to telling the story, he or she whispered, chanted, sang, or wept the dialogue for each puppet in the play. A musical accompanist provided music and sound effects to simulate rain, wind, and so on.

Today Bunraku is enjoying a revival. In 1985, The National Bunraku Theatre was granted a permanent home in the city of its origin, Osaka, where it produces four shows a year. Bunraku masters and puppet-makers are aging, however, and there is some question as to whether there will be sufficient interest from the younger generation to continue the Bunraku tradition.

A Bunraku puppetry performance.

For More Information

Books

Ando, Tsuruo, *Bunraku: The Puppet Theatre*, Walker/Weatherhill, 1970.

Currell, David, *Making and Manipulating Marionettes*, Crowood Press, 2005.

Other Media

Visit the Bread and Puppet Theatre at www.breadandpuppet.org.

Visit the Puppeteers of American at www.puppeteers.org.

Bread & Puppet Theater: Today's Political Puppetry

Peter Schumann founded the Bread & Puppet Theater in 1963. During the Vietnam War era, Schumann and his collaborators staged outdoor performances on New York City's Lower East Side. These were often in the form of block-long processions of papier-mâché puppets depicting anti-war themes. Bread & Puppet's figures moved hypnotically. They also varied greatly in scale: the smallest puppets fit on one finger. The largest were more than eight feet tall and were designed to be held high above the audience by means of long poles draped with fabric and manipulated by several puppeteers.

The Bread & Puppet Theater became widely known for its unique brand of puppet-and-mask political theatre, and its work has inspired and influenced a generation of artists. In 1974, the group moved to Vermont and settled on a farm just outside the tiny village of Glover. One of the outbuildings became a museum for the retired puppets, masks, and paintings once used by the company. The museum is open to the public from May through October, and admission is free, in keeping with Bread & Puppet's egalitarian philosophy.

Members of Bread & Puppet Theatre display their creations.

A typical puppet from the Bread & Puppet Theater collection

One of the oldest nonprofit, self-supporting theatre companies in the United States, Bread & Puppet Theater tours its shows all over the world. During the summer months, visitors can often catch a performance at the farm. The theatre company celebrated its 50th anniversary in 2013.

Other Cultures, Other Times
Punch and Judy

Punch and Judy go back hundreds of years in British history, and prior to that, Punch is believed to have been based on a character in Italian *commedia dell' arte*. He may even go back as far as the ancient Romans and Greeks. His persona is aligned with that of mischief-makers and trickster figures found in most cultures.

Punchinello, as he was originally named, was at first a puppet on strings. The slapstick-swinging hand puppet that became known as Mr. Punch developed later. No one knows exactly when he teamed up with Judy, but the duo has been battling it out for decades. Recently there has been some opposition to Punch's violent attacks on all the puppets around him, particularly his better half, but the Punch and Judy College of Professors and the Punch and Judy Fellowship, both located in Great Britain, are sworn to keep Punch and Judy puppetry true to its historical form—whacks, smacks, and all.

For more information on these organizations and their namesakes, visit *www.punchandjudy.com* and *www.punchandjudy.org*.

Notes

Chapter 28

Film

This chapter will give students some tools to evaluate a film and to understand the impact and influence of film on society.

Objectives

1 to identify and distinguish between conventions and structure of film and theatre

2 to evaluate film orally and in writing

3 to recognize and use film terminology

4 to identify the impact and influence of film on society

5 to identify innovations in film technology

Project Specs

This project stretches students' skills in evaluation as well as collaboration. One key aspect of the project is the understanding students will gain of the way in which group discussion can generate, develop, and refine ideas. Students also need to collaborate for their actual presentation.

On Your Feet

Time each flash critique with a stopwatch. Tell students their goal is to keep talking for the entire sixty seconds. They should aim to share just the main points of their impressions, not every detail, to stay within the time frame.

---

28 Film

Film and theatre share many common characteristics. They are both based on story and character, and they both have a lot to tell us about the human condition. Films, however, approach storytelling in their own unique way. This chapter will help you review a film and understand the impact of film on society.

Project Specs

Project Description As part of a group, you will write a review of a film. Then the group will give an eight- to ten-minute presentation of the review.

Purpose to understand and critique the elements of film

Materials an outline or the Film Review Activity Sheet your teacher provides

On Your Feet

Choose a recent hit movie you have seen and evaluate it for the class in a one-minute "flash critique." You only have sixty seconds, so keep your comments brief and to the point. Try to mention elements and ideas that affected you either negatively or positively. What moved you, made you laugh, or made you think? Then call on a classmate to present his or her flash critique.

Theatre Terms

3D film
cinematographer
computer-generated imagery (CGI)
film editing
motion capture
pan
pull quotes
screenplay
special effects
rave review

James Cameron's 1997 film *Titanic*, with Leonardo DiCaprio and Kate Winslet, used spectacular special effects.

Theatre Terms

3D film a film technique that gives the viewer the impression of three-dimensionality

cinematographer chief artist and overseer of a film's lighting and camera crews

computer-generated imagery (CGI) computer graphics that create or contribute to images in film and other media

film editing the creative process of putting a film together once it has been shot

motion capture a film process of recording patterns of movement digitally

pan a very negative review

pull quotes a (usually positive) quote excerpted from an article or review and used in advertising

screenplay the written script of a film

special effects illusions used to create a specific cinematic or virtual world

rave review very positive review

PREVIEW

When was the last time you saw a movie? If you're like most people, it wasn't too long ago. Where were you? At a movie theatre? In a classroom? In your living room? Maybe you were watching it on TV or on your computer. You might have been viewing it on a tablet or even on a cell phone. Technology has changed the way we interact with film, but it hasn't changed our love for it. (See page 412.)

Theatrical Conventions in Film

Today, seeing a movie is a very different experience from watching a live performance. But in the early years of film, moviemakers borrowed heavily from the theatre—a dramatic art form that could translate easily to this new medium. In fact, films made in the early 1900s were nothing more or less than plays captured on film. The camera sat in for the audience, remaining in a fixed position and taking in all the action from the limited perspective of its viewfinder. The camera could only look ahead, a little to the left, or a little to the right. Like stage actors, film stars played to their audience—the camera.

The Language of
THEATRE

Express spoken opinions using a variety of sentence types and connecting words.

- Use individual words or simple phrases to express your opinion of a film in the On Your Feet exercise. Decide if you will give a *rave review* or *pan* it. Try to use connecting words: *and, or, but.*

- Use complete simple sentences to express your opinion of a film in the On Your Feet exercise. Decide if you will give a *rave review* or *pan* it. Try to use connecting words: *and, or, but.*

- Use a variety of sentence types (simple, compound, complex) and connecting words as you discuss your opinion of a dramatic performance, including the screenplay or script, with your group.

- Use a full range of sentence types, including compound-complex, and connecting words as you discuss your opinion of a dramatic performance. Does your review contain good *pull quotes*?

Chapter 28 Film **379**

PREVIEW
Theatrical Conventions in Film

Because of the comparatively primitive nature of early camera and lighting equipment, the first movies were filmed on sets constructed outdoors with no ceilings, so that the filmmakers could take advantage of natural lighting. Some of the best and most consistent natural lighting in the United States was on the Pacific coast, which is one reason the film industry moved early in its development to California and the area that would become Hollywood.

 **Visual Cue**

In this scene from *Titanic,* the ship is beginning to sink. The following prompts can be used to exercise **critical viewing skills.**

- What are these people doing?

- How might this same scene be represented on the stage?

- From what you can see in the photo, what are some further prop pieces that might be appropriate in this setting?

Resource Binder

- Film Activity Sheet, p. 137
- Analyze Camera Techniques Worksheet, p. 138
- Critique Sheet: Film Review Presentation, p. 139
- Film Test, p. 140

Handbook Connections
pages 565 and 586

Going Further

Using extremely realistic special effects, *Titanic* re-created in graphic detail the sinking of the famous luxury liner along with many of its passengers. Big-budget blockbusters like *Titanic* are often referred to as "big-screen films" because the larger-than-life screen of a movie theatre shows the film off to its greatest advantage. Ask students to think of more recent examples of big-screen movies.

Never again would the stage and screen be so closely aligned as they were in those early days of the movies. By the 1920s, innovations had revolutionized film. Film editing became an art, which meant scenes could be shortened, rearranged, or cut out entirely. By that time, cameras could move in many directions. They could track up and down or move in close enough to give the audience an intimate look as an actor's face lit up with joy or crumpled in despair. New types of lighting technology were created for the sole purpose of illuminating movies. Indeed, a brand new industry was born to supply filmmakers with all the technical equipment they needed. As film technology advanced, the differences between theatre and film became ever more pronounced.

Theatrical conventions also appear in television and other media. But as each medium has matured, its conventions grew apart from those of theatre in key ways. For more on distinguishing theatrical conventions in television and other media, see pages 396, 398, and 418.

What Theatre Does That Film Can't

- *Theatre is active.* While film and television audiences tend to be passive viewers, theatre audiences are active participants, as their responses to the action affect the performances onstage.
- *Theatre is multidimensional.* When attending a theatrical production, audiences have to look around. There can be quite a lot taking place on the stage, which requires the audience members to look wherever the action is.
- *Theatre is a multimedia event.* Many stage productions use visual arts in the production of a set and costumes. Some may use video, film, live or recorded music, and dance.
- *Every performance is unique.* Because theatrical events are live, each performance is a bit different, which opens it up to new understanding and new opportunity for improvisation.

Many films have been adapted from stage plays and musicals, but in recent years there has been a reverse trend of films being adapted into musicals. The 2013 Tony Award-winning Broadway musical *Kinky Boots* was adapted from a small 2005 British film of the same title.

Film version of *Kinky Boots*

Broadway play version of *Kinky Boots*

Backstage Gossip: Unresponsiveness of Film

Critic Walter Kerr says that the difference between theatre and movies is the way a live audience reacts to the actors and how the actors respond to the audience.

"This never happens at a film because the film is already built, finished, sealed, incapable of responding to us [the audience] in any way. The actors can't hear us or feel our presence; nothing WE do in our liveness, counts. We could be dead and the film would purr out its appointed course, flawlessly, indifferently."

- *Film has intimacy.* Stage actors are taught to project their voices to fill the auditorium. In a film, an actor can speak softly and make subtle gestures. The camera picks up small but telling changes in facial expression.
- *Film plays the angles.* In film, the camera can be angled first one way and then the other to show exactly the movement the director intends. The audience's vision is focused by the camera's lens. As a result, the audience sees only what the director and cinematographer intend them to see.
- *Film's picture is worth a thousand words.* The expression on an actor's face can convey his or her innermost feelings more clearly than a monologue would. In general, a film accomplishes as much with its visual world as a play does with its verbal world.
- *Film transcends time and space.* Film can jump time and place in a matter of a single second. In the 2006 film *Babel*, for example, a tragedy involving an American couple on vacation in Morocco sets in motion an interlocking story that weaves together the lives of four families in four different countries.

Structure: Film vs. Theatre

Most contemporary films are between ninety minutes and two hours long, although some are a bit shorter and a few clock in at over three hours. Like a

Cate Blanchett and Brad Pitt in a scene from *Babel*. As directed by Alejandro Gonzàlez Iñàrritu, the action seesaws back and forth between very different worlds, using time and place to pull the audience along on a cinematic roller coaster.

play, a film's storytelling typically is built on a three-act structure—the exposition (act one), the rising action (act two), and the resolution (act three). The audience is typically unaware of when the plot moves from the first act into the second because, unlike plays, films do not have to stop for a break between acts—instead they run straight through from beginning to end. This allows film to use streamlined storytelling and move at a fast pace.

What Film Does That Theatre Can't

Once students have read through this section, ask them to come up with a list of films that they believe offer strong examples of each of the film elements listed as it is differentiated from theatre.

Intimacy or Mumblecore?

Mumblecore is a subgenre of American film characterized by low production values, amateur actors, and improvised naturalistic dialogue. Mumblecore films are usually filmed in black and white in natural locations and tend to focus on a single twenty-something character. Although the style has its roots in the 1960s, the term *mumblecore* was coined in the early 2000s to describe a handful of quiet independent films that were long on atmosphere and short on plot, such as Andrew Bujalski's *Funny Ha Ha* and *Mutual Appreciation* and *The Puffy Chair* by Mark and Jay Duplass.

Totally Quotable

"Ironically, film actors can work very quickly to put a scene together in a film that then exists forever while theatre actors may work for months to achieve a performance that only lasts as long as the run of the show."

—Playwright and screenwriter Conor McPherson

Film and New Media

Shooting a film in which one of the main characters is a Bengal tiger presents its share of real-world challenges. As *Life of Pi's* visual effects supervisor put it: "We didn't want our actor to get eaten." To achieve both a highly realistic version of a tiger and the freedom to tell a complex cinematic story, the production company opted for a digital tiger rendered by the special effects house Rhythm & Hues. You can see a slide show of how they accomplished it at http://www.nytimes.com/2012/11/18/movies/creating-a-tiger-for-life-of-pi.html.

CGI and the Uncanny Valley

While CGI is a great solution for many film shots involving scenic or magical backgrounds, enormous crowd scenes, or bizarre creatures, the technology has so far fallen short when it comes to simulating actual human beings. So far, digital renderings of humans tend to fall into what social scientists refer to as an "uncanny valley." This means that the digitally rendered characters intended to seem human seem instead to be both human and alien, and, at least to this point in the ever-changing technology, that gives many viewers the creeps.

Life of Pi (2013), set on a small boat shared by a young man and a ferocious Bengal tiger, won multiple Academy Awards, including one for Ang Lee as Best Director. Lee received sharp criticism from the special effects industry for failing to acknowledge the film's special effects team in his acceptance speech.

Film and New Media

In one form or another, **special effects**—the optical and mechanical illusions that allow filmmakers to re-create hurricanes, train wrecks, or other eye-popping visuals—have always been part of moviemaking. In the early days, effects were created using mechanical technologies like hand-cranked wind machines and scale models. But since the 1990s, **computer-generated imagery** (CGI) has been on a steady rise in film production. The results for the industry have been profound. CGI gives filmmakers more control over visual spectacle than ever before, allowing them to create magical or terrifying effects with minimal danger and maximum believability.

American film production is at the forefront of this technology. Companies like Lucasfilm, creator of the Star Wars films, are working to take CGI to the next level—creating real-time computer-generated images using a technology called **motion capture**—which could revolutionize the filmmaking process. Recent years have also brought advances in the realm of three-dimensional, or **3D film**, production. Although 3D has been intermittently popular ever since it was first introduced to American film audiences in the 1950s, the improved quality of the technology in recent years has brought a big jump in popular demand for 3D films.

From the Field: It's the Tale, Not the Technology

Periodically, I am asked how I think the "digital revolution" will change the role of the cinematographer. It's true that advances in digital camera and postproduction technologies have made images more accessible and easier to manipulate . . . . Digital technology might make it easier to record moving images, but it is the skill of the people who have mastered the art of cinematography that will create the most powerful images—which will endure. In my experience, the best films have always been those that used great imagery to tell good stories in ways that had the greatest emotional impact on an audience. The technology or tools used to tell the story may have been sophisticated or simple, but it was the storyteller that made the real difference.

John Toll, Cinematographer

An *indie* is an independent film turned out by an independent filmmaker. (The filmmaker may also be referred to as an indie.) Indies are people who have broken away from the multimillion-dollar Hollywood machine to make smaller films on smaller budgets, often on topics that interest them, rather than topics considered commercial. In recent years independent filmmakers have received more awards and more attention, and there are now festivals devoted to them, such as Robert Redford's Sundance Film Festival.

Film and Society

The American film industry has been reinforcing cultural values ever since the cameras started rolling more than a hundred years ago. Early silent films often featured the strong, handsome hero saving the beautiful, innocent girl from the forces of evil. During the Great Depression, movie audiences wanted to be comforted with idealistic and hopeful stories. *Gone with the Wind*, for example, even though it dealt with the devastation of the Civil War, portrayed a beautiful and genteel version of the South with strong, self-sufficient characters who learned how to solve their own problems. Shirley Temple made people sing and tap dance, the Marx Brothers made people howl with laughter, and that classic Depression-era film *The Wizard of Oz* encouraged audiences to forget their troubles and travel down the "yellow brick road" to a better future.

In the 1940s and 50s, Westerns gave life to the American ideals of rugged individualism and self-reliance. Films about World War II reinforced the patriotism of the American public, in stark contrast to the darker films of the Vietnam War era and beyond.

As Thomas Sherak, president of the Academy of Motion Picture Arts and Sciences, said, "Movies are a form of communication, and that communication, those stories, come from society—not just where society is presently and what it's doing now—but where society has been." This, then, is why America continues its love affair with the movies—to see who they are now and who they may yet become.

Born on the Fourth of July

Chapter 28 Film **383**

From the Field: An Indie Film Festival

I think the modern student will respond quite favorably to the possibility of making a movie for under $1,000. The challenge to Spielberg and Lucas, et al., is fascinating. Perhaps a film challenge on a local level would be a nice project for a high school . . . . connect local bands, local individual music artists, actors, visual artists, set and costume designers, and writers. A nominal entry fee and then a charge for the screening, followed by the awards, would put a school on the arts map and fulfill a very important arts gap.

John Landers, University of Miami, Coral Gables, Florida

Impact on Contemporary Society

Lead a class discussion of recent or current blockbuster film series that feature youthful characters in primary, heroic roles. Examples include Harry Potter and company in the *Harry Potter* films, Katniss Everdeen and others in the *Hunger Games* series, and Tris Prior and others in *Divergent*. Ask students to think about what makes these stories, which are typically set in fictional realms, relevant to contemporary audiences. Ask questions such as:

- What social issues are highlighted in these films?
- How are the forces of good and evil portrayed?
- How does youth factor into the story?
- What is the overall statement about society?

Buzz Lightyear and Woody quickly become beloved characters in *Toy Story*, the pioneering CGI animated film from 1995.

Impact on Contemporary Society

You can identify the short-term impact of a film simply by learning how many people see it, write about, and talk about it with others. But to identify and fully understand the larger impact of a film, you need to go deeper. The following approaches will help you deepen your understanding of a film's impact on society

Analyze the Impact. As demographics and social dynamics continue to change, new ideas make their way into films, which in turn can serve to drive further changes in values and behaviors in everything from politics to law and from fashion to music. For example, 2008's *Food, Inc.* changed many people's understanding about how their food is grown, processed, and distributed. In the 2006 comedy *The Devil Wears Prada*, actress Meryl Streep's sleek, silver haircut gave rise to a new, more natural standard of beauty for middle-aged and older women. And in 2013, the hit 3D concert film *This Is*

Us, about the well-known tween group One Direction, brought the already famous band an even greater global fan base. These and other films tap into society's often unspoken zeitgeist, or the underlying spirit of the times, and drive it forward into the future.

Evaluate the Impact. Of course, just because something is popular doesn't mean it's necessarily providing any great benefit for society. There is, for example, a continuing national discussion about whether onscreen violence leads to offscreen violence—or at least a lack of empathy—in real life. As you evaluate the role of film in contemporary society, you might consider the impact of film on social roles, political viewpoints, environmental attitudes, and basic values. Also consider the impact, if any, the film has on the art of film itself. Did it break new ground in any way? For example, *Toy Story* (1995) was the first feature film made completely on computers, heralding a new age of digital possibilities.

From the Field: Is It Over Yet?

Are movies getting longer? Though many contemporary films are less than ninety minutes long, a 2013 *Business Insider* report revealed that viewers who attended all three of the hit 2012 films *Django Unchained*, *Les Misérables*, and *The Hobbit: An Unexpected Journey* spent a total of *492 minutes* in the theatre (or 537 minutes for viewers who were also on hand for the fifteen minutes of previews preceding each film). That's almost nine hours of film viewing—not bad for a public often accused of having a short attention span.

Synthesize the Impact. To synthesize the impact of film on contemporary society, pull together the analysis and evaluation you have done into a whole concept. Consider the immediate, short-term impact as well as the longer-term impact on society in general and on the art of film itself. Also, seek out the views of others. Reading professional film reviews, film forum posts, and books about the history and future of film will help you merge new information with your own ideas and opinions to gain the broadest possible understanding.

Articulate the Impact. Put your views into words to articulate the impact you have analyzed, evaluated, and synthesized. Many filmgoers find that even informal discussions after a movie are valuable in sharpening insights into a film's impact. Another suggestion is to write a blog, inviting comments, guest postings, and discussion. Or you might consider joining or starting an online forum for young film reviewers to discuss their impressions and ideas with one another.

Employ the Impact. With the availability of digital tools, nearly everybody, including you, has the ability to make movies. Use your understanding about the impact of film on contemporary society to make a positive and beneficial contribution to the culture.

Evaluating a Film

Film criticism is something nearly everyone takes part in from time to time. Audiences are quick to evaluate and judge. In so doing, they state their opinions about artistic products. But opinions vary, and different people often have starkly conflicting views. One of your classmates may give a film a **rave review**; another may **pan** it, that is, give it an extremely negative review.

How, then, are you to know which opinions to respect? You might begin with the simple question "Why?" "Why did you think the film was good (or mediocre or awful)?" The viewer who answers with a shrug, or with a statement such as "I don't know—it just was," should probably not be taken too seriously. But the viewer who can back up his or her opinion with intelligent reasons and insights deserves more consideration. Of course, the best way to decide the worth of a film is to see it.

Some critics have a reputation for being derogatory or overly harsh. However, if you read film or theatre reviews regularly, you will find that many critics have positive things to say as well. In fact, theatre and movie producers often use **pull quotes,** quotes that are pulled directly from the reviews, to advertise. Unfortunately, unethical advertisers sometimes use a pull quote but leave out significant parts of the quote, replacing them with ellipses. The resulting statement can completely misrepresent the critic's actual views.

Evaluating a Film

Have students use Internet resources such as rottentomatoes.com to find examples of critical raves or pans of current or recent films they have seen. Then challenge them to use Goethe's Principles of Criticism (Chapter 18, page 216) as a set of guidelines to evaluate the reviews they selected. They should be able to answer the three questions:

- What was the filmmaker trying to do?
- How well did the filmmaker accomplish this goal?
- Was it worth doing?

Encourage students to discuss their views together in small groups.

Hot Air: The Sometimes Dubious Ethics of Pull Quotes

In creating pull quotes, advertisers sometimes use the words of a film review out of context, resulting in an inaccurate or sometimes downright dishonest rendering of the critic's original statement. For example, consider this quote: "*The Longest Ride* is stunning!" Now here's the actual quote from the review: "*The Longest Ride* is stunning for its altogether absurd lack of both plot and substance." Students might have fun creating a few of these falsified pull quotes for movies they have seen.

PREPARE

Work on Your Film Review

You may wish to assign students particular films to review instead of allowing them to select their own. Choose films that can be easily accessed on DVD, so that students can view their film either as a group at school or on their own at home or elsewhere.

PART ONE: Preparing Your Portion of the Review

Remind students that although they will be assigned only one of the film's many elements to focus on, it is vital for them to pay close attention and be familiar with the entire film—the details of its acting, direction, design elements, and cinematography. They should think about why a particular element stands out as good or bad. For example, if the dialogue sounds forced, do they believe the problem is related to the writing, to the performance, or to both?

As they move through the preparation process, some groups may benefit from using both the Film Review Activity Sheet and a group-created outline.

In Chapter 18 you began developing critical tools to evaluate a dramatic production—in either oral or written form. By so doing you took a big step toward becoming an intelligent, discerning critic. Now you can use those same tools, with a few modifications, to review a film. (Review pages 216–219 for the criteria for evaluating a dramatic production.) Overall:

- **Evaluate the filmmaker's intent.** What type of film did the director set out to make? What genre does it fall into? Does it meet the expectations of that genre?

- **Evaluate the effectiveness of the effort.** How well did the filmmaker and all involved in the production accomplish their purpose? Did they use all the tools of the medium—such as lighting, camera work, special effects, music and other sound, acting—to achieve their effect?

- **Evaluate the worth of the effort.** Was the resulting film worth the effort? What impact might it have on viewers? On society as a whole?

As you work on your review, be sure to use precise and specific observations, and express yourself in vocabulary appropriate for evaluation. Also, be aware of the similarities and differences between a film review and a review of a theatrical production.

PREPARE

Work on Your Film Review

Divide into groups of four. As a group, choose the film you would like to evaluate. You will all review the entire film, but each of you will also be required to give special consideration to one particular aspect of the film. Decide which person will be responsible for reviewing the film's screenplay, acting, direction, design elements (set, lights, costumes, soundtrack, makeup, technical execution), and cinematography.

Once you have designated these responsibilities, use the Film Review Activity Sheet or create an outline to help you focus on your assignment. Then follow these steps to work on the first part of this project.

PART ONE: Preparing Your Portion of the Review

1 Enjoy the movie, but take notes about what you see and how you feel. Pay particular attention to your specific assigned production element.

2 Write your review. Cover the overall quality of the film—screenplay, performance, direction, and technical elements. Then devote several paragraphs to analyzing your assigned production aspect. Back up your opinions with reasons and specific examples from the movie. You'll use this written report later when your group gives its presentation.

Off-Screen Gossip: David Denby and "the Paulines"

Stanford University-trained film critic David Denby writes for *The New Yorker* magazine, where he shares a weekly column with critic Anthony Lane. He has made a very good name for himself as a sharp and perceptive critic in one of the nation's most respected publications. However, when he first began his career in the early 1970s, he was part of a school of bright, young film critics who were said to model their reviewing style on that of *The New Yorker*'s then head critic Pauline Kael—to the point where they were often referred to collectively in film circles by the tongue-in-cheek nickname "the Paulines."

In addition to the questions on pages 216–219, consider these topics. Two of them, cinematography and editing, are unique to film.

Cinematography: Like photography, cinematography involves the use of color, light, focus, and framing. Unlike still photography, it also involves how the camera tracks movements. What elements of cinematography contributed to your response to the film?

Mise-en-scene: Everything that appears in a scene is called *mise-en-scene*, from the French "placing on stage." All choices about what appears in a frame are deliberate, and they are the result of collaboration among many artists who work on a film.

Editing: How are the scenes and shots pieced together? In what ways does the editing contribute to continuity? In what ways does it disrupt continuity? How does the editing affect your response?

PART TWO: Putting It All Together

Use the following steps to guide you as you work with your group to create a cohesive critique.

1 Have a group discussion. Discuss your impressions of the entire film, focusing on the plot, theme, direction, and acting. What do you all agree on? What are some issues you disagree about? Make note of these.

2 Read aloud the review you each wrote about your specific aspect of the production. Discuss how your opinions connect and how they vary. Take notes.

3 Listen for overlap. For example, if the person reviewing the script brings up a point about the acting, there may be a way to use this area as a transition into the portion of the review dedicated to the actors' performances.

4 Write and edit your presentation. Collaborate to revise and edit your presentation. Use the transitions that have come up in your discussions to create a smooth, seamless flow from one aspect of the production to the next. This will help you decide the order of the presentation.

5 Rehearse your presentation. Be aware that your individual parts of the review don't have to agree with one another. Practice presenting your review together. Make sure the transitions are clear and that each of you knows exactly when to begin reading. Be sure that the presentation can fit in the eight- to ten-minute time slot. If it is too long, decide together where to cut text. If it is too short, go over your notes and add pertinent information.

Part Two: Putting It All Together
Circulate among the groups as they are preparing and putting their presentations together.

Remind students that while it is important to note both good points and flaws within a film, they do not have to make comments as to how they themselves might change those elements. Critics are not filmmakers. Their job is to respond as fairly and objectively as possible to what they see and hear, not to change or revise the film to their own specifications or review the film they would rather have seen.

Participants should avoid getting into long repetitive discussions of plot points unless those points have a direct bearing on their assigned element.

A Few Cinematography Terms

jump cut in film editing, when two sequential shots of the same thing are taken from only a slightly different position, giving the effect of jumping ahead in time

dissolve an instance of fading from one image into another

smash cut a technique where one scene cuts very abruptly to another without a transition; usually intended to startle or excite the audience

split screen visible division of the screen, often in half but sometimes into several different images, breaking the illusion that the screen's frame is a seamless view of reality

PRESENT

Read Your Group Film Review

Remind students to double-check all their presentation materials in advance to make sure they are all ready to go, both individually and as a group.

CRITIQUE

Review the Reviewers

Class discussion of the presentations might be simplified by asking two main questions:

- What was the single best aspect of this presentation?

- What was one aspect of this presentation that needed improvement?

After you have reviewed student critiques, trim off the evaluator's name and hand out the sheets to the groups of subjects of the evaluations, discussing with them any issues you feel are important.

PRESENT

Read Your Group Review of a Performance

When your group is called, walk together to the playing area. Don't forget to bring your reviews and Film Review Activity Sheets with you, as you will be reading from them.

When your turn comes, read your portion of the review with expression, just the way you rehearsed it. Try to leave as few gaps as possible between the sections. Remember that this is a performance. The idea is to try to present the collaborative review as a unified whole. When your group has finished presenting its review, take a short pause before leaving the playing area. Hand your materials to your teacher on your way back to your seat.

Career Focus

The camera is the central technology of film. Read about the career of cameraperson on page 402. Then research the career of cinematographer in both print and online sources. Write a brief description of a cinematographer's job, how it differs from that of a cameraperson's, and the talent, skills, and experience needed to perform well as a cinematographer, either as a career or an avocation. Evaluate your own interests and skills and make a judgment about how well suited you may be for this career. Refer to the chart on page 10 for other ways to evaluate this career.

CRITIQUE

Review the Reviewers

Choose one of the group presentations to evaluate. Remember that it is best to begin with the positives. Rate the presentation on a scale of 1 to 5, with 1 being "needs much improvement" and 5 being "outstanding." Ask yourself the following questions as you listen to the presentation.

- Were the group members able to present their material in a well-organized and well-structured way?

- How well was the group able to articulate ideas and concepts?

- Did the individuals in the group use clear and pleasant vocal projection and expression?

  - Did the group members convince you that their opinions were well supported?

  - Did presenters seem poised and comfortable in their presentations, both as individuals and as a group?

  - Did the group pace their presentation to avoid falling short or going over the allotted time?

Write a paragraph that explains why you rated this group as you did.

The Film Critics of Tomorrow

In 2014, the late film critic Roger Ebert's company Ebert Digital and the civil rights empowerment organization Chicago Urban League teamed up to offer opportunities to aspiring high school and college-age film critics. Through a series of education initiatives and panel discussions, students received training in the fundamentals of film criticism. Then as part of the Urban League's Black History Month Film Festival, these students were invited to post on Rogerebert.com their reviews of films about or created by African Americans.

Changing Elements and Methods of Communication in Film

Today's movies are a feast for the senses: colorful, eye-popping visuals and special effects, sometimes even 3D, and a soundtrack that "surrounds" the audience so viewers feel fully immersed in the experience. If you compare these to the movies of the silent era, you might see little resemblance. There are dramatic differences, to be sure, but there are fundamental similarities as well in the elements of each type of film and their methods of communication.

Similarities: Both silent movies and today's blockbusters rely on certain conventions of filmmaking. These include

- continuity editing (editing so there is a smooth transition between shots)
- three-point lighting (the standard way to illuminate a subject)
- the 180 degree rule (having the camera stay on one side of an imaginary line between characters so it doesn't appear they have switched places)

Differences:

- use of sound
- use of color
- predominant type of shot. Silent movies relied on the medium close-up; contemporary movies use actual close-up. This difference places more emphasis on facial expression in contemporary films and less on subtle body movements and gestures.
- movement of camera. Contemporary films use a free-ranging camera, sometimes in a prolonged shot that follows a character; sometimes just circling around a dinner table.
- blocking. Movement in early films was often motivated and expressive, so directors carefully crafted their movement. As one Hollywood agent said, "In the old days, directors moved their actors. Now they move their cameras."

If possible, show students a short film featuring one or more stars of the silent film era, such as Charlie Chaplin or Buster Keaton. Encourage them to take notes on what they see, and to think about the film in comparison to contemporary films, paying attention to specific elements listed in this section. Afterward, have them discuss thoughts and impressions either orally or in writing. Ask them the following questions:

- What storytelling techniques does this film rely on?
- How do you feel about the main character? What specific elements made you feel that way?
- If this film were shot using contemporary techniques and elements, what do you think the differences would be?

D.W. Griffith's *The Birth of a Nation*

In many ways American filmmaking as we know it evolves from D.W. Griffith's 1915 silent Civil War epic, *The Birth of a Nation*. It was the first film to use such techniques as close-ups or camera pans. The result of these new techniques heightened both the drama and the audience's feelings of empathy. But sadly, it also elicited much controversy over its racist depictions of blacks in post-Civil War America. Still, it is often considered a must-see in film history circles due to its use of groundbreaking camera techniques.

Film Test

The test for this chapter is available in blackline master form in the Resource Binder, page 140.

For More Information

For tips on films and the people who create them:

Books

Ascher, Steven, and Edward Pincus, *The Filmmaker's Handbook: A Comprehensive Guide for the Digital Age, 2013 Edition,* Penguin Group, 2012.

Ebert, Roger, *Life Itself,* Grand Central Publishing, 2012.

Ferrell, William K., *Literature and Film as Modern Mythology,* Praeger Publishers, 2000.

Maltin, Leonard, *Leonard Maltin's 2014 Movie Guide: The Modern Era,* Penguin Group, 2013.

Thomson, David. *New Biographical Dictionary of Film,* Alfred A. Knopf, 2010.

Vineyard, Jeremy, *Setting Up Your Shots: Great Camera Moves Every Filmmaker Needs to Know,* Michael Wiese Productions, 2008.

Other Media

www.filmsite.org
www.imdb.com
www.rottentomatoes.com
www.totalfilm.com

Apps

Flixster
IMDb
Movie Vault

Additional Projects

1 Compare reviews by two different professional critics concerning the same film. Suggested sources include the *New York Times, The Washington Post, The New Yorker*, and *Time*. There are also good sites online for comparing movie reviews. Notice the differences between the two points of view—and the similarities. Do both reviews appear to use the criteria presented in this chapter? Create a chart or a Venn diagram to depict where the opinions overlap and where they diverge.

2 Write a review of a current film. Provide precise and specific observations about the film and use the vocabulary of criticism introduced in Chapter 18 and this chapter. Read your review to the class and discuss other interpretations.

3 What is your favorite movie genre? Do you like science fiction, romantic comedies, or thrillers? Research your favorite genre and identify key films of that genre. Identify, analyze, evaluate, synthesize, and articulate the impact of those films on contemporary society. Use specific examples from the films to back up your interpretations. Include consideration of the role the films might play in everyday life and their influence on our values and behavior.

4 Choose a small group to review a current 3D or CGI film. Each of you will write a complete review, including a section focused specifically on the technical elements. Then get together to present and discuss your impressions.

5 Form a small group discussion with classmates to make predictions about the future of American innovation and contributions to the art of filmmaking. Use evidence from research or from films you have seen to back up your predictions.

6 Read about treatments of Homer's *The Odyssey* on pages 392–393. With additional research, identify theatrical conventions they have in common as well as the conventions that distinguish them. Also read a review of both Mary Zimmerman's play and the Coen brothers' film.

Compare and contrast the reviews, noting the criteria each uses to form a judgment.

7 Using examples from plays and movies you know, compare and contrast the structure of film and theatre. Write your analysis in a brief essay.

8 Reread page 389. Then research changes in elements and methods of communication between theatre in the early 1900s and theatre today. Present your findings clearly and coherently using a technology tool such as PowerPoint.

9 Research three careers or avocations in film. After learning about them, write a brief essay in which you make judgments about those careers or avocations and your potential to achieve success and satisfaction in them.

10 **Theatre Journal** If there were discord in your school over some social issue, what film would you choose to show to students to employ the effect film has on contemporary society? Explain your choice.

Substitute Teacher Activities

The suggestions below are for one or more days when you will be out of the classroom.

- Assign the Analyze Camera Techniques Worksheet on page 138 of the Resource Binder.
- Teach the Film section of the Student Handbook, pp. 565 and 586.
- Assign students one or more of the Additional Projects on this page.

- Have students use their personal reactions to create blurbs for a current or recent film of their choice.
- Have students use online research to access film reviews of current or recent films. Then ask them to use those reviews to create effective pull quotes.

Master of the Craft

Spike Lee: On the Scene with a Wake-up Call

When Spike Lee first came to the attention of the film world in 1986, young African-American filmmakers were a rarity. But Lee quickly made a name for himself, not only because of his impressive skills, but also because of his reputation as an independent, outspoken black artist.

Lee's New York University thesis film, *Joe's Bed-Stuy Barbershop: We Cut Heads*, won a Student Academy Award in 1984 (Bed Stuy is short for Bedford Stuyvesant, a neighborhood in Brooklyn, New York). Lee later said: "I thought that now that I had this plaque on top of my television that Columbia, Warner Brothers. . . Spielberg, Lucas, would call me. So I just sat by the phone. Then the phone got turned off.

That's when I decided to try to do it more independently."

Lee's stylish and ably directed independent feature debut, *She's Gotta Have It*, used what he later described as "guerrilla filmmaking." He focused on controversial social issues in a unique, unorthodox, and even combative way. Lee's second feature, *School Daze*, released in 1988, secured backing from Columbia Pictures, who offered him a third of what they typically paid filmmakers. Despite lukewarm reviews, *School Daze* earned more than twice what it had cost to make. It satirized issues of class and race differentiation at an all-black college in the form of a musical comedy, establishing Lee

as a director who would not compromise his vision. Lee's 1989 film *Do the Right Thing* scored him an artistic and commercial success. Many films followed, including *Mo' Better Blues* (1990), *Malcolm X* (1992), *He Got Game* (1998), *Bamboozled* (2001), and *25th Hour* (2002).

In all his films Lee focuses on the divisions within American society as well as in the black community. He continues to make films with his production company, 40 Acres and a Mule, in which he asks viewers to wake up and open up their minds.

Spike Lee

Spike Lee appears in his own film *Do the Right Thing*.

Master of the Craft
More About Spike Lee

In 2012, Lee co-wrote and directed *Red Hook Summer*, the sixth film in his "Chronicles of Brooklyn" series, which also includes *She's Gotta Have It*, *Do the Right Thing*, *Crooklyn* (1994), *Clockers* (1995), and *He Got Game* (1998).

During the more than three decades of his career, Lee has worked in an eclectic variety of media and genres— from starring opposite Michael Jordan in a popular series of 1990s television commercials for Nike to directing the 2006 documentary about life in post-Hurricane Katrina New Orleans *When the Levees Broke: A Requiem in Four Acts*. With his wife Tonya Lewis Lee, he even wrote a children's book entitled *Please, Baby, Please* (2006), a humorous take on the common parental difficulty of getting babies to fall asleep. Along the way, Lee has racked up an impressive list of awards and honors, including, in 2013, the prestigious Dorothy and Lillian Gish Prize, which came with a cash award of $300,000.

Spike Lee's Essential Films List

Spike Lee is a filmmaker, but he is also a huge fan of the medium. He regularly distributes his "Essential Films List" to film students in the master's program at New York University, where he teaches. A cursory glance at this list reveals that he has a number of favorite directors. Among them are Akira Kurosawa, Alfred Hitchcock, Federico Fellini, John Huston, and Stanley Kubrick. After repeated

criticism that his list contained virtually no women filmmakers, Lee updated the list in 2013 to include five women: Jane Campion, Euzhan Palcy, Julie Dash, Kathryn Bigelow, and Lina Wertmuller. Lee's complete list is available at www. slate.com/blogs/browbeat/2013/08/20/ spike_lee_s_essential_films_list_revised_ the_director_adds_more_women_ filmmakers.html.

Theatre **Then** and **Now**

Poem to Play to Film

The two Homeric epics, *The Iliad* and *The Odyssey* are so rich in complex characters, thrilling actions, and evocative cultural icons that they have stimulated the imaginations of story-tellers and other artists for centuries. Two famous 20th-century novelizations are Nikos Kazantzakis's *The Odyssey: A Modern Sequel* and James Joyce's *Ulysses,* which transposes the story to 1904 Dublin, Ireland. Two musical stage versions are *The Odyssey* and *The Golden Apple,* which places the story in the state of Washington.

Theatre **Then** and **Now**

Poem to Play to Film

Homer's *The Odyssey*

The Odyssey is an epic poem attributed to an author we call Homer. The story is probably 3000 years old, and the written version is about 1000 years old. *The Odyssey* was written to be recited—and perhaps read. Though not written as a play, it has nevertheless inspired many a poet, playwright, and filmmaker to adapt and expand its themes and plot.

The Odyssey tells the story of Ulysses, a hero of the Trojan War, who attempts to return to his home in Ithaca after the war. Unfortunately, he has angered the gods, who present him with a series of obstacles. During his ten-year journey, Ulysses encounters a land with a flower that causes deep sleep; a one-eyed monster called the Cyclops; Circe, the enchantress who turns men into beasts; and many others. All the while, his wife, Penelope, waits patiently for his return.

Homer's epic is exciting and beautifully written and should certainly be read for its own sake as well as for an understanding of all the poems, paintings, plays, and films that allude to it.

"Every day in rehearsal there are moments that I feel . . . the presence and the weight of this text and its history and its long life, and how we're the part of this telling that has gone on for twenty-seven hundred years."

–Mary Zimmerman

Mary Zimmerman's *The Odyssey*

Mary Zimmerman's adaptation of *The Odyssey* tells a tale much like the original poem. While Ulysses battles monsters and escapes the deadly sirens' call, his wife is being heavily pressured by suitors to forget him.

Like the poem, Zimmerman's play uses flashback and interesting details to tell the story. It also takes advantage of

Ulysses and Penelope

Notes

Master of the Craft
Spike Lee: On the Scene with a Wake-up Call

When Spike Lee first came to the attention of the film world in 1986, young African-American filmmakers were a rarity. But Lee quickly made a name for himself, not only because of his impressive skills, but also because of his reputation as an independent, outspoken black artist.

Lee's New York University thesis film, *Joe's Bed-Stuy Barbershop: We Cut Heads*, won a Student Academy Award in 1984 (Bed Stuy is short for Bedford Stuyvesant, a neighborhood in Brooklyn, New York). Lee later said: "I thought that now that I had this plaque on top of my television that Columbia, Warner Brothers. . . Spielberg, Lucas, would call me. So I just sat by the phone. Then the phone got turned off.

That's when I decided to try to do it more independently."

Lee's stylish and ably directed independent feature debut, *She's Gotta Have It*, used what he later described as "guerrilla filmmaking." He focused on controversial social issues in a unique, unorthodox, and even combative way. Lee's second feature, *School Daze*, released in 1988, secured backing from Columbia Pictures, who offered him a third of what they typically paid filmmakers. Despite lukewarm reviews, *School Daze* earned more than twice what it had cost to make. It satirized issues of class and race differentiation at an all-black college in the form of a musical comedy, establishing Lee

as a director who would not compromise his vision. Lee's 1989 film *Do the Right Thing* scored him an artistic and commercial success. Many films followed, including *Mo' Better Blues* (1990), *Malcolm X* (1992), *He Got Game* (1998), *Bamboozled* (2001), and *25th Hour* (2002).

In all his films Lee focuses on the divisions within American society as well as in the black community. He continues to make films with his production company, 40 Acres and a Mule, in which he asks viewers to wake up and open up their minds.

Spike Lee

Spike Lee appears in his own film *Do the Right Thing.*

In 2012, Lee co-wrote and directed *Red Hook Summer,* the sixth film in his "Chronicles of Brooklyn" series, which also includes *She's Gotta Have It, Do the Right Thing, Crooklyn* (1994), *Clockers* (1995), and *He Got Game* (1998).

During the more than three decades of his career, Lee has worked in an eclectic variety of media and genres—from starring opposite Michael Jordan in a popular series of 1990s television commercials for Nike to directing the 2006 documentary about life in post-Hurricane Katrina New Orleans *When the Levees Broke: A Requiem in Four Acts.* With his wife Tonya Lewis Lee, he even wrote a children's book entitled *Please, Baby, Please* (2006), a humorous take on the common parental difficulty of getting babies to fall asleep. Along the way, Lee has racked up an impressive list of awards and honors, including, in 2013, the prestigious Dorothy and Lillian Gish Prize, which came with a cash award of $300,000.

Spike Lee's Essential Films List

Spike Lee is a filmmaker, but he is also a huge fan of the medium. He regularly distributes his "Essential Films List" to film students in the master's program at New York University, where he teaches. A cursory glance at this list reveals that he has a number of favorite directors. Among them are Akira Kurosawa, Alfred Hitchcock, Federico Fellini, John Huston, and Stanley Kubrick. After repeated

criticism that his list contained virtually no women filmmakers, Lee updated the list in 2013 to include five women: Jane Campion, Euzhan Palcy, Julie Dash, Kathryn Bigelow, and Lina Wertmuller. Lee's complete list is available at www.slate.com/blogs/browbeat/2013/08/20/spike_lee_s_essential_films_list_revised_the_director_adds_more_women_filmmakers.html.

Theatre **Then** and **Now**

Poem to Play to Film

The two Homeric epics, *The Iliad* and *The Odyssey* are so rich in complex characters, thrilling actions, and evocative cultural icons that they have stimulated the imaginations of story-tellers and other artists for centuries. Two famous 20th-century novelizations are Nikos Kazantzakis's *The Odyssey: A Modern Sequel* and James Joyce's *Ulysses,* which transposes the story to 1904 Dublin, Ireland. Two musical stage versions are *The Odyssey* and *The Golden Apple,* which places the story in the state of Washington.

Theatre **Then** and **Now**

Poem to Play to Film

Homer's *The Odyssey*

The Odyssey is an epic poem attributed to an author we call Homer. The story is probably 3000 years old, and the written version is about 1000 years old. *The Odyssey* was written to be recited—and perhaps read. Though not written as a play, it has nevertheless inspired many a poet, playwright, and filmmaker to adapt and expand its themes and plot.

The Odyssey tells the story of Ulysses, a hero of the Trojan War, who attempts to return to his home in Ithaca after the war. Unfortunately, he has angered the gods, who present him with a series of obstacles. During his ten-year journey, Ulysses encounters a land with a flower that causes deep sleep; a one-eyed monster called the Cyclops; Circe, the enchantress who turns men into beasts; and many others. All the while, his wife, Penelope, waits patiently for his return.

Homer's epic is exciting and beautifully written and should certainly be read for its own sake as well as for an understanding of all the poems, paintings, plays, and films that allude to it.

"Every day in rehearsal there are moments that I feel . . . the presence and the weight of this text and its history and its long life, and how we're the part of this telling that has gone on for twenty-seven hundred years."
—Mary Zimmerman

Mary Zimmerman's *The Odyssey*

Mary Zimmerman's adaptation of *The Odyssey* tells a tale much like the original poem. While Ulysses battles monsters and escapes the deadly sirens' call, his wife is being heavily pressured by suitors to forget him.

Like the poem, Zimmerman's play uses flashback and interesting details to tell the story. It also takes advantage of

Ulysses and Penelope

Notes

Hermes and his men march onstage in Mary Zimmerman's 2000 production of *The Odyssey*.

contemporary technology. For example, gigantic video projections help create the setting for the underworld. And the lighting designed by Daniel Ostling represents settings ranging from "rosy-fingered dawn" to stormy seas.

The production draws on traditions in dancing and music and the lyrical poetry of the original to communicate the breadth of Homer's epic tale.

O Brother, Where Art Thou?

Joel and Ethan Coen also owe much of their film *O Brother, Where Art Thou?* to Homer. They don't try to hide the fact—their references to the ancient epic are fairly easy to spot. But someone who didn't know a thing about Homer would think it was a modern tale.

The movie is a quirky comedy set in 1930s Mississippi. It tells the story of a chain-gang escapee, appropriately named Ulysses, who endures a series of trials as he makes his way home. It comes complete with sirens, a cyclops, and suitors for his estranged wife. In the end, Ulysses is restored to his family.

In the Coen brothers' adaptation, *The Odyssey* is not only retold in a new medium—it is given a new translation and a new audience.

John Turturro, Tim Blake Nelson, and George Clooney star in *O Brother, Where Art Thou?*, the contemporary film based on *The Odyssey*.

Chapter 28 Film **393**

For More Information

Books

Ferrell, William K., *Literature and Film as Modern Mythology*, Greenwood Publishing Group, Inc., 2000.

Hamilton, Edith, *Mythology: Timeless Tales of Gods and Heroes*, Warner Books, 1999.

Homer, *The Odyssey*, tr. Robert Fitzgerald, Noonday Press, 1998.

Zimmerman, Mary, *The Odyssey: A Play*, Northwestern University Press, 2003.

Other Media

Homer's Odyssey, from Book I through Book XXIV and translated by Samuel Butler, can be read on the Internet by visiting *http://classics.mit.edu/Homer/odyssey.html*.

Visit *www.pbs.org/now/transcript/transcript_zimmerman2.html* for the transcript of an interview with Mary Zimmerman conducted by Bill Moyers.

Chapter 29

Television

This chapter discusses early TV, daytime TV, controversial TV, public TV, and satellite and cable technologies. Students will explore writing for television and will present a proposal for a television show.

Objectives

1. to identify and distinguish between conventions and structure of television, film, and theatre
2. to evaluate television orally and in writing
3. to recognize and use television terminology
4. to identify the impact and influence of television on society
5. to identify innovations in television technology

Project Specs

Not all students may have discretionary access to a television set at the times when their chosen program airs, so you may want to provide recordings of episodes of several favorite series and arrange a time and a place for viewing.

Special Needs Students

The episode outline described on page 403 requires paying attention to several elements at once during viewing. Suggest that students concentrate on who the characters are and where the scenes take place. Then they can create an original scene.

On Your Feet

This activity could be a class game. Stick to contemporary shows or the real classics; not everyone watches enough reruns to be familiar with their theme songs or signature lines.

Chapter

29 Television

When we watch TV, we often see the same personalities or characters one or more times a week. Eventually, we come to know and care about the people we see on our household screens.

Project Specs

Project Description You will write an outline for an episode of a well-known television drama or situation comedy, then present your outline in five to ten minutes.

Purpose to explore the unique aspects of television and to understand the demands of writing for this medium

Materials paper or the Television Activity Sheet provided by your teacher

Theatre Terms

demographic
digital TV (DTV)
high-definition TV (HDTV)
pilot
Public Broadcasting System (PBS)
reality TV
sitcom
syndication
target audience
teleplay

On Your Feet

How influential is television? Does it really have an effect on people's thoughts? Take turns with your classmates humming a theme song or saying a signature line from a popular television show from the past or present. Challenge your classmates to identify the show from the song or line you've provided.

TV has come to play a dominant role in American life.

Theatre Terms

demographic an advertising term used for a group of people

digital TV (DTV) transmission of audio and video by digitally processed and multiplexed signal

high-definition TV (HDTV) television that features a very high-resolution image

pilot first episode of a television show

Public Broadcasting System (PBS) a group of television stations that specialize in educational programming

reality TV a genre of television

sitcom situation comedy programming that documents unscripted situations and actual occurrences and typically features a previously unknown cast

syndication when a television show that has already aired on a network is sold to several stations at once for reruns

target audience a group of people that advertisers have determined a television show is most relevant to

teleplay a television script

Early Television and Beyond

When television emerged through American ingenuity and innovation, it did not borrow heavily from the conventions or structure of theatre as early film had done. Instead, because TV relied on both recorded sound and moving picture, it proved more of a threat to the recording industries of radio and film. So the first effect of TV's broad selection of audiovisual programming—news, sports, and variety shows—was to pull audiences away from their radios. Later TV offered a viable alternative to film through dramas, comedies, and documentary presentations. For example, *Playhouse 90* (1956–1961) used theatre conventions and structure to present classically

George Burns and Gracie Allen

structured **teleplays** such as *Judgment at Nuremburg* and *Requiem for a Heavyweight*. TV was versatile in that it could be broadcast live or taped for later presentation. Perhaps most significantly, viewers could watch and enjoy it in the convenient privacy of their own homes.

Like radio, the structure of television was driven in part by advertising dollars from corporate sponsors who paid to have their products touted on the air during commercial breaks.

Programming soon gave rise to realistic episodic dramas and situation comedies, or **sitcoms**. Among the most-watched early sitcoms were *The George*

PREVIEW

Early Television and Beyond

This chapter's preview provides a brief history of television and descriptions of several different kinds of television programs. Students may not be familiar with some of these shows. Encourage discussion of programs that students know about or substitute the names of additional programs that fit into the various categories outlined here. Ask: What is it about the show you're describing that makes it a sitcom (or other genre)?

Visual Cue

The picture of George Burns and Gracie Allen on this page is typical of a publicity still of that time. Contrast that image to the production still of *Ozzie and Harriet* on page 408. Use the following prompts for both images in order to exercise **critical viewing skills** as well as to make comparisons.

- Compare the actors' costumes and hairstyles in both pictures.

- What is Gracie supposed to be doing? What does this imply about her character and about their show?

- What do the characters on *Ozzie and Harriet* seem to be doing? What might this imply about their show?

ACTivity To reinforce the meaning of sitcoms, or situation comedies, have students list and describe shows they watch today that fit that category.

Resource Binder

- Television Activity Sheet, p. 141
- Television Episode Worksheet, p. 142
- Critique Sheet: Television Episode Outline, p. 143
- Television Test, p. 144

Handbook Connections
pages 576–577

To Have on Hand

- One or more episodes of several comedy, drama, crime, etc., series for students to research
- TV monitor and VCR or DVD player

Daytime TV

Most students probably don't have much opportunity to watch daytime TV. If possible, record and bring in some typical fare from the major networks, including game shows, talk shows, soaps, specialty shows like *Judge Judy* or *Dr. Phil*, educational fare, and reality shows. Ask students to discuss the differences in today's programming based on what they have learned about early daytime TV.

Quiz Show Scandal

Twenty One was an American quiz show that ran during the late 1950s. A highly rated and popular program, its reputation took a nosedive when evidence came to light that the show was rigged and that popular contestants had been given the answers in advance of the broadcast. The ensuing scandal led to a congressional investigation into game show practices, which very nearly brought down the entire game show industry. The 1994 Robert Redford–directed film *Quiz Show* depicted this dramatic moment in television history. You may wish to select a scene from this film to play for the class.

ACTivity Despite the quiz show scandal, American game shows survived and still thrive today. As another experiment with students' familiarity with TV, divide the class into two teams and have each team list as many contemporary game show titles as they can think of.

Vanna White spins the big letters on *Wheel of Fortune*.

Burns and Gracie Allen Show and *The Jack Benny Show* (both of which had their roots in radio). Another hit show, *The Goldbergs*, brainchild of writer-producer Gertrude Berg, had enjoyed a seventeen-year run on the radio (as *Meet the Goldbergs*) before jumping to television in 1949. Berg, who also played the family matriarch Molly Goldberg, focused her show on an ordinary lower-middle-class Jewish family living in a New York tenement. Berg's control over the writing, casting, and production elements of her show paved the way for such female producer-superstars as Lucille Ball and Carol Burnett.

Daytime TV

In television's infancy, the daytime viewer had little to choose from. Viewers watched programs structured in fifteen-minute episodes. They ranged from talk shows to music and dance recitals to dramas. The dramas, often employing the structural elements and conventions of theatre, such as melodrama, came to be known as "soap operas." This nickname came from the heyday of radio, when laundry soap companies had sponsored similar shows, and the name stuck. Over time, these shows became longer, more dramatic, and complex, with convoluted plots and characters of all ages and socioeconomic levels.

Soon producers added game shows and children's programming to the daytime mix. Shows such as *The Price Is Right* became popular, and soon offerings such as *The $64,000 Question, Jeopardy!, Wheel of Fortune,* and *Family Feud* became popular nighttime fare as well. Programming in each of these areas expanded until around-the-clock television was no longer a novelty, but the norm.

Television for the Public Good

Educational programming made its debut in 1953, when a Los Angeles station set aside one hour of "public service time" on Saturdays to present a show about Shakespeare. The result, *Shakespeare on TV*, surprised everyone by becoming a hit. Soon, with government and corporate sponsorship and the dedication of various producers, educational programming expanded into a community of stations that became known as the **Public Broadcasting Service**, or **PBS**.

Backstage Gossip: An "Enchanted Sense of Play

When discussing her feelings about working in television, legendary TV producer and star Lucille Ball once made the following comment: "It is so important to have what I like to call the enchanted sense of play. Many, many times you should think and react as a child in doing comedy. All the inhibitions and embarrassments disappear. We did some pretty crazy things in *I Love Lucy*, but we believed every minute of them. It's like getting drunk without taking a drink."

In the beginning, public television offered only instructional programming. But in 1961, the series *An Age of Kings* used theatre conventions and structure to win a loyal TV audience for Shakespeare's history plays. In the years since, PBS has used vivid and varied storytelling to create dramatic series such as *Masterpiece* (formerly *Masterpiece Theatre*) and its smash hit *Downton Abbey*.

Public television today also offers a wide variety of educational programming including news, cooking shows, documentaries, and more. Its charming and innovative kids' fare— such as the long-running *Sesame Street* and the CGI-animated show *Super Why!*—continues to set the standard for children's programming in both public and commercial television.

The Language of
THEATRE

Show that you understand the main points of spoken language by taking notes.

- Listen to a few minutes of a program with simple language on PBS and take notes to identify any familiar words or phrases. Write down a word or phrase to identify the main point of what you heard.

- As you listen to short segments of programs on PBS on familiar and unfamiliar topics, take notes to identify the main points.

- Listen to two programs on PBS, one on a familiar topic and one that is unfamiliar. Take notes as you listen to each program to identify the main points.

- Listen to two programs on PBS, one on a familiar topic and one that is unfamiliar. Take notes as you listen to identify the main points and to help you evaluate the programs as outlined on pages 401-402.

PBS is known for its innovative programming, such as the animated shows *Super Why!*, *Curious George*, and the gold standard of educational kids' shows, *Sesame Street*.

The Mass Appeal of *Downton Abbey*

The hit PBS series *Downton Abbey* takes place at an English country estate during World War I. It looks at the lives of both a very wealthy family and their many servants. In 2012, when he was asked about *Downton Abbey*'s huge success with American audiences, the show's creator Julian Fellowes responded: "You will probably ask about class division and so on, but class, as a topic, is of far less interest to the Americans than the British. Good for them. What Americans want to see is life in their drama. Life of all sorts: hard lives, easy lives, or lives which, like most of ours, are a mixture of the two." Ask students who have seen the show to respond with their own impressions and ideas about why it has been so successful.

The Language of
THEATRE

Anyone who has ever tried to learn a foreign language and then visited a country where that language is spoken knows the disorientation of engaging a native speaker who communicates too rapidly. As you take your class through new television terms and other unfamiliar vocabulary, remember that what you consider a normal rate of speech will sound very different to ELL or hearing-impaired students.

Go Back in Time

If possible, show students a YouTube clip from the 1960s television show *An Age of Kings*. William Shakespeare's *Henry V* is among the plays available, featuring an appearance by a youthful Judi Dench. After students have viewed the clip, ask them to discuss both similarities and difference between it and contemporary PBS shows they may have seen. http://www.youtube.com/watch?v=WYNQOczcHWY&list=PL5F3D4A55168C5031

Digital Evolution

The Rise of Streaming Media

Ask students to look into and discuss streaming media devices such as Roku, Apple TV, and Chromecast, which can open up an extremely wide world of viewing options for a single price. These devices are currently taking a huge bite out of cable and satellite markets. Digital media and digital convergence are discussed at length in Chapter 30, but students may already know and be able to share quite a bit about the various options available for media streaming beyond cable and satellite TV.

Vocabulary Enhancement

A **spinoff** is a television show that derives from an existing work. For example, in 2013, the AMC network announced plans to air *Better Call Saul*, a spinoff from AMC's smash hit *Breaking Bad* focusing on the character of a lawyer played by Bob Odenkirk in a popular episode from season two.

Digital Evolution

Digital TV, often shortened to **DTV**, represents the latest major technological advance for broadcast television, replacing the previous analog infrastructure. (See Chapter 30 for more on analog versus digital technologies.) In 2009, when the U.S. switched over from analog to DTV, millions had to replace their televisions or buy a converter box to run the technology, as analog was completely phased out. DTV is considered the most significant innovation in television broadcasting since color television was introduced in the 1950s. **High-definition TV** (HDTV) is a **DTV** quality standard. The digital format offers much better picture and sound quality.

Scene from *Breaking Bad*

Even before the full conversion to digital, however, the television landscape was permanently altered by cable and satellite television, offered by subscription. From the beginning, cable and satellite provided far more varied programming than network TV. In addition, the ability to record shows, or for that matter get them on DVD—another digital advance—allowed for "time-shifting." This is the term for watching shows at a time other than their broadcast slot, a practice which has eroded broadcast networks' fundamental base: viewers who tune in at predictable times and see advertisements, which pay for the programming. (See page 418 for more on time-shifting and other impacts of the digital evolution.)

Netflix, long a leader in subscription DVD services, has in recent years transformed itself into a television "network" that "transmits" via the Internet and that competes with both standard networks and other cable networks. Hulu and Amazon On Demand have also created programming. Like HBO and Showtime, Netflix, Hulu, and Amazon Instant Video offer original serialized shows, miniseries, and movies. Hour-long cable dramas such as *House of Cards, Mad Men,* and *Homeland* have explored little-known subsets of American culture, fostering strong viewer emotions—from repulsion to empathy and from laughter to tears. *House of Cards* also experimented with theatrical conventions, having the main character "break the fourth wall" and speak directly to the audience. *Breaking Bad*, which ended its five-season run in 2013, gave us an antihero in Bryan Cranston's Walter White, who seemed a

Totally Quotable

"One thing I won't do in television is a sitcom. I find that world to be so neurotic and bizarre. My plays are comedies, but my work is character-centric. I don't belong in television comedy; I'm not a joke writer."

—Theresa Rebeck, playwright and television writer/producer

logical progression from James Gandolfini's Tony Soprano in the long-running series *The Sopranos* (1999–2007). Overall, cable, satellite, and Internet-based content providers like Netflix and Hulu are more innovative than broadcast networks, and satellite television is able to broadcast programs from nearly anywhere around the world.

Impact of Television on Contemporary Society

Because it depends on a wide audience base, network television has often taken the safe road and avoided programming risks. Nevertheless, innovative American television writers and producers through the years have both reflected and influenced the culture by pushing the boundaries of content and dramatic form. The landmark 1971 sitcom *All in the Family*, for example, brought controversial contemporary social issues to television by presenting in a humorous way the conflicts between a bigoted middle-aged man and his liberal son-in-law. *The Mary Tyler Moore Show* presented positive images of professional women at a time when the idea was still fairly novel. *The Jeffersons, Good Times*, and *Chico and the Man* brought minority issues to the mainstream.

Since the 1990s, progressive comedies such as *Seinfeld* and *Friends* have given way to contemporary sitcoms like *Weeds, Shameless*, and *Modern Family*. With their frank discussion of sexuality, drugs, and other issues, these newer shows sometimes serve to stretch public perceptions of what is suitable for home viewing.

Learn to analyze the ways television influences values. By examining the elements of a show's content—its characters, setting, and situation—you can identify the values a show expresses. For example, the 1977 miniseries *Roots* was one of the first television shows to present African Americans as well-developed characters rather than stereotypes. The settings and situations in this slave saga offered a new perspective to viewers and promoted the value of social equality.

Also learn to analyze the ways television, particularly advertising, influences our behaviors. Identify the purpose of ads and the strategies they use to influence consumers. For example, an advertisement for a pain reliever might give statistics about its effectiveness. To create positive feelings, it might also show a beautiful woman and a handsome man laughing together. The message: This product will relieve your pain and make you attractive and happy!

Impact of Television on Contemporary Society

Television often relies on a collection of situations, phrases, or behaviors that seem to pop up and travel from show to show. A real-life situation can become a pop culture cliche when it is used to excess on TV. Discuss with students the following examples of cliche moments in TV sitcoms:

- A character speaks in nonsense or gibberish to prove that another character is not really listening.
- Someone mistakes a character's sibling for his or her spouse.
- A character (usually a teenager, but not always) is reprimanded for speaking in text abbreviations.
- A character throws his back out and can't move at all throughout an entire episode.

Ask students to think of more stock dialogue or situations common to television. Tell them that some of the most popular TV shows today make a point of upending these tropes or avoiding them altogether.

Totally Quotable

"It's very easy for me to say what success is. I think success is connecting with an audience who understands you and having a dialogue with them. I think success is continuing to push yourself forward creatively and not sort of becoming a caricature of yourself."

—*Girls* creator Lena Dunham

Here's How

Ask students to take turns reading this chart out loud. Tell them to jot down any points they strongly agree with as well as those whose validity they may question. Have students discuss their impressions of these points and how they might impact their television and film viewing in the future.

Ready for Their Close-up

Ask pairs of students to stand face to face about ten feet apart. Then have one of them make a fictional statement about himself of herself as the other student takes a cell phone video. This speaker should try to sell the fictional statement as fact. Then have them repeat the process while standing only three feet apart as the cameraperson shoots the same statement in a close-up. What, if any, differences do they notice between the two versions? Which performance is more believable for the cameraperson? For the speaker? Once they have discussed their responses, have them switch roles and try the exercise again.

Here's How
Television Differs from Film

Whether you're an actor, director, producer, or crew member, you'll find that working in television is different from working in film. Here are some of the ways they differ:

	Television	Film
Performance	• Programming can be presented live. • It lends itself to intimate, confessional styles. • It requires hooks and cliff-hangers to grab audiences. • Audiences are casual and expectations are low. • Many shows have a laugh track; the soundtrack is minimal.	• Film is not presented live. • It lends itself to dramatic, heroic styles. • It can build slowly toward a climactic event. • Audiences buy tickets, therefore expectations are higher. • There is no laugh track; the soundtrack is important.
Structure	• Programs vary in length—most are about 30 minutes; some are three hours. • Programs are interrupted by commercials. • Many programs are weekly or daily serials.	• Programs vary in length from about 1 1/2 to 3 1/2 hours. • Programs usually run uninterrupted. • Though sequels exist, each movie must stand on its own.
Technical Elements	• Close-ups are less effective. • Mid-range shots are effective. • Panoramic shots are rarely effective. • Characters tend to seem approachable and real.	• Close-ups can be very effective. • Mid-range shots are effective. • Panoramic shots can be extremely effective. • Characters and topics sometimes seem larger than life.

Totally Quotable

The theater is the actor's medium. Movies are the director's medium. Television is nobody's medium.

Lee J. Cobb, Actor, quoted in *TV Guide,* 1963

Television is so much a part of our lives that we may be unaware of just how much it influences our values and behavior. Learn to analyze the influence of its content and advertising in all areas of your lives—social mores, language, food, fashion, and politics, to name only a few. The strategies below can give you some additional basic tools to deepen your understanding.

Understanding the Impact of Television

Analyze Try to think about what you watch. Ask analytical questions about the feelings and thoughts you are left with afterward. For example: Is it pure escapism? What is going on under the story? What does that mean in your world?

Evaluate Once you've analyzed what you've watched, evaluate it by asking how it might affect you or others you know. For example, how might it affect the way you dress, interact socially, or spend time?

Synthesize Synthesize your analysis and evaluation with those of professional TV reviews or TV-related podcasts to form a unique perspective.

Articulate Share your understandings with others. One way might be to create an online journal or brief TV reviews, or to join an online forum or an after-school discussion group.

Employ How might you put to use what you have learned about the impact of television in a production of your own? Explore possibilities with a local cable station.

A Critic's Perspective

With the same tools you developed and sharpened in Chapters 18 and 28, you can critically evaluate television or any of the arts and media. Developing a critical foundation for analyzing and evaluating what you watch can make the experience more challenging and rewarding by giving you some sense of the underlying message. To clarify your thoughts, evaluate the creators' intent, use of structure, effectiveness, and overall value. Ask yourself the following questions to help you fairly assess what you watch on TV.

- *What is the intent?* What did the show set out to do? What were the writers and producers trying to accomplish? Was the show intended to be a comedy? a drama? a documentary about the future of the planet? To criticize anything, first make every attempt to understand the creators' intent.

What criteria did critics use to pronounce *Game of Thrones*, the wildly popular fantasy series, an artistic success?

Chapter 29 Television   **401**

Notes

_____

_____

_____

_____

_____

_____

_____

Career Focus

Being a cameraperson for motion pictures may be a dream job for many high school students, but the assistant cameraperson is also in an enviable position. The assistant is responsible for setting up the camera and seeing that the camera is in focus, which can be quite a challenge on an active set with all kinds of crew walking around. The assistant can learn a lot about camerawork from those around him or her. And an added bonus is the potential for exotic and interesting locations, sometimes quite challenging, such as jungles with wild animals close by, highways with cars zooming by, helicopters flying immediately overhead, and so on.

Show, Don't Tell Many students will probably be old hands at handling video cameras and recorders, but if there are some who have never had hands-on experience with a video camera, give them a chance. Arrange for a video camera in your classroom and allow time for every student (who wants to) to do some filming. Viewing the resulting tape later, you can point out such things as: How fast should a pan move? How close is a closeup? What results can you get from unusual camera angles?

- *How is it structured?* Of course, intent on its own is not enough. There must be a structure that allows the artists to succeed. Given the intent, did the structure help to put it across? What structural elements worked or didn't work?

- *Is it effective?* Many elements go into the making of a television product. So consider whether the artists' use of the medium and all technical elements (sound, lighting, cinematography, and so on) worked well.

- *Does it have value?* Although this question is subjective, once you have responded to a work's intent, structure, and effectiveness, you will be much more prepared to make an informed judgment on that work.

Career Focus

Cameraperson

Camera crew members in television, film, and other media straddle the line between technical theatre and art. They must know about lighting, camera shots, and angles, but they must also understand creative composition and visual styles.

You can gain an introduction to all these things through classes in photography, television, and film. Most camera operators now have a college degree in a film or broadcast field. You can easily appraise the value of the visual skills, creativity, and experiences with digital media and software to higher education and many careers.

It is still important to master these skills through experience by working as a camera operator. That is, try it out on your own time. Cameraperson Sidney Lubbitch explains, "The most important thing is to learn the language of the viewfinder." By that, he means that you must learn how the camera frames images and action.

Many professional camera operators now prefer to work with digital cameras because they are inexpensive and flexible. So start by working with a digital camera taking still photos. Learn about light and speed and how to focus a lens. Experiment with camera angles and composition.

Then you can progress to video. You can film family occasions, produce your own documentaries, or collaborate with someone who has a story to tell. A local access cable station may provide equipment and training or opportunities to apply your skills.

Review and learn from your still shots and video. You can also use the successful pieces to construct a portfolio of works created in technical theatre. Considering what you know about this career and your own skills, talents, and discipline, make a judgment about this career. Is it something you might pursue for yourself as either a career or an avocation? Refer to the chart on page 10 for more ways to evaluate this career.

Totally Quotable

"Statisticians report that television is watched over six hours a day in the average American household. I don't know any fiction writers who live in average American households. ... Actually, I have never seen an average American household. Except on TV."

—David Foster Wallace, *A Supposedly Fun Thing I'll Never Do Again*

PREPARE

Outline Your Proposed Episode for a TV Show

For this project, you will develop an outline for an episode of a broadcast television show with which you are very familiar—a drama or a comedy.

Before you begin your outline, try to obtain a copy of the program's writer's guidelines. These can help you understand what producers are looking for in scripts for their particular show. If this is not possible, use a writer's handbook with guidelines for writing scripts and screenplays. Be sure you consider the following points as you write your outline.

Your Outline Should Reflect:

- **The TV Category** Your proposal will be easier to sell if you can identify it as part of a specific kind of programming, such as a sitcom, an adult cartoon, a family drama, a medical drama, a crime drama, an action series, or a law and justice series.

- **The Correct Tone** Each TV series has its own distinctive tone. *Friends,* for example, is breezy, but *The X-Files* is dark science fiction. Producers are apt to buy scripts in keeping with the usual tone of the show.

- **The Right Plot Elements** Some shows feature a continuing plot thread, while others are self-contained. As an outside writer, you must show an understanding of plot developments that have happened so far without imposing any new plot line.

- **Familiar Character Types** Characters in most television programs have specific roles. Many characters feature one or two defining characteristics, such as bossy, fun-loving, goofy, predatory, spacey, suspicious, innocent, sweet, malicious, and so on.

- **A Target Audience** Most shows are aimed at a specific **demographic,** or group of people (for advertising purposes), such as white males who are 18–35 years old. This would be called your **target audience.** If you know a particular show's demographic, you can include references and topics that appeal to this group.

- **Commercial Breaks** Think about the time slot your particular episode is likely to fill. Then find out where commercials are inserted into programming for that time slot. Structure your script so that suspenseful moments fall just before commercials. This will reel your audience in—and hold them during the commercial break.

PREPARE

Outline Your Proposed Episode for a TV Show

Show, Don't Tell Many television series make writer's guidelines available to prospective writers. If possible, obtain at least one to show students what is specified in such guidelines and what is left open to a writer's imagination.

Consideration of the time slot is crucial. Most obviously, there is a great difference between a half-hour program and a full-hour program in terms of how many characters can be featured and how many plot elements or subplots can be introduced. (In a sense, it is like the difference between a one-act and a full-length play.) Less obviously, the programming time slot may hold implications for program content. Although what is permissible in prime time has changed greatly over the years, many audience members still have expectations for language, sexual references, and so on—especially during "family" viewing hours.

Vocabulary Enhancement

Screenwriters often write *on spec,* or on the speculation of payment, without any contract or specific promise of payment.

A Word About Binge-Watching . . .

"As it turns out, the entire connotation of 'binge'—a term tinged with the shame of eating an entire roll of cookie dough—has changed into something prideful and brag-worthy. Finally some people get that there's something ironic about the term. People aren't watching *Dukes of Hazard.* They're watching great TV, not bad TV."

—Grant McCracken, cultural anthropologist

PRESENT

Share Your Outline for a Proposed TV Episode

Before students present their outlines, go over with them one last time the six points that their outline should reflect. Write each on the board and suggest that they give a minute to their introductions, a minute to each of the points, a minute for the conclusion, and a minute for questions from you or the audience.

CRITIQUE

Evaluate a Classmate's Outline

You can choose whether every student will evaluate every other classmate's outline or whether every student will evaluate only one other student, so as to make possible a more thoughtful, more detailed evaluation. If the latter, you will have to assign evaluators so that everyone receives at least one critique from a classmate.

After you have reviewed student critiques, trim off the evaluator's name and hand out the sheets to the subjects of the evaluations.

PRESENT

Share Your Outline for a Proposed TV Episode

When your name is called, step to the front of the room and share your outline with the class. First, give the name of the television program to which your episode pertains. Then read your outline. Be sure to stay within the ten-minute time limit.

When your presentation is complete, hand your outline or your Activity Sheet to your teacher and return to your seat.

CRITIQUE

Evaluate a Classmate's Outline

You will choose one outline and rate it on a scale of 1 to 5, with 1 being "needs much improvement" and 5 being "outstanding." Ask yourself the following questions as you evaluate your classmate's presentation.

- In what ways did the outlined episode seem suitable (or unsuitable) for this particular TV series?

- Did the plot and characters seem to fit in smoothly with the TV program as you have experienced it?

- In what way would the episode outlined in this presentation draw in the target audience of this show?

- Did the presentation seem well researched and well thought out in terms of the time slot, demographics, and style of the show?

Write a short paragraph explaining why you gave this outline the rating you did.

Notes

Reality TV

CBS unveiled the first show in the reality format more than forty years ago. It was called *Wanted,* and it focused on alleged criminals in much the same way that *America's Most Wanted* and *Cops* do today. Allen Funt's *Candid Camera* revealed long ago how people act under stressful circumstances—and this same premise is found today updated in *America's Funniest Home Videos* and other similar shows.

PBS aired its first reality show, called *An American Family,* in 1973. It featured the Louds, a seemingly typical family, who opened up their home to video cameras for a period of seven months. This footage was heavily edited, but the resulting twelve-hour program included the breakup of the Louds' marriage and the coming out of their son Lance. Viewers found it riveting. In 2007, *Jon and Kate Plus 8,* a show about the Gosselins, a couple struggling to raise their eight very young children, traveled similar ground—with similar results. By 2009, the show was chronicling the Gosselins' ugly divorce.

An American Family was the inspiration in 1992 for MTV's *The Real World,* in which people video their lives together for a period of weeks. In 2014, *The Real World* was approved for yet another consecutive season. The action-oriented competition show *Survivor,* introduced in 1997, challenges people to live and compete under various difficult conditions. Similar in nature are the romance-inspired shows *The Bachelor, Blind Date,* and *The Bachelorette.* Reality shows such as these are popular with networks because they are less costly to produce than regular programming. The shows' novelty and unpredictability draw strong ratings. The downside of these types of programs is that they will likely not make money in syndication. That is, the network will likely not be able to resell reality programs as highly lucrative reruns (as they have such huge fictional series as *Battlestar Galactica, Seinfeld,* and *The Sopranos*).

In recent years, a broad constellation of reality TV shows has evolved, including *The Biggest Loser* (in which people compete to see who can lose the most weight), *America's Top Model, So You Think You Can Dance, Cupcake Wars,* and *Top Chef.* Reality TV explores fame (or the quest for it), bizarre behavior of all kinds, and just about any niche subject imaginable. Many offer elements of sitcom and drama, as real people encounter various challenges while followed by (and playing to) the camera. Often criticized for poor aesthetic quality and lack of taste, these shows nonetheless draw huge audiences and continue to have an overwhelming effect on mainstream television.

Candid Camera actually has its roots in radio! Allen Funt began his career by taping the complaints of his fellow servicemen and airing them for a broadcast audience.

Spotlight on

Reality TV

ACTivity **Beginning Students**
Have students research and compare a reality television show seen in America to a reality program offered in another country. Have students present their findings to the class.

ACTivity **Advanced Students**
Ask these students to choose two countries to analyze in terms of their television production. Comparisons should include production practices and theatrical traditions.

Backstage Gossip: Reality TV's Granddaddy

The granddaddy of the reality TV genre is *Candid Camera,* which has been on television on and off since 1948 (yep, almost since the dawn of the medium itself). The show actually has its roots in radio. When Allen Funt taped and broadcast his fellow servicemen on Armed Forces Radio and took his idea to network radio in 1947, it was called *Candid Microphone.* The television version followed a year later. Funt was still active on the show when he died in 1999.

Beth Rowen in *History of Reality TV* on *infoplease.com,* 2000.

Television Test

The test for this chapter is available in blackline master form in the Resource Binder, page 144.

For More Information

Block, Bruce, *The Visual Story: Creating the Visual Structure of Film, TV and Digital Media,* 2nd ed., Focal Press, 2009.

DiMaggio, Madeline, *How to Write for Television,* Fireside, 2008.

Rabkin, William, *Writing the Pilot,* moon & sun & whiskey, 2011.

Silvers, Dean, *Secrets of Breaking into the Film and TV Business: Tools and Tricks for Today's Directors, Writers, and Actors,* William Morrow Books, 2014.

Smith, Evan S., *Writing Television Sitcoms* (revised edition), Perigree Books, 2009.

Other Media

abc.go.com
www.aetv.com
www.aspiringtvwriter.blogspot.com
www.hbo.com
www.mtv.com
www.nbc.com
www.netflix.com
www.paleycenter.org
www.pbs.org

Additional Projects

1 With a partner, prepare a presentation using technology that shows how you analyze, evaluate, articulate, and synthesize the impact of television on contemporary society. For each of those tasks, include specific examples that make your point. For example, when you analyze the impact, refer to specific television shows and specific impacts. When you evaluate the impact, refer to the same or additional shows to support your evaluation. Conclude by explaining how television creators can employ the powerful impact of television for a good cause.

2 Prepare a timeline, either on paper or using a computer, showing the innovations in television over the years of its lifetime. Then write a paragraph identifying and showing appreciation of the contribution to television made by the United States.

3 Work with a partner. In a television interview format, offer a critique of a television show. One person should be the talk show host and ask the questions.

As you prepare answers, be sure to use the vocabulary of criticism with such terms as intent, structure, effectiveness, and worth.

4 In a small group, analyze ways in which television influences values and behavior, addressing both content and advertising. Then improvise a scene in which you reveal those influences on everyday life. Be creative in your approach.

5 Experiment! Develop a plan for a mixed-genre program, such as a news/game show or a reality/sitcom.

6 Read a teleplay by a playwright such as Paddy Chayefsky or Arthur Miller, and write a plan for a sequel.

7 Research the career and life of an early television pioneer such as Lucille Ball, Ernie Kovacks, Ed Sullivan, or Sid Caesar. Share your findings with the class using technology.

8 In an essay, analyze and evaluate the training and skills needed to pursue career opportunities as a camera operator in film, television, and other media.

Also appraise the value of these skills and experiences to higher education and careers outside of the theatre. Make a judgment about the possible careers and avocational opportunities in television that seem best suited to you and your talents and interests.

9 Choose an existing television series, and write a short script for this program based on one of the scenes found in Unit Eight of this book. You must adapt the scene so that it will appeal to the people who typically watch this TV show. In your adaptation, take into account the differences in structure between television and theatre.

10 **Theatre Journal** Keep a running journal of the television shows you watch during one week. During commercial or station breaks, make a few notes about each show you watch. What do you like and dislike about the show? What theatre conventions can you identify in the shows?

Substitute Teacher Activities

The suggestions below are for one or more days when you will be out of the classroom.

• Assign the Television Episode Worksheet on page 142 of the Resource Binder.

• Teach the Television section of the Student Handbook, pp. 576–577.

• Assign students one or more of the Additional Projects on this page.

• Assist students as they interview each other about viewing habits.

• **Play a game of TV charades.** Divide the class into teams (either two teams or small groups of four to five students). Ask them to write the titles of several television shows on separate slips of paper. Check the slips to make sure there is no duplication, and then begin the game. A member of one group picks one of the other team's titles and has three minutes to pantomime it for his or her team.

Master of the Craft
David Simon: From Reporter to Producer

David Simon started out as a reporter for the *Baltimore Sun*, where he worked for thirteen years, mostly on the crime beat. In 1991, while still on staff, he published a book titled *Homicide: A Year on the Killing Streets*, based on his connections with members of the police department's homicide division. The book was a brainy and heartfelt examination of Baltimore's law enforcement and criminal element. That book led to a TV show in 1993 which ran until 1999.

Simon left his job at the *Sun* in 1995, but he didn't slow his pace a bit. While continuing to write for *Homicide*, he wrote another book, 1997's *The Corner: A Year in the Life of an Inner City Neighborhood*. Simon later transformed that book into an HBO miniseries called *The Corner*, which aired in 2000. *The Corner* contained the seeds of Simon's future

work—ideas, characters, and situations he would develop further to create perhaps the most brilliantly complex crime series in television history, *The Wire*.

The Wire aired on HBO from 2002 until 2008. Its structure was a departure from that of earlier crime dramas in that each of the show's five seasons focused on a different area of urban crime or decay, including housing projects, inner-city schools, and the news media. The show's long-form narrative structure featured a number of concurrent storylines that probed deeply into the lives of characters at all different levels of society. Despite enormous critical acclaim, *The Wire* did not score huge audiences during its five years on the air. Since the final season ended, however, it has

gone on to a robust life on DVD, picking up many thousands of fans along the way.

After *The Wire*, Simon's next major TV venture was a drama called *Treme* (HBO). Set in New Orleans three months after Hurricane Katrina, *Treme* premiered in 2010 and ended just three years later. "I love these *(Treme)* characters," Simon said. "They're the most complex human beings I've been able to write."

He is sometimes frustrated with the limitations of television. "I think it's time to look at the medium and say, 'What is possible?'. . . ." Simon has begun to find some answers in his closely observed shows.

David Simon (left) in a panel for HBO's *Treme*

Master of the Craft
David Simon's Musical Side

Music has been a touchstone in Simon's work. *The Wire's* theme song, "Way Down in the Hole," for example, opened every episode. Written by Tom Waits, the song was sung by a different singer or band each season. In the series itself, Simon used a number of songs by the Irish band The Pogues, and he made no secret of being a big fan of the band. In late 2013, five years after *The Wire* went off the air, *Rolling Stone* reported that Simon was creating a new musical featuring the songs of The Pogues. He had been collaborating on the project with Phil Chevron, the band's guitarist, who died of cancer in October 2013. The project was in development at Ireland's Druid Theatre.

Totally Quotable

"The trick to making a story matter is that every now and then, somebody you care about has to go. If it's somebody that you don't care about, then it doesn't really have—the stakes aren't there. But if you do that every now and then, then the story matters to people. And there are actual stakes involved, emotional stakes."

—David Simon on writing for television

Theatre **Then** and**Now**

Theatre and Television: The Odd Couple

The days of the television anthology series, which featured plays written for television—often by some of the country's finest playwrights—and performed live, are called television's "Golden Age." Many of these plays have been anthologized. Suggest that students find and read TV plays by Paddy Chayefsky, Horton Foote, Reginald Rose, and Rod Serling (*The Twilight Zone*).

Theatre **Then** and**Now**

Theatre and Television: The Odd Couple

Theatre and television have had a love-hate relationship from the start, but, when they share their expertise with each other, both are enriched.

Theatre on the Small Screen

Theatre's early influence on television came in the form of the anthology series—plays written for television and performed live by both rising theatrical stars and hopeful unknowns.

Early television series such as *Philco Television Playhouse, Goodyear Television Playhouse, Kraft Television Theatre,* and *Revlon Theatre* opened a new door for writers, and they responded with timeless TV dramas such as Paddy Chayefsky's *Marty,* Horton Foote's *A Young Lady of Property,* and Reginald Rose's *Twelve Angry Men.* Each of these teleplays dealt with what Chayefsky called "the marvelous world of the ordinary."

During the 1950s, sponsors became increasingly uncomfortable with the controversy some of the early teleplays aroused. These theatrically-based shows were then replaced with an era of shorter action shows and a myriad of sitcoms. Most of these new programs catered to sponsors who preferred to underwrite light entertainment.

New programs featured dashing, unsullied heroes like the eligible young Dr. Kildare or the dedicated detective Ellery Queen. Situation comedies such as *Ozzie and Harriet* presented a sweet, comforting view of family life as television settled into an entertainment routine, with the occasional game show, news show, or mini-drama thrown in. For a time, authentic drama was all but forgotten.

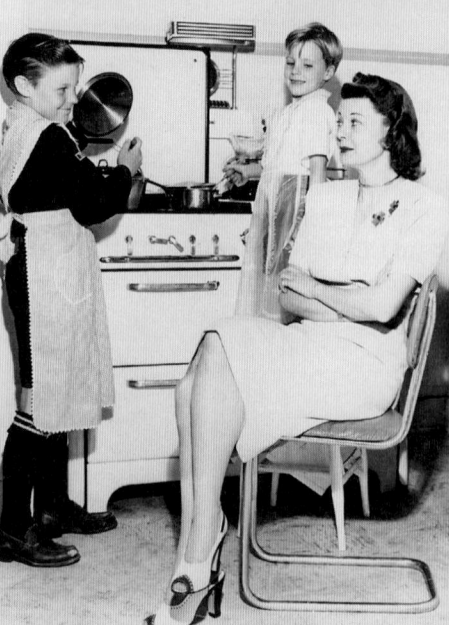

David, Ricky, and their mom, Harriet Nelson, in *Ozzie and Harriet.*

For More Information

Books

Hoopes, Ned E., and Patricia Neale Gordon, editors, *Great Television Plays, Volume 2,* Dell, 1975.

Kaufman, William I., editor, *Best Television Plays,* Harcourt Brace, 1957.

LaKuke, Dee, *Making Great Television: Four Essential Ingredients,* Gardner, 2004.

Vidal, Gore, *Best Television Plays,* Ballantine, 1970.

Other Media

Adventures of Ozzie and Harriet—Vol. 1 Platinum Edition, Good Times Home Video, DVD, 2009.

The Twilight Zone—Collections 1–4, Rod Serling, et al., Image Entertainment, DVD, 2002.

The X-Files: The Complete Collector's Edition, Twentieth Century Fox Home Video, DVD, 2007.

Small Screens Onstage

These days, playwrights creating television drama is not as common as it once was. Theatre's influence on television is perhaps more subtle, while film techniques have become more obvious.

It should not come as a surprise to learn that over the years television has influenced theatre to some degree. Some theatrical professionals have used television as a dramatic tool.

At their most ordinary, televisions are just set pieces with characters watching them onstage. But TV sets have also been used as a technical element of theatre. They are sometimes featured as alternative narrators or as symbolic characters. American directors have begun to incorporate television technology into their dramatic images. The Wooster Group in New York used television monitors in its staging of *Our Town* by Thornton Wilder. The group feels it plays "a pivotal role in bringing technically sophisticated and evocative uses of sound, film, and video into the realm of contemporary theater."

Television also has fostered audience participation by moving theatrical professionals to offer what television

Tony Hernandez of the Actors Gymnasium's Flying Griffin Circus in Evanston, Illinois.

cannot. It has spurred theatrical productions to be daring in order to woo audiences away from their TV sets, and it has inspired productions based on television, from tributes to *Gilligan's Island* and *The Brady Bunch* to Green Mamba's satirical take on *Big Brother*.

Playwrights Who Work in TV

Many of today's leading playwrights divide their time between writing for the theatre and writing for television. Here is a small sampling of recent writers who have made this leap:

- Roberto Aguirre-Sacasa, *Big Love*
- Jon Robin Baitz, *Brothers & Sisters*
- Carlie Mensch, *Weeds*
- Eric Overmeyer, *The Wire, Treme*
- Adam Rapp, *In Treatment*
- Theresa Rebeck, *Law & Order, Smash*
- Tanya Saracho, *Girls*
- Craig Wright, *Six Feet Under, Dirty Sexy Money*

Chapter **30**

Electronic Media

Objectives

1 to identify the influence of digital media on everyday life

2 to identify the impact of digital media on contemporary society

3 to evaluate new media orally and in writing

Project Specs

Digital media have given us instant access to a vast constellation of information across multiple platforms. This project allows students to make imaginative predictions about electronic media while expanding on information from the chapter.

On Your Feet

Before students create their lists, tell them that one way to think of as many examples as possible is to imagine themselves waking up in the morning, going through the morning routine (making and/or eating breakfast), leaving the house, getting to school, and so on.

Chapter

30 Electronic Media

Now more than ever, electronic media play a pivotal role in our lives. Being an active and savvy media consumer means keeping pace with current digital technology—and understanding something about its effects on you and your world.

Project Specs

Project Description With a partner, you will create and present a humorous three- to five-minute scene from the future, illustrating the evolution and impact of technology

Purpose to understand the impact of technology and use digital technology in a scene

Materials an outline or the Electronic Media Activity Sheet your teacher provides

On Your Feet

How many forms of digital technology do you encounter in a given day—at home, at school, and elsewhere? Write down as many as you can think of in one minute. Then exchange lists with a classmate and discuss any differences.

Theatre Terms

analog
cloud computing
digital convergence
digital divide
spectatorship
Web 2.0

Theatre Terms

analog using signals or information in the form of a continuously variable quality such as position or voltage

cloud computing information technology purchased as a service rather than a collection of hardware

digital convergence the conversion of four separate electronic media formats on one device

digital divide the division between those who are able to use information technologies and those who are not

spectatorship the fundamental ways people consume and interact with media

Web 2.0 the user environment that allows collaboration and sharing on the Internet

The Digital Convergence

The rise of digital media has revolutionized our world. Twenty-five years ago, nearly all media was **analog**. In analog media there is a direct physical relationship between the original message and the reproduction of that message. For example, with a book or other hardcopy print media there is a one-to-one relationship between the print and the message it represents. The same is true of musical sounds and the iron particles responsible for reproducing them on an audiotape. During the analog days, each technology—radio, computer, television, telephone—operated completely independently. Each was transmitted on its own network unconnected to the networks of other media forms.

Today, with digitized content, you can consume the same media on a variety of devices because all information can flow along the same network and can be stored or viewed on the same kinds of equipment. For example, you can now read e-mail on your mobile phone, or stream a movie via a home theatre connected to the Internet. The interconnectedness of four once-separate enterprises—information technologies, telecommunications, consumer electronics,

and entertainment—into a single system of converged, networked technologies that can run on any device is referred to as the **digital convergence**.

Influence of Electronic Media on Everyday Life

Our concept of media is in the process of a radical shift, and everything from large computers and televisions to small personal wallets and cell phones will one day to be hooked up to a vast global network that will replace the current Internet. In the not-too-distant future, separate technologies will likely merge into a single media provider that may even be worn as clothing.

Following are just a few specific developments in the convergence of electronic media that influence everyday life. **Web 2.0,** the dynamic user environment that allows for collaboration and sharing on the Internet, has been a foundation for many of the changes.

- Information technology: **cloud computing**, allowing users to buy information technology as a service rather than a collection of hardware and manage it through increasingly smaller and portable devices

- Telecommunications: replacement of landlines with cell phones capable of texting, connecting to the Internet, storing and sending photos and music, and sending e-mails;

Chapter 30 Electronic Media **411**

PREVIEW

The Digital Convergence

A number of contemporary fiction writers have imagined worlds where books are a nearly forgotten thing of the past. In Gary Steynghart's novel *Super Sad True Love Story*, people are completely connected to a digital technology channel that carries shopping, reality shows, and porn. In the novel, people actually believe that the few paper (analog) books left in the world give off a bad smell. Use the idea of a world without books as a jumping off point for a student discussion about the place of books in current culture and in the future.

Influence of Electronic Media on Everyday Life

The rise of electronic media has changed the way we work, learn, and socialize. For example, more and more businesses are beginning to realize that they can forgo brick-and-mortar office and retail spaces in favor of online linkups and file transfer protocols for their employees. Have students do Internet research on the pros and cons of telecommuting and teleshopping for both employees and employers.

Resource Binder

- Electronic Media Activity Sheet, p. 145

- Media Literacy Worksheet, p. 146

- Critique Sheet: Futuristic Scene, p. 147

- Electronic Media Test, p. 148

Handbook Connections
page 571

Impact on Contemporary Society

Today's "always-on" technologies allow students more opportunity than ever to stay connected. The following are statistics from a Pew Research study entitled "Teens and Technology, 2013," published in March 2013:

- 95 percent of teens are online, a statistic that has remained consistent since 2006

- one in four teens are "cell-mostly" Internet users, meaning they tend to access the internet by means of their mobile phones

- 78 percent of teens currently have a cell phone; of those, 47 percent own smartphones

- nine out of ten teens have a computer or have home access to one

- 23 percent of teens have a tablet or have home access to one

- among teens aged 12–17, smartphone ownership rose to 37 percent, up from just 23 percent in 2011

For more information from the Pew study, visit www.pewinternet.org/files/old-media/Files/Reports/2013/PIP_TeensandTechnology2013.pdf

videoconferencing; global positioning systems (GPS)

- Consumer electronics: increasingly smaller and more portable computers; e-readers; mp3 players; digital television (see pages 398–399)

- Entertainment: digital music and digital marketplaces for it; movies on DVD and streaming video, related to a decline in moviegoing; video file-sharing sites; Internet-based multiplayer video games

- Social media: popular sites for connecting with friends and family; new channels for businesses to reach customers

Impact on Contemporary Society

To analyze how media convergence affects society, think of convergence as a two-part transition. First, there is the ongoing technological advancement, which has exploded since the turn of the twenty-first century. As technology has advanced, the cost of technological tools and processes has dropped dramatically. That deep price reduction has led to the second major transition, a shift in **spectatorship**, the basic way we consume and interact with our media. Today's fast-moving media culture allows us to move beyond passive consumption. Today, nearly everyone can be a content producer, because the cost of even powerful tools to create, record, edit, and transmit content is within

reach of many ordinary people—not just networks or big studios. At the very least, people can be co-creators and participants through their interactions with media. Following are key ways the new media are making an impact.

Interactivity A video game with the look and feel of a big screen movie—in fact, often tied to a blockbuster release—along with interactivity that puts you in the middle of the action has become commonplace. But what about interactivity in an actual movie theatre? Some media developers have been experimenting with the so-called "second screen" to add a dimension of interactivity to movies and television. For some specially developed movies, for example, moviegoers are encouraged to bring their cell phones or tablets so that at designated times during the movie they can interact with the movie via extensions such as games and trivia questions. Some sports broadcasters are using the second screen to give home viewers an extended experience on a second device, such as an iPad or computer, via different camera angles on the playing field or extra features that are accessed through a special app. Live tweets are already established as a way to add interactivity to otherwise passive consumption of media. For example, by only the 5th day of Olympics in Sochi, Russia, in 2014, users had already generated more than

The GPS Dot

In 2012 Todd Humphries gave a TED Talk on his theory that in the not-too-distant future, personal GPS tracking systems will be used in our daily lives to locate anything from mislaid car keys to a missing child. He was talking about the "GPS dot," a tiny GPS tracking device, which he claimed would eventually be sold in bulk and used for a variety of purposes by just about every person every single day. The GPS dot would differ from current large-scale GPS systems in that putting a dot on a person, place, or thing would show its location within a single millimeter. Many experts believe that this technology has huge implications for the future of personal privacy. Humphries's complete TED Talk is available at http://www.ted.com/talks/todd_humphreys_how_to_fool_a_gps.html.

10 million tweets on the topic of the Olympics.

Social Media As the Olympics example shows, consumers have more power than ever before to respond to and interact directly (and instantly) with the media they consume—and to communicate their responses with an enormous circle of friends, peers, and family members. For many people, social networking sites have become a regular part of daily life. The world of social media offers users the opportunity to engage with others and to foster a sense of community. It can also provide advertisers and businesses the opportunity to connect with consumers in ways that can serve to increase loyalty and increase sales. Social media cut across age, ethnicity, and income barriers. Through social media, we are sharing with others more and more information that in the past would have been deemed strictly private. Today, many use social networking sites to share photos, romance, recipes, job information, and more.

Olympians at Sochi, most of whom grew up entirely in an online world, provide an example of other uses for social media as well. Some athletes used "crowd-funding"—raising money online through small individual donations—to support their Olympic bid. Some also knew that social media fame at the Olympics would raise their profile and, coupled with a winning performance, possibly lead to lucrative endorsement deals. U.S. bobsledder Johnny Quinn raised his profile after getting stuck in a bathroom in his Sochi hotel room. Quinn broke through the door—and tweeted a picture of the hole he had made. It went viral. He went from 14,751 followers before the incident to 25,000 right after and got appearances on major television networks.

Mobility Quinn's story shows another impact of new media—the ability to create (or consume) content anywhere and at any time. With a mobile phone, Quinn easily both created and transmitted the photo that made such a splash.

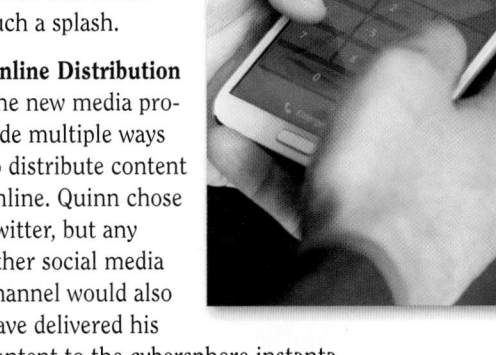

Online Distribution The new media provide multiple ways to distribute content online. Quinn chose Twitter, but any other social media channel would also have delivered his content to the cybersphere instantaneously. On YouTube, one of the most

Notes

Analyze the Impact Have students choose an online game, social media site, or well-known news blog to visit and take notes on the quality of their experience.

Evaluate Ask students to think critically about the relative worth of their experience. Was it worthwhile? Can they recommend that others visit it? Why or why not?

Synthesize Have students use a search engine to compare how others, including professional media critics, discuss the media they have selected.

Articulate Have students discuss their experiences in small groups and come up with a set of guidelines for viewing and evaluating online media effectively.

trafficked websites in the world, users can upload content at no cost using a Smartphone, tablet, or desktop or laptop computer to share with the world.

Mix of Content Mobility and the capability of instant online distribution have led to another impact of new media—a mix of user-generated and professional content. From sporting events like the Olympics to natural disasters or political uprisings, broadcast journalists often invite amateurs to submit photos, videos, and other media, and then feature these prominently in the broadcast where only professionally produced content would have been offered before.

Reviews Consumers are also increasingly relied on for their "real person" review of services and products online. If you want to see a movie, you can check what other viewers, not just professional reviewers, thought of it. Looking for a new doctor? Check the patient reviews online. Trying to decide which computer to buy? Read the user reviews. The authority to determine the worth of a product or service is shifting from professionals to ordinary people.

In the past, media shaped our culture. In today's dynamic media environment, though, consumers have the power to reshape culture simply through their participation.

Use the following strategies for further understanding the impact of electronic media on contemporary society.

Analyze the Impact. Think about what you are drawn to online. Do you see a pattern? Question yourself about what you view or share. How do your choices make you feel about yourself or others? Do the media encourage engagement? Do they have any lasting value?

Evaluate the Impact. Evaluate your new media preferences by thinking about how specific media might affect your future. For example, how might they affect your other interests, your daily activities, your social interactions, or your free time? Would those effects be mainly positive or mainly negative?

Synthesize the Impact. After you've articulated your responses to the media you interact with, you can compare and synthesize them with the responses of other media consumers and professional media experts through online or text sources that focus on media culture.

Articulate the Impact. Share your analysis, evaluation, and synthesis. For example, you might create a media

Backstage Gossip: "I Can Take It"

Noel Coward, playwright, songwriter, actor, and author renowned for his wit, once claimed, "I can take any amount of criticism, as long as it is unqualified praise."

awareness blog and ask other students to post comments. Use theatre vocabulary to articulate your understanding.

Employ the Impact. As you create your own digital products, use what you've learned about the impact of electronic media on contemporary society to make a positive contribution.

Evaluating New Media

If you have ever fallen for an Internet hoax or read an erroneous listing on Wikipedia, you know all too well not to believe everything you read. To increase your media literacy, develop a critical foundation for analyzing and evaluating what you read and watch. The same questions you have used to evaluate theatre, film, and television apply here as well.

- *What is the intent?* What did the content creator set out to do? Was it a hilarious story to be shared among friends? A critique of society or a call to action? A news update relevant to life in your country, state, or area? Begin by trying to understand intent.

- *How is it structured?* The structure must allow the content to successfully connect with the consumer— whether it is a long article on an online news site or a 140-character tweet. Given the intent, what structural elements worked (or didn't)?

How does the structure compare to the structure of theatre?

- *Is it effective?* Given the intent and structure, was the content effective? Did it make its point well?

- *Does it have value?* Are you and/or the world at large better off for having experienced this?

The Language of THEATRE

Use support from a teacher or classmate along with visuals and context clues to help you read.

- Work with a partner to help you read the theatre terms on page 410. Then look for visuals to help you develop background knowledge to understand the terms *digital convergence* and *digital divide*.

- With a partner, read aloud the section The Digital Convergence on page 411. Look for visuals or context clues that give you background to understand the terms *analog* and *digital convergence*.

- Read the section Influence of Electronic Media on Everyday Life on pages 411–412. Use context clues to gain background on the terms *Web 2.0* and *cloud computing*. Then discuss with a classmate.

- Read the chapter on your own, using visuals and context to develop background knowledge for the project. Then discuss the concept of changing *spectatorship* with a classmate.

Evaluating New Media

Many students do their homework on a laptop computer while at the same time watching TV and keeping track of social media and texts on their phone. This diversity of available information channels can lead to a situation called *media fragmentation.* Users control the way they interact with a wide variety of digital media channels, shifting back and forth among them, which creates a kind of echo chamber of user preferences. According to Brooke Gladstone, host of the National Public Radio show *On the Media*, although digital media is an accelerated version of media fragmentation, "People were always in echo chambers of one kind or another. The difference is that you have the option to use an already filtered site that you think offers high-quality information, or you use your Twitter feed, which aggregates information from people whose interests overlap with your yours."

Totally Quotable

"Think about what people are doing on Facebook today. They're keeping up with their friends and family, but they're also building an image and identity for themselves, which in a sense is their brand. They're connecting with the audience they want to connect to. It's almost a disadvantage if you're not on it now."

—Mark Zuckerberg

- Some suggestions of technology students might consider: GPS pin-point tracking to locate phone and other objects, fingerprint identification to leave or enter buildings, driverless car, and so on.

- Remind students to include enough detail in their scenarios to keep them on track during their presentations, but not so much as to create an actual script.

- Once students have nailed down the key elements, ask them to go through their scenario again to think about how each element will connect to the others.

- After they have rehearsed the presentation once, students should make any necessary edits before their second time through.

Remind students that most digital interactions are driven by personal preferences. Interacting on social media and the Internet leaves a complex trail of digital breadcrumbs for advertisers and content providers to follow. Students should consider this while creating their presentations.

PREPARE

For this assignment you will mine both your understanding of currently available digital media technologies and your own imagination. Read the sample scenario below, and then dig in.

Research the history and development of holograms for a good understanding of their current uses and their potential for the future.

You awake to an earsplitting commotion from your bedside table. A crowing rooster suddenly looms up over you. You bolt up and press your thumb into a fingerprint reader, and the rooster instantly disappears as the clock resets for the next day. You shake your head; you thought that 3D hologram rooster clock would be a lot more fun when you first had it teleported from Brazil. From the small, flexible screen on the sleeve of your pajamas, your preprogrammed news media beeps, so you blink your eye at the sensor to scan through the most important stories of the day.

1 With your partner brainstorm several examples of media technologies that currently exist. Think about how they might change in the future. Use your combined imaginations to take your ideas even further.

2 Write out a scenario that illustrates the ideas you had. The basis of the scenario should be a fairly simple activity like the one outlined above—for example, getting to school or work, or ordering dinner in a restaurant. You can create your scenario in any way you like, but one suggestion is that one of you will play a person and the other will portray the various types of technology.

3 Decide what digital technology to include to enhance your scene. It could be a video, a digital audio recording, an Internet site, or digital graphic. Decide how you will use the technology in your scene.

4 Although you do not have to script the scene, you'll need to select and write out a very specific scenario with all the moments you plan to present during your planned scene.

5 Rehearse your scene together at least twice with the chosen technology. Make sure your scenario will fit within the three-minute time frame.

About Net Neutrality

Net neutrality refers to a series of "open Internet" principles that mandate a level playing field for consumers to make their own choices as to what they view, create, and share on the Internet. But this free and open Internet access is in the midst of change. Major Internet providers like Verizon, Comcast, and now Google, claim that the government's current position on net neutrality presents them with overly strict regulatory guidelines. Time will tell what future versions of the Internet will be.

PRESENT

When the time comes for your presentation, calmly walk to the playing area with your partner. Give yourself a moment to breathe and center yourself. Make eye contact with your audience. Then make eye contact with your partner and introduce the title of your presentation.

Perform the scene as you rehearsed it, but don't be so rigid that you fail to be in the moment. You want your audience to laugh, so try to pace your presentation to allow for laughter. On the other hand, don't wait for laughter if the audience doesn't laugh. When you have finished, take a brief pause and then quietly leave the playing area. Remember that your presentation is not complete until you have returned to your seat.

Career Focus

Because of the nature of the digital environment, you are already a participant in the world of electronic media. You already create content and communicate in a variety of ways. Ask yourself what you are especially good at in this digital environment. Are you a social media expert, clever meme creator, accomplished Web designer, or effective blogger? Consider your skills and talents and research careers and avocational opportunities in electronic media that might match your skillset and interests. Based on what you learn, make a judgment about a career or avocation in electronic media you may wish to learn more about or even pursue. Refer to the chart on page 10 for additional ways to evaluate careers in electronic media.

CRITIQUE

As you watch your classmates' presentations, take notes on how effectively they put across their version of a futuristic technological world. Choose one presentation to evaluate. Consider both the successful and the not-so-successful aspects of the performance. Your evaluation should be based on a scale of 1 to 5, in which 1 means "needs much improvement" and 5 means "outstanding." As you craft your evaluation, ask yourself questions like the ones below.

- Did the presentation show a logical extension of current technology?

- Did the presentation use humor effectively?

- Was the presentation focused and well paced?

  - How effectively was the digital media incorporated into the scene?

  - Did the presenters speak clearly? Did their gestures and movements help you understand the ideas behind the presentation?

  - Was the presentation the correct length?

PRESENT

Students' presentations are intended to be humorous. Therefore, remind them that if during their presentation the audience laughs loudly, they may need to hold for a moment or two so as not to step on the laugh. If they don't wait at least briefly for the laughter to subside, the laughs will stop coming altogether because the audience will begin to fear missing something.

CRITIQUE

One way to move efficiently through a post-presentation discussion is to ask students to comment on the single strongest element of each presentation, and the element that was most in need of improvement.

Once you have reviewed students' critiques, trim off the evaluator's name and hand out all applicable sheets to the pairs of presenters, pointing out to them any issues or ideas you feel are of particular note.

Notes

_____

_____

_____

_____

_____

_____

_____

Spotlight on

Digital Convergence and Theatre, Film, and Television

The Turing Test Lead a class discussion on the Turing Test. In 1950, English code breaker Alan Turing predicted that during the twenty-first century, people would come to believe that machines could think on their own. Machines convincingly human enough to communicate with humans without being detected would, in so doing, pass the Turing Test. So far no single machine has completely passed. Yet today, we interact with more and more sophisticated programs that simulate human conversation; some of the most commonplace are Apple's iPhone application Siri as well as programs that mimic human speech and dialogue across various channels including chat rooms, customer service interfaces, and email.

Vocabulary Enhancement

A **chatbot** or cleverbot is a computer application designed to simulate intelligent conversation with one or more human users via text or auditory means.

Spotlight on

Digital Convergence and Theatre, Film, and Television

As in other aspects of contemporary life, digital convergence has blurred some of the lines between theatre, film, and television.

Theatre As a live medium, theatre has probably experienced less of an impact from the digital convergence than film and television. Nonetheless, companies such as BroadwayHD are screening HD recordings of theatrical productions in movie theatres around the country. Other theatre companies are also exploring innovative ways to use the digital convergence. New Paradise Laboratories (NPL) in Philadephia, for example, incorporates social media—YouTube, Sound Cloud, Facebook, and Skype, for example—in their productions. Before even stepping into a theatre for an NPL production, audience members get to know the fictional characters through their made-up social media profiles. The difference between fiction and reality is sometimes blurred in the process.

Film The availability of relatively inexpensive on-demand movies through television, DVDs, and streaming services has led to a decline in movie attendance. Hollywood has responded by trying to upgrade the moviegoing experience through such technologies as 3D and IMAX to market the moviegoing experience as a premium event and try to justify the higher cost of going to the movies rather than watching them at home.

Television The rise of Netflix and Amazon Instant Video has encouraged new ways of consuming TV shows, including time shifting and binge watching, or watching entire seasons of television shows such as *Breaking Bad* or the cult comedy *Arrested Development* in back-to-back marathon viewings. In large part because of these new viewing habits, some television shows have experimented with storytelling conventions and structures. In the Netflix-created final season of *Arrested Development*, for example, each episode centers on a character rather than a plot, so they all tell the same basic story but with overlapping perspectives. Binge watching also allows creators to present complex plotlines without confusing viewers for whom a week goes by before the next installment. Cable-produced *Damages* (2007–2012) also experimented with storytelling structure, employing a dual timeline and a distinctive flash-forward technique to tell its story in a unique way.

Love in the Digital Age

Spike Jonze's 2013 futuristic romantic comedy *Her* takes the idea of the chatbot to a logical extreme. In the film, a middle-aged man falls in love with a computer application that converses with him whenever, wherever, and about whatever he likes. Over the course of the film, the application and the film's protagonist learn from each other and their relationship deepens to the point of being nearly human. By the end of the film, however, the application's capacity grows so vast that it eventually transcends the protagonist's human capabilities and moves on.

Additional Projects

1 With a small group, prepare a presentation using technology that shows how you analyze, evaluate, articulate, and synthesize the impact of electronic media on contemporary society. For each of those tasks, include specific examples that make your point. For example, when you analyze the impact, refer to specific electronic media and specific impacts. When you evaluate the impact, refer to the same or additional media examples to support your evaluation. Conclude your presentation by showing how creators of electronic media products can employ the impact of the media on contemporary society for social good.

2 Prepare a video showing the innovations in electronic media over the last 20 years, with an emphasis on the contribution to electronic media made by the United States.

3 Work with a partner to choose a YouTube video to evaluate. In your review, be sure to include such terms as *intent, structure, effectiveness,* and *worth.*

Identify any theatrical conventions you notice and their effectiveness. Compare the structure and conventions to those of theatre and explain any differences.

4 Using computer graphics or art supplies, create a poster or chart evaluating how media technology can be used by directors, designers, or actors in a theatrical process.

5 Adapt a scene from a classic play such as Henrik Ibsen's *A Doll's House* by updating to a contemporary setting. Think about how technology might factor into—and change—the plot.

6 Write a proposal for a sitcom based on the futuristic world from your presentation. Design it to take advantage of consumers' binge watching.

7 Do further research on the careers or avocations in electronic media you identified as possibly interesting to you. You have already made judgments about their suitability to your interests and talents. Now make judgments about these careers based on

research about expected job growth or decline and the likelihood of your finding a job after appropriate training.

8 Expand on the scenario you created for this chapter's project to create a futuristic play that identifies and questions cultural, global, and historic belief systems, as many futuristic works do. Then create a setting for the play. Use text and graphics to create details and label technology in a room or other location.

9 **Theatre Journal** Take a reflective look at the influence electronic media has had on your everyday life. Explain it in detail, and then explore whether you think your experience is typical or not, and why.

Ordinary people have become the creators of wildly popular videos and other media content.

Chapter 30 Electronic Media **419**

Electronic Media Test

The test for this chapter is available in blackline master form in the Resource Binder, page 148.

For More Information

Books

Blaine, Mark, *The Digital Reporter's Notebook,* Routledge, 2013.

Gardner, Howard, and Katie Davis, *The App Generation: How Today's Youth Navigate Identity, Intimacy, and Imagination in a Digital World,* Yale University Press, 2013.

Jenkins, Henry, *Convergence Culture: Where Old and New Media Collide,* New York University Press, 2008.

McCullough, Malcolm, *Ambient Commons: Attention in the Age of Embodied Information,* MIT Press, 2013.

Thompson, Clive, *Smarter Than You Think: How Technology is Changing Our Minds for the Better,* 2013.

Other Media

http://mediasmarts.ca/digital-media-literacy/educational/

Frontine, "digital_nation," 2010, www.pbs.org/wgbh/pages/frontline/digitalnation/view/

Frontline, "Growing Up Online," 2007, www.pbs.org/wgbh/pages/frontline/kidsonline/

www.primaryaccess.org

Substitute Teacher Activities

The suggestions below are for one or more days when you will be out of the classroom.

- Assign the Media Literacy Worksheet on page 146 of the Resource Binder.

- Teach the Networking section of the Student Handbook, p. 571.

- Assign one or more of the Additional Projects on this page.

Cultural
Heritage

Cultural Heritage: The Digital Divide

Worldwide Internet Usage

- Africa: 7% (population 1,073,380,925)
- Asia: 44.8% (population 3,922,066,987)
- Europe: 21.5% (population 820,918,446)
- Middle East: 3.7% (population 223,608,203)
- North America: 11.4% (population 348,280,154)
- Latin America/Caribbean: 10.6% (population 593,688,638)
- Oceania/Australia: 1.0% (population 35,903,569)

Source: Internet World Stats

Cultural
Heritage

Global Heritage: The Digital Divide

Early in the digital media boom, some people predicted that media convergence would usher in a brand new era of worldwide access, bringing with it huge benefits for all humankind. The reality is that convergence, while granting access for many, has at the same time led to what's known as a **digital divide** between those who are able to use information technologies and those who, for whatever reason, are not. For some, the divide stems from a simple lack of access to online services and technology. For others it a lack of education or computer know-how. In either case, income inequality is a strong contributing factor.

Global Haves and Have Nots

The widest gap in the digital divide occurs between developing nations and the developed world. In Africa, for example, only 7 percent of the continent's massive population has the knowledge and/or the technology to access the Internet. While many more people across Africa have mobile phones, only 18 percent of all African mobile phones are equipped with Internet capability.

Governments and aid organizations in many nations are striving to bridge the global digital divide. For example, in Jamaica, community access points—in post offices, schools, and libraries—have been created to improve the national online literacy rate. At these centers, citizens can learn basic online skills and connect to the Internet free of charge. As of January 2014, 163 community access points had been created in Jamaica, with many more planned for the future. Yet for Jamaica, and many other nations, universal access is a long way away.

Even in some nations with significant availability of the Internet, the culture prevents full access. Nations with a strong central government with a high degree of control tend to censor political and social discussions as well as matters related to conflict and security. China's censorship, for example, is considered "pervasive" by the OpenNet Initiative organization. In contrast, the United States with its culture of free speech has little Internet censorship.

From the Field . . .

A 2013 Neilson study found that in Australia, which has traditionally made up the smallest piece of the world's regional-Internet-use pie chart, the media landscape is exploding. Back in 2003, for example, Australians spent an average 6.7 hours per week online. By 2012, they were averaging more than three and a half times that much—spending an average of 23.3 hours online (that's nearly one full day) per week.

In 2013, the U.S. government unrolled the ConnectED Initiative, with a goal of bridging the digital divide by making Internet connectivity available to 99% of the nation's students by 2018.

U.S. Haves and Have Nots

Nonetheless, Internet access in the United States is not universal, despite all the mobile phones, e-readers, laptops, and tablets in the classrooms and hallways of many American schools.

According to a 2013 Pew Research survey, 84 percent of middle and secondary school teachers expressed the view that the proliferation of mobile technology in the schools actually contributes to the digital divide, because lower-income schools are often left out. The survey showed that 56 percent of teachers of upper- and middle-income students use tablet computers in their classrooms. For teachers of lower-income students, that figure slides to 37 percent. Fifty-two percent of teachers of upper and middle-income students claimed their students use cell phones to check or look up information during classroom assignments. Compare that to only 35 percent of teachers who work at schools in lower-income communities. The disparity between the digital haves and have nots continues to be a major challenge to education in the United States—and around the globe.

Cross-Media Consumption

In 2013, the research company Scarborough published an infographic that illustrated some telling facts about the evolution of cross-platform media consumers (meaning those who get their media from multiple sources, in this case, social, traditional, and digital).

- Between 2009 and 2012, social media use expanded by 238 percent.

- 42 percent of American adults claimed the Internet as their main source of entertainment.

- Traditional media platforms declined or flatlined, yet 68 percent of adults claimed to still read a newspaper.

- From 2006 to 2012, the number of households owning a smartphone went from 8 percent to 44 percent.

Notes

_____

_____

_____

_____

_____

_____

_____

PREVIEW

1 The music director works with the actors, prepares the cast for the musical portions of the show, and often conducts the orchestra. The onstage director casts, directs, and collaborates with the staff to assure a smooth-running performance.

2 The important considerations are: c) money d) space e) cast f) audience.

3 Bunraku is an ancient Japanese puppetry form that relies heavily on tradition and unique conventions of puppet manipulation, recitation, and music.

4 Yes, writing about topics you care about allows you to bring more of yourself—your deepest thoughts and feelings—into your writing, which results in more sincerity and often more vivid language.

5 Cameras allow for quick changes in time and place. That means that characters can appear in widely separated and elaborate scenes that flash on the screen within seconds of each other. Neither the stage nor the film is confined to straightforward, chronological storytelling, but a movie can make far greater use of flashbacks, quick-cuts, and so on. The stage remains grounded in the practical need of time for scene changes, costume changes, makeup changes, and so on.

6 Television reflects society and everyday life by presenting subject matter that relates to current concerns. In the 1970s, for example, shows such as the *Mary Tyler Moore Show* showed women in professional roles, highlighting a changing view of women. At the same time, it influenced society by popularizing and reinforcing this image of women.

Unit Six Review

PREVIEW

Examine the following key concepts previewed in Unit Six.

1 What is the difference between the Director of a musical and the Music Director?

2 Which of the following are important considerations when choosing a musical for your school?
a. length   b. humor   c. money
d. space   e. cast   f. audience

3 What is Bunraku?

4 Is it important to write poetry about things you care about? Why or why not?

5 Compare the dramatic structure of a movie to that of live theatre.

6 In what ways does television both reflect and influence society and everyday life?

7 Explain how film, TV, electronic media, and the theatre may be interdependent.

8 Explain *spectatorship* in terms of media consumption and the impact of new media on it.

PREPARE

Assess your response to the preparation process for projects in this unit.

9 Did you find it more difficult to write character sketches or the plot synopsis for your musical? Why?

10 As you prepared your performance poem, did the ideas and images flow freely or was it a struggle to find the right words? Were you satisfied with the additional media form you used? Give details.

11 Compare and contrast the criteria and processes for evaluating film with those for theatre.

12 How is television changing, and what is responsible for those changes?

13 In what ways has the explosion of new media affected society and individuals?

---

7 Film, TV, electronic media, and the theatre may be interdependent in that each medium can borrow from the others. These borrowings may be of story elements, since all media are involved in telling stories; these borrowings may be of reference, in which television screens are shown in movies and theatrical performances are shown on TV; or they may be of technology, in which any of the media may share lighting effects, montages, or split-screen or simultaneous scene effects, music and sound effects, and so on.

8 *Spectatorship* refers to the stance consumers have in relation to media. Instead of being just passive consumers, new media gives individuals the chance to interact with media as well as produce and distribute it at very low cost.

PRESENT

Analyze the experience of presenting your work to the class.

14 In creating your presentations, which medium did you find the most interesting—musical theatre, other theatre forms, film, television, or other electronic media? Why?

15 Were you able to remember all the important points you wanted to make in presenting your proposal for a new musical? Explain.

16 What were your impressions of sharing your poetry in a slam format? Would you like to do it again? Why or why not?

17 How did you present your movie review? Would you do it differently next time? Explain.

18 Were you able to use any unusual or inventive ways to make any of your presentations? Discuss them.

CRITIQUE

Evaluate how you go about critiquing your work and the work of others.

19 Did the comments, questions, and other feedback after presenting your outline for a TV episode encourage you to write the episode?

20 What did you learn about your own work while critiquing the work of others?

21 Do you feel that most students are sensitive and fair in their evaluations of classmates' work? Explain.

EXTENSIONS

- Choose any art form that interests you and create a short performance piece based upon it.

- Create a ten-minute video using only inanimate objects as your characters.

- Write and perform a theme song for a new television show about a ten-year-old who finds a tiny universe of aliens dressed in formal attire in her bedroom closet.

Unit Six Review **423**

Resource Binder

Unit Six Test, p. 149

PREPARE

Questions **9–13** should be answered honestly and thoughtfully by students. Talk to students about any answers you find unsatisfactory.

PRESENT

Questions **14–18** should contain honest accounts of each student's experiences while presenting the projects in this unit. Discuss with students any problems or disappointments they may have experienced.

CRITIQUE

Questions **19–21** should show some insight into the critiquing process and how it impacts not only the student's work but the work he or she is evaluating.

EXTENSIONS

- Before students begin their performance pieces, make sure all content is suitable for performance in the classroom.

- Suggest to students that before beginning this extension project they read up on videography and filmmaking.

- Give students the option of choosing another subject for the TV show. Have any students who write a theme song share it with you before performing it for the class.

Unit **Seven**

Exploring Drama and Theatre History

Note: Although this unit has been placed near the end of the text so that students begin their study of drama with a more action-oriented focus, it is possible that some instructors will prefer to begin the year with theatre history. In this case, simply begin with Unit Seven, which has been written in a manner that allows it to be taught at any time.

The Theatre Then and Now features in this text have shown students how elements of historical and contemporary theatre are connected. These connections are a preview to the more focused academic approach in this unit, where students will study the span of theatre history from early cultures to today.

Unlike previous units in the text, this unit is divided into three parts with suggested projects at the end of each section.

Part One
The Dawn of Theatre
This section covers the theatre of early peoples as well as the early theatre of Egypt, Judea, Greece, Rome, China, India, and Japan.

Part Two
The Middle Ages to 1800
In this section Medieval, Renaissance, Elizabethan, Restoration, and 18th-century theatre is explored.

Part Three
1800 to the Present
Part Three begins with the 19th-century theatre of Europe and America and ends with theatre of the 20th century and beyond.

Unit **Seven**
Exploring Drama and Theatre History

What distinguishes drama and theatre? *Drama* means "to do" or "to act" in Greek; *theatre*, from the Greek *theatron*, means "seeing place." Sometimes the words are used interchangeably, but, generally, drama, or dramatic literature, refers to the written text of plays, which may be serious, comic, or musical. That's why playwrights are also called *dramatists. Drama* may also refer to unscripted creative processes with no final production. *Theatre* refers to the whole production of a play or to the places where plays are staged and viewed.

To know the development and historical underpinnings of drama and theatre is to understand the development of the human race. As the theatre grows, civilization grows; when theatre flourishes, human culture flourishes; when theatre is suppressed, people live in darkness. Study the theatre of a particular era and you will learn the religious, social, political, and economic influences of that time. You will learn the people's desires, their ideals, and their needs. Perhaps more importantly, looking into the past helps give you insight into the present. A comparison of past eras not only emphasizes the evolution of drama, but also furthers your understanding of the theatre of today, and it points the way to the theatre of tomorrow.

Quotables
Use the quotes below as journal writing prompts, discussion starters, or for your own enjoyment.

The story of theatre is the story of humankind, because in its essential form theatre belongs to no one race, age, or culture.

Joy H. Reilly and M. Scott Phillips
from *Introducing Theatre*

. . . there may be somebody in any theatre at any time to whom you are opening a new door, a new gateway to beauty.

Gabrielle Réjane, Actor

425

Discussion Questions

The following questions are intended to tap into students' **prior knowledge** and attitudes about the subject matter of the unit.

- What do you think of when you hear the words drama and theatre? What are the differences between the two terms? Does one term interest you more than the other?

- What do you already know about some aspect of theatre history? Think about information you have gotten from your travels, movies, books, and studies in other classes.

- Why might it be important to know about the history of the theatre in a drama class?

- Think about the Theatre Then and Now and Cultural Heritage features presented in earlier chapters of this book. Which ones did you find most interesting? Why?

- Based on what you have learned so far about theatre history, score your potential interest level in this unit by using the following guide. Rate your interest on a scale from one to five, with five being "very interesting" and one being "boring." What is your theatre history interest level?

- In what way might studying the theatre history of a country help you understand its culture?

Visual Cue

The image above is a painting by 17th-century artist Jan Miel of *commedia dell'arte* players. *Commedia* is a theatrical form that originated in Italy during the Renaissance. It featured a traveling troupe of actors who played stock characters in improvised comic performances. Use the following questions to discuss the image with your students.

- Describe the characters pictured in the wagon. How are they interacting with the people on the street?

- What might be the intent of the character in black on the right?

Part **One**

The Dawn of Theatre

This section of the unit will introduce students to the beginnings of theatre and its growth and refinement in various cultures.

Objectives

1 to learn about the origins of theatre

2 to appreciate the cultural heritages of world drama and theatre, especially the contributions of the early Greeks to the development of theatre

3 to identify key figures, works, and trends in dramatic literature and technical theatre of the period

4 to compare and contrast early theatre in both Western and Eastern cultures

Key Trends in Dramatic Literature
Review the four trends and explain that students should look for evidence of these trends as they read Part One. Engage students in a discussion about the relationships or tensions between formal, literary drama and theatrical spectacle and entertainment. Ask if they see evidence of these two trends today.

Key Figures and Works in Dramatic Literature Ask students if they are familiar with any of these key figures or works. Invite students with prior knowledge to share it with the class. Encourage students to notice how these key figures and works are connected to the trends.

Part **One** The Dawn of Theatre

In this section, you will have the opportunity to understand and appreciate the cultural heritage of world drama and theatre from their earliest connections with religious ritual in early peoples and in Egyptian and Hebrew theatre to the drama and theatre of Classical Greece and Rome. You will also explore early theatres of India, China, and Japan.

You will read about these **key trends in dramatic literature** during this period.

- Drama moves beyond religious ritual to scripted plays.
- Greek literary drama becomes more entertaining and sensationally spectacular in Rome.
- Chinese dramas become more action-oriented after the Mongol invasion.
- Japanese drama develops the formal Noh plays and the more popular and melodramatic Kabuki.

You will read about these **key figures and works** that helped shape the trends.

- Aeschylus: *Oresteia* trilogy
- Sophocles: *Electra, Oedipus Rex, Antigone*
- Euripides: *Medea, Alcestis*
- Aristophanes: *The Birds, The Frogs, The Clouds*
- Menander: *The Curmudgeon*
- Seneca: closet dramas (read rather than performed)
- Plautus: *Menaechmi, Pot of Gold*
- Chinese Emperor Ming Huang
- Mongolian Chinese: *The Chalk Circle, The Lute Song*
- Peking Opera
- Japanese Noh Drama
- Japanese Kabuki
- Indian Sanskrit: *Mahabharata*

c. 240 BC Rome: Huge wooden amphitheatres, first use of stage curtain

475 AD Fall of Rome, A dark period of theatre in Europe follows

c. 3000 BC Egypt: Rituals similar to a play

500-400 BC Greece: Golden Age period, Outdoor stone amphitheatres; "deus ex machine," crane to raise and lower gods

---

Resource Binder

Architects and designers of early theatres are unknown. But you will read about these **key trends in technical theatre** as well as the development, discoveries, and periods in theatre architecture and stage technology shown in the timeline below.

- Greek and Roman amphitheatres include simple painted scenery and basic stage technology, such as a crane to raise and lower gods onto the playing area.
- Theatre in China and Japan uses symbolic props, costumes, and makeup.
- Noh and Kabuki theatres use specific, distinctive architecture and innovative stagecraft, including ramps, trapdoors, and later, revolving stages.
- Greeks use the *skene* and Hindu theatre the greenroom as a place for actors to change costumes.

Use technology to help you document, communicate, and present information and findings and demonstrate your knowledge in a clear and coherent way.

To document information, use a notetaking, journaling, or word processing program. Look for ways to group information meaningfully. With theatre history, for example, you might document information according to geographic region, or you might group notes into such categories as key figures, works, and trends, or theatre architecture and technology.

Much theatre preparation work is research. Use technology, such as an online platform for collaboration, to communicate the findings of your research with your artistic team. Be sure your work is clear and coherent so that others can understand.

Use technology to present your findings more formally as well. Use a program such as PowerPoint or one of many other programs that allow you to create, capture, and mix media. Be sure to use the technology to present your findings in a clear and coherent manner.

Here's How

Discuss with students the kinds of technology they currently use to document, communicate, and present information. Invite them to share any tips about the most effective ways they have found to use technology. Make them aware of resources available at the school or in the community, for example in the media lab or the public library.

Key Trends in Technical Theatre
Review the four trends and ask students to compare and contrast them with the trends in dramatic literature. Invite students to discuss any examples of how these trends from ancient theatre are still influencing contemporary theatre.

1600s AD Japan: Kabuki stage technology includes entrance ramp and trapdoors.

1793 AD Japan: First Kabuki revolving stage

1300s AD Japan: Noh drama uses specific architecture and stagecraft.

Part One The Dawn of Theatre **427**

Notes

Early Peoples

Timeless Rituals Tribal ceremonies of the sort that gave rise to theatre are not only still practiced but are still respected for their potency. According to the *Seattle Times,* Native American soldiers prepared for the Iraq War by participating in shamanic rituals designed to protect them from harm. Washington's *Tri-City Herald* reported in May 2001 that the Yakama tribe billed the Bonneville Power Administration $32,000 for two rain dances that the Yakamas contend broke a local drought.

Early Peoples

Although our word for drama comes from the Greek, drama itself is much older than the Greek civilization. It was born out of the dance ceremonies of primitive people, when instinctive rhythmic movements and the desire to imitate evolved into pantomimes that told of various tribal traditions or rites of passage.

> **Theatre Terms**
> pacify
> ritual
> shaman

There were initiation dances to teach the tribe's customs to boys approaching manhood, war dances to kindle bravery in young warriors, story dances to enact events of a hunt or a great battle, and religious dances to **pacify** or try to satisfy the numerous unseen spirits that these tribes believed controlled the world.

From these religious dances evolved a **ritual.** The chief representative of the gods—the medicine man, **shaman,** witch doctor, or priest—donned a mask believed to have powerful magic and prayed, chanted, and danced in an attempt to drive away evil spirits while the tribe assisted or watched. Out of this religious ritual, performed in a circle in front of the temple, drama began to emerge.

Today, we can still see some of these dramatic forms in the dances of South African and Australian tribes. Remnants of ancient ritual are equally evident in Hawaiian hula and American Indian dances, such as the snake dance, the corn dance, and the sun dance.

Egyptian Theatre

As far as we know, the Egyptians were the first people whose ritualistic rites took a form very similar to our idea of a play, performing them as early as 3000 B.C. The Egyptian people were very concerned with life after death. The rulers of Egypt,

> **Theatre Terms**
> hieroglyphics
> pharaohs

> ## Theatre Terms
>
> **pacify** to soothe, satisfy, or make tranquil
>
> **ritual** the established form or order for a ceremony
>
> **shaman** a priest or priestess who uses magic to cure the sick or predict the future
>
> **hieroglyphics** a system of writing using pictures
>
> **pharaohs** the rulers of ancient Egypt
>
> **Book of Job** 18th book in the Bible's Old Testament, which confronts the problem of good and evil in the world
>
> **Old Testament** the first portion of the Christian Bible

called **pharaohs,** and other wealthy citizens built huge pyramids and furnished them with great splendor, for they intended to dwell there in the afterworld. This philosophy of life and death is illustrated in their dramas, which were sometimes written in **hieroglyphics** on the walls of tombs.

Plays were often written for important events, such as the coronation of a new pharaoh or an important year in the pharaoh's rule. Some plays revolved around magical healing, and some were religious dramas written on tomb walls and enacted by priests.

The hieroglyphics adorning the hallowed walls of this Egyptian tomb display one of the first forms of theatre.

Hebrew Theatre

Although dance and ritual are mentioned in the **Old Testament,** there is no reference to a definite theatre in Judea. However, two books of the Bible read as dramatic literature. *The Song of Solomon,* which was probably chanted at wedding festivals, contains beautiful poetic dialogue spoken by a bride and groom.

> **Theatre Terms**
> Book of Job
> Old Testament

The play *J.B.,* by Archibald MacLeish, is based on the Book of Job.

The **Book of Job** has many of the elements of a five-act drama with a prologue and epilogue. There is no record, though, of its having ever been performed in ancient times. Today it is usually classified as dramatic poetry rather than drama. However, there have been several modern versions of the story that have been successfully adapted for the stage.

Part One The Dawn of Theatre **429**

sual Cues

The image above left shows Egyptian hieroglyphics.

- What event do you think is being dramatized on this tomb wall?

The image above right is from the award-winning play *J.B.* by Archibald MacLeish.

- What do the characters' costumes tell you about the play?

- Describe the set and type of stage in the picture. Could your school mount a similar production? Why or why not?

Hebrew Theatre

Song of Solomon Here is a portion of "The Song of Solomon" (chapter five, King James Version), set up in script form, with three speaking parts: Groom, Bride, and Chorus of Women.

GROOM

> *I am come into my garden, my sister, my spouse: I have gathered my myrrh with my spice; I have eaten my honeycomb with my honey; I have drunk my wine with my milk: eat, O friends; drink, yea, drink abundantly, O beloved.*

BRIDE

> *I sleep, but my heart waketh: it is the voice of my beloved that knocketh, saying, Open to me, my sister, my love, my dove, my undefiled: for my head is filled with dew, and my locks with the drops of the night. . . . I rose up to open to my beloved; and my hands dropped with myrrh, and my fingers with sweet smelling myrrh, upon the handles of the lock. I opened to my beloved; but my beloved had withdrawn himself, and was gone: my soul failed when he spake: I sought him, but I could not find him; I called him, but he gave me no answer. The watchmen that went about the city found me, they smote me, they wounded me; the keepers of the walls took away my veil from me. I charge you, O daughters of Jerusalem, if ye find my beloved, that ye tell him, that I am sick of love.*

CHORUS

> *What is thy beloved more than another beloved, O thou fairest among women? What is thy beloved more than another beloved, that thou dost so charge us?*

The Book of Job Perhaps the most successful stage version of the Job story was Archibald MacLeish's *J.B.,* which ran for 364 performances at the American National Theatre and Academy (ANTA) in New York. A 1959 Pulitzer Prize winner, this dramatic poem places the story in a modern-day circus where Mr. Zuss the balloon vendor is God and Nickles the popcorn man is Satan.

Part One The Dawn of Theatre **429**

Greek Theatre

Plato and Aristotle No less an authority than the Greek philosopher Plato rejected the arts, including drama. In book ten of *The Republic* he argues that there are three levels of reality: the loftiest is that of the ideal, then comes the actual, and finally imitations of the actual. Artists, he said, work at the lowest level: Producing imperfect copies of a reality that already consists of imperfect copies, they are far removed from the truth of things. What's worse, he said, artists undermine morality by depicting bad behavior. Aristotle's *Poetics,* with its theory of catharsis, was written to rebut Plato's polemic.

Greek Theatre

The legacy of the ancient Greek theatre has never been surpassed. Only the Elizabethans came close to achieving such a wealth of plays. The Classic, or Golden Age, of Greece (500–400 B.C.) brought human civilization the greatest tragedies of all time, as well as outstanding creativity in such fields as architecture and government.

A Festival of Theatre

Greek theatre had its beginnings in the religious rites that paid homage to Dionysus, the god of wine and fertility. These public celebrations were held around stone altars at the foot of hilly vineyards. There was much dancing and singing of hymns, called **dithyrambs,** to honor Dionysus, and as these religious celebrations gained popularity, choral groups were organized with vocal contests among them.

Out of these dithyrambic rituals developed tragedy, which literally means "goat song" (*tragos* in Greek). There is disagreement among scholars as to why it was called this. There are several possibilities. Perhaps the chorus wore goatskins, or they draped the altar with one. Another theory is that a goat was sacrificed at the end of the festival as an offering to the gods. It is possible that all of these were true.

Of the four Dionysian festivals, the one held in March, the **City Dionysia,** developed into a festival of tragedies, where a coveted prize was awarded to the best series of plays. The festival, which took place in Athens, was both a national and religious ceremony. Since business was suspended for a week, everyone participated. Crowds came from the surrounding villages, and if someone could not afford the nominal ticket price, the state would pay their entrance fee. Both men and women attended, although theatre production and acting were restricted to males (as was the case worldwide for many centuries).

The annual festival lasted five or six days. The first day included a procession that carried the image of Dionysus to the city limits where people spent their time performing religious rites, drinking wine, singing, and making merry. At night the image was returned to the theatre (*theatron* in Greek, or "seeing place") by candlelight.

The final three days were reserved for the play contests. Each day a different dramatist was featured, offering four plays: a trilogy of tragedies and a satire that provided comic relief after the three heavier plays. At the end of the festival, the winning author and his financial backer (*choregus*) were allowed to wear the coveted ivy garland on their heads.

> ### Theatre Terms
> City Dionysia
> deus ex machina
> dithyrambs
> mantle
> periaktois
> skene
> thespian

Theatre Terms

City Dionysia one of several drama festivals held in ancient Greece

deus ex machina literally "the god in the machine." In ancient Greek theatre, a giant crane used to "fly" actors into the playing area

dithyrambs songs of praise to honor the god Dionysus

mantle a long cloak

periaktois in scenery, three flats that form a triangle and are mounted on a revolving platform

skene a small building near the stage used by actors for dressing or relaxing

thespian an actor

Dug out of the slope under the south side of the Acropolis in the late 6th century B.C., the Theatre of Dionysus was the center for presenting the works of the great Greek playwrights Euripides, Aeschylus, and Sophocles. It was rebuilt many times, so its original shape is difficult to determine.

Comedies (from *komos,* meaning "a band of revelers") were sometimes performed in the afternoon during the City Dionysia. However, most comedies were performed at the Lenaea Festival (in early February), where prizes were awarded for the best comic writer.

Greek Plays in Performance

Plays were performed outdoors. At first, the theatre consisted of crude benches placed on a sloping hill and looking down on a circle of hard-packed ground where the chorus performed around an altar. Later, the side of the mountain was scooped out into a bowl shape, something like our amphitheatres today, and tiers of stone seats in concentric semicircles were built on the hill. These theatres provided seating for up to 20,000, with a special first row reserved for dignitaries. The acting area, called the *orchestra*, was the circular space marked out on the ground at the foot of the hill. It varied from 65 feet to 85 feet in diameter.

 **Visual Cue**

The image above shows the ruins of an early Greek theatre.

• What do you think it might have been like to see a play in an ancient amphitheatre such as the one pictured?

• Compare and contrast attending a theatrical performance in ancient Greece to attending a modern event in an outdoor arena such as a football or baseball game.

Stages The proscenium creates a frame around the stage, through which we see the narrative unfold as a series of apparently two-dimensional images. In order to create a rounder, more realistic effect, such standard variations as the thrust and "in-the-round" stages evolved. Twentieth century experimentalists went further. A good example is Jerzy Grotowski, the Polish director who started staging work in the 1950s. Hoping to strip away everything but what he regarded as the indispensable performer-spectator relationship, Grotowski created staging arrangements in which the action might literally encircle or even engulf the audience.

The actors changed costumes in the **skene,** a small building first situated at the side of the orchestra and later permanently placed behind it. The skene, from which we derive the word *scene,* had three doors through which actors would enter. To the right and left between the skene and the orchestra was a wide passageway, called the *parodos,* which was used for the chorus to enter and exit. Eventually, a platform called a *proskenion* (from which we get the term *proscenium*) was placed in front of the skene for the actors. On each side, two wings called the *paraskenia* were introduced.

Since the theatre was large and the distance between audience and playing area was great, the actors used broad gestures and a declamatory vocal style. To be seen by the audience, the actor made himself taller by wearing thick-soled shoes, called *cothurnus,* and a high headpiece, called an *onkus*. In addition, he wore a wooden, cork, or linen mask that fit over his entire head. These masks not only denoted character, station in life, and emotion, they also projected the actor's voice through a type of inside megaphone.

Actors perform a Greek drama in traditional masks.

sual Cue

The image above shows a modern production of a Greek tragedy.

• What emotion do the masks convey?

• Compare these costumes to the drawings at the top of page 433. How authentic are the modern costumes?

From left to right, the *chiton, himation,* and *chlamys* of the ancient Greek attire.

Costumes of both the actor and the chorus consisted of standard Greek attire: the sleeveless *chiton,* or tunic, belted below the breast; the *himation,* or long **mantle,** draped around the right shoulder; and the *chlamys,* or short cloak. These costumes were very colorful and often featured elaborately embroidered patterns.

Staging was accomplished simply with the use of *pinakes,* or scenery painted on boards and placed against the skene, and *periaktois,* triangular prisms that could be revolved for scenery changes. A few properties were also used. Drums were sounded for thunder, and the *eccyclema,* a small wagon platform, was wheeled on to show a corpse to the audience (all killing had to occur off-stage and be reported to the audience by the chorus or a messenger). The *deus ex machina,* or "god in the machine," was a unique mechanical crane used for lowering and raising gods. The term is still used today for any plot device, such as the death of a rich uncle, that unexpectedly occurs to assist the main character in the convenient solution of a major problem.

The Great Greek Playwrights

The Greek tragedies were based on ancient myths, which were well known to the audience. Most of the plays encompassed certain elements that Aristotle (384–322 B.C.) later identified in his *Poetics.* (See pages 139–140 for more about Aristotle's *Poetics.*)

The first tragedian to win the City Dionysia playwriting prize was Thespis.

The Legacy of Plato and Aristotle

The ideas of both Plato and Aristotle have had enormous influence on the theatre, albeit in opposite directions. On the one hand, the Platonic view of art as false and immoral has been invoked throughout the centuries—sometimes consciously, sometimes not—to close theatres. (The fact that Greek drama originated as part of the orgiastic rites of Dionysus didn't help.) On the other hand, Aristotlean notions about the nature and rules of drama have guided the work of playwrights from Jean Racine (1639–1699) to Eugene O'Neill (1888–1953). Aristotle's authority was so great during and after the Renaissance that it wasn't until the 20th century that his precepts met with serious theoretical opposition.

German playwright-provocateur Bertolt Brecht attacked catharsis, saying it discouraged audiences from thinking critically by appealing to—and exhausting—their emotions.

In a 1966 essay called "Against Interpretation," Susan Sontag argued that Plato and Aristotle together had all but destroyed Western art by creating a cultural environment in which art could not be appreciated for itself but had to justify its existence by demonstrating its usefulness. The process has gone so far, she said, that the justifications have finally overwhelmed the art entirely.

Backstage Gossip: The Drama of Politics

Thespis was beginning to act in tragedies, and the people flocked to see the novelty .... Solon the great lawmaker went to see Thespis act. After the play, Solon went backstage and asked the actor if he was not ashamed to tell so many lies before such a large crowd. When Thespis replied that it was no harm to do so in a play, Solon vehemently struck his staff against the ground: "Ah, but if we commend lies on the stage, some day we will find it in politics."

from *Theatrical Anecdotes* by Peter Hay

Aeschylus According to the ancient Greek travel writer, Pausanias, Aeschylus's career in the theatre was ordained by a god. When the future tragedian was a child, the story goes, he was sent out to tend grapes. Falling asleep in the vineyard, he dreamed he saw Dionysus, who told him to write plays. Another, more irreverent legend has it that Aeschylus died when an eagle, attempting to crack a turtle's shell, mistook the playwright's bald head for a rock.

The Oresteia trilogy follows the often horrific fortunes of the descendants of two brothers, Atreus and Thyestes, who fought each other for control of the throne of Mycenae. In *Agamemnon,* the eponymous son of Atreus has no sooner returned from his victory over Troy than he is assassinated by his wife, Clytemnestra, and her lover, Aegisthus (who is Thyestes' son by his own daughter, Pelopia). In *Choephori* (The Libation Bearers) Agamemnon's son, Orestes, avenges his father by killing Clytemnestra and Aegisthus. In the *Eumenides,* Orestes is tried and exonerated for his crime. The essential trajectory of the three plays, then, takes us from crime through punishment to redemption.

Sophocles Sophocles won his first victory in the City Dionysia play competition by beating no less a rival than Aeschylus.

Euripides Sophocles is reputed to have said that while he depicted people as they ought to be, Euripides depicted them as they are. Unfortunately, Euripides' psychological realism did not go over very well with many of his peers. Apparently alienated by his comparative lack of success and the harassment meted out to him by satirists like Aristophanes, Euripides left Athens in 409 B.C. to live at the court of King Archelaus of Macedonia. Following Euripides' death in 405 B.C., his son, Euripides the Younger, returned to Athens with the script of *The Bacchae.* It was performed at the City Dionysia and won first prize.

In his plays that year (534 B.C.), he introduced a leader for the chorus. The leader spoke, and the chorus responded in chants. Thus, the leader became the first Greek actor. Thespis also instigated another first in his drama: the use of masks. It is from his name that the word *thespian* comes—another way of saying *actor.*

Three great writers of tragedy developed during the Golden Age. Some of their plays have survived and are still performed today.

Aeschylus (525–456 B.C.) has been called the Father of Tragedy. He is considered by many scholars to be the greatest tragic poet of all time. Aeschylus frequently participated in the City Dionysia, winning first prize thirteen

The Colosseum, Rome's ancient arena of death and slaughter, reopened its gates for the first time in 1500 years for this performance of *Oedipus Rex.*

times. He is credited with inventing the trilogy and adding a second actor to the plays. He reduced the chorus from fifty to twelve, but that honored group still handled most of the play, relating the events and setting the mood. Aeschylus loved spectacle, and his plays abounded with it. He had one character, Prometheus (who steals fire and gives it to humans), fall from a cliff. He dressed the Furies (spirits of revenge who chase down those who do not atone for their sins) in such frightful masks that women and children fainted at the sight of them. Of Aeschylus's ninety plays, only seven survive, of which the Oresteia trilogy may be the most enduring.

Sophocles (496–406 B.C.) is the second great writer of tragedies. He was a handsome, well-educated man of many talents: musician, singer, and athlete. He was also interested in civic affairs, becoming the treasurer of Athens. Sophocles, like Aeschylus, had a brilliant career in theatre. He wrote more than a hundred scripts and won eighteen Dionysia festivals. In his plays, he introduced a third actor and changed the number of chorus members to fifteen. Sophocles was a polished literary craftsman who had keen theatrical sense. His plays feature beautiful language, a well-balanced plot, and excellent character development. Today his work is considered the essence of great Greek drama. The best known of his seven surviving plays are *Electra, Oedipus Rex,* and *Antigone.*

Notes

_____

_____

_____

_____

_____

_____

_____

Euripides (480–406 B.C.), although apparently good at boxing and painting, confined himself to a literary life. He would often retire to a cave overlooking the sea, and there he would meditate and write. Euripides was an unorthodox thinker who questioned traditional religious ideas. His plays emphasize psychological motivations and social consciousness, particularly accentuating the plight of women and the problem of the outsider. He was the first to humanize drama with little household details and events that appealed to the emotions. His *Medea* is a potent tragedy that shows the mental anguish of Medea, a woman driven mad by jealousy. In *Alcestis*, Euripides created a play that combined both the serious and the humorous.

Besides these three great tragedians, two writers of comedy gained note.

Aristophanes (circa 448–380 B.C.) is considered the finest comic writer of ancient Greece. His biting, bawdy satires, such as *The Birds, The Frogs,* and *The Clouds* abound with humorous ideas and bold attacks.

Menander (circa 342–291 B.C.) was also a celebrated writer of comedy. Unlike Aristophanes, who wrote about aspects of public life, Menander lampooned domestic or private life. His plays are filled with cunning servants, parasitic relatives, protective fathers, and young lovers. Until the 20th century, only fragments of Menander's plays were known; our

knowledge of his work was understood mainly from ancient Roman writers who copied him extensively. But in 1957, the complete work of Menander's *The Curmudgeon,* a farce full of physical and slapstick humor, was discovered.

Greek drama began to deteriorate as Caesar's armies marched over the land. From the seeds of Greek drama, the victorious Romans established their theatre.

Roman Theatre

As the Romans invaded, they began to take special interest in Greek literature and art. Soon, Rome's crude native drama was replaced by translations and adaptations of Greek plays.

The Roman aristocracy frowned upon theatre, so audiences consisted mainly of the lower classes. They wanted entertainment. Scoffing at the art-loving and intellectual, they demanded spectacle and vulgarity. Thus, the imitated Greek theatre became decadent and hollow. Tragedies gradually degenerated and comedies slipped into common slapstick.

The Stage and the Playwrights

Because the Roman senate was hostile to theatre, the Roman playhouses were merely portable wooden platforms around which the audience stood. But in 61 B.C., the Roman leader Pompey had a huge outdoor auditorium built. In order to make it legal, he erected a small statue of Venus at the top and

Aristophanes Aristophanes is credited with writing the world's first antiwar play, *The Acharnians,* in which a farmer concludes his own peace with the Spartans and goes on to have a great time while his more warlike neighbor ends up limping home.

Greek Comedy Scholars distinguish three eras of classical Greek comedy: old, middle, and new. The differences among them are not merely chronological; they have to do with style, subject matter, political realities, and the evolution of the City Dionysia itself from an orgiastic ritual honoring Dionysus to an entertainment for Athens' upper classes.

Old Comedy was the raucous, vulgar, often scathing child of Athenian democracy—formally unrefined and politically outspoken. Middle Comedy arrived in the wake of the catastrophic defeat of Athens at the hands of Sparta (404 B.C.), when demoralized Athenians wanted, as one commentator put it, "to be amused, not lectured." Playwrights—including Aristophanes—abandoned the harsh social criticism so essential to Old Comedy while moving toward greater decorum in language and greater naturalism in style. The era of the New Comedy began when Athenian independence was crushed entirely under Macedonian rule. Whether by choice or compulsion, Menander and his contemporaries steered clear of politics, focusing instead on the comic possibilities of thwarted love and mistaken identity—and thereby providing the pattern for the modern comedy of manners.

Notes

Roman Theatre

Slaves The Romans owed their slaves an enormous cultural debt. After all, it was a Roman slave of Greek origin, Livius Andronicus (284–204 B.C.), who gave Rome access to the masterpieces of classical Greece by translating plays—and the *Odyssey,* as well—into Latin. Livius Andronicus wrote the first original Latin tragedy and comedy. He was in such demand as a performer that, according to the Roman historian Livy, he lost his voice and had to have a young assistant sing his part while he acted it. The elegant comic writer, Terence, was also a slave, as was an accomplished author of mime farces named Publilius Syrus.

Mime Theatre The Roman mime theatre was famously degenerate. Female actors appeared in the nude. Sex scenes were not just graphic but literal, and so were death scenes. When the play called for a character to be executed, a condemned criminal was substituted for the actor playing that role, and dispatched onstage. By contrast, pantomime was a more exalted form in which a single masked performer would silently act out a narrative to the accompaniment of an orchestra and chorus.

Plautus Plautus's comedies continue to provide inspiration. His *Pseudolus* provided the basis for the 1962 hit musical, *A Funny Thing Happened on the Way to the Forum.*

called it a temple of worship. The steps of this temple, of course, served as seats for the theatre.

Not to be outdone, the next Roman emperor, Caesar, ordered a playhouse built that was in the shape of two wooden theatres, back to back, each of which could be revolved to face the other. After a play presentation, the seats could be swung around into an amphitheatre for chariot races and gladiatorial contests.

> **Theatre Terms**
> claque
> closet drama

Among their discoveries in technical theatre, the Romans were the first to use a front curtain. It rolled up and down from a trough in the downstage floor. Roman theatre also instigated the **claque,** a person or persons paid to arouse the audience into clapping and shouting. (For more on Roman theatre

The Circus Maximus, where charioteers raced around the track.

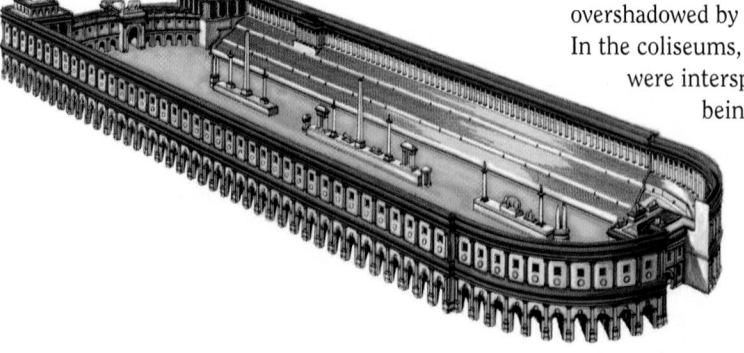

architecture and stage technology and their influence on audiences, see page 206.)

Seneca (circa 4 B.C.–65 A.D.) was a key figure in Roman dramatic literature. His plays are so bombastic and full of gory details, however, that they are more effective as **closet drama** (plays to be read rather than performed).

The comic writer **Plautus** (254–184 B.C.) is important mainly because his plays served as a pattern for later writers. His *Menaechmi* influenced Shakespeare's *Comedy of Errors,* and his *Pot of Gold* served as Molière's pattern for *The Miser.*

The Fall of Roman Theatre

Soon Roman theatrical activity gained impetus, with plays and other entertainment being presented for every holiday—and there were many Roman holidays—up to 175 at one point, which would have occupied about six months' time.

The production of plays was eventually overshadowed by sensational spectacles. In the coliseums, gladiatorial contests were interspersed with Christians being fed to lions.

Theatre Terms

claque a person or group hired to applaud at a performance

closet drama drama more suited for reading than performance

interpretive dance dance that tells a story

Peking Opera Chinese drama that features chanting, singing, and music

AMPHITHEATRES.

Vespasian's Amphitheatre, which contained eightyseven thousand spectators.

This ancient amphitheatre seated 80,000 spectators.

Special arenas called *naumachiaes* were filled with water, and slaves on ships fought until all hands were killed.

Finally, theatre entertainment became so base that when Rome fell in 475 A.D., the Christian church banned all theatrical activity. For hundreds of years afterward, theatre lay dormant throughout the continent. The East, however, did not suffer the darkness of Europe. Instead, theatrical forms that had been nurtured from years past, gained momentum throughout India and other parts of Asia.

Chinese Theatre

The beginning of Chinese drama dates back to 2000 B.C., when **interpretative dance,** that is, dance that tells a story, became more dramatic in form as ancestor worship and military celebrations were staged. These early performances, however, were not presented as entertainment. The Chinese revered their ancestors; dramatic ritual was solely religious with only the emperor, the priests, and the court as participants and audience.

> **Theatre Terms**
> interpretive dance
> Peking Opera

The Blossoming of Chinese Drama
Later, the religious rituals developed into definite plays, but it was not until the 8th and 9th centuries A.D. that Chinese drama blossomed, led by Emperor Ming Huang (713–756 A.D.), who founded a school for actors in his garden. The school was so successful that Chinese actors are traditionally called "Children of the Pear Tree Garden." Ming Huang continues as the patron saint of Chinese theatre, and actors traditionally burn incense to his statue before they begin a performance.

Chinese Theatre

Masks It is said that a general serving under Emperor Wu of the Han dynasty (141–87 B.C.) used to wear a fierce mask to intimidate his adversaries. Actors therefore wore masks to portray this general in plays, and the tradition of wearing masks was born.

Backstage Gossip: When in Rome . . .

In Greek theatres, refreshments were sold during the performance, as they are at today's sporting events. This was apparently not the custom in Roman theatres. Augustus is said to have been surprised to see a knight drinking during the show, and sent a messenger to tell him: "When the Emperor wants a drink, he goes home." "Ah," said the knight between swigs, "but the Emperor isn't afraid of losing his seat."

The Pear Tree Garden The Chinese poet Tu Fu, an almost exact contemporary of Emperor Ming Huang, wrote the following poem in memory of an artist of the Pear Tree Garden:

On Seeing the Pupil of Kung-sun Dance the Sword Dance

Of old times there was a beautiful courtesan Kung-sun,
When she danced the sword dance everyone was moved;
Those who saw her were massed like the hills tense with emotion;
Heaven and earth swayed in sympathy up and down.
For she flashed like the arrow with which the archer Yi shot down the nine suns
And soared as a crowd of spirit kings astride their winged dragons.
She began like a thunderclap with all the anger of rolling echoes,
She finished like the waters of the river and sea shining calm and still on a summery day.
Her red lips, her pearl sleeves are things of the past,
But in the evening of her life there was a pupil to carry on her fragrant traditions.
When the beautiful dancer of Lin-ying, now her successor, danced in Po Ti
She danced wonderfully to the music and her skill triumphed.
When I talked with her we found a common background of memory . . . .
The children of the pear garden have drifted away like smoke,
The remnant of that galaxy of beauty look forward to the bright cold of a winter's day.

From *Selections from Three Hundred Poems of the T'ang Dynasty* [London: John Murray, 1940], translated by Soame Jenyns. Thanks to *Dancezine*.

The drama of Ming Huang's time was highly formal. It dealt primarily with three themes: ancestor worship, military glory, and faithfulness to a husband. It was written in classical Chinese that only the exceptionally well educated could understand. This classical tradition changed, however, when the Mongols invaded in 1280 A.D. Lacking in cultural background, the Mongols demanded action, acrobatic stunts, songs, and dances. It was in this period that such plays as *The Chalk Circle* and *The Lute Song* were written.

The dramas associated with the Mongolian influence became traditional theatre, and throughout the centuries, they were enacted in their original form until the Communists took over China after World War II. After 1949, the Communist government rewrote many of the classical plays using them to preach government policy.

The Peking Opera
Because Chinese drama features chanting, singing, and musical accompaniment, Westerners began calling it **Peking Opera**. Traditional Peking Opera can still be seen today, along with new trends that reveal the influences of the West. Although Chinese drama may seem unusual and exotic to the Western world, its symbolic quality has influenced the writing of many plays, including Thornton Wilder's *Our Town*. (See page 330 for more on the Peking Opera.)

A Peking Opera production being performed in present-day Beijing.

Notes

Most of the acting is done by men, who also take women's parts. Acting is regarded as a life study. It uses movements and poses that are highly symbolic. The stylized traditional movements are graceful, and every gesture means something specific. For example, a sleeve passed over the eye denotes weeping; a shaking of the shoulders signifies grief.

Props also have symbolic meaning. White paper falling from a red umbrella means snow; a man with a whip indicates that he is on horseback; an actor carrying a flag indicates an army; a flag with wavy lines symbolizes a river. An onstage prop man, dressed in black, hands properties to the actor. The actors wear dazzling costumes and thick makeup in which color signifies character: red means faithfulness; blue, cruelty; white, evil; and so on. The greatest influence of Chinese drama has been on the theatre of Japan.

Japanese Theatre

Early drama in Japan was probably based on the ritualistic dance of the Shinto religion, but in the 14th century the Japanese **Noh** plays appeared. Similar in form and content to Chinese drama, these pieces were written in a formal, classical language meant only for the aristocrats. They remain remarkably unchanged and are still performed in Japan today. They are short, serious, philosophical studies that combine poetry with dance and music. The dance is completely unlike Western dance, which tends to feature vigorous movements. Instead, Japanese Noh movements comprise a series of sedate postures in which a specific attitude is expressed.

Noh Drama and Theatre

Noh stages are always built to specific measurements. They are wooden 18-foot squares, with the audience sitting on three sides. The stage's pointed roof, a carryover from the early days when Noh plays were performed outside, is similar to that of a Shinto shrine and is supported by four pillars. The floor is of highly polished Japanese cypress, specially constructed with large empty jars underneath to provide a unique resonant sound when the actor thumps his feet at a climactic moment.

The characters enter from a room off stage right by means of a narrow upstage corridor. As each character enters, he bows to the audience, announces his name, where he has come from, and what he will do. The chorus, which consists of six to eight men, sits on stage left and provides chanting background music.

> **Theatre Terms**
> Bunraku
> flowerway
> Kabuki
> Kyogen
> Noh

The Chalk Circle tells the story of a young woman named Chang Hai-tang who becomes the second wife of a tax collector, Ma Chun-Shing, and bears him a son. Jealous and afraid that Hai-tang will take her position and fortune away from her, Ma Chun-Shing's first wife poisons Ma Chun-Shing, blames Hai-tang, and claims the baby as her own. The case is brought to the emperor, who orders that a chalk circle be drawn on the ground and the baby placed at its center. He then tells the two women to grab hold of the child and pull; the one who drags him out of the circle wins. The first wife does as she's told, but Hai-tang refuses for fear of hurting her son. The emperor recognizes Hai-tang's maternal gesture and not only awards her the baby but the opportunity to do as she pleases with the first wife. In 1945, Bertolt Brecht adapted this story into his socialist parable, *The Caucasian Chalk Circle*.

Recent History A notorious figure in the cultural life of communist China was Jiang Qing (1914–1991), the actress who became Mao Ze Dong's second wife in 1939. As a member of the Gang of Four, she helped mastermind the fanatical purges of the Cultural Revolution (1966–1976). She also attempted to remake the Beijing Opera, replacing its traditional depictions of "emperors, kings, generals, chancellors, literati, and beauties" with paeans to the revolution. She was sentenced to death in 1981, freed in 1991, and reputed to have committed suicide ten days after her release.

Japanese Theatre

Kyogen The word *kyogen* means "wild words" and alludes to a passage in the writings of the Chinese poet, Po Chu-i (772–846 A.D.): "May the vulgar trade of letters that I have plied in this life, all the folly of wild words and fine phrases, be transformed into a hymn of praise that shall celebrate the Buddha in age on age to come, and cause the Great Wheel of Law to turn."

Theatre Terms

Bunraku Japanese puppet theatre

flowerway in a Kabuki theatre, a ramp from the back of the audience to the stage

Kabuki a melodramatic, sensational Japanese drama with song and dance, intended for the common man

Kyogen a short comedy presented before or after a Noh drama to offset its serious tone

Noh Japanese dramatic tragedy in classical style performed with poetry, dance, and music

Actors From the introduction to Arthur Waley's groundbreaking collection, *The No Plays of Japan:* "The training of actors began at seven years old. . . . After twelve the various branches of impersonation are gradually imparted. . . . The danger at twenty-four and twenty-five . . . is that the actor's friends will overpraise him. If he gains applause in his own theatre and happens one day to win in a competition with another troupe, people will begin telling him that he is a master. But such persons are doing him a very ill service; for such temporary success is not the 'true flower.' Thirty-five is the actor's prime. . . . If at forty-five he still retains his 'flower,' it is certain that it is the 'true flower.'"

A Japanese woodcut by Okumura Masanobu of a Kyogen play being performed before a large audience in the 1700s.

Scenery consists of a pine tree tapestry hung on the back wall. Only essential properties are used, and they are often a suggestion rather than an actual representation of the object. For example, a folding fan the actor uses for his various acting poses may at times suggest a dagger, a tray, or a letter, depending on what is needed.

Costumes are ornate silks, worn by all characters whether they are rich or poor. The cut of the costume and the makeup differentiate social class. Major actors wear carved wooden masks that have stereotyped expressions from one of the fifteen standard masks allowed in Noh plays. To offset the often depressing, foreboding quality of the Noh plot, the **Kyogen** was developed to serve as a comic interlude. Kyogens are farcical comedies performed without music and without masks. Usually five Nohs are presented at one performance, inter-

spersed with three Kyogens. (For more on technical theatre aspects of Noh drama, see page 310.)

Bunraku
In the 17th century another form of Japanese theatre became popular. **Bunraku,** or doll theatre, features four-foot-tall, full-body wooden marionettes, carved in such realistic detail that eyelids, eyebrows, mouth, and fingers can all be moved. Each doll is elaborately costumed. While narrators read the dialogue and a musician plays, three attendants dressed in black and wearing gauze masks (a convention that tells the audience to regard them as invisible) manipulate the dolls. (See page 342 for more on Bunraku.)

Kabuki Theatre
The Japanese drama of the common man is called **Kabuki,** which incorporates song and dance, and is thought to be more melodramatic and sensational than Noh drama. Kabukis,

Visual Cue

The woodcut on this page shows a Japanese Kyogen theatre. To make connections between this and theatres in other countries, have students discuss the following questions:

• Compare this theatre to the inn-yard stage on page 454 and the Globe on page 455. What similarities and differences do you see?

• How attentive is the Kyogen audience? How do audience members meet or not meet the rules for "audience etiquette" as expected in the United States today?

which began in the 1600a, have a wide range of subject matter. There are heavy, tension-filled historical tragedies that realistically portray scenes of suicide, murder, and torture; there are domestic love triangles; and there are unspoken dance dramas that often feature grotesque demons.

The Kabuki playhouse uses a wide extended platform, but it dispenses with the roof, pillars, and bridge of the Noh theatre. Actors enter from a **flowerway,** a ramp that extends through the audience from the back of the auditorium up to the stage. The stage floor contains trapdoors where actors may also make spectacular entrances and exits.

Kabuki utilizes colorful, extravagant scenery. Since 1793, most Kabuki theatres have been equipped with a revolving stage, which allows quick and impressive scene shifting. In recent years, theatrical devices such as the ramp, trapdoor, and revolving stage have been borrowed from Japan by the Western world.

Kabuki is noted for its lavish use of elaborate and colorful silk costumes. Although Kabuki actors do not use masks, they apply stylized masklike makeup. The actors wear wigs that denote their character's station, personality, and age; these wigs can weigh as much as twenty-five pounds. (For more about Kabuki, see page 40.)

In both Kabuki and Noh, acting skill is all-important. Actors are traditionally men who are versatile at impersonating women. Today, it is legal for women to act in Kabuki, although few do. For centuries the torch of the acting profession in Japan has been passed along family lines, with children as young as five sometimes appearing onstage as they begin their lifelong profession.

Acting follows the Chinese tradition. It is highly symbolic, presentational, and rhythmic, moving slowly from one studied pose to another. Even the tilt of the finger or the flutter of an eyelash has meaning and can evoke a certain mood in the audience.

Hindu Theatre

Dramatic form in India is ancient, dating back to 1500 B.C., when dialogue was used in religious hymns. According to Hindu mythology, Brahma invented theatre and commanded the first playhouse be built; but real theatre did not emerge until the 5th century B.C. Plays were composed in **Sanskrit,** the literary language used and understood only by the aristocrats. In fact, most Hindu drama was for the upper classes, being performed in either the gardens or courtyards of the palaces or in specially built palace playhouses.

> **Theatre Terms**
> greenroom
> Sanskrit

Bunraku The word *bunraku* is derived from the name of a puppeteer, Uemura Bunrakuken, whose eponymous theatre flourished in 19th-century Osaka. The generic term for the form is *ningyo-joruri,* designating the union of puppetry (*ningyo*) with a particular style of chanted storytelling (*joruri*).

Japan's Shakespeare Japan's first professional playwright is also widely acknowledged to have been her greatest. And he achieved this distinction by writing mostly for puppets. Called the Shakespeare of Japan, Chikamatsu Monzaemon (1653–1725) helped found the form that came to be known as Bunraku when he teamed up with another pivotal figure, Takemoto Gidayu, in 1705. His fame is not based entirely on this innovation, however; he is also credited with being the first to write dramas about common people, using the language of the streets. Monzaemon's *The Love Suicides at Sonezaki* deals, for instance, with the star-crossed love of an apprentice clerk and a prostitute. The play was not only popular but notorious, inspiring a spate of love suicides. Monzaemon is said to have written 110 Bunraku and 30 Kabuki plays. Like Shakespeare, he did not shy away from the lurid; his work includes onstage scenes of torture, violent death, and even a Caesarean delivery.

Hindu Theatre

The *Natyasastra* The Hindu equivalent of Aristotle's *Poetics* is the *Natyasastra*. Attributed to the legendary Brahman priest and sage, Bharata, its many chapters set out the rules and practices of stagecraft with an encyclopedic comprehensiveness Aristotle does not attempt.

> **Theatre Terms**
> greenroom a room where actors can relax when they are not onstage
> Sanskrit a classical language of India

The *Natyaveda* The Natyasastra says that theatre was invented by the gods during a time of human degeneracy. People were, as one source puts it, "addicted to sensual pleasures, and jealousy; anger, desire and greed filled their hearts." Led by Indra, a delegation of gods asked Brahma, the creator of the universe, to devise an entertainment that would please and inspire everyone. Brahma took elements from the four Vedas (holy books) and combined them to create a fifth: the *Natyaveda,* or holy book of dance. He gave the new Veda to the gods, but they complained that they were incapable of putting it into practice. Brahma therefore revealed it to the sage Bharata, who, together with his hundred sons, produced the first drama. This premiere of premieres did not go well. The demons in the audience were offended by the story; they took revenge by paralyzing the actors' speech, movement, and memory, which in turn incited the gods to kill many of the demons.

The Language of
THEATRE

Create a word wall of basic sight vocabulary routinely used in written classroom materials. Invite students with varying levels of English proficiency to find words in the text that they recognize and write them on sticky notes or index cards to add to the wall as the year progresses.

The stage was situated at one end of the room with the audience sitting around. The only scenery was a decorated wall with doors leading to the **greenroom,** a place where the actors changed and relaxed before and after performances. The tradition continues, and today almost every theatre and TV studio has a greenroom.

Theatre patrons had a great love of beauty, and Hindu theatre is very intimate, delicate, and restrained. It is performed strictly for pleasant entertainment, with the plays always ending happily. As far as we know, Hindu theatre was the first to permit women to act onstage. (For more on Sanskrit drama, see page 298.)

Lord Shiva, disguised as a hunter, in the Sanskrit drama *Mahabharata.*

The Language of
THEATRE

Develop basic sight vocabulary routinely used in the textbook.

- Point to these basic vocabulary words when you see them on page 443: *discuss, draw, make, read, show, study, use.*
- As you read the Suggested Projects on page 443, identify the basic vocabulary routinely used for such assignments, such as analyze, discuss, research and report, and use an Internet site.
- Read the Suggested Projects on page 443. If there are any words that you do not recognize on sight, use a dictionary to help build your vocabulary.
- Read the Suggested Projects on page 443. Notice which words and phrases are commonly used for classroom assignments and which ones are specific for this chapter.

Notes

Suggested Projects

1 From current articles online or in print, such as those in *National Geographic* magazine, research and report on the theatre of another culture. Show pictures to portray theatre as a reflection of life in a particular time, place, and culture.

2 Write an essay in which you analyze and relate the historical and cultural influences on different periods of Chinese theatre before 1800. Refer to specific works.

3 Demonstrate your understanding and appreciation of the cultural heritages of world theatre by creating a presentation to explain the influences of Asian Noh and Kabuki theatre on modern theatre.

4 Read and report on one of the plays below by key figures in Greek dramatic literature. Analyze the physical, emotional, and social dimensions of the characters. Consider the purpose of and audience for the play as well.

Agamemnon, Libation Bearers, The Furies, or *Prometheus Bound* by Aeschylus
Oedipus Rex, Antigone, or *Electra* by Sophocles
Medea or *Alcestis* by Euripides
The Curmudgeon by Menander

5 With one or two classmates, present a panel discussion on the trends in dramatic literature from the Golden Age of Greece to the fall of Rome.

6 Study the puppets of East and South Asia, including the Japanese doll theatre, Bunraku, and Indian puppet theatre. Create a visual presentation on the historical development of these influences on stage technology.

7 Analyze and report on contemporary trends in dramatic literature and technical theatre in China, including recent developments in Peking Opera.

8 Use an Internet site to learn all you can about the innovations, or discoveries, in architecture and stage technology of ancient Greek theatres. Based on your findings, demonstrate a working knowledge of this subject by creating a model or drawing of one of the theatres. Present your model or drawing to the class and explain the influences of these theatres on modern theatre.

9 With two or three classmates, show your understanding and appreciation of the cultural heritages of world drama by working on a scene from a key work in Sanskrit drama, such as *The Fatal Ring* or *Little Clay Cart.* Refine your scene as you rehearse, and then act out the scene for the class.

For More Information

Books

Beacham, Richard, *Spectacle Entertainments of Early Imperial Rome,* Yale University Press, 1999.

Hadas, Moses (trans.), *Ten Plays by Euripides,* Bantam Classics,1990.

Hutton, James (trans.), *Aristotle's Poetics,* W.W. Norton, 1982.

Roche, Paul, (trans.), *Aristophanes: The Complete Plays,* NAL Trade, 2005.

Waley, Arthur (trans.), *The Noh Plays of Japan,* Turtle Publishing, 2009.

Other Media

Behind the Mask, DVD, Insight Media, 1990.

A Casebook on Sanskrit Theater, DVD, Insight Media, 1994.

Chinese Opera, DVD, Insight Media, 1992.

Fellini Satyricon (film based on *Petronius*), adapted by Federico Fellini and Bernardino Zapponi, directed by Federico Fellini, DVD, 1970.

Jowett, Benjamin (trans.), *The Republic of Plato,* The Internet Classics Archive, 1994–2000. *classics.mit.edu/Plato/republic.html*

Peter Brook's *The Mahabharata* (stage version of Indian epic), adapted by Peter Brook, Jean-Claude Carrière, and Marie-Helene Estienne, directed by Peter Brook, DVD, 2002.

Masterpieces of Ancient Greek Literature, DVD, The Teaching Company Great Courses, 2007.

Oedipus Rex, DVD, Insight Media, 2003.

The Tradition of Performing Arts in Japan, DVD, Insight Media, 1990.

www.theatrehistory.com/

www.tctwebstage.com/oftheatre.htm

www.cwu.edu/~robinsos/ppages/resources/Theatre_History/

Part **Two**

The Middle Ages to 1800

This section of the unit begins with the liturgical plays of the Middle Ages and proceeds through Renaissance, Elizabethan (including Shakespeare), and Restoration drama.

Objectives

1 to learn about Medieval and Renaissance theatre, including *commedia dell'arte*

2 to gain appreciation of Elizabethan playwrights, actors, and theatres, especially Shakespeare and the Globe

3 to understand Restoration and 18th-century theatre, especially the comedy of manners

4 to identify key figures, works, and trends in dramatic literature and technical theatre of the period

Key Trends in Dramatic Literature

Review the four trends and explain that students should look for evidence of these trends as they read Part Two. Invite students to give current examples of plays that mix comic and serious themes or that satirize pompous behavior.

The classic unities of time and place refer to the principles first described in Aristotle's Poetics. French Renaissance dramatists followed these principles more strictly than Aristotle had intended. In the plays of Pierre Corneille and Jean Racine, there was a single action that occurred in one place in the course of a single day or even in the real time that it took for the play to be performed. English dramatists rarely followed these ideas, including multiple plots and locations as they mixed serious and comic scenes.

Key Figures and Works in Dramatic Literature
Ask students if they are familiar with any of these key figures or works. Invite students with prior knowledge to share it with the class. Encourage students to notice how these key figures and works are connected to the trends.

Part
Two The Middle Ages to 1800

In Part Two, The Middle Ages to 1800, you will have the opportunity to analyze and evaluate historical and cultural influences on theatre in Europe and learn more about key figures, works, and trends. The major periods are the Medieval, the continental Renaissance, the Elizabethan, the Restoration, and 18th-century theatre.

Christian teachings dominated the theatre of the Middle Ages, but more worldly themes and innovations in staging developed in the Renaissance that began in the 1400s. You will read about this and the following other **key trends in dramatic literature** during this period.

- Religious influence gave way to an emphasis on humanism.
- Mixture of comic and serious began in the Middle Ages and continued in *commedia dell'arte* and Elizabethan plays.
- Over time, there was movement away from observing the classic unities of time and place and rigid dramatic rules.

- Comedies of manners in the Restoration and 18th century wittily satirized artificial and pompous behavior.

You will read about these **key figures and works** that helped shape the trends.

- Medieval mystery, miracle, and morality plays: *Everyman;* Hrosvitha, religious comedies
- Renaissance: Italian, *Commedia dell'arte*; Spanish, Miguel de Cervantes, *Entremeses*; Lope de Vega, Calderone; French, Molière: *The Doctor in Spite of Himself, Tartuffe, The Imaginary Invalid*
- Elizabethan: Christopher Marlowe: *Tamburlaine, Edward II, The Jew of Malta, Dr. Faustus*; Ben Jonson: *Everyman in His Humour, Volpone, The Alchemist*; William Shakespeare: 38 plays, including *Hamlet, Romeo and Juliet, King Lear, As You Like It, A Midsummer Night's Dream, Julius Caesar, Macbeth, Othello, Richard III*
- Restoration: John Dryden: *All for Love*; George Etherege: *Love in a Tub*; William

c. 1415: Renaissance period: Brunelleschi's discovery of perspective

1508: Renaissance period: first use of painted perspective backdrop in a theatre

1545: Renaissance period: Serlio publishes *Architetura*

800s–1300s: Medieval period: Elaborate stage devices, pageant wagons

ACTivity Have students work in small groups to research and identify additional figures and events in technical theatre history that could be added to the timeline. Have each group share its findings. You may wish to create a wall timeline to which these additional items can be inserted, or you may want to display a timeline on a whiteboard and let students add their new items.

Wycherly: *The Country Wife*; George Farquhar: *The Beaux Stratagem*; William Congreve: *The Way of the World*
- 18th Century England: Oliver Goldsmith: *She Stoops to Conquer*; Richard Brinsley Sheridan: *The Rivals, The School for Scandal, The Critic*

You will also read about these and other **key figures in technical theatre** as well as the development, discoveries, and periods in theatre architecture and stage technology shown in the timeline below.

- Filippo Brunelleschi: discovers how to use linear perspective to create illusion of three-dimensional space on a flat surface, which revolutionizes stage scenery
- Andrea Palladio: designs *Teatro Olimpico*, which reflects classical Roman theatre design

- Pellegrino da San Danielle: first uses perspective backdrop for staging of Ariosto's *The Casket*
- James Burbage: constructed The Theatre, first public Elizabethan playhouse, in the Wooden O style
- Inigo Jones: introduced movable perspective scenery, proscenium arch, and colored lighting to English theatre

You will follow theses **trends in technical theatre.**

- In the Middle Ages, elaborate stage devices developed; pageant wagons brought action closer to the audience.
- Beginning in the Renaissance, there was increasing use of movable perspective scenery and a raked stage, a proscenium arch, and mechanized staging.
- Open-air Elizabethan playhouses changed to circular or octagonal
- Elaborate indoor Restoration theatres featured a pit, tiers of galleries with box seats, and a wide apron in front of the curtain.

1576: Elizabethan period: The Theatre built in London

1584: Late Renaissance period: Palladio's Teatro Olimpico, only surviving Renaissance theatre

1598: Elizabethan period: Globe Theatre built in London

1605: English Renaissance: Inigo Jones introduces perspective scenery in England none

After 1660: Restoration period: Theatres built in the Baroque style

Part Two The Middle Ages to 1800 **445**

Key Figures and Works in Technical Theatre
Filippo Brunelleschi (1377–1446) was an architect of the early Italian Renaissance, most known for the dome of the Cathedral of Santa Maria del Fiore (the Duomo) in Florence. The principles of perspective had been known to the Greeks and Romans but lost during the Middle Ages. Brunelleschi's early perspective drawings showed that he understood the principle of the vanishing point: two parallel lines seem to converge in the distance and objects appear to become smaller as they recede. Brunelleschi's discovery of these principles, probably around 1415, was described in a treatise on painting *(Della pittura)* by Brunelleschi's friend and fellow architect, Leon Battista Alberti.

Find examples of perspective drawing and Renaissance painting online or in fine art books to share with students. Then discuss with students why the discovery of perspective might have had such a big effect on stage scenery.

Key Trends in Technical Theatre

Show, Don't Tell Display images of the different types of theatre architecture and stage technology mentioned in the student book to allow students to preview the trends. Or invite students to search for images of The Globe (page 454) and a Restoration theatre (page 457). A pageant wagon is shown in the Theatre Then and Now feature on page 244 in Chapter 19, Set Design.

Notes

Medieval Theatre

Opposition The early church fathers made no secret of their opposition to the theatre. In a disquisition called *De Spectaculis* (*Of Spectacles*), Tertullian (c. 160–225) wrote, "No, we certainly nowhere find it enjoined with the same clearness as 'Thou shalt not kill,' 'Thou shalt not worship an idol,' 'Thou shalt not commit adultery' or 'fraud'; we nowhere find it expressly laid down, 'Thou shalt not go to the circus, thou shalt not go to the theatre, thou shalt not look on the contest or spectacle.' But we find relevant to this type of thing that first word of David; 'Happy is the man,' he says, 'who has not gone to the gatherings of the impious, who has not stood in the way of sinners, nor sat in the chair of pestilences.'"

English translation by T. R. Glover.

Medieval Theatre

The Middle Ages in Europe was a period often called the Dark Ages because there was little or no cultural activity. The Middle Ages began with the fall of Rome in 476 A.D. and continued until the 15th century. **Feudalism,** in which peasants worked land and paid rent to land-owning lords, was the political system of the time. Poverty and illiteracy among the masses was common. Travel and the exchange of ideas all but vanished. For approximately 400 years there was no theatre, except for sparse folk festivals and a few wandering jugglers and minstrels, who managed to stir the theatrical coals that were routinely extinguished by the church.

Theatre Born of the Church

Strange as it may seem, the church that buried drama in the 5th century resurrected that same art sometime during the 9th century when it introduced the **trope,** short dramatized scenes, into the mass. The trope began in France, but the idea soon spread throughout the European subcontinent. At first, brief Easter and Nativity tableaus (representations of a scene performed by motionless people in costume) were given to help the illiterate congregation understand the service. Pantomimes developed, which soon gave way to dialogue, first in Latin and then in the common language. Priests and choirboys enacted this religious drama. The scenes became so popular that whole stories began to be enacted. Small platforms called **mansions,** or stations, were placed within the cathedral. Separate scenes were performed on these with the crowd moving from one mansion to another until they had seen the whole story.

Theatre Terms

cycles
feudalism
guilds
mansions
miracle play
morality play
mystery play
passion play
trope

Theatre Terms

cycles a series of short plays based on religious history, often performed on pageant wagons in Medieval times

feudalism a social system whereby peasants worked the land and paid rent to the landowning nobles

guilds trade unions

mansions small platforms on which short scenes are played

miracle play drama about the life of a saint

morality play drama that teaches moral lessons

mystery play drama based on a biblical story

passion play drama based on episodes of Christ's life

trope short dramatized scenes added to the Catholic mass

Three types of plays were presented in the Middle Ages.

1 **Mystery plays** Bible stories re-enacted

2 **Miracle plays** Enacting the lives of the saints

3 **Morality plays** Stories teaching right from wrong in which characters personified abstract qualities.

An excellent example of a morality play is *Everyman,* which is still performed today. As Everyman journeys to Death, his Friends, Worldly Goods, and so on, all leave him. Only Good Deeds accompanies him to the grave.

In the 10th century, a nun, Hrosvitha, wrote religious comedy that was performed on the cathedral mansions.

An early artist's interpretation of a scene from a miracle play.

Drama in the church became boisterous when comedy was added, and the crowds became so large that in the 13th or 14th century, the mansions were moved outside to the marketplace. The comedy vein persisted: Herod became a devil and the audience laughed at his antics; Noah's wife stubbornly refused to enter the ark and had to be carried inside kicking and screaming; devils with pitchforks prodded the wicked.

Staging the Plays

Elaborate staging devices were contrived, such as Hell's Mouth, which would open and close amid smoke and flames, as well as a rack that exhibited tortured souls, complete with realistic screams. Eventually, the trade **guilds** (unions) sponsored the plays, with each guild presenting an applicable episode. The shipbuilders staged Noah's Ark; the

A recent European passion play is presented just as it was in the Middle Ages.

"Feast" plays The Middle Ages had its own form of guerrilla theatre. Secret societies produced annual "feasts"—such as the Feast of Fools, the Feast of the Ass, and the Feast of the Boy Bishop—that used vulgarity, nonsense, and a touch of paganism to satirize the Mass and temporarily invert the social order. Possibly older than the mystery plays themselves, these events occurred throughout Europe but enjoyed a special popularity in France, where troupes included Les Enfant sans Souci (The Carefree Children). Though it was argued that the feasts served as an important societal safety valve, they were outlawed by the Council of Basel in 1435.

Hrosvitha (c. 935–1002) According to Adolphus William Ward, Hrosvitha's plays "were devised on the simple principle that the world, the flesh, and the devil should not have all the good plays to themselves." She wrote six of them, occasionally employing rhyme and even elements of farce to illuminate sacred themes. Her plots tend to focus on saints undergoing conversion or enduring martyrdom. Called the "strong voice of Gandersham," Hrosvitha is thought to have been Europe's first female playwright.

Visual Cue

The image at the left shows Martin Norz as Jesus in the Oberammergau passion play of May 2000. Use the following questions to discuss the image with students:

• What episode of Christ's life is pictured?

• Do you think these are professional or amateur actors? Why?

• How might this scene have been different when performed in the 1600s?

Backstage Gossip: Deadly Dominoes

A play given in Sweden in the late Middle Ages set a dismal record for quick deceases. It was a religious drama called *The Passion of Our Savior,* and an actor named Lengis plunged his lance into the side of the actor on the cross and killed him. The dead man, falling from the cross, struck the actress playing the Virgin Mary, and she was fatally injured. The King of Sweden, John the Second, who was in the audience, swung a scimitar at Lengis and killed him; and the audience, who liked Lengis rather more than they liked their King, rose in their wrath and killed John the Second.

from *All Wrong on the Night* by Maurice Dolbier

Oberammergau The present-day Oberammergau Passion Play takes five and a half hours to perform, involves a cast and crew of 2,200 (nearly half the town's population), and takes place in a theatre that seats 4,700.

Anti-Semitism In 1984, Samuel Weintraub of the American Jewish Committee evaluated six American passion plays and found various degrees of anti-Semitism present in all of them. The plays, Weintraub said, tend to demean and stigmatize Jews while excusing the conduct of the Roman curate, Pontius Pilate, and obscuring the Jewish cultural context out of which Jesus arose.

The report calls one play "deliberately and maliciously anti-Semitic," but praises the producers of another for working to rid it of bias. (According to a *Chicago Tribune* story dated July 2, 2000, even the original Bavarian passion play has changed in this respect: "The . . . text used since 1860 has been reworked this year," the article says, "to erase implications that the Jews killed Jesus and that women played only a minor role in Jesus' life.")

cooks handled Hell's Mouth, since they were used to smoke and flames. Each scene was prepared in great detail and was carefully rehearsed. The productions, which were often quite spectacular, were presented to throngs of people on festival days in an atmosphere of gaiety and fun.

In England, France, and the Netherlands, pageant wagons were often used instead of stationary mansions. These were double-decker wagons. The lower story was curtained off and served as a changing room. The play's action was staged on the upper level and sometimes on the street around the wagon. Audience members would find vantage points and remain there as the wagons were brought to them, episode by episode—something like our parade floats today. In England the plays performed on pageant wagons were called **cycles,** and they were given in the spring on Corpus Christi day. Four of these cycles still exist: those of York, Chester, Wakefield, and Coventry. These old plays are periodically performed today in England during special summer festivals. (For more about medieval staging and pageant wagons, see page 230.)

The **passion play** evolved during the late Middle Ages. It depicted scenes from Christ's life, particularly the last days of his suffering and his resurrection. Of these, the passion play at Oberammergau,

Germany, is still performed. More than 300 years ago, residents of that small village prayed that if they were spared the black plague that was laying waste to the continent, they would periodically dramatize a passion play. Their village was spared, and they kept their vow. In 1633 they presented their first play. Since then, the Oberammergau Passion Play has been performed every ten years, at the turn of the decade. Only in 1940, during WWII, were the townspeople unable to give a show. Today thousands throng to see this intriguing play from the past. Similar passion plays, though on a smaller scale, are enacted in the United States in Spearfish, South Dakota; Lake Wales, Florida; and Eureka Springs, Arkansas.

The effects of medieval theatre would be felt in later drama. Because audience members were brought close to the performers, and because the playing area provided increased freedom, the art of acting became as important as the dialogue. Medieval drama also brought in a mixture of the comic and the serious, a combination that would be imitated by both the improvisational players in Italy and the Elizabethan writers in England.

Renaissance Theatre

The Renaissance, which means "rebirth" in French, took place largely in the 15th and 16th centuries, and was an exciting

Notes

A scene from a recent American production of a *commedia dell'arte* play by Molière.

time for theatre. As the ancient classic writers were rediscovered, a rebirth of learning occurred throughout Europe, with vigorous activity in all of the arts and sciences. The Renaissance started in Italy, and men such as Petrarch, Leonardo da Vinci, Michelangelo, and Machiavelli contributed to a great flowering of knowledge and ideas.

Italian Theatre of the Renaissance

An important form of theatre that originated in Italy at this time was the *commedia dell'arte.* Developed years before from mimes and pantomimes that may have been remnants of ancient Roman comedy, this art was flourishing by 1550. *Commedia dell'arte* was professional improvised comedy performed in the streets for the masses. A company, consisting usually of seven men and three women, would ad lib action, dialogue, song, and dance around a scenario that usually involved love and intrigue. To improvise effectively, actors had to be inventive, clever, and witty, with agile bodies for the many acrobatic stunts, fights, and dances.

Stock characters developed: Harlequin, who wore patches that later evolved into the stylized diamond costume still used today, was the clever, witty servant; Pierrot was lovelorn and moody; Columbine was flirtatious and pretty; Pantalone, who wore baggy trousers (and from whom we derive the word *pantaloons*), was the gullible father. The cast of a *commedia dell'arte,* which included the first women on the stage since Indian drama, wore half masks. The popularity of this art form spread throughout Europe and was particularly well received in France, where it would later influence the writings of Molière. (For more on *commedia dell'arte,* see page 38.)

> **Theatre Terms**
> *commedia dell'arte*
> neoclassicism

Renaissance Theatre

Arte In his book, *The Tricks of the Trade,* Italian Nobel laureate and comic genius Dario Fo reminds us that *arte,* as in *commedia dell'arte,* does not necessarily translate as "art." "In the Middle Ages," he says, "*arte* also meant 'guild,' and there existed an arte, or guild, of woolworkers, of silkworkers, of masons, and so on . . . . *Commedia dell'arte,* then, means primarily comedy staged by professional actors."

Zanni One *commedia* character was a comic servant named Giovanni but known by his nickname, Zanni. It is from him that we get the word *zany.*

Lazzi Also from *The Tricks of the Trade:* "The [*commedia*] actors had at their disposal an incredible store of stage business, called *lazzi*—situations, dialogues, gags, rhymes, and rigamaroles which they could call up at a moment's notice to give the impression of on-stage improvisation . . . . The players were past masters at dismantling and re-assembling the different elements, and in this style the most unlikely twists and turns could be extended over the entire script."

Goldoni and Gozzi Though he borrowed heavily from *commedia* story lines and characters, Carlo Goldoni (1707–1793) disdained the form's cartoonishness and brought a transformation to the Italian stage by writing more naturalistic, dimensional, character-based comedy in the manner of Molière. Goldoni's primary opponent was Count Carlo Gozzi (1720–1806), who championed traditional Tuscan culture. Gozzi's fantasies, *Turandot* and *The Love of Three Oranges* (the latter written—in *commedia* style—to lampoon Goldoni and Pietro Chiari [1700–1788]), have inspired operas by the likes of Puccini and Prokofiev.

Theatre Terms

commedia dell'arte improvised comedy with stock characters which began in Renaissance Italy

neoclassicism a form in which dramatists follow the classic unities and write in verse

Spanish Theatre Called *Monstruo de la Naturaleza*—"Prodigy of Nature"—by Miguel de Cervantes (1547–1616), Lope de Vega (1562–1635) was as prodigal as he was prolific. He quarrelled, loved, soldiered, and reproduced with remarkable gusto even as he was writing more plays than any single individual is known to have written either before or since. Nor did he slow down when he joined the priesthood in 1614. Where the plays of Calderon de la Barca (1600–1681) tend to be abstract and contemplative in tone, Lope's are given to action and often draw on contemporary events. In his based-on-fact drama, *Fuenteovejuna,* for instance, the lord of the eponymous village rapes a young woman and is murdered by angry villagers; when King Ferdinand's judge arrives to investigate, he finds that, even under torture, the villagers will say only that Fuenteovejuna killed him. Ultimately, their courage earns them the pardon and protection of the king.

French Theatre The two titans of French neoclassicism were Pierre Corneille (1606–1684) and Jean Racine (1639–1699). The paths of their careers were remarkably similar. Each was born into a bourgeouis setting and received a solid, religiously based, classically oriented education (although Corneille's was Jesuit and Racine's Jansenist). Each came early under the wing of an important patron (Corneille's was Cardinal Richelieu; Racine's, Molière) from whom each soon became alienated. Each had a blockbuster, epoque-making hit (Corneille's: *Le Cid,* Racine's: *Andromaque*) followed by a series of successes in the tragic mode, characterized by stylistic rigor and emotional power. And each finally turned his back on the theatre (Racine, because of attacks against his greatest play, *Phédre;* Corneille, at least partly because of Racine).

Spanish Theatre of the Renaissance

While Italy was developing its *commedia* and opera, Spain became interested in drama. From about 1550 to 1680, Spanish theatre flourished. It was influenced by both *commedia dell'arte* and Italian court staging. Three major playwrights evolved at this time: Miguel de Cervantes (1547–1616), who is better known today for the novel *Don Quixote* than for his 30 plays; Lope de Vega (1562–1635), who wrote a phenomenal 2000 plays, many of them full of beautiful poetry, vigorous action, and dashing romance; and Calderon (1600–1681), who created 200 plays, which were distinguished by their spiritual emphasis and elevated poetry.

These dramatists were all successful in establishing an original art form, free from the classical rules that fettered so many Italian and French writers. Spanish dramatists, ignoring the unities of time and place, wrote beautiful flowing dialogue and centered their action around adventure, romance, and chivalry.

French Renaissance Theatre

Because of France's many wars, and because one theatre group had exclusive rights to the public playhouse, the Renaissance came late to French theatre, reaching its height during the 17th century. At that time the increased theatre activity gave rise to **neoclassicism,** a form in which dramatists were supposed to observe the classic unities and write in a restricted verse form. This French drama developed into entertainment mainly for royalty. Playhouses were ornate, with carvings washed in gold, velvet-covered seats, and lavish drapes, following the Italian

A scene from *O Soldado Vigilante*, a farce by Miguel de Cervantes, performed at the Teatro da Rainha in Portugal.

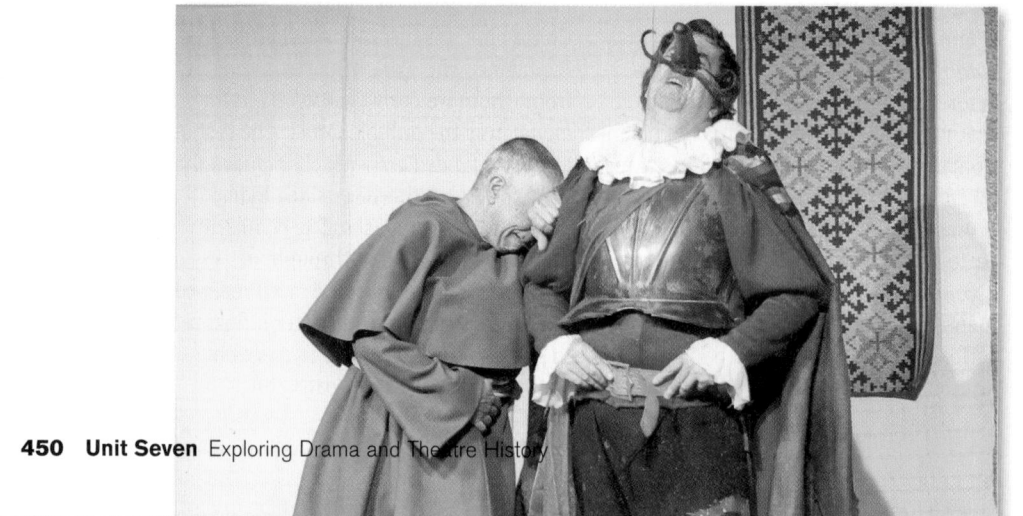

Visual Cue

Use the following questions to discuss the production pictured above:

- What details in the actors' poses suggest the farcical nature of this play, whose title translates as *The Vigilant Sentinel*?

- What details of costuming suggest that the play is a farce?

- The characters shown here are the sacristan (left) and the sentinel, both of whom desire the love of a kitchen maid, Cristina, What does the photo suggest about the relationship between these two suitors? Does it appear that one has the upper hand with winning Cristina's heart?

tradition of luxurious surroundings for the nobles.

Molière (1622–1673) represents the high point of French Renaissance drama. He wrote such witty satire that his plays continue to entertain audiences around the world. Molière's real name was Jean-Baptiste Poquelin, but when he chose the theatre as his life's work, he also chose another name so that his parents would not be disgraced by having an actor in the family.

Molière toured for twelve years as an actor in a *commedia dell'arte* company. As he began to write comedies, he drew from the *commedia's* farcical style. His many plays, performed both for the public and for the court of Louis XIV, are masterpieces of satire, a perfect blend of the humorous and the caustic. In *The Doctor in Spite of Himself,* Molière lampoons the field of medicine; in *Tartuffe* he satirizes hypocrisy; in *The Imaginary Invalid* he spoofs hypochondria. Throughout his writing career, Molière continued to act. In his last years he was ill from tuberculosis, and, ironically, he died onstage just after completing a performance of *The Imaginary Invalid.* (For more about Molière, see page 132.)

Although the theatrical activity in Italy and Spain (and later, in France) advanced Renaissance drama, it was not in these countries where drama realized its greatest potential. Instead, we look to England for a unique form that reached staggering heights.

Elizabethan Theatre

Elizabeth and the Playwrights

There was great vitality, zest, and intellectual curiosity throughout England during Queen Elizabeth I's reign (1558–1603). Her country swelled with national pride over its voyages of discovery, its defeat of the Spanish armada, its expanding trade markets, and its increased literary vistas—the result of the introduction of printed books in 1475.

When Elizabeth became queen of England, the theatre gained a friend, for even though the Lord Mayor and other civil authorities were hostile to drama (because of the fear that the crowds would spread disease and start fights), Elizabeth loved the theatre. She commanded many court performances, protected groups of players through court sponsorship, and looked upon London's feverish dramatic activity with approval.

The Elizabethan period was an age of literary enlightenment. There were many brilliant playwrights, and most of them wrote with great freedom, disregarding the classic unities of time and place, and the rule—left over from the ancient Greeks—that violence

> **Theatre Terms**
> discovery space
> groundlings
> masques
> soliloquies
> tiring house
> Wooden O's

Interestingly, in attempting to describe the difference between Corneille and Racine, one observer felt compelled to paraphrase Sophocles' remark about the difference between himself and Euripides: Corneille depicted people as they ought to be while Racine depicted them as they are.

Corneille's *Le Cid* made such a strong impression on Parisian society that "Beautiful as *Le Cid*" became a catchphrase.

Molière produced Racine's first two tragedies. Racine repaid him by seducing one of his leading ladies and coaxing her to jump to a rival company. Molière reputedly never spoke to Racine again.

Elizabethan Theatre

The Role of Age A sidelight: The greatest figures of the Italian, Spanish, and French Renaissances lived to be very old men. Goldoni, Gozzi, Chiari, and Calderon reached their 80s; Lope de Vega and Corneille lived into their 70s; Cervantes saw his 69th birthday; and Racine died relatively young at 60. The tendency for writers of the English Renaissance is exactly opposite. Of the eleven leading writers listed in this section, only three made it out of their 50s, with Thomas Heywood the grand old man at 67. Shakespeare and John Lyly both died at 52; Greene, Kyd, Peele, Webster, Beaumont, and Fletcher were all spent by their 30s or early 40s. And, of course, Marlowe famously lost his life at 29. One wonders if there is a correlation between the greater vigor of the English Renaissance and the shorter life spans of its participants. Did the expectation of death paradoxically enliven their work? Did the long lives of the Italian, Spanish, and French lions discourage competition and therefore innovation?

Theatre Terms

discovery space in an Elizabethan theatre, a space at the back of the stage used for small interior settings

groundlings audience members who stood in the pit around the Elizabethan stage

masques extravagant court entertainments that included dance, music, and poetry

soliloquies types of monologues that reveal the character's inner thoughts

tiring house in an Elizabethan theatre, a backstage area where actors changed clothes

Wooden O's Elizabethan theatres which were usually round or octagonal

Christopher Marlowe was the adventurer par excellence. It is thought that he spied for the English crown during his college years, keeping tabs on its Catholic adversaries in France, and that after taking his M.A. he went to the Low Countries (the present-day Netherlands and Belgium) to fight alongside Protestant rebels. Back in London, he was an outspoken, ostentatiously dressed dandy before the term was coined. His incautious, irreverent mouth made him the target of charges of heresy, for which he might have been prosecuted if he had not been killed first in a fight over a bar tab. (Some think the fight was intentionally provoked in order to get Marlowe out of the way.)

Marlowe's roommate, Thomas Kyd, was arrested for heresy and tortured into informing against Marlowe. He died a year later.

Ben Jonson's valediction "To the Memory of Shakespeare" compares the Bard favorably not only to his contemporaries but to the greatest writers of the Classical period. It contains these lines: "Soul of the age!/ The applause! delight! the wonder of our stage! . . . /He was not of an age, but for all time!" Jonson himself is the only person buried vertically under the floor at Westminster Abbey. His headstone reads, "O rare Ben Johnson" (sic). Legend has it that this epitaph was an afterthought, requested and paid for by an admirer who happened to be present when masons were closing the grave.

Like so many other theatre artists of the Renaissance, Ben Jonson (1572–1637) did time in jail. In 1597, he was imprisoned for cowriting—with Thomas Nashe—a seditious satire called *The Isle of Dogs*.

The following year he killed an actor named Gabriel Spencer in a duel and was convicted of murder. He escaped hanging but forfeited his possessions and was literally branded (on the thumb) as a felon.

should not be seen on stage. Moreover, they mixed poetry with prose and interspersed comedy with tragedy. Competent though they were, Thomas Kyd, John Lyly, Robert Greene, George Peele, John Webster, Thomas Dekker, Thomas Heywood, and Beaumont and Fletcher were overshadowed by the three giants of Elizabethan theatre: Christopher Marlowe, Ben Jonson, and William Shakespeare.

Christopher Marlowe (1564–1593)
Next to Shakespeare, Marlowe is considered the greatest dramatist of tragedy in England, even though he lived only to the age of twenty-nine. Marlowe's blank verse is often termed "Marlowe's Mighty Line." In his short life, he wrote seven plays. *Tamburlaine, Edward II, The Jew of Malta,* and *Dr. Faustus* became his best known.

Ben Jonson (1572–1637)
Like Marlowe, Jonson scorned Shakespeare at first because Shakespeare knew "small Latin and less Greek." Jonson was a classic writer, always correct, always abiding by the Aristotelian unities. Much of his work is biting, humorous satire. *Everyman in His Humour, Volpone,* and *The Alchemist* are but a few of his plays. When James I inherited the throne, Jonson entertained the court with

masques, great extravaganzas of song, dance, and recitation. It is said that on one Jonson production alone, James spent the equivalent of $500,000 on lavish costumes and sets designed by Inigo Jones, who had studied perspective scenery in Italy.

William Shakespeare (1564–1616)
Considered the greatest of all English dramatists, it is strange and unfortunate that we know so little about Shakespeare's life. Born in Stratford-upon-Avon, where his father was a glover and, for a time, a respected town official, Shakespeare attended grammar school, his only formal education. At eighteen, he married Anne Hathaway, eight years his senior. Although the exact reason is not known, he left his wife and three children and went to London, where he began working in the theatre world as an actor, manager, and writer. By 1596, he was well established and in royal favor, for Queen Elizabeth granted him a coat of arms.

In the thirty-eight plays attributed to him, Shakespeare created histories, comedies, tragedies, and fantasies. His plays combined skillful plot and character development with majestic use of language. Among his masterful creations are the melancholy Hamlet,

Notes

Prince of Denmark; the fat, braggart Falstaff; the impish Puck; the boyish Rosalind; the impetuous Hotspur; the youthfully passionate Juliet; and the jealous Othello.

Shakespeare's luminous **soliloquies** (speeches where actors talk alone to reveal their thoughts aloud) encompass great breadth of emotion and intellect and are beloved throughout the world.

But his less grand phrases are a part of our world as well. We quote Shakespeare without even knowing it. Phrases such as "grim necessity," "as luck would have it," "Greek to me," "the short and long of it," "a rose by any other name," "haven't slept a wink," "all the world's a stage," "the unkindest cut of all," and "eating out of house and home" are straight out of Shakespeare's playful, compelling, and inventive language.

Shakespeare is as popular today as he was over 400 years ago, as can be seen in this lively and imaginative scene from a recent production of his *Twelfth Night*.

William Shakespeare There are those who argue that Shakespeare's plays are too great to have been written by Shakespeare. They claim that the historical Shakespeare—whom they prefer to call the Stratford Man (for his hometown of Stratford-upon-Avon), or Will Shakespeare (for the way he signed documents)—was too unschooled, untraveled, and plebian to have given the world the profundity of *Hamlet,* the sophistication of *As You Like It,* the humanity of *King Lear,* or the sweetness of *A Midsummer Night's Dream.* (Apparently it escapes them that Marlowe was the son of a shoemaker and Jonson was raised by a bricklayer.) They have therefore written fat books purporting to prove that Shakespeare was a front for someone else who could not afford to be associated directly with the seamy world of the theatre. Candidates include Francis Bacon, Edward de Vere, King James I, and Queen Elizabeth. Christopher Marlowe has been put forward, also, on the theory that he faked his death in order to confound his enemies, and then continued his career in secret.

For an entertaining and sensible refutation of the "anti-Stratfordian" argument, see William M. Murphy's 1964 lecture, "Thirty-Six Plays in Search of an Author."

Shakespeare's children were a daughter named Susanna and a pair of twins, Hamnet and Judith. On August 11, 1596, 11-year-old Hamnet died of unknown causes.

Visual Cue

Ask students to study the image from the *Twelfth Night* production above. Discuss the concept of Shakespeare in modern dress with your students.

- The photo caption says that Shakespeare plays are as popular today as they were 400 years ago. Do you agree with this statement? Why or why not?

- What is your opinion about Shakespeare in modern dress? Does it help with comprehension, or does it detract from the majesty of the plays?

- What would you think of a modern-language Shakespeare along with the modern dress? In other words, changing the language to contemporary English?

Lord Pembroke's Men performed some of Shakespeare's earliest plays, including the lurid *Titus Andronicus.* By the 1590s Shakespeare was a principal member of the Lord Chamberlain's Men, the company that built the Globe Theatre. When James I succeeded Queen Elizabeth to the throne in 1603, he became their patron and the company was renamed the King's Men.

The Theatres The Globe Theatre's motto was *"Totus mundus agit histrionem,"* or "an entire world of players." The converse, of course, is, "All the world's a stage."

From the Web site of the Rose Theatre Trust: "Built in 1587 by Philip Henslowe, the Rose was the first theatre on London's [Thames] Bankside. In 1989 its remains were discovered and partially excavated amidst a blaze of international press coverage. Despite their huge archaeological and cultural significance, they were promptly covered up again for conservation reasons. Nearly ten years later, the theatre site was reopened to the public as part of an historical exhibition. Meanwhile, thanks primarily to the efforts of the late American actor Sam Wanamaker, the Globe has been rebuilt as faithfully as possible and reopened as a performance venue."

The Theatres

The first public playhouse to be erected during this time was The Theatre, constructed by James Burbage in 1576, accommodating about 1,500 people. It was placed outside of London to escape the city's jurisdiction. Other theatres, including The Rose, The Fortune, The Swan, Blackfriars, and The Globe, were soon built. Although we do not know the exact nature of Elizabethan theatre structure, we know that the playhouses were modeled upon the inn yards where earlier plays had been presented. Called **Wooden O's,** the theatres were usually round or octagonal with two or three tiers of thatched roof galleries surrounding an open court on three sides. One end served as a multiple acting area with a large platform (equipped with trapdoors), which was elevated by four to six feet and extended into the open court. Each theatre also had a **discovery space** located between two doors at the back of the stage and used for small interior settings, such as Juliet's burial vault. The two doors at the back of the stage led to the **tiring house,** or backstage area, where the actors would go to change costumes.

On the second level of the stage facade, there was another acting space (an "inner above"), as well as balcony windows and a terrace. A third level could also provide a playing area but was used mainly for the musicians as they

Stage in an inn yard, around 1565. Portable platforms upon which plays were performed were set up in the inn yards. This image is based on a sketch from the 16th century by Pieter Breughel the Younger.

accompanied songs and dances and played musical interludes. A fourth level was a structure called the hut, which housed stage machinery for the special effects.

Plays were held in the afternoon (with the daylight serving as lighting system), and to announce performances, a flag—white for comedy, black for tragedy—was raised at the top of the theatre. All classes of people attended, for the theatre was to Elizabethans not only their drama, but also their movies, novels, radio, television, and newspapers rolled into one. The **groundlings**—usually tradespeople, soldiers, apprentices, and servants—paid a penny and stood in the pit around the acting platform. Lords

Notes

and ladies paid more and had seats in the gallery. A few rich, young gallants might even occupy a portion of the stage. The whole atmosphere was joyful and at times boisterous. Peddlers sold oranges and nuts that were noisily eaten—and sometimes thrown—by the audience.

There was no scenery. The spectators used their imaginations as they listened to the playwright's descriptions and the characters' dialogue. Some properties were used, and so were certain sound effects. In fact, the burning of The Globe Theatre in 1613 was the result of the thatch roof catching a spark from the cannon shots that announced the king's entrance in Shakespeare's *Henry VIII*. By June of 1614 it was rebuilt and in use again.

Since costumes were usually handsome styles of the day donated by patrons, there was little attempt made toward historical accuracy. Julius Caesar, along with Dr. Faustus, wore Renaissance clothes on the Elizabethan stage. Only a few stylized costumes, those for fairies, witches, lawyers, and churchmen, were used.

The modern Globe, an open-air theatre reconstructed through the efforts of many, including American actor Sam Wanamaker. The original Globe was destroyed in 1644.

Backstage Gossip: Cockney Catastrophe

When a "super" [extra] graduates to a "bit part," the margin for error is sizably increased. In an early nineteenth-century provincial production of *Richard III,* an amateur actor entered toward the end of the first act and told the astonished king, "My Lord, I 'ave cut off the Dook of Buckingham's 'ead." "Oh, you 'ave, 'ave you?" King Richard retorted. "Well, you've gone and spoiled the 'ole bloomin' play, that's wot you've done!"

from *All Wrong on the Night* by Maurice Dolbier

Edward Alleyn became very wealthy as an entertainment entrepreneur. One of his businesses was the Bear Garden, a venue for bearbaiting.

Will Kempe was the great theatrical clown of his day, famous for jigging the entire way from London to Norwich—a distance of about 100 miles as the crow flies. Some scholars think that part of Hamlet's famous speech to the Players (". . . and let those that play your clowns speak no more than is set down for them, for there be of them that will themselves laugh, to set on some quantity of barren spectators to laugh too, though in the mean time some necessary question of the play be then to be considered. That's villainous and shows a most pitiful ambition in the fool that uses it.") was Shakespeare's not-so-subtle gibe at Kempe.

The Jacobean Age The reign of James I was called the Jacobean Age. In the theatre it was characterized by cynicism, melancholy, and a preoccupation with evil. *Hamlet,* Webster's *The Duchess of Malfi,* and Jonson's *Volpone* embody the Jacobean mood.

The Language of
THEATRE

Prepare students for understanding more complex imperative sentences such as those in the Suggested Projects by having them read these sentences that you write on the board: Read [write] this word [sentence]. Point out that *you* is understood as the subject of the sentence.

The Language of
THEATRE

Comprehend English vocabulary and language structures routinely used in the textbook.

- Work with a teacher or classmate to read the first word in each of the Suggested Projects on page 429. Say what you think each one means. Notice that they are all verbs that tell you to do something.
- Read the Suggested Projects on page 459 with a partner. Discuss what each one asks you to do. Identify proper nouns and possessives.
- Read the Suggested Projects on page 459, using a dictionary as needed to comprehend the instructions. Notice how the structure of the sentences helps you identify the steps of each project.
- Read the Suggested Projects on page 459. Identify any English vocabulary or structures of words or sentences that are still challenging for you to understand.

The Players
Actors were all men, with the women's parts being taken by boys whose voices had not yet changed to masculine lowness or by men with higher-than-usual voices. Acting was a strenuous life, for often roles required singing, dancing, fighting, and fencing. Three great actors emerged during this period:

Richard Burbage (1567–1619, son of the man who built The Theatre in 1576) Born, like Shakespeare, in Stratford-upon-Avon, Burbage played many of Shakespeare's tragic figures, including Hamlet, Othello, Richard III, and King Lear. He and his brother Cuthbert built The Globe Theatre in London.

Edward Alleyn (1566–1626) Alleyn played the title roles in *Tamburlaine* and *Dr. Faustus* as well as Barabas in *The Jew of Malta,* all written by Christopher Marlowe. In 1600, Alleyn and his partner Philip Henslowe constructed The Fortune Theatre north of London to compete with the Globe.

William Kemp or Will Kempe (circa 1560–about 1603) Kemp's greatest success came from the role of Nick Bottom in *A Midsummer Night's Dream.* Shakespeare created this character with the supposed intention of ridiculing the scene-stealing actor, but Kemp made the character his own, even down to Bottom's donkey ears. In early manuscripts Shakespeare inadvertently identifies Bottom as "Kempe."

James I (1603–1625) reigned after the death of Elizabeth I. The political unrest that had been brewing throughout his reign continued after Charles I was crowned in 1625.

Backstage Gossip: Will vs. Richard

This story comes from an actor in Shakespeare's company, who noted the following in his diary under March 13, 1601:

Upon a time when Burbage played Richard III, there was a citizen grew so far in liking with him that before she went from the play she appointed him to come that night unto her, by the name of "Richard the Third." Shakespeare, overhearing their conclusion, went before, was entertained, and at his game ere Burbage came. Then, message being brought that Richard the Third was at the door, Shakespeare caused return to be made, that William the Conqueror was before Richard the Third.

from *Theatrical Anecdotes* by Peter Hay

Eventually, civil war broke out, and Oliver Cromwell, the Puritan leader, gained control. Charles was beheaded, and the rest of the Stuart line fled to France. The Puritans, always against the theatre, closed what they considered "dens of iniquity" in 1642. Public theatre died in England until Charles II regained control of England in 1660. During Cromwell's time, however, plays were performed surreptitiously, as the historical record of arrests of actors and audience members shows.

Restoration and 18th-Century Theatre

The Restoration came about with the reestablishing of the monarchy in England in 1660 under Charles II. When Charles returned from France and was restored to the English throne, he started a new era of drama that was fashioned after the theatre he had seen in Paris.

Since the Elizabethan playhouses had been torn down by the Puritans, new indoor

The Restoration

Aphra Behn A sometime English spy with the code name "Astrea," Aphra Behn (1640–1689) became one of the most prolific playwrights of the Restoration and the first European woman to earn her living by writing. Though she also wrote fiction and poetry, she was well known for racy comedies with titles like *The Forced Marriage, The Amorous Prince, The Feigned Courtesans,* and *The Lucky Chance.*

"All women together ought to let flowers fall upon the tomb of Aphra Behn...," Virginia Woolf wrote, "for it was she who earned them the right to speak their minds. It is she—shady and amorous as she was—who makes it not quite fantastic for me to say to you tonight: Earn five hundred a year by your wits."

Theatre design in the 18th century featured box seats, a pit, a wide apron in front of the curtain, and a gallery for the audience. The scene depicted here is the wrestling match in Shakespeare's *As You Like It* at the Drury Lane Theatre, London, 1841.

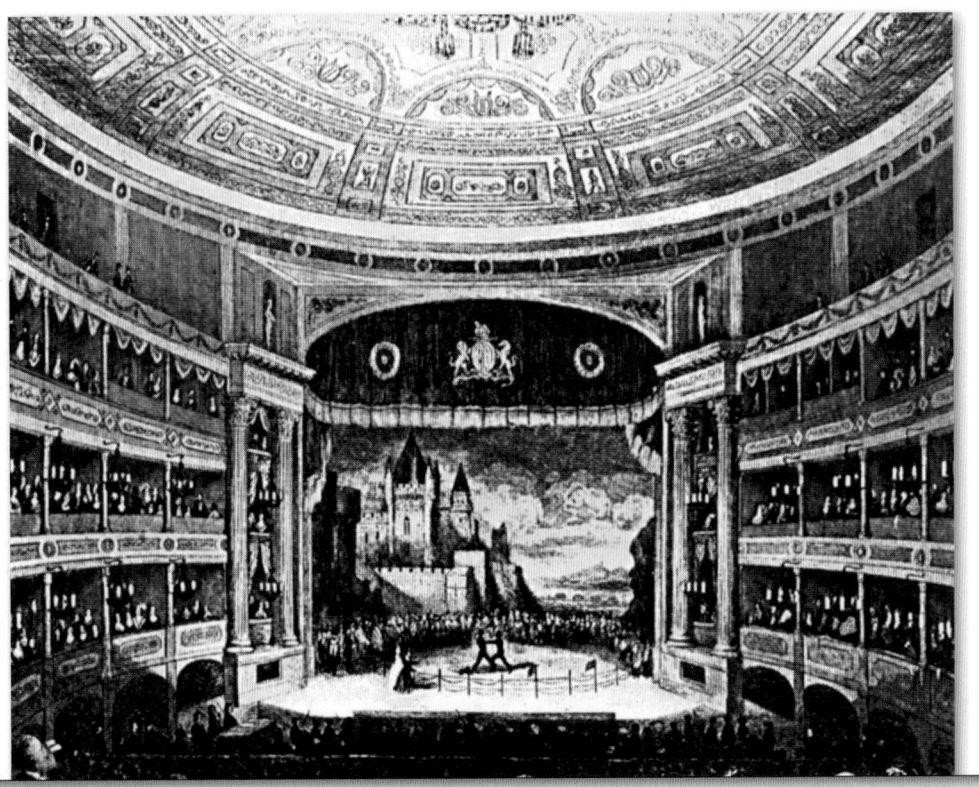

Theatre Terms

bombastic pompous and high-flown language

legitimate theatre a term originally based on England's Licensing Act of 1737 in which plays could only be performed in two specific playhouses

the Restoration an era that began with the restoration of the British monarchy in 1660 under Charles II

Sarah Kemble Siddons was especially famous for her portrayal of Lady Macbeth, and she chose the role for her farewell performance in 1812. It is said that the audience at that performance was so taken with Siddons in the sleepwalking scene that they would not let the play proceed beyond it.

theatres were built with a deep apron on which to act and with a proscenium arch, behind which a series of flats were painted in perspective and were set parallel to the curtain. These flats were spaced upstage of each other to give the illusion of distance. Candles and oil lamps provided lighting in these indoor theatres, and women were allowed to perform.

> **Theatre Terms**
> bombastic
> legitimate theatre
> the Restoration

The audience was the sophisticated aristocracy. Broadly generalized, this crowd was witty, insincere, and apt to indulge in foolish pleasures. The plays staged at this time were comedies of manners that satirized the artificiality of the day, and so they, too, were witty and concerned with foolish pleasures.

Plays of the Restoration include John Dryden's *All for Love,* George Etherege's *Love in a Tub,* William Wycherley's *The Country Wife,* George Farquhar's *The Beaux' Stratagem,* and William Congreve's *The Way of the World.*

The Restoration ended in 1737, when Parliament passed the Licensing Act, which limited London's public playhouses to two: Covent Garden and Drury Lane. All others were illegal. Thus, evolved the term legitimate theatre, which today has changed meaning and refers to all live play performances (as opposed to film).

The Comedy of Manners

Later in the century and roughly corresponding to the period of the American Revolution, two other English dramatists carried on the comedy of manners tradition with a brilliance and inoffensiveness that must have pleased the licensing board. Oliver Goldsmith (1728–1774) unveiled his witty, upbeat *She Stoops to Conquer,* and Richard Brinsley Sheridan (1751–1816) fashioned the best English comedies since those of Shakespeare, such as *The School for Scandal* and *The Rivals.*

During this period, some great actors made their names on the English stage. David Garrick (1717–1779), both actor and director, is credited with establishing a less **bombastic** style of acting, that is, one that didn't appear pompous or overdone. He did many Shakespearean revivals, often rewriting, deleting, or adding scenes. The tragic actress Sarah Kemble Siddons (1755–1831) and her brother John Philip Kemble (1757–1823) were also famous stage personalities. Later, Edmund Kean (1787–1833) achieved great acclaim, particularly for his role as Shylock in Shakespeare's *The Merchant of Venice.*

Backstage Gossip: The Worst Audience Award

Restoration audiences have a fair claim to being considered the worst that any actors in the world have had to play to—the theatre being looked on as a place to eat, drink, brawl, pick up prostitutes or merchants' wives and, from time to time, damn the play and the players loudly. On several occasions, fights that broke out in the audience were carried to the stage itself and ended in fatal sword thrusts.

from *All Wrong on the Night* by Maurice Dolbier

Suggested Projects

1 Read, analyze, and evaluate one of the following plays, and discuss the historical and cultural influences on theatre in the Middle Ages based on the example you choose. Verify how your example communicates for a specific purpose and audience.

   The Second Shepherd's Play
   Everyman
   Gammer Gurton's Needle

2 Research and write a report on the influences of world drama and theatre by using the Internet to present and support an opinion about the Oberammergau Passion Play today and how it connects to the original Passion Play.

3 Read Simonson's description of medieval staging in his book *The Stage Is Set* and demonstrate a working knowledge of stage technology in this period by using the information to stage a scene from *Everyman*.

4 Create sketches or computer drawings showing a set design for a Renaissance play in order to demonstrate a working knowledge of the discoveries in stage technology related to perspective.

5 Research *commedia dell'arte* characters and draw costumes for each. Apply historical or cultural accuracy from research in your designs.

6 Write an original scenario for a *commedia dell'arte* troupe to improvise. Mix comic and serious elements to reflect the trends in dramatic literature in this period.

7 Rehearse and present a scene or soliloquy from a Shakespeare play. Read the complete play to understand your character's motivation. Then discuss how the experience helped you appreciate Shakespeare as a key figure in world drama and theatre.

8 Demonstrate a working knowledge of theatre architecture and stage technology in the periods of Elizabethan England and Renaissance Spain by creating a PowerPoint presentation comparing the two periods. (See *The Living Stage* by Macgowan and Melnitz or use Internet resources.)

9 Read and act out scenes from one of Molière's comedies, such as *The Doctor in Spite of Himself, The Would-Be Gentleman, The Miser,* or *Tartuffe*. Then in a discussion analyze Molière's role in the cultural heritage of world drama.

10 Learn more about The Globe by visiting www.shakespearesglobe.com/about-us/virtual-tour. Synthesize this research with your previous knowledge and articulate the impact of the Globe in the context of the cultural heritage of world drama and theatre. Discuss your findings with your classmates.

For More Information

Books

Cawley, A.C. (ed.), *Everyman and Medieval Miracle Plays,* Everyman Paperback Classics, 1993.

Everyman, with Other Interludes, Including Eight Miracle Plays, BiblioBazaar, 2007.

Fields, Bertram, *Players: The Mysterious Identity of William Shakespeare,* Harper Perennial, 2006.

Gordon, Mel, *Lazzi: The Comic Routines of the Commedia dell'Arte,* PAJ Publications, 2001.

Slater, Maya (trans.), *Molière: The Misanthrope, Tartuffe, and Other Plays,* Oxford University Press, 2008.

Spencer, Jane (ed.), *Aphra Behn: The Rover and Other Plays,* Oxford University Press, 2008.

Other Media

Commedia by Fava: The Commedia dell'Arte Step by Step, 2 DVDs, Insight Media, 2006.

Commedia dell'Arte: The Story, the Style, DVD, Insight Media, 2007.

Doctor Faustus, DVD, Insight Media, 2009.

Everyman, DVD, Insight Media, 1991.

Modern Molière: Tartuffe, DVD, Insight Media, 2007.

The N-Town Passion Play (Ludus Coventriae), DVD, Insight Media, 1990.

Period Movement: Restoration, DVD, Insight Media, 2005.

The Way of the World, DVD, Insight Media, 1977.

www.perseus.tufts.edu/hopper/searchresults.jsp?q=christopher+marlowe

Part **Three**

1800 to the Present

The third part of Unit Seven addresses 19th-century theatre on the continent and in America and concludes with an overview of theatre in the 20th and 21st centuries.

Objectives

1 to understand and appreciate the cultural heritages of world drama and theatre from the period

2 to understand realism and romanticism and the playwrights who dominated these movements

3 to identify key figures, works, and trends in dramatic literature and technical theatre of the period

4 to understand and appreciate the multicultural heritage of United States drama and theatre and identify key figures, works, and trends in dramatic literature and technical theatre

Key Trends in Dramatic Literature

Review the four trends and explain that students should look for evidence of these trends as they read Part Three. Discuss with students how a move to more realism in theatre is connected to plays that challenge audiences to think about social and political issues. Invite students to give current examples of plays about such issues.

Key Figures and Works in Dramatic Literature

Ask students if they are familiar with any of these key figures or works. Invite students with prior knowledge to share it with the class. Point out that the first five names on the list are from world drama and the last five names represent playwrights from the United States. Encourage students to notice how these key figures and works are connected to the trends.

Part **Three** 1800 to the Present

In Part Three, 1800 to the present, you will relate theatre to history, society, and culture in Europe and the United States over a period of more than 200 years. You will also have an opportunity to understand and appreciate the multicultural heritage of drama and theatre, including technical theatre, in the United States.

During this period, Romanticism gave way to realistic and experimental drama and staging starting in the 19th century and continuing into the 21st century. You will read about this and the following other **key trends in dramatic literature** during this period.

- Romanticism gave way to realism.
- Plays challenged audiences to think about social and political issues.

- Avant-garde theatre, including absurdism, developed in the second half of the 20th century.
- The United States began developing its own unique theatre in the 20th century.

You will read about these **key figures and works** that helped shape the trends.

- Henrik Ibsen: *A Doll's House, Hedda Gabler, An Enemy of the People*
- George Bernard Shaw: *Pygmalion, Major Barbara, Arms and the Man*
- Bertolt Brecht: *Mother Courage, The Caucasian Chalk Circle, The Three Penny Opera*
- Tom Stoppard: *Rosencrantz and Guildenstern Are Dead, Arcadia*
- Samuel Beckett: *Endgame, Waiting for Godot*

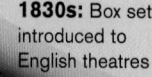

1830s: Box set introduced to English theatres

1874: Duke of Saxe-Meiningen uses historic sets and costumes

1880: Incandescent lighting first used in theatres

1895: Appia introduces ideas that become the New Stagecraft

Notes

- Eugene O'Neill: *A Long Day's Journey into Night, Mourning Becomes Electra*
- Thornton Wilder: *Our Town, The Skin of Our Teeth*
- Tennessee Williams: *The Glass Menagerie, A Streetcar Named Desire*
- Arthur Miller: *Death of a Salesman, The Crucible*
- Neil Simon: *The Odd Couple, Brighton Beach Memoirs*

You will also read about these and other **key figures and works in technical theatre.**

- Charles Kean and the Duke of Saxe-Meiningen: historical accuracy in sets and costumes
- Adolphe Appia and Gordon Craig: New Stagecraft (3-dimensional sets and directional lighting)

- Bertolt Brecht: emphasis on theatricality by making technical elements visible to audiences
- Robert Edmond Jones: "father" of American scene design

You will follow theses **trends in technical theatre.**

- Smaller auditoriums with narrow aprons, realistic box sets (instead of wings and painted backdrops)
- Historical accuracy in sets and costumes
- New technology affecting all aspects of theatre design, from incandescent lights to computerized design and controls allowing for more elaborate stage movement
- Use of impressionistic settings rather than realistic painted sets

1939: Penthouse Theatre in Seattle, WA, first modern theatre in the round

1947: Jo Mielziner pioneers use of projections in scenic design

1970s: Construction of adaptable spaces for multiple theatre forms

1990s: Performing arts complexes

1800 to the Present **461**

Key Figures and Works in Technical Theatre

Charles Kean(1811–1868) was a popular actor-manager in London known for mounting historically accurate productions of Shakespeare's plays. Recall that in Shakespeare's time, costumes were often donated by well-to-do patrons and so reflected the Elizabethan period rather than the period in which the plays were set. Kean felt that making settings and costumes more historically accurate could allow the theatre to be educational as well as entertaining.

Robert Edmond Jones (1887–1954) studied the New Stagecraft of Adolphe Appia and Gordon Craig in Europe after his graduation from Harvard in 1910. His simple presentational set for the 1915 production of *The Man Who Married a Dumb Wife* was a shock to American audiences. He is most known for his work with the Provincetown Players and the Theatre Guild, including dramatic lighting in several Shakespearean plays. Jo Mielziner later apprenticed with Jones. See the following pages for additional information on other key figures: Duke of Saxe-Meiningen, page 178; Adolphe Appia, page 285; and Bertolt Brecht, page 345.

Key Trends in Technical Theatre

Invite students to find references to the key trends in the timeline. Lead a discussion about how rapidly technology has affected theatre design.

Visual Cue

The timeline highlights the historical development, discoveries, and periods in theatre architecture and stage technology influences. The following prompts can be used to exercise students' **critical viewing skills.**

- What is most striking in the visual of the 1895 set by Adolphe Appia?

- What do you notice about the historical development of performance spaces throughout this period?
- How would you compare the theatre architecture of the 20th century with earlier periods? Refer to earlier timelines.

Multicultural Heritage of the United States

In addition to the information in Part Three of Unit 7, the multicultural heritage of the United States in drama and theatre is covered in features on pages 41, 83, 95, 145, 161, 163, 333, 365, and 391.

 **Advanced Students**

Have students choose one of the key figures listed on pages 462–463 and conduct research to present more information to classmates. Encourage them to synthesize this information with information on the key trends in dramatic literature.

Visual Cue

The following prompts can be used to exercise students' critical viewing skills.

- What can you tell about the cultural and social aspects of the play based on the photo?
- Based on the characters' body language, what do you think might be happening in the scene?

Multicultural Heritage of the United States

In the 20th century, the United States began developing its own unique theatre. The nation's multicultural heritage was a key factor in making the theatre of the United States unique. You will read about these **key trends in dramatic literature.**

- Ethnic theatres provided opportunities for ethnic playwrights and actors to tell their stories.
- Plays explored diverse immigrant experiences, broke down cultural stereotypes.

- Plays reflected the increasingly mixed nature of the American population and experience.

You will read about these **key figures and works** that helped shape the trends in United States multicultural theatre.

- Sholom Aleichem: *The Dybbuk*; Tevye stories, basis of *Fiddler on the Roof*
- Lorraine Hansberry: *A Raisin in the Sun*

The 2013 Pulitzer Prize-winning play *Disgraced* by Ayed Akhtar centers on a Pakistani-American lawyer who hides his ethnic identity because he works for a Jewish law firm and a dinner party that falls apart when two couples clash on religion and racial discrimination.

Quotable

"I believe . . . that the proliferation of works dealing with stories from a variety of cultural backgrounds will continue, thus eventually making the term 'ethnic theater' irrelevant."

—David Henry Wang in an interview on *US Asians* Web site

Tony Award-winning costume designer Santo Loquasto is shown here with the masks he created for the Mardi Gras section in the Twyla Tharp ballet *Waiting at the Station*, which has music by iconic New Orleans musician Allen Toussaint.

(Ken Lambert / The Seattle Times)

- August Wilson: *The Piano Lesson, Fences*
- David Henry Hwang: *M. Butterfly, Yellow Face*
- Nilo Cruz: *Anna in The Tropics*
- Quiara Alegría Hudes: *In the Heights, Water by the Spoonful*
- Ayad Akhtar: *Disgraced*

You will also read about these and other **key figures and works in technical theatre** representing the multicultural heritage of the United States.

- Jo Mielziner: set and lighting design for plays such as *Glass Menagerie* and *Death of a Salesman* and musicals by Rogers and Hammerstein
- Ming Cho Lee: scenic design in regional theatres, Joseph Papp's Shakespeare in the Park, Tonys for *K2* (1983) and lifetime achievement (2013).

- Santo Loquasto: numerous Tony and Drama Desk awards and nominations for set and costume design, as well as Academy Award nominations for costume and production design for films

You will follow theses **trends in technical theatre** representing the multicultural heritage of the United States.

- Regional theatres provide opportunities for theatre designers from diverse cultures.
- Designers blend elements from diverse heritages of world drama and theatre.
- Designers from diverse cultures are well represented on award-winning Broadway shows.

1800 to the Present **463**

Visual Cue

Twyla Tharp's Waiting at the Station premiered at Pacific Northwest Ballet in 2013. Tharp wanted music that would suggest Mardi Gras in the mid-20th century. Loquasto's costumes reflect the same setting and the idea that Mardi Gras is a time when the supernatural and the everyday coexist. The following prompts can be used to exercise students' critical viewing skills.

- What similarities and differences do you see among the masks in the photograph?
- What elements of the masks suggest the supernatural?

Key Figures and Works in Technical Theatre

Santo Loquasto (1944–) earned his first Tony nomination for set design in 1972 for That Championship Season and was nominated in 2013 for The Assembled Parties, reflecting his talent over a career of more than 40 years. He also worked on costume and production design for more than 20 films by Woody Allen, winning Oscar nominations for Bullets Over Broadway and Radio Days. See more information on Ming Cho Lee on page 245 and on Jo Mielzener on page 265.

Key Trends in Technical Theatre

Discuss with students why technical theatre artists from diverse cultural backgrounds might have greater opportunities in mainstream theatre than actors from similar backgrounds.

Notes

_____
_____
_____
_____
_____
_____
_____
_____

Continental Theatre in the 19th Century

August Strindberg According to one account, August Strindberg's ferocious talent was set loose by a dose of opium he thought would kill him. Despondent, young Strindberg (1849–1912) attempted suicide but fell into a deep sleep instead. When he awoke he found he'd released a torrent of repressed memories and began to write. Even in his naturalist period, the sense of a torrent is vivid. *Miss Julie,* his drama about the sexual power struggle between a young countess and her father's servant, is fraught with a barely socialized energy. Later works like *A Dream Play* bypass the social aspect and attempt to access the unconscious source of that energy directly.

Henrik Ibsen kept Strindberg's portrait above his desk. It is reported that he once said, "I cannot write a line without that madman standing and staring down at me with those mad eyes."

Continental Theatre in the 19th Century

Romance and Realism

The dramatic style that firmly established itself in the early 19th century was **romanticism,** an emotional escape into adventure, beauty, and sentimental idealism. Started by Goethe (1749–1832) and Schiller (1759–1805) in Germany, the movement blossomed in France with the works of Victor Hugo (1802–1885) and Alexander Dumas (1802–1870), who adapted for the stage his well-loved adventure stories, such as *The Three Musketeers.*

In the mid-19th century, however, drama radically changed direction. **Realism,** which depicts a selected view of real life, emerged. The dominant figure in this theatre movement was Henrik Ibsen (1828–1906), a Norwegian who is often called the father of realism. His work was well written and constructed, and it had keen insight into characterization. Although his plays seem mild to today's audiences, his themes completely revolutionized the theatre of his day, shocking the spectators and bringing on a storm of criticism about the way his plays dealt with social problems. In *A Doll's House,* Nora leaves her husband and children; this single action presented to the world a new position of women in society. Ibsen's other plays, among them *Hedda Gabler, The Master Builder, An Enemy of the People,* and *Ghosts,* have equally provocative themes that realistically revealed the problems of Ibsen's time and place. His work influenced other dramatists, such as August Strindberg of Sweden, who wrote expressionistic drama that became the forerunner of today's avant-garde theatre. (For more about Henrik Ibsen, see page 98.) Anton Chekhov's *The Cherry Orchard* and Maxim Gorki's *Lower Depths* continued the movement away from romanticism. Konstantin Stanislavski (1863–1938), the great Russian director, also contributed to the movement with his experimental Moscow Art Theatre, where he trained actors in a technique of realistic acting. (For more on Stanislavski, see page 28.)

In England, George Bernard Shaw (1856–1950) introduced Ibsen to the larger theatre world by producing *Ghosts.*

Theatre Terms
realism
romanticism

Theatre Terms

realism a type of literature that depicts life objectively and accurately

romanticism a literary movement of the late 18th and early 19th centuries that emphasized imagination and emotions

Shaw then continued his own realistic bent by writing comic satire in which he attacked all cherished beliefs, leaving little untouched by his caustic yet delightful wit. Considered the finest English playwright since Shakespeare, Shaw was also very prolific. *Androcles and the Lion, Pygmalion, Major Barbara, The Devil's Disciple, Arms and the Man, The Doctor's Dilemma,* and *Candida* are but a few of his successes. Shaw hoped that his comic writings would reform the world. That they failed to do so, he felt, was no fault of his own.

Although realism grew to great heights, many authors around the world continued to write noteworthy romantic, symbolic, or mystical plays. In England, Oscar Wilde (1854–1900) produced witty farces. *The Importance of Being Earnest* is in the best 18th-century comedy of manners style. Sir William Gilbert (1836–1911) and Sir Arthur Sullivan (1842–1900) wrote hugely popular operettas such as *The Mikado, HMS Pinafore,* and many others. In France, Edmond Rostand (1868–1918) wrote *Cyrano de Bergerac* in 1897; and in Russia in 1836, Nikolai Gogol (1809–1852) wrote *The Inspector General.*

Konstantin Stanislavski In 1907 Stanislavski tried breaking away from realism, staging an expressionist version of Leonid Andreyev's *The Life of Man.* The show was a popular success, but Stanislavski believed it failed to challenge his actors. As James Roose-Evans reports in his book, *Experimental Theatre: From Stanislavsky to Today,* the experience marked a turning point. "From that moment on," Roose-Evans writes, "[Stanislavski's] work and his attention were devoted almost completely to the study and teaching of inner creativeness" as opposed to scenic show.

Anti-Stanislavski In Russian and early Soviet theatre, Vsevolod Meyerhold (1874–1940) was the anti-Stanislavski. A former actor with impeccable realist credentials (he originated the role of Treplev in Chekhov's *The Seagull*), Meyerhold became a proponent of the "Theater Theatrical," which exalted spectacle. His 1920 production of *The Storming of the Winter Palace* involved 8,000 performers and a cannon blast from a warship.

Bernard Shaw A thoroughgoing pedant, albeit an entertaining one, Bernard Shaw never lost a chance to educate the public. He was famous for publishing his plays with introductory essays that might exceed the play in length.

Ubu Roi In 1896 Alfred Jarry staged the premiere of *Ubu Roi,* a grotesque, gleefully coarse travesty of *Macbeth* in which a pear-shaped king of Poland tries to take over the world. It caused an uproar and supplied a prototype for post-World War II absurdism. It was originally written as a school prank, to burlesque a mathematics teacher.

Ian McKellen performs with a young actor in Ibsen's *An Enemy of the People,* at the Royal National Theatre.

Quotable

The nineteenth century was a time of change in Europe. Of all centuries, it was the century of revolution—political revolution and industrial revolution . . . . The outcome of all these upheavals was a slow march towards political and social democracy . . . . The theatre was greatly affected by the peculiar nature of the 19th century. There was revolution in playwriting . . . . The story of the theatre throughout the full 19th century is a story of definite and important progress. Playwrights moved from classicism to romanticism to realism.

from *The Theatre and Its Continuing Social Function* by William Melnitz

American Theatre in the 19th Century

Royall Tyler Aside from writing plays, fiction, and poetry, Royall Tyler (1757–1826) was Chief Justice of the Vermont Supreme Court. *The Contrast* is a satire on city and country manners. It includes a scene in which Jonathon, a country Yankee, goes to the theatre and watches an entire performance of *The School for Scandal* without realizing it's a play. He thinks all the houses in New York must have curtains that rise, to "let us look right into the next neighbor's house." One reason for President Washington's enthusiasm over the play (aside from Tyler's stature as a jurist) might have been the fact that the hero of the piece, Colonel Manly, appears to have been modeled after him.

Edwin Booth, of course, was the older brother of presidential assassin John Wilkes Booth (1838–1865). Before he made his treasonous appearance in President Lincoln's box at Ford's Theatre on April 14, 1865, John Wilkes had appeared there onstage in thirteen productions. Lincoln himself had seen him perform at the Ford, in a play called *The Marble Heart.*

The Barrymores Mrs. Drew's daughter, Georgiana (1856–1893), was a popular comedienne who married Maurice Barrymore (1847–1905), a popular leading man. Their three children, Lionel, Ethel, and John, were among the preeminent stage and film actors of their generation. Drew Barrymore of *Charlie's Angels* fame is Georgiana and Maurice's great-grand-daughter. The story is told that "when Maurice Barrymore was being laid to rest, the straps supporting the lowered coffin became twisted and the coffin had to be raised again for an adjustment to be made. 'How like Father,' Lionel Barrymore whispered as the coffin reappeared, 'a curtain call!' "

Among the famous continental actors of the 19th century were France's Sarah Bernhardt and Coquelin; Italy's Eleanora Duse; and England's Sir Henry Irving and his leading lady, Ellen Terry, who together were largely responsible for returning the acting profession once again to respectability.

American Theatre in the 19th Century

Early American Theatre

The theatre of the American colonies had been sparse, as most people regarded the entire art form as sinful. In fact, in the New York colony the governor's council passed an act in 1709 forbidding "play-acting and prizefighting." Theatre fared better in the Virginia colony, where students at the College of William and Mary performed a play in 1702, and where the first playhouse in America was built in Williamsburg in 1716.

> **Theatre Terms**
> minstrel shows
> vaudeville

The first American play worthy of consideration was written by Royall Tyler in 1787. Called *The Contrast,* it was a pleasing comedy dealing with American problems. Apparently, the play was most successful, for when it was published, President George Washington's name was first on the subscription list. In fact, Washington was a theatre lover and periodically attended plays where he saw Shakespearean and other classic revivals.

American Theatre Comes into Its Own

It was not until the 19th century, however, that theatre blossomed in America. By then, most of the moralist opposition had disappeared. Numerous showboats entertained up and down the Mississippi. Playhouses were built in major American cities. These buildings followed the new trend of smaller auditoriums, narrow aprons, box settings (instead of wings and backdrops), and after 1880, incandescent lighting.

Powerful managers formed stock companies where groups of actors received excellent training in repertory theatre. This was the age of the actor, and many outstanding stars found fame. Edwin Booth (1833–1893) was considered to be America's greatest actor; appearing as Hamlet, he played one hundred nights, a record broken by few other Hamlets. Joseph Jefferson (1829–1905) made a name for himself with his many performances as Rip Van Winkle; the brilliant Richard Mansfield (1857–1907) starred in many productions; Maude Adams delighted audiences in such plays as *Peter Pan;* and Mrs. John Drew, whose daughter married a Barrymore and started that famous acting family, found success in Sheridan's *The Rivals.*

Many of these beloved actors toured America with their shows playing frequent one-night stands. During this time, touring shows did great business.

Theatre Terms

minstrel shows shows performed in black face makeup featuring African American songs and jokes

vaudeville variety shows featuring singers, acrobats, comedians, animal acts, and other types of entertainment

absurdism a belief that life is meaningless and that searching for order only brings conflict

epic theatre drama that asks the audience to think seriously about a political or social issue and in which theatricality overrides realism

impressionistic in painting, the use of color and line to suggest mood and setting rather than realistic representations

regional theatres theatres in major American cities other than New York

For more than fifty years, road companies traversed the country until the competition of radio and movies and the increased railroad rates brought about a decline in business. With the disappearance of road shows and repertory companies, the long-run performances on Broadway began, and New York City became the theatrical center of the United States. There, the theatre again burgeoned into big business.

Three major types of native theatrical activity developed in 19th-century America. The **minstrel shows,** performed in black face and featuring African-American songs and jokes, were exceptionally popular throughout America and England. **Vaudeville** was even more popular. It was a variety show featuring everything: trained seals, singers, acrobats, jugglers, dancers, comedians, and animal acts. Shows were relatively inoffensive so the whole family could enjoy the entertainment. Vaudeville was an important part of the American entertainment scene for many years until movie and radio competition made it obsolete. Now it is almost a lost art, except for a few nightclub variety shows. **Melodrama** that dripped with sentimentality also thrived during this time, as audiences throughout the country wept at the plight of poverty-stricken heroines in the clutches of evil villains.

Theatre in the 20th Century and Beyond

At the beginning of the 20th century, new stagecraft methods revolutionized the theatre. Through the creativity of such innovative designers as Switzerland's Adolphe Appia and England's Gordon Craig, the theatre was introduced to **impressionistic** settings that used color and line to evoke the mood of a place rather than realistic painting. Also implemented were revolving stages, projected scenery, and a variety of amazing lighting effects.

Theatre Terms
absurdism
epic theatre
impressionistic
regional theatres

Theatre on the Continent
Continental playwrights made numerous contributions. In Germany, Bertolt Brecht (1898–1956) developed his **epic theatre,** where he hoped to encourage audience members to think critically and to promote social reform through political action. To do so, Brecht purposely broke the realistic illusion and stressed theatricality. He deliberately inserted narration and songs between episodic scenes; he made stage light units visible to the audience; he used placards, projections, and any other effect to get the spectator to think and ask questions that would encourage societal changes. His most popular plays include *Mother Courage,*

New Vaudeville In the late 1960s and 1970s, vaudeville-style performance made a comeback in the form of what came to be known as New Vaudeville. Peaking in the mid-80s, when a New Vaudeville version of Shakespeare's *The Comedy of Errors* played Chicago's Goodman Theatre and traveled to the Olympic Arts Festival in Los Angeles, the playful, slapstick, tongue-in-cheek style attracted seriously skilled artists like Bill Irwin, the Flying Karamazov Brothers, Avner the Eccentric, and juggler Michael Moschen.

Theatre in the 20th Century and Beyond

Audience Response "The dramatic theatre's spectator says: Yes, I have felt that way too—Just like me—It's only natural—It'll never change—The sufferings of this man appal me, because they are inescapable—That's great art; it all seems the most obvious thing in the world—I weep when they weep, I laugh when they laugh."

"The epic theatre's spectator says: I'd never have thought it—That's not the way—That's extraordinary, hardly believable—It's got to stop—The sufferings of this man appal me, because they are unnecessary—That's great art: nothing obvious in it—I laugh when they weep; I weep when they laugh."

Bertolt Brecht, in an essay called "Theatre for Pleasure or Theatre for Instruction" (translated by John Willett), describing the difference in audience response between Aristotlean theatre and his own.

Quotable

It is not enough to demand insight and informative images of reality from the theater. Our theater must stimulate a desire for understanding, a delight in changing reality. Our audience must experience not only the ways to free Prometheus, but be schooled in the very desire to free him. Theater must teach all the pleasures and joys of discovery, all the feelings of triumph associated with liberation.

from "Essays on the Art of Theater," by Bertolt Brecht

Theatre of Cruelty In 1938 the mad French theatrician Antonin Artaud published a series of essays under the title *Le Théâtre et son Double (The Theater and Its Double)* that became the manifesto of the Theatre of Cruelty, a postlinguistic theatre of communal ritual and spectacle calculated to free people from the empty tyranny of things and restore the "magic relation to reality and danger." "If there is still one hellish, truly accursed thing in our time," Artaud declared, "it is our artistic dallying with forms, instead of being like victims burnt at the stake, signaling through the flames." Artaud spent nine years in an asylum for the insane; when he emerged in 1946, two years before his death, the greatest names in the French theatre honored him at the Theatre Sarah Bernhardt in Paris.

The Caucasian Chalk Circle, The Good Woman of Setzuan, and *The Three Penny Opera.* (For more on Bertolt Brecht, see pages 123 and 345.)

In France, Jean Giraudoux (1882–1944) wrote the popular *Tiger at the Gates, Ondine,* and *The Madwoman of Chaillot.* Jean Anouilh (1910–1987) wrote a modern version of *Antigone* and a play about Joan of Arc called *The Lark.* In each, he showed an uncompromising protagonist maintaining integrity by choosing death.

In Spain, Federico García Lorca (1898–1936) achieved acclaim with themes of love and honor in *Blood Wedding* and *The House of Bernarda Alba.* In Italy, Luigi Pirandello (1867–1936) wrote about appearance versus reality in *Six Characters in Search of an Author.*

Ireland's John M. Synge (1871–1909) wrote in poetic prose about the Irish people and the conflict between a desire for freedom and an oppressive way of life in his plays *The Playboy of the Western World* and *In the Shadow of the Glenn.* Sean O'Casey (1880–1964) dealt with the effects of the Irish rebellion on ordinary people in *The Shadow of a Gunman, Juno and the Paycock,* and *The Plough and the Stars.*

Popular English dramatists in the first half of the century include: T. S. Eliot (1888–1965), who wrote poetic drama in *The Cocktail Party* and *Murder in the Cathedral;* Christopher Fry (1907–2005), who created intellectual comic verse plays with *The Lady's Not for Burning* and *Venus Observed;* and J. B. Priestly (1894–1984), who wrote mysteries such as *An Inspector Calls.* James M. Barrie (1860–1937) wrote *Peter Pan,* and Noel Coward (1899–1973) developed witty, sophisticated comedies including *Blithe Spirit* and *Private Lives.*

Post-War Drama and the Absurdists
Opening up a new post-World War II era of English drama, John Osborne's *Look Back in Anger* became a rallying cry for a group of playwrights who became known collectively as the "angry young men." In the 1950s and '60s innovative playwrights such as Peter Shaffer *(Black Comedy, Five Finger Exercises, Equus,* and *Amadeus)* and Tom Stoppard *(Rosencrantz and Guildenstern Are Dead, Travesties, Hapgood,* and *Arcadia)* came to prominence. Many of the playwrights of this period have become even more prolific in recent years. Tom Stoppard, in particular, has created a phenomenal series of plays covering everything from love to astrophysics to mathematics to world history.

One school of playwrights are often combined together, not because of nationality, but because they are exponents of the avant-garde theatre

Notes

called **absurdism.** In their plays, the absurdists argue that all life is meaningless. Characters speak and act at random with no societal (or theatrical) rules. Proponents of the Theatre of the Absurd include Samuel Beckett (1906–1989), whose plays *Endgame, Happy Days,* and *Waiting for Godot* concern the sense of loneliness and alienation that results when people face the task of establishing real communication with one another. Eugene Ionesco (1912–1994) in *Rhinoceros, The Chairs,* and *The Bald Soprano,* rejected traditional plot lines and consistent characters and instead wrote comic plays about the meaninglessness of a life ruled by chance. Other examples are Jean Genet's *The Balcony,* Harold Pinter's *The Dumb Waiter,* Dario Fo and Franca Rame's *Accidental Death of an Anarchist* and *We Won't Pay! We Won't Pay!,* and Edward Albee's *The Sandbox.*

The American Scene
The United States began developing its own unique theatre, largely through the efforts of Professor George Pierce Baker and his playwriting course at Harvard. This remarkable teacher nurtured many of the century's most notable American dramatists, including Phillip Barry, Robert Sherwood, Sidney Howard, S. H. Behrman, and Eugene O'Neill. These playwrights were aided by Baker and two major theatre companies willing to stage their work, the Washington Square Players and the Provincetown Players.

Eugene O'Neill
Of these new writers, Eugene O'Neill (1888–1953) became the leading American dramatist in the first part of the 20th century. His plays were both realistic and expressionistic, often dealing with difficult psychological truths. After mastering the one-act form, O'Neill turned to writing longer scripts. *The Emperor Jones, The Hairy Ape, Strange Interlude, A Long Day's Journey into Night, Mourning Becomes Electra,* and many other plays made him—and the American theatre scene—famous throughout the world.

Other U.S. playwrights who came to prominence were George S. Kaufman and his comedies *You Can't Take It with You* and *The Man Who Came to Dinner;* Lillian Hellman with *The Little Foxes* and *The Children's Hour;* Robert Sherwood with *Idiot's Delight* and *Abe Lincoln in Illinois;* Maxwell Anderson, who penned the poetic dramas *Winterset* and *Elizabeth the Queen;* and Clifford Odets with *Waiting for Lefty* and *Golden Boy.*

Special attention should be given to the following four American dramatists:

Thornton Wilder (1897–1975)
Wilder contributed to dramatic literature

The Bald Soprano A classic scene in Ionesco's "anti-play" *The Bald Soprano* has a man and a woman sitting in the drawing room of a home to which they have been invited for dinner. "Excuse me," says the man, "but haven't we met before?" It seems possible, but how? They discover they both come from Manchester. "How curious!" they say. Not only that, but they both left Manchester about five weeks ago in the same car of the same train. "That is curious! How very bizarre! And what a coincidence!" Could that be where they met? Perhaps, but they don't recall it. Now it also happens that they live on the same floor in the same building on the same street. And not only that, but they sleep in the same bed in the same room. "How curious it is, how curious it is, how curious it is, and what a coincidence!" Perhaps it is there that they met, suggests the man. "How curious it is and what a coincidence!" the woman replies. "It is indeed possible that we have met there, and perhaps even last night. But I do not recall it, dear sir!" "Well," says the man, "I have a little girl, my little daughter, she lives with me, dear lady. She is two years old, she's blonde, she has a white eye and a red eye, she is very pretty, her name is Alice, dear lady." Amazingly, the woman has a daughter with precisely the same attributes. They cannot avoid concluding that they are husband and wife, and fall into each other's arms.

Voodoo Macbeth During the Great Depression, President Roosevelt instituted the Works Progress Administration to provide jobs for the unemployed. The WPA had a cultural wing that hired 40,000 artists representing all disciplines, including the theatre. In 1936, under the direction of a 20-year-old Orson Welles, the Negro Unit of the Federal Theater Project mounted an all-black "Voodoo" *Macbeth* set in 19th-century Haiti. The show sold out in Harlem, then transferred downtown before touring to Bridgeport, Hartford, Dallas, Indianapolis, Chicago, Detroit, Cleveland, and Syracuse.

Backstage Gossip: Not My Cup of Tea

Memories of the opening run of *Waiting for Godot* still haunt Peter Bull, who played Pozzo. Not everyone who went to see Beckett's masterpiece enjoyed it. Cries of "Rubbish," "It's a disgrace," and "Take it off," were commonplace. One night when Vladimir said to his companion, "I am happy," and Estragon replied, "I am happy too," a man in the stalls called out, "Well, I'm bloody well not." Attempts to silence the protester simply provoked him further: "And nor are you. You've been hoaxed like me."

from *Great Theatrical Disasters* by Gyles Brandreth

Tennessee Williams had his first literary success at the age of 16, when he won third prize and $5 for an essay titled, "Can a Good Wife Be a Good Sport?" He would later win two Pulitzer Prizes, one for *A Streetcar Named Desire* and the other for *Cat on a Hot Tin Roof.*

Tennessee Williams

one of the world's best-loved and most frequently produced plays—*Our Town*. This play depicts American small-town life in the early 1900s and shows the eternal patterns of human existence. In *The Skin of Our Teeth* Wilder exhibits zany humor and great passion in portraying humanity's ability to overcome disaster.

Tennessee Williams (1911–1983)
Southern characters that were often neurotic and nearly always desperate were his specialty, but Williams's unique form of poetic realism got inside the hearts and minds of these characters, telling universal truths. This has continued to make an indelible impression on audiences. His best-known works include *The Glass Menagerie, A Streetcar Named Desire,* and *Cat On a Hot Tin Roof.*

Arthur Miller (1915–2005)
Miller wrote of the dilemma of American families and the tragedy of common citizens in such plays as the classic *Death of a Salesman* and the WWII morality play *All My Sons.* In *The Crucible* Miller used the historical setting of the Salem Witch Trials to criticize the methods of Senator Joe McCarthy and the House Un-American Activities Committee. (To read more about Arthur Miller, see page 111.)

Neil Simon (1927–)
Simon remains one of the world's most popular and prolific writers of comedy. He combines wisecracks and barbed wit with family realism and serious themes. Some of his best-known works are *The Odd Couple, Lost in Yonkers, Brighton Beach Memoirs,* and *Biloxi Blues.* (For more information on Neil Simon, see page 145.)

Other Playwrights
Other notable living American playwrights include Sam Shepard (*Buried Child, Fool for Love*), David Mamet (*American Buffalo, Glengarry Glen Ross*), Marsha Norman (*'Night, Mother*), Beth Henley (*Crimes of the Heart*), Lanford Wilson (*Tally's Folly, The Fifth of July*), Tony Kushner (*Angels in America*), Christopher Durang (*Sister Mary Ignatius Explains It All for You*), Arthur Kopit (*Wings, Y2K*), A. R. Gurney, Jr. (*The Dining Room*), Wendy Wasserstein (*An American Daughter*), Rebecca Gilman (*Spinning into Butter*), Kia Corthron (*Breath, Boom*), and Julie Jenson (*Two-Headed*).

Playwrights from the diverse multicultural heritage of the United States made significant contributions to its dramatic literature. For example, African

Quotable

Arthur Miller describes the moment during the first production of *Death of a Salesman* when actor Lee J. Cobb truly transformed himself into the character of Willy Loman.

The theatre vanished. The stage vanished. The chill of an age-old recognition shuddered my spine; a voice was sounding in the dimly lit air up front, a created spirit, an incarnation . . . a new human being was being formed before all our eyes . . . In an empty and dusty theatre, he cast the shadow of a being that was not himself but the distillation of all he had ever observed. . . .

American theatre has been enriched by the work of Lorraine Hansberry (1930–1965), who wrote *A Raisin in the Sun,* and by August Wilson (1945–2005), who wrote a history of black America with a cycle of plays set in different decades of the 20th century. Known as the "Pittsburgh Cycle," these plays include *Ma Rainey's Black Bottom, Fences, The Piano Lesson, King Hedley II,* and *Radio Golf.* (To read more about August Wilson, see page 161.) Charles Fuller (1939–) won success with *A Soldier's Play.* He is writing a series of plays about African Americans since the freeing of the slaves. Suzan-Lori Parks, with her vibrant language and overtly political themes, won the 2002 Pulitzer Prize for her play *Topdog/Underdog.* Lynn Nottage focuses on stories of African American women and women from the African diaspora. She won a 2007 MacArthur Genius Grant and 2009 Pulitzer Prize for her play *Ruined.*

Beyond Broadway

Today, the theatre is alive with activity. Broadway is still considered the hub of professional theatre in the United States, but rising costs have kept producers away from many newer, more risky ventures. Most Broadway shows are comedies or musicals with mass appeal to ensure their status as commercial hits. Consequently, new plays have had to find homes elsewhere. Off-Broadway theatre (New York theatres seating fewer than 299 people) welcomes new names

Lorraine Hansberry

and plays because shows can be produced less expensively—and therefore at less risk to investors. Not being tied so tightly to the box office allows for the staging of experimental productions. Some of these shows become hits and occasionally move to Broadway. Professional productions also thrive outside of New York City. In the 1960s, **regional theatres** were established in many major cities across the United States. One of the first began under the direction of Tyrone Guthrie in 1963 in Minneapolis, Minnesota. The Guthrie Theatre remains among the top regional theatres in the country. Later, other companies opened in San Francisco, Chicago, Louisville, Seattle, Dallas, Los Angeles, and Denver, to mention a few.

These resident companies encourage new technical talent and playwrights, including those who represent various ethnic groups and social minorities. For example, David Henry Hwang writes about the Chinese and Chinese American culture, as do Frank Chin and James Yoshimura. Hwang's *M Butterfly* drew on the traditions of Italian opera, Kabuki stagecraft, and choreography from the Beijing Opera. It received Tony

Viola Spolin Not all of contemporary American theatre is playwright-centered. Organizations like The Second City build shows through improvisational ensemble work. The Second City approach grew out of games Viola Spolin invented during the 1930s while working with immigrant teenagers at a settlement house. Having noticed that the structure of a game gives people permission to put aside their inhibitions, she created a bunch of them for her shy young clients to play. Her son, Paul Sills, subsequently worked with her to adapt the games for theatrical use. The same principle applies in either case: The game establishes a free zone for creative interaction.

Regional Theatre As an indication of the vigor of American theatre, consider that the League of Chicago Theatres reports a membership of more than 200 professional companies, big and small.

Notes

awards for best play, director, and featured actor as well as nominations for best costume and set design for Eiko Ishioka. Among recent Pulitzer Prize–nominees and winners who concern themselves with Hispanic issues and culture are Quiara Alegría Hudes, Lin-Manuel Miranda, Kristoffer Diaz, and Nilo Cruz. José Rivera, Migdalia Cruz, Maria Irene Fornes, and Edwin Sanchez concern themselves with Hispanic issues and culture. John Belluso and others focus on disability issues. Still other playwrights concentrate on plays for children.

Laura Esping and Judson Pearce Morgan in *Comedy of Errors* at the Guthrie Theatre in Minneapolis.

Nonprofessional community theatre is strong almost everywhere. Community theatres usually perform New York

successes several years after the original run. Most also produce musicals and sometimes classical plays. They attempt to involve townspeople, and their enthusiasm and imagination help them to overcome the barriers of insufficient funding and/or facilities. By drawing on the creativity of its diverse communities, the United States will continue to innovate and contribute to the performing arts in exciting and unexpected ways. Understanding theatre history and current trends helps you to predict what those future innovations and contributions might be.

Quotable

Fortunately for the theatre, it does not have to keep pushing to the edge of human experience. It must be remembered that the most popular forms of theatre are light comedy, farce, murder mystery, and musical comedy—the musical without a message. These are some of the ways audiences enjoy themselves . . . There is no exclusive form of theater. It is not now, and never has been, the preserve of some intellectual minority.

from *All the World's a Stage* by Ronald Harwood

Suggested Projects

1 Create a PowerPoint presentation in which you analyze and articulate the impact of the cultural heritage of world theatre and identify key figures, works, and trends in technical theatre since 1800.

2 Research the influences of world drama by reading and reporting on *Six Characters in Search of an Author* by Luigi Pirandello or *The Inspector General* by Nikolai Gogol.

3 Demonstrate a working knowledge of the historical development, discoveries, and periods of theatre architecture and stage technology and their influences on modern theatre by creating a multimedia presentation.

4 Create and stage a class vaudeville show to demonstrate a working knowledge of the innovations and contributions of the United States to the performing arts. Be sure to evaluate and refine your dramatic concept before presenting it.

5 Understand, appreciate, analyze, and articulate the impact of the multicultural heritage of the United States in order to hold a panel discussion on key figures, works, and trends in dramatic literature and technical theatre.

6 Read a play by a 20th-century author. Create a visual presentation in which you demonstrate a working knowledge of historical or cultural accuracy from research in theatrical design for the chosen play. Give your presentation, and defend the historical or cultural accuracy of your design ideas.

7 Attend a community or university theatre production. Arrange to visit backstage. Find out about the theatre's use of advanced technology in set, light, costume, and sound design. Take notes to identify how these implementations reflect key trends in technical theatre. Discuss your findings in class.

8 Explain how the Elizabethan stages have influenced the style of our modern thrust stages.

9 Review what you have learned about the innovations and contributions of the United States to the performing arts. Then write an opinion piece for a theatre publication predicting future innovations and contributions.

10 Research and analyze the influences of the multicultural heritage of the United States on a current playwright and give an oral report in which you articulate the impact of that heritage on that person's dramatic work. Be sure to consider how community ideas and personal beliefs impact the work.

For More Information

Books

Artaud, Antonin (translated by Mary Caroline Richards), *The Theater and Its Double,* Grove Press, 1994.

Bartow, Arthur, *The Director's Voice: Twenty-One Interviews*, Theatre Communications Group, 1993.

Brook, Peter; *The Empty Space,* Reprint ed. Touchstone, 1995.

Callow, Simon, *Being an Actor,* Grove Press, 2003.

Fo, Dario (translated by Joe Farrell), *Tricks of the Trade,* Routledge, 1991.

Innes, Christopher, *Avant Garde Theatre 1892–1992,* Routledge, 1993.

Loewith, Jason, *The Director's Voice: Twenty Interviews, Vol. 2,* Theatre Communications Group, 2012.

Savran, David, *In Their Own Words: Contemporary American Playwrights,* Theatre Communications Group, 1993.

Spolin, Viola, *Improvisation for the Theatre,* 3rd ed., Northwestern University Press, 1999.

Sweet, Jeffrey (ed.), *Something Wonderful Right Away: An Oral History of The Second City and The Compass Players,* Avon Books, 2004.

Other Media

American Musical Theater, DVD, Insight Media, 1986.

The Cherry Orchard, DVD, Insight Media, 1999.

College Brecht, DVD, Insight Media, 2012.

Dario Fo and Franca Rame: A Nobel for Two, DVD, Insight Media, 1998.

The Federal Theatre, Project 891, and the Mercury Theatre, DVD, Insight Media, 1999.

Theater in the Modern World, DVD, Insight Media, 2011.

Ubu Roi, DVD, Insight Media, 1977.

Many vaudeville videos are available on YouTube.

The Studio:
Monologues and Scenes
for Study and Performance

Welcome to The Studio, a library of dramatic excerpts you can use to practice a variety of theatrical skills—from script analysis and acting to casting and directing, and more. You may already have become familiar with some of these selections through the Additional Projects at the end of each chapter. Now you can dig in deeper to bring these excerpts from exemplary plays to life. Like the studio theatres often associated with drama schools and universities, let this unit serve to provide a means for honing your skills and experimenting.

Monologues

Monologues for a Woman

Monologues for a Man

How to Use These Monologues

Approach the monologues in this section as an opportunity to explore all the creative processes that go into analyzing, interpreting, embodying, and communicating the richness of complex characters through the application of theatrical skills.

Script Analysis Skills The monologues in this section come from a range of genres and styles, from Shakespeare to contemporary playwrights, from tragedy to comedy. Using your understanding of the genre and style of the play in which a monologue appears, as well as the social, cultural, and political climate of the time and place the play was written, analyze and interpret the character delivering the monologue. Describe his or her physical, intellectual, emotional, and social dimensions as clearly as you can based on your reading of the text and understanding of the period. Read the whole play and learn as much about it as you can.

Rehearsal Skills Prepare your monologue thoughtfully, pairing up with a partner to practice and rehearse. Develop and practice your own memorization skills (see page 118), and then model your memorization skills for your partner and share techniques.

Experiment with stage movement. What movements and gestures can you use to express the thoughts, feelings, and actions of your character effectively? Devise the movement you want to use for your monologue and model it for your partner. Ask for suggestions for improving your movements and revise as appropriate.

Also work on proper techniques in the use of effective voice, such as diction, inflection, and projection, to express thoughts, feelings, and actions. Model these for your partner as well, inviting constructive criticism so your performance can be the best it can be.

Performance Skills Review what you have learned about safety and performance so you can identify and recognize the importance of safe theatre practices. As always, apply theatre warm-up and preparation skills effectively before your performance. Review the information on safe and appropriate physical expression (pages 18, 54–59, and 207), vocal expression (pages 75–79), and emotional expression (pages 18 and 54–57). Employ and model these and any other safe and appropriate expressive techniques so that you are in full control of your performance.

Charlotte Randle as Juliet in the National Theatre production of *Romeo and Juliet*

Monologues   477

Romeo and Juliet
by William Shakespeare

Attending a dance, Juliet meets Romeo, and they fall in love. Later, Romeo hides in her garden. When she walks onto her balcony and romantically speaks aloud to herself about Romeo, he discloses his presence. Embarrassed, Juliet addresses him.

JULIET.   Thou know'st the mask of night is
   on my face,
Else would a maiden blush bepaint
   my cheek
For that which thou hast heard me speak
   tonight.
Fain would I dwell on form, fain,
   fain deny
What I have spoke; but farewell
   compliment!
Dost thou love me? I know thou wilt say "Ay,"
And I will take thy word; yet, if thou swear'st,
   Thou mayst prove false: at lovers'
   perjuries
They say, Jove laughs. O gentle Romeo,
If thou dost love, pronounce it faithfully;
Or if thou think'st I am too quickly won,
I'll frown and be perverse and say
   thee nay,
So thou wilt woo; but else, not for
   the world.
In truth, fair Montague, I am too fond,
And therefore thou mayst think my 'haviour
   light;
But trust me, gentleman, I'll prove more true
Than those that have more cunning to be
   strange.

I should have been more strange,
   I must confess,
But that thou overheard'st, ere I
   was ware,
My true love's passion; therefore
   pardon me,
And not impute this yielding to light love,
Which the dark night hath so discovered.

Saint Joan by George Bernard Shaw

Joan of Arc has been sentenced to life in prison, instead of burning at the stake, for leading soldiers into battle based on voices she has heard from Heaven. When she realizes that she is to be continually confined, she recants her confession and boldly addresses her inquisitors.

JOAN.   Yes: they told me you were fools *[the word gives great offence],*
and that I was not to listen to your fine words nor trust to your charity. You promised me my life; but you lied *[indignant exclamations].* You think that life is nothing but not being stone dead. It is not the bread and water I fear: I can live on bread; when have I asked for more? It is no hardship to drink water if the water be clean. Bread has no sorrow for me, and water no affliction. But to shut me from the light of the sky and the sight of the fields and flowers; to chain my feet so that I can never again ride with the soldiers nor climb the hills; to make me breathe foul damp darkness, and keep from me everything that brings me back

to the love of God when your wickedness and foolishness tempt me to hate Him: all this is worse than the furnace in the Bible that was heated seven times. I could do without my war-horse; I could drag about in a skirt; I could let the banners and the trumpets and the knights and soldiers pass me and leave me behind as they leave the other women, if only I could still hear the wind in the trees, the larks in the sunshine, the young lambs crying through the healthy frost, and the blessed, blessed church bells that send my angel voices floating to me on the wind. But without these things I cannot live; and by your wanting to take them away from me, or from any human creature, I know that your counsel is of the devil, and that mine is of God.

"Trudy" from The Search for Signs of Intelligent Life in the Universe
by Jane Wagner

In this one-woman show written for Lily Tomlin, the playwright investigates the lives of many characters, including Trudy, a bag woman with a mind of her own.

TRUDY.   Here we are, standing on the corner of "Walk, Don't Walk."
You look away from me, tryin' not to catch my eye, but you didn't turn fast enough, *did* you?

You don't like my *raspy* voice, do you?
I got this raspy voice
'cause I have to yell all the time
'cause nobody around here ever
LISTENS to me.

You don't like that I scratch so much; yes, and excuse me,
I scratch so much
'cause my neurons are
on *fire*.

And I admit my smile is not at its Pepsodent best
'cause I think my
caps must've somehow got
osteo*porosis.*

And if my eyes seem to be twirling around like fruit flies—
the better to see you with, my dears!

Look at me,
you mammalian-brained LUNKHEADS!
I'm not just talking to myself.
I'm talking to you, too.
And to you
and you
and you
and you and you and you!

I know what you're thinkin'; you're thinkin' I'm crazy.
You think I give a hoot? You people
look at my shopping bags,
call me crazy 'cause I save this junk. What should we call the
ones who
buy it?

It's my belief we all, at one time or another, secretly ask ourselves the question,

"Am *I* crazy?"
In my case, the answer came back:
A resounding
YES!

You're thinkin': How does a person know if
they're crazy or not?
Well, sometimes you don't know. Sometimes
you can go through
life suspecting you *are*
but never really knowing for sure.
Sometimes you know for sure
'cause you got so many people tellin' you
you're crazy
that it's your word against
everyone else's.

Another sign is when you see life so clear
sometimes
you black out.
This is your typical visionary variety
who has flashes of insight
but can't get anyone to listen to 'em
'cause their insights make 'em sound
so *crazy*!

In my case,
the symptoms are subtle
but unmistakable to the trained eye. For
instance, here I am,
standing at the corner of
"Walk, Don't Walk,"
waiting for these aliens from outer space to
show up.
I call that crazy, don't you?
If I were sane,
I should be waiting for the light like
everybody else.

They're late
as usual.

You'd think,
as much as they know about time travel,
they could be on time *once* in a while.

I could kick myself.
I told 'em I'd meet 'em on the corner of "Walk,
Don't Walk"
'round lunchtime.
Do they even know what
"lunch" means?
I doubt it.

And "'round." Why did I say "'round?" Why
wasn't I more specific? This is so typical of
what I do.

Now they're probably stuck somewhere in
time, wondering what I meant by
"'round lunchtime." And when they get here,
they'll be dying to know what "lunchtime"
means. And when they
find out it means going to Howard Johnson's
for fried clams, I wonder,
will they be just a bit let down?

I dread having to explain
tartar sauce.

This problem of time just points out
how far apart we really are.
See, our ideas about time and space are
different from theirs.
When we think of time, we tend to think of
clock radios, coffee breaks, afternoon naps,
leisure time,
halftime activities, parole time,

doing time, Minute Rice, instant tea, mid-life
crises, that time of the month, cocktail hour.
And if I should suddenly
mention *space*—aha! I bet most of
you thought of your closets.
But when they think of time and space, they
really think
of
Time and Space.

They asked me once my thoughts on infinity
and I told 'em
with all I had to think about,
infinity was not on my list
of things to think about.
It could be time on an ego trip,
for all I know. After all, when you're pressed for
time,
infinity may as well
not be there.
They said, to them, infinity is
time-released time.

Frankly, infinity doesn't affect
me personally one way or the other.

You think too long about infinity,
you could go stark raving mad.
But I don't ever want to sound
negative about going crazy.
I don't want to overromanticize
it either, but frankly,
goin' crazy was the *best* thing ever
happened to me.
I don't say it's for everybody;
some people couldn't cope. . . . .

Clear Glass Marbles by Jane Martin

*A young woman is standing next to an end
table with a lamp on it, holding a crystal bowl
filled with ninety clear glass marbles.*

LAURIE.   The day my mother found out she
was dying she asked me to go out and buy her
these clear glass marbles. Dad and I hadn't even
known she was ill which was nothing new.
Whenever you asked my mother if she was ill
she would throw things at you, sesame buns,
the editorial page, a handful of hair ribbons.
"Do not," she would say, "suggest things to
suggestible people." Anyway, I brought her the
marbles and she counted ninety of them out
and put them in this old cut-glass bowl which
had been the sum total of great Aunt Helena's
estate. Apparently, the doctor had given her
three months and she set great store by
doctors. She said she always believed them
because they were the nearest thing to the Old
Testament we had. "I wouldn't give you two bits
for these young smiley guys," she'd say, "I go
for a good, stern-furrowed physician." She
wouldn't even have her teeth cleaned by a
dentist under fifty. So she counted out ninety
clear glass marbles and set them in the bowl on
her bedside table. Then she went out and spent
twelve hundred dollars on nightgowns. She
said, "In my family you are only dying when
you take to your bed, and that, my darlings, is
where I am going." And she did. Oh we hashed
it around. Dad said she couldn't possibly be
dying but the doctors convinced him. I told her
it seemed a little medieval to lie in state up
there but she said she didn't want to be

distracted from what she loved, us, and what she wanted to mull. . . And she said there was nothing outside except drugstores and supermarkets and drycleaners and that given her situation they were beneath her dignity. I asked her what she intended to do up there and she said study French, visit with us, generally mull and maybe call a few pals. Study French. She said she had made a pledge to herself years ago that she would die bilingual. Dad and I cried a lot, but she didn't. He was fun to cry with. From then on the doctors had to come see *her* because, as she put it, she *came in* with a house call and she was *going out* with a house call. And all day, every day, she would hold one of these marbles in her hand. Why? She said it made the day longer. Mother had her own bedroom. That was the way it always was, for as long as I can remember. She called my father "The Thrasher." Dad could really get into a nightmare. Apparently early on in the marriage he had flipped over and broken her nose and that was it. Separate beds. Her room was very spare really. Wooden floors, an old steel-and-brass bed, oak dresser, bedside table, and don't ask me why, a hat rack. No pictures on the walls. She never understood how people could look at the same darn thing day after day. She said it was bound to "deflate the imagination." We'd sit with her after dinner and talk about "issues." She told us she was too far gone for gossip or what we ate for lunch. Then we'd all turn in and in a little while, just before I'd drift off I'd hear this. . . *(She rolls one of the marbles across the stage floor.)* Happened every night. After the third or fourth day I saw one on the floor and started to pick it up but she said "leave it." She said it very sharply. I asked, "How come?" She said she was "learning to let go of them." *(From now on the actress frequently rolls marbles across the stage, indicated hereafter by an asterisk, ending up at last with only one.)* Oh, she passed the time. There were things she wanted. She made out a list of children's books from her own childhood and we got as many of them as we could find from the library. She said they were still the only good books she'd ever read.

She wrote notes to, I don't know, maybe sixty or seventy people, and they told us later on that they were sort of little formal goodbyes, each of them recalling some incident or shared something, not very significant, but the odd thing was that in each one she included a recipe. A recipe in every one of them.

We got out the big cookie tin full of snapshots that somehow never became a scrapbook. She liked that. She showed my father how to do the medical insurance and how she handled the accounts. We went through her jewelry.* She wrote down the names of the roofers and plumbers and air-conditioning people. She called it "wrapping it up." "Well, this is good," she'd say, "I'm wrapping it up."

She had the television moved up in her room and she called me aside to say that it was entirely possible that she might reach a stage where she really wouldn't know what she was watching but that I must promise her that I'd keep it on PBS.

Later on, when it started getting hard,* she told Dad and me that she would like to spend more time alone. "I'm afraid," she said, "that I'm going to have to do this more or less by myself." She said that she was glad, and she hoped we would be, that this was arranged so that you got less attached to the people you loved at the end. The next period isn't worth going into, it was just. . . hard. *(She picks up the bowl of marbles.)* Do you know that from the very beginning down to the very last she never admitted to any pain. Never. She called it "the chills." The last thing she asked for was a picture we had in the front entrance hall of a Labrador retriever she and Dad had owned when they were first married. He was, she said, a perfectly dreadful dog. "When you are young," she said, "you believe in the perfectibility of dogs."

I was in bed two weeks ago Wednesday toward dawn, then this. . . *(She pours the rest of the marbles on the floor. When they have stopped rolling, she speaks.)* Dad and I ran in there. The bedside table was turned over and she was gone. Dead. When the emergency medical people got there they found this. . . *(She opens her hand to disclose one more marble.)* The rest spilled when the table fell, but this one was still in her hand.

I keep it.

I keep it in my hand all day.

It makes the day longer.

Real Women Have Curves
by Josefina López

Ana is a top-notch student who wants to attend college, but her mother insists that she help in her sister Estela's struggling dress factory. Ana sees that the factory employees work very hard for their pay and that dresses that cost little to make are sold in stores for hundreds and hundreds of dollars. Ana awakens her mother, sister, and coworkers to the idea that they shouldn't be misled by the body image promoted by these stores. In the end, Ana too learns a lesson.

ANA.   I always took their work for granted, to be simple and unimportant. I was not proud to be working there at the beginning. I was only glad to know that because I was educated, I wasn't going to end up like them. I was going to be better than them. And I wanted to show them how much smarter and liberated I was. I was going to teach them about the women's liberation movement, about sexual liberation and all the things a so-called educated American woman knows. But in their subtle ways they taught me about resistance. About a battle no one was fighting for them except themselves. About the loneliness of being women in a country that looks down on us for being mothers and submissive wives. With their work that seems simple and unimportant, they are fighting. . . Perhaps the greatest thing I learned from them is that women are powerful, especially when working together. . . As for me, well, I settled for a secondhand typewriter and I wrote an essay on my experience and I was awarded a fellowship. So I went to New York and was a starving writer for some time before I went to New York University. When I came back, the plans for making the boutique were no longer a dream, but a reality. *(Ana picks up a beautiful designer jacket and puts it on.)* Because I now wear original designs from Estela Garcia's boutique, "Real Women Have Curves."

(The lights come on and all the women enter the door wearing new evening gowns and accessories designed by Estela. The women parade down the theatre aisles voguing in a fashion-show style. They take their bows, continue voguing, and slowly exit. Lights slowly fade out.)

Hamlet by William Shakespeare

Polonius, who is the Danish court's Lord Chamberlain, bids good-bye to his son Laertes, who is returning to a French university. Polonius gives some fatherly advice.

POLONIUS.   Yet here, Laertes? Aboard, aboard, for shame!
The wind sits in the shoulder of your sail,
And you are stayed for. There—my blessing with thee,
And these few precepts in thy memory
Look thou character. Give thy thoughts no tongue,
Nor any unproportioned thought his act.
Be thou familiar, but by no means vulgar.
Those friends thou hast, and their adoption tried,

Grapple them unto thy soul with hoops of steel;
But do not dull thy palm with entertainment
Of each new-hatched, unfledged courage. Beware
Of entrance to a quarrel, but being in,
Bear't that th' opposed may beware of thee.
Give every man thy ear, but few thy voice;
Take each man's censure, but reserve thy judgment.
Costly thy habit as thy purse can buy,
But not expressed in fancy; rich not gaudy,
For the apparel oft proclaims the man,
And they in France of the best rank and station
Are of a most select and generous chief in that.
Neither a borrower nor a lender be,
For loan oft loses both itself and friend,
And borrowing dulls th' edge of husbandry.
This above all, to thine own self be true,
And it must follow as the night the day
Thou canst not then be false to any man.
Farewell. My blessing season this in thee!

Cyrano de Bergerac by Edmond Rostand

Although charming and witty, Cyrano de Bergerac, a 17th-century poet, has an exceptionally large nose that brings him excessive ridicule. Tiring of mundane comments about his nose, he imaginatively describes various remarks that could be made about it by a clever person.

CYRANO.   I'm afraid your speech was a little short, young man. You could have said . . . oh, all sorts of things, varying your tone to fit your words. Let me give you a few examples.

In an aggressive tone. "If I had a nose like that, I'd have it amputated!"

Friendly. "The end of it must get wet when you drink from a cup. Why don't you use a tankard?"

Descriptive. "It's a rock, a peak, a cape! No, more than a cape: a peninsula!"

Curious. "What do you use that long container for? Do you keep your pens and scissors in it?"

Gracious. "What a kind man you are! You love birds so much that you've given them a perch to roost on."

Truculent. "When you light your pipe and the smoke comes out your nose, the neighbors must think a chimney has caught fire!"

Solicitous. "Be careful when you walk; with all that weight on your head, you could easily lose your balance and fall."

Thoughtful. "You ought to put an awning over it, to keep its color from fading in the sun."

Pedantic. "Sir, only the animal that Aristophanes calls the hippocam-pelephantocamelos could have had so much flesh and bone below its forehead."

Flippant. "That tusk must be convenient to hang your hat on."

Grandiloquent. "No wind but the mighty Arctic blast, majestic nose, could ever give you a cold from one end to the other!"

Dramatic. "When it bleeds, it must be like the Red Sea!"

Admiring. "What a sign for a perfume shop!"

Lyrical. "Is that a conch, and are you Triton risen from the sea?"

Naïve. "Is that monument open to the public?"

Respectful. "One look at your face, sir, is enough to tell me that you are indeed a man of substance."

Rustic. "That don't look like no nose to me. It's either a big cucumber or a little watermelon."

Military. "The enemy is charging! Aim your cannon!"

Practical. "A nose like that has one advantage: it keeps your feet dry in the rain". . . .

There, now you have an inkling of what you might have said to me if you were witty and a man of letters.

Death of a Salesman by Arthur Miller

Biff has returned home for a short time. With his brother, Happy, as a sounding board, Biff confesses that he has wasted his life and still does not know what to do. He is torn between the demands of his father and his own self-desires. [If Happy's speech is omitted, the speech becomes a monologue.]

BIFF.   Well, I spent six or seven years after high school trying to work myself up. Shipping clerk, salesman, business of one kind or another. And it's a measly manner of existence.

To get on that subway on the hot mornings in summer. To devote your whole life to keeping stock, or making phone calls, or selling or buying. To suffer fifty weeks of the year for the sake of a two-week vacation, when all you really desire is to be outdoors, with your shirt off. And always to have to get ahead of the next fella. And still—that's how you build a future.

[HAPPY.   Well, you really enjoy it on a farm? Are you content out there?]

BIFF.   Hap, I've had twenty or thirty different kinds of jobs since I left home before the war, and it always turns out the same. I just realized it lately. In Nebraska when I herded cattle, and the Dakotas, and Arizona, and now in Texas. It's why I came home now, I guess, because I realized it. This farm I work on, it's spring there now, see? And they've got about fifteen new colts. There's nothing more inspiring or—beautiful than the sight of a mare and a new colt. Add it's cool there now, see? Texas is cool now, and it's spring. And whenever spring comes to where I am, I suddenly get the feeling, my God, I'm not gettin' anywhere! What the hell am I doing, playing around with horses, twenty-eight dollars a week! I'm thirty-four years old, I ought to be makin' my future. That's when I come running home. And now, I get here, and I don't know what to do with myself. *(After a pause)* I've always made a point of not wasting my life, and every time I come back here I know that all I've done is to waste my life.

The Drummer by Athol Fugard

A pile of rubbish is seen on the pavement, waiting to be cleared away. This consists of an over-filled trash can and a battered old chair with torn upholstery on which is piled card- board boxes and plastic bags full of junk. Distant and intermittent city noises are heard.

At RISE: A BUM enters. He walks over to the pile of rubbish and starts to work his way through it . . . looking for something useful in terms of that day's survival. He has obviously just woken up and yawns from time to time. After a few seconds he clears the chair, sits down, makes himself comfortable, and contin- ues his search. One of the boxes produces a drumstick. He examines it and then abandons it. A little later he finds a second drumstick. He examines it. Remembers! He scratches around in the pile of rubbish at his feet and retrieves the first. Two drumsticks! His find intrigues him. Another dip into the rubbish but it produces nothing further of interest. Two drumsticks! He settles back in his chair and surveys the world.

An ambulance siren approaches and recedes stage right. He observes indifferently. A fire engine approaches and recedes stage left. He observes. While this is going on, he taps idly on the lid of the trash can with one of the drumsticks. He becomes aware of this little action. Two drumsticks and a trash can! It takes him a few seconds to realize the potential. He straightens up in his chair and with a measure of caution, attempts a little tattoo on the lid of the can. The result is not very impressive. He makes a second attempt, with the same result. Problem. Solution! He gets up and empties the trashcan of its contents, replaces the lid, and makes a third attempt. The combination of a serious intention and the now resonant bin produces a decided effect. He develops it and in doing so starts to enjoy himself. His excitement gets him onto his feet. He has one last flash of inspiration. He removes the lid from the can, up-ends it, and with great bravura drums out a final tattoo . . . virtually an accompaniment to the now very loud and urgent city noises all around him. Embellishing his appearance with some item from the rubbish . . . a cape? . . . and holding his drumsticks ready, he chooses a direction and sets off to take on the city. He has discovered it is full of drums . . . and he has got drumsticks.

The Beginning

The Janitor by August Wilson

Sam, a janitor, enters an empty ballroom. He is pushing a broom near the lectern. He stops and reads the sign hanging across the ballroom.

SAM. NATIONAL . . . CONFERENCE . . . ON . . . YOUTH. *(He nods his approval and continues sweeping. He gets an idea, stops, and approaches the lectern. He clears his throat and begins to speak. His speech is delivered with the literacy of a janitor. He chooses his ideas carefully. He is a man who has approached life honestly, with both eyes open.)*

I want to thank you all for inviting me here to speak about youth. See . . . I's fifty-six years old and I knows something about youth. The first thing I knows . . . is that youth is sweet before flight . . . its odor is rife with speculation, and its resilience—that means bounce back—is remarkable. But it's that sweetness that we victims of. All of us. Its sweetness . . . and its flight. One of them fellows in that Shakespeare stuff said, "I'm not what I am." See. He wasn't like Popeye. This fellow had a different understanding. "I am not what I am." Well, neither are you. You are just what you have been . . . whatever you are now. But what you are now ain't what you gonna become. . . even though it is with you now. . . it's inside you now this instant. Time. . . see, this is how you get to this. . . Time ain't changed. It's just moved. Or maybe it ain't moved . . . maybe it just changed. It don't matter. We are all victims of the sweetness of youth and the time of its flight.

See. . . just like you I forgot who I am. I forgot what happened first. But I know the river I step into now. . . is not the same river I stepped into twenty years ago. See, I know that much. But I have forgotten the name of the river. . . I have forgotten the name of the gods. . . and like everybody else I have tried to fool them with my dancing . . . and guess at their faces. It's the same with everybody. We don't have to mention no names. Ain't nobody innocent. We are all victims of ourselves. We have all had our hand in the soup . . . and made the music play just so.

See now... this is what I call wrestling with Jacob's angel. You lay down at night and that angel come to wrestle with you. When you wrestling with that angel, you bargaining for your future. See. And what you need to bargain with is that sweetness of youth. So... to the youth of the United States I says... don't spend that sweetness too fast! 'Cause you gonna need it. See. I's fifty-six years old and I done found that out.

But it's all the same. It all comes back on you... just like sowing and reaping. Down and out ain't nothing but being caught up in the balance of what you put down. If you down and out and things ain't going right for you... you can bet you done put down a payment on your troubles. Now you got to pay up on the balance. That's as true as I'm standing here. Sometimes you can't see it like that. The last note on Gabriel's horn always gets lost when you get to realizing you done heard the first. So, it's just like—

[MR. COLLINS *(entering).*   Come on, Sam... let's quit wasting time and get this floor swept. There's going to be a big important meeting here this afternoon.]

SAM.   Yessuh, Mr. Collins. Yessuh. *(He goes back to sweeping, as the lights go down to black.)*

For More Practice

1 Choose another monologue from this section or from any other source, including online sources. Use your understanding of the genre and style of the play from which the monologue is taken to analyze and interpret the character delivering the monologue. Describe his or her physical, intellectual, social, and emotional dimensions. Also take into account the social, cultural, and political environment of the play. Write a character description conveying your analysis and interpretation.

2 Pair up with a new partner. For the monologue you chose in the first activity, model the following:

- your memorization skills. How would you go about memorizing the monologue?

- the stage movement you might experiment with and devise to express the character's thoughts, feelings, and actions

- proper, appropriate, and safe techniques for warm-ups and for effective vocal, physical, and emotional expression that conveys the character's thoughts, feelings, and actions

3 Compare and contrast the effect of the genre and style on the two monologues you have studied—the one you performed and the one you analyzed in the previous two activities. How do the genre and style affect the way you interpret and evaluate the character? Prepare a brief explanation to present to the class.

Steve Martin in *Roxanne*

Scenes

Scenes for One Man and One Woman

Scenes for Two Men

Scenes for Two Women

Scenes for Mixed Groups

How to Use These Scenes

The collection of scenes on the following pages includes a variety of genres and styles. As an actor, it provides you an opportunity to **interpret and experiment with scripted scenes** of various styles to portray believable characters. It also provides an opportunity to hone your skills in **analyzing and evaluating dramatic texts,** whether you are acting, directing, designing, or contributing to another aspect of technical theatre.

The scenes also afford you an opportunity to **cast and direct,** giving you practice in developing directorial skills. Begin with casting and directing the duet scenes (pages 493–521). Apply everything you have learned about dramatic texts, characterization, and technical considerations to convey meaning.

As you get ready to direct and cast a duet, analyze the characters you are casting and identify their chief characteristics. Ask yourself what qualities actors should demonstrate to portray those characters effectively and what types of looks and voices might help represent those characters. If you are in a situation that includes auditions, observe each audition with an open mind. After initial auditions, you may want to call back actors for reading scenes together to see how they interact.

Analyzing and Evaluating Dramatic Texts: Technical Considerations   Use these scenes to gain experience in analyzing scripts to determine artistic roles and technical assignments and elements. Following are some categories of analysis and useful questions.

- **Characters** What kinds of actors does the play seem to require? What actor might play each part best? What special technical needs, such as makeup, costuming, and props, might the characters need, and who is able to fill those technical assignments?

- **Themes** What are the play's themes? How can they be best expressed through direction, acting, and technical aspects? Who might be best able to express the themes effectively in acting, directing, and technical aspects?

- **Duties** What challenges and duties are inherent in the script for the director, actors, designers, and the tech crew?

- **Elements** The elements of a script include such features as character names, actions, scene headings, and parenthetical notes about how to read a line. What do the script's elements tell you about the artistic roles and

technical assignments that would most effectively bring the script to life?

Evaluate the answers to your questions to help you determine artistic roles and technical assignments.

Another way to approach the analysis and evaluation of dramatic texts is to consider the following topics in relation to technical elements.

- **Setting** Where does the play take place, both broadly (France, for example) and specifically (a living room, for example)? What technical elements will be needed to create the setting effectively?

- **Times** When does the action take place? What technical aspects can help portray the times?

- **Literary Style** What is the literary style of the play? Is it realistic or nonrealistic? Is it Shakespearean or is it a Broadway comedy? What technical elements and decisions will enhance the literary style effectively?

- **Genre** Is the play a comedy or tragedy? Is it a murder mystery, or is it experimental? Is it a fantasy or from the theatre of the absurd? How can you use technical elements in the service of the play's genre?

Evaluate the setting, times, literary style, and genre, as well as the characters and themes, as the basis for technical discussions to determine the most effective technical treatment for a scene and the play from which it is cut.

Performing a Role in Collaboration After analyzing and evaluating a dramatic text, you can demonstrate leadership while performing a role in collaboration with others by **directing a brief**

scene and **casting and directing** one of the longer scenes in this collection, producing a unified theatrical product with the resources at your disposal. At least one of the scenes you choose should be a duet. Review Chapter 15 so that you can perform your role as a director effectively, demonstrating your responsibility, artistic discipline, and creative problem solving.

The Imaginary Invalid

by Molière, adapted by Fran Tanner

In this 17th-century French satire, the young girl Louison is teasing her father, Argan, by refusing at first to disclose that her older sister, Angelique, is seeing a gentleman. When forced to speak, she enjoys embellishing her story.

(Louison, a girl of twelve or thirteen, enters.)

LOUISON.   Did you call me, papa?

ARGAN.   Yes, little one. Come here. *(She advances part way.)*

ARGAN.   *(Beckoning slyly.)* A little closer.

(Louison comes closer.)

ARGAN.   Now then. Look at me.

LOUISON.   *(With seeming innocence.)* Yes, papa?

ARGAN.   Don't you have something to tell me?

LOUISON.   *(Sweetly.)* Well, I can tell you a story. Would you like to hear the Donkey's Skin or the fable of the Raven and the Fox?

ARGAN.   *(Angrily.)* That's not what I had in mind.

LOUISON.   My apologies, papa.

ARGAN.   Don't you obey your father?

LOUISON.   Of course, papa.

ARGAN.   And didn't I ask you to report all that you see?

LOUISON.   Yes, papa.

ARGAN.   Have you told me everything?

LOUISON.   *(With some doubt.)* Yes, papa.

ARGAN.   Haven't you seen something today?

LOUISON.   No, papa.

ARGAN.   No?

LOUISON.   *(Quite doubtful.)* No . . .

ARGAN.   Aha. Then I shall have to renew your memory.

(Picks up his cane and starts toward LOUISON.)

LOUISON.   *(Frightened.)* Oh, papa.

ARGAN.   Is it not true that you saw a man with your sister Angelique?

LOUISON.   *(Crying.)* Oh, dear.

ARGAN.   *(Raising his cane to hit her.)* I shall teach you to lie.

LOUISON.   Oh, forgive me, papa. Angelique made me promise not to tell. But I'll tell you now.

ARGAN.   Very well. You shall tell me, but only after I have punished you for telling a lie.

LOUISON.   Don't whip me, dear papa. Please don't whip me.

ARGAN.   I shall! *(Raises his cane and strikes once.)*

Scenes   493

LOUISON. *(LOUISON backs against the couch, crying loudly, pretending to be hurt.)* Oh, I'm hurt. Papa, stop. I'm hurt. Oh, I'm dying, I'm dead. *(She falls on couch, pretending to be dead, but keeping one eye open to see what her father will do.)*

ARGAN. What's this? Louison, my little one. Louison, what have I done to you? Oh, dear. My poor Louison. Oh, my poor child.

LOUISON. *(No longer able to hide her laughter, sits up suddenly.)* Come, come, papa. It's all right. I'm not quite dead.

ARGAN. *(Surprised, but relieved.)* Oh, you imp, you. What a rascal I have. Well, I'll overlook it this once, but you must tell me everything.

LOUISON. Yes, papa. But don't tell Angelique I told.

ARGAN. Of course not.

LOUISON. *(Looks to be sure no one is listening.)* Well, while I was in Angelique's sitting room, a handsome man came, looking for her.

ARGAN. *(Eagerly.)* Yes?

LOUISON. When I asked what he wanted, he said he was her new music teacher.

ARGAN. Aha. So that is their little plan. Continue.

LOUISON. Then Angelique came and when she saw him she said *(Over dramatically.)* "Oh, go away, for my sake, leave."

ARGAN. *(Disappointed.)* Oh.

LOUISON. But he didn't leave. He stayed and talked to her.

ARGAN. *(Eagerly.)* What did he say?

LOUISON. He told her . . . *(Teasing her father.)* many things.

ARGAN. Yes?

LOUISON. That he loved her passionately, and that she was the most glorious creature in the world.

ARGAN. And then?

LOUISON. And then he fell on his knees before her—

ARGAN. *(Excitedly.)* Yes, yes.

LOUISON. *(Dramatically.)* And kissed her hand— *(Giggles.)*

ARGAN. *(Eagerly.)* And then?

LOUISON. And then—*(Pause full of suspense, followed by a matter of fact.)* Mama came and he ran away.

ARGAN. *(Disappointed.)* That's all? Nothing more?

LOUISON. No, papa. There was nothing more. *(She giggles and runs out. Argan groans and sinks into a chair.)*

A Doll's House

by Henrik Ibsen,
translated by Michael Meyer

In this Norwegian play written in 1879, the question of women's rights is addressed. Nora is a wife who is treated as a child by Torvald Helmer, her husband. In this scene, Nora realizes what she must do to achieve her own identity.

NORA. *(Looks at her watch.)* It isn't that late. Sit down here, Torvald. You and I have a lot to talk about. *(She sits down on one side of the table.)*

HELMER. Nora, what does this mean? You look quite drawn—

NORA. Sit down. It's going to take a long time. I've a lot to say to you.

HELMER. *(Sits down on the other side of the table.)* You alarm me, Nora. I don't understand you.

NORA. No, that's just it. You don't understand me. And I've never understood you—until this evening. No, don't interrupt me. Just listen to what I have to say. You and I have got to face facts, Torvald.

HELMER. What do you mean by that?

NORA. *(After a short silence.)* Doesn't anything strike you about the way we're sitting here?

HELMER. What?

NORA. We've been married for eight years. Does it occur to you that this is the first time that we two, you and I, man and wife, have ever had a serious talk together?

HELMER. Serious? What do you mean, serious?

NORA. In eight whole years—no, longer—ever since we first met—we have never exchanged a serious word on a serious subject.

HELMER. Did you expect me to drag you into all my worries—worries you couldn't possibly have helped me with?

NORA. I'm not talking about worries. I'm simply saying that we have never sat down seriously to try to get to the bottom of anything.

HELMER. But, my dear Nora, what on earth has that got to do with you?

NORA. That's just the point. You have never understood me. A great wrong has been done to me, Torvald. First by Papa, and then by you.

HELMER. What? But we two have loved you more than anyone in the world!

NORA. *(Shakes her head.)* You have never loved me. You just thought it was fun to be in love with me.

HELMER. Nora, what kind of a way is this to talk?

NORA. It's the truth, Torvald. When I lived with Papa, he used to tell me what he thought about everything, so that I never had any opinions but his. And if I did have any of my own, I kept them quiet, because he wouldn't have liked them. He called me his little doll, and he played with me just the way I played with my dolls. Then I came here to live in your house—

HELMER.   What kind of a way is that to describe our marriage?

NORA.   *(Undisturbed.)* I mean, then I passed from Papa's hands into yours. You arranged everything the way you wanted it, so that I simply took over your taste in everything—or pretended I did—I don't really know—I think it was a little of both—first one and then the other. Now I look back on it, it's as if I've been living here like a pauper, from hand to mouth. I performed tricks for you, and you gave me food and drink. But that was how you wanted it. You and Papa have done me a great wrong. It's your fault that I have done nothing with my life.

HELMER.   Nora, how can you be so unreasonable and ungrateful? Haven't you been happy here?

NORA.   No; never. I used to think I was; but I haven't ever been happy.

HELMER.   Not—not happy?

NORA.   No. I've just had fun. You've always been very kind to me. But our home has never been anything but a playroom. I've been your doll-wife, just as I used to be Papa's doll-child. And the children have been my dolls. I used to think it was fun when you came in and played with me, just as they think it's fun when I go in and play games with them. That's all our marriage has been, Torvald.

HELMER.   There may be a little truth in what you say, though you exaggerate and romanticize. But from now on it'll be different. Playtime is over. Now the time has come for education.

NORA.   Whose education? Mine or the children's?

HELMER.   Both yours and the children's, my dearest Nora.

NORA.   Oh, Torvald, you're not the man to educate me into being the right wife for you.

HELMER.   How can you say that?

NORA.   And what about me? Am I fit to educate the children?

HELMER.   Nora!

NORA.   Didn't you say yourself a few minutes ago that you dare not leave them in my charge?

HELMER.   In a moment of excitement. Surely you don't think I meant it seriously?

NORA.   Yes. You were perfectly right. I'm not fitted to educate them. There's something else I must do first. I must educate myself. And you can't help me with that. It's something I must do by myself. That's why I'm leaving you.

HELMER.   *(Jumps up.)* What did you say?

NORA.   I must stand on my own feet if I am to find out the truth about myself and about life. So I can't go on living here with you any longer.

HELMER.   Nora, Nora!

NORA.   I'm leaving you now, at once. Christine will put me up for tonight—

HELMER.   You're out of your mind! You can't do this! I forbid you!

NORA.   It's no use your trying to forbid me any more. I shall take with me nothing but what is mine. I don't want anything from you, now or ever.

HELMER.   What kind of madness is this?

NORA.   Tomorrow I shall go home— I mean, to where I was born. It'll be easiest for me to find some kind of a job there.

HELMER.   But you're blind! You've no experience of the world—

NORA.   I must try to get some, Torvald.

HELMER.   But to leave your home, your husband, your children! Have you thought what people will say?

NORA.   I can't help that. I only know that I must do this.

HELMER.   But this is monstrous! Can you neglect your most sacred duties?

NORA.   What do you call my most sacred duties?

HELMER.   Do I have to tell you? Your duties towards your husband, and your children.

NORA.   I have another duty which is equally sacred.

HELMER.   You have not. What on earth could that be?

NORA.   My duty towards myself.

Blood Wedding
by Federico García Lorca

This opening scene, set in Spain in the early 1900s, suggests the lyrical gloom that envelopes the bridegroom's family and his upcoming wedding to a woman who loves another.

BRIDEGROOM.   *(entering)* Mother.

MOTHER.   What?

BRIDEGROOM.   I'm going.

MOTHER.   Where?

BRIDEGROOM.   To the vineyard.
(He starts to go.)

MOTHER.   Wait.

BRIDEGROOM.   You want something?

MOTHER.   Your breakfast, son.

BRIDEGROOM.   Forget it. I'll eat grapes. Give me the knife.

MOTHER. What for?

BRIDEGROOM. *(laughing)* To cut the grapes with.

MOTHER. *(muttering as she looks for the knife)* Knives, knives. Cursed be all knives, and the scoundrel who invented them.

BRIDEGROOM. Let's talk about something else.

MOTHER. And guns and pistols and the smallest little knife—and even hoes and pitchforks.

BRIDEGROOM. All right.

MOTHER. Everything that can slice a man's body. A handsome man, full of young life, who goes out to the vineyards or to his own olive groves—his own because he's inherited them . . .

BRIDEGROOM. *(lowering his head)* Be quiet.

MOTHER. . . . and then that man doesn't come back. Or if he does come back it's only for someone to cover him over with a palm leaf or a plate of rock salt so he won't bloat. I don't know how you dare carry a knife on your body—or how I let this serpent *(She takes a knife from a kitchen chest.)* stay in the chest.

BRIDEGROOM. Have you had your say?

MOTHER. If I live to be a hundred I'd talk of nothing else. First your father; to me he smelled like a carnation and
I had him for barely three years. Then your brother. Oh, is it right—how can it be—that a small thing like a knife or a pistol can finish off a man—a bull of a man? No, I'll never be quiet. The months pass and the hopelessness of it stings in my eyes and even to the roots of my hair.

BRIDEGROOM. *(forcefully)* Let's quit this talk!

MOTHER. No. No. Let's not quit this talk. Can anyone bring me your father back? Or your brother? Then there's the jail. What do they mean, jail? They eat there, smoke there, play music there! My dead men choking with weeds, silent, turning to dust. Two men like two beautiful flowers. The killers in jail, carefree, looking at the mountains.

BRIDEGROOM. Do you want me to go kill them?

MOTHER. No . . . If I talk about it it's because . . . Oh, how can I help talking about it, seeing you go out that door? It's . . . I don't like you to carry a knife. It's just that . . . that I wish you wouldn't go out to the fields.

BRIDEGROOM. *(laughing)* Oh, come now!

MOTHER. I'd like it if you were a woman. Then you wouldn't be going out to the arroyo now and we'd both of us embroider flounces and little woolly dogs.

BRIDEGROOM. *(He puts his arm around his mother and laughs.)* Mother, what if I should take you with me to the vineyards?

MOTHER. What would an old lady do in the vineyards? Were you going to put me down under the young vines?

BRIDEGROOM. *(lifting her in his arms)* Old lady, old lady—you little old, little old lady!

MOTHER. Your father, he used to take me. That's the way with men of good stock; good blood. Your grandfather left a son on every corner. That's what I like. Men, men; wheat, wheat.

BRIDEGROOM. And I, Mother?

MOTHER. You, what?

BRIDEGROOM. Do I need to tell you again?

MOTHER. *(seriously)* Oh!

BRIDEGROOM. Do you think it's bad?

MOTHER. No.

BRIDEGROOM. Well, then?

MOTHER. I don't really know. Like this, suddenly, it always surprises me. I know the girl is good. Isn't she? Well behaved. Hard working. Kneads her bread, sews her skirts, but even so when I say her name I feel as though someone had hit me on the forehead with a rock.

BRIDEGROOM. Foolishness.

MOTHER. More than foolishness. I'll be left alone. Now only you are left me—I hate to see you go.

BRIDEGROOM. But you'll come with us.

MOTHER. No. I can't leave your father and brother here alone. I have to go to them every morning and if I go away it's possible one of the Felix family, one of the killers, might die—and

they'd bury him next to ours. And that'll never happen! Oh, no! That'll never happen! Because I'd dig them out with my nails and, all by myself, crush them against the wall.

BRIDEGROOM. *(sternly)* There you go again.

MOTHER. Forgive me. *(pause)* How long have you known her?

BRIDEGROOM. Three years. I've been able to buy the vineyard.

MOTHER. Three years. She used to have another sweetheart, didn't she?

BRIDEGROOM. I don't know. I don't think so. Girls have to look at what they'll marry.

MOTHER. Yes. I looked at nobody. I looked at your father, and when they killed him I looked at the wall in front of me. One woman with one man, and that's all.

BRIDEGROOM. You know my girl's good.

MOTHER. I don't doubt it. All the same, I'm sorry not to have known what her mother was like.

BRIDEGROOM. What difference does it make now?

MOTHER. *(looking at him)* Son.

BRIDEGROOM. What is it?

MOTHER. That's true! You're right! When do you want me to ask for her?

BRIDEGROOM. Does Sunday seem all right to you?

MOTHER. *(seriously)* I'll take her the bronze earrings, they're very old—and you buy her...

BRIDEGROOM. You know more about that...

MOTHER. ... you buy her some open-work stockings—and for you, two suits—three! I have no one but you now!

BRIDEGROOM. I'm going. Tomorrow I'll go see her.

MOTHER. Yes, yes—and see if you can make me happy with six grand-children—or as many as you want, since your father didn't live to give them to me.

BRIDEGROOM. The first-born for you!

MOTHER. Yes, but have some girls. I want to embroider and make lace, and be at peace.

Driving Miss Daisy
by Alfred Uhry

Miss Daisy's son has hired Hoke to drive the elderly Miss Daisy wherever she needs to go. Miss Daisy is a proud, opinionated white woman, and the idea does not sit right with her. In Hoke, an equally determined black man, she has met her match.

DAISY. Good morning.

HOKE. Right cool in the night, wadn't it?

DAISY. I wouldn't know. I was asleep.

HOKE. Yassum. What yo plans today?

DAISY. That's my business.

HOKE. You right about dat. Idella say we runnin' outa coffee and Dutch Cleanser.

DAISY. We?

HOKE. She say we low on silver polish too.

DAISY. Thank you. I will go to the Piggly Wiggly on the trolley this afternoon.

HOKE. Now, Miz Daisy, how come you doan' let me carry you?

DAISY. No thank you.

HOKE. Ain't that what Mist' Werthan hire me for?

DAISY. That's his problem.

HOKE. All right den. I find something to do. I tend yo zinnias.

DAISY. Leave my flower bed alone.

HOKE. Yassum. You got a nice place back beyond the garage ain' doin' nothin' but sittin' there. I could put you in some butterbeans and some tomatoes and even some Irish potatoes could we get some ones with good eyes.

DAISY. If I want a vegetable garden, I'll plant it for myself.

HOKE. Well, I go out and set in the kitchen, then, like I been doin' all week.

DAISY. Don't talk to Idella. She has work to do.

HOKE. Nome. I jes sit there till five o'clock.

DAISY. That's your affair.

HOKE.   Seem a shame, do. That fine Oldsmobile sittin' out there in the garage. Ain't move a inch from when Mist' Werthan rode it over here from Mitchell Motors. Only got nineteen miles on it. Seem like that insurance company give you a whole new car for nothin'.

DAISY.   That's your opinion.

HOKE.   Yassum. And my other opinion is a fine rich Jewish lady like you doan b'long draggin' up the steps of no bus, luggin' no grocery store bags. I come along and carry them fo' you.

DAISY.   I don't need you. I don't want you. And I don't like you saying I'm rich.

HOKE.   I won' say it, then.

DAISY.   Is that what you and Idella talk about in the kitchen? Oh, I hate this! I hate being discussed behind my back in my own house! I was born on Forsyth Street and, believe you me, I knew the value of a penny. My brother Manny brought home a white cat one day and Papa said we couldn't keep it because we couldn't afford to feed it. My sisters saved up money so I could go to school and be a teacher. We didn't have anything!

HOKE.   Yassum, but look like you doin' all right now.

DAISY.   And I've ridden the trolley with groceries plenty of times!

HOKE.   Yassum, but I feel bad takin' Mist' Werthan's money for doin' nothin'. You understand?

(She cuts him off in the speech.)

DAISY.   How much does he pay you?

HOKE.   That between me and him, Miz Daisy.

DAISY.   Anything over seven dollars a week is robbery. Highway robbery!

HOKE.   Specially when I doan do nothin' but set on a stool in the kitchen all day long. Tell you what, while you goin' on the trolley to the Piggly Wiggly, I hose down yo' front steps. *(Daisy is putting on her hat.)*

DAISY.   All right.

HOKE.   All right I hose yo' steps?

DAISY.   All right the Piggly Wiggly. And then home. Nowhere else.

HOKE.   Yassum.

DAISY.   Wait. You don't know how to run the Oldsmobile!

HOKE.   Miz Daisy, a gear shift like a third arm to me. Anyway, thissun automatic. Any fool can run it.

DAISY.   Any fool but me, apparently.

HOKE.   Ain' no need to be so hard on yoseff now. You cain' drive but you probably do alota things I cain' do. It all work out.

DAISY.   *(Calling offstage.)* I'm gone to the market, Idella.

HOKE.   *(Also calling.)* And I right behind her! *(Hoke puts on his cap and helps Daisy into the car. He sits at the wheel and backs the car down the driveway. Daisy, in the rear, is in full bristle.)* I love a new car smell. Doan' you? *(Daisy slides over to the other side of the seat.)*

DAISY. I'm nobody's fool, Hoke.

HOKE. Nome.

DAISY. I can see the speedometer as well as you can.

HOKE. I see dat.

DAISY. My husband taught me how to run a car.

HOKE. Yassum.

DAISY. I still remember everything he said. So don't you even think for a second that you can—Wait! You're speeding! I see it!

HOKE. We ain' goin' but nineteen miles an hour.

DAISY. I like to go under the speed limit.

HOKE. Speed limit thirty-five here.

DAISY. The slower you go, the more you save on gas. My husband told me that.

HOKE. We barely movin'. Might as well walk to the Piggly Wiggly.

DAISY. Is this your car?

HOKE. Nome.

DAISY. Do you pay for the gas?

HOKE. Nome.

DAISY. All right then. My fine son may think I'm losing my abilities, but I am still in control of what goes on in my car. Where are you going?

HOKE. To the grocery store.

DAISY. Then why didn't you turn on Highland Avenue?

HOKE. Piggly Wiggly ain' on Highland Avenue. It on Euclid, down there near—

DAISY. I know where it is and I want to go to it the way I always go. On Highland Avenue.

HOKE. That three blocks out of the way, Miz Daisy.

DAISY. Go back! Go back this minute!

HOKE. We in the wrong lane! I cain' jes—

DAISY. Go back I said! If you don't, I'll get out of this car and walk!

HOKE. We movin'! You cain' open the do'!

DAISY. This is wrong! Where are you taking me?

HOKE. The sto'.

DAISY. This is wrong. You have to go back to Highland Avenue!

HOKE. Mmmm Hmmmm.

DAISY. I've been driving to the Piggly Wiggly since the day they put it up and opened it for business. This isn't the way! Go back! Go back this minute!

HOKE.   Yonder the Piggly Wiggly.

DAISY.   Get ready to turn now.

HOKE.   Yassum.

DAISY.   Look out! There's a little boy behind that shopping cart!

HOKE.   I see dat.

DAISY.   Pull in next to the blue car.

HOKE.   We closer to the do' right here.

DAISY.   Next to the blue car! I don't park in the sun! It fades the upholstery.

HOKE.   Yassum. *(He pulls in, and gets out as Daisy springs out of the back seat.)*

DAISY.   Wait a minute. Give me the car keys.

HOKE.   Yassum.

DAISY.   Stay right here by the car. And you don't have to tell everybody my business.

HOKE.   Nome. Don' forget the Dutch Cleanser now. *(She fixes him with a look meant to kill and exits. Hoke waits by the car for a minute, then hurries to the phone booth at the corner.)* Hello? Miz McClatchey? Hoke Coleburn here. Can I speak to him? *(Pause.)* Mornin sir, Mist' Werthan. Guess where I'm at? I'm at dishere phone booth on Euclid Avenue right next to the Piggly Wiggly. I jes drove yo' Mama to the market. *(Pause.)* She flap a little on the way. But she all right. She in the store. Uh oh. Miz Daisy look out the store window and doan' see me, she liable to throw a fit right there by the checkout. *(Pause.)* Yassuh, only took six days.

Same time it take the Lawd to make the worl'. *(Lights out on him.)*

FOB
by David Henry Hwang

In this play, Steve has entered the back room of a Chinese restaurant in Torrance, California, and asked Grace, who sits at a table, if they have a certain dish. She tells him they are not yet open, and he proceeds to tell her that he is the legendary Chinese hero Gwan Gung.

STEVE.   Tell me, how do people think of Gwan Gung in America? Do they shout my name while rushing into battle, or is it too sacred to be used in such ostentatious display?

GRACE.   Uh—no.

STEVE.   No—what? I didn't ask a "no" question.

GRACE.   What I mean is, neither. They don't do either of those.

STEVE.   Not good. The name of Gwan Gung has been restricted for the use of leaders only?

GRACE.   Uh—no. I think you better sit down.

STEVE.   This is very scandalous. How are the people to take my strength? Gwan Gung might as well not exist, for all they know.

GRACE.   You got it.

STEVE.   I got what? You seem to be having trouble making your answers fit my questions.

GRACE. No, I think you're having trouble making your questions fit my answers.

STEVE. What is this nonsense? Speak clearly, or don't speak at all.

GRACE. Speak clearly?

STEVE. Yes. Like a warrior.

GRACE. Well, you see, Gwan Gung, no one gives a wipe about you 'round here. You're dead.

(Pause.)

STEVE. You . . . you make me laugh.

GRACE. You died way back . . . hell, no one even noticed when you died—that's how bad off your PR was. You died and no one even missed a burp.

STEVE. You lie! The name of Gwan Gung must be feared around the world—you jeopardize your health with such remarks. *(Pause.)* You—you have heard of me, I see. How can you say—?

GRACE. Oh, I just study it a lot—Chinese-American history, I mean.

STEVE. Ah. In the schools, in the universities, where new leaders are born, they study my ways.

GRACE. Well, fifteen of us do.

STEVE. Fifteen. Fifteen of the brightest, of the most promising?

GRACE. One wants to be a dental technician.

STEVE. A man studies Gwan Gung in order to clean teeth?

GRACE. There's also a middle-aged woman that's kinda bored with her kids.

STEVE. I refuse—I don't believe you—your stories. You're just angry at me for treating you like a servant. You're trying to sap my faith. The people—the people outside—they know me— they know the deeds of Gwan Gung.

GRACE. Check it out yourself.

STEVE. Very well. You will learn—learn not to test the spirit of Gwan Gung.

(Steve exits. Grace picks up the box. She studies it.)

GRACE. Fa Mu Lan sits and waits. She learns to be still while the emperors, the dynasties, the foreign lands flow past, unaware of her slender form, thinking it a tree in the woods, a statue to a goddess long abandoned by her people. But Fa Mu Lan, the Woman Warrior, is not ashamed. She knows that the one who can exist without movement while the ages pass is the one to whom no victory can be denied. It is training, to wait. And Fa Mu Lan, the Woman Warrior, must train, for she is no goddess, but girl—girl who takes her father's place in battle. No goddess, but woman—warrior-woman *(She breaks through the wrapping, reaches in, and pulls out another box, beautifully wrapped and ribboned.)*—and ghost. *(She puts the new box on the shelf, goes to the phone, dials.)* Hi, Dale? Hi, this is Grace . . . Pretty good. How 'bout you? . . . Good, good. Hey, listen, I'm sorry to ask you at the last minute and every-thing, but are you doing anything tonight? . . . Are you sure? . . . Oh, good. Would you like to go out with me and some of my friends? . . . Just out to dinner, then maybe we were think-ing of going to a movie or something . . . Oh, good . . . Are you sure? . . . Yeah, okay. Um, we're all going to meet at the restaurant . . . No, *our* restaurant . . . right—as soon as possi-ble. Okay, good . . . I'm really glad that you're coming. Sorry it's such short notice. Okay. Bye, now . . . Huh? Frank? Oh, okay. *(Pause.)* Hi, Frank . . . Pretty good . . . Yeah? . . . No, I don't think so . . . Yeah . . . No, I'm sorry, I'd still rather not . . . I don't want to, okay? Do I have to be any clearer than that? . . . You are not! . . . You don't even know when they come—you'd have to lie on those tracks for hours . . . Forget it, okay? . . . Look, I'll get you a schedule so you can time it properly . . . It's not a favor, damn it. Now goodbye! *(She hangs up.)* Jesus!

(Steve enters.)

STEVE.   Buncha weak boys, what do they know? One man—ChinaMan—wearing a lei-sure suit—green! I ask him, "You know Gwan Gung?" He says, "Hong Kong?" I say, "No, no. Gwan Gung." He says, "Yeah. They got sixty thousand people living on four acres. Went there last year." I say, "No, no. Gwan Gung." He says, "Ooooh! Gwan Gung?" I say, "Yes, yes, Gwan Gung." He says, "I never been there before."

GRACE.   See? Even if you didn't die—who cares?

STEVE.   Another kid—blue jeans and a T-shirt—I ask him, does he know Gwan Gung? He says, he doesn't need it, he knows Jesus Christ. What city is this now?

GRACE.   Los Angeles.

STEVE.   This isn't the only place where a new ChinaMan can land, is it?

GRACE.   I guess a lot go to San Francisco.

STEVE.   Good. This place got a bunch of weirdos around here.

GRACE.   Yeah.

STEVE.   They could never be followers of Gwan Gung. All who follow me must be loyal and righteous.

GRACE.   Maybe you should try some other state.

STEVE.   Huh? What you say?

GRACE.   Never mind. You'll get used to it—like the rest of us.

(Pause. Steve begins laughing.)

STEVE.   You are a very clever woman.

GRACE.   Just average.

STEVE.   No. You do a good job to make it seem like Gwan Gung has no followers here. At the university, what do you study?

GRACE.   Journalism.

STEVE.   Journalism—you are a writer, then?

GRACE. Of a sort.

STEVE. Very good. You are close to Gwan Gung's heart.

GRACE. As close as I'm gonna get.

STEVE. I would like to go out tonight with you.

GRACE. I knew it. Look, I've heard a lot of lines before, and yours is very creative, but . . .

STEVE. I will take you out.

GRACE. You will, huh?

STEVE. I do so because I find you worthy to be favored.

GRACE. You're starting to sound like any other guy now.

The Importance of Being Earnest
by Oscar Wilde

In this 19th-century English comedy, Algernon is quizzing Jack about the latter's proposal of marriage to Gwendolen. The two men spar with clever remarks, for which author Oscar Wilde is famous.

ALGERNON. Didn't it go off all right, old boy? You don't mean to say Gwendolen refused you? I know it is a way she has. She is always refusing people. I think it is most ill-natured of her.

JACK. Oh, Gwendolen is as right as a trivet. As far as she is concerned, we are engaged. Her mother is perfectly unbearable. Never met such a gorgon . . . I don't really know what a gorgon is like, but I am quite sure that Lady Bracknell is one. In any case, she is a monster, without being a myth, which is rather unfair . . . I beg your pardon, Algy, I suppose I shouldn't talk about your own aunt in that way before you.

ALGERNON. My dear boy, I love hearing my relations abused. It is the only thing that makes me put up with them at all. Relations are simply a tedious pack of people who haven't got the remotest knowledge of how to live, nor the smallest instinct about when to die.

JACK. Oh, that is nonsense!

ALGERNON. It isn't.

JACK. Well, I won't argue about the matter. You always want to argue about things.

ALGERNON. That is exactly what things were originally made for.

JACK. Upon my word, if I thought that, I'd shoot myself. *(A pause.)* You don't think there is any chance of Gwendolen becoming like her mother in about a hundred and fifty years, do you Algy?

ALGERNON. All women become like their mothers. That is their tragedy. No man does. That's his.

JACK. Is that clever?

ALGERNON. It is perfectly phrased! And quite as true as any observation in civilized life should be.

JACK.   I am sick to death of cleverness. Everybody is clever nowadays. You can't go anywhere without meeting clever people. The thing has become an absolute public nuisance. I wish to goodness we had a few fools left.

ALGERNON.   We have.

JACK.   I should extremely like to meet them. What do they talk about?

ALGERNON.   The fools? Oh, about the clever people, of course.

JACK.   What fools!

ALGERNON.   By the way, did you tell Gwendolen the truth about your being Ernest in town, and Jack in the country?

JACK.   (In a very patronizing manner.) My dear fellow, the truth isn't quite the sort of thing one tells to a nice sweet refined girl. What extraordinary ideas you have about the way to behave to a woman!

ALGERNON.   The only way to behave to a woman is to make love to her, if she is pretty, and to someone else if she is plain.

JACK.   Oh, that is nonsense.

ALGERNON.   What about your brother? What about the profligate Ernest?

JACK.   Oh, before the end of the week I shall have got rid of him. I'll say he died in Paris of apoplexy. Lots of people die of apoplexy, quite suddenly, don't they?

ALGERNON.   Yes, but it's hereditary, my dear fellow. It's a sort of thing that runs in families. You had much better say a severe chill.

JACK.   You are sure a severe chill isn't hereditary, or anything of that kind?

ALGERNON.   Of course it isn't.

JACK.   Very well, then. My poor brother Ernest is carried off suddenly in Paris, by a severe chill. That gets rid of him.

ALGERNON.   But I thought you said that . . . Miss Cardew was a little too much interested in your poor brother Ernest? Won't she feel his loss a good deal?

JACK.   Oh, that is all right. Cecily is not a silly romantic girl, I am glad to say. She has got a capital appetite, goes for long walks, and pays no attention at all to her lessons.

ALGERNON.   I would rather like to see Cecily.

JACK.   I will take very good care you never do. She is excessively pretty, and she is only just eighteen.

ALGERNON.   Have you told Gwendolen yet that you have an excessively pretty ward who is only just eighteen?

JACK.   Oh! One doesn't blurt these things out to people. Cecily and Gwendolen are perfectly certain to be extremely great friends. I'll bet you anything you like that half an hour after they have met, they will be calling each other sister.

ALGERNON.   Women only do that when they have called each other a lot of other things first. Now, my dear boy, if we want to get a good table at Willis's, we really must go and dress. Do you know it is nearly seven?

JACK. *(Irritably.)* Oh! It always is nearly seven.

ALGERNON. Well, I'm hungry.

JACK. I never knew you when you weren't . . .

ALGERNON. What shall we do after dinner? Go to the theatre?

JACK. Oh, no! I loathe listening.

ALGERNON. Well, let us go to the Club.

JACK. Oh, no! I hate talking.

ALGERNON. Well, we might trot round to the Empire at ten?

JACK. Oh, no! I can't bear looking at things. It is so silly.

ALGERNON. Well, what shall we do?

JACK. Nothing!

ALGERNON. It is awfully hard work doing nothing. However, I don't mind hard work where there is no definite object of any kind.

You Can't Take It with You
by Moss Hart and George S. Kaufman

In this American comedy, the Sycamore family is considered eccentric because of their unusual philosophy. Grandpa Sycamore explains to the stalwart Mr. Kirby that people should not work at jobs they dislike.

KIRBY. *(Outraged.)* I beg your pardon, Mr. Vanderhof. I am a very happy man.

GRANDPA. Are you?

KIRBY. Certainly I am.

GRANDPA. *(Sits.)* I don't think so. What do you think you get your indigestion from? Happiness? No, sir. You get it because most of your time is spent in doing things you don't want to do.

KIRBY. I don't do anything I don't want to do.

GRANDPA. Yes, you do. You said last night that at the end of a week in Wall Street you're pretty near crazy. Why do you keep on doing it?

KIRBY. Why do I keep on—why, that's my business. A man can't give up his business.

GRANDPA. Why not? You've got all the money you need. You can't take it with you.

KIRBY. That's a very easy thing to say, Mr. Vanderhof. But I have spent my entire life building up my business.

GRANDPA. And what's it got you? Same kind of mail every morning, same kind of deals, same kind of meetings, same dinners at night, same indigestion. Where does the fun come in? Don't you think there ought to be something more, Mr. Kirby? You must have wanted more than that when you started out. We haven't got too much time, you know—any of us.

KIRBY. What do you expect me to do? Live the way you do? Do nothing?

GRANDPA. Well, I have a lot of fun. Time enough for everything—read, talk, visit the zoo now and then, practice my darts, even have time to notice when spring comes around. Don't see anybody I don't want to, don't have six hours of things I have to do every day before I get one hour to do what I like in—and I haven't taken bicarbonate of soda in thirty-five years. What's the matter with that?

KIRBY. The matter with that? Suppose we all did it? A fine world we'd have, everybody going to zoos. Don't be ridiculous, Mr. Vanderhof. Who would do the work?

GRANDPA. There's always people that like to work—you can't stop them. Inventions, and they fly the ocean. There're always people to go down to Wall Street, too—because they like it. But from what I've seen of you I don't think you're one of them. I think you're missing something.

KIRBY. I am not aware of missing anything.

GRANDPA. I wasn't either, till I quit. I used to get down to that office nine o'clock sharp no matter how I felt. Lay awake nights for fear I wouldn't get that contract. Used to worry about the world, too. Got all worked up about whether Cleveland or Blaine was going to be elected President—seemed awful important at the time, but who cares now? What I'm trying to say, Mr. Kirby, is that I've had thirty-five years that nobody can take away from me, no matter what they do to the world. See?

KIRBY. *(Crossing to table.)* Yes, I do see. And it's a very dangerous philosophy, Mr. Vanderhof. It's—it's un-American.

"Dead Parrot" from The Complete Monty Python's Flying Circus

by Graham Chapman, John Cleese, Terry Gilliam, Eric Idle, Terry Jones, and Michael Palin

Mr. Praline walks into the pet shop carrying a dead parrot in a cage. He walks to counter where shopkeeper tries to hide below cash register.

PRALINE. Hello, I wish to register a complaint. . . Hello? Miss?

SHOPKEEPER. What do you mean, miss?

PRALINE. Oh, I'm sorry, I have a cold. I wish to make a complaint.

SHOPKEEPER. Sorry, we're closing for lunch.

PRALINE. Never mind that my lad, I wish to complain about this parrot that I purchased not half an hour ago from this very boutique.

SHOPKEEPER. Oh yes, the Norwegian Blue. What's wrong with it?

PRALINE. I'll tell you what's wrong with it. It's dead, that's what's wrong with it.

SHOPKEEPER. No, no it's resting, look!

PRALINE. Look my lad, I know a dead parrot when I see one and I'm looking at one right now.

SHOPKEEPER. No, no sir, it's not dead. It's resting.

PRALINE. Resting?

SHOPKEEPER. Yeah, remarkable bird the Norwegian Blue, beautiful plumage, innit?

PRALINE. The plumage don't enter into it—it's stone dead.

SHOPKEEPER. No, no—it's just resting.

PRALINE. All right then, if it's resting I'll wake it up. *(Shouts into cage.)* Hello Polly! I've got a nice cuttlefish for you when you wake up, Polly Parrot!

SHOPKEEPER. *(Jogging cage.)* There it moved.

PRALINE. No he didn't. That was you pushing the cage.

SHOPKEEPER. I did not.

PRALINE. Yes, you did. *(Takes parrot out of cage, shouts.)* Hello Polly, Polly. *(Bangs it against counter.)* Polly Parrot, wake up. Polly. *(Throws it in the air and lets it fall to the floor.)* Now that's what I call a dead parrot.

SHOPKEEPER. No, no it's stunned.

PRALINE. Look my lad, I've had just about enough of this. That parrot is definitely

deceased. And when I bought it not half an hour ago, you assured me that its lack of movement was due to it being tired and shagged out after a long squawk.

SHOPKEEPER. It's probably pining for the fiords.

PRALINE. Pining for the fiords, what kind of talk is that? Look, why did it fall flat on its back the moment I got it home?

SHOPKEEPER. The Norwegian Blue prefers kipping on its back. Beautiful bird, lovely plumage.

PRALINE. Look, I took the liberty of examining that parrot, and I discovered that the only reason that it had been sitting on its perch in the first place was that it had been nailed there.

SHOPKEEPER. Well of course it was nailed there. Otherwise it would muscle up to those bars and voom.

PRALINE. Look matey *(Picks up parrot.)*, this parrot wouldn't voom if I put four thousand volts through it. It's bleeding demised.

SHOPKEEPER. It's not, it's pining.

PRALINE. It's not pining, it's passed on. This parrot is no more. It has ceased to be. It's expired and gone to meet its maker. This is a late parrot. It's a stiff. Bereft of life, it rests in peace. If you hadn't nailed it to the perch, it would be pushing up the daisies. It's rung down the curtain and joined the choir invisible. This is an ex-parrot.

SHOPKEEPER. Well, I'd better replace it then.

PRALINE. *(To camera.)* If you want to get anything done in this country you've got to complain till you're blue in the mouth.

SHOPKEEPER. Sorry guv, we're right out of parrots.

PRALINE. I see. I see. I get the picture.

SHOPKEEPER. I've got a slug.

PRALINE. Does it talk?

SHOPKEEPER. Not really, no.

PRALINE. Well, it's scarcely a replacement, then is it?

SHOPKEEPER. Listen, I'll tell you what, *(Handing over a card.)* tell you what, if you go to my brother's pet shop in Bolton he'll replace your parrot for you.

PRALINE. Bolton eh?

SHOPKEEPER. Yeah.

PRALINE. All right.

(He leaves, holding the parrot.)

(CAPTION: 'A SIMILAR PET SHOP in BOLTON, LANCS')

(Close-up of sign on door reading: 'Similar Pet Shops Ltd.' Pull back from sign to see same pet shop. Shopkeeper now has moustache. Praline walks into shop. He looks around with interest, noticing the empty parrot cage still on the floor.)

PRALINE. Er, excuse me. This is Bolton, is it?

SHOPKEEPER. No, no it's, er, Ipswich.

PRALINE. *(To camera.)* That's Inter-City Rail for you. *(Leaves.)*

(Man in porter's outfit standing at complaints desk for railways. Praline approaches.)

PRALINE. I wish to make a complaint.

PORTER. I don't have to do this, you know.

PRALINE. I beg your pardon?

PORTER. I'm a qualified brain surgeon. I only do this because I like being my own boss.

PRALINE. Er, excuse me, this is irrelevant, isn't it?

PORTER. Oh yeah, it's not easy to pad these out to thirty minutes.

PRALINE. Well I wish to make a complaint. I got on the Bolton train and found myself deposited here in Ipswich.

PORTER. No, this is Bolton.

PRALINE. *(To camera.)* The pet shop owner's brother was lying.

PORTER. Well you can't blame British Rail for that.

PRALINE. If this is Bolton, I shall return to the pet shop.

(CAPTION: 'A LITTLE LATER LTD')

(Praline walks into the shop again.)

PRALINE.   I understand that this is Bolton.

SHOPKEEPER.   Yes.

PRALINE.   Well, you told me it was Ipswich.

SHOPKEEPER.   It was a pun.

PRALINE.   A pun?

SHOPKEEPER.   No, no, not a pun, no. What's the other thing which reads the same backwards as forwards?

PRALINE.   A palindrome?

SHOPKEEPER.   Yes, yes.

PRALINE.   It's not a palindrome. The palindrome of Bolton would be Notlob. It don't work.

SHOPKEEPER.   Look, what do you want?

PRALINE.   No I'm sorry, I'm not prepared to pursue my line of enquiry any further as I think this is getting too silly.

The Giver

by Eric Coble, based on the book by Lois Lowry

When Jonas turns 12, he is chosen for special training by The Giver, the only person who holds the memories for the dystopian community in this dark story.

GIVER.   You're one minute late—

JONAS.   I apologize—

GIVER.   Ah ah ah.

JONAS.   I'm one minute late because it just happened again. What I think you call "seeing beyond."

GIVER.   Describe it.

JONAS.   It started with an apple a few weeks ago—one second it was a regular old apple, and then one second it had changed. The same thing happened at the ceremony, the faces of the crowd changed, just for second. And just now, outside with Fiona—her hair . . .

GIVER.   *(Nods.)* Lie down.

(JONAS does, but the GIVER merely sits beside him.)

Call back the memory of the ride in the sled. Just the beginning of it.

(JONAS sits . . . the snow begins to fall, he opens his eyes, pulls up the rope as the bed becomes the sled again . . .)

SHOPKEEPER.   Well, I'd better replace it then.

PRALINE.   *(To camera.)* If you want to get anything done in this country you've got to complain till you're blue in the mouth.

SHOPKEEPER.   Sorry guv, we're right out of parrots.

PRALINE.   I see. I see. I get the picture.

SHOPKEEPER.   I've got a slug.

PRALINE.   Does it talk?

SHOPKEEPER.   Not really, no.

PRALINE.   Well, it's scarcely a replacement, then is it?

SHOPKEEPER.   Listen, I'll tell you what, *(Handing over a card.)* tell you what, if you go to my brother's pet shop in Bolton he'll replace your parrot for you.

PRALINE.   Bolton eh?

SHOPKEEPER.   Yeah.

PRALINE.   All right.

(He leaves, holding the parrot.)

(CAPTION: 'A SIMILAR PET SHOP in BOLTON, LANCS'

(Close-up of sign on door reading: 'Similar Pet Shops Ltd.' Pull back from sign to see same pet shop. Shopkeeper now has moustache. Praline walks into shop. He looks around with interest, noticing the empty parrot cage still on the floor.)

PRALINE.   Er, excuse me. This is Bolton, is it?

SHOPKEEPER.   No, no it's, er, Ipswich.

PRALINE.   *(To camera.)* That's Inter-City Rail for you. *(Leaves.)*

(Man in porter's outfit standing at complaints desk for railways. Praline approaches.)

PRALINE.   I wish to make a complaint.

PORTER.   I don't have to do this, you know.

PRALINE.   I beg your pardon?

PORTER.   I'm a qualified brain surgeon. I only do this because I like being my own boss.

PRALINE.   Er, excuse me, this is irrelevant, isn't it?

PORTER.   Oh yeah, it's not easy to pad these out to thirty minutes.

PRALINE.   Well I wish to make a complaint. I got on the Bolton train and found myself deposited here in Ipswich.

PORTER.   No, this is Bolton.

PRALINE.   *(To camera.)* The pet shop owner's brother was lying.

PORTER.   Well you can't blame British Rail for that.

PRALINE.   If this is Bolton, I shall return to the pet shop.

(CAPTION: 'A LITTLE LATER LTD')

(Praline walks into the shop again.)

PRALINE.   I understand that this is Bolton.

SHOPKEEPER.   Yes.

PRALINE.   Well, you told me it was Ipswich.

SHOPKEEPER.   It was a pun.

PRALINE.   A pun?

SHOPKEEPER.   No, no, not a pun, no. What's the other thing which reads the same backwards as forwards?

PRALINE.   A palindrome?

SHOPKEEPER.   Yes, yes.

PRALINE.   It's not a palindrome. The palindrome of Bolton would be Notlob. It don't work.

SHOPKEEPER.   Look, what do you want?

PRALINE.   No I'm sorry, I'm not prepared to pursue my line of enquiry any further as I think this is getting too silly.

The Giver

by Eric Coble, based on the book by Lois Lowry

When Jonas turns 12, he is chosen for special training by The Giver, the only person who holds the memories for the dystopian community in this dark story.

GIVER.   You're one minute late—

JONAS.   I apologize—

GIVER.   Ah ah ah.

JONAS.   I'm one minute late because it just happened again. What I think you call "seeing beyond."

GIVER.   Describe it.

JONAS.   It started with an apple a few weeks ago—one second it was a regular old apple, and then one second it had changed. The same thing happened at the ceremony, the faces of the crowd changed, just for second. And just now, outside with Fiona—her hair . . .

GIVER.   *(Nods.)* Lie down.

(JONAS does, but the GIVER merely sits beside him.)

Call back the memory of the ride in the sled. Just the beginning of it.

(JONAS sits . . . the snow begins to fall, he opens his eyes, pulls up the rope as the bed becomes the sled again . . .)

GIVER (con'td).   Look down at the sled.

(JONAS does—the sled is now distinctly . . .
RED. He whirls to the GIVER—lights shift,
snow stops.)

JONAS.   Yes! I saw it! In the sled!

JONAS.   I apologize—

GIVER.   Look at the bookcase, the very top
row of books—

(JONAS looks—the uppermost row of books
flashes red—then back to its muted grays.)

JONAS.   It happened.

GIVER.   You're beginning to see the color red.

JONAS.   The what?

GIVER.   Back in the time of the memories
everything had a shape and size, but they also
had a quality called color. There were lots of
colors and one of them was red. Your friend
Fiona has red hair—quite distinctive actually.

JONAS.   And the faces of the people at the
ceremony?

GIVER.   Flesh is not red, but it has red tones
in it. There was a time actually—you'll see it in
the memories—when flesh was many different
colors. Before we went to Sameness.

JONAS.   The red was so beautiful.

GIVER.   It is.

JONAS.   Do you see it all the time?

GIVER.   I see all of them. All the colors.

JONAS.   Why can't everyone? Why did colors
disappear?

GIVER.   (Shrugs.) Our people made that
choice. Before my time, before the previous
time, back and back and back. We gave up
color when we gave up sunshine. We gained
control of many things. But we had to let go of
others.

JONAS.   We shouldn't have!

GIVER.   (Beat; smiles.) You've come very
quickly to that conclusion. It took me many
years. Lie back down. We have so much to do.

Othello
by William Shakespeare

*Othello believes that his wife, Desdemona, has
been unfaithful. Jealous with rage, he sends
her to her room with the intent of killing her.
Desdemona is blameless and cannot
understand Othello's anger. As she
prepares for bed, she discusses the situation
with Emilia, her maid.*

EMILIA.   How goes it now? He looks gentler
than he did.

DESDEMONA.   He says he will return
   incontinent;
And hath commanded me to go to bed,
And bade me to dismiss you.

EMILIA.   Dismiss me?

DESDEMONA. It was his bidding; therefore, good Emilia,
Give me my nightly wearing, and adieu.
We must not now displease him.

EMILIA. I would you had never seen him!

DESDEMONA. So would not I: my love doth so approve him,
That even his stubbornness, his checks, his frowns—
Prithee, unpin me—have grace and favor in them.

EMILIA. I have laid those sheets you bade me on the bed.

DESDEMONA. All's one.
Good faith, how foolish are our minds!
If I do die before thee, prithee, shroud me
In one of those same sheets.

EMILIA. Come, come, you talk.

DESDEMONA. My mother had a maid call'd Barbara:
She was in love, and he she lov'd prov'd mad
And did forsake her.
She had a song of "willow";
An old thing 't was but it express'd her fortune,
And she died singing it. That song tonight
Will not go from my mind; I have much to do
But to go hang my head all at one side
And sing it like poor Barbara.
Prithee, dispatch.

EMILIA. Shall I go fetch your nightgown?

DESDEMONA. No, unpin me here.
This Lodovico is a proper man.

EMILIA. A very handsome man.

DESDEMONA. He speaks well.

EMILIA. I know a lady in Venice would have walked barefoot to Palestine for a touch of his nether lip.

DESDEMONA. (Singing.)
"The poor soul sat sighing by a sycamore tree,
Sing all a green willow;
Her hand on her bosom, her head on her knee
Sing willow, willow, willow.
The fresh streams ran by her, and murmur'd her moans;
Sing willow, willow, willow;
Her salt tears fell from her, and soften'd the stones;
Sing willow, willow, willow."
Lay by these—
(Singing.)
"Willow"—
Prithee, hie thee; he'll come anon —
(Singing.)
"Sing all a green willow must be my garland.
Let nobody blame him, his scorn I approve—"
Nay, that's not next—
Hark! Who is 't that knocks?

EMILIA. It's the wind.

DESDEMONA. (Singing.)
"I call'd my love false love; but what said he then?
Sing willow, willow, willow.
If I court moe women, you'll couch with moe men—"
So, get thee gone; good-night.
Mine eyes do itch;
Doth that bode weeping?

EMILIA.   'T is neither here nor there.

DESDEMONA.   I have heard it said so. O, these men, these men!
Dost thou in conscience think—tell me, Emilia—
That there be women do abuse their husbands
In such gross kind?

EMILIA.   There be some such, no question.

DESDEMONA.   Wouldst thou do such a deed for all the world?

EMILIA.   Why, would not you?

DESDEMONA.   No, by this heavenly light!

EMILIA.   Nor I neither by this heavenly light; I might do't as well i' th' dark.

DESDEMONA.   Wouldst thou do such a deed for all the world?

EMILIA.   The world's a huge thing; it is a great price
For a small vice.

DESDEMONA.   In troth, I think thou wouldst not.

EMILIA.   In troth, I think I should; and undo't when I had done. Marry, I would not do such a thing for a joint-ring, nor for measures of lawn, nor for gowns, petticoats, nor caps, nor any petty exhibition; but, for all the whole world— 'ud's pity, who would not make her husband a cuckold to make him a monarch? I should venture purgatory for it.

DESDEMONA.   Beshrew me,
if I would do such a wrong
For the whole world.

EMILIA.   Why, the wrong is but a wrong i' th' world; and having the world for your labour, 't is a wrong in your own world, and you might quickly make it right.

DESDEMONA.   I do not think there is any such woman.

EMILIA.   Yes, a dozen; and as many to th' vantage as would store the world they play'd for.

But I do think it is their husbands' faults
If wives do fall. Say that they slack their duties
And pour our treasures into foreign laps,
'Or else break out in peevish jealousies.
Throwing restraint upon us; or say they strike us.
Or scant our former having in despite;
Why, we have galls, and though we have some grace,
Yet have we some revenge. Let husbands know
Their wives have sense like them; they see and smell
And have their palates both for sweet and sour
As husbands have. What is it that they do
When they change us for others? Is it sport?
I think it is. And doth affection breed it?
I think it doth. Is 't frailty that thus errs?
It is so too. And have not we affections,
Desires for sport, and frailty, as men have?
Then let them use us well; else let them know,
That ills we do, their ills instruct us so.

DESDEMONA.   Good-night, good-night.
Heaven me such uses send,
Not to pick bad from bad,
but by bad amend.

The Glass Menagerie

by Tennessee Williams

In an attempt to help her daughter, Laura, gain skills for the job market, Amanda scrapes up the money to send Laura to typing school. But in her shyness, Laura quits the school without telling her mother. In the following scene, Amanda confronts her daughter about her deceit.

LAURA.   Mother, I was just . . .

AMANDA.   I know. You were just practicing your typing, I suppose. *(Behind chair R.)*

LAURA.   Yes.

AMANDA.   Deception, deception, deception!

LAURA.   *(Shakily.)* How was the D.A.R. meeting, Mother?

AMANDA.   *(Crosses to Laura.)* D.A.R. meeting!

LAURA.   Didn't you go to the D.A.R. meeting, Mother?

AMANDA.   *(Faintly, almost inaudibly.)* No, I didn't go to any D.A.R. meeting. *(Then more forcibly.)* I didn't have the strength—I didn't have the courage. I just wanted to find a hole in the ground and crawl in it and stay there the rest of my entire life. *(Tears type charts, throws them on floor.)*

LAURA.   *(Faintly.)* Why did you do that, Mother?

AMANDA.   *(Sits on R. end of day-bed.)* Why? Why? How old are you, Laura?

LAURA.   Mother, you know my age.

AMANDA.   I was under the impression that you were an adult, but evidently I was very much mistaken. *(She stares at Laura.)*

LAURA.   Please don't stare at me, Mother! *(Amanda closes her eyes and lowers her head. Pause.)*

AMANDA.   What are we going to do? What is going to become of us? What is the future? *(Pause.)*

LAURA.   Has something happened, Mother? Mother, has something happened?

AMANDA.   I'll be all right in a minute. I'm just bewildered—by life . . .

LAURA.   Mother, I wish that you would tell me what's happened!

AMANDA.   I went to the D.A.R. this afternoon, as you know; I was to be inducted as an officer. I stopped off at Rubicam's Business College to tell them about your cold and to ask how you were progressing down there.

LAURA.   Oh . . .

AMANDA.   Yes, oh-oh-oh. I went straight to your typing instructor and introduced myself as your mother. She didn't even know who you were. "Wingfield," she said? "We don't have any such scholar enrolled in this school." I assured her she did. I said my daughter Laura's been coming to classes since early January. "Well, I don't know," she said, "unless you mean that terribly shy little girl who dropped out of school after a few days' attendance?" No, I said,

I don't mean that one. I mean my daughter, Laura, who's been coming here every single day for the past six weeks! "Excuse me," she said. And she took down the attendance book and there was your name, unmistakable, printed, and all the dates you'd been absent. I still told her she was wrong. I still said, "No there must have been some mistake! There must have been some mix-up in the records!" "No," she said, "I remember her perfectly now. She was so shy and her hands trembled so that her fingers couldn't touch the right keys! When we gave a speed-test—she just broke down completely— was sick at the stomach and had to be carried to the washroom! After that she never came back. We telephoned the house every single day and never got any answer." *(Rises from daybed, crosses R.C.)* That was while I was working all day long down at that department store, I suppose, demonstrating those—*(With hands indicates brassiere.)* Oh! I felt so weak I couldn't stand up! *(Sits in armchair.)* I had to sit down while they got me a glass of water! *(Laura crosses up to phonograph.)* Fifty dollars' tuition. I don't care about the money so much, but all my hopes for any kind of future for you—gone up the spout, just gone up the spout like that. *(Laura winds phonograph up.)* Oh, don't do that, Laura!— Don't play that victrola!

LAURA.   Oh! *(Stops phonograph, crosses to typing table, sits.)*

AMANDA.   What have you been doing every day when you've gone out of the house pretending that you were going to business college?

LAURA.   I've just been going out walking.

AMANDA.   That's not true!

LAURA.   Yes, it is, Mother, I just went walking.

AMANDA.   Walking? Walking? In winter? Deliberately courting pneumonia in that light coat? Where did you walk to, Laura?

LAURA.   All sorts of places—mostly in the park.

AMANDA.   Even after you'd started catching that cold?

LAURA.   It was the lesser of two evils, Mother. I couldn't go back. I threw up on the floor!

AMANDA.   From half-past seven till after five every day you mean to tell me you walked around in the park, because you wanted to make me think that you were still going to Rubicam's Business College?

LAURA.   Oh, Mother, it wasn't as bad as it sounds. I went inside places to get warmed up.

AMANDA.   Inside where?

LAURA.   I went in the art museum and at the birdhouses at the Zoo. I visited the penguins every day! Sometimes I did without lunch and went to the movies. Lately I've been spending most of my afternoons in the Jewel-box, that big glass house where they raise the tropical flowers.

AMANDA. You did all that to deceive me, just for deception! Why? Why? Why? Why?

LAURA. Mother, when you're disappointed, you get that awful suffering look on your face, like the picture of Jesus' mother in the Museum!

(Rises.)

AMANDA. Hush!

LAURA. *(Crosses R. to menagerie.)* I couldn't face it. I couldn't.

AMANDA. *(Rising from day-bed.)* So what are we going to do now, honey, the rest of our lives? Just sit down in this house and watch the parades go by? Amuse ourselves with the glass menagerie? Eternally play those worn-out records your father left us as a painful reminder of him? *(Slams phonograph lid.)* We can't have a business career. No, we can't do that—that just gives us indigestion. *(Around R. day-bed.)* What is there left for us now but dependency all our lives? I tell you, Laura, I know so well what happens to unmarried women who aren't prepared to occupy a position in life. *(Crosses L., sits on day-bed.)* I've seen such pitiful cases in the South— barely tolerated spinsters living on some brother's wife or a sister's husband—tucked away in some mousetrap of a room— encouraged by one in-law to go on and visit the next in-law—little birdlike women—without any nest—eating the crust of humility all their lives! Is that the future that we've mapped out for ourselves? I swear I don't see any other alternative. And I don't think that's a very pleasant alternative. Of course—some girls do marry. My goodness, Laura, haven't you ever liked some boy?

LAURA. Yes, Mother, I liked one once.

AMANDA. You did?

LAURA. I came across his picture a while ago.

AMANDA. He gave you his picture, too? *(Rises from day-bed, crosses to chair R.)*

LAURA. No, it's in the yearbook.

AMANDA. *(Sits in armchair.)* Oh—a high-school boy.

LAURA. Yes. His name was Jim.

The Effect of Gamma Rays on Man-in-the-Moon Marigolds by Paul Zindel

Act I

This 1964 play is about a dysfunctional family including a single mother, Beatrice, and her two daughters, Ruth and Tillie, who struggle with their circumstances and status in life. Tillie prepares her science fair project, which involves the raising of marigolds from seeds exposed to radioactivity.

Scene 1

(As the house lights fade, a music theme fades in. A light picks up Tillie sitting on the floor R. of the sofa, she is holding a small white rabbit).

TILLIE'S VOICE. *(Recorded.)* He told me to look at my hand for a part of it came from a star that exploded too long ago to imagine.

This part of me was formed from a tongue of fire that screamed through the heavens until there was our sun. And this part of me—this tiny part of me—was on the sun when it itself exploded and whirled in a great storm until the planets came to be. *(The lights in the room begin to fade up slowly.)* And this small part of me was then a whisper of the earth. When there was life perhaps this part of me got lost in a fern that was crushed and covered until it was coal. And then it was a diamond millions of years later—it must have been a diamond as beautiful as the star from which it had first come. *(The tape begins to fade and Tillie continues the speech.)* Or perhaps this part of me got lost in a terrible beast, or became part of a huge bird that flew above the primeval swamps. And he said this thing was so small— this part of me was so small it couldn't be seen—but it was there from the beginning of the world. And he called this bit of me an atom. And when he wrote the word, I fell in love with it. Atom. Atom. What a beautiful word. *(Pause. Telephone rings. The lights in the room fade up.)*

BEATRICE.   *(Off upstairs.)* Will somebody get that please? *(Phone continues to ring.)* Aaaaa! *(She enters, crosses downstairs.)* No help! Never any help! *(She answers the phone.)* Hello? Yes it is. Who's this? *(Pause.)* I hope there hasn't been any trouble at school? Oh, she's always been like that. She hardly says a word around here either. I always say some people were born to speak and others just to listen. *(Pause.)* You know I've been meaning to call you to thank *you* for that lovely rabbit you gave Matilda. She and I just adore it and it's gotten so big. *(Pause.)* Well, it certainly was thoughtful. Mr. Goodman, I don't mean to change the subject but aren't you that delightful young man Tillie said hello to a couple of months back at the A & P? You were by the lobster tank and I was by the frozen foods? That delightful and handsome young man? *(Pause.)* Why, I would very much indeed use the expression handsome. Yes, and . . . *(Pause.)* Well, I encourage her at every opportunity at home. Did she say I didn't? Both my daughters have their own desks and I put 75 watt bulbs right near them. *(She crosses to the D. end of the counter, turns her back to the audience and puts instant coffee into a cup.)* Yes. . . yes. . . *(She turns front.)* I think those tests are very much overrated, anyway, Mr. Goodman. Well believe me she's nothing like that around this house. *(She crosses to the L. of the table, pulls the chair out, and sits. Pause.)* Now I don't want you to think I don't appreciate what you're trying to do, Mr. Goodman, but I'm afraid it's simply useless. I'd say as long as she's doing well in your class that's all you should be concerned about. I'm sure with all those modern techniques you must have, you can bring her out—that is the phrase, isn't it?—just as well as anyone. *(Pause.)* I've tried just everything, but she isn't a pretty girl—I mean, let's be frank about it—she's going to have her problems. But with all your charm and patience I'm sure she'll respond and improve to your satisfaction. Are you married, Mr. Goodman? Oh, that's too bad. I don't know what's the matter with women today letting a handsome young man like you get away. *(Long pause.)* Well, some days she just doesn't feel like going to school. You just said how bright she is, and I'm really afraid to put too much of a strain on her after what happened to her sister. You know, too much strain is the worst thing in this modern world, Mr. Goodman, and I can't afford to have another convulsive on my hands, now can I? *(She rises, and crosses to the bottom of the stairs.)* I can't tell you how happy I am that you called. Why, believe it or not you're the first teacher that's ever taken the trouble to call me as a preventative measure. And I truly appreciate that, Mr. Goodman. Oh, the others call you when the damage has been done, but I doubt that Ruth would have had that breakdown, if those teachers down there had taken the trouble to call me... Well, she never acted strange at home. But don't you worry about Matilda. There will be some place for her in this world. And, like I said, some were born to speak and others just to listen... and do call again, Mr. Goodman, it's been a true pleasure speaking with you. Goodbye. *(She hangs up the phone, and crosses D. C. Tillie puts the rabbit in its cage.)* Matilda, that wasn't very nice of you to tell them I was forcibly detaining you from school. Why the way that Mr. Goodman spoke he must think I'm running a concentration camp. Do you have any idea how embarrassing it is to be accused of running a concentration camp for your own children? Well, it isn't embarrassing at all. *(She crosses U. of the kitchen table, to the counter, pours water into the cup with instant coffee, turns the hotplate off, and turns to Tillie.)* That school of yours is forty years behind the times anyway, and believe me you learn more around here than that ugly Mr. Goodman can teach you! You know, I really feel sorry for him. Of course, he's not as bad as Miss Hanley. The idea of having her teach girl's gym is staggering. And you have to place me in the embarrassing position of giving them a reason to call me at eight-thirty in the morning, no less.

TILLIE.   *(Rising.)* I didn't say anything...

BEATRICE.   What do you tell them when they want to know why you stay home once in a while?

TILLIE.   I tell them I'm sick.

BEATRICE.   *(Crosses U. C., gets the pillow from the window ledge, crosses to U. of the L. sofa unit, puts the pillow on the sofa, and pushes the sofa next to the other section. She sits and drinks her coffee. Tillie picks up her school book from the sofa.)* Oh, you're sick all right, the exact nature of the illness is not fully realized, but you're sick all right. Any daughter that would turn her mother in as the administrator of a concentration camp has got to be suffering from something very peculiar.

TILLIE.   *(Pause, as she crosses U. of the sofa, to the kitchen table.)* Can I go in today, mother? *(She picks up a second book, and crosses to the L. of Beatrice.)*

BEATRICE.   You'll go in, all right...

TILLIE.   Mr. Goodman said he was going to do an experiment...

BEATRICE. Why, he looks like the kind that would do his experimenting after sundown. . .

TILLIE. On radioactivity. . .

BEATRICE. On radioactivity? That's all that high school needs!

TILLIE. He's going to bring in the cloud chamber. . .

BEATRICE. Why, what an outstanding event. If you would've warned me I would've gotten dressed to kill and gone with you today. I just love seeing cloud chambers being brought in. . .

TILLIE. You can actually see. . .

BEATRICE. You're giving me a headache.

TILLIE. *(Pause as she crosses to U. of the end table.)* Please?

BEATRICE. No, my dear, the fortress of knowledge is not going to be blessed by your presence today. I have a good number of exciting duties for you to take care of, not the least of which is rabbit droppings.

TILLIE. Oh, mother, please. . . I'll do it after school.

BEATRICE. If we wait one minute longer this house is going to ferment. I found rabbit droppings in my bedroom even this time and if you don't start moving you're going to smell hasenpfeffer.

TILLIE. *(Crosses to the small table U. of Nanny's door, puts her books on the table, picks up the rabbit cage, crosses to the R. of*

the sofa, holding the cage between herself and Beatrice.) I could do it after Mr. Goodman's class. I'll say I'm ill and ask for a sick pass.

BEATRICE. Do you want me to chloroform that thing right this minute?

TILLIE. No!

BEATRICE. Then shut up.

Jar the Floor
by Cheryl L. West

Vennie and her friend Raisa have come to visit Vennie's mother MayDee and her grandmother MaDear, although the mother and daughter have long been at odds. Vennie and MayDee can't seem to avoid arguing.

MAYDEE. I find it so astounding that you never fail to make sure everything careens out of control every time you come home.

VENNIE. So this is all my fault?

MAYDEE. Who said anything about fault? Let's just table this. I want MaDear to have a good day. We have plenty of time to discuss this later. How long are you two planning to stay?

VENNIE. You started it.

MAYDEE. Started what? What did I start this time? All I asked you was how long you plan to stay. How is that an invitation for conflict?

VENNIE. Mother please! It's what you start every time I come home . . .

MAYDEE.   I have not started one thing today . . . all I asked . . .

VENNIE.   You and your little ice pick . . . soon's you see me, you go to town. Pick, pick, pick. My clothes ain't right, pick, my hair ain't right, pick, pick, my grammar ain't right. . .triple pick. . . sum it up, I ain't right. . .

MAYDEE.   Whine . . . whine . . . whine . . . grow up, Vennie.

VENNIE.   I would if you'd let me.

MAYDEE.   That's not true.

VENNIE.   *(Sarcastically, but delivered calmly with a smile.)* Oh, let's get real. Y'all have performed for the company so let's take it on down to Front Street. See Raisa, I'm something to be bought for, organized and then laid out so others can marvel at how wonderful MayDee Lakeland is . . . how she overcame every obstacle to get her three degrees in one hand and raise me single-handedly in the other. . . and what's that commercial. . . never let 'em see you sweat. Well that's MayDee Lakeland . . . you'll never see her sweat, queen of control . . . that's what we all love about her . . . *(Feigned innocence, as if the thought just occurred to her.)* Um, do we have an itinerary this weekend, Mother? I was telling Raisa that you always made sure I participated in every activity: karate, dance, art, gymnastics. So did the secretary remember to outline Vennie's activities, you know in those fifteen minute increments. . . what Mother-dear is going to do with daughter-dear this weekend. *(MayDee quietly disposes of the itinerary.)* Oh come on now, you didn't leave our time together to chance. 'Cause then maybe you would have to enjoy me. And that would be too much like right, wouldn't it Mother? S'pecially given that you don't even like me.

MAYDEE.   *(Pausing, embarrassed to have this conversation in front of Raisa, MayDee laughs.)* You're just like your grandmother, such a wicked sense of humor. I love you, Vennie. All I ever wanted was to protect you. Don't you know how much I love you, whatever you do?

VENNIE.   What I know is being your daughter hurts . . . bad, or should I say badly. . .

MAYDEE.   You can't mean that. *(Exits with hair stuff.)*

Macbeth
by William Shakespeare

After helping her husband kill King Duncan, Lady Macbeth is obsessed with her terrible deed. In this sleepwalking scene, her gentlewoman asks the doctor to observe and diagnose the problem.

GENTLEWOMAN.   Lo you, here she comes! This is her very guise, and upon my life, fast asleep. Observe her. Stand close.

DOCTOR.   How came she by that light?

GENTLEWOMAN.   Why, it stood by her. She has light by her continually, 'tis her command.

DOCTOR. You see, her eyes are open.

GENTLEWOMAN. Aye, but their sense is shut.

DOCTOR. What is it she does now? Look how she rubs her hands.

GENTLEWOMAN. It is an accustomed action with her to seem thus washing her hands. I have known her to continue in this a quarter of an hour.

LADY MACBETH. Yet, here's a spot.

DOCTOR. Hark! She speaks. I will set down what comes from her, to satisfy my remembrance the more strongly.

LADY MACBETH. Out, damned spot! Out I say! One, two—why, then 'tis time to do 't. Hell is murky. Fie, my lord, fie! A soldier, and afeard? What need we fear who knows it, when none can call our power to account? Yet who would have thought the old man to have had so much blood in him?

DOCTOR. Do you mark that?

LADY MACBETH. The Thane of Fife had a wife. Where is she now? What, will these hands ne'er be clean? No more o' that, my lord, no more o' that. You mar all with this starting.

DOCTOR. Go to, go to. You have known what you should not.

GENTLEWOMAN. She has spoke what she should not, I am sure of that. Heaven knows what she has known.

LADY MACBETH. Here's the smell of the blood still. All the perfumes of Arabia will not sweeten this little hand. Oh, oh, oh!

DOCTOR. What a sigh is there! The heart is sorely charged.

GENTLEWOMAN. I would not have such a heart in my bosom for the dignity of the whole body.

DOCTOR. Well, well, well—

GENTLEWOMAN. Pray God it be, sir.

DOCTOR. This disease is beyond my practice. Yet I have known those which have walked in their sleep who have died holily in their beds.

LADY MACBETH. Wash your hands, put on your nightgown, look not so pale. I tell you yet again, Banquo's buried, he cannot come out on's grave.

DOCTOR. Even so?

LADY MACBETH. To bed, to bed, there's knocking at the gate. Come, come, come, come, give me your hand. What's done cannot be undone. To bed, to bed, to bed. *(Exit.)*

Blithe Spirit

by Noël Coward

After holding a seance for research on his book, Charles finds that the spirit of his dead wife, Elvira, has appeared. Since only Charles (and the audience) can see her, his present wife, Ruth, thinks he is crazy. In trying to convince Ruth that the spirit of Elvira is indeed present, the following humorous scene ensues.

(Elvira enters by the windows, carrying a bunch of grey roses. She crosses to the writing-table up stage R., and throws the zinnias into the wastepaper basket and puts her roses into the vase. The roses are as grey as the rest of her.)

ELVIRA.   You've absolutely ruined that border by the sundial. It looks like a mixed salad.

CHARLES.   Oh, my God!

RUTH.   What's the matter now?

CHARLES.   She's here again!

RUTH.   What do you mean? Who's here again?

CHARLES.   Elvira.

RUTH.   Pull yourself together and don't be absurd.

ELVIRA.   It's all those nasturtiums; they're so vulgar.

CHARLES.   I like nasturtiums.

RUTH.   You like what?

ELVIRA.   *(Putting her grey roses into the vase.)* They're all right in moderation, but in a mass like that they look beastly.

RUTH.   *(Crosses over to R. of Charles, C.)* What did you mean about nasturtiums?

CHARLES.   *(Takes Ruth's hands and comes round to the L. of her.)* Never mind about that now. I tell you she's here again.

ELVIRA.   *(Comes to above the sofa.)* You have been having a nice scene, haven't you? I could hear you right down the garden.

CHARLES.   Please mind your own business.

RUTH.   If you behaving like a lunatic isn't my business, nothing is.

ELVIRA.   I expect it was about me, wasn't it? I know I ought to feel sorry, but I'm not. I'm delighted.

CHARLES.   Ruth—darling—please . . .

RUTH.   I've done everything I can to help. I've controlled myself admirably. And I should like to say here and now that I don't believe a word about your damned hallucination. You're up to something, Charles—there's been a certain furtiveness in your manner for weeks. Why don't you be honest and tell me what it is?

CHARLES.   You're wrong—you're dead wrong! I haven't been in the least furtive—I—

RUTH.   You're trying to upset me. *(She moves away from Charles.)* For some obscure reason you're trying to goad me into doing something that I might regret. *(She bursts into tears.)* I won't stand for it any more. You're making me utterly miserable! *(She crosses to the sofa and falls into the R. end of it.)*

CHARLES.   *(Crosses to Ruth.)* Ruth—please—

RUTH.   Don't come near me!

ELVIRA.   Let her have a nice cry. It'll do her good. *(She saunters round to down stage L.)*

CHARLES.   You're utterly heartless!

RUTH.   Heartless!

CHARLES.   *(Wildly.)* I was not talking to you! I was talking to Elvira.

RUTH.   Go on talking to her then, talk to her until you're blue in the face, but don't talk to me.

CHARLES.   *(Crosses to Elvira.)* Help me, Elvira—

ELVIRA.   How?

CHARLES.   Make her see you or something.

ELVIRA.   I'm afraid I couldn't manage that. It's technically the most difficult business—frightfully complicated, you know—it takes years of study—

CHARLES.   You are here, aren't you? You're not an illusion?

ELVIRA.   I may be an illusion, but I'm most definitely here.

CHARLES.   How did you get here?

ELVIRA.   I told you last night—I don't exactly know—

CHARLES.   Well, you must make me a promise that in future you only come and talk to me when I'm alone.

ELVIRA.   *(Pouting.)* How unkind you are, making me feel so unwanted. I've never been treated so rudely.

CHARLES.   I don't mean to be rude, but you must see—

ELVIRA.   It's all your own fault for having married a woman who is incapable of seeing beyond the nose on her face. If she had a grain of real sympathy or affection for you she'd believe what you tell her.

CHARLES.   How could you expect anybody to believe this?

ELVIRA.   You'd be surprised how gullible people are; we often laugh about it on the Other Side.

(Ruth, who has stopped crying and been staring at Charles in horror, suddenly rises.)

RUTH.   *(Gently.)* Charles!

CHARLES.   *(Surprised at her tone.)* Yes, dear—*(Charles crosses to her, R.)*

RUTH.   I'm awfully sorry I was cross.

CHARLES.   But, my dear—

RUTH.   I understand everything now. I do really.

CHARLES.   You do?

RUTH.   *(Patting his arm reassuringly.)* Of course I do.

ELVIRA.   Look out—she's up to something.

CHARLES.   Will you please be quiet?

RUTH. Of course, darling. We'll all be quiet, won't we? We'll be as quiet as little mice.

CHARLES. Ruth dear, listen—

RUTH. I want you to come upstairs with me and go to bed.

ELVIRA. The way that woman harps on bed is nothing short of erotic.

CHARLES. I'll deal with you later.

RUTH. Very well, darling—come along.

CHARLES. What are you up to?

RUTH. I'm not up to anything. I just want you to go quietly to bed and wait there until Doctor Bradman comes.

CHARLES. No, Ruth, you're wrong—

RUTH. *(Firmly.)* Come, dear—

ELVIRA. She'll have you in a straitjacket before you know where you are.

CHARLES. *(Comes to Elvira—frantically.)* Help me—you must help me—

ELVIRA. *(Enjoying herself.)* My dear, I would with pleasure, but I can't think how.

CHARLES. I can. *(Back to Ruth.)* Listen, Ruth—

RUTH. Yes, dear?

CHARLES. If I promise to go to bed, will you let me stay here for five minutes longer?

RUTH. I really think it would be better—

CHARLES. Bear with me, however mad it may seem, bear with me for just five minutes longer.

RUTH. *(Leaving go of him.)* Very well. What is it?

CHARLES. Sit down.

RUTH. *(Sitting down.)* All right. There!

CHARLES. Now listen, listen carefully—

ELVIRA. Have a cigarette; it will soothe your nerves.

CHARLES. I don't want a cigarette.

RUTH. *(Indulgently.)* Then you shan't have one, darling.

CHARLES. Ruth, I want to explain to you clearly and without emotion that beyond any shadow of doubt, the ghost or shade or whatever you like to call it of my first wife Elvira is in this room now.

RUTH. Yes, dear.

CHARLES. I know you don't believe it and are trying valiantly to humor me, but I intend to prove it to you.

RUTH. Why not lie down and have a nice rest and you can prove anything you want to later on?

CHARLES. She may not be here later on.

ELVIRA. Don't worry—she will!

CHARLES. Oh God!

RUTH.   Hush, dear.

CHARLES.   *(To Elvira.)* Promise you'll do what I ask?

ELVIRA.   That all depends what it is.

CHARLES.   *(Between them both, facing upstage.)* Ruth—you see that bowl of flowers on the piano?

RUTH.   Yes, dear, I did it myself this morning.

ELVIRA.   Very untidily, if I may say so.

CHARLES.   You may not.

RUTH.   Very well—I never will again. I promise.

CHARLES.   Elvira will now carry that bowl of flowers to the mantelpiece and back again. You will, Elvira, won't you? Just to please me.

ELVIRA.   I don't really see why I should. You've been quite insufferable to me ever since I materialized.

CHARLES.   Please!

ELVIRA.   *(Goes over to the piano.)* All right, I will just this once. Not that I approve of all these Maskelyne and Devant carryings-on.

CHARLES.   *(Crosses to the mantelpiece.)* Now, Ruth—watch carefully!

RUTH.   *(Patiently.)* Very well, dear.

CHARLES.   Go on, Elvira—take it to the mantelpiece and back again.

(Elvira takes a bowl of pansies off the piano and brings it slowly down stage, below the armchair to the fire; then suddenly pushes it towards Ruth's face, who jumps up and faces Charles, who is at the mantelpiece.)

RUTH.   *(Furiously.)* How dare you, Charles! You ought to be ashamed of yourself.

CHARLES.   What on earth for?

RUTH.   *(Hysterically.)* It's a trick. I know perfectly well it's a trick. You've been working up to this. It's all part of some horrible plan. . .

CHARLES.   It isn't—I swear it isn't. Elvira— do something else, for God's sake!

ELVIRA.   Certainly—anything to oblige.

RUTH.   *(Becoming really frightened.)* You want to get rid of me—you're trying to drive me out of my mind—

CHARLES.   Don't be so silly.

RUTH.   You're cruel and sadistic and I'll never forgive you.

(Elvira picks up the chair from down stage L., holds it in midair as if to hit Ruth, Ruth flinches, then Elvira puts it back, and stands above the windows. Ruth makes a dive for the door, moving between the armchair and sofa. Charles follows and catches her.)

I'm not going to put up with this any more.

CHARLES.   *(Holding her.)* You must believe it—you must—

RUTH.   Let me go immediately.

CHARLES.   That was Elvira—I swear it was.

RUTH. *(Struggling.)* Let me go.

CHARLES. Ruth—please—

(Ruth breaks away to the windows. Elvira shuts them in her face and crosses quickly to the mantelpiece. Ruth turns at the windows to face Charles.)

RUTH. *(Looking at Charles with eyes of horror.)* Charles—this is madness—sheer madness—it's some sort of autosuggestion, isn't it?—Some form of hypnotism, swear to me it's only that—*(She rushes to Charles, C.)* Swear to me it's only that.

ELVIRA. *(Taking an expensive vase from the mantelpiece and crashing it into the grate.)* Hypnotism my foot!

A Raisin in the Sun
by Lorraine Hansberry

Walter and his wife Ruth and sister Beneatha all live with Walter and Beneatha's mother in a cramped apartment in a black neighborhood in a large city. Because some money has come into the family, their mother has put a down payment on a house in a white section of town. Mr. Lindner comes to talk to them about "problems" he foresees in their move.

LINDNER. How do you do.

WALTER. *(Amiably, as he sits himself easily on a chair, leaning with interest forward on his knees and looking expectantly into the newcomer's face.)* What can we do for you, Mr. Lindner!

LINDNER. *(Some minor shuffling of the hat and briefcase on his knees.)* Well—I am a representative of the Clybourne Park Improvement Association—

WALTER. *(Pointing.)* Why don't you sit your things on the floor?

LINDNER. Oh—yes. Thank you. *(He slides the briefcase and hat under the chair.)* And as I was saying—I am from the Clybourne Park Improvement Association and we have had it brought to our attention at the last meeting that you people—or at least your mother—has bought a piece of residential property at—*(He digs for the slip of paper again.)*—four o six Clybourne Street.

WALTER. That's right. Care for something to drink? Ruth, get Mr. Lindner a beer.

LINDNER. *(Upset for some reason.)* Oh—no, really. I mean thank you very much, but no thank you.

RUTH. *(Innocently.)* Some coffee?

LINDNER. Thank you, nothing at all.

(Beneatha is watching the man carefully.)
LINDNER. Well, I don't know how much you folks know about our organization. *(He is a gentle man; thoughtful and somewhat labored in his manner.)* It is one of these community organizations set up to look after—oh, you know, things like block upkeep and special projects and we also have what we call our New Neighbors Orientation Committee...

BENEATHA. *(Drily.)* Yes—and what do they do?

LINDNER. *(Turning a little to her and then returning the main force to Walter.)* Well—it's what you might call a sort of welcoming committee, I guess. I mean they, we, I'm the chairman of the committee—go around and see the new people who move into the neighborhood and sort of give them the lowdown on the way we do things out in Clybourne Park.

BENEATHA. *(With appreciation of the two meanings, which escape Ruth and Walter.)* Un-huh.

LINDNER. And we also have the category of what the association calls—*(He looks elsewhere.)*—uh—special community problems . . .

BENEATHA. Yes—and what are some of those?

WALTER. Girl, let the man talk.

LINDNER. *(With understated relief.)* Thank you. I would sort of like to explain this thing in my own way. I mean I want to explain to you in a certain way.

WALTER. Go ahead.

LINDNER. Yes. Well. I'm going to try to get right to the point. I'm sure we'll all appreciate that in the long run.

BENEATHA. Yes.

WALTER. Be still now!

LINDNER. Well—

RUTH. *(Still innocently.)* Would you like another chair—you don't look comfortable.

LINDNER. *(More frustrated than annoyed.)* No, thank you very much. Please. Well—to get right to the point I—*(A great breath, and he is off at last.)* I am sure you people must be aware of some of the incidents which have happened in various parts of the city when colored people have moved into certain areas—*(Beneatha exhales heavily and starts tossing a piece of fruit up and down in the air.)* Well—because we have what I think is going to be a unique type of organization in American community life—not only do we deplore that kind of thing—but we are trying to do something about it. *(Beneatha stops tossing and turns with a new and quizzical interest to the man.)* We feel—*(Gaining confidence in his mission because of the interest in the faces of the people he is talking to.)*—we feel that most of the trouble in this world, when you come right down to it—*(He hits his knee for emphasis.)*—most of the trouble exists because people just don't sit down and talk to each other.

RUTH. *(Nodding as she might in church, pleased with the remark.)* You can say that again, mister.

LINDNER. *(More encouraged by such affirmation.)* That we don't try hard enough in this world to understand the other fellow's problem. The other guy's point of view.

RUTH. Now that's right.

(Beneatha and Walter merely watch and listen with genuine interest.)

LINDNER.   Yes—that's the way we feel out in Clybourne Park. And that's why I was elected to come here this afternoon and talk to you people. Friendly like, you know, the way people should talk to each other and see if we couldn't find some way to work this thing out. As I say, the whole business is a matter of *caring* about the other fellow. Anybody can see that you are a nice family of folks, hardworking and honest I'm sure. *(Beneatha frowns slightly, quizzically, her head tilted regarding him.)* Today everybody knows what it means to be on the outside of *something*. And of course, there is always somebody who is out to take advantage of people who don't always understand.

WALTER.   What do you mean?

LINDNER.   Well—you see our community is made up of people who've worked hard as the dickens for years to build up that little community. They're not rich and fancy people; just hardworking, honest people who don't really have much but those little homes and a dream of the kind of community they want to raise their children in. Now, I don't say we are perfect and there is a lot wrong in some of the things they want. But you've got to admit that a man, right or wrong, has the right to want to have the neighborhood he lives in a certain kind of way. And at the moment the overwhelming majority of our people out there feel that people get along better, take more of a common interest in the life of the community, when they share a common background. I want you to believe me when I tell you that race

prejudice simply doesn't enter into it. It is a matter of the people of Clybourne Park believing, rightly or wrongly, as I say, that for the happiness of all concerned that our Negro families are happier when they live in their *own* communities.

BENEATHA.   *(With a grand and bitter gesture.)* This, friends, is the Welcoming Committee!

WALTER.   *(Dumbfounded, looking at Lindner.)* Is this what you came marching all the way over here to tell us?

LINDNER.   Well, now we've been having a fine conversation. I hope you'll hear me all the way through.

WALTER.   *(Tightly.)* Go ahead, man.

LINDNER.   You see—in the face of all things I have said, we are prepared to make your family a very generous offer. . .

BENEATHA.   Thirty pieces and not a coin less!

WALTER.   Yeah?

LINDNER.   *(Putting on his glasses and drawing a form out of the briefcase.)* Our association is prepared, through the collective effort of our people, to buy the house from you at a financial gain to your family.

RUTH.   Lord have mercy, ain't this the living gall!

WALTER.   All right, you through?

LINDNER.   Well, I want to give you the exact terms of the financial arrangement—

WALTER. We don't want to hear no exact terms of no arrangements. I want to know if you got any more to tell us 'bout getting together?

LINDNER. *(Taking off his glasses.)* Well—I don't suppose that you feel...

WALTER. Never mind how I feel—you got any more to say 'bout how people ought to sit down and talk to each other?... Get out of my house, man.

(He turns his back and walks to the door.)

LINDNER. *(Looking around at the hostile faces and reaching and assembling his hat and briefcase.)* Well—I don't understand why you people are reacting this way. What do you think you are going to gain by moving into a neighborhood where you just aren't wanted and where some elements—well—people can get awful worked up when they feel that their whole way of life and everything they've ever worked for is threatened.

WALTER. Get out.

LINDNER. *(At the door, holding a small card.)* Well—I'm sorry it went like this.

WALTER. Get out.

LINDNER. *(Almost sadly regarding Walter.)* You just can't force people to change their hearts, son.

(He turns and puts his card on a table and exits. Walter pushes the door to with stinging hatred, and stands looking at it. Ruth just sits and Beneatha just stands. They say nothing. . . .)

The Actor's Nightmare
by Christopher Durang

To his utter dismay, George finds himself onstage with a role in a play he does not know. In this scene, the famous actress Sarah Siddons is playing the female lead in a play very much like one by Noël Coward. She is in a glamorous evening gown, and she is holding a cocktail glass. After a moment, George arrives onstage, practically pushed on. He is dressed as Hamlet—black leotard and large gold medallion around his neck. As soon as he enters, several flash photos are taken, which disorient him greatly. When he can, he looks out and sees the audience and is very taken aback. We hear music.)

SARAH. Extraordinary how potent cheap music is.

GEORGE. What?

SARAH. Extraordinary how potent cheap music is.

GEORGE. Yes, that's true. Am I supposed to be Hamlet?

SARAH. *(Alarmed; then going on.)* Whose yacht do you think that is?

GEORGE. Where?

SARAH. The Duke of Westminster, I expect. It always is.

GEORGE. Ah, well, perhaps. To be or not to be. I don't know any more of it. *(She looks irritated at him; then she coughs three times. He remembers and unzips her dress; she slaps him.)*

SARAH. Elyot, please. We are on our honeymoons.

GEORGE. Are we?

SARAH. Yes. *(Irritated, being over-explicit)* Me with Victor, and you with Sibyl.

GEORGE. Ah.

SARAH. Tell me about Sibyl.

GEORGE. I've never met her.

SARAH. Ah, Elyot, you're so amusing. You're married to Sibyl. Tell me about her.

GEORGE. Nothing much to tell really. She's sort of nondescript, I'd say.

SARAH. I bet you were going to say that she's just like Lady Bundle, and that she has several chins, and one blue eye and one brown eye, and a third eye in the center of her forehead. Weren't you?

GEORGE. Yes. I think so.

SARAH. Victor's like that too. *(Long pause)* I bet you were just about to tell me that you travelled around the world.

GEORGE. Yes I was. I travelled around the world.

SARAH. How was it?

GEORGE. The world?

SARAH. Yes.

GEORGE. Oh, very nice.

SARAH. I always feared the Taj Mahal would look like a biscuit box. Did it?

GEORGE. Not really.

SARAH. *(She's going to give him the cue again.)* I always feared the Taj Mahal would look like a biscuit box. Did it?

GEORGE. I guess it did.

SARAH. *(Again).* I always feared the Taj Mahal would look like a biscuit box. Did it?

GEORGE. Hard to say. What brand biscuit box?

SARAH. I always feared the Taj Mahal would look like a biscuit box. Did it? *(Pause)* Did it? Did it?

GEORGE. I wonder whose yacht that is out there.

SARAH. Did it? Did it? Did it? Did it? *(Enter Meg. She's put on an apron and maid's hat and carries a duster, but is otherwise still in her stage manager's garb.)*

MEG. My, this balcony looks dusty. I think I'll just clean it up a little. *(Dusts and goes to George and whispers in his ear; exits.)*

GEORGE. Not only did the Taj Mahal look like a biscuit box, but women should be struck regularly like gongs. *(Applause.)*

SARAH. Extraordinary how potent cheap music is.

GEORGE. Yes. Quite extraordinary.

SARAH. How was China?

GEORGE. China?

SARAH. You travelled around the world. How was China?

GEORGE. I liked it, but I felt homesick.

SARAH. *(Again this is happening; gives him cue again.)* How was China?

GEORGE. Lots of rice. The women bind their feet.

SARAH. How was China?

GEORGE. I hated it. I missed you.

SARAH. How was China?

GEORGE. I hated it. I missed . . . Sibyl.

SARAH. How was China?

GEORGE. I . . . miss the maid. Oh, maid!

SARAH. How was China?

GEORGE. Just wait a moment please. Oh, maid! *(Enter Meg.)* Ah, there you are. I think you missed a spot here. *(She crosses, dusts, and whispers in his ear; exits.)*

SARAH. How was China?

GEORGE. *(With authority.)* Very large, China.

SARAH. And Japan?

GEORGE. *(Doesn't know, but makes a guess.)* Very . . . small, Japan.

SARAH. And Ireland?

GEORGE. Very . . . green.

SARAH. And Iceland?

GEORGE. Very white.

SARAH. And Italy?

GEORGE. Very . . . Neapolitan.

SARAH. And Copenhagen?

GEORGE. Very . . . cosmopolitan.

SARAH. And Florida?

GEORGE. Very . . . condominium.

SARAH. And Perth Amboy?

GEORGE. Very . . . mobile home, I don't know.

SARAH. And Sibyl?

GEORGE. What?

SARAH. Do you love Sibyl?

GEORGE. Who's Sibyl?

SARAH. Your new wife, who you married after you and I got our divorce.

GEORGE. Oh, were we married? Oh yes, I forgot that part.

SARAH. Elyot, you're so amusing. You make me laugh all the time. *(Laughs.)* So, do you love Sibyl?

GEORGE.   Probably. I married her. *(Pause. She coughs three times, he unzips her dress, she slaps him.)*

SARAH.   Oh, Elyot, darling, I'm sorry. We were mad to have left each other. Kiss me. *(They kiss. Enter Dame Ellen Terry as Sibyl, in an evening gown.)*

ELLEN.   Oh, how ghastly.

SARAH.   Oh dear. And this must be Sibyl.

ELLEN.   Oh how ghastly. What shall we do?

SARAH.   We must all speak in very low voices and attempt to be civilized.

ELLEN.   Is this Amanda? Oh, Elyot, I think she's simply obnoxious.

SARAH.   How very rude.

ELLEN.   Oh, Elyot, how can you treat me like this?

GEORGE.   Hello, Sibyl.

ELLEN.   Well, since you ask, I'm very upset. I was inside writing a letter to your mother and wanted to know how to spell apothecary.

SARAH.   A-P-O-T-H-E-C-A-R-Y.

ELLEN. *(Icy.)*   Thank you. *(Writes it down; Sarah looks over her shoulder.)*

SARAH.   Don't scribble, Sibyl.

ELLEN.   Did my eyes deceive me, or were you kissing my husband a moment ago?

SARAH.   We must all speak in very low voices and attempt to be civilized.

ELLEN.   I was speaking in a low voice.

SARAH.   Yes, but I could still hear you.

ELLEN.   Oh. Sorry. *(Speaks too low to be heard.)*

SARAH. *(Speaks inaudibly also.)*

ELLEN. *(Speaks inaudibly.)*

SARAH. *(Speaks inaudibly.)*

ELLEN. *(Speaks inaudibly.)*

SARAH.   I can't hear a bloody word she's saying. The woman's a nincompoop. Say something, Elyot.

GEORGE.   I couldn't hear her either.

ELLEN.   Elyot, you have to choose between us immediately—do you love this creature, or do you love me?

GEORGE.   I wonder where the maid is.

ELLEN & SARAH. *(Together, furious.)* Forget about the maid, Elyot! *(They look embarrassed.)* You could never have a lasting relationship with a maid. Choose between the two of us.

GEORGE.   I choose. . . oh God, I don't know my lines. I don't know how I got here. I wish I *weren't* here. I wish I had joined the monastery like I almost did right after high school. I almost joined, but then I didn't.

A Waitress in Yellowstone or Always Tell the Truth

by David Mamet

Following is the beginning of the play. A narrator takes the stage. He is dressed as a park ranger.

RANGER.   Winnie was a waitress. She worked for tips. Here is a tip: a bad situation generally grows worse.

Things which can get no worse improve. There are exceptions: here is not one. Winnie caught a guy lifting a tip off of her table. Told him "who do you think you are?" and she read him out to the onlooking crowd, what sort of a you-fill-in-the-blank that he *was*... which he was.

It turns out this man was a congressman. In an election year. He had to keep a shining image in the public eye, which is exactly where he kept it.

Would have been better off to be what he wished to seem, but barring that he took the secondary course, lived like a thief and made the Public Pay.

Winnie and her son Doug. Had planned a trip to Yellowstone. To celebrate his Tenth Birthday. He'd, as you might imagine, looked forward to that trip all year. And it was the object of much of their talk and much of their joint happiness.

At the restaurant.

WAITRESS.   Hey, Winnie, quit dreaming, table number three wants the check!

(Old Couple)

OLD MAN.   Could I have the check, please.

WINNIE.   Here you are.

OLD MAN.   Thank you. See you tomorrow, Winnie...

WINNIE.   No you won't, sir. Tomorrow my boy and I leave for our vacation. I'll see you in two weeks.

OLD MAN.   Where are you going?

WINNIE.   Yellowstone Park.

OLD MAN.   That's right, you told me. Here's a little extra, you have a fine trip.

(The Old Couple starts up to leave.)

WINNIE.   That's *very* generous of you, sir... thank you... *(Before she can gather the money, etc., she is called to another table.)*

CONGRESSMAN.   Miss!

WINNIE *(to Old Man)*.   Thank you very much.

CONGRESSMAN.   Miss!

WINNIE.   I'm coming. *(to Congressman)* Yes, sir?

CONGRESSMAN *(of check)*.   What is the meaning of this?

WINNIE *(checking bill)*.   Ninety-five cents, for a substitution. You had beans instead of the creamed spinach.

CONGRESSMAN.   You never told me that.

WINNIE.   Yes, sir, I did.

CONGRESSMAN. You certainly did *not*. You did *not* tell me that.

WINNIE. Yes, sir, I am certain, you said "I'll have the Special." Look: It's not important. If you take the check to the boss, I'm sure that he'll. . .

CONGRESSMAN. Well, that's not the point, is it? The point is that you never *told* me. . .

WINNIE. Well, if that's true, I'm sorry, sir.

CONGRESSMAN. No: *say* you never told me. . .

WINNIE. Excuse me. . .

CONGRESSMAN. You owe me an apology.

WINNIE. I think that I apologized, excuse me. . . *(She walks away. To another waitress.)* Some people have too much salt in their diet. . . *(to Congressman)* WAIT A SECOND WAIT A SECOND WAIT A SECOND: *WAIT* A SECOND THERE!

(She walks back to his table, which he has gotten up from. He is standing near the table vacated by the Old Couple. To Congressman.)

You wanna put something back? *(Pause)* You wanna put something back, or you want me to call the police.

CONGRESSMAN. I don't know what you're talking about.

WINNIE. I'm talking about you just lifted my tip off of that table. Now: you put it back or I call the cops.

CONGRESSMAN. You're saying. . . *(Pause)* You're saying I did whhh. . . ? Get out of my way. *(Tries to push past her)*

WINNIE. In a pig's *eye* I will. Somebody call the cops! Somebody call the cops, this guy took my tip off the. . . *(To Congressman)* You aren't going anywhere!

BOSS. What's the trouble?

WINNIE. This guy took my tip off the table.

CONGRESSMAN. Lady, you're in a world of trouble here.

WINNIE. Well, we're just going to see. . .

COP. What seems to be the trouble?

WINNIE. This guy lifted my tip off the table.

CONGRESSMAN. Not only is it not true, but I want to tell you you've just caused yourself a lot of pain. What's your name, Officer? I'm John Larue, I am the congressman for this district, and this deranged and sick individual has just slandered me. Pick her *tip* off the table? You know WHO I *AM*???

(The Congressman sings about the exalted position he enjoys. He finishes singing.)

CONGRESSMAN. Now: I'll give you one last chance to retract what you said and take back your vicious lie, or you're going to wish you never were born.

WINNIE. Well, to wish you never were born you have to be born. Which gives you the option, and I think I'll stick with the truth. You should be ashamed of yourself. Good-bye.

(The Cop takes the Congressman away.)

WINNIE.   What kind of a world is it? That guy should be setting an example...

(Winnie and the assembled customers sing "What Kind of a World Is It?" peppering the song with examples from their own lives. The second verse is: "On the Other Hand," where Winnie sings about some of the good things which may be had simply in life, in her case, the trip with her son to Yellowstone Park.

As the clock strikes twelve she sings "My Day Is Done, and I'm Going on Vacation," and leaves the restaurant. She walks home.)

WINNIE.   Look at the stars, what a beautiful night it is. Always various. *(She walks into her house.)* Look at my son, isn't he gorgeous. And now we have all this vacation time to be alone together. All the rest is basically illusion.

RANGER.   And so she fell asleep, and she and her son dreamed the same dream. In which they were in Yellowstone Park, high upon a ridge, upon a summit, looking down, and they saw mountain sheep, and they saw deer, and when the rain came unexpectedly they made a shelter from a fallen tree. And as in the wild of sleep and as in the wild of the forest their cares fell away. And when Winnie awoke, she saw her son, already dressed, sitting at the breakfast table, and he had made her a cup of tea.

(N.B. They are both dressed in full camp regalia.)

WINNIE.   Good morning. What are you doing up so early?

DOUG.   Oh, I couldn't sleep.

WINNIE.   Why? You worried about school, shouldn't you be off to school?

DOUG.   Well, I thought I wouldn't go to school today.

WINNIE.   Wouldn't go to school? Why, of course, you have to go to school today, why wouldn't you?

DOUG.   'CAUSE WE'RE GOING TO YELLOWSTONE PARK!!!!!

(They jump up and down and sing a song about how they must make sure they've taken the right things. They sing about the contents of a rucksack, and emergency gear, which they inspect on each other's person. This gear includes: waxed matches in a waterproof container [several containers secreted in various parts of the clothing and generally high up to keep them dry should one fall into waist-high water], a compass, a spare compass, a topographic map of the area to be camped in. A candle for helping to light fires, needle and thread, steel wool which, though it is not generally known, is, in its superfine variety, great tinder and can just be wrung out when wet, extra clothing, rain gear, pencil and paper, fishing line and hook, bandages, whistle, etc. They finish the song, and, having checked each other out, decide that they are ready to proceed to the bus, which they have ten minutes to catch. In deciding which coat to wear, they turn on the radio to catch a weather report.)

DOUG.   I can't believe we're really going.

WINNIE.   Have I ever lied to you?

DOUG.   No!

WINNIE.   Well, then, there you are.

RADIO ANNOUNCER *(voice over)*.
In other news, Congressman John Larue, up for reelection, yesterday was accosted for the misdemeanor of Attempting to Defraud of Services or, to put it simply, a waitress at a restaurant he frequents accused the Congressman of lifting her tip off her table.

WINNIE.   . . .come on, let's get out of here. . .

CONGRESSMAN *(voice over)*.   You know, it's easy to accuse, and I think by far the simplest thing would be to let this sick accusation pass, and go my way, but there comes a time. . .

WINNIE.   Turn that creep off, let's go to the *country. . .*

DOUG *(turns off radio)*.   What'd he do?

WINNIE.   The creep. Lifted a tip off of a waitress's table. Can you believe that?

DOUG *(opening door)*.   What a life.

WINNIE.   On to the Wilds!

(In the door are two burly plainclothes policemen.)

POLICEMAN.   Winnie Magee?

WINNIE.   I. . . uh, what is it?

POLICEMAN.   Are you Ms. Winnie Magee?

WINNIE.   I can't talk to you now, we have to catch a bus.

POLICEMAN.   ARE YOU WIN. . . ?

WINNIE.   Yes, but I can't talk. . .

POLICEMAN *(simultaneously with "talk")*.
You're under arrest. Would you come with us, please?

WINNIE.   I. . .

DOUG.   Wait, you can't, what's this all. . . ?

POLICEMAN.   Slander, Malicious Mischief, Defamation of Character, would you please. . . ?

WINNIE.   Who, what. . . ?

DOUG.   What are you doing to my mother?

SECOND POLICEMAN.   She insulted a congressman, kid.

WINNIE.   But we. . . we just have ten minutes to catch the bus. . .

(They are in a court of law.)

And we're going to Yellowstone P. . . what is this, what's going on here. . . ?

JUDGE.   You are accused of wantonly, maliciously, and with malice aforethought having verbally assaulted, insulted, and impugned the character of one John Larue, Congressman for the Seventh District of. . .

WINNIE.   HOLD ON A SECOND.
I insulted wh. . . ?

JUDGE.   You have no voice in this court, would you please, who is your counsel?

WINNIE.   Say that again?

BAILIFF.   Who's your lawyer?

WINNIE.   I don't have a lawyer, why should... What's going on here? *(Pause)* Come on, I have to catch a bus. *(Pause)*

JUDGE.   You are accused by the congressman here *(Congressman stands.)* of, in simple terms, of lying about him in such a way as to damage his reputation.

WINNIE.   Ah.

JUDGE.   When you said that he stole your tip.

WINNIE.   He *did* steal my tip.

JUDGE.   The court will now appoint you a lawyer.

WINNIE.   I don't need a lawyer, I don't *want* one. Let's settle this here and now, 'cause I'm on my vacation time, alright? You tell me how you want to do this, and let's get this done.

JUDGE.   You wish to act as your own lawyer?

WINNIE.   That's... okay. *(Pause)* Okay.

JUDGE.   You're making a mistake.

WINNIE.   I've made them before. Nothing to be scared of. Now, what is the thing?

DOUG.   Mom, what's going on...?

(Winnie and Doug hold a whispered consultation while the Bailiff and the Judge sing about the charge and the procedure in this case. They are joined by the Lawyer for the Congressman and the Congressman, who sing about her heinous behavior and the grave damage that has been done. They stop. Pause.)

WINNIE.   Now what?

JUDGE.   You may present your case.

A Star Ain't Nothin' But a Hole in Heaven
by Judi Ann Mason

The Lorraine Hansberry award, of which this play is a recipient, is established for the best plays on the black experience in America. The following scene is set in Louisiana, 1969. Pokie, a high school senior who lives with her senile, dying aunt Mamie and her aged, blind uncle Lemuel, struggles to overcome tradition and her family's disapproval to go north to get a good college education.

MAMIE.   Lemuel, Lemuel. That man is a great man, Pokie. Good man.

POKIE.   I know.

MAMIE.   Sometimes you don't understand him. He is hard to understand sometimes.

POKIE.   He treats me like I'm a little baby.

MAMIE.   He tryin' to protect you.

POKIE.   From what?

MAMIE.   What he had to go through.

POKIE.   Things ain't like that no more. There's a lotta things I have to do and he won't let me. I think he don't want me to graduate.

MAMIE.   Aw, Pokie . . .

POKIE.   Every time I ask him for something I need, he tells me that I don't need it.

MAMIE.   You got to try real hard to make him see.

POKIE.   I told him I needed a white dress—

MAMIE.   He's always been like that. Like the time I told him I needed some new shoes for my sister's wedding.

POKIE.   I wouldn't ask him for the dress if I didn't have to have it. . .

MAMIE.   All the time before that, all the money had to be spent on things for his pappy.

POKIE.   Do you think he'll let me buy it?

MAMIE.   "Lemuel, the shoes don't cost but $2. And I'll take good care of them. You won't have to buy me no more. . ."

POKIE.   I saw a dress that cost only $12 up at the Woolworth.

MAMIE.   He told me that we didn't have the money. But I knew we had the money cause I had worked five days straight down to Miss Blema's store that week and I gived him all the money. . .

POKIE.   Aint Mamie, will you listen to me?

MAMIE.   So I tells him I had the money and he gets mad at me. "You ain't grateful for all I done for you. Who else gon marry a woman like you? You be thankful for me marrying you . . ."

POKIE.   Will you listen to me?

MAMIE.   I told him that he didn't have to marry me. If he had to wipe my brow with it, he didn't have to marry me.

POKIE.   I got problems, too! But nobody around here never listens to me talk. . .

MAMIE.   It was just like talkin' to myself. "You told me you didn't make no mind about children. You told me I was just as much a woman cause I couldn't make babies. Lotsa women can't make babies. I ain't the only one, Lemuel."

POKIE.   (Unable to control her moment of disgust.) For once can't you hear me? Come back and talk to me!

MAMIE.   "I love you, Lemuel. I love Jesus, too. Jesus is the Savior! Save me, Lord! Take this curse from my womb!"

POKIE.   Come back and talk Aint Mamie!

MAMIE.   Too old now. Life done creeped up on me. It done snatched my breath from my lungs. I'm still a woman.

POKIE.   Listen to me! (Mamie bursts into a fit of tears. Pokie goes to her and starts to shake her.) Listen! You come back here and listen!

MAMIE.   Turn me loose! Jesus gonna remember me! Turn Jesus loose! Take the cross from his back! He's the Son of God! Turn the Lord aloose!

LEMUEL.   (At door.) Mamie, what's the matter? (Seeing Pokie.) Pokie, let her be! You trying to kill her? What you doing? Stop hollin' at her! Turn her loose!

POKIE. *(She releases Mamie and stands back staring at Lemuel.)* You saw that?

LEMUEL. It's alright Mamie. All right.

POKIE. How did you see what I was doing to her?

LEMUEL. She was hollin'.

POKIE. No, you saw it. Joretta was right. You can see.

LEMUEL. Girl, stop that barking and help me get her to bed.

POKIE. Do it yourself.

LEMUEL. What you say?

POKIE. Do it yourself. You saw well enough a minute ago. . .

LEMUEL. Go get the alum so you can rub her down.

POKIE. I ain't gonna do it!

LEMUEL. Is this the thank-you we get after all we done for you? You musta forgot we didn't have to take you in. . .

POKIE. I'm leaving, Uncle Lemuel.

LEMUEL. Pokie, shut up that noise.

POKIE. Me and Joretta going up north to college.

LEMUEL. Help me get Mamie to bed.

POKIE. I ain't coming back here. You done all this to keep me here, but I'm going to college. And I'm gonna be an artist!

LEMUEL. Then what we suppose to do?

POKIE. You can move to town.

LEMUEL. This is my land.

POKIE. You can sell it and buy somewhere in town.

LEMUEL. Who gon take care of Mamie? She's your ainnie and you talking about leaving her. A decent girl would stay as close to her kin as she could—

POKIE. I ain't willing to sacrifice my life.

LEMUEL. You know we can't take care of ourselves. We subject to die in this house.

POKIE. I can't stay here. I won't.

LEMUEL. If you think I'll let you leave—

POKIE. How you gon stop me? You can't see, remember? All I got to do is walk out of here.

LEMUEL. You shut up! *(He comes toward her.)*

POKIE. I'm leaving. I don't owe nobody nothing but me.

(Lemuel tries to grab her. Pokie dashes out of the way. Lemuel stumbles on the chair. Pokie rushes to the door and exits.)

LEMUEL.   Pokie! Come back here! Pokie!

(Pokie runs toward the tree, lays her head against it and cries. Lemuel looks after the door.)

MAMIE.   Lemuel, we need to get Pokie a white dress to graduate in. A nice white dress, with ruffles and a big collar. Lemuel, Pokie needs a white dress. . .

(lights dim)

"Baucis and Philemon" *from Metamorphoses*

by Mary Zimmerman

Following is the entire segment of "Baucis and Philemon" from Mary Zimmerman's play, Metamorphoses, *which is based on the writings of Ovid. Be aware that much of the play takes place in a pool of water.*

(Music. Transition. The raft and candelabra are struck.)

NARRATOR ONE.   It happened that one night, Zeus, the lord of the heavens, and Hermes, his son, came down to earth to see what people were really like. They disguised themselves as two old beggars, stinking and poor, ragged and filthy. They knocked on a thousand doors.

(Zeus knocks on the surface of the deck. Both adopt supplicating poses.)

ZEUS.   Hello, do you have any spare—?

OFFSTAGE VOICE.   Get out of here! Get the hell out of here! I work hard for my money!

NARRATOR ONE.   And a thousand doors were slammed on them.

(They knock on the deck, and a woman opens the door.)

HERMES.   Hello, we're tired, we live on the street, and we hoped that you might—

WOMAN AT THE DOOR.   I'm sorry, I'm. . . um. . . soooo sorry. Sorry. *(She slams the door shut.)*

NARRATOR ONE.   At last they came to a little hut on the outskirts of town.

HERMES.   Why bother knocking here? We've knocked on houses of all kinds, the homes of people with plenty to spare. Whoever lives here obviously has nothing.

ZEUS.   Let's give it a try all the same. We've come all this way.

(He knocks.)

HERMES.   This is hopeless. Let's just go ho—

BAUCIS.   *(Entering.)* Poor strangers! Philemon, there are guests at our door!

ZEUS.   Hello. We are strangers to these parts. We've lost our way and—

PHILEMON.   *(Entering.)* Baucis, why are you standing there! We must bring our guests inside.

ZEUS.   Do you know us?

PHILEMON.   Of course.

HERMES.   You do?

PHILEMON. Yes—

HERMES. Then who are we?

PHILEMON. Why, you are children of God. Come in, come in.

(At this point, the narrative divides among several members of the company. They enter and exit variously, carrying illuminated candles in wooden bowls, which stand in for all the items they will mention. They hand these bowls to Baucis and Philemon, or place them in the water themselves. The scene is active: The entire surface of the water becomes the "table" being set with illuminated candles.)

NARRATOR TWO. The two immortals, satisfied that their disguises had not been seen through, entered the house, lowering their heads to fit through the door.

BAUCIS. No, don't sit on the floor! Sit on chairs, as quality people do.

NARRATOR THREE. Philemon ran to get another chair.

NARRATOR FOUR. And Baucis fetched two pieces of cloth to pad them so the strangers might rest easy.

NARRATOR FIVE. She stirred the coals in the hearth and fanned the fire to cook them a meal.

NARRATOR ONE. Philemon set out the embroidered cloth that they saved for feast days.

NARRATOR TWO. Baucis saw that one of the legs of the chair was short and she propped it up with a shard of a pot.

NARRATOR THREE. Philemon set out a plate of olives, green ones and black, and a saucer of cherry plums.

NARRATOR FOUR. Then there was cabbage and some roasted eggs . . .

NARRATOR FIVE. For dessert there were nuts, figs, dates, and plums.

NARRATOR ONE. And a basket of ripe apples.

NARRATOR TWO. Remember how apples smell?

(A pause. Everyone inhales and remembers. Then they continue.)

NARRATOR ONE. At last, with a show of modest pride, they brought out a bit of honeycomb for sweetness.

NARRATOR TWO. Philemon poured wine from a bottle, but as he filled the glasses of the guests, he saw that the bottle remained full.

ALL NARRATORS. And then they knew.

(Narrators exit.)

BAUCIS. Oh, mercy! Mercy!

(She runs with her husband to kneel in front of the gods.)

PHILEMON. You are divine and we've served you such a simple meal. Baucis, go and kill the goose!

ZEUS. Let it live. We are gods and we thank you. You've done enough, more than your nasty neighbors thought to do.

(The original narrator of the scene enters with three other members of the company, all carrying bowls of candles. As she speaks, they come forward, kneel in the water, and set the bowls floating. There is music under the next line of Narrator One.)

NARRATOR ONE. Suddenly, everything was changing. The poor little house, their simple cottage, was becoming grander and grander, a glittering marble-columned temple. The straw and reeds of the thatched roof metamorphosed into gold, and gates with elaborate carvings sprang up, as ground gave way to marble paving stones.

HERMES. Old man, old woman, ask of us what you will. We shall grant whatever request you make of us.

(Baucis and Philemon whisper to each other.)

BAUCIS. Having spent all our lives together, we ask that you allow us to die at the same moment.

PHILEMON. I'd hate to see my wife's grave, or have her weep at mine.

NARRATOR TWO. The gods granted their wish. Arrived at a very old age together, the two stood at what had been their modest doorway and now was a grandiose facade.

ZEUS. And Baucis noticed her husband was beginning to put forth leaves, and he saw that she, too, was producing leaves and bark. They were turning into trees. They stood there, held each other, and called, before the bark closed over their mouths:

PHILEMON AND BAUCIS. Farewell.

NARRATOR ONE. Walking down the street at night, when you're all alone, you can still hear, stirring in the intermingled branches of the trees above, the ardent prayer of Baucis and Philemon. They whisper:

ALL. Let me die the moment my love dies.

NARRATOR ONE. They whisper:

ALL. Let me not outlive my own capacity to love.

NARRATOR ONE. They whisper:

ALL. Let me die still loving, and so, never die.

Promenade
by Maria Irene Fornes

In this excerpt from her offbeat, bright-spirited play, Maria Irene Fornes's every word is a new surprise. With characters named 106, 105, Miss U, and Mr. R, you are instantly aware that this play is a bit out of the ordinary. And don't expect linear plot lines and obvious themes. Do expect intelligence and philosophical insight wrapped in zaniness.

Scene 2

The Banquet. There are ladies and gentlemen in evening clothes around the table. The servant sweeps. The waiter serves the guests.

105 and 106 enter. They put on top hats and tails. They sit at the table and eat.

MR. R.   Speech . . . speech . . .

MR. S.   Let's play croquet . . .

MR. R.   Speeches and music . . .

MR. T.   Let's call Mr. Lipschitz . . .

MR. S.   No speeches . . . No speeches . . .

MR. R.   Let's have a song . . .

(105 and 106 clear their throats.)

MISS O.   Mr. T, was that you I saw on the corner of Fifth and Tenth?

MR. T.   Perhaps.

MISS O.   With Mrs. Schumann and her newly clipped poodle?

MR. T.   Oh, no, it wasn't I. Friday night I was out of town.

MISS O.   Ah! And how did you know it was Friday night I saw you on the corner of Fifth?

(They all laugh.)

MR. T.   Well, I must confess. The lady loves me.

(They all laugh.)

MISS U.   She shows good taste.

MR. R.   Then, introduce us. She'll surely fall for me.

(The ladies giggle.)

(Mr. R writes in a notebook.) Mrs. Schumann . . . lady of taste . . . Bring dog biscuit.
(To Mr. T.) What is her address?

MR. T.   Tch-Tch.

MISS I.   Oh, Mr. R, what perspicacity.

MISS O.   Are you sure that's what you mean?

(Miss I looks a little embarrassed.)

MR. S.   Let's have a song.

(105 and 106 stand and get ready to sing.)

MISS O.   And who are these? Dear me.

(105 and 106 realize they have been indiscreet. They sit back at the table and pretend not to hear the others.)

MISS I.   They must be friends of Mr. S.

MISS U.   My dear. You go right to the point . . .

MISS I.   Mr. S does frequent rather unearthly places, doesn't he?

MR. T.   What do you mean?

MISS I.   I mean the lower depths.

MR. T.   Oh, yes.

MR. S.   If I am sometimes in the company of this and that, my dear, it's only because I like to study life . . . I am what you might call a student of life . . . This . . . and that.

MISS U.   Oh, how incredibly personal you are, Mr. S. Have I not always said you have the artist in you?

MR. S.   I am neither more than I seem to be, nor more than I am, and no less, also.

SERVANT.   *(Mimicking in a low voice.)* And no less . . . also.

MR. R.   Miss I . . .

MISS I.   Yes?

MR. R.   Last Saturday I waited for a certain lady who never arrived.

MISS I.   You did?

MR. R.   Yes.

MISS I.   Oh, she couldn't come. She spent all afternoon walking up and down a certain street where a gentleman *(Referring to Mr. T.)* who shall remain nameless lives. She was hoping to have an accidental meeting. . . a sort of unexpected encounter with him. But he never left his house . . . nor did he enter it.

(Miss O and Miss U giggle. The servant is bored by the ladies' and gentlemen's repartee. Through the following speeches she pantomimes their gestures.)

MR. T.   He didn't, Madam . . . he didn't. He saw the lady from his window and she did indeed walk up and down his street. But he couldn't receive her . . . his heart was torn. You see, he received a letter from the one he loves *(Referring to Miss U.)* telling him his love was unrequited. He spent all afternoon sitting by his window plucking petals from flowers, and the answer always was . . . she loves me not.

MISS O.   And who is this he speaks of?

MISS U.   She is not free to love. Her heart belongs to he *(Referring to Mr. S.)* whose glance drives her to a frenzy, and whose mere presence brings color to her cheeks.

MR. S.   The man who puts you in such a state has eyes only for O. Oh, Miss O.

MISS I.   Oh! What tension! A name has been mentioned.

MISS U.   And what have you to say to that, O?

MISS O.   I regret I cannot speak since Mr. S has mentioned me by name. But do you wonder why O shuns you when you are so indiscreet? *(Taking a step toward R.)* And besides, she loves R.

(R takes a step toward I.)
(I takes a step toward T.)
(T takes a step toward U.)
(U takes a step toward S.)
(S takes a step toward O.)
(O takes a step toward R.)

MISS U.   You were there when I was not.
I was there when you were not.
Don't love me, sweetheart,
Or I might stop loving you.
Unrequited love,
Unrequited love.

MISS O.   Passionate lips are sweet.
But oh, how much sweeter
Are lips that refuse.
Don't love me, sweetheart,
Or I might stop loving you.

MISS I.   Inviting lips,
Alluring lips

Which shape the word no
No no no no no no.
Don't love me, sweetheart,
Or I might stop loving you.

MR. R.   You know nothing of life,
You know nothing of love
Till you have tasted
Of unrequited love.
Don't love me, sweetheart,
Or I might stop loving you.

ALL.   Unrequited love,
Unrequited love.
There is no love
Like unrequited love.

MISS I.   Oh! We sang that well.

MR. R.   He who scrubs the pot finds it
most shiny.

MR. S.   *(To Mr. R.)* And he who soils it, turns
up his nose. Mr. R, you were flat.

MISS I.   Touché!

MISS U.   What a marvelous mind.

MR. S.   Just frank.

SERVANT.   *(Mimicking.)* Just frank.

(They all look at the servant, shocked.)

MISS I.   Mr. S, it's up to you to think of a
rejoinder.

MR. S.   Dear me, I'm speechless. Wait! Listen
to my answer. *(He improvises the following:)*

My frankness, my dear,
My wit, my veneer,
Are something you should revere.

LADIES.   A rhyme! A rhyme!

MR. S.   Instead, you just think it queer.
Your unprosperous status
Produces a dubious,
Fallacious, and tedious
Outlook on life.
(The servant makes a face at him.)
You do not know what we're about
We do not know what you're about
Or care to know.
(The servant lowers her head.)
It's sad your career
Depends on our whim.
On with your work, my dear,
Or you'll get thin.
You see, even if you're here,
And we're also here,
You are not near.
Isn't that clear?

MISS U.   Oh, Mr. S, how well you rhyme.

MR. S.   Not difficult, dear. Just keep the
ending of the word in mind. . . it will come.

MISS U.   *Incendo, incendis, incendit,
incendimos, incenditis, incendunt.*

MR. S.   No, dear, the ending, not the
beginning.

Icarus

by Edwin Sánchez

A brother and sister, Primitivo and Altagracia, are living in a remote beachside cabin. Each day Primitivo swims farther and farther out to sea and back again. His sister is helping him train to become a celebrity. Soon the two are joined by Mr. Ellis, his dog Betty, Miss the Gloria, and Beau. Beau challenges Primitivo to a race. Following is a conversation among the members of the small community.

PRIMITIVO.   I was kind of afraid of you before but not anymore. You're going to become exhausted out there. Your lungs will collapse, and they'll fill with water, and the only person who can save you will be me, but I'll be too busy touching the sun. *(Pointing to the ocean.)* She's all yours. I'm sure you'll want to practice. I should warn you, she's a little choppy and watch out for her undertow, she doesn't let go easily.

(Primitivo and Altagracia exit. Beau goes to the Gloria. Lights up on the Gloria. She is wearing a facial masque and has a strapped-on ice pack around her eyes.)

the GLORIA.   Halt, who goes there?

BEAU.   It's just me, Miss the Gloria.

the GLORIA.   Ah, my fan. But you shouldn't see me like this. I'm a work in progress. Turn away.

BEAU.   You look fine.

the GLORIA.   Turn away! Have you?

BEAU.   Yes. *(He hasn't.)*

the GLORIA.   I'll have to take your word as a gentleman that indeed you have.

(Beau turns around.)

the GLORIA.   You're here much too early. The Gloria is best seen under man-made illumination. Nonetheless, I'm so glad you're here. I have so much to tell you.

BEAU.   Has it ever occurred to you that every time I see you we only talk about you?

the GLORIA.   You say that as if it were a bad thing.

BEAU.   Do you ever wonder what I look like?

the GLORIA.   You're going to give me frown lines. I won't like you anymore if I get frown lines.

BEAU.   Do you ever ask yourself, "Why you?" "Why are you so beautiful?"

the GLORIA.   Massage my feet, please.

(Beau does.)

the GLORIA.   Because I can handle the stress. Not everyone could, you know. The weight, the burden, the responsibility that comes from being everybody's fantasy.

BEAU.   I have my mask off. Do you wanna see me?

the GLORIA.   Of course not. I already have my image of you. Whatever you do, whatever it takes, maintain the illusion. It's hard work, it's a full-time job, but it's worth it.

BEAU.   And what will you do when your beauty is gone?

(Panic-stricken, the Gloria stops him.)

the GLORIA.   I haven't faded, have I? This is the only currency I have.

BEAU.   No, you're still perfect.

the GLORIA.   You frightened me. I mean, who would ever want me without my face?

BEAU.   Goodbye now.

the GLORIA.   Bye-bye.

(Beau exits. Mr. Ellis sits on the beach, a pair of baby shoes by his side. He is too tired to dig.)

MR. ELLIS.   I'm not staring, I'm not staring, I'm not staring, I'm not staring, am I staring? I'm not staring, I'm not staring, I'm not staring, I'm not staring, I'm... not... I don't like to remember. I don't.

(Beau stops. He sits by Mr. Ellis and takes his shovel and begins to dig for him. Mr. Ellis grabs his wrists and stops him.)

MR. ELLIS.   You weren't invited to help. If you have something you don't want to remember, go find your own beach.

(Altagracia brings Primitivo downstairs to the beach.)

PRIMITIVO.   We should be sending out press releases.

ALTAGRACIA.   I'm on it.

PRIMITIVO.   And we'll need V I P seating.

ALTAGRACIA.   Uh-huh.

PRIMITIVO.   And maybe baton twirlers.

MR. ELLIS.   What do you think his losing will do to her?

BEAU.   Are you so sure I'm gonna win?

MR. ELLIS.   You're not gonna win. You're just gonna beat him.

ALTAGRACIA.   I need to talk to you. We need to discuss the terms of the race.

PRIMITIVO.   The rules.

ALTAGRACIA.   Yeah, the rules.

BEAU.   We get in the water and swim. One of us wins—

PRIMITIVO.   Me.

BEAU.   —and one of us loses.

PRIMITIVO.   You.

ALTAGRACIA.   Primi, let management manage, okay? That's why I'm getting the big bucks. Why don't you practice your victory speech?

PRIMITIVO.   Okay, but don't give away the foreign distribution rights. Remember, I'm right here.

(Altagracia sits on a step.)

ALTAGRACIA. Step into my office.

(Beau sits next to Altagracia, who finds herself too close to him so she moves up a step.)

BEAU. Well, it's almost race time. Primitivo seems really excited.

ALTAGRACIA. Yeah.

BEAU. How's that?

ALTAGRACIA. I said, "Yeah."

BEAU. Are you talking to me or to your feet?

ALTAGRACIA. Why are you doing this?

BEAU. I thought this is what you wanted.

ALTAGRACIA. I wanted Primitivo to swim.

BEAU. He's not swimming?

ALTAGRACIA. Farther and better than ever. No complaining, either.

BEAU. Then what's the problem? You still believe he can touch the sun, right?

ALTAGRACIA. Sure I do.

BEAU. Then you should be grateful I'm staying. I'll give him a chance to prove it.

ALTAGRACIA. You're right.

BEAU. If anybody can, he can. You just lost your faith for a second, that's all.

ALTAGRACIA. Yeah.

BEAU. I guess I should go practice.

(Altagracia grabs his arm.)

ALTAGRACIA. Are you really gonna go through with this?

(Beau nods his head and strips down to his bathing trunks as he goes into the water. Primitivo does his sun touch, stretched arm with splayed fingers as he watches Beau swimming. Altagracia sits next to Mr. Ellis, who opens his suitcase and retrieves a brooch from it. He holds it up.)

ALTAGRACIA. Pretty.

MR. ELLIS. Cheap. My wife's one piece of Christmas jewelry. She'd wear it exactly from December first to January seventh. I didn't even know I had it.

(Mr. Ellis drops the brooch in the hole and buries it.)

ALTAGRACIA. You know, in the summer, some little kid with a sand shovel is gonna find it.

MR. ELLIS. It might be her. Reincarnated.

ALTAGRACIA. Oh, please.

MR. ELLIS. She'll have a feeling of déjà vu.

ALTAGRACIA. I can barely survive going through this once. Let alone over and over again.

MR. ELLIS. Next time it would be different.

ALTAGRACIA. I'd want it in writing, notarized, and blessed by the Pope.

(She picks up Betty and holds her close.)

Does My Head Look Big in This?

by Jeff Gottesfeld and Elizabeth Wong
based on the novel by Randa Abdel-Fattah

Amal Abdel-Hakim, 16, makes a decision to wear her hijab, the headscarf worn by many Muslim women, in public, even though her parents warn her of the taunting she might face. In a tense situation on a bus, Amal's grouchy Greek neighbor, Mrs. Vaselli (Mrs. Vee), stands up for her. Amal realizes that practicing her faith is deeply important, even if it means telling Adam, her debate opponent and the boy she likes, that she does not want to hold hands. During the final scene, her friends—Eileen, Leila, Leila's mother (both hijab-wearing Muslims as well), Simone, Josh (Simone's boyfriend), and Adam—gather at her home for a holiday party.

AMAL *(to audience).*   So Adam is talking to me again. He succumbed to my charms, sparkling personality and the fact that I had just gone head-to-head with him in a debate. Or maybe he'd thought about what I'd said at the party. Because it was true. What was right for Josh and Simone didn't have to be right for me. Does that mean I still don't lay in bed at night and wonder about what if? Of course I do. Come on guys, I'm not just Muslim, I'm human! *(A beat.)* Anyway, the school year droned on. I kept up my grades, hung with my friends, visited Mrs. Vee and started thinking about colleges with pre-law programs. Before I knew it, it was Muslim New Year . . . which fell right near Christmas and Hanukkah. I know. Multicultural to the max. Muslim New Year is no big deal—it's no Ramadan—but since it was close to the other holidays, my folks decided to have a get-together. Any excuse for my mother to make enough *fatoosh, mansaf* and *makloba* to feed the western hemisphere.

(EILEEN, JOSH, SIMONE, ADAM, and LEILA are at the Abdel-Hakim household. LEILA'S MOTHER is also there, helping with the table.)

DAD.   Welcome, everyone! Welcome to our celebration. Welcome to our home.

MOM.   We call it *Hijiri*. New Year; it comes at the start of the Muslim month *Muharram.*

DAD.   It's not a big deal holiday, but we still wish each other *"Kul'am wa enta bi-khair,"* which means "May every year find you in good health."

EILEEN.   And eat a lot of stuff you guys can't pronounce.

AMAL.   But we don't celebrate with drinking and partying.

SIMONE.   I have something momentous to say. I'm hungry.

JOSH.   Hey, Hanukkah started tonight, too. I lit candles and ate potato latkes. That's what we Jews call a big blowout.

LEILA'S MOTHER.   You light candles?

JOSH.   Yeah. Jews light candles a lot. Two on Friday night, and eight for Hanukkah.

SIMONE.   One candle for every night of the holiday. Did I get that right, pooh bear?

JOSH.   You were perfect, hunny bunny.

Scenes   551

(SIMONE and JOSH gaze goofily at each other. Clearly in l-u-v.)

EILEEN.   You guys are nauseating.

(Meanwhile, AMAL is a million miles away, thinking. Then, she zeroes in on JOSH like a laser.)

AMAL.   Did you say Jews light two candles every Friday night?

JOSH.   Sure. And we bless a glass of wine—

(A realization strikes AMAL.)

AMAL.   Ya Allah!

(AMAL jumps up and dashes for the door.)

DAD.   Amal!

LEILA/JOSH/EILEEN/SIMONE.   Where are you going, Amal?/You need some backup?/Amal, where you going?

AMAL.   I'll be right back!

MOM.   Amal! You have guests!

(Too late. She's already gone.)

AMAL (to audience).   I went straight to Mrs. Vaselli's house.

(AMAL sounds the doorbell. MRS VASELLI answers.)

MRS. VASELLI.   Hello, Amal.

AMAL.   Hello, Mrs. Vee. Happy Hanukkah.

MRS. VASELLI.   Huh? What you say?

AMAL.   Happy Hanukkah!

MRS. VASELLI.   Goodbye!

(MRS. VASELLI slams the door or turns away. AMAL stops her.)

AMAL.   Please don't. Look, I don't know how to say this, so I'll just say it. I think you're Jewish.

MRS. VASELLI.   No! I am Greek Orthodox, what makes you say such a thing.

AMAL.   When I came over to thank you for what you did on the bus . . . I saw you lighting two candles.

MRS. VASELLI.   You saw nothing.

AMAL.   It was a Friday night. There was wine, too. In a beautiful silver goblet. I think it was for the Jewish sabbath.

MRS. VASELLI.   Go home, Amal!

AMAL.   You don't have to hide from me. I'm your friend.

MRS. VASELLI.   No! Stop saying something, I am not.

AMAL.   The Nazis. The Nazis killed your family. That's why they were gone. Am I right?

MRS. VASELLI.   Don't! You hear me? Never say that outloud. (A beat.) Bad things happen once, they happen again.

AMAL.   I think you want everyone to believe you are Christian because that makes you feel safer. You do all your Jewish stuff in secret.

MRS. VASELLI.   This crazy talk. You on drugs like all kids!

AMAL.   Mrs. Vee. It's fine if you are Jewish!

MRS. VASELLI.   You need to go home.

AMAL.   Mrs. Vaselli, look at me. Look how I dress. I go to school. I go to the mall. I ride the bus. I am who I am. *(A beat.)* Remember on the bus? You told me I wasn't alone. You're not alone, either.

(A fraught moment. Then MRS. VASELLI acknowledges the truth.)

MRS. VASELLI.   How did you know?

AMAL.   Those candles. The wine. But mostly it was the story about Solinika. It's horrible—horrible what they did.

MRS. VASELLI.   So many Jews to the camps. So—so many.

AMAL.   You're safe with me. And my family. And my friends.

MRS. VASELLI.   I don't know.

AMAL.   Come to our house. We're celebrating Muslim New Year.

MRS. VASELLI.   No, no I can't.

AMAL.   Please come. There's plenty of food. Please.

MRS. VASELLI.   You know it's the first night on Hanukkah.

AMAL.   I do. My friend Josh is over. He lit candles tonight. You were going to light yours in secret, weren't you?

MRS. VASELLI.   No. Yes. Yes, of course.

AMAL.   Can you light them with me?

MRS. VASELLI.   I don't know.

AMAL.   Come to our house. We're celebrating Muslim New Year.

MRS. VASELLI.   No, no I can't.

AMAL.   Please come. There's plenty of food. Please.

(MRS. VASELLI hesitates, then walks to a sideboard where she has hidden a simple Hanukkah menorah with two pre-placed candles. She takes out the menorah.)

MRS. VASELLI.   I do this because of you, Amal. *(Sings in Hebrew, as she kindles the sha-mush.) Baruch Atoh Adonai, Elohenu melech Ha-olam. Asher kidishshanu b'mitzvatav vitzi-vahnum l'hadlik ner shel Channukah.*

(As MRS. VASELLI sings, and uses the lit shamush *to ignite the first candle on the menorah, AMAL puts an arm around her. The blessing ends; they contemplate the flickering candles.*

AMAL turns to the audience.)

AMAL *(to audience).*   Turns out Mrs. Vaselli is an absolute fiend for my mother's *makloba.*

(AMAL might change hijabs during the follow-ing.)

AMAL *(cont'd).*   I'm not going to lie and say the new year brought peace, love and understanding. Tia stayed a Grade-A beeyotch. Leila and I still got hassled by strangers. But my hijab stayed on. We're lucky to live in a country where you're allowed to be yourself, whoever you might be. Me? I'm a Palestinian-American-Muslim girl who loves Allah, checking my notifications, hanging out at the mall, visiting Mrs. Vee, going to the mosque and, of course, the unmistakable smell of a brand new Toyota Prius. Fingers crossed! Add to the list, my mom, Jamila; my dad, Mohammed; my friends Leila, Simone, Josh, and Adam; and my cellphone. Oh, and I love Ellen DeGeneres. And that's my official list of "Can't Live Without It," not necessarily all in that order. You wouldn't think it all fits, right? But it does somehow. Maybe I'll talk about it someday when I'm promoting my new talk show. Maybe I'll be interviewing a certain young Palestinian-American-Muslim civil rights attorney fighting for a world where everyone can be free to be who they really are. *(Starts to walk away; then stops.)* Oh! What do you think? Tell me—be brutal. *(Readjusts her new hijab.)* Does my head look big in this?

For More Practice

1 With a partner, choose three scenes of various styles in which you would enjoy acting. Interpret and experiment with these scripted scenes to portray believable characters in creative ways.

2 Choose one brief and one longer scene from this unit that you would like to direct. At least one should be a duet. Analyze and evaluate each one and the full play from which it is taken.

For the shorter one, use the following questions as a guide to analyzing and evaluating the scene as you take technical questions into consideration. Write out answers to the questions and be prepared to discuss them in class.

What is the setting? What technical elements will help bring that setting to life? Consider set design and construction, lighting, sound, costumes, makeup, and props. Create a complete design for the scene that incorporates all elements of stage technology, using researched technical elements to increase the impact. Review Unit Five to create a light and sound plot.

What is the time of the action? How can you use technical elements to portray that time? Again, consider each aspect of technical theatre and how it might contribute.

What is the literary style? What does the style suggest about appropriate and effective technical theatre elements?

What is the genre? How can you make the most of the genre's characteristics through creative use of technical elements?

How can technical elements help reveal character? How can you cleverly use technical elements to add insight into characters?

What technical elements seem appropriate to the **theme**?

For the longer scene, use the following as a template for analyzing and evaluating the script.

Artistic Roles	Technical Assignments
The **characters** in this play/scene suggest the following artistic roles:	The **characters** in this play/scene suggest the following technical assignments:
The **themes** suggest these artistic roles:	The **themes** suggest these technical assignments:
The **duties** inherent in the script suggest that these are appropriate artistic roles:	The **duties** inherent in the script suggest that these are appropriate technical assignments:
The **elements** in the script point to these artistic roles:	The **elements** in the script point to these technical assignments:

3 For the shorter scene, in addition to the analysis and evaluation you did in the above activity, analyze the characters fully, describing physical, social, intellectual, and emotional dimensions. Demonstrate your leadership, responsibility, artistic discipline, and creative problem solving by planning ahead very carefully before the first rehearsal. Think through the blocking and be prepared with a promptbook to convey the blocking to your actors. Read through the lines carefully, making notes about expression that seems appropriate. Direct your actors with sensitivity and clarity so you support their efforts and achieve the effects you seek.

4 For the longer scene, follow the same process, but also spend time thinking about your casting and be able to justify your decisions based on details in the script. Analyze the characters you are casting and identify their chief characteristics. Ask yourself what qualities actors should demonstrate to portray those characters effectively and what types of looks and voices might help represent those characters. If you are in a situation that includes auditions, observe each audition with an open mind. After initial auditions, you may want to call back actors for reading scenes together to see how they interact.

Also recruit a technical team. Meet with your technical team to explain the vision you have for the scene and accept input from them on how to achieve that with materials and equipment in the classroom or in the theatre, if you have access to it. Meet with your cast as well, expressing the vision you have for the scene and how the cast might help you achieve it. Show your leadership by planning a rehearsal schedule and setting expectations for all participants to bring needed materials to each rehearsal. Encourage the actors to call on their emotional and sensory memories to bring a character and the scene to life. Give the cast notes after each rehearsal. Help them plan a final bow to finish off the performance.

Unit Nine

Student Handbook
for Performance and Production

Taking part in a theatrical production can be one of the most rewarding experiences of high school. Whether you are playwriting, acting, directing, designing, working on a technical crew, or working with the stage and theatre management teams, you will have a chance to develop and apply your expertise in a specialized area of theatre. This handbook will help you refresh and extend your knowledge of each main aspect of a theatrical production.

557

Part One Acting

Apply Your Expertise

You got the part! Whether you have the lead role or a bit part, you have a chance as an actor in a production to grow in many ways. Make the most of your experience by focusing on the following attributes of an outstanding cast member who displays a high level of technical proficiencies.

Responsibility Develop and demonstrate your responsibility as an actor by coming to rehearsals on time and well prepared. Analyze the production plans, including the research, blocking, technical designs, and rehearsal schedules, so you are prepared with knowledge and organization. Keep your script up to date with acting notes, and mark cues clearly. Use your memorization skills to nail down your lines. The director and the rest of the cast and crew depend on you—demonstrate responsibility at every opportunity.

Artistic Discipline Good actors make acting look easy. But as any actor knows, effective acting requires artistic discipline and the hard work of careful preparation. You may, for example, need to learn an accent to portray your character effectively, or you may need to learn stage combat or some other physical movement. All of these require the artistic discipline of daily practice. You may also need to spend time outside of rehearsal drawing on your sensory and emotional memories, researching the time and place of the play, and learning more about a topic related to the play, such as an illness if your character is afflicted. While you might want to socialize with other cast members before rehearsals, develop and demonstrate your artistic discipline by instead inviting a castmate to warm up with you, or to run through some lines. Discipline yourself to keep a straight face even if something funny happens during rehearsal. Take every opportunity available to you to develop and demonstrate your artistic discipline.

Creative Problem Solving In a way, every word of a script is a problem to be solved. What are the character's motivation, obstacles, thoughts, and feelings? What movements and gestures best express the character's state of mind? If a character has a long speech to deliver, what stage business can add interest to the scene? All of these are problems that actors and directors working together can solve creatively. Try these different approaches.

- Take a break and get a fresh start.
- Reframe the problem: what are you really trying to solve?
- Brainstorm. The more ideas you come up with, the more likely you are to find a good solution.

Creativity You are a creative being. Demonstrate your creativity through imaginative acting choices in addition to problem solving.

Safe and Appropriate Acting Techniques As always, employ and model safe and appropriate techniques for vocal, emotional, and physical expression. Model stage movement to express concepts about your character, his or her relationships, and the environment of the scene.

Acting Styles

There are two main approaches to acting.

Method Acting Actors who have worked or prefer to work by "becoming" the character are influenced by the tradition of Method acting, originated by Konstantin Stanislavski (1863–1938) and currently taught by schools such as the Actors Studio in New York and Los Angeles. This approach asks actors to fully immerse themselves in the general world of the play and the specific world of their characters. Method work is also called *internal* or *subjective* work because actors build the character from within, tapping into the parts of themselves that relate to the character.

Technical Acting Actors who work technically tend to approach a role from a much more objective viewpoint. The technical actor uses powerful vocal and physical work to bring a character to life. The interpretation of the character is often more intellectual or stylized than emotional. Technical work is sometimes called *external* or *objective* work, because the actor builds the character through pacing, projection, vocalization, movement, and emotion. These are intellectualized from the script, but not necessarily "felt" by the actor. Technical acting is an important part of contemporary theatre because it emphasizes the disciplined training of the voice and body.

Are you a method or a technical actor? Your style will be determined partly by type and temperament and partly by the teachers, directors, training methods, and acting companies with which you work. You will also be influenced by the styles of plays in which you are cast. Both approaches will be useful to you as an actor in certain roles and productions. Research various acting styles and draw from your research when developing a character.

To prepare for work in either style of acting, the actor must still employ a combination of research and imagination. Actors research the *given circumstances* of the play, and imagination fills in the gaps. Given circumstances include:

- What the playwright says about the character.
- What other characters say about the character.
- What the character says about himself or herself.
- What the character does.

This research should be attuned to both the obvious and direct statements, such as one character saying, "You're so selfish," or the more subtle, "What do you expect from her?" The first example is direct text and the second is *subtext,* or what may lie beneath the surface meaning of the dialogue.

Acting Types

In the theatre, and particularly in movies and television, appearance and stage presence have much to do with an actor's ability to be cast and to work. A role can be, and often is, a combination of the following types:

Antagonist The character who opposes the objectives of the protagonist, or main character.

Bit Part A smaller role, such as GUARD #1 or a chorus member.

Character Part Usually a parental, comic, threatening, or eccentric figure. This person often has odd characteristics or personality quirks that serve as a *foil,* or contrast, to the protagonist. Character parts provide comic relief, dramatic tension, and/or color to a play. They are often challenging "stretch" roles for younger actors.

Foil A character that serves as either an antagonist or as a significant character to whom the protagonist may be compared.

Ingenue [AHN•juh•nu] A young female love interest, sometimes the protagonist, and in older plays, an example of idealized womanhood.

Juvenile A young male love interest, sometimes a protagonist or hero. In older plays he is often an example of perfect manhood.

Principal A main or leading role, usually the protagonist, antagonist, or love interest in a play.

Protagonist The main character with whom the audience sympathizes. Usually the character who changes the most during the course of the play.

Supporting Role A smaller role, often a sidekick or secondary love interest.

Straight Part A role that can fulfill some of the same functions as a character part but without the eccentricity. A straight part will not be played as broadly as a character part but may still provide comic relief, dramatic tension, and/or color. Straight roles demand less of a stretch for young actors.

Characterization

There are five basic areas to explore when preparing for a role. They are based on the journalistic questions *Who? What? When? Where?* and *Why?* Try to find the answers by analyzing the script. If the answers are not in the script, create the answers from your imagination.

Who is your character? To understand the world of the play and, therefore, the world of a character, an actor must explore the character's personality. This understanding is formed by a variety of influences: genetics, environment, and social influences, among others. Here are some questions to ask and answer about a character:

- Where were you born?
- Does this location affect your behavior? The way you speak?
- How important are social institutions such as school, government, and church in your world?
- What are your prejudices, if any?
- What is your attitude toward the opposite sex?
- In what way do you have professional power? Personal power? How well do you use what power you have?
- How would you describe your home life? What was your family life like when you were growing up? How has it affected your present life?
- How do you want to appear to other characters in the play?

What is going on in the script? First, read the entire play. Then read it again, focusing on your character. Take notes on the following questions:

- What does the playwright say about your character?
- What do other characters say about your character?
- What does your character say about him/herself?
- What does your character do? (Remember that actions speak louder than words.) Does your character say one thing and do another?
- What does your character want and need as written in the script?

- What changes does your character go through over the course of the play?
- What is the playwright trying to communicate? What is the play about?

When? What's going on before, during, and after you are onstage? For every scene you are involved in, you need to be able to answer the following questions:

- Where have I just come from?
- What am I thinking about as I walk into the room?
- How much of my history do I bring into the room with me?
- As I walk into this room, what are my immediate expectations and goals?
- What are my long-range expectations and goals?
- What do I need to accomplish before I leave this room?
- As I leave, where am I going? How do I feel about what just happened? What will I do next?

Where? How do surroundings affect your behavior? If there is more than one setting, ask these questions about each location. People behave differently in different places.

- Where am I and what time is it?
- What kind of room or area is it?
- How does the space I am in impact my behavior?

Why do you do what you do? Every play has a main idea or "spine." In addition to independent character study, you will analyze the play with your director. Once you have a clear concept of the main idea, ask yourself these questions, first for the play as a whole, and then for each scene in which you appear.

- What do I want?
- What am I willing to do to get what I want?
- What is in my way?

Scoring a Role

The term *scoring* has various definitions depending on your instructor. For some teachers, the scoring of a role relates to the character analysis detailed above. For others, scoring is the literal marking in the script of notes and reminders about line delivery and blocking. Each actor develops his or her own personal shorthand for marking a script. The following elements are usually noted:

- Pauses
- Pitch
- Emphasis
- Speed or Tempo
- Movement
- Character Revelation or Discovery
- Stage Business

Another important aspect to scoring is to break scenes into sections and give them names using concrete noun titles for specific actions. Examples of names for scenes might include:

- The Courtship
- The Denial
- The Rejection
- The Request
- The Secret
- The Illusion
- The Trick

Next, define how your character will fit into the scene using the infinitive verb form. What does your character want at this moment, and how will he or she go about getting it? Examples of infinitives to use within scenes are:

- To Romance
- To Seduce
- To Deny
- To Conquer
- To Conceal
- To Beg
- To Criticize
- To Excuse
- To Supplicate
- To Hide

Auditions

There are two main types of auditions:

- **The audition for a specific role or play.** If possible, read the full play before the audition. This will give you a clear advantage when you approach the role for which you are reading. The director may request a specific type of audition piece, such as one of the types of monologues listed on page 563, or he or she may simply ask you to read from the play itself (see **Cold Reading** on page 563). The more you know about the play, the easier it will be for you to make meaning from even the smallest section or scene.

- **The prepared professional audition.** Most audition situations allow you to prepare beforehand. You are expected to keep the audition material short, usually one to two minutes, and you are often called upon to provide two contrasting monologues—one comic or character and the other dramatic or period—all within the allotted time period. Directors know what they are looking for and are used to assessing actors quickly. An experienced director will immediately spot the qualities needed for the role—which means that the professionalism of your approach in that very short amount of time may make the difference between being cast or forever waiting in the wings.

At most auditions, you will be asked to fill out a form with information about yourself. Take the time to fill in the information clearly and completely; you don't want anything to stand in the way of your success. You will then be given a number or a time, or told to wait until your name is called.

When you are called, make a strong cross to center stage or the center of the audition room and smile. When it is clear that the auditors are ready, state your name clearly. Some auditors will expect you to state the name of your audition piece and its source; however, many auditors only need to hear your name (and talent agency if you have representation) and then will expect you to proceed. At the end of your audition, pause in case the director wishes to ask you any questions, give direction, or invite you to do more. Then say, "Thank you," and leave.

The Audition Résumé The résumé gives the director a thumbnail sketch of who you are and what sort of work you have done. Your résumé reflects how much you care about your acting career, so be sure it looks clean and professional.

The résumé begins with your name, contact information, and any personal information you wish to share. This is followed by a listing of your educational background, then your professional credits, and finally any special abilities that might help you in your work. There are a variety of formats, many of which are detailed in library books, textbooks, and even such handbooks as *Résumés for Dummies.* Here are some basic rules:

- Don't leave anything out you want the director to know.
- Don't exaggerate or fabricate experiences.
- Don't list anything more than ten years old.

Audition Selections Every actor should have between four and ten monologues memorized at all times, including contemporary and classical pieces. Try to find selections that are not overused, but avoid monologues that do not originate from published plays. Talk to teachers, directors, and other actors about which monologues might be right for you. Following are the general categories:

- **Dramatic Monologue** Preferably a recent work featuring a character close to your age and range of experience.

- **Comic Monologue** Again, try to choose something from contemporary literature that relates to your own experience and your "type." Comedy and drama will both work if you enjoy and feel comfortable with the piece.

- **Shakespearean Monologue** Choose something that you enjoy and understand. Analyze the scene carefully so that the language makes sense, and don't allow yourself to be trapped in the iambic pentameter (poetry) of the piece. Read for content and meaning. Many thoughts and sentences expand beyond one line and bridge several poetic phrases. Read the entire play, and be sure the character is within your range.

- **Classical Monologue** Choose a selection from classical literature, ranging from ancient Greek to Restoration comedy to Ibsen and Chekov. Having this material in your repertory will show that you are well versed in theatre styles and history.

Callbacks During the audition process, the director will begin to sort out combinations of people who will make the production the best and most cohesive possible. These actors will be called back to read again, usually for specific roles in the play.

Educational institutions and community theatres will post callbacks. If you are not called back by an educational institution, it is acceptable to wait until the casting process is over and then approach the director for feedback. Be sure to check both the callback sheet *and* the final cast list. Even though you are not called back, you may still be cast.

In a professional situation, most callbacks and casting are done via phone calls or e-mail. Be sure to check your messages. Producers rarely make any contact if you are not cast, and it is considered unprofessional to ask the producer for feedback on your audition. Just keep trying.

The best way to handle a callback audition is to treat the event as if it were a rehearsal. Behave as though you already had the part. Watch for clues about how the director sees the character. If the audition or callback involves a group of people and you are able to stay in the room, listen carefully to what the director is asking from each actor.

Cold Reading Some auditions are *cold,* or unprepared, readings. Many callbacks operate in this manner. You will usually have only a few moments to prepare, sometimes with a partner or two. Use whatever time you have to become as familiar as possible with the material. The best preparation for such an audition is to read plays out loud as often as possible—alone, in class, or with friends.

Musical Audition For musical theatre, you will be required to prepare either sixteen bars of music, or a song of a specific type, such as "Broadway belt," "standard musical comedy," ballad, or even contemporary rock.

Avoid using operatic-type material unless the audition specifically calls for it. Bring the music for your audition piece(s) with you and be sure it:

- Is in the key that best fits your voice.
- Has a clearly marked introduction.
- Shows what *tempo* (speed) you want.
- Indicates where you wish to start and stop.

Be prepared to sing more than sixteen bars if you are asked and have at least one additional song ready in case the director or musical director wants an "on the spot" callback. Most musical theatre actors keep a notebook of ten to twenty contrasting songs that are well-rehearsed and memorized.

Preparation

- **Memorize your audition pieces.** Nothing will kill an actor's chance of being cast more quickly than "going up" or "blanking" (forgetting your lines). The director will immediately wonder whether you have the discipline to memorize an entire script.
- **Rehearse your material.** Have your material in a notebook. Work with a teacher, director, or your peers to make sure your audition plays as strongly as possible.
- **Read the directions.** Auditions are almost always announced with a simple set of expectations. One of the easiest ways to impress a director is to prove that you can follow directions. If the audition calls for one sixty-second monologue, give exactly that and no more. Find out something about the play or company for which you are auditioning. Don't audition with a David Ives comic monologue for a production of

Macbeth. If the company does only contemporary dramas, audition with pieces that show your ability to tackle David Mamet or Tom Stoppard. Make sure you know your audition time and location and never, ever arrive late.

- **Dress professionally and appropriately.** You will be dressing for both the character and the audition. You do not need to audition in costume, but what you wear should be compatible with the character you are portraying. How you dress also reflects how much respect you have for the director and the audition process. If you show up in sloppy, wrinkled clothes, the assumption may be made that your life is in similar shape.

Difficult Acting Scenes

"I have to cry?"
"I have to kiss him?"

If you are a method actor, you solve these problems with substitution—imagine who you'd really like to kiss, or find something from your life to cry about. If you're a technical actor, you address these situations by showing that you know how to kiss or how to cry because you've practiced the technique and it's something actors are called upon to do.

Crying In order to cry on stage, you can practice the principal of substitution by thinking of something sad in your life that will bring up strong enough emotions to generate tears. A more technical approach is to use eye drops just prior to a scene—as long as it's possible to establish that the crying began offstage. Entering with "tears" in your eyes will appear realistic. Technically, crying shows in the voice and body as much as in the eyes. People who are crying often have to catch their breath and fight to keep their voice from wavering or their shoulders from shaking.

Kissing First, check with your director to see if a real kiss is necessary or if an illusion will do. Once this is decided, there are techniques to make a stage kiss simple and believable. The taller partner, usually the man, should stand in front of the woman with his back slightly to the audience. He can then lean in and either actually kiss her or place his cheek against her cheek. His head will keep the audience from actually seeing whether a real kiss takes place. The kiss should last at least three to five seconds, depending on the amount of passion that is to be shown. Getting into and out of the kiss is as important as the event itself. The buildup and response show the level of emotion and nature of the relationship.

Film

Acting Much of what you learn about theatrical acting technique has to be re-learned for film and television. Many of the skills are the same, and a good actor can be accomplished at both, but the small screen (television) and the big screen (movies) can look at the actor so closely that every acting moment must become smaller and more subtle. Actors who excel in a large theatre can easily be "too big" for the screen. In order to learn to act for television and film, every actor should study with teachers who understand the style. There are classes in all the major regional and national theatre centers. Check the credentials of whomever you study under. Make sure that former students really do get work.

The best piece of advice for an actor who wants to work in television and film is to start doing so on any level. Be an extra, work on the production team, get a job as a driver—just stay close to where films are being made.

The Business of Film

Most actors rely on their agents, managers, and/or entertainment lawyers to serve as buffers and negotiators for their work in motion pictures. While the major studios provide the biggest budgets and the best and most lucrative work for actors, independent films are the wave of the late 20th and early 21st centuries. Many independent films are made "on spec." The actors work at the SAG (Screen Actors Guild) minimum wage and donate the remainder of their normal salary to the production budget in the hopes that once the film makes the round of independent film festivals, it will be picked up for distribution. If this happens, everyone involved in the film stands to make a great deal of money. The success of an independent film can also make a sudden star out of a relatively unknown actor or generate "heat" for the screenwriter or director. Independent films account for much of the new talent in the industry.

Improvisation

Improvisation is the spontaneous exploration of the journalistic *W's*—the same ones that appear in the section under Characterization on page 560. The three principal *W*'s that govern an improv are *Who? Where?* and *What?*

Who? An improvisation can be character-centered. The *who* can provide the most important imaginative content. *Who* might be an old lady, a skunk, a preacher, and so forth.

Where? An improvisation can be location-centered. The *where* can be the basis for much of the comedy or drama of the scene. *Where* could be in a zoo, in an elevator, by the shore of a farm pond, or at a funeral parlor.

What? An improvisation can be situation-centered. The *what* can be an event that provides the imaginative content that drives the direction of the improv. *What* might be a wedding, a robbery, a funeral, or a game show.

An improv based on these examples could end up being the "wedding of an old lady and a skunk in an elevator."

Improvisations will be too short or die out quickly unless there is conflict involved. If there is a situation where one of the characters wants something and the other will not let him or her have it (motivation and obstacle), then these characters are in conflict and the conversation can become quite heated and animated. The basis of energy in improvisation is conflict, either provided in the setup or created by the characters themselves.

Dos and Don'ts of Improvisation

- **Do accept every offer.** Whatever some-one else says is an offer to move forward. If an improv partner says, "You wrecked the car," your response might be, "You wanted a new one anyway, and now you have the insurance money to get it."

- **Do accept what is said as fact.** Again, when a partner says, "You wrecked the car," you did! There are a million explanations, or "yes, . . . ands" available to you, such as, "Yeah it's wrecked, but it's not my fault. Your mother was talking on her cell phone, and she rear-ended me!"

- **Do stay in the world you create.** If you establish the roles of a parent and teenager, stay in that world. "You were out awfully late last night," says the parent, to which you might respond, "Oh, I was with Brian, and his parents were downstairs. Didn't they call you?"

- **Do keep focused on your motivation.** (Work to achieve your objective in the improv.)

- **Do listen, observe, and respond as the character you've created.**

- **Don't dead-end an improv with the word "No."**

- **Don't reject offers.** When your partner says, "You wrecked the car," the response, "No, I didn't" leaves little room to maneuver.

- **Don't reject what is said as fact.** Again, when a partner says, "You wrecked the car," the response, "Huh-uh, you did it. You were driving," creates an almost insurmountable obstacle for your partner.

- **Don't stray from the world you create.** If you are a parent and teenager arguing, remember your world. If your response to "You were out awfully late last night" is "You said I could stay out as late as I wanted, and you didn't come home on time either," we lose the sense of the balance of power in the relationships.

- **Don't spend time explaining.** Theatre is action. Use action statements when-ever possible.

Motivation

Finding and using motivation is an extension of character development. It is the most important key to how a character responds to a situation in both improvisations and in written dramatic text. Why does your character act the way he or she does? What does your character truly want? How can you figure these things out and apply them to your acting scenes?

Finding motivation comes from analysis of the script, or in the case of improvised scenes, from creating wants and needs for a character. When you break a script into acting units, even the smallest unit will involve the motivation of your character. When you are perfectly clear as to what your character wants, that clarity drives your actions, inflection, and even movement.

Motivation also creates *subtext,* that which is not said or is hidden between the lines. A good playwright will generally not state a character's motivation directly but will cloak it, just as people do in actual conversation. For example, at the crises of Arthur Miller's *The Crucible,* there is a moment when the characters are virtually screaming out between and beneath the lines. John Proctor wants to prove his abiding love for Elizabeth and to seek her forgiveness by being honest, but Elizabeth wants John to lie just this one time in order to save his life. They are completely trapped by the situation and cannot say what they truly wish to have happen when the other onstage characters are listening. The audience knows the motivation that drives each one, empathizes with both, and is drawn into the tragedy of the moment.

Whether you are preparing for an audition, doing scene work, or rehearsing for a play, be sure you know and play your character's motivation. If you are having trouble, discuss it with your director or teacher. Once you have found your motivation, it will be easier to memorize lines and develop stage business, because you will know the reasons behind your words, thoughts, and actions.

Movement

Physical work is extremely important in theatre. Actors spend a great deal of time warming up and looking for ways to fine-tune working with their bodies. In addition to basic stage crosses and knowledge of stage directions, there are several important terms to remember:

- **Counter** This is the term for a move that allows another actor to take the stage or make a clear and forceful movement. Because that actor is moving, the stage picture might become unbalanced, and another actor may need to counter the move by stepping back or out of the way.

- **Dress** This term refers to the idea of an actor as a set piece or decoration. The director "dresses" the set with actors as he moves them about. For this reason, the director will sometimes tell an actor to "dress right" or "dress left" (move stage right or stage left) to balance the position of another actor.

- **Gesture** "What do I do with my hands?" Beginning actors tend to work with their minds first. They understand a character intellectually but cannot make physical the traits of the character. Observe people and other good actors, then imitate what they are doing. The skill of observation is very important when seeking to find the right stance or gesture.

- **Leading Center** Each character has an essential "center" to her or his physical being. An overbearing Henry VIII might feel his center in his belly and lead from that center. An intellectual Thomas More from *A Man for All Seasons* might lead with his forehead. Snoopy in *You're a Good Man, Charlie Brown* might lead with his fast-moving feet or lapping and yapping mouth. Whatever your character's center, leading with that in your mind will help your character take on a look and movement that is individual and unique.

- **Master Gesture** Technical actors may plan and method actors discover a master gesture for their characters. This gesture is a distinctive movement that helps separate the character from the actor playing the character. The gesture might be a walk, a twitch, a stance, or the pulling of a strand of hair—some significant act that reflects the inner life and nature of the character. The master gesture also separates one character from another as the audience watches each come to life in the same play. The more stylized the play, the larger the master gesture. In an intense realistic drama, the gesture might be as simple as tapping a pencil nervously. In a broad comedy, the gesture might be a funny walk or an exaggerated expression.

- **Stage Picture** The director looks at each moment on stage and sees a picture made up of characters and set pieces. Each actor not only creates an individual role, but also becomes part of this picture.

Creating Believable Action

- **Use all of your senses and your sense memory.** Where are you in the play? When were you in a similar situation in real life? How did you move? What did you do?

- **Register the environment in your brain.** Let it sink in. This may take a split second or several seconds, depending on the situation, but don't react like you already know how you're supposed to act. The reaction must be in real time. Acting is active rather than reactive. The audience needs to sense you making a discovery rather than simply following what's said in the script or reacting to the other actors on stage.

- **Respond physically to the stimulus.** If your scene takes place in a pizzeria, think about what it smells like and how it makes you feel. Whatever the environment, you should have a physical reaction that the audience can perceive.

- **Respond orally.** How you move and speak will be different depending on whether you are hungry, angry, lonely, hot, cold, or tired. Your posture, your physical and verbal reactions, including tone of voice, will be affected by the environment, just as it is in real life. Physical and vocal response to the environment creates belief and represents an opportunity to use your sense of observation in order to be a stronger actor.

Fighting, Slapping, and Physical Force

The principal rule in stage combat is that the victim does all the work. If you are flung to the floor, you are actually flinging yourself. The aggressor in any physical stage work or stage combat starts the blow or attack and then "pulls the punch" in a manner imperceptible to the audience. The reaction of the audience is based on the reaction from the actor receiving the blow or attack.

When an abusive husband character grabs his wife by the arm and flings her down, he simply takes hold of her arm and she makes a rapid movement back and forth, then falls to the ground. If the actor then reaches down to slap her, she may hold up a hand which receives a "slap" from the husband, but at the same time snaps her head to one side to create the illusion that he has slapped her face. The audience will watch and believe the victim.

In another example, when the monster in a production of *Frankenstein* picks the doctor up by the throat, the actor playing the doctor simply grabs the arm of the monster with both hands and does a pull up while moving his head back and forth and gasping for air. Virtually no work is done by the monster, but the audience perceives him as having great strength.

Swordplay and Stage Combat Rule one is "Be safe." Stage combat is very technical and requires much discipline and practice from both the method and technical actor. Any combat involving props should be choreographed. The director, more experienced actors, or a stage combat or martial arts professional should work with the actors to plot out every beat and every stroke of any swordplay, fistfight, violent chase sequence, or other form of elaborate fight. There is no room for improvisation in stage combat. Both combatants must have a clear idea of where the fight is going.

Training Many actors attend physical theatre schools such as those mentioned in the following section on mime and pantomime. They also study aerobics, dance, Pilates, and/or yoga. All actors should take some basic dance courses including beginning ballet, tap, and modern dance. This training is good for coordination, and most actors at some time or another are required to do some dancing in connection with a role.

Mime and Pantomime

These terms are often used interchangeably and both imply essentially the same thing—the art of telling a story through body movement and facial gestures alone.

Mime is an art form that involves creating moments of drama and theatricality through movement without vocalization. It is more formal than pantomime. Mimes do not speak, though they may sometimes vocalize. They usually wear simple clown white makeup, often with a touch of personalization such as a tear, a smile, or a frown. Classical mimes usually have extensive physical training and can create tricks and complete environments with their bodies. Some classical mime movements or illusions include creating a wall, ascending and descending stairs, climbing a rope, blowing up a balloon, as well as entire scenes and stories.

Pantomime, strictly speaking, is simply creating a situation or movement that represents something, such as going fishing or sweeping the floor, usually without props and often without sound. Pantomime is very useful in many theatre situations. In much of what is known as "transformational" theatre, the actors create much of the set and the props with their bodies or they use representational objects such as a hanger, piece of fabric, or small box, that can become anything because of the way the actor works with it. For example, a stick can become a fishing pole, a bat, a fly swatter, a cane, an antenna, or anything else the actor imagines.

Some plays have a combination of pantomimed and realistic props. There might be a real bowl for cooking, but the egg that goes into the bowl is pantomimed.

Each play will have its own set of rules for the use of realistic versus pantomime props and situations. A simple example of this is the standard children's theatre production of *Peter Pan* in which the main character may actually "fly" using wire rigging or simply pantomime flying. Again, depending on the rules for the given production, all flying may be pantomimed, but all sword fights might use "real" prop swords.

Training Mimes are well grounded in physical theatre. Mime training is related to clown and new vaudeville training, which is taught in specialized schools. Three of the principal schools of physical theatre training are Le Coq in Paris, started by Jacques Le Coq; Decroux in Paris, founded by Etienne Decroux; and in America, the Dell'Arte school in Blue Lake, California, founded by Carlo Mazzone-Clementi.

Musical Theatre

Musical theatre in its present form—a play driven by songs and music—is one of the most uniquely American theatrical institutions. From early works such as *Babes in Toyland,* to Rodgers and Hammerstein's epic *The Sound of Music,* and from classically derived *West Side Story* through Bob Fosse's *A Chorus Line* to *The Lion King, Rent,* and *Kinky Boots,* the world of theatre is enriched by plays with memorable music.

An actor in musical theatre needs to be a "triple threat"—one part actor, one part singer, and one part dancer. Many theatre programs offer specialty degrees in each area, but an actor who intends to be successful in musical theatre should have a working knowledge of all three.

Acting Everything in the previous sections on acting applies to musical theatre. However, the actor must be prepared to convey a role with a minimal amount of dialogue, some of which is sung rather than spoken.

Choreography Every musical has a choreographer. The choreographer's vision is sometimes of equal importance to that of the director. Occasionally, they will be the same person. *Chicago* is as much a product of the genius of choreographer Bob Fosse as it is of all the stage directors (and even film directors) who have since interpreted the show. Choreography is the art of creating and directing not only the specific dance combinations of any given piece, but also of bringing to life the "look" of the entire production. Some musicals are jazz-based, some modern, and some, like *The King and I,* owe much to the beauty of the waltz and ballroom dancing. In order to learn dance numbers, the actor needs a dance vocabulary. This is achieved through taking basic dance classes and fearlessly trying everything suggested by the choreographer.

Music Voice lessons are important for most actors who seek a professional career but are absolutely necessary for actors who wish to participate in musical theatre. Most colleges will offer voice as part of their curriculum, but there are also excellent private vocal coaches and voice teachers. In addition, you should learn to play a musical instrument, one that requires you to read music. Piano helps you learn the structure and theory of music. Guitar is excellent because it gives you an instrument with which to accompany yourself when you sing. If you don't read music, be prepared to keep a small tape recorder with you at all times so that you can record your parts, both harmonies and solos, and practice them outside of regular rehearsal time.

Networking

Young actors need to be supportive of one another. The good and bad relationships you develop in your career will come back to help or hinder your progress. Theatre is a business of relationships and connections. Many theatre companies are started by frustrated actors who are not getting cast and branch out to become self-producers. The innovative and experimental work created at these theatres often becomes a part of the mainstay theatre scene. Your relationship to such actors becomes important when one of them suddenly becomes the director or playwright of a hit show.

Your teachers, directors, and their peers are also important connections. The acting profession is actually quite a small industry, and cultivating friendships and professional relationships with those who have gone before can pay the dual dividends of increased knowledge of your craft for the present and unique opportunities in the future. Establish a presence on social media. Promote your work intelligently and post short videos from recent performances. As in your face-to-face relationships, be helpful, courteous, and collaborative in developing your connections.

Also look for opportunities to give back to others. Join professional organizations. Work for free on occasion. Make outreach a part of your theatrical life—outreach to youth, to the aged, to those challenged or less fortunate. Volunteer to share what you've learned and the talent you've cultivated. All that you give, you will receive back, and all that you receive is a gift from those who have gone before in this very small and occasionally brutal business.

Performance Art

Another form of acting is performance art. Performance art is almost always inter-disciplinary. Multimedia and mixed media complement and enhance the theatrical aspects of the presentation, which is often called an *installation*.

During the late 1950s and into the 1960s, performance art was developed as a defiant alternative to more traditional theatrical events. Music was often improvised, slide projection was commonplace, and the performer would express himself or herself in an abstract or absurd manner. Some of the best known early performance artists were John Cage and Yoko Ono. John Cage still has a tremendous influence in the field of classical music, and one of his performance art pieces is still ongoing. This piece adds a brick per year to play a specific pedal note on a German organ. This musical piece will take over 1000 years to complete. Other examples of performance art installations could include:

- Creating a living room in which the artist simply goes about daily life in front of the viewing public.
- Reading from classical plays or literature while dance is going on in response to the reading.
- Musicians improvising while a theatrical artist responds with poetry.

Performance art is all about concept. There is usually no director—the artist fulfills that function. As a result, performance art sometimes has a random or unplanned feel. Although it may appear spontaneous and simple, creating an interesting, multi-disciplined environment is easily as difficult as creating an evening of good theatre. The art in both cases is dependent upon content, thought, audience response, timeliness, relevance, and creativity. Being involved in performance art gives the theatre actor a wonderful opportunity to be exposed to new and exciting artists and art forms.

Physical Warm-ups

There is not a sport in the world that doesn't require the athlete to warm up. While theatre is not a sport, it is a very physical process. Most educational and training theatre ensembles will have a group warm-up. Sometimes this is led by the director, at other times by one of the company members. Professional actors are expected to warm up on their own rather than taking up paid rehearsal time.

Because the tools of the acting trade are voice, body, and imagination, all three should be exercised during a warm up. You can develop your own warm-up routines, but you should also be open to learning them from other actors and even other disciplines. Remember to warm up the voice along with the body. Vocal warm-ups can include tongue twisters, over-enunciation, experimenting with your lines from the play, and singing vocalizations. Physical warm-ups should include the entire body, starting slowly and increasing in intensity. Your mental warm-up should include at least a little improvisation, even if it's only by talking with yourself or your character in the mirror. Meditation and

guided imagery are other types of mental warm-ups that help clear the mind in preparation for its use onstage.

Radio

Before television, there was radio. The Golden Age of Radio featured nearly as many comedies, news shows, adventure programs, serials, soap operas, and musical revues as there are on television today. Some of the great stars and stories of early television began their careers on the radio, including Jack Benny, Burns and Allen, and *The Lone Ranger*. With the advent of television as the principal media in the American household, radio has become predominantly a vehicle for music, sports, news, and talk or opinion shows. Radio is generally not as lucrative as television for the actor. Jobs include disc jockey, sportscaster, news or weather forecaster, talk radio personality, and voice-over actors for advertising commercials. Each of these requires extensive use of the voice. Actors with very unique and distinct voices tend to find work on radio most easily. A quick wit and improvisational ability also contribute to success in this field.

Because of a recent resurgence of interest in radio, many stations are now broadcasting "made-for-radio" comedy, mystery, adventure, and variety shows. One of the most successful of these is *A Prairie Home Companion,* featuring the wit, wisdom, and storytelling of Garrison Keillor.

Most universities with a television and film department provide courses in radio work, and many of these universities allow students to get hands-on experience by working with the university's local FM or AM radio station.

Readers Theatre

Readers Theatre is just that—an opportunity to read a play without memorization. This allows a play to reach an audience in a shorter time period, allows actors to gain valuable experience getting to know plays, and allows audiences to engage their imaginations and discover new material.

Readers Theatre is used for educational purposes, for new play development, and for pure entertainment. In this medium, the level of blocking or movement is up to the director and/or cast members. Much of Readers Theatre is done with actors seated on stools with their scripts on music stands. Words rather than actions are the stars of the show. Performance in this genre is therefore dependent upon a clear commitment by the actor to the vocal work involved in creating a character or characters. (It is possible to reduce a ten-character play to a reading by four or five actors through the doubling of parts.)

Readers Theatre usually, but not always, has a director who also serves as a producer, assigning roles, guiding rehearsals, and planning the evening's reading. Either the director or a stage manager reads any stage directions in the script. Following are ways to stage these performances:

Platform Readings are done with a clear distinction between audience and actors. The actors sit in front of the audience on a bare stage.

Monodrama is the reading of a play or selections from a play by a single actor. Clarity of character and the ability to quickly shift from one voice to the next are essential to maintaining interest during this sort of presentation. Monodrama is also defined as "memorized work that is written for or by a single actor, such as a one-man or one-woman show." Historical figures are often the subjects of monodramas. A prime example is Hal Holbrook's *Evening with Mark Twain.*

Choral Readings involve more than one person reading at the same time. Choral reading is often done to great effect at large events. Actors on one side of the room might read a poem by an American poet such as Walt Whitman, while those on the other side might read excerpts from the daily news in a "call and response" manner. In choral reading, the actors must be keenly sensitive to one another and to the rhythms of the work being read. Choral reading is hard but can be very effective. Many people are familiar with choral reading through their own religious institutions. There is a profound unity of purpose achieved through choral reading, which is why it is so prevalent in religion and also why the chorus was such an important part of early Greek theatre.

Group Readings One of the most entertaining ways to learn about theatre is to start a play-reading group. The group meets and chooses plays, then reads them, taking turns or choosing roles, sections, or otherwise dividing the material. Group readings are done mostly for the entertainment, education, and artistic development of the group doing the reading.

Chamber Theatre Chamber theatre takes its name from chamber music. Usually smaller than fully staged theatre, Chamber Theatre often involves some staging. Actors may still carry scripts, but they do the work "on their feet."

Rehearsals

Rehearsals can be both the most exciting and most challenging part of the theatrical process. As an actor, the time you are not on stage may move very slowly. Be sure to use your time wisely. Study your lines and make sure you are ready for your entrances.

There are several types of rehearsals, each with a specific purpose.

Blocking Rehearsals are used to work out stage movement. Actors carry their scripts, carefully writing down stage directions. Nothing frustrates a director, assistant director, or stage manager more than having to go through blocking a second or third time for an actor who was either inattentive or who didn't write down what he or she was to do the first time the direction was given. A pencil and eraser are the best tools for this job, since the second time through, things may change. The director may see a better way to play or stage a scene, and in the case of a new play, the playwright may change a line or even an entire scene.

Working and Polishing Rehearsals follow blocking rehearsals and can be the most fun for both actor and director. When the rehearsal period is long enough, this is the time for exploration and discovery. The play is analyzed, subjected to experimentation, developed, dissected, and put back together.

Technical Rehearsals are not about the actor. During a technical rehearsal, the actor takes a backseat to the sound, lights, stage management, cues, and other elements that will allow the production to shine in its full theatricality. Actor discipline is extremely important during tech rehearsals. The actor must be prepared to start and stop, wait, wait, and probably wait some more–and yet be able to start again with full emotion and clear purpose the moment the rehearsal continues. Some technical rehearsals go "cue by cue," meaning that large chunks of dialogue during which there are no sound or light cues may be skipped. Again, the actor must be ready for this and give a clear and precise performance of the cues so that the technicians can recognize their cues and be prepared to do their part to support the production.

Dress Rehearsals are often difficult for actors. Added to performances that seemed "set" are the sudden distractions of unfamiliar clothing and makeup. This can be especially difficult for a *period* (not contemporary) play that requires elaborate costumes and/or complex makeup. Concentration becomes the most important skill an actor can use during this time—that and a positive attitude. "Make it an acting problem," is one of the favorite responses of a costumer, stage manager, or director to actor complaints about wigs that don't feel right or clothes that seem too big or appear unflattering. Actors need to remind themselves that costumes and makeup are similar to personal props. There are often discoveries to be made about characters based on the vision the costume designer and director had when wardrobes were planned. If the fabric of a costume is especially reflective or shiny, that character may also shine and reflect. If a costume flows, then the actor wearing it should give it every opportunity to do so. If costumes include accessories such as kerchiefs, lace, monocle, glasses, pocket watch, or pockets, characters should find ways to use them.

Making these discoveries when first wearing the costume is part of what makes the dress rehearsal feel so different. An experienced director knows that during a dress rehearsal some of the old work will be left behind as characters catch up with their costumes.

Final Rehearsal All elements of the production should be in place during the final rehearsal. Even though every actor will continue to make some new discoveries during the run of a show, the expectation of the production team is that at the final rehearsal they can see how the production will appear to the audience. This rehearsal is their final opportunity to give notes and to tweak the show before the public adds the most important dimension of response.

Previews In professional theatres with long runs, the final rehearsal is often followed by a series of preview rehearsals, which are actually performances of the show in front of an audience. These are especially important for new plays and are always done for shows that plan to move to a major theatre on Broadway, or even onto one of the many strong regional theatre stages. Previews give the production team time to make changes based on how the audience reacts to the material. Comedy can be clarified, timing cleaned up, and dramatic moments crafted for the maximum possible effect.

Press Night is the last preview or first performance depending on the theatre involved. Press night is when the critics are invited in to review the play. Major commercial theatre projects often live and die by the success of their previews and press nights.

Script

Actors create their own working script in a variety of manners. Many actors photocopy the script onto pages that can be put in a notebook. Some actors, like directors, prefer to have the script copied on only one side of each sheet, so the back becomes available for notes. These can be notes on staging and blocking, character notes, or notes received from the director during the course of the show. The actor traditionally highlights his or her lines so that they are easy to find during working rehearsals and for purposes of memorization. The notebook also provides a good place to keep rehearsal schedules and other handouts the actor receives from the stage manager, assistant director, director, producer, and other members of the production team.

Storytelling

Storytellers practice their craft by performing at various venues on the professional storytelling circuit. They may also belong to professional organizations and/or take part in national competitions. In addition, storytellers are in high demand in the world of theatre for youth.

A good storyteller uses the same tools as an actor—voice, body, and imagination. A storyteller combines a strong narrative voice that sets the scene and strong character voices that propel the story through dialogue. The storyteller is really multiple actors in one, creating each character and building the story through the combination of character and dramatic action. Storytellers who create their own stories must work much like playwrights, creating a story structure that includes conflict, rising action, crisis, and climax.

Storytellers usually tell more than one story during a session, and these should have some variety so that the entire session shows a dramatic build and a rhythmic ebb and flow. The strongest stories are usually saved for last.

Television

Next to the movie industry, television provides the most lucrative possibilities for the young actor. Since more "product" is created for television, there are more opportunities for acting jobs.

Most television programs are designed to appeal to the broadest possible audience. For this reason, some actors feel they compromise their "art" when they work in television. Such actors must weigh the relative values of great art with a full refrigerator. Some television shows, made-for-TV movies, and even series are works by important artists and exhibit great artistry.

On the other hand, there is no doubt that some programming is sensationalistic and driven solely by ratings—the industry's determination of what people are watching most frequently. Television reflects the mass culture of our country, while theatre generally reflects the cultural life of artists and their vision. This is not meant to be judgmental. People enjoy comedy, sports, news, and sentimental stories, and the industry is able to provide such fare. The comparison is similar to discussing the relative values of a newspaper and a novel. Fewer people will read the novel, but it may have a longer lasting effect on the aesthetic (artistic) history and strength of a culture.

Most television programming can be grouped into the following categories:

Children's Programming Since the 1950s with its *Captain Kangaroo* and Saturday morning cartoons, television has produced fare for children. In the early years, most programming was commercially driven by sponsors of breakfast cereals and toys. Since then, however, the advent of public television has opened the door for shows with educational as well as entertainment value. Programs such as *Sesame Street* and *Super Why* play an important role in the national education process.

Dramatic Series Television dramas range from action-adventure, such as *Game of Thrones*, to police and courtroom series, such as *Suits*. Drama series and sitcoms (situation comedies) usually include a stock (regular) cast of characters and many featured roles around whom each week's drama revolves. Dramatic series tend to choose topical themes and reflect the world as it is. For this reason, most series last anywhere from two to six seasons before the taste of the public and the nature of current events bring new work forward.

Educational and Informational Television Public television and channels such as the History Channel and the Discovery Channel have done much to make historical and factual events entertaining and available to the general public.

Reality TV Reality TV has always been a part of television programming. Early shows such as *The Dating Game, This Is*

Your Life, and Candid Camera all dealt with reality-based incidents. Currently, however, reality-type programs dominate TV fare. The onslaught of such offerings is due in part to recent strikes by the actors' and writers' unions. Without scripts or actors, producers and networks looked for other ways to fill the holes in their schedules. The result was the development of reality programming such as *Survivor, American Idol,* and *The Bachelor.* Networks were delighted to discover that such shows drew large audiences (and thus, sponsors) and, for the most part, avoided the need for expensive professional talent. In fact, the acting industry has suffered because of the popularity of such shows. The artistic value of reality television is an easy target, but the fact that such shows remain popular is a strong statement about the current cultural climate in America.

Science Fiction
From the movie houses of the 1930s, serialized adventures of *Flash Gordon* and *Superman* quickly made their way to the small screen. These were followed by such shows as *The Twilight Zone, Alfred Hitchcock Presents,* and *Star Trek.* Recent science fiction series have included further editions of *Star Trek* and newer, edgier shows such as *Almost Human* and *Arrow.*

Situation Comedies (sitcoms)
From *I Love Lucy, The Beverly Hillbillies,* and *All in the Family* to *Seinfeld, The Simpsons,* and *Community,* the sitcom is one of the mainstays of television. In historical derivation, the sitcom most resembles commedia dell'arte—comedy based on larger-than-life stock characters in situations that reflect our lives and allow us to laugh at our own mistakes and weaknesses.

Soap Operas
Soap operas are the melodramas of today's media. Viewers thrive on the sensationalistic surrealism of characters suffering even more than people do in real life. *Days of Our Lives, The Guiding Light,* which ran from 1952 to 2009, and others kept their audiences for decades by airing hyper-dramatic situations and the difficulties of both rich and poor.

Sporting Events
Some of the highest ratings go to the industry that also consumes the most entertainment dollars—professional sporting events. The NFL, NBA, and collegiate athletics take up a good portion of airtime on commercial channels. These events also provide jobs for those who wish to work in the industry either on camera or behind the scenes.

Voice
Caring for and cultivating the voice take up much of the training time of the professional actor. Without clear diction and a strong instrument, an actor cannot hope to have a successful career in this very competitive business. Some actors and actresses are born with a particularly powerful or unique voice, but others may still aspire to success through diligent work and training.

Actors must develop vocal control of the following elements:

Accents
Accents may seem easy, but they are very hard to do correctly. In some comedies, actors will "fake" an accent, having fun with the sound of "pretend"

British, French, or German. This is fine for burlesque or broader comedy, but it is not acceptable when trying to create a real character. Some plays, and certainly many movie and television production companies, hire phonetic or diction experts as accent coaches. Actors without such resources can purchase tapes and guides for different dialects and accents. Nothing shouts "amateur" more than a bad accent, and nothing can enrich a play more than a well-researched one. Some actors and actresses have a talent or an "ear" for accents; for others, diction and accents are just another part of the hard work that is the discipline of the professional actor.

Emphasis and Subordination Some words are more important than others, as are some phrases. Your director might ask you to "point" a portion of your speech so that a crucial piece of information is not missed. On the other hand, some speeches or parts of lines are less important and can be "thrown away." This can be done to move quickly through material or even for comic intent.

Where the emphasis in a line is placed will also have a definite impact on what the line means. Sometimes the playwright will underline or boldface a word or phrase to help make it clear where he or she is going with the line. Note how the emphasis of different words changes the meaning in the following sentences.

> **I'll** take the money to town.
> I'll **take** the money to town.
> I'll take the **money** to town.
> I'll take the money to **town**.

Final Consonants Some beginning actors drop the ends of individual words, not truly finishing consonants. "Give me the hat back, won't you, Fred?" might become "Gimme eh ha ba, on u, Fre?"

Practice speaking your lines, making sure that every consonant is crisp and clear. This may feel unnatural at first, but the more it becomes second nature to you, the easier it will be to command an audience with the clarity of your voice and line delivery.

Pause and Rate Attention to pauses and speaking rates can make vocal acting stronger and more natural-sounding.

Pauses are an important part of speaking. On the positive side, a pause creates emphasis. The audience will literally hold its collective breath waiting to hear what you say next. On the negative side, too long a pause can indicate that you've forgotten your next line! Although long pauses occur naturally during real conversation, in the theatre, it often appears like a missed cue or a late entrance. If an actor leaves too many long pauses in between sentences or before starting his or her line, the scene will begin to drag.

Rate of delivery is also important. The actor needs to speak clearly and concisely at a pace that allows the audience to follow what's said but not become bored. Picking up cues does not always mean speaking faster—it can mean to speak sooner, one line after the other.

The opposite problem to dragging is rushing. Some actors learn their lines so well that they rattle them off without giving them full meaning. In more declamatory styles, including certain passages of Shakespeare, the actor can actually slow down and play with the poetry of the language. Most of the time, however, it is important to speak naturally but at a reasonable rate of speed.

Swallowing Words Beginning actors who lack experience with breath control, may swallow words—often at the end of sentences. An actor might have a line such as "I'm off and I won't be back until sunrise." If the actor swallows the end of the line it might sound like "I'm off and I won't be b--k t-l s--rse." Although difficult to show on paper, it is easy to spot when an actor rushes the end of a line, dropping pitch and volume while increasing rate.

Apply Your Expertise: Extension

After you have been cast, analyze the production plans to learn about the blocking, technical designs, rehearsal schedules, and the research into the play's historical and cultural setting. In your journal, write a reflection after analyzing the plans to set your mind for the work ahead. Then, after each rehearsal or even private practice/preparation session, use your theatre journal to evaluate how well you applied your acting expertise. Use the evaluation questions below.

Actor's Self-Evaluation
Responsibility In what ways did I develop and demonstrate responsibility in today's rehearsal/practice session? How can I improve on my responsibility?
Artistic Discipline In what ways did I develop and demonstrate artistic discipline? What benefits did I receive from that? How can I improve my artistic discipline?
Creative Problem Solving How effectively did I develop and demonstrate creative problem solving in today's work? What techniques did I use?
Creativity How did I demonstrate creativity as it relates to myself?
Safe and Appropriate Techniques What safe and appropriate techniques did I use for: <ul><li>vocal expression?</li><li>physical expression?</li><li>emotional expression?</li></ul>

Part Two Directing and Producing

Apply Your Expertise

Even though the director controls the production and develops its artistic vision, he or she is first and foremost the principal collaborator. A good director establishes unity of purpose through a spirit of cooperation and respect.

A good producer, in turn, makes it possible for the director to realize his or her vision. A producer must demonstrate an understanding of management skills in order to bring in and allocate the financial backing for a production.

The charts that follow summarize traits to develop and demonstrate in these two theatrical roles.

Growing as a Director

Responsibility Develop and demonstrate your responsibility as a director by reviewing and putting into practice the director's responsibilities outlined on page 165.

Artistic Discipline Keep your artistic vision clearly focused so that the whole team knows the play's direction. Adhere to schedules you create and be respectful of each person's time and talents.

Creative Problem Solving In a collaborative spirit, but always modeling leadership, challenge yourself to find creative solutions to perplexing problems in the production.

Growing as a Producer

Responsibility Develop and demonstrate your responsibility as a producer by reviewing and putting into practice the producer's duties outlined on pages 166–167.

Discipline Producers need to focus on the business end of a theatrical production, raising money to cover costs and making sure bills are all paid. A disciplined approach to finances will help keep the production afloat and make sure all necessary permissions are in place.

Creative Problem Solving How do I raise money for the show? How do I advertise the show? How do I fill the seats in the theatre so the show covers its expenses? All of these questions require the producer to develop and demonstrate creative problem solving.

The section that follows delves into the roles of director and producer in more detail.

The Director

Below are aspects of the director's work.

Choosing the Play There are several factors that guide the choice of a play. Some of these are artistic and some are practical.

- **Artistic Preference** The director may choose a play based on his or her passion for the specific play or playwright. The director may feel a period piece must be presented because only contemporary plays were done during the previous season. The director may want to explore the unique worlds of David Mamet or Maria Irene Fornes. The director might be committed to new works and may even hold a contest for new plays or select a new play from one of the many play development workshops across the country. Or, the director may simply choose a play because he or she has always wanted to direct it.

- **Box Office** The box office is a big and not always artistic factor in choosing a play. Even in educational theatre, filling the house can make a difference in the ongoing success of the program. Sometimes a theatre can support experimental or edgy work that brings in a smaller audience as long as they are willing to do one or two "box-office hits." Musicals and plays such as *West Side Story, The Odd Couple, Into the Woods, Oliver, A Christmas Carol, My Fair Lady, Camelot,* and many others are almost sure to fill the house.

- **Performance Space** The three main types of performance space are:

  1 **Proscenium** The proscenium is the classic theatre framed by the *proscenium arch*—the well-defined sides and top that border the front of the stage. Most proscenium stages have a main front curtain and then a playing area with *wings* (areas on the sides of the stage for the exit and entrance of actors and scenery). The proscenium stage establishes the "fourth wall" through which the audience watches the production.

  2 **Thrust** A thrust stage is any configuration in which the stage is built out so that the audience surrounds it on three sides.

  3 **Arena** Arena staging is theatre-in-the-round with the audience on all sides of the actors. This is the most intimate of theatre settings, but it presents obvious challenges to actors, the design team, and the director.

After analyzing a script, the producer and the director may decide that they want to present the play in the intimate space of an arena or thrust stage. On the other hand, when doing a production with a large cast and complex sets, they may opt for a full proscenium theatre.

Even when there is only one choice of space, it can sometimes be reconfigured. High schools with full proscenium stages may seat the audience on the stage in order to present theatre-in-the-round or three-quarter-round.

The choice of space may also be a financial one. If producing a big budget Broadway musical, the theatre must have enough seats to guarantee the income necessary to meet expenses.

The director may also choose a play based on the strengths of available talent. If he or she has a very strong African American actor who is ready for a large role, the director may choose to showcase that actor by doing *Othello.* If the director has a large number of very talented singers who are strong physical actors, he or she may decide on a show such as *Sweeney Todd* or *Candide.* If the company has its own rock band, the director might consider *Rent* or *Grease* with the band onstage during the performance.

The size of the cast is also a criterion. High school producers may need to use thirty to fifty people and so may have to choose a large musical or Shakespearean production. Most schools have more female actors than male, so a director might look for plays such as *Steel Magnolias* that feature strong female casts.

Developing the Artistic Vision As the director reads and analyzes a script, he or she begins to develop an aesthetic vision. Sometimes this is a concept, such as setting *Romeo and Juliet* during the Civil War. Sometimes the vision is more technical, such as doing *The Glass Menagerie* in the round with as few set pieces and props as possible.

Along with the artistic vision, the director must also consider functional aspects of the script, such as:

- What acting areas are required?
- How many different locations are needed?
- How many entrances and exits occur?
- What levels might be used for various settings?
- What special effects or technical needs are required?

The director shares his or her initial vision and set of requirements with the production team members and then listens to input from them. Their ideas will help to shape, fulfill, and even add to the director's vision. In subsequent design meetings, and during the rehearsal process, the designers for costumes, sets, makeup, and lights will bring in sketches, plots, models, and renderings and share them with the rest of the team.

Planning the Blocking and Stage Composition As a director works with the actors, he or she moves them around the stage forming stage "pictures," or arrangements. Stage pictures show the relative power and importance of the characters. Audience focus will always go to the actor in the strongest position. Center stage and downstage right are the most dominant positions. Movement and stage pictures are dictated by issues of appropriateness, feasibility, genre, and intent.

- **Appropriateness** Moving actors around merely for the sake of movement will read as unnatural and unrealistic. In fact, moving people around as a means of holding the audience's interest does just the opposite. The movement becomes diluted and unimportant. All movement should relate to the content of the scene and be appropriate to the motivation of and relationships among the characters.

- **Feasibility** Actors must not be asked to do something that makes them uncomfortable or puts them in danger. An elderly actor cannot suddenly spring across the room. An unskilled actor should not be asked to participate in stage combat or swordplay.

- **Genre** A director responds to genre and style when blocking movement patterns. Classical theatre may require adherence to a different set of rules than modern drama. Melodrama is often very stylized, comedy very broad, and drama very reserved. Sometimes the best movement is no movement at all.

- **Intent** What is the director trying to say with the movement and stage pictures he or she creates? How do these elements reflect relationships among characters as well as the mood and theme of the play?

The blocking developed by the director should be flexible. Actors bring to a production varying amounts of experience as well as their own character research and motivation. Often, after the initial blocking session, the actor may feel that his or her character would move in a manner other than the director has indicated. All such ideas should be explored. Although the final decision remains with the director, actors often provide new and interesting ways to block scenes based on their characters' motivations and impulses.

The Producer

In professional terms, a producer has both the best and worst of all possible jobs. The producer has the greatest possibility of realizing profit and recognition for artistic success as well as the greatest financial risk. Producers are often idea people who provide the backing and backbone for a production. Some are very hands-on, helping to decide which directors, designers, or actors to hire as well as choosing the play. A producer in high school theatre is often the drama teacher and occasionally a fine arts administrator or even the bookkeeper. The producer in a community or not-for-profit theatre setting is often the board of directors. In community theatre, if the production is profitable there will be money to fund the next production and perhaps increase production values as the theatre becomes more successful.

The producer is the money person in professional theatre, gathering the funding to get the show on its feet. Since theatre receives all money on the "back end" (revenue comes only after the production money has been spent), the producer is also the risk-taker. If the show should flop, the producer is the one left holding the bag. Everyone else gets paid for the work done. If the show makes a profit, so does the producer. The following people report to the producer:

The Business Manager The business manager in a high school production may be the school's treasurer or financial officer. In a small theatre, the producer often handles the business manager's duties, which include:

- Working with the producer and director to create a budget.
- Maintaining, updating, and reporting on the budget.
- Collecting and banking receipts.
- Making sure the play does not go over budget.
- Getting approval from the director or producer to go over budget.
- Authorizing and tracking expenses.
- Paying bills.
- Handling the payroll of contract labor and employees.
- Overseeing the box office.

The House Manager The house manager is responsible for the seating and comfort of the audience. He or she sees that the auditorium is a comfortable temperature, that the doors are open early for audience seating at each performance, and that programs are available for distribution. The house manager also supervises the ushers by helping them become familiar with the seating arrangements. Ushers hand out programs and escort audience members to their seats.

Publicity, Ticket, and Program Personnel Members of these crews design and procure printed materials such as posters, ads, and tickets; create advertising campaigns; sell paid advertising for programs; arrange for cast photos; write and place announcements about the show on the radio or in newspapers; distribute flyers; arrange for reviewers; sell tickets; and so forth.

The Production Team

One of the most critical jobs of the producer and director is to bring together an effective production team. In schools, this team may consist of both students and professionals. Students who have a considerable amount of technical experience can often be stage managers and, when given training and the benefit of experience, can even serve as costume or set designers.

Some or all of the following personnel may be part of the production team. Their roles will be discussed further in Parts Three through Eight of this handbook.

- **Choreographer** Plans and teaches all dance and stylized movement for a production.
- **Costume Designer** Designs, supervises, and/or builds the costumes.
- **Fight Choreographer** Plans fight and swordplay scenes and teaches fight techniques.
- **Music Director** If the production has live music, a musical director contacts, hires, trains, and conducts the musicians and works with the singers and sound designer.

- **Set Designer** Designs and supervises set construction and painting.
- **Sound Designer** Designs the sound-scape for the show, including sound effects and incidental music.
- **Stage Manager** The stage manager is the unsung hero in theatre. In a good production, the director and stage manager seek to be invisible, allowing the actors and ultimately the play to take center stage. The director technically finishes his or her job on opening night. From that point on, the stage manager is responsible for everything that happens, both on and off the stage. A partial list of the stage manager's duties includes:

- Attending all production meetings.
- Preparing the prompt book.
- Posting the auditions, callbacks, and casting notices.
- Assisting in the selection of crew members.
- Preparing the cast and crew contact sheets.
- Setting up, posting, and updating the rehearsal schedule.
- Marking the ground plan on the stage or rehearsal area floor.
- Keeping track of time during breaks.
- Coordinating all tech and dress rehearsals.
- Calling light, sound, and music cues during the show.

A stage manager usually highlights cues in the prompt book since they are his or her "lines" for running the show. A stage manager also usually writes in a "warn" or "ready" cue so that when calling the show, the lighting and sound operators can be alerted before the cue actually runs. For example, the stage manager would call

"Ready lights cue 1," "Ready sound cue 2," "Go cue 1," "Go cue 2," and so on. Sound cues and light cues are often written in different colors so that they are easy to spot.

A positive attitude from all members of the production team will create a positive attitude from the cast and crews serving under them.

The Prompt Book

The prompt book is the place where the director breaks the script down into units, names the units, indicates cues, and pre-plans the blocking. As blocking is given and/or changed and cues are added, the assistant director or stage manager keeps the book up to date. The prompt book should be easy to work with and functional for the duration of the rehearsal and production process. Usually, each page of the script is duplicated on three-hole-punched notebook paper. (The script should already have been paid for so there is no danger of copyright infringement.) In addition, some directors put a copy of the ground plan between each page of the script so that they can visualize the playing area and mark blocking and stage pictures.

The prompt book becomes the most comprehensive record of an individual production. When they are first produced, many plays contain few or no stage directions. In such cases, the prompt book notations become part of the manuscript when the play is published. Many directors and theatres keep copies of their prompt books in case they decide to repeat a production.

The Script

When choosing a script, it is important to consider what type of play you wish to live with as a producer or director. Producers generally choose plays based on box office receipts and profitability. Directors more often choose what appeals to them artistically. The best producer/director teams find a convergence of these two visions. When preparing to choose a script, the team must look at both genre and style. The team must also evaluate theatrical conventions of various cultural and historic periods to understand what would be involved in producing a play from a different cultural or historic period.

The Comedy Genre Comedy can be broken down into several categories. *Low comedy* is physical and exaggerated and includes burlesque and farce. *Middle comedy* relies more on situations and mental aerobics than on the physical. Romantic comedy and parody fall into this group. *High comedy* is intellectual in form, often mocking the upper classes. This group includes satire and comedy of manners.

The Dramatic Genre Drama includes the most classical form of Greek tragedy, but also refers to many other types of plays dealing with serious or realistic subjects, but not necessarily with the unhappy ending of tragedy. Drama can deal with social issues, family situations, or historical events. Categories include classic and Shakespearean tragedy, melodrama, psychological and social drama, and fantasy.

Experimental Style *Avant garde* or experimental theatre are catchall expressions that encompass whatever is current, new, and exciting in off-Broadway, off-off-Broadway, or street theatre. Once a style is accepted, it is no longer experimental.

Historical Style The style of a script can be defined in historical terms. Major historical styles include: *commedia dell'arte,* Elizabethan, Restoration, romanticism, realism, expressionism, theatre of the absurd, theatre of involvement, and transformational theatre.

Presentational Style When the "fourth wall" is broken and an actor speaks directly to the audience, the style is called *presentational.*

Representational Style Representational plays are those in which the actors seem unaware of an audience, The audience watches as though through a "fourth wall."

Post Production

This term has two different meanings. One is theatrical and the other is for film and video work.

In Theatre The show is over. Now what? You *strike*—which means all the company members help take apart and put away sets, props, costumes, etc., and return the theatre to a state of readiness for the next production. The stage manager runs the strike and is usually responsible for putting together a strike duty sheet that everyone follows. In professional companies, each group of workers has its own strike duties. Actors clean up their areas and return their props and costumes. Set crews take apart and store the set; costume crews clean and store the costumes; props crews return or put away props. In most nonprofessional theatres, strike involves everyone who participated in the production.

In Television and Film Post production has a completely different meaning in film and television. In these areas, post production is everything that happens to a film after the footage has been shot and the actors' work is over. Post production includes the following tasks:

- Edit and review the *dailies* and *rushes* (film from each day of shooting).
- Edit the video/film.
- Add sound effects and music.
- Add special effects.
- Create a rough cut for the director's approval.
- Add credits.
- Make and screen the final cut of the film.
- Distribute and promote the film.

Apply Your Expertise: Extension

You are the director of a play looking at scripts. Two that interest you especially are *The Emperor of the Moon,* a Restoration farce by Aphra Behn based on commedia dell'arte; and *The Chip Woman's Fortune,* by Harlem Renaissance playwright Willis Richardson. From a director's perspective, research and evaluate the theatrical conventions from the culture and period of these plays. Write up your evaluation and a statement about which play you would prefer to direct and why. Then repeat the evaluation, this time from the perspective of a producer. How would the choice of plays affect your ability to do your job as producer successfully? Write a separate statement evaluating the theatrical conventions of each and stating and explaining your preference as a producer.

Part Three Costumes

Apply Your Expertise

As in all other aspects of a theatrical production, participants involved in costumes should develop and demonstrate responsibility, artistic discipline, and creative problem solving as they apply their expertise. The information that follows, as well as the information in Chapter 23, provides specific ways to accomplish these goals.

Costume crew members also need to articulate and defend the importance of both leadership and collaboration skills. Modeling collaboration with other costume crew members is essential, as is working collaboratively with the whole production team as well as the actors, directors, and designers. Despite the importance of collaboration, however, leadership is still a desired quality, even in a crew member. Demonstrate and model leadership skills as you take the initiative in finding, buying, renting, and borrowing costumes, or in preventing accidents through safety reminders, or even in putting supplies back where they belong.

Define the standard vocabulary of costumes, including the terms below, in your role on the crew, using the terms regularly to demonstrate their proper use.

building	notions
costume parade	pinking shears
costume plot	silhouette
crinolines	swatches
modified authenticity	trim

Costume Crew

The size of the costume crew for a particular show varies based on the production values of the theatre and the scale of the play being produced. The crew works with the costume designer prior to production week and under the stage manager from that point on. Crew members assist with:

- Organizing available costumes.
- Measuring actors.
- Finding, buying, renting, and borrowing costumes.
- *Building* (making) costumes: sewing, painting, gluing, etc.
- Creating and updating the costume plot and acquisitions list.
- Fitting and altering costumes.
- Serving as "dressers" for actors or actresses who have fast changes.
- Washing, repairing, ironing, and maintaining costumes.
- Keeping the dressing rooms clean.
- Returning any borrowed items after the show closes.

The costume crew *call* (the time to be at the theatre) is usually fifteen minutes to one-half hour before the actor call. Some members of the crew may be able to leave once everyone is dressed, but other crew members will stay for the entire show in order to be available for any emergency sewing or repair. The crew also does a check at the end of each performance to determine laundry and repair needs.

Costume Design

Before working on a costume plan, the costume designer will analyze the play to answer the following questions:

- When does the play take place (period)?
- How many characters are there?
- Who are the characters?
- How are their clothes described?
- Are they rich? poor?
- Over what period of time does the play take place?
- Do characters need to change clothes?
- Are there any special needs, e.g., accommodating a body mic or including pockets, bows, or other things mentioned in the script?

At the first production meeting, the costume designer will listen to the producer and director's vision for the show. Next, the designer will create costume *renderings,* sketches of characters in costume that enable the team to visualize the designer's concept. *Swatches* (small pieces of fabric selected for the costume) often accompany renderings. With the director's approval, the designer begins to supervise the gathering and building of the costumes.

Costume Considerations
The creativity of costuming should follow some practical considerations in addition to the artistic concept for the play.

- **Action** What will the actor be doing in this costume: dancing, fighting, loving, falling, running?
- **Changeability** How easy is the costume to put on and take off, especially if the actor has fast changes, wears multiple costumes for different scenes, or plays multiple characters?
- **Comfort** Will the actor be able to work during the entire performance without worrying about the costume?
- **Durability** How well will the costume hold up? (Consider the fabric as well as the assembly.)
- **Historical Accuracy** Does the costume look as though it is truly from the play's historical period?
- **Coordinated Effect** How will all the costumes look with each other?

Costume Efficiency

- Look for ways to layer costumes. Does each change have to be full, or can a change be effected by adding or removing pieces of clothing?
- Plan for an actor's fast changes by having a member of the costume crew waiting in the wings to help.
- Use Velcro™ fasteners instead of buttons and snaps.
- Use reversible clothing. This is a quick way to create more than one look for the same actor.

Costume Plot

The costume designer will track all characters through the entire play, noting what each one will wear in any given scene as well as any changes the character might need to make. This costume plot allows the designer to make a clear list of all needed costumes. He or she then determines which are already available in the school or company's costume shop, which need to be borrowed, rented, or purchased, and which may be altered or built.

Decoration

Fabrics and trims can help create a period look. Gold braid, lace, velvet capes, "jeweled" clasps, leather or faux leather fabric, burlap, felt, and other specialty fabrics can transform a simple garment into anything from a peasant girl's dress to a Roman soldier's tunic and cape. Trims can be sewn on or applied with a hot glue gun. Some decorations are painted on with fabric paint or markers. Stenciling or sponging the material can create other effects.

"Distressing"

Often a costume needs to appear well worn, or *distressed*. Using sandpaper or a wire brush on the elbows, knees, collars, cuffs, and hems of the garment for this effect. Stretching clothing until it is baggy and out of shape also adds to the effect. Fabric can also be distressed by simply putting it on the ground and walking on it!

Dyeing

At one time or another, every costume department will find it necessary to dye fabric. Dyes such as Rit™ and Tintex™ are available in fabric stores, as well as grocery and discount department stores. For the deepest shades, you may have to use a unified aniline dye or a disperse dye available from theatrical supply houses. Costumes that need to be the same color should be dyed at the same time. Different batches seem to take to the dye in different ways. Wash all dyed material in cold water or have it dry-cleaned.

Measurements

The important measurements for women and men differ. You should create a standard measurement chart for both genders. Make and date charts for each actor and keep them on file. An actor who does a show two months later may not need a new chart. A year later, however, the actor might have different measurements. Although hair and eye color are not true "measurements," they are often helpful to the costumer in terms of matching costume color to a particular actor and should be added to the chart. Whenever possible, measurements should be taken by persons of the same sex as the actor— especially in school settings.

Patterns

When building costumes, it is often useful to begin with a commercial pattern. These are available in various sizes at any fabric store. Although some "period" patterns are available, you may have to adjust a contemporary pattern to achieve the look you need. Wedding dresses and formal wear often lend themselves to adaptation. Features such as sleeves, vest lengths, hemlines, and necklines can be modified to achieve the necessary silhouette.

Sewing

Sewing is simply a matter of creating a *seam*—which is a line of stitches that joins two or more pieces of fabric. It is necessary to leave some fabric free between the edge of the fabric and the seam—this is called the *seam allowance*—which is traditionally ⅝" wide. Whether stitching by hand or using a machine, use pins to hold the fabric in place while stitching along the seam allowance. To be an effective machine sewer, you have to learn to sew a straight line and keep a steady, medium speed to avoid fabric bunching up. Finish your seams by trimming the seam allowance with pinking shears to create a zigzag cut. This will keep the edges from fraying.

Wardrobe Room

Sometimes called a *costume room* or *costume shop*, the wardrobe room, depending on size, may be used for both the building and storage of costumes. A wardrobe room that is used for building costumes should have the following tools and supplies available:

- **Measuring Tools** Flexible measuring tape, sewing gauge for hems, measurement charts.
- **Marking Tools** Tracing paper and tracing wheel for moving markings from pattern to fabric; chalk for marking fabric during fittings.
- **Cutting Tools** Scissors and pinking shears.
- **Seam Ripper** For taking stitches out.
- **Long Cutting Table**
- **Fitting Equipment** Dress form or dressmaker's dummy.
- **Full-length Mirror**
- **Sewing Machine**
- **Steam Iron, Ironing Board, and Portable Steamer**
- **Storage Bins** For fabrics, scraps, accessories, patterns, and sewing notions.
- **Movable Clothes Rack**
- **Hot Glue Gun and Glue Sticks**
- **Notions** Needles, fasteners, thimbles, pins, snaps, hooks and eyes, Velcro™, buttons, etc.

Apply Your Expertise: Extension

1 Work with a partner. One of you is the manager of the costume crew. The other is a member of the costume crew who balks at the idea of a meeting with the costume designers, who want to discuss the overall plan for the costumes and the historical research behind them, because it seems unnecessary. As the manager, prepare some notes that might guide you in articulating and defending the importance of working collaboratively with all members of the production team. Enact your conversation in front of the class to model your articulation and defense of collaboration.

2 Switch roles. This time, a member of the crew has taken the initiative to find a fabric supplier that will give the school a discount. The costume crew manager wants to recognize the leadership skills demonstrated by this crew member. Prepare a conversation to model for the class demonstrating, articulating, and defending the importance of leadership skills.

3 In both conversations, demonstrate proper use of the standard vocabulary of costumes by using at least three words from the list on page 587. Define them ahead of time so you are sure of their meaning.

4 In your journal, explain ways in which a member of the costume crew can develop and demonstrate responsibility, artistic discipline, and creative problem solving. If you are on a costume crew, apply the explanation to your own work.

Part Four Lighting

Apply Your Expertise

Review Chapter 21 and the information in this section for ways to develop and demonstrate responsibility, artistic discipline, and creative problem solving as they apply to lighting.

As a technical crew member, you will be expected to use established theatre systems, such as the production calendar, tech rehearsal schedule, and production staff roles, to stay on top of progress. Pay attention to these systems and the documents that convey information about them so you can be a fully responsible technical crew member. Model effective communication through the use of such documents as the production calendar and light plot.

Being a responsible member of a technical team also requires demonstrating and modeling appropriate behavior at various types of live performances. The lighting operator, for example, should check equipment at call times to make sure everything is in good working order. The lighting crew helps the light board operator as needed during performance. Other responsibilities include keeping the control booth well organized and being on

hand to solve any problems that may come up during performance.

Before, during, and after performances, always use and model safe theatre practices to avoid injury with lighting equipment and electricity. Be sure the equipment is hung securely and that cables are not tripping hazards. Wear gloves to protect your hands from hot bulbs. Know the theory behind electricity so that you can safely connect cables and outlets.

As a member of a lighting crew, know the definitions of the standard vocabulary of lights, including the terms below, and use the terms regularly to demonstrate their proper use.

barn doors	gelatins
batten	gobo
border strips, or strip lights	roundels
dimmers	scoops
ERS (ellipsoidal reflector spotlight)	spill
floodlights	spotlights
followspots	tableau
Fresnel	

Color Effects

Besides its use for illumination, lighting provides design opportunities through the effect of color—including the gel color of the lights and the effects these have on objects being lighted. In addition, certain colors have an emotional effect on the audience. These colors have traditionally been associated with the following qualities:

- Yellow = joyful, youthful, cowardly
- Orange = exhilarating, lively, wealthy
- Red = bloody, passionate, angry, strong, warlike
- Pink = romantic, fantastic
- White = innocent, truthful, virginal, peaceful, pure
- Blue = calm, spiritual, formal, cold, depressing
- Purple = mystical, royal, mournful
- Soft Green = soothing, waterlike, tranquil
- Green = young, natural, springlike, jealous
- Gray = neutral, serious, cloudy, negative
- Brown = poor, earth-bound, peasantlike
- Black = tragic, deathly, somber, eerie

When beginning to plan a lighting design, it is important to know what happens when one color is placed over another. See page 328 of this text for an illustration of the effect of colored lights on a color wheel. While the lighting designer can work ahead of time with the set and costume designers to plan for effect, final adjustments cannot be made until tech rehearsals when the actors can be seen in costume and makeup under lights.

Light Crew

The light crew usually consists of the lighting designer, several technicians, one or more followspot operators (if necessary), and a dimmer board operator. The light crew:

- Maintains the lighting instruments.
- Hangs the instruments according to the plot.
- Gels and focuses the lighting instruments.
- Makes adjustments during technical rehearsals.
- *Strikes* (takes down) and stores the lights when the production closes.

Hanging and Focusing The light crew works under the supervision of the lighting designer to hang the lights according to the light plot. Lights are hung on the proper battens, which usually have different names. The battens are sometimes called *rails* and are numbered or labeled according to their position.

- **Balcony Rail** is a beam or batten at balcony level.
- **House Rail** #1 might be over the house, but closer to the stage than the balcony rail.
- **First Electric** is a rail or batten with plugs, usually found just behind the proscenium.
- **Second Electric** is the next upstage batten.
- **Third Electric** is further upstage.

Most electrical rails can be lowered for the initial hanging of the lights. Preliminary focus may be done at this time. Because it is difficult to focus lights exactly until they are in place, ladders are still used to focus the lights when the electrics are raised back up above the stage. Once all the lights are hung and focused and the lighting designer approves the look, the gels are inserted.

The lighting crew then works with the director, stage manager, and lighting designer to do a *dry tech* of the production. The dry tech is simply an opportunity to run through the show from one light cue to the next to make sure that all the cues are in order and that the lighting looks as good as possible without actors or costumes to illuminate. This is a troubleshooting rehearsal during which the lighting designer and director may choose to add or subtract cues.

Most theatres built or renovated after 1993 have computerized light boards. These make the world of lighting much easier. Each light that is plugged in is patched through the computer into a dimmer. Dimmers can then be combined and levels set to create specific looks for each cue. Once programmed, the intensity and duration of each cue can be changed with just the touch of a few buttons.

Older theatres may work from manual dimmers and a manual patch board. A manual patch board has a number for each lighting plug that corresponds to another numbered plug in the light booth which is then plugged into a specific dimmer. These dimmer controls can then be combined on submasters (several of the dimmers put together) and brought up and down (raised and lowered in intensity).

Really old theatres may simply have a way to bring the lights up and down. The potential level of sophistication in your lighting plot will be directly proportional to the quality of the lighting system your school or theatre can provide.

Running the Show A running crew will usually consist of a lightboard operator, one or two followspot operators, a backstage lighting operator or, if necessary, a specials operator. *Specials* are windows, sunlight, lamps, special effects moments, or emphasis lighting.

Followspots are used more frequently in musicals than in any other form of theatre. Usually one followspot is enough to accentuate a singer during a solo. A second followspot is sometimes used to bathe the singer in light or to light two singers during a duet. Most followspots have color wheels so that they can illuminate the singers in a variety of colors that enhance costume, mood, and setting.

Homemade Lights
A drama department on a limited budget can make adequate spotlights for mounting on a teaser batten. Purchase 150-watt PAR-38 spots and screw them into clamp-on swivel sockets that can be mounted on a batten. (To be safe, use wire as well as clamps to attach the spots to the batten.) By using swivel sockets, you can adjust the lamps to any angle. Reflector spots are available in several colors, or you can use a clear lamp and attach spring tension

holders that house special glass color filters. For greater color diversity, buy clear lamps and make frames for holding gelatin or plastic. Cut each frame from a large tin can or from sheet aluminum available at the lumberyard or at a metal shop. Fold the frame double, place the gelatin between the frames, and close them with brads at the top. Then wire the frame to the socket with a coat hanger or other heavy-duty wire, allowing space for ventilation between the lamp and the gel. Without such ventilation, the heat will burn or melt the gelatin.

Portable Lighting Systems Many rock bands use small portable lighting systems consisting of PARs mounted on a folding light stand. Most theatrical lighting companies make the stands, or "trees," for such lights and also sell small dimmer packs. These packs can either be plugged directly into a wall outlet or the lights themselves can be plugged in and then controlled from the dimmer board with microphone-type cable. A lighting system such as this usually consists of four lights per tree and most school "gymnatoriums" and multipurpose rooms can support two such trees. These lights can be gelled to provide color.

Lighting Design

The lighting designer must prepare for a production in the same way every other member of the production design team does—by first analyzing the script. The lighting designer looks for answers to the following questions:

- What scenes happen at night? during the day?
- What sources of light are mentioned (lamps, windows, etc.)?
- What sort of day is it? rainy? sunny? foggy? stormy?
- What season is it?
- What is the theme of the play?
- How does the mood change throughout the play?
- What areas must be well-lighted?

After hearing from the director and the other designers, the lighting designer will have new elements to consider:

- What "specials" are needed? (As you know, specials are specific lights used for monologues or to accentuate a certain speech or action. In *Macbeth*, the lighting of the dagger that hangs in midair is an example of a special.)
- What color choices have been made by the director, costumer, and/or set designer, and how may lights accentuate or contrast with those choices?

The Lighting Plan With input from the script, the director, and the other designers, the lighting designer develops a basic lighting plan. The plan shows which instruments will light specific parts of the stage. Each area should be covered by a minimum of two instruments, one from each side. Usually these are a contrast of warm and cool colors to provide depth. A third light can provide a front wash or fill in a color designed to give emotional power to the scene.

As a rule of thumb, lighting designers break the proscenium stage into six areas that must be lighted: upstage left, center, and right and downstage left, center, and right. Lighting instruments are then assigned to these areas. Additional instruments may be added to provide sidelighting, backlighting, color, and additional wash. After these playing areas have been covered, the lighting designer adds instruments to cover the specials. The complete lighting plan is shown visually in a diagram called the *light plot*, which is illustrated on page 274 of this text.

The Hanging Plot This is the compilation of the lighting plot with the instrument list. It provides an organized method of showing which instrument has to go to which position and be placed into which specific circuit or dimmer. The hanging plot is used by the light crew to hang, focus, and gel the lights for the production.

Apply Your Expertise: Extension

After you have been assigned to the lighting crew, use all the established theatre systems, such as the production and tech rehearsal schedules, to stay on track. Analyze the production plans to learn about the blocking, technical designs, general rehearsal schedules, and the research into the play's historical and cultural setting. Get to know the light plot and hanging plot inside and out, so you can always be ready with each cue. In your journal, write a reflection after analyzing the plans to set your mind for the work ahead. Then, after each rehearsal or even private practice/preparation session, use your theatre journal to evaluate how well you applied

your lighting crew expertise. Use the evaluation questions below. Define the vocabulary terms associated with lighting and demonstrate their proper use by using at least five of them in your regular self-evaluations.

Lighting Crew Self-Evaluation
Responsibility In what ways did I develop and demonstrate responsibility in today's session? How can I improve on my responsibility?
Artistic Discipline In what ways did I develop and demonstrate artistic discipline? How well did I model effective communication between designers and directors by using the light plot and other technical theatre documents?
Creative Problem Solving How effectively did I develop and demonstrate creative problem solving in today's work? What techniques did I use?
Appropriate Behavior How did I demonstrate appropriate behavior for a technical crew member at rehearsals and performances?
Safe Theatre Practices How did I use and model safe theatre practices in: • hanging and focusing lights? • dealing with electricity? • protecting my hands from heat?

Part Five Makeup

Apply Your Expertise

Review Chapter 24 and the information in this section for ways to develop and demonstrate responsibility, artistic discipline, and creative problem solving as they apply to makeup.

Like other technical crew members, you will be expected to use established theatre systems, such as the production calendar, tech rehearsal schedule, and production staff roles, to be ready to do your job well. Apply and model appropriate behavior at various types of live performances by helping with makeup or hairstyle/wig changes for actors and any unexpected problems that may arise. Other responsibilities include keeping the makeup area well organized.

Expand your expertise by seeking out opportunities where you can use makeup in a variety of theatrical styles and genres. Learn the various makeup styles that go with different types of shows.

As a member of a makeup crew, know the definitions of the standard vocabulary of props, including the terms below, and use the terms regularly to demonstrate their proper use.

acetone	makeup morgue
cake makeup	putty wax
character makeup	spirit gum
collodion	stippling
complementary colors	straight makeup
creme foundation	water-soluble foundation
crepe hair	

The Makeup Crew

This crew will vary in size depending on the production. For a simple, realistic play, the crew could consist of one or two crew members whose duties will include:

- Ordering, buying, or otherwise supplying all nonpersonal makeup and special effects items (such as crepe hair, nose putty, and spirit gum).
- Setting up the makeup room in advance of makeup call.
- Making sure that all actors have their makeup charts and/or sketches.
- Assisting actors with makeup.
- Cleaning up the makeup area.
- Performing emergency re-application of makeup during the production.
- Striking and restocking makeup at the end of the production.

Makeup Design

The bigger the budget of the theatre, the more likely it is that there will be a makeup designer. Makeup is an intensely personal thing, however, and should be learned by the actor, who is usually expected to be able to do simple "street" makeup. Actors are also expected to provide their own basic makeup kit.

Like other members of the production team, makeup designers begin with an analysis of the script, looking for the theme of the play as well as the following:

- How many characters are there?
- When does the play take place?
- What style of makeup was prevalent during this time period?
- How old are the characters?
- What special features or attributes are mentioned in the script? (e.g., age, scars, coloration, significant features)

Character Makeup Sketches At the first production meeting, the makeup designer will listen to the director's overall production vision and will then begin to work on a plot for each character based on the expectations of the director and the requirements of the script. The designer may decide to sketch out how some characters should look. This is especially important if there are clowns, elves, or other fantastical characters.

Unusual Makeup Designs In fantasy productions such as *The Wiz, Cats,* or *The Lion King* and in many children's theatre productions, it is essential to create a sketch and a plan for animal or creature makeup. These designs can be suggestive or realistic. Suggestive makeup might include feathers, mop heads, fake teeth, and so on. Realistic makeup can be created using crepe hair, latex, and a life mask of the actor's face.

Life Masks A life mask can be made from plaster bandage strips one-inch wide and six to eight inches long. Apply petroleum jelly to the actor's face, then put the bandages on one at a time. Leave breathing holes and cover the eyes with waxed paper. When two to three layers have covered the face, use a blow dryer for fifteen to twenty minutes to set the mask. Remove the mask and allow it to dry.

Apply Your Expertise: Extension

After each rehearsal, use your theatre journal to evaluate how well you applied your makeup crew expertise. Use the evaluation questions below. Define the vocabulary terms associated with makeup and demonstrate their proper use by using at least five of them in your regular self-evaluations.

Makeup Crew Self-Evaluation
Responsibility In what ways did I develop and demonstrate responsibility in today's work? How can I improve on my responsibility?
Artistic Discipline In what ways did I develop and demonstrate artistic discipline? How artfully did I apply makeup or style hair?
Creative Problem Solving How effectively did I develop and demonstrate creative problem solving in today's work? What am I most proud of?
Appropriate Behavior How did I demonstrate appropriate behavior for a technical crew member at rehearsals and performances?
Other Styles and Genres What opportunities did I take to use makeup in other theatrical styles and genres? What other opportunities would help me stretch my makeup skills?

Part Six Props

Apply Your Expertise

Review Chapter 25 and the information in this section for ways to develop and demonstrate responsibility, artistic discipline, and creative problem solving as they apply to props.

Safety is a very important concern for the props crew, especially when you are making props. Be sure everyone on the props construction crew is familiar with the safety rules for the shop. Always model safe and effective use of tools and materials involved in props construction. Review the safety precautions in Chapter 20 on Set Construction and in Chapter 25, Props, on page 339 and make them part of your routine.

As a member of a props crew, know the definitions of the standard vocabulary of props, including the terms below, and use the terms regularly to demonstrate their proper use.

decorative props	pull
hand props	set dressing
prop plot	set props
props master	

Prop is an abbreviation of the word *property*. A prop is the "property" of the actor. As such, directors will often say that every actor is responsible for making sure his or her props are available when going on stage. However, props are ultimately the responsibility of a props master, or if the theatre is small, the set designer with help from the stage manager. Props are most closely related to set design, as they are part of the visual aspect of the play.

Consumable Props such as food items must be handled carefully. Remember to consider what actors have to do or say after eating or drinking a certain prop. If their mouths are filled with something dry, there must be water available on stage as well. Make sure whatever you prepare is fresh and kept covered and sanitary. Avoid using something for a prop that will tempt cast or crew members to help themselves. Instead, try to find items that are not particularly desirable but still achieve the effect and look you need.

Making or Finding Props Although it is always preferable to use the real thing, most theatre budgets don't allow the purchase of antiques or even replicas of certain items. The props master's job is to create, borrow, purchase, or otherwise dress the set and provide the actors with working and then final props. Many things can be made quite easily from wood, carved Styrofoam covered with plaster, or papier-mâché. The set crew and set designer can help with particularly difficult or large props to make sure they are in the same style as the set.

The Props Crew Again, depending on the scope of the show and the number of students/actors/volunteers involved, the props crew can be just the props master (who may also be the stage manager), or a complete crew. In small productions, props may be handled by the stage crew under the direction of the stage manager. Along with making or procuring props, the props crew is responsible for:

- Setting up the props table.
- Checking the prop list before and after every scene, act, and performance.
- Re-supplying and making consumable props for each show.
- Assisting the actors with finding props and returning them to the table.
- Striking the props at the end of the production and returning those that were borrowed.

The Prop Table is one of the most important backstage locations. Set up and designed by the props master and/or stage manager, the table will often have a location outlined and labeled for each prop. Actors are responsible for picking up their props from the table before making an entrance and returning them to the table if they exit the stage with a prop.

Apply Your Expertise: Extension

After each rehearsal, use your theatre journal to evaluate how well you applied your props crew expertise. Use the evaluation questions below. Define the vocabulary terms associated with props and demonstrate their proper use by using at least five of them in your regular self-evaluations.

Props Crew Self-Evaluation
Responsibility In what ways did I develop and demonstrate responsibility in today's work? How can I improve on my responsibility?
Artistic Discipline In what ways did I develop and demonstrate artistic discipline? How did I artfully design, make, repair, or manage props?
Creative Problem Solving How effectively did I develop and demonstrate creative problem solving in today's work? What am I most proud of?
Appropriate Behavior How did I demonstrate appropriate behavior for a technical crew member at rehearsals and performances?
Safety Did I model safe and effective use of tools and materials in property construction?

Part
Seven Sets

Apply Your Expertise

If you are working on **set design** for a school production, chances are your talents and creativity thrive in the visual arts. Though obviously part of the art of theatre, set design is an art form unto itself. As you work on set design, apply the design and technical elements of theatre *as an art form* to create the most effective and expressive sets and scenery. To fully appreciate the artistry of scenic design, defend set design—and, for that matter, any of the technical aspects of theatre—as an art form in your mind, noting all the ways in which it qualifies as an art. With this clear framework in mind, you will give your work the artistic discipline it requires and deserves.

As a scenic designer, model creativity as it relates to your personal expression in technical theatre and design. Evaluate yourself as a creative being so you know where your strengths are and how you can best put them to use in your set design. Also evaluate your results. Stand back from your design and construction work and offer yourself constructive criticism of it. Re-imagine and revise your design choices during rehearsal as needed to support the story and emotional impact of the play.

At the same time, recognize that collaboration will make your work better. Ask for feedback from peers on your design and construction projects, analyze and compare artistic choices based on your experiences in theatre, and accept constructive criticism

from them. In the same spirit, offer constructive criticism to your peers on their designs and construction projects. In the course of evaluating your design work or having it evaluated by others, be prepared to defend the historical or cultural accuracy built into your design. In order to defend it, do the necessary research and make your design as accurate as possible in its reflection of the historical and cultural period it portrays. Through research, identify the technical elements in the various styles and genres of the plays you are working on, recognize the function of those elements, and use those elements in your design. (See page 238.)

Although primarily an artist, a scenic designer needs to wear other hats as well. As a set designer, you will need to serve as a conduit between the director and the production team. Model communication methods with the various directors, making full use of the prompt book and the light, costume, and props plot to be sure everyone is working toward the same goal. Work collaboratively with the production team, including the crew members and stage manager, but also be able to manage them as needed to keep the play and the director's vision on track.

As in all other theatrical roles, develop and demonstrate your responsibility, artistic discipline, and creative problem solving.

Growing as a Set Designer

Responsibility Understand and fulfill your responsibilities to the director and the production team.

Artistic Discipline Do your research carefully and apply the principles of design and composition artfully.

Creative Problem Solving Look at challenges as an opportunity to stretch your creativity and your collaboration skills.

If you are working on the **set construction crew,** be able to articulate the importance of both collaboration and leadership, and strive to be models of both. Offer and receive constructive feedback on your construction projects, and evaluate your own projects with constructive criticism as well.

Safety is of special importance in your field. Review the safety tips, precautions, and guidelines in Chapter 20 and make them part of your working routine. Always:

- Model the **safe and effective use of tools** in scenery construction. Your model will help protect both your own safety and the safety of other crew (and cast) members.

- Model the **safe and effective use of materials** in scenery construction. Know the materials with which you are working and any special considerations associated with them. For painting, for example, follow all guidelines on proper ventilation so fumes do not become hazardous.

- Use **safe theatre practices**, such as personal safety, fire safety, tool safety, shop safety, and handling emergencies in the theatre, and be a model for others in how you employ these practices.

At appropriate times, and no matter what field of technical theatre is your specialty, compile materials for your **portfolio**. Take photographs of your work. For example, photograph the sturdily constructed platform you helped build, or the elegantly painted impressionistic landscape you helped create. Use your **résumé** and portfolio to help open doors for future work in set construction.

Review and define the standard vocabulary terms of scenery on pages 230 and 246 and use them regularly in your role on the set design or construction team.

As always, keep working to improve responsibility, artistic discipline, and creative problem solving.

Growing in Set Construction

Responsibility Know your duties to the set designer and the rest of the construction crew. Make safety your number one priority.

Artistic Discipline Take the time to do things right. Measure carefully and accurately, making sure you are always true to scale. Hone your construction skills; work on artistry in your painting techniques.

Creative Problem Solving Look at challenges as an opportunity to stretch your creativity and your collaboration skills.

Design

Pre-planning Before the process of design begins, there are several things the set designer must consider. These have to do more with the facility than with artistic considerations. Necessary information includes:

- **Aprons, Fly Loft, and Wings** Where is the storage area for what you build? Is there room to take scenery off and on the stage? Is there tracking? Is there fly space? Is it a full fly? Can you fly your scenery in and out? Is the system manual or automatic? Will the fly system make any noise when it operates?

- **Equipment** What does the theatre have in terms of construction equipment and supplies for building? How many pre-existing flats, drops, and scrims are there? What are the heights and widths of the flats? Is there a permanent cyclorama, or cyc, curtain?

- **The Shop** How big is the shop? When is it available? When can you work? What other shows are being built? What tools are there and are they all fully operational?

- **The Stage** Is there a revolving stage floor? Are there trapdoors? Are there pre-constructed permanent steps, ramps, thrusts, pits, or rakes that you must work around?

The answers to these questions help the designer prepare a plan and budget for the set. If existing equipment can be used, money will be saved, and perhaps spent instead on an interesting design choice that will further the artistry of the production.

Script Analysis The set designer will analyze the play for several specifics before beginning to map out a design. These include:

- What is the director's artistic vision for the play?
- What locations does the play call for?
- When does the play take place?

Design Principles Keeping all these things in mind and based on the pre-design planning, apply the following principles of design to your plans:

- **Line** Lines in columns, costume, draperies, and positioning or height of flats have a psychological and emotional effect on the audience. General principles of line include:

  Crooked lines = chaos, pain, conflict

  Curves and angles = intensity, danger, excitement

  Curved lines = wealth, expanse, comfort

  Diagonal lines = force, strife, conflict, or discord

  Horizontal lines = stability, calmness, peace

  Long vertical lines = dignity, hope, spirituality

- **Shape** This is the outline provided by the set. The background can appear circular, triangular, pointed, or linear in order to create a sense of realism, impressionism, or expressionism as fits the genre of the play.

- **Mass** Bulk and weight have a profound effect. Both can bring the play closer to audience members, making them feel closed in.

- **Measure** Measure is another word for size, the length, width, and height of something. It relates to the composition principle of proportion (see below), since size on stage is always relative.

- **Position** The placement of elements will determine where the audience focus is directed and what is emphasized.

- **Color** The use of light and pigment has an enormous effect on the tone of a set; be sure the colors you choose reflect the mood of the work and offer insights into the play and the characters.

- **Texture** What surface qualities best portray your central ideas for a set? If the feel of the set is cold and distant, glossy surfaces might help reflect that. If the feel is warm and inviting, you may want to use softer textures.

Also apply the following principles of composition to your set design.

- **Unity** Although all the parts are separate, a set should have unity, a oneness and cohesion.

- **Harmony** Create a harmonious set, one in which the separate parts are artfully arranged.

- **Contrast** Use contrast—the highlighting of differences—to illuminate aspects of the time and place of the play and even the characters.

- **Variation** Strive for enough variety so that the set does not appear monotonous

- **Balance** There will be a focal point to the design, called the central axis, usually slightly off center. This can be the highest or lowest point on stage, the bulkiest or sparsest point of the set. This focal point will be balanced by the director's choice of how to populate the stage and space the actors. Actors effectively become part of the stage picture. There must be some balance from one side of the stage to the other. A large double door stage right might be balanced by a large chest of drawers or a stairway stage left. If everything is on one side of the stage, it "tips the boat." Most sets, however, exercise some asymmetrical or informal balance rather than perfect symmetry. (The exception is extreme stylization.)

- **Proportion** The set will appear realistic if all elements are scaled to a six-foot-tall person. Nonrealistic sets can have people overshadowed by high peaks, tall buildings, or, when the person is more important than the background, placed in abstract settings such as pipe grids.

- **Emphasis** Where is your center of attention? Be aware of the design elements that draw a viewer's eye; be sure you control where the emphasis will be.

Final Design When the design concept is complete, the designer will create *renderings* (drawings) and a three-dimensional model of the set. Once this is accepted by the director, the designer puts together the working drawings so that the construction and stage crews can begin to build the sets. The stage manager often has input into the practicality of these working drawings and renderings.

The Crew

The stage crew works directly for the stage manager and may be responsible for:

- Building and painting scenery.
- Making and painting props.
- Organizing props with the props crew.
- Erecting and bracing scenery.
- Shifting, flying, or rolling scenery in and out during the production.
- Placing props and setting the stage between acts and scenes.
- Operating special effects such as smoke machines, flash pots, trapdoors, revolving stages, etc.
- Re-setting all scenery at the end of the performance.
- Sweeping the stage and backstage areas.

The stage crew customarily dresses in all black so that they will not be noticed when they change scenery in minimal lights or blackouts. The stage crew, along with the stage manager, forms the backbone of successful theatre production.

Set Construction

Sets consist not only of backdrops and flats, but also things such as ramps, platforms, boxes, and stairs. Muslin or canvas flats are still sometimes used, but many theatres have shifted to lightweight lauan or plywood. However the set is created, it must be safe and stable as well as functional and visually interesting.

Constructing Flats Sets are often built in pieces and then assembled on the set. They can be moved into place by stagehands who either lift one edge up and then tilt it into place or who "walk" the flat up by having one crew member place a foot against the bottom while another lifts the top and slowly walks it into place. Flats can also be flown into place by lifting them up on a flyline, swinging them to where they need to be, and lowering them into position. This method is called *floating* and is the most time-consuming but easiest on the stagehands.

Joining and Bracing Flats Once in place, flats can be joined by either lashing them together using cleat hooks and rope, or hinging them. Using loose pin hinges will allow for easy removal, especially if the set is designed for touring or repeat usage. When the flats are all in place, *dutchman* (muslin strips dipped in sizing) is applied to cover the seams. If flats are perfectly matched, a strip of masking tape can be substituted. For plywood or lauan flats, a small amount of wood putty, caulking, or sheetrock mud can cover the seams.

Flats are kept upright with stage braces. Commercial, adjustable stage braces can be used that are anchored to the floor with screws. If there are restrictions against nails or screws, you can build a plywood floor plate with a rubber adhesive bottom and then attach the stage brace to that. Such a plate should be weighted with stage weights in order to make it sturdy and slip-proof. You can also use a simple triangular wooden bracing, called a *jack*. This brace consists of three pieces of wood that form a triangle: one going up the back of the flat, one extending out at a right angle from the bottom of the flat, and a third on an angle connecting the first two. The jack should also be weighted with sandbags, or stage weights, or screwed into the floor with a foot iron.

Changing the Set Sets can be constructed in ways to make set changes go smoothly. Here are three useful methods:

- **Revolves** You must have a stage with a large, built-in revolve or build a round platform that will serve as a revolve. The revolve allows you to build up to three "looks" that can be revealed as the set is turned mechanically or by hand. Revolves give a very distinct and dramatic look, especially if the change occurs as an actor walks "into a scene."

- **Wagons** Platforms on wheels, from 4' x 8' to 8' x 16', can be preset in the wings, depending on available wing space. Called *wagons,* they can be furnished or "dressed" backstage during a prior scene. The same wagon can be used for multiple locations depending on what furniture, props, or flats are set on it and what scenic units may be flown in to join the wagon once it is in place. Many high-tech theatres have hydraulic wagons that can roll sets in from all sides as well as the back of the stage.

- **Jackknifing** This involves either two wagons on either side of the stage or simply braced scenery on sliders that are easy to move. One scene is simply pivoted out from right or left as the other scene is pivoted into place. When the scenery is in place, it is flush with the proscenium. When it is out of the way, it rests flat against the stage right or stage left side of backstage. The full set is pivoted so the previous set cannot be seen. This is best done in a blackout or when the main curtain is down as it is not as smooth a transition

Set Painting

Base Coat All flats need a primer and a base coat of color. With some careful planning, you can change the color of the base coat to match the details of the set. For example, blue paint might be used where windows will be created, a brick-red color could be used for the fireplace, and beige for the rest of walls.

Kinds of Paint There are several types of paint that make scenic painting easy, including:

1 **Casein paints** These are used for professional scenery and will hold up outdoors or in dampness.

2 **Latex paint** This covers well, cleans up easily, and is cheap and readily available. Painting with latex on muslin may reduce the life of the flat as the paint tends to crack as the cloth absorbs it.

3 **Vinyl- and acrylic-based scenic paints** These have pure colors and strong durability.

Texturing A painted set can look far more interesting if you use one of the following methods of texturing to add depth and dimension:

- **Dry brushing** Use a dry brush lightly coated with paint. Move it quickly back and forth. Change colors and do the same in a different direction.

- **Feather dusting** This quick-texturing technique involves dipping an inexpensive feather duster into paint, brushing off the excess, and pressing the duster against the flat. Turn the duster gently and you will get a different pattern each time it moves. This effect can look like leaves or brush.

- **Rag rolling** A rag or rolled-up piece of frayed burlap dipped in paint can be rolled over the base coat in order to make it look like plaster.

- **Spattering** Use two or more colors, one lighter and the other a shade darker than the base. Fill the brush with paint and remove the excess. Stand a short distance from the flat and strike the brush handle with a hand, a board, or other surface so that the paint spatters onto the flat. Spattering may take some practice.

- **Stippling** This is done using a sponge or crumpled rag pressed against the base coat. Stippling should create a random pattern—do not make it look uniform.

Production Design

Each production has its own look or style. The production design is a composite of the visions of the producer, the director, and all the principal designers. The best production designs are based on these four qualities:

1 **Informative** Lets us know something about the piece, such as time and place.

2 **Expressive** Shows us something about the theme and mood of the play.

3 **Appropriate** Fits the world of the play, based on elements taken from the play.

4 **Usable** The set must have levels and be flexible and dramatically dynamic.

Technical Considerations for Three Types of Theatre Spaces

	Scenery	Lights	Sound	Makeup
Proscenium	Has the most options—sets can be flown in, rolled in from sides, turned, and set while mid-drop is down. This is most flexible for large sets and period shows.	Front lights (side possible). Easy to accomplish. The audience is never "in the light." Flexible.	Audience is at a distance, so sound must be clear. Floor or hanging mics often used. Need monitors. Most difficult to create sound in this space.	Most difficult because of space between actor and audience. All effects must read from a distance, but not seem unrealistic close up.
Thrust	Backdrops are possible, but most set pieces must be low because sightlines become a problem. Actors may be blocked by sets.	Light is from front. Side light is more difficult. Must be careful not to shine light on audience. Can do effects on back wall.	Actors are easier to amplify, closer to audience. Orchestra can be a problem; no pit. Floor mics helpful. Monitors helpful.	Less makeup needed, as audience is closer (except for special makeup).
Arena	Most difficult, but very freeing. No drops. Unit sets work best; must be small because of sightlines. Everything must be brought on in full view of audience.	Most difficult to light, but light is important to delineate areas. Lights from above and sides. Must be careful not to shine light in eyes of audience.	In a smaller theatre, less amplification is needed. Speakers can "surround" the audience for effect, or sound can come from above.	Little makeup needed, as audience is so close (with the exception of special makeup).

The production design can also be concept-driven, for example, setting *Romeo and Juliet* during the Civil War with the Montagues as a rich Southern family and the Capulets as a poorer family from the North. This concept begins to rule all aspects of the production. During meetings, the production team may make variations on the original design, perhaps deciding to do costumes in traditional antebellum period style but setting all the action in the middle of a battlefield, representing the war that separates the two families. The production design is an element that emphasizes theatre as a collaborative art form. The set in this case still remains informative, expressive, appropriate, and usable.

Apply Your Expertise: Extension

Serve on a set crew for a school or community theatre production. Review the safety information in Chapter 20, and as a set crew member always use safe theatre practices in matters of personal safety, fire safety, tool safety, shop safety, and handling emergencies in the theatre. After your experience, use the evaluation questions below. Define the vocabulary terms associated with scenery and demonstrate their proper use by using at least five of them in your reflection.

Evaluation Questions for the Set Crew

1. What examples show how I modeled safe and effective use of tools?

2. What examples show how I modeled safe and effective use of materials?

3. Overall, what safe theatre practices, such as those related to fire safety and emergencies, did I use and model?

Evaluation Questions for Set Designers

1. How well did I serve as a model in creativity? in communication with directors?

2. How did I evaluate myself as a creative being and apply that evaluation to my set design?

3. Did I offer and receive constructive criticism to and from my peers? What did I learn from these exchanges?

4. Did I offer constructive criticism to myself after gaining some distance on my work?

5. How well did I apply design and technical elements as an art form, using the principles of design and composition?

6. How would I defend my design as an art form if someone questioned me about that?

7. How well can I defend the historical and cultural accuracy of my design?

8. Did I manage the production team well and at the same time work collaboratively with them?

9. How did I identify the technical elements of various styles and genres, recognize their function, and use them in my designs?

Questions for Both Designers and Crew

1. Did I compile materials for a technical theatre portfolio and résumé and then use them to look for other opportunities?

2. In what areas can I expand my experience to increase future opportunities?

Part
Eight Sound

Apply Your Expertise

If you are working on a **sound team** for a school production—whether as sound designer or crew member—your talents probably include a knack for working with technology as well as an interest in music. Value your creativity, and model it in relation to your personal expression in technical theatre. The more you model creativity, the more others around you will tap into their own creativity.

Growing as a Sound Crew Member
Responsibility Analyze, apply, and model appropriate behavior for a sound crew during performances, always paying attention.
Artistic Discipline Open your mind to creative possibilities and record and collect your sound effects and music artfully.
Creative Problem Solving Review the creative solutions for sound challenges that technicians found long before technology to help you think of new possibilities.

As a member of a sound crew, know the definitions of the standard vocabulary of sound including the terms below, and use the terms regularly to demonstrate their proper use.

acoustics	equalizer
amplifier	public domain
body mic, or lavalier mic	sound board, console, or mixer
CD-R (compact disc, recordable)	transmitter
digital audio software	

Sound Crew

The head of the sound crew usually runs the cues called by the stage manager. There may be more than one crew member if the sound is coming from multiple sources. The microphone mixer or board operator hooks up the wireless mics, sets the floor mics, and makes sure that they all have batteries and are turned on and off at the appropriate moments.

Guidelines

1 Be sure that the sound operator is in the house where the balance can actually be heard. Placing a sound operator in a booth with glass doors and expecting him or her to adjust sound based on what is heard through a headset is a recipe for disaster.

2 Replace the batteries in all cordless microphones every night. Make sure the actors know how to turn their microphones off and on and that they keep them on during the show so that all control is done by the soundboard operator.

3 Never leave a wireless microphone turned up after an actor leaves the stage.

4 Make sure there are monitors for musical productions. Singers may be off-key if they cannot hear each other or the orchestra accompaniment.

5 Balance live music with the amplified voices. Orchestras in contemporary musicals are often slightly amplified so that the sound can be balanced and equalized between voices and instruments.

6 Don't touch the equalizers. These should not be used to increase amplification. The professionals who installed the equipment or who are hired to set up the sound design for a show will adjust the equalizers, which should then be left at those levels unless there is a serious problem with either feedback or highs and lows.

7 Every performance will be unique. The sound operator must be aware of where laugh lines are and how the audience might react. The operator should also watch carefully because actors may unexpectedly change positions and deliver their lines at different places on stage relative to fixed hanging or floor microphones. The sound operator's job is to follow the action with the microphone levels.

8 Make sure a sound check is done every night. Each actor should do a few lines and all microphones should be tested.

9 Sound operators must play the mics like musical instruments. They should know when a performer is going to enter, speak, and leave. The sound operator should not be afraid to speak with actors about correcting anything that affects sound quality.

10 When touring, or even in an auditorium where additional sound is used, be sure to tape cords and cables down with gaffer's tape.

Sound Design

Like all other designers, the sound designer does an analysis of the play for meaning as well as needed sound effects and then begins to develop a *soundscape* for the production. The sound designer will attend the initial production meeting and amend the original concept to fit the overall production design. At the next production meeting, the sound designer should have examples of music choices and important sound effects as well as a chart of microphone placement and wireless microphone usage.

Soundscape A soundscape is the "color palette" of the sound designer. It contains his or her interpretation of the overall feel of the production design. For example, in a recent production of *Frankenstein,* the powerful soundscape consisted of a combination of odd and organic laboratory sounds and industrial 1980s music between scenes. The soundscape for *The Robber Bridegroom* might consist of bluegrass music with a few electronically altered versions of the same pieces threaded throughout the show.

Sound Recording and Construction

The sound crew gathers the sounds to be used in the play and puts them together in a logical and simple playback method. Occasional sounds like the crashing or breaking of glass can be constructed, but most of these sounds are available either on recordings or on many sound effects sources on the Internet. Today's digital technology makes it easy to compile sounds and use digital editing to create a CD or even a playlist that will have all the cues lined up one after the other so that sound operation is done by push-button control. Digital editing is so precise that the simplest changes can be made in tempo, pitch, and volume and a new sound file or CD burned or made quickly from one rehearsal to the next. If your school or theatre does not have such technology, you can usually find a student or professional who has the necessary equipment and will be willing to help create a sound score for your production.

Analyzing Appropriate Behavior of Technical Staff

The guidelines on pages 608–609 include some directives for appropriate behavior for the sound crew. No matter what technical crew you are on, take time to analyze and apply appropriate behavior for technical staff at various types of live performances. To analyze staff behavior, break it down into the following categories.

Cast Identify ways the cast depends on you and your behavior during a live performance. For example, are you paying full attention, and do you stand ready to do your part so the play can advance without a hitch?

Crew Identify the ways your fellow crew members rely on you and your behavior. If technical problems arise, for example, are you prepared to handle them quickly? Are you willing to help someone on a different crew if necessary? Are you a good team member?

Tools and Equipment Identify appropriate behavior in relation to the tools and equipment associated with your crew. For example, are you completely compliant with safety procedures, and do you have backup plans and equipment available? Are you dressed appropriately to handle the equipment?

Types of Performances Analyze how appropriate behavior in each of the above categories differs at a variety of live performance types—from a studio improv show to a fully-staged musical.

Apply Your Expertise: Extension

After each rehearsal or preparation session, use your theatre journal to evaluate how well you applied your sound expertise. Use the evaluation questions below. Define the vocabulary terms associated with sound and demonstrate their proper use by using at least five of them in your regular self-evaluations.

Sound Crew Self-Evaluation

Responsibility In what ways did I develop and demonstrate responsibility in today's work? How can I improve on my responsibility?

Artistic Discipline In what ways did I develop and demonstrate artistic discipline? How artfully did I work with sounds and sound equipment? How did I model creativity as it relates to personal expression?

Creative Problem Solving How effectively did I develop and demonstrate creative problem solving in today's work?

Appropriate Behavior How did I apply and model appropriate behavior for a technical crew member at rehearsals and performances?

Other Styles and Genres What opportunities did I take to use sound in other theatrical styles and genres? What other opportunities would help me stretch my sound skills?

Agents, Lawyers, and Managers

Agents In the early days of your career, an agent can help you become "marketable." You still have to the do the essential work of proving yourself in auditions, but the agent can get you through the door for movies, television, and stage acting. And an agent will certainly help you in negotiations once success starts to come your way. Agents also represent writers and directors in both the film and television industries. Agents receive a percentage (generally ten percent) of every contract they negotiate for you.

Lawyers Entertainment lawyers serve a more specific function than agents do. They negotiate contracts and help protect the actor/director. Entertainment lawyers usually work for a fee rather than a percentage. Many very successful artists have both a lawyer and an agent.

Managers Some actors also find it helpful to have a manager. Managers are concerned with all aspects of an actor's career, often serving as counselor, friend, image consultant, and career guide. Like an agent, managers receive a percentage of what the actor earns.

Auditions

In larger cities, audition calls are listed in trade and industry magazines and newspapers. New York and Los Angeles have trade magazines such as *Backstage* and *Onstage,* as well as Web sites that list auditions. In other areas you may need to do some investigating to discover how and where auditions are held. Read the local newspapers and study the theatre scene where you are living. Attend shows and introduce yourself. If you see a theatre company that you like, ask them if and when they hold open auditions and always check listings and bulletin boards at local Actors' Equity Association offices.

Some auditions are open and others are exclusive. Exclusive auditions require you to have an agent set up the appointment. If you don't have an agent, the best thing to do is to attend every possible open audition that seems to fit your age and type. Don't waste the time of directors and producers by showing up for auditions where you clearly won't be cast. You may also hear about auditions for talent "showcases" or volunteer/internship programs. Study all of these carefully. Doing some work for free in hopes that it may lead to money and publicity later is a gamble that sometimes pays big dividends, but too much free work can devalue you as an actor.

"Foot-in-the-Door" Jobs

Following is a list of jobs that may help you make the connections you need to move up the industry ladder.

- *Box Office Worker* Sells tickets.
- *Drama Specialist* If you have some training, particularly college or university training, you might find work at a youth program or camp that needs a drama

specialist. You may be expected to teach theatre, direct, or even act with young people ranging from the very privileged and experienced to at-risk students.

- *Dresser* Like a costume assistant, a dresser helps a principal actor with quick costume changes.
- *Extra* Extras get paid next to nothing, but they do get screen time and once in a while are picked out for speaking roles or extra on-camera opportunities.
- *Food Service Provider* This can range from working in a concession stand to working a catering job for a company that provides meals for production personnel.
- *Grip* This term comes from "gripping" equipment—moving things on location, holding microphones, pulling cables, and otherwise assisting on a movie set.
- *Intern* An intern is sometimes paid a minimal amount but often works for free in order to learn some aspect of the trade.
- *Production Assistant* This is a catchall title that can include jobs as diverse as appointment book manager, errand runner, props collector, script-reader, or even tutor.
- *Receptionist* This person answers phones and greets visitors for directors, producers, or production companies.
- *Stagehand* Although these jobs are usually held for trained technical people, it is sometimes possible to get hired as a stagehand. Technical theatre people probably have the easiest time finding work in the industry.
- *Stand-in* Most television and movie stars do not stand and wait while the camera angles are set and lights arranged. They have a stand-in of the approximate height, build, and hair color who "stands in" the position until it's time to do the scene. Although this can be very boring work, it puts your face in front of directors on a regular basis.

Headshots, Portfolios, Demo Videos, and Résumés

Headshots When you go to an audition, you will be expected to bring a *headshot,* a photo of your head and shoulders. Most actors have at least one current headshot—as recent as two years for a young person and within five years for an adult. Some actors have several photos. They choose whichever one is most appropriate to the audition or job interview at hand.

Headshots should be done by a professional photographer. Ask a fellow actor or a talent agent to recommend someone. Once you've had your sitting, the photographer will give you contact sheets from which you will pick your favorite shot. Get help in choosing the image that will best serve you. If possible, ask a director and/or casting director for feedback on how your photo compares to other actors' and how well it reflects your appearance. Glamour shots that give a false impression can work against you. You then need prints made of your headshot. Don't scrimp here. You need plenty of photos so that you are not afraid to leave a trail of them at auditions and with directors and theatre companies.

A Portfolio A portfolio is a very useful tool. Most directors, educators, and designers use a portfolio to show examples of their work when a "live" audition isn't appropriate. The portfolio consists of sketches, photographs, programs, drawings, and other documentation of your work. It is a good tool for actors looking for work with a company, though rarely is such evidence called for in an audition.

Demo Video The *demo video* is a video portfolio featuring clips from television or motion picture work you have done. As with headshots, ask other people in the industry to recommend professionals who can help you put together your demo reel.

Résumés You must have a résumé. (See pages 562–563 of this handbook.) In fact, you might want to have multiples—each designed to showcase the aspect of your work most likely to get you a specific job. For example, if you are auditioning for film, list your film and/or video credits first. If you are auditioning for a Shakespearean play, be sure to place prior Shakespeare credits early in the résumé.

Networking and Connecting

Networking is one of the greatest keys to success. Try to find ways to get close to people who are having success. Often people who are successful in the business are very willing to serve as mentors to others. Apprenticeships and opportunities to further others in the business can only help you later on.

Organizations and Unions

Larger cities offer alumni groups from universities or colleges you might join. These groups provide a valuable service, allowing you to meet others who may work in the industry and who may have experiences to share. Join any such organizations that you can. It is also an excellent idea to join professional

organizations such as TCG (Theatre Communications Group), ASSITEJ/USA (The United States Center for the Association of Theater for Children and Young People), or AATE (The American Alliance for Theatre and Education). You may also soon qualify for the various unions including AEA (Actors' Equity Association), SAG-–AFTRA (Screen Actors' Guild–American Federation of Television and Radio Actors), IATSE (International Alliance of Theatrical Stage Employees), WGA (Writers Guild of America), or DGA (Dramatists Guild of America).

Joining a union will take money and time and is not always the best decision. Many companies have a certain number of union versus nonunion jobs and young actors can price themselves out of the market by becoming union members too soon. On the other hand, the union provides a safety net in terms of pay scale and health insurance as well as connecting the young actor to others in the business. Certain large film or television roles may require actors to join SAG–AFTRA.

Finances You should always have a "fall-back" trade in case you become frustrated with your progress in the theatre. The best advice is to find a job that is flexible enough to allow you to audition and perform, but still lucrative enough to support you when you are not employed in theatre. Waiting tables is the obvious parallel profession to acting, but there are other jobs that will allow you time to audition as well.

Glossary

3D film a film that gives the viewer the impression of three-dimensionality

accent the sound and patterns of speech from a specific region

acetone (ASS•ih•tohn) a solvent similar to nail polish remover used to remove spirit gum

acoustics the science of sound waves

act the main sections of a play

active listening using what you hear to build meaning

adrenaline a hormone that produces the feel of sudden increased energy

amphitheater a round structure arranged around an open space with tiered seating

amplifier a device that provides the power supply to sound equipment

analog using signals or information in the form of a continuously variable quality such as position or voltage

antagonist a main character who opposes the protagonist

apron the stage floor between the front edge of the stage and front curtain

archetype (AR•kih•typ) a character who represents a certain type or idea

arena stage staging in the center of a room with the audience sitting on all sides of the playing area; also called *theatre-in-the-round*

articulation clearly pronouncing words

artistic selectivity selecting the minimal amount of information needed to portray a character while still communicating necessary ideas and emotions

aside words spoken by a character to the audience rather than to the other characters who supposedly do not hear the speech

audible able to be heard

audience participation when the audience takes part in the action of the play

auditions tryouts for a part in a play

auditorium the part of a theatre where the audience sits

auditors the people conducting auditions

avant garde (ah•vahn•GARD) experimental new work; unorthodox

backstage the area behind the scenery not visible to the audience

barn door an accessory for Fresnel lighting instruments that houses moveable flaps to control the light beam

base foundation color used for stage makeup

base coat a layer of foundational paint applied after the prime coat

batten a horizontal pipe suspended over the stage, from which scenery, lights, or curtains are hung

bit part a role with very few lines

black box stage a stage consisting of a large empty square with black walls; also called *flexible stage*

blackout when all stage lights go off simultaneously

blocking the director's planned movement for the characters

blueprints reproductions of technical drawings documenting a design

body language using expressions and body movement to communicate rather than words

body mic a small microphone that can be hidden in the performer's clothing or hair

book the written script for a musical

border lights long, narrow, metal enclosures that house a row of lamps and reflectors; also called *strip lights*

box office 1. where tickets are purchased for theatrical events 2. the amount taken in for ticket sales

box set a set representing the walls of a room, sometimes with a ceiling

build 1. to make a costume from scratch **2.** the increase of vocal intensity toward a climactic point

Bunraku (bun•RAH•koo) traditional Japanese puppetry

burlesque (bur•LESK) physical comedy that uses exaggeration that is directed at a person, custom, artifact, or event

business detailed bits of action such as knitting, setting the table, etc., as distinguished from broad stage movement; also called *stage business*

business manager the person in charge of finance, publicity, ticket sales, programs, and other business relating to a theatrical production

call posted announcement of rehearsals, etc., placed on the call-board near stage entrance

callback a second audition at which only those actors under serious consideration for roles are called in

cameo a one-scene part

casting the process of selecting actors for various roles

catharsis (kuh•THAR•sis) emotional purging or an uplifting release that the audience feels during a play, particularly at the end of a tragedy

CD-R (compact disc, recordable) a compact disk used for recording and playing back sound

character a role that an actor portrays in a play

character makeup makeup that changes an actor's appearance drastically

character role a role in which character traits and appearance differ from that of the actor

cheating out playing a bit toward the audience while conversing with others on stage

choreographer the person responsible for designing a show's dance numbers

chorus 1. In Greek drama, a group of actors who speak in unison and comment on the action of the play **2.** the singers in a musical other than the principal performers

cinematographer chief artist and overseer of a film's lighting and camera crews

climax the high point of the play at which the protagonist makes an irrevocable decision; also called the *turning point*

closed audition an audition open only to union members or those represented by an agent

close-up a camera shot that shows only an actor(s) head

cloud computing information technology purchased as a service rather than a collection of hardware

clown white white makeup often used by mimes

cold reading when an actor auditions for a role without having read the script

collaborate to work jointly with another person or group to create something

collodion (kuh•LOH•dee•un) a clear, thick liquid used on the skin to make scars

comedy a play that ends happily and arouses laughter through humorous treatment of an aspect of life

comedy of manners comedy that originated in the late 1600s which makes fun of upper-class pretentiousness and the attitudes of the wealthy

commedia dell'arte (kuh•MAY•dee•uh del•AR•tay) improvised comedy featuring stock characters that began in Renaissance Italy

computer generated imagery (CGI) computer graphics that create or contribute to images in film and other media

conflict the dramatic opposition of the protagonist with society, with his or her peers, or with him- or herself

console See *sound board.*

costume parade when actors walk onstage in full costume for the purpose of determining comfort, utility, movement, and proper lighting

costume plot a list of every character and his or her costume for each scene

costume shop the place where costumes are built and stored

counter-cross moving in the opposite direction— and out of the way—of another actor who is moving across the stage

Glossary 615

Glossary

counterweight system a system that uses lines, cables, and weights to raise and lower the battens that hold scenery, drops, and lights

creativity ability to discover or invent something

creme foundation a makeup foundation with an oil base

crepe hair artificial hair made of wool used for making beards and mustaches

crinolines full, stiff underskirts

crisis an event that occurs just when it seems things could either resolve or worsen; the crisis leads to the climax

cross an actor's move from one side of the stage to another

cross light when two spotlights are placed on opposite sides of the stage at a 45-degree angle to minimize shadows on an actor's face

cue 1. the last words or action of one actor that immediately precede another actor's speech 2. signal for light changes, curtain, etc.

cue pickup the term for when a character begins to speak

cut 1. delete 2. a command to stop action and dialogue

cyc or **cyclorama (sy•kluh•RAH•mah)** a curtain or wall at the back and sides of the stage

dead zone an area of the stage without adequate lighting

decorative props details on stage such as paintings, newspapers, or window curtains; also called *set dressing*

demographic an advertising term meaning a group of people

denouement (day•noo•MAH) the outcome of the main problem in a drama

deus ex machina (DAY•us eks MAH•kih•nah) literally, "god in the machine"; a mechanical crane used to lower and raise gods in ancient Greek theatre

dialogue conversation among characters

diaphragm (DY•uh•fram) the muscle below the rib cage

diction the vocal style, dialect, rhythm, and words of the characters

digital audio software computer software that allows the user to mix sounds

dimmers controls that change the level of lighting intensity

director the person who interprets a play, casts, blocks, and helps actors develop their characters

discovery space in Elizabethan theatres, the space located between two doors at the back of the stage used for small interior settings

dissolve in film and TV, when one shot is faded out and another is faded in

double cast selecting two actors for each role; the casts then split the performances

downstage the area of the stage closest to the audience

dramatic criticism the act of reviewing a dramatic work

dramaturg a person who performs a variety of tasks to assist with the production of a play, including reading and evaluating scripts, researching historical and societal issues, and sharing pertinent information with the director and cast

dress rehearsals the final rehearsals before opening night run without stopping; actors are in full makeup and costume and all production elements are in place

dress the stage keep the stage picture balanced

drop a canvas or muslin curtain that forms part of the scenery

dry tech a rehearsal run without actors in order to check technical cues

dual role the actor's two realities onstage—the actor-as-character and the actor-as-actor

dutchman thin strips of muslin used to cover the gap between flats

elevations different views of a three-dimensional area or object

elevation sketch a drawing that shows how the stage will look from the perspective of the audience

ellipsoidal (ih•lip•SOY•dul) reflector spotlight (ERS) a spotlight with an ellipsoidal reflector, usually hung from the auditorium ceiling to light downstage acting areas; also called a *Leko*

emoting expressing emotions

emotional recall recall that uses remembered feelings to recapture an experience

empathy ability to relate to feelings that are experienced by someone else

ensemble a group that performs together to achieve an overall effect

epic a long narrative poem that tells the story of a legendary hero

epic theatre a drama in which the audience is encouraged to think critically about political and social issues; theatricality overrides realism

equalizer a device on the sound board that balances high, medium, and low frequencies to achieve a desired blend of sounds

etiquette appropriate conduct

exposition information that gives you an idea about what has happened before the play began and what is happening as the play begins

external traits characteristics that make up physical appearance, such as posture, gestures, mannerisms, voice, and clothing

fall when the actor does not stay in character

farce a physical comedy that exaggerates situations until they are hardly believable

flats pieces of canvas stretched over wooden frames that are painted and linked together to create scenery such as walls and doorways

flexible stage See *black box stage*.

floodlights lights that illuminate broad areas of the stage

floor plan a diagram that shows the walls, doors, windows, furniture, and other important architectural details on the stage drawn to scale; also called *ground plan*

fly space the area above the stage where scenery, drops, and lights are hung when not in use

foil a character whose personal attributes contrast sharply with the main character or protagonist

followspots spotlights that produce strong beams of light that follow an actor onstage

foundation makeup the color of one's skin

fourth wall the imaginary wall through which the audience views the play

Fresnel (fruh•NEL) a spotlight with a step-lens that throws an efficient and soft beam, usually hung from a batten to light upstage areas

full back/full front facing completely away from or completely toward the audience

gelatins (gels) transparent color sheets inserted into a frame in front of a spotlight or floodlight

genre a type or classification of literature

gestures movements of separate parts of the body such as waving an arm or shrugging a shoulder

gobo a template of thin metal inserted into an ellipsoidal reflector spotlight to create a light pattern on stage

going up forgetting one's lines during a rehearsal or performance

grand drape the front curtain on a proscenium stage, usually made of a heavy, luxurious fabric

greasepaint heavy, oil-based theatrical makeup

greenroom a room where actors relax before and after performances

grid or gridiron the framework high over the stage that supports the curtain and scenery riggings

groundlings (in Elizabethan times) tradespeople and lower class citizens who stood in the pit around the stage to watch a performance

Glossary

ground plan See *floor plan*.

hand props items handled and/or carried on stage by actors during the show, such as letters, books, guns, dishes, and so forth

hanging plot the plan created by the lighting designer that shows where the crew should hang the lighting instruments

high comedy comedy such as satire or comedy of manners that makes fun of political situations, cultural habits, and accepted social standards

high-definition TV (HDTV) television that features a very high-resolution image

hold the pause required after a character delivers a funny line

Hollywood flats hard-covered flats with a frame that is perpendicular to the paint surface

hot spot a place where too much light hits a small area of the stage

house another name for auditorium; the place where the audience sits

house lights auditorium lights used before and after the play and during intermission

house manager the person who oversees the box office, supervises the ushers, and attends to conditions in the auditorium

illusion of the first time the actor's ability to perform in a show over and over while making it appear that the dialogue and situations are happening for the first time

impressionistic relying on colors and lines to create mood and setting rather than on realistic representations

improvise to make up the dialogue and action of a scene as you go along

inciting incident the first event that suggests the situation of the drama will change; the event to which all other actions in the play can be traced

incubation the phase of the design process during which ideas simmer, recombine, or develop into new creative solutions

inflection variety of vocal pitch

ingenue (AHN•juh•nu) a young female lead character, often the love interest in the play

installation a presentation of performance art

instrument the term used to refer to a stage light

internal traits the characteristics that make up personality, such as family circumstances, environment, occupation, level of education, interests, and so on

interplay interaction between characters

joinery fasteners, bindings, and adhesives used to join together wooden or metal construction elements

Kabuki (kuh•BOO•kee) stylized Japanese drama which originated in the 1600s

kill eliminate; for example, "kill the noise" means to be quiet

Kyogen (ky•O•gen) a short Japanese comedy performed without music and masks

lamp the bulb for a lighting instrument

larynx (LAR•inks) the part of the throat that contains the vocal cords

lavalier (lah•vuh•LEER) mic See *body mic*

left the left side of the stage from the actor's perspective when facing the audience; also called *stage left*

legitimate theatre originally evolved from England's Licensing Act of 1737, in which plays could only be performed in two specific playhouses, today the term refers to all live play performances (as opposed to film)

lighting designer the person responsible for creating a lighting plan for a theatrical production

light plot a plan showing the position of lighting instruments

low comedy comedy that is physical and sometimes vulgar; it includes outlandish behavior and oddly harmless violence

lauan a type of inexpensive plywood

makeup morgue a collection of portrait pictures or photos used as a reference when creating a character's makeup

mansions small platforms or stations where scenes of plays were performed, and viewers moved from place to place to view the entire story

masques extravagant entertainments held at court that included dance, song, and recitation

master gesture a distinctive gesture used to establish a character's personality

melodrama an overly dramatic play that focuses more on cliff-hanging action and intense emotions than on character development or real problems

Method acting an acting approach that calls on the actor to use personal experience and sense memory to develop a character

middlebrow comedy comedy based on plot and sentimental situations; often used in romantic and situation comedies

mime an actor who communicates through movements of the body and face, but does not speak; a more formal and disciplined version of pantomime

miracle play a drama depicting the lives of the saints

mixer See *sound board*

modified authenticity the idea that a costume does not have to replicate a historical design exactly, but rather give the impression of that design

monologue a long speech by one character

morality play a drama that teaches right from wrong

motion capture a film process of recording patterns of movement digitally

motivation a specific reason for saying or doing something; to show a character's desires through voice and movement

moving light a programmable light able to make rapid lighting changes

multimedia using more than one medium onstage, including TV, film, dance, etc.

muscular memory when you know the role so well that your actions become effortless and appear completely natural

musical a dramatic production accompanied by song and dance

music director the person who directs the actors, singers, and often the orchestra in a musical

musical comedy a comedic drama featuring song and dance

muslin thin fabric sometimes used to cover flats

mystery play a drama based on a Bible story

neoclassicism with regard to drama, a form of writing in which playwrights were to observe classical influences and adapt them to their work

Noh traditional Japanese theatre in which the story is communicated through poetry, dance, and music

nonrealistic play a play in which the characters and/ or events are exaggerated

objectives goals or needs

observation recognizing a fact or event

obstacle anything that gets in the way of an objective

off book having a part memorized so that a script is no longer needed

offstage any part of the stage that the audience cannot see

onstage any part of the stage that is visible to the audience

open stance when an actor faces the audience; full front

outcome result

pan a very negative review

pancake makeup makeup that is pressed into a hard round cake and applied with a wet sponge

pantomime telling a story or presenting an idea through bodily movement and expression rather than words

parody imitate in a humorous way

Glossary

passion play a drama depicting scenes from Christ's life, especially the days of his suffering and resurrection

PBS Public Broadcasting System, a group of television stations that specializes in educational and arts programming; partly funded by government money and private donations

Peking Opera Chinese drama that features chanting, singing, and musical accompaniment

performance art unstructured dramatic events in which movement, music, improvisation, and games are presented, often with the purpose of making a political statement

performing arts artistic processes that are performed in front of an audience

periaktoi (pair•ee•AK•toy) the Greek word for a triangle of flats that can be revolved for scenery changes

pilot the first episode of a television show that introduces a potential new series

pinking shears a kind of scissors that cuts a zigzag edge, used to prevent fabrics from unraveling

pitch 1. the relative highness or lowness of a voice **2.** to present a plan or idea in hopes of convincing others to invest in or accept it

pliable 1. adaptable to varying conditions **2.** flexible

plot the story of a play from beginning to end

poetry slam a competitive poetry reading in which poets present short, original poems that are judged by the audience

practical light a light that actually works onstage, such as a lamp or candle

presentational a style of play in which the actor may speak directly to the audience

prime coat first layer of paint

principals actors in major roles

producer a person who secures financial backing for a play or film, chooses the director, and oversees the day-to-day business of the production

production numbers elaborate song-and-dance sequences in which most of the cast takes part

profile facing sideways to the audience so that they only see one side of your body

project to increase voice or actions so they will carry to the audience

prompt book a book (usually a three-ring binder) that contains the script annotated with the director's ideas about details such as movement, as well as technical cues for lights, sound, etc.

prop plot a list of props needed for each scene

props or properties set furnishings including furniture, pictures, ornaments, drapes, and so on. See *hand props* and *set props*

props master the person in charge of obtaining and organizing all of the props for a play

prop table a backstage location where hand props are kept

proscenium stage a stage with a permanent framed opening through which the audience sees the play

protagonist the main character with whom audience empathy lies

public domain a work that belongs to the public; royalty-free

pull to retrieve costumes or props from storage

pull quotes a (usually positive) quote excerpted from an article or review and used in advertising

putty wax a pliable substance used in a character's makeup to build a false nose, chin, or forehead

quarter turn a 90-degree turn

quick study one who can memorize a part rapidly

rail 1. the top or bottom board of a flat **2.** another term for *batten*

raked stage a slanted stage, where upstage is slightly higher than downstage

rate the speed at which one speaks

rave review a very positive review

Readers Theatre a form of drama in which actors are seated and read aloud from scripts

realism a type of literature that depicts life objectively and accurately

realistic play a play that imitates real life

reality TV a form of television programming in which nonprofessional participants speak and act as they would in real life

recall to remember a fact or event so as to re-create it

regional accent the sound of speech from a particular region

rehearsal a session where the play is practiced in preparation for performance

rendering a colored drawing of a set or costume

repertory a group of plays presented in rotation over a period of time by the same company of actors

representational a theatrical style, in which the actors are "unaware" that the audience is watching

resolution the end of a plot when the conflict is resolved

resonance a rich, warm vocal tone

Restoration comedy See *comedy of manners*

rhetorical involving speech (rather than action)

right the stage area to the actor's right as he or she faces the audience; also called *stage right*

role a part in a play

romanticism a literary, artistic, and philosophical movement of the late 18th and early 19th centuries that emphasized the imagination and emotions

roundels colored glass disks used in border lights

royalties the fees paid to the rights holder of a play, other literature, or music in order to use or perform it

rule of three the belief that pratfalls, accidents, and misunderstandings designed to make the audience laugh are only funny three times in a row

run through a rehearsal without interruption

satire comedy that makes fun of people to try to change their foolish behavior

scenario an outline of a play

scene a part or division of an act of a play

scenery the background pieces such as flats and drops that create the play's setting

scene shop the place where scenery and props are constructed

scoops lights that illuminate broad areas

scoring a role 1. marking the script with notes on blocking and delivery 2. analyzing the script as an aid to character development

screenplay a script for a film

scrim a loose-weave curtain on a batten used for "visions," "flashbacks," and so on, opaque when lighted from the front, transparent when the set behind it is lighted

script a printed copy of the play

sensory recall recall that uses all the senses to recapture an experience

set the scenery used onstage

set designer the person in charge of creating a plan for the set(s) of a production

set dressing anything on stage that adds to the visual representation, including actors

set piece a three-dimensional scenery piece that stands by itself, such as a rock or tree

set props items used to dress the set, such as furniture, carpets, and lighting fixtures

sightlines imaginary lines indicating visibility of stage areas from different areas of the house

sitcoms situation comedies

skene (SKEE•nee) in ancient theatres, a building behind the stage used by the actors

social drama a play that focuses on serious, real-life problems of ordinary people

solid-state lighting lighting that uses LEDs rather than incandescent or arc sources

Glossary 621

Glossary

soliloquies speeches in which one actor speaks aloud, revealing his or her inner thoughts

sound board a device that controls sound sources and allows them to be manipulated and balanced; also called a *mixer*

sound designer the person responsible for planning the sound for a show

soundscape the sound designer's artistic vision for a production's sound

spectacle everything the audience sees, including scenery, costuming, dance, pantomime, and swordplay

special effects illusions used to create a specific cinematic or virtual world

spectatorship the fundamental ways people consume and interact with media

spiking marking the rehearsal area with masking tape to show the positions of furniture, doors, etc.

spill light leakage from stage lights

spirit gum an adhesive used for applying items such as a false beard or nose putty

spotlights lights that produce concentrated illumination

stage business See *business*

staged reading the reading of a drama in which actors use manuscripts and rough blocking

stage fright feeling nervous before a performance

stage left/stage right See *left, right*

stage manager the person who directs the backstage crews and runs the show once it goes into performance

stakes the level or degree of importance in getting objectives met

stealing the scene taking audience attention away from the proper focal point

step on to cut off or interrupt another character by speaking over his or her lines

stiles the vertical boards that make up the sides of a flat

stippling adding color and texture by using small, short strokes in applying makeup or paint

stock character a character with a set of recognizable traits, such as the young lover, the irate father, the clever servant, and so on—often seen in *commedia dell'arte* productions

straight makeup makeup that enhances natural features and coloring

strike 1. to remove something from the set; 2. to take down set and props after the show's final performance

strip lights See *border lights*

subtext information that is implied in the dialogue but not stated

supporting roles roles that support a leading role

suspend disbelief the ability of a viewer to accept what he or she sees and hears as real

swatch a small sample of fabric

symbol an object that is used to represent an abstract concept or principle

syndication when a television program that has already aired on a network is sold to other stations

tableau a visual effect in which actors create a picture by standing in a frozen position

tag line the final line of a play or scene

target audience the group of people to whom advertisers believe a television show or film is most relevant

teaser the overhead curtain that masks the first batten of lights and adjusts the height of the proscenium opening

technical acting an acting approach that calls on the actor to use learned techniques for movement, speech, and character development rather than emotions and sense memory

technical elements effects in a performance that are not created by the onstage performers, including lighting, recorded sound, costuming, etc.

teleplay a television script

theatre-in-the-round See *arena stage*

theatre of the absurd a type of drama based on the idea that life is meaningless and that searching for order only brings about confusion and conflict

theme the underlying message or meaning of a play or other piece of literature

thespian an actor

three-quarter turn a 270-degree turn

thrust stage a stage that juts into the audience area, with the audience usually sitting around its three sides

timing to move and say one's lines at the most effective moment

tiring house in an Elizabethan theatre, the backstage area where actors would go to change costumes

toggle cross brace

tormentors side curtains or flats that adjust the proscenium width

tragedy a drama in which a protagonist struggles against some force, usually making an ennobling sacrifice before going down in defeat (usually death)

tragic flaw a weakness of character that ultimately causes the protagonist's destruction

transmitter a device that sends a signal from the microphone to the receiver

trapdoor an opening in the stage floor that allows actors to enter and exit

travesty a humorous imitation

trilogy three related works of literature

trim decorative items such as buttons, lace, ribbon, jewelry, etc.

tryouts auditions for parts in a play

turning point See *climax*

typecasting casting someone over and over again in the same type of role

understudy an actor who learns a role in case a lead actor cannot perform

unit set a set made of several pieces that can be rearranged to produce more than one scene

unity a balance in the variety and kinds of movement in a play

upstage the stage area farthest away from the audience, toward the backstage wall

upstaging drawing the audience's attention to yourself when it should be focused on another character

vaudeville (VAWD•vil) a variety show featuring many acts, including trained animals, singers, acrobats, dancers, and comedians

villain a despicable character, especially in a melodrama

visualize to picture in one's mind

vocalizing singing without words

voice-over the voice of an unseen narrator

volume the relative loudness of a voice

wagon stage platforms on which scenery is placed and rolled onto the stage

walk-on a part in which the actor walks on and off stage without having any lines to say

warn to notify that a cue is approaching

Web 2.0 the user environment that allows collaboration and sharing on the Internet

wings offstage to right and left of the acting area

Wooden O's round or octagonal theatres, such as Shakespeare's Globe, with two or three tiers of thatched roof galleries on three sides of an open court

work lights white lights used solely for rehearsal

Glossary 623

Acknowledgments

624 Acknowledgments

Acknowledgments

Image Credits

2,3: © Robbie Jack/CORBIS; 4: Photos.com; 6: Anna Henson, Projection Design by Anna Henson; 7: Bruce Gilkas / FilmMagic / Getty Images; 8: © Igor Terekhov / Dreamstime.com, © Sergey Skleznev / Dreamstime.com, © Yurly Chaban / Dreamstime.com; 9: © Lunary / Dreamstime.com; 11: © Simone Van Den Berg / Dreamstime.com; 12: © Photomyeye / Dreamstime.com; 13: © Eagleflying / Dreamstime.com; 14, 15: Blend Stock Photos / Fotosearch; 16: William Burlingham Photographs; 17: William Burlingham Photographs; 22,23: © Donald Cooper/Photostage; 23: Michael Lutch; 25: William Burlingham Photographs; 27: Photofest; 28: © Bettmann/CORBIS; 29: © Bettmann/CORBIS; 30,31: © Reuters NewMedia Inc./CORBIS; 32: William Burlingham Photographs; 33: William Burlingham Photographs; 34: William Burlingham Photographs; 35: William Burlingham Photographs; 37: Photos.com; 38: © Monkey Business Images Ltd / Deamstime.com; 39: Corel; 40: © Charles & Josette Lenars/CORBIS; 40 bottom: © Michael S. Yamashita/CORBIS; 41: © Stephen Lovekin / WireImage /Getty Images; 41 bottom: © Joe McNally / Getty Images Entertainment / Getty Images; 42,43: Michael Brosilow; 45: William Burlingham Photographs; 47: William Burlingham Photographs; 48 left: © Leonard de Selva/CORBIS; 48 right: Michael Brosilow; 49: The Black Version; 50: ArtToday; 52,53: © Robbie Jack/CORBIS; 54,55: © Robbie Jack/ CORBIS; 56: William Burlingham Photographs; 58: Corel; 59: Burdette Parks, Roundlake Studios; 62: Corel; 63 top: © Randy Miramontez / Dreamstime.com; 63 bottom: MICHAEL HALSBAND/Landov; 64, 65: Chris Bennion/Theatre Pix; 66: Mike Aspengren; 67: William Burlingham Photographs; 68: Mike Aspengren; 71: William Burlingham Photographs; 72,73: The Newark Museum / Art Resource, NY; 73: Des Moines Community Playhouse; 74,75: © Robbie Jack/CORBIS; 75 top: Mike Aspengren; 76: Corel; 77: © Robbie Jack/ CORBIS; 79: William Burlingham Photographs; 81: © G0r3cki / Dreamstime.com; 83: Anthony Neste / TIME & LIFE Images Collection / Getty Images; 84: Connie Verkade; 85: © Jason Falchook / The Moth; 86,87: Michael Brosilow; 89: iStockphoto; 90: Donald Cooper, Photostage; 94: Ebright; 95: Jeffery St. Mary Sunrise Foundation, photograph by Jeffery St. Mary; 95 bottom: Community members Lorinda Hawkins and Renée Günter starred in Cornerstone Theater Company's production of SEED: A Weird Act of Faith. Oct. 25 - Nov. 18, 2012 @ Chuco's Justice Center. Written by Sigrid Gilmer. Directed by Shishir Kurup. Photo by Kevin Michael Campbell.; 96: Burdette Parks, Roundlake Studios; 98, 99: © Robbie Jack/ CORBIS; 100, 101: © Robbie Jack/CORBIS; 103: Michael Brosilow; 105: Franck Caillet / Thinkstock; 106: William Burlingham Photographs; 107: Michael Brosilow; 109: Library of Congress; 110: The Sydney Morning Herald / Fairfax Media / Getty Images; 111: CBS/Landov; 112, 113: Kevin Berne; 114 bottom: Mike Aspengren; 114 top: Western Michigan University; 116: Utah Shakespearean Festival; 118: College of Southern Idaho; 119: © Robbie Jack/CORBIS; 122 top and bottom: ArtToday; 123 bottom: © Robbie Jack/CORBIS; 124, 125: © Geraint Lewis / Alamy; 126: Alan Youngbood / Oscala Star-Banner / Landov; 127: Burdette Parks, Roundlake Studios; 131: City of Westminster Archive Centre, London, UK/ Bridgeman Art Library; 133 top: The Kobal Collection at Art Resource, NY / CASTLE ROCK ENTERTAINMENT; 133 bottom: The Kobal Collection at Art Resource, NY / RENAISSANCE FILMS / BBC / CURZON; 134, 135: J. Gurney & Son / Library of Congress; 135: © Bettmann/CORBIS; 136, 137: Corel; 137 top: Des Moines Community Playhouse; 138: © Robbie Jack/CORBIS; 139: The Kobal Collection at Art Resource, NY / ODYSSEY; 143: AP Photo/E Pablo Kosmicki; 144: © Leonard de Selva/CORBIS; 145 left: Huton Archive / Getty Images; 145 right: Time Life Pictures / Getty Images; 147: Corel; 148, 149: RAFAEL PEREZ/Reuters /Landov; 150, 151: AP Photo/Alan Solomon; 152: Richard Feldman; 155: William Burlingham Photographs; 157: Mike Aspengren; 159: A. Vincent Scarano; 161: AP Photo/Tina Fineberg; 162 top: ArtToday; 162 bottom: © Lindsay Hebberd/CORBIS; 163: Annie Paladino; 164,165: © Micheline Pelletier/CORBIS SYGMA; 168: William Burlingham Photographs; 171: © G0r3cki / Dreamstime.com; 172: artsfuse.org / Mark S. Howard; 174,175 : William Burlingham Photographs; 177 left: The Kobal Collection at Art Resource, NY / MARAT SADE / UNITED ARTISTS; 177 left: © Colita/CORBIS; 178: © adoc-photos/CORBIS; 179 top: © Jacques M. Chenet/CORBIS; 179 bottom: AP Photo/ Ted S. Warren; 180,181: © Robbie Jack/CORBIS; 183: William Burlingham Photographs; 186: William Burlingham Photographs; 193: Western Michigan University; 194: The Harvard Theatre Collection, The Houghton Library; 195: Richard Feldman; 196,197: The Flying Karamazov Brothers; 198: Mike Aspengren; 199: Mike Aspengren; 200 top: Corel; 200: Mike Aspengren; 201: Burdette Parks, Roundlake Studios;

202: Mike Aspengren; 203, 204: Mike Aspengren; 207: William Burlingham Photographs; 208: De Agostini / Getty Images; 209: Richard Feldman;

210 top: Corel; 210,211: Western Michigan University; 212,213: Digital Vision; 215: Neo Futurists; 217: © Bettina Strenske / Alamy; 220: Burdette Parks, Roundlake Studios; 222: William Burlingham Photographs; 224: Top Photo Corporation / Thinkstock; 225: Steven Rosenbaum / Flickr; 227: ArtToday; 227,228: Donald Cooper/ Photostage; 230,231: Andrew H. Walker / Getty Images Entertainment; 232: Wayne Kischer; 233: Nic McPhee / flickr; 233: Mike Aspengren; 235: Mike Aspengren; 236: Mike Aspengren; 236: Mike Aspengren; 237: Mike Aspengren; 238: Richard Feldman; 239: Mike Aspengren; 240: Richard Feldman; 243: G.W. Mercier; 224: North Wind Archives; 245: Tallahassee Little Theatre, Susan Stripling photography; 246,247: Michael Le Poer Trench/ ArenaPAL; 248: Wikimedia Commons / Pajameson; 250: Photos.com; 252: Photos.com; 253: Photos.com; 254: Mike Aspengren; 255: Mike Aspengren; 257: Mike Aspengren; 258: © Lenny712 / Dreamstime.com; 258: © Tonyz20 / Dreamstime. com; 258: © Louella38 / Dreamstime.com; 259: © Walter McBride/Corbis; 259: Mike Aspengren; 260: Photos.com; 263: © Peter M. Fisher/Corbis; 264 bottom: Thinkstock; 264 top: Mary Ann Evans Picture Library; 265: © Robbie Jack/Corbis; 266,267: Richard Feldman; 268: Strand; Strand; Guy Currier, Altman Lighting;Lighting Innovation; Strand; Oasis Stage Werks; 269: University of Indianapolis; PLC Collection; PLC Collection; PLC Collection; DHA Lighting Limited; PLC Collection; 270: Corel; 271: Western Michigan University; 272: Goodman Theatre, Eric Y. Exit; 274: Mike Aspengren; 275: Mike Aspengren; 276: Wallace Photography; 279: Photos. com; 282: © Bidouze Stephane / Dreamstime.com; 284: Wikimedia Commons; 285: Beinecke Rare Book and Manuscript Library, Yale University; 285: Richard Feldman; 286, 287: © Robbie Jack/CORBIS; 288, 289: Liquid Library; 290: iStockphoto.com; 291: ArtToday; 295: The Kobal Collection at Art Resource, NY / COLUMBIA; 296: Mike Aspengren; 297 bottom: The Kobal Collection at Art Resource, NY; 297 top: Michael Brosilow; 298,299: © RobbieJack/CORBIS; 300: William Burlingham Photographs; 301: William Burlingham Photographs; 302: William Burlingham Photographs; 303: Royal Shakespeare Theatre / Royal Shakespeare Company / Photostage; 306: PLC Collection; 308: Nan Zabriskie; 308: © 1996 Liz Lauren; 311: © MAIMAN RICK/CORBIS SYGMA; 312: The Devonshire Collection, Chatsworth. Reproduced by permission of the Duke of Devonshire and the Chatsworth Settlement Trustees; 313: Mummenschanz; 313: © Sergio Perez/Reuters/Corbis; 314,315: © Robbie Jack/CORBIS; 315: Des Moines Community Playhouse; 316: Rich Addicks / Associated Press; 317: William Burlingham Photographs; 318: William Burlingham Photographs; 319: Mike Aspengren; 320:

William Burlingham Photographs; 321: William Burlingham Photographs; 322: William Burlingham Photographs; 324: William Burlingham Photographs; 325: William Burlingham Photographs; 326: William Burlingham Photographs; 327: William Burlingham Photographs; 328: Mike Aspengren; 332: Cynthia Clampitt; 333: NAATC; 334,335: Corel; 336: Corel; 338,339: Photos.com; 339: Corel; 340: Photos.com; 341: Photos.com; 343: William Burlingham Photographs; 344 left: Photos.com; 344 right: ArenaPAL; 345: Henrietta Butler/ ArenaPAL; 346: Mike Aspengren; 348,349: AP Photo/ Denis Doyle; 350,351: © Kelly-Mooney Photography/CORBIS; 351 top: © Geraint Lewis / Alamy; 352: Carol Rosegg/ArenaPAL; 354: © Bob King / CORBIS; 355: © Walter McBride / CORBIS; 362: The Kobal Collection at Art Resource, NY / MIRAMAX / JAMES, DAVID; 363: AP Photo/Stephen Chernin; 364: © Liu Liqun/CORBIS; 365: Scott

Mike Aspengren Illustrations: 56, 58, 65 top, 102, 145, 184, 185, 186 bottom, 188, 189, 190, 214, 215, 217, 218, 219, 222, 223, 224 top, 225, 240, 241, 262, 285, 294, 405 left and right

William Burlingham Photographs: back cover, 6, 7, 22, 23, 24, 25, 35, 37, 46, 57, 61, 69, 94, 143, 154, 156, 160–161, 169, 172, 193, 228, 258, 259, 266, 267, 268, 283, 284, 286, 287, 289, 290, 291, 292, 293, 304–305, 309

The editors wish to thank the playwrights, publishers, and agents who have allowed their copyrighted materials to be used in this book. Every effort has been made to contact all copyright holders. If we have omitted anyone, please let us know and we will include a suitable acknowledgment in subsequent editions.

Index

Index

Index

Greek tragedy, 110, 125
  melodrama in, 127–128,
    353, 396, 467, 582, 583
  Noh, 162, 344, 439–440,
    441
  origin of term, 424, 428
  plot of, 151
  political aspects of, 172
  regional accents and, 128
  sanskrit, 332
  serious, 126–127
  Shakespearean tragedies in,
    125–126
  social, 126
  social aspects of, 172
  sound in, 152
  spectacle in, 152
  styles of, 172
  symbolic elements of, 171
  technical elements of,
    172–173
  theme in, 151
  writing a, 151
Drama specialist, 611–612
Dramatic miniseries, 353
Dramatic monologue, 563
Dramatic poetry, 429
Dramatic roles, 124–131
  building, 126
Dramatic series on TV, 576
Dramaturg, 166, 169
Dress, 567
Dressers, 612
Dress rehearsals, 186–188
  stage lighting for, 278–279
Dress right/dress left, 567
Drew, Mrs. John, 466
Dreyfuss, Richard, 139
Drills, 249
Driving Miss Daisy, scene from,
  500–503
Drop, 234, 259
The Drummer, monologue from,
  486–487
Drury Lane Theatre, 457
Dry brushing, 605
Dryden, John, 458
Dry tech, 186, 593
Dual role, 101
Dumas, Alexander, 464
The Dumb Waiter, 469
Dunham, Lana, 399
Durang, Christoper, 113, 291,
  470, 531
Duration, 209
Duse, Eleanora, 466
Dutchman, 604

DVT, 398
The Dybbuk, 145
Dying, 207

E

East West Players, 41
Eccyclema, 433
Edison, Thomas, 353
Editing of film, 380, 387
Educational and informational
  television, 576
Edward II, 452
Egyptian theatre, 426, 428–429
Electra, 434
Electrical theory and safety, 277
Electronic media, 353,
  410–421
  digital convergence and,
    411, 418
  digital divide and, 420–421
  evaluating new, 415
  impact on society, 412–415
  influence on everyday life,
    411–412
  Web 2.0 and, 411
Elevations, 251
Elevation sketch, 234
Eliot, T. S., 363, 468
Elizabethan theatre, 122,
  451–457
  actors in, 94, 456–457
  playwrights in, 451–453
  theatres in, 454–455, 457
Elizabeth I, Queen of England,
  451, 452, 456
Elizabeth the Queen, 469
Ellipsoidal reflector spotlights,
  591
Emoting, 91
Emotion, using, 127
Emotional recall, 24, 129
Empathy, 9
The Emperor Jones, 469
The Emperor of the Moon, 586
Emphasis, 578
Endgame, 126, 469
An Enemy of the People,
  464–465
English National Opera, 55
Ensemble, 4, 43, 86–95
  acting in, 87
  choosing situation, 88
  contemporary, 95
  developing relationships in,
    89
  in Elizabethan period, 94
  etiquette in, 91
  keeping on track, 92

  in 19th century, 94
  safety net in, 87
  working alone, 89
  working with group, 89–90
Ensemble ethic, 87, 89
Ensemble Theatre of Houston,
  93
Entering on stage, 55
Entremeses, 450
Ephemeral art forms, 5
Epic, defined, 151
Epic theatre, 123, 467
Equalizers, 289, 609
Equus, 468
E-readers, 412
ERS (ellipsoidal reflector
  spotlight), 268, 270, 276,
  285
Esping, Laura, 472
Etherage, George, 458
Ethics
  critical, 218
  ensemble, 87, 89
Ethnic theatres, 462
Etiquette, audience, 215,
  220–221
Euripides, 162, 435
Evening with Mark Twain, 573
Everyman, 447
Everyman in His Humour, 452
Evita, 179, 363
Exercises
  vocal, 18, 80–81
  warm-up, 16–17, 19
Exiting, 56
Experimental theatre, 313, 585
Experimention, 46
Experiment with an Airpump, 87
Exposition in a plot, 154, 156,
  381
External traits, 103–104
External work, 559
Extras, 612
Eyebrow pencils, 326
Eyebrows
  common character, 319
  makeup for, 318, 326
Eye focus, 199
Eye pouches, 323

F

Fabric for costumes, 303
Face, aging of, 322–325
Facebook, 418
Fall, 87
Falling, 207
Falling action in a plot, 115, 156
Falling inflection, 78

Falsettoland, 333
Falstaff, 453
Family Feud, 396
Far Away, 113
Farce, 137, 585
Farquhar, George, 458
Feather dusting, 605
Fences, 161, 471
Ferrell, Will, 49
Feudalism, 446
Fey, Tina, 49
The Fifth of July, 470
Fight choreographers, 584
Fighting, 568–569
Files, 249
Film, 5, 353, 367, 378–393
  acting in, 565
  audiences for, 381, 400
  blocking in, 389
  business of, 565
  changing elements and
    methods of
    communication in, 389
  comparison of television with,
    400
  computer-generated imagery
    in, 382, 384
  digital convergence and, 418
  editing of, 380, 387
  evaluating, 385–388
  exposition in, 381
  expressions on faces in, 381
  flashbacks in, 392
  intimacy of, 381
  motion capture in, 382
  movement of camera in, 389
  180 degree rule in, 389
  playing of angles in, 381
  plot in, 381
  post production in, 586
  resolution in, 381
  rising action in, 381
  society and, 383–385
  special effects in, 382
  structure of, 381
  technology and, 379
  television, 586
  theatrical conventions in,
    379–381
  3D, 382, 384, 389
  three-point lighting in, 389
  in transcending time and
    space, 381
Filmmaker, evaluating intent of,
  386
Final consonants, 578
Final rehearsal, 575

Index

Index 635

Index

Index

staging for, 244
tragedies in, 435
Romantic comedy, 585
Romanticism, 460, 464
Romeo and Juliet, 131, 303, 352, 418, 477, 582, 607
monologue from, 478
Room to Improv, 49
"Roots," 84
Rosalind, 453
Rose, Reginald, 408
Rosencrantz and Guildenstern Are Dead, 139, 468
Rostand, Edmond, 113, 465, 484
Roth, Tim, 139
Rouge, 326
Roundels, 269, 273, 591
Routine, 15
Roxanne, 489
Royal Academy of Dramatic Art, 133
Royal Shakespeare Company, 133, 177
Royalties, 166–167
Rubbing alcohol, 326
Ruined, 471
Rule of three, 138
Rulers, 279
Rumble carts, 296
Running crews, 168–169, 593
Running the show, 593
Rushing, 578–579
Russell Simmons Del Poetry Jam, 366

S

Saar, David, 114
Sabratha, theatre at, 224
Sabre saw, 250
Safety
in costume construction, 306
lighting and, 277–278
makeup and, 327
in scene shops, 256, 263
in set construction, 256
in the theatre, 18
SAG-AFTRA (Screen Actors' Guild-American Federation of Television and Radio Actors), 613
SAG (Screen Actors Guild)
minimum wage, 565
Saint Joan, monologue from, 478–479
Sakuntala, 332
Salach, Cin, 371

Salsation Theater Company, 49
Sanchez, Edwin, 159, 472, 548
San Danielle, Pellegrino da, 445
The Sandbox, 469
Sanskrit drama, 332, 441
Satin, 304
Saturday Night Live, 7, 49
Saws, 249
Scaffolding, 245
Scale models, 232
Scars, 322
Scenario, 57
creating, 57
creating high-stakes, 106–107
evaluating, 158
gathering ideas for, 153–154
sharing, 158
thinking about, 155–156
writing, 156–157
Scenery, 231
in Kabuki theatre, 441
in Noh drama, 440
Scenes
acting in dramatic, 130
casting and rehearsing, 293
for mixed groups, 522–554
for one man and one woman, 493–506
performing, using stage movement, 60
playing, with sound effects, 293
recording, 292
rehearsing, 58, 119
sounds of the, 291
for two men, 506–513
for two women, 513–522
working out the, 57
Scene shifts, 187
Scene shops, 249
safety in, 256, 263
Scene study groups, 90
Schechner, Richard, 178
Schiller, 464
School Daze, 391
The School for Scandal, 137
The School for Wives, 144
Schtick, 138
Schumann, Peter, 377
Science fiction on televison, 577
Scoop floodlight, 268
Scoops, 271, 591
Scoring of role, 561–562
Screwdrivers, 249
Screws, 252
Scrims, 284

Script analysis, 477, 602
Scripts, 585–586
actor creation of own, 575
analyzing, for props, 336
for comedy genre, 585
defined, 150
director's notations on, 67
for dramatic genre, 585
experimental style, 585–586
focusing on character in, 560–561
historical style of, 586
presentational style, 586
reading of, by sound designer, 288
representational style, 586
stage business in, 58
Scrumbling, 258
Seam allowances, 589
Seams, 589
Search for Signs of Intelligent Life in the Universe, 143
monologue from, 479–481
Seascape, 329
The Second City, 43, 49
Second electric, 592
Second screen, 412
Section elevation, 251
Secular drama, 312
Seed: A Weird Act of Faith, 93
Seinfeld, 399, 405, 577
Self-evaluation
for actors, 579
for lighting crew, 595
for makeup crew, 597
for props crew, 599
for sound crew, 610
Seneca, 436
Sense memory, improving your, 25
Sensory recall, 24, 129
Sesame Street, 397, 576
Set construction, 246–265, 604
building flats in, 253–254
growing in, 601
joining flats in, 255
knowing theatre in, 248–250
measurements in, 250–251
painting sets in, 258, 605–606
personnel involved in, 247
platforms in, 257
putting together, 252
rigging in, 259
safety in, 256

Set crews, 586
evaluation questions for, 607
Set design, 230–245, 602
art of, 239
comunication and, 233–234
creativity in technical design in, 232
current, 245
defined, 231
design requirements in, 238
evaluating, 241
history of, 244
incubation in, 231
principles of, 231, 603
setting the mood in, 239
stage elements in, 234–235
types of stages in, 232–233
working on, 240–241
working with space in, 236–237
Set designers, 230, 243, 584
evaluation questions for, 607
growing as, 600
Set dressing, 335
Set pieces, 236
Set props, 335
Sets, 5, 600–607
changing, 605
painting, 258, 605–606
strike of, 168
Setting, 171
Seven Guitars, 161
Sewing, 589
The Shadow of a Gunman, 468
Shadow puppets, 368
Shaffer, Peter, 468
Shakespeare, William, 46, 75, 80, 110, 113, 122, 212, 243, 311, 436, 452–453, 458, 478, 484, 522
tragedies of, 125–126
Shakespearean monologue, 563
Shakespeare on TV, 396
Shamanism, 62
Shamans, 428
Shameless, 399
"Shampapi," 375
Shape, 602
Shaw, George Bernard, 128, 259, 464–465
Shepard, Sam, 470
Sherak, Thomas, 383
Sheridan, Richard Brinsley, 137, 458, 466
Sherwood, Robert, 469
She's Gotta Have It, 391

Index

Index

Training, 569
  for mime and pantomime, 570
Transmitters, 289
Trap, 235
Traveler, 234
Travesties, 468
Travesty, 137
Treme, 407
Trim, 303
Trope, 446
Tungsten lamps, 273
Turning on stage, 55
Turning point in plots, 115, 156
Turturro, John, 393
Twelfth Night, 133, 308, 453
Twelve Angry Men, 408
25th Hour, 391
The Twilight Zone, 577
Twist-lock connectors, 269, 273
Twitter, 413
Two-by-fours, 250–251
Two-Headed, 470
Two Trains Running, 161
Tyler, Royal, 466

U

Uhry, Alfred, 500
Unbleached muslin, 303
Underwear for period costume, 302
Unions, 613
United States. *See also* American theatre
  innovations of, to performance arts, 353
  multicultural heritage of, 462
Unit set, 236
Unity, 201
  set design and, 603
Universality, 333
Upstage, 59, 65
Ushers, 171

V

Value, personal, of theatre, 9
Variation, set design and, 603
Variations, 363
Vaudeville, 353, 467
Vega, Lope de, 450
Velvet, 304
Venus Observed, 468
Video, 367
Vincent, Jean-Pierre, 164
Vinyl paints, 605
Visibility, 267
Vision of directors, 175

Visual arts, 5
Visualization, 24
  in pantomime, 36
Vocal exercises, 18, 80
Vocalization, 15
Vocal training, 76
Voice, 75, 103, 577–579
  inflection of, 78
  pitch of, 78
  production and articulation of, 74–85
  protection of, 76
  volume of, 75, 78, 80
  warming up, 76
Voice-overs, 81, 288
Volpone, 452
Volume, 75, 78, 80

W

Wagner, Jane, 143, 479
Wagner, Richard, 285, 314
Wagons, 605
Waiting at the Station, 463
Waiting for Godot, 101, 126, 469
Waiting for Lefty, 469
A Waitress in Yellowstone or Always Tell the Truth, scene from, 535–539
Walking, 55
Wang, David Henry, 41
Wanted, 405
Wardrobe room, 590
War Horse, 265
Warm ups, 14–20
  exercises for, 16–17
  physical, 572
  reasons for, 15–16
  relaxation techniques in, 16
  routines for, 19–20
  stage fright and, 20
  vocal exercises in, 18
  of voice, 76
Warner Brothers, 391
Washington Square Players, 469
Washinton, George, 466
Wasserstein, Wendy, 145, 470
Water-soluble foundation, 316
Way of Snow, 311
The Way of the World, 458
Webber, Andrew Lloyd, 46, 363
Webster, John, 452
Weeds, 399
West, Cheryl L., 113
West, Dominic, 90
West End, 133

Westerns, 383
West Side Story, 352, 365, 570, 581
West Virginia Formula, 277
The West Wing, 143
We Won't Pay! We Won't Pay!, 469
WGA (Writers Guild of America), 613
Wheel of Fortune, 396
Whistle Down the Wind, 363
White, Vanna, 396
White, Walter, 398
Whitman, Walt, 573
Wicked, 73, 316
Wiggle lights, 271
Wiig, Kristin, 49
Wilde, Oscar, 138–139, 202, 465
Wilder, Thornton, 409, 438, 469–470
Williams, Tennessee, 6, 23, 29, 470
Wilson, August, 159, 161, 171, 333, 471, 487
Wilson, Lanford, 470
Wingfield, Amanda, 6
Wingfield, Laura, 23
Wingfield, Tom, 6
Wings, 235, 581
Wings, 470
Winslet, Kate, 133, 378
Winterset, 469
The Wire, 407
Wisocky, Rebecca, 112
The Wiz, 597
The Wizard of Oz, 383
The Woman in White, 363
Women
  men in playing roles of, 194
  monologues for, 478–483
  scenes for one, and one man, 493–506
  scenes for two, 513–522
Wong, Elizabeth, 551
Wooden O's, 454
Wooster Group, 409
Work gloves, 279
Working and polishing rehearsals, 574
Wrenches, 249
Wrinkles, 323
Wycherly, William, 458

X

The X-Files, 403

Y

Y2K, 470
Yale Repertory, 7
The Yellow Boat, 114
"Yes, and. . .," 43, 104
Yiddish theatre, 145
Yoke, 270
Yoshimitsu, 162
Yoshimura, James, 471
You Can't Take It with You, 469
A Young Lady of Property, 408
You're a Good Man, Charlie Brown, 568
You Tube, 353, 413–414, 418

Z

Zellweger, Renee, 362
Zero Dark Thirty, 383
Zeta-Jones, Catherine, 362
Zimmerman, Mary, 392–393, 542

Bibliography

ACTING

Adler, Stella. *The Art of Acting.* Applause Books, 2000.

Barton, Robert. *Style for Actors.* 2nd ed. Routledge, 2009.

Benedetti, Robert. *The Actor at Work.* 10th ed. Pearson, 2008.

Bernard, Ian. *Film and Television Acting.* 2nd ed. Focal Press, 1997.

Berry, Mick and Michael Edelstein. *Stage Fright: 40 Stars Tell You How They Beat America's #1 Fear.* See Sharp Press, 2009.

Boleslavsky, Richard. *Acting: The First Six Lessons.* Martino Fine Books, 2013.

Chekhov, Michael. *To The Actor.* Rev. ed. Routledge, 2002.

_____. *On the Technique of Acting.* Harper Perennial, 1993.

Callow, Simon. *Being an Actor.* Rev. ed. Picador, 2003.

Cohen, Robert. *Acting Power.* Routledge, 2013.

Cole, Toby, editor. *Acting: A Handbook of the Stanislavski Method.* Rev. Sub ed. Three Rivers Press, 1995.

Cole, Toby and Helen Chinoy. *Actors on Acting.* Rev. ed. Kessinger, 2010.

Crawford, Jerry and Joan Snyder. *Acting in Person and in Style.* 5th ed. Waveland, 2010.

Felner, Mira. *Free to Act: An Integrated Approach to Acting.* 2nd ed. Pearson, 2003.

Franklin, Miriam. *Rehearsal.* Literary Licensing, 2012.

Hagen, Uta. *A Challenge for the Actor.* Scribner's, 1991.

Hagen, Uta, and Haskel Frankel. *Respect for Acting.* 2nd ed. Wiley, 2008.

Harrop, John, and Sabin Epstein. *Acting With Style.* 3rd ed. Pearson, 1999.

Jesse, Anita. *Let the Part Play You: A Practical Approach to the Actor's Creative Process.* 4 Rev. Sub ed. Wolf Creek Press; 1998.

Kahan, Stanley. *Introduction to Acting.* 4th ed. Pearson, 1997.

Kassel, Paul. *Acting: An Introduction to the Art and Craft of Playing.* Pearson, 2006.

Lewis, Robert. *Advice to the Players.* Theatre Communications Group, 1993.

McGaw, Charles. *Acting Is Believing.* 11th ed. Cengage Learning, 2011.

Morris, Eric. *Being and Doing: A Workbook for Actors.* Ermor Enterprises, 2005.

Moore, Sonia. *The Stanislavski System.* 2nd ed. Viking Penguin, 1984.

_____. *Training an Actor.* Rev. ed. Viking Penguin, 1979.

Sonenberg, Janet. *The Actor Speaks: Twenty-four Actors Talk About Process and Technique.* Three Rivers Press, 1996.

Spolin, Viola. *Improvisation for the Theatre: A Handbook of Teaching and Directing Techniques.* 3rd ed. Northwestern University Press, 1999.

_____. *Theatre Game File.* Northwestern University Press, 1989.

Stanislavski, Konstantin. *An Actor Prepares.* Reprint ed. Routledge, 1989.

_____. *Building a Character.* Reprint ed. Routledge, 1989.

Thomas, James. *Script Analysis for Actors, Directors and Designers.* 5th ed. Focal Press, 2013.

ACTING IN SHAKESPEARE

Barton, John. *Playing Shakespeare.* Anchor, 2001.

Bate, Jonathan, and Dora Thornton. *Shakespeare: Staging the World.* Oxford University Press, 2012. Insight into Shakespeare's London and the places and characters in his plays through historic artifacts.

Brine, Adrian, and Michael York. *A Shakespearean Actor Prepares.* Smith and Krause, 2000.

Chute, Marchette. *Shakespeare of London.* Viking Penguin, 1991. Background and feel of Elizabethan times.

Gielgud, John. *Acting Shakespeare.* Applause Books, 2000.

Hodges, Walter. *Shakespeare and the Players.* Coward McCann, 1967. Elizabethan actors and acting.

Linklater, Kristin. *Freeing Shakespeare's Voice: The Actor's Guide to Talking the Text.* Theatre Communications Group, 1993.

Maher, Mary Z. *Modern Hamlets and Their Soliloquies.* University of Iowa Press, 1992.

Rodenburg, Patsy. *Speaking Shakespeare.* Palgrave Macmillan, 2004.

Silverbush, Rhona. *Speak the Speech! Shakespeare's Monologues Illuminated.* Faber and Faber, 2002.

Van Tassel, Wesley. *Clues to Acting Shakespeare.* Allworth Press, 2006.

AUDITIONS

Black, David. *Actor's Audition.* Vintage, 1990.

Callen, K. *How to Sell Yourself as an Actor.* 6th ed. Sweden Press, 2008.

Dennard, Mary Anna. *I GOT IN! The Ultimate College Audition Guide For Acting And Musical Theatre.* 2014 Updated Ed. Mary Anna Austin Dennard, Inc., 2010.

Flom, Jonathon. *Get the Callback: The Art of Auditioning for Musical Theatre.* Scarecrow Press, 2009.

Hunt, Gordon. *How to Audition.* 2nd Sub ed. Collins Reference, 1995.

Merlin, Joanna. *Auditioning: An Actor-Friendly Guide.* Vintage Books, 2001.

Oliver. Donald. *How to Audition for the Musical Theatre.* Rev. Sub ed. Smith and Kraus, 1995.

Richardson, Randall. *The Audition Sourcebook: Do's, Don'ts, and an Online Guide to 2100+ Monologues and Musical Excerpts.* Heinemann, 2002.

Shurtleff, Michael. *Audition: Everything an Actor Needs to Get the Part.* Walker and Company, 2003.

CAREERS

Alterman, Glenn. *Promoting Your Acting Career.* Allworth Press, 2004.

Cohen, Robert. *Acting Professionally: Raw Facts About Careers.* 7th ed. Palgrave Macmillan, 2009.

Fridell, Squire. *Acting in Television Commercials for Fun and Profit.* 4th ed. Three Rivers Press, 2009.

Henry, Mari Lynn, and Lynne Rogers. *How to Be a Working Actor,* 5th ed. Back Stage Books, 2007.

Lawler, Mike. *Careers in Technical Theater.* Allworth Press, 2007.

Logan, Tom. *How to Act and Eat at the Same Time.* Limelight Editions, 2004.

Loveland, Elaina. *Creative Careers.* 2nd ed. Supercollege, 2009.

McKay, Dawn Rosenberg. "Careers in the Performing Arts." About.com http://careerplanning.about.comod/occupations/a/perf_arts.htm

Moore, Dick. *Opportunities in Acting Careers.* McGraw-Hill, 2005.

Volz, Jim. *Working in American Theatre.* 2nd Rev. ed. Bloomsbury Methuen Drama, 2011.

COSTUMES

Baker, Georgia, and Helen Pullen. *A Handbook of Costume Drawing.* 2nd ed. Focal Press, 2000.

Bicât, Tina. *Making Stage Costumes: A Practical Guide.* Crowood, 2001.

Cassin-Scott, Jack. *The Illustrated Encyclopedia of Costumes and Fashion from 1066 to the Present.* Cassell, 2006.

Cunningham, Rebecca. *The Magic Garment.* 2nd ed. Waveland, 2009.

Cumming, Valerie, and Aileen Ribeiro. *The Visual History of Costume.* Rev. ed. Quite Specific Media Group, 1997.

Dial, Tim. *Basic Millinery for the Stage.*

Heinemann Drama, 2002.

Fernald, Mary, and Eileen Shenton. *Historic Costumes and How to Make Them*. Dover, 2006.

Hunnisett, Jean. *Period Costume for Stage and Screen*. Players Press, 1991.

Jackson, Sheila. *Costumes for the Stage: A Complete Handbook for Every Kind of Play*. 2nd ed. New Amsterdam Books, 2001.

Ingham, Rosemary, and Elizabeth Covey. *The Costume Technician's Handbook*. 3rd ed. Heinemann Drama, 2003.

Kidd, Mary. *Stage Costume: Step By Step*. 2nd ed. Betterway, 2002.

LaMotte, Richard. *Costume Design 101*. 2nd Rev. ed. Michael Wiese Productions. 2010.

Litherland, Janet, and Sue McAnally, *Broadway Costumes on a Budget: Big-Time Ideas for Amateur Producers*. Meriwether, 1996.

Musgrove, Jan, *Make-up, Hair, and Costume for Film and Television*. Focal Press, 2003.

Strand-Evans, Katherine. *Costume Construction*. Waveland, 1999.

Tan Huaixiang. *Costume Craftwork on a Budget*. Focal Press, 2007.

Wilcox, Ruth Turner. *Five Centuries of American Costume*. Dover, 2011.

_____. *The Mode in Costume*. 2nd ed. Dover, 2008.

DIRECTING

Ball, William. *A Sense of Direction*. Drama Pub, 1984.

Benedetti, Robert. *The Director at Work*. Prentice Hall, 1985.

Bloom, Michael. *Thinking Like a Director: A Practical Handbook*. Faber & Faber, 2001.

Bogart, Anne. *A Director Prepares: Seven Essays on Art and Theatre*. Routledge, 2001.

Catron, Louis E. *The Director's Vision: Play Direction from Analysis to Production*. Waveland, 2010.

Clurman, Harold. *On Directing*. Touchstone, 1997.

Cole, Toby. *Directors on Directing*. Pearson, 1963.

Converse, Terry John. *Directing for the Stage: A Workshop Guide of Creative Exercises and Projects*. Meriwether, 1995.

Dean, Alexander, and Lawrence Carra. *Fundamentals of Play Directing*. 5th ed. Waveland, 2009.

Deer, Joe. *Directing in Musical Theatre*. Routledge, 2014.

Hauser, Frank, and Russell Reich. *Notes on Directing: 130 Lessons in Leadership from the Director's Chair*. Reprint ed. Walker, 2008.

Hodge, Francis. *Play Directing*. 7th ed. Pearson, 2009.

Kirk, John, Christina Kirk, and Ralph Bellas. *The Art of Directing*. Xlibris, 2004.

Robinson, Mary B. *Directing Plays, Directing People, A Collaborative Art*. Smith & Kraus, 2012.

IMPROVISATION & THEATRE GAMES COLLECTIONS

Barker, Clive. *Theatre Games*. A&C Black, 2010. Includes a DVD showing Barker at work.

Frost, Anthony, and Ralph Yarrow. *Improvisation in Drama*. 2nd ed. Palgrave Macmillan, 2007.

Hodgson, John, and Ernest Richards. *Improvisation*. Grove Press, 1994.

Libera, Anne. *The Second City Almanac of Improvisation*. Northwestern University Press, 2004.

Napier, Mick. *Improvise.: Scene from the Inside Out*. Heinemann Drama, 2004.

Polsky, Milton. *Let's Improvise*. 3rd ed. Applause Books, 2000.

Spolin, Viola. *Improvisation for the Theatre*. 3rd ed. Northwestern University Press, 1999.

_____. *Theatre Games for Rehearsal*. Northwestern University Press, 1985.

LEISURE READING & THEATRE HUMOR

Brandreth, Gyles. *Great Theatrical Disasters*. St. Martin's Press, 1983.

Brook, Peter. *The Empty Space*. Reprint ed. Touchstone, 1995.

Coleman, Terry. *Olivier*. Henry Holt, 2006.

Dolbier, Maurice. *All Wrong on the Night*. Walker, 1966. Vignettes of humorous theatrical errors.

Funke, Lewis and John Booth. *Actors Talk About Acting*. Avon, 1961. Very good for the serious drama student.

Gielgud, John. *Stage Directions*. Sceptre, 1992.

Gillmore, Margalo. *Four Flights Up*. Houghton Mifflin, 1964. Most entertaining.

Grotowski, Jerzy. *Towards a Poor Theatre*. Routledge, 2002.

Guthrie, Tyrone. *Life in the Theatre*. Talman, 1987.

Hart, Moss. *Act One*. 2nd ed. St. Martin's Griffin, 2014. Excellent.

Hay, Peter. *Broadway Anecdotes*. Oxford University Press, 1990.

_____. *Theatrical Anecdotes*. Oxford University Press, 1987.

Hayes, Helen. *My Life in Three Acts*. Harcourt,

Brace, Jovanovich, 1990.

Holbrook, Hal. *Mark Twain Tonight*. Pyramid Books, 1967.

Houseman, John. *Unfinished Business*. Applause Books, 2000.

Lewes, George. *On Actors and the Art of Acting*. Forgotten Books, 2012.

Martin, Mary. *My Heart Belongs*. William Morrow, 1976.

Mosel, Tad, and Gertrude Macy. *Leading Lady: Katharine Cornell*. Little, Brown, 1978.

Nightingale, Benedict. *Great Moments in the Theatre*. Oberon Books, 2013.

Redgrave, Michael. *The Actor's Ways and Means*. 2nd ed. Routledge, 1995.

Shaw, George Bernard. *Shaw on Theatre*. Hill and Wang, 1967.

Sherrin, Ned. *Voices from the Wings: A Connoisseur's Collection of Great Theatrical & Showbiz Anecdotes*. Rev. and enlarged ed. JR Books, 2008.

Stanislavski, Konstantin. Jean Benedetti, trans. *My Life in Art*. Routledge, 2008.

MAKEUP

Corson, Richard. *Fashions in Hair*. 3rd ed. Peter Owen, 2005.

_____. *Stage Makeup*. 10th ed. Pearson, 2009.

Davis, Gretchen, and Mindy Hall. *The Makeup Artist Handbook*. 2nd ed. Focal Press, 2012.

Swinfield, Rosemarie. *Stage Makeup Step-by-Step*. Betterway Books, 1995.

_____. *Period Makeup for the Stage: Step-by-Step*. Betterway Books, 1997.

Thudium, Laura. *Stage Makeup: The Actor's Complete Guide*. Backstage Books, 1999.

MONOLOGUE COLLECTIONS

Aston, Irene Ziegler, ed. *The Ultimate Audition Book: 222 Comedy Monologues, 2 Minutes And Under*. Smith & Kraus, 2005.

Beard, Jocelyn A., et. al., eds. *The Ultimate Audition Book: 222 Monologues 2 Minutes and Under*. Smith & Kraus, 1997.

Capecci, John, et. al., eds. *The Ultimate Audition Book: 222 Monologues, 2 Minutes and Under from Literature*. Smith & Kraus, 2002.

Catalano, Frank. *The Art of the Monologue: Monologues They Haven't Heard Yet*. BookSurge Publishing, 2007.

Coen, Stephanie. *American Theatre Book of Monologues for Men*. Theatre Communications Group, 2001.

_____. *American Theatre Book*

of Monologues for Women. Theatre Communications Group, 2001.

Depner, Mary. Echo Booming Monologues: 100 Monologues for Teens. Jelliroll, 2007.

_____. 50/50 Monologues for Student Actors. Meriwether, 2011.

Edwards, Gus. 50 African American Audition Monologues. Heinemann, 2002.

_____. Monologues on Black Life. Heinemann, 1997.

_____. More Monologues on Black Life. Heinemann, 2000.

Henry, Joyce E., et. al., eds. One on One: The Best Men's Monologues for the 21st Century. Applause Books, 2008.

_____. One on One: The Best Women's Monologues for the 21st Century. Applause Books, 2007.

Johnson, Phyllis C. Just Me: 100 Monologues for Teens. Meriwether, 2013.

Price, Lindsay. Competition Monologues. Theatrefolk, Vol. 1, 2004; Vol 2, 2012.

Rudnicki, Stefan. The Actor's Book of Classical Monologues. Penguin Books, 1988.

_____. The Actor's Book of Monologues for Women. Viking Penguin, 1991.

Slaight, Craig, and Jack Sharrar. Great Monologues for Young Actors.

Smith and Kraus, Vol I, 1992; Vol 2, 1999; Vol III, 2009.

Smith, Marisa, and Kristin Graham. Monologues from Literature. Fawcett, 1990.

Uno, Roberta. Monologues for Actors of Color. Routledge, 2000.

MOVEMENT & MIME

Aubert, Charles. The Art of Pantomime. Dover, 2003.

Davies, Gill. Staging a Pantomime. A&C Black, 1996.

Hobbs, William. Stage Combat: The Action to the Word. St. Martin's, 1981.

Howell, Jonathan. Stage Fighting: A Practical Guide. Crowood Press, 2009.

Kipnis, Claude. The Mime Book. Meriwether, 1988.

Lust, Annette. Bringing the Body to the Stage and Screen. Scarecrow Press, 2011.

Martinez, J. D. Combat Mime: A Non-Violent Approach to Stage Violence. Rowan & Littlefield, 1982.

Oxenford, Lyn. Playing Period Plays. Dramatic Publishing, 1995.

Sabatine, Jean. Movement Training for Stage and Screen. Watson-Guptill, 1995.

Snow, Jackie. Movement Training for Actors.

Bloomsbury Methuen Drama. 2013. Includes a DVD.

Stolzenberg, Mark. Be a Mime. Sterling, 2001.

OTHER THEATRE FORMS

Alpert, Hollis. Broadway, 125 Years of Musical Theatre. Arcade Publishing, 1991.

Baird, Bil The Art of the Puppet, Bonanza Books, 1973.

Beddow, Margery. Bob Fosse's Broadway. Heinemann, 1996.

Bell, John. Puppets, Masks, and Performing Objects. MIT Press, 2001.

_____. Strings, Hands, Shadows: A Modern Puppet History. Detroit Institute of Arts, 2000.

Bloom, Ken. American Song: The Complete Musical Theatre Companion. Schirmer Books, 1996.

Bloom, Ken, and Frank Vlastnik. Broadway Musicals. Black Dog & Leventhal, 2010.

Conrad, Christine. Jerome Robbins: That Broadway Man, That Ballet Man. Booth Clibborn Editions, 2000.

Currell, David. Puppets and Puppet Theatre. Crowood Press, 1999.

Davis, Lee. Bolton and Wodehouse and Kern, The Men Who Made Musical Comedy. Heinemann, 1993.

Deer, Joe. Directing in Musical Theatre. Routledge, 2014.

DeVenney, David P. The New Broadway Song Companion, An Annotated Guide to Musical Theatre Literature by Voice Type and Song Title. 2nd ed. Scarecrow Press, Inc., 2009.

Eleveld, Mark, editor. The Spoken Word Revolution: Slam, Hip Hop & the Poetry of a New Generation, Sourcebooks, 2005.

Filichia, Peter. Let's Put on a Musical!: How to Choose the Right Show for Your School. Watson-Guptill, 2004.

Hobbs, William. Stage Combat: The Action to the Word. St. Martin's, 1981.

Jones, Stanleigh H. Jr. The Bunraku Puppet Theater of Japan. University of Hawaii Press, 2012.

Mandelbaum, Ken. A Chorus Line and the Musicals of Michael Bennett. St. Martin's Press, 1989.

Miletich, Leo N. Broadway's Prize-Winning Musicals, An Annotated Guide for Libraries and Audio Collectors. Routledge, 1993.

Mordden, Ethan. Anything Goes: A History of American Musical Theatre. Oxford University Press, 2013.

Novak, Elaine A., and Deborah. Staging Musical Theatre, A Complete Guide for Directors, Choreographers and Producers.

Better Way Books, 1996.

Shepard, Aaron. Readers on Stage: Resources for Readers Theater. Shepard Publications, 2004.

PLAY ANTHOLOGIES – THREE-ACT

Allison, Alexander, Arthur Carr, and Arthur Eastman. Masterpieces of Drama. 6th ed. Longman, 1990.

Barnes, Clive. Best American Plays: Ninth Series 1983-1992 Complete. Crown, 1993.

Barnet, Sylvan, Morton Berman, and William Burto. Types of Drama: Plays and Essays. 8th ed. Longman, 2001.

Cerf, Bennett, and Van Cartmell. Plays of Our Time. Random House, 1967.

Gainor, J. Ellen, et. al, eds. The Norton Anthology of Drama (Vol. 1 & 2). W. W. Norton, 2009.

Gassner, John. Best American Plays. Crown Publishers. Eight in the series from 1918 to 1982.

_____. Best Plays of the Early American Theater. Dover, 2000. Includes 16 plays from 1787 to 1911.

_____. Treasury of the Theatre. Simon and Schuster. Series 1935, 1940, 1951, 1963, 1967, 1970.

_____. Twenty-Five Best Plays of the Modern American Theatre. Crown, 1980.

Godinez, Henry, and Ramon H. Rivera-Servera, eds. The Goodman Theatre's Festival Latino: Six Plays. Northwestern University Press, 2013.

Goldman, Mark, and Isadore Traschen. The Drama: Traditional and Modern. Allyn and Bacon, 1969.

Goodman, Randolph. From Script to Stage: Eight Modern Plays. Rinehart Press, 1971. Plays and discussions on their staging.

_____. Drama on Stage. 2nd ed. Harcourt College, 1978.

Hatlen, Theodore. Drama Principles and Plays. 2nd ed. Prentice-Hall, 1975.

Hay, David, and James Howell. Contact With Drama. Science Research Associates, 1974.

Jones, Douglas A. Jr., and Harry J. Elam Jr. The Methuen Drama Book of Post-black Plays. Bloomsbury Methuen Drama, 2013.

Perfection Learning Corporation. Page to Stage: Plays from Classic Literature, 2002.

_____. Drama for Reading and Performance, Collection One, 2002.

_____. Drama for Reading and Performance, Collection Two, 2002.

Perrine, Laurence. Dimensions of Drama. Harcourt College, 1973. Comments and study questions.

Pickering, Jerry. *A Treasury of Drama: Classical Through Modern.* West, 1975.

Roudane, Matthew. *Drama Essentials: An Anthology of Plays.* Cengage Learning, 2007.

PLAY ANTHOLOGIES — ONE-ACT

Barlow, Judith E. *Women Writers of the Provincetown Players: A Collection of Short Works.* State University of New York Press, 2009.

Bert, Norman A. and Deb. *More One-Act Plays for Acting Students.* 2nd ed. Meriwether, 2003.

_____. *New One-Act Plays for Acting Students.* Meriwether, 2003.

Bruchac, Joseph. *Pushing Up the Sky: Seven Native American Plays for Children.* Dial Books, 2000.

Cerf, Bennett, and Van Cartmell. *Thirty Famous One-Act Plays.* Modern Library, Random House, 1979.

_____. *Twenty-Four Favorite One-Act Plays.* Broadway Books, 1963.

Coleman, Wim. *Nine Muses: Modern Plays from Classic Myths.* Perfection Learning Corporation, 2001.

France, Rachel. *A Century of Plays by American Women.* Rosen, 1979.

Gassner, John, and Frederick Little. *Reading and Staging the Play.* Holt, Rinehart and Winston, 1967. Excellent plays with notes on production, setting, and interpretation.

Halpern, Dan. *Plays in One Act.* 2nd ed. Harper Perennial, 2005.

Kozelka, Paul. *Fifteen American One-Act Plays.* Washington Square Press, 1971. Excellent plays.

Lewis, Jacquie J. and Diane Warren. *Eureka! 7 One-Act Plays for Secondary Schools.* Coteau Books, 1996.

Pizzarello, Jason. *Random Acts of Comedy: 15 Hit One-Act Plays for Student Actors.* Playscripts, 2011.

Richards, Stanley. *Best Short Plays.* Chilton. Series from 1969 to present.

_____. *Best Short Plays of the World Theatre.* Crown. Three series from 1958 to 1973.

Scanlan, Michael. *Inside/Out.* Bakers Plays, Boston, 1984. Features issues important to teens.

Shepard, Sam. *Fifteen One-Act Plays.* Reprint ed. Vintage, 2012.

Sweetkind, Morris. *Ten Great One-Act Plays.* Bantam, 1972.

Waldrep, Mary Carolyn, ed. *Twelve Classic One-Act Plays.* Dover, 2010.

Weiss, Jerry. *Ten Short Plays.* Dell, 1972.

Zachar, Irwin. *Plays as Experience: One-Act Plays for the Secondary Schools.* 2nd Rev. ed. Odyssey Press, 1979.

PLAY INDEXES

Logasa, Hanna. *Index to One-Act Plays.* F. W. Faxon Company. 1966.

Keller, Dean. *Index to Plays in Periodicals, 1977–1987.* Scarecrow Press, 1990.

Greenfieldt, John. *Play Index 2003-2007: An Index to 2,792 Plays.* H. W. Wilson, 2009.

Montgomery, Denise L. *Ottemiller's Index to Plays in Collections.* 8th ed. Scarecrow Press, 2011.

Slaight, Craig, et. al., eds. *The Smith and Kraus Play Index for Young Actors Grades 6-12.* Smith & Kraus, 2000. Yaakov, Juliette, ed. *Play Index.* H. W. Wilson. 1993 (1988–1992) and (1998) 1993–1997.

Play indexes are also available in online databases through many libraries, such as H. W. Wilson's *Play Index* through Ebsco. See www.ebscohost.comacademic/play-index

SCENE COLLECTIONS

Beard, Jocelyn A., ed. *Scenes from Classic Plays.* Smith & Kraus, 1994.

Bert, Norman. *The Scenebook for Actors.* Meriwether, 1990.

Brown, John R. *Shakescenes: Shakespeare for Two.* Applause Books, 2000.

Cassady, Marshall. *The Book of Cuttings for Acting and Directing.* NTC, 1991.

_____. *The Book of Scenes for Acting Practice.* Glencoe/McGraw-Hill, 2001.

Cohen, Lorraine. *Scenes for Young Actors.* Avon Books, 1990.

Elkind, Samuel. *Scenes for Acting and Directing Volume 3.* Players Press, 2003.

Franklin, Miriam. *Rehearsal.* Literary Licensing, 2012.

Harbison, Lawrence, ed. *The Best Men's Stage Monologues & Scenes 2012.* Smith & Kraus, 2013.

_____. *The Best Women's Stage Monologues & Scenes 2012.* Smith & Kraus, 2013.

Henry, Joyce E., et. al., eds. *Duo!: The Best Scenes for Two for the 21st Century.* Applause Books, 2009.

Hooks, Ed, ed. *The Ultimate Scene and Monologue Sourcebook.* 2nd ed. Back Stage Books, 2007.

King, Woodie, Jr. *Voices of Color 50 Scenes & Monologues.* Applause Books, 2000.

Kluger, Garry Michael. *Fifty Professional Scenes for Student Actors.* Meriwether, 1993.

Nicholas, Angela. *99 Film Scenes for Actors.* Avon, 1999.

Pizzarello, Jason, ed. *Actor's Choice: Scenes for Teens.* Playscripts, 2010.

Schulman, Michael, and Eva Mekler. *Play the Scene: The Ultimate Collection of Contemporary and Classic Scenes and Monologues.* St. Martin's Griffin, 2004.

Stevens, Chambers. *Sensational Scenes for Teens.* Sandcastle, 2001.

Steffensen, James. *Great Scenes from the World Theatre.* Avon Books, 1987.

Wilson, Michael. *Scenes from Shakespeare.* Meriwether, 1993.

_____. *More Scenes from Shakespeare.* Meriwether, 1999.

SCENERY, LIGHTING, & PRODUCTION

Adler, Phoebe, ed. *Behind the Scenes: Contemporary Set Design.* Black Dog Publishing, 2014.

Arnold, Richard. *Scene Technology.* 3rd ed. Prentice Hall, 1993.

Boger, Louise. *The Complete Guide to Furniture Styles.* Waveland, 1997.

Blurton, John. *Scenery: Drafting and Construction.* Routledge, 2001.

Carver, Rita Kogler. *Stagecraft Fundamentals.* 2nd ed. Focal Press, 2012.

Fraser, Neil. *Stage Lighting Explained.* Crowood Press, 2002.

Gassner, John, and Frederick Little. *Reading and Staging the Play.* Holt, Rinehart and Winston, 1967.

Gillette, Michael J. *Designing With Light.* 6th ed. McGraw-Hill, 2013.

_____. *Theatrical Design and Production.* 7th ed. McGraw-Hill, 2012.

Glerum, J. O. *Stage Rigging Handbook.* 3rd ed. Southern Illinois University Press, 2007.

Wilson, Andy. *Making Stage Props: A Practical Guide.* Crowood Press, 2003.

Hays, David. *Light on the Subject: Stage Lighting for Directors and Actors.* Rev. ed. Limelight, 2004.

Kelly, Thomas. *A Backstage Guide to Stage Management.* 3rd ed. Back Stage Books, 2009.

Langley, Stephen. *Theatre Management and Production in America.* Drama Book Publishers, 2006.

Gardyne, John. *Producing Musicals: A Practical Guide.* Crowood Press, 2004.

Wolf, R. Craig, and Dick Block. *Scene Design and Stage Lighting.* 10th ed. Cengage Learning, 2013.

Swift, Charles I. *Introduction to Stage*

Lighting: The Fundamentals of Theatre Lighting Design. Meriwether, 2004.

Winslow, Colin. *The Handbook of Techniques for Theatre Designers.* Crowood Press, 2011.

STORYTELLING

Greene, Ellin, and Joyce M. Del Negro. *Storytelling: Art and Technique.* 4th ed. Libraries Unlimited, 2010.

Breneman, Lucille and Bren. *Once Upon a Time: A Storytelling Handbook.* Burnham, 1983.

Bryant, Sara. *How to Tell Stories to Children.* Sophia Institute Press, 2008.

Lipman, Doug. *Improving Your Storytelling.* August House, 1999.

MacDonald, Margaret Read. *The Storyteller's Start-Up Book.* August House, 2006.

Mellon, Nancy. *Storytelling with Children.* Hawthorn Press, 2000.

Mooney, Bill, and David Holt. *Storyteller's Guide.* August House, 2005.

Pellowski, Anne. *The World of Storytelling.* Rev. ed. H. W. Wilson, 1991.

Philips, Sarah. *Drama with Children.* Oxford University Press, 1999.

Sawyer, Ruth. *The Way of the Storyteller.* Rev. ed. Penguin Books, 1977.

Warren, Liz. *The Oral Tradition Today: An Introduction to the Art of Storytelling.* Pearson Learning Solutions, 2008.

Zipes, Jack. *Speaking Out: Storytelling and Creative Drama for Children.* Routledge, 2004.

THEATRE APPRECIATION & CRITICISM

Barranger, M. S. *Theatre: A Way of Seeing.* 7th ed. Cengage Learning, 2014.

Blurn, Daniel, and John Willis. *A Pictorial History of American Theatre.* 6th Rev. ed. Crown Publishers, 1986.

Brockett, Oscar G., and Robert J. Ball. *The Essential Theatre, Enhanced.* 10th ed. Cengage Learning, 2013.

Brustein, Robert. *Rants and Raves, Opinions, Tributes and Elegies.* Smith & Kraus, 2011.

_____. *Siege of the Arts: Collected Writings, 1994-2001.* Ivan R. Dee, 2001.

Cohen, Robert. *Theatre.* 9th ed. McGraw-Hill Humanities, 2010.

Downs, William Missouri, et. al. *The Art of Theatre: A Concise Introduction.* 3rd ed. Cengage Learning, 2012.

Forrest, Tim. *The Bulfinch Anatomy of Antique Furniture.* Little, Brown and Company, 1996.

Haymon, Ronald. *How to Read a Play.* Rev. Upd ed. Grove Press, 1999.

Pickering, Kenneth, and Mark Woolgar.

Theatre Studies. Palgrave Macmillan, 2009.

Porter, Tom, and Sue Goldman. *Designer Primer,* Architectural Press, 2000.

Wilson, Edwin. *The Theatre Experience.* 10th ed. New York: McGraw-Hill Humanities, 2005.

_____, and Alvin Goldfarb. *Theatre: The Lively Art.* 8th ed. McGraw-Hill Humanities, 2012.

THEATRE HISTORY

Allen, John. *Great Moments in the Theatre.* Phoenix House, 1958. Interesting true stories about important happenings in the theatre; good for reading aloud or to use as lecture sidelights.

Benedetti, Jean. *The Art of the Actor: The Essential History of Acting.* Routledge, 2007.

Blum, Daniel. *A Pictorial History of the American Theatre, 1860–1985.* 6th ed. Crown, 1986.

Brockett, Oscar G., and Franklin J. Hildy. *History of the Theatre.* 10th ed. Pearson, 2007.

Duer, Edwin. *The Length and Depth of Acting.* Holt, Rinehart and Winston, 1963. A history of acting.

Ernst, Earle. *The Kabuki Theatre.* University of Hawaii Press, 1974.

Haar, Frances. *Japanese Theatre in Highlight.* 2nd ed. Charles Tuttle, 1971. Excellent pictures.

Hamilton, Edith. *The Greek Way. Reissue ed.* W. W. Norton, 1993. (Abridged in National Geographic, March 1944.)

_____. *The Roman Way. Reissue ed.* W. W. Norton, 1993.

Hartnol, Phyllis, and Enoch Brater. *The Theatre: A Concise History.* 4th ed. Thames & Hudson, 2012.

Hill, Errol G., and James V. Hatch. *A History of African American Theatre.* Cambridge University Press, 2006.

Kitto, H. D. F. *Greek Tragedy.* 2nd ed. Routledge, 2002.

Kuritz, Paul. *The Making of Theatre History.* Prentice Hall, 1988.

Macgowan, Kenneth. *The Living Stage: A History of World Theatre.* Prentice-Hall, 1955. Very good.

_____. and William Melnitz. *Golden Ages of the Theatre.* 2nd ed. Prentice-Hall, 1979.

_____. and Herman Rosse. *Masks and Demons.* Reprint ed. Kessinger, 2003. Readings on primitive theatre.

McDonald, Marianne, and Michael Walton. *The Cambridge Companion to Greek and Roman Theatre.* Cambridge University Press, 2007.

Meserve, Walter and Mollie. *A Chronological Outline of World Theatre.* Feedback Theatre Books, 1992.

Mordden, Ethan. *Anything Goes: A History of American Musical Theatre.* Oxford University Press, 2013.

Nightingale, Benedict. *Great Moments in the Theatre.* Oberon Books, 2013.

Ortolani, Benito. *The Japanese Theatre.* Rev. ed. Princeton University Press, 1995.

Wilmeth, Don B., and Christopher Bigsby, eds. *The Cambridge History of American Theatre.* Cambridge University Press, Vol 1, 1998; Vol 2, 2006.

Wilson, Edwin, and Alvin Goldfarb. *Living Theatre: A History.* 5th ed. McGraw-Hill Humanities, 2006.

Zarilli, Phillip B., et. al. *Theatre Histories: An Introduction.* 2nd ed. Routledge, 2009.

VOICE & ORAL INTERPRETATION, DIALECT, DICTION, & PRONUNCIATION

Alburger, James. *The Art of Voice Acting.* 4th ed. Focal Press, 2010.

Berry, Cecily. *Voice and the Actor.* Wiley, 1991.

Blumenfeld, Robert. *Accents: A Manual for Actors.* Rev. ed. Limelight, 2004.

Blunt, Jerry. *Stage Dialects.* Dramatic Publishing, 1994.

_____. *More Stage Dialects.* Dramatic Publishing, 1996.

Bowen, Elbert, and others. *Communicative Reading.* 4th ed. Macmillan, 1990.

Crannell, Kenneth. *Voice and Articulation.* 5th ed. Cengage Learning, 2011.

Eisenson, Jon, and Arthur M. *Voice and Diction: A Program for Improvement.* 7th ed. Pearson, 1996.

Hobbs, Bob. *Teach Yourself Transatlantic.* Mayfield, 1986.

King, Robert and Eleanor DiMichael. *Voice and Diction Handbook.* Waveland, 1991.

Lee, Charlotte, and Timothy Gura. *Oral Interpretation.* 12th ed. Pearson, 2009.

Lessac, Arthur. *The Use and Training of the Human Voice.* 3rd ed. McGraw-Hill, 1996.

Linklater, Kristan. *Freeing the Natural Voice.* Rev. Exp ed. Drama Publishers, 2006.

Machlin, Evangeline. *Speech for the Stage.* 2nd ed. Routledge, 1992.

Meier, Paul. *Accents & Dialects for Stage and Screen.* 22nd ed. Paul Meier Dialect Services, 2012.

Shepard, Aaron. *Readers on Stage: Resources for Readers Theater.* Shepard Publications, 2004.

Tanner, Fran. *Readers Theatre Fundamentals.* 2nd ed. Clark Publishing, 1993.

Turner, J. Clifford, and Jane Boston. *Voice and Speech in the Theatre.* 6th ed. Bloomsbury Methuen Drama, 2007.

Yordon, Judy. *Roles in Interpretation.* 5th ed. McGraw-Hill Humanities, 2001.

PLAY PUBLISHERS

Dramatic Publishing Co.
311 Washington St.
Woodstock, IL 60098
www.dramaticpublishing.com

Dramatists Play Service
440 Park Ave. S.
New York, NY 10016
www.dramatists.com

Eldridge Plays and Musicals
P.O. Box 14367
Tallahassee, FL 32317
http://www.histage.com

Samuel French, Inc.
235 Park Avenue South, 5th Floor
New York, NY 10003
Phone (866) 598-8449 Fax (212) 206-1429
www.samuelfrench.com

New Plays, Inc.,
1026 Highlands Drive
Charlottesville, VA 22901
Phone (434) 823-7555

Perfection Learning Corp.,
1000 North Second Avenue, P.O. Box 500,
Logan, IA 51546
www.perfectionlearning.com

Pioneer Drama Service, Inc.
PO Box 4267
Englewood, CO 80155-4267
www.pioneerdrama.com

Players Press, Inc.
P.O. Box 1132
Studio City, CA 91614
Phone (818) 789-4980

Plays, the Drama Magazine for Young People
897 Washington St. #600160
Newton, MA 02460
www.playsmagazine.com

Playscripts, Inc.
450 Seventh Ave., Suite 809
New York, NY 10123
www.playscripts.com

Smith and Kraus Publishers, Inc.
40 Walch Drive
Portland, ME 04103
www.smithandkraus.com

www.stageplays.com

SUGGESTED PLAYS FOR SCHOOL PRODUCTIONS

The following listings include these abbreviations:

DPC: Dramatic Publishing Company
DPS: Dramatists Play Service
French: Samuel French

Three-Act Plays
Classics

Arms and the Man. George Bernard Shaw. Comic satire. 5m 3w. French. 1885 costumes. Raina, the romantic daughter of an Hungarian major, assists an enemy soldier who hides in her home. After the war, the soldier returns to add amusing complications to Raina's planned life.

The Doctor in Spite of Himself. Molière. Comic satire. 8m 5w. French. 17th century French costumes. To spite her lazy husband, Martine tells some strangers that he is a wonderful doctor, but will never admit it until he has been beaten. After a beating Sganarelle not only agrees to being a doctor, but "cures" a very sick maiden by arranging for her to elope with her lover.

The Imaginary Invalid. Molière. Comic satire. 8m 4w. DPC. 17th century French costumes. Argan thinks himself ill and wishing to have a doctor with him at all times, decides to have his daughter marry a doctor. She refuses because she is in love with another. Comic disguises on the part of her lover and servant cure her father, and he agrees to her desired marriage.

The Importance of Being Earnest. Oscar Wilde. Farce. 4m 4w. French. Victorian costumes. When Jack courts Gwendolen, he faces numerous problems because he doesn't have the name of Ernest. Merry complications evolve. Excellent farce.

The Inspector General. Gogol. Farce. 19m 9w (many can be doubles). French. 19th century costumes. The crooked politicians of a small Russian town mistake a young braggart for an important government official. Only after they have wined and dined him and have nothing left, do they discover the real government inspector.

Lady Precious Stream. Hsiung. Romantic drama. 16m 8w. Extras. French. When Lady Precious Stream, the daughter of a nobleman, marries a humble gardener, her family disowns her. After years of hardship and adventure, her husband becomes king of the western regions and they again live the noble life. Done in traditional Chinese style.

The Miser. Molière. Comic satire. 11m 5w. French. 17th century French costumes. A greedy father refuses to allow his children to marry as they wish, until he loses his money chest. Delightful situations occur before he regains his money and the children get their wishes.

The Rivals. Richard Brinsley Sheridan. Comedy. 8m 4w. French. 18th century costumes. Lydia is attracted to a young

man, Beverley, because she believes he is a romantic peasant. Her aunt disapproves because she wants Lydia to marry the wealthy Jack Absolute. Humorous complications result when Beverley turns out to be Jack in disguise, and Lydia refuses to marry him because of his money.

School for Scandal. Richard Brinsley Sheridan. Comedy. 12m 4w. French. 18th century costumes. Intrigues of an artificial society are humorously brought to life as we learn the real character of two brothers who are trying to impress their wealthy uncle.

She Stoops to Conquer. Oliver Goldsmith. Comedy. 15m 4w. French. 18th century costumes. A merry intrigue as the Hardcastles attempt to marry off their two children.

Shakespeare, William
As You Like It
Taming of the Shrew
Midsummer Night's Dream
Twelfth Night
Comedy of Errors
(acting editions and *Romeo and Juliet* streamlined versions are available through French)

Comedies & Farces

Many classic plays, including those by Shakespeare, are available as free e-books through Project Gutenberg at www.gutenberg.org/. Be sure to determine if fees must be paid if you use these scripts for public performances.

Ah Wilderness! Eugene O'Neill. 9m 6w. French. 1910 costumes. A small-town family becomes involved with the antics of its teenage son as he asserts his independence. Length needs cutting.

Almost, Maine Jon Cariani. 2m 2w. DPS. On a winter's night, residents of an isolated, mythical town in Maine fall in and out of love in surprising ways with often hilarious results.

Charley's Aunt. Brandon Thomas. 6m 4w. French. 1892 costumes. Farcical fun begins when an Oxford university student disguises himself as a friend's aunt, so that his friends may entertain their lady loves, properly chaperoned. When the real aunt appears, the frolic becomes even more involved.

Cheaper By The Dozen. Christopher Setgel from the book by Ernestine and Frank Gilbreth. 9m 7w. DPC. Father, an efficiency expert, runs his family of 12 children with efficient factory methods that lead to many humorous events. Good family comedy.

The Curious Savage. John Patrick. 5m 6w. DPS. Mrs. Savage has been left a fortune by her late husband. Because she will not give it to her greedy stepchildren, they commit her to a sanitarium. She meets delightful people there and decides to help them with her money.

The Happiest Millionaire. Kyle Crichton. 9m 6w. DPS. 1916 costumes. A millionaire father's zest for life creates many humorous events as he lunges from one interest into another, including "testing" his daughter's boyfriend.

Ladies of the Jury. Fred Ballard. Comedy-drama. 12m 10w. French. Jury members in a murder trial gradually reverse their decisions through the subtle suggestions of a keenly intelligent lady juror.

Life With Father. Howard Lindsay and Russel Crouse. 8m 8w. DPS. 1880 costumes. Amusing family life as Vinnie enlists her children and relatives to help in getting Father baptized against his wishes.

The Loud Red Patrick. John Boruff. 4m 5w. French. 1912 costumes. An Irish widower who has always taught his four daughters the importance of intellectual freedom finds his democratic family council going against him when his oldest daughter decides to substitute marriage for college.

The Madwoman of Chaillot. Jean Giraudoux. 17m 8w. DPS. A "madwoman" decides to free the world of financiers and other materialists whose worship of money breeds unhappiness. She traps them in a unique way and thus saves Paris.

The Matchmaker. Thornton Wilder. 9m 7w. French. 1880 costumes. A rich merchant hires a lady to arrange for him a marriage with a young girl. The farcical events end with his marrying the lady he hired. Light and fun.

Nuts in May. Kristen Sergel from the book by Cornelia Otis Skinner. 6m 10w. DPC. It is the opening of Miss Skinner's new Broadway play, but instead of a quiet day of rest, she is besieged by well wishing family and friends who are more nervous than she. The fun continues when Cornelia's teenage son reveals that he has accidently asked two dates to the opening.

Our Hearts Were Young and Gay. Jean Kerr, adapted from Cornelia Otis Skinner's novel. 9m 8w. DPC. 1920 costumes. The merry adventures of two girls as they sail for Europe and "discover" Paris. Length needs cutting.

Romanoff and Juliet. Peter Ustinov. 9m 4w. DPS. When the son of a Russian ambassador and the daughter of an American ambassador fall in love, humorous trouble ensues.

Scapino. Frank Dunlop, Jim Dale, and Molière. 10m 4w. DPC. The comic romps of Scapino lead to hilarious situations.

The Solid Gold Cadillac. Teichmann and Kaufman. 13m 5w. DPS. When a little old lady with her ten shares of stock attends a stockholders' meeting of a big company, her questions so worry the directors that they hire her to keep her quiet. But she is not easily subjugated. Needs some editing.

The Star-Spangled Girl. Neil Simon. 2m 1w. French. Two earnest young men, struggling to put out a "protest" magazine, spin into romance when an all-American girl moves next door. Witty lines and humorous situations.

You Can't Take It With You. Moss Hart and George Kaufman. 9m 7w. DPS. A delightful family, each pursuing different hobbies, lives a pleasing, unorthodox life that almost breaks up the daughter's romance when her boyfriend's family arrives unexpectedly and is shocked by the activities. Excellent.

Was He Anyone? N. F. Simpson. 3m 4w. DPC. A comic "absurdist" satire on organized charity and bureaucracy as various organizations decide how best to help a man drowning in the Mediterranean.

Dramas

The Barretts of Wimpole Street. Rudolph Besier. 12m 5w. Romantic drama. DPS. 1850 costumes. The romance of Elizabeth Barrett and Robert Browning, against the background of Elizabeth's tyrannical father whom she finally resists. Difficult but worthwhile.

The Crucible. Arthur Miller. 10m 10w. DPS. An exciting historical drama about the Puritan purge of witchcraft in old Salem. A classic.

The Diary of Anne Frank. Goodrich and Hackett. 5m 5w. DPS. The story of a Jewish family who goes into hiding in World War II and the shining spirit of the young teenage Anne.

The Dining Room. A. R. Gurney. 3m 3w. DPS. Cast portrays a wide array of characters. The action embodies humorous as well as touching scenes that show the vanishing lifestyle of the upper middle class where the now neglected dining room was once a vital center of family life.

The Diviners. James Leonard. 6m 5w. French. A compelling story of the 1930s when a disenchanted preacher makes friends with a disturbed young man who is afraid of water in any form.

I Remember Mama. John VanDruten, adapted from Katharine Forbes' *Mama's Bank Account.* 9w 13w. DPS. Costumes 1900–1910. (Special version for high schools is available.) Life of a Scandinavian immigrant family who meets its problems with humor and pathos, as the children grow up, graduate, and launch careers. Excellent characterizations.

Inherit the Wind. Jerome Lawrence and Robert Lee. 21m 6w. (Many parts can be doubled.) DPS. 1920 costumes. A poignant, meaningful drama of the Scope's trial concerning the legality of teaching Darwin's Theory of Evolution in the schools. Excellent dialogue.

The Night Thoreau Spent in Jail. Lawrence and Lee. 11m 5w. French. Thoreau as a young man struggling with the principles he stands for and learning from Emerson; all placed in montage for a single night's experience.

Our Town. Thornton Wilder. 17m 7w. French. 1901 costumes. A beautiful play of American life in a small village at the turn of the century. The Gibbs and Webbs watch their children grow up, marry, and then meet death. A deeply moving play in all its simplicity.

The Rainmaker. Richard Nash. Romantic drama. 6m 1w. French. A man who says he can bring rain comes to a drought area and sells his plan to a family. Through him they learn the value of a dream and their plain sister, who is doomed an old maid, learns to believe she is pretty and becomes so. Terrific pace.

Twelve Angry Men. Reginald Ross. 13m. (Also women's version: *Twelve Angry Women,* or mixed cast version: *Twelve Angry Jurors.*) DPC. Jurors in a murder case attempt to reach a verdict, and in so doing, learn much about themselves.

Fantasies

Alice in Wonderland. Lewis Carroll's classic adapted by The Manhattan Project at NYU as directed by Andre Gregory. 4m 2w. DPS. Alice's familiar adventures are presented with some startling differences as the play explores the human psyche in its humorous and horrible aspects with appearances by Freud, Jung, Kafka, and Dali.

Berkeley Square. John Balderston. Drama 7m 8w. French. Some 18th century costumes. A modern American goes to England when he inherits an old English ancestral house in London. There he finds he can step into his ancestor's life in the 18th century.

Captain Applejack. Walter Hackett. Mystery fantasy. 7m 4w. French. Pirate adventures develop when Applejohn learns that his late night visitors are trying to find a pirate's treasure hidden in the house. Applejohn's dream on stage as a pirate later becomes an actuality.

Gramercy Ghost. John Holm. Mystery fantasy. 6m 6w. DPS. A young woman inherits the ghost of a Revolutionary soldier and finds that she is the only one who can see and hear him. Entanglements result until the ghost's secret is discovered and his conditions met.

Green Valley. Frank Waltron. Comic fantasy. 11m 7w. French. Elden Berry, the last of a long line of Berrys who pioneered California's Green Valley, is losing his land to an unscrupulous promoter who wants the area because vegetables grow to giant size. The spirits of Elden's ancestors return to help him keep the land. Uniquely refreshing story. Good production notes on making special properties.

Harvey. Mary Chase. Comic fantasy. 6m 6w. DPS. Complications arise when Veta Dowd tries to commit her brother Elwood to a sanitarium after he introduces his imaginary friend Harvey, a six-and-a-half-foot rabbit, to her friends at a society party. Elwood's delusion affects Veta and the doctors in strange ways. This play continues to be among the most popular and successful for nonprofessional companies.

Mrs. McThing. Mary Ellen Chase. Comic fantasy. 8m 9w. DPS. When a rich woman deprives her son of playing with a witch's daughter, strange things happen that teach her life's values.

Noah. Andre Obey. Drama fantasy. 5m 4w and 3 as animals. French. Stylized Biblical costumes. The story of Noah and his family as they prepare for and meet the flood.

Mysteries

Angel Street (or Gaslight). Patrick Hamilton. 4m 3w. French. 1880 costumes. A murderer almost succeeds in making his wife believe she is insane, when an amiable man from Scotland Yard begins investigating. Exciting action emerges as the detective proves the husband's guilt.

The Bat. Rinehart and Hopwood. 7m 3w. French. Houseguests attempt to solve the mysterious happenings in the home of a deceased bank president whose bank was recently robbed. Excellent mystery, but with exacting light cues.

Double Door. Elizabeth McFadden. 7m 5w. French. 1910 costumes. Victoria dominates her sister's and brother's lives with tyrannical firmness. Disapproving her brother's bride, Victoria makes plans for murder. Suspense develops.

A Murder Has Been Arranged. Emlyn Williams. 3m 6w. French. On the night he is to inherit a large fortune, a man is murdered after he has been tricked into writing his own suicide note. Tension mounts as the others learn what has happened and prepare to obtain a confession from the murderer.

A Perfect Alibi. A. A. Milne. 8m 3w. French. In full view of the audience, an English gentleman is murdered by two houseguests. The police declare the death was suicide, but the dead man's nephew and ward prove differently.

Ten Little Indians. Agatha Christie. 8m 3w. French. Ten strangers who are guests at an island house are each accused of a different murder, and then one by one they too are murdered, according to the rhyme "Ten Little Indians." Suspense mounts as each of the remaining tries to determine who the murderer is.

One-Act Plays
Comedies & Farces

13 Ways to Screw Up Your College Interview. Ian McWethy. 6m 7w 3 either (4–16 actors possible). Playscripts (www.playscripts.com/play/1815 www.playscripts.com/play/1815). Thirteen wacky high school seniors try to impress two college recruiters trying to fill one final spot at their prestigious university. These hilarious interviews vividly illustrate what not to do. There is also a sequel, *14 More Ways to Screw Up Your College Interview.*

Antic Spring. Robert Nail. 3m 3w. French. High school students go on a pantomimed picnic.

Apollo of Bellac. Jean Giraudoux. 9m 3w. French. A girl learns the secret of getting along in the world – telling every man he is handsome. She does, with amazing results.

The Boor. Anton Chekhov. 2m 1w. French. In his attempts to collect a bill from his debtor's widow, a man gets the widow instead.

Check Please. Jonathan Rand. 7m 7w (2–13 each m and w actors possible). Playscripts (www.playscripts.com/play/202 www.playscripts.com/play/202) . A series of blind dinner dates goes from bad to worse with dates ranging from a blind kleptomaniac to a grandmother's bridge partner. Sequels include *Check Please: Take 2* and *Check Please: Take 3.*

Box and Cox. John Morton. 2m 1w. French. The same room is rented to two different men; one by day and one by night. The men are at first unaware of the situation, so humorous events evolve.

Dear Departed. Stanley Houghton. 3m 3w. French. A family is quarreling over their dead father's possessions when he walks in, very much alive.

Family Album. Noel Coward. Comedy with music. 5m 4w. French. Gathered together after their father's funeral, a family feigns sorrow until the oldest admits their father was no good. Memories of childhood and many revelations unfold. Some parts charmingly set to music, but may be used without.

Flattering Word. George Kelly. 2m 3w. French. When he is told that he looks like a great actor, a minister who is against the theatre accepts an invitation to attend a play.

The Florist Shop. Winifred Hawkridge. 3m 2w. French. A salesgirl in a florist shop arranges a wedding between a spinster and a bachelor by sending flowers to the lady from an "unknown" admirer.

The Ghost Story. Booth Tarkington. 5m 5w. French. A young man, unhappy with the crowd around his girl, decides to tell a ghost story and scare them away so that he can have the girl to himself. A humorous ending ensues.

Goodbye to the Lazy K. Robert Finch. 5m 1w. Chilton Company (East Washington Square, Philadelphia, Pennsylvania 19106). (Non-royalty play; script appears in Zachar's *Plays as Experience.*) The cowboy hero decides to leave his girl and go to the city where he hopes to become rich. Parting is difficult and his friends make matters worse. Song and dance mixed with the comedy.

The Happy Journey. Thornton Wilder. Comedy-drama. 3m 3w. French. Ma and Pa and two children journey to see a married daughter. A simple story, but dramatically and touchingly told. No scenery.

In the Suds. Barnard and Rose Hewitt. 1m 2w. French. A henpecked husband gains revenge upon his shrewish wife when she falls into a tub of suds and can't get out.

I'm a Fool. Christopher Sergel from Sherwood Anderson's story. 4m 4w. DPC. To impress an attractive girl, a boy who works at a race track pretends he is a wealthy heir. The girl promises to write him, but unhappily her letters will go to the person he is impersonating.

Ladies Alone. Ryerson and Clements. 3w. French. Three roommates vow to spend a night home together until the telephone rings and each accepts a date.

The Lost Princess. Dan Totheroh. Comedy in Chinese tradition. Sequel to *The Stolen Prince.* 8m 4w, extras. (Or all women or men.) French. The twin sister of the stolen prince is rescued and reared by a notorious outlaw. The girl reforms him and saves his life when she is recognized as the lost princess.

The Lost Silk Hat. Lord Dunsany. 5m. French. When a young man leaves his hat at his girl's house, he sends different people to retrieve it, with an amusing result.

The Man Who Married a Dumb Wife. Anatole France. 7m 3w. French. A French gentleman marries a woman who cannot speak. When he has his doctor cure his wife, he discovers that life was better when she was silent.

The Marriage Proposal. Anton Chekhov. 2m 1w. French. A man comes to propose but ends up in a violent quarrel over land and a dog.

Master Pierre Patelin. Merritt Stone, tran. 4m 1w. French. A lawyer participates in some underhanded business that proves hilarious.

The Neighbors. Zona Gale. Comedy-drama. 2m 6w. French. When a spinster receives word that she is being sent a homeless nephew, the neighbors pitch in to help. A touching story.

Opening Night. Roland Fernand from the story by Cornelia Otis-Skinner. 1m 10w. DPC. The day that she is to open in a Broadway play, Miss Skinner's family wants her to rest, but she is besieged by well wishers and nervous family who are so worried about her that they fail to let her relax.

Overtones. Alice Gerstenberg. 4w. French. While two women carry on a polite conversation, their inner selves reveal their true thoughts and feelings.

The Princess Marries the Page. Edna St. Vincent Millay. 6m 1w. French. A princess falls in love with a neighboring king who is disguised as a page.

The Romancers. Edmond Rostand. 5m 1w. French. Two young people flirt over a garden wall while their fathers pretend disapproval, knowing that if they approve, their children will not marry. A fake abduction brings about the marriage. Delightful and self-contained although it is Act I of a 3-act play.

The Still Alarm. George Kaufman. 5m. French. There is a fire in a hotel, but the men are exceedingly unconcerned about it; and there the fun lies.

Spreading the News. Lady Gregory. 7m 3w. French. When one man forgets his pitchfork at a country fair in Ireland, another runs after him. Nosy townspeople add up misinformation and an exaggerated story of a murder is circulated.

The Stolen Prince. Dan Totheroh. Comedy in Chinese tradition. 9m 3w. (Or all men or women.) French. A prince is stolen in infancy and raised by a poor couple. Brought before the Emperor for punishment, the young prince's true identity is discovered. See *The Lost Princess* as a sequel.

A Sunny Morning. Quinteros. 2m 2w. French. Two people, who were formerly sweethearts, meet again when they are old.

Sure Thing. David Ives. 1m 1w. DPS. Humorous satire of the dating game in which a young man tries and tries again to engage a young woman in conversation. A bell rings each time he goes astray, and he picks up the conversation once more.

This Is a Test. Stephen Gregg. 13–15 actors, either gender. DPC. A student faces many people's worst nightmare: trying to take a high-stakes test for which one is totally unprepared, including an essay question in Chinese. As the clock ticks down, the student deals with a hostile teacher, cheating classmates, and inner voices that describe a disastrous personal life.

The Trysting Place. Booth Tarkington. 4m 3w. French. Humorous complications arise when several pairs of lovers try to meet in a hotel.

The Ugly Duckling. A. A. Milne. 4m 3w. French. A prince and princess are betrothed by their families, sight unseen. Each family in turn arranges a "stand-in" until the wedding, because of their "plain" children. But the real prince and princess meet and fall in love.

Dramas–Serious Plays, Mysteries, Melodramas

The Clod. Lewis Beach. 4m 1w. French. During the Civil War a farm woman is insulted beyond her endurance by two Southern soldiers who are searching for a Northern soldier.

Cathleen ni Houlihan. William Butler Yeats. 3m 3w. French. 1798 Irish peasant costumes. A young man who is about to be married leaves his fiancee and home to fight for his native Ireland. Excellent symbolic drama.

The Game of Chess. Kenneth Goodman. 4m. French. A pre-revolutionary governor of a Russian province is interrupted at chess by an assassin. Through cunning trickery, the governor saves himself.

Ile. Eugene O'Neill. 5m 1w. DPS. A captain of a whale ship obstinately remains at sea while his wife goes insane.

Jacob Comes Home. William Kozlenko. 2m 3w. French. A Jewish family in the 1930s await the return of their father who is to be released by the Nazis. Suspense builds to the horrifying climax. Well written.

The Last of the Loweries. Paul Green. 1m 3w. French. An outlaw son returns to the mountains to see his mother, but he is killed.

The Long Christmas Dinner. Thornton Wilder. Comedy-drama. 5m 7w. French. Spans a family's history of Christmas dinners by showing the changing times and American life in general. A moving story.

The Lottery. Brainerd Duffield from a story by Shirley Jackson. 8m 5w. DPC. From a seemingly happy situation of families gathering for a lottery, we gradually suspect the horrible nature of the lottery.

A Minuet. Louis Parker. Poetic-drama. 2m 1w. French. During the French Revolution, a nobleman who has been separated from his wife meets her as both await the guillotine. A show of moral courage that is handled well.

Moonshine. Arthur Hopkins. 2m. French. A revenue officer who discovers a group of dangerous moonshiners is able to trick them into letting him go. Full of suspense.

Night at the Inn. Lord Dunsany. 8m. French. The thieves who have stolen the ruby eye from an Eastern idol are visited by the idol. A thriller.

The Old Lady Shows Her Medals. James M. Barrie. 2m 5w. French. A childless old woman invents a war hero son who surprisingly materializes. Play can be adapted for modern times.

Pawns. Percival Wilde. 6m. French. Ignorant but sensitive peasants learn from a crude Army sergeant that they are to be "mobilized" and sent to kill their next-door neighbors who are "enemies" because of a boundary line. Powerful.

Riders to the Sea. John M. Synge. 1m 3w. French. The sea triumphs as the wife of a fisherman buries her last son, drowned at sea.

The Ring of General Macias. Josefina Niggle. 3m 2w. Music Corporation of America (598 Madison Avenue, New York, New York 10022). During the Mexican Revolution of 1912, the wife of a Federal general is held captive by two Revolutionary soldiers. She succeeds in "saving" her husband's honor by arranging for his death. Exciting melodrama.

The Sandbar. Edward Albee. 3m 2w. DPS. Comedy and drama mix in play about old age.

Submerged. Cottman and Shaw. 6m. French. When a submarine crew is trapped on the ocean floor, one of them must be shot through the torpedo tube so rescue workers will find the crew. How the choice of man is made and what happens is exciting.

The Sun Is a Dead Man's Weapon. Robert Carroll. 2m 2w. French. When their tyrannical father dies, two sisters and a brother think they can pick up life where they left it. The older sister learns something about their past, however, that alters their future.

The Valiant. Hollworthy Hall and Robert Middlezuss. 5m 1w. French. A girl visits a man in prison, hoping he is her long lost brother.

Trifles. Susan Glaspell. 3m 3w. French. While the police are searching for clues that will convict a woman of murdering her husband, two friends discover items that would convict her. By keeping still about their discovery, their friend is released. Powerful story.

Two Crooks and a Lady. Eugene Pillot. 3m 3w. French. Two thieves are about to steal an old woman's jewels, but she is cleverly able to get them fighting between themselves.

Where the Cross Is Made. Eugene O'Neill. 6m 1w. DPS. An old man dies and his son is driven insane through a search for a non-existent treasure.

The Will. James M. Barrie. 6m 1w. French. 1915 and modern costumes. The life of a husband and wife is revealed through the years as they have their will drawn up, first as poor newlyweds; later in middle life; and finally, by the old, wealthy husband who has no one to leave his money to because his wife is dead.

Fantasies

The Actor's Nightmare. Christopher Durang. Fantasy-comedy. 2m 3w. Grove/Atlantic, Inc. (841 Broadway, New York, N.Y. 10003). To his dismay, George finds himself onstage with no idea what part he is playing. Hilarious antics ensue.

Aria da Capo. Edna St. Vincent Millay. Fantasy-drama. 4m 1w. French. Pierrot and Columbine in a play written in protest about war and selfishness.

The Devil and Daniel Webster. Stephen Vincent Benèt. Fantasy-drama. 6m 1w. DPS. Daniel Webster pleads a case against the Devil for a man who has sold his soul to the Devil.

Dust of the Road. Kenneth Goodman. Fantasy-drama. 3m 1w. French. A man, who is about to steal from his friend's son, meets Judas who is walking the earth on Christmas Eve.

Early Frost. Douglas Parkhirst. Fantasy-mystery.

4w. French. When a young girl comes to live with her two old aunts and begins to rummage around the attic, the horrible secret of her "strange" aunt is revealed.

Jest of Hahalaba. Lord Dunsany. 4m. Fantasy-drama. French. An old gentleman, through the powers of an alchemist who conjures spirits, is allowed to see into the forthcoming year. What he sees is a terrible shock—notice of his own death the very next day.

Maker of Dreams. Oliphant Down. Fantasy-comedy. 2m 1w. French. Pierrot, searching for his ideal woman, is assisted by the Maker of Dreams.

Three Pills in a Bottle. Rachel Field. Fantasy-drama. 5m 3w. French. The souls of three people come to play with a sick child, who gives them each a magic pill to cure their particular pains.

This Way to Heaven. Douglas Parkhirst. Fantasy-comedy. 2m 3w. French. A mysterious man appears in Gram's kitchen and makes several bungling attempts to take Gram with him to heaven, where he wants her to cook for his section so he can earn his wings. Finally he decides to leave Gram, but there is a surprise ending.

The Wonder Hat. Hecht and Goodman. Fantasy-comedy. 3m 2w. French. Harlequin buys a hat that makes him invisible, and Columbine buys a slipper that makes her attractive to men. Humorous situations and a surprising end.

SOURCES & ADDRESSES DECLAMATION MATERIAL

Orations, monologues, readings, pageants, blackouts, stunts, skits, sketches, etc.

Contemporary Drama Service
885 Elkton Drive
Colorado Springs, CO 80907
www.contemporarydrama.com

Hansen Drama Shop
Phone (801) 685-221
www.dramashop.com

PLAYS

To keep informed on new plays, have your name put on the mailing list for current catalogues published by these companies or check their Web sites for new titles.

Brooklyn Publishers
P.O. Box 248
Cedar Rapids, IA 52406
(888) 473-8521
www.brookpub.com

Dramatic Publishing Company (DPC)
3ll Washington St.
Woodstock, IL 60098-3308
www.dramaticpublishing.com

Dramatists Play Service, Inc. (DPS)
440 Park Avenue South
New York, NY 10016
www.dramatists.com

Samuel French, Inc. (French)
235 Park Avenue South,
5th Floor, New York, NY 10003
www.samuelfrench.com

Samuel French Bookshop
7623 Sunset Blvd.
Hollywood, CA 90046

Drama Book Shop
250 W. 40th St.
New York, NY 10018
www.dramabookshop.com
(handles most theatre books)

Perfection Learning Corporation
1000 North Second Avenue
P.O. Box 500
Logan, IA 51546
(800) 831-4190
www.perfectionlearning.com

Quite Specific Media Group
www.quitespecificmedia.com
(publishes books on many theatre aspects)

Richard Stoddard
Out-of-Print Theatre Books
43 East 10th Street #6-D
New York, NY 10013
(212) 598-9421
www.richardstoddard.com

MUSICALS

Also try other companies listed in this section.

Music Theatre International
421 West 54th St., 2nd Floor
New York, NY 10019
www.mtishows.com

Rodgers and Hammerstein Library
229 West 28th St. 11th floor
New York, NY 10001
www.rnh.com

Tams-Witmark Music Library
560 Lexington Ave.
New York, NY 10022
www.tamswitmark.com

MELODRAMAS

Also try other companies listed in this section.

Pioneer Drama Service
P.O. Box 4267
Englewood, CO 80155-4267
www.pioneerdrama.com

THEATRE SUPPLY HOUSES

These are just a few of the larger supply houses.

COSTUMES

Broadway Costumes

1100 West Cermak Road
Second Floor
Chicago, IL 60608
www.broadwaycostumes.com

Costume World
950 South Federal Highway
Deerfield Beach, FL 33441
www.costumeworld.com

The Costumer
Catalog/Internet Department
1995 Central Avenue
Albany, NY 12205
www.thecostumer.com

Lost Eras
1511 West Howard Street
Chicago, IL 60626
773-764-7400
www.losteras.com

Morris Costumes
4300 Monroe Road
Charlotte, NC 28205
www.morriscostumes.com

Rubies Costume
(516) 326–1500
www.rubies.com

The TDF Costume Collection
(Located at the Kaufman Astoria Studios)
34-12 36th Street
Lower Level, Suite 1
Astoria, NY 11106
www.tdf.org/costumes (costumes for non-profit theatre groups)

The Theatre Company
1400 North Benson Avenue
Upland, CA 91786
www.theatreco.com

Theatre House, Inc
400 West 3rd Street
Covington, KY 41011
www.theatrehouse.com

COSTUME SPECIALTIES

Amazon Drygoods
125 South Buckeye Street
Osgood, IN 47037
www.amazondrygoods.com

(historical patterns, clothing, and accessories)

Backstage Dancewear
380 West 3rd Avenue
Eugene, OR 97401
(541) 686-2671
(wigs, accessories, hats)

Cloak and Corset
www.cloakandcorset.com
(resources for making 19th-century historical clothing)

Costume Armour
2 Mill Street
Building 1 Suite 101
Cornwell, NY 12518
www.costumearmour.com

Weapons of Choice
4075 Browns Valley Rd.
Napa, CA 94558-4144
www.weaponsofchoice.com

Richard the Thread Costume Shop Supplier
1960 S. La Cienega Blvd.
Los Angeles, CA 90034
www.richardthethread.com

FABRIC
(For costumes, drapes, and scenery)

Associated Fabrics
15-01 Pollitt Drive, Unit 7
Fair Lawn, NJ 07410
www.afcfabrics.com

Dazian
18 Central Boulevard
South Hackensack, NJ 07606
www.dazian.com

Rose Brand
4 Emerson Lane
Secaucus, NJ 07094
www.rosebrand.com

LIGHTING

Grand Stage Lighting Company
630 West Lake Street
Chicago, IL 60661
www.grandstage.com

GAM Products, Inc.
A Division of Rosco Laboratories Inc.
52 Harbor View
Stamford, CT 06902
www.gamonline.com

Lee Filters
2237 North Hollywood Way
Burbank, CA 91505
www.leefilters.com

Premier Lighting & Production Co.
12023 Victory Blvd.
North Hollywood, CA 91606-3318
www.premier-lighting.com

Rosco Laboratories, Inc.
52 Harbor View Avenue
Stamford, CT 06902
www.rosco.com

Stagecraft Industries
P.O. Box 4442
Portland, OR 97208
www.stagecraftindustries.com

Strand Lighting
10911 Petal Street
Dallas, TX 75238
www.strandlighting.com

MAKEUP HOUSES
(Check Web sites or send for catalogs)

Alcone Company
5-45 49th Avenue
Long Island City, NY 11101

www.alconeco.com
(excellent catalog)

Joe Blasco Cosmetics
Training centers in Hollywood, CA and
Orlando, FL
www.joeblasco.com

Kryolan Corp.
132 Ninth Street
San Francisco, CA 94103
www.kryolan.com

Mehron, Inc.
100 Red Schoolhouse Rd.
Chestnut Ridge, NY 10977
www.mehron.com

Ben Nye
3655 Lenawee Avenue
Los Angeles, CA 90016
www.bennyemakeup.com

PUBLICITY
See Play Publishers in this section to inquire
about visuals and posters related to various
plays.

RECORDINGS & CDs DIALECTS
CDs are available with Blunt's *Stage
Dialects*, Machlin's *Dialects for the Stage*,
and Meier's *Accents & Dialects for Stage and
Screen*.

Various accent and dialect recordings are
available from:

Dialect Accent Specialists, Inc.
P.O. Box 44
Lyndonville, VT 05851
www.dialectaccentspecialists.com
(instructional recordings by Dr. David Alan
Stern)

The Dialect Resource
www.dialectresource.com

International Dialects of English Archive
www.dialectsarchive.com

Videos of dialects for actors may also be found
on YouTube.

SOUND EFFECTS
Films for the Humanities and Sciences
132 West 31st Street
17th Floor
New York, NY 10001
(audio CD collections)
www.ffh.films.com

MediaCollege.com
www.mediacollege.comdownloads/sound-
effects/
(free sound effects)

Valentino Music
www.tvmusic.com
(extensive library of production music and
sound effects for digital download)

SCENE PAINT
Rosco Laboratories, Inc.
52 Harbor View Avenue
Stamford, CT 06902
www.rosco.com
(products sold at dealers throughout the
country)

Rose Brand
4 Emerson Lane
Secaucus, NJ 07094
www.rosebrand.com

STAGE HARDWARE
J. R. Clancy, Inc.
7041 Interstate Island Road
Syracuse, NY 13209
www.jrclancy.com

Mutual Hardware
36–27 Vernon Boulevard
Long Island City, NY 11106
www.mutualhardware.com

THEATRICAL SUPPLIES

These houses handle lights, makeup, stage
hardware, fabrics, paints, costumes, tools,
draperies, etc.

Globe Theatrical Resource
813 Pearl St.
Sioux City, IA 51101
www.globetheatricalresource.com

Norcostco
825 Rhode Island Ave. South
Minneapolis, MN 55426
www.norcostco.com

Hollywood Rentals
(800) 233-7830
www.hollywoodrentals.com

Theatre House
400 W. 3rd St.
Covington, KY 41011
www.theatrehouse.com

Tobins Lake Studios
7030 Whitmore Lake Rd.
Brighton, MI 48116
www.tobinslake.com

TICKETS PRINTED
Worldwide Ticketcraft
3606 Quantum Blvd.
Boynton Beach, FL 33426
www.worldwideticketcraft.com

Weldon, Williams & Lick
(800) 643-2598
www.wwlinc.com

SPECIAL EFFECTS
(projections, lighting, fog, etc.)

GAM Products, Inc.
A Division of Rosco Laboratories Inc.
52 Harbor View
Stamford, CT 06902

www.gamonline.com

J & M Special Effects
524 Sackett Street
Brooklyn, NY 11217
www.jmfx.net

StageSpot
(888) 567-8243
www.stagespot.com

VIDEOS & FILMS

Many state universities offer rental videos and films on drama. Many libraries have films of plays on DVD. Films of many plays are available for download or on DVD from www.amazon.com

The New York Public Library maintains the Theatre on Film and Tape Archive www.nypl.org/locations/lpa/theatre-film-and-tape-archive

The following companies offer DVDs and streaming media on theatre history, Shakespeare and his plays, acting, voice training, movement, stage combat, script analysis, auditioning, characterization, makeup, lighting, set construction, etc.

Films for the Humanities & Sciences
132 West 31st Street
17th Floor
New York, NY 10001
www.ffh.films.com

First Light Video Publishing
2321 Abbot Kinney Blvd., Top Floor
Venice, CA 90291
www.firstlightvideo.com

Insight Media
2162 Broadway
New York, NY 10024
www.insight-media.com

Theatre Arts Video Library
174 Andrew Avenue
Leucadia, CA 92024
www.theatreartsvideo.com

THEATRE ORGANIZATIONS & PERIODICALS

Affiliation with any of the following groups will keep you abreast of new events in the profession. Membership will also entitle you to receive the organization's bulletin and to attend the conferences.

ORGANIZATIONS

Actors Equity
165 West 46Th Street
New York, NY 10036
(212) 869-8530
www.actorsequity.org

Alpha Psi Omega/Delta Psi Omega
Wichita State University
1845 Fairmount St.
Box 153

Wichita, KS 67260
www.alphapsiomega.org
(drama honorary for college and junior college students)

American Alliance for Theatre and Education
Alexis Truitt
Operations Manager
4908 Auburn Ave.
Bethesda, MD 20814
(301) 200-1944
www.aate.com

Association for Theatre in Higher Education
P.O. Box 1290
Boulder, CO 80306-1290
www.athe.org

ASCAP
1900 Broadway
New York, NY 10023
(212) 621-6000
www.ascap.com

BMI
7 World Trade Center
250 Greenwich Street
New York, NY 10007-0030
(212) 220-3000
www.bmi.com

Dramatists Guild
1501 Broadway
Suite 101
New York, NY 10036
(212) 398-9366
www.dramatistsguild.com

Educational Theatre Association & International Thespian Society
2343 Auburn Avenue
Cincinnati, OH 45219
(513) 421-3900
www.schooltheatre.org
www.schooltheatre.org/ITS
(for secondary school students)

National Communication Association
1765 N Street NW
Washington, DC 20036
www.natcom.org

U. S. Center of the International Theatre Institute
Theatre Communications Group
520 Eighth Avenue, 24th Floor
New York, NY 10018-4156
www.tcg.org

PERIODICALS – EDUCATIONAL

Communication Education
National Communication Association
1765 N Street NW
Washington, DC 20036
www.natcom.org/journals.aspx

Dramatics Magazine
Educational Theatre Assoc. & International Thespian Society
2343 Auburn Avenue

Cincinnati, OH 45219
www.schooltheatre.org/publications/dramatics

New Theatre Quarterly
Cambridge University Press
32 Avenue of the Americas
New York, NY 10013-2473
www.cambridge.org/

The Playbill
Alpha Psi Omega
Wichita State University
1845 Fairmount St.
Box 153
Wichita, KS 67260
www.alphapsiomega.org

Stage Directions
6000 S. Eastern Ave., Suite J-14
Las Vegas, NV 89119
(for academic and community theatre)
www.stage-directions.com
Also publishes the online Theatre Resources Directory
www.trd.stage-directions.com

PERIODICALS – COMMERCIAL

American Theatre
520 8th Ave., 24th Floor
New York, NY 10018
www.tcg.org/publications

Live Design
1166 Avenue of the Americas, 10th Floor
New York, NY 10036
(866) 505-7173
www.livedesignonline.com
(creative and technical journal for live entertainment professionals in lighting, sound, staging, and projection)

Playbill.com
37-15 61st St.
Woodside, NY 11377
www.playbill.com
(Broadway, Off-Broadway, and London news)

Plays
897 Washington St. #600160
Newton, MA 02460
www.playsmagazine.com
(magazine with scripts and skits for teenagers)